ACCOUNTING

Horngren, Harrison, Bamber
Custom Edition for Moraine Valley Community College

Taken from:
Accounting, Sixth Edition
by Charles T. Horngren, Walter T. Harrison Jr., and Linda Smith Bamber

Taken from:

Accounting, Sixth Edition
by Charles T. Horngren, Walter T. Harrison Jr., and Linda Smith Bamber
Copyright © 2005, 2002, 1999, 1996, 1993 Pearson Education, Inc.
Published by Prentice Hall, Inc.
Upper Saddle River, New Jersey 07458

This special edition published in cooperation with Pearson Custom Publishing.

Printed in the United States of America

10 9 8 7 6 5 4 3 2 1

ISBN 0-536-25947-X

2006160278

LG

Please visit our web site at *www.pearsoncustom.com*

PEARSON CUSTOM PUBLISHING
75 Arlington Street, Suite 300, Boston, MA 02116
A Pearson Education Company

Brief Contents

■Contents

CHAPTER 14   Retained Earnings, Treasury
Stock, and the Income
Statement   542

CHAPTER 15   Long-Term Liabilities   578

■ About the Authors

Charles T. Horngren is the Edmund W. Littlefield Professor of Accounting, Emeritus, at Stanford University. A graduate of Marquette University, he received his MBA from Harvard University and his Ph.D. from the University of Chicago. He is also the recipient of honorary doctorates from Marquette University and DePaul University.

A Certified Public Accountant, Horngren served on the Accounting Principles Board for six years, the Financial Accounting Standards Board Advisory Council for five years, and the Council of the American Institute of Certified Public Accountants for three years. For six years, he served as a trustee of the Financial Accounting Foundation, which oversees the Financial Accounting Standards Board and the Government Accounting Standards Board.

Horngren is a member of the Accounting Hall of Fame.

A member of the American Accounting Association, Horngren has been its President and its Director of Research. He received its first annual Outstanding Accounting Educator Award.

The California Certified Public Accountants Foundation gave Horngren its Faculty Excellence Award and its Distinguished Professor Award. He is the first person to have received both awards.

The American Institute of Certified Public Accountants presented its first Outstanding Educator Award to Horngren.

Horngren was named Accountant of the Year, Education, by the national professional accounting fraternity, Beta Alpha Psi.

Professor Horngren is also a member of the Institute of Management Accountants, from whom he has received its Distinguished Service Award. He was a member of the Institute's Board of Regents, which administers the Certified Management Accountant examinations.

Horngren is the author of other accounting books published by Prentice-Hall: *Cost Accounting: A Managerial Emphasis*, Eleventh Edition, 2003 (with Srikant Datar and George Foster); *Introduction to Financial Accounting*, Eighth Edition, 2002 (with Gary L. Sundem and John A. Elliott); *Introduction to Management Accounting*, Thirteenth Edition, 2005 (with Gary L. Sundem and William Stratton); *Financial Accounting*, Fifth Edition, 2004 (with Walter T. Harrison, Jr.).

Horngren is the Consulting Editor for Prentice-Hall's Charles T. Horngren Series in Accounting.

Walter T. Harrison, Jr. is Professor of Accounting at the Hankamer School of Business, Baylor University. He received his B.B.A. degree from Baylor University, his M.S. from Oklahoma State University, and his Ph.D. from Michigan State University.

Professor Harrison, recipient of numerous teaching awards from student groups as well as from university administrators, has also taught at Cleveland State Community College, Michigan State University, the University of Texas, and Stanford University.

A member of the American Accounting Association and the American Institute of Certified Public Accountants, Professor Harrison has served as Chairman of the Financial Accounting Standards Committee of the American Accounting Association, on the Teaching/Curriculum Development Award Committee, on the Program Advisory Committee for Accounting Education and Teaching, and on the Notable Contributions to Accounting Literature Committee.

Professor Harrison has lectured in several foreign countries and published articles in numerous journals, including *The Accounting Review, Journal of Accounting Research, Journal of Accountancy, Journal of Accounting and Public Policy, Economic Consequences of Financial Accounting Standards, Accounting Horizons, Issues in Accounting Education,* and *Journal of Law and Commerce.*

He is co-author of *Financial Accounting*, Fifth Edition, 2004 (with Charles T. Horngren), published by Prentice Hall. Professor Harrison has received scholarships, fellowships, and research grants or awards from PriceWaterhouse Coopers, Deloitte & Touche, the Ernst & Young Foundation, and the KPMG Foundation.

Linda Smith Bamber holds the J.M. Tull Chair of Accounting at the J.M. Tull School of Accounting at the University of Georgia. She graduated summa cum laude from Wake Forest University, where she was a member of Phi Beta Kappa. She is a Certified Public Accountant, and received an Elijah Watt Sells Award as well as the North Carolina Bronze Medal for her performance on the CPA examination. Before returning to graduate school, Professor Bamber gained professional experience working in management accounting at R.J. Reynolds, Inc. She then earned an MBA from Arizona State University, and a Ph.D. from The Ohio State University.

Professor Bamber has received numerous teaching awards from The Ohio State University, the University of Florida, and the University of Georgia.

She has lectured in Canada and Australia, in addition to the U.S., and her research has appeared in numerous journals, including *The Accounting Review, Journal of Accounting Research, Journal of Accounting and Economics, Journal of Finance, Contemporary Accounting Research, Accounting Horizons, Issues in Accounting Education,* and *The CPA Journal.* She also developed the annotations for the *Annotated Instructor's Edition* of Horngren, Foster, and Datar's *Cost Accounting: A Managerial Emphasis,* Seventh, Eighth, and Ninth Editions.

A member of the Institute of Management Accounting, the American Accounting Association (AAA) and the AAA's Management Accounting Section and Financial Accounting and Reporting Section, Professor Bamber has chaired the AAA New Faculty Consortium and the AAA Competitive Manuscript Award Committees, served on the AAA Council, the AAA Research Advisory Committee, the AAA Nominations Committee, and numerous other AAA and section committees. She served as Associate Editor of *Accounting Horizons*, and as editor of *The Accounting Review.*

■ Preface

From The Authors

This new sixth edition of *Accounting* has been tailored to meet instructors' needs and to help students master accounting. We think our efforts have made this revision much easier for instructors to teach and students to learn from. Throughout the text, we have streamlined the presentation and focused the content on the core topics of first-year accounting. To better prepare students for the business world, wherever possible we have used actual documents and real situations.

The text revisions and the new design, combined with an outstanding resource package, provide excellent tools for success in accounting. We hope you agree.

Charles Horngren ★ **Tom Harrison** ★ **Linda Bamber**

For The Student

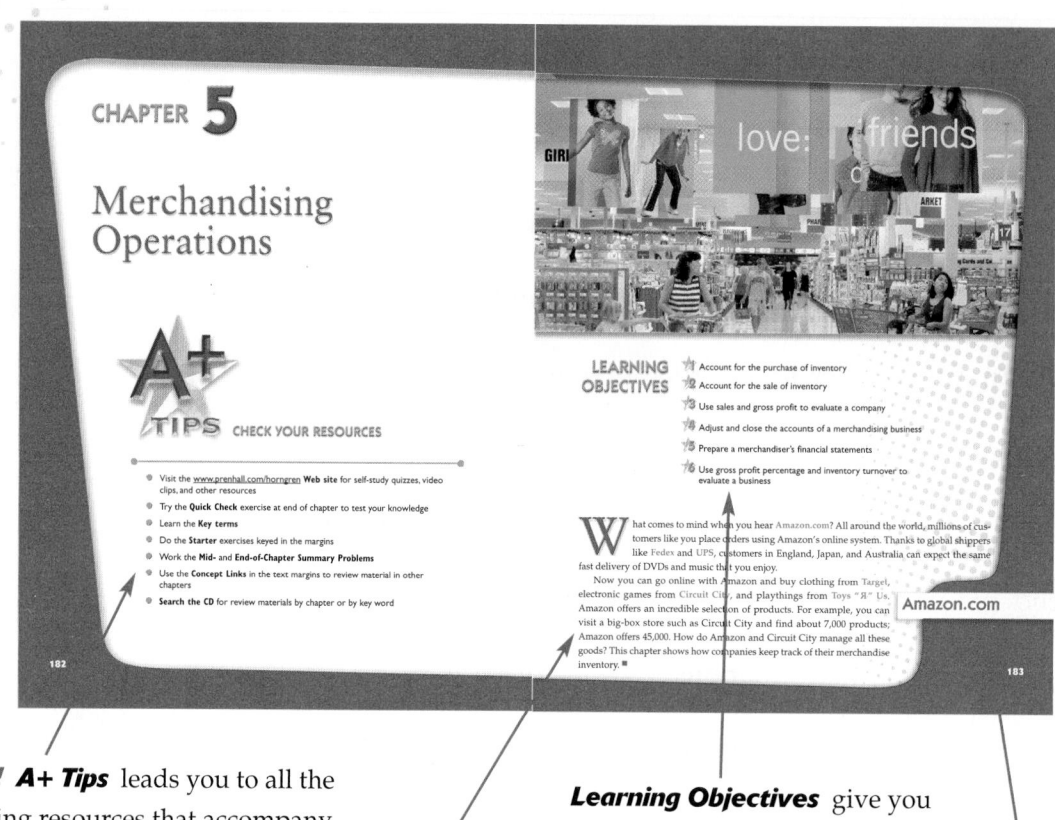

New! A+ Tips leads you to all the learning resources that accompany the text. Follow the A+ Tips to improve your understanding—and your course grade!

Learning Objectives give you an overview of the skills you will learn in the chapter.

Chapter-opening vignettes take you into the real world of accounting—where business decisions affect the future of actual organizations. Each vignette introduces you to the central issues covered in the chapter. Many of the vignettes—on Jelly Belly, Oracle, Dell—are linked to unique, custom-created *On Location!* **Videos** available on the **Student and Instructor Resource CD-ROMs**.

New feature company: Amazon.com Amazon.com's annual report is bound into the book; Amazon is also the feature company in several chapter-opening vignettes, and in end-of-chapter financial statement cases.

Features

New! *Sitemaps* appear at the beginning of each chapter and at main headings throughout the chapter as a roadmap to show you where you are and what is coming next.

New! An open and reader-friendly **text design** includes many new exhibits and infographics.

A Running Glossary provides a full definition when a term is introduced. A list of terms appears at the end of each chapter, and there is a complete Glossary at the end of the book.

Unique! Concept Links help you remember material learned earlier. Concept links in the side margins point you to relevant topics covered earlier: they provide both a rationale for the material and a chapter and text page cross reference.

---

184   Chapter 5

■ Sitemap

■ Merchandising Operations

■ Accounting for Inventory: Perpetual System

■ Adjusting and Closing Accounts

■ Preparing Financial Statements

■ Key Decision-Making Ratios

We shift gears in Chapter 5. The first four chapters focused on service companies such as Gay Gillen eTravel, the San Francisco Giants, and eBay. Here we begin working with merchandisers such as Amazon.com, Target, and Circuit City. A merchandiser differs from a service business in two important ways. A merchandiser sells *products*, whereas a service company provides a *service*. A merchandiser has an asset called *merchandise inventory*, such as DVDs, videos, and clothing. A service company carries no inventory.

Inventory includes all the goods a company owns and holds for sale in the normal course of operations. Throughout the remainder of the book we refer to merchandise inventory simply as inventory. It is a merchandiser's most important asset. This chapter demonstrates the central role of inventory in a business that sells merchandise. We illustrate accounting for the purchase and sale of inventory, and we also illustrate how to adjust and credi-

What Are Merchandising Operations?

Merchandising is the business activity of buying and selling products rather than services. Accounting for merchandising operations requires us to deal with these balance sheet and income statement items.

Balance Sheet:
■ Inventory, an asset

Income Statement:
■ Sales revenue (often abbreviated as Sales), a revenue
■ Cost of goods sold, an expense

These items are italicized in Exhibit 5-1 for Merchandising Co. Let's begin with the operating cycle of a merchandising business.

■ **Merchandising Operations**
☐ Accounting for Inventory: Perpetual System
☐ Adjusting and Closing Accounts
☐ Preparing Financial Statements
☐ Key Decision-Making Ratios

🔘 Student Resource CD
periodic system, perpetual system

TRANSPORTATION COSTS   The transportation cost of moving inventory from seller to buyer can be significant. The purchase agreement specifies FOB terms to indicate who pays the shipping charges. *FOB* means *free on board*. FOB terms govern (1) when legal title to the goods passes from seller to buyer and (2) who pays the freight. Exhibit 5-4 summarizes FOB terms.

Exhibit 5-4   FOB Terms Determine Who Pays Freight

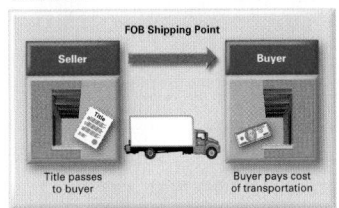

FOB Shipping Point — Seller — Buyer — Title passes to buyer — Buyer pays cost of transportation

FOB Destination — Seller — Buyer — Seller pays cost of transportation — Title passes to buyer

Freight costs are either *Freight in* or *Freight out*.

■ Freight in is the transportation cost on *purchased goods*.
■ Freight out is the transportation cost on *goods sold*.

Freight In   FOB shipping point terms are most common, so the buyer pays the freight. Freight in becomes part of the cost of inventory. The buyer debits Inventory and credits Cash or Accounts Payable for the freight. Suppose Austin Sound pays a $60 shipping bill. Austin Sound's entry to record payment of the freight charge is

June 1	Inventory	60	
	Cash		60
	Paid a freight bill.		

Sales Returns and Allowances
Decreases in the seller's receivable from a customer's return of merchandise or from granting the customer an allowance from the amount owed to the seller. A contra account to Sales Revenue.

Sales Discount
Reduction in the amount receivable from a customer, offered by the seller as an incentive for the customer to pay promptly. A contra account to Sales Revenue.

Net Sales Revenue
Sales revenue less sales discounts and sales returns and allowances.

SALES DISCOUNTS AND SALES RETURNS AND ALLOWANCES   We just saw that purchase returns and allowances and purchase discounts decrease the cost of inventory purchases. In the same way, **sales returns and allowances** and **sales discounts**, which are contra accounts to Sales Revenue, decrease the net amount of revenue earned on sales.

CREDIT-BALANCE ACCOUNT		DEBIT-BALANCE ACCOUNTS			CREDIT SUBTOTAL (NOT A SEPARATE ACCOUNT)
Sales Revenue	−	Sales Returns and Allowances	−	Sales Discounts	= Net sales revenue[1]

Companies maintain separate accounts for Sales Discounts and Sales Returns and Allowances. Now let's examine a sequence of JVC sale transactions. Assume JVC is selling to Austin Sound Center.

On July 7, JVC sells stereo components for $7,200 on credit terms of 2/10 n/30. These goods cost JVC $4,700. JVC's entries to record this credit sale and the related cost of goods sold are

July 7   Accounts Recei...

Because Austin Sound sold goods, the business also must decrease the Inventory balance. Suppose these goods cost the seller $1,900. A second journal entry is needed to transfer the $1,900 cost of the goods from the Inventory account to Cost of Goods Sold, as follows:→

June 9	Cost of Goods Sold	1,900	
	Inventory		1,900
	Recorded the cost of goods sold.		

← *The recording of cost of goods sold along with sales revenue is an example of the matching principle (Chapter 3, p. 95)*

This Stop & Think example is exactly like the preceding one, but with freight in. On September 15, Austin Sound purchased $1,000 of merchandise, with *$80 freight added*, for an invoice total of $1,080. Austin returns $100 of the goods for credit on September 20 and pays the account payable in full on September 25. Journalize these transactions.

Answer

Purchase: Sept. 15	Inventory ($1,000 + $80)	1,080	
	Accounts Payable.		1,080
Return: Sept. 20	Accounts Payable.	100	
	Inventory.		100
Payment: Sept. 25	Accounts Payable ($1,080 − $100).	980	
	Inventory [($1,000 − $100 × 0.02].		18
	Cash ($1,000 + $80 − $100 − $18)		962

There is no discount on freight.

Stop & Think exercise boxes appear within the text in every chapter. The exercises encourage you to assess your understanding of concepts by providing immediate practice of what you have just learned.

Amazon.com: For E-Tailers Free Shipping Isn't Free, But It's Not a Cost, Either

Like most accounting students, Jennifer didn't have time to go Christmas shopping. She cruised the online mall and ended up buying all her presents from Amazon.com, the largest player in online retailing. Jennifer was lured by Amazon.com's huge selection and an offer of free shipping for all orders over $25.

Amazon.com views free shipping as a key factor in boosting its growth—revenue jumped 233% to $851 million in one year. Yet, the company doesn't send packages via eight trusty reindeer. Amazon has to pay freight companies to deliver DVD players, books, and blenders to customers around the world. How does an e-tailer—one that is just barely making a profit—account for these shipping and handling costs?

Fortunately for Amazon and other e-tailers, in the process of revolutionizing business, e-commerce has also bent certain accounting rules. One such rule is that the cost of products sold to customers is usually recorded as Cost of Goods Sold, a merchandiser's major expense. But online powerhouses like Amazon.com and Buy.com count some of this cost as "sales and marketing expenses." By listing these "fulfillment costs" as marketing expenses, both e-tailers and catalog houses such as L. L. Bean don't have to subtract the expense in arriving at gross profit.

Small wonder that this controversial approach came under investigation by the Financial Accounting Standards Board (FASB). The dot-com bubble had burst, and e-tailers were poised to reclassify shipping and handling costs as costs of goods sold. That would restate gross profit downward. However, the Emerging Issues Task Force of the FASB recommended that shipping and handling *revenue* should be included in sales, without giving any guidance about how to account for shipping and handling *costs*. So Amazon and other e-tailers are free to continue including shipping and handling costs under marketing expense. The result: Gross profits are still high.

Based on: Nick Winfield, "Survival Strategy: Amazon Takes Page from Wal-Mart to Prosper on Web—Internet Retailer Cuts Prices and Keeps Eye on Costs in Bid for High Volumes—Betting Big on Free Shipping," The Wall Street Journal, November 22, 2002, p. A1. Saul Hansell, "Amazon's Loss in Quarter Shows a Sharp Decrease," The New York Times, October 25, 2002, p. 8. Katherine Hobson, "Silver Lining: FASB Spares E-Tailers in Cost Ruling," The Street.com, August 8, 2000.

Accounting.com boxes Nothing has changed business more in recent years than the Internet. Horngren/Harrison/Bamber's Accounting.com boxes identify accounting issues affecting companies doing business on the Web.

MID-CHAPTER Summary Problem

Suppose Amazon.com engaged in the following transactions during June of the current year:

June 3 Purchased inventory on credit terms of 1/10 net eom (end of month), $1,600.
     9 Returned 40% of the inventory purchased on June 3. It was defective.
    12 Sold goods for cash, $920 (cost, $550).
    15 Purchased goods for $5,000. Credit terms were 3/15 net 30.
    16 Paid a $260 freight bill on goods purchased.
    18 Sold inventory on credit terms of 2/10 n/30, $2,000 (cost, $1,180).
    22 Received returned goods from the customer of the June 18 sale, $800 (cost, $480).
    24 Borrowed money from the bank to take advantage of the discount

A+ TIPS
CHECK YOUR RESOURCES

Summary Problems This unique Horngren/Harrison/Bamber feature enables you to pause and assess your progress at two locations within each chapter—midway and again at the end of the chapter text. Solutions appear with the problems for immediate feedback.

END-OF-CHAPTER Summary Problem

A+ TIPS
CHECK YOUR RESOURCES

The adjustment data and trial balance of Jan King Distributing Company follow. (The solution to Requirement 1 is on page 208.)

Adjustment data at December 31, 20X6.

a. Supplies used during the year, $2,580.
b. Prepaid rent in force, $1,000.
c. Unearned sales revenue still not earned, $2,400.
d. Depreciation. The furniture and fixtures' estimated useful life is 10 years, and they are expected to be worthless when they are retired from service.
e. Accrued salaries, $1,300.
f. Accrued interest expense, $600.
g. Inventory on hand, $65,800.

Required

1. Enter the trial balance on a work sheet and complete the work sheet.
2. Journalize the adjusting and closing entries at December 31. Post to the Income Summary account as an accuracy check on the entries affecting that account. The credit balance closed out of Income Summary should equal net income computed on the work sheet.
3. Prepare the company's multi-step income statement, statement of owner's equity, and balance sheet in account format. Draw arrows linking the statements.
4. Compute the inventory turnover for 20X6. Inventory at December 31, 20X5, was $61,000. Turnover for 20X5 was 2.1 times. Would you expect Jan King Distributing Company to be more profitable or less profitable in 20X6 than in 20X5? Give your reason.

A+ Tips reminders appear with both Mid-Chapter and End-of-Chapter review problems.

Unique! Decision Guidelines show when, why, and how managers—not just accountants—use accounting information to make good business decisions.

Excel Application Exercises Every business professional must know how to use Excel, and Horngren/Harrison/Bamber provides the tools you need to master it. Excel Application Exercises appear in each chapter, with instructions for creating your own spreadsheets. Spreadsheet templates appear on the CD.

Decision Guidelines

MERCHANDISING OPERATIONS AND THE ACCOUNTING CYCLE

Amazon.com and Kinko's Copy Centers are two very different companies. How do Amazon and Kinko's differ? How are they similar? The Decision Guidelines answer these questions.

Decision	Guidelines
How do merchandisers differ from service entities?	• Merchandisers, such as Amazon.com, buy and sell *merchandise inventory*. • Service entities, such as Kinko's, perform a *service*.
How do a merchandiser's financial statements differ from the statements of a service business?	

Income Statement:

Merchandiser

Sales revenue	$XXX
−Cost of goods sold	(X)
= Gross profit	XX
−Operating expenses	(X)
= Net income	$ X

Statements of Owner's Equity:
Which type of inventory system to use?

Balance sheet:
• Merchandiser has *inventory*, an asset.
• Service business has no inventory.

Service Business

Service revenue	$ XX
−Operating expenses	(X)
= Net income	$ X

No difference

• *Perpetual system* shows the amount of *inventory* on hand (the asset) and the cost of goods sold (the expense) at all times.
• *Periodic system* shows the correct balances of inventory and cost of goods sold only after a physical count of the inventory, which occurs at least once each year.

Excel Application Exercise

Goal: Create a spreadsheet to compute Amazon.com's gross profit percentage and inventory turnover for the past three years.

Scenario: You are intrigued by Amazon's ability to sell merchandise via the Internet and would like to invest in such a venture. Before doing so, however, you remember from your accounting course that ratio analysis is an important part of making an investment decision. You decide to calculate two key ratios: gross profit percentage and inventory turnover. (You may need to visit Amazon.com on the Web to find inventory data from past years. Look under Investor Relations at the bottom of the Home page.) When you have completed your worksheet, answer the following questions:

1. What has happened to Amazon's gross profit percentage over the past three years?
2. What can you tell about Amazon's inventory operations from its inventory turnover ratio for the past two years?

Step-by-Step:
1. Open a new Excel spreadsheet.
2. In column 1, create a bold-faced heading as follows:
   a. Chapter 5 Excel Application Exercise
   b. Evaluating Amazon Inventory Operations
   c. Today's Date
3. Two rows down and two columns over, create bold and underlined headings for the most recent three years (e.g., 2002, 2001, and 2000).
4. In column A, enter the following (one per row):
   a. Net Sales (in thousands)
   b. Cost of Goods Sold (Cost of Sales)
   c. Gross Profit
   d. Inventory
   e. Gross Profit Percentage
   f. Inventory Turnover
5. Locate the data for items a-d in the Amazon.com annual report (or on the Web) and enter it in the appropriate columns.
6. Calculate gross profit percentage and inventory turnover. To help visualize the data trends, use the Chart Wizard to create a bar graph of performance.
7. Format all columns, rows, and data as needed. Save your work and print a copy for your files.

Assignment Materials

New! Starters Starters serve as warm-ups and confidence builders at the beginning of the assignment material. Try to solve these easy, single-concept exercises. Each Starter is referenced within the chapter so that if you need more guidance, you know exactly what material to review to complete the exercise.

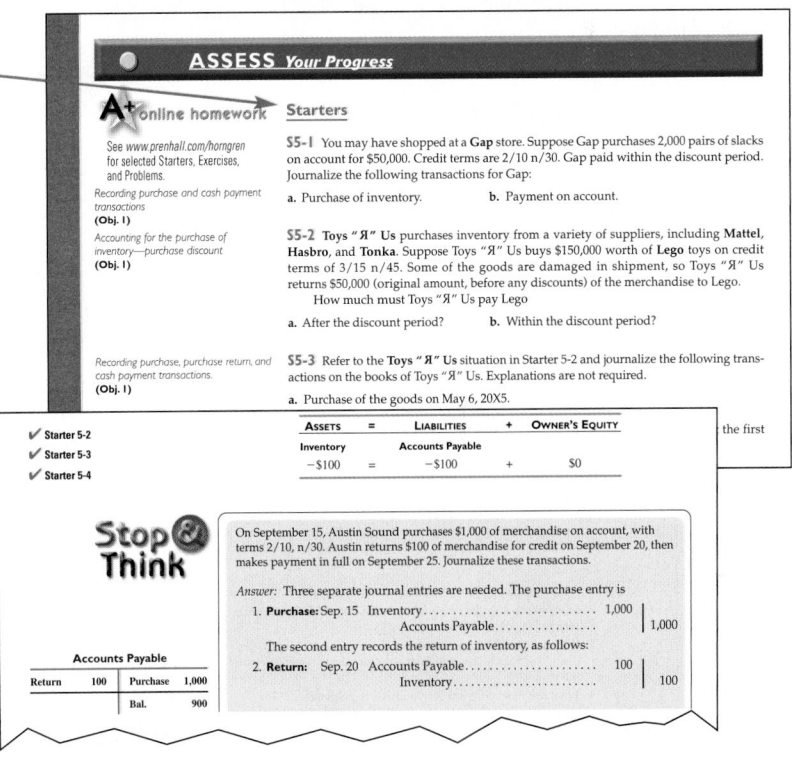

ASSESS Your Progress

A+ online homework

See www.prenhall.com/horngren for selected Starters, Exercises, and Problems.

Recording purchase and cash payment transactions
(Obj. 1)

Accounting for the purchase of inventory—purchase discount
(Obj. 1)

Recording purchase, purchase return, and cash payment transactions.
(Obj. 1)

Starters

S5-1 You may have shopped at a **Gap** store. Suppose Gap purchases 2,000 pairs of slacks on account for $50,000. Credit terms are 2/10 n/30. Gap paid within the discount period. Journalize the following transactions for Gap:

a. Purchase of inventory.   b. Payment on account.

S5-2 **Toys "Я" Us** purchases inventory from a variety of suppliers, including **Mattel**, **Hasbro**, and **Tonka**. Suppose Toys "Я" Us buys $150,000 worth of **Lego** toys on credit terms of 3/15 n/45. Some of the goods are damaged in shipment, so Toys "Я" Us returns $50,000 (original amount, before any discounts) of the merchandise to Lego.
How much must Toys "Я" Us pay Lego

a. After the discount period?   b. Within the discount period?

S5-3 Refer to the **Toys "Я" Us** situation in Starter 5-2 and journalize the following transactions on the books of Toys "Я" Us. Explanations are not required.

a. Purchase of the goods on May 6, 20X5.

✔ Starter 5-2
✔ Starter 5-3
✔ Starter 5-4

ASSETS	=	LIABILITIES	+	OWNER'S EQUITY
Inventory		Accounts Payable		
−$100	=	−$100	+	$0

the first

Stop & Think

On September 15, Austin Sound purchases $1,000 of merchandise on account, with terms 2/10, n/30. Austin returns $100 of merchandise for credit on September 20, then makes payment in full on September 25. Journalize these transactions.

Answer: Three separate journal entries are needed. The purchase entry is

1. **Purchase:** Sep. 15 Inventory.............................. 1,000
                              Accounts Payable................. 1,000

The second entry records the return of inventory, as follows:

2. **Return:** Sep. 20 Accounts Payable....................... 100
                              Inventory........................ 100

Accounts Payable

Return	100	Purchase	1,000
		Bal.	900

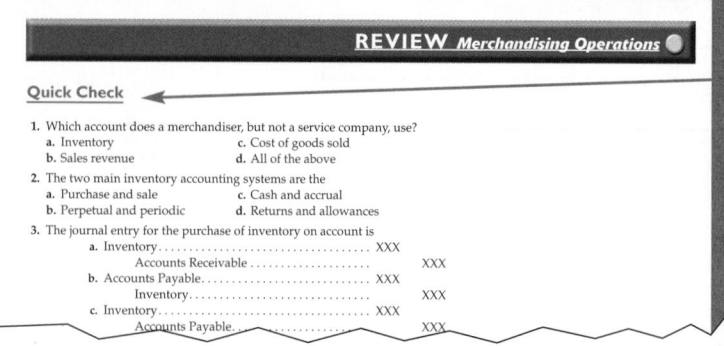

REVIEW *Merchandising Operations*

Quick Check

1. Which account does a merchandiser, but not a service company, use?
   a. Inventory   c. Cost of goods sold
   b. Sales revenue   d. All of the above
2. The two main inventory accounting systems are the
   a. Purchase and sale   c. Cash and accrual
   b. Perpetual and periodic   d. Returns and allowances
3. The journal entry for the purchase of inventory on account is
   a. Inventory.................................... XXX
        Accounts Receivable   XXX
   b. Accounts Payable........................... XXX
        Inventory..............................   XXX
   c. Inventory.................................... XXX
        Accounts Payable......................   XXX

New! Quick Check These new multiple-choice questions appear at the ends of chapters so you can test your understanding of material before taking multiple-choice exams. Answers to Quick Checks appear in Appendix D at the end of the book

Exercises and Problems Exercises and Problems give you plenty of practice in solving accounting dilemmas and checking your understanding of major concepts in the chapter.

E5-14 Marcia Walker's consulting practice performs systems consulting. Walker has also begun selling accounting software. During January, the business completed these transactions:

Accounting for both merchandising and service operations
(Obj. 1, 2, 4, 5)

Student Resource CD
General Ledger, Peachtree, QuickBooks

Jan. 2   Completed a consulting engagement and received cash of $7,200.
    2   Prepaid three months' office rent, $1,500.
    7   Purchased accounting software inventory on account, $4,000.
  16   Paid employee salary, $1,400.

A+ online homework

Explaining the perpetual inventory system
(Obj. 1, 2)

Problems
(Group A)

P5-1A Lens Masters is a regional chain of optical shops. The company offers a large selection of eyeglass frames, and Lens Masters stores provide while-you-wait service. The company has launched a vigorous advertising campaign to promote two-for-the-price-of-one frame sales.

Required

Lens Masters expects to grow rapidly and to increase its level of inventory. As the chief accountant of this company, you wish to install a perpetual inventory system. Write a one-paragraph business memo to the company president to explain how that system would work for the purchase and sale of eyeglasses. Use the following heading for your memo:

Cases A variety of cases, plus **Team Projects**—and **Comprehensive Problems** at the ends of groups of chapters—give you opportunities to practice decision-making in real business situations. Cases include **Decision Cases**, **Ethical Issues**, and **Financial Statement Cases** that use the **Amazon.com** annual report at the end of the book.

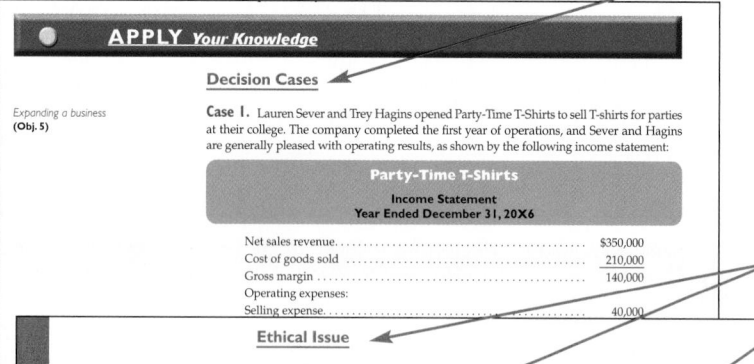

APPLY *Your Knowledge*

Decision Cases

Expanding a business
(Obj. 5)

Case 1. Lauren Sever and Trey Hagins opened Party-Time T-Shirts to sell T-shirts for parties at their college. The company completed the first year of operations, and Sever and Hagins are generally pleased with operating results, as shown by the following income statement:

Party-Time T-Shirts
Income Statement
Year Ended December 31, 20X6

Net sales revenue...	$350,000
Cost of goods sold	210,000
Gross margin	140,000
Operating expenses:	
Selling expense...	40,000

Ethical Issue

Hunter Glass Company makes all sales under terms of FOB shipping point. The company usually receives orders for sales approximately one week before shipping inventory to customers. For orders received late in December, Donny Hunter, the owner, decides when

Financial Statement Case

This case uses both the income statement (statement of operations) and the balance sheet of Amazon.com in Appendix A. It will help you understand the closing process of a business.

Closing entries and the gross profit percentage
(Obj. 4, 6)

Required

1. Journalize Amazon.com's closing entries for the revenues and expenses of 2002. Show all amounts in thousands as in the Amazon financial statements. You may be unfamiliar with certain revenues and expenses, but treat each item on the income statement as either a revenue or an expense. For example, Net Sales is the first revenue, and Interest Income is also a revenue. The last revenue is Cumulative Effect of Change in Accounting Principle. A loss is like an expense. In your closing entries

Team Project

With a small team of classmates, visit one or more merchandising businesses in your area. Interview a responsible official of the company to learn about its inventory policies and accounting system. Obtain answers to the following questions, write a report, and be prepared to make a presentation to the class if your instructor so directs:

Required

1. What merchandise inventory does the business sell?
2. From whom does the business buy its inventory? Is the relationship with the supplier new or longstanding?
3. What are the FOB terms on inventory purchases? Who pays the freight, the buyer or the seller? Is freight a significant amount? What percentage of total inventory cost is the freight?
4. What are the credit terms on inventory purchases—2/10 n/30, or other? Does the business pay early to get purchase discounts? If so, why? If not, why not?
5. How does the business actually pay its suppliers? Does it mail a check or pay elec-

Comprehensive Problem for Chapters 1–7

COMPLETING THE ACCOUNTING CYCLE FOR A MERCHANDISING ENTITY— USING SPECIAL JOURNALS

Digital Meter Company closes its books and prepares financial statements at the end of each month. Digital uses the perpetual inventory system. The company completed the following transactions during August:

Aug. 1   Issued check no. 682 for August office rent of $1,000. (Debit Rent Expense.)
    2   Issued check no. 683 to pay the salary payable of $1,250 from July 31.
    2   Issued invoice no. 503 for sale on account to R. T. Loeb, $600. Digital's cost of this merchandise was $190.
    3   Purchased inventory on credit terms of 1/15 n/60 from Grant, Inc., $1,400.

Study Aids And Resources

Throughout the book, margin icons indicate resources available on the **Student Resource CD**. Selected end-of-chapter problems appear in **spreadsheet templates** on the CD, and also in **General Ledger (GL)**, **QuickBooks (QB)**, and **Peachtree (PT)** formats. Other assignments are linked to Prentice Hall's new online homework program that includes a variety of assignments whose results feed directly into the grading program. The program includes algorithm-based problems, to give you extensive practice on a single concept.

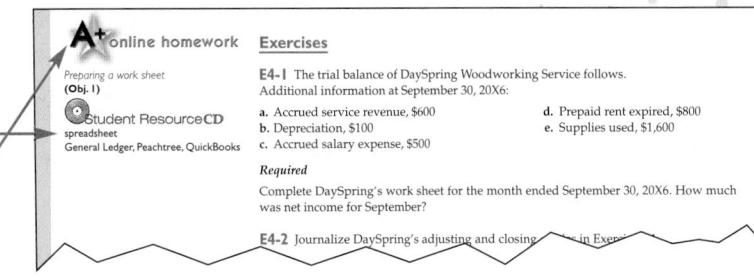

New Student and Instructor Resource CD-ROMs This innovative product includes all resources for the text—Powerpoint files, video clips, spreadsheet templates, tutorial software, General Ledger software, and Peachtree and QuickBooks software. You can access resources by chapter or by keyword (like "LIFO"). The student version of the CD allows you to create your own individualized review program. Free with new texts.

Text Icons

Study Guide This chapter-by-chapter learning aid systematically and effectively helps you study accounting and get the maximum benefit from study time. Each chapter provides a Chapter Overview and Review, a Featured Exercise that covers in a single exercise all of the most important topics in the chapter, and Review Questions and Exercises that test your understanding of the material.

Powerpoint slides help you review concepts by providing a summary of important points. *Remember!* You can choose to review **Powerpoints** by chapter or by keyword.

Video Clips include a series of **tutorial videos** designed to help you review concepts, plus **On Location! Videos** that take you inside companies such as **Jelly Belly** and **It's Just Lunch** to show you how managers use accounting information to make everyday business decisions. *Remember!* You can choose to review **videos** by chapter or by keyword.

Spreadsheet templates Selected end-of-chapter exercises and problems appear on pre-created templates for you to use in solving these assignments. If you need additional help in using Excel, you may opt to review the tutorial segment.

More Study Aids

General Ledger Software enables you to complete homework assignments using a general ledger software package. You may also enter and solve your own problems. E-Working Papers are available for each chapter.

New! Getting Started If your professor has chosen to package one of the Getting Started series manuals with your text, you may access the data files to use with the manuals.

Companion Website www.prenhall.com/horngren Prentice Hall's Learning on the Internet Partnership offers extensive Internet-based support. Our Web sites provide a wealth of free resources for you, including Student Study Hall, Online Tutorial Assistance, Study Guide with Quizzes, Internet Exercises, and much more.

For The Instructor

(A complete list of chapter-by-chapter highlights follows this overview)

Text & Assignment Material

- *New Amazon.com Annual Report & Financial Statement Analysis Cases!* New copies of the text now include the Amazon.com annual report. This is linked to many of the chapter-opening vignettes, and end-of-chapter financial statement analysis cases.

- *New Theme: Show More. Say Less.* Throughout the text, the authors have worked hard to tighten and focus the content on core topics in first year accounting.

- *New, more open and student-friendly design* includes many new exhibits to aid in student understanding.

- *New Chapter Organization.* The chapters on merchandising and inventory (previously Chapters 5 & 9) are now Chapters 5-6 to enable students to link these topics more easily.

- *New A+Tips* at each chapter opening list resources to help students learn key concepts; reminders appear within the chapter.

- *New Quick Check Questions.* New multiple-choice exercises at the ends of chapters enable students to test their understanding before taking multiple-choice examinations. Answers appear in Appendix D.

- *New Starters* (previously called "Daily Exercises") serve as warm-ups/ confidence builders at the beginning of the assignment material. Students solve these easy, single-concept exercises (many using real companies). Each problem is referenced to material within the chapter so that if students need more guidance, they know exactly what to review to complete the exercise.

- *New Excel Application Exercises*, now for each chapter in the book, with spreadsheet solutions.

Grading & Practice

- *New Peachtree, QuickBooks, and General Ledger Assignments.* Selected end-of-chapter problems are available on templates for Peachtree, QuickBooks, and General Ledger software. In addition, instructors may opt to package a brief introductory manual on the latest release of Peachtree or QuickBooks at no charge with new texts.

- *New Manual and Computerized Practice Sets* include optional exercises using Peachtree and QuickBooks. Package any Practice Set at 50% off with new texts.

- *New Automatic Homework Grading!* Prentice Hall's online homework program includes a variety of in-text assignments for students to complete online— and results feed directly into the grading program. The program includes

algorithm-based problems that enable students to have extensive practice on a single concept. They *reduce cheating* because two students sitting next to one another could see different versions of the problem (the instructor determines whether the problem is viewed in static or algorithm-based format). Students get extensive feedback to help them understand where they went wrong.

The New CD

Student ResourceCD

- *New Instructor and Student Resource CD-ROMs:* This innovative CD-ROM includes all resources for the text and allows instructors to create custom multi-media lectures in less than 5 minutes! Access the resources by chapter or keyword (e.g., "LIFO"). A student version of the CD enables students to create individualized review programs. Free with new texts.

Chapter-by-Chapter Highlights

CHAPTER 1   Accounting and the Business Environment

- New chapter opener focuses on **Amazon.com**, the feature company for this edition.
- Discussion of ethics in accounting features **Enron**, **WorldCom**, and **Xerox**.
- New illustration of the effects of transactions on balance sheet and income statement.

CHAPTER 2   Recording Business Transactions

- New chapter opener features **Frito-Lay**.
- New notations for journal entries clarify the rules of debit and credit.
- New roadmap shows how accounts, ledgers, journals, and the trial balance fit together.

CHAPTER 3   The Adjusting Process

- New notations for adjusting entries clarify the rules of debit and credit.
- New graphic shows the difference between the accrual basis and the cash basis.

CHAPTER 4   Completing the Accounting Cycle

- New chapter opener features the **Chicago Cubs** baseball team.
- New exhibit illustrates the closing process.
- Dell Computer's balance sheet illustrates the accounts covered to date.

CHAPTER 5   Merchandising Operations

- New chapter opener features **Amazon.com**.
- This completely revised chapter begins with purchase of merchandise, then moves to sales, all based on the perpetual system.

- Appendix on the periodic system.

CHAPTER 6   Merchandise Inventory

- New chapter opener features **Columbia Sportswear** and the **International Balloon Festival**.
- New exhibits! One shows the effect of merchandising on the financial statements; another shows FIFO, LIFO, and average costing; and others show the relationship between transactions in a perpetual system and related journal entries.
- New, streamlined coverage of accounting for inventory in a periodic system.

CHAPTER 7   Accounting Information Systems

- New discussion of Enterprise Resource Planning (ERP) systems.
- New explanation of the relationship between manual and computerized systems.

CHAPTER 8   Internal Control and Cash

- Discussion of the Sarbanes-Oxley Act and internal controls.
- Streamlined discussion of the bank reconciliation.
- New graphics: internal controls for cash receipts and cash payments.
- New: Enron examples to illustrate ethics in accounting.

CHAPTER 9   Receivables

- Simplified examples to illustrate accounting for uncollectibles.
- New graphics: integration of order entry, shipping, and billing of receivables.

CHAPTER 10 Plant Assets and Intangible Assets

- New chapter opener features airlines and their assets.
- New exhibit: relationship between plant assets and related expenses.
- New graphic: relative-sales-value method.
- Streamlined coverage of Depreciation and Income Taxes.
- Simplified coverage of Partial-Year Depreciation.
- Updated accounting for goodwill.

CHAPTER 11 Current Liabilities and Payroll

- New chapter opener features General Motors, Sony, and Goodyear.
- New graphic: how to allocate interest expense to the appropriate period.
- Streamlined accounting for sales tax payable.
- Beefed up—and streamlined—coverage of accounting for contingencies.
- Simplified payroll illustrations.
- Added Form 941, Employer's Quarterly Federal Tax Return.

CHAPTER 12 Partnerships

- New chapter opener on the fragility of partnerships, featuring the Arthur Andersen debacle.
- New graphics illustrate the various ways to start a partnership.

CHAPTER 13 Corporations: Paid-in Capital and the Balance Sheet

- New discussion of closing net income for a corporation.
- Streamlined accounting for income tax by a corporation.

CHAPTER 14 Retained Earnings, Treasury Stock, and the Income Statement

- New chapter opener features Coca-Cola, Dell Computer, and Pier 1 Imports.
- New graphic: retained earnings are not cash.
- New coverage of stock dividends.
- Scaled-down treatment of the corporate income statement.
- Simplified treatment of earnings per share.

CHAPTER 15 Long-term Liabilities

- Revised chapter opener features Amazon.com.

- New roadmap guides students through issuing bonds payable to borrow money.
- Deleted sections on Leases and Pensions.

CHAPTER 16 Investments and International Operations

- New chapter opener features McDonald's, Panasonic, and Nokia.
- Scaled-down coverage of accounting for international operations.

CHAPTER 17 The Statement of Cash Flows

- New chapter opener features eBay.
- Completely revised chapter: Two distinct sections for the indirect method and the direct method. Each section features step-by-step preparation of the statement.
- Scaled-down level of complexity for both methods—fewer accounts to analyze.
- New graphics: how cash is affected by changes in the other current accounts.

CHAPTER 18 Financial Statement Analysis

- New chapter opener features Bristol-Myers Squibb.
- Revised chapter organized around decisions and the need for financial statement analysis.
- New graphics illustrate horizontal analysis and vertical analysis.
- Scaled-down financial statements—fewer accounts to analyze.
- Revised discussions of the ratios—shorter paragraphs, fewer words.
- New section on Red Flags in Financial Statement Analysis.
- New section on Analyzing Nonfinancial Data.

CHAPTER 19 Introduction to Management Accounting

- New chapter opener and On Location! video on Regal Marine.
- New infographics.
- New exhibit simplifies and clarifies the distinction between merchandisers' and manufacturers' income statements.
- Simplified discussion of cost of goods manufactured, linking the flow of activities.
- Brief new discussion of ERP systems.

CHAPTER 20 Job Costing

- Updated chapter opener: why and how Dell figures the cost of a built-to-order computer.
- Emphasis on why all managers need to know how much it costs to produce a product or to serve a customer.
- Reorganized and simplified discussion of accounting for materials and labor.
- Exciting new team project asks students to compare the cost (and profits) of regular airlines' versus budget airlines' flights, using real-world data.

CHAPTER 21 Process Costing

- New chapter opener and **On Location!** video feature Jelly Belly.
- Text discussion uses Jelly Belly to illustrate key process costing principles.
- *First half* of chapter enables students to grasp the basics of process costing without complications caused by the presence of beginning work in process inventory. Instructors who prefer to introduce the basics of process costing can assign just the first half of the chapter. There is plenty of relevant assignment material.
- The *second half* of the chapter allows for beginning inventories. Scaled-back coverage focuses on the process costing method students find easiest to grasp—weighted average.
- Full and self-contained coverage of the more complex FIFO method appears in a new appendix. Instructors can add—or substitute—the FIFO-based appendix for the second half of the chapter.
- Several new Decision Guidelines emphasize the big picture—job versus process costing, the checks and balances in the 5-step process costing approach illustrated in the chapter, the goal of process costing, and how managers use the production cost report.

CHAPTER 22 Cost-Volume-Profit Analysis

- Streamlined presentation of variable, fixed, and mixed costs.
- Significantly reorganized chapter: Illustrations proceed from cost behavior, to basic CVP analysis, to using CVP analysis for profit planning, to conducting sensitivity analyses with CVP.
- Chapter midpoint now follows basic CVP analysis. This speed bump prompts students to reinforce their understanding of the basics.
- Significantly revised discussion of sensitivity analyses includes realistic business decision contexts for changing various components of the CVP analysis, covers the margin of safety, and explains how managers use information technology.

CHAPTER 23 The Master Budget and Responsibility Accounting

- New chapter opener features Amazon.com CEO Jeff Bezos' use of budgets to control costs.
- Focus on Amazon.com throughout chapter, including new Decision Guidelines contexts, new end-of-chapter multiple-choice questions, and several new infographics.
- New pedagogy moves from students' personal budgets, to a simple budget for a small company, to the main example featuring a retail store's budget, to how large companies use software to roll up individual unit budgets into the companywide budget.
- Emphasizes how managers *use* the budget to plan and control, and also considers behavioral issues such as tips for increasing employees' acceptance of the budget.
- New infographic organization chart coupled with a new exhibit showing a responsibility performance report illustrate how responsibility accounting works in a real-world context.

CHAPTER 24 The Flexible Budget and Standard Costs

- New introductory example based on students' daily life shows why variances are important guides to future action.
- Mid-chapter Decision Guidelines and new Excel exercise show how students can use flexible budgets and variances to plan and control costs in start-up businesses.
- New discussion of how managers set price and quantity standards.
- Significantly streamlined discussion of allocating manufacturing overhead in a standard costing system
- Streamlined explanation of overhead variances: more visuals, fewer words.

CHAPTER 25 Activity Based Costing and Other Cost Management Tools

- Streamlined and updated discussion of how managers use activity-based management in pricing, product mix, and cost-cutting decisions.

(continued)

(Chapter 25 continued)

- Streamlined discussion of when ABC passes the cost-benefit test.
- Simplified discussion of the just-in-time philosophy and total quality management.
- New Financial Statement Case highlights Amazon.com's unique activities as an e-tailer.

CHAPTER 26 Special Business Decisions and Capital Budgeting

- New graphics: decision rules for special short-term decisions such as special orders, product mix, and sell or process further.
- Simplified coverage of special sales orders.
- Discussion and new examples of the trend toward outsourcing all kinds of business functions.
- Simplified illustration of opportunity costs in the context of decisions on best use of facilities and outsourcing.
- New graphics: decision rules for long-term capital budgeting decisions.
- Simplified coverage of net present value.
- New Financial Statement Case asks students to apply payback, accounting rate of return, and discounted cash flow techniques to Amazon.com's investments.

Instructor Resources

Everything you need where you need it. The Prentice Hall Instructor Resource Center/CD-ROM increases your effectiveness and saves you time and effort. Harness the power of having all of your resources in one well-organized place. Because resources should simplify, not overwhelm.

Technology Resources: How Horngren Makes It Easier for You to Test and Grade

NEW! INSTRUCTOR AND STUDENT RESOURCE CD-ROMs

These CD's are powerful teaching and learning tools. They first serve as a roadmap through the chapters to identify key concepts and then guide students to other resources on the CD-ROM, where they can further develop their skills.

- Available in separate versions for faculty and students, this unique tool enables faculty to **save time** and **quickly prepare highly effective and interactive multimedia classroom presentations**.
- Using a **highly accessible menu**, students and faculty can easily customize study programs or presentations. By simply clicking on a chapter or keyword, they can access an interactive library of resources.
- Instructor's CD-ROM contains all ancillaries. Student CD-ROM contains tutorial software, On Location! video clips, PowerPoints, General Ledger software, Excel tutorial, spreadsheet templates, and much more.

These CD-ROMs also contain a special option for instructors who wish to build their own online courses! Faculty can pick and choose from the various supplements (organized by chapter and topic), and export them to their hard drive in HTML. From hard drive to online course is an easy step!

The IRCD contains all print and technology (e.g., spreadsheets, videos) supplements on a single CD-ROM. Enjoy the freedom to transport the entire package from office, to home, to classroom. This enables you to customize any of the ancillaries, print only the chapters or materials you wish to use, or access any item from the package within the classroom!

NEW! COMPUTERIZED ACCOUNTING PRACTICE SETS

Containing lots of simulated real-world examples, the **A-1 Photography** and **Runners Corporation** practice sets are available complete with data files for Peachtree, QuickBooks, and PH General Ledger. Each practice set also includes business stationery for manual entry work.

NEW! PRENTICE HALL AUTOMATIC HOMEWORK GRADING!

An outstanding Web-based homework solution. Students can work end-of-chapter problems at their own pace online. In addition, the algorithmically generated numbers ensure that problems are never repetitive.

NEW! GETTING STARTED SERIES

Upon request, faculty may package their choice of one of these approximately 70-page manuals on the latest professional accounting software packages with **Accounting, 6th ed.**, at no charge. Each manual introduces students to the concepts of Excel, Peachtree, QuickBooks, or PH General Ledger.

NEW! SPECIAL OFFERS - PROFESSIONAL ACCOUNTING SOFTWARE PACKAGES

Package your choice of the latest software releases of Peachtree or QuickBooks, for less than $15, with new text purchases.

- **General Ledger Software** General Ledger software enables students to complete homework assignments using a general ledger software package. Students may also enter and solve their own problems. Available on the Student CD-ROM, Instructor CD-ROM, and downloadable from Companion Web site.

- **Working Papers and e-Working Papers** Working Papers contain tailormade spreadsheets for all end-of-chapter Excel problems. A sample set of working papers is packaged free with every Student Resource CD-ROM.

- **INNOVATION! Standard Online Courses in WebCT, CourseCompass, and BlackBoard** Teach a complete online course or a Web-enhanced course. Add your own course materials, take advantage of online testing and Gradebook opportunities, and utilize the bulletin board and discussion board functions. Free upon request. This is an excellent time to build your own course using our CD-ROMs with your choice of platform.

- **Companion Web site www.prenhall.com/horngren** Prentice Hall's Learning on the Internet Partnership offers extensive Internet-based support. Our Web site provides a wealth of resources for students and faculty including: Student Study Hall, Online Tutorial Assistance, Study Guide with Quizzes, Internet Exercises, and much more.

More Instructor Resources: Horngren makes it easier for you to prepare your classes!

- **Annotated Instructor's Edition** Replete with teaching tips, real-world examples, short exercises, ethical insights, and discussion, this annotated edition is ideal for instructors wishing to augment their classroom discussions.

- **Instructor's Resource Manual** Each chapter of this comprehensive resource consists of a list of the student learning objectives, a narrative overview of main topics, and an outline with teaching tips interspersed.

- **Test Item File** The printed Test Item File consists of over 2,900 questions, including true/false questions, conceptual and quantitative multiple-choice questions, critical thinking problems, and exercises. Each question identifies the difficulty level and the corresponding learning objective. Prentice Hall TestGenEQ can create exams, and evaluate and track student results. New to this edition are algorithmically generated conceptual questions integrated throughout the TestGen.

- **Solutions Manual** In addition to fully worked-out and accuracy-checked solutions for every question, exercise, problem, and case in the text, this manual provides a categorization of assignment material. In addition, every page of the Solutions Manual has been reproduced in acetate form for use on the overhead projector.

- **On Location! Videos** These brief videos take students "on location" to real companies where real accounting situations are discussed and explained.

Acknowledgments

Special Thanks to:

Professor Michael Bamber of the University of Georgia for his substantive contributions to the ethics cases and team projects in Chapters 19–26.

Professor Lynn Mazzola of Nassau Community College for her help in checking assignment material and reading the text of Chapters 19–26.

Professors Becky Jones and Betsy Willis for writing the Instructor's Manual and Professor Jones for coordinating the accuracy checking of the Solutions Manual.

Professor Robert Bauman of Allan Hancock College for providing the annotations for the Instructor's Edition.

Pradeep Nagar at the University of Georgia for helping ensure the clarity and accuracy of all the assignments in Chapters 19–26.

Writer Nancy Brandwein for the Accounting.com boxes.

We also want to thank the reviewers of the Sixth Edition and the Focus Group participants, who gave of their time and talents to help us streamline the new edition and focus on the essentials. We especially want to thank the reviewers of Chapters 5 and 6, who provided so many useful comments and suggestions.

Finally, we want to thank the hard-working members of our Prentice Hall team, all of whom contributed so much to this edition: P. J. Boardman, editor-in-chief; Jeannine Ciliotta, senior development editor; Beth Toland, executive marketing manager; Sam Goffinet, assistant editor; Jane Avery, senior editorial assistant; Melene Kubat, administrative assistant; Steve Frim, designer; Anne Graydon, production editor; Arnold Vila, production manager; Christy Mahon, manager, multimedia production; and Nancy Welcher, media project manager.

Reviewers of Accounting, 6th ed.

[alphabetized by school]

Jenny Davis *Angelo State University*
Paulette Ratliff *Arkansas State University*
Frank Marino *Assumption College*
Terry Willyard *Baker College*
Charles Birnberg *Bergen Community College*
Robert D. Collmier *Bloomfield College*
Bonnie Giraldi *Cecil Community College*
Jeffrey Jones *Community College of Southern Nevada*
Kimberly Smith *County College of Morris*
Patty Holmes
Tom Turner *DesMoines Area Community College*
Rachel Ezelle *East Mississippi Community College*
John L. Stancil *Florida Southern College*
Rebecca Floor *Greenville Tech*
Linda Tarrago *Hillsborough Community College*
Judy Isonhood *Hinds Community College*
Cynthia Beier-Greeson
Warren Smock
Cynthia Vanoosterum *Ivy Tech State College*
Suzie Cordes *Johnson County Community College*
Tara Laken *Joliet Junior College*
Ron Carlin *Lamar University-Pt. Arthur*
Susan Logorda *Lehigh Carbon Community College*
Fred R. Jex *Macomb Community College*
David Grooms *Maui Community College*
Bruce Swindle *McNeese State University*
Josie Mathias *Mercer County Community College*

Judith Garcia *Miami Dade Community College—ESL*
Pamela Bogart *University of Michigan—ESL*
Joe Flynn *Moraine Valley Community College*
Cheryl McKay *Monroe County Community College*
Laura Prosser *National American University*
Laura Ilcisin *University of Nebraska*
Toni Clegg *Palm Beach Community College*
Randy Kidd *Penn Valley*
Shifei Chung
Stephanie Weidman *Rowan Community College*
Merrily Hoffman
Jeff Jackson
Randall Whitmore *San Jacinto College Central*
Patricia Halliday *Santa Monica College*
Ann Gregory *South Plains College*
Patricia Novak *Southeast Community College*
Gloria Worthy *Southwest Tennessee Community College*
Jack Fatica *Terra Community College*
Tracy Burdis *Sylvan Learning Center*
Julie Dailey *Tidewater Community College*
Michael Stemkoski *Utah Valley State College*
Chuck Bunn *Wake Tech*
Clyde Galbraith *West Chester University*
Jerry Kreuze *Western Michigan University*
Jim Murray *Western Wisconsin Technical College*
Rajeev Parikh *Wilmington College*

Focus Group Participants

Sheila Arnouts
Thomas Badley *Baker College*
Janet Grange *Chicago State University*
William Harvey *Henry Ford Community College*
Linda Tarrago *Hillsborough Community College*
Dennis Valenti *Hudson County Community College*
Shirley Glass
Fred R. Jex *Macomb Community College*

Cheryl McKay *Monroe County Community College*
Nashwa George *Montclair State University*
Zach Holmes
Meg Costello Lambert *Oakland Community College*
Daniel Clark *Owens Community College*
Patricia Halliday *Santa Monica College*
Ruth Henderson *Union County College*
Michael Stemkoski *Utah Valley State College*

Resource Authors and Technical Reviewers

Instructor's Manual

Becky Jones, *Baylor University*

Betsy Willis, *Baylor University*

Alice Sineath, *Forsyth Technical Community College*

Solutions Manual & Solutions Transparencies

Charles T. Horngren, *Stanford University*

Walter T. Harrison, *Baylor University*

Linda Smith Bamber, *University of Georgia*

Working Papers

Ellen Sweatt, *Georgia Perimeter College*

Test Item File

Alice Sineath, *Forsyth Technical Community College*

Study Guide

Ann B. DeCapite

A1 Photography & Runner's Corporation Practice Sets

Jean Insinga, *Middlesex Community College*

On Location! Videos

Beverly Amer, *Northern Arizona University*

Companion Web site Online Student Self-Tests

Timothy Carse

Online Courses (WebCT, Blackboard, CourseCompass)

PowerPoints by Timothy Carse, with audio developed and created by Beverly Amer, *Northern Arizona University*. Original course content by Tony Fortini, *Camden Community College*, revised by Beverly Amer

Prentice Hall's Online Homework Program

Larry Kallio of the *Universtiy of Minnesota at Mankato*, with many thanks to Nancy Welcher of PH Business Publishing for extensive project coordination and support.

TestGenEQ Software

Alice B. Sineath, with algorithms selected and created by Alfonse Oddo of *Niagara University*. Software by Tamarack Software, Inc.

Student Resource CD-ROM

Instructor's Resource CD-ROM

PowerPoint Presentations by Olga Quintana of the *University of Miami*.
PH General Ledger by Jean Insinga and Carol Goetters. Spreadsheet Templates by Al Fisher of the *Community College of Southern Nevada*. Instructions to the templates provided by Diane Fisher & Associates.

Technical Reviewers

Lynn Mazzola, *Nassau Community College*; Robert Bauman, *Allan Hancock College*; Carolyn Stroebel; Becky Jones, *Baylor University*; Timothy Carse; Tom How; Pradeep Nagar, *University of Georgia*

Accounting and the Business Environment

TIPS CHECK YOUR RESOURCES

- Visit the www.prenhall.com/horngren **Web site** for self-study quizzes, video clips, and other resources

- Try the **Quick Check** exercise at the end of the chapter to test your knowledge

- Learn the **key terms**

- Do the **Starter** exercises keyed in the margins

- Work the **end-of-chapter summary problems**

- Use the **Concept Links** to review material in other chapters

- Search the **CD** for review materials by chapter or by key word

- Watch the **tutorial videos** to review key concepts

- Watch the **On Location Accounting and Business** video for an overview of the accounting function.

LEARNING OBJECTIVES

1 Use accounting vocabulary

2 Apply accounting concepts and principles

3 Use the accounting equation

4 Analyze business transactions

5 Prepare the financial statements

6 Evaluate business performance

Like most other people, you've probably bought Amazon.com products by shopping online. And like most other people, you've probably been amazed at how easy it is. Amazon.com is one of the most interesting organizations on earth. Consider these facts about the company:

- Amazon.com opened its virtual doors in 1995.
- In only a few years, millions of people in 220 countries have made it the world's leading online shopping site.
- It offers the world's largest selection of products.
- On Amazon.com's busiest shopping day of 2002, customers ordered 1.7 million units. That's 20 items per second, around the clock.
- There is still no Amazon.com store anywhere except online.

Amazon.com

Amazon.com continues to add partners and merchandise at breakneck speed. But it took from 1995 to 2002 for the company to post a profit. And it reported the figures using standard accounting methods.

What does all this mean? What does "profitable" mean? What are standard accounting methods? How can a company keep growing if it isn't making money? Lots of questions: And here's where accounting comes in. "Profitable" means that the company earns more revenue than its expenses. Accounting methods govern how companies keep track of their activities. This book will help you understand revenues, expenses, profit and loss, and other business concepts. After completing this first accounting course, you will be able to decide whether a company is a good (or bad) investment. You will be able to evaluate an auto loan and manage your own money. You will also be able to use accounting in your business career. ■

■Sitemap

Student ResourceCD

financial statements

⭐ *Use accounting vocabulary*

Accounting
The information system that measures business activities, processes that information into reports, and communicates the results to decision makers.

Financial Statements
Documents that report on a business in monetary amounts, providing information to help people make informed business decisions.

We'll start our study with a small, single-person business known as a proprietorship. We need to begin by asking exactly what accounting is.

Accounting: The Language of Business

Accounting is the information system that measures business activity, processes the information into reports, and communicates the results to decision makers. Accounting is "the language of business." The better you understand the language, the better your decisions will be, and the better you can manage your finances. For example, how will you decide whether to borrow money? You had better consider your income: The concept of income comes straight from accounting.

A key product of accounting is a set of documents called financial statements. **Financial statements** report on a business in monetary terms. Is Amazon.com making a profit? Should Amazon expand? Answering these questions calls for Amazon's financial statements.

Exhibit 1-1 illustrates the role of accounting in business. The process starts and ends with people making decisions.

| Exhibit 1-1 | The Accounting System: The Flow of Information |

People make decisions | Business transactions occur | Businesses prepare reports to show the results of their operations

Decision Makers: The Users of Accounting Information

Decision makers need information. The bigger the decision, the greater the need. Here are some decision makers who use accounting information.

INDIVIDUALS You use accounting information to manage your bank account, evaluate a new job prospect, and decide whether to rent or buy a house. Amazon.com employees in Seattle, Washington, make the same decisions that you do.

BUSINESSES Managers use accounting information to set goals for their organizations. They also evaluate progress toward those goals, and they take corrective action when it's needed. For example, Amazon must decide which software to purchase, how many DVDs and books to keep on hand, and how much money to borrow. Accounting provides the information for making these decisions.

INVESTORS Investors provide the money to get a business going. To decide whether to invest, a person predicts the amount of income on the investment. This means analyzing the financial statements and keeping up with company developments—using, for example, www.yahoo.com (click on Finance), www.hoovers.com (click on Companies), the SEC's EDGAR database, and *The Wall Street Journal*.

CREDITORS Before lending money, a bank evaluates the borrower's ability to make the payments. This evaluation includes a report on the borrower's financial position and predicted income. To borrow money before striking it rich, Jeff Bezos, the president of Amazon.com, probably had to document his income and financial position.

GOVERNMENT REGULATORY AGENCIES Most organizations face government regulation. For example, the Securities and Exchange Commission (SEC), a federal agency, requires businesses to report their financial information to the public.

TAXING AUTHORITIES Local, state, and federal governments levy taxes. Income tax is figured using accounting information. Sales tax depends upon a company's sales.

NONPROFIT ORGANIZATIONS Nonprofit organizations—churches, hospitals, and colleges—use accounting information the same way as Amazon.com and The Coca-Cola Company.

Financial Accounting and Management Accounting

Accounting can be divided into two fields—financial accounting and management accounting.

Financial accounting provides information for people outside the company. Lenders and outside investors are not part of day-to-day management. These people use the company's financial statements. Chapters 2–18 of this book deal primarily with financial accounting.

Financial Accounting
The branch of accounting that focuses on information for people outside the firm.

Management accounting focuses on information for internal decision makers, such as the company's executives and the administrators of a hospital. Chapters 19 through 26 cover management accounting. Exhibit 1-2 illustrates the difference between financial accounting and management accounting.

Management Accounting
The branch of accounting that focuses on information for internal decision makers of a business.

Exhibit 1-2   Financial Accounting and Management Accounting

Investors:	Amazon.com	Creditors:
Should we invest in Amazon.com? Is the company profitable? Investors use financial accounting information to measure profitability.	Jeff Bezos, president, and other managers use management accounting information to operate the company.	Should we lend money to Amazon.com? Can the company pay us back? Creditors use financial accounting information to decide whether to make a loan.

Student Resource**CD**

ethics

Financial Accounting Standards Board (FASB)
The private organization that determines how accounting is practiced in the United States.

Certified Public Accountant (CPA)
A licensed accountant who serves the general public rather than one particular company.

Exhibit 1-3

Key Accounting Organizations

Regulating Accounting

All professions have regulations. Let's see the organizations that most influence the accounting profession.

Governing Organizations

In the United States, a private organization called the **Financial Accounting Standards Board (FASB)** formulates accounting standards. The FASB works with a governmental agency, the SEC, and two private groups, the American Institute of Certified Public Accountants (AICPA) and the Institute of Management Accountants (IMA). **Certified public accountants**, or **CPAs**, are professional accountants who are licensed to serve the general public. **Certified management accountants**, or **CMAs**, are professional accountants who work for a single company. Both groups of accountants have passed qualifying exams.

The rules that govern public accounting information are called *generally accepted accounting principles (GAAP)*. Exhibit 1-3 diagrams the relationships among the various accounting organizations.

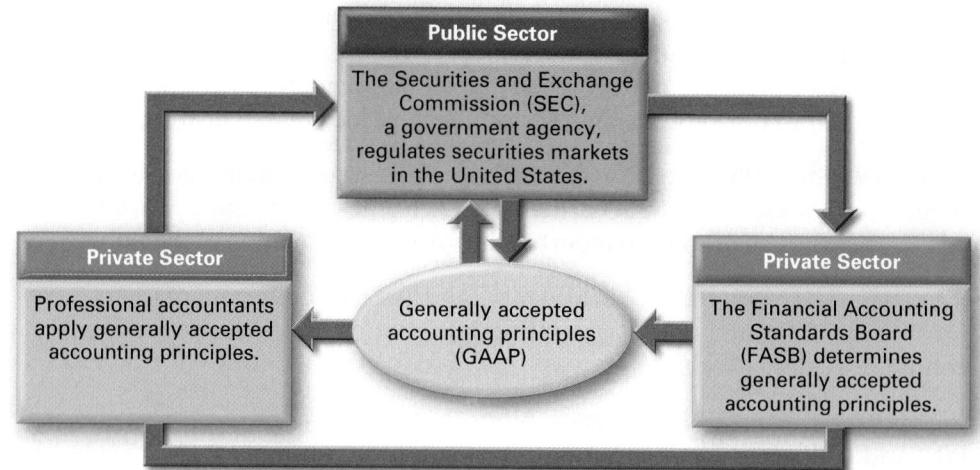

Certified Management Accountant (CMA)
A licensed accountant who works for a single company.

Audit
An examination of a company's financial situation.

Ethics in Accounting and Business

Ethical considerations affect everything accountants do. Investors and creditors need relevant and reliable information about a company such as Amazon.com or General Motors. The companies naturally want to make themselves look as good as possible in order to attract investors. There is potential for conflict here. To provide reliable information for the public, the SEC requires companies to have their financial statements audited by independent accountants. An **audit** is a financial examination. The accountants then certify that the financial statements give a true picture of the company's situation.

The vast majority of accountants do their jobs quietly, professionally, and ethically. We never hear about them. Unfortunately, only those who bend the rules make the headlines. In recent years we've seen more accounting scandals than at any time since the 1920s.

Enron Corp., for example, was the seventh-largest company in the United States before the company admitted reporting fewer debts than it really owed. WorldCom, a major long-distance telephone provider, admitted accounting for expenses as though they were assets (resources). Xerox Corp. was accused of manipulating reported profits. These and other scandals rocked the business community and hurt investor confidence. Innocent people lost their jobs, and the stock market suffered. The courts are still sorting out who was responsible for the flawed information and its consequences.

The New Economy: Pumping Up Revenue via Round-Trip Trades

The stock market can get obsessed with revenue, and that can put intense pressure on companies to boost their revenue figures. "Round-trip trades" are one technique for reporting high revenues. These deals typically involve a swap of assets or services without any real gains. Two companies get together and set a price for advertising on each other's Web sites at, say, $1 million. They then swap banners and each declares $1 million as revenue and $1 million for expenses—but not a single penny changes hands. Here are some examples:

- In 1999, the women's Web site iVillage revealed that 20% of its revenue came from round-trip trades of online advertising.
- In 2001, CMS Energy and Dynegy completed two electricity trades worth $1.7 billion on Dynegy's online trading platform. The trades cancelled each other out, but the companies cited the artificially boosted revenues in their press releases.
- With revenues lagging, telecom companies Global Crossing and Qwest began booking revenue from capacity swaps in 1999.

The SEC began investigating round-trip trades when it learned that many of the transactions served only to inflate revenue, and in 2002 it barred telecom trades that inflate revenue. Earlier, in 1999, the FASB forced companies to disclose online advertising swaps as "barter revenue." Yet, scrutiny from shareholders and accounting regulatory agencies hasn't stopped everyone.

Homestore, Inc., an online real estate company, and America Online are now under investigation for complex multiparty deals in which Homestore allegedly bought products from a third company, which then bought ads on America Online. The days of round-trip trades may be over.

Based on: Dennis K. Berman, Julia Angwin, and Chip Cummins, "What's Wrong?—Tricks of the Trade: As Market Bubble Neared End, Bogus Swaps Provided a Lift," *The Wall Street Journal*, December 23, 2002, p. A1. David Wessel, "What's Wrong?—Venal Sins: Why the Bad Guys of the Boardroom Emerged en Masse," *The Wall Street Journal*, June 20, 2002, p. A1. Susan Pulliam and Rebecca Blumenstein, "SEC Broadens Investigation into Revenue-Boosting Tricks," *The Wall Street Journal*, May 16, 2002, p. A1.

Standards of Professional Conduct

The AICPA's Code of Professional Conduct for Accountants provides guidance to CPAs in their work. Ethical standards are designed to produce relevant and reliable information for decision making. The preamble to the Code states: "[A] certified public accountant assumes an obligation of self-discipline above and beyond the requirements of laws and regulations . . . [and] an unswerving commitment to honorable behavior. . . . "

The opening paragraph of the Standards of Ethical Conduct of the Institute of Management Accountants (IMA) states: "Management accountants have an obligation to the organizations they serve, their profession, the public, and themselves to maintain the highest standards of ethical conduct." The requirements are similar to those in the AICPA code.

Most corporations also set standards of ethical conduct for employees. For example, The Boeing Company, a leading manufacturer of aircraft, has a highly developed set of business conduct guidelines. The chairperson of the board states: "We owe our success as much to our reputation for integrity as we do to the quality and dependability of our products and services. This reputation is

Student ResourceCD

corporation, partnership, proprietorship

Proprietorship
A business with a single owner.

Partnership
A business with two or more owners.

Corporation
A business owned by stockholders; it begins when the state approves its articles of incorporation. A corporation is a legal entity, an "artificial person," in the eyes of the law.

Stockholder
A person who owns stock in a corporation. Also called a **shareholder**.

fragile and can easily be lost." As one chief executive has stated, "Ethical practice is simply good business."

Truth is always better than dishonesty—in accounting, in business, and in life.

Types of Business Organizations

A business can have one of three forms of organization: proprietorship, partnership, or corporation. You should understand the differences among the three.

PROPRIETORSHIPS A **proprietorship** has a single owner, called the proprietor, who is often the manager. Proprietorships tend to be small retail stores or professional businesses, such as physicians, attorneys, and accountants. From the accounting viewpoint, each proprietorship is distinct from its proprietor: The accounting records of the proprietorship do *not* include the proprietor's personal financial records. However, from a legal perspective, the business *is* the proprietor. In this book, we begin the accounting process with a proprietorship.

PARTNERSHIPS A **partnership** joins two or more individuals as co-owners. Each owner is a partner. Many retail establishments and professional organizations of physicians, attorneys, and accountants are partnerships. Most partnerships are small or medium-sized, but some are gigantic, exceeding 2,000 partners. Accounting treats the partnership as a separate organization, distinct from the personal affairs of each partner. But again, from a legal perspective, a partnership *is* the partners.

CORPORATIONS A **corporation** is a business owned by **stockholders**, or **shareholders**. These are the people who own shares of ownership in the business. A business becomes a corporation when the state approves its articles of incorporation. A corporation is a legal entity that conducts business in its own name. Unlike the proprietorship and the partnership, the corporation is not defined by its owners.

Corporations differ significantly from proprietorships and partnerships in another way. If a proprietorship or a partnership cannot pay its debts, lenders can take the owners' personal assets—their cash—to satisfy the business's obligations. But if a corporation goes bankrupt, lenders cannot take the personal assets of the stockholders. This *limited liability* of stockholders for corporate debts explains why corporations are so popular: People can invest in corporations with limited personal risk.

Another factor in corporate growth is the division of ownership into individual shares. The Coca-Cola Company, for example, has billions of shares of stock owned by many stockholders. An investor with no personal relationship to Coca-Cola can become a stockholder by buying 50, 100, 5,000, or any number of shares of its stock.

Exhibit 1-4 summarizes the differences among the three types of business organization.

Exhibit 1-4 Comparison of the Three Forms of Business Organization

	Proprietorship	Partnership	Corporation
1. Owner(s)	Proprietor—there is only one owner	Partners—there are two or more owners	Stockholders—there are generally many owners
2. Life of the organization	Limited by the owner's choice, or death	Limited by the owners' choices, or death	Indefinite
3. Personal liability of the owner(s) for the business's debts	Proprietor is personally liable	Partners are personally liable	Stockholders are not personally liable
4. Legal status of the organization	The proprietorship is the proprietor	The partnership is the partners	The corporation is separate from the stockholders

Accounting Concepts and Principles

The rules that govern accounting fall under the heading **GAAP**, which stands for **generally accepted accounting principles**. GAAP is the "law" of accounting— rules for providing the information that is acceptable to the majority of Americans.

GAAP rests on a conceptual framework written by the FASB: *The primary objective of financial reporting is to provide information useful for making investment and lending decisions*. To be useful, information must be relevant, reliable, and comparable. We begin the discussion of GAAP by introducing basic accounting concepts and principles.

Student ResourceCD

accounting principles

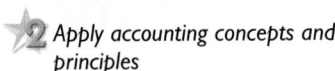

Apply accounting concepts and principles

The Entity Concept

The most basic concept in accounting is that of the **entity**. An accounting entity is an organization or a section of an organization that stands apart as a separate economic unit. In accounting, boundaries are drawn around each entity so as not to confuse its affairs with those of other entities.

Consider Amazon.com. Assume Jeff Bezos started Amazon.com on his own. Suppose he began with $5,000 obtained from a bank loan. Following the entity concept, Bezos would account for the $5,000 separately from his personal assets, such as his clothing, house, and automobile. To mix the $5,000 of business cash with his personal assets would make it difficult to measure the financial position of Amazon.com.

Consider Toyota, a huge organization with several divisions. Toyota management evaluates each division as a separate accounting entity. If sales in the Lexus division are dropping, Toyota can find out why. But if sales figures from all divisions of the company are combined, management will not know that Lexus sales are going down. Thus, the entity concept applies *to any economic unit that needs to be evaluated separately*.

Generally Accepted Accounting Principles (GAAP)
Accounting guidelines, formulated by the Financial Accounting Standards Board, that govern how accountants measure, process, and communicate financial information.

Entity
An organization or a section of an organization that, for accounting purposes, stands apart from other organizations and individuals as a separate economic unit.

The Reliability (Objectivity) Principle

Accounting information is based on the most reliable data available. This guideline is the *reliability principle*, also called the *objectivity principle*. Reliable data are verifiable. They may be confirmed by any independent observer. For example, an Amazon.com bank loan is supported by a promissory note. This is objective evidence of the loan. Without the reliability principle, accounting data might be based on whims and opinions.

Suppose you want to open an electronics store. For a store location, you transfer a small building to the business. You believe the building is worth $150,000. To confirm its cost to the business, you hire two real estate appraisers, who value the building at $140,000. Which is the more reliable estimate of the building's value, your estimate of $150,000 or the $140,000 professional appraisal? The appraisal of $140,000 is more reliable because it is supported by an independent observation. The business should record the building cost as $140,000.

The Cost Principle

The *cost principle* states that acquired assets and services should be recorded at their actual cost (also called *historical cost*). Even though the purchaser may believe the price is a bargain, the item is recorded at the price actually paid and not at the "expected" cost. Suppose your electronics store purchases TV equipment from a supplier who is going out of business. Assume that you get a good deal and pay only $2,000 for equipment that would have cost you $3,000 elsewhere. The cost principle requires you to record the equipment at its actual cost of $2,000, not the $3,000 that you believe the equipment is worth.

The cost principle also holds that the accounting records should maintain the historical cost of an asset over its useful life. Why? Because cost is a reliable measure. Suppose your store holds the TV equipment for six months. During that time TV prices rise, and the equipment can be sold for $3,500. Should its accounting value—the figure "on the books"—be the actual cost of $2,000 or the current market value of $3,500? By the cost principle, the accounting value of the equipment remains at actual cost: $2,000.

You are considering the purchase of land for future expansion. The seller is asking $50,000 for land that cost her $35,000. An appraisal shows a value of $47,000. You first offer $44,000. The seller counteroffers with $48,000, and you agree on a price of $46,000. What dollar value for this land is reported on your financial statement? Which accounting concept or principle guides your answers?

Answer: According to the cost principle, assets and services should be recorded at their actual cost. You paid $46,000 for the land, so report the land at $46,000.

The Going-Concern Concept

Another reason for measuring assets at historical cost is the *going-concern concept*. This concept assumes that the entity will remain in operation for the foreseeable future. Under the going-concern concept, accountants assume that the business will remain in operation long enough to use existing resources for their intended purpose.

To understand the going-concern concept better, consider the alternative—which is to go out of business. A store holding a going-out-of-business sale is trying to sell everything. In that case, instead of historical cost, the relevant measure is current market value. But going out of business is the exception rather than the rule.

The Stable-Monetary-Unit Concept

In the United States, we record transactions in dollars because the dollar is the medium of exchange. British accountants record transactions in pounds sterling. French and German transactions are measured in euros. The Japanese record transactions in yen. The value of a dollar or a Mexican peso changes over time. A rise in the price level is called *inflation*. During inflation, a dollar will purchase less milk, less gas for your car, and less of other goods. When prices are stable—when there is little inflation—the purchasing power of money is also stable.

Accountants assume that the dollar's purchasing power is stable. It allows us to add and subtract dollar amounts as though each dollar has the same purchasing power as any other dollar at any other time.

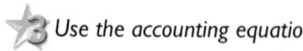
Student ResourceCD

accounting equation, asset, liability, owner's equity

⭐ *Use the accounting equation*

Accounting Equation
The basic tool of accounting, measuring the resources of the business and the claims to those resources: Assets = Liabilities + Owner's Equity.

Asset
An economic resource that is expected to be of benefit in the future.

The Accounting Equation

The basic tool of accounting is the **accounting equation**. It measures the resources of a business and the claims to those resources.

Assets and Liabilities

Assets are economic resources that are expected to be of benefit in the future. Cash, merchandise inventory, furniture, and land are assets.

Claims to those assets come from two sources. **Liabilities** are *outsider* claims—debts that are payable to outsiders. These outside parties are called *creditors*. For example, a creditor who has loaned money to Amazon.com has a claim to some of Amazon's assets until Amazon pays the debt.

Exhibit 1-5

11

The Accounting Equation

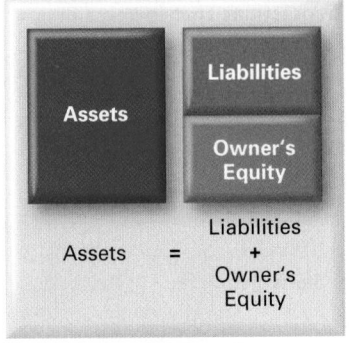

Insider claims to Amazon.com's assets are called **owner's equity**, or **capital**. These insider claims are held by the owners of the business. Owners have a claim to some of the assets because they have invested in the business.

The accounting equation shows how assets, liabilities, and owner's equity are related. Assets appear on the left side of the equation, and the liabilities and owner's equity appear on the right side. Exhibit 1-5 shows that the two sides must always be equal:

(Economic Resources)		(Claims to Economic Resources)
ASSETS	=	LIABILITIES + OWNER'S EQUITY

1. If the assets of a business are $170,000 and the liabilities total $80,000, how much is the owner's equity?
2. If the owner's equity in a business is $22,000 and the liabilities are $36,000, how much are the assets?

Answers: To answer both questions, use the accounting equation:

1.

ASSETS	–	LIABILITIES	=	OWNER'S EQUITY
$170,000	–	$80,000	=	$90,000

2.

ASSETS	=	LIABILITIES	+	OWNER'S EQUITY
$58,000	=	$36,000	+	$22,000

Liability
An economic obligation (a debt) payable to an individual or an organization outside the business.

Owner's Equity
The claim of a business owner to the assets of the business. Also called **capital**.

Here is an example that illustrates the elements of the accounting equation. Sony supplies cell phones to Amazon.com. Amazon may buy the cell phones on credit and promise to pay Sony later. Sony's claim against Amazon.com is an **account receivable**, an asset that will benefit Sony. A *written* promise for future collection is called a **note receivable**.

Amazon.com has a debt to pay Sony. This liability is an **account payable**. It is backed only by the reputation and the credit standing of Amazon. A written promise of future payment is called a **note payable**.

All receivables are assets. All payables are liabilities. Most businesses have both receivables and payables.

Owner's Equity

Owner's equity is the amount of an entity's assets that remain after its liabilities are subtracted.

$$\text{ASSETS} - \text{LIABILITIES} = \text{OWNER'S EQUITY}$$

The purpose of business is to increase owner's equity through revenues. **Revenues** are increases in owner's equity earned by delivering goods or services to customers. Revenues also increase assets, or they decrease liabilities. As a result, the owner's share of the business's assets increases. Exhibit 1-6 shows that owner investments and revenues increase the owner's equity of the business.

Account Receivable
A promise to receive cash from customers to whom the business has sold goods or for whom the business has performed services.

Note Receivable
A written promise for future collection of cash.

Account Payable
A liability backed by the general reputation and credit standing of the debtor.

Note Payable
A written promise of future payment.

Revenue
Amounts earned by delivering goods or services to customers. Revenues increase owner's equity.

Exhibit 1-6

Transactions That Increase or
Decrease Owner's Equity

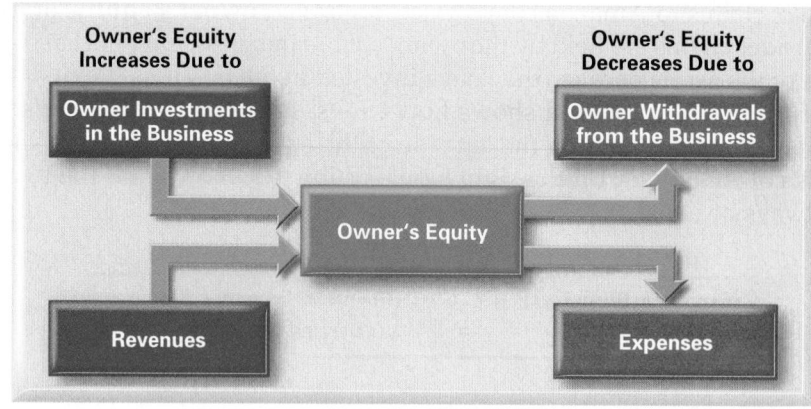

✔ Starter 1-1

✔ Starter 1-2

Owner Withdrawals
Amounts removed from the business
by an owner.

Expense
Decrease in owner's equity that occurs
from using assets or increasing
liabilities in the course of delivering
goods or services to customers.

✔ Starter 1-3

✔ Starter 1-4

Student ResourceCD

transaction analysis

Transaction
An event that affects the financial
position of a particular entity and can
be recorded reliably.

Exhibit 1-6 also shows that owner withdrawals and expenses decrease owner's equity. **Owner withdrawals** are amounts removed from the business by the owner. Withdrawals are the opposite of owner investments. **Expenses** are decreases in owner's equity that occur from using assets or increasing liabilities to deliver goods and services to customers. Expenses are the cost of doing business; they are the opposite of revenues. Expenses include the cost of:

- Office rent
- Salaries of employees
- Advertisements
- Utility payments

- Interest on loans
- Insurance
- Property taxes
- Supplies used up

Accounting for Business Transactions

Accounting records are based on actual transactions. A **transaction** is any event that affects the financial position of the business *and* can be recorded reliably. Many events affect a company, including elections and economic booms. Accountants do not record the effects of those events because they can't be measured reliably. An accountant records only those events with effects that can be measured reliably, such as the purchase of a building, a sale of merchandise to a customer, and the payment of rent. The dollar amounts of these events can be measured reliably, so accountants record these transactions.

What are some of your personal transactions? You may have bought a DVD player. Your purchase was a transaction. If you are making payments on an auto loan, your payments are also transactions. You need to record all your business transactions just as Amazon.com does in order to manage your personal affairs.

To illustrate accounting for a business, let's use Gay Gillen eTravel. Gillen operates a travel agency. Online customers plan and pay for their trips through the Gillen Web site. The Web site is linked to airlines, hotels, and cruise lines, so clients can obtain the latest information 24 hours a day, 7 days a week. Gillen's Web site allows the agency to transact more business than it could through the phone, fax, or e-mail. As a result, Gillen can operate with few employees, and this saves on expenses. She can pass along the cost savings to clients by charging them lower commissions. That builds up her business.

Now let's analyze some of Gillen eTravel's transactions.

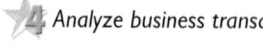

Analyze business transactions

TRANSACTION 1: STARTING THE BUSINESS   Gay Gillen invests $30,000 of her own money to start the business. She deposits $30,000 in a bank account titled Gay Gillen eTravel. The effect of this transaction on the accounting equation of the Gay Gillen eTravel business entity is

ASSETS		LIABILITIES		OWNER'S EQUITY	TYPE OF OWNER'S EQUITY TRANSACTION
Cash	=		+	Gay Gillen, Capital	
(1) +30,000				+30,000	Owner investment

For every transaction, the amount on the left side of the equation must equal the amount on the right side. The first transaction increases both the assets (in this case, Cash) and the owner's equity (Gay Gillen, Capital) of the business. To the right of the transaction, we write "Owner investment" to keep track of the source of the owner's equity.

Immediately after this first transaction, Gay Gillen eTravel can prepare a balance sheet. A **balance sheet** reports the assets, liabilities, and owner's equity of the business. Gillen's initial balance sheet would appear as follows on April 1, 20X5:

Balance Sheet
An entity's assets, liabilities, and owner's equity as of a specific date. Also called the **statement of financial position**.

Gay Gillen eTravel
Balance Sheet
April 1, 20X5

Assets		=	Liabilities	
Cash..................	$30,000		None..................	$0
			+	
			Owner's Equity	
			Gay Gillen, capital	30,000
			Total liabilities and	
Total assets	$30,000		owner's equity	$30,000

A balance sheet reports the financial position of the entity at a moment in time—in this case at the stroke of midnight on April 1. Gay Gillen eTravel has $30,000 of cash, owes no liabilities, and has owner's equity of $30,000.

TRANSACTION 2: PURCHASE OF LAND   Gillen purchases land for an office location, paying cash of $20,000. The effect of this transaction on the accounting equation is

	ASSETS				LIABILITIES	+	OWNER'S EQUITY	TYPE OF OWNER'S EQUITY TRANSACTION
	Cash	+	Land				Gay Gillen, Capital	
(1)	30,000			=			30,000	Owner investment
(2)	−20,000	+	20,000					
Bal.	10,000		20,000				30,000	
	30,000						30,000	

✔ Starter 1-5

The cash purchase of land increases one asset, Land, and decreases another asset, Cash, by the same amount. After the transaction is completed, Gillen's business has cash of $10,000, land of $20,000, no liabilities, and owner's equity of $30,000. Note that the sums of the balances (abbreviated Bal.) on both sides of the equation must always be equal.

✔ Starter 1-6

✔ Starter 1-7

With software, such as QuickBooks and Peachtree, a business can print a balance sheet at any time to see where it stands financially. Gillen can use QuickBooks to prepare a balance sheet—this time after two transactions. The business's balance sheet on April 2 follows:

Gay Gillen eTravel
Balance Sheet
April 2, 20X5

Assets		Liabilities	
Cash.	$10,000	None.	$0
Land	20,000		
		Owner's Equity	
		Gay Gillen, capital	30,000
		Total liabilities and	
Total assets	$30,000	owner's equity	$30,000

Now the business holds two assets, with the liabilities and owner's equity unchanged. After we move through a sequence of transactions, we will return to Gillen's balance sheet. It's most common to prepare a balance sheet at the end of the accounting period. Now let's account for additional transactions of Gay Gillen eTravel.

TRANSACTION 3: PURCHASE OF OFFICE SUPPLIES Gillen buys stationery and other office supplies, agreeing to pay $500 within 30 days. This transaction increases both the assets and the liabilities of the business. Its effect on the accounting equation is

	ASSETS					LIABILITIES	+	OWNER'S EQUITY
	Cash	+	**Office Supplies**	+	**Land**	**Accounts Payable**	+	**Gay Gillen, Capital**
Bal.	10,000				20,000			30,000
(3)			+500			+500		
Bal.	10,000		500		20,000	500		30,000
		30,500					30,500	

Office Supplies is an asset, not an expense, because the supplies can be used in the future. The liability created by this transaction is an account payable. Recall that a *payable* is a liability.

Prepare the balance sheet of Gay Gillen eTravel on April 9, after transaction 3.

Answer:

Gay Gillen eTravel
Balance Sheet
April 9, 20X5

Assets		Liabilities	
Cash	$10,000	Accounts payable	$500
Office supplies	500	**Owner's Equity**	
Land	20,000	Gay Gillen, capital	30,000
		Total liabilities and	
Total assets	$30,500	owner's equity	$30,500

TRANSACTION 4: EARNING OF SERVICE REVENUE Gay Gillen eTravel earns service revenue by providing travel services for clients. She earns $5,500 revenue and collects this amount in cash. The effect on the accounting equation is an increase in the asset Cash and an increase in Gay Gillen, Capital, as follows:

	ASSETS					LIABILITIES	+	OWNER'S EQUITY	TYPE OF OWNER'S EQUITY TRANSACTION
	Cash	+	Office Supplies	+	Land	Accounts Payable	+	Gay Gillen, Capital	
Bal.	10,000		500		20,000	500		30,000	
(4)	+5,500							+5,500	*Service revenue*
Bal.	15,500		500		20,000	500		35,500	
		36,000					36,000		

A revenue transaction grows the business, as shown by the increases in assets and owner's equity. A company like Amazon.com or Wal-Mart that sells goods to customers is a merchandising business. Its revenue is called *sales revenue*. By contrast, Gay Gillen eTravel performs services for clients; Gillen's revenue is called *service revenue*.

✔ Starter 1-8

TRANSACTION 5: EARNING OF SERVICE REVENUE ON ACCOUNT
Gillen performs services for clients who do not pay immediately. In return for her travel services, Gillen receives clients' promises to pay $3,000 within one month. This promise is an asset to Gillen, an account receivable because she expects to collect the cash in the future. In accounting, we say that Gillen performed this service *on account*. When the business performs service for a client, the business earns the revenue.

The act of performing the service, not collecting the cash, earns the revenue. This $3,000 of service revenue increases the wealth of Gillen's business just like the $5,500 of revenue that she collected immediately in transaction 4. Gillen records $3,000 of revenue on account as follows:

	ASSETS							LIABILITIES	+	OWNER'S EQUITY	TYPE OF OWNER'S EQUITY TRANSACTION
	Cash	+	Accounts Receivable	+	Office Supplies	+	Land	Accounts Payable	+	Gay Gillen, Capital	
Bal.	15,500				500		20,000	500		35,500	
(5)			+3,000							+3,000	*Service revenue*
Bal.	15,500		3,000		500		20,000	500		38,500	
			39,000						39,000		

TRANSACTION 6: PAYMENT OF EXPENSES
During the month, Gillen pays $3,300 in cash expenses: lease expense on a computer, $600; office rent, $1,100; employee salary, $1,200 (part-time assistant); and utilities, $400. The effects on the accounting equation are

	ASSETS							LIABILITIES	+	OWNER'S EQUITY	TYPE OF OWNER'S EQUITY TRANSACTION
	Cash	+	Accounts Receivable	+	Office Supplies	+	Land	Accounts Payable	+	Gay Gillen, Capital	
Bal.	15,500		3,000		500		20,000	500		38,500	
(6)	− 600									− 600	*Lease expense, computer*
(6)	− 1,100									− 1,100	*Rent expense, office*
(6)	− 1,200									− 1,200	*Salary expense*
(6)	− 400									− 400	*Utilities expense*
Bal.	12,200		3,000		500		20,000	500		35,200	
			35,700						35,700		

Expenses have the opposite effect of revenues. Expenses cause the business to shrink, as shown by the decreased balances of assets and owner's equity.

Each expense is recorded separately. The expenses are listed together here for simplicity. We could record the cash payment in a single amount for the sum of the four expenses: $3,300 ($600 + $1,100 + $1,200 + $400). In all cases, the "balance" of the equation holds, as we know it must.

After any transaction, the business can prepare a balance sheet, as we illustrated earlier. Click on "Print Balance Sheet" and the software will produce the document.

After Gillen's revenue and expense transactions, Gay Gillen will want to know how well the travel agency is performing. Is the business profitable, or is it losing money? To answer this important question, Gillen can use QuickBooks to print an income statement. An income statement reports revenues and expenses to measure profits (called **net income**, **net earnings**, or **net profit**) and losses (called **net loss**). Gillen's income statement for the month ended April 30 would appear as follows:

Net Income
Excess of total revenues over total expenses. Also called **net earnings** or **net profit**.

Net Loss
Excess of total expenses over total revenues.

Gay Gillen eTravel		
Income Statement		
Month Ended April 30, 20X5		
Revenue:		
Service revenue ($5,500 + $3,000)		$8,500
Expenses:		
Salary expense	$1,200	
Rent expense, office.	1,100	
Lease expense, computer	600	
Utilities expense.	400	
Total expenses.		3,300
Net income		$5,200

The business had more revenues than expenses, so it was profitable during April. It earned net income of $5,200—not bad for a start-up company. We will revisit the income statement later.

TRANSACTION 7: PAYMENT ON ACCOUNT   Gillen pays $300 to the store where she purchased $500 worth of office supplies in transaction 3. In accounting, we say that she pays $300 *on account*. The effect on the accounting equation is a decrease in the asset Cash and a decrease in the liability Accounts Payable, as shown next.

		ASSETS					**LIABILITIES**	+	**OWNER'S EQUITY**
	Cash	+	Accounts Receivable	+	Office Supplies	+	Land	Accounts Payable	+	Gay Gillen, Capital
Bal.	12,200		3,000		500		20,000	=	500		35,200
(7)	− 300							−300		
Bal.	11,900		3,000		500		20,000		200		35,200
			35,400						35,400	

The payment of cash on account has no effect on Office Supplies because the payment does not affect the supplies available to the business. Likewise, the payment on account does not affect expenses. Gillen was paying off a liability, not an expense.

TRANSACTION 8: PERSONAL TRANSACTION   Gillen remodels her home at a cost of $40,000, paying cash from personal funds. This event is *not* a transaction of Gay Gillen eTravel. It has no effect on the travel agency and therefore is not recorded by the business. It is a transaction of the Gay Gillen *personal* entity, not Gay Gillen eTravel. This transaction illustrates the *entity concept.*

TRANSACTION 9: COLLECTION ON ACCOUNT   In transaction 5, Gillen performed services for a client on account. The business now collects $1,000 from the client. We say that Gillen collects the cash *on account*. Gillen will record an increase in the asset Cash. Should she also record an increase in service revenue? No, because she already recorded the revenue when she earned it in transaction 5. The phrase "collect cash on account" means to record an increase in Cash and a decrease in Accounts Receivable. The effect on the accounting equation of Gay Gillen eTravel is

	ASSETS				LIABILITIES	+	OWNER'S EQUITY
Cash +	Accounts Receivable +	Office Supplies +	Land	=	Accounts Payable +		Gay Gillen, Capital
Bal. 11,900	3,000	500	20,000	=	200		35,200
(9) + 1,000	−1,000						
Bal. 12,900	2,000	500	20,000		200		35,200
	35,400					35,400	

Total assets are unchanged from the preceding total. Why? Because Gillen merely exchanged one asset for another. Also, total liabilities and owner's equity are unchanged.

✔ Starter 1-9

TRANSACTION 10: SALE OF LAND   Gillen sells some land owned by the travel agency. The sale price of $9,000 is equal to Gillen's cost of the land. Gillen's business receives $9,000 cash. The effect on the accounting equation of the travel agency follows:

	ASSETS				LIABILITIES	+	OWNER'S EQUITY
Cash +	Accounts Receivable +	Office Supplies +	Land	=	Accounts Payable +		Gay Gillen, Capital
Bal. 12,900	2,000	500	20,000	=	200		35,200
(10) + 9,000			− 9,000				
Bal. 21,900	2,000	500	11,000		200		35,200
	35,400					35,400	

TRANSACTION 11: WITHDRAWAL OF CASH   Gillen withdraws $2,000 cash from the business for personal use. The effect on the accounting equation is

	ASSETS					LIABILITIES	+	OWNER'S EQUITY	TYPE OF OWNER'S EQUITY TRANSACTION
Cash +	Accounts Receivable +	Office Supplies +	Land		=	Accounts Payable +		Gay Gillen, Capital	
Bal. 21,900	2,000	500	11,000		=	200		35,200	
(11) − 2,000								− 2,000	*Owner withdrawal*
Bal. 19,900	2,000	500	11,000			200		33,200	
	33,400						33,400		

Gillen's withdrawal of $2,000 cash decreases the asset Cash and also the owner's equity of the business. *The withdrawal does not represent an expense because the cash is used for the owner's personal affairs.* We record this decrease in owner's equity as Withdrawals or as Drawings. The double underlines below each column indicate a final total.

✔ Starter 1-10

Evaluating Business Transactions

Exhibit 1-7 summarizes Gay Gillen eTravel's transactions. Panel A lists the details of the transactions, and Panel B shows the analysis. As you study the exhibit, note that every transaction maintains the equality

---

ASSETS = LIABILITIES + OWNER'S EQUITY

⭐5 *Prepare the financial statements*

The Financial Statements

After analyzing transactions, we need a way to present the results. We look now at the *financial statements*, which report the entity's financial information to interested parties such as Gay Gillen. If Gillen ever needs a loan, her banker will also want to see her financial statements. Earlier we prepared Gillen's income statement and balance sheet after a few transactions. Now we are ready to examine all the business's financial statements at the end of the period.

💿Student Resource**CD**

balance sheet, financial statements, income statement, statement of cash flows, statement of owner's equity

The financial statements are the

- Income statement
- Statement of owner's equity
- Balance sheet
- Statement of cash flows

INCOME STATEMENT The **income statement** presents a summary of an entity's revenues and expenses for specific period of time, such as a month or a year. The income statement, also called the **statement of earnings** or **statement of operations**, is like a video—it presents a moving picture of operations during the period. The income statement holds one of the most important pieces of information about a business—whether it earned:

Income Statement
Summary of an entity's revenues, expenses, and net income or net loss for a specific period. Also called the **statement of earnings** or the **statement of operations**.

- *Net income* (total revenues greater than total expenses) or
- *Net loss* (total expenses greater than total revenues)

Net income is good news about operations. A net loss is bad news. What was the result of Gay Gillen eTravel's operations during April? Good news—the business earned net income (see the top part of Exhibit 1-8, page 21).

STATEMENT OF OWNER'S EQUITY The **statement of owner's equity** shows the changes in *owner's equity* during a specific time period, such as a month or a year, as follows:

Increases in owner's equity come from:

Statement of Owner's Equity
Summary of the changes in an entity's owner's equity during a specific period.

- Owner investments
- Net income

Decreases in owner's equity result from:

- Owner withdrawals
- Net loss

BALANCE SHEET The *balance sheet* lists all the entity's assets, liabilities, and owner's equity as of a specific date, usually the end of a month or a year. The balance sheet is like a snapshot of the entity. For this reason, it is also called the *statement of financial position* (see the middle of Exhibit 1-8, page 21).

Statement of Cash Flows
Reports cash receipts and cash payments during a period.

STATEMENT OF CASH FLOWS The **statement of cash flows** reports the cash coming in (cash receipts) and the amount of cash going out (*cash payments*) during a period. Business activities result in a net cash inflow (receipts greater than payments) or a net cash outflow (payments greater than receipts). The statement of cash flows shows the net increase or decrease in cash during the period and the ending cash balance. (We focus on the statement of cash flows in Chapter 17.)

| Exhibit 1-7 | Analysis of Transactions, Gay Gillen eTravel |

PANEL A—Details of Transactions

(1) Gillen invested $30,000 cash in the business.

(2) Paid $20,000 cash for land.

(3) Bought $500 of office supplies on account.

(4) Received $5,500 cash from clients for service revenue earned.

(5) Performed travel service for clients on account, $3,000.

(6) Paid cash expenses: computer lease, $600; office rent, $1,100; employee salary, $1,200; utilities, $400.

(7) Paid $300 on the account payable created in transaction 3.

(8) Remodeled Gillen's personal residence. This is *not* a transaction of the business.

(9) Collected $1,000 on the account receivable created in transaction 5.

(10) Sold land for cash at its cost of $9,000.

(11) Withdrew $2,000 cash for personal expenses.

PANEL B—Analysis of Transactions

	ASSETS						LIABILITIES	+	OWNER'S EQUITY	TYPE OF OWNER'S EQUITY TRANSACTION
	Cash	+	Accounts Receivable	+	Office Supplies	+ Land	Accounts Payable	+	Gay Gillen, Capital	
(1)	+30,000								+30,000	Owner investment
Bal.	30,000								30,000	
(2)	−20,000					+20,000				
Bal.	10,000					20,000			30,000	
(3)	_____				+500	_____	+500		_____	
Bal.	10,000				500	20,000	500		30,000	
(4)	+ 5,500					_____	_____		+ 5,500	Service revenue
Bal.	15,500				500	20,000	500		35,500	
(5)	_____		+3,000		_____	_____	_____		+ 3,000	Service revenue
Bal.	15,500		3,000		500	20,000	500		38,500	
(6)	− 600								− 600	Lease expense, computer
(6)	− 1,100								− 1,100	Rent expense, office
(6)	− 1,200								− 1,200	Salary expense
(6)	− 400		_____		_____	_____	_____		− 400	Utilities expense
Bal.	12,200		3,000		500	20,000	500		35,200	
(7)	− 300		_____		_____	_____	−300		_____	
Bal.	11,900		3,000		500	20,000	200		35,200	
(8)	Not a transaction of the business									
(9)	+ 1,000		−1,000		_____	_____				
Bal.	12,900		2,000		500	20,000	200		35,200	
(10)	+ 9,000					− 9,000			_____	
Bal.	21,900		2,000		500	11,000	200		35,200	
(11)	− 2,000		_____		_____	_____			− 2,000	Owner withdrawal
Bal.	19,900		2,000		500	11,000	200		33,200	
			33,400						33,400	

=

✔ Starter 1-11

Financial Statement Headings

Each financial statement has a heading giving three pieces of data:

- Name of the business (such as Gay Gillen eTravel)
- Name of the financial statement (income statement, balance sheet, and so on)
- Date or time period covered by the statement (April 30, 20X5, for the balance sheet; month ended April 30, 20X5, for the income statement)

An income statement (or a statement of owner's equity) that covers a year ended in December 20X5 is dated "Year Ended December 31, 20X5." A monthly income statement (or statement of owner's equity) for September 20X4 shows "Month Ended September 30, 20X4," or "For the Month of September 20X4." Income must be identified with a particular time period.

 *Evaluate business performance*

Relationships Among the Financial Statements

Exhibit 1-8 illustrates all four financial statements. Their data come from the transaction analysis in Exhibit 1-7 which covers the month of April 20X5. Study the exhibit carefully. Specifically, observe the following in Exhibit 1-8:

1. The *income statement* for the month ended April 30, 20X5:
   a. Reports April's revenues and expenses. Expenses are listed in decreasing order of their amount, with the largest expense first.
   b. Reports *net income* of the period if total revenues exceed total expenses. If total expenses exceed total revenues, a *net loss* is reported instead.

2. The *statement of owner's equity* for the month ended April 30, 20X5:
   a. Opens with the owner's capital balance at the beginning of the period.
   b. Adds *investments by the owner* and also adds net income (or subtracts net loss, as the case may be). Net income or net loss come directly from the income statement (see arrow ① in Exhibit 1-8).
   c. Subtracts withdrawals by the owner. Parentheses indicate a subtraction.
   d. Ends with the owner's capital balance at the end of the period.

3. The *balance sheet* at April 30, 20X5:
   a. Reports all assets, all liabilities, and owner's equity at the end of the period.
   b. Reports that total assets equal total liabilities plus total owner's equity.
   c. Reports the owner's ending capital balance, taken directly from the statement of owner's equity (see arrow ②).

4. The *statement of cash flows* for the month ended April 30, 20X5:
   a. Reports cash flows from three types of business activities (*operating, investing,* and *financing activities*) during the month. Each category of cash-flow activities includes both cash receipts (positive amounts), and cash payments (negative amounts denoted by parentheses).
   b. Reports a net increase in cash during the month and ends with the cash balance at April 30, 20X5. This is the amount of cash to report on the balance sheet (see arrow ③).

Have you ever thought of having your own business? The Decision Guidelines feature shows how to make some of the decisions that you will face if you start a business. Decision Guidelines appear in each chapter.

Exhibit 1-8

Financial Statements of Gay Gillen eTravel

Gay Gillen eTravel
Income Statement
Month Ended April 30, 20X5

Revenue		
Service revenue		$8,500
Expenses:		
Salary expense	$1,200	
Rent expense, office	1,100	
Lease expense, computer	600	
Utilities expense	400	
Total expenses		3,300
Net income		$5,200

Gay Gillen eTravel
Statement of Owner's Equity
Month Ended April 30, 20X5

Gay Gillen, capital, April 1, 20X5		$ 0
Add: Investments by owner		30,000
Net income for the month		5,200
		35,200
Less: Withdrawals by owner		(2,000)
Gay Gillen, capital, April 30, 20X5		$33,200

①

Gay Gillen eTravel
Balance Sheet
April 30, 20X5

②

Assets		Liabilities	
Cash	$19,900	Accounts payable	$ 200
Accounts receivable	2,000		
Office supplies	500	**Owner's Equity**	
Land	11,000	Gay Gillen, capital	33,200
		Total liabilities and	
Total assets	$33,400	owner's equity	$33,400

✔ Starter 1-12

✔ Starter 1-13

✔ Starter 1-14

✔ Starter 1-15

Gay Gillen eTravel
Statement of Cash Flows*
Month Ended April 30, 20X5

③

Cash flows from **operating** activities:		
Receipts:		
Collections from customers ($5,500 + $1,000)		$ 6,500
Payments:		
To suppliers ($600 + $1,100 + $400 + $300)	$ (2,400)	
To employees	(1,200)	(3,600)
Net cash inflow from operating activities		2,900
Cash flows from **investing** activities:		
Acquisition of land	$(20,000)	
Sale of land	9,000	
Net cash outflow from investing activities		(11,000)
Cash flows from **financing** activities:		
Investment by owner	$30,000	
Withdrawal by owner	(2,000)	
Net cash inflow from financing activities		28,000
Net increase in cash		19,900
Cash balance, April 1, 20X5		0
Cash balance, April 30, 20X5		$19,900

*Chapter 17 shows how to prepare this statement.

Decision Guidelines

MAJOR BUSINESS DECISIONS

Suppose you open a business to take photos at parties at your college. You hire a professional photographer and line up suppliers for party favors and photo albums. Here are some factors you must consider if you expect to be profitable.

Decision	Guidelines
How to organize the business?	If a single owner—a *proprietorship*.
	If two or more owners, but not incorporated—a *partnership*.
	If the business issues stock to stockholders—a *corporation*.
What to account for?	Account for the business, a separate entity apart from its owner *(entity concept)*.
	Account for transactions and events that affect the business and can be measured reliably.
How much to record for assets and liabilities?	Actual historical amount *(cost principle)*.
How to analyze a transaction?	The accounting equation:

$$\text{Assets} = \text{Liabilities} + \text{Owner's Equity}$$

How to measure profits and losses?	Income statement:

$$\text{Revenues} - \text{Expenses} = \text{Net Income (or Net Loss)}$$

Did owner's equity increase or decrease?	Statement of owner's equity:

Beginning capital
+ Owner investments
+ Net income (or − Net loss)
− Owner withdrawals
= Ending capital

Where does the business stand financially?	Balance sheet (accounting equation):

$$\text{Assets} = \text{Liabilities} + \text{Owner's Equity}$$

Excel Application Exercise

Goal: Create a simple spreadsheet that a stockholder or creditor could use to quickly analyze the financial performance of a company.

Scenario: After buying some books and DVDs from **Amazon.com**, you are thinking about investing some of your savings in the company's stock. Before doing so, however, you want to perform a quick check of the company's financial performance. Use the Amazon.com Annual Report in Appendix A to gather your data (also found online at www.amazon.com, Investor Relations).

When you have completed your worksheet, answer the following question [Hint: See Amazon's Consolidated Balance Sheets, Consolidated Statements of Operations (income statement), and Consolidated Statements of Cash Flows]:

1. Net income (loss) affects both stock prices and dividends. What changes have occurred in Amazon's net income (loss) over the past two years? If you were in management at Amazon, would you include such a chart in your annual report? Why or why not?

Step-by-step:

1. Open a new Excel spreadsheet.
2. In column 1, create a bold-faced heading as follows:
   a. Chapter 1 Excel Application Exercise
   b. Amazon Financial Performance
   c. Today's Date
3. Two rows down, enter the following labels (one in each row):
   a. Income Statement Data (bold)
   b. Net Income (Loss) (in 000's)
   c. Percentage Change
4. Two rows below your heading, starting in the second column, set up three column headings, beginning with 2000 and ending with 2002 (or the last three fiscal years, if different from these).

5. Using the Amazon annual report, enter the net income (loss) data for the past three years, and use formulas to calculate the percentage change from year to year.
6. Enter the current assets and current liabilities data for at least two years.
7. Use the Chart Wizard to create a column chart showing how net income has changed (in percent). Title the chart "Net Income (Loss) Trend" and use the "percentage change" data for the chart data range. Position the chart appropriately on your worksheet.
8. Format all cells appropriately (width, dollars, percent, decimal places).
9. Save your worksheet and print a copy for your files.

END-OF-CHAPTER *Summary Problem*

Jill Smith opens an apartment-locater business near a college campus. She is the sole owner of the proprietorship, which she names Campus Apartment Locators. During the first month of operations, July 20X6, she engages in the following transactions:

a. Smith invests $35,000 of personal funds to start the business.
b. She purchases on account office supplies costing $350.
c. Smith pays cash of $30,000 to acquire a lot next to the campus. She intends to use the land as a future building site for her business office.
d. Smith locates apartments for clients and receives cash of $1,900.
e. She pays $100 on the account payable she created in transaction (b).
f. She pays $2,000 of personal funds for a vacation.
g. She pays cash expenses for office rent, $400, and utilities, $100.
h. The business sells office supplies to another business for its cost of $150.
i. Smith withdraws cash of $1,200 for personal use.

Required

1. Analyze the preceding transactions in terms of their effects on the accounting equation of Campus Apartment Locators. Use Exhibit 1-7 as a guide, but show balances only after the last transaction.
2. Prepare the income statement, statement of owner's equity, and balance sheet of the business after recording the transactions. Use Exhibit 1-8 as a guide.

Solution

Requirement 1

PANEL A—Details of transactions

    (a)   Smith invested $35,000 cash to start the business.

    (b)   Purchased $350 of office supplies on account.

    (c)   Paid $30,000 to acquire land as a future building site.

    (d)   Earned service revenue and received cash of $1,900.

    (e)   Paid $100 on account.

    (f)   Paid for a personal vacation, which is not a transaction of the business.

    (g)   Paid cash expenses for rent, $400, and utilities, $100.

    (h)   Sold office supplies for cost of $150.

    (i)   Withdrew $1,200 cash for personal use.

TIPS

CHECK YOUR RESOURCES

PANEL B—Analysis of transactions:

	ASSETS					LIABILITIES	+	OWNER'S EQUITY	TYPE OF OWNER'S EQUITY TRANSACTION
	Cash	+	Office Supplies	+	Land	Accounts Payable	+	Jill Smith, Capital	
(a)	+35,000							+35,000	*Owner investment*
(b)			+350			+350			
(c)	−30,000				+30,000				
(d)	+ 1,900							+ 1,900	*Service revenue*
(e)	− 100					−100			
(f)	Not a transaction of the business								
(g)	− 400							− 400	*Rent expense*
	− 100							− 100	*Utilities expense*
(h)	+ 150		−150						
(i)	− 1,200							− 1,200	*Owner withdrawal*
Bal.	5,250		200		30,000	250		35,200	

Assets total: 35,450 = Liabilities + Owner's Equity: 35,450

Requirement 2: **Financial Statements of Campus Apartment Locators**

Campus Apartment Locators

Income Statement
Month Ended July 31, 20X6

Revenue:		
Service revenue		$1,900
Expenses:		
Rent expense	$400	
Utilities expense	100	
Total expenses		500
Net income		$1,400

Campus Apartment Locators

Statement of Owner's Equity
Month Ended July 31, 20X6

Jill Smith, capital, July 1, 20X6	$ 0
Add: Investment by owner	35,000
Net income for the month	1,400
	36,400
Less: Withdrawals by owner	(1,200)
Jill Smith, capital, July 31, 20X6	$35,200

Campus Apartment Locators

Balance Sheet
July 31, 20X6

Assets		Liabilities	
Cash	$ 5,250	Accounts payable	$ 250
Office supplies	200	**Owner's Equity**	
Land	30,000	Jill Smith, capital	35,200
		Total liabilities and	
Total assets	$35,450	owner's equity	$35,450

REVIEW *Accounting and the Business Environment*

Quick Check

1. Generally accepted accounting principles (GAAP) are formulated by the
   a. Securities and Exchange Commission (SEC)
   b. Financial Accounting Standards Board (FASB)
   c. Institute of Management Accountants (IMA)
   d. American Institute of Certified Public Accountants (AICPA)

2. Which type of business organization is owned by its stockholders?
   a. Proprietorship   c. Corporation
   b. Partnership   d. All the above are owned by stockholders

3. Which accounting concept or principle specifically states that we should record transactions at amounts that can be verified?
   a. Entity concept   c. Cost principle
   b. Reliability principle   d. Going-concern concept

4. **Fossil** is famous for fashion wristwatches and leather goods. At the end of a recent year, Fossil's total assets added up to $381 million, and owners' equity was $264 million. How much did Fossil owe creditors?
   a. Cannot determine from the data given   c. $264 million
   b. $381 million   d. $117 million

   $381,000,000 = X + 264000000$
   $264\,000\,000$ -264000000
   $117,000,000 = X$

5. Assume that Fossil sold watches for $50,000 to a department store on account. How would this transaction affect Fossil's accounting equation?
   a. Increase both assets and owners' equity by $50,000
   b. Increase both assets and liabilities by $50,000
   c. Increase both liabilities and owners' equity by $50,000
   d. No effect on the accounting equation because the effects cancel out

   $381050000 = X + 264,050000$
   -264050000
   $264050000 =$
   $\overline{17000\,000} = X$

6. Refer to Fossil's sale of watches on account in the preceding question. Which parts of the accounting equation does a sale on account affect?
   a. Accounts Receivable and Accounts Payable
   b. Accounts Payable and Cash
   c. Accounts Payable and Owner, Capital
   d. Accounts Receivable and Owner, Capital

7. Assume that Fossil paid expenses totaling $35,000. How does this transaction affect Fossil's accounting equation?
   a. Increases assets and decreases liabilities
   c. Decreases both assets and owners' equity
   b. Increases both assets and owners' equity
   d. Decreases assets and increases liabilities

   $50,000 - 35,000$
   Net Income
   $15,000$

8. Consider the overall effects of transactions 5 and 7 on Fossil. What is Fossil's net income or net loss?
   a. Net income of $50,000   c. Net income of $15,000
   b. Net loss of $35,000   d. Cannot determine from the data given

9. The balance sheet reports
   a. Financial position on a specific date   c. Financial position for a specific period
   b. Results of operation on a specific date d. Results of operations for a specific period

10. The income statement reports
    a. Financial position on a specific date   c. Financial position for a specific period
    b. Results of operations on a specific date d. Results of operations for a specific period

Accounting Vocabulary

Accounting has a special vocabulary and it is important that you understand the following terms.
They appear in the text and in the margins, and also in the glossary at the end of the book.

account payable (p. 11)

account receivable (p. 11)

accounting (p. 4)

accounting equation (p. 10)

asset (p. 10)

audit (p. 6)

balance sheet (p. 13)

capital (p. 11)

certified management accountant (CMA) (p. 6)

certified public accountant (CPA) (p. 6)

corporation (p. 8)

entity (p. 9)

expense (p. 12)

financial accounting (p. 5)

Financial Accounting Standards Board (FASB) (p. 6)

financial statements (p. 4)

generally accepted accounting principles (GAAP) (p. 9)

income statement (p. 18)

liability (p. 11)

management accounting (p. 5)

net earnings (p. 16)

net income (p. 16)

net loss (p. 16)

net profit (p. 16)

note payable (p. 11)

note receivable (p. 11)

owner's equity (p. 11)

owner withdrawals (p. 12)

partnership (p. 8)

proprietorship (p. 8)

revenue (p. 11)

shareholder (p. 8)

statement of cash flows (p. 18)

statement of earnings (p. 18)

statement of financial position (p. 13)

statement of operations (p. 18)

statement of owner's equity (p. 18)

stockholder (p. 8)

transaction (p. 12)

● ASSESS *Your Progress*

See *www.prenhall.com/horngren* for selected Starters, Exercises, and Problems.

Explaining assets, liabilities, owner's equity
(Obj. 1)

Explaining revenues, expenses
(Obj. 1)

Applying accounting concepts and principles
(Obj. 2)

Applying accounting concepts and principles
(Obj. 2)

Starters

S1-1 Suppose you need a bank loan in order to purchase office equipment for **Jan's Perfect Presents,** which you own. In evaluating your loan request, the banker asks about the assets and liabilities of your business. In particular, the banker wants to know the amount of your owner's equity. In your own words, explain the meanings of *assets, liabilities,* and *owner's equity.* Also give the mathematical relationship among assets, liabilities, and owner's equity.

S1-2 Gay Gillen eTravel has been open for one year, and Gillen wants to know the amount of the business's profit (net income) or net loss for the year. First, she must identify the revenues earned and the expenses incurred during the year. What are *revenues* and *expenses*? How do revenues and expenses enter into the determination of net income or net loss?

S1-3 Suppose you are starting a business, Web Master, to design Web sites for small businesses in your city. In organizing the business and setting up its accounting records, consider the following:

1. In keeping the books of the business, you must decide the amount to record for assets purchased and liabilities incurred. At what amount should you record assets and liabilities? Which accounting concept or principle provides guidance?

2. Should you account for your personal assets and personal liabilities along with the assets and the liabilities of the business, or should you keep the two sets of records separate? Why? Which accounting concept or principle provides guidance?

S1-4 Mac Mendelsohn owns and operates Mac's Floral Designs. He proposes to account for the shop's assets at current market value in order to have realistic amounts on the books if he must liquidate the business. Which accounting concept or principle does Mendelsohn's view violate? How should Mendelsohn account for the assets of the business? Which concept or principle governs this decision?

SI-5 You begin Job-Link Employment Service by investing $10,000 of your own money in a business bank account. Before starting operations, you borrow $8,000 cash by signing a note payable to Summit Bank. Write the business's accounting equation (Exhibit 1-5, page 11) after completing these transactions.

Using the accounting equation
(Obj. 3)

SI-6 Alex Briggs owns 1-800-Fly-Europe, a travel agency near the campus of Tidewater Community College. The business has cash of $5,000 and furniture that cost $12,000. Debts include accounts payable of $8,000 and a $6,000 note payable. How much equity does Briggs have in the business? Using Briggs' figures, write the accounting equation (page 11) of the travel agency.

Using the accounting equation
(Obj. 3)

SI-7 Review transaction 2 of Gay Gillen eTravel, on page 13. In that transaction, the business purchased land for $20,000. To buy the land, Gillen was obligated to pay for it. Why, then, did the business record no liability in this transaction?

Analyzing transactions
(Obj. 4)

SI-8 Study Gay Gillen's transaction 4 on pages 14–15. Gillen recorded revenues earned by providing travel service for clients. Suppose the amount of revenue earned in transaction 4 was $4,000 instead of $5,500. How much are the business's cash and total assets after the transaction? How much is Gay Gillen, Capital?

Analyzing transactions
(Obj. 4)

SI-9 Review transaction 9 of Gay Gillen eTravel, on page 17. Gillen collected cash from a client for whom she had provided travel services earlier. Why didn't the travel agency record any revenue in transaction 9?

Analyzing transactions
(Obj. 4)

SI-10 Clements Auction Co. earns service revenue by selling antique furniture for customers. Clements' main expenses are the salaries paid to employees. Write the accounting equation to show the effects of

Analyzing transactions
(Obj. 4)

a. Clements' earning $10,000 of service revenue on account and
b. Clements' $6,000 payment of salaries for October.

Show all appropriate headings, starting with the accounting equation. Also list the appropriate item under each heading. Assume Clements began with an adequate cash balance.

SI-11 Examine Exhibit 1-7 on page 19. The exhibit summarizes the transactions of Gay Gillen eTravel for the month of April 20X5. Suppose Gillen has completed only the first seven transactions and needs a bank loan on April 21. The vice president of the bank requires financial statements to support all loan requests.

    Prepare the income statement, statement of owner's equity, and balance sheet that Gay Gillen would present to the banker after completing the first seven transactions on April 21, 20X5. Exhibit 1-8, page 21, shows the format of these statements.

Preparing the financial statements
(Obj. 5)

SI-12 Gay Gillen wishes to know how well her business performed during April. The income statement in Exhibit 1-8, page 21, helps answer this question. Write the formula for measuring net income or net loss on the income statement.

Format of the income statement
(Obj. 5)

SI-13 Bellmead Auto Repair has just completed operations for the year ended December 31, 20X8. This is the third year of operations for the company. As the proprietor, you want to know how well the business performed during the year. You also wonder where the business stands financially at the end of the year. To address these questions, you have assembled the following data:

Preparing the income statement
(Obj. 6)

Insurance expense	$ 4,000	Salary expense	$42,000
Service revenue	101,000	Accounts payable	8,000
Accounts receivable	7,000	Owner, capital,	
Supplies expense	1,000	December 31, 20X7	13,000
Cash	16,000	Supplies	2,000
Fuel expense	6,000	Withdrawals by owner	36,000
Rent expense	8,000		

Prepare the income statement of Bellmead Auto Repair for the year ended December 31, 20X8. Follow the format shown in Exhibit 1-8, page 21.

Preparing the statement of owner's equity
(Obj. 6)

S1-14 Use the data in Starter 1-13 to prepare the statement of owner's equity of Bellmead Auto Repair for the year ended December 31, 20X8. Follow the format in Exhibit 1-8. Compute net income from the data in Starter 1-13.

Preparing the balance sheet
(Obj. 6)

S1-15 Use the data in Starter 1-13 to prepare the balance sheet of Bellmead Auto Repair at December 31, 20X8. The year-end balance sheet will show where the business stands financially at the end of the year. Follow the format in Exhibit 1-8. Owner's equity (Owner, capital) at December 31, 20X8, is $17,000.

A⁺online homework

Exercises

Deciding on an investment
(Obj. 1)

E1-1 Suppose you have saved some money and you are considering an investment in **Amazon.com**. What accounting information will you use to decide whether or not to invest in Amazon? Which accounting principle do you hope Amazon's accountants follow closely? Explain your answer.

Explaining the income statement and the balance sheet
(Obj. 1)

E1-2 Shelly Herzog publishes a travel magazine. In need of cash, she asks Central Bank for a loan. The bank requires borrowers to submit financial statements to show results of operations and financial position. With little knowledge of accounting, Herzog doesn't know how to proceed. Explain to her the information provided by the balance sheet and the income statement. Indicate why a lender would require this information.

Business transactions
(Obj. 2)

E1-3 As manager of a **Kinko's Copies** store, you must deal with a variety of business transactions. Give an example of a transaction that has the described effect on the accounting equation:

a. Increase an asset and increase owner's equity.
b. Increase an asset and increase a liability.
c. Increase one asset and decrease another asset.
d. Decrease an asset and decrease owner's equity.
e. Decrease an asset and decrease a liability.

Transaction analysis
(Obj. 2)

E1-4 **Automatic Chef**, a proprietorship, supplies snack foods. The business experienced the following events. State whether each event (1) increased, (2) decreased, or (3) had no effect on the total assets of the business. Identify any specific asset affected.

a. Automatic Chef received a cash investment from the owner.
b. Cash purchase of land for a building site.
c. Paid cash on accounts payable.
d. Purchased machinery and equipment for a manufacturing plant; signed a promissory note in payment.
e. Performed service for a customer on account.
f. The owner withdrew cash from the business for personal use.
g. Received cash from a customer on account receivable.
h. The owner used personal funds to purchase a swimming pool for his home.
i. Sold land for a price equal to the cost of the land; received cash.
j. Borrowed money from the bank.

Accounting equation
(Obj. 3)

E1-5 Compute the missing amount in the accounting equation for each entity:

	Assets	Liabilities	Owner's Equity
Autozone	$?	$61,800	$21,000
Army-Navy Surplus	72,000	?	34,000
Amy's Hallmark	102,700	79,800	?

E1-6 Oracle Web Sites started 20X4 with total assets of $25,000 and total liabilities of $11,000. At the end of 20X4, Oracle's total assets stood at $31,000, and total liabilities were $14,000.

Accounting equation
(Obj. 3)

Required

1. Did the owner's equity of Oracle increase or decrease during 20X4? By how much?
2. Identify two possible reasons for the change in owner's equity during the year.

E1-7 Avis Rentals' balance sheet data at May 31, 20X6, and June 30, 20X6, follow:

Accounting equation
(Obj. 3)

	May 31, 20X6	June 30, 20X6
Total assets	$150,000	$195,000
Total liabilities	109,000	131,000

Required

Following are three assumptions about investments and withdrawals by the owner of the business during June. For each assumption, compute the amount of net income or net loss during June 20X6.

1. The owner invested $10,000 in the business and made no withdrawals.
2. The owner made no additional investments in the business but withdrew $5,000 for personal use.
3. The owner invested $30,000 in the business and withdrew $6,000 for personal use.

E1-8 Indicate the effects of the following business transactions on the accounting equation of an **Enterprise Rent-a-Car** location. Transaction (a) is answered as a guide.

Transaction analysis
(Obj. 4)

a. Received cash of $25,000 from the owner, who was investing in the business.
   Answer: Increase asset (Cash)
              Increase owner's equity (Capital)
b. Paid $700 cash to purchase supplies.
c. Earned rental revenue on account, $500.
d. Purchased on account office furniture at a cost of $600.
e. Received cash on account, $900.
f. Paid cash on account, $250.
g. Sold land for $12,000, which was the cost of the land.
h. Rented automobiles and received cash of $680.
i. Paid monthly office rent of $800.

E1-9 Ken Luikhart opens a medical practice. During the first month of operation, July, the business, titled Ken Luikhart, M.D., experienced the following events.

Transaction analysis; accounting equation
(Obj. 4)

Student ResourceCD

spreadsheet

July 6   Luikhart invested $60,000 in the business by opening a bank account in the name of K. Luikhart, M.D.

   9   Luikhart paid $55,000 cash for land. He plans to build an office building on the land.

   12   He purchased medical supplies for $2,000 on account.

   15   Luikhart officially opened for business.

15–31   During the rest of the month, he treated patients and earned service revenue of $7,000, receiving cash.

15–31   He paid cash expenses: employees' salaries, $1,400; office rent, $1,000; utilities, $300.

   28   He sold supplies to another physician for the cost of those supplies, $500.

   31   He paid $1,500 on account.

Required

Analyze the effects of these events on the accounting equation of the medical practice of K. Luikhart, M.D. Use a format similar to that of Exhibit 1-7, with headings for Cash; Medical Supplies; Land; Accounts Payable; and K. Luikhart, Capital.

Business transactions and net income
(Obj. 4)

E1-10 The analysis of Marstaller TV Service's first eight transactions follows. The owner of the business made only one investment to start the business and no withdrawals.

	Cash +	Accounts Receivable +	Equipment =	Accounts Payable +	Note Payable +	Owner Capital
1.	+50,000					+50,000
2.	−750		+750			
3.			+100,000		+100,000	
4.		+800				+800
5.	−2,000					−2,000
6.	+2,200					+2,200
7.	−10,000			−10,000		
8.	+150	−150				

Required

1. Describe each transaction.
2. If these transactions fully describe the operations of Marstaller TV Service during the month, what was the amount of net income or net loss?

Business organization, balance sheet
(Obj. 5)

E1-11 The balances of the assets and liabilities of JD's Graphic Design at November 30, 20X9, follow. Also included are the revenue and expense figures of this service business for November.

Service revenue	$9,100	Office equipment	$15,500
Accounts receivable	6,900	Supplies	600
Accounts payable	2,500	Note payable	8,000
J.D. Power, capital	?	Rent expense	500
Salary expense	2,000	Cash	2,000

Required

1. What type of business organization is JD's Graphic Design? How can you tell?
2. Prepare the balance sheet of the business at November 30, 20X9.
3. What does the balance sheet report—financial position or operating results? Which financial statement reports the other information?

Income Statement
(Obj. 5)

Student ResourceCD

spreadsheet

E1-12 The assets, liabilities, owner's equity, revenues, and expenses of Award Specialties, an engraving business, at December 31, 20X6, the end of its first year of operation, have the following balances. During the year, T. Kershaw, the owner, invested $15,000 in the business.

Office furniture	$ 45,000	Note payable	$41,000
Utilities expense.	6,800	Rent expense	24,000
Accounts payable	3,300	Cash	3,600
T. Kershaw, capital	27,100	Office supplies	4,800
Service revenue	161,200	Salary expense	60,000
Accounts receivable	9,000	Salaries payable	2,000
Supplies expense.	4,000	Property tax expense	1,200

Required

1. Prepare the income statement of Award Specialties for the year ended December 31, 20X6. What is the result of operations for 20X6?

2. What was the amount of the proprietor's withdrawals during the year?

E1-13 In this exercise you will practice using the data of a well-known company. The 20X1 annual report of **Fedex**, the overnight shipping company, reported revenue of $19.6 billion. Total expenses for the year were $19.0 billion. Fedex ended the year with total assets of $13.3 billion, and it owed debts totaling $7.4 billion. At year-end 20X0, Fedex reported total assets of $11.5 billion and total liabilities of $6.7 billion.

Evaluating the performance of a real company
(Obj. 6)

Required

1. Compute Fedex's net income for 20X1.

2. Did Fedex's owners' equity increase or decrease during 20X1? By how much?

3. How would you rate Fedex's performance for 20X1—good or bad? Give your reason.

E1-14 Compute the missing amount for Mars Company. You will need to prepare a statement of owner's equity.

Using the financial statements
(Obj. 6)

Mars Co.	
Beginning:	
Assets	$ 50,000
Liabilities	20,000
Ending:	
Assets	$ 70,000
Liabilities	35,000
Owner's Equity:	
Investments by owner	$ 0
Withdrawals by owner	40,000
Income Statement:	
Revenues	$230,000
Expenses	?

Did Mars earn a net income or suffer a net loss for the year? Compute the amount.

Problems

(Group A)

P1-1A Lynn Greenspan practiced law with a partnership for 10 years. Recently she opened her own law office, which she operates as a proprietorship. The name of the new entity is Lynn Greenspan, Attorney. Greenspan experienced the following events during the organizing phase of the new business and its first month of operation. Some of the events were personal and did not affect the law practice. Others were business transactions and should be accounted for by the business.

Entity concept, transaction analysis, accounting equation
(Obj. 2, 3, 4)

July 1	Sold 1,000 shares of **Eastman Kodak** stock, which she had owned for several years, receiving $68,000 cash.
2	Deposited the $68,000 cash from sale of the Eastman Kodak stock in her personal bank account.
3	Received $170,000 cash from former law partners.
5	Deposited $100,000 cash in a new business bank account titled Lynn Greenspan, Attorney.
6	A representative of a large company telephoned Greenspan and told her of the company's intention to transfer its legal business to Lynn Greenspan, Attorney.

(continued)

7 Paid $500 cash for letterhead stationery for the new law office.

9 Purchased office furniture for the law office, agreeing to pay the account, $9,500, within 3 months.

23 Finished court hearings on behalf of a client and submitted her bill for legal services, $3,000.

30 Paid office rent, $1,900.

31 Withdrew $10,000 cash from the business for personal use.

Required

1. Analyze the effects of the preceding events on the accounting equation of the proprietorship of Lynn Greenspan, Attorney. Use a format similar to Exhibit 1-7.

2. At July 31, compute the business's
   a. Total assets
   b. Total liabilities
   c. Total owner's equity
   d. Net income or net loss for the month

Transaction analysis, accounting equation, financial statements
(Obj. 3, 4, 5)

P1-2A Daniel Peavy owns and operates an architectural firm called Peavy Design. The following amounts summarize the financial position of his business on April 30, 20X5:

	Assets			=	Liabilities	+	Owner's Equity
Cash +	Accounts Receivable +	Supplies +	Land =		Accounts Payable	+	Daniel Peavy, Capital
Bal. 1,720	3,240		24,100		5,400		23,660

During May 20X5, the following events occurred.

a. Peavy received $12,000 as a gift and deposited the cash in the business bank account.
b. Paid off the beginning balance of accounts payable.
c. Performed services for a client and received cash of $1,100.
d. Collected cash from a customer on account, $750.
e. Purchased supplies on account, $720.
f. Consulted on the interior design of a major office building and billed the client for services rendered, $5,000.
g. Invested personal cash of $1,700 in the business.
h. Recorded the following business expenses for the month:
   1. Paid office rent, $1,200.
   2. Paid advertising, $660.
i. Sold supplies to another interior designer for $80 cash, which was the cost of the supplies.
j. Withdrew cash of $4,000 for personal use.

Required

1. Analyze the effects of the preceding transactions on the accounting equation of Peavy Design. Adapt the format of Exhibit 1-7.

2. Prepare the income statement of Peavy Design for the month ended May 31, 20X5. List expenses in decreasing order by amount.

3. Prepare the statement of owner's equity of Peavy Design for the month ended May 31, 20X5.

4. Prepare the balance sheet of Peavy Design at May 31, 20X5.

Business transactions and analysis
(Obj. 3, 4)

P1-3A Jacobs-Cathey Heating & Cooling was recently formed. The balance of each item in the company's accounting equation follows for August 4 and for each of the nine following days:

	Cash	Accounts Receivable	Supplies	Land	Accounts Payable	Owner's Equity
Aug. 4	$2,000	$7,000	$ 800	$11,000	$3,800	$17,000
9	6,000	3,000	800	11,000	3,800	17,000
14	4,000	3,000	800	11,000	1,800	17,000
17	4,000	3,000	1,100	11,000	2,100	17,000
19	5,000	3,000	1,100	11,000	2,100	18,000
20	3,900	3,000	1,100	11,000	1,000	18,000
22	9,900	3,000	1,100	5,000	1,000	18,000
25	9,900	3,700	400	5,000	1,000	18,000
26	9,300	3,700	1,000	5,000	1,000	18,000
28	4,200	3,700	1,000	5,000	1,000	12,900

Required

A single transaction took place on each day. Describe briefly the transaction that most likely occurred on each day, beginning with August 9. Indicate which accounts were increased or decreased and by what amount. No revenue or expense transactions occurred on these dates.

P1-4A Collins Photographic Studio provides pictures for high-school yearbooks. The capital balance of L. Collins, owner of the company, was $50,000 at December 31, 20X8. During 20X9 he withdrew $16,000 for personal use. At December 31, 20X9, the business's accounting records show these balances:

Preparing the financial statements—simple situation
(Obj. 5)

Accounts receivable	$ 8,000	Rent expense	$ 7,000
Note payable	12,000	Cash	16,000
L. Collins, capital	?	Accounts payable	6,000
Salary expense	22,000	Advertising expense	4,000
Equipment	65,000	Service revenue	70,000

Prepare the following financial statements for Collins Photographic Studio:

a. Income statement for the year ended December 31, 20X9
b. Statement of owner's equity for the year ended December 31, 20X9
c. Balance sheet at December 31, 20X9

P1-5A The amounts of (a) the assets and liabilities of Vail Financial Consultants at December 31, 20X4, and (b) the revenues and expenses of the company for the year ended on that date follow. The items are listed in alphabetical order.

Income statement, statement of owner's equity, balance sheet
(Obj. 5, 6)

Accounts payable	$12,000	Note payable	$31,000
Accounts receivable	3,000	Property tax expense	2,000
Building	56,000	Rent expense	14,000
Cash	7,000	Salary expense	38,000
Equipment	21,000	Service revenue	108,000
Interest expense	4,000	Supplies	7,000
Interest payable	1,000	Utilities expense	3,000
Land	8,000		

The capital balance of Matthew Vail, the owner, was $43,000 at December 31, 20X3. During 20X4, Vail withdrew $32,000 for personal use.

Required

1. Prepare the income statement of Vail Financial Consultants for the year ended December 31, 20X4.

2. Prepare the company's statement of owner's equity for the year ended December 31, 20X4.

3. Prepare the company's balance sheet at December 31, 20X4.

4. Answer these questions about the company.
   a. Was the result of operations for the year a profit or a loss? How much?
   b. Did Vail drain off all the earnings for the year, or did he increase the company's capital during the period? How would his actions affect the company's ability to borrow?
   c. How much in total economic resources does the company have as it moves into the new year? How much does the company owe? What is the dollar amount of Vail's equity interest in the business at the end of the year?

Balance sheet, entity concept
(Obj. 2, 3, 5)

P1-6A Helen Chuy is a realtor. Chuy organized the business as a proprietorship on March 10, 20X6. Consider the following facts at March 31, 20X6:

a. Chuy had $15,000 in her personal bank account and $17,000 in her business bank account.
b. Office supplies on hand at the real estate office totaled $1,000.
c. Chuy's business spent $15,000 for an **Electronic Realty Associates** (ERA) franchise, which entitled Chuy to represent herself as an ERA agent. This franchise is an asset.
d. Chuy owed $34,000 on a note payable for some land that had been acquired by the business for a total price of $60,000.
e. Chuy owed $90,000 on a personal mortgage on her personal residence, which she acquired in 20X1 for a total price of $175,000.
f. Chuy owed $950 on her personal VISA credit card.
g. Chuy acquired business furniture for $12,000 on March 26. Of this amount, Chuy's business owed $6,000 on account at March 31.

Required

1. Prepare the balance sheet of the real estate business of Helen Chuy, Realtor, at March 31, 20X6.

2. Identify the personal items that would not be reported on the balance sheet of the business.

Correcting a balance sheet
(Obj. 5)

P1-7A The bookkeeper of Electronic Tax Service prepared the balance sheet of the company while the accountant was ill. The balance sheet contains numerous errors. In particular, the bookkeeper knew that the balance sheet should balance, so he plugged in the owner's equity amount to achieve this balance. The owner's equity amount, however, is not correct. All other amounts are accurate, but some are out of place.

Electronic Tax Service
Balance Sheet
Month Ended October 31, 20X7

Assets		Liabilities	
Cash	$ 5,400	Notes receivable	$ 3,000
Insurance expense.	300	Interest expense	2,000
Land	31,500	Office supplies	800
Salary expense.	3,300	Accounts receivable	2,600
Office furniture	6,700	Note payable	21,000
Accounts payable	3,000		
Utilities expense	2,100	**Owner's Equity**	
		Owner's equity	22,900
Total assets.	$52,300	Total liabilities.	$52,300

Required

1. Prepare the correct balance sheet, and date it correctly. Compute total assets, total liabilities, and owner's equity.

2. Identify the accounts that should *not* be presented on the balance sheet. State why you excluded them from the correct balance sheet you prepared. Where should these items be reported?

Problems

(Group B)

PI-IB Jerry Ford practiced law with a partnership for five years. Recently he opened his own law office, which he operates as a proprietorship. The name of the new entity is Jerry Ford, Attorney. Ford experienced the following events during the organizing phase of his new business and its first month of operations. Some of the events were personal and did not affect his law practice. Others were business transactions and should be accounted for by the business.

Entity concept, transaction analysis, accounting equation
(Obj. 2, 3, 4)

Feb. 4	Received $100,000 cash from former law partners.
5	Deposited $80,000 cash in a new business bank account titled Jerry Ford, Attorney.
6	Paid $300 cash for letterhead stationery for the new law office.
7	Purchased office furniture for the law office. Ford agreed to pay the account payable, $7,000, within 3 months.
10	Sold 500 shares of **Intel** stock, which he had owned for several years, receiving $75,000 cash.
11	Deposited the $75,000 cash from sale of the Intel stock in his personal bank account.
12	A representative of a large company telephoned Ford and told him of the company's intention to transfer its legal business to Jerry Ford, Attorney.
18	Finished court hearings on behalf of a client and submitted a bill for legal services, $5,000. Ford expected to collect from this client within two weeks.
25	Paid office rent, $1,000.
28	Withdrew $10,000 cash from the business for personal use.

Required

1. Analyze the effects of the events on the accounting equation of the proprietorship of Jerry Ford, Attorney. Use a format similar to Exhibit 1-7 on page 19.

2. At February 28, compute:
   a. Total assets
   b. Total liabilities
   c. Total owner's equity
   d. Net income or net loss for February

PI-2B Monica Bass owns and operates an interior design studio called Enchanting Designs. The following amounts summarize the financial position of her business on August 31, 20X2:

Transaction analysis, accounting equation, financial statements
(Obj. 3, 4, 5)

	Assets				=	Liabilities	+	Owner's Equity
		Accounts				Accounts		Monica Bass,
	Cash	+ Receivable	+ Supplies	+ Land	=	Payable	+	Capital
Bal.	2,250	1,500		12,000		8,000		7,750

During September 20X2, the following events occurred.

a. Bass inherited $20,000 and deposited the cash in the business bank account.
b. Performed services for a client and received cash of $700.

c. Paid off the beginning balance of accounts payable.
d. Purchased supplies on account, $1,000.
e. Collected cash from a customer on account, $1,000.
f. Invested personal cash of $1,000 in the business.
g. Consulted on the interior design of a major office building and billed the client for services rendered, $2,400.
h. Recorded the following business expenses for the month:
   1. Paid office rent, $900.
   2. Paid advertising, $100.
i. Sold supplies to another business for $150 cash, which was the cost of the supplies.
j. Withdrew cash of $2,000 for personal use.

Required

1. Analyze the effects of the preceding transactions on the accounting equation of Enchanting Designs. Adapt the format of Exhibit 1-7, page 19.
2. Prepare the income statement of Enchanting Designs for the month ended September 30, 20X2. List expenses in decreasing order by amount.
3. Prepare the entity's statement of owner's equity for the month ended September 30, 20X2.
4. Prepare the balance sheet at September 30, 20X2.

Business transactions and analysis
(Obj. 3, 4)

P1-3B Little People Day Care Center was recently formed. The balance of each item in the company's accounting equation is shown for March 10 and for each of the nine following business days.

	Cash	Accounts Receivable	Supplies	Land	Accounts Payable	Owner's Equity
Mar. 10	$ 4,000	$4,000	$1,000	$ 8,000	$4,000	$13,000
11	13,000	4,000	1,000	8,000	4,000	22,000
12	6,000	4,000	1,000	15,000	4,000	22,000
15	6,000	4,000	3,000	15,000	6,000	22,000
16	5,000	4,000	3,000	15,000	5,000	22,000
17	7,000	2,000	3,000	15,000	5,000	22,000
18	15,000	2,000	3,000	15,000	5,000	30,000
19	12,000	2,000	3,000	15,000	2,000	30,000
22	11,000	2,000	4,000	15,000	2,000	30,000
23	3,000	2,000	4,000	15,000	2,000	22,000

Required

A single transaction took place on each day. Briefly describe the transaction that most likely occurred on each day, beginning with March 11. Indicate which accounts were increased or decreased and by what amounts. No revenue or expense transactions occurred on these dates.

Preparing the financial statements—
simple situation
(Obj. 5)

P1-4B Robinson Chauffeur Service works weddings and prom-type parties. The capital balance of J. Robinson, the owner of the company, was $56,000 at December 31, 20X4. During 20X5 he withdrew $50,000 for personal use. At December 31, 20X5, the business's accounting records show these balances:

Accounts receivable	$ 3,000	Insurance expense	$ 4,000
Note payable	35,000	Cash	5,000
J. Robinson, capital	?	Accounts payable	1,000
Salary expense	14,000	Advertising expense	2,000
Automobiles	80,000	Service revenue	66,000

Prepare the following financial statements for Robinson Chauffeur Service:

a. Income statement for the year ended December 31, 20X5
b. Statement of owner's equity for the year ended December 31, 20X5
c. Balance sheet at December 31, 20X5

P1-5B Presented here are (a) the assets and liabilities of Ping Technology Consultants at December 31, 20X7, and (b) the revenues and expenses of the company for the year ended on that date. The items are listed in alphabetical order.

Income statement, statement of owner's equity, balance sheet
(Obj. 5, 6)

Accounts payable	$ 19,000	Land	$ 60,000
Accounts receivable	12,000	Note payable	85,000
Advertising expense	13,000	Property tax expense	4,000
Building	170,000	Rent expense	23,000
Cash	14,000	Salary expense	63,000
Equipment	20,000	Salary payable	1,000
Insurance expense	2,000	Service revenue	178,000
Interest expense	9,000	Supplies	3,000

The capital balance of Brian Sartor, the owner, was $150,000 at December 31, 20X6. During 20X7, Sartor withdrew $40,000 for personal use.

Required

1. Prepare Ping's income statement for the year ended December 31, 20X7.
2. Prepare the company's statement of owner's equity for the year ended December 31, 20X7.
3. Prepare the company's balance sheet at December 31, 20X7.
4. Answer these questions about the company:
   a. Was the result of operations for the year a profit or a loss? How much?
   b. Did Sartor drain off all the earnings for the year, or did he increase the company's capital during the period? How will his actions affect the company's ability to borrow?
   c. How much in total economic resources does the company have as it moves into the new year? How much does the company owe? What is the dollar amount of Sartor's equity interest in the business at the end of the year?

P1-6B Lou Phillips is a realtor. She organized her business as a proprietorship on November 24, 20X4. Consider the following facts at November 30, 20X4.

Balance sheet, entity concept
(Obj. 2, 3, 5)

a. Phillips owed $55,000 on a note payable for some undeveloped land that had been acquired by her business for a total price of $100,000.
b. Phillips' business had spent $20,000 for a **Century 21** real estate franchise, which entitled her to represent herself as a Century 21 agent. This franchise is a business asset.
c. Phillips owed $60,000 on a personal mortgage on her personal residence, which she acquired in 20X1 for a total price of $150,000.
d. Phillips had $8,000 in her personal bank account and $7,000 in her business bank account.
e. Phillips owed $1,800 on a personal charge account with the **Neiman-Marcus** store.
f. Phillips acquired business furniture for $17,000 on November 25. Of this amount, her business owed $6,000 on account at November 30.
g. Office supplies on hand at the real estate office totaled $1,000.
   1. Prepare the balance sheet of the real estate business of Lou Phillips, Realtor, at November 30, 20X4.
   2. Identify the personal items that would not be reported on the balance sheet of the business.

P1-7B The bookkeeper of Epson Printing Co. prepared the company's balance sheet while the accountant was ill. The balance sheet contains numerous errors. In particular, the bookkeeper knew that the balance sheet should balance, so he plugged in the owner's equity amount needed to achieve this balance. The owner's equity amount, however, is not correct. All other amounts are accurate, but some are out of place.

Correcting a balance sheet
(Obj. 5)

Epson Printing Co.

Balance Sheet
Month Ended July 31, 20X3

Assets		Liabilities	
Cash	$ 12,000	Accounts receivable.	$ 23,000
Office supplies.	1,000	Service revenue	68,000
Land	44,000	Property tax expense.	800
Salary expense.	2,500	Accounts payable	9,000
Office furniture	8,000		
Note payable	36,000	**Owner's Equity**	
Rent expense	4,000	Owner's equity	6,700
Total assets.	$107,500	Total liabilities.	$107,500

Required

1. Prepare the correct balance sheet, and date it correctly. Compute total assets, total liabilities, and owner's equity.

2. Identify the accounts that should *not* be presented on the balance sheet. State why you excluded them from the correct balance sheet you prepared. Where should these items be reported?

APPLY *Your Knowledge*

Decision Cases

Measuring net income
(Obj. 5, 6)

Case 1. Jimmy and Virginia Campbell saved all their married life with the dream of opening a bed and breakfast (B&B) in a quiet village in New England. They invested $300,000 of their own money and also got a $200,000 bank loan to round out the $500,000 they needed to get started. The Campbells bought a beautiful old Victorian home in Stowe, Vermont, for $200,000. It cost another $150,000 to renovate. They found most of the furniture at antique shops and flea markets—total cost was $50,000. Kitchen equipment cost $10,000, and a **Dell** computer set them back another $2,000.

Prior to the grand opening, the banker requests a report on their activities thus far. Jimmy and Virginia examine their bank statement and find it shows a cash balance of $88,000. They feel pretty good with that much net income in only six months. To better understand how well they are doing, they prepare the following income statement for presentation to the bank:

Old Victorian Bed and Breakfast

Income Statement
Six Months Ended June 30, 20X5

Revenues:	
Investments by owner	$300,000
Bank loan	200,000
Total revenues	500,000
Expenses:	
Cost of the house	$200,000
Repairs to house	150,000
Furniture expense	50,000
Kitchen equipment expense	10,000
Computer expense	2,000
Total expenses	412,000
Net income	$ 88,000

1. Suppose you are the Campbells' banker, and they have given you this income statement. Would you congratulate them on their net income? If so, explain why. If not, how would you advise them to measure the net income of the business? Does the amount of cash in the bank measure net income? Explain.

2. Show the Campbells how to prepare Old Victorian's balance sheet from their data.

Case 2. The proprietors of two businesses, James Dobson Company and O'Reilly Public Relations, have sought business loans from you. To decide whether to make the loans, you have requested their balance sheets.

Using financial statements to evaluate a loan request
(Obj. 1, 2, 6)

James Dobson Company
Balance Sheet
August 31, 20X4

Assets		Liabilities	
Cash	$ 9,000	Accounts payable	$ 12,000
Accounts receivable	14,000	Note payable	18,000
Merchandise inventory	85,000	Total liabilities	30,000
Store supplies	500		
Furniture and fixtures	9,000	**Owner's Equity**	
Building	80,000	James Dobson, capital	181,500
Land	14,000	Total liabilities	
Total assets	$211,500	and owner's equity	$211,500

O'Reilly Public Relations
Balance Sheet
August 31, 20X4

Assets		Liabilities	
Cash	$ 11,000	Accounts payable	$ 6,000
Accounts receivable	7,000	Note payable	168,000
Office supplies	1,000	Total liabilities	174,000
Office furniture	56,000	**Owner's Equity**	
Land	169,000	Bill O'Reilly, capital	70,000
		Total liabilities and	
Total assets	$244,000	owner's equity	$244,000

Required

1. Solely on the basis of these balance sheets, to which entity would you be more comfortable lending money? Explain fully, citing specific items and amounts from the balance sheets.

2. In addition to the balance sheet data, what other information would you require? Be specific.

Ethical Issues

Ethical Issue 1. The board of directors of McLane Wholesale Grocery is meeting to discuss the past year's results before releasing financial statements to the public. The discussion includes this exchange: Rebecca Stone, company president: "This has not been a good year! Revenue is down and expenses are way up. If we're not careful, we'll report a loss for the third year in a row. I can temporarily transfer some land that I own into the company's name, and that will beef up our balance sheet. Grant, can you save $500,000 from expenses? Then we can probably get the bank loan that we need."

Grant Tye, company chief accountant: "Rebecca, you are asking too much. Generally accepted accounting principles are designed to keep this sort of thing from happening."

Required

1. What is the fundamental ethical issue in this situation?
2. Discuss how Stone's proposals violate generally accepted accounting principles. Identify each specific concept or principle involved.

Ethical Issue 2. The tobacco companies have paid billions because of smoking-related illnesses. In particular, **Philip Morris**, a leading cigarette manufacturer, paid over $3 billion in one year.

Required

1. Suppose you are the chief financial officer (CFO) responsible for the financial statements of Philip Morris. What ethical issue would you face as you consider what to report in your company's annual report about the cash payments? What is the ethical course of action for you to take in this situation?
2. What are some of the negative consequences to Philip Morris for not telling the truth? What are some of the negative consequences to Philip Morris for telling the truth?

Financial Statement Case

Identifying items from a company's financial statements
(Obj. 3, 4)

This and similar cases in later chapters focus on the financial statement of a real company—**Amazon.com, Inc.**, the Internet shopping leader. As you work each case, you will gain confidence in your ability to use the financial statements of real companies.

Refer to Amazon.com's financial statements in Appendix A at the end of the book.

Required

1. How much in cash (including cash equivalents) did Amazon have on December 31, 2002?
2. What were the company's total assets at December 31, 2002? At December 31, 2001?
3. Write the company's accounting equation at December 31, 2002, by filling in the dollar amounts:

ASSETS = LIABILITIES + STOCKHOLDERS' EQUITY

---

4. Identify Net sales (revenue) for the year ended December 31, 2002. How much did total revenue increase or decrease from 2001 to 2002?
5. How much net income or net loss did Amazon experience for 2002 and for 2001? Was 2002 better or worse than 2001? State your reasons.

Team Projects

Project I. You are opening a pet kennel. Your purpose is to earn a profit, so you will need to establish the business. Assume you organize as a proprietorship.

1. Make a detailed list of 10 factors you must consider to establish the business.
2. Identify 10 or more transactions that your business will undertake to open and operate the kennel.
3. Prepare the kennel's income statement, statement of owner's equity, and balance sheet at the end of the first month of operations before you have had time to pay all the business's bills. Use made-up figures and include a complete heading for each financial statement. Date the balance sheet as of August 31, 20XX.
4. Discuss how you will evaluate the success of your business and how you will decide whether to continue its operation.

Project 2. You are promoting a rock concert in your area. Your purpose is to earn a profit, so you will need to establish the business. Assume you organize as a proprietorship.

Required

1. Make a detailed list of 10 factors you must consider to establish the business.
2. Describe 10 of the items your business must arrange in order to promote and stage the rock concert.
3. Prepare your business's income statement, statement of owner's equity, and balance sheet on August 31, 20XX, immediately after the rock concert and before you have had time to pay all the business's bills and to collect all receivables. Use made-up amounts, and include a complete heading for each financial statement. For the income statement and the statement of owner's equity, assume the period is the three months ended August 31, 20XX.
4. Assume that you will continue to promote rock concerts if the venture is successful. If it is unsuccessful, you will terminate the business within three months after the concert. Discuss how you will evaluate the success of your venture and how you will decide whether to continue in business.

For Internet Exercises, go to the Web site www.prenhall.com/horngren.

APTER **2**

Recording Business Transactions

TIPS CHECK YOUR RESOURCES

- Visit the www.prenhall.com/horngren **Web site** for self-study quizzes, video clips, and other resources

- Try the **Quick Check** exercise at the end of the chapter to test your knowledge

- Learn the **key terms**

- Do the **Starter** exercises keyed in the margins

- Work the **mid-** and **end-of-chapter summary problems**

- Use the **Concept Links** to review material in other chapters

- Search the **CD** for review materials by chapter or by key word

- Watch the **tutorial videos** to review key concepts.

- Watch the **On Location Three Dog Bakery** video for the role of accounting in manufacturing and retail business.

LEARNING OBJECTIVES

1. Use accounting terms

2. Apply the rules of debit and credit

3. Record transactions in the journal

4. Post from the journal to the ledger

5. Prepare and use a trial balance

6. Analyze transactions without a journal

What is your favorite snack food? If you are like most people, it may be Doritos, Sun Chips, or plain potato chips. All of these are Frito-Lay products. Year in and year out, Frito-Lay leads the prepared-snack-food industry. How does this company deliver fresh quantities of chips to thousands of stores every day of the year?

One of Frito-Lay's great advantages is its accounting system. Route managers use handheld computers to record how many products are sold each day. The data are relayed to company headquarters, and managers can see instantly which products are moving and where. Suppose Doritos are selling well and potato chips are currently out of favor. Frito-Lay managers know to buy more corn for Doritos and less potatoes for chips. The company avoids waste by buying only what it needs to meet consumer demand.

Frito-Lay

The result? Frito-Lay is very profitable. This chapter shows how Frito-Lay and other companies record their business transactions. The procedures outlined here are followed by entities ranging from giants like Frito-Lay to a local travel agency such as Gay Gillen eTravel. ■

 Use accounting terms

Account
The detailed record of the changes in a particular asset, liability, or owner's equity during a period. The basic summary device of accounting.

In Chapter 1, p. 10, we learned that the accounting equation is the basic tool in all of accounting. It measures the assets of the business and the claims to those assets.

The following diagram summarizes the accounting process covered in this chapter.

Accounting begins and ends with accounts.

The Account, the Ledger, and the Journal

The basic summary device of accounting is the **account**. This is the detailed record of all the changes that have occurred in a particular asset, liability, or owner's equity during a period. As we saw in Chapter 1, business transactions— such as buying and selling—cause the changes.

Accountants record transactions first in a **journal**. The journal is the chronological record of the transactions. Accountants then copy (post) the data to the accounts in a record called the **ledger**. A list of all the ledger accounts, along with their balances, is called a **trial balance**.

Take a moment to memorize these important terms. You will be using them over and over again.

- *Account* —the detailed record of the changes in a particular asset, liability, or owner's equity
- *Ledger* —the record holding all the accounts
- *Journal* —the chronological record of transactions
- *Trial balance* —the list of all the accounts with their balances

Accounts are grouped in three broad categories, according to the accounting equation ←:

ASSETS = LIABILITIES + OWNER'S EQUITY

Suppose you bought a $20,000 Pontiac Grand Am and had to borrow $12,000 to pay for it. Can you write your personal accounting equation for this transaction?

Answer

ASSETS	=	LIABILITIES	+	OWNER'S EQUITY
$20,000	=	$12,000	+	$8,000

Assets

Assets are economic resources that will benefit the business in the future. Most firms use the following asset accounts.

CASH The Cash account is a record of the cash effects of transactions. Cash includes money, such as a bank account balance, paper currency, coins, and checks. Successful companies such as Frito-Lay have plenty of cash.

NOTES RECEIVABLE A business may sell goods or services and receive a *promissory note*. A note receivable is a written pledge that the customer will pay a fixed amount of money by a certain date. Notes Receivable is a record of the promissory notes the business expects to collect in cash. If you loan money to a friend and get him to sign a note, you have a note receivable from your friend.

ACCOUNTS RECEIVABLE A business may sell goods or services in exchange for an oral or implied promise of future cash receipt. Such sales are made on credit ("on account"). The Accounts Receivable account holds these amounts. Most sales in the United States and in other developed countries are made on account receivable. A receivable from your friend, if not supported by a formal note, could be an account receivable.

PREPAID EXPENSES A business often pays certain expenses, such as rent and insurance, in advance. A *prepaid expense* is an asset because the prepayment provides a future benefit for the business. The ledger has a separate asset account for each prepaid expense. Prepaid Rent, Prepaid Insurance, and Office Supplies are prepaid expense accounts. Your prepaid rent on your apartment or dorm room is an asset to you.

LAND The Land account is a record of the cost of land a business owns and uses in its operations. Land held for sale is accounted for separately—in an investment account.

BUILDING The cost of a business's buildings—office, warehouse, store, and the like—appear in the Buildings account. Frito-Lay owns buildings around the country, where it makes Doritos and other snack foods. But buildings held for sale are separate assets accounted for as investments.

EQUIPMENT, FURNITURE, AND FIXTURES A business has a separate asset account for each type of equipment—Computer Equipment, Office Equipment, and Store Equipment, for example. The Furniture and Fixtures account shows the cost of this asset. Frito-Lay has lots of manufacturing equipment.

Liabilities

Recall that a *liability* is a debt. A business generally has fewer liability accounts than asset accounts because a business's liabilities are summarized in a few accounts.

NOTES PAYABLE The Notes Payable account is the opposite of Notes Receivable. Notes Payable represents amounts the business must pay because it signed promissory notes to borrow money or to purchase goods or services.

ACCOUNTS PAYABLE The Accounts Payable account is the opposite of Accounts Receivable. The oral or implied promise to pay a debt arising from a credit purchase appears in the Accounts Payable account. Such a purchase is said to be made on account. All companies, including Frito-Lay, Coca-Cola, and eBay, have accounts payable.

Journal
The chronological accounting record of an entity's transactions.

Ledger
The record holding all the accounts.

Trial Balance
A list of all the accounts with their balances.

Student ResourceCD

asset, expenses, liability, owner's equity, revenues

ACCRUED LIABILITIES An *accrued liability* is a liability for an expense that has not been paid. Taxes Payable, Interest Payable, and Salary Payable are liability accounts of Frito-Lay and most other companies.

Owner's Equity

The owner's claim to the assets of the business is called *owner's equity*. In a proprietorship or a partnership, owner's equity is split into separate accounts for the owner's capital balance and the owner's withdrawals.

CAPITAL The Capital account shows the owner's claim to the assets of the business. Consider Gay Gillen eTravel. Subtracting total liabilities from total assets computes the travel agency's capital. The Capital balance equals the owner's investments in the business plus net income and minus any net losses and owner withdrawals. ←

See the statement of owner's equity in Chapter 1, Exhibit 1-8. →

WITHDRAWALS When Gay Gillen withdraws cash from the business for personal use, the travel agency's assets and owner's equity decrease. The amounts taken out of the business appear in a separate account titled Gay Gillen, Withdrawals, or Gay Gillen, Drawing. If withdrawals were recorded directly in the Capital account, the amount of owner withdrawals would not show up and the data might be lost. The Withdrawals account *decreases* owner's equity.

REVENUES The increase in owner's equity created by delivering goods or services to customers is called *revenue*. The ledger contains as many revenue accounts as needed. Gay Gillen eTravel needs a Service Revenue account for amounts earned by providing travel services. If Gay Gillen eTravel lends money to an outsider, it needs an Interest Revenue account for the interest earned on the loan. If the business rents a building to a tenant, it needs a Rent Revenue account.

EXPENSES Expenses use up assets or create liabilities in the course of operating a business. Expenses have the opposite effect of revenues; expenses *decrease* owner's equity. A business needs a separate account for each type of expense, such as Salary Expense, Rent Expense, Advertising Expense, and Utilities Expense. Businesses strive to minimize their expenses in order to maximize net income—whether it's General Electric or Gay Gillen eTravel.

Exhibit 2-1 shows how asset, liability, and owner's equity accounts can be grouped in the ledger.

✔ Starter 2-1

✔ Starter 2-2

Exhibit 2-1

The Ledger (Asset, Liability, and Owner's Equity Accounts)

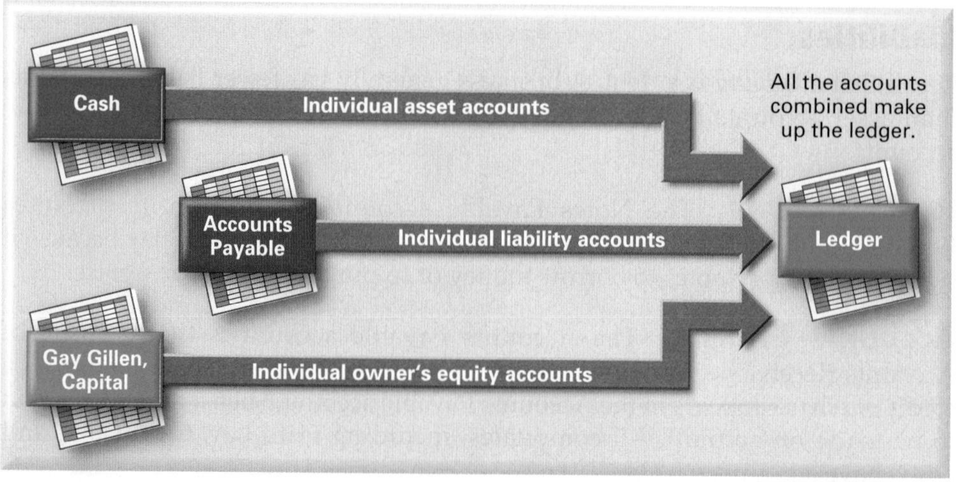

Double-Entry Accounting

Accounting is based on a *double-entry system*, which means that we record the *dual effects* of a business transaction. *Each transaction affects at least two accounts.* For example, Gay Gillen eTravel's $30,000 cash receipt from the owner increased both the Cash and the Capital of the business. It would be incomplete to record only the increase in cash without recording the increase in owner's equity.

Consider a cash purchase of supplies. What are the dual effects? The purchase (1) decreases cash and (2) increases supplies. A credit purchase of supplies (1) increases supplies and (2) increases accounts payable.

The T-Account

The most widely used account format is called the *T-account* because it takes the form of the capital letter "T." The vertical line in the T-account divides the account into its left and right sides, with the title at the top. For example, the Cash account of a business appears as follows.

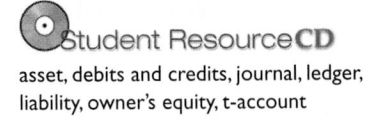

Student Resource CD

asset, debits and credits, journal, ledger, liability, owner's equity, t-account

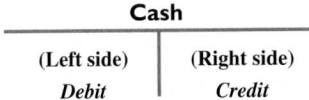

Cash

(Left side)	(Right side)
Debit	*Credit*

The left side of the account is called the **debit** side, and the right side is called the **credit** side. The words *debit* and *credit* are new. To become comfortable using them, remember that

Debit
The left side of an account.

Credit
The right side of an account.

Debit = Left side   Credit = Right side

The terms *debit* and *credit* are deeply entrenched in business.[1] Debit and credit are abbreviated as follows:

Dr = Debit   Cr = Credit

Increases and Decreases in the Accounts

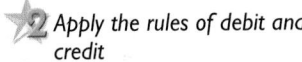

Apply the rules of debit and credit

The account category (asset, liability, equity) governs how we record increases and decreases. For any given account, increases are recorded on one side, and decreases are recorded on the other side. The following T-accounts provide a summary.

Assets

Increases **are recorded** on the left (debit) **side.**	Decreases **are recorded** on the right (credit) **side.**

Liabilities and Owner's Equity

Decreases **are recorded** on the left (debit) **side.**	Increases **are recorded** on the right (credit) **side.**

These are the *rules of debit and credit*.

In your study of accounting, forget the general usage of credit and debit. Remember that *debit means left side* and *credit means right side*. Whether an account is increased or decreased by a debit or a credit depends on the type of account.

In a computerized accounting system, the computer interprets debits and credits as increases or decreases by account category. For example, a computer reads a debit to Cash as an increase. The computer reads a debit to Accounts Payable as a decrease.

---

[1]The words *debit* and *credit* abbreviate the Latin terms *debitum* and *creditum*. Luca Pacioli, the Italian monk who wrote about accounting in the 15th century, popularized these terms.

This pattern of recording debits and credits is based on the accounting equation:

Assets = Liabilities + Owner's Equity
Debits = Credits

Assets are on the opposite side of the equation from liabilities and owner's equity. Therefore, increases and decreases in assets are recorded in the opposite manner from increases and decreases in liabilities and owner's equity. Liabilities and owner's equity are on the same side, so they are treated in the same way. Exhibit 2-2 shows the relationship between the accounting equation and the rules of debit and credit.

Exhibit 2-2

The Accounting Equation and the
Rules of Debit and Credit

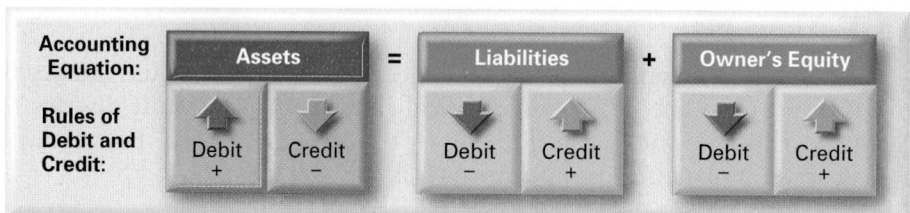

To illustrate the ideas diagrammed in Exhibit 2-2, reconsider the first transaction from Chapter 1. Gay Gillen eTravel received $30,000 cash from Gillen and gave her the owner's equity in the business. We are accounting for the business entity Gay Gillen eTravel. We are not accounting for Gay Gillen, the person. Which accounts of the business are affected? By what amounts? On what side (debit or credit)?

The answer: The business's Assets and Capital would increase by $30,000, as the T-accounts show.

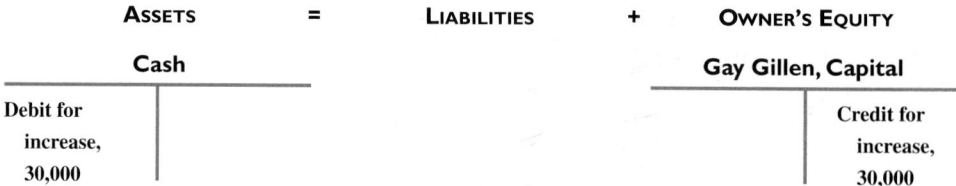

The amount remaining in an account is called its *balance*. The first transaction gives Cash a $30,000 debit balance and Gay Gillen, Capital a $30,000 credit balance.

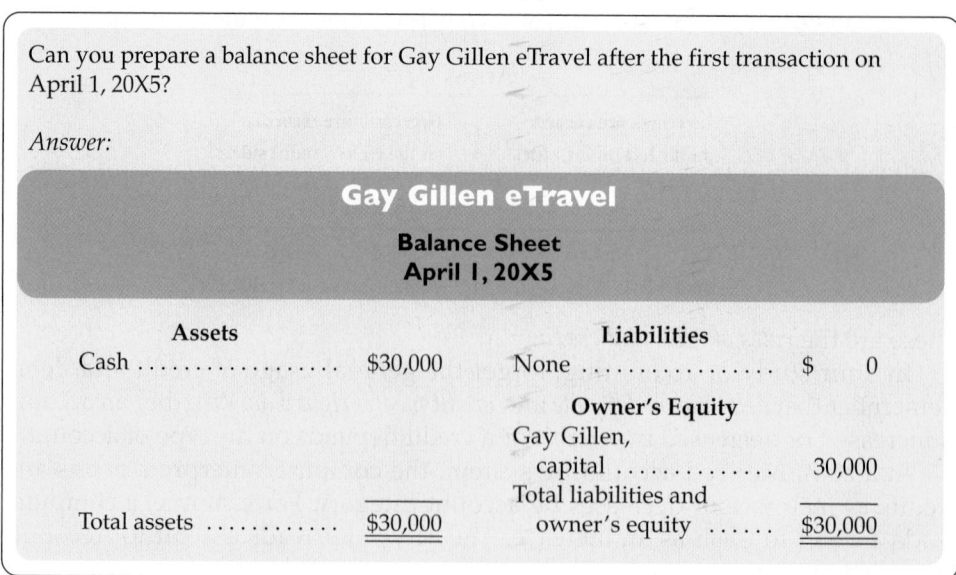

Can you prepare a balance sheet for Gay Gillen eTravel after the first transaction on April 1, 20X5?

Answer:

Gay Gillen eTravel

Balance Sheet
April 1, 20X5

Assets		Liabilities	
Cash	$30,000	None	$ 0
		Owner's Equity	
		Gay Gillen,	
		capital	30,000
		Total liabilities and	
Total assets	$30,000	owner's equity	$30,000

Notice that Assets = Liabilities + Owner's Equity *and* that total debit amounts = total credit amounts. Exhibit 2-3 illustrates the accounting equation and Gay Gillen eTravel's first three transactions.

Exhibit 2-3   The Accounting Equation and the First Three Transactions of Gay Gillen eTravel

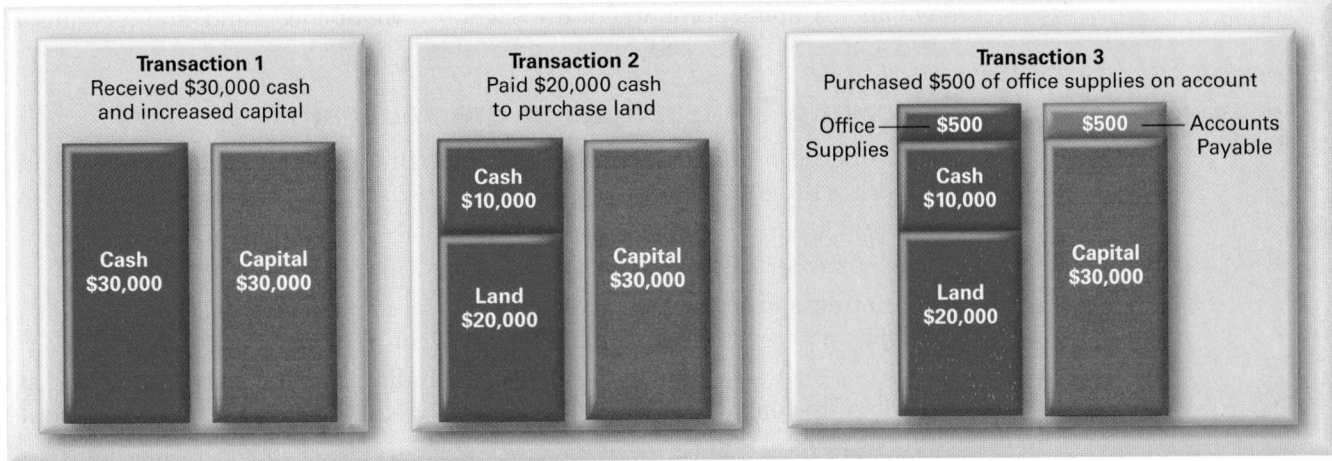

The second transaction is a $20,000 cash purchase of land. This transaction decreases (credits) Cash and increases (debits) Land, as shown in the T-accounts:

ASSETS	**=**	**LIABILITIES**	**+**	**OWNER'S EQUITY**

Cash

Balance	30,000	Credit for
		decrease,
		20,000
Balance	10,000	

Land

Debit for	
increase,	
20,000	
Balance	20,000

Gay Gillen, Capital

	Balance	30,000

After this transaction, Cash has a $10,000 debit balance ($30,000 debit minus $20,000 credit), Land has a debit balance of $20,000, and Gay Gillen, Capital has a $30,000 credit balance.

Transaction 3 is a $500 purchase of office supplies on account. This transaction increases the asset Office Supplies and the liability Accounts Payable, as shown in the following accounts and in the right side of Exhibit 2-3 (labeled transaction 3):

ASSETS	**=**	**LIABILITIES**	**+**	**OWNER'S EQUITY**

Cash

Balance	10,000	

Office Supplies

Debit for	
increase,	500
Balance	500

Land

Balance	20,000

Accounts Payable

	Credit for
	increase, 500
	Balance 500

Gay Gillen, Capital

	Balance 30,000

We create accounts as needed. The process of creating a new T-account is called *opening the account*. For transaction 1, we opened the Cash account and the Gay Gillen, Capital account. For transaction 2, we opened Land, and for transaction 3, Office Supplies and Accounts Payable.

Recording Transactions in the Journal

⭐ 3 *Record transactions in the journal*

In practice, accountants record transactions first in a *journal*. The journalizing process has three steps:

1. Specify each account affected and classify each account by type (asset, liability, or owner's equity).
2. Determine whether each account is increased or decreased. Use the rules of debit and credit to debit or credit each account.
3. Record the transaction in the journal, including a brief explanation. The debit side of the entry is entered first and the credit side last. Total debits should always equal total credits.

Step 3, "Recording the transaction in the journal," is also called "making the journal entry" or "journalizing the transaction."

These steps are the same in a computerized system or a manual system. In step 3, the journal entry is generally entered into the computer by account number, and the account name pops up automatically.

Let's journalize the first transaction of Gay Gillen eTravel—the receipt of Gillen's $30,000 cash investment in the business.

STEP 1 The accounts affected by the receipt of cash from the owner (Exhibit 2-3) are *Cash* and *Gay Gillen, Capital*. Cash is an asset. Gay Gillen, Capital is an owner's equity account.

STEP 2 Both accounts increase by $30,000. Therefore, we debit Cash, the asset account, and we credit Gay Gillen, Capital, the owner's equity account.

STEP 3 The journal entry is

Journal			Page 1
Date	Accounts and Explanation	Debit	Credit
Apr. 1[a]	Cash[b] (↑ asset; debit)	30,000[d]	
	Gay Gillen, Capital[c] (↑ equity; credit) .		30,000[e]
	Received investment from owner.[f]		

Alongside Cash and Gay Gillen, Capital, we show an arrow to indicate an increase or a decrease in the account. We also give the type of account and the related debit or credit rule. These parenthetical notations are *not* part of the formal journal entry and are *not required*. But they will help you learn how to make journal entries.[2]

The journal entry includes (a) the date of the transaction, (b) the title of the account debited (printed flush left), (c) the title of the account credited (indented), the dollar amounts of the (d) debit and (e) credit, and (f) a short explanation of the transaction. Dollar signs are omitted in the money columns because it is understood that the amounts are in dollars. The journal presents the full story for each transaction. Exhibit 2-4 shows how Journal page 1 looks after Gillen has recorded the first transaction (without the extra notation).

Exhibit 2-4 **The Journal**

Journal			Page 1
Date	Accounts and Explanation	Debit	Credit
Apr. 1	Cash	30,000	
	Gay Gillen, Capital		30,000
	Received investment from owner.		

---

[2]We thank Michael Stemkoski for suggesting these aids to student learning.

Copying Information (Posting) from Journal to Ledger

Posting in accounting means to copy the amounts from the journal to the ledger. Debits in the journal are posted as debits in the ledger, and credits in the journal are credits in the ledger. Debits never become credits, and credits never become debits. The investment transaction of Gay Gillen eTravel is posted to the ledger in Exhibit 2-5.

Post from the journal to the ledger

Posting
Copying amounts from the journal to the ledger.

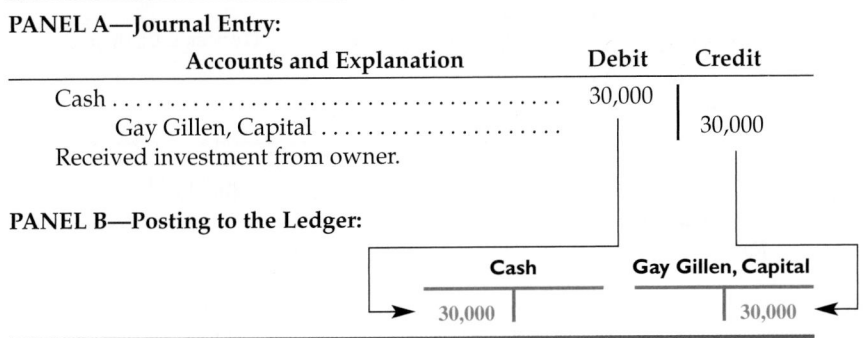

Exhibit 2-5

Making a Journal Entry and Posting to the Ledger

- The Account, the Ledger, and the Journal
- Double-Entry Accounting
- **Flow of Accounting Data**
- Details of Journals and Ledgers
- Expanding the Accounting Equation
- Expanded Problem: Revenues and Expenses
- Quick Decision Making

Student Resource CD
account, debits and credits, journal, ledger, transaction analysis, trial balance

The Flow of Accounting Data

Exhibit 2-6 summarizes the flow of data through the accounting system. In the pages that follow, we account for six of Gay Gillen eTravel's early transactions. In this first half of the chapter we do not account for any revenue or expense transactions. Those we save for the second half of the chapter. Keep in mind that we are accounting for the travel agency. We are *not* accounting for Gay Gillen's *personal* transactions.

Exhibit 2-6   Flow of Accounting Data from the Journal to the Ledger

Transaction Analysis, Journalizing, and Posting to the Accounts

TRANSACTION 1 ANALYSIS   The business received $30,000 cash that Gay Gillen invested to begin her travel agency. The business increased its asset cash, so we debit Cash. The business also increased owner's equity, so we credit Gay Gillen, Capital.

Accounting Equation	ASSETS	=	LIABILITIES	+	OWNER'S EQUITY
	Cash				Gay Gillen, Capital
	+30,000	=	0	+	+30,000

Journal Entry

Cash (↑ asset; debit)   30,000
    Gay Gillen, Capital (↑ equity; credit) . . .   30,000
Received investment from owner.

Ledger Accounts

Cash		Gay Gillen, Capital	
(1) 30,000		(1) 30,000	

TRANSACTION 2 ANALYSIS   Gillen paid $20,000 cash for land. The purchase decreased cash; therefore, credit Cash. The asset, land, increased, so we debit the Land account.

Accounting Equation	ASSETS		=	LIABILITIES	+	OWNER'S EQUITY
	Cash	Land				
	−20,000	+20,000	=	0	+	0

Journal Entry

Land (↑ asset; debit)   20,000
    Cash (↓ asset; credit)   20,000
Paid cash for land.

Ledger Accounts

Cash			Land	
(1) **30,000**	(2) 20,000		(2) 20,000	

TRANSACTION 3 ANALYSIS   Gillen purchased $500 of office supplies on account. The asset office supplies increased, so we debit Office Supplies. The liability accounts payable also increased, so we credit Accounts Payable.

Accounting Equation	ASSETS	=	LIABILITIES	+	OWNER'S EQUITY
	Office Supplies		Accounts Payable		
	+500	=	+500	+	0

Journal Entry

Office Supplies (↑ asset; debit)   500
    Accounts Payable (↑ liability; credit) . . .   500
Purchased supplies on account.

Ledger Accounts

Office Supplies		Accounts Payable	
(3) 500		(3) 500	

TRANSACTION 4 ANALYSIS   Gillen paid $300 on the account payable created in transaction 3. The payment decreased cash; therefore, credit Cash. The payment decreased the liability accounts payable, so we debit Accounts Payable.

Accounting Equation	ASSETS	=	LIABILITIES	+	OWNER'S EQUITY
	Cash		Accounts Payable		
	−300	=	−300	+	0

Journal Entry

Accounts Payable (↓ liability; debit) 300
    Cash (↓ asset; credit)................. | 300
Paid cash on account.

Ledger Accounts

	Cash					Accounts Payable		
(1)	30,000	(2)	20,000		(4)	300	(3)	500
		(4)	300					

TRANSACTION 5 ANALYSIS   Gay Gillen remodeled her home with personal funds. This is not a transaction of the travel agency, so we make no entry on its books.

TRANSACTION 6 ANALYSIS   Gillen withdrew $2,000 cash for personal living expenses. The withdrawal decreased the entity's cash; therefore, credit Cash. The transaction also decreased owner's equity. Decreases in equity that result from owner withdrawals are debited to a separate account, Withdrawals. Therefore, debit Gay Gillen, Withdrawals.

Accounting Equation	ASSETS	=	LIABILITIES	+	OWNERS' EQUITY
	Cash				Gay Gillen, Withdrawals
	−2,000	=	0		−2,000

Journal Entry

Gay Gillen, Withdrawals (↓ equity; debit)...... 2,000
    Cash (↓ asset; credit)................. | 2,000
Withdrawal by owner.

Ledger Accounts

	Cash					Gay Gillen, Withdrawals	
(1)	30,000	(2)	20,000		(6)	2,000	
		(4)	300				
		(6)	2,000				

Each journal entry posted to the ledger is keyed by date or by transaction number. In this way, any transaction can be traced from the journal to the ledger and back to the journal. This linking allows you to locate any information you may need.

Accounts After Posting

We next show the accounts after posting the preceding transactions. The accounts are grouped under their headings.

Each account has a balance, denoted *Bal*. An account balance is the difference between the account's total debits and its total credits. For example, the $7,700 balance in the Cash account is the difference between

- Total debits, $30,000
- Total credits, $22,300 ($20,000 + $300 + $2,000)

The balance is the amount of cash left over after the journal entries have been posted to the account. We set an account balance apart from the transaction amounts by a horizontal line. The final figure in an account, below the horizontal line, is the balance.

ASSETS		=	LIABILITIES		+	OWNER'S EQUITY	

Cash			Accounts Payable			Gay Gillen, Capital	
(1) 30,000	(2) 20,000	(4) 300	(3) 500			(1) 30,000	
	(4) 300		Bal. 200			Bal. 30,000	
	(6) 2,000						
Bal. 7,700							

Office Supplies						Gay Gillen, Withdrawals	
(3) 500						(6) 2,000	
Bal. 500						Bal. 2,000	

Land	
(2) 20,000	
Bal. 20,000	

If the sum of an account's debits is greater than the sum of its credits, that account has a debit balance, as Cash does. If the sum of the credits is greater, the account has a credit balance, as for Accounts Payable.

The Normal Balance of an Account

Normal Balance
The balance that appears on the side of an account—debit or credit—where we record increases.

An account's **normal balance** appears on the side of the account—debit or credit—where we record *increases*. For example, Cash and other assets normally have a debit balance, so assets are called *debit-balance accounts*. Conversely, liabilities and owner's equity normally have a credit balance, so they are *credit-balance accounts*. Exhibit 2-7 illustrates the normal balances of assets, liabilities, and owner's equity.

Exhibit 2-7

Normal Balances of the Balance Sheet Accounts

Assets		=	Liabilities		+	Owner's Equity	
Normal Bal. Debit			Normal Bal. Credit			Normal Bal. Credit	

An account that normally has a debit balance may occasionally have a credit balance. That indicates a negative amount of the item. For example, Cash will have a temporary credit balance if the business overdraws its bank account. Similarly, the liability Accounts Payable—normally a credit-balance account—will have a debit balance if the entity overpays its account. In other instances, an odd balance indicates an error. For example, a credit balance in Office Supplies, Office Furniture, or Buildings reveals an error because negative amounts of these assets make no sense.

✔ Starter 2-3

✔ Starter 2-4

✔ Starter 2-5

As we saw earlier, owner's equity contains the Capital account and the Withdrawals account. In total, these accounts show a normal credit balance. An individual owner's equity account with its normal credit balance is Gay Gillen, Capital. This account represents an *increase* in owner's equity. An owner's equity account that carries a normal debit balance is Gay Gillen, Withdrawals. Withdrawals represent a *decrease* in equity.

Revenues increase owner's equity, so the normal balance of a revenue is a credit. Expenses decrease equity, so the normal balance of an expense is a debit.

⭐5 *Prepare and use a trial balance*

The Trial Balance

A trial balance lists all the accounts with their balances taken from the ledger—assets first, followed by liabilities and then owner's equity. In a manual accounting system, the trial balance provides a check on accuracy by showing whether total debits equal total credits. In all types of systems, the trial balance is a useful summary of the accounts and their balances. A trial balance may be taken at any time. The most common time is at the end of the accounting period. Exhibit 2-8 is the trial balance of Gay Gillen eTravel after the first six transactions.

Gay Gillen eTravel

Trial Balance
April 30, 20X5

Exhibit 2-8

Trial Balance

Account Title	Balance	
	Debit	Credit
Cash	$ 7,700	
Office supplies	500	
Land	20,000	
Accounts payable		$ 200
Gay Gillen, capital		30,000
Gay Gillen, withdrawals	2,000	
Total	$30,200	$30,200

MID-CHAPTER *Summary Problem*

On August 1, 20X6, Liz Shea opens Shea's Research Service. She owns the proprietorship. During its first 10 days of operations, the business completes these transactions:

a. To begin operations, Shea deposits $40,000 of personal funds in a bank account titled Shea's Research Service. The business receives the cash and gives Shea capital (owner's equity).
b. Pays $30,000 cash for a small building to be used as an office.
c. Purchases office supplies for $500 on account.
d. Pays cash of $6,000 for office furniture.
e. Pays $150 on the account payable created in transaction (c).
f. Withdraws $1,000 cash for personal use.

Required

1. Give the accounting equation for each transaction. Then journalize these transactions and post to the accounts. Key the journal entries by letter.
2. Show all the T-accounts after posting.
3. Prepare the trial balance of Shea's Research Service at August 10, 20X6.

CHECK YOUR RESOURCES

Solution

Requirement 1

a. Accounting Equation

ASSETS	=	LIABILITIES	+	OWNER'S EQUITY
Cash				Liz Shea, Capital
+40,000	=	0	+	$40,000

Journal Entry

Cash 40,000
 Liz Shea, Capital 40,000
Received investment from owner.

Ledger Accounts

Cash	Liz Shea, Capital
(a) 40,000	(a) 40,000

b. Accounting Equation

	ASSETS		=	LIABILITIES	+	OWNER'S EQUITY
	Cash	Building				
	−30,000	+30,000	=	0	+	0

Journal Entry

Building 30,000
    Cash............................   30,000
Purchased building.

Ledger Accounts

Cash				Building		
(a)	40,000	(b)	30,000	(b)	30,000	

c. Accounting Equation

	ASSETS	=	LIABILITIES	+	OWNER'S EQUITY
	Office Supplies		Accounts Payable		
	+500	=	+500	+	0

Journal Entry

Office Supplies....................... 500
    Accounts Payable   500
Purchased office supplies on account.

Ledger Accounts

Office Supplies			Accounts Payable		
(c)	500			(c)	500

d. Accounting Equation

	ASSETS		=	LIABILITIES	+	OWNER'S EQUITY
		Office				
	Cash	Furniture				
	−6,000	+6,000	=	0	+	0

Journal Entry

Office Furniture...................... 6,000
    Cash............................   6,000
Purchased office furniture.

Ledger Accounts

Cash				Office Furniture		
(a)	40,000	(b)	30,000	(d)	6,000	
		(d)	6,000			

e. Accounting Equation

	ASSETS	=	LIABILITIES	+	OWNER'S EQUITY
	Cash		Accounts Payable		
	−150	=	−150	+	0

Journal Entry

Accounts Payable 150
    Cash............................   150
Paid cash on account.

Ledger Accounts

Cash				Accounts Payable			
(a)	40,000	(b)	30,000	(e)	150	(c)	500
		(d)	6,000				
		(e)	150				

f. Accounting Equation

	ASSETS	=	LIABILITIES	+	OWNER'S EQUITY
	Cash				Liz Shea, Withdrawals
	−1,000	=	0	+	−1,000

Journal Entry

Liz Shea, Withdrawals 1,000
    Cash............................   1,000
Withdrawal by owner.

Ledger Accounts

	Cash					Liz Shea, Withdrawals	
(a)	40,000	(b)	30,000	(f)	1,000		
		(d)	6,000				
		(e)	150				
		(f)	1,000				

Requirement 2

ASSETS		=	LIABILITIES	+	OWNER'S EQUITY

Cash

(a)	40,000	(b)	30,000
		(d)	6,000
		(e)	150
		(f)	1,000
Bal.	2,850		

Office Furniture

(d)	6,000	
Bal.	6,000	

Accounts Payable

(e)	150	(c)	500
		Bal.	350

Liz Shea, Capital

		(a)	40,000
		Bal.	40,000

Liz Shea, Withdrawals

(f)	1,000	
Bal.	1,000	

Office Supplies

(c)	500	
Bal.	500	

Building

(b)	30,000	
Bal.	30,000	

Requirement 3

Shea's Research Service

Trial Balance
August 10, 20X6

Account Title	Debit	Credit
Cash	$ 2,850	
Office supplies	500	
Office furniture	6,000	
Building	30,000	
Accounts payable		$ 350
Liz Shea, capital		40,000
Liz Shea, withdrawals	1,000	
Total	$40,350	$40,350

Details of Journals and Ledgers

To focus on the main points of journalizing and posting, we have omitted certain data. In practice, the journal and the ledger provide details to create a "trail" through the records. For example, a supplier may bill us twice for an item that we purchased. To prove we paid the first bill, we would search the records to find our payment. To see how this process works, let's take a closer look at the journal and the ledger.

DETAILS IN THE JOURNAL Exhibit 2-9, Panel A, describes a transaction, and Panel B shows the journal. The page number appears in the upper right corner, and the journal displays the following information:

■ The *date* when the transaction occurred, April 1, 20X5.

■ The *accounts* debited and credited and an explanation.

Student ResourceCD

chart of accounts, journal, ledger

Exhibit 2-9

Journalizing and Posting

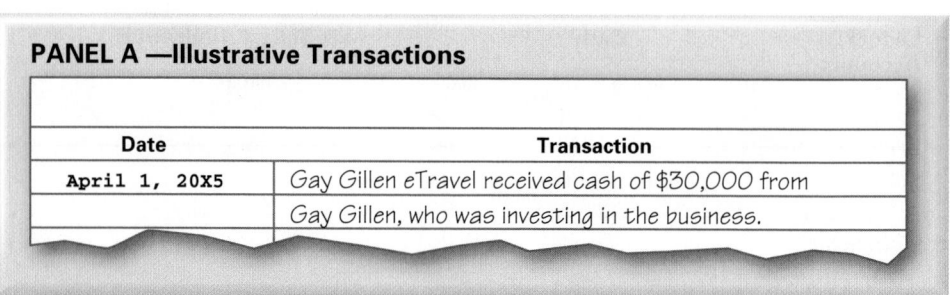

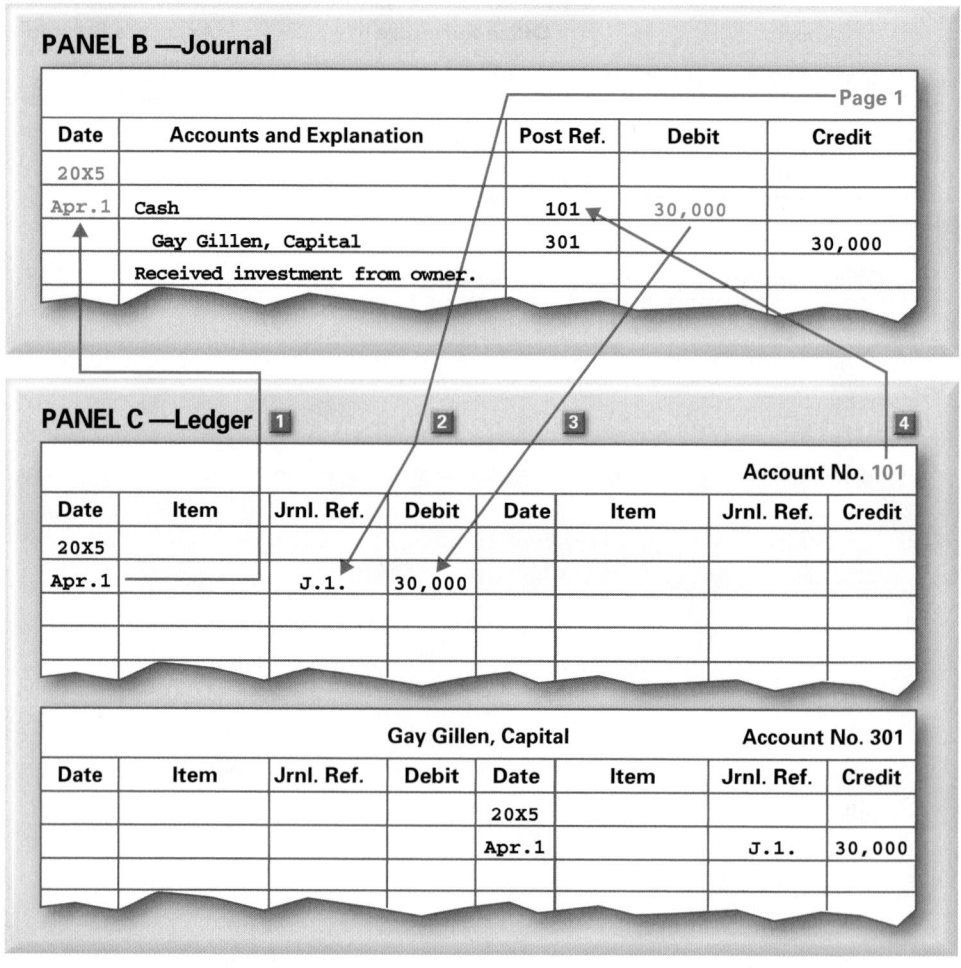

- The *posting reference*, abbreviated Post. Ref. Use of this column will become clear when we discuss posting.
- The *debit* column, for the dollar amount debited.
- The *credit* column, for the dollar amount credited.

DETAILS IN THE LEDGER   Exhibit 2-9, Panel C, shows the T-accounts affected by the first transaction: Cash and Gay Gillen, Capital. The account number appears at the upper right corner of each account. Each account has a separate column for

- The Date.
- The Item column, which can be used for any special notation.
- The Journal Reference column, abbreviated Jrnl. Ref. The use of this column will become clear when we discuss posting.
- The Debit column, with the amount debited.
- The Credit column, with the amount credited.

Posting from the Journal to the Ledger

Posting means copying information from the journal to the ledger. But how do we handle the details? Exhibit 2-9 illustrates the steps. Panel A describes the first transaction of the business entity, Gay Gillen eTravel; Panel B gives the journal; and Panel C shows the ledger.

The posting process includes four steps. After recording the transaction in the journal:

Arrow ①—Copy (post) the transaction **date** from the journal to the ledger.

Arrow ②—Copy (post) the journal page number from the journal to the ledger. **Jrnl. Ref.** means Journal Reference. **J.1** refers to Journal page 1. This step records where the data came from: Journal page 1.

Arrow ③—Copy (post) the dollar amount of the debit **($30,000)** from the journal as a debit to the Cash account in the ledger. Likewise, post the dollar amount of the credit (also **$30,000**) from the journal to the appropriate account in the ledger. Now the ledger accounts have their correct amounts.

Arrow ④—Copy (post) the account number **(101)** from the ledger back to the journal. This step records that the $30,000 debit to Cash has been posted to the Cash account in the ledger. Also, copy the account number **(301)** for Gay Gillen, Capital, back to the journal to show that the credit has been posted to the ledger. **Post. Ref.** is the abbreviation for Posting Reference.

After posting, you can prepare the trial balance.

The Four-Column Account: An Alternative to the T-Account

The ledger accounts illustrated in Exhibit 2-9 appear in T-account format, with the debit on the left and the credit on the right. The T-account clearly separates debits from credits and is used for teaching, where there isn't much detail. Another account format has four amount columns, as illustrated in Exhibit 2-10.

Account Cash					Account No. 101	
		Jrnl.			Balance	
Date	Item	Ref.	Debit	Credit	Debit	Credit
20X5						
Apr. 1		J.1	30,000		30,000	
3		J.1		500	29,500	

Exhibit 2-10

Account in Four-Column Format

The first pair of amount columns are for the amounts posted from individual entries, such as the $30,000 debit. The second pair of amount columns are for the account balance. The four-column format keeps a running balance in the account. For this reason, it is used more often in practice than the T-account format. In Exhibit 2-10, Cash has a debit balance of $30,000 after the first transaction and a debit balance of $29,500 after the second transaction.

Chart of Accounts

As you know, the ledger contains the accounts grouped under these headings:

- Balance sheet accounts: Assets, Liabilities, and Owner's Equity
- Income statement accounts: Revenues and Expenses

Organizations use a **chart of accounts** to list all their accounts along with the account numbers. Account numbers serve as posting references, illustrated by arrow 4 in Exhibit 2-9.

Chart of Accounts
List of all the accounts and their account numbers in the ledger.

Account numbers usually have two or more digits. Assets are often numbered beginning with 1, liabilities with 2, owner's equity with 3, revenues with 4, and expenses with 5. The second and third digits in an account number indicate where the account fits within the category. For example, Cash may be account number 101, the first asset account. Accounts Receivable may be account number 111, the second asset. Accounts Payable may be number 201, the first liability. All accounts are numbered by this system.

The chart of accounts for Gay Gillen eTravel appears in Exhibit 2-11. Notice the gap in account numbers between 111 and 141. Gillen may need to add another category of receivables—for example, Notes Receivable, which she might number 121. Or she may start selling some type of inventory, account number 131.

Exhibit 2-11

**Chart of Accounts—
Gay Gillen eTravel**

Balance Sheet Accounts

Assets	Liabilities	Owner's Equity
101 Cash	201 Accounts Payable	301 Gay Gillen, Capital
111 Accounts Receivable	231 Notes Payable	311 Gay Gillen, Withdrawals
141 Office Supplies		
151 Office Furniture		
191 Land		

**Income Statement Accounts
(Part of Owner's Equity)**

Revenues	Expenses
401 Service Revenue	501 Rent Expense
	502 Salary Expense
	503 Utilities Expense

Appendix B gives expanded charts of accounts that you will find helpful throughout this course. The first chart lists the typical accounts of a *service* proprietorship, such as Gay Gillen eTravel. The second chart is for a *merchandising* corporation, one that sells a product rather than a service. The third chart lists the accounts for a *manufacturing* company. You will use the manufacturing accounts in Chapters 19 through 26. Study the service proprietorship now, and refer to the other charts of accounts as needed later.

Expanding the Accounting Equation: Revenues and Expenses

As we have noted, *revenues* are increases in owner's equity that result from delivering goods or services to customers. *Expenses* are decreases in equity that occur from using up assets or increasing liabilities in the course of operations. Therefore, we must expand the accounting equation. In Exhibit 2-12, revenues and expenses appear under equity because their net effect equals net income, which increases owner's equity. If expenses exceed the revenues, there is a net loss, which decreases owner's equity.

We can now express the rules of debit and credit in final form, as shown in Exhibit 2-13, Panel A. Panel B shows the *normal* balances of the five types of accounts: *Assets; Liabilities;* and *Owner's Equity* and its subparts, *Revenues and Expenses*. All of accounting is based on these five types of accounts.

Exhibit 2-12

The Accounting Equation Includes Revenues and Expenses

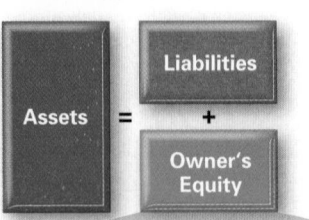

Before proceeding make sure you know the rules of debit and credit. Also make sure you know the normal balances of the five types of accounts.

Exhibit 2-13

Final Rules of Debit and Credit and the Normal Balance of Accounts

PANEL A—Rules of Debit and Credit

Assets	=	Liabilities	+	Capital

Debit for increase	Credit for decrease	Debit for decrease	Credit for increase	Debit for decrease	Credit for increase

Withdrawals

Debit for increase	Credit for decrease

PANEL B—Normal Balances

Revenues

	Debit for decrease	Credit for increase
Assets................. Debit		
Liabilities.............. Credit		
Owner's equity—overall.. Credit		
Capital .... Credit		

Expenses

Debit for increase	Credit for decrease

Withdrawals .... Debit
Revenues............. Credit
Expenses .... Debit

Student Resource CD

debits and credits, expenses, revenues

Stop & Think

Compute the missing amount in each account.

1. Cash		2. Accounts Receivable		3. Annie Todd, Capital	
Bal. 10,000		Bal. 12,800			Bal. X
20,000	13,000	45,600	X	22,000	56,000
					15,000
Bal. X		Bal. 23,500			Bal. 73,000

Answers:

1. The ending balance (X) for Cash is

$$X = \$10,000 + \$20,000 - \$13,000$$
$$X = \$17,000$$

2. We are given the beginning and ending balances. We can compute the credit entry (X) as follows for Accounts Receivable:

$$\$12,800 + \$45,600 - X = \$23,500$$
$$\$58,400 - \$23,500 = X$$
$$X = \$34,900$$

3. The Capital account has an ending credit balance of $73,000. We can figure the beginning credit balance (X), as follows:

$$X + \$56,000 + \$15,000 - \$22,000 = \$73,000$$
$$X = \$73,000 - \$56,000 - \$15,000 + \$22,000$$
$$X = \$24,000$$

☐ The Account, the Ledger, and the Journal
☐ Double-Entry Accounting
☐ Flow of Accounting Data
☐ Details of Journals and Ledgers
☐ Expanding the Accounting Equation
■ Expanded Problem: Revenues and Expenses
☐ Quick Decision Making

Expanded Problem Including Revenues and Expenses

Let's account for the revenues and expenses of the law practice of Brett Wilkinson, Attorney, for the month of July 20X7. We follow the same steps illustrated earlier in this chapter: Analyze the transaction, journalize, post to the ledger, and prepare the trial balance. To aid your learning of the journalizing process, we include the extra notation for each account debited or credited. Again, these notations are *not required*.

Student Resource CD

debits and credits, expenses, revenues, transaction analysis, trial balance

Transaction Analysis, Journalizing, and Posting

TRANSACTION 1 ANALYSIS Brett Wilkinson invested $10,000 cash in a business bank account to open his law practice. The business received the cash and gave Wilkinson owner's equity. The business's cash is increased; therefore, debit Cash. The owner's equity of the business increased, so credit Brett Wilkinson, Capital.

Journal Entry

```
Cash (↑ asset; debit)........................ 10,000
      Brett Wilkinson, Capital (↑ equity; credit) ..        10,000
Received investment from owner.
```

Ledger Accounts

Cash		Brett Wilkinson, Capital	
(1) 10,000			(1) 10,000

TRANSACTION 2 ANALYSIS Wilkinson performed service for a client and collected $3,000 cash. The asset cash is increased, so debit Cash. Revenue is increased; credit Service Revenue.

Journal Entry

```
Cash (↑ asset; debit)........................ 3,000
      Service Revenue (↑ revenue; credit) .......        3,000
Performed service and received cash.
```

Ledger Accounts

Cash		Service Revenue	
(1) 10,000			(2) 3,000
(2) 3,000			

TRANSACTION 3 ANALYSIS Wilkinson performed service for a client and billed the client for $500 on account receivable. Wilkinson expects to collect the $500 later. The asset accounts receivable is increased; therefore, debit Accounts Receivable. Service revenue is increased; credit Service Revenue. Remember that revenues are credit-balance accounts.

Journal Entry

```
Accounts Receivable (↑ asset; debit)............ 500
      Service Revenue (↑ revenue; credit) .......        500
Performed service on account.
```

Ledger Accounts

Accounts Receivable		Service Revenue	
(3) 500			(2) 3,000
			(3) 500

TRANSACTION 4 ANALYSIS Wilkinson earned $700 service revenue by advising a client. Wilkinson received $300 cash immediately and billed the remaining $400 to the client. The assets cash and accounts receivable are increased; therefore, debit both asset accounts. Service revenue is increased; credit Service Revenue for the total amount earned.

Journal Entry

```
Cash (↑ asset; debit)........................ 300
Accounts Receivable (↑ asset; debit)............ 400
      Service Revenue (↑ revenue; credit) .......        700
Performed service for cash and on account.
```

Note: A transaction that debits or credits more than two accounts at the same time requires a *compound entry*. **As always, total debits must equal total credits.**

Ledger Accounts

Cash		Accounts Receivable		Service Revenue	
(1) 10,000		(3) 500			(2) 3,000
(2) 3,000		(4) 400			(3) 500
(4) 300					(4) 700

TRANSACTION 5 ANALYSIS   Wilkinson paid the following cash expenses: office rent, $900; employee salary, $1,500; and utilities, $500. The asset cash is decreased; therefore, credit Cash for the sum of the three expense amounts. The expenses are increased, and each expense account is debited separately. Remember that expenses are debit-balance accounts, the opposite of revenues.

Journal Entry

Rent Expense (↑ expense; debit).............	900	
Salary Expense (↑ expense; debit)	1,500	
Utilities Expense (↑ expense; debit)...........	500	
Cash (↓ asset; credit)		2,900
Paid cash expenses.		

Note: In practice, the business would record these three transactions separately. But we can record them together in a compound journal entry.

Ledger Accounts

	Cash				Rent Expense	
(1)	10,000	(5)	2,900	(5)	900	
(2)	3,000					
(4)	300					

	Salary Expense			Utilities Expense	
(5)	1,500		(5)	500	

TRANSACTION 6 ANALYSIS   Wilkinson received a telephone bill for $100 and will pay this expense next week. There is no cash payment now. Utilities expense is increased, so debit this expense. The liability accounts payable is increased, so credit Accounts Payable.

Journal Entry

Utilities Expense (↑ expense; debit)...........	100	
Accounts Payable (↑ liability; credit)......		100
Received utility bill.		

Ledger Accounts

	Accounts Payable				Utilities Expense	
		(6)	100	(5)	500	
				(6)	100	

TRANSACTION 7 ANALYSIS   Wilkinson collected $200 cash from the client in transaction 3. Cash is increased, so debit Cash. Accounts receivable is decreased; credit Accounts Receivable.

Journal Entry

Cash (↑ asset; debit)	200	
Accounts Receivable (↓ asset; credit)......		200
Received cash on account.		

Note: This transaction has no effect on revenue; the related revenue was recorded in transaction 3.

Ledger Accounts

	Cash				Accounts Receivable		
(1)	10,000	(5)	2,900	(3)	500	(7)	200
(2)	3,000			(4)	400		
(4)	300						
(7)	200						

TRANSACTION 8 ANALYSIS   Wilkinson paid the telephone bill from transaction 6. Cash is decreased, so credit Cash. Accounts payable is decreased; therefore, debit Accounts Payable.

Journal Entry

Accounts Payable (↓ liability; debit)	100	
Cash (↓ asset; credit)		100
Paid cash on account.		

Note: This transaction has no effect on expense because the related expense was recorded in transaction 6.

Ledger Accounts	Cash				Accounts Payable			
	(1)	10,000	(5)	2,900	(8)	100	(6)	100
	(2)	3,000	(8)	100				
	(4)	300						
	(7)	200						

TRANSACTION 9 ANALYSIS   Wilkinson withdrew $1,000 cash for personal use. The asset cash decreased; credit Cash. The withdrawal decreased owner's equity; therefore, debit Brett Wilkinson, Withdrawals.

✔ Starter 2-6

✔ Starter 2-7

Journal Entry

Brett Wilkinson, Withdrawals (↓ equity; debit) . .   1,000
    Cash (↓ asset; credit)   1,000
Withdrew cash for personal use.

✔ Starter 2-8

✔ Starter 2-9

Ledger Accounts	Cash				Brett Wilkinson, Withdrawals			
	(1)	10,000	(5)	2,900	(9)	1,000		
	(2)	3,000	(8)	100				
	(4)	300	(9)	1,000				
	(7)	200						

Ledger Accounts After Posting

ASSETS
Cash

(1)	10,000	(5)	2,900
(2)	3,000	(8)	100
(4)	300	(9)	1,000
(7)	200		
Bal.	9,500		

Accounts Receivable

(3)	500	(7)	200
(4)	400		
Bal.	700		

LIABILITIES
Accounts Payable

(8)	100	(6)	100
		Bal.	0

OWNER'S EQUITY
Brett Wilkinson, Capital

	(1)	10,000
	Bal.	10,000

Brett Wilkinson, Withdrawals

(9)	1,000	
Bal.	1,000	

REVENUE
Service Revenue

	(2)	3,000
	(3)	500
	(4)	700
	Bal.	4,200

EXPENSES
Rent Expense

(5)	900	
Bal.	900	

Salary Expense

(5)	1,500	
Bal.	1,500	

Utilities Expense

(5)	500	
(6)	100	
Bal.	600	

Trial Balance

The trial balance lists the balance of each account.

✔ Starter 2-10

✔ Starter 2-11

Brett Wilkinson, Attorney
Trial Balance
July 31, 20X7

	Balance	
Account Title	Debit	Credit
Cash	$ 9,500	
Accounts receivable	700	
Accounts payable		$ 0
Brett Wilkinson, capital		10,000
Brett Wilkinson, withdrawals	1,000	
Service revenue		4,200
Rent expense	900	
Salary expense	1,500	
Utilities expense	600	
Total	$14,200	$14,200

Correcting Trial Balance Errors

In a trial balance, total debits and total credits should always be equal. If they are not, there is an error. Computerized accounting systems eliminate most errors because most software won't let you make a journal entry that doesn't balance. But computers cannot *eliminate* all errors because humans can input the wrong data.

Errors can be detected by computing the difference between total debits and total credits on the trial balance. Then perform one or more of the following actions:

1. Search the trial balance for a missing account. For example, suppose the accountant omitted Brett Wilkinson, Withdrawals, from Wilkinson's trial balance. The total amount of the debits would be $13,200 ($14,200 − $1,000). Trace each account from the ledger to the trial balance, and you will locate the missing account.

2. Divide the difference between total debits and total credits by 2. A debit treated as a credit, or vice versa, doubles the amount of error. Suppose Brett Wilkinson's accountant posted a $100 credit as a debit. Total debits contain the $100, and total credits omit the $100. The out-of-balance amount is $200. Dividing the difference by 2 identifies the $100 amount of the transaction. Then search the journal for a $100 transaction and trace to the account affected.

✔ **Starter 2-12**

✔ **Starter 2-13**

3. Divide the out-of-balance amount by 9. If the result is evenly divisible by 9, the error may be a *slide* (example: writing $300 as $30) or a *transposition* (example: treating $65 as $56). Suppose Wilkinson printed his $1,000 Withdrawal as $10,000 on the trial balance—a slide-type error. Total debits would differ from total credits by $9,000 ($10,000 − $1,000 = $9,000). Dividing $9,000 by 9 yields $1,000, the correct amount of withdrawals. Trace $1,000 through the ledger until you reach the Brett Wilkinson, Withdrawals account. You have then found the error.

A warning: Do not confuse the trial balance with the balance sheet. A trial balance is an internal document used only by company insiders. The public never sees a trial balance. Outsiders get only the company's financial statements.

The Seven Trillion Dollar Mistake

"If we can send missiles to a bull's-eye at a . . . training camp in Afghanistan, we ought to be able to set up an accounting system at the Defense Department. . . . " This is what Senator Charles Grassley (R-Iowa) said in 1998 after embezzlements at U.S. military installations were allowed to occur because of weaknesses in the Pentagon's accounting system.

A year later, precision was still lacking at the Department of Defense. Pentagon money managers required almost $7 trillion of accounting adjustments to make their books balance. Each adjustment represents an accountant's correction of a discrepancy. The lesson of the $7 trillion mistake is this: Computers don't keep books; people do.

These bookkeeping errors affect all our pocketbooks. Without sound costing data, military managers simply can't make good decisions—like whether to close a base or keep it open. The public never knows the real cost of defense programs such as the missile defense shield or the cost of health care for military retirees. With more reliable accounting data, we would know how to vote on these issues.

Sources: Julia Malone, "Auditors cite failings in 11 of 24 agencies," *Atlanta Constitution*, March 31, 2000, p. A; 20. John M. Donnelly, "Pentagon's Finances Just Don't Add Up," *Los Angeles Times*, March 5, 2000, p. 8. Ralph Vartabedian, "Thefts Reveal Flawed Pentagon Contract System," *Los Angeles Times*, September 28, 1998, p. 1.

Accounting.com

Student Resource CD

transaction analysis

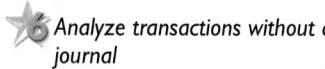

Analyze transactions without a journal

✔ **Starter 2-14**

Quick Decision Making

Often people must make quick decisions. Sometimes they can't take the time to follow all the steps in an accounting system. For example, suppose the Frito-Lay route manager needs more storage space to meet customer demand. He can purchase a small building for $70,000, or he can rent a building at an annual cost of $10,000. Whether to buy or rent depends on the financial effects of the two options.

The route manager doesn't need a full-blown accounting system to make this decision. If he knows a little accounting, he can figure out how the two options will affect his business. The following accounts summarize the effects of renting versus buying the building.

RENT THE BUILDING		BUY THE BUILDING	
Cash	**Rent Expense**	**Cash**	**Building**
10,000	10,000	70,000	70,000

The accounts make it clear that buying will require more cash. But buying the building adds an asset to the business. This may motivate the route manager to borrow cash and buy the building. A low cash balance may force the manager to rent.

Companies do not actually keep their records in this short-cut fashion. But a decision maker who needs information immediately can quickly analyze the effects of a transaction on the financial statements. Simply record the transactions directly in the T-accounts.

Now you have seen how to account for transactions. Solidify your understanding of the accounting process by reviewing the Decision Guidelines.

Decision Guidelines

ANALYZING AND RECORDING TRANSACTIONS

Suppose the Frito-Lay route manager in the chapter-opening story stocks the shelves of 20 stores and earns service revenue. He opens a small office, hires a helper, and has a few other expenses. QuickBooks software is used for the accounting.

The route manager offers you a job as accountant for this small business. The pay is good. Can you answer the manager's questions, which are outlined in the Decision Guidelines? If so, you may get the job.

Decision	Guidelines
• Has a transaction occurred?	If the event affects the entity's financial position and can be reliably recorded—*Yes*
	If either condition is absent—*No*
• Where to record the transaction?	In the *journal*, the chronological record of transactions
• What to record for each transaction?	Increases and/or decreases in all the accounts affected by the transaction
• How to record an increase/decrease in a (an)	Rules of debit and credit:

	Increase	*Decrease*
Asset	Debit	Credit
Liability	Credit	Debit
Owner's Equity	Credit	Debit
Revenue	Credit	Debit
Expense	Debit	Credit

Decision Guidelines *(continued)*

Decision	Guidelines
• Where to store all the information for each account?	In the *ledger*, the record holding all the accounts
• Where to list all the accounts and their balances?	In the *trial balance*
• Where to report the results of operations?	In the income statement (Revenues − Expenses = Net income or Net loss)
• Where to report financial position?	In the balance sheet (Assets = Liabilities + Owner's equity)

Excel Application Exercise

Goal: Create an Excel spreadsheet to calculate total assets, total liabilities, total owner's equity, and net income (or loss) from the Brett Wilkinson, Attorney trial balance found in your text on page 64.

Scenario: In your interview with Wilkinson, he asks you to prepare a trial balance for his law practice. Your task is to create a simple spreadsheet to calculate total assets, total liabilities, total owner's equity, and net income (or loss) from a trial balance. When finished, answer these questions:

1. What are Brett Wilkinson's total assets?
2. What are Brett Wilkinson's total liabilities?
3. What is Brett Wilkinson's total owner's equity?
4. What is Brett Wilkinson's net income (or net loss) for the period?

Step-by-Step:

1. Open a new Excel spreadsheet.
2. Create a bold-faced heading for your spreadsheet that contains the following:

a. Chapter 2 Excel Application Exercise
b. Brett Wilkinson, Attorney
c. Trial Balance
d. July 31, 20X7

3. Two rows down from your worksheet heading, copy the heading format of the Brett Wilkinson trial balance. Make "Account Title" your first column (sized appropriately). Make two separate columns for the "Debit" and "Credit" balances.
4. Enter the account titles (without periods) and data from the trial balance under the correct headings. Create formulas for the column totals for the debit and credit balances. Format the data in each column.
5. Beginning two rows under the trial balance in the first column, enter the following descriptions:
a. Total Assets
b. Total Liabilities
c. Total Owner's Equity
d. Total Net Income (Loss)
6. In column two, across from each description, enter the formula to calculate the item.
7. Save your work to disk, and print a copy for your files.

END-OF-CHAPTER *Summary Problem*

The trial balance of Tomassini Computer Service Center on March 1, 20X2, lists the entity's assets, liabilities, and owner's equity on that date.

	Balance	
Account Title	**Debit**	**Credit**
Cash..	$26,000	
Accounts receivable.............................	4,500	
Accounts payable.................................		$ 2,000
Larry Tomassini, capital		28,500
Total	$30,500	$30,500

TIPS

CHECK YOUR RESOURCES

During March, the business engaged in the following transactions:

a. Borrowed $45,000 from the bank and signed a note payable in the name of the business.
b. Paid cash of $40,000 to a real estate company to acquire land.
c. Performed service for a customer and received cash of $5,000.
d. Purchased supplies on credit, $300.
e. Performed customer service and earned revenue on account, $2,600.
f. Paid $1,200 on account.
g. Paid the following cash expenses: salaries, $3,000; rent, $1,500; and interest, $400.
h. Received $3,100 on account.
i. Received a $200 utility bill that will be paid next week.
j. Withdrew $1,800 for personal use.

Required

1. Open the following accounts, with the balances indicated, in the ledger of Tomassini Computer Service Center. Use the T-account format.
   ■ Assets—Cash, $26,000; Accounts Receivable, $4,500; Supplies, no balance; Land, no balance
   ■ Liabilities—Accounts Payable, $2,000; Note Payable, no balance
   ■ Owner's Equity—Larry Tomassini, Capital, $28,500; Larry Tomassini, Withdrawals, no balance
   ■ Revenues—Service Revenue, no balance
   ■ Expenses—(none have balances) Salary Expense, Rent Expense, Utilities Expense, Interest Expense
2. Journalize each transaction. Key journal entries by transaction letter.
3. Post to the ledger.
4. Prepare the trial balance of Tomassini Computer Service Center at March 31, 20X2.

Solution

Requirement 1

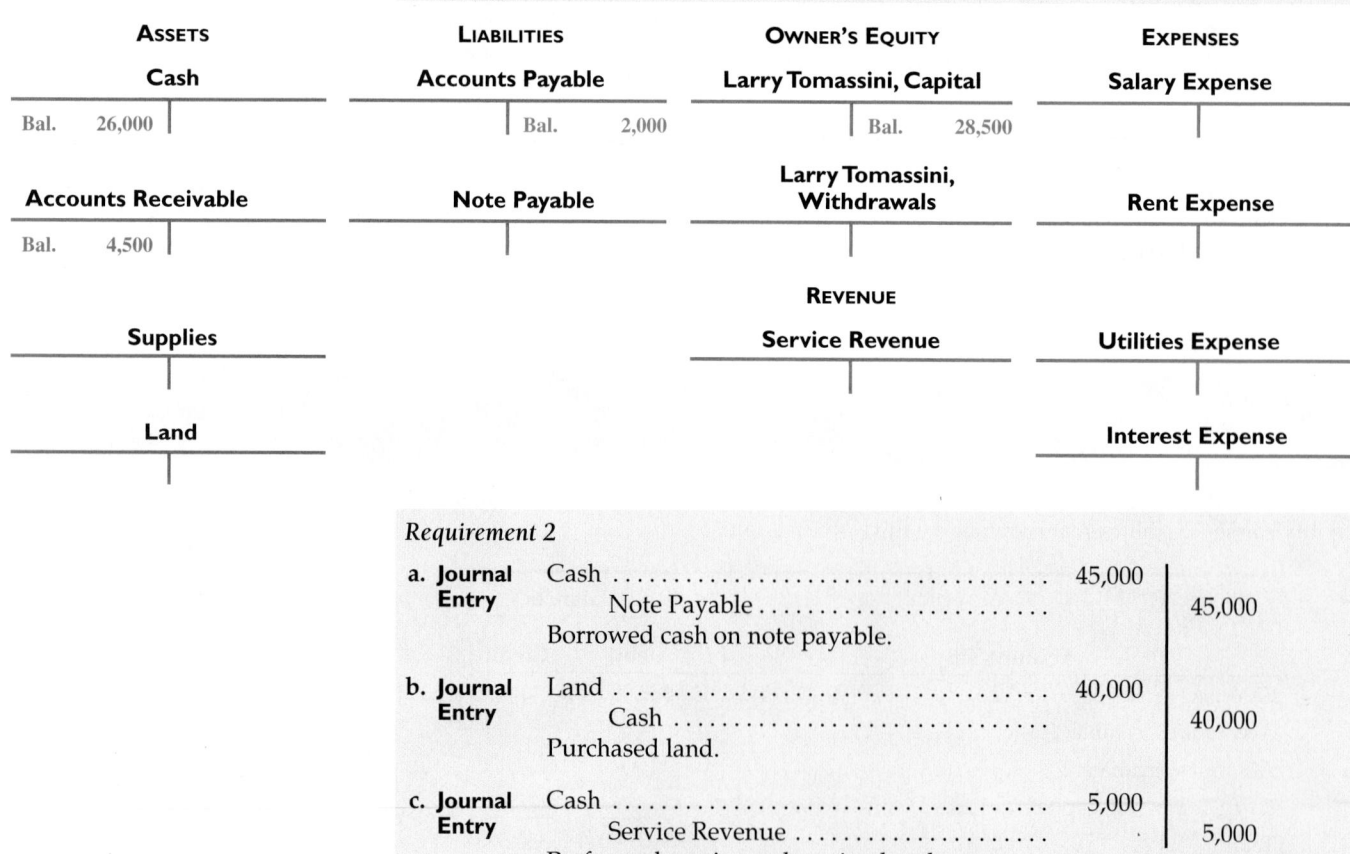

ASSETS	LIABILITIES	OWNER'S EQUITY	EXPENSES
Cash	**Accounts Payable**	**Larry Tomassini, Capital**	**Salary Expense**
Bal. 26,000	Bal. 2,000	Bal. 28,500	
Accounts Receivable	**Note Payable**	**Larry Tomassini, Withdrawals**	**Rent Expense**
Bal. 4,500			
Supplies		**REVENUE**	**Utilities Expense**
		Service Revenue	
Land			**Interest Expense**

Requirement 2

a. Journal Entry	Cash	45,000	
	Note Payable		45,000
	Borrowed cash on note payable.		
b. Journal Entry	Land	40,000	
	Cash		40,000
	Purchased land.		
c. Journal Entry	Cash	5,000	
	Service Revenue		5,000
	Performed service and received cash.		

d. Journal Entry	Supplies	300	
	Accounts Payable		300
	Purchased supplies on account.		

e. Journal Entry	Accounts Receivable.......................	2,600	
	Service Revenue		2,600
	Performed service on account.		

f. Journal Entry	Accounts Payable	1,200	
	Cash		1,200
	Paid on account.		

g. Journal Entry	Salary Expense	3,000	
	Rent Expense............................	1,500	
	Interest Expense	400	
	Cash		4,900
	Paid expenses.		

h. Journal Entry	Cash	3,100	
	Accounts Receivable.................		3,100
	Received cash on account.		

i. Journal Entry	Utilities Expense	200	
	Accounts Payable		200
	Received utility bill.		

j. Journal Entry	Larry Tomassini, Withdrawals	1,800	
	Cash		1,800
	Owner withdrawal.		

Requirement 3

ASSETS

Cash

Bal.	26,000	(b)	40,000
(a)	45,000	(f)	1,200
(c)	5,000	(g)	4,900
(h)	3,100	(j)	1,800
Bal.	31,200		

Accounts Receivable

Bal.	4,500	(h)	3,100
(e)	2,600		
Bal.	4,000		

Supplies

(d)	300	
Bal.	300	

Land

(b)	40,000	
Bal.	40,000	

LIABILITIES

Accounts Payable

(f)	1,200	Bal.	2,000
		(d)	300
		(i)	200
		Bal.	1,300

Note Payable

		(a)	45,000
		Bal.	45,000

OWNER'S EQUITY

Larry Tomassini, Capital

	Bal.	28,500

Larry Tomassini, Withdrawals

(j)	1,800	
Bal.	1,800	

REVENUE

Service Revenue

		(c)	5,000
		(e)	2,600
		Bal.	7,600

EXPENSES

Salary Expense

(g)	3,000	
Bal.	3,000	

Rent Expense

(g)	1,500	
Bal.	1,500	

Interest Expense

(g)	400	
Bal.	400	

Utilities Expense

(i)	200	
Bal.	200	

Requirement 4

Tomassini Computer Service Center

Trial Balance
March 31, 20X2

Account Title	Balance Debit	Credit
Cash	$31,200	
Accounts receivable	4,000	
Supplies	300	
Land	40,000	
Accounts payable		$ 1,300
Note payable		45,000
Larry Tomassini, capital		28,500
Larry Tomassini, withdrawals	1,800	
Service revenue		7,600
Salary expense	3,000	
Rent expense	1,500	
Interest expense	400	
Utilities expense	200	
Total	$82,400	$82,400

REVIEW *Recording Business Transactions*

Quick Check

1. Which sequence of actions correctly summarizes the accounting process?
   a. Prepare a trial balance, journalize transactions, post to the accounts
   b. Post to the accounts, journalize transactions, prepare a trial balance
   c. Journalize transactions, post to the accounts, prepare a trial balance
   d. Journalize transactions, prepare a trial balance, post to the accounts

2. The left side of an account is used to record
   a. Debits
   b. Credits
   c. Debit or credit, depending on the type of account
   d. Increases

3. Suppose a **Target** store has cash of $50,000, receivables of $60,000, and furniture and fixtures totaling $200,000. The store owes $80,000 on account and has a $100,000 note payable. How much is the store's owner equity?
   a. $20,000
   b. $310,000
   c. $180,000
   d. $130,000

4. A Target store purchased supplies of $1,000 on account. The journal entry to record this transaction is

   a.
Inventory	1,000	
Accounts Payable		1,000

   b.
Accounts Payable	1,000	
Supplies		1,000

   c.
Supplies	1,000	
Accounts Payable		1,000

   d.
Supplies	1,000	
Accounts Receivable		1,000

5. Posting a $1,000 purchase of supplies on account appears as follows:

a.	Supplies	Accounts Receivable	c.	Supplies	Accounts Payable
	1,000	1,000		1,000	1,000

b.	Supplies	Accounts Payable	d.	Cash	Supplies
	1,000	1,000		1,000	1,000

6. Which journal entry records Target's payment for the supplies purchased in transaction 4?

a.	Accounts Payable..........................	1,000	
	Accounts Receivable		1,000
b.	Accounts Payable..........................	1,000	
	Cash.....................................		1,000
c.	Cash	1,000	
	Accounts Payable.....................		1,000
d.	Supplies...................................	1,000	
	Cash.....................................		1,000

7. A Target store paid $500 for supplies and purchased additional supplies on account for $700. The store paid $300 of the accounts payable. What is the balance in the Supplies account?

a. $500   c. $1,200
b. $900   d. $1,500

8. **Kinko's Copies** recorded a cash collection on account by debiting Cash and crediting Accounts Payable. What will the trial balance show for this error?

a. Too much for liabilities   c. The trial balance will not balance
b. Too much for assets   d. Both a and b

9. Brett Wilkinson, Attorney, began the year with total assets of $120,000, liabilities of $70,000, and owner's equity of $50,000. During the year he earned revenue of $110,000 and paid expenses of $30,000. He also invested an additional $20,000 in the business and withdrew $60,000 for living expenses. How much is the law firm's equity at year-end?

a. $90,000   c. $130,000
b. $120,000   d. $160,000

10. How would Brett Wilkinson record his expenses for the year in the preceding question?

a.	Expenses..............................	30,000	
	Cash................................		30,000
b.	Expenses..............................	30,000	
	Accounts Payable		30,000
c.	Cash	30,000	
	Expenses...........................		30,000
d.	Accounts Payable	30,000	
	Cash................................		30,000

Accounting Vocabulary

account (p. 44)
chart of accounts (p. 59)
credit (p. 47)

debit (p. 47)
journal (p. 45)
ledger (p. 45)

normal balance (p. 54)
posting (p. 51)
trial balance (p. 45)

●ASSESS *Your Progress*

See *www.prenhall.com/horngren* for selected Starters, Exercises, and Problems.

Using accounting terms
(Obj. 1)

Starters

S2-1 Review basic accounting definitions by completing the following crossword puzzle.

Down:

1. Left side of an account
4. Record holding the grouping of accounts
5. An economic resource
7. Record of transactions

Across:

2. Records an increase in a liability
3. List of accounts with their balances
6. Another word for liability

Using accounting terms
(Obj. 1)

S2-2 Tighten your grip on accounting by filling in the blanks to review some key definitions.

Lynn Bratton is describing the accounting process for a friend who is a philosophy major. Lynn states, "The basic summary device in accounting is the _____. The left side is called the _____ side, and the right side is called the _____ side. We record transactions first in a _____. Then we post (copy the data) to the _____. It is helpful to list all the accounts with their balances on a _____ _____."

Using accounting terms
(Obj. 1)

S2-3 Accounting has its own vocabulary and basic relationships. Match the accounting terms at left with the corresponding definitions at right.

_____ 1. Posting	A. Record of transactions
_____ 2. Normal balance	B. Always an asset
_____ 3. Payable	C. Left side of an account
_____ 4. Journal	D. Side of an account where increases are recorded
_____ 5. Receivable	E. Copying data from the journal to the ledger
_____ 6. Capital	F. Using up assets in the course of operating a business
_____ 7. Debit	G. Always a liability
_____ 8. Expense	H. Revenues – Expenses
_____ 9. Net income	I. Grouping of accounts
_____ 10. Ledger	J. Owner's equity in the business

Explaining the rules of debit and credit
(Obj. 2)

S2-4 Art Sudan is tutoring Nick Mull, who is taking introductory accounting. Art explains to Nick that *debits* are used to record increases in accounts and *credits* record decreases. Nick is confused and seeks your advice.

- When are credits increases? When are credits decreases?
- When are debits increases? When are debits decreases?

Exhibit 2-13, page 61, gives the rules of debit and credit.

S2-5 The accounting records of all businesses include three basic categories of accounts: assets, liabilities, and owner's equity. In turn, owner's equity holds the following categories: capital, withdrawals, revenues, and expenses. Identify which categories of all the accounts—including the subparts of owner's equity—have a normal debit balance and which categories of accounts have a normal credit balance. Exhibit 2-13, Panel B, on page 62, gives the normal balance in each category of account.

Normal account balances
(Obj. 2)

S2-6 Liana Garcia opened a medical practice in San Diego. Record the following transactions in the journal of Liana Garcia, M.D. Include an explanation with each journal entry.

Recording transactions
(Obj. 3)

September 1	Garcia invested $30,000 cash in a business bank account to start her medical practice. The business received the cash and gave Garcia owner's equity in the business.
2	Purchased medical supplies on account, $10,000.
2	Paid monthly office rent of $4,000.
3	Recorded $5,000 revenue for service rendered to patients. Received cash of $2,000 and sent bills to patients for the remainder.

S2-7 After operating for a month, Liana Garcia, M.D., completed the following transactions during the latter part of October:

Recording transactions
(Obj. 3)

October 15	Borrowed $50,000 from the bank, signing a note payable.
22	Performed service for patients on account, $3,600.
30	Received cash on account from patients, $2,000.
31	Received a utility bill, $200, which will be paid during November.
31	Paid monthly salary to nurse, $3,000.
31	Paid interest expense of $200 on the bank loan.

Journalize the transactions of Liana Garcia, M.D. Include an explanation with each journal entry.

S2-8 Stuart Deng purchased supplies on account for $5,000. Two weeks later, Deng paid half on account.

Journalizing transactions; posting
(Obj. 3, 4)

1. Journalize the two transactions for Stuart Deng. Include an explanation for each transaction.
2. Open the Accounts Payable T-account and post to Accounts Payable. Compute the balance, and denote it as *Bal.*

S2-9 Lance Alworth performed legal service for a client who could not pay immediately. Alworth expected to collect the $6,000 the following month. Later, he received $3,500 cash from the client.

Journalizing transactions; posting
(Obj. 3, 4)

1. Record the two transactions for Lance Alworth, Attorney. Include an explanation for each transaction.
2. Open these accounts: Cash; Accounts Receivable; Service Revenue. Post to all three accounts. Compute each account's balance, and denote as *Bal.*
3. Answer these questions based on your analysis:
   a. How much did Alworth earn? Which account shows this amount?
   b. How much in total assets did Alworth acquire as a result of the two transactions? Show the amount of each asset.

Note: Starter 2-10 should be used in connection with Starter 2-6.

Posting; preparing a trial balance
(Obj. 4, 5)

S2-10 Use the September transaction data for Liana Garcia, M.D., given in Starter 2-6.

1. Open the following T-accounts: Cash; Accounts Receivable; Medical Supplies; Accounts Payable; Liana Garcia, Capital; Service Revenue; Rent Expense.

2. After making the journal entries in Starter 2-6, post to the ledger. No dates or posting references are required. Compute the balance of each account, and denote it as *Bal.*

3. Prepare the trial balance, complete with a proper heading, at September 3, 20X8. Use the trial balance on page 64 as a guide.

Preparing a trial balance
(Obj. 5)

S2-11 **Interfax Corporation** reported the following summarized data at December 31, 20X3. Accounts appear in no particular order; dollar amounts are in millions.

Revenues.............	$29	Other liabilities........	$19
Other assets	40	Cash.................	12
Accounts payable	1	Expenses	22
Capital..............	25		

Prepare the trial balance of Interfax Corporation at December 31, 20X3. List the accounts in proper order, as on page 64.

Correcting a trial balance
(Obj. 5)

S2-12 Brett Wilkinson, Attorney, prepared his trial balance on page 64. Suppose Wilkinson made an error: He erroneously listed his capital balance of $10,000 as a debit rather than a credit.

Compute the incorrect trial balance totals for debits and credits. Then refer to the discussion of correcting errors on page 65, and show how to correct this error.

Correcting a trial balance
(Obj. 5)

S2-13 Return to Brett Wilkinson's trial balance on page 64. Assume that Wilkinson accidentally listed his withdrawals as $100 instead of the correct amount of $1,000. Compute the incorrect trial balance totals for debits and credits. Then show how to correct this error, which is called a *slide*.

Analyzing transactions without a journal
(Obj. 6)

S2-14 Jane Avery established Bodyfit, a health club, with an initial cash investment of $100,000. The business immediately purchased equipment on a note payable for $80,000. Avery needs to know her account balances immediately and doesn't have time to journalize the transactions.

1. Open the following T-accounts on the books of Bodyfit. Cash; Equipment; Note Payable; Jane Avery, Capital.

2. Record the first two transactions directly in the T-accounts without using a journal.

3. Compute the balance in each account and show that total debits equal total credits.

Exercises

Using accounting vocabulary
(Obj. 1)

E2-1 Sharpen your use of accounting terms by working this crossword puzzle.

Down:

1. Records a decrease in a liability
4. Bottom line of an income statement
7. Revenue – net income = _____

Across:

2. Amount collectible from a customer
3. Statement of financial position
5. Copy data from the journal to the ledger
6. Records a decrease in an asset

E2-2 → *Link Back to Chapter 1 (Accounting Equation).* **Coca-Cola** is famous worldwide for soft drinks. At the end of 20X1, Coca-Cola had total assets of $22 billion and liabilities totaling $11 billion.

Using debits and credits with the accounting equation
(Obj. 1, 2)

Required

1. Write the company's accounting equation, and label each amount as a debit or a credit.
2. Coca-Cola's total revenues for 20X1 were $20 billion, and total expenses for the year were $16 billion. How much was Coca-Cola's net income (or net loss) for 20X1? Write the equation to compute Coca-Cola's net income, and indicate which element is a debit and which is a credit. Does net income represent a net debit or a net credit? Does net loss represent a net debit or a net credit? Review Exhibit 1-8, page 21, if needed.
3. During 20X1, the owners of Coca-Cola withdrew $2 billion in the form of dividends (same as owner Withdrawals). Did the dividends represent a debit or a credit?

E2-3 Record the following transactions in the journal of Elzinga Enterprises. Explanations are not required. Follow the pattern given for the December 1 transaction.

Analyzing and journalizing transactions
(Obj. 2, 3)

Dec. 1 Paid interest expense of $500.

    1 Interest Expense (↑ expense; debit) 500
          Cash (↓ asset; credit)   500

    5 Purchased office furniture on account, $800.
   10 Performed service on account for a customer, $1,600.
   12 Borrowed $7,000 cash, signing a note payable.
   19 Sold for $29,000 land that had cost this same amount.
   21 Purchased building for $140,000; signed a note payable.
   27 Paid the liability from December 5.

E2-4 This exercise should be used only in connection with Exercise 2-3. Refer to the transactions of Elzinga Enterprises in Exercise 2-3.

Applying the rules of debit and credit; posting
(Obj. 2, 4)

Required

1. Open the following T-accounts with their December 1 balances: Cash, debit balance $3,000; Land, debit balance $29,000; Ken Elzinga, Capital, credit balance $32,000.
2. Post the transactions of Exercise 2-3 to the T-accounts affected. Use the dates as posting references. Start with December 1.
3. Compute the December 31 balance for each account, and prove that total debits equal total credits.

Student ResourceCD

General Ledger, Peachtree, QuickBooks

E2-5 Westview Landscaping completed the following transactions during March 20X8, its first month of operations:

Journalizing transactions
(Obj. 3)

Mar. 1 Ray Hawk invested $70,000 of cash to start the business.
    2 Purchased supplies of $200 on account.
    4 Paid $60,000 cash for a building to use for storage.
    6 Performed service for customers and received cash, $3,000.
    9 Paid $100 on accounts payable.
   17 Performed service for customers on account, $1,600.
   23 Received $1,200 cash from a customer on account.
   31 Paid the following expenses: salary, $1,200; rent, $500.

Student ResourceCD

GL, PT, QB

Required

Record the preceding transactions in the journal of Westview Landscaping. Key transactions by date and include an explanation for each entry, as illustrated in the chapter. Use the following accounts: Cash; Accounts Receivable; Supplies; Building; Accounts Payable; Ray Hawk, Capital; Service Revenue; Salary Expense; Rent Expense.

Posting to the ledger and preparing a trial balance
(Obj. 4, 5)

E2-6 Refer to Exercise 2-5 for the transactions of Westview Landscaping.

Required

1. After journalizing the transactions of Exercise 2-5, post to the ledger, using T-account format. Key transactions by date. Date the ending balance of each account Mar. 31.
2. Prepare the trial balance of Westview Landscaping at March 31, 20X8.

Describing transactions and posting
(Obj. 2, 3)

E2-7 The journal of Vogue Career Services includes the following entries for May 20X6.

Required

1. Describe each transaction.
2. Set up the ledger using the following account numbers: Cash, 110; Accounts Receivable, 120; Supplies, 130; Accounts Payable, 210; Note Payable, 230; Laura Edwards, Capital, 310; Service Revenue, 410; Rent Expense, 510; Advertising Expense, 520; Utilities Expense, 530.
3. Post to the accounts. Write dates and journal references in the accounts, as illustrated in Exhibit 2-9, page 58. Compute the balance of each account after posting.
4. Prepare the trial balance of Vogue Career Services at May 31, 20X6.

	Journal			**Page 5**
Date	**Accounts and Explanation**	**Post Ref.**	**Debit**	**Credit**
May 2	Cash		20,000	
	Laura Edwards, Capital..........			20,000
5	Cash		25,000	
	Note Payable....................			25,000
9	Supplies		200	
	Accounts Payable...............			200
11	Accounts Receivable..............		2,600	
	Service Revenue			2,600
14	Rent Expense.....................		3,200	
	Cash			3,200
22	Accounts Payable		300	
	Cash			300
25	Advertising Expense		400	
	Cash			400
27	Cash		1,400	
	Accounts Receivable			1,400
31	Utilities Expense		100	
	Accounts Payable..............			100

Journalizing transactions
(Obj. 3)

E2-8 The first five transactions of The Mane Event, a styling salon, have been posted to the accounts as follows:

	Cash				**Supplies**		**Equipment**		**Building**	
(1)	22,000	(3)	40,000	(2)	400	(5)	6,000	(3)	40,000
(4)	37,000	(5)	6,000						

	Accounts Payable		**Note Payable**		**Liz Adeva, Capital**	
	(2)	400	(4)	37,000	(1)	22,000

Required

Prepare the journal entries that served as the sources for the five transactions. Include an explanation for each entry as illustrated in the chapter.

E2-9 Prepare the trial balance of The Mane Event at October 31, 20X4, using the account data from Exercise 2-8.

Preparing a trial balance
(Obj. 5)

E2-10 The accounts of SW Bell Advertising follow with their normal balances at December 31, 20X4. The accounts are listed in no particular order.

Preparing a trial balance
(Obj. 5)

Student ResourceCD
spreadsheet

Account	Balance
S. W. Bell, capital	$ 48,800
Insurance expense	700
Accounts payable	4,300
Service revenue	86,000
Land	29,000
Supplies expense	300
Cash	5,000
Salary expense	6,000
Building	125,000
Rent expense	2,000
S. W. Bell, withdrawals	6,000
Utilities expense	400
Accounts receivable	9,500
Note payable	45,000
Supplies	200

Required

Prepare the company's trial balance at December 31, 20X4, listing accounts in proper sequence, as illustrated in the chapter. For example, Supplies comes before Building and Land. List the largest expense first, the second-largest expense next, and so on.

E2-11 The trial balance of Harvey Spark, M.D., at March 31, 20X9, does not balance:

Correcting errors in a trial balance
(Obj. 5)

Cash	$ 3,000	
Accounts receivable	2,000	
Supplies	600	
Land	66,000	
Accounts payable		$21,500
Harvey Spark, capital		41,600
Service revenue		9,700
Salary expense	1,700	
Rent expense	800	
Utilities expense	300	
Total	$74,400	$72,800

Investigation of the accounting records reveals that the bookkeeper

a. Recorded a $400 cash revenue transaction by debiting Accounts Receivable. The credit entry was correct.
b. Posted a $1,000 credit to Accounts Payable as $100.
c. Did not record utilities expense or the related account payable in the amount of $200.
d. Understated Harvey Spark, Capital, by $700.

Required

Prepare the correct trial balance at March 31, complete with a heading; journal entries are not required.

Recording transactions without a journal
(Obj. 6)

E2-12 Open the following T-accounts of Mike Reitmeier, CPA: Cash; Accounts Receivable; Office Supplies; Office Furniture; Accounts Payable; Mike Reitmeier, Capital; Mike Reitmeier, Withdrawals; Service Revenue; Salary Expense; Rent Expense.

Record the following transactions directly in the T-accounts without using a journal. Use the letters to identify the transactions. Compute the balance of each account.

a. Reitmeier opened an accounting firm by investing $15,000 cash and office furniture valued at $5,400.
b. Paid monthly rent of $1,500.
c. Purchased office supplies on account, $700.
d. Paid employee's salary, $1,800.
e. Paid $400 of the account payable created in transaction (c).
f. Performed accounting service on account, $1,600.
g. Withdrew $7,000 for personal use.

Preparing a trial balance
(Obj. 5)

E2-13 After recording the transactions in Exercise 2-12, prepare the trial balance of Mike Reitmeier, CPA, at May 31, 20X7.

Student ResourceCD
GL, PT, QB
Analyzing transactions without a journal
(Obj. 6)

E2-14 Northern Starr Telecom began when Suzanne Starr invested $50,000 cash in a business bank account. During the first week, the business purchased supplies on credit for $8,000 and paid $12,000 cash for equipment. Starr later paid $5,000 on account.

Required

1. Open the following T-accounts: Cash; Supplies; Equipment; Accounts Payable; Suzanne Starr, Capital.
2. Record Starr's four transactions directly in the T-accounts without using a journal.
3. Compute the balance in each account, and show that total debits equal total credits. The T-accounts on page 54 provide a guide.

Analyzing accounting errors
(Obj. 2, 3, 4, 5)

E2-15 Kamran Saddiqi has trouble keeping his debits and credits equal. During a recent month, he made the following errors:

a. In journalizing a receipt of cash for service revenue, Saddiqi debited Cash for $80 instead of the correct amount of $800. Saddiqi credited Service Revenue for $80, the incorrect amount.
b. Saddiqi recorded a $120 purchase of supplies on account by debiting Supplies and crediting Accounts Payable for $210.
c. In preparing the trial balance, Saddiqi omitted a $50,000 note payable.
d. Saddiqi posted a $700 utility expense as $70. The credit posting to Cash was correct.
e. In recording a $400 payment on account, Saddiqi debited Supplies and credited Accounts Payable.

Required

1. For each of these errors, state whether total debits equal total credits on the trial balance.
2. Identify each account with an incorrect balance, and indicate the amount and direction of the error (such as "Accounts Receivable $500 too high").

Computing financial statement amounts
without a journal
(Obj. 7)

E2-16 The owner of Specialty Medical Services needs to compute the following summary information from the accounting records:

a. Net income for the month of March
b. Total cash paid during March
c. Cash collections from customers during March
d. Cash paid on a note payable during March

The quickest way to compute these amounts is to analyze the following accounts:

	Balance		Additional Information
Account	Feb. 28	Mar. 31	for the Month of March
a. Owner, Capital	$ 9,000	$22,000	Withdrawals, $7,000
b. Cash.	7,000	2,000	Cash receipts, $70,000
c. Accounts Receivable . .	24,000	26,000	Revenues on account, $90,000
d. Note Payable	11,000	20,000	New borrowing on a note payable, $15,500

The net income for March can be computed as follows:

Owner, Capital

		Feb. 28 Bal.	9,000
March Withdrawals	7,000	March Net Income	X = $20,000
		March 31 Bal.	22,000

Use a similar approach to compute the other three items.

Continuing Exercise

Exercise 2-17 is the first exercise in a sequence that begins an accounting cycle. The cycle is completed in Chapter 5.

E2-17 Marsha Walker completed these transactions during the first half of December:

Recording transactions and preparing a trial balance
(Obj. 2, 3, 4, 5)

Dec. 2 Invested $14,000 to start a consulting practice titled Marsha Walker, Consultant. *debit Cash, credit M. Walker, capital*

2 Paid monthly office rent, $500. *debit rent expense, credit cash*

3 Paid cash for a Dell computer, $2,000. The computer is expected to remain in service for five years. *credit asset debit Cash*

4 Purchased office furniture on account, $3,600. The furniture should last for five years. *Debit asset, credit accounts payable*

5 Purchased supplies on account, $300. *Debit asset, credit accounts payable*

9 Performed consulting service for a client on account, $1,700. *Debit Accounts recievable, credit Service Revenue*

12 Paid utility expenses, $200. *Credit cash, debit expense*

18 Performed service for a client and received cash for the full amount of $800. *debit cash, credit service revenue.*

Student ResourceCD

GL, PT, QB

Required

1. Open T-accounts in the ledger: Cash; Accounts Receivable; Supplies; Equipment; Furniture; Accounts Payable; Marsha Walker, Capital; Marsha Walker, Withdrawals; Service Revenue; Rent Expense; Utilities Expense; and Salary Expense.

2. Journalize the transactions. Explanations are not required.

3. Post to the T-accounts. Key all items by date, and denote an account balance as *Bal.* Formal posting references are not required.

4. Prepare a trial balance at December 18. In the Continuing Exercise of Chapter 3, we will add transactions for the remainder of December and prepare a trial balance at December 31.

Problems

(Group A)

P2-1A → *Link Back to Chapter 1 (Balance Sheet, Income Statement).* Avery Patel, owner of Hillsboro Emergency Service, is selling the business. He offers the following trial balance to prospective buyers. Your best friend is considering buying the company. He seeks your advice in interpreting this information.

Using accounting terms and analyzing a trial balance
(Obj. 1)

Hillsboro Emergency Service		
Trial Balance		
December 31, 20X4		
Cash	$ 7,000	
Accounts receivable	6,000	
Prepaid expenses	4,000	
Automobiles	251,000	
Accounts payable		$ 31,000
Note payable		180,000
Avery Patel, capital		33,000
Avery Patel, withdrawals	21,000	
Service revenue		112,000
Wage expense	38,000	
Fuel expense	14,000	
Rent expense	8,000	
Supplies expense	7,000	
Total	$356,000	$356,000

Required

Help your friend decide whether to buy Hillsboro Emergency Service by answering the following questions.

1. How much are the firm's total assets? total liabilities? net income or net loss?

2. Suppose Hillsboro earned all the service revenue on account. Make a single journal entry to record the revenue, set up the T-accounts affected, and post to the accounts. Then write a sentence to explain where the trial balance amount for Service Revenue comes from.

3. In your own words, describe the accounting process that results in Hillsboro's $7,000 balance for Cash. Use the following terms in your explanation: account, balance, journal, ledger, post, and trial balance.

4. If your friend were to join Avery Patel as a co-owner of Hillsboro Emergency Service, what form of business organization would the firm then take? If necessary, review Chapter 1.

Analyzing and journalizing transactions
(Obj. 2, 3)

P2-2A Art Levitt practices medicine under the business title Art Levitt, M.D. During June, his medical practice engaged in the following transactions:

GL, PT, QB

June 1	Levitt deposited $55,000 cash in the business bank account. The business gave Levitt owner's equity in the firm.
5	Paid monthly rent on medical equipment, $700.
9	Paid $22,000 cash to purchase land for an office site.
10	Purchased supplies on account, $1,200.
19	Borrowed $20,000 from the bank for business use. Levitt signed a note payable to the bank in the name of the business.
22	Paid $1,000 on account.
30	Revenues earned during the month included $6,000 cash and $5,000 on account.
30	Paid employees' salaries ($2,400), office rent ($1,500), and utilities ($400).
30	Withdrew $10,000 from the business for personal use.

Levitt's business uses the following accounts: Cash; Accounts Receivable; Supplies; Land; Accounts Payable; Notes Payable; Art Levitt, Capital; Art Levitt, Withdrawals; Service Revenue; Salary Expense; Rent Expense; Utilities Expense.

Required

Journalize each transaction, as shown for June 1. Show all notations as follows:

June 1 Cash (↑ asset; debit)..................... 55,000
           Art Levitt, Capital (↑ equity; credit) ..   55,000

P2-3A Monica Kaska opened a law office on December 2 of the current year. During the first month of operations, the business completed the following transactions:

Journalizing transactions, posting to T-accounts, and preparing a trial balance
(Obj. 2, 3, 4, 5)

Dec. 2	Kaska deposited $30,000 cash in the business bank account Monica Kaska, Attorney.
3	Purchased supplies, $500, and furniture, $2,600, on account.
4	Performed legal service for a client and received cash, $1,500.
7	Paid cash to acquire land for a future office site, $22,000.
11	Prepared legal documents for a client on account, $900.
15	Paid secretary's salary, $570.
16	Paid for the furniture purchased December 3 on account.
18	Received $1,800 cash for helping a client sell real estate.
19	Defended a client in court and billed the client for $800.
29	Received partial collection from client on account, $400.
31	Paid secretary's salary, $570.
31	Paid rent expense, $700.
31	Withdrew $2,200 for personal use.

Required

Open the following T-accounts: Cash; Accounts Receivable; Supplies; Furniture; Land; Accounts Payable; Monica Kaska, Capital; Monica Kaska, Withdrawals; Service Revenue; Salary Expense; Rent Expense.

1. Record each transaction in the journal, using the account titles given. Key each transaction by date. Explanations are not required.

2. Post the transactions to the ledger, using transaction dates as posting references in the ledger. Label the balance of each account *Bal.*, as shown in the chapter.

3. Prepare the trial balance of Monica Kaska, Attorney, at December 31 of the current year.

P2-4A The trial balance of Robert Quiroga, Registered Dietician, at November 15, 20X3, follows.

Journalizing transactions, posting to accounts in four-column format, and preparing a trial balance
(Obj. 2, 3, 4, 5)

Robert Quiroga, Registered Dietician

Trial Balance
November 15, 20X3

Account Number	Account	Debit	Credit
11	Cash	$ 3,000	
12	Accounts receivable	8,000	
13	Supplies	600	
14	Equipment	15,000	
21	Accounts payable		$ 4,600
31	Robert Quiroga, capital		20,000
32	Robert Quiroga, withdrawals	2,300	
41	Service revenue		7,100
51	Salary expense	1,800	
52	Rent expense	1,000	
	Total	$31,700	$31,700

During the remainder of November, Quiroga completed the following transactions:

Nov. 16	Collected $6,000 cash from a client on account.
17	Performed a nutritional analysis for a hospital on account, $1,700.
21	Used personal funds to pay for the renovation of private residence, $55,000.
22	Purchased supplies on account, $800.
23	Withdrew $2,100 for personal use.
23	Paid on account, $2,600.
24	Received $1,900 cash for consulting with **Kraft Foods**.
30	Paid rent, $700.
30	Paid employees' salaries, $2,100.

Required

1. Record the transactions that occurred November 16 to November 30 on page 6 of the journal. Include an explanation for each entry.
2. Post the transactions to the ledger, using dates, account numbers, journal references, and posting references. Open the ledger accounts listed in the trial balance together with their balances at November 15. Use the four-column account format illustrated in the chapter (Exhibit 2-10). Enter *Bal.* (for previous balance) in the Item column, and place a check mark (✓) in the journal reference column for the November 15 balance of each account.
3. Prepare the trial balance of Robert Quiroga, Registered Dietician, at November 30, 20X3.

Correcting errors in a trial balance
(Obj. 2, 5)

P2-5A ← *Link Back to Chapter 1 (Income Statement).* The trial balance for Online Cable Service does not balance. The following errors were detected:

a. The cash balance is understated by $400.
b. Rent expense of $350 was erroneously posted as a credit rather than a debit.
c. An $8,300 credit to Service Revenue was not posted.
d. A $600 debit to Accounts Receivable was posted as $60.
e. The balance of Utilities Expense is understated by $60.
f. A $100 purchase of supplies on account was neither journalized nor posted.
g. Office furniture should be listed in the amount of $21,300.

Online Cable Service

Trial Balance
March 31, 20X1

Cash	$ 6,200	
Accounts receivable	2,000	
Supplies	500	
Office furniture	22,300	
Computers	46,000	
Accounts payable		$ 2,700
Note payable		18,300
Meredith Ballard, capital		50,800
Meredith Ballard, withdrawals	5,000	
Service revenue		4,900
Salary expense	1,300	
Rent expense	500	
Advertising expense	300	
Utilities expense	200	
Total	$84,300	$76,700

Required

1. Prepare the correct trial balance at March 31. Journal entries are not required.

2. Prepare Online Cable Service's income statement for the month ended March 31, 20X1, to determine whether the business had a net income or a net loss for the month. Refer to Exhibit 1-8, page 21, if needed.

P2-6A Vince Serrano started Serrano Carpet Installers, and during the first month of operations (January 20X7), he completed the following selected transactions:

Recording transactions directly in T-accounts; preparing a trial balance **(Obj. 2, 5, 6)**

a. Serrano began the business with an investment of $18,000 cash and a van (automobile) valued at $13,000. The business gave Serrano owner's equity in the firm.

b. Borrowed $25,000 from the bank; signed a note payable.

c. Paid $32,000 for equipment.

d. Purchased supplies on account, $400.

e. Paid employee's salary, $1,300.

f. Received $800 for a carpet installation job performed for a bank.

g. Received an $800 bill for advertising expense that will be paid in the near future.

h. Paid $100 of the account payable created in transaction (d).

i. Installed carpet for a hotel on account, $3,300.

j. Received cash on account, $1,100.

k. Paid the following cash expenses:
   (1) Rent, $1,000.   **(2)** Insurance, $600.

l. Withdrew $2,600 for personal use.

Required

1. Open the following T-accounts: Cash; Accounts Receivable; Supplies; Equipment; Automobile; Accounts Payable; Note Payable; Vince Serrano, Capital; Vince Serrano, Withdrawals; Service Revenue; Salary Expense; Rent Expense; Advertising Expense; Insurance Expense.

2. Record the transactions directly in the T-accounts without using a journal. Use the letters to identify the transactions.

3. Prepare the trial balance of Serrano Carpet Installers at January 31, 20X7.

Note: Problem 2-7A should be used in conjunction with Problem 2-6A.

P2-7A → *Link Back to Chapter 1 (Income Statement, Statement of Owner's Equity, Balance Sheet).* Refer to Problem 2-6A. After completing the trial balance in Problem 2-6A, prepare the following financial statements for Serrano Carpet Installers:

Preparing the financial statements **(Obj. 5)**

1. Income statement for the month ended January 31, 20X7.

2. Statement of owner's equity for the month ended January 31, 20X7.

3. Balance sheet at January 31, 20X7.

Draw arrows to link the statements. If needed, use Exhibit 1-8, page 21, as a guide for preparing the financial statements.

Problems

(Group B)

P2-1B → *Link Back to Chapter 1 (Balance Sheet, Income Statement).* Letrice Simkin, owner of the Simkin Law Firm, is considering adding another lawyer to the firm. Michelle McGuire is considering joining Simkin and asks to see Simkin's financial information. Simkin gives McGuire the firm's trial balance, which follows. Help McGuire decide whether to join the firm by answering these questions for her.

Using accounting terms and analyzing a trial balance **(Obj. 1)**

1. How much are the firm's total assets? total liabilities? net income or net loss?

2. Suppose Simkin earned all the service revenue on account. Make a single journal entry to record the revenue, set up the T-accounts affected, and post to the accounts. Then write a sentence to explain where the trial balance amount for Service Revenue comes from.

3. In your own words, describe the accounting process that results in Simkin's $12,000 balance for Cash. Use the following terms in your explanation: account, balance, journal, ledger, post, and trial balance.

4. If McGuire joins Simkin as a co-owner of the law firm, what form of business organization will the firm take? If necessary, review Chapter 1.

Simkin Law Firm

Trial Balance
December 31, 20X8

Cash	$ 12,000	
Accounts receivable	27,000	
Prepaid expenses	4,000	
Land	63,000	
Accounts payable		$ 35,000
Note payable		32,000
Letrice Simkin, capital		30,000
Letrice Simkin, withdrawals	48,000	
Service revenue		116,000
Rent expense	26,000	
Advertising expense	3,000	
Wage expense	23,000	
Supplies expense	7,000	
Total	$213,000	$213,000

Analyzing and journalizing transactions
(Obj. 2, 3)

Student ResourceCD

GL, PT, QB

P2-2B Hollywood Theaters owns movie theaters in the shopping centers of a major metropolitan area. Its owner, James Stevens, engaged in the following business transactions:

April 1	Stevens invested $500,000 personal cash in the business by depositing that amount in a bank account titled Hollywood Theaters. The business gave Stevens owner's equity in the company.
2	Paid $400,000 cash to purchase a theater building.
5	Borrowed $220,000 from the bank. Stevens signed a note payable to the bank in the name of Hollywood Theaters.
10	Purchased theater supplies on account, $1,700.
15	Paid $800 on account.
15	Paid property tax expense on theater building, $1,200.
16	Paid employee salaries, $2,800, and rent on equipment, $1,800.
17	Withdrew $6,000 from the business for personal use.
30	Received $20,000 cash from revenue and deposited that amount in the bank. Label the revenue as Sales Revenue.

Hollywood Theaters uses the following accounts: Cash; Supplies; Building; Accounts Payable; Notes Payable; James Stevens, Capital; James Stevens, Withdrawals; Sales Revenue; Salary Expense; Rent Expense; Property Tax Expense.

Required

Journalize each transaction of Hollywood Theaters as shown for April 1. Show all notations as follows:

Apr. 1 Cash (↑ asset; debit)		500,000
James Stevens, Capital (↑ equity; credit)		500,000

P2-3B Emily Smith started her practice as a registered dietician on September 3 of the current year. During the first month of operations, the business completed the following transactions:

Journalizing transactions, posting to T-accounts, and preparing a trial balance
(Obj. 2, 3, 4, 5)

Sep. 3	Smith transferred $20,000 cash from her personal bank account to a business account titled Emily Smith, Registered Dietician. The business gave Smith owner's equity in the firm.
4	Purchased supplies, $200, and furniture, $1,800, on account.
6	Performed services for a hospital and received $4,000 cash.
7	Paid $15,000 cash to acquire land for a future office site.
10	Performed a nutritional analysis for a hotel and received its promise to pay the $800 within one week.
14	Paid for the furniture purchased September 4 on account.
15	Paid secretary's salary, $600.
17	Received partial collection from client on account, $500.
20	Prepared a nutrition plan for a school on account, $800.
28	Received $1,500 cash for consulting with **Procter & Gamble**.
30	Paid secretary's salary, $600.
30	Paid rent expense, $500.
30	Withdrew $2,900 for personal use.

Required

Open the following T-accounts: Cash; Accounts Receivable; Supplies; Furniture; Land; Accounts Payable; Emily Smith, Capital; Emily Smith, Withdrawals; Service Revenue; Salary Expense; Rent Expense.

1. Record each transaction in the journal, using the account titles given. Key each transaction by date. Explanations are not required.

2. Post the transactions to the ledger, using transaction dates as posting references in the ledger. Label the balance of each account *Bal.*, as shown in the chapter.

3. Prepare the trial balance of Emily Smith, Registered Dietician, at September 30 of the current year.

P2-4B The trial balance of Mark Power, CPA, is dated February 14, 20X3:

Journalizing transactions, posting to accounts in four-column format, and preparing a trial balance
(Obj. 2, 3, 4, 5)

Mark Power, CPA
Trial Balance
February 14, 20X3

Account Number	Account	Debit	Credit
11	Cash	$ 2,000	
12	Accounts receivable	9,500	
13	Supplies	800	
14	Land	18,600	
21	Accounts payable		$ 3,000
31	Mark Power, capital		26,500
32	Mark Power, withdrawals	1,200	
41	Service revenue		7,200
51	Salary expense	3,600	
52	Rent expense	1,000	
	Total	$36,700	$36,700

During the remainder of February, Power completed the following transactions:

Feb. 15	Power collected $3,500 cash from a client on account.
16	Performed tax services for a client on account, $700.
20	Paid on account, $1,000.
21	Purchased supplies on account, $100.
21	Withdrew $1,200 for personal use.
21	Paid for a deck for private residence, using personal funds, $9,000.
22	Received cash of $5,500 for consulting work just completed.
28	Paid rent, $800.
28	Paid employees' salaries, $1,800.

Required

1. Record the transactions that occurred from February 15 to February 28 in page 3 of the journal. Include an explanation for each entry.
2. Open the ledger accounts listed in the trial balance, together with their balances at February 14. Use the four-column account format illustrated in the chapter (Exhibit 2-10). Enter *Bal.* (for previous balance) in the Item column, and place a check mark (✓) in the journal reference column for the February 14 balance in each account. Post the transactions to the ledger using dates, account numbers, journal references, and posting references.
3. Prepare the trial balance of Mark Power, CPA, at February 28, 20X3.

Correcting errors in a trial balance
(Obj. 2, 5)

P2-5B ← *Link Back to Chapter 1 (Income Statement).* The trial balance for Feelgood Fitness Center does not balance. The following errors were detected:

a. The cash balance is understated by $700.
b. The cost of the building was $93,000, not $96,000.
c. A $200 purchase of supplies on account was neither journalized nor posted.
d. The balance of Utilities Expense is overstated by $70.
e. Rent expense of $200 was erroneously posted as a credit rather than a debit.
f. A $300 debit to Accounts Receivable was posted as $30.
g. A $4,300 credit to Service Revenue was not posted.

Feelgood Fitness Center
Trial Balance
June 30, 20X2

Cash..	$ 3,000	
Accounts receivable	10,000	
Supplies......................................	900	
Equipment	85,100	
Building	96,000	
Accounts payable		$ 55,000
Note payable		72,000
Rob Rylander, capital		62,500
Rob Rylander, withdrawals......................	2,900	
Service revenue		6,500
Salary expense................................	2,100	
Rent expense	1,000	
Advertising expense...........................	600	
Utilities expense..............................	400	
Total..	$202,000	$196,000

Required

1. Prepare the correct trial balance at June 30. Journal entries are not required.
2. Prepare the company's income statement for the month ended June 30, 20X2, in order to determine the business's net income or net loss for the month. Refer to Exhibit 1-8, page 21, if needed.

P2-6B Christie Clinton started a consulting service and during the first month of operations (June 20X3) completed the following selected transactions:

Recording transactions directly in T-accounts; preparing a trial balance **(Obj. 2, 5, 6)**

a. Clinton began the business with an investment of $5,000 cash and a building valued at $50,000. The business gave Clinton owner's equity in the business.
b. Borrowed $30,000 from the bank; signed a note payable.
c. Purchased office supplies on account, $2,100.
d. Paid $18,000 for office furniture.
e. Paid employee's salary, $2,200.
f. Performed consulting service on account for client, $5,100.
g. Paid $800 of the account payable created in transaction (c).
h. Received a $600 bill for advertising expense that will be paid in the near future.
i. Performed consulting service for customers and received cash, $1,600.
j. Received cash on account, $1,200.
k. Paid the following cash expenses:
   (1) Rent on equipment, $700.   (2) Utilities, $400.
l. Withdrew $7,500 for personal use.

Required

1. Open the following T-accounts: Cash; Accounts Receivable; Office Supplies; Office Furniture; Building; Accounts Payable; Note Payable; Christie Clinton, Capital; Christie Clinton, Withdrawals; Service Revenue; Salary Expense; Advertising Expense; Rent Expense; Utilities Expense.
2. Record each transaction directly in the T-accounts without using a journal. Use the letters to identify the transactions.
3. Prepare the trial balance of Clinton Consulting at June 30, 20X3.

Note: Problem 2-7B should be used in conjunction with Problem 2-6B.

P2-7B → *Link Back to Chapter 1 (Income Statement, Statement of Owner's Equity, Balance Sheet).* Refer to Problem 2-6B. After completing the trial balance in Problem 2-6B, prepare the following financial statements for Clinton Consulting Service:

Preparing the financial statements **(Obj. 5)**

1. Income statement for the month ended June 30, 20X3.
2. Statement of owner's equity for the month ended June 30, 20X3.
3. Balance sheet at June 30, 20X3.

Draw arrows to link the statements. If needed, use Exhibit 1-8, page 21, as a guide for preparing the financial statements.

●APPLY *Your Knowledge*

Decision Cases

Case 1. You have been requested by a friend named Stephanie Bernina to advise her on the effects certain transactions will have on her business. Time is short, so you cannot journalize the transactions. Instead, you must analyze the transactions without a journal. Bernina will continue the business only if she can expect to earn monthly net income of $5,000. The following transactions occurred during March:

Recording transactions directly in T-accounts, preparing a trial balance, and measuring net income or loss **(Obj. 2, 5, 6)**

a. Bernina deposited $8,000 cash in a business bank account to start the company.
b. Paid $300 cash for supplies.
c. Incurred advertising expense on account, $700.
d. Paid the following cash expenses: secretary's salary, $1,400; office rent, $1,150.
e. Earned service revenue on account, $8,800.
f. Collected cash from customers on account, $1,200.

Required

1. Open the following T-accounts: Cash; Accounts Receivable; Supplies; Accounts Payable; Stephanie Bernina, Capital; Service Revenue; Salary Expense; Rent Expense; Advertising Expense; Utilities Expense; Interest Expense.
2. Record the transactions directly in the accounts without using a journal. Key each transaction by letter.
3. Prepare a trial balance at March 31, 20X9. List the largest expense first, the next largest second, and so on. The business name is Bernina Travel Planners.
4. Compute the amount of net income or net loss for this first month of operations. Would you recommend that Bernina continue in business?

Using the accounting equation
(Obj. 2)

Case 2. Answer the following questions. Consider each question separately.

1. When you deposit money in your bank account, the bank credits your account. Is the bank misusing the word *credit* in this context? Why does the bank use the term *credit* to refer to your deposit, and not *debit?*
2. Explain the advantages of double-entry bookkeeping over single-entry bookkeeping to a friend who is opening a used book store.
3. Your friend asks, "When revenues increase assets and expenses decrease assets, why are revenues credits and expenses debits and not the other way around?" Explain to your friend why revenues are credits and expenses are debits.

Ethical Issue

Brave Hearts, a charitable organization in Panama City, Florida, has a standing agreement with De Leon State Bank. The agreement allows Brave Hearts to overdraw its cash balance at the bank when donations are running low. In the past, Brave Hearts managed funds wisely and rarely used this privilege. Jacob Henson has recently become the president of Brave Hearts. To expand operations, Henson acquired office equipment and spent large amounts on fund-raising. During Henson's presidency, Brave Hearts has maintained a negative bank balance of approximately $6,000.

Required

What is the ethical issue in this situation? State why you approve or disapprove of Henson's management of Brave Hearts' funds.

Financial Statement Case

Journalizing transactions for a company
(Obj. 2, 3)

This problem helps you develop skill in recording transactions by using a company's actual account titles. Refer to the **Amazon.com** financial statements in Appendix A. Assume that Amazon completed the following selected transactions during December 2002:

Dec. 5	Earned sales revenue and collected cash, $110,000.
9	Borrowed $500,000 by signing a note payable.
12	Purchased equipment on account, $50,000.
17	Paid $100,000 of the note payable, plus interest expense of $8,000.
22	Paid half the account payable from December 12.
28	Paid a home-office electricity bill for $3,000 (this is an administrative expense).

Required

Journalize these transactions, using the following account titles taken from the Amazon.com financial statements: Cash; Equipment; Accounts Payable; Note Payable; Sales Revenue; Administrative Expense; and Interest Expense. Explanations are not required.

Team Project

Contact a local business and arrange with the owner to learn what accounts the business uses.

Required

1. Obtain a copy of the business's chart of accounts.
2. Prepare the company's financial statements for the most recent month, quarter, or year. You may use either made-up account balances or balances supplied by the owner.

If the business has a large number of accounts within a category, combine related accounts and report a single amount on the financial statements. For example, the company may have several cash accounts. Combine all cash amounts and report a single Cash amount on the balance sheet.

You will probably encounter numerous accounts that you have not yet learned. Deal with these as best you can. The chart of accounts given in Appendix B at the end of the book will be helpful.

Keep in mind that the financial statements report the balances of the accounts listed in the company's chart of accounts. Therefore, the financial statements must be consistent with the chart of accounts.

For Internet Exercises, go to the Web site www.prenhall.com/horngren.

CHAPTER 3

The Adjusting Process

A+ TIPS CHECK YOUR RESOURCES

- Visit the www.prenhall.com/horngren **Web site** for self-study quizzes, video clips, and other resources

- Try the **Quick Check** exercise at the end of the chapter to test your knowledge

- Learn the **key terms**

- Do the **Starter** exercises keyed in the margins

- Work the **end-of-chapter summary problems**

- Use the **Concept Links** to review material in other chapters

- Search the **CD** for review materials by chapter or by key word

- Watch the **tutorial videos** to review key concepts

- Watch the **On Location It's Just Lunch** video for an overview of accounting in business

LEARNING OBJECTIVES

1 Distinguish accrual accounting from cash-basis accounting

2 Apply the revenue and matching principles

3 Make adjusting entries

4 Prepare an adjusted trial balance

5 Prepare the financial statements from the adjusted trial balance

What do dating and accounting have in common? Lots, if you are the owner of It's Just Lunch. Andrea McGinty founded It's Just Lunch as a service company and, in the process, turned dating into dollars. For a fee, It's Just Lunch will arrange lunch dates for busy professionals. After 10 years in business, McGinty's company is earning several million dollars a year in revenues and generating healthy profits.

According to It's Just Lunch,

- The average single professional has 8 first dates in a year.
- 78% of men will take 15 minutes on a first date to decide whether to see the person again.
- After 24 hours, the chance that a first date will call you again is 1 in 8.

For more information, you can visit the company's Web site at **www.itsjustlunch.com**. ■

It's Just Lunch

⊙Student Resource**CD**

accrual basis, cash basis, matching principle, revenue principle, time-period concept

Distinguish accrual accounting from cash-basis accounting

Accrual Accounting
Accounting that records the impact of a business event as it occurs, regardless of whether the transaction affected cash.

Cash-Basis Accounting
Accounting that records transactions only when cash is received or paid.

How does It's Just Lunch use accounting? How does McGinty know whether or not she is making money? It's Just Lunch measures assets, liabilities, revenues, and expenses like any other company. It records transactions and then prepares its financial statements at the end of the period.

In Chapter 2 we saw how to record transactions, post to the accounts, and prepare a trial balance. Here we take the accounting process a step further. It's Just Lunch comes to the end of the period, and the company's accounts must be updated. Its computers have depreciated, and It's Just Lunch owes some services to customers. This chapter shows how to adjust the books and ready the accounts for the financial statements.

Financial Statements and Adjusting Entries

One step in financial statement preparation is the trial balance that we covered in Chapter 2. To measure income, a business must bring the records up to date at the end of the period. This process is called *adjusting the books*, and it requires special journal entries called *adjusting entries*. This chapter focuses on the adjustments that are needed to measure income.

Accountants have concepts and principles to guide the measurement of income. Chief among these are accrual accounting, the accounting period, the revenue principle, and the matching principle. In this chapter, we apply these principles to Gay Gillen eTravel for the month of April. It's Just Lunch and all other companies follow the same principles.

Accrual versus Cash-Basis Accounting

There are two ways to do accounting:

- ■ **Accrual accounting** records the effect of each transaction as it occurs. Most businesses use the accrual basis as covered in this book.

- ■ **Cash-basis accounting** records only cash receipts and cash payments. It ignores receivables, payables, and depreciation. Only very small businesses use the cash basis of accounting.

Suppose It's Just Lunch purchased $2,000 of office supplies on account. On the accrual basis, It's Just Lunch records Office Supplies and Accounts Payable as follows:

Office Supplies (↑ asset; debit)	2,000	
Accounts Payable (↑ liability; credit)		2,000
Purchased supplies on account.		

To help you learn to make journal entries, we repeat the special notations that we began in Chapter 2. As before, the arrows and the debit/credit notations are not required.

In contrast, cash-basis accounting ignores this transaction because It's Just Lunch paid no cash. The cash basis records only cash receipts and cash payments. In the cash basis,

- ■ *Cash receipts are treated as revenues.*

- ■ *Cash payments are treated as expenses.*

Under the cash basis, It's Just Lunch would record each cash payment as an expense and not as an asset. This is faulty accounting: It's Just Lunch acquired supplies, which are assets because they provide future benefit to the company.

Now let's see how differently the accrual basis and the cash basis account for a revenue. Suppose It's Just Lunch performed service and earned the revenue but collected no cash. Under the accrual basis, It's Just Lunch records $10,000 of revenue on account as follows:

Accounts Receivable (↑ asset; debit).	10,000	
Service Revenue (↑ revenue; credit)		10,000
Earned revenue on account.		

Under the cash basis, It's Just Lunch would not even bother to record any revenue earned *on account* because there is no cash receipt. Instead, it would wait until the company receives the cash. Then it would record the cash receipt as revenue. As a result, cash-basis accounting never reports accounts receivable from customers. It shows the revenue in the wrong accounting period, when the cash is received. Revenue should be recorded when it is earned, and that is how the accrual basis operates.

Exhibit 3-1 illustrates the difference between the accrual basis and the cash basis. Keep in mind that the accrual basis is the correct way to do accounting. Panel A of the exhibit illustrates a revenue, and Panel B covers an expense.

Exhibit 3-1 Accrual Accounting versus Cash-Basis Accounting

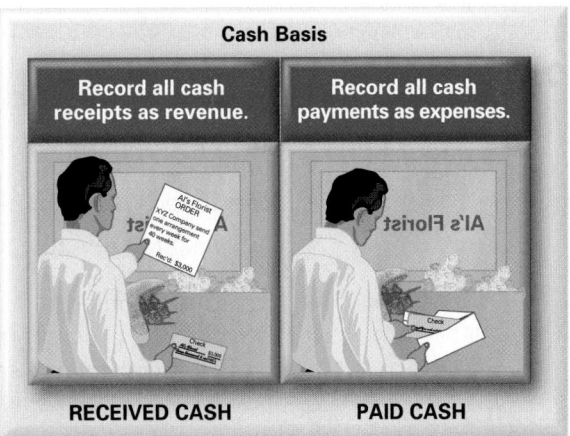

Now let's apply what you've learned. Work the Stop & Think.

Suppose **It's Just Lunch** collects $3,000 from customers on January 1. The company will earn the $3,000 of revenue evenly during January, February, and March. How much service revenue will It's Just Lunch report each month under (a) accrual accounting and (b) cash-basis accounting?

Answer:

		Jan.	Feb.	Mar.
(a) *Accrual accounting:*	Service revenue	$1,000	$1,000	$1,000
(b) *Cash-basis accounting:*	Service revenue	$3,000		

Now suppose It's Just Lunch prepays $6,000 for TV advertising. The ads will run during October, November, and December. How much advertising expense will It's Just Lunch report each month under the two methods of accounting?

Answer:

		Oct.	Nov.	Dec.
(a) *Accrual accounting:*	Advertising expense . . .	$2,000	$2,000	$2,000
(b) *Cash-basis accounting:*	Advertising expense . . .	$6,000		

Observe the vast differences between accrual accounting and the cash basis. The accrual basis is the correct way to do the accounting.

✔ Starter 3-1

✔ Starter 3-2

The Accounting Period

The only way to know for certain how successfully a business has operated is to close its doors, sell the assets, pay the liabilities, and give any leftover cash to the owners. This process of going out of business is called *liquidation*. It is not practical to measure income this way. Instead, businesses need periodic reports on their affairs. Accountants slice time into small segments and prepare financial statements for specific periods.

The basic accounting period is one year, and all businesses prepare annual financial statements. For about 60% of large companies in a recent survey, the annual accounting period runs the calendar year from January 1 through December 31. Other companies use a *fiscal year*, which ends on a date other than December 31. The year-end date is usually the low point in business activity for the year. Retailers are a notable example. For instance, Wal-Mart, Target, and most other retailers use a fiscal year that ends on January 31 because the low point in their activity falls after Christmas.

Companies also prepare financial statements for *interim* periods, so monthly statements are common. A series of monthly statements can be combined for quarterly and semiannual periods. Most of our discussions are based on an annual accounting period, but everything can be applied to interim periods as well.

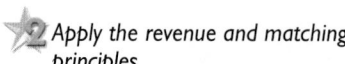 *Apply the revenue and matching principles*

Revenue Principle
The basis for recording revenues; tells accountants when to record revenue and the amount of revenue to record.

Revenue, defined in Chapter 1, p. 11, is the increase in owner's equity from delivering goods and services to customers in the course of operating a business.

The Revenue Principle

The **revenue principle** tells accountants

- *When* to record revenue—that is, when to make a journal entry
- The *amount* of revenue to record.

←"Recording" something in accounting means to make an entry in the journal. That is where the process starts.

The revenue principle says to record revenue when it has been earned—but not before. In most cases, revenue is earned when the business has delivered a good or service to the customer. The company has done everything required by the sale agreement, including transferring the item to the customer.

Exhibit 3-2 shows two situations that provide guidance on when to record revenue for Gay Gillen eTravel. The first situation illustrates when *not* to record revenue—because the client merely states his plan. Situation 2 illustrates when revenue should be recorded—after the travel agency has performed a service for the client.

Exhibit 3-2

Recording Revenue: The Revenue Principle

 **Starter 3-3**

The revenue principle says to record revenue for the cash value of the item transferred to the customer. Suppose that to obtain a new client, Gillen performs travel service for the cut-rate price of $500. Ordinarily, Gillen would have charged $600 for this service. How much revenue should Gillen record? The answer is $500, because that was the value of the transaction. Gillen will not receive $600, so that is not the amount of revenue to record. She will receive only $500 cash, so she records that amount of revenue. The Accounting.com box entitled "Grossing Up the Revenue: Priceline.com" shows how Internet service companies, such as Priceline.com, have attempted to rewrite the accounting rules for recording their revenues.

The Matching Principle

The **matching principle** guides accounting for expenses. → Recall that expenses—such as rent, utilities, and advertising—are the costs of operating a business. Expenses are the costs of assets used up and liabilities incurred to earn revenue. The matching principle directs accountants to

1. Identify all expenses incurred during the period and measure the expenses.
2. Match the expenses against the revenues earned during the period.

To match expenses against revenues means to subtract expenses from revenues. The goal is to compute net income or net loss. Exhibit 3-3 illustrates the matching principle.

There is a natural link between revenues and some expenses. For example, Gay Gillen may pay sales commissions to employees who sell the travel agency's services. *Cost of goods sold* is another example. If Ford Motor Company sells no automobiles, Ford has no cost of goods sold.

An expense, defined in Chapter 1, p. 12, is a decrease in owner's equity that occurs from using assets or increasing liabilities in the course of operating a business.

Matching Principle
Guide to accounting for expenses. Identify all expenses incurred during the period, measure the expenses, and match them against the revenues earned during that same time period.

Grossing Up the Revenue: Priceline.com

Suppose you're going to Australia. You want a cheap air ticket, and Priceline.com lets you "name your price" for airline tickets and hotel rooms. Your bid of $975 is accepted, and Priceline pockets the spread between your price and the amount Priceline pays the airline company. What should Priceline claim as revenue—the fee it earns, or the full price of your ticket?

Priceline.com and other Internet service companies record the entire value of the products sold through their sites. Priceline has defended this practice by saying it operates differently from a travel agency, which earns a fixed commission. Priceline purchases the airline ticket outright, assumes the full risk of ownership, and controls the profit on each sale. The Securities and Exchange Commission (SEC) and the Financial Accounting Standards Board (FASB) call this practice "grossing up" revenue.

Grossing up may be legal, but the SEC and the FASB are considering placing restrictions on it. The FASB now has added a project on revenue recognition to its agenda. "Revenue usually is the largest item in [a company's] financial statements, and revenue recognition issues top the list of reasons for financial restatements," say L. Todd Johnson, FASB senior project manager. "The FASB's proposed project would address such matters by developing one accounting standard that would apply to a broad range of industries."

Sources: Elizabeth McDonald, "Plump from Web Sales, Some Dot.Coms Face Crash Diet of Restriction on Booking Revenue," The Wall Street Journal, February 28, 2000, p. C4. Jeremy Kahn, "Presto Chango! Sales Are Huge!" Fortune, March 21, 2000, pp. 90–96. Also, http://www.fasb.org/news/nr052002.shtml.

| Exhibit 3-3 | Recording Expenses: The Matching Principle |

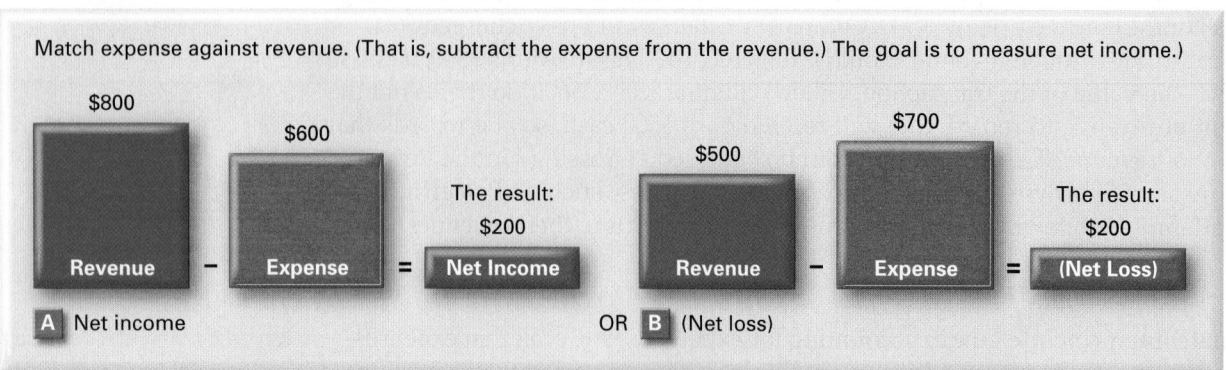

Match expense against revenue. (That is, subtract the expense from the revenue.) The goal is to measure net income.)

A Net income   OR   **B** (Net loss)

✔ **Starter 3-4**

Other expenses are not so easy to link to sales. For example, Gay Gillen eTravel's monthly rent expense occurs regardless of the revenues earned that month. The matching principle says to identify those expenses with a particular time period, such as a month or a year. Gay Gillen eTravel will record rent expense each month based on the lease agreement. Gillen also pays monthly salaries to some employees.

How does Gay Gillen account for a travel plan that begins in April and ends in May? How does she bring accounts up to date for the financial statements? To answer these questions, accountants use the time-period concept.

The Time-Period Concept

Time-Period Concept
Ensures that information is reported at regular intervals.

Managers need periodic readings on the business. The **time-period concept** ensures that information is reported often. To measure income accurately, companies update their accounts at the end of each period. Fossil, the fashion watch company, provides an example of an expense accrual. At December 31, 2002, Fossil recorded employee compensation of $11 million that the company owed its workers at year-end. The company's accrual entry, adapted and in millions of dollars, was

2002			
Dec. 31	Salary Expense (↑ expense; debit)	11	
	Salary Payable (↑ liability; credit)		11
	Accrued salary expense.		

This entry assigns the salary expense to 2002, the year when the employees worked for the company. Without this entry, 2002's expenses would be understated, and net income would be overstated. The accrual entry also records the liability for the balance sheet at December 31, 2002. Without this entry, total liabilities would be understated.

The remainder of the chapter shows how to adjust the accounts and bring the books up to date. What are the final products of the accounting process? The financial statements: the income statement, the balance sheet, and so on.

☐ Financial Statements and
    Adjusting Entries
■ **Adjusting the Accounts**
☐ Prepaids and Accruals
☐ Adjusted Trial Balance
☐ The Financial Statements
☐ Ethical Issues
☐ Appendix: Alternative
    Treatment of Prepaid Expenses
    and Unearned Revenues

Student Resource**CD**

adjusting entries, adjustments,
trial balance

3 Make adjusting entries

Adjusting the Accounts

At the end of the period, the accountant prepares the statements. The end-of-period process begins with the trial balance. ← Exhibit 3-4 is the trial balance of Gay Gillen eTravel at April 30, 20X5. This *unadjusted trial balance* lists most of the revenues and expenses of the travel agency for April. But these trial balance amounts are incomplete because they omit certain revenue and expense transactions. That is why the trial balance is *unadjusted*. Usually, however, we refer to it simply as the trial balance, without the label "unadjusted."

Under cash-basis accounting, there is no need for adjustments to the accounts because all April cash transactions have already been recorded. However, accrual accounting requires adjusting entries at the end of the period. We must have correct balances for the financial statements. To see why, consider the Supplies account in Exhibit 3-4.

Exhibit 3-4

Unadjusted Trial Balance

Gay Gillen eTravel
Unadjusted Trial Balance
April 30, 20X5

Cash	$24,800	
Accounts receivable	2,250	
Supplies	700	
Prepaid rent	3,000	
Furniture	16,500	
Accounts payable		$13,100
Unearned service revenue		450
Gay Gillen, capital		31,250
Gay Gillen, withdrawals	3,200	
Service revenue		7,000
Salary expense	950	
Utilities expense	400	
Total	$51,800	$51,800

Gay Gillen eTravel uses supplies during the month. This reduces the quantity of supplies on hand and creates an expense, just like salary or rent. It is a waste of time to record supplies expense more than once a month. But by the end of the month, the $700 of Supplies on the unadjusted trial balance (Exhibit 3-4) is out of date. So how does Gillen account for supplies expense? Gillen must adjust the accounts at April 30 in order to show correct amounts for supplies and supplies expense. The adjusting process requires adjusting journal entries.

Adjusting entries assign revenues to the period when they are earned and expenses to the period when they are incurred. Adjusting entries also update the asset and liability accounts. Adjustments are needed to properly measure (1) the period's income on the income statement, and (2) the assets and the liabilities on the balance sheet. Adjusting entries are key to accrual accounting. This end-of-period process is called *adjusting the accounts, making the adjusting entries*, or *adjusting the books*. The two basic categories of adjustments are *prepaids* and *accruals*.

Adjusting Entry
Entry made at the end of the period to assign revenues to the period in which they are earned and expenses to the period in which they are incurred. Adjusting entries help measure the period's income and bring the related asset and liability accounts to correct balances for the financial statements.

Prepaids and Accruals

In a *prepaid* adjustment, the cash transaction occurs before an expense or revenue is recorded. *Accrual*-type adjustments are the opposite of prepaids. Accruals record an expense or a revenue before the cash settlement.

Adjusting entries can be further divided into five categories:

1. Prepaid expenses
2. Depreciation
3. Accrued expenses
4. Accrued revenues
5. Unearned revenues

The core of this chapter shows how to account for these five types of adjusting entries. Study this material carefully, because it is the most challenging topic in all of introductory accounting.

Student ResourceCD

accruals, depreciation, prepaid expenses

Prepaid Expenses

Prepaid expenses are advance payments of expenses. Prepaid rent and prepaid insurance are examples of expenses that are paid in advance. All companies, large and small, must adjust their prepaid expenses. For example, McDonald's Corporation, the restaurant chain, makes prepayments for rent, insurance, and supplies. Keep in mind that prepaid expenses are assets, not expenses.

PREPAID RENT   Landlords require tenants to pay rent in advance. This prepayment creates an asset for the renter. Suppose Gay Gillen eTravel prepays three months' office rent on April 1, 20X5. If the lease specifies a monthly rental of $1,000, the entry to record the payment is

Apr. 1	Prepaid Rent ($1,000 × 3)		
	(↑ asset; debit)	3,000	
	Cash (↓ asset; credit)		3,000
	Paid rent in advance.		

After posting, Prepaid Rent has a $3,000 debit balance.

ASSETS

Prepaid Rent

Apr. 1	3,000

The trial balance at April 30, 20X5, lists Prepaid Rent with a debit balance of $3,000. Throughout April, Prepaid Rent maintains this beginning balance (Exhibit 3-4). But $3,000 is *not* the amount to report for Prepaid Rent on the balance sheet at April 30. Why?

At April 30, Prepaid Rent should be decreased for the amount of the asset that has been used up. The used-up portion is one-third of the prepayment. Recall that an asset that has expired is an *expense*. The adjusting entry transfers $1,000 ($3,000 × 1/3) of the Prepaid Rent to Rent Expense. The adjusting entry is

Apr. 30	Rent Expense ($3,000 × 1/3)		
	(↑ expense; debit)	1,000	
	Prepaid Rent (↓ asset; credit) . . .		1,000
	To record rent expense.		

After posting, Prepaid Rent and Rent Expense show correct ending balances:

ASSETS   **EXPENSES**

Prepaid Rent   ⟶   **Rent Expense**

Apr. 1	3,000	Apr. 30	1,000	Apr. 30	1,000		
Bal.	2,000			Bal.	1,000		

Correct asset amount: **$2,000**	→	**Total accounted for: $3,000**	←	**Correct expense** amount: **$1,000**

The same analysis applies to the prepayment of three months of insurance. The only difference is in the account titles, which would be Prepaid Insurance instead of Prepaid Rent and Insurance Expense instead of Rent Expense. In a computerized system, the adjusting entry is programmed to recur automatically each accounting period.

The chapter appendix shows an alternative treatment of prepaid expenses. The end result on the financial statements is the same as illustrated here.

SUPPLIES   Supplies are accounted for in the same way as prepaid expenses. On April 2, Gay Gillen paid $700 for office supplies:

> Apr. 2   Supplies (↑ asset; debit)............... 700
> Cash (↓ asset; credit)............. | 700
> Paid cash for supplies.

The April 30 trial balance, therefore, lists Supplies with a $700 debit balance, as shown in Exhibit 3-4. But Gillen's April 30 balance sheet should *not* report supplies of $700. Why?

During April, Gillen used supplies to conduct business. The cost of the supplies used becomes *supplies expense*. To measure supplies expense, Gillen counts the supplies on hand at the end of April. This is the amount of the asset still available to the business. Assume that supplies costing $400 remain at April 30. Subtracting the supplies on hand at the end of April ($400) from the supplies available ($700) measures supplies expense for the month ($300).

Cost of asset available	−	Cost of asset on hand at the end of the period	=	Cost of asset used (expense) during the period
$700	−	$400	=	$300

The April 30 adjusting entry to update the Supplies account and to record Supplies Expense for the month follows:

> Apr. 30   Supplies Expense ($700 – $400)
> (↑ expense; debit).................... 300
> Supplies (↓ asset; credit) .... | 300
> To record supplies expense.

After posting, Supplies and Supplies Expense hold correct ending balances: ✔ **Starter 3-5**

ASSETS				**EXPENSES**		
Supplies				**Supplies Expense**		
Apr. 2	700	Apr. 30	300	Apr. 30	300	
Bal.	400			Bal.	300	

Correct asset amount: $400	→	Total accounted for: $700	←	Correct expense amount: $300

The Supplies account then enters May with a $400 balance, and the adjustment process is repeated each month.

At the beginning of the month, Supplies were $5,000. During the month, the company purchased $7,000 of supplies. At month's end, $3,000 of supplies were still on hand.

1. What was the cost of supplies used during the month? Where is this item reported?
2. What is the ending balance of Supplies? Where is this item reported?
3. Make the adjusting entry to update the Supplies account at the end of the month.

Answers:

1.	Beginning balance	$ 5,000
	+Purchases	7,000
	=Supplies available	12,000
	–Ending balance	(3,000)
	=Expense (supplies used)	$ 9,000

Report supplies expense among the expenses on the *income statement*.

2. The ending balance of Supplies is $3,000.

3. Adjusting entry: Report supplies among the assets on the *balance sheet*.

```
Supplies Expense  .......  9,000
      Supplies  ..........          9,000
```

Depreciation

Plant Asset
Long-lived tangible assets—such as land, buildings, and equipment—used in the operation of a business.

Accrual accounting is clearly illustrated by depreciation. **Plant assets** are long-lived tangible assets used in the operation of a business. Examples include land, buildings, equipment, and furniture and fixtures. As one accountant said, "All assets but land are on a march to the junkyard" because they decline in usefulness. This decline is an expense, and accountants systematically spread the cost of a plant asset over its useful life. This allocation of cost to expense is called **depreciation**. Land is the exception. We record no depreciation for land.

Depreciation
The allocation of a plant asset's cost to expense over its useful life.

SIMILARITY TO PREPAID EXPENSES The concept underlying accounting for plant assets is the same as for a prepaid expense. The major difference between a prepaid expense and a plant asset is the length of time it takes for the asset to wear out. Prepaid expenses usually expire within a year, while most plant assets remain useful for several years. Consider Gay Gillen eTravel. Suppose that on April 3 Gillen purchased furniture on account for $16,500 and made this journal entry:

```
Apr. 3  Furniture (↑ asset; debit)............... 16,500
            Accounts Payable (↑ liability; credit)..       16,500
        Purchased furniture on account.
```

After posting, the Furniture account has a $16,500 balance:

ASSETS

Furniture

Apr. 3 16,500	

Gillen believes the furniture will remain useful for 5 years and will be worthless at the end. One way to compute depreciation is to divide the cost of the asset ($16,500) by its expected useful life (5 years). This procedure—called the straight-line method—computes depreciation of $3,300 per year ($16,500/5 years). Depreciation for the month of April is $275 ($3,300/12 months = $275 per month).

THE ACCUMULATED DEPRECIATION ACCOUNT Depreciation expense for April is recorded by this entry:

```
Apr. 30  Depreciation Expense—Furniture
             (↑ expense; debit)........................ 275
             Accumulated Depreciation—Furniture
             (↓ asset; credit) .....................        275
         To record depreciation on furniture.
```

Accumulated Depreciation is credited instead of the Furniture account because it is helpful to keep the original cost in the Furniture account. Managers can then refer to the Furniture account to see how much the asset cost. This information may aid a decision about how much to pay for new furniture.

Depreciation is an estimate. The Accumulated Depreciation account holds the sum of all the depreciation recorded for the asset. The Accumulated Depreciation account increases over the life of the asset.

Accumulated Depreciation is a contra asset, which means an asset account with a normal credit balance. A **contra account** has two main characteristics:

- A contra account follows a companion account.
- A contra account's normal balance (debit or credit) is opposite that of the companion.

Accumulated Depreciation
The cumulative sum of all depreciation expense recorded for an asset.

Accumulated Depreciation is the contra account that follows Furniture. Furniture has a debit balance, so Accumulated Depreciation, a contra asset, has a credit balance. *All contra assets have credit balances.*

A business carries an accumulated depreciation account for each depreciable asset. If Gay Gillen eTravel has both building and furniture, it will carry two accounts: Accumulated Depreciation—Building and Accumulated Depreciation—Furniture.

Contra Account
An account that always has a companion account and whose normal balance is opposite that of the companion account.

After posting the depreciation entry, Gay Gillen's accounts appear as follows:

ASSETS		EXPENSES	
NORMAL ASSET	**CONTRA ASSET**		
Furniture	**Accumulated Depreciation—Furniture**	**Depreciation Expense—Furniture**	
Apr. 3 16,500	Apr. 30 275	Apr. 30 275	
Bal. 16,500	Bal. 275	Bal. 275	

BOOK VALUE The balance sheet reports both Furniture and Accumulated Depreciation. Because it's a contra account, the balance of Accumulated Depreciation is subtracted from Furniture. The resulting net amount of a plant asset (cost minus accumulated depreciation) is called its **book value**, as follows for Furniture:

Book value of plant assets:	
Furniture	$16,500
Less: Accumulated depreciation	(275)
Book value of the furniture	$16,225

Book Value (of a Plant Asset)
The asset's cost minus accumulated depreciation.

Suppose Gillen also owns a building that cost $48,000, with annual depreciation of $2,400 ($48,000/20 years). The amount of depreciation for one month would be $200 ($2,400/12), and the following entry records depreciation for April:

Apr. 30	Depreciation Expense—Building		
	(↑ expense; debit).......................	200	
	Accumulated Depreciation—Building		
	(↓ asset; credit).....................		200
	To record depreciation on building.		

✔ **Starter 3-6**

The April 30 balance sheet would report plant assets as shown in Exhibit 3-5.

Exhibit 3-5

Plant Assets on the Balance Sheet of Gay Gillen eTravel (April 30)

Plant Assets:		
Furniture	$16,500	
Less: Accumulated depreciation	(275)	$16,225
Building	$48,000	
Less: Accumulated depreciation	(200)	47,800
Plant assets, net		$64,025

Exhibit 3-6 shows how Fossil, the fashion watch company, reported Property, Plant, and Equipment as adapted from its annual report. The only new items are the last two. Leasehold improvements show Fossil's cost of changes made to assets that Fossil leases. An example would be the cost to paint the Fossil logo on delivery trucks that Fossil leases. The last item reports the cost of Fossil's plant assets that are under construction.

Exhibit 3-6

Fossil Reports Property, Plant, and Equipment

	Millions
Land	$ 8
Buildings	16
Furniture and fixtures	33
Computer equipment	19
Leasehold improvements	20
Construction in progress	27
	123
Less: Accumulated depreciation	(33)
	$ 90

Fossil's cost of plant assets was $123 million. Of this total cost, Fossil has depreciated $33 million. The book value of the company's plant assets is, therefore, $90 million.

Now let's return to Gay Gillen eTravel.

Accrued Expenses

Accrued Expense
An expense that the business has incurred but not yet paid.

Businesses often have expenses before they pay them. Consider an employee's salary. Gillen's salary expense grows as the employee works, so the expense is said to *accrue*. Another accrued expense is interest expense on a note payable. Interest accrues as the clock ticks. The term **accrued expense** refers to an expense the business has incurred but not yet paid. An accrued expense always creates a liability.

Companies don't make weekly journal entries to accrue expenses. That would be a waste of time. Instead they wait until the end of the period. They make an adjusting entry to bring each expense (and the related liability) up to date for the financial statements.

Remember the key differences between a prepaid expense and an accrued expense:

- A *prepaid expense* is paid first and expensed later.
- An *accrued expense* is expensed first and paid later.
- Prepaids and accruals are opposites.

Now let's see how to account for accrued expenses.

SALARY EXPENSE   Suppose Gay Gillen pays her employee a monthly salary of $1,900, half on the 15th and half on the last day of the month. Here is a calendar for April with the two paydays circled:

			April			
S	M	T	W	T	F	S
					1	2
3	4	5	6	7	8	9
10	11	12	13	14	(15)	16
17	18	19	20	21	22	23
24	25	26	27	28	29	(30)

To illustrate a salary accrual, assume that if either payday falls on a weekend, Gillen pays the following Monday. During April, Gillen paid the first half-month salary on Friday, April 15, and made the following entry:

Apr. 15	Salary Expense (↑ expense; debit).......... 950	
	Cash (↓ asset; credit)	950
	To pay salary.	

After posting, Salary Expense shows its balance:

EXPENSES

Salary Expense

Apr. 15 950	

The trial balance at April 30 (Exhibit 3-4) includes Salary Expense, with a debit balance of $950. This is Gillen's salary expense for only the first half of April. The second half-month amount of $950 will be paid in May, so Gillen must accrue salary expense for the second half of April. At April 30, Gillen makes an adjusting entry as follows:

Apr. 30	Salary Expense (↑ expense; debit).......... 950	
	Salary Payable (↑ liability; credit)	950
	To accrue salary expense.	

This is accrual accounting in action. After posting, Salary Expense and Salary Payable hold their April 30 balances:

EXPENSES   **LIABILITIES**

Salary Expense   **Salary Payable**

Apr. 15 950			Apr. 30 950
Apr. 30 950			Bal. 950
Bal. 1,900			

Salary Expense holds a full month's salary, and Salary Payable shows the liability the company owes at April 30.

Weekly salaries for a five-day workweek total $3,500, payable on a Friday. This month, November 30 falls on a Tuesday.

1. Which accounts require adjustment at November 30?

2. Make the adjusting entry.

Answers:

1. Salary Expense and Salary Payable require adjustment

2. Salary Expense ($3,500 × 2/5)   1,400
          Salary Payable.   1,400
       To accrue salary expense.

Accrued Revenues

Accrued Revenue
A revenue that has been earned but not yet collected in cash.

As we have just seen, some expenses occur before the cash payment, and that creates an accrued expense. Likewise, businesses also earn revenue before they receive the cash. This calls for an **accrued revenue**, which is a revenue that has been earned but not yet collected in cash.

Assume that Gay Gillen eTravel is hired on April 15 to perform travel services for **It's Just Lunch**. Under this agreement, Gillen will earn $500 monthly. During April, Gillen will earn half a month's fee, $250, for work April 15 through April 30. On April 30, Gillen makes the following adjusting entry to accrue the revenue earned during April 15 through 30:

Apr. 30 Accounts Receivable ($500 × 1/2)
             (↑ asset; debit)   250
                 Service Revenue (↑ revenue; credit) . .   250
         To accrue service revenue.

The unadjusted trial balance in Exhibit 3-4 shows that Accounts Receivable has an unadjusted balance of $2,250. Service Revenue's unadjusted balance is $7,000. Posting the adjustment increases both accounts to their correct balances at April 30.

ASSETS		REVENUES	
Accounts Receivable		**Service Revenue**	
	2,250		7,000
Apr. 30	250	Apr. 30	250
Bal.	2,500	Bal.	7,250

Without the adjustment, Gillen's financial statements would be incomplete and misleading: They would understate both Accounts Receivable and Service Revenue. All accrued revenues are accounted for similarly: Debit a receivable and credit a revenue.

Now we turn to the final category of adjusting entries.

Unearned Revenues

Unearned Revenue
A liability created when a business collects cash from customers in advance of doing work. Also called **deferred revenue**.

Some businesses collect cash from customers in advance. Receiving cash before earning it creates a liability called **unearned revenue**, and the company owes a product or a service to the customer. Only when the job is completed will the business *earn* the revenue.

Suppose **Intel Corporation** engages Gillen to provide travel services, agreeing to pay her $450 monthly, beginning immediately. Gillen collects the first amount from Intel on April 20. Gillen records the cash receipt and a liability as follows:

Apr. 20 Cash (↑ asset; debit).   450
             Unearned Service Revenue
                 (↑ liability; credit)   450
         Collected revenue in advance.

Now the liability account Unearned Service Revenue shows that Gillen owes $450.

LIABILITIES

Unearned Service Revenue

	Apr. 20 450

Unearned Service Revenue is a liability because it represents Gillen's obligation to perform service for Intel.

The April 30 trial balance (Exhibit 3-4) lists Unearned Service Revenue with a $450 credit balance. During the last 10 days of the month—April 21 through April 30—Gillen will *earn* one-third (10 days divided by April's 30 days) of the $450, or $150. Therefore, Gillen makes the following adjustment to account for earning $150 of the revenue:

Apr. 30	Unearned Service Revenue ($450 × 1/3)	
	(↓ liability; debit)	150
	Service Revenue (↑ revenue; credit) . .	150
	To record service revenue that was collected in advance.	

This adjusting entry shifts $150 of the total from liability to revenue. Service Revenue increases by $150, and Unearned Service Revenue decreases by $150. Now both accounts are up to date at April 30:

LIABILITIES

Unearned Service Revenue

Apr. 30	150	Apr. 20	450
		Bal.	300

REVENUES

Service Revenue

		7,000
	Apr. 30	250
	Apr. 30	150
	Bal.	7,400

Correct liability amount: $300 → Total accounted for: $450 ← Correct revenue amount: $150

All revenues collected in advance are accounted for this way.

An unearned revenue to one company is a prepaid expense to the company that paid in advance. Consider Intel in the preceding example. Intel had prepaid travel expense—an asset. Gay Gillen eTravel had unearned service revenue—a liability. Remember this key point:

✔ Starter 3-9

An unearned revenue is a liability, not a revenue.

Consider the tuition you pay your college or university. Assume that one semester's tuition costs $1,500 and that you make a single payment up front. Can you make the journal entries to record the tuition transactions on your own books and on the books of your college or university?

Answer:

	Your Books			**Your College's Books**		
Start of Semester	Prepaid Tuition	1,500		Cash	1,500	
	Cash		1,500	Unearned Tuition		
	Paid semester tuition.			Revenue		1,500
				Collected revenue in advance.		
End of Semester	Tuition Expense	1,500		Unearned Tuition		
	Prepaid Tuition . . .		1,500	Revenue	1,500	
	To record tuition expense.			Tuition Revenue . .		1,500
				To record tuition revenue that was collected in advance.		

Exhibit 3-7 summarizes the timing of prepaid and accrual adjustments. The chapter appendix shows an alternative treatment for unearned revenues.

Exhibit 3-7 **Prepaid and Accrual Adjustments**

PREPAIDS—Cash transaction comes first.

First ———————————————————————————→ Later

Prepaid	*Pay cash and record an asset:*			*Record an expense and decrease the asset:*	
Expenses	Prepaid Rent......................... XXX			Rent Expense......................... XXX	
	Cash..............................	XXX		Prepaid Rent......................	XXX
Unearned	*Receive cash and record a liability:*			*Record a revenue and decrease the liability:*	
Revenues	Cash................................. XXX			Unearned Service Revenue.............. XXX	
	Unearned Service Revenue	XXX		Service Revenue..................	XXX

ACCRUALS—Cash transaction comes later.

First ———————————————————————————→ Later

Accrued	*Accrue an expense and the related payable:*			*Pay cash and decrease the payable:*	
Expenses	Salary Expense........................ XXX			Salary Payable........................ XXX	
	Salary Payable.....................	XXX		Cash..............................	XXX
Accrued	*Accrue a revenue and the related receivable:*			*Receive cash and decrease the receivable:*	
Revenues	Interest Receivable.................... XXX			Cash................................. XXX	
	Interest Revenue...................	XXX		Interest Receivable................	XXX

Source: The authors thank Darrel Davis and Alfonso Oddo for suggesting this exhibit.

CHECK YOUR RESOURCES

Summary of the Adjusting Process

The adjusting process has two purposes:

1. Measure net income or net loss on the *income statement*. Every adjusting entry affects a *Revenue* or an *Expense*.

2. Update the *balance sheet*. Every adjusting entry affects an *Asset* or a *Liability*.

No adjusting entry debits or credits Cash because the cash transactions are recorded before the end of the period. Exhibit 3-8 summarizes the effects of the various adjusting entries.

Exhibit 3-8

Summary of Adjusting Entries

Category of Adjusting Entry	Debit	Credit
Prepaid expense...........................	Expense	Asset
Depreciation	Expense	Contra asset
Accrued expense	Expense	Liability
Accrued revenue	Asset	Revenue
Unearned revenue	Liability	Revenue

Source: Adapted from material provided by Beverly Terry.

Exhibit 3-9 summarizes the adjusting entries of Gay Gillen eTravel at April 30. Panel A gives the data for each adjustment, Panel B shows the adjusting entries, and Panel C gives the accounts after posting. The adjustments are keyed by letter.

Exhibit 3-9 Journalizing and Posting the Adjusting Entries of Gay Gillen eTravel

PANEL A—Information for Adjustments at April 30, 20X5

(a) Prepaid rent expired, $1,000.

(b) Supplies on hand, $400.

(c) Depreciation on furniture, $275.

(d) Accrued salary expense, $950.

(e) Accrued service revenue, $250

(f) Service revenue that was collected in advance and now has been earned, $150.

PANEL B—Adjusting Entries

(a)	Rent Expense (↑ expense; debit)	1,000	
	Prepaid Rent (↓ asset; credit)		1,000
	To record rent expense.		
(b)	Supplies Expense (↑ expense; debit)	300*	
	Supplies (↓ asset; credit)		300
	To record supplies used.		
(c)	Depreciation Expense—Furniture (↑ expense; debit)	275	
	Accumulated Depreciation—Furniture (↓ asset; credit)		275
	To record depreciation on furniture.		
(d)	Salary Expense (↑ expense; debit)	950	
	Salary Payable (↑ liability; credit)		950
	To accrue salary expense.		
(e)	Accounts Receivable (↑ asset; debit)	250	
	Service Revenue (↑ revenue; credit)		250
	To accrue service revenue.		
(f)	Unearned Service Revenue (↓ liability; debit)	150	
	Service Revenue (↑ revenue; credit)		150
	To record revenue that was collected in advance.		

*Supplies available ($700) − supplies on hand ($400) = supplies expense ($300).

PANEL C—Ledger Accounts

ASSETS

Cash
Bal. 24,800		

Accounts Receivable
2,250		
(e) 250		
Bal. 2,500		

Supplies
700	(b)	300
Bal. 400		

Prepaid Rent
3,000	(a)	1,000
Bal. 2,000		

Furniture
Bal. 16,500		

Accumulated Depreciation— Furniture
	(c)	275
	Bal.	275

LIABILITIES

Accounts Payable
	Bal.	13,100

Salary Payable
	(d)	950
	Bal.	950

Unearned Service Revenue
(f) 150		450
	Bal.	300

OWNER'S EQUITY

Gay Gillen, Capital
	Bal.	31,250

Gay Gillen, Withdrawals
Bal. 3,200		

REVENUE

Service Revenue
		7,000
	(e)	250
	(f)	150
	Bal.	7,400

EXPENSES

Rent Expense
(a) 1,000		
Bal. 1,000		

Salary Expense
950		
(d) 950		
Bal. 1,900		

Supplies Expense
(b) 300		
Bal. 300		

Depreciation Expense— Furniture
(c) 275		
Bal. 275		

Utilities Expense
Bal. 400		

Student ResourceCD

adjustments, trial balance

 *Prepare an adjusted trial balance*

Adjusted Trial Balance
A list of all the accounts with their
adjusted balances.

✔ **Starter 3-10**

✔ **Starter 3-11**

✔ **Starter 3-12**

✔ **Starter 3-13**

The Adjusted Trial Balance

This chapter began with the trial balance before any adjustments—the unadjusted trial balance (Exhibit 3-4). After the adjustments, the accounts appear as shown in Exhibit 3-9, Panel C. A useful step in preparing the financial statements is to list the accounts, along with their adjusted balances, on an **adjusted trial balance**. Exhibit 3-10 shows how to prepare the adjusted trial balance.

Exhibit 3-10 is a *work sheet*. We will continue this work sheet into Chapter 4. For now, simply note how clear this format is. The Account Titles and the Trial Balance are copied directly from the trial balance. The two Adjustments columns show the adjustment Debits and Credits. Each debit is identified by a letter keyed to Exhibit 3-9.

The Adjusted Trial Balance columns give the adjusted account balances. Each amount in these columns is computed by combining the trial balance amounts plus or minus the adjustments. For example, Accounts Receivable starts with a debit balance of $2,250. Adding the $250 debit from adjustment (e) gives Accounts Receivable an adjusted balance of $2,500. Supplies begins with a debit balance of $700. After the $300 credit adjustment, Supplies has a $400 balance. More than one entry may affect a single account, such as for Service Revenue. An account unaffected by the adjustments will show the same amount on both trial balances. For example, Cash, Furniture, Accounts Payable, Capital, and Withdrawals do not change.

Exhibit 3-10 Preparation of Adjusted Trial Balance

Gay Gillen eTravel
Preparation of Adjusted Trial Balance
April 30, 20X5

Account Title	Trial Balance Debit	Trial Balance Credit	Adjustments Debit	Adjustments Credit	Adjusted Trial Balance Debit	Adjusted Trial Balance Credit	
Cash.	24,800				24,800		⎫
Accounts receivable	2,250		(e) 250		2,500		
Supplies	700			(b) 300	400		
Prepaid rent	3,000			(a) 1,000	2,000		
Furniture.	16,500				16,500		*Balance Sheet*
Accumulated depreciation				(c) 275		275	*(Exhibit 3-13)*
Accounts payable		13,100				13,100	
Salary payable				(d) 950		950	
Unearned service revenue		450	(f) 150			300	⎭
Gay Gillen, capital.		31,250				31,250	*Statement of*
Gay Gillen, withdrawals	3,200				3,200		*Owner's Equity*
Service revenue		7,000		(e) 250		7,400	*(Exhibit 3-12)*
				(f) 150			
Rent expense			(a) 1,000		1,000		*Income*
Salary expense.	950		(d) 950		1,900		*Statement*
Supplies expense.			(b) 300		300		*(Exhibit 3-11)*
Depreciation expense			(c) 275		275		
Utilities expense	400				400		⎭
	51,800	51,800	2,925	2,925	53,275	53,275	

The Financial Statements

The April financial statements of Gay Gillen eTravel can be prepared from the adjusted trial balance in Exhibit 3-10. In the right margin, we see how the accounts are distributed to the financial statements. As always, the income statement (Exhibit 3-11) reports the revenues and the expenses. The statement of owner's equity (Exhibit 3-12) shows why owner's capital changed during the period. Finally, the balance sheet (Exhibit 3-13) reports the assets, liabilities, and owner's equity.

 Student ResourceCD

financial statements

Preparing the Statements

The financial statements should be prepared in this order:

1. Income statement—to determine net income
2. Statement of owner's equity—to compute ending capital
3. Balance sheet—which needs the ending capital amount to achieve its balancing feature

⭐ *Prepare the financial statements from the adjusted trial balance*

Exhibit 3-11

Income Statement

Gay Gillen eTravel
Income Statement
Month Ended April 30, 20X5

Revenue:		
Service revenue.		$7,400
Expenses:		
Salary expense	$1,900	
Rent expense	1,000	
Utilities expense	400	
Supplies expense	300	
Depreciation expense.	275	
Total expenses.		3,875
Net income		$3,525

Exhibit 3-12

Statement of Owner's Equity

Gay Gillen eTravel
Statement of Owner's Equity
Month Ended April 30, 20X5

Gay Gillen, capital, April 1, 20X5	$31,250
Add: Net income	3,525
	34,775
Less: Withdrawals	(3,200)
Gay Gillen, capital, April 30, 20X5	$31,575

Exhibit 3-13

Balance Sheet

Gay Gillen eTravel
Balance Sheet
April 30, 20X5

Assets			Liabilities		
Cash		$24,800	Accounts payable		$13,100
Accounts			Salary payable		950
receivable		2,500	Unearned service		
Supplies.		400	revenue		300
Prepaid rent		2,000	Total liabilities		14,350
Furniture	$16,500				
Less:			**Owner's Equity**		
Accumulated			Gay Gillen, capital		31,575
depreciation	(275)	16,225	Total liabilities and		
Total assets		$45,925	owner's equity		$45,925

All financial statements include these elements:

Heading

- Name of the entity—such as Gay Gillen eTravel
- Title of the statement—income statement, balance sheet, and so on
- Date, or period, covered by the statement—April 30, 20X5, or Month ended April 30, 20X5

Body of the statement

The income statement should list expenses in descending order by amount, as shown in Exhibit 3-11. However, Miscellaneous Expense, a catchall category, usually comes last.

Relationships Among the Financial Statements

The relationships among the financial statements were introduced in Chapter 1, p. 21.

The arrows in Exhibits 3-11, 3-12, and 3-13 show how the financial statements relate to each other. ←

1. Net income from the income statement increases owner's equity in Exhibit 3-12. A net loss decreases owner's equity.
2. Ending capital from the statement of owner's equity is transferred to the balance sheet. The owner's ending capital is the final balancing amount for the balance sheet.

To solidify your understanding of these relationships, trace net income from the income statement to the statement of owner's equity. Then trace ending capital to the balance sheet.

Stop & Think

Student Resource**CD**

depreciation, ethics

Examine Gay Gillen eTravel's adjusted trial balance in Exhibit 3-10. Suppose Gillen forgot to record the $1,000 of rent expense at April 30. What net income would the travel agency then report for April? What amounts of total assets, total liabilities, and owner's equity would Gay Gillen eTravel report at April 30?

Answer: Omitting the rent expense would produce these effects:

1. Net income would have been $4,525 ($3,525 + $1,000). See Exhibit 3-11.
2. Total assets would have been $46,925 ($45,925 + $1,000). See Exhibit 3-13.
3. Total liabilities (Exhibit 3-13) would have been unaffected by the error.
4. Owner's equity (Gay Gillen, Capital) would have been $32,575 ($31,575 + $1,000). See Exhibit 3-13.

Ethical Issues in Accrual Accounting

Like all areas of business, accounting poses ethical challenges. Accountants must be honest in their work. Only with complete and accurate information can people make wise decisions. An example will illustrate.

It's Just Lunch has done well as a business. The company has opened offices in most major cities in the United States. At this time, It's Just Lunch actually wishes to open an office in Nashville, Tennessee. Assume the company needs to borrow $100,000 to open the office. Suppose It's Just Lunch understated expenses in order to inflate net income on the income statement. A banker could be tricked into lending the company money. Then if It's Just Lunch could not pay the loan, the bank would lose—all because the banker relied on incorrect accounting information.

Accrual accounting provides opportunities for unethical accounting. It would be easy for a dishonest businessperson to overlook depreciation expense at the end of the year. Failing to record depreciation would overstate net income and paint a rosy picture of the company's financial situation. It is important for accountants to prepare accurate and complete financial statements because people rely on the data for their decisions.

Decision Guidelines

THE ACCOUNTING PROCESS

Take the role of Andrea McGinty, who founded **It's Just Lunch**. Assume it's now the end of the first year of operation, and McGinty wants to know where the business stands financially. The Decision Guidelines give a map of the accounting process to help McGinty manage the business.

Decision	Guidelines
Which basis of accounting better measures business income?	*Accrual basis*, because it provides more-complete reports of operating performance and financial position
How to measure revenues?	Revenue principle—Record revenues only after they're earned
How to measure expenses?	Matching principle—Subtract expenses from revenues in order to measure net income
Where to start with the measurement of income at the end of the period?	Unadjusted trial balance, usually referred to simply as the *trial balance*
How to update the accounts for the financial statements? What are the categories of adjusting entries?	*Adjusting entries* at the end of the period

Prepaid expenses   Accrued revenues

Depreciation of plant assets   Unearned revenues

Accrued expenses

Decision	Guidelines

How do the adjusting entries differ from other journal entries?	**1.** Adjusting entries are made only at the end of the period.
	2. Adjusting entries never affect cash.
	3. All adjusting entries debit or credit
	  • At least one *income statement* account (a revenue or an expense), and
	  • At least one *balance sheet* account (an asset or a liability)

Where are the accounts with their adjusted balances summarized?	*Adjusted trial balance*, which aids preparation of the financial statements

Excel Application Exercise

Goal Create a spreadsheet that contains an income statement, a statement of owner's equity, and a balance sheet, complete with the formula relationships among all three statements.

Scenario The three financial statements are related. The relationships show up when net income changes. Using Exhibits 3-11, 3-12, and 3-13, replicate the income statement, statement of owner's equity, and balance sheet for Gay Gillen eTravel. When you are finished, you will change just two related variables, but you will see the effect ripple through all the statements you have created.

  I. Change service revenue from $7,400 to $10,900 and cash from $24,800 to $28,300 (remember, every transaction

requires at least one debit entry and one credit entry). What is the new net income figure?

2. What is the new balance for Gay Gillen, Capital on April 30, 20X5?

3. Did any other amounts change? If so, which ones?

Step-by-Step

I. Open a new Excel spreadsheet.

2. In column 1, create a bold-faced heading as follows:
  a. Chapter 3 Excel Application Exercise
  b. Gay Gillen eTravel
  c. Today's Date

Excel Application Exercise *(continued)*

3. Refer to Exhibit 3-11. Prepare the income statement as it appears in the text near the top of your spreadsheet, formatting and using formulas as appropriate. When finished, put a border around the income statement.
4. Refer to Exhibit 3-12. In your spreadsheet, prepare the statement of owner's equity as it appears in the text, to the right of the income statement. Be sure "Net Income" is a cell reference to your income statement's net income. Format and use formulas as appropriate. When finished, put a border around the statement of owner's equity.

5. Refer to Exhibit 3-13. Prepare the balance sheet as it appears in the text, below the income statement in your spreadsheet. Be sure "Gay Gillen, Capital" is a cell reference to the ending capital balance in your statement of owner's equity. When finished, put a border around the balance sheet.
6. Make the two changes in scenario question 1. Save your file to disk, and print a copy for comparison with Exhibits 3-11, 3-12, and 3-13.

● END-OF-CHAPTER *Summary Problem*

TIPS

CHECK YOUR RESOURCES

The trial balance of Clay Employment Services pertains to December 31, 20X9, which is the end of Clay's annual accounting period. Data needed for the adjusting entries include

a. Supplies on hand at year-end, $2,000.
b. Depreciation on furniture and fixtures, $20,000.
c. Depreciation on building, $10,000.

d. Salaries owed but not yet paid, $5,000.
e. Accrued service revenue, $12,000.
f. $32,000 of the unearned service revenue has been earned.

Required

1. Open the ledger accounts with their unadjusted balances. Show dollar amounts in thousands, as for Accounts Receivable:

Accounts Receivable	
370	

2. Journalize Clay's adjusting entries at December 31, 20X9. Key entries by letter, as in Exhibit 3-9.
3. Post the adjusting entries.
4. Write the trial balance on a work sheet, enter the adjusting entries, and prepare an adjusted trial balance, as shown in Exhibit 3-10.
5. Prepare the income statement, the statement of owner's equity, and the balance sheet. Draw arrows linking the three financial statements.

Clay Employment Services

Trial Balance
December 31, 20X9

Cash	$ 198,000	
Accounts receivable	370,000	
Supplies	6,000	
Furniture and fixtures	100,000	
Accumulated depreciation—furniture and fixtures		$ 40,000
Building	250,000	
Accumulated depreciation—building		130,000
Accounts payable		380,000
Salary payable		
Unearned service revenue		45,000
Jay Clay, capital		293,000
Jay Clay, withdrawals	65,000	
Service revenue		286,000

Salary expense	172,000	
Supplies expense		
Depreciation expense—furniture and fixtures		
Depreciation expense—building.		
Miscellaneous expense	13,000	
Total.	$1,174,000	$1,174,000

Solution

Requirements 1 and 3 (amounts in thousands)

ASSETS

Cash

Bal.	198	

Accounts Receivable

	370	
(e)	12	
Bal.	382	

Supplies

	6	(a)	4
Bal.	2		

Furniture and Fixtures

Bal.	100	

Accumulated Depreciation—Furniture and Fixtures

			40
		(b)	20
		Bal.	60

Building

Bal.	250	

Accumulated Depreciation—Building

			130
		(c)	10
		Bal.	140

LIABILITIES

Accounts Payable

		Bal.	380

Salary Payable

		(d)	5
		Bal.	5

Unearned Service Revenue

(f)	32		45
		Bal.	13

OWNER'S EQUITY

Jay Clay, Capital

		Bal.	293

Jay Clay, Withdrawals

Bal.	65	

REVENUE

Service Revenue

			286
		(e)	12
		(f)	32
		Bal.	330

EXPENSES

Salary Expense

	172	
(d)	5	
Bal.	177	

Supplies Expense

(a)	4	
Bal.	4	

Depreciation Expense— Furniture and Fixtures

(b)	20	
Bal.	20	

Depreciation Expense— Building

(c)	10	
Bal.	10	

Miscellaneous Expense

Bal.	13	

Requirement 2

20X9

a. Dec. 31	Supplies Expense ($6,000 – $2,000)	4,000	
		Supplies		4,000
		To record supplies used.		
b. 31	Depreciation Expense—Furniture and Fixtures	20,000	
		Accumulated Depreciation—Furniture and Fixtures		20,000
		To record depreciation expense on furniture and fixtures.		
c. 31	Depreciation Expense—Building	10,000	
		Accumulated Depreciation—Building		10,000
		To record depreciation expense on building.		
d. 31	Salary Expense	5,000	
		Salary Payable		5,000
		To accrue salary expense.		
e. 31	Accounts Receivable	12,000	
		Service Revenue		12,000
		To accrue service revenue.		
f. 31	Unearned Service Revenue	32,000	
		Service Revenue		32,000
		To record service revenue that was collected in advance.		

Requirement 4

Clay Employment Services

Preparation of Adjusted Trial Balance
December 31, 20X9 (amounts in thousands)

Account Title	Trial Balance		Adjustments				Adjusted Trial Balance	
	Debit	Credit	Debit		Credit		Debit	Credit
Cash..............................	198						198	
Accounts receivable....................	370		(e)	12			382	
Supplies..............................	6				(a)	4	2	
Furniture and fixtures.................	100						100	
Accumulated depreciation— furniture and fixtures		40			(b)	20		60
Building.............................	250						250	
Accumulated depreciation—building		130			(c)	10		140
Accounts payable.....................		380						380
Salary payable					(d)	5		5
Unearned service revenue		45	(f)	32				13
Jay Clay, capital		293						293
Jay Clay, withdrawals	65						65	
Service revenue		286			(e)	12		330
					(f)	32		
Salary expense	172		(d)	5			177	
Supplies expense			(a)	4			4	
Depreciation expense— furniture and fixtures			(b)	20			20	
Depreciation expense—building.........			(c)	10			10	
Miscellaneous expense	13						13	
	1,174	1,174	83		83		1,221	1,221

Requirement 5

Clay Employment Services

Income Statement
Year Ended December 31, 20X9 (amounts in thousands)

Revenue:
Service revenue... $330

Expenses:
Salary expense.. $177
Depreciation expense—furniture and fixtures............ 20
Depreciation expense—building 10
Supplies expense 4
Miscellaneous expense 13
Total expenses...................................... 224

Net income $106

Clay Employment Services
Statement of Owner's Equity
Year Ended December 31, 20X9 (amounts in thousands)

Jay Clay, capital, January 1, 20X9	$293
Add: Net income	106
	399
Less: Withdrawals	(65)
Jay Clay, December 31, 20X9	$334

Clay Employment Services
Balance Sheet
December 31, 20X9 (amounts in thousands)

Assets			Liabilities		
Cash.		$198	Accounts payable.		$380
Accounts receivable .		382	Salary payable.		5
Supplies		2	Unearned service revenue . .		13
Furniture and fixtures	$100		Total liabilities.		398
Less: Accumulated					
depreciation	(60)	40			
Building	$250		**Owner's Equity**		
Less: Accumulated			Jay Clay, capital		334
depreciation	(140)	110	Total liabilities and		
Total assets		$732	owner's equity		$732

REVIEW *The Adjusting Process*

Quick Check

1. What are the features of accrual accounting and cash-basis accounting?
   a. Accrual accounting records all transactions.
   b. Cash-basis accounting records only cash receipts and cash payments.
   c. Accrual accounting is superior because it provides more information.
   d. All the above are true.

2. The revenue principle says
   a. Record revenue only after you have earned it.
   b. Record revenue only when you receive cash.
   c. Measure revenues and expenses in order to compute net income.
   d. Divide time into annual periods to measure revenue properly.

3. Adjusting the accounts is the process of
   a. Recording transactions as they occur during the period
   b. Updating the accounts at the end of the period
   c. Zeroing out account balances to prepare for the next period
   d. Subtracting expenses from revenues to measure net income

4. Which types of adjusting entries are natural opposites?
   a. Prepaids and depreciation
   b. Expenses and revenues
   c. Prepaids and accruals
   d. Net income and net loss

5. Assume that the weekly payroll of **It's Just Lunch** is $5,000. December 31, end of the year, falls on Monday, and the company will pay employees on Friday for the full week. What adjusting entry will It's Just Lunch make on Monday, December 31?

    a. Salary Expense.   1,000
        Salary Payable   1,000
    b. Salary Expense.   1,000
        Cash.   1,000
    c. Salary Payable   1,000
        Salary Expense.   1,000
    d. No adjustment is needed because the company will pay the payroll on Friday.

6. Assume It's Just Lunch gains a client who prepays $600 for a package of six dates. It's Just Lunch collects the $600 in advance and will provide the date arrangements later. After setting up two dates for the client, what should It's Just Lunch report on its income statement?

    a. Cash of $600   **c.** Service revenue of $200
    b. Service revenue of $600   **d.** Unearned service revenue of $400

7. Unearned revenue is always a (an)

    a. Liability   **c.** Asset
    b. Revenue   **d.** Owners' equity because you collected the cash in advance

8. Assume you prepay It's Just Lunch for a package of six dates. Which type of account should you have in your records?

    a. Accrued expense   **c.** Accrued revenue
    b. Prepaid expense   **d.** Unearned revenue

9. The adjusted trial balance shows

    a. Amounts that may be out of balance   **c.** Assets, liabilities, and owner's equity only
    b. Revenues and expenses only   **d.** Amounts ready for the financial statements

10. The accounting data flow from the

    a. Income statement to the statement of owner's equity
    b. Statement of owner's equity to the balance sheet
    c. Both a and b are correct
    d. None of the above is correct

Accounting Vocabulary

accrual accounting (p. 92)
accrued expense (p. 102)
accrued revenue (p. 104)
accumulated depreciation (p. 101)
adjusted trial balance (p. 108)
adjusting entry (p. 97)

book value (of a plant asset) (p. 101)
cash-basis accounting (p. 92)
contra account (p. 101)
deferred revenue (p. 104)
depreciation (p. 100)
matching principle (p. 95)

plant asset (p. 100)
prepaid expense (p. 98)
revenue principle (p. 94)
time-period concept (p. 96)
unearned revenue (p. 104)

◯ASSESS *Your Progress*

Comparing accrual accounting and cash-basis accounting
(Obj. 1)

Starters

S3-1 Suppose you work summers mowing lawns. Most of your customers pay you immediately after you cut their grass. A few ask you to send them a bill at the end of each month. It is now June 30 and you have collected $900 from cash-paying customers. Your remaining customers owe you $300. How much service revenue would you have under the (a) cash basis and (b) accrual basis? Which method of accounting provides more information about your lawn-service business? Explain your answer.

Accrual accounting versus cash-basis accounting for expenses
(Obj. 1)

S3-2 It's Just Lunch, the business featured at the beginning of this chapter, uses client databases to help clients meet. Suppose It's Just Lunch paid $3,000 for a **Dell** computer. Review pages 92 and 93, and then describe how It's Just Lunch would account for the $3,000 expenditure under (a) the cash basis and (b) the accrual basis. State in your own words why the accrual basis is more realistic for this situation.

Applying the revenue principle
(Obj. 2)

S3-3 **Intel Corporation** produces Pentium© processors that drive many computers. Suppose Intel has completed production of 1,000 processor units that it expects to sell to **Gateway**. Assume that Intel's cost to manufacture each processor is $140 and that Intel sells each processor for $375.

Apply the revenue principle to determine (1) when Intel should record revenue for this situation and (2) the amount of revenue Intel should record for the sale of 1,000 processors.

Applying the matching principle
(Obj. 2)

S3-4 Return to the **Intel Corporation** situation described in Starter 3-3. Suppose Intel has sold 1,000 Pentium© processors to **Gateway**. What will Intel record in order to apply the matching principle? Give the name of the expense that Intel will record, and specify its amount.

Adjusting prepaid expenses
(Obj. 3)

S3-5 Answer the following questions.

1. Prepaid expenses are discussed beginning on page 98. Focus on the accounting for prepaid rent. Assume that Gay Gillen's initial $3,000 prepayment of rent on April 1 (page 98) was for 6 months rather than 3. Give the adjusting entry to record rent expense at April 30. Include the date of the entry and an explanation. Then post to the two accounts involved, and show their balances at April 30.
2. Refer to the supplies example on pages 99–100. Assume that Gillen's travel agency has $500 of supplies on hand (rather than $400) at April 30. Give the adjusting entry, complete with date and explanation, at April 30. Post to the accounts and show their balances at April 30.

Recording depreciation
(Obj. 3)

S3-6 It's Just Lunch uses computers for data searches. Suppose that on May 1 the company paid cash of $24,000 for **Dell** computers that are expected to remain useful for two years. At the end of two years, the value of the computers is expected to be zero.

1. Make journal entries to record (a) purchase of the computers on May 1 and (b) depreciation on May 31. Include dates and explanations, and use the following accounts: Computer Equipment; Accumulated Depreciation—Computer Equipment; and Depreciation Expense—Computer Equipment.
2. Post to the accounts listed in requirement 1, and show their balances at May 31.
3. What is the equipment's book value at May 31?

Accruing and paying interest expense
(Obj. 3)

S3-7 Suppose Gay Gillen borrowed $50,000 on October 1 by signing a note payable to Community One Bank. Gillen's interest expense for each month is $300.

1. Make Gillen's adjusting entry to accrue interest expense at December 31. Date the entry and include its explanation.
2. Post to the two accounts affected by the adjustment.

Accruing and receiving cash from interest revenue
(Obj. 3)

S3-8 Return to the situation of Starter 3-7. Suppose you are accounting for the same transactions on the books of Community One Bank, which lent the money to Gay Gillen eTravel. Perform both requirements of Starter 3-7 for Community One Bank using its own accounts: Interest Receivable and Interest Revenue.

Accounting for unearned revenues
(Obj. 3)

S3-9 **Yankee Clipper Magazine** collects cash from subscribers in advance and then mails the magazines to subscribers over a one-year period. Give the adjusting entry that Yankee Clipper makes to record the earning of $8,000 of Subscription Revenue that was collected in advance. Include an explanation for the entry, as illustrated in the chapter.

Contrasting the unadjusted and the adjusted trial balances
(Obj. 4)

S3-10 Study the T-accounts in Exhibit 3-9, Panel C, on page 107. Focus on the Supplies account. Which amount in the Supplies account appeared on the *unadjusted* trial balance

(Exhibit 3-10, page 108)? Which amount will appear on the *adjusted* trial balance? Which amount will be reported on the balance sheet at April 30? Under what balance sheet category will Gillen report Supplies? Under what category, and on which financial statement, will Gillen report supplies used up?

Using the adjusted trial balance
(Obj. 4)

S3-11 In the Adjustments columns of Exhibit 3-10, page 108, two adjustments affected Service Revenue.

1. Make journal entries for the two adjustments. Date each entry and include an explanation.
2. The journal entries you just made affected three accounts: Accounts Receivable; Unearned Service Revenue; and Service Revenue. Show how Gay Gillen eTravel will report all three accounts in its financial statements at April 30. For each account, identify its (a) financial statement, (b) category on the financial statement, and (c) balance.

Preparing the balance sheet
(Obj. 5)

S3-12 Refer to the adjusted trial balance in Exhibit 3-10, page 108.

1. Focus on the *adjusted* figures. Compute Gillen's total assets and total liabilities at April 30. Compare your totals to the balance sheet amounts in Exhibit 3-13, page 109. Are they the same?
2. Why does a business need to make adjusting entries at the end of the period?

Preparing the income statement
(Obj. 5)

S3-13 Refer to the adjusted trial balance in Exhibit 3-10, page 108.

1. Focus on the *adjusted* figures. Compute Gillen's total revenues, total expenses, and net income for April. Compare your totals to the income statement amounts in Exhibit 3-11, page 109. Are they the same?
2. Why does a business need to make adjusting entries at the end of the period?

 **online homework**

Exercises

Cash basis versus accrual basis
(Obj. 1)

E3-1 Lexington Inn completed the following selected transactions during July:

July 1	Prepaid rent for three months, $3,000
5	Paid electricity expenses, $800.
9	Received cash for the day's room rentals, $2,600.
14	Paid cash for six television sets, $3,000.
23	Served a banquet, receiving a note receivable, $1,600.
31	Made the adjusting entry for rent (from July 1).
31	Accrued salary expense, $900.

Show how each transaction would be handled using the accrual basis. Give the amount of revenue or expense for July. Journal entries are not required. Use the following format for your answer, and show your computations:

Amount of Revenue (Expense) for July		
		Accrual-Basis
Date	Revenue (Expense)	Amount

Accrual accounting concepts and principles
(Obj. 1)

E3-2 Identify the accounting concept or principle (there may be more than one) that gives the most direction on how to account for each of the following situations:

a. Expenses of $1,200 must be accrued at the end of the period to measure income properly.
b. A customer states her intention to switch health clubs. Should the new health club record revenue based on this intention? Give the reason for your answer.

c. The owner of a business desires monthly financial statements to measure the progress of the entity on an ongoing basis.
d. Expenses of the period total $6,700. This amount should be subtracted from revenue to compute the period's net income.

E3-3 Suppose you start up your own photography business to shoot videos at college parties. The freshman class pays you $300 in advance just to guarantee your services for its party. The sophomore class promises you a minimum of $250 for filming its formal, and you end up collecting cash of $350 for this party. Answer the following questions about the correct way to account for your revenue under the accrual basis.

Cash versus accrual; applying the revenue principle
(Obj. 1, 2)

1. In addition to cash, what type of account was created when you received $300 from the freshman class? Name the new account.
2. When did you earn your revenue for both parties? What actually caused you to earn the revenue? Did you earn the revenue at the moment you received cash?

E3-4 Compute the amounts indicated by question marks for each of the following Prepaid Rent situations. For situation A, journalize the needed entry. Consider each situation separately.

Allocating prepaid expense to the asset and the expense
(Obj. 2, 3)

Student ResourceCD
spreadsheet

		Situation		
	A	**B**	**C**	**D**
Beginning Prepaid Rent.................	$ 400	$500	$ 900	$ 600
Payments for Prepaid Rent during the year	1,400	?	1,100	?
Total amount to account for..............	?	?	2,000	1,500
Ending Prepaid Rent	300	400	?	700
Rent Expense.........................	$?	$900	$1,200	$ 800

E3-5 Journalize the adjusting entries for the following adjustments at January 31, end of the accounting period.

Journalizing adjusting entries
(Obj. 3)

a. Employee salaries owed for Monday through Thursday of a five-day workweek; weekly payroll, $10,000.
b. Unearned service revenue earned, $500.
c. Depreciation, $3,000.
d. Prepaid rent expired, $300.
e. Interest revenue accrued, $3,800.

E3-6 Suppose the adjustments required in Exercise 3-5 were not made. Compute the overall overstatement or understatement of net income as a result of the omission of these adjustments.

Analyzing the effects of adjustments on net income
(Obj. 3)

E3-7 Journalize the adjusting entry needed at December 31 for each of the following independent situations.

Journalizing adjusting entries
(Obj. 3)

a. On October 1, we collected $6,000 rent in advance. We debited Cash and credited Unearned Rent Revenue. The tenant was paying one year's rent in advance.
b. Interest revenue of $800 has been earned but not yet received. The business holds a $20,000 note receivable.
c. Salary expense is $1,500 per day—Monday through Friday—and the business pays employees each Friday. This year December 31 falls on a Wednesday.
d. The unadjusted balance of the Supplies account is $3,100. Supplies on hand total $1,200.
e. Equipment was purchased last year at a cost of $10,000. The equipment's useful life is four years. Record the year's depreciation.
f. On September 1, when we prepaid $1,200 for a two-year insurance policy, we debited Prepaid Insurance and credited Cash.

Recording adjustments in T-accounts
(Obj. 3)

E3-8 The accounting records of Randall Roberts, Architect, include the following unadjusted balances at March 31: Accounts Receivable, $1,000; Supplies, $600; Salary Payable, $0; Unearned Service Revenue, $400; Service Revenue, $4,700; Salary Expense, $1,200; Supplies Expense, $0. Roberts' accountant develops the following data for the March 31 adjusting entries:

a. Service revenue accrued, $2,000.
b. Unearned service revenue that has been earned, $200.
c. Supplies on hand, $100.
d. Salary owed to employee, $400.

Open a T-account for each account and record the adjustments directly in the accounts, keying each adjustment by letter. Show each account's adjusted balance. Journal entries are not required.

Adjusting the accounts
(Obj. 3, 4)

E3-9 The adjusted trial balance of Stephen Perdue, Craftsman, is incomplete. Enter the adjustment amounts directly in the adjustment columns of the text.

Stephen Perdue, Craftsman
Preparation of Adjusted Trial Balance
May 31, 20X8

Account Title	Trial Balance Debit	Trial Balance Credit	Adjustments Debit	Adjustments Credit	Adjusted Trial Balance Debit	Adjusted Trial Balance Credit
Cash	3,000				3,000	
Accounts receivable.	4,500				7,600	
Supplies.	1,000				800	
Equipment.	32,300				32,300	
Accumulated depreciation		14,000				14,400
Salary payable						900
S. Perdue, capital		26,400				26,400
S. Perdue, withdrawals.	5,100				5,100	
Service revenue		9,600				12,700
Salary expense	2,700				3,600	
Rent expense.	1,400				1,400	
Depreciation expense					400	
Supplies expense					200	
	50,000	50,000			54,400	54,400

Journalizing adjustments
(Obj. 3, 4)

E3-10 Make the journal entry for each adjustment needed to complete the adjusted trial balance in Exercise 3-9. Date the entries and include explanations.

Student ResourceCD
General Ledger, Peachtree, QuickBooks

Preparing the financial statements
(Obj. 5)

E3-11 Refer to the adjusted trial balance in Exercise 3-9. Prepare the Stephen Perdue, Craftsman, income statement and statement of owner's equity for the month ended May 31, 20X8, and its balance sheet on that date. Draw arrows linking the three statements.

Preparing the income statement
(Obj. 5)

E3-12 The accountant for Bill Glaze, Attorney, has posted adjusting entries (a) through (e) to the accounts at December 31, 20X6. Selected balance sheet accounts and all the revenues and expenses of the entity follow in T-account form.

Accounts Receivable

23,000	
(e) 1,000	

Supplies

4,000	(a) 1,000

Accumulated Depreciation—Equipment

	5,000
	(b) 2,000

Accumulated Depreciation—Building

	33,000
	(c) 5,000

Salary Payable

	(d) 1,500

Service Revenue

	105,000
	(e) 1,000

Salary Expense

28,000	
(d) 1,500	

Supplies Expense

(a) 1,000	

Depreciation Expense—Equipment

(b) 2,000	

Depreciation Expense—Building

(c) 5,000	

Required

1. Prepare the income statement of Bill Glaze, Attorney, for the year ended December 31, 20X6. List expenses in order from the largest to the smallest.
2. Were 20X6 operations successful? Give the reason for your answer.

E3-13 Blackhawk Data Processing began the year with capital of $90,000. On July 12, Kent Black (the owner) invested $12,000 cash in the business. On September 26, he transferred to the company land valued at $70,000. The income statement for the year ended December 31, 20X5, reported a net loss of $28,000. During this fiscal year, Black withdrew $1,500 each month for personal use.

Preparing the statement of owner's equity
(Obj. 5)

Required

1. Prepare Blackhawk's statement of owner's equity for the year ended December 31, 20X5.
2. Did the owner's equity of the business increase or decrease during the year? What caused this change?

E3-14 The adjusted trial balances of Quartz Control Corporation at December 31, 20X7, and December 31, 20X6, include these amounts:

Computing financial statement amounts
(Obj. 5)

	20X7	20X6
Supplies	$ 2,100	$ 1,500
Salary payable	3,100	3,700
Unearned service revenue	14,200	16,300

Analysis of the accounts at December 31, 20X7, reveals these transactions for 20X7:

Purchases of supplies.............................	$ 8,400
Cash payments for salaries	84,600
Cash receipts in advance for service revenue..........	180,200

Compute the amount of supplies expense, salary expense, and service revenue to report on the Quartz Control income statement for 20X7.

Continuing Exercise

Exercise 3-15 continues the Marsha Walker, Consultant, situation begun in Exercise 2-17 of Chapter 2.

Adjusting the accounts, preparing an adjusted trial balance, and preparing the financial statements
(Obj. 3, 4, 5)

E3-15 Refer to Exercise 2-17 of Chapter 2. Start from the trial balance and the posted T-accounts that Marsha Walker, Consultant, prepared for her business at December 18, as follows:

Student Resource CD

GL, PT, QB

Marsha Walker, Consultant
Trial Balance
December 18, 20XX

Account	Debit	Credit
Cash..	$12,100	
Accounts receivable...............................	1,700	
Supplies..	300	
Equipment	2,000	
Furniture.......................................	3,600	
Accounts payable................................		$ 3,900
Marsha Walker, capital		14,000
Marsha Walker, withdrawals.......................	—	
Service revenue		2,500
Rent expense....................................	500	
Utilities expense................................	200	
Salary expense		
Total...	$20,400	$20,400

Later in December, the business completed these transactions, as follows:

Dec. 21	Received $900 in advance for client service to be performed evenly over the next 30 days.	
21	Hired a secretary to be paid $1,500 on the 20th day of each month. The secretary begins work immediately.	
26	Paid $300 on account.	
28	Collected $600 on account.	
30	Withdrew $1,600 for personal use.	

Required

1. Open these additional T-accounts: Accumulated Depreciation—Equipment; Accumulated Depreciation—Furniture; Salary Payable; Unearned Service Revenue; Depreciation Expense—Equipment; Depreciation Expense—Furniture; Supplies Expense.

2. Journalize the transactions of December 21 through 30.

3. Post to the T-accounts, keying all items by date.

4. Prepare a trial balance at December 31. Also set up columns for the adjustments and for the adjusted trial balance, as illustrated in Exhibit 3-10.

5. At December 31, Walker gathers the following information for the adjusting entries:
   a. Accrued service revenue, $400.
   b. Earned a portion of the service revenue collected in advance on December 21.
   c. Supplies on hand, $100.
   d. Depreciation expense—equipment, $50; furniture, $60.
   e. Accrued expense for secretary's salary—10 days worked.

   Make these adjustments directly in the adjustments columns, and complete the adjusted trial balance at December 31. Throughout the book, to avoid rounding errors, we base adjusting entries on 30-day months and 360-day years.

6. Journalize and post the adjusting entries. Denote each adjusting amount as *Adj.* and an account balance as *Bal.*

7. Prepare the income statement and the statement of owner's equity of Marsha Walker, Consultant, for the month ended December 31, and prepare the balance sheet at that date. Draw arrows linking the statements.

Problems

(Group A)

Cash basis versus accrual basis
(Obj. 1, 2)

P3-1A The Española Medical Clinic completed these transactions during May:

May 2	Prepaid insurance for May through July, $900.
4	Paid water bill, $550.
5	Performed services on account, $3,000.
9	Purchased medical equipment for cash, $1,400.
12	Received cash for services performed, $7,400.
14	Purchased office equipment on account, $300.
28	Collected $500 on account from May 5.
29	Paid salary expense, $1,100.
30	Paid account payable from May 14.
31	Recorded adjusting entry for May insurance expense (see May 2).
31	Debited unearned revenue and credited revenue in an adjusting entry, $700.

Required

1. Show how each transaction would be handled using the accrual basis of accounting. Give the amount of revenue or expense for May. Journal entries are not required. Use the following format for your answer, and show your computations:

Amount of Revenue (Expense) for May		
Date	Revenue (Expense)	Accrual-Basis Amount

2. Compute May net income or net loss under the accrual basis of accounting.

3. Why is the accrual basis of accounting preferable to the cash basis?

Applying accounting principles
(Obj. 1, 2)

P3-2A Assume you own and operate Westview Nursery. Your greenhouse is quite large, and you employ 10 people. Write a business memo to your assistant manager to explain the difference between the cash basis of accounting and the accrual basis. Mention the roles of the revenue principle and the matching principle in accrual accounting. The format of a business memo follows.

Date: _____
To: Assistant Manager
From: (Student Name)
Subject: Difference between the cash basis and the accrual basis of accounting

Journalizing adjusting entries
(Obj. 3)

P3-3A Journalize the adjusting entry needed on December 31, end of the current accounting period, for each of the following independent cases affecting Colorado River Rafting.

Student ResourceCD
GL, PT, QB

a. Details of Prepaid Insurance are shown in the account:

Prepaid Insurance	
Mar. 31 2,400	

Colorado pays liability insurance each year on March 31. Record insurance expense for the year ended December 31.

b. Colorado pays employees each Friday. The amount of the weekly payroll is $2,000 for a five-day workweek. The current accounting period ends on Monday.

c. Colorado has borrowed money, signing a note payable. For the current year, Colorado accrued interest expense of $600 that it will pay next year.

d. The beginning balance of Supplies was $2,600. During the year, Colorado purchased supplies for $6,100, and at December 31 the supplies on hand total $2,100.

e. Colorado is providing river-rafting trips for a large tour operator from Denver. The tour operator paid Colorado $12,000 as the annual service fee and Colorado recorded this amount as Unearned Service Revenue. The owner determines that Colorado has earned one-fourth the total fee during the current year.

f. Depreciation for the current year includes Canoe Equipment, $3,850; and Trucks, $1,300. Make a compound entry, as illustrated in Chapter 2.

Analyzing and journalizing adjustments **(Obj. 3)**

GL, PT, QB

P3-4A Assume a U-Haul location's unadjusted and adjusted trial balances at April 30, 20X7, show the following data:

	U-Haul Adjusted Trial Balance April 30, 20X7				
Account Title	**Trial Balance** Debit	Credit	**Adjusted Trial Balance** Debit	Credit
Cash	6,200		6,200	
Accounts receivable	6,000		6,700	
Interest receivable...............			300	
Note receivable	4,100		4,100	
Supplies	1,000		300	
Prepaid rent....................	2,400		1,600	
Equipment.....................	66,400		66,400	
Accumulated depreciation		16,000		17,200
Accounts payable		6,900		6,900
Wages payable..................				300
Paul Olen, capital		59,500		59,500
Paul Olen, withdrawals..........	3,600		3,600	
Rental revenue..................		9,500		10,200
Interest revenue.................				300
Wage expense	1,600		1,900	
Rent expense			800	
Depreciation expense............			1,200	
Insurance expense...............	400		400	
Supplies expense................			700	
Utilities expense	200		200	
	91,900	91,900	94,400	94,400

Required

Journalize the adjusting entries that account for the differences between the two trial balances.

Journalizing and posting adjustments to T-accounts; preparing the adjusted trial balance
(Obj. 3, 4)

GL, PT, QB

P3-5A The trial balance of Smoky Mountain Lodge at December 31, 20X5, and the data needed for the month-end adjustments follow.

Adjustment data:

a. Prepaid insurance still in force at December 31, $600.

b. Supplies used during the month, $600.

c. Depreciation for the month, $900.

d. Accrued advertising expense at December 31, $300. (Credit Accounts Payable.)

e. Accrued salary expense at December 31, $100.

f. Unearned service revenue still unearned at December 31, $1,100.

Smoky Mountain Lodge

Trial Balance
December 31, 20X5

Cash	$ 12,200	
Accounts receivable	14,100	
Prepaid insurance	3,100	
Supplies	800	
Building	412,700	
Accumulated depreciation		$311,600
Accounts payable		1,900
Salary payable		
Unearned service revenue		2,300
Rocky Rivers, capital		125,000
Rocky Rivers, withdrawals	2,900	
Service revenue		7,900
Salary expense	2,100	
Insurance expense		
Depreciation expense		
Advertising expense	800	
Supplies expense		
Total	$448,700	$448,700

Required

1. Open T-accounts for the accounts listed in the trial balance, inserting their December 31 unadjusted balances.
2. Journalize the adjusting entries and post them to the T-accounts. Key the journal entries and the posted amounts by letter.
3. Prepare the adjusted trial balance.
4. How will the company use the adjusted trial balance?

P3-6A The adjusted trial balance of Air & Sea Travel at December 31, 20X6, follows.

Preparing the financial statements from an adjusted trial balance

(Obj. 5)

Air & Sea Travel

Adjusted Trial Balance
December 31, 20X6

Cash	$ 1,300	
Accounts receivable	4,900	
Supplies	2,300	
Prepaid rent	1,600	
Office furniture	37,700	
Accumulated depreciation—office furniture		$ 4,800
Accounts payable		4,500
Unearned service revenue		600
Cindy Sorrel, capital		26,000
Cindy Sorrel, withdrawals	29,000	
Service revenue		106,000
Depreciation expense—office furniture	2,300	
Salary expense	39,900	
Rent expense	17,400	
Utilities expense	2,600	
Supplies expense	2,900	
Total	$141,900	$141,900

Required

1. Prepare Air & Sea Travel's 20X6 income statement, statement of owner's equity, and year-end balance sheet. List expenses in decreasing order on the income statement and show total liabilities on the balance sheet. Draw arrows linking the three financial statements.
2. **a.** Which financial statement reports Air & Sea Travel's results of operations? Were operations successful during 20X6? Cite specifics from the financial statements to support your evaluation.
   b. Which statement reports the company's financial position? Does Air & Sea Travel's financial position look strong or weak? Give the reason for your evaluation.

Preparing an adjusted trial balance and the financial statements
(Obj. 3, 4, 5)

P3-7A The unadjusted trial balance of Pat Patillo, CPA, at July 31, 20X6, and the related month-end adjustment data follow.

Student ResourceCD
GL, PT, QB

Pat Patillo, CPA		
Trial Balance **July 31, 20X6**		
Cash	$ 8,900	
Accounts receivable	11,600	
Prepaid rent	4,000	
Supplies	800	
Furniture	28,800	
Accumulated depreciation		$ 3,500
Accounts payable		3,400
Salary payable		
Pat Patillo, capital		39,100
Pat Patillo, withdrawals	4,000	
Accounting service revenue		15,000
Salary expense	2,400	
Rent expense		
Utilities expense	500	
Depreciation expense		
Supplies expense		
Total	$61,000	$61,000

Adjustment data:

a. Accrued accounting service revenue at July 31, $900.
b. Prepaid rent expired during the month. The unadjusted balance of prepaid rent relates to the period July through October.
c. Supplies on hand at July 31, $400.
d. Depreciation on furniture for the month. The estimated useful life of the furniture is 4 years.
e. Accrued salary expense at July 31 for 1 day only. The 5-day weekly payroll is $1,000.

Required

1. Using Exhibit 3-10 as an example, write the trial balance on a work sheet and prepare the adjusted trial balance of Pat Patillo, CPA, at July 31, 20X6. Key each adjusting entry by letter.
2. Prepare the income statement and the statement of owner's equity for the month ended July 31, 20X6, and the balance sheet at that date. Draw arrows linking the three statements.

Problems

(Group B)

Cash basis versus accrual basis
(Obj. 1, 2)

P3-1B Brazos Medical Clinic completed the following selected transactions during January:

Jan. 1	Prepaid insurance for January through March, $600.
4	Performed medical service on account, $4,000.
5	Purchased office furniture on account, $150.
8	Paid property tax expense, $450.
11	Purchased office equipment for cash, $800.
19	Performed medical service and received cash, $700.
24	Collected $400 on account.
26	Paid account payable from January 5.
29	Paid salary expense, $900.
31	Recorded adjusting entry for January insurance expense (see Jan. 1).
31	Debited unearned revenue and credited revenue to adjust the accounts, $600.

Required

1. Show how each transaction would be handled using the accrual basis of accounting. Give the amount of revenue or expense for January. Journal entries are not required. Use the following format for your answer, and show your computations:

Amount of Revenue (Expense) for January		
Date	Revenue (Expense)	Accrual-Basis Amount

2. Compute January net income or net loss under the accrual basis of accounting.

3. State why the accrual basis of accounting is preferable to the cash basis.

Applying accounting principles
(Obj. 1, 2)

P3-2B As the controller of Genie Car Wash, you have hired a new bookkeeper, whom you must train. He objects to making an adjusting entry for accrued salaries at the end of the period. He reasons, "We will pay the salaries within a week or two. Why not wait until payment to record the expense? In the end, the result will be the same." Write a business memo to explain to the bookkeeper why the adjusting entry for accrued salary expense is needed. The format of a business memo follows.

Date: _____	
To: New Bookkeeper	
From: (Student Name)	
Subject: Why the adjusting entry for salary expense is needed	

Journalizing adjusting entries
(Obj. 3)

Student ResourceCD
GL, PT, QB

P3-3B Journalize the adjusting entry needed on December 31, the end of the current accounting period, for each of the following independent cases affecting Metz Marketing Concepts.

a. Each Friday, Metz pays employees for the current week's work. The amount of the payroll is $5,000 for a five-day workweek. The current accounting period ends on Thursday.

b. Details of Prepaid Insurance are shown in the account:

Prepaid Insurance	
April 30 3,000	

Metz pays insurance each year on April 30. Record insurance expense for the year ended December 31.

c. Metz has received notes receivable from some clients for professional services. During the current year, Metz has earned accrued interest revenue of $170, which will be collected next year.

d. The beginning balance of Supplies was $3,800. During the year, Metz purchased supplies costing $5,500, and at December 31, the supplies on hand total $2,900.

e. Metz designed a marketing campaign, and the client paid Metz $36,000 at the start of the project. Metz recorded this amount as Unearned Service Revenue. The campaign will run for several months. Metz estimates that the company has earned three-fourths of the total fee during the current year.

f. Depreciation for the current year includes: Office Furniture, $5,500; and Building, $3,700. Make a compound entry, as illustrated in Chapter 2.

Analyzing and journalizing adjustments
(Obj. 3)

P3-4B Howe Investment Brokers' unadjusted and adjusted trial balances at December 31, 20X7, follow.

Student Resource CD
GL, PT, QB

Howe Investment Brokers
Adjusted Trial Balance
December 31, 20X7

Account Title	Trial Balance Debit	Trial Balance Credit	Adjusted Trial Balance Debit	Adjusted Trial Balance Credit
Cash	4,100		4,100	
Accounts receivable	5,200		13,200	
Supplies	1,200		300	
Prepaid insurance...............	2,600		2,300	
Office furniture	21,600		21,600	
Accumulated depreciation..................		8,200		9,800
Accounts payable		6,400		6,400
Salary payable..................				1,000
Interest payable.................				400
Note payable		13,800		13,800
Sandy Howe, capital.............		13,500		13,500
Sandy Howe, withdrawals	29,400		29,400	
Commission revenue		66,900		74,900
Depreciation expense............			1,600	
Supplies expense................			900	
Utilities expense	5,000		5,000	
Salary expense..................	26,600		27,600	
Rent expense	12,200		12,200	
Interest expense.................	900		1,300	
Insurance expense...............			300	
	108,800	108,800	119,800	119,800

Journalizing and posting adjustments to T-accounts; preparing the adjusted trial balance
(Obj. 3, 4)

Student Resource CD
GL, PT, QB

Required

Journalize the adjusting entries that account for the differences between the two trial balances.

P3-5B The trial balance of Unistar Alarm Systems at August 31, 20X6, and the data needed for the month-end adjustments follow.

Unistar Alarm Systems
Trial Balance
August 31, 20X6

Cash	$ 7,100	
Accounts receivable	19,800	
Prepaid rent	2,400	
Supplies	1,200	
Furniture	19,700	
Accumulated depreciation		$ 3,600
Accounts payable		3,300
Salary payable		
Unearned service revenue		2,800
John Wilhelm, capital		35,500
John Wilhelm, withdrawals	5,300	
Service revenue		15,600
Salary expense	3,800	
Rent expense		
Depreciation expense		
Advertising expense	1,500	
Supplies expense		
Total	$60,800	$60,800

Adjustment data:

a. Unearned service revenue still unearned at August 31, $1,600.
b. Prepaid rent still in force at August 31, $600.
c. Supplies used during the month, $700.
d. Depreciation for the month, $400.
e. Accrued advertising expense at August 31, $600. (Credit Accounts Payable.)
f. Accrued salary expense at August 31, $500.

Required

1. Open T-accounts for the accounts listed in the trial balance, inserting their August 31 unadjusted balances.
2. Journalize the adjusting entries and post them to the T-accounts. Key the journal entries and the posted amounts by letter.
3. Prepare the adjusted trial balance.
4. How will Unistar use the adjusted trial balance?

P3-6B The adjusted trial balance of Doc's Recreation Center at December 31, 20X8, follows.

Preparing the financial statements from an adjusted trial balance
(Obj. 3, 4, 5)

Doc's Recreation Center
Adjusted Trial Balance
December 31, 20X8

Cash	$ 2,340	
Accounts receivable	50,490	
Prepaid rent	1,350	
Supplies	970	
Equipment	75,690	
Accumulated depreciation—equipment		$ 22,240
Furniture	29,100	

(continued)

Accumulated depreciation—furniture		3,670
Accounts payable.		13,600
Unearned service revenue		4,520
Interest payable		2,130
Salary payable.		930
Note payable.		45,000
D. Brooks, capital		32,380
D. Brooks, withdrawals.	48,000	
Service revenue.		209,790
Depreciation expense—equipment	11,300	
Depreciation expense—furniture.	2,410	
Salary expense	87,800	
Rent expense.	12,000	
Interest expense	4,200	
Utilities expense	3,770	
Insurance expense	3,150	
Supplies expense	1,690	
Total	$334,260	$334,260

Required

1. Prepare Doc's 20X8 income statement and statement of owner's equity and year-end balance sheet. List expenses in decreasing order on the income statement and show total liabilities on the balance sheet. Draw arrows linking the three financial statements.

2. a. Which financial statement reports Doc's results of operations? Were 20X8 operations successful? Cite specifics from the financial statements to support your evaluation.

 b. Which statement reports the company's financial position? Does Doc's financial position look strong or weak? Give the reason for your evaluation.

Preparing an adjusted trial balance and the financial statements
(Obj. 3, 4, 5)

Student Resource CD
GL, PT, QB

P3-7B Consider the unadjusted trial balance of Progressive Limo Service at October 31, 20X7, and the related month-end adjustment data.

Progressive Limo Service
Trial Balance
October 31, 20X7

Cash	$ 6,300	
Accounts receivable.	8,000	
Prepaid rent.	6,000	
Supplies	600	
Automobiles	120,000	
Accumulated depreciation		$ 3,000
Accounts payable.		2,800
Salary payable.		
Jack Dicorte, capital		131,000
Jack Dicorte, withdrawals.	3,600	
Service revenue.		9,400
Salary expense	1,400	
Rent expense.		
Fuel expense	300	
Depreciation expense.		
Supplies expense		
Total	$146,200	$146,200

Adjustment data:

a. Accrued service revenue at October 31, $2,000.

b. One-fourth of the prepaid rent expired during the month.

c. Supplies on hand October 31, $200.

d. Depreciation on automobiles for the month. The autos' expected useful lives are five years.

e. Accrued salary expense at October 31 for one day only. The five-day weekly payroll is $2,000.

Required

1. Write the trial balance on a work sheet, using Exhibit 3-10 as an example, and prepare the adjusted trial balance of Progressive Limo Service at October 31, 20X7. Key each adjusting entry by letter.

2. Prepare the income statement and the statement of owner's equity for the month ended October 31, 20X7, and the balance sheet at that date. Draw arrows linking the three financial statements.

APPLY *Your Knowledge*

Decision Cases

Valuing a business on the basis of its net income
(Obj. 3, 4)

Case 1. Chance Wayne has owned and operated Chance Wayne Advertising since its beginning 10 years ago. The company has prospered. Recently, Wayne mentioned that he has lost his zest for the business and would consider selling it for the right price.

Assume that you are interested in buying this business. You obtain its most recent monthly trial balance, which follows. Revenues and expenses vary little from month to month, and April is a typical month. Your investigation reveals that the trial balance does not include monthly revenues of $3,800 and expenses totaling $1,100. If you were to buy Chance Wayne Advertising, you would hire a manager so you could devote your time to other duties. Assume that this person would require a monthly salary of $4,000.

Chance Wayne Advertising		
Trial Balance		
April 30, 20XX		
Cash..	$ 9,700	
Accounts receivable	4,900	
Prepaid expenses..............................	2,600	
Plant assets..................................	221,300	
Accumulated depreciation......................		$189,600
Land..	158,000	
Accounts payable		13,800
Salary payable		
Unearned advertising revenue		56,700
Chance Wayne, capital		137,400
Chance Wayne, withdrawals.....................	9,000	
Advertising revenue		12,300
Rent expense		
Salary expense	3,400	
Utilities expense............................	900	
Depreciation expense		
Supplies expense		
Total..	$409,800	$409,800

Required

1. Assume that the most you would pay for the business is 25 times the monthly net income *you could expect to earn* from it. Compute this possible price.

2. Wayne states that the least he will take for the business is his capital balance on April 30. Compute this amount.

3. Under these conditions, how much should you offer Wayne? Give your reason.

Completing the accounting cycle to compute net income
(Obj. 3, 5)

Case 2. One year ago, Bob Cervenka founded Total Restoration Service. Cervenka remembers that you took an accounting course while in college and comes to you for advice. He wishes to know how much net income the business earned during the past year in order to decide whether to keep the company going. His accounting records consist of the T-accounts from his ledger, which were prepared by an accountant who moved to another city. The ledger at December 31 follows. The accounts have *not* been adjusted.

Cash			Accounts Receivable			Prepaid Rent			Supplies	
Dec. 31 5,830			Dec. 31 12,360			Jan. 2 2,800			Jan. 2 2,600	

Equipment			Accumulated Depreciation						Accounts Payable	
Jan. 2 36,600										Dec. 31 21,540

Unearned Service Revenue			Salary Payable							
	Dec. 31 4,130									

Bob Cervenka, Capital			Bob Cervenka, Withdrawals						Service Revenue	
	Dec. 31 20,000		Dec. 31 28,420							Dec. 31 60,740

Salary Expense			Depreciation Expense			Rent Expense			Utilities Expense	
Dec. 31 17,000									Dec. 31 800	

Supplies Expense	

Cervenka indicates that at year-end, customers owe him $1,600 of accrued service revenue. These revenues have not been recorded. During the year, he collected $4,130 service revenue in advance from customers, but he earned only $600 of that amount. Rent expense for the year was $2,400, and he used up $2,100 of the supplies. Cervenka estimates that depreciation on his equipment was $5,900 for the year. At December 31, he owes his employee $1,200 accrued salary.

Required

Help Cervenka compute his net income for the year. Advise him whether to continue operating Total Restoration Service.

Ethical Issue

The net income of Bynum & Hobbs, a department store, decreased sharply during 2004. Ron Bynum, owner of the store, anticipates the need for a bank loan in 2005. Late in 2004, Bynum instructs the store's accountant to record a $6,000 sale of furniture to the Bynum family, even though the goods will not be shipped from the manufacturer until January 2005. Bynum also tells the accountant *not* to make the following December 31, 2004, adjusting entries:

Salaries owed to employees.	$900
Prepaid insurance that has expired	400

Required

1. Compute the overall effects of these transactions on the store's reported income for 2004.

2. Why is Bynum taking this action? Is his action ethical? Give your reason, identifying the parties helped and the parties harmed by Bynum's action.

3. As a personal friend, what advice would you give the accountant?

Financial Statement Case

Journalizing and posting transactions and tracing account balances to the financial statements
(Obj. 3, 5)

Amazon.com—like all other businesses—makes adjusting entries prior to year-end in order to measure assets, liabilities, revenues, and expenses properly. Examine Amazon's balance sheet and Note 3. Pay particular attention to Accumulated Depreciation, Interest Payable, and Unearned Revenue.

1. Open T-accounts for the following accounts with their balances at December 31, 2001 (amounts in thousands, as in the Amazon.com financial statements):

Accumulated Depreciation..........................	$166,392
Interest Payable	68,632
Unearned Revenue	87,978

2. Assume that during 2002 Amazon.com completed the following transactions (amounts in thousands). Journalize each transaction (explanations are not required).
   a. Recorded depreciation expense, $76,946.
   b. Paid the beginning balance of interest payable.
   c. Accrued interest expense, $71,661.
   d. Earned sales revenue that had been collected in advance, $40,062.

3. Post to the three T-accounts. Then the balance of each account should agree with the corresponding amount reported in the December 31, 2002, balance sheet. Check to make sure they do agree with Amazon's actual balances. You can find Accumulated Depreciation in Note 3.

Team Project

Return to the chapter-opening story, which describes **It's Just Lunch**. Suppose your group is opening an It's Just Lunch office in your area. You must make some important decisions—where to locate, how to advertise, and so on—and you must also make some accounting decisions. For example, what will be the end of your business's accounting year? How often will you need financial statements to evaluate operating performance and financial position? Will you use the cash basis or the accrual basis? When will you account for the revenue that the business earns? How will you account for the expenses?

Required

Write a report (or prepare an oral presentation, as directed by your professor) to address the following considerations:

1. Will you use the cash basis or the accrual basis of accounting? Give a complete explanation of your reasoning.

2. How often do you want financial statements? Why? Discuss how you will use each financial statement.

3. What kind of revenue will you earn? When will you record it as revenue? How will you decide when to record the revenue?

4. Prepare a made-up income statement for It's Just Lunch for the year ended December 31, 20X5. List all the business's expenses, starting with the most important (largest dollar amount) and working through the least important (smallest dollar amount). Try to come as close as you can to the actual figures, as follows: Net revenues, $20,175,920; Net income, $2,018,516.

5. Using made-up dollar amounts, prepare all the adjusting entries your business will need at the end of the year. Identify the date of your adjustments.

For Internet Exercises, go to the Web site www.prenhall.com/horngren.

APPENDIX *to Chapter 3*

Alternative Treatment of Prepaid Expenses and Unearned Revenues

Chapters 1 through 3 illustrate the most popular way to account for prepaid expenses and unearned revenues. This appendix illustrates an alternative approach.

Prepaid Expenses

Prepaid expenses are advance payments of expenses such as Prepaid Insurance, Prepaid Rent, and Prepaid Advertising. Supplies are also accounted for as prepaid expenses.

When a business prepays an expense—rent, for example—it can debit an *asset* account (Prepaid Rent), as illustrated on page 98.

Aug. 1	Prepaid Rent (↑ asset; debit)............ xxx	
	Cash (↓ asset; credit)	xxx

Alternatively, it can debit an *expense* account to record this cash payment:

Aug. 1	Rent Expense (↑ expense; debit) xxx	
	Cash (↓ asset; credit)	xxx

Either way, the business must adjust the accounts at the end of the period to report the correct amounts of the expense and the asset.

Prepaid Expense Recorded Initially as an Expense Prepaying an expense creates an asset. However, the asset may be so short-lived that it will expire in the current accounting period—within one year or less. Thus, the accountant may decide to debit the prepayment to an expense account at the time of payment. A $6,000 cash payment for rent (one year, in advance) on August 1 may be debited to Rent Expense:

20X6		
Aug. 1	Rent Expense (↑ expense; debit)...... 6,000	
	Cash (↓ asset; credit)...........	6,000

At December 31, only five months' prepayment has expired (for August through December), leaving seven months' rent still prepaid. In this case, the accountant must transfer 7/12 of the original prepayment of $6,000, or $3,500, to the asset account Prepaid Rent. At December 31, 20X6, the business still has the benefit of the prepayment for January through July of 20X7. The adjusting entry at December 31 is

Adjusting Entries

20X6
Dec. 31   Prepaid Rent ($6,000 × 7/12)
             (↑ assets; debit).   3,500
                   Rent Expense (↓ expense; credit). .   3,500

After posting, the two accounts appear as follows (where CP = cash payment entry; Adj = adjusting entry):

Prepaid Rent				Rent Expense		
20X6				**20X6**		**20X6**
Dec. 31 Adj.	**3,500**			Aug. 1 CP	**6,000**	Dec. 31 Adj. **3,500**
Dec. 31 Bal.	3,500			Dec. 31 Bal.	2,500	

The balance sheet at the end of 20X6 reports Prepaid Rent of $3,500, and the income statement for 20X6 reports Rent Expense of $2,500, regardless of whether the business initially debits the prepayment to an asset account or to an expense account.

Unearned (Deferred) Revenues

Unearned (deferred) revenues arise when a business collects cash before earning the revenue. Unearned revenues are liabilities because the business that receives cash owes the other party goods or services to be delivered later.

Unearned (Deferred) Revenue Recorded Initially as a Revenue   Receipt of cash in advance creates a liability, as recorded on page 104. Another way to account for the receipt of cash is to credit a *revenue account*. If the business has earned all the revenue within the same period, no adjusting entry is needed at the end of the period. However, if the business earns only part of the revenue at the end of the period, it must make an adjusting entry.

Suppose on October 1, 20X2, a law firm records as revenue the receipt of cash for a nine-month fee of $9,000 received in advance. The cash receipt entry is

20X2
Oct. 1   Cash (↑ asset; debit)   9,000
                 Legal Revenue (↑ revenue, credit)   9,000

At December 31, the attorney has earned only 3/9 of the $9,000, or $3,000, for the months of October, November, and December. Accordingly, the firm makes an adjusting entry to transfer the unearned portion (6/9 of $9,000, or $6,000) from the revenue account to a liability account, as follows:

Adjusting Entries

20X2
Dec. 31   Legal Revenue ($9,000 × 6/9)
             (↓ revenue; debit)   6,000
                   Unearned Legal Revenue
                   (↑ liability; credit).   6,000

The adjusting entry transfers the unearned portion (6/9, or $6,000) of the original amount to the liability account because the law firm still owes legal service to the client during January through June of 20X3. After posting, the total amount ($9,000) is properly divided between the liability account ($6,000) and the revenue account ($3,000), as follows (where CR = cash receipt entry and Adj. = adjusting entry).

Unearned Legal Revenue		
	20X2	
	Dec. 31 Adj.	6,000
	Dec. 31 Bal.	6,000

Legal Revenue				
20X2		20X2		
Dec. 31 Adj.	6,000	Oct. 1 CR	9,000	
		Dec. 31 Bal.	3,000	

The attorney's 20X2 income statement reports legal revenue of $3,000, and the balance sheet at December 31, 20X2, reports the unearned legal revenue of $6,000 as a liability. The result is the same whether the business initially credits a liability account or a revenue account.

Appendix Assignments

Exercises

Recording supplies transactions two ways

E3A-1 At the beginning of the year, supplies of $1,190 were on hand. During the year, Damon Air Conditioning Service paid $5,400 cash for supplies. At the end of the year, Damon has $860 of supplies on hand.

Required

1. Assume that Damon records supplies by initially debiting an *asset* account. Therefore, place the beginning balance in the Supplies T-account, and record the preceding entries directly in the accounts without using a journal.
2. Assume that Damon records supplies by initially debiting an *expense* account. Therefore, place the beginning balance in the Supplies Expense T-account, and record the preceding entries directly in the accounts without using a journal.
3. Compare the ending account balances under both approaches. Are they the same?

Recording unearned revenues two ways

E3A-2 At the beginning of the year, Avant Garde Advertising owed customers $2,750 for unearned service revenue collected in advance. During the year, Avant Garde received advance cash receipts of $7,000. At year-end, the liability for unearned revenue is $3,700.

Required

1. Assume that Avant Garde records unearned revenues by initially crediting a *liability* account. Open T-accounts for Unearned Service Revenue and Service Revenue, and place the beginning balance in Unearned Service Revenue. Journalize the cash collection and adjusting entries, and post their dollar amounts. As references in the T-accounts, denote a balance by *Bal.*, a cash receipt by *CR*, and an adjustment by *Adj.*
2. Assume that Avant Garde records unearned revenues by initially crediting a *revenue* account. Open T-accounts for Unearned Service Revenue and Service Revenue, and place the beginning balance in Service Revenue. Journalize the cash collection and adjusting entries, and post their dollar amounts. As references in the T-accounts, denote a balance by *Bal.*, a cash receipt by *CR*, and an adjustment by *Adj.*
3. Compare the ending balances in the two accounts.

Problem

Recording prepaid rent and rent revenue collected in advance two ways

P3A-1 Smart Pages Pack'n Mail completed the following transactions during 20X4:

Oct. 1	Paid $4,500 store rent covering the 6-month period ending March 31, 20X5.
Dec. 1	Collected $3,200 cash in advance from customers. The service revenue will be earned $800 monthly over the period ending March 31, 20X5.

Required

1. Journalize these entries by debiting an asset account for Prepaid Rent and by crediting a liability account for Unearned Service Revenue. Explanations are unnecessary.
2. Journalize the related adjustments at December 31, 20X4.
3. Post the entries to the ledger accounts, and show their balances at December 31, 20X4. Posting references are unnecessary.
4. Repeat requirements 1 through 3. This time, debit Rent Expense for the rent payment and credit Service Revenue for the collection of revenue in advance.
5. Compare the account balances in requirements 3 and 4. They should be equal.

CHAPTER 4

Completing the Accounting Cycle

TIPS CHECK YOUR RESOURCES

- Visit the www.prenhall.com/horngren **Web site** for self-study quizzes, video clips, and other resources

- Try the **Quick Check** exercise at the end of the chapter to test your knowledge

- Learn the **key terms**

- Do the **Starter** exercises keyed in the margins

- Work the **mid-** and **end-of-chapter summary problems**

- Use the **Concept Links** to review material in other chapters

- Search the **CD** for review materials by chapter or by key word

- Watch the **On Location Merchandisers** video to review sale of inventory issues

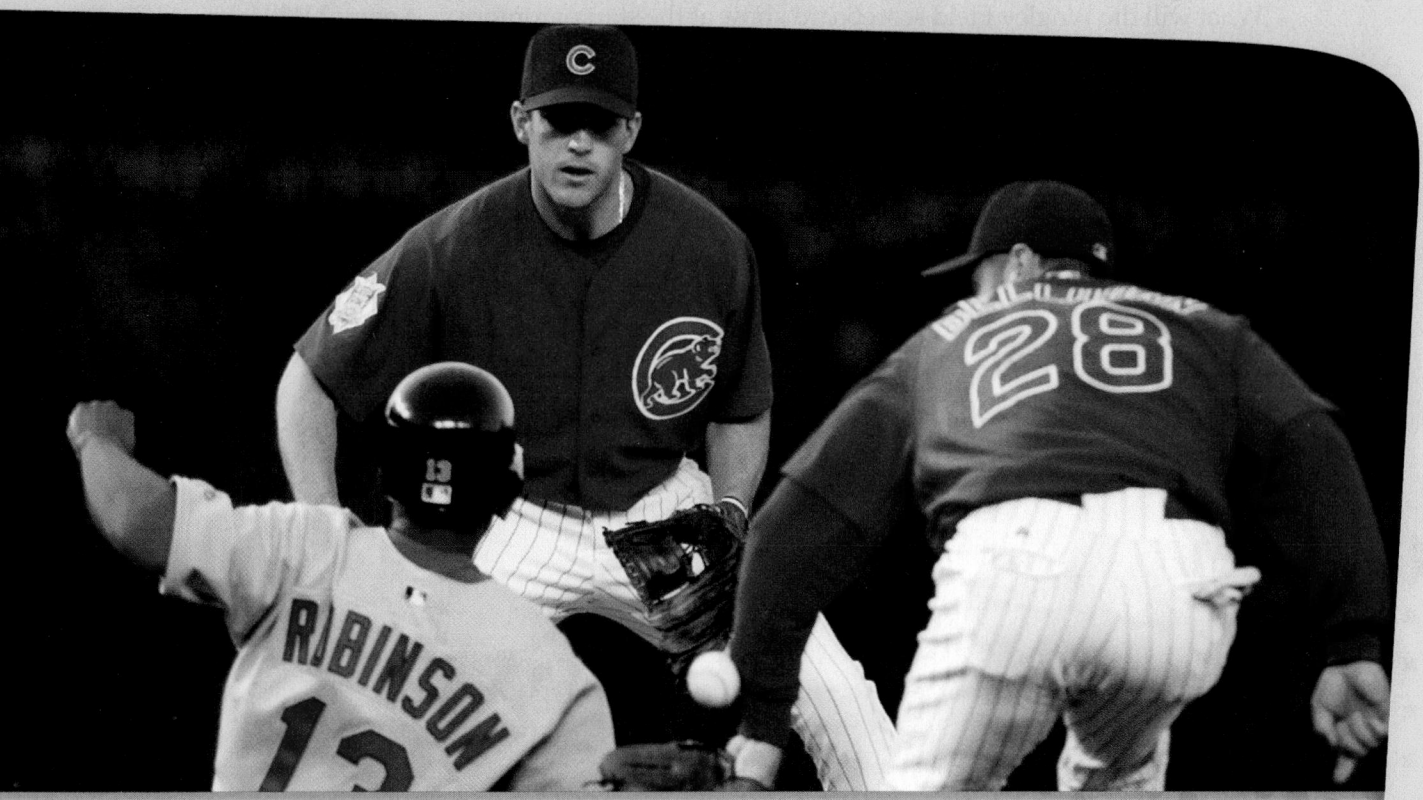

LEARNING OBJECTIVES

1. Prepare an accounting work sheet

2. Use the work sheet to complete the accounting cycle

3. Close the revenue, expense, and withdrawal accounts

4. Classify assets and liabilities as current or long-term

5. Use the current ratio and the debt ratio to evaluate a company

It's a beautiful day in Chicago. You are enjoying being at Wrigley Field, home of the Chicago Cubs. The St. Louis Cardinals are in town for a three-game series—one of the great sports rivalries in America. The bratwurst, pretzels, and drinks are refreshing, and the baseball should be even better.

St. Louis jumps to an early lead and stays up by two runs for most of the game. But then Chicago ties the score in the bottom of the ninth. Now the game goes into extra innings. How will it turn out?

In the top of the tenth inning, the Cardinals are shut out: three batters are up and down. Fortunately, the Cubs' Sammy Sosa is up next. And today, as at so many other Cubs games, Sammy hits a home run, a solo shot over the left-field wall, to win the game for Chicago. The final score is 6–5. Faithful Cubs fans go home happy.

Chicago Cubs

What will the Wrigley Field scoreboard show at the start of tomorrow's game? Will it be 6–5 to carry over the score from the first game? Or will the scoreboard be set back to zero? The answer is obvious: After a game is finished, the scoreboard is always set back to zero.

In the same way, the accounting process sets the scoreboard back to zero at the end of each period. The process is called closing the books, and it is the main topic of this chapter. Here we show how companies close their books. The logic behind the closing process in accounting is the same as setting the scoreboard back to zero after a game. The final step in the process is to report the financial statements to the public.

Next period, we will repeat the accounting process outlined here. And the Cubs will travel to St. Louis, where the Busch Stadium scoreboard will start out with a score of 0–0.

Sitemap

- The Accounting Cycle
- The Work Sheet
- Completing the Cycle
- Classifying Assets and Liabilities
- Accounting Ratios
- Appendix: Reversing Entries

Thus far, we have prepared financial statements from an adjusted trial balance. That approach works well for quick decision making, but companies take the process a step further. At the end of each period, after adjusting the accounts, they close their books. Whether the company is the Chicago Cubs baseball organization, Amazon.com, or Gay Gillen eTravel, the closing process follows the same pattern. Closing the books marks the end of the *accounting cycle* for a given period.

Accountants often use a document known as the *work sheet*. There are many different types of work sheets—in fact, as many as there are needs for data. Work sheets are useful because they summarize lots of data.

■ The Accounting Cycle
☐ The Work Sheet
☐ Completing the Cycle
☐ Classifying Assets and
   Liabilities
☐ Accounting Ratios
☐ Appendix: Reversing Entries

🖸 Student ResourceCD
accounting cycle

Accounting Cycle
Process by which companies produce their financial statements for a specific period.

The Accounting Cycle

The **accounting cycle** is the process by which companies produce their financial statements. For the Chicago Cubs, Amazon.com, or any other business, the first accounting step is to open the accounts. After a business has operated for one period, some of the account balances carry over to the next period. Therefore, the accounting cycle starts with the beginning asset, liability, and owner's equity account balances left over from the preceding period. Exhibit 4-1 outlines the complete accounting cycle of Gay Gillen eTravel and every other business. The boldface items in Panel A indicate the new concepts we introduce in this chapter. Accounting takes place at two different times:

- During the period—Journalizing transactions
  Posting to the accounts in the ledger
- End of the period — Adjusting the accounts, including journalizing and posting the adjusting entries
  Closing the accounts, including journalizing and posting the closing entries
  Preparing the financial statements (income statement, statement of owner's equity, and balance sheet)

The end-of-period work also readies the accounts for the next period. In Chapters 3 and 4, we cover the end-of-period accounting for a service business such as the Chicago Cubs and Gay Gillen eTravel. Chapter 5 shows how a merchandising entity such as Wal-Mart or Target adjusts and closes its books.

Exhibit 4-1 The Accounting Cycle

PANEL A

During the Period	End of the Period
1. Start with the account balances at the beginning of the period.	4. Compute the unadjusted balance in each account at the end of the period.
2. Analyze and journalize transactions as they occur.	5. Enter the trial balance on the work sheet, and complete the work sheet (optional).
3. Post journal entries to the accounts.	6. Using the adjusted trial balance or the full work sheet as a guide,
	a. Prepare the financial statements.
	b. Journalize and post the adjusting entries.
	c. **Journalize and post the closing entries.**
	7. Prepare the postclosing trial balance. This trial balance becomes step 1 for the next period.

PANEL B

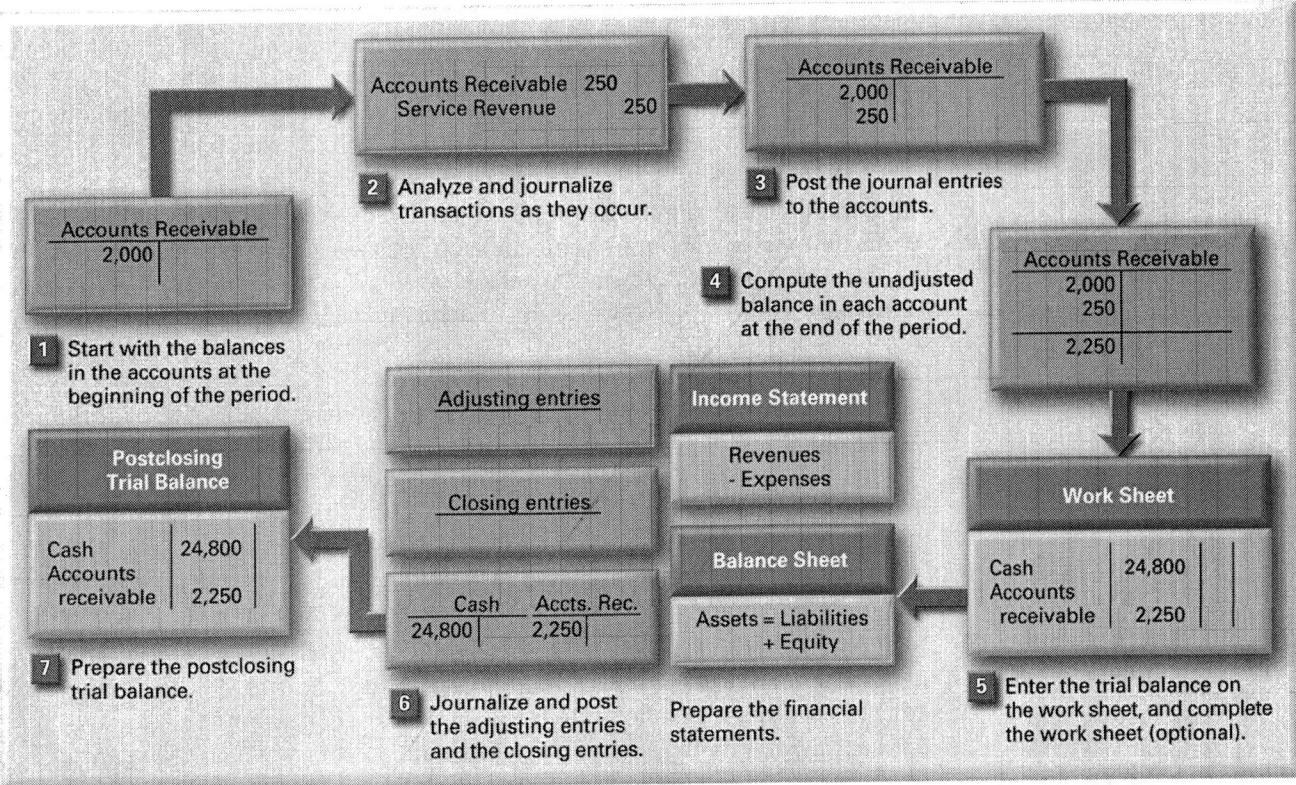

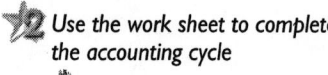
Use the work sheet to complete the accounting cycle

The financial statements can be prepared directly from the adjusted trial balance; see p. 108. This is why completion of the work sheet is optional.

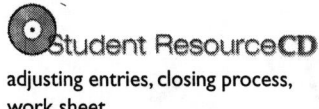
Student ResourceCD

adjusting entries, closing process, work sheet

Completing the Accounting Cycle

The work sheet helps accountants prepare the financial statements, make the adjusting entries, and close the accounts. First, let's prepare the financial statements.

Preparing the Financial Statements

The work sheet shows the amount of net income or net loss for the period, but we still must prepare the financial statements. ← Exhibit 4-7 shows the April financial statements for Gay Gillen eTravel (based on data from the work sheet in Exhibit 4-6). We can prepare Gillen's financial statements immediately after completing the work sheet.

Recording the Adjusting Entries

Adjusting the accounts requires journal entries and posting to the accounts. Panel A of Exhibit 4-8 repeats the April adjusting entries of Gay Gillen eTravel that we journalized in Chapter 3. Panel B shows the revenue and the expense

Exhibit 4-7

April Financial Statements of Gay Gillen eTravel

Gay Gillen eTravel
Income Statement
Month Ended April 30, 20X5

Revenue:		
Service revenue		$7,400
Expenses:		
Salary expense	$1,900	
Rent expense	1,000	
Utilities expense.	400	
Supplies expense	300	
Depreciation expense	275	
Total expenses	3,875	
Net income	$3,525	

Gay Gillen eTravel
Statement of Owner's Equity
Month Ended April 30, 20X5

Gay Gillen, capital, April 1, 20X5	$31,250
Add: Net income	3,525
	34,775
Less: Withdrawals	(3,200)
Gay Gillen, capital, April 30, 20X5	$31,575

Gay Gillen eTravel
Balance Sheet
April 30, 20X5

Assets			Liabilities		
Cash		$24,800	Accounts payable		$13,100
Accounts receivable		2,500	Salary payable..........		950
Supplies		400	Unearned service		
Prepaid rent............		2,000	revenue.............		300
Furniture	$16,500		Total liabilities..........		14,350
Less:					
Accumulated			**Owner's Equity**		
depreciation ..	(275)	16,225	Gay Gillen, capital		31,575
			Total liabilities and		
Total assets............		$45,925	owner's equity		$45,925

accounts after all adjustments have been posted. *Adj.* denotes an amount posted from an adjusting entry. The adjusting entries should be journalized after they are entered on the work sheet. Only the revenue and expense accounts are presented in the exhibit in order to focus on the closing process.

Accountants can use the work sheet to prepare monthly or quarterly statements without journalizing and posting the adjusting entries. Many companies journalize and post the adjusting entries (as in Exhibit 4-8) only once annually—at the end of the year.

| Exhibit 4-8 | Journalizing and Posting the Adjusting Entries |

PANEL A—Journalizing: Page 4

Adjusting Entries

Apr. 30	Accounts Receivable	250	
	Service Revenue		250
30	Supplies Expense	300	
	Supplies		300
30	Rent Expense	1,000	
	Prepaid Rent		1,000
30	Depreciation Expense	275	
	Accumulated Depreciation		275
30	Salary Expense	950	
	Salary Payable		950
30	Unearned Service Revenue	150	
	Service Revenue		150

PANEL B—Posting the Adjustments to the Revenue and Expense Accounts:

REVENUE   **EXPENSES**

Service Revenue

		7,000
	Adj.	250
	Adj.	150
	Bal.	7,400

Rent Expense

Adj.	1,000	
Bal.	1,000	

Salary Expense

	950	
Adj.	950	
Bal.	1,900	

Supplies Expense

Adj.	300	
Bal.	300	

Depreciation Expense

Adj.	275	
Bal.	275	

Utilities Expense

	400	
Bal.	400	

Adj. = Amount posted from an adjusting entry   Bal. = Balance

Close the revenue, expense, and withdrawal accounts

Closing the Accounts
Step in the accounting cycle at the end of the period. Closing the accounts consists of journalizing and posting the closing entries to set the balances of the revenue, expense, and withdrawal accounts to zero for the next period.

Temporary Accounts
The revenue and expense accounts that relate to a particular accounting period and are closed at the end of the period. For a proprietorship, the owner withdrawal account is also temporary.

Permanent Accounts
Accounts that are *not* closed at the end of the period—the asset, liability, and capital accounts.

Closing the Accounts

Closing the accounts is the end-of-period process that gets the accounts ready for the next period. Closing consists of journalizing and posting the closing entries. The closing process zeroes out all the revenues and all the expenses in order to measure each period's net income separately from all other periods.

Recall that the income statement reports net income for only one period. For example, net income for the Chicago Cubs baseball organization for 2005 relates exclusively to 2005. At December 31, 2005, the Chicago Cubs' accountants close the company's revenue and expense accounts for that year. The revenue and expense account balances relate to only one accounting period and are therefore closed at the end of the period (December 31, 2005). For this reason, revenues and expenses are called **temporary accounts**. For example, Gay Gillen's balance of Service Revenue at April 30, 20X5, is $7,400. This balance relates exclusively to April and must be zeroed out before Gillen records revenue for May.

The owner's Withdrawal account is also a temporary account because it measures the owner's withdrawals for only one period. The Withdrawals account is also closed at the end of the period.

To better understand the closing process, contrast the temporary accounts with the **permanent accounts**—the asset, liability, and capital accounts. The asset, liability, and capital accounts are *not* closed at the end of the period because their balances are not used to measure income. Consider Cash, Accounts Receivable, Accounts Payable, and Gay Gillen, Capital. These accounts do not represent business *activity* for a single period, so they are not closed at the end of the period. Their balances carry over to the next period. For example, the Cash balance at December

31, 20X5, becomes the beginning balance for 20X6. The Accounts Receivable balance at December 31, 20X5, becomes the beginning balance for 20X6. The same is true for all the other assets, all the liabilities, and the owner's capital account.

Closing entries transfer the revenue, expense, and owner withdrawal balances to the capital account. As you know,

Closing Entries
Entries that transfer the revenue, expense, and owner withdrawal balances to the capital account.

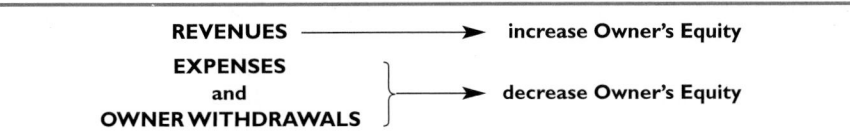

Posting the closing entries transfers all the revenues, all the expenses, and the owner's withdrawals to the Capital account.

As an intermediate step, the revenues and the expenses are transferred first to an account titled **Income Summary**. This temporary account collects the sum of all the expenses (a debit) and the sum of all the revenues (a credit). The Income Summary account is like a "holding tank." The balance of Income Summary is then transferred to capital. Exhibit 4-9 gives a picture of the closing process. Observe that Owner's Capital is the final account in the closing process.

Income Summary
A temporary "holding tank" account into which revenues and expenses are transferred prior to their final transfer to the capital account.

The Closing Process

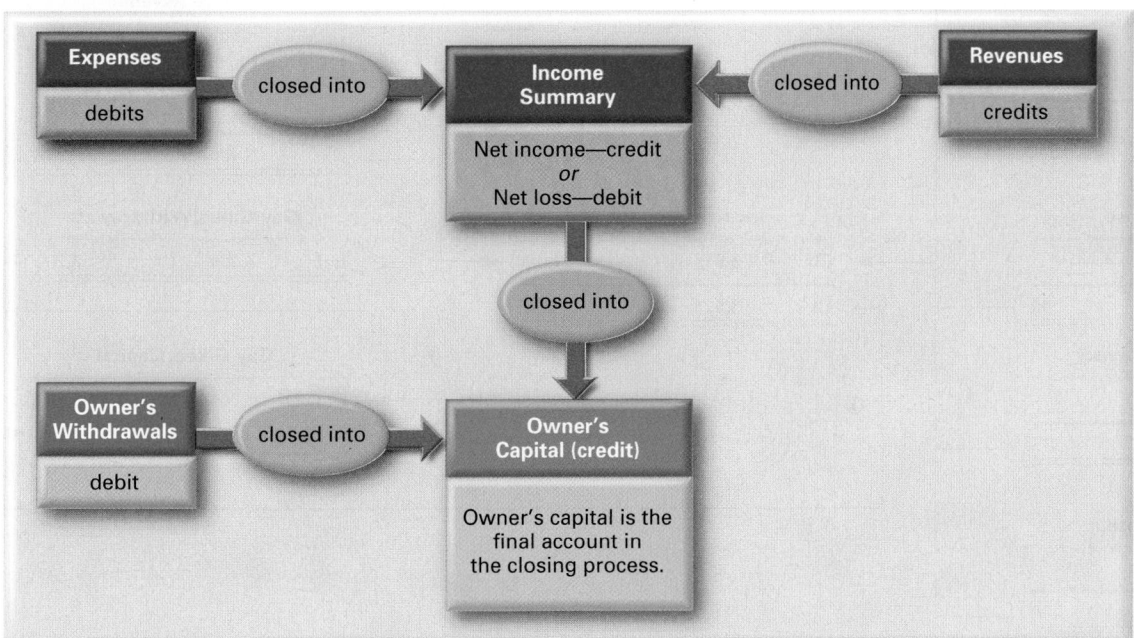

CLOSING STEPS   The steps in closing the books follow (the circled numbers are keyed to Exhibit 4-10).

① Debit each *revenue* account for the amount of its credit balance. Credit Income Summary for the total of the revenues. This closing entry transfers total revenues to the *credit* side of Income Summary.

② Credit each *expense* account for the amount of its debit balance. Debit Income Summary for the total of the expenses. This closing entry transfers total expenses to the *debit* side of Income Summary.

③ The Income Summary account now holds the net income (or net loss) of the period, but only for a moment. To close net income, we debit Income Summary for the amount of its *credit balance,* and credit the Capital account. This closing entry transfers net income to the owner's Capital account.

Exhibit 4-10 Journalizing and Posting the Closing Entries

PANEL A—Journalizing   Page 5

Closing Entries

①	Apr. 30	Service Revenue	7,400	
		Income Summary.....................		7,400
②	30	Income Summary	3,875	
		Rent Expense		1,000
		Salary Expense......................		1,900
		Supplies Expense....................		300
		Depreciation Expense		275
		Utilities Expense		400
③	30	Income Summary ($7,400 – $3,875)	3,525	
		Gay Gillen, Capital		3,525
④	30	Gay Gillen, Capital.......................	3,200	
		Gay Gillen, Withdrawals		3,200

PANEL B—Posting

Rent Expense

Adj.	1,000		
Bal.	1,000	Clo.	1,000

Salary Expense

	950		
Adj.	950		
Bal.	1,900	Clo.	1,900

Supplies Expense

Adj.	300		
Bal.	300	Clo.	300

Depreciation Expense

Adj.	275		
Bal.	275	Clo.	275

Utilities Expense

	400		
Bal.	400	Clo.	400

Income Summary

② Clo.	3,875	Clo.	7,400
Clo.	3,525	Bal.	3,525

Service Revenue

			7,000
		Adj.	250
		Adj.	150
Clo.	7,400	Bal.	7,400

Gay Gillen, Withdrawals

Bal.	3,200	Clo.	3,200

Gay Gillen, Capital

Clo.	3,200		31,250
		Clo.	3,525
		Bal.	31,575

Adj. = Amount posted from an adjusting entry   Clo. = Amount posted from a closing entry   Bal. = Balance

✔ Starter 4-4
✔ Starter 4-5
✔ Starter 4-6
✔ Starter 4-7

④   Credit the *Withdrawals* account for the amount of its debit balance. Debit the owner's Capital account. This entry transfers the owner's withdrawals to the *debit* side of the Capital account.

These steps are best illustrated with an example. Suppose Gay Gillen closes the books at the end of April. Exhibit 4-10 shows the complete closing process for Gillen's travel agency. Panel A gives the closing journal entries, and Panel B shows the accounts after posting.

After the closing entries, Gay Gillen, Capital ends with a balance of $31,575. Trace this balance to the statement of owner's equity and also to the balance sheet in Exhibit 4-7.

CLOSING A NET LOSS What would the closing entries be if Gillen's travel agency had suffered a net *loss* during April? Suppose expenses totaled $7,700 and revenues remained $7,400. In that case, Gillen's business suffered a net loss of $300 for April. The loss shows up as a debit balance in Income Summary, as follows:

Income Summary

Clo.	7,700	Clo.	7,400
Bal.	300		

Closing entry ③ would then credit Income Summary and debit Gay Gillen, Capital, as follows:

③ Apr. 30	Gay Gillen, Capital	....	300	
	Income Summary.............			300

Then Income Summary would be closed out and Gay Gillen, Capital has its ending balance, as follows:

Income Summary

Clo.	7,700	Clo.	7,400
Bal.	300	Clo.	300

Gay Gillen, Capital

Clo.	300	31,250

Finally, the Withdrawals balance would be closed to Capital, as before. The double underline in an account means that the account has a zero balance; nothing more will be posted to the account in the current period.

Postclosing Trial Balance

The accounting cycle can end with a **postclosing trial balance** (Exhibit 4-11). This optional step lists the accounts and their adjusted balances after closing.

Postclosing Trial Balance
List of the accounts and their balances at the end of the period after journalizing and posting the closing entries. This last step of the accounting cycle ensures that the ledger is in balance to start the next accounting period.

Exhibit 4-11

Postclosing Trial Balance

✔ **Starter 4-8**

Gay Gillen eTravel
Postclosing Trial Balance
April 30, 20X5

Cash	$24,800	
Accounts receivable	2,500	
Supplies	400	
Prepaid Rent	2,000	
Furniture	16,500	
Accumulated depreciation		$ 275
Accounts payable		13,100
Salary payable		950
Unearned service revenue		300
Gay Gillen, capital		31,575
Total	$46,200	$46,200

Only assets, liabilities, and capital appear on the postclosing trial balance. No temporary accounts—revenues, expenses, or withdrawal accounts—are included because they have been closed. The ledger is up-to-date and ready for the next period's transactions.

Reversing entries are special journal entries that key off the adjustments at the end of the period. Reversing entries ease the accounting of the next period. They are optional, and we cover them in the appendix at the end of this chapter.

Reversing Entries
Special journal entries that ease the burden of accounting for transactions in the next period.

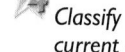

Student Resource CD

classified balance sheet, current assets, current liabilities, long-term liabilities

4 *Classify assets and liabilities as current or long-term*

Liquidity
Measure of how quickly an item can be converted to cash.

Current Asset
An asset that is expected to be converted to cash, sold, or consumed during the next 12 months, or within the business's normal operating cycle if the cycle is longer than a year.

Operating Cycle
Time span during which cash is paid for goods and services, which are then sold to customers from whom the business collects cash.

Long-Term Asset
An asset other than a current asset.

Plant or Fixed Asset
Another name for property, plant, and equipment.

Current Liability
A debt due to be paid with cash or with goods and services within one year or within the entity's operating cycle if the cycle is longer than a year.

Long-Term Liability
A liability other than a current liability.

✔ **Starter 4-9**

Classifying Assets and Liabilities

Assets and liabilities are classified as either *current* or *long-term* to indicate their relative liquidity. **Liquidity** measures closeness to cash, which is the most liquid asset. Accounts receivable is a relatively liquid asset because the receivables will be collected in the near future. Supplies are less liquid than receivables, and furniture and buildings are even less liquid because of their long lives.

Managers are interested in liquidity because business difficulties arise from a shortage of cash. How quickly can Amazon.com convert an asset to cash? How soon must Amazon pay a liability? These are questions of liquidity. A classified balance sheet helps to answer these questions.

Assets

CURRENT ASSETS   **Current assets** will be converted to cash, sold, or used up during the next 12 months or within the business's normal operating cycle if the cycle is longer than a year. The **operating cycle** is the time span during which

1. Cash is used to acquire goods and services.
2. These goods and services are sold to customers.
3. The business collects cash.

For most businesses, the operating cycle is a few months. Cash, Accounts Receivable, Notes Receivable due within a year or less, and Prepaid Expenses are current assets. Merchandising entities such as Intel, Sears, and Dell Computer have another current asset: Inventory. Inventory holds the cost of the goods the business is holding for sale to customers.

LONG-TERM ASSETS   **Long-term assets** are all assets other than current assets. One category of long-term assets is **plant assets** (also called **fixed assets**). Another name for plant assets is Property, Plant, and Equipment. Land, Buildings, Furniture and Fixtures, and Equipment are plant assets. Of these, Gay Gillen eTravel has only Furniture.

Other categories of long-term assets include Long-Term Investments and Other Assets (a catchall category). We discuss these categories in later chapters.

Liabilities

Business owners and managers need to know when they must pay their liabilities. Liabilities that must be paid immediately create a strain on cash. Therefore, the balance sheet lists liabilities in the order in which they must be paid. Balance sheets report two liability categories: *current liabilities* and *long-term liabilities*.

CURRENT LIABILITIES   **Current liabilities** must be paid with cash or with goods and services within one year or within the entity's operating cycle if the cycle is longer than a year. Accounts Payable, Notes Payable due within one year, Salary Payable, Unearned Revenue, and Interest Payable are current liabilities.

LONG-TERM LIABILITIES   All liabilities that are not current are classified as **long-term liabilities**. Many notes payable are payable after one year or the entity's operating cycle if the cycle is longer than a year. Some notes payable are paid in installments, with the first installment due within one year, the second installment due the second year, and so on. The first installment is a current liability, and the remaining installments are long-term liabilities. A $100,000 note payable to be paid $10,000 per year over 10 years would include:

■ A current liability of $10,000 for next year's payment, and
■ A long-term liability of $90,000.

A Detailed Balance Sheet

Thus far we have presented the *unclassified* balance sheet of Gay Gillen eTravel. Now we move up to the form of the balance sheet actually used in practice — called a classified balance sheet. Exhibit 4-12 presents Gillen's classified balance sheet.

Exhibit 4-12

Classified Balance Sheet of Gay Gillen eTravel

Gay Gillen eTravel
Balance Sheet
April 30, 20X5

Assets			Liabilities		
Current assets:			**Current liabilities:**		
Cash		$24,800	Accounts payable		$13,100
Accounts receivable		2,500	Salary payable		950
Supplies		400	Unearned service revenue		300
Prepaid rent		2,000	Total current liabilities		14,350
Total current assets		29,700	Long-term liabilities (None)		0
Fixed assets:			Total liabilities		14,350
Furniture	$16,500				
Less: Accumulated			**Owner's Equity**		
depreciation	(275)	16,225	Gay Gillen, capital		31,575
			Total liabilities and		
Total assets		$45,925	owner's equity		$45,925

Gillen classifies each asset and each liability as current or long-term. She could have labeled fixed assets as *long-term assets*, or as *plant assets*.

The classified balance sheet in Exhibit 4-12 reports more information—totals for current assets and current liabilities, which do not appear on an unclassified balance sheet. This is why actual balance sheets always classify the assets and the liabilities.

Why is the classified balance sheet in Exhibit 4-12 more useful than an unclassified balance sheet (Exhibit 4-7) to (a) Gay Gillen and (b) a banker considering whether to lend $10,000 to Gillen?

Answer: A classified balance sheet indicates to Gillen and a banker

- Which of Gillen's liabilities, and the dollar amounts, that Gillen must pay within the next year
- Which of Gillen's assets are the most liquid and thus available to pay the liabilities
- Which assets and liabilities are long-term

Exhibit 4-13 presents a detailed balance sheet. To illustrate, we use the actual balance sheet of Dell Computer Corporation. You can understand all of Dell's account titles. Among the Current Assets are Short-term investments, which are investments that Dell expects to sell within one year. These assets are very liquid, which is why they come immediately after cash. Dell also reports inventory for the computers the company sells. And Dell has several different types of plant (fixed) assets. Everything else on Dell's balance sheet is similar to that of Gay Gillen eTravel.

Balance Sheet Forms

The balance sheet of Dell Computer in Exhibit 4-13 lists the assets at the top and the liabilities and owner equity below. This arrangement is known as the *report form*. The balance sheet of Gay Gillen eTravel in Exhibit 4-7 lists the assets at the left and the liabilities and the owner's equity at the right. That arrangement is known as the *account form*. Either form is acceptable; the report form used by Dell is more popular.

Exhibit 4-13

Dell Computer's
Classified Balance Sheet

Dell Computer Corporation

Balance Sheet (Adapted)
January 31, 2002

Assets

		(millions)
Current assets:		
Cash..		$ 3,641
Short-term investments........................		273
Accounts receivable............................		2,269
Inventories		278
Prepaid expenses..............................		1,416
Total current assets		7,877
Property, plant, and equipment:		
Land and buildings	$ 374	
Computer equipment	627	
Machinery and other equipment..................	437	
Total cost of property, plant, and equipment........	1,438	
Less: Accumulated depreciation	(612)	
Property, plant, and equipment, net		826
Other assets..................................		4,832
Total assets		$13,535

Liabilities

Current liabilities:	
Accounts payable.............................	$ 5,075
Salary payable	384
Taxes payable	264
Unearned revenue	322
Other current liabilities.......................	1,474
Total current liabilities......................	7,519
Long-term notes payable	520
Other long-term liabilities	802
Total liabilities	8,841

Owner Equity

Owner capital....................................	4,694
Total liabilities and owner equity	$13,535

✔ **Starter 4-10**

☐ The Accounting Cycle
☐ The Work Sheet
☐ Completing the Cycle
☐ Classifying Assets and
   Liabilities
■ **Accounting Ratios**
☐ Appendix: Reversing Entries

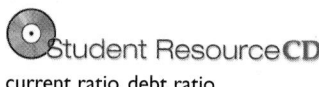

Student Resource**CD**

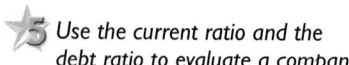

current ratio, debt ratio

⭐ *Use the current ratio and the
debt ratio to evaluate a company*

Current Ratio
Current assets divided by current
liabilities. Measures the company's
ability to pay current liabilities from
current assets.

Accounting Ratios

Accounting is designed to provide information for decision making by business owners, managers, and lenders. A bank considering lending money to Gay Gillen must predict whether she can repay the loan. If Gillen already has a lot of debt, repayment is less certain than if she doesn't owe much money. To measure Gillen's (or **Dell Computer's**) financial position, decision makers use ratios that they compute from the company's financial statements. Two of the most widely used decision aids in business are the current ratio and the debt ratio.

Current Ratio

The **current ratio** measures a company's ability to pay its current liabilities. This ratio is computed as follows:

$$\text{Current ratio} = \frac{\text{Total current assets}}{\text{Total current liabilities}}$$

A company prefers to have a high current ratio because that means it has plenty of current assets to pay current liabilities. An increasing current ratio indicates improvement in ability to pay current debts.

A rule of thumb: A strong current ratio is 1.50, which indicates that the company has $1.50 in current assets for every $1.00 in current liabilities. A company with a current ratio of 1.50 would probably have little trouble paying its current liabilities. Most successful businesses operate with a current ratio of 1.50 or more. A current ratio of 1.00 is considered low.

> Compute **Dell Computer's** current ratio. Use the company's balance sheet in Exhibit 4-13 and show dollar amounts in millions.
>
> *Answer:* $\text{Current} = \dfrac{\text{Total current assets}}{\text{Total current liabilities}} = \dfrac{\$7,877}{\$7,519} = 1.05$
>
> How much in current assets does Dell have for every dollar the company owes in current liabilities?
>
> *Answer:* $1.05
>
> Is Dell's current ratio high or low? Is this ratio value risky?
>
> *Answer:* Dell's current ratio is low, which makes it look risky. However, Dell operates successfully with a low current ratio because the company sells computers so fast.

Debt Ratio

A second decision aid is the **debt ratio**, which measures overall ability to pay debts. The debt ratio is computed as follows:

$$\text{Debt ratio} = \frac{\text{Total liabilities}}{\text{Total assets}}$$

Debt Ratio
Ratio of total liabilities to total assets. Tells the proportion of a company's assets that it has financed with debt.

The debt ratio indicates the proportion of a company's assets that are financed with debt. This ratio measures a business's overall ability to pay both current and long-term debts—total liabilities. The debt ratio measures debt-paying ability differently than the current ratio.

A *low* debt ratio is safer than a high debt ratio. Why? Because a company with low liabilities has low required payments. This company is unlikely to get into financial difficulty. By contrast, a business with a high debt ratio may have trouble paying its liabilities. When a company fails to pay its debts, the creditors can take the business away from its owner. The largest retail bankruptcy in history, Federated Department Stores, the parent company of Bloomingdale's, was due to high debt during an economic recession. People put off clothing purchases. Federated couldn't weather the downturn and had to declare bankruptcy.

A rule of thumb: A debt ratio below 0.60, or 60%, is considered safe for most businesses. A debt ratio above 0.80, or 80%, borders on high risk. Most companies have debt ratios in the range of 0.60 to 0.80.

✔ Starter 4-11

✔ Starter 4-12

> We saw that **Dell Computer** has a low current ratio, but Dell nevertheless operates successfully (profits are high, cash is plentiful, and the company grows steadily). Now compute Dell's debt ratio from the company's balance sheet in Exhibit 4-13. Show dollar amounts in millions.
>
> *Answer:* $\text{Debt ratio} = \dfrac{\text{Total liabilities}}{\text{Total assets}} = \dfrac{\$8,841}{\$13,535} = 0.65, \text{ or } 65\%$
>
> For each dollar of its total assets, how much does Dell owe in total liabilities?
>
> *Answer:* $0.65
>
> What percentage of Dell's total assets is financed with debt?
>
> *Answer:* 0.65, or 65%
>
> If you owed $0.65 for every dollar of your total assets, would you worry about your ability to pay your debts?
>
> *Answer:* Probably not. A debt ratio of 65% is pretty safe.

Dell Computer Corp.: Where Customer Focus Equals Solid Financials

Michael Dell dropped out of The University of Texas in 1984 to start **Dell Computer Corporation**. As he puts it, "My parents were upset, until I showed them my first financial statement." Dell began with $1,000 in seed money, and it was profitable from day one.

Today Dell is No. 1 in desktop PCs, No. 1 in the United States in low-end servers, and the country's No. 1 Internet retailer. Even with the PC industry in a slump, the company is on track to earn $2 billion net income in 2003. And while many technology stocks fell 80% from their 2000 peak, Dell's was down just 8% in 2002.

One of the main reasons Michael Dell was featured in *Business Week's* January 13, 2003, issue as one of "The Best Managers of the Year" is that he does not let the market valuation of his business cloud his vision. "There are two pieces of financials," says Dell. "One is the market's interpretation . . . stock price [and] credit ratings. Another is financial results. We don't have control of the market's reaction. We can focus on [keeping] our costs in line and [on having] the right mix of products." This focus fits with the company's mandate: ". . . The most important thing is to satisfy our customers. The second most important is to be profitable. If we don't do the first one well, the second one won't happen."

Dell has made a science of shaving costs from the PC-assembly process. Its process is so efficient that it rarely needs more than two hours' worth of parts inventory. Parts storage takes up a space no larger than your bedroom. Operating costs ate up only 10% of Dell's $35 billion revenue in 2002—compared with 21% at **Hewlett-Packard**, 25% at **Gateway**, and 46% at **Cisco**.

The direct-to-customer model has worked so well in PCs that Michael Dell wants to expand it into several other product lines, such as handhelds, servers, and storage systems. He knows that PCs alone will not keep his profit machine growing. Hewlett-Packard, Gateway, Cisco, and **IBM**: Watch out!

Based on: Kathryn Jones, "The Dell Way," *Business 2.0,* February 2003, www.business2.com/articles/mag/. Anonymous, "Michael Dell, Dell Computer," *Business Week,* January 13, 2003, p. 62. Del Jones, "Dell: Take Time to Build; Computer Chief Says Company Puts Its Focus on Customers," *USA Today,* October 10, 2002, p. B.06.

Managing Both the Current Ratio and the Debt Ratio

In general,

- A *high* current ratio is preferable to a low current ratio.
- A *low* debt ratio is preferable to a high debt ratio.

Which ratio gives the more reliable signal? Experienced lenders and investors examine a large number of ratios over several years to spot trends and turning points. They also consider other factors, such as the company's trend of net income.

As you progress through your study of accounting, we will introduce key ratios that people use for decision making. Chapter 18 summarizes all the ratios discussed in this book. It provides an overview of the more common ratios used to evaluate the success of a business.

Now study the Decision Guidelines feature, which summarizes what you have learned in this chapter, and do the Excel Application Exercise.

Decision Guidelines

COMPLETING THE ACCOUNTING CYCLE

Suppose you own the **Chicago Cubs** baseball organization, or suppose you are Michael Dell, working hard to get **Dell Computer** off the ground. How can you measure the success of your business? The Decision Guidelines describe the accounting process you will use to provide the information for your decisions.

Decision	Guidelines
How (where) to summarize the effects of all the entity's transactions and adjustments throughout the period?	Accountant's *work sheet* with columns for • Trial balance • Income statement • Adjustments • Balance sheet • Adjusted trial balance
What is the last *major* step in the accounting cycle?	*Closing entries* for the *temporary accounts:* • Revenues ⎫ • Expenses ⎬ Income statement accounts • Owner's withdrawals
Why close out the revenues, expenses, and owner withdrawals?	Because these *temporary accounts* have balances that relate only to one accounting period and do *not* carry over to the next period.
Which accounts do *not* get closed out?	*Permanent (balance sheet) accounts:* • Assets • Owner's capital • Liabilities The balances of these accounts *do* carry over to the next period.
How do businesses classify their assets and liabilities for reporting on the balance sheet?	*Current* (within one year or the entity's operating cycle if longer than a year) *Long-term* (not current)
How do decision makers evaluate a company?	There are many ways, such as the company's net income (or net loss) on the income statement and the trend of net income from year to year. Another way to evaluate a company is based on the company's *financial ratios.* Two key ratios: $$\text{Current ratio} = \frac{\text{Total current assets}}{\text{Total current liabilities}}$$ The *current ratio* measures the ability to pay current liabilities with current assets. $$\text{Debt ratio} = \frac{\text{Total liabilities}}{\text{Total assets}}$$ The *debt ratio* measures the overall ability to pay liabilities. The debt ratio shows the proportion of the entity's assets that are financed with debt.

Excel Application Exercise

Goal: Create an Excel spreadsheet to calculate the current ratio and debt ratio for different companies, and use the results to answer questions about the companies. Requires Web research on **Amazon.com** and **Barnes & Noble.com**.

Scenario: You are deciding whether to buy the stock of two well-known online companies: Amazon.com and Barnes & Noble.com. You know that the current ratio and the debt ratio measure whether a company has the assets to cover its liabilities.

Your task is to create a simple spreadsheet to compare the current ratio and the debt ratio for each company. When done, answer these questions:

1. Do both companies have an acceptable current ratio? How can you tell?
2. Do both companies have an acceptable debt ratio? How can you tell?
3. What is the trend (up or down) for the ratios of both companies? Is the trend for each company positive or negative? Explain your answer.
4. Which company has the "better" current ratio? The "better" debt ratio?

Step-by-Step:

1. Locate the following current and prior-year information for Amazon.com and Barnes & Noble.com (found on the "Consolidated Balance Sheets"). For Amazon, use the annual report packaged with this text, or go to www.amazon.com, look under Services, click on "Investor Relations," then "Annual Reports." For Barnes & Noble.com, go to www.bn.com, click on "Investor Relations," then "Investor Information," and then "SEC Filings," and then "Annual Reports."
   a. Current Assets
   b. Total Assets

c. Current Liabilities
d. Long-Term Liabilities (You may have to compute this on the spreadsheet.)
e. Total Liabilities (You may have to compute this on the spreadsheet.)
f. Total Shareholders' Equity (Deficit)
g. Total Liabilities and Shareholders' Equity

2. Open a new Excel spreadsheet.
3. Create a bold-faced heading for your spreadsheet that contains the following:
   a. Chapter 4 Excel Application Exercise
   b. The Current Ratio and Debt Ratio
   c. Amazon.com and Barnes & Noble.com Comparison
   d. Today's date
4. Two rows down from your worksheet heading, create a column heading titled "Amazon.com (in 000's)." Make it bold and underline the heading.
5. One row down from Amazon's column heading, create a row with the following bold, underlined column titles:
   a. Account
   b. FYxx (xx = the most recent fiscal year, for example, 02)
   c. FYyy (yy = the prior fiscal year, for example, 01)
6. Starting with the "Account" column heading, enter the data found in No. 1, above. You should have seven rows of data, with row descriptions (for example, "Current Assets"). Format the columns as necessary.
7. Skip a row at the end of your data, and then create a row titled "Current Ratio" and another row titled "Debt Ratio."
8. Enter the formula for each ratio in the "FYxx" and "FYyy" columns. You should have four formulas. Make both rows bold.
9. Repeat steps 4 through 8, substituting the Barnes & Noble.com title and data as appropriate.
10. Save your work to disk, and print a copy for your files.

○ END-OF-CHAPTER *Summary Problem*

CHECK YOUR RESOURCES

Refer to the data in the Mid-Chapter Summary Problem (Clay Employment Services, page 145–146).

Required

1. Journalize and post the adjusting entries. (Before posting to the accounts, enter into each account its balance as shown in the trial balance. For example, enter the $370,000 balance in the Accounts Receivable account before posting its adjusting entry.) Key adjusting entries by *letter*, as shown in the work sheet solution to the Mid-Chapter Summary Problem. You can take the adjusting entries straight from the work sheet on page 146.
2. Journalize and post the closing entries. (Each account should carry its balance as shown in the adjusted trial balance.) To distinguish closing entries from adjusting entries, key the closing entries by *number*. Draw arrows to illustrate the flow of data, as shown in Exhibit 4-10. Indicate the balance of the Capital account after the closing entries are posted.
3. Prepare the income statement for the year ended December 31, 20X9. List Miscellaneous Expense last among the expenses, a common practice.
4. Prepare the statement of owner's equity for the year ended December 31, 20X9. Draw an arrow linking the income statement to the statement of owner's equity.

5. Prepare the classified balance sheet at December 31, 20X9. Use the report form. All liabilities are current. Draw an arrow linking the statement of owner's equity to the balance sheet.

Solution

Requirement 1

Adjusting Entries

a.	Dec. 31	Supplies Expense.....................................	4,000	
		Supplies...		4,000
b.	31	Depreciation Expense—Furniture and Fixtures	20,000	
		Accumulated Depreciation—Furniture and Fixtures. .		20,000
c.	31	Depreciation Expense—Building.....................	10,000	
		Accumulated Depreciation—Building..............		10,000
d.	31	Salary Expense......................................	5,000	
		Salary Payable		5,000
e.	31	Accounts Receivable.................................	12,000	
		Service Revenue.................................		12,000
f.	31	Unearned Service Revenue	32,000	
		Service Revenue................................		32,000

Accounts Receivable			**Supplies**			**Accumulated Depreciation— Furniture and Fixtures**			**Accumulated Depreciation—Building**	
370,000			6,000	(a) 4,000			40,000			130,000
(e) 12,000						(b)	20,000		(c)	10,000

Salary Payable		**Unearned Service Revenue**			**Service Revenue**	
	(d) 5,000	(f) 32,000	45,000			286,000
					(e)	12,000
					(f)	32,000
					Bal.	330,000

Salary Expense		**Supplies Expense**		**Depreciation Expense— Furniture and Fixtures**		**Depreciation Expense—Building**	
172,000		(a) 4,000		(b) 20,000		(c) 10,000	
(d) 5,000		Bal. 4,000		Bal. 20,000		Bal. 10,000	
Bal. 177,000							

Requirement 2

Closing Entries

1.	Dec. 31	Service Revenue	330,000	
		Income Summary............................		330,000
2.	31	Income Summary...............................	224,000	
		Salary Expense		177,000
		Supplies Expense		4,000
		Depreciation Expense—Furniture and Fixtures .		20,000
		Depreciation Expense—Building		10,000
		Miscellaneous Expense		13,000
3.	31	Income Summary ($330,000 – $224,000)............	106,000	
		Capital		106,000
4.	31	Capital	65,000	
		Withdrawals		65,000

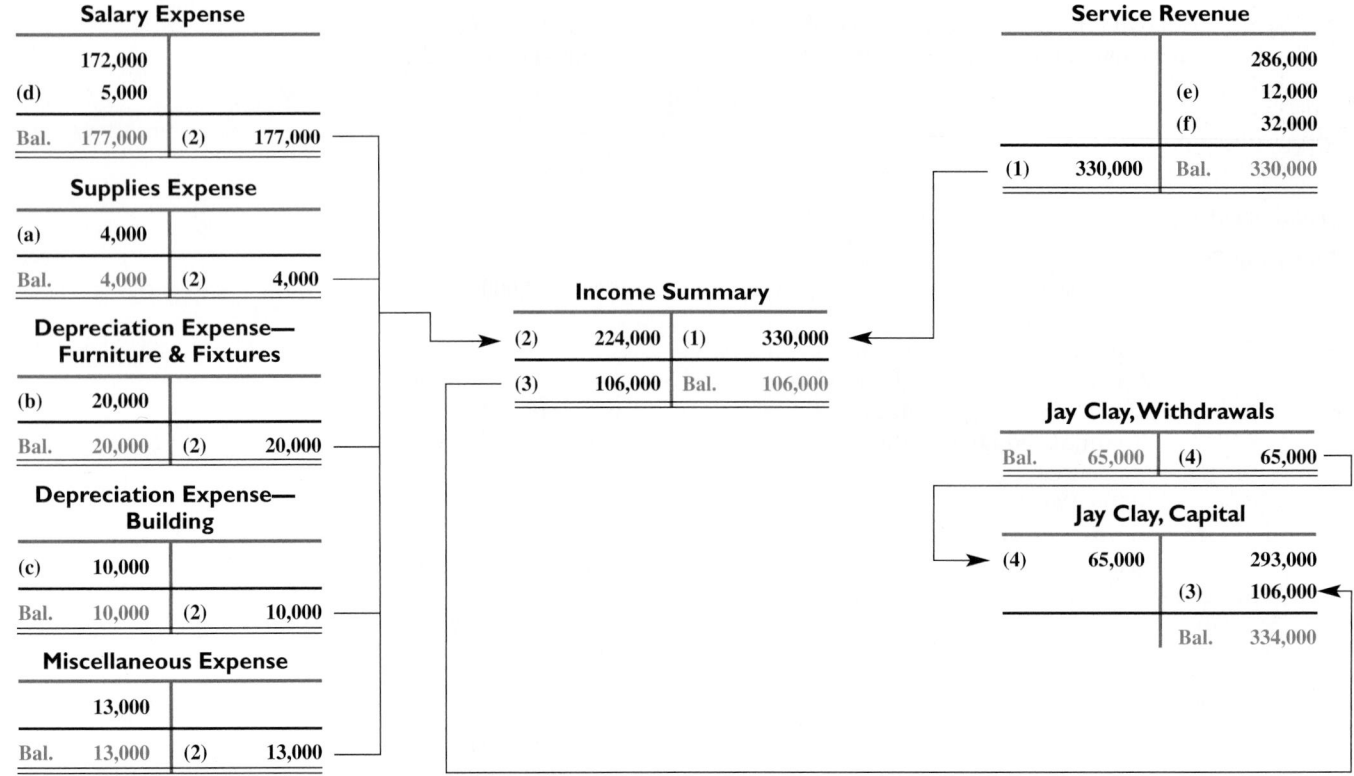

Salary Expense

	172,000		
(d)	5,000		
Bal.	177,000	(2)	177,000

Supplies Expense

(a)	4,000		
Bal.	4,000	(2)	4,000

Depreciation Expense—Furniture & Fixtures

(b)	20,000		
Bal.	20,000	(2)	20,000

Depreciation Expense—Building

(c)	10,000		
Bal.	10,000	(2)	10,000

Miscellaneous Expense

	13,000		
Bal.	13,000	(2)	13,000

Income Summary

(2)	224,000	(1)	330,000
(3)	106,000	Bal.	106,000

Service Revenue

			286,000
		(e)	12,000
		(f)	32,000
(1)	330,000	Bal.	330,000

Jay Clay, Withdrawals

Bal.	65,000	(4)	65,000

Jay Clay, Capital

(4)	65,000		293,000
		(3)	106,000
		Bal.	334,000

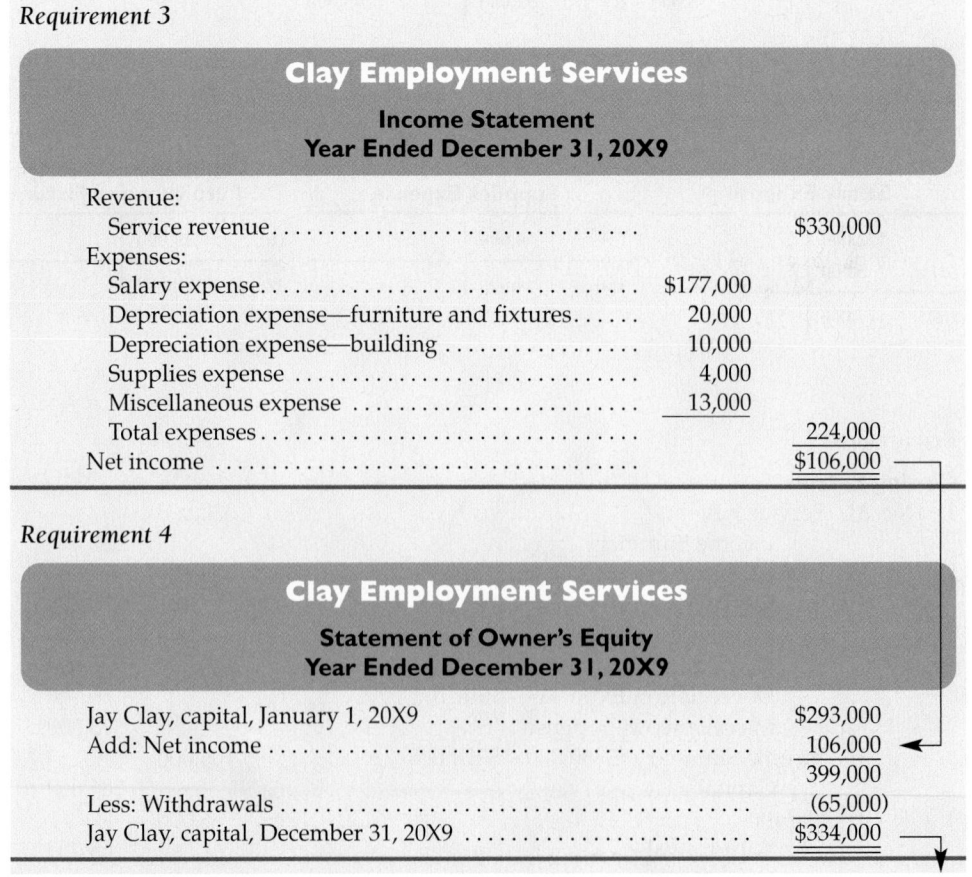

Requirement 3

Clay Employment Services

Income Statement
Year Ended December 31, 20X9

Revenue:		
Service revenue...............................		$330,000
Expenses:		
Salary expense.................................	$177,000	
Depreciation expense—furniture and fixtures......	20,000	
Depreciation expense—building	10,000	
Supplies expense	4,000	
Miscellaneous expense	13,000	
Total expenses................................		224,000
Net income		$106,000

Requirement 4

Clay Employment Services

Statement of Owner's Equity
Year Ended December 31, 20X9

Jay Clay, capital, January 1, 20X9	$293,000
Add: Net income	106,000
	399,000
Less: Withdrawals	(65,000)
Jay Clay, capital, December 31, 20X9	$334,000

Requirement 5

Clay Employment Services

Balance Sheet
December 31, 20X9

Assets

Current assets:

Cash	$198,000
Accounts receivable	382,000
Supplies	2,000
Total current assets	582,000

Long-term assets:

Furniture and fixtures	$100,000	
Less: Accumulated depreciation	(60,000)	40,000
Building	$250,000	
Less: Accumulated depreciation	(140,000)	110,000
Total assets		$732,000

Liabilities

Current liabilities:

Accounts payable	$380,000
Salary payable	5,000
Unearned service revenue	13,000
Total current liabilities	398,000

Owner's Equity

Jay Clay, capital	334,000
Total liabilities and owner's equity	$732,000

REVIEW *Completing the Accounting Cycle*

Quick Check

1. Consider the steps in the accounting cycle in Exhibit 4-1, page 141. Which part of the accounting cycle provides information to help a bank decide whether to lend money to a company?
   a. Financial statements
   b. Adjusting entries
   c. Closing entries
   d. Postclosing trial balance

2. Which columns of the accounting work sheet show unadjusted amounts?
   a. Trial balance
   b. Adjustments
   c. Income Statement
   d. Balance Sheet

3. Which columns of the work sheet show net income?
   a. Adjusted Trial Balance
   b. Income Statement
   c. Balance Sheet
   d. Both b and c

4. Which situation indicates a net loss on the income statement?
   a. Total debits equal total credits
   b. Total debits exceed total credits
   c. Total credits exceed total debits
   d. None of the above

5. Assume that Supplies has a $6,000 unadjusted balance on the Trial Balance of **Dell Computer's** accounting work sheet. At year-end Dell counts supplies of $2,000. What adjustment will appear on Dell's work sheet?

a.	Supplies	4,000	
	Supplies Expense		4,000
b.	Supplies Expense	4,000	
	Supplies		4,000
c.	Supplies Expense	2,000	
	Supplies		2,000

   d. No adjustment is needed because the Supplies account already has a correct balance.

6. Which of the following accounts is not closed?
    a. Salary Expense
    b. Service Revenue
    c. Accumulated Depreciation
    d. Owner, Withdrawals

7. What do closing entries accomplish?
    a. Transfer revenues, expenses, and owner withdrawals to the capital account
    b. Zero out the revenues, expenses, and owner withdrawals to prepare these accounts for the next period
    c. Bring the capital account to its correct ending balance
    d. All of the above

8. Which of the following is not a closing entry?
    a. Income Summary XXX
          Rent Expense.   XXX
    b. Salary Payable. XXX
          Income Summary . .   XXX
    c. Service Revenue XXX
          Income Summary   XXX
    d. Owner, Capital XXX
          Owner, Withdrawals . .   XXX

9. Assets and liabilities are listed on the balance sheet in order of their
    a. Purchase date
    b. Liquidity
    c. Market value
    d. Adjustments

10. Examine Gay Gillen eTravel's classified balance sheet in Exhibit 4-12, page 153. Gillen's current ratio at April 30, 20X5, is
    a. 3.20
    b. 0.31
    c. 0.48
    d. 2.07

Accounting Vocabulary

accounting cycle (p. 140)
closing the accounts (p. 148)
closing entries (p. 149)
current asset (p. 152)
current liability (p. 152)
current ratio (p. 154)
debt ratio (p. 155)

fixed asset (p. 152)
Income Summary (p. 149)
liquidity (p. 152)
long-term asset (p. 152)
long-term liability (p. 152)
operating cycle (p. 152)
permanent accounts (p. 148)

plant asset (p. 152)
postclosing trial balance (p. 151)
reversing entries (p. 151)
temporary accounts (p. 148)
work sheet (p. 142)

⬤ASSESS *Your Progress*

See *www.prenhall.com/horngren*
for selected Starters, Exercises,
and Problems.

Explaining items on the work sheet
(Obj. 1)

Explaining items on the work sheet
(Obj. 1, 2)

Starters

S4-1 ← *Link Back to Chapter 3 (Adjusting Entries).* Return to the trial balance in Exhibit 4-2 on the acetate pages. In your own words, explain why the following accounts must be adjusted:

a. Salary payable
b. Unearned service revenue
c. Supplies
d. Prepaid rent
e. Accumulated depreciation

S4-2 ← *Link Back to Chapters 1, 2, and 3 (Definitions of Accounts).* Examine the Adjusted Trial Balance columns of Exhibit 4-4 on the acetate pages. Explain what the following items mean:

a. Accounts receivable
b. Supplies
c. Prepaid rent
d. Furniture
e. Accumulated depreciation
f. Accounts payable
g. Unearned service revenue
h. Service revenue
i. Rent expense

S4-3 Consider the Income Statement columns and the Balance Sheet columns of the work sheet in Exhibit 4-6 on the acetate pages. Answer the following questions:

Using the work sheet
(Obj. 1, 2)

1. What type of balance does the Owner's Capital account have—debit or credit?
2. Which Income Statement account has the same type of balance as the Capital account?
3. Which Income Statement accounts have the opposite type of balance?
4. What do we call the difference between total debits and total credits on the Income Statement? Into what account is the difference figure closed at the end of the period?

S4-4 Study Exhibit 4-5 on the acetate pages.

Making closing entries
(Obj. 3)

1. Journalize the closing entries for
   a. Owner's withdrawals
   b. Service revenue
   c. All the expenses (make a single closing entry for all the expenses)
   d. Income Summary
2. Set up all the T-accounts affected by requirement 1 and insert their adjusted balances (denote as *Bal.*) at April 30. Also set up a T-account for Income Summary. Post the closing entries to the accounts, denoting posted amounts as *Clo.*

S4-5 This exercise should be used in conjunction with Starter 4-4.

Analyzing the overall effect of the closing entries on the owner's capital account
(Obj. 3)

1. Return to Exhibit 4-5 on the acetate pages. Without making any closing entries or using any T-accounts, compute the ending balance of Gay Gillen, Capital.
2. Trace Gay Gillen's ending capital balance to its two appropriate places in Exhibit 4-7 (page 147). In which two financial statements do you find Gay Gillen, Capital? Where on each statement?

S4-6 Oracle Corporation reported the following items, adapted from its financial statements at May 31 (amounts in millions):

Making closing entries
(Obj. 3)

Sales and marketing expense	$2,622	Cash	$1,786
Other assets	477	Service revenue	5,139
Interest expense	21	Accounts payable	284
Long-term liabilities	382	Accounts receivable	2,238

Make Oracle's closing entries, as needed, for these accounts.

S4-7 This exercise should be used in conjunction with Starter 4-6. Use the data in Starter 4-6 to set up T-accounts for those accounts that **Oracle Corporation** closed out at May 31. Insert their account balances prior to closing, post the closing entries to these accounts, and show each account's ending balance after closing. Also show the Income Summary T-account. Denote a balance as *Bal.* and a closing entry amount as *Clo.*

Posting closing entries
(Obj. 3)

S4-8 After closing its accounts at May 31, 20XX, **Oracle Corporation** had the following account balances (adapted) with amounts given in millions:

Preparing a postclosing trial balance
(Obj. 3)

Long-term liabilities	$ 518	Property	$ 988
Other assets	825	Cash	1,786
Accounts receivable	2,479	Service revenue	0
Total expenses	0	Owners' equity	3,695
Accounts payable	284	Other current assets	1,182
Other current liabilities	2,759	Short-term notes payable	4

Prepare Oracle's postclosing trial balance at May 31, 20XX. List accounts in proper order, as shown in Exhibit 4-11.

Classifying assets and liabilities as
current or long-term
(Obj. 4)

S4-9 **Lands' End** had sales of $1,320 million during the year ended January 31, 20X0, and total assets of $456 million at January 31, 20X0, the end of the company's fiscal year. The financial statements of Lands' End reported the following (all amounts in millions):

Sales revenue............	$1,320	Land and buildings........	$ 103
Inventory	162	Accounts payable..........	75
Receivables..............	18	Total expenses............	1,073
Interest expense...........	2	Accumulated depreciation..	117
Equipment	176	Accrued liabilities (such as	
Prepaid expenses..........	22	Salary payable)..........	44

1. Identify the assets (including contra assets) and liabilities.
2. Classify each asset and each liability as current or long-term.

Classifying assets and liabilities as
current or long-term
(Obj. 4)

S4-10 ← *Link Back to Chapter 3 (Book Value).* Examine **Dell Computer's** balance sheet in Exhibit 4-13. Identify or compute the following amounts for Dell:

a. Total current assets   d. Total long-term assets
b. Total current liabilities   e. Total long-term liabilities
c. Book value of Property, plant, and equipment

Computing the current ratio and the
debt ratio
(Obj. 5)

S4-11 Montez Printing Company has these account balances at December 31, 20X7:

Accounts payable	$ 5,000	Note payable, long-term....	$ 9,000
Accounts receivable	6,000	Prepaid rent	1,000
Cash....................	3,000	Salary payable	2,000
Depreciation expense......	4,000	Service revenue	31,000
Equipment	12,000	Supplies..................	2,000

Compute Montez's current ratio and debt ratio.

Computing and using the current ratio
and the debt ratio
(Obj. 5)

S4-12 This exercise should be used in conjunction with Starter 4-8. Use the postclosing trial balance that you prepared for Starter 4-8 to compute **Oracle Corporation's** current ratio and debt ratio.

1. How much in *current* assets does Oracle have for every dollar of *current* liabilities that it owes? What ratio measures this relationship?
2. What percentage of Oracle's total assets are financed with debt? What is the name of this ratio?
3. What percentage of Oracle's total assets do the owners of the company actually own?

Exercises

Preparing a work sheet
(Obj. 1)

E4-1 The trial balance of DaySpring Woodworking Service follows on page 165. Additional information at September 30, 20X6:

Student ResourceCD
spreadsheet
General Ledger, Peachtree, QuickBooks

a. Accrued service revenue, $600   d. Prepaid rent expired, $800
b. Depreciation, $100   e. Supplies used, $1,600
c. Accrued salary expense, $500

Required

Complete DaySpring's work sheet for the month ended September 30, 20X6. How much was net income for September?

Journalizing adjusting and closing entries
(Obj. 2, 3)

E4-2 Journalize DaySpring's adjusting and closing entries in Exercise 4-1.

DaySpring Woodworking Service		
Trial Balance September 30, 20X6		
Cash	$ 3,500	
Accounts receivable	3,400	
Prepaid rent	1,200	
Supplies	3,300	
Equipment	32,600	
Accumulated depreciation		$ 1,800
Accounts payable		3,600
Salary payable		
Gail Pfeiffer, capital		36,000
Gail Pfeiffer, withdrawals	2,000	
Service revenue		7,100
Depreciation expense		
Salary expense	1,800	
Rent expense		
Utilities expense	700	
Supplies expense		
Total	$48,500	$48,500

E4-3 Set up T-accounts for those accounts affected by the adjusting and closing entries in Exercise 4-2. Post the adjusting and closing entries to the accounts; denote adjustment amounts by *Adj.*, closing amounts by *Clo.*, and balances by *Bal.* Double underline the accounts with zero balances after you close them, and show the ending balance in each account.

Posting adjusting and closing entries **(Obj. 2, 3)**

Student ResourceCD

E4-4 After completing Exercises 4-1, 4-2, and 4-3, prepare the postclosing trial balance of DaySpring Woodworking Service at September 30, 20X6.

Preparing a postclosing trial balance **(Obj. 2)**

E4-5 ← *Link Back to Chapter 2 (Adjusting Entries).* Pioneer Travel's accounting records include the following account balances:

Adjusting the accounts **(Obj. 2)**

	December 31,	
	20X1	20X2
Prepaid insurance	$1,400	$1,600
Unearned service revenue	4,100	3,100

During 20X2, Pioneer recorded the following:

a. Paid the annual insurance premium of $4,800.
b. Made the year-end adjustment to record insurance expense for the year. You must compute this amount.
c. Collected $17,000 cash in advance for service revenue to be earned later.
d. Made the year-end adjustment to record the earning of $18,000 service revenue that had been collected in advance.

Required

1. Set up T-accounts for Prepaid Insurance, Insurance Expense, Unearned Service Revenue, and Service Revenue. Insert beginning and ending balances for Prepaid Insurance and Unearned Service Revenue.
2. Journalize entries a through d above, and post to the T-accounts. Explanations are not required. Ensure that the ending balances for Prepaid Insurance and Unearned Service Revenue agree with the December 31, 20X2, balances given above.

E4-6 Refer to the Pioneer Travel data in Exercise 4-5. After making the adjusting entries in Exercise 4-5, journalize Pioneer's closing entries at the end of 20X2. Also set up T-accounts for Insurance Expense and Service Revenue and post the closing entries to these accounts. What are their balances after closing?

Closing the books **(Obj. 3)**

Identifying and journalizing entries
(Obj. 3)

E4-7 From the following selected accounts of Daewoo Energy at June 30, 20X4, prepare the entity's closing entries:

Park Daewoo, capital	$ 21,600	Interest expense	$ 2,200
Service revenue	110,000	Accounts receivable	14,000
Unearned revenues	1,300	Salary payable	800
Salary expense	12,500	Depreciation expense	10,200
Accumulated depreciation	35,000	Rent expense	5,900
Supplies expense	1,700	Park Daewoo, withdrawals	40,000
Interest revenue	700	Supplies	1,400

What is Daewoo's ending capital balance at June 30, 20X4?

Identifying and journalizing closing entries
(Obj. 3)

E4-8 The accountant for MichiganTechnology.com has posted adjusting entries (a) through (e) to the following accounts at December 31, 20X8.

Accounts Receivable	
126,000	
(a) 9,500	

Supplies	
4,000	(b) 2,000

Accumulated Depreciation—Furniture	
	5,000
	(c) 1,100

Accumulated Depreciation—Building	
	33,000
	(d) 6,000

Salary Payable	
	(e) 700

Felix Rohr, Capital	
	52,400

Felix Rohr, Withdrawals	
61,400	

Service Revenue	
	108,000
	(a) 9,500

Salary Expense	
26,000	
(e) 700	

Supplies Expense	
(b) 2,000	

Depreciation Expense—Furniture	
(c) 1,100	

Depreciation Expense—Building	
(d) 6,000	

Required

1. Journalize MichiganTechnology.com's closing entries at December 31, 20X8.
2. Determine Felix Rohr's ending capital balance at December 31, 20X8.

Preparing a statement of owner's equity
(Obj. 3)

E4-9 From the following accounts of Chang Realty, prepare Chang's statement of owner's equity for the year ended December 31, 20X2.

Alvin Chang, Capital	
Clo. 72,000	Jan. 1 164,000
	Clo. 143,000
	Bal. 235,000

Alvin Chang, Withdrawals	
Mar. 31 19,000	
Jun. 30 17,000	
Sep. 30 19,000	
Dec. 31 17,000	
Bal. 72,000	Clo. 72,000

Income Summary	
Clo. 85,000	Clo. 228,000
Clo. 143,000	Bal. 143,000

Identifying and recording adjusting and closing entries
(Obj. 2, 3)

E4-10 The trial balance and adjusted income statement amounts from the April work sheet of The Megan Price Decorator Guild follow:

Account Title	Unadjusted Trial Balance	Income Statement
Cash	$14,200	
Supplies	2,400	
Prepaid rent	1,100	
Equipment	51,100	
Accumulated depreciation	$ 6,200	
Accounts payable	4,600	
Salary payable		
Unearned service revenue	4,400	

(continued)

Account Title	Unadjusted Trial Balance		Income Statement	
Long-term note payable		10,000		
Megan Price, capital...........		34,800		
Megan Price, withdrawals	1,000			
Service revenue...............		14,800		16,000
Salary expense	3,000		$ 3,800	
Rent expense.................	1,200		1,400	
Depreciation expense..........			300	
Supplies expense			400	
Utilities expense.............	800		800	
	$74,800	$74,800	6,700	16,000
Net income or net loss.........			?	
			$16,000	$16,000

Required

1. Journalize Price's adjusting and closing entries at April 30.
2. How much net income or net loss did Price earn for April? How can you tell?

E4-11 Refer to Exercise 4-10.

Preparing a classified balance sheet
(Obj. 4, 5)

Required

1. After solving Exercise 4-10 use the data in that exercise to prepare the classified balance sheet of The Megan Price Decorator Guild at April 30 of the current year. Use the report format.
2. Compute Price's current ratio and debt ratio at April 30. One year ago, the current ratio was 1.50 and the debt ratio was 0.30. Indicate whether Price's ability to pay debts has improved, deteriorated, or remained the same during the current year.

E4-12 Data for the unadjusted trial balance of Joy's Dance Studio at December 31, 20X7, follow:

Computing financial statement amounts
(Obj. 2, 4)

Cash....................	$ 3,000	Service revenue	$ 93,600
Property, plant,		Salary expense	42,700
and equipment	66,200	Depreciation expense	
Accumulated depreciation .	21,800	Supplies expense	
Accounts payable	6,100	Insurance expense	

Adjusting data for 20X7 are

a. Accrued service revenue, $8,100.
b. Supplies used in operations, $600.
c. Accrued salary expense, $1,400.

d. Insurance expense, $1,800.
e. Depreciation expense, $2,900.

Joy Maddox, the owner, has received an offer to sell the company. She needs to know the net income for the year covered by these data.

Required

Without opening accounts, making journal entries, or using a work sheet, give Maddox the requested information. Prepare an income statement, and show all computations.

Continuing Exercise

This exercise continues the Marsha Walker, Consultant, situation begun in Exercise 2-17 of Chapter 2 and continued in Exercise 3-15 of Chapter 3.

E4-13 Refer to Exercise 3-15 of Chapter 3. Start from the posted T-accounts and the adjusted trial balance that Marsha Walker, Consultant, prepared for her business at December 31:

Closing the books and preparing a classified balance sheet
(Obj. 3, 4, 5)

Marsha Walker, Consultant		
Adjusted Trial Balance December 31, 20XX		

	Adjusted Trial Balance	
Account	**Debit**	**Credit**
Cash	$11,700	
Accounts receivable	1,500	
Supplies	100	
Equipment	2,000	
Accumulated depr.—equipment		$ 50
Furniture	3,600	
Accumulated depr.—furniture...................		60
Accounts payable		3,600
Salary payable.................................		500
Unearned service revenue......................		600
Marsha Walker, capital.........................		14,000
Marsha Walker, withdrawals	1,600	
Service revenue................................		3,200
Rent expense	500	
Utilities expense	200	
Salary expense.................................	500	
Depreciation expense—equipment	50	
Depreciation expense—furniture................	60	
Supplies expense...............................	200	
Total	$22,010	$22,010

Required

1. Journalize and post the closing entries at December 31. Denote each closing amount as *Clo.* and an account balance as *Bal.*
2. Prepare a classified balance sheet at December 31.
3. If your instructor assigns it, complete the accounting work sheet at December 31.

Problems

(Group A)

P4-1A The trial balance of Lane's Interiors at May 31, 20X8, follows.

Preparing a work sheet
(Obj. 1)

Lane's Interiors		
Trial Balance May 31, 20X8		

Cash..	$ 4,300	
Notes receivable............................	10,300	
Interest receivable		
Supplies....................................	500	
Prepaid insurance	1,700	
Furniture...................................	27,400	
Accumulated depreciation—furniture..........		$ 1,400
Building....................................	53,900	
Accumulated depreciation—building		34,500
Land.......................................	18,700	
Accounts payable		14,700
Interest payable		
Salary payable		
Unearned service revenue		8,800

(continued)

Note payable, long-term..........................		18,700
K. Lane, capital.................................		29,900
K. Lane, withdrawals	3,800	
Service revenue		16,800
Interest revenue................................		
Depreciation expense—furniture		
Depreciation expense—building...................		
Salary expense	2,100	
Insurance expense..............................		
Interest expense................................		
Utilities expense................................	1,100	
Advertising expense............................	1,000	
Supplies expense		
Total.......................................	$124,800	$124,800

Additional data at May 31, 20X8:

a. Depreciation: furniture, $500; building, $400.
b. Accrued salary expense, $600.
c. Supplies on hand, $400.
d. Prepaid insurance expired, $300.
e. Accrued interest expense, $200.
f. Unearned service revenue earned during May, $4,400.
g. Accrued advertising expense, $100 (credit Accounts Payable).
h. Accrued interest revenue, $200.

Required

Complete Lane's work sheet for May. Key adjusting entries by letter.

Preparing a work sheet and the financial statements
(Obj. 1, 2)

Student ResourceCD

General Ledger, Peachtree, QuickBooks

P4-2A The unadjusted T-accounts of Ross Reagan, M.D., at December 31, 20X5, and the related year-end adjustment data follow.

Cash	Accounts Receivable	Supplies	Equipment
Bal. 29,000	Bal. 44,000	Bal. 6,000	Bal. 102,000

Accumulated Depreciation	Accounts Payable	Salary Payable	Unearned Service Revenue
Bal. 12,000	Bal. 16,000		Bal. 2,000

Note Payable, Long-Term		Ross Reagan, Capital	Ross Reagan, Withdrawals
Bal. 40,000		Bal. 41,000	Bal. 54,000

Service Revenue		Salary Expense	Supplies Expense
Bal. 175,000		Bal. 36,000	

Depreciation Expense	Interest Expense	Insurance Expense
	Bal. 5,000	Bal. 10,000

Adjustment data at December 31, 20X5:

a. Depreciation for the year, $5,000.
b. Supplies on hand, $2,000.
c. Accrued service revenue, $4,000.
d. Unearned service revenue earned during the year, $2,000.
e. Accrued salary expense, $4,000.

Required

1. Enter the trial balance on a work sheet, and complete the work sheet. Key each adjusting entry by the letter corresponding to the data given. List all the accounts, including those with zero balances. Leave a blank line under Service Revenue.

2. Prepare the income statement, the statement of owner's equity, and the classified balance sheet in account form.

3. Did Reagan have a good or a bad year during 20X5? Give the reason for your answer.

Journalizing adjusting and closing entries
(Obj. 2, 3)

Student ResourceCD
GL, PT, QB

P4-3A The *unadjusted* trial balance of TexasOnline Service at April 30, 20X8, follows. Adjusting data at April 30, 20X8, consist of

a. Accrued service revenue, $2,200.
b. Depreciation for the year: equipment, $6,900; building, $3,700.
c. Accrued wage expense, $800.
d. Unearned service revenue earned during the year, $4,100.
e. Additional supplies used, $500.
f. Prepaid insurance expired, $700
g. Accrued interest expense, $1,200.

Required

1. Journalize the adjusting entries.
2. Journalize the closing entries.

TexasOnline Service
Adjusted Trial Balance
April 30, 20X8

Cash	$ 14,500	
Accounts receivable.	43,700	
Supplies.	3,600	
Prepaid insurance	2,200	
Equipment	63,900	
Accumulated depreciation—equipment		$ 28,400
Building.	74,300	
Accumulated depreciation—building		18,200
Land.	30,600	
Accounts payable.		19,500
Interest payable		2,000
Wages payable		800
Unearned service revenue		3,600
Note payable, long-term.		69,900
Jeff Trichel, capital		77,100
Jeff Trichel, withdrawals.	27,500	
Service revenue		98,500
Depreciation expense—equipment.		
Depreciation expense—building.		
Wage expense.	32,800	
Insurance expense	5,100	
Interest expense	8,100	
Utilities expense.	4,900	
Supplies expense	6,800	
Total	$318,000	$318,000

Preparing an income statement
(Obj. 3)

P4-4A Refer to the data for TexasOnline Service in Problem 4-3A. After journalizing TexasOnline's adjusting and closing entries, prepare the company's income statement for the year ended April 30, 20X8. List expenses in descending order—that is, largest first, second-largest next, and so on.

Completing the accounting cycle
(Obj. 2, 3, 4)

Student ResourceCD
GL, PT, QB

P4-5A The trial balance of Lange Party Productions at October 31, 20X6, follows, along with the data for the month-end adjustments.

Account			
Lange Party Productions			
Trial Balance			
October 31, 20X6			

Account Number	Account Title	Debit	Credit
11	Cash	$ 4,900	
12	Accounts receivable	15,310	
13	Prepaid rent	2,200	
14	Supplies	840	
15	Equipment	26,830	
16	Accumulated depreciation—equipment		$ 3,400
21	Accounts payable		7,290
22	Salary payable		
23	Unearned service revenue		5,300
31	Melanie Lange, capital		28,290
32	Melanie Lange, withdrawals	3,900	
41	Service revenue		12,560
51	Salary expense	2,860	
52	Rent expense		
54	Depreciation expense—equipment		
56	Supplies expense		
	Total	$56,840	$56,840

Adjusting data at October 31:

a. Unearned service revenue still unearned, $800.

b. Prepaid rent still in force, $2,000.

c. Supplies used, $770.

d. Depreciation on equipment for the month, $250.

e. Accrued salary expense, $310.

Required

1. Open the accounts listed in the trial balance, inserting their October 31 unadjusted balances. Also open the Income Summary account, number 33. Use four-column accounts. Date the balances of the following accounts October 1: Prepaid Rent, Supplies, Equipment, Accumulated Depreciation—Equipment, Unearned Service Revenue, and Melanie Lange, Capital.

2. Enter the trial balance on a work sheet and complete the work sheet of Lange Party Productions for the month ended October 31, 20X6.

3. Prepare the income statement, statement of owner's equity, and classified balance sheet in report form.

4. Using the work sheet data that you prepare, journalize and post the adjusting and closing entries. Use dates and posting references. Use 12 as the journal page number.

5. Prepare a postclosing trial balance.

P4-6A Selected accounts of Mark Tynes, Architect, at December 31, 20X3, follow.

Preparing a classified balance sheet in report form
(Obj. 4, 5)

Required

1. Prepare Tynes's classified balance sheet in report form at December 31, 20X3. Show totals for total assets, total liabilities, and total liabilities and owner's equity.

Accounts payable	$34,700	Insurance expense..........	$ 600
Accounts receivable	41,500	Note payable, long-term.....	3,200
Accumulated depreciation—		Other assets	2,300
building...............	47,300	Other current liabilities......	1,100
Accumulated depreciation—		Prepaid insurance	600
equipment............	7,700	Prepaid rent	4,700
Building	55,900	Salary expense.............	17,800
Cash....................	3,400	Salary payable	2,400
Depreciation expense	1,900	Service revenue	71,100
Mark Tynes, capital.......	38,300	Supplies..................	3,800
Equipment	24,200	Unearned service revenue ...	1,700

2. Compute Tynes's current ratio and debt ratio at December 31, 20X3. At December 31, 20X2, the current ratio was 1.28 and debt ratio was 0.52. Did Tynes's ability to pay debts improve, deteriorate, or remain the same during 20X3?

P4-7A ← *Link Back to Chapter 2 (Accounting Errors).* The accountant of Vivid Image Photography encountered the following situations while adjusting and closing the books at February 28. Consider each situation independently.

a. The accountant failed to make the following adjusting entries at February 28:
   1. Depreciation of equipment, $700.
   2. Earned service revenue that had been collected in advance, $2,700.
   3. Accrued service revenue, $1,400.
   4. Insurance expense, $360.
   5. Accrued interest expense on a note payable, $520.
   Compute the overall net income effect of these omissions.
b. Record each of the adjusting entries identified in item a.
c. A $1,400 debit to Supplies was posted as $4,100.
   1. At what stage of the accounting cycle will this error be detected?
   2. What is the name of this type of error? Explain how to identify the error.
d. The $1,300 balance of Computer Software was entered as $13,000 on the trial balance.
   1. What is the name of this type of error?
   2. Assume that this is the only error in the trial balance. Which will be greater, the total debits or the total credits, and by how much?
   3. How can this type of error be identified?

Problems

(Group B)

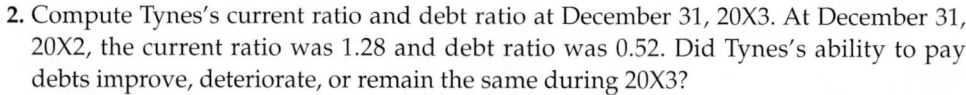
P4-1B The trial balance of Roadster Tune Center at June 30, 20X3, follows.

Roadster Tune Center		
Trial Balance		
June 30, 20X3		
Cash.	$ 21,200	
Accounts receivable	37,800	
Supplies	17,600	
Prepaid insurance	2,300	
Equipment	32,600	
Accumulated depreciation—equipment		$ 26,200
Building	42,800	
Accumulated depreciation—building		10,500
Land	28,300	
Accounts payable		22,600
Interest payable		
Wages payable		
Unearned service revenue		10,500
Note payable, long-term		22,400
Dan Runyan, capital		79,100
Dan Runyan, withdrawals.	4,200	
Service revenue		20,100
Depreciation expense—equipment		
Depreciation expense—building		
Wage expense	3,200	
Insurance expense.		
Interest expense.		
Utilities expense	1,100	
Advertising expense.	300	
Supplies expense.		
Total.	$191,400	$191,400

Additional data at June 30, 20X3:

a. Depreciation: equipment, $600; building, $300.
b. Accrued wage expense, $200.
c. Supplies on hand, $14,300.
d. Prepaid insurance expired during June, $500.

e. Accrued interest expense, $100.
f. Unearned service revenue earned during June, $4,900.
g. Accrued advertising expense, $100 (credit Accounts Payable).
h. Accrued service revenue, $1,100.

Required

Complete Roadster Tune Center's work sheet for June. Key adjusting entries by letter.

P4-2B The unadjusted T-accounts of Lake Air Studio, at December 31, 20X6, and the related year-end adjustment data follow.

Preparing a work sheet and the financial statements
(Obj. 1, 2)

Adjustment data at December 31, 20X6:

a. Unearned service revenue earned during the year, $5,000.
b. Supplies on hand, $1,000.

c. Depreciation for the year, $9,000.
d. Accrued salary expense, $1,000.
e. Accrued service revenue, $2,000.

Student ResourceCD
GL, PT, QB

Required

1. Enter the trial balance on a work sheet, and complete the work sheet. Key each adjusting entry by the letter corresponding to the data given. List all the accounts, including those with zero balances. Leave a blank line under Service Revenue.
2. Prepare the income statement, the statement of owner's equity, and the classified balance sheet in account format.
3. Did Lake Air Studio have a good or a bad year during 20X6? Give the reason for your answer.

Cash	Accounts Receivable	Supplies	Equipment
Bal. 15,000	Bal. 36,000	Bal. 9,000	Bal. 99,000

Accumulated Depreciation	Accounts Payable	Salary Payable	Unearned Service Revenue
Bal. 13,000	Bal. 6,000		Bal. 5,000

Note Payable, Long-Term		Betsy Willis, Capital	Betsy Willis, Withdrawals
Bal. 60,000		Bal. 36,000	Bal. 62,000

Service Revenue		Salary Expense	Supplies Expense
Bal. 182,000		Bal. 53,000	

Depreciation Expense	Interest Expense	Rent Expense	Insurance Expense
	Bal. 6,000	Bal. 15,000	Bal. 7,000

P4-3B The *unadjusted* trial balance of Oriental Rug Repair at June 30, 20X9 follows on the next page.

Journalizing adjusting and closing entries
(Obj. 2, 3)

Adjusting data at June 30, 20X9:

a. Prepaid insurance expired, $2,200.
b. Accrued interest expense, $500.
c. Accrued service revenue, $900.
d. Accrued wage expense, $700.
e. Depreciation for the year: equipment, $7,300; building, $3,900.
f. Additional supplies used, $200.

Student ResourceCD
GL, PT, QB

Required

1. Journalize Oriental Rug Repair's adjusting entries.
2. Journalize the closing entries.

Oriental Rug Repair

Trial Balance
June 30, 20X9

Cash	$ 12,300	
Accounts receivable	26,400	
Supplies	31,200	
Prepaid insurance	3,200	
Equipment	135,800	
Accumulated depreciation—equipment		$ 16,400
Building	34,900	
Accumulated depreciation—building		16,800
Land	30,000	
Accounts payable		39,100
Interest payable		1,400
Wages payable		
Note payable, long-term		97,000
Linda Gallo, capital		49,400
Linda Gallo, withdrawals	45,300	
Service revenue		139,800
Depreciation expense—equipment		
Depreciation expense—building		
Wage expense	21,400	
Insurance expense	3,100	
Interest expense	8,500	
Utilities expense	4,300	
Supplies expense	3,500	
Total	$359,900	$359,900

Preparing an income statement
(Obj. 3)

P4-4B Refer to the data for Oriental Rug Repair in Problem 4-3B. After journalizing Oriental's adjusting and closing entries, prepare the company's income statement for the year ended June 30, 20X9. List expenses in descending order—that is, largest first, second-largest next, and so on.

Completing the accounting cycle
(Obj. 2, 3, 4)

Student ResourceCD
GL, PT, QB

P4-5B The trial balance of Revere Silver Plating at August 31, 20X9, and the data for the month-end adjustments follow:

Revere Silver Plating

Trial Balance
August 31, 20X9

Account Number	Account Title	Debit	Credit
11	Cash	$ 3,800	
12	Accounts receivable	15,560	
13	Prepaid rent	1,290	
14	Supplies	20,900	
15	Equipment	15,350	
16	Accumulated depreciation—equipment		$ 12,800
17	Building	89,900	
18	Accumulated depreciation—building		28,600
21	Accounts payable		4,240
22	Salary payable		
23	Unearned service revenue		8,900
31	Paul Revere, capital		71,920
32	Paul Revere, withdrawals	4,800	
41	Service revenue		27,300
51	Salary expense	2,160	
52	Rent expense		
54	Depreciation expense—equipment		
55	Depreciation expense—building		
57	Supplies expense		
	Total	$153,760	$153,760

Adjustment data:

a. Unearned commission revenue still unearned at August 31, $6,500.

b. Prepaid rent still in force at August 31, $1,050.

c. Supplies used during the month, $5,340.

d. Depreciation on equipment for the month, $370.

e. Depreciation on building for the month, $130.

f. Accrued salary expense at August 31, $460.

Required

1. Open the accounts listed in the trial balance and insert their August 31 unadjusted balances. Also open the Income Summary account, number 33. Use four-column accounts. Date the balances of the following accounts as of August 1: Prepaid Rent, Supplies, Equipment, Accumulated Depreciation—Equipment, Building, Accumulated Depreciation—Building, Unearned Service Revenue, and Paul Revere, Capital.

2. Enter the trial balance on a work sheet and complete the work sheet of Revere Silver Plating for the month ended August 31, 20X9.

3. Prepare the income statement, the statement of owner's equity, and the classified balance sheet in report form.

4. Using the work sheet data that you prepare, journalize and post the adjusting and closing entries. Use dates and posting references. Use 7 as the journal page number.

5. Prepare a postclosing trial balance.

P4-6B Selected accounts of Noteworthy Communications at December 31, 20X6, follow:

Preparing a classified balance sheet in report form
(Obj. 4, 5)

Accounts payable	$ 15,100	Lori Stone, capital	$67,100
Accounts receivable	6,600	Note payable, long-term	27,800
Accumulated depreciation—		Other assets	3,600
equipment	37,800	Other current liabilities	4,700
Accumulated depreciation—		Prepaid insurance	1,100
computers	11,600	Prepaid rent	6,600
Equipment	114,400	Salary expense	24,600
Cash	16,500	Salary payable	3,900
Service revenue	93,500	Supplies	2,500
Computers	22,700	Unearned service revenue	5,400
Interest payable	600		

Required

1. Prepare Noteworthy's classified balance sheet in report form at December 31, 20X6. Show totals for total assets, total liabilities, and total liabilities and owner's equity.

2. Compute Noteworthy's current ratio and debt ratio at December 31, 20X6. At December 31, 20X5, the current ratio was 1.52 and the debt ratio was 0.39. Did the company's ability to pay debts improve or deteriorate during 20X6?

P4-7B ← *Link Back to Chapter 2 (Accounting Errors).* The accountant for River Square Retail Center encountered the following situations while adjusting and closing the books at December 31. Consider each situation independently.

Analyzing errors and journalizing adjusting entries
(Obj. 2)

a. The accountant failed to make the following adjusting entries at December 31:
1. Accrued property tax expense, $200.
2. Supplies expense, $1,090.
3. Accrued interest revenue on a note receivable, $1,650.
4. Depreciation of equipment, $400.
5. Earned rent revenue that had been collected in advance, $1,100.
Compute the overall net income effect of these omissions.

b. Record each adjusting entry identified in item a.

c. A $500 credit to Accounts Receivable was posted as a debit.
1. At what stage of the accounting cycle will this error be detected?
2. Describe the technique for identifying the amount of the error.

d. The $16,000 balance of Equipment was entered as $1,600 on the trial balance.

    1. What is the name of this type of error?

    2. Assume that this is the only error in the trial balance. Which will be greater, the total debits or the total credits, and by how much?

    3. How can this type of error be identified?

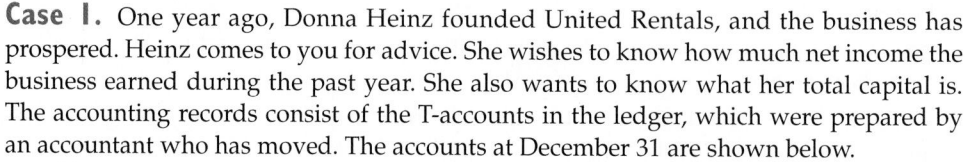

APPLY *Your Knowledge*

Decision Cases

Completing the accounting cycle to develop the information for a bank loan
(Obj. 3, 4)

Case 1. One year ago, Donna Heinz founded United Rentals, and the business has prospered. Heinz comes to you for advice. She wishes to know how much net income the business earned during the past year. She also wants to know what her total capital is. The accounting records consist of the T-accounts in the ledger, which were prepared by an accountant who has moved. The accounts at December 31 are shown below.

Heinz indicates that, at year-end, customers owe her $1,600 accrued rent revenue, which she expects to collect early next year. These revenues have not been recorded. During the year, she collected $4,130 rent revenue in advance from customers, but the business has earned only $2,500 of that amount. Advertising expense for the year was $2,400, and she used up $2,100 of the supplies. Heinz estimates that depreciation on equipment was $5,900 for the year. At December 31, she owes her employee $1,200 accrued salary.

Heinz expresses concern that her withdrawals during the year might have exceeded the business's net income. To get a loan to expand the business, Heinz must show the bank that her capital account has grown from its original $40,000 balance. Has it? You and Heinz agree that you will meet again in one week.

Required

Prepare the financial statement that is needed to answer Heinz's question. Can Heinz expect to get the loan? Give your reason.

Cash		Accounts Receivable		Prepaid Rent		Supplies	
Dec. 31 5,850		Dec. 31 12,360		Jan. 2 2,800		Jan. 2 2,600	

Equipment		Accumulated Depreciation				Accounts Payable	
Jan. 2 42,000							Dec. 31 18,540

Salary Payable		Unearned Rent Revenue		Donna Heinz, Capital		Donna Heinz, Withdrawals	
			Dec. 31 4,130		Jan. 2 40,000	Dec. 31 60,000	

Rent Revenue				Salary Expense		Depreciation Expense	
	Dec. 31 80,740			Dec. 31 17,000			

Advertising Expense		Utilities Expense		Supplies Expense			
		Dec. 31 800					

Finding an error in the work sheet
(Obj. 1)

Case 2. You are preparing the financial statements for the year ended October 31, 20X5, for Zadell Software Company.

- You began with the trial balance of the ledger, which balanced, and then made the required adjusting entries.
- To save time, you omitted preparing an adjusted trial balance.
- After making the adjustments on the work sheet, you extended the balances from the trial balance, adjusted for the adjusting entries, and computed amounts for the income statement and the balance sheet columns.

Required

a. When you added the total debits and the total credits on the income statement, you found that the credits exceeded the debits by $45,000. Did the business have a profit or a loss?

b. You took the balancing amount from the income statement columns to the debit column of the balance sheet and found that the total debits exceeded the total credits in the balance sheet. The difference between the total debits and the total credits on the balance sheet is $90,000. What is the cause of this difference? (Except for these errors, everything else is correct.)

Ethical Issue

← *Link Back to Chapter 3 (Revenue Principle)*. Lords & Ladies Boutique wishes to expand and has borrowed $250,000. As a condition for making this loan, the bank requires that the store maintain a current ratio of at least 1.50.

Business has been good but not great. Expansion costs have brought the current ratio down to 1.40 at December 15. Josh Hemingway, owner of the boutique, is considering what might happen if the business reports a current ratio of 1.40 to the bank. One course of action for Hemingway is to record in December some revenue that the business will earn in January of next year. The contract for this job has been signed.

Required

1. Journalize the revenue transaction, and indicate how recording this revenue in December would affect the current ratio.
2. State whether it is ethical to record the revenue transaction in December. Identify the accounting principle relevant to this situation.
3. Propose a course of action that is ethical for Hemingway.

Financial Statement Case

This case, based on the balance sheet of **Amazon.com** in Appendix A, will familiarize you with some of the assets and liabilities of that company. Use the Amazon balance sheet to answer the following questions.

Using a balance sheet
(Obj. 4, 5)

Required

1. Which balance sheet format does Amazon.com use?
2. Name the company's largest current asset and largest current liability at December 31, 2002.
3. Compute Amazon's current ratios at December 31, 2002 and 2001. Did the current ratio improve, worsen, or hold steady during 2002?
4. Under what category does Amazon report furniture, fixtures, and equipment?
5. What was the cost of the company's fixed assets at December 31, 2002? What was the amount of accumulated depreciation? What was the book value of the fixed assets? See Note 3 for the data.

Team Project

Aaron Grant formed a lawn service business as a summer job. To start the business on May 1, he deposited $1,000 in a new bank account in the name of the proprietorship. The $1,000 consisted of a $600 loan from his father and $400 of his own money. Aaron rented lawn equipment, purchased supplies, and hired other students to mow and trim customers' lawns.

At the end of each month, Aaron mailed bills to his customers. On August 31, he was ready to dissolve the business and return to Blue Mountain Community College. Because he was so busy, he kept few records other than his checkbook and a list of receivables from customers.

At August 31, Aaron's checkbook shows a balance of $2,000, and his customers still owe him $500. During the summer, he collected $5,500 from customers. His checkbook lists payments for supplies totaling $400, and he still has gasoline, weedeater cord, and other supplies that cost a total of $50. He paid his employees $1,800, and he still owes them $300 for the final week of the summer.

Aaron rented some equipment from Ludwig's Machine Shop. On May 1, he signed a six-month lease on mowers and paid $600 for the full lease period. Ludwig's will refund the unused portion of the prepayment if the equipment is in good shape. In order to get the refund, Aaron has kept the mowers in excellent condition. In fact, he had to pay $300 to repair a mower.

To transport employees and equipment to jobs, Aaron used a trailer that he bought for $300. He figures that the summer's work used up one-third of the trailer's service potential. The business checkbook lists a payment of $500 for cash withdrawals by Aaron during the summer. Aaron paid his father back during August.

Required

1. Prepare the income statement of Grant Lawn Service for the four months May through August.
2. Prepare the classified balance sheet of Grant Lawn Service at August 31.
3. Was Grant's summer work successful? Give the reason for your answer.

For Internet Exercises, go to the Web site www.prenhall.com/horngren.

APPENDIX *to Chapter 4*

Reversing Entries: An Optional Step

Reversing entries are special journal entries that ease the burden of accounting for transactions in a later period. Reversing entries are the exact opposites of certain adjusting entries at the end of the prior period. Reversing entries are used most often in conjunction with accrual-type adjustments, such as accrued salary expense and accrued service revenue. *Generally accepted accounting principles do not require reversing entries. They are used only for convenience and to save time.*

Accounting for Accrued Expenses

To see how reversing entries work, return to Gay Gillen's unadjusted trial balance at April 30 (Exhibit 4-2, page 144). Salary Expense has a debit balance of $950 for salaries paid during April. At April 30, the business still owes its employee an additional $950 for the last half of the month, so Gillen makes this adjusting entry:

Adjusting Entries		
Apr. 30 Salary Expense	950	
Salary Payable		950

After posting, the accounts are updated at April 30.[1]

Salary Payable			
	Apr. 30 Adj.	950	
	Apr. 30 Bal.	950	

Salary Expense			
Paid during			
April, CP	950		
Apr. 30 Adj.	950		
Apr. 30 Bal.	1,900		

After the adjusting entry,

- The April income statement reports salary expense of $1,900.
- The April 30 balance sheet reports salary payable of $950.

The $1,900 debit balance of Salary Expense is closed at April 30, 20X5, with this closing entry:

Closing Entries		
Apr. 30	Income Summary	1,900	
	Salary Expense		1,900

After posting, Salary Expense has a zero balance as follows:

Salary Expense			
Paid during			
April, CP	950		
Apr. 30 Adj.	950		
Apr. 30 Bal.	1,900	Apr. 30 Clo.	1,900

Zero balance

Assume for this illustration that on May 5, the next payday, Gillen will pay the $950 of accrued salary left over from April 30 plus $100 of salary for the first few days of May. Gillen's next payroll payment will be $1,050 ($950 + $100).

Accounting Without a Reversing Entry

On May 5, the next payday, Gillen pays the payroll of $1,050 and makes this journal entry:

May 5	Salary Payable.	950	
	Salary Expense	100	
	Cash		1,050

This method of recording the cash payment is correct. However, it wastes time because Gillen must refer back to the April 30 adjustments. Otherwise, she does not know the amount of the debit to Salary Payable (in this example, $950). Searching April's adjusting entries wastes time and money. To save time, accountants use reversing entries.

---

[1]Entry explanations used throughout this discussion are

Adj. = entry	CP = Cash payment entry—a credit to Cash
Bal. = Balance	CR = Cash receipt entry—a debit to Cash
Clo. = Closing entry	Rev. = Reversing entry

Making a Reversing Entry

Reversing Entry
An entry that switches the debit and the credit of a previous adjusting entry. The reversing entry is dated the first day of the new period.

A **reversing entry** switches the debit and the credit of a previous adjusting entry. *A reversing entry, then, is the exact opposite of a prior adjusting entry.* The reversing entry is dated the first day of the new period.

To illustrate reversing entries, recall that on April 30, Gillen made the following adjusting entry to accrue Salary Payable:

	Adjusting Entries		
Apr. 30	Salary Expense	950	
	Salary Payable.		950

The reversing entry simply reverses the debit and the credit of the adjustment:

	Reversing Entries		
May 1	Salary Payable.	950	
	Salary Expense		950

Observe that the reversing entry is dated the first day of the new period. It is the exact opposite of the April 30 adjusting entry. Ordinarily, the accountant who makes the adjusting entry also prepares the reversing entry at the same time. Gillen dates the reversing entry as of May 1 so that it affects only the new period. Note how the accounts appear after Gillen posts the reversing entry:

Salary Payable				**Salary Expense**			
May 1 Rev.	950	Apr. 30	Bal. 950	Apr. 30 Bal. 1,900		Apr. 30	Clo. 1,900
	Zero balance				Zero balance		
						May 1	Rev. 950

The arrow shows the transfer of the $950 credit balance from Salary Payable to Salary Expense. This credit balance in Salary Expense does not mean that the entity has negative salary expense, as you might think. Instead, the odd credit balance in the Salary Expense account is merely a temporary result of the reversing entry. The credit balance is eliminated on May 5, when Gillen pays the payroll and debits Salary Expense in the customary manner:

May 5	Salary Expense	1,050	
	Cash		1,050

Then this cash payment entry is posted as follows:

Salary Expense			
May 5 CP	1,050	May 1 Rev.	950
May 5 Bal.	100		

Now Salary Expense has its correct debit balance of $100, which is the amount of salary expense incurred thus far in May. The $1,050 cash disbursement also pays the liability for Salary Payable so that Salary Payable has a zero balance, which is correct.

Appendix Assignment
Problem

P4A-1 Refer to the data in Problem 4-5A, pages 170–171.

Required

1. Open accounts for Salary Payable and Salary Expense. Insert their unadjusted balances at October 31, 20X6.

2. Journalize adjusting entry (e) and the closing entry for Salary Expense at October 31. Post to the accounts.

3. On November 5, Lange Party Productions paid the next payroll amount of $500. This payment included the accrued amount at October 31, plus $190 for the first few days of November. Journalize this cash payment, and post to the accounts. Show the balance in each account.

4. Using a reversing entry, repeat requirements 1 through 3. Compare the balances of Salary Payable and Salary Expense computed using a reversing entry with those balances computed without the reversing entry (as they appear in your answer to requirement 3).

CHAPTER 5

Merchandising Operations

TIPS CHECK YOUR RESOURCES

- Visit the www.prenhall.com/horngren **Web site** for self-study quizzes, video clips, and other resources

- Try the **Quick Check** exercise at end of chapter to test your knowledge

- Learn the **Key terms**

- Do the **Starter** exercises keyed in the margins

- Work the **Mid-** and **End-of-Chapter Summary Problems**

- Use the **Concept Links** in the text margins to review material in other chapters

- **Search the CD** for review materials by chapter or by key word

LEARNING OBJECTIVES

1 Account for the purchase of inventory

2 Account for the sale of inventory

3 Use sales and gross profit to evaluate a company

4 Adjust and close the accounts of a merchandising business

5 Prepare a merchandiser's financial statements

6 Use gross profit percentage and inventory turnover to evaluate a business

What comes to mind when you hear Amazon.com? All around the world, millions of customers like you place orders using Amazon's online system. Thanks to global shippers like Fedex and UPS, customers in England, Japan, and Australia can expect the same fast delivery of DVDs and music that you enjoy.

Now you can go online with Amazon and buy clothing from Target, electronic games from Circuit City, and playthings from Toys "Я" Us. Amazon offers an incredible selection of products. For example, you can visit a big-box store such as Circuit City and find about 7,000 products; Amazon offers 45,000. How do Amazon and Circuit City manage all these goods? This chapter shows how companies keep track of their merchandise inventory. ■

Amazon.com

Sitemap

- **Merchandising Operations**
- **Accounting for Inventory: Perpetual System**
- **Adjusting and Closing Accounts**
- **Preparing Financial Statements**
- **Key Decision-Making Ratios**

Inventory
All the goods that the company owns and expects to sell in the normal course of operations.

We shift gears in Chapter 5. The first four chapters focused on service companies such as Gay Gillen eTravel, the San Francisco Giants, and eBay. Here we begin working with merchandisers such as Amazon.com, Target, and Circuit City. A merchandiser differs from a service business in two important ways. A merchandiser sells *products*, whereas a service company provides a *service*. A merchandiser has an asset called *merchandise inventory*, such as DVDs, videos, and clothing. A service company carries no inventory.

Inventory includes all the goods a company owns and holds for sale in the normal course of operations. Throughout the remainder of the book we refer to merchandise inventory simply as inventory. It is a merchandiser's most important asset. This chapter demonstrates the central role of inventory in a business that sells merchandise. We illustrate accounting for the purchase and sale of inventory, and we also illustrate how to adjust and close the books of a merchandiser. The chapter also covers two ratios investors and creditors use to evaluate companies.

Before launching into merchandising, let's compare service entities, with which you are familiar, to merchandising companies. Exhibit 5-1 shows how the financial statements of a service entity (on the left) differs from a merchandiser (on the right).

Exhibit 5-1

Financial Statements of a Service Company and a Merchandiser

<table>
<tr><th colspan="2">Service Co. *
Balance Sheet
June 30, 20XX</th><th colspan="2">Merchandising Co. **
Balance Sheet
June 30, 20XX</th></tr>
<tr><td colspan="2" align="center">**Assets**</td><td colspan="2" align="center">**Assets**</td></tr>
<tr><td colspan="2">Current assets:</td><td colspan="2">Current assets:</td></tr>
<tr><td>Cash . . . .</td><td>$X</td><td>Cash. . . . .</td><td>$X</td></tr>
<tr><td>Short-term investments. . . .</td><td>X</td><td>Short-term investments . . . .</td><td>X</td></tr>
<tr><td>Accounts receivable, net . . .</td><td>X</td><td>Accounts receivable, net. . . .</td><td>X</td></tr>
<tr><td>Prepaid expenses . . . .</td><td>X</td><td>*Inventory* . . . .</td><td>X</td></tr>
<tr><td></td><td></td><td>Prepaid expenses. . . . .</td><td>X</td></tr>
<tr><td colspan="2" align="center">*Such as Gay Gillen e-Travel</td><td colspan="2" align="center">**Such as Amazon.com</td></tr>
</table>

<table>
<tr><th colspan="2">Service Co.
Income Statement
Year Ended June 30, 20XX</th><th colspan="2">Merchandising Co.
Income Statement
Year Ended June 30, 20XX</th></tr>
<tr><td>Service revenue. . . . .</td><td>$XXX →</td><td>*Sales revenue* . . . .</td><td>$X,XXX</td></tr>
<tr><td>Expenses: ⟶</td><td></td><td>*Cost of goods sold* . . . .</td><td>X</td></tr>
<tr><td>Salary expense. . . . .</td><td>X</td><td>*Gross profit* . . . .</td><td>XXX</td></tr>
<tr><td>Depreciation expense. . .</td><td>X</td><td>Operating expenses:</td><td></td></tr>
<tr><td>Income tax expense . . . .</td><td>X</td><td>Salary expense. . . . .</td><td>X</td></tr>
<tr><td>Net income. . . . .</td><td>$ X</td><td>Depreciation expense. .</td><td>X</td></tr>
<tr><td></td><td></td><td>Income tax expense . . .</td><td>X</td></tr>
<tr><td></td><td></td><td>Net income. . . . .</td><td>$ X</td></tr>
</table>

What Are Merchandising Operations?

Merchandising is the business activity of buying and selling products rather than services. Accounting for merchandising operations requires us to deal with these balance sheet and income statement items.

Balance Sheet:
- Inventory, an asset

Income Statement:
- Sales revenue (often abbreviated as Sales), a revenue
- Cost of goods sold, an expense

These items are italicized in Exhibit 5-1 for Merchandising Co. Let's begin with the operating cycle of a merchandising business.

■ Merchandising Operations
☐ Accounting for Inventory: Perpetual System
☐ Adjusting and Closing Accounts
☐ Preparing Financial Statements
☐ Key Decision-Making Ratios

Student ResourceCD
periodic system, perpetual system

The Operating Cycle of a Merchandising Business

The operating cycle of a business is different from the accounting cycle. The operating cycle begins when a merchandiser buys inventory. The company then sells the goods to customers and collects cash. Exhibit 5-2 diagrams the operating cycle for *sales on account*.

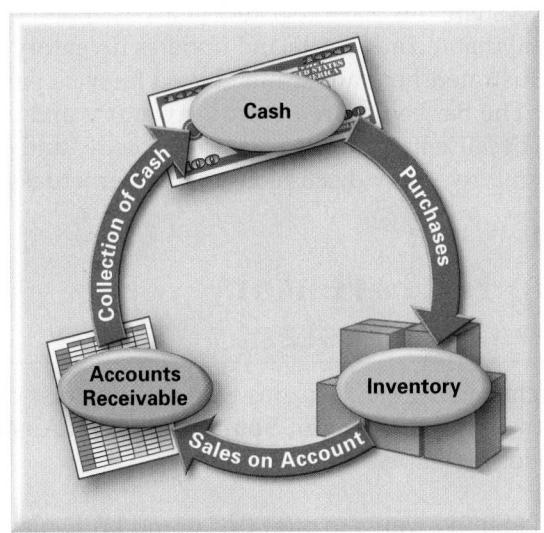

Exhibit 5-2

Operating Cycle of a Merchandiser

   Now let's see how companies account for their inventory. The accounting cycle begins with journal entries, posts journal entries to the ledger accounts, and ends with the financial statements.

Inventory Systems: Perpetual and Periodic

There are two main types of inventory accounting systems:

- Periodic system
- Perpetual system

The **periodic inventory system** is used for relatively inexpensive goods. A convenience store without optical-scanning cash registers does not keep a daily running record of every loaf of bread and every key chain that it sells. Instead, the business counts its inventory at some regular interval to determine the quantities on hand. Restaurants and small retail stores also use the periodic system. Chapter 6 covers this system, which is becoming less and less popular as more businesses keep their inventory records by computer.

Periodic Inventory System
A system in which the business does not keep a continuous record of inventory on hand. At the end of the period, it makes a physical count of on-hand inventory and uses this information to prepare the financial statements.

Perpetual Inventory System
The accounting inventory system in which the business keeps a running record of inventory and cost of goods sold.

The **perpetual inventory system** keeps a running record of inventory and cost of goods sold. This system achieves control over the inventory. Even in a perpetual system, the business counts inventory at least once a year. The physical count establishes the correct amount of ending inventory for the financial statements and also serves as a check on the perpetual records.

The following chart compares the perpetual and periodic systems:

Perpetual Inventory System
- Keeps a running record of all goods bought and sold.
- Inventory counted at least once a year.

Periodic Inventory System
- Does *not* keep a running record of all goods bought and sold.
- Inventory counted at least once a year.

Integrated Inventory Systems

An integrated inventory system records units purchased, units sold, and the quantities of goods on hand. Inventory systems are integrated with accounts receivable and sales. For example, Amazon.com's computers keep up-to-the-minute records, so managers can call up current inventory information at any time.

In a perpetual system, the "cash register" at a Target or a Circuit City store is a computer terminal that records a sale and updates inventory records. Bar codes such as the one illustrated here are scanned by a laser as part of the perpetual inventory system. The bar coding represents inventory and cost data that keep track of each item. Because most businesses use bar codes and computerized cash registers, we base our inventory discussions on the perpetual system.

Bar code

☐ Merchandising Operations
■ **Accounting for Inventory: Perpetual System**
☐ Adjusting and Closing Accounts
☐ Preparing Financial Statements
☐ Key Decision-Making Ratios

Student ResourceCD
cost of goods sold, gross profit, purchase of inventory, sale of inventory, sales revenue

Invoice
A seller's request for cash from the purchaser.

Accounting for Inventory in the Perpetual System

The cycle of a merchandising entity begins with the purchase of inventory. In this section, we trace the steps that Austin Sound Center, in Austin, Texas, takes to purchase and pay for inventory.

1. Suppose Austin Sound wants to offer JVC brand DVD players. Austin Sound orders DVD players from JVC.
2. JVC ships the goods and sends the invoice in Exhibit 5-3 to Austin Sound the same day. The **invoice** is the seller's request for a cash payment by the buyer. An invoice is also called a *bill*. To Austin Sound, the document is a purchase invoice.
3. After the inventory is received, Austin Sound pays JVC the invoice amount.

Account for the purchase of inventory

Purchase of Inventory

Here we use the actual invoice in Exhibit 5-3 — a $700 purchase of inventory—to illustrate the purchasing process. Suppose Austin Sound receives the goods on May 30. Austin Sound records this purchase on account as follows:

May 30	Inventory	700	
	Accounts Payable		700
	Purchased inventory on account.		

Exhibit 5-3 An Actual Invoice (Adapted)

		Invoice	
		Date	Number
[3]		5/27/05	410

JVC SOUTHWEST BRANCH
P.O. BOX 100876
HOUSTON, TX 77212

Shipped To: AUSTIN SOUND CENTER
[2]   305 WEST MLK BLVD.
         AUSTIN, TX 78701

Terms of Sale			[5]			
3% 15, NET 30 DAYS [4]						
Quantity Ordered	Description	Model No.	Quantity Shipped	Unit Price	Total
7	DVD PLAYER	QLA200	7	$100.00	$700.00
				[7] Pd.	06-10-05

Due Date & Due Amount			Sub Total	$700.00
06/11/05	06/26/05		Ship. or Handl. Chg.	–
$679 00	$700 00		Tax (3%)	–
[8]			Total(s)	$700.00
				[6]

Explanations:

[1] The seller is JVC.

[2] The purchaser is Austin Sound Center.

[3] The invoice date, needed for determining whether the purchaser gets a discount for prompt payment (see 4).

[4] Credit terms of the transaction: If it pays within 15 days of the invoice date, Austin Sound may deduct a 3% discount. Otherwise, the full amount—net—is due in 30 days. (The discussion of discounts starts on page 187.)

[5] JVC shipped 7 DVD players to Austin Sound.

[6] Total invoice amount is $700.

[7] Austin Sound's payment date. How much did Austin pay? (See 8, which follows.)

[8] Payment occurred 14 days after the invoice date—within the discount period—so Austin paid $679 ($700 – 3% discount).

The purchase of inventory on account increases Austin Sound's assets (Inventory) and liabilities (Accounts Payable), as shown by the accounting equation:

ASSETS	**=**	**LIABILITIES**	**+**	**OWNER'S EQUITY**
Inventory		**Accounts Payable**		
$700	=	$700	+	$0

The Inventory account is used only for goods purchased for resale. Supplies, equipment, and other assets are recorded in their own accounts. Inventory is an asset until sold.

PURCHASE DISCOUNTS   Many businesses offer customers a purchase discount for early payment. JVC's credit terms of 3% 15, NET 30 DAYS mean that Austin Sound may deduct 3% of the total debt if Austin pays within 15 days of the invoice date. Otherwise, the full amount—NET—is due in 30 days. These credit terms can also be expressed as 3/15 n/30.

Terms of n/30 mean that no discount is offered and payment is due 30 days after the invoice date. Terms of *eom* mean that payment is due at the end of the current month.

Austin Sound paid within the discount period, so its cash payment entry is

June 10	Accounts Payable........................	700	
	Cash ($700 × 0.97)		679
	Inventory ($700 × 0.03)		21
	Paid within discount period.		

✔ **Starter 5-1**

Note that the discount is credited to the Inventory account. Why? Because the discount decreases Austin Sound's cost of goods, as shown in the Inventory account:

Inventory

May 30	700	June 10	21
Bal.	**679**		

But if Austin Sound pays this invoice after the discount period, Austin Sound must pay the full amount of $700. In that case, the payment entry is

June 24	Accounts Payable....	700	
	Cash		700
	Paid after discount period.		

Inventory

May 30	700	

PURCHASE RETURNS AND ALLOWANCES   Businesses allow customers to *return* merchandise that is defective, damaged, or otherwise unsuitable. Or the seller may deduct an *allowance* from the amount the buyer owes. Both purchase returns and purchase allowances decrease the buyer's cost of the inventory.

Suppose one DVD player purchased by Austin Sound (Exhibit 5-3) was damaged in shipment. Austin returns the merchandise to the seller and records the purchase return as follows:

June 3	Accounts Payable......................	100	
	Inventory.......................		100
	Returned inventory to seller.		

A purchase return decreases Austin Sound's assets and its liabilities, as shown by the accounting equation:

ASSETS	=	LIABILITIES	+	OWNER'S EQUITY
Inventory		Accounts Payable		
−$100	=	−$100	+	$0

✔ **Starter 5-2**
✔ **Starter 5-3**
✔ **Starter 5-4**

Accounts Payable

Return	100	Purchase	1,000
		Bal.	**900**

On September 15, Austin Sound purchases $1,000 of merchandise on account, with terms 2/10, n/30. Austin returns $100 of merchandise for credit on September 20, then makes payment in full on September 25. Journalize these transactions.

Answer: Three separate journal entries are needed. The purchase entry is

1. **Purchase:** Sep. 15   Inventory............................ 1,000
         Accounts Payable................   1,000

The second entry records the return of inventory, as follows:

2. **Return:**   Sep. 20   Accounts Payable...................... 100
         Inventory........................   100

The third entry records the payment of $882, as follows: Purchase amount, $1,000, minus the $100 return equals the net payable of $900. Now subtract the 2% discount ($900 × 0.02 = $18) to arrive at the final payment of $882.

3. **Payment:** Sep. 25   Accounts Payable   900

                            Cash.   882

                            Inventory   18

TRANSPORTATION COSTS   The transportation cost of moving inventory from seller to buyer can be significant. The purchase agreement specifies FOB terms to indicate who pays the shipping charges. *FOB* means *free on board*. FOB terms govern (1) when legal title to the goods passes from seller to buyer and (2) who pays the freight. Exhibit 5-4 summarizes FOB terms.

Exhibit 5-4   **FOB Terms Determine Who Pays Freight**

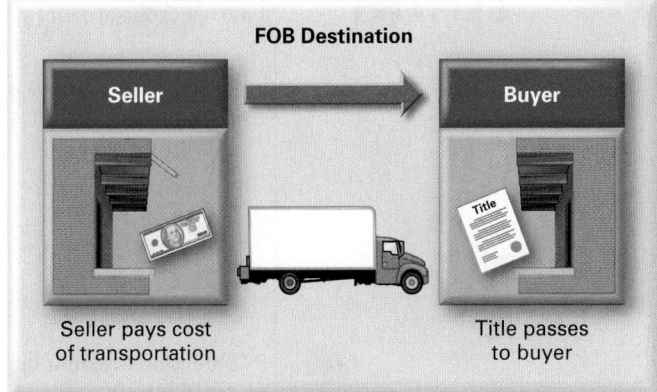

Freight costs are either *Freight in* or *Freight out*.

- Freight in is the transportation cost on *purchased goods.*
- Freight out is the transportation cost on *goods sold.*

Freight In   FOB shipping point terms are most common, so the buyer pays the freight. Freight in becomes part of the cost of inventory. The buyer debits Inventory and credits Cash or Accounts Payable for the freight. Suppose Austin Sound pays a $60 shipping bill. Austin Sound's entry to record payment of the freight charge is

June 1   Inventory   60

             Cash   60

             Paid a freight bill.

The freight charge increases the cost of the inventory to $660, as follows:

Inventory					
May 30	Purchase	700	June 3	Return	100
June 1	Freight in	60			
Bal.	Net cost	660			

Discounts are computed only on the account payable to the seller ($600), not on the transportation costs, because there is no discount on freight.

Under FOB shipping point terms, the seller sometimes prepays the transportation cost as a convenience and lists this cost on the invoice. A $5,000 purchase of goods, coupled with a related freight charge of $400, would be recorded as follows:

Mar. 12	Inventory ($5,000 + $400).............	5,400	
	Accounts Payable		5,400
	Purchased inventory on account, including freight.		

If the buyer pays within the discount period, the discount will be computed on the $5,000 merchandise cost, not on the $5,400. For example, a 2% discount would be $100 ($5,000 × 0.02).

Freight Out Freight charges paid to ship goods sold to customers are called *freight out*. Freight out is delivery expense to the seller. Delivery expense is an operating expense. It is debited to the Delivery Expense account.

This Stop & Think example is exactly like the preceding one, but with freight in. On September 15, Austin Sound purchased $1,000 of merchandise, with *$80 freight added*, for an invoice total of $1,080. Austin returns $100 of the goods for credit on September 20 and pays the account payable in full on September 25. Journalize these transactions.

Answer

Purchase:	Sept. 15	Inventory ($1,000 + $80)	1,080	
		Accounts Payable.......................		1,080
Return:	Sept. 20	Accounts Payable.............................	100	
		Inventory................................		100
Payment:	Sept. 25	Accounts Payable ($1,080 − $100)................	980	
		Inventory [($1,000 − $100) × 0.02]..........		18
		Cash ($1,000 + $80 − $100 − $18)		962

There is no discount on freight.

ACCOUNTING FOR PURCHASE RETURNS AND ALLOWANCES, DISCOUNTS, AND TRANSPORTATION COSTS Suppose Austin Sound buys $35,000 of audio/video inventory, takes a discount, and returns some of the goods. Austin Sound also pays some freight in. The following summary shows Austin Sound's total cost of this inventory. All amounts are assumed for this illustration.

Inventory

Price paid for inventory	35,000	Purchase ret. & allow.	700
Freight in	2,100	Purchase discount	800
Balance	35,600		

DEBIT - BALANCE ACCOUNT		CREDITS TO INVENTORY					DEBIT TO INVENTORY		TOTAL COST OF THE INVENTORY
Inventory	−	Purchase Returns and Allowances	−	Purchase Discounts	+		Freight in	=	Inventory
$35,000	−	$700	−	$800	+		$2,100	=	$35,600

⭐ *② Account for the sale of inventory*

Sales Revenue
The amount that a merchandiser earns from selling its inventory. Also called **sales.**

Cost of Goods Sold
The cost of the inventory that the business has sold to customers. Also called **cost of sales**.

Sale of Inventory

After a company buys inventory, the next step is to sell the goods. We shift now to the selling side and follow Austin Sound Center through a sequence of selling transactions. The amount a business earns from selling merchandise inventory is called **sales revenue** (often abbreviated as **sales**). A sale also creates an expense, Cost of Goods Sold, as the seller gives up the asset Inventory. **Cost of goods sold** is the entity's cost of its inventory that has been sold to customers. Cost of goods sold (often abbreviated as **cost of sales**) is the merchandiser's major expense.

After making a sale on account, Austin Sound may experience any of the following:

- *A sales return:* The customer may return goods to Austin Sound.
- *A sales allowance:* Austin Sound may grant a sales allowance to reduce the cash to be collected from the customer.
- *A sales discount:* If the customer pays within the discount period—under terms such as 2/10 n/30—Austin Sound collects the discounted amount.
- *Freight out:* Austin Sound may have to pay delivery expense to transport the goods to the buyer.

Let's begin with a cash sale.

CASH SALE   Sales of retailers, such as Austin Sound, grocery stores, and restaurants, are often for cash. Cash sales of $3,000 are recorded by debiting Cash and crediting Sales Revenue as follows:

June 9	Cash	3,000	
	Sales Revenue		3,000
	Cash sale.		

Because Austin Sound sold goods, the business also must decrease the Inventory balance. Suppose these goods cost the seller $1,900. A second journal entry is needed to transfer the $1,900 cost of the goods from the Inventory account to Cost of Goods Sold, as follows: →

June 9	Cost of Goods Sold	1,900	
	Inventory		1,900
	Recorded the cost of goods sold.		

The recording of cost of goods sold along with sales revenue is an example of the matching principle (Chapter 3, p. 95)

The Cost of Goods Sold account keeps a current balance throughout the period. In this example, cost of goods sold is not $3,000, because that's the selling price of the goods. Cost of goods sold is always based on the entity's cost, not the selling price.

After posting, the Cost of Goods Sold account holds the cost of the merchandise sold ($1,900 in this case):

Inventory		Cost of Goods Sold	
Purchases 50,000	Cost of sales 1,900 ◄──────►	June 9 1,900	
(amount assumed)			

The computer automatically records the cost of goods sold entry. The cashier keys in the code number of the inventory that is sold, and optical scanners perform this task.

SALE ON ACCOUNT   Most sales in the United States are made on account (on credit). A $5,000 sale on account is recorded as follows:

June 11	Accounts Receivable	5,000	
	Sales Revenue		5,000
	Sale on account.		

These goods cost the seller $2,900, so the related cost of goods sold entry is

June 11	Cost of Goods Sold	2,900	
	Inventory		2,900
	Recorded the cost of goods sold.		

When the cash comes in, the seller records the cash receipt on account as follows:

June 19	Cash	5,000	
	Accounts Receivable		5,000
	Collection on account.		

How does the January 19 collection of cash affect revenue?

Answer: It doesn't affect revenue at all. The business recorded the revenue back when it made the sale.

SALES DISCOUNTS AND SALES RETURNS AND ALLOWANCES We just saw that purchase returns and allowances and purchase discounts decrease the cost of inventory purchases. In the same way, **sales returns and allowances** and **sales discounts**, which are contra accounts to Sales Revenue, decrease the net amount of revenue earned on sales.

Sales Returns and Allowances
Decreases in the seller's receivable from a customer's return of merchandise or from granting the customer an allowance from the amount owed to the seller. A contra account to Sales Revenue.

Sales Discount
Reduction in the amount receivable from a customer, offered by the seller as an incentive for the customer to pay promptly. A contra account to Sales Revenue.

Net Sales Revenue
Sales revenue less sales discounts and sales returns and allowances.

CREDIT-BALANCE ACCOUNT	DEBIT-BALANCE ACCOUNTS		CREDIT SUBTOTAL (*NOT A SEPARATE* ACCOUNT)
Sales Revenue −	Sales Returns and Allowances −	Sales Discounts =	Net sales revenue[1]

Companies maintain separate accounts for Sales Discounts and Sales Returns and Allowances. Now let's examine a sequence of JVC sale transactions. Assume JVC is selling to Austin Sound Center.

On July 7, JVC sells stereo components for $7,200 on credit terms of 2/10 n/30. These goods cost JVC $4,700. JVC's entries to record this credit sale and the related cost of goods sold are

July 7	Accounts Receivable	7,200	
	Sales Revenue		7,200
	Sale on account.		
July 7	Cost of Goods Sold..................	4,700	
	Inventory		4,700
	Recorded cost of goods sold.		

Sales Returns Assume that the buyer returns $600 of the goods. JVC, the seller, records the sales return as follows:

July 12	Sales Returns and Allowances	600	
	Accounts Receivable		600
	Received returned goods.		

Accounts Receivable decreases because JVC will not collect cash for the returned goods. JVC receives the returned merchandise and updates inventory records. JVC must also decrease Cost of Goods Sold as follows (these goods cost JVC $400):

July 12	Inventory	400	
	Cost of Goods Sold.............		400
	Placed goods back in inventory.		

---

[1]Often abbreviated as Net sales.

Sales Allowances   Suppose JVC grants a $100 sales allowance for damaged goods. A sales allowance is recorded as follows:

```
July 15   Sales Returns and Allowances . . . . . . . . . . . .   100
                Accounts Receivable . . . . . . . . . . . . . .          100
          Granted a sales allowance for damaged goods.
```

There is no inventory entry for a sales allowance because the seller receives no returned goods from the customer.

After these entries are posted, Accounts Receivable has a $6,500 debit balance, as follows:

Accounts Receivable

July 7	Sale	7,200	July 12	Return	600
			15	Allowance	100
Bal.		6,500			

Sales Discounts   On July 17, the last day of the discount period, JVC collects $4,000 of this receivable. Assume JVC allows customers to take discounts on all amounts JVC receives within the discount period. JVC's cash receipt is $3,920 [$4,000 − ($4,000 × 0.02)], and the collection entry is

✔ **Starter 5-5**

```
July 17   Cash . . . . . . . . . . . . . . . . . . . . . . . . . . .   3,920
          Sales Discounts ($4,000 × 0.02) . . . . . . . .      80
                Accounts Receivable. . . . . . . . . . . .              4,000
          Cash collection within the discount period.
```

Suppose that JVC collects the remaining $2,500 on July 28. That date falls after the discount period, so there is no sales discount. JVC records this collection on account as follows:

```
July 28   Cash ($6,500 − $4,000) . . . . . . . . . . . . . .   2,500
                Accounts Receivable. . . . . . . . . . . .              2,500
          Cash collection after the discount period.
```

Now, JVC's Accounts Receivable balance is zero:

Accounts Receivable

July 7	Sale	7,200	July 12	Return	600
			15	Allowance	100
			17	Collection	4,000
			28	Collection	2,500
Bal.		–0–			

Evaluating Profitability: Sales Revenue, Cost of Goods Sold, and Gross Profit

⭐ *Use sales and gross profit to evaluate a company*

Managers and investors evaluate a business's profitability based on its net sales revenue, cost of goods sold, and gross profit. Net sales revenue minus cost of goods sold is called **gross profit**, or **gross margin**.

Gross Profit
Excess of net sales revenue over cost of goods sold. Also called **gross margin**.

| Net sales revenue (abbreviated as Sales) | − | Cost of goods sold (same as Cost of sales) | = | Gross profit (same as Gross margin) |

or, more simply,

$$\text{Sales} - \text{Cost of sales} = \text{Gross profit}$$

Gross profit, along with net income, is a measure of business success. A sufficiently high gross profit is vital to a merchandiser. Amazon.com's operations were quite successful during 2001. Amazon's gross profit was almost $800 million.

The following example will clarify the nature of gross profit. Suppose Amazon's cost to purchase a DVD is $15 and Amazon sells the DVD for $20. Amazon's gross profit per unit is $5, computed as follows:

Sales revenue earned by selling one DVD	$20
Less: Cost of goods sold for the DVD	
(what the DVD cost Amazon).	(15)
Gross profit on the sale of one DVD	$ 5

✔ Starter 5-6

✔ Starter 5-7

Accounting.com

Amazon.com: For E-Tailers Free Shipping Isn't Free, But It's Not a Cost, Either

Like most accounting students, Jennifer didn't have time to go Christmas shopping. She cruised the online mall and ended up buying all her presents from Amazon.com, the largest player in online retailing. Jennifer was lured by Amazon.com's huge selection and an offer of free shipping for all orders over $25.

Amazon.com views free shipping as a key factor in boosting its growth—revenue jumped 233% to $851 million in one year. Yet, the company doesn't send packages via eight trusty reindeer. Amazon has to pay freight companies to deliver DVD players, books, and blenders to customers around the world. How does an e-tailer—one that is just barely making a profit—account for these shipping and handling costs?

Fortunately for Amazon and other e-tailers, in the process of revolutionizing business, e-commerce has also bent certain accounting rules. One such rule is that the cost of products sold to customers is usually recorded as Cost of Goods Sold, a merchandiser's major expense. But online powerhouses like Amazon.com and Buy.com count some of this cost as "sales and marketing expenses." By listing these "fulfillment costs" as marketing expenses, both e-tailers and catalog houses such as L. L. Bean don't have to subtract the expense in arriving at gross profit.

Small wonder that this controversial approach came under investigation by the Financial Accounting Standards Board (FASB). The dot-com bubble had burst, and e-tailers were poised to reclassify shipping and handling costs as costs of goods sold. That would restate gross profit downward. However, the Emerging Issues Task Force of the FASB recommended that shipping and handling *revenue* should be included in sales, without giving any guidance about how to account for shipping and handling *costs*. So Amazon and other e-tailers are free to continue including shipping and handling costs under marketing expense. The result: Gross profits are still high.

Based on: Nick Winfield, "Survival Strategy: Amazon Takes Page from Wal-Mart to Prosper on Web—Internet Retailer Cuts Prices and Keeps Eye on Costs in Bid for High Volumes—Betting Big on Free Shipping," *The Wall Street Journal,* November 22, 2002, p. A1. Saul Hansell, "Amazon's Loss in Quarter Shows a Sharp Decrease," *The New York Times,* October 25, 2002, p. 8. Katherine Hobson, "Silver Lining: FASB Spares E-Tailers in Cost Ruling," *The Street.com,* August 8, 2000.

The gross profit reported on Amazon.com's 2001 income statement is the sum of the gross profits on all the DVDs and other products the company sold during the year.

Let's put into practice what you've learned in the first half of this chapter.

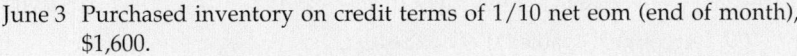

MID-CHAPTER *Summary Problem*

Suppose Amazon.com engaged in the following transactions during June of the current year:

TIPS

CHECK YOUR RESOURCES

June 3 Purchased inventory on credit terms of 1/10 net eom (end of month), $1,600.

  9 Returned 40% of the inventory purchased on June 3. It was defective.

  12 Sold goods for cash, $920 (cost, $550).

  15 Purchased goods for $5,000. Credit terms were 3/15 net 30.

  16 Paid a $260 freight bill on goods purchased.

  18 Sold inventory on credit terms of 2/10 n/30, $2,000 (cost, $1,180).

  22 Received returned goods from the customer of the June 18 sale, $800 (cost, $480).

  24 Borrowed money from the bank to take advantage of the discount offered on the June 15 purchase. Signed a note payable to the bank for the net amount.

  24 Paid supplier for goods purchased on June 15, less the discount.

  28 Received cash in full settlement of the account from the customer who purchased inventory on June 18, less the return on June 22.

  29 Paid the amount owed on account from the purchase of June 3, less the June 9 return.

Required

1. Journalize the preceding transactions. Explanations are not required.
2. Set up T-accounts and post the journal entries to show the ending balances in the Inventory and the Cost of Goods Sold accounts.
3. Assume that the note payable signed on June 24 requires the payment of $95 interest expense. Was borrowing funds to take the cash discount a wise or unwise decision?

Solution

Requirement 1

June 3	Inventory	1,600	
	Accounts Payable.		1,600
9	Accounts Payable ($1,600 × 0.40)	640	
	Inventory.		640
12	Cash.	920	
	Sales Revenue		920
12	Cost of Goods Sold	550	
	Inventory.		550
15	Inventory	5,000	
	Accounts Payable.		5,000
16	Inventory	260	
	Cash		260
18	Accounts Receivable.	2,000	
	Sales Revenue		2,000
18	Cost of Goods Sold	1,180	
	Inventory.		1,180

(continued)

June 22	Sales Returns and Allowances	800	
	Accounts Receivable		800
22	Inventory	480	
	Cost of Goods Sold		480
24	Cash [$5,000 − 0.03 ($5,000)].....................	4,850	
	Note Payable..........................		4,850
24	Accounts Payable	5,000	
	Inventory ($5,000 × 0.03)...................		150
	Cash ($5,000 × 0.97).......................		4,850
28	Cash [($2,000 − $800) × 0.98]	1,176	
	Sales Discounts [($2,000 − $800) × 0.02]	24	
	Accounts Receivable ($2,000 − $800)		1,200
29	Accounts Payable ($1,600 − $640)	960	
	Cash		960

Requirement 2

Inventory					Cost of Goods Sold			
June 3	1,600	June 9	640		June 12	550	June 22	480
15	5,000	12	550		18	1,180		
16	260	18	1,180		Bal.	1,250		
22	480	24	150					
Bal.	4,820							

Requirement 3

Amazon's decision to borrow funds was wise because the discount ($150) exceeded the interest paid ($95). Thus Amazon was $55 better off.

Student ResourceCD

adjusting, cost of goods sold, inventory, inventory turnover, work sheet

4 *Adjust and close the accounts of a merchandising business*

Adjusting and Closing the Accounts of a Merchandiser

A merchandiser adjusts and closes accounts the same way a service entity does. If a work sheet is used, the trial balance is entered, and the work sheet is completed to determine net income or net loss. The work sheet aids the adjusting and closing processes and preparation of the financial statements.

Adjusting Inventory Based on a Physical Count

The inventory account should stay current at all times. However, the actual amount of inventory on hand may differ from what the books show. Theft, damage, and errors occur. For this reason, businesses, like the bookstore chain Barnes & Noble, take a physical count of inventory at least once a year. The most common time to count inventory is at the end of the fiscal year. The business then adjusts the Inventory account based on the physical count.

Exhibit 5-5, Austin Sound's work sheet for the year ended December 31, 20X5, lists a $40,500 balance for inventory on the trial balance (first two columns). With no shrinkage—due to theft or error—the business should have inventory costing $40,500. But on December 31, when Austin Sound counts the inventory, the total cost of the goods on hand comes to only $40,200.

ACTUAL INVENTORY ON HAND	−	INVENTORY BALANCE BEFORE ADJUSTMENT	=	ADJUSTING ENTRY TO THE INVENTORY ACCOUNT
$40,200	−	$40,500	=	Credit of $300

Austin Sound then records this adjusting entry for inventory shrinkage:

Dec. 31	Cost of Goods Sold.....................	300	
	Inventory ($40,500 − $40,200)		300

This entry brings Inventory and Cost of Goods Sold to their correct balances.

Exhibit 5-5 Accounting Work Sheet

Austin Sound Center
Accounting Work Sheet
Year Ended December 31, 20X5

Account Title	Trial Balance Debit	Trial Balance Credit	Adjustments Debit	Adjustments Credit	Income Statement Debit	Income Statement Credit	Balance Sheet Debit	Balance Sheet Credit
Cash	2,850						2,850	
Accounts receivable	4,600						4,600	
Note receivable, current	8,000						8,000	
Interest receivable			(a) 400				400	
Inventory	40,500			(b) 300			40,200	
Supplies	650			(c) 550			100	
Prepaid insurance	1,200			(d) 1,000			200	
Furniture and fixtures	33,200						33,200	
Accumulated depreciation		2,400		(e) 600				3,000
Accounts payable		47,000						47,000
Unearned sales revenue		2,000	(f) 1,300					700
Wages payable				(g) 400				400
Interest payable				(h) 200				200
Note payable, long-term		12,600						12,600
C. Ernest, capital		25,900						25,900
C. Ernest, withdrawals	54,100						54,100	
Sales revenue		168,000		(f) 1,300		169,300		
Sales discounts	1,400				1,400			
Sales returns and allowances	2,000				2,000			
Interest revenue		600		(a) 400		1,000		
Cost of goods sold	90,500		(b) 300		90,800			
Wage expense	9,800		(g) 400		10,200			
Rent expense	8,400				8,400			
Depreciation expense			(e) 600		600			
Insurance expense			(d) 1,000		1,000			
Supplies expense			(c) 550		550			
Interest expense	1,300		(h) 200		1,500			
	258,500	258,500	4,750	4,750	116,450	170,300	143,650	89,800
Net income					53,850			53,850
					170,300	170,300	143,650	143,650

The physical count can also reveal that more inventory is present than the books show. In that case, the adjusting entry debits Inventory and credits Cost of Goods Sold.

To illustrate a merchandiser's adjusting and closing process, let's use Austin Sound's 20X5 work sheet in Exhibit 5-5. All the new accounts—Inventory, Cost of Goods Sold, and the contra accounts—are highlighted for emphasis.

Adjustment data at December 31, 20X5:

a. Interest revenue earned but not yet collected, $400.

b. Inventory on hand, $40,200.

c. Supplies on hand, $100.

d. Prepaid insurance expired during the year, $1,000.

e. Depreciation, $600.

f. Unearned sales revenue earned during the year, $1,300.

g. Accrued wage expense, $400.

h. Accrued interest expense, $200.

Preparing and Using the Work Sheet

The Exhibit 5-5 work sheet is similar to the work sheets we have seen so far, but there are a few differences. This work sheet does not include adjusted trial balance columns. ← In most accounting systems, a single operation combines trial balance amounts with the adjustments. The adjusted balances go directly to the income statement and balance sheet columns.

This work sheet is slightly different from the one introduced in the Chapter 4 acetates following p. 144—this work sheet contains four pairs of columns, not five.

Account Title Columns The trial balance lists the unadjusted amount for each account. There are a few accounts without balances. These accounts are affected by the adjusting process. Examples include Interest Receivable, Wages Payable, and Depreciation Expense. Accounts are listed in the order they appear in the ledger.

Trial Balance Columns Examine the Inventory account in the trial balance. Inventory has a balance of $40,500 before the physical count at the end of the year. Any difference between the Inventory amount on the trial balance ($40,500) and the correct amount based on the physical count ($40,200) is debited or credited to Cost of Goods Sold, as we just saw.

Adjustments Columns The adjustments are similar to those discussed in Chapters 3 and 4. The debit amount of each entry should equal the credit amount, and total debits should equal total credits.

Income Statement Columns The income statement columns in Exhibit 5-5 show adjusted amounts for the revenues and the expenses. Sales Revenue, for example, has an adjusted balance of $169,300.

The income statement totals indicate a net income or net loss.

■ Net income: Total credits > Total debits   ■ Net loss: Total debits > Total credits

Austin Sound's total credits of $170,300 exceed the total debits of $116,450, so the company earned a net income.

Balance-Sheet Columns The only new item in the balance sheet columns is Inventory. The $40,200 balance is determined by the physical count at the end of the period.

Journalizing the Adjusting and Closing Entries

Exhibit 5-6 presents Austin Sound's adjusting entries, which are similar to those you have seen previously, except for the inventory adjustment [entry (b)]. → The closing entries in the exhibit also follow the pattern illustrated in Chapter 4.

Chapter 4, p. 148, explains closing entries in more detail.

The *first closing entry* debits the revenue accounts for their ending balances. The offsetting credit of $170,300 transfers the sum of total revenues to Income Summary. This amount comes directly from the credit column of the income statement (Exhibit 5-5).

The *second closing entry* credits Cost of Goods Sold, the contra revenue accounts (Sales Discounts and Sales Returns and Allowances), and all the expense accounts. The offsetting $116,450 debit to Income Summary represents the amount of total expenses plus the contra revenues. These amounts come from the debit column of the income statement.

The *last two closing entries* close net income to the Capital account and also close Withdrawals into the Capital account.

Journal

Adjusting Entries

a.	Dec. 31	Interest Receivable............................	400	
		Interest Revenue		400
b.	31	Cost of Goods Sold	300	
		Inventory..................................		300
c.	31	Supplies Expense ($650 – $100)	550	
		Supplies...................................		550
d.	31	Insurance Expense............................	1,000	
		Prepaid Insurance		1,000
e.	31	Depreciation Expense	600	
		Accumulated Depreciation		600
f.	31	Unearned Sales Revenue	1,300	
		Sales Revenue............................		1,300
g.	31	Wage Expense	400	
		Wages Payable		400
h.	31	Interest Expense.............................	200	
		Interest Payable		200

Closing Entries

1.	Dec. 31	Sales Revenue................................	169,300	
		Interest Revenue	1,000	
		Income Summary.......................		170,300
2.	31	Income Summary.............................	116,450	
		Sales Discounts		1,400
		Sales Returns and Allowances..............		2,000
		Cost of Goods Sold		90,800
		Wage Expense		10,200
		Rent Expense		8,400
		Depreciation Expense		600
		Insurance Expense.......................		1,000
		Supplies Expense........................		550
		Interest Expense.........................		1,500
3.	31	Income Summary ($170,300 – $116,450)	53,850	
		C. Ernest, Capital.........................		53,850
4.	31	C. Ernest, Capital............................	54,100	
		C. Ernest, Withdrawals...................		54,100

Exhibit 5-6

Adjusting and Closing Entries for a Merchandiser

✔ **Starter 5-8**

✔ **Starter 5-9**

✔ **Starter 5-10**

Study Exhibits 5-5 and 5-6 carefully because they show the end-of-period process that leads to the financial statements.

Here is an easy way to remember the closing process. First, look at the work sheet. Then:

1. Debit all income statement accounts with a credit balance. Credit Income Summary for the total.
2. Credit all income statement accounts with a debit balance. Debit Income Summary for the total.
3. Compute the balance in the Income Summary account. A debit balance indicates a net loss; to close a net loss, credit Income Summary and debit Capital. If Income Summary has a credit balance, there is a net income; to close net income, debit Income Summary and credit Capital.
4. Withdrawals has a debit balance. Credit Withdrawals to close its balance, and debit Capital for the same amount. This is the final closing entry.

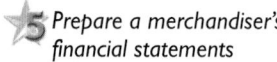

income statement

⭐5 *Prepare a merchandiser's financial statements*

Operating Expenses
Expenses, other than cost of goods sold, that are incurred in the entity's major line of business. Examples include rent, depreciation, salaries, wages, utilities, and supplies expense.

Operating Income
Gross profit minus operating expenses plus any other operating revenues. Also called **income from operations**.

Other Revenue
Revenue that is outside the main operations of a business, such as a gain on the sale of plant assets.

Other Expense
Expense that is outside the main operations of a business, such as a loss on the sale of plant assets.

Preparing a Merchandiser's Financial Statements

Exhibit 5-7 shows Austin Sound's financial statements for 20X5.

Income Statement The income statement begins with sales, cost of goods sold, and gross profit. Then come the **operating expenses,** which are those expenses other than cost of goods sold that occur in the entity's major line of business.

Many companies report operating expenses in two categories:

■ *Selling expenses* are expenses related to marketing the company's products—sales salaries; sales commissions; advertising; depreciation, rent, and utilities on store buildings; and delivery expense.

■ *General expenses* include office expenses, such as the salaries of the company president and office employees; depreciation; rent; utilities; and property taxes on the home office building.

Gross profit minus operating expenses plus any other operating revenues equals **operating income**, or **income from operations**. Operating income measures the results of the entity's major ongoing activities.

The last section of Austin Sound's income statement is **other revenue and expense**. This category reports revenues and expenses that fall outside its main operations. Examples include gains and losses on the sale of plant assets (not inventory) and gains and losses on lawsuits.

The bottom line of the income statement is net income:

$$\text{Net income} = \text{Total revenues and gains} - \text{Total expenses and losses}$$

We often hear the term *bottom line*, that is, a final result. The *bottom line* is net income on the income statement.

Statement of Owner's Equity A merchandiser's statement of owner's equity looks exactly like that of a service business.

Balance Sheet If the business is a merchandiser, the balance sheet shows inventory as a major current asset. Service businesses usually have no inventory.

Exhibit 5-7

Financial Statements of Austin
Sound Center

Austin Sound Center

Income Statement
Year Ended December 31, 20X5

Sales revenue		$169,300
Less: Sales discounts	$ (1,400)	
Sales returns and allowances	(2,000)	(3,400)
Net sales revenue		$165,900
Cost of goods sold		90,800
Gross profit		75,100
Operating expenses:		
Wage expense	$ 10,200	
Rent expense	8,400	
Insurance expense	1,000	
Depreciation expense	600	
Supplies expense	550	20,750
Operating income		54,350
Other revenue and (expense):		
Interest revenue	$ 1,000	
Interest expense	(1,500)	(500)
Net income		$ 53,850

✔ Starter 5-11

Austin Sound Center

Statement of Owner's Equity
Year Ended December 31, 20X5

C. Ernest, capital, December 31, 20X4	$25,900
Add: Net income	53,850
	79,750
Less: Withdrawals	(54,100)
C. Ernest, capital, December 31, 20X5	$25,650

Austin Sound Center

Balance Sheet
December 31, 20X5

Assets			Liabilities		
Current:			Current:		
Cash		$ 2,850	Accounts payable . . .		$47,000
Accounts receivable		4,600	Unearned sales		
Note receivable		8,000	revenue		700
Interest receivable		400	Wages payable		400
Inventory		40,200	Interest payable		200
Prepaid insurance		200	Total current		
Supplies		100	liabilities		48,300
Total current assets		56,350	Long-term:		
Plant:			Note payable		12,600
Furniture and fixtures . .	$33,200		Total liabilities		60,900
Less: Accumulated					
depreciation	(3,000)	30,200	**Owner's Equity**		
			C. Ernest, capital		25,650
			Total liabilities and		
Total assets		$86,550	owner's equity . . .		$86,550

✔ Starter 5-12

For a review of balance sheet formats, see Chapter 4, p. 153.

Income Statement Formats: Multi-Step and Single-Step

←The balance sheet appears in two formats:

- The report format (assets on top, . . . , owner's equity at bottom)
- The account format (assets at left, liabilities and owner's equity at right)

There are also two formats for the income statement:

- The multi-step format
- The single-step format

The multi-step format is by far the more popular.

Multi-Step Income Statement
Format that contains subtotals to highlight significant relationships. In addition to net income, it reports gross profit and operating income.

MULTI-STEP INCOME STATEMENT   The **multi-step format** lists important subtotals. In addition to net income, it also reports gross profit and income from operations. This format reports a merchandiser's results of operations especially well because gross profit and income from operations are important to investors. The income statements presented thus far in this chapter have been multi-step. Austin Sound's multi-step income statement for the year ended December 31, 20X5, appears in Exhibit 5-7.

Single-Step Income Statement
Format that groups all revenues together and then lists and deducts all expenses together without drawing any subtotals.

SINGLE-STEP INCOME STATEMENT   The **single-step format** groups all revenues together and all expenses together without drawing any subtotals. IBM and Wal-Mart use this format. The single-step format clearly distinguishes revenues from expenses, as Exhibit 5-8 shows. This format works well for service entities because they have no gross profit to report.

Exhibit 5-8

Single-Step Income Statement

Austin Sound Center	
Income Statement	
Year Ended December 31, 20X5	
Revenues:	
Net sales (net of sales discounts, $1,400, and returns and allowances, $2,000)	$165,900
Interest revenue	1,000
Total revenues	166,900
Expenses:	
Cost of goods sold	90,800
Wage expense	10,200
Rent expense	8,400
Interest expense	1,500
Insurance expense	1,000
Depreciation expense	600
Supplies expenses	550
Total expenses	113,050
Net Income	$ 53,850

☐ Merchandising Operations
☐ Accounting for Inventory:
   Perpetual System
☐ Adjusting and Closing Accounts
☐ Preparing Financial Statements
■ Key Decision-Making Ratios

Student ResourceCD

gross profit, inventory turnover

Two Key Ratios for Decision Making

Merchandise inventory is the most important asset for a merchandising business. Owners and managers use several ratios to evaluate operations, among them the gross profit percentage and the rate of inventory turnover.

The Gross Profit Percentage

A key decision tool highlights gross profit, which is net sales minus cost of goods sold. Merchandisers strive to increase the **gross profit percentage**, which is computed as follows:

**For Austin Sound Center
(Exhibit 5-7)**

$$\text{Gross profit percentage} = \frac{\text{Gross profit}}{\text{Net sales revenue}} = \frac{\$75{,}100}{\$165{,}900} = 0.453 = 45.3\%$$

Gross Profit Percentage
Gross profit divided by net sales revenue. A measure of profitability. Also called **gross margin percentage**.

The gross profit percentage (also called the *gross margin percentage*) is one of the most carefully watched measures of profitability. A 45% gross margin means that each dollar of sales generates 45 cents of gross profit. On average, the goods cost the seller 55 cents. For most firms, the gross profit percentage changes little from year to year. A small increase may signal an important rise in income, and vice versa for a decrease.

Exhibit 5-9 compares Austin Sound's gross margin to that of Target and Amazon.com.

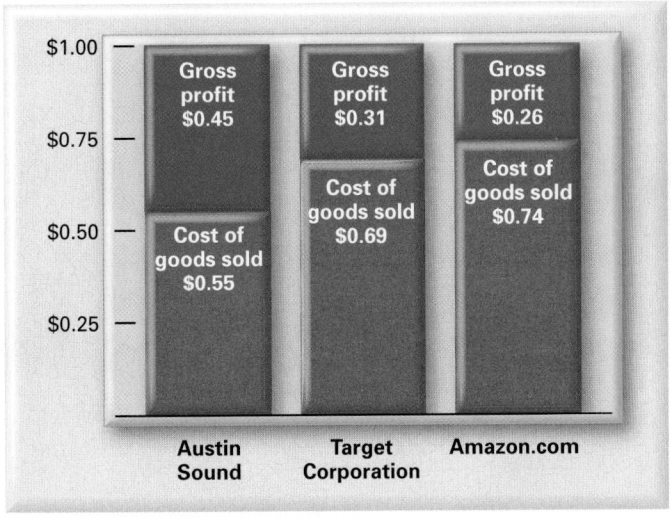

Exhibit 5-9

Gross Profit on $1 of Sales for Three Merchandisers

The Rate of Inventory Turnover

Owners and managers strive to sell inventory quickly because the inventory generates no profit until it is sold. The faster the sales, the higher the income. The slower the sales, the lower the income. Ideally, a business could operate with zero inventory. Most businesses, however, including Amazon.com and Target, must keeps goods on hand. **Inventory turnover**, the ratio of cost of goods sold to average inventory, indicates how rapidly inventory is sold. It is computed as follows:

Inventory Turnover
Ratio of cost of goods sold to average inventory. Measures the number of times a company sells its average level of inventory during a year.

**For Austin Sound Center
(Exhibit 5-7)**

$$\frac{\text{Inventory}}{\text{turnover}} = \frac{\text{Cost of goods sold}}{\text{Average inventory}} = \frac{\text{Cost of goods sold}}{(\text{Beginning inventory} + \text{Ending inventory})/2}$$

$$= \frac{\$90{,}800}{(\$38{,}600^* + \$40{,}200)/2} = 2.3 \text{ times per year}$$

---
*Taken from balance sheet at the end of the preceding period.

✔ **Starter 5-13**

✔ **Starter 5-14**

Inventory turnover is usually computed for an annual period, so the cost-of-goods sold figure is the amount for the entire year. Average inventory is computed from the beginning and ending balances. Austin Sound's beginning inventory would be taken from the balance sheet at the end of the preceding year.

A high turnover rate is desirable, and an increase in the turnover rate usually means higher profits. Inventory turnover varies from industry to industry. Grocery stores, for example, turn their goods over much faster than automobile dealers do. Retailers of electronic products, such as Austin Sound, have an average turnover of 3.6 times per year. A turnover rate of 2.3 times per year suggests that Austin Sound is not very efficient. Exhibit 5-10 compares the inventory turnover rate of Austin Sound and Amazon.com.

Exhibit 5-10 tells an interesting story. Amazon.com moves its merchandise six times as fast as Austin Sound.

In fact, the trick for merchandisers is in keeping enough goods to sell but not so much that inventory becomes a financial drain. According to analysts, disappointing sales from Home Depot show that the home improvement giant has not quite mastered the inventory balancing act. After Home Depot cut its inventory way back, customers started shopping at Home Depot's rival, Lowe's. Home Depot's sales dropped by 2%, and now the company is working hard to keep enough inventory on hand.[2]

Exhibit 5-10

Rate of Inventory Turnover for Two Merchandisers

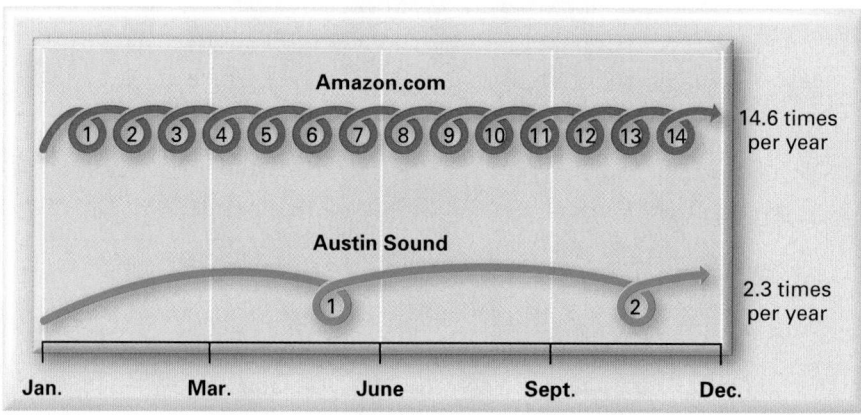

Calculate the rate of inventory turnover for Safeway, Inc., the large grocery chain (amounts in millions).

Beginning inventory	$ 1,856
Ending inventory	2,445
Cost of goods sold	20,349

Answer

$$\text{Inventory turnover} = \frac{\text{Cost of goods sold}}{(\text{Beginning inventory} + \text{Ending inventory})/2}$$

$$= \frac{\$20,349}{(\$1,856 + \$2,445)/2} = 9.5 \text{ times per year}$$

---

[2]Chad Terhune, "Home Depot Earnings Fall 3.4% Amid First Quarterly Sales Drop, *The Wall Street Journal,* February 26, 2003, p. A.11.

Decision Guidelines

MERCHANDISING OPERATIONS AND THE ACCOUNTING CYCLE

Amazon.com and Kinko's Copy Centers are two very different companies. How do Amazon and Kinko's differ? How are they similar? The Decision Guidelines answer these questions.

Decision	Guidelines
How do merchandisers differ from service entities?	• Merchandisers, such as Amazon.com, buy and sell *merchandise inventory*. • Service entities, such as Kinko's, perform a *service*.
How do a merchandiser's financial statements differ from the statements of a service business?	**Balance sheet:** • Merchandiser has *inventory*, an asset. • Service business has no inventory.

Income Statement:

Merchandiser

Sales revenue	$XXX
−Cost of goods sold	(X)
= Gross profit	XX
−Operating expenses	(X)
= Net income	$ X

Service Business

Service revenue	$ XX
−Operating expenses	(X)
= Net income	$ X

No difference

Statements of Owner's Equity:

Decision	Guidelines
Which type of inventory system to use?	• *Perpetual system* shows the amount of *inventory* on hand (the asset) and the cost of goods sold (the expense) at all times. • *Periodic system* shows the correct balances of inventory and cost of goods sold only after a physical count of the inventory, which occurs at least once each year.
How do the adjusting and closing procedures of merchandisers and service entities differ?	Very little. The merchandiser may have to *adjust* the Inventory account for shrinkage. The merchandiser must *close* the Cost of Goods Sold account. Service entities have no inventory to adjust and no cost of goods sold to close.

How to format the merchandiser's income statement?

Multi-Step Format

Sales revenue	$ XXX
−Cost of goods sold	(X)
= Gross profit	XX
−Operating expenses	(X)
= Operating income	X
+ Other revenues	X
−Other expenses	(X)
= Net income	$ XX

Single-Step Format

Revenues:

Sales revenue	$ XXX
Other revenues	X
Total revenues	XXXX

Expenses:

Cost of goods sold	(X)
Operating expenses	(X)
Other expenses	(X)
Total expenses	XX
Net income	$ XX

How to evaluate inventory operations?

Two key ratios

$$\text{Gross profit percentage*} = \frac{\text{Gross profit}}{\text{Net sales revenue}}$$

$$\text{Inventory turnover*} = \frac{\text{Cost of goods sold}}{\text{Average inventory}}$$

*In most cases—the higher, the better.

Excel Application Exercise

Goal: Create a spreadsheet to compute Amazon.com's gross profit percentage and inventory turnover for the past three years.

Scenario: You are intrigued by Amazon's ability to sell merchandise via the Internet and would like to invest in such a venture. Before doing so, however, you remember from your accounting course that ratio analysis is an important part of making an investment decision. You decide to calculate two key ratios: gross profit percentage and inventory turnover. (You may need to visit Amazon.com on the Web to find inventory data from past years. Look under Investor Relations at the bottom of the Home page.) When you have completed your worksheet, answer the following questions:

1. What has happened to Amazon's gross profit percentage over the past three years?
2. What can you tell about Amazon's inventory operations from its inventory turnover ratio for the past two years?

Step-by-Step:

1. Open a new Excel spreadsheet.
2. In column 1, create a bold-faced heading as follows:
   a. Chapter 5 Excel Application Exercise
   b. Evaluating Amazon Inventory Operations
   c. Today's Date
3. Two rows down and two columns over, create bold and underlined headings for the most recent three years (e.g., 2002, 2001, and 2000).
4. In column A, enter the following (one per row):
   a. Net Sales (in thousands)
   b. Cost of Goods Sold (Cost of Sales)
   c. Gross Profit
   d. Inventory
   e. Gross Profit Percentage
   f. Inventory Turnover
5. Locate the data for items **a-d** in the Amazon.com annual report (or on the Web) and enter it in the appropriate columns.
6. Calculate gross profit percentage and inventory turnover. To help visualize the data trends, use the Chart Wizard to create a bar graph of performance.
7. Format all columns, rows, and data as needed. Save your work and print a copy for your files.

END-OF-CHAPTER *Summary Problem*

CHECK YOUR RESOURCES

The adjustment data and trial balance of Jan King Distributing Company follow. (*The solution to Requirement 1 is on page 208.*)

Adjustment data at December 31, 20X6:

a. Supplies used during the year, $2,580.
b. Prepaid rent in force, $1,000.
c. Unearned sales revenue still not earned, $2,400.
d. Depreciation. The furniture and fixtures' estimated useful life is 10 years, and they are expected to be worthless when they are retired from service.
e. Accrued salaries, $1,300.
f. Accrued interest expense, $600.
g. Inventory on hand, $65,800.

Required

1. Enter the trial balance on a work sheet and complete the work sheet.
2. Journalize the adjusting and closing entries at December 31. Post to the Income Summary account as an accuracy check on the entries affecting that account. The credit balance closed out of Income Summary should equal net income computed on the work sheet.
3. Prepare the company's multi-step income statement, statement of owner's equity, and balance sheet in account format. Draw arrows linking the statements.
4. Compute the inventory turnover for 20X6. Inventory at December 31, 20X5, was $61,000. Turnover for 20X5 was 2.1 times. Would you expect Jan King Distributing Company to be more profitable or less profitable in 20X6 than in 20X5? Give your reason.

Jan King Distributing Company

Trial Balance
December 31, 20X6

Cash	$ 5,670	
Accounts receivable	37,100	
Inventory	60,500	
Supplies	3,930	
Prepaid rent	6,000	
Furniture and fixtures	26,500	
Accumulated depreciation		$ 21,200
Accounts payable		46,340
Salary payable		
Interest payable		
Unearned sales revenue		3,500
Note payable, long-term		35,000
Jan King, capital		23,680
Jan King, withdrawals	48,000	
Sales revenue		346,700
Sales discounts	10,300	
Sales returns and allowances	8,200	
Cost of goods sold	171,770	
Salary expense	82,750	
Rent expense	7,000	
Depreciation expense		
Utilities expense	5,800	
Supplies expense		
Interest expense	2,900	
Total	$476,420	$476,420

Solution

Requirement 2 (starts here; continues on p. 209)

Adjusting Entries

20X6

Dec. 31	Supplies Expense.		2,580	
	Supplies.			2,580
31	Rent Expense		5,000	
	Prepaid Rent.			5,000
31	Unearned Sales Revenue ($3,500 − $2,400)		1,100	
	Sales Revenue.			1,100
31	Depreciation Expense ($26,500/10)		2,650	
	Accumulated Depreciation			2,650
31	Salary Expense.		1,300	
	Salary Payable			1,300
31	Interest Expense.		600	
	Interest Payable			600
31	Inventory ($65,800 − $60,500)		5,300*	
	Cost of Goods Sold			5,300

*Excess of inventory on hand over the balance in the Inventory account. This adjustment brings Inventory to its correct balance.

Requirement 1

Jan King Distributing Company
Accounting Work Sheet
Year Ended December 31, 20X6

Account Title	Trial Balance Debit	Trial Balance Credit	Adjustments Debit	Adjustments Credit	Income Statement Debit	Income Statement Credit	Balance Sheet Debit	Balance Sheet Credit
Cash	5,670						5,670	
Accounts receivable . . .	37,100						37,100	
Inventory	60,500		(g) 5,300				65,800	
Supplies	3,930			(a) 2,580			1,350	
Prepaid rent	6,000			(b) 5,000			1,000	
Furniture and fixtures	26,500						26,500	
Accumulated depreciation		21,200		(d) 2,650				23,850
Accounts payable		46,340						46,340
Salary payable				(e) 1,300				1,300
Interest payable				(f) 600				600
Unearned sales revenue		3,500	(c) 1,100					2,400
Note payable, long-term		35,000						35,000
Jan King, capital		23,680						23,680
Jan King, withdrawals	48,000						48,000	
Sales revenue		346,700		(c) 1,100		347,800		
Sales discounts	10,300				10,300			
Sales returns and allowances	8,200				8,200			
Cost of goods sold	171,770			(g) 5,300	166,470			
Salary expense	82,750		(e) 1,300		84,050			
Rent expense	7,000		(b) 5,000		12,000			
Depreciation expense			(d) 2,650		2,650			
Utilities expense	5,800				5,800			
Supplies expense			(a) 2,580		2,580			
Interest expense	2,900		(f) 600		3,500			
	476,420	476,420	18,530	18,530	295,550	347,800	185,420	133,170
Net income					52,250			52,250
					347,800	347,800	185,420	185,420

Closing Entries

20X6

Dec. 31	Sales Revenue		347,800	
	Income Summary			347,800
31	Income Summary		295,550	
	Sales Discounts			10,300
	Sales Returns and Allowances			8,200
	Cost of Goods Sold			166,470
	Salary Expense			84,050
	Rent Expense			12,000
	Depreciation Expense			2,650
	Utilities Expense			5,800
	Supplies Expense			2,580
	Interest Expense			3,500
31	Income Summary ($347,800 − $295,550)		52,250	
	Jan King, Capital			52,250
31	Jan King, Capital		48,000	
	Jan King, Withdrawals			48,000

Income Summary

Clo.	295,550	Clo.	347,800
Clo.	52,250	Bal.	52,250

Requirement 3

Jan King Distributing Company

Income Statement
Year Ended December 31, 20X6

Sales revenue		$347,800	
Less: Sales discounts	$(10,300)		
Sales returns and allowances	(8,200)	(18,500)	
Net sales revenue		$329,300	
Cost of goods sold		166,470	
Gross profit		162,830	
Operating expenses:			
Salary expense	$ 84,050		
Rent expense	12,000		
Utilities expense	5,800		
Depreciation expense	2,650		
Supplies expense	2,580	107,080	
Income from operations		55,750	
Other expense:			
Interest expense		3,500	
Net income		$ 52,250	

(*continued*)

Jan King Distributing Company

Statement of Owner's Equity
Year Ended December 31, 20X6

Jan King, capital, December 31, 20X5	$23,680
Add: Net income	52,250
. . . .	75,930
Less: Withdrawals	(48,000)
Jan King, capital, December 31, 20X6	$27,930

Jan King Distributing Company

Balance Sheet
December 31, 20X6

Assets		Liabilities	
Current:		Current:	
Cash	$ 5,670	Accounts payable	$46,340
Accounts receivable	37,100	Salary payable	1,300
Inventory	65,800	Interest payable	600
Supplies	1,350	Unearned sales revenue . .	2,400
Prepaid rent	1,000	Total current liabilities . . .	50,640
Total current assets	110,920	Long-term:	
Plant:		Note payable	35,000
Furniture and			
fixtures $26,500		Total liabilities	85,640
Less:			
Accumulated			
depreciation . . (23,850)	2,650	**Owner's Equity**	
		Jan King, capital	27,930
		Total liabilities and	
Total assets	$113,570	owner's equity	$113,570

Requirement 4

$$\frac{\text{Inventory}}{\text{turnover}} = \frac{\text{Cost of goods sold}}{\text{Average inventory}} = \frac{\$166,470}{(\$61,000 + \$65,800)/2} = 2.6 \text{ times}$$

The increase in the rate of inventory turnover from 2.1 to 2.6 suggests higher profits in 20X6 than in 20X5.

REVIEW *Merchandising Operations*

Quick Check

1. Which account does a merchandiser, but not a service company, use?
  a. Inventory
  b. Sales revenue
  c. Cost of goods sold
  d. All of the above

2. The two main inventory accounting systems are the
  a. Purchase and sale
  b. Perpetual and periodic
  c. Cash and accrual
  d. Returns and allowances

3. The journal entry for the purchase of inventory on account is

  a. Inventory................................... XXX
          Accounts Receivable   XXX
  b. Accounts Payable.......................... XXX
          Inventory..............................   XXX
  c. Inventory................................. XXX
          Accounts Payable.......................   XXX
  d. Inventory................................. XXX
          Cash...................................   XXX

4. Amazon.com purchased inventory for $5,000 and also paid a $300 freight bill. Amazon returned half the goods to the seller and took a 2% purchase discount. What is Amazon's cost of the inventory that it kept?
  a. $2,750
  b. $2,800
  c. $2,700
  d. $2,500

5. Suppose Amazon.com had sales of $4.0 billion and sales returns of $0.9 billion. Cost of goods sold was $2.3 billion. How much gross profit did Amazon report?
  a. $0.8 billion
  b. $1.7 billion
  c. $2.6 billion
  d. Cannot be determined from the data given

6. Suppose Amazon.com's Inventory account showed a balance of $141 million before the year-end adjustments. The physical count of goods on hand totaled $144 million. To adjust the accounts, Amazon would make this journal entry (amounts in millions):

  a. Inventory................................... 3
          Accounts Receivable   3
  b. Accounts Payable.......................... 3
          Inventory..............................   3
  c. Inventory................................. 3
          Cost of Goods Sold   3
  d. Cost of Goods Sold 3
          Inventory..............................   3

7. Which account in question 6 would Amazon.com close at the end of the year?
  a. Inventory
  b. Accounts Receivable
  c. Accounts Payable
  d. Cost of Goods Sold

8. The final closing entry for a proprietorship is

  a. Owner, Withdrawals XXX
          Owner, Capital   XXX
  b. Sales Revenue............................. XXX
          Income Summary........................   XXX
  c. Owner, Capital XXX
          Owner, Withdrawals   XXX
  d. Income Summary........................... XXX
          Expenses   XXX

9. Which subtotals appear on a multi-step income statement, but not on a single-step income statement?
   a. Net sales and Cost of goods sold
   b. Gross Profit and Income from operations
   c. Cost of goods sold and net income
   d. Operating expenses and net income

10. Amazon.com made net sales of $3.12 billion, and cost of goods sold totaled $2.32 billion. Average inventory was $0.16 billion. What was Amazon.com's rate of inventory turnover for this period?
    a. 34%   c. 19.5 times
    b. 14.5%   d. 14.5 times

Accounting Vocabulary

cost of goods sold (p. 190)
cost of sales (p. 190)
gross margin (p. 193)
gross margin percentage (p. 203)
gross profit (p. 193)
gross profit percentage (p. 203)
income from operations (p. 200)
inventory (p. 184)

inventory turnover (p. 203)
invoice (p. 186)
multi-step income statement (p. 202)
net purchases (p. 233)
net sales revenue (p. 192)
operating expenses (p. 200)
operating income (p. 200)
other expense (p. 200)

other revenue (p. 200)
periodic inventory system (p. 185)
perpetual inventory system (p. 186)
sales (p. 190)
sales discount (p. 192)
sales returns and allowances (p. 192)
sales revenue (p. 190)
single-step income statement (p. 202)

ASSESS *Your Progress*

 online homework

See *www.prenhall.com/horngren* for selected Starters, Exercises, and Problems.

Recording purchase and cash payment transactions
(Obj. 1)

Accounting for the purchase of inventory—purchase discount
(Obj. 1)

Recording purchase, purchase return, and cash payment transactions.
(Obj. 1)

Starters

S5-1 You may have shopped at a **Gap** store. Suppose Gap purchases 2,000 pairs of slacks on account for $50,000. Credit terms are 2/10 n/30. Gap paid within the discount period. Journalize the following transactions for Gap:

a. Purchase of inventory.   b. Payment on account.

S5-2 **Toys "Я" Us** purchases inventory from a variety of suppliers, including **Mattel**, **Hasbro**, and **Tonka**. Suppose Toys "Я" Us buys $150,000 worth of **Lego** toys on credit terms of 3/15 n/45. Some of the goods are damaged in shipment, so Toys "Я" Us returns $50,000 (original amount, before any discounts) of the merchandise to Lego.
    How much must Toys "Я" Us pay Lego

a. After the discount period?   b. Within the discount period?

S5-3 Refer to the **Toys "Я" Us** situation in Starter 5-2 and journalize the following transactions on the books of Toys "Я" Us. Explanations are not required.

a. Purchase of the goods on May 6, 20X5.
b. Return of the damaged goods on May 13.
c. Payment on May 15. Before journalizing this transaction, it is helpful to post the first two transactions to the Accounts Payable T-account.

S5-4 Suppose a **Lord & Taylor** store purchases $140,000 of women's sportswear on account from **Liz Claiborne, Inc.** Credit terms are 2/10 net 30. Lord & Taylor pays electronically, and Liz Claiborne receives the money on the tenth day.

    Journalize Lord & Taylor's (a) purchase and (b) payment transactions. What was Lord & Taylor's net cost of this inventory?

    Note: Starter 5-5 covers this same situation for the seller.

Recording purchase transactions
(Obj. 1)

S5-5 **Liz Claiborne, Inc.**, sells $140,000 of women's sportswear to a **Lord & Taylor** store under credit terms of 2/10 net 30. Liz Claiborne's cost of the goods is $82,000, and Claiborne receives the appropriate amount of cash from Lord & Taylor on the tenth day.

    Journalize Liz Claiborne's (a) sale, (b) cost of goods sold, and (c) cash receipt.

    Note: Starter 5-4 covers the same situation for the buyer.

Recording sales, cost of goods sold, and cash collections
(Obj. 2)

S5-6 Suppose **Prentice Hall,** the publisher, sells 1,000 books on account for $15 each (cost of these books is $8,000). One hundred of these books (cost, $800) were damaged in shipment, so Prentice Hall later received the damaged goods as sales returns. Then the customer paid the balance within the discount period. Credit terms were 2/15 net 30.

    Journalize Prentice Hall's (a) sale, (b) sale return, and (c) cash collection transactions. How much gross profit did Prentice Hall earn on this sale?

Recording sales, sales return, and collection entries
(Obj. 2, 3)

S5-7 **Intel Corporation**, famous for the Pentium© processor that powers personal computers, offers sales discounts to customers. Intel also allows its customers to return defective processors. Suppose that Intel made sales of $600,000 on credit terms of 3/10 net 30. Assume that Intel received sales returns of $12,000. Later, Intel collected cash within the discount period. Cost of goods sold for the period was $255,000 after all sales returns.

    For this particular period, compute Intel's

a. Net sales revenue   **b.** Gross profit

Computing net sales and gross profit
(Obj. 3)

S5-8 Examine the work sheet of **Austin Sound Center** in Exhibit 5-5, page 197. Focus on adjusting entries (a) and (b). Which entry is exactly the same as for a service company? Which entry relates to a merchandiser only? Explain the reason for the merchandiser's adjusting entry.

Adjusting the accounts of a merchandiser
(Obj. 4)

S5-9 Refer to the work sheet of **Austin Sound Center** in Exhibit 5-5, page 197. Based solely on the Income Statement columns of the work sheet, make two closing entries, as follows:

Making closing entries
(Obj. 4)

- Journalize the closing entry for the *first account* listed that must be closed at the end of the period.
- Journalize the closing entry for the *last account* listed on the work sheet (not net income, which is not an account).

All closing entries for revenues and expenses follow the pattern of the closing entries you just made. Now make the final two closing entries of Austin Sound Center:

- Journalize the closing entry for net income.
- Journalize the closing entry for the Owner's Withdrawals account.

    Set up a T-account for the Owner's Capital account, and insert the balance from the work sheet. Then post your closing entries to the Capital account. Its ending balance should be the same as the amount reported on Austin Sound's balance sheet in Exhibit 5-7 on page 201. Is it?

Closing the accounts
(Obj. 3)

S5-10 Refer to the income statement of Merchandising Co. in Exhibit 5-1, page 184.

1. Make two closing entries for Merchandising Co. at June 30, 20XX:

   • Close the revenue   • Close the expenses

2. Which of Merchandising Co.'s balance sheet accounts will the company close at June 30, 20XX? Give your reason.

Preparing a merchandiser's income statement
(Obj. 5)

S5-11 **Dell Computer Corporation** reported these figures in its January 31, 20X1, financial statements (adapted, and in millions):

Cash	$ 3,809
Total operating expenses	3,552
Accounts payable	3,538
Owners' equity	5,308
Long-term liabilities	971
Inventory	391
Cost of goods sold	20,047
Other assets (long-term)	3,025
Other current liabilities	1,654
Property and equipment, net	765
Net sales revenue	25,265
Other current assets	873
Accounts receivable	2,608

Prepare Dell's multi-step income statement for the year ended January 31, 20X1.

Preparing a merchandiser's balance sheet
(Obj. 5)

S5-12 Use the data in Starter 5-11 to prepare **Dell Computer's** classified balance sheet at January 31, 20X1. Use the report format with all headings, and list accounts in proper order.

Computing the gross profit percentage and the rate of inventory turnover
(Obj. 6)

S5-13 Refer to the **Dell Computer** situation in Starter 5-12. Compute Dell's gross profit percentage and rate of inventory turnover for 20X1. One year earlier, at January 31, 20X0, Dell's inventory balance was $320 million.

Contrasting gross profit and cash flows
(Obj. 6)

S5-14 **Lands' End**, the catalog merchant, reported the following for the year ended January 31, 20X0 (adapted, with amounts in millions):

Cash collections from customers	$1,323
Selling, general, and administrative expenses	529
Cost of sales	727
Net sales revenue	1,320
Cash payments to suppliers	682

As an investor, you wonder which was greater, Lands' End's (a) gross profit, or (b) the company's excess of cash collections from customers over cash payments to suppliers? Compute both amounts to answer this question.

Exercises

E5-1 As the proprietor of Davis Tire Co., you receive the following invoice from a supplier:

Journalizing transactions from a purchase invoice
(Obj. 1)

 **WHOLESALE DISTRIBUTORS, INC.**
2600 Commonwealth Avenue
Boston, Massachusetts 02215

Invoice date: May 14, 20X6   **Payment terms:** 3/10 n/30

Sold to: Davis Tire Co.
4219 Crestwood Parkway
Lexington, Mass. 02173

Description	Quantity Shipped	Price	Amount
P135–X4 Radials.....................................	4	$37.14	$ 148.56
L912 Belted-bias	8	41.32	330.56
R39 Truck tires.......................................	10	60.02	600.20
Total...			$1,079.32

Due date:	**Amount:**
May 24, 20X6	$1,046.94
May 25 through June 13, 20X6	$1,079.32

Required

1. Davis received the invoice on May 15. Record the May 15 purchase on account. Carry amounts to the nearest cent throughout.
2. The R39 truck tires were ordered by mistake and were therefore returned to Wholesale Distributors. Journalize the return on May 19.
3. Record the May 22 payment of the amount owed.

E5-2 On April 30, Stanley & Weaver Jewelers purchased inventory of $8,000 on account from Intergem Jewels, a jewelry importer. Terms were 3/15 net 45. On receiving the goods, Stanley & Weaver checked the order and found $1,000 of unsuitable merchandise. Stanley & Weaver returned the unsuitable merchandise to Intergem on May 4.

Journalizing purchase transactions
(Obj. 1)

To pay the remaining amount owed, Stanley & Weaver borrowed the net amount of the invoice from the bank. On May 14, Stanley & Weaver signed a short-term note payable to the bank and immediately paid the borrowed funds to Intergem. On June 14, Stanley & Weaver paid the bank the net amount of the invoice, plus 1% monthly interest (rounded to the nearest dollar).

Required

Record the indicated transactions in the journal of Stanley & Weaver Jewelers. Explanations are not required.

Journalizing sales transactions
(Obj. 2)

E5-3 Refer to the business situation in Exercise 5-2. Journalize the transactions of Intergem Jewels. Intergem's gross profit is 40%, so cost of goods sold is 60% of sales. Explanations are not required.

Journalizing purchase and sales
transactions
(Obj. 1, 2)

E5-4 Journalize, without explanations, the following transactions of Jan's Perfect Presents during the month of September:

Sept. 3	Purchased $1,900 of inventory on account under terms of 2/10 n/eom (end of month) and FOB shipping point.
7	Returned $300 of defective merchandise purchased on September 3.
9	Paid freight bill of $30 on September 3 purchase.
10	Sold inventory on account for $3,100. Payment terms were 3/15 n/30. These goods cost Jan's $1,700.
12	Paid amount owed on credit purchase of September 3, less the discount and the return.
16	Granted a sales allowance of $800 on the September 10 sale.
23	Received cash from September 10 customer in full settlement of her debt, less the allowance and the discount.

Computing gross profit and net income
(Obj. 3)

E5-5 **General Electric (GE)**, the giant company known for home appliances and engines for jet aircraft, reported these figures for 2001 and 2000 (adapted and in billions):

	2001	2000
Net sales..	$52.7	$54.8
Cost of sales.....................................	35.7	39.3
Total operating expenses and other expenses	3.3	2.8

Compute GE's (a) gross profit and (b) net income for each year. Which year was more successful?

Give your reason.

Evaluating a company's revenues, gross
profit, and net income
(Obj. 3)

E5-6 **Toys "Я" Us** reported the following (adapted):

Toys "Я" Us, Inc.
Statements of Earnings (adapted)

	Fiscal Years Ended	
(In millions)	January 31, 20X1	January 31, 20X0
Net sales	$11,862	$11,170
Cost and expenses:		
Cost of sales	8,321	8,191
Other expenses	3,262	3,111
Net earnings (net loss)	$ 279	$ (132)

Toys "Я" Us, Inc.
Balance Sheets (partial, adapted)

Assets (In millions)	January 31, 20X1	January 31, 20X0
Current Assets:		
Cash and cash equivalents	$ 584	$ 410
Accounts and other receivables	182	204
Merchandise inventories	2,027	1,902
Prepaid expenses and other current assets	80	81
Total Current Assets	$2,873	$2,597

Required

1. Is Toys "Я" Us a merchandising entity, service business, or both? How can you tell? List the items in the Toys "Я" Us financial statements that influence your answer.

2. Compute Toys "Я" Us's gross profit for fiscal years 20X1 and 20X0. Did the gross profit increase or decrease in 20X1? Is this a good sign or a bad sign about the company?

3. Write a brief memo to investors advising them of Toys "Я" Us's trend of sales, gross profit, and net income. Indicate whether the outlook for Toys "Я" Us is favorable or unfavorable, based on this trend. Use the following memo format:

Date: _____
To: Investors
From: Student Name
Subject: Trend of sales, gross profit, and net income for Toys"Я" Us

E5-7 Supply the missing income statement amounts in each of the following situations:

Computing inventory and cost of goods sold amounts
(Obj. 3)

Sales	Sales Discounts	Net Sales	Cost of Goods Sold	Gross Profit
$98,300	(a)	$92,800	(b)	$33,000
62,400	$2,100	(c)	$44,100	(d)
91,500	1,800	89,700	59,400	(e)
(f)	3,000	(g)	72,500	39,600

E5-8 **Home Depot's** accounting records carried the following accounts (adapted, with amounts in millions) at January 31, 20X1:

Making closing entries
(Obj. 4)

Inventory	$ 5,489
Interest revenue	37
Accounts payable	1,993
Cost of goods sold	27,023
Other expense	1,597
Owner withdrawals	255
Selling expense	6,832
Sales revenue	38,434
Interest expense	28
Receivables	587
General and administrative expense	671

Required

1. Journalize all of Home Depot's closing entries at January 31, 20X1. Use an Owner Capital account.

2. Set up T-accounts for the Income Summary account and the Owner Capital account. Post to these accounts and take their ending balances. One year earlier, at January 31, 20X0, the Owner Capital balance was $8,740 million.

Journalizing closing entries
(Obj. 4)

E5-9 The trial balance and adjustments columns of the work sheet of Southside Development at March 31, 20X6 follow.

Account Title	Trial Balance		Adjustments	
	Debit	**Credit**	**Debit**	**Credit**
Cash	2,000			
Accounts receivable	8,500		(a) 12,000	
Inventory	36,100			(b) 4,290
Supplies	13,000			(c) 8,600
Equipment	42,470			
Accumulated depreciation		11,250		(d) 2,250
Accounts payable		9,300		
Salary payable				(e) 1,200
Note payable, long-term		7,500		
Jack Potter, capital		33,920		
Jack Potter, withdrawals	45,000			
Sales revenue		233,000		(a) 12,000
Sales discounts	2,000			
Cost of goods sold	111,600		(b) 4,290	
Selling expense	21,050		(c) 5,200	
			(e) 1,200	
General expense	10,500		(c) 3,400	
			(d) 2,250	
Interest expense	2,750			
Total	294,970	294,970	28,340	28,340

Compute the adjusted balance for each account that must be closed. Then journalize Southside's closing entries at March 31, 20X6. How much was Southside's net income or net loss?

Preparing a multi-step income statement
(Obj. 5)

Student ResourceCD
spreadsheet

E5-10 Use the data in Exercise 5-9 to prepare the multi-step income statement of Southside Development for the year ended March 31, 20X6.

Preparing a merchandiser's multi-step income statement to evaluate the business
(Obj. 5, 6)

Student ResourceCD
spreadsheet

E5-11 Selected amounts from the accounting records of Persnikity Tim's Coffee Shops are listed in alphabetical order.

Accounts payable.................................	$ 16,200
Accumulated depreciation	18,700
Cost of goods sold	99,300
General expenses	23,500
Interest revenue	1,500
Inventory, December 31, 20X5	21,000
Inventory, December 31, 20X6	19,400
Owner's equity, December 31, 20X6..............................	126,070
Sales discounts	9,000
Sales returns	4,600
Sales revenue....................................	204,000
Selling expenses	37,800
Unearned sales revenue	6,500

Required

1. Prepare the business's multi-step income statement for the year ended December 31, 20X6.

2. Compute the rate of inventory turnover for the year. Last year the turnover rate was 3.8 times. Does this two-year trend suggest improvement or deterioration in inventory turnover?

E5-12 Prepare Persnikity Tim's Coffee Shops' single-step income statement for 20X6, using the data from Exercise 5-11. Compute the gross profit percentage, and compare it with last year's gross profit percentage of 50%. Does this two-year trend in the gross percentage suggest better or worse profitability during the current year?

Preparing a single-step income statement to evaluate the business
(Obj. 5, 6)

Student ResourceCD
spreadsheet

E5-13 **Motorola Systems** earned sales revenue of $55 million in 20X4. Cost of goods sold was $33 million, and net income reached $8 million, Motorola's highest ever. Total current assets included inventory of $6 million at December 31, 20X4. Last year's ending inventory was $4 million. The managers of Motorola need to know the company's gross profit percentage and rate of inventory turnover for 20X4. Compute these amounts.

Computing gross profit percentage and inventory turnover
(Obj. 6)

Continuing Exercise. *This exercise completes the Marcia Walker, Consultant, situation from Exercise 2-17 of Chapter 2, Exercise 3-15 of Chapter 3, and Exercise 4-13 of Chapter 4.*

E5-14 Marcia Walker's consulting practice performs systems consulting. Walker has also begun selling accounting software. During January, the business completed these transactions:

Accounting for both merchandising and service operations
(Obj. 1, 2, 4, 5)

Student ResourceCD
General Ledger, Peachtree, QuickBooks

Jan. 2	Completed a consulting engagement and received cash of $7,200.
2	Prepaid three months' office rent, $1,500.
7	Purchased accounting software inventory on account, $4,000.
16	Paid employee salary, $1,400.
18	Sold accounting software on account, $1,100 (cost $700).
19	Consulted with a client for a fee of $900 on account.
21	Paid on account, $2,000.
24	Paid utilities, $300.
28	Sold accounting software for cash, $600 (cost $400).
31	Recorded these adjusting entries:
	Accrued salary expense, $1,400.
	Accounted for expiration of prepaid rent.
	Depreciation of office furniture, $200.

Required

1. Open the following selected T-accounts in the ledger: Cash; Accounts Receivable; Accounting Software Inventory; Prepaid Rent; Accumulated Depreciation; Accounts Payable; Salary Payable; Marcia Walker, Capital; Income Summary; Service Revenue; Sales Revenue; Cost of Goods Sold; Salary Expense; Rent Expense; Utilities Expense; and Depreciation Expense.

2. Journalize and post the January transactions. Key all items by date. Compute each account balance, and denote the balance as *Bal.* Journalize and post the closing entries. Denote each closing amount as *Clo.* After posting all closing entries, prove the equality of debits and credits in the ledger.

3. Prepare the January income statement of Marcia Walker, Consultant. Use the single-step format.

Explaining the perpetual inventory system
(Obj. 1, 2)

Problems

(Group A)

P5-1A Lens Masters is a regional chain of optical shops. The company offers a large selection of eyeglass frames, and Lens Masters stores provide while-you-wait service. The company has launched a vigorous advertising campaign to promote two-for-the-price-of-one frame sales.

Required

Lens Masters expects to grow rapidly and to increase its level of inventory. As the chief accountant of this company, you wish to install a perpetual inventory system. Write a one-paragraph business memo to the company president to explain how that system would work for the purchase and sale of eyeglasses. Use the following heading for your memo:

> **Date:** _____
>
> **To:** Company president
>
> **From:** Chief Accountant
>
> **Subject:** How a perpetual inventory system works for purchases and sales

Accounting for the purchase and sale of inventory
(Obj. 1, 2)

P5-2A Assume the following transactions occurred between **Walgreen Co.**, the pharmacy chain, and Procter & Gamble (P&G), the consumer products company, during June of the current year:

> June 8 P&G sold $6,000 worth of merchandise to Walgreen on terms of 2/10 n/30, FOB shipping point. P&G prepaid freight charges of $200 and included this amount in the invoice total. (P&G's entry to record the freight payment debits Accounts Receivable and credits Cash.) These goods cost P&G $2,100.
>
> 11 Walgreen returned $1,000 of the merchandise purchased on June 8. P&G accounted for the sales return and placed the goods back in inventory (P&G's cost, $400).
>
> 17 Walgreen paid $2,000 of the invoice amount owed to P&G for the June 8 purchase, less the discount. This payment included none of the freight charge.
>
> 26 Walgreen paid the remaining amount owed to P&G for the June 8 purchase.

Required

Journalize these transactions, first on the books of Walgreen Co. and, second, on the books of Procter & Gamble.

Journalizing purchase and sale transactions
(Obj. 1, 2)

P5-3A Hawkeye Electric company engaged in the following transactions during July:

> July 2 Purchased inventory for cash, $800.
>
> 5 Purchased store supplies on credit terms of net eom, $600.
>
> 8 Purchased inventory of $3,000, plus freight charges of $230. Credit terms are 3/15 n/30.
>
> 9 Sold goods for cash, $1,200. Hawkeye's cost of these goods was $700.
>
> 11 Returned $200 of the inventory purchased on July 8. It was damaged.
>
> 12 Purchased inventory on credit terms of 3/10 n/30, $3,330.

(continued)

July 14   Sold inventory on credit terms of 2/10 n/30, $9,600 (cost $5,000).

16   Paid utilities expense, $275.

20   Received returned inventory from the July 14 sale, $400. Hawkeye shipped the wrong goods by mistake. Hawkeye's cost of the inventory received was $250.

21   Borrowed the amount owed on the July 8 purchase. Signed a note payable to the bank for $2,946, which takes into account the return of inventory on July 11.

21   Paid supplier for goods purchased on July 8 less the return and the discount.

23   Received $6,860 cash in partial settlement of his account from the customer who purchased inventory on July 14. Granted the customer a 2% discount and credited his account receivable for $7,000.

30   Paid for the store supplies purchased on July 5.

Required

1. Journalize the preceding transactions on the books of Hawkeye Electric Company.

2. Compute the amount of the receivable at July 31 from the customer to whom Hawkeye sold inventory on July 14. What amount of cash discount applies to this receivable at July 31?

P5-4A The accounting records of Academy Security Systems at June 30, 20X8, list the following:

Computing net sales, gross profit, and net income
(Obj. 3)

Cash	$ 13,600
Accounts receivable	8,100
Note payable	4,300
Sales revenue	199,100
Salary payable	1,800
Luke Stover, capital	36,000
Sales returns and allowances	12,100
Selling expenses	19,800
Luke Stover, withdrawals	30,400
Inventory: June 30, 20X7	23,800
June 30, 20X8	28,500
Equipment	44,700
Cost of goods sold	95,000
Accumulated depreciation— equipment	6,900
Sales discounts	3,400
General expenses	16,300
Accounts payable	23,800

Required

1. Prepare a multi-step income statement to show the computation of Academy Security Systems' net sales, gross profit, and net income for the year ended June 30, 20X8.

2. Luke Stover, owner of the business, strives to earn gross profit of $90,000 and net income of $50,000. Did he achieve these goals? Write a couple of sentences to explain.

P5-5A TravelMaster Supply Co.'s trial balance pertains to December 31, 20X7.

TravelMaster Supply Co. Trial Balance December 31, 20X7		
Cash	$ 2,910	
Accounts receivable.	10,190	
Inventory.	101,760	
Store supplies	1,990	
Prepaid insurance	3,200	
Store fixtures.	63,900	
Accumulated depreciation		$ 37,640
Accounts payable.		29,770
Salary payable		
Interest payable		
Note payable, long-term.		37,200
Elaine Lorens, capital		63,120
Elaine Lorens, withdrawals	36,300	
Sales revenue		290,000
Cost of goods sold	161,090	
Salary expense	46,580	
Rent expense.	14,630	
Utilities expense.	6,780	
Depreciation expense		
Insurance expense	5,300	
Store supplies expense		
Interest expense	3,100	
Total	$457,730	$457,730

Adjustment data at December 31, 20X7:

a. Insurance expense for the year, $6,090.
b. Store fixtures have an estimated useful life of 10 years and are expected to be worthless when they are retired from service.
c. Accrued salaries at December 31, $1,260.
d. Accrued interest expense at December 31, $870.
e. Store supplies on hand at December 31, $760.
f. Inventory on hand at December 31, $94,780.

Required

Complete TravelMaster's accounting work sheet for the year ended December 31, 20X7. Key adjusting entries by letter.

Journalizing the adjusting and closing entries of a merchandising business
(Obj. 4)

P5-6A Refer to the data in problem 5-5A.

Required

1. Journalize the adjusting and closing entries of TravelMaster Supply Co.
2. Determine the December 31, 20X7, balance of Elaine Lorens, Capital.

Preparing a multi-step income statement and a classified balance sheet
(Obj. 3, 5)

P5-7A → *Link Back to Chapter 4 (Classified Balance Sheet).* Selected accounts of Omega Electronics are listed along with their balances before closing at July 31, 20X5.

Accounts payable	$127,300
Accounts receivable	48,600
Accumulated depreciation—store equipment	16,400
A. L. Carson, capital, June 30	69,100
A. L. Carson, withdrawals	11,000
Cash	24,300
Cost of goods sold	360,900
General expense	75,800
Interest payable	3,000
Interest revenue	1,200
Inventory	187,300
Note payable, long-term	160,000
Salary payable	6,100
Sales discounts	8,300
Sales returns and allowances	17,900
Sales revenue	556,600
Selling expense	84,600
Store equipment	126,000
Supplies	4,300
Unearned sales revenue	9,300

Required

1. Prepare Omega Electronics' *multi-step* income statement for the month ended July 31, 20X5.
2. Prepare Omega's classified balance sheet in *report format* at July 31, 20X5. Show your computation of the July 31 balance of A. L. Carson, Capital.

Preparing a single-step income statement and a classified balance sheet
(Obj. 3, 5)

P5-8A → *Link Back to Chapter 4 (Classified Balance Sheet).*

Required

1. Use the data of Problem 5-7A to prepare Omega Electronics' *single-step* income statement for the month ended July 31, 20X5.
2. Prepare Omega's classified balance sheet in *report format* at July 31, 20X5. Show your computation of the July 31 balance of A. L. Carson, Capital.

Using trial balance and adjustment data to prepare financial statements and evaluate the business; multi-step income statement
(Obj. 4, 5, 6)

P5-9A The trial balance and adjustment data of Bonds Baseball Cards at September 30, 20X9, follow:

Account Title	Trial Balance Debit	Trial Balance Credit	Adjustments Debit	Adjustments Credit
Cash	7,300			
Accounts receivable	4,360		(a) 1,400	
Inventory	9,630		(b) 2,100	
Supplies	10,700			(c) 7,940
Equipment	99,450			
Accumulated depreciation		29,800		(d) 9,900
Accounts payable		13,800		
Salary payable				(f) 200
Unearned sales revenue		3,780	(e) 2,600	
Note payable, long-term		10,000		
B. Bonds, capital		58,360		
B. Bonds, drawing	39,000			
Sales revenue		216,000		(a) 1,400
				(e) 2,600
Sales returns	3,100			
Cost of goods sold	95,600			(b) 2,100
Selling expense	40,600		(c) 7,940	
			(f) 200	
General expense	21,000		(d) 9,900	
Interest expense	1,000			
Total	331,740	331,740	24,140	24,140

Required

1. Without completing a formal accounting work sheet, prepare the company's multi-step income statement for the year ended September 30, 20X9.
2. Compute the gross profit percentage and the inventory turnover for 20X9. Inventory on hand at September 30, 20X8, was $10,250. For 20X8 Bonds' gross profit percentage was 50% and the inventory turnover rate was 7.8 times. Does the two-year trend in these ratios suggest improvement or deterioration in profitability?

Problems

(Group B)

Explaining the perpetual inventory system
(Obj. 1, 2)

P5-1B **Wal-Mart Stores, Inc.,** is the largest retailer in the world, with almost 4,000 stores. A key Wal-Mart advantage is its sophisticated perpetual inventory accounting system.

Required

You are the manager of a Wal-Mart store in Fort Lauderdale, Florida. Write a one-paragraph business memo to a new employee explaining how the company accounts for the purchase and sale of merchandise inventory. Use the following heading for your memo.

> **Date:** _____
>
> **To:** New Employee
>
> **From:** Store Manager
>
> **Subject:** Wal-Mart's perpetual inventory accounting system

P5-2B Assume the following transactions occurred between **Bristol-Myers Squibb (BMS)**, the health-care products company, and Walgreen Co., the pharmacy chain, during February of the current year:

Accounting for the purchase and sale of inventory
(Obj. 1, 2)

Feb. 6 BMS sold $8,000 worth of merchandise to Walgreen on terms of 3/10 n/30, FOB shipping point. BMS prepaid freight charges of $500 and included this amount in the invoice total. (BMS's entry to record the freight payment debits Accounts Receivable and credits Cash). These goods cost BMS $6,100.

10 Walgreen returned $900 of the merchandise purchased on February 6. BMS accounted for the $900 sales return and placed the goods back in inventory (BMS's cost, $590).

15 Walgreen paid $3,000 of the invoice amount owed to BMS for the February 6 purchase, less the discount. This payment included none of the freight charge.

27 Walgreen paid the remaining amount owed to BMS for the February 6 purchase.

Required

Journalize these transactions, first on the books of Walgreen and second on the books of Bristol-Myers Squibb.

P5-3B Belmont Software engaged in the following transactions during May:

Journalizing purchase and sale transactions
(Obj. 2)

May 3 Purchased office supplies for cash, $300.

7 Purchased inventory on credit terms of 3/10 net eom, $2,000.

8 Returned half the inventory purchased on May 7. It was not the inventory ordered.

10 Sold goods for cash, $450 (cost, $250).

13 Sold inventory on credit terms of 2/15 n/45, $3,900 (cost, $1,800).

16 Paid the amount owed on account from the purchase of May 7, less the return and the discount.

17 Received defective inventory as a sales return from May 13 sale, $900. Belmont's cost of the inventory received was $600.

18 Purchased inventory of $5,000 on account. Payment terms were 2/10 net 30.

26 Borrowed $4,900 from the bank to take advantage of the discount offered on the May 18 purchase. Signed a note payable to the bank for this amount.

28 Received cash in full settlement of the account from the customer who purchased inventory on May 13, less the return and the discount.

29 Purchased inventory for cash, $2,000, plus freight charges of $160.

Required

1. Journalize the preceding transactions on the books of Belmont Software.

2. The note payable signed on May 26 requires Belmont to pay $30 interest expense. Was the decision to borrow funds in order to take advantage of the cash discount wise or unwise? Support your answer by comparing the discount to the interest paid.

Computing net sales, gross profit, and net income
(Obj. 3)

P5-4B The accounting records of Copeland Appliance list the following at November 30, 20X7:

Accounts receivable	$ 18,000
Selling expenses	28,800
Furniture	37,200
Sales returns and allowances	3,200
Salary payable.	300
Jim Copeland, capital.	52,800
Sales revenue.	199,600
Accounts payable	13,200
Inventory: November 30, 20X6.	41,700
November 30, 20X7.	41,500
Cash	29,000
Notes payable	21,600
Accumulated depreciation—furniture	13,600
Cost of goods sold	132,000
Sales discounts	2,100
General expenses	9,300

Required

1. Prepare a multi-step income statement to show the computation of Copeland's net sales, gross profit, and net income for the month ended November 30, 20X7.

2. Jim Copeland, owner of the company, strives to earn gross profit of $60,000 and net income of $20,000 each month. Did he achieve these goals? Write a sentence to explain.

Preparing a merchandiser's work sheet
(Obj. 4)

Student Resource CD
GL, PT, QB

P5-5B China Palace Restaurant's trial balance pertains to December 31, 20X9.

China Palace Restaurant		
Trial Balance		
December 31, 20X9		
Cash.	$ 1,270	
Accounts receivable	4,430	
Inventory	73,900	
Prepaid rent	4,400	
Fixtures.	22,100	
Accumulated depreciation.		$ 8,380
Accounts payable		6,290
Salary payable		
Interest payable		
Note payable, long-term		18,000
Jacob Xiang, capital.		55,920
Jacob Xiang, withdrawals	39,550	
Sales revenue		170,150
Cost of goods sold.	67,870	
Salary expense.	24,700	
Rent expense	7,700	
Advertising expense.	4,510	

(continued)

Utilities expense	3,880	
Depreciation expense		
Insurance expense....................................	2,770	
Interest expense.......................................	1,660	
Total..	$258,740	$258,740

Adjustment data at December 31, 20X9:

a. Total rent expense for the year, $10,200.

b. Store fixtures have an estimated useful life of 10 years and are expected to be worthless when they are retired from service.

c. Accrued salaries at December 31, $900.

d. Accrued interest expense at December 31, $360.

e. Inventory on hand at December 31, $71,000.

Required

Complete China Palace's accounting work sheet for the year ended December 31, 20X9. Key adjusting entries by letter.

P5-6B Refer to the data in problem 5-5B.

1. Journalize the adjusting and closing entries.

2. Determine the December 31, 20X9, balance of Jacob Xiang, Capital.

Journalizing the adjusting and closing entries of a merchandising business
(Obj. 4)

P5-7B → *Link Back to Chapter 4 (Classified Balance Sheet).* Selected accounts of Nature's Best Organic Products are listed along with their balances before closing at May 31, 20X9.

Preparing a multi-step income statement and a classified balance sheet
(Obj. 3, 5)

Accounts Payable..........	$ 16,900	Interest revenue	$ 400
Accounts receivable........	33,700	Inventory..................	45,500
Accumulated depreciation—		Note payable, long-term....	45,000
equipment..............	38,000	Salary payable	2,800
P. Debruge, capital,		Sales discounts............	10,400
April 30, 20X9...........	73,900	Sales returns and	
P. Debruge, withdrawals....	9,000	allowances	18,000
Cash	7,800	Sales revenue	701,000
Cost of goods sold	362,000	Selling expenses...........	137,900
Equipment................	146,000	Supplies..................	5,900
General expenses	116,700	Unearned sales revenue	13,800
Interest payable	1,100		

Required

1. Prepare the Nature's Best *multi-step* income statement for the month ended May 31, 20X9.

2. Prepare the Nature's Best classified balance sheet in *report format* at May 31, 20X9. Show your computation of the May 31 balance of P. Debruge, Capital.

P5-8B → *Link Back to Chapter 4 (Classified Balance Sheet).*

Preparing a single-step income statement and a classified balance sheet
(Obj. 3, 5)

Required

1. Use the data of Problem 5-7B to prepare a *single-step* income statement for the month ended May 31, 20X9.

2. Prepare the Nature's Best classified balance sheet in *report format* at May 31, 20X9. Show your computation of the May 31 balance of P. Debruge, Capital.

Using trial balance and adjustment data to prepare financial statements and evaluate the business; multi-step income statement
(Obj. 4, 5, 6)

P5-9B The trial balance and adjustments data of Mozart Music Company include the following accounts and balances at November 30, 20X4:

Account Title	Trial Balance Debit	Trial Balance Credit	Adjustments Debit	Adjustments Credit
Cash	24,000			
Accounts receivable	14,500		(a) 4,000	
Inventory	36,330		(b) 1,010	
Supplies	2,800			(c) 2,400
Furniture	39,600			
Accumulated depreciation		6,300		(d) 2,450
Accounts payable		12,600		(f) 1,000
Salary payable				
Unearned sales revenue		13,570	(e) 6,700	
Note payable, long-term		15,000		
W. Mozart, capital		60,310		
W. Mozart, drawing	42,000			
Sales revenue		174,000		(a) 4,000
				(e) 6,700
Sales returns	7,700			
Cost of goods sold	72,170			(b) 1,010
Selling expense	28,080		(f) 1,000	
General expense	13,100		(c) 2,400	
			(d) 2,450	
Interest expense	1,500			
Total........................	281,780	281,780	17,560	17,560

Required

1. Without entering the preceding data on a formal work sheet, prepare the company's multi-step income statement for the year ended November 30, 20X4.

2. Compute the gross profit percentage and the rate of inventory turnover for 20X4. Inventory on hand one year ago, at November 30, 20X3, was $32,650. For 20X3, Mozart's gross profit percentage was 55%, and inventory turnover was 1.91 times during the year. Does the two-year trend in these ratios suggest improvement or deterioration in profitability?

APPLY *Your Knowledge*

Decision Cases

Expanding a business
(Obj. 5)

Case 1. Lauren Sever and Trey Hagins opened Party-Time T-Shirts to sell T-shirts for parties at their college. The company completed the first year of operations, and Sever and Hagins are generally pleased with operating results, as shown by the following income statement:

Party-Time T-Shirts
Income Statement
Year Ended December 31, 20X6

Net sales revenue...	$350,000
Cost of goods sold	210,000
Gross margin	140,000
Operating expenses:	
Selling expense...	40,000
General expense..	25,000
Net income	$ 75,000

Sever and Hagins are considering how to expand the business. They each propose a way to increase profits to $100,000 during 20X7.

a. Sever believes they should advertise more heavily. She believes additional advertising costing $20,000 will increase net sales by 30% and leave general expense unchanged.
b. Hagins proposes selling higher-margin merchandise, such as party dresses. An importer can supply a minimum of 1,000 dresses for $40 each; Party-Time can mark these dresses up 100% and sell them for $80. Hagins realizes they will have to advertise the new merchandise, and this advertising will cost $5,000. Party-Time can expect to sell only 80% of these dresses during the coming year.

Required

Help Sever and Hagins determine which plan to pursue. Prepare a single-step income statement to show the expected net income under each plan.

Case 2. → *Link Back to Chapter 4 (Classified Balance Sheet. Current Ratio; Debt Ratio).* Judy Brooks owns Heights Pharmacy, which has prospered during its second year of operation. In deciding whether to open another pharmacy in the area, Brooks has prepared the current financial statements of the business (below and on page 230). Brooks read in an industry trade journal that a successful pharmacy meets all of these criteria:

Using the financial statements to decide on a business expansion
(Obj. 5, 6)

a. Gross profit percentage is at least 60%.
b. Current ratio is at least 2.0.
c. Debt ratio is no higher than 0.50.
d. Inventory turnover rate is at least 3.40. (Heights Pharmacy's inventory one year ago, at December 31, 20X7 was $16,390.)

Brooks believes the business meets all four criteria. She intends to go ahead with the expansion plan and asks your advice on preparing the pharmacy's financial statements in accordance with generally accepted accounting principles. When you point out that the statements include errors, Brooks assures you that all amounts are correct. But some items are listed in the wrong place.

Required

1. Compute the four ratios based on the Heights Pharmacy financial statements prepared by Brooks. Does the business appear to be ready for expansion?
2. Prepare a correct multi-step income statement and a correct classified balance sheet in report format.
3. On the basis of the corrected financial statements, compute correct measures of the four ratios listed in the trade journal.
4. Make a recommendation about whether Brooks should undertake the expansion.

Heights Pharmacy

Income Statement
Year Ended December 31, 20X8

Sales revenue	$195,000
Gain on sale of land	24,600
Total revenue	219,600
Cost of goods sold	85,200
Gross profit	134,400
Operating expenses:	
Salary expense	30,690
Interest expense	6,000
Depreciation expense	4,900
Utilities expense	3,730
Total operating expense	45,320
Income from operations	89,080

(continued)

Other expense:

Sales returns	10,700
Net income	$ 78,380

Heights Pharmacy
Statement of Owner's Equity
Year Ended December 31, 20X8

J. Brooks, capital, December 31, 20X7	$ 30,000
Net income	78,380
J. Brooks, capital, December 31, 20X8	$108,380

Heights Pharmacy
Balance Sheet
December 31, 20X8

Assets

Current:

Cash	$15,030
Inventory	32,860
Store fixtures	63,000
Total current assets	110,890

Other:

Withdrawals	65,000
Total assets	$175,890

Liabilities

Current:

Accumulated depreciation—store fixtures	$ 6,300
Accounts payable	10,310
Salary payable	900
Total current liabilities	17,510

Other:

Note payable due in 90 days	50,000
Total liabilities	67,510

Owner's Equity

J. Brooks, capital	108,380
Total liabilities and owner's equity	$175,890

Ethical Issue

Hunter Glass Company makes all sales under terms of FOB shipping point. The company usually receives orders for sales approximately one week before shipping inventory to customers. For orders received late in December, Donny Hunter, the owner, decides when to ship the goods. If profits are already at an acceptable level, Hunter delays shipment until January. If profits for the current year are lagging behind expectations, Hunter ships the goods during December.

Required

1. Under Hunter's FOB policy, when should the company record a sale?
2. Do you approve or disapprove of Hunter's manner of deciding when to ship goods to customers and record the sales revenue? If you approve, give your reason. If you disapprove, identify a better way to decide when to ship goods. (There is no accounting rule against Hunter's practice.)

Financial Statement Case

This case uses both the income statement (statement of operations) and the balance sheet of Amazon.com in Appendix A. It will help you understand the closing process of a business.

Closing entries and the gross profit percentage
(Obj. 4, 6)

Required

1. Journalize Amazon.com's closing entries for the revenues and expenses of 2002. Show all amounts in thousands as in the Amazon financial statements. You may be unfamiliar with certain revenues and expenses, but treat each item on the income statement as either a revenue or an expense. For example, Net Sales is the first revenue, and Interest Income is also a revenue. The last revenue is Cumulative Effect of Change in Accounting Principle. A loss is like an expense. In your closing entries ignore all subtotals such as Gross Profit, Total Operating Expenses, and Net Loss.
2. Create a T-account for Income Summary, post to that account, and then close Income Summary (debit Retained Earnings and credit Income Summary for $149,132). For this purpose, Retained Earnings is similar to the Owner's Capital account. How much was closed to Retained Earnings? How is this amount labeled on the income statement?

Team Project

With a small team of classmates, visit one or more merchandising businesses in your area. Interview a responsible official of the company to learn about its inventory policies and accounting system. Obtain answers to the following questions, write a report, and be prepared to make a presentation to the class if your instructor so directs:

Required

1. What merchandise inventory does the business sell?
2. From whom does the business buy its inventory? Is the relationship with the supplier new or longstanding?
3. What are the FOB terms on inventory purchases? Who pays the freight, the buyer or the seller? Is freight a significant amount? What percentage of total inventory cost is the freight?
4. What are the credit terms on inventory purchases—2/10 n/30, or other? Does the business pay early to get purchase discounts? If so, why? If not, why not?
5. How does the business actually pay its suppliers? Does it mail a check or pay electronically? What is the actual payment procedure?
6. Which type of inventory accounting system does the business use—perpetual or periodic? Is this system computerized?
7. How often does the business take a physical count of its inventory? When during the year is the count taken? Describe the count procedures followed by the company.
8. Does the owner or manager use the gross profit percentage and the rate of inventory turnover to evaluate the business? If not, show the manager how to use these ratios in decision making.
9. Ask any other questions your group considers appropriate.

APPENDIX *to Chapter 5*

Accounting for Merchandise in a Periodic Inventory System

After studying this appendix to Chapter 5, you should be able to:

A1. Account for purchase and sale of inventory

A2. Compute cost of goods sold

A3. Adjust and close the accounts of a merchandising business

A4. Prepare a merchandiser's financial statements

Purchasing Merchandise

Some businesses find it uneconomical to invest in a perpetual inventory system. These businesses use a periodic system.

Account for the purchase and sale of inventory

Recording Purchases of Inventory All inventory systems use the Inventory account. But in a periodic system, purchases, purchase discounts, purchase returns and allowances, and transportation costs are recorded in separate accounts. Let's account for **Austin Sound Center's** purchase of the **JVC** goods in Exhibit 5A-1.

Exhibit 5A-1 An Actual Invoice (Adapted)

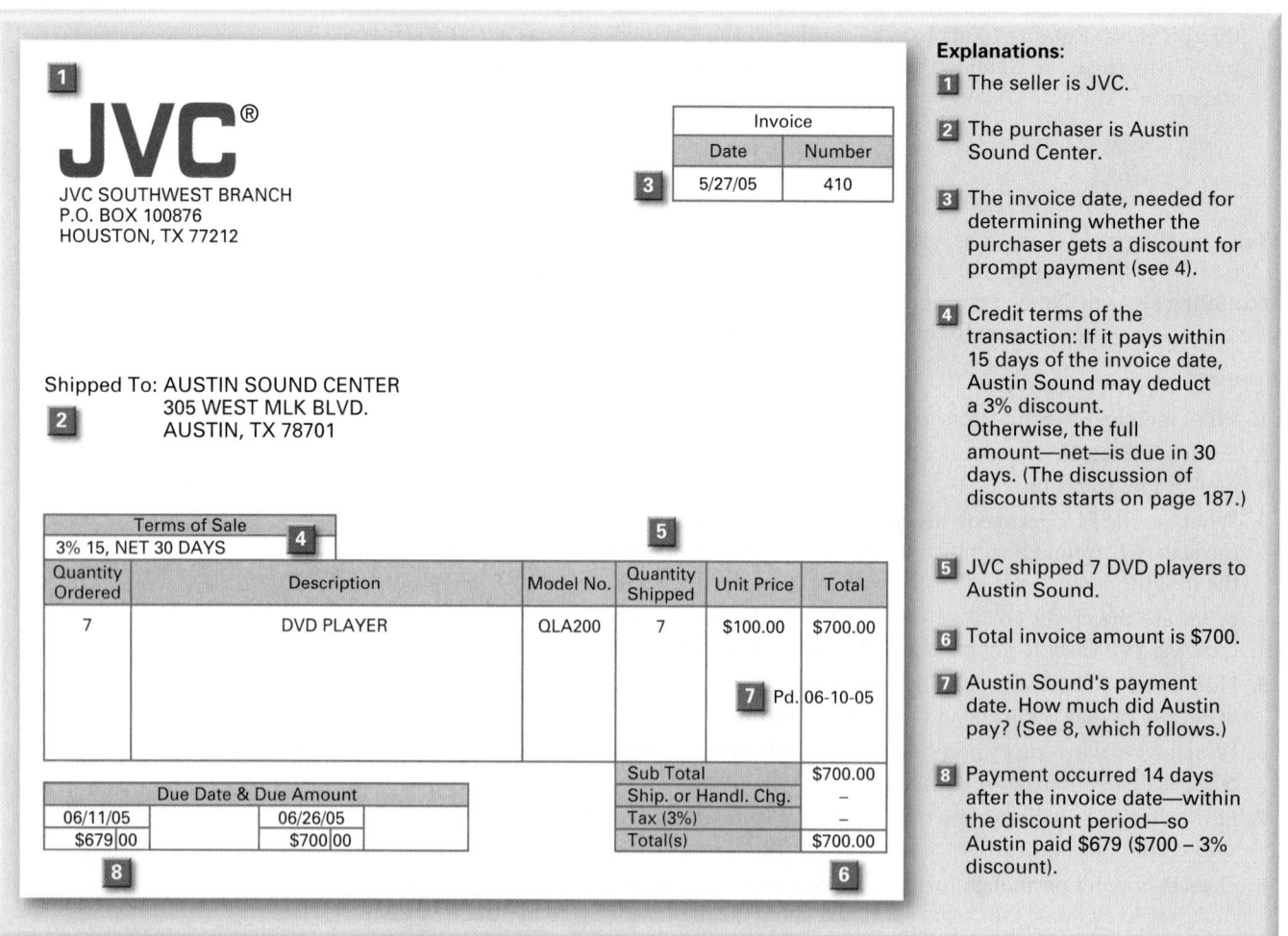

The following entries record the purchase and payment on account within the discount period. Assume that Austin Sound received the goods on May 30.

May 30	Purchases	700	
	Accounts Payable		700
	Purchased inventory on account		

June 10	Accounts Payable......................	700	
	Cash ($700 × 0.97)		679
	Purchase Discounts ($700 × 0.03) ...		21
	Paid on account.		

Recording Purchase Returns and Allowances Suppose that, prior to payment, Austin Sound returned to JVC goods costing $100 and also received from JVC a purchase allowance of $10. Austin Sound would record these transactions as follows:

June 3	Accounts Payable	100	
	Purchase Returns and Allowances..		100
	Returned inventory to seller.		

June 4	Accounts Payable.....................	10	
	Purchase Returns and Allowances..		10
	Received a purchase allowance.		

During the period, the business records the cost of all inventory bought in the Purchases account. The balance of Purchases is a *gross* amount because it does not include subtractions for discounts, returns, or allowances. **Net purchases** is the remainder after subtracting the contra accounts from Purchases:

> **Net Purchases**
> Purchases less purchase discounts and purchase returns and allowances.

>   Purchases (*debit*)
> − Purchase Discounts (*credit*)
> − Purchase Returns and Allowances (*credit*)
> _____
> = Net purchases (a *debit* subtotal, not a separate account)

Recording Transportation Costs Under the periodic system, costs to transport purchased inventory from seller to buyer are debited to the Freight In account, as shown for a $60 freight bill:

June 1	Freight In	60	
	Cash		60
	Paid a freight bill.		

Recording the Sale of Inventory

Recording sales is streamlined in the periodic system. With no running record of inventory to maintain, we can record a $3,000 sale as follows:

June 5	Accounts Receivable................	3,000	
	Sales Revenue		3,000
	Sale on account.		

There is no accompanying entry to Inventory and Cost of Goods Sold in the periodic system.

Cost of goods sold (also called *cost of sales*) is the largest single expense of most businesses that sell merchandise, such as **Gap Inc.** and **Austin Sound**. It is the cost of the inventory the business has sold to customers. In a periodic system, cost of goods sold must be computed as in Exhibit 5A-2.

> 2 *Compute cost of goods sold*

PANEL A:

Beginning inventory
+ Net purchases ◄──────
+ Freight in
= Cost of goods available for sale
− Ending inventory
= Cost of goods sold

Purchases of inventory
− Purchase discounts
− Purchase returns and allowances
= Net purchases

PANEL B:

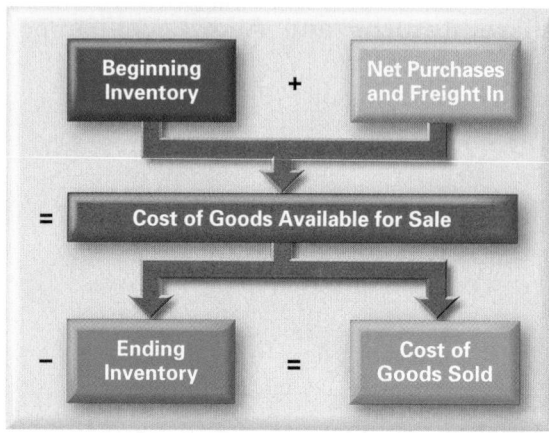

Exhibit 5A-3 summarizes the first half of this appendix by showing Austin
Sound's net sales revenue, cost of goods sold, and gross profit on the income
statement for the periodic system. (All amounts are assumed.)

Austin Sound Center
Income Statement
Year Ended December 31, 20X5

PANEL A—Detailed Gross Profit Section

Sales revenue			$169,300
Less: Sales discounts	$(1,400)		
Sales returns and allowances	(2,000)	(3,400)	
Net sales			$165,900
Cost of goods sold:			
Beginning inventory		$38,600	
Purchases		$91,400	
Less: Purchase discounts	$(3,000)		
Purch. returns & allow.	(1,200)	(4,200)	
Net purchases		87,200	
Freight in			5,200
Cost of goods available for sale		131,000	
Less: Ending inventory		(40,200)	
Cost of goods sold			90,800
Gross profit			$ 75,100

**PANEL B—Gross Profit Section
(Streamlined in Annual Reports to Outsiders)**

Net sales	$165,900
Cost of goods sold	90,800
Gross profit	$ 75,100

Adjusting and Closing the Accounts

A merchandising business adjusts and closes the accounts much as a service entity does. The steps of this end-of-period process are the same: If a work sheet is used, the trial balance is entered and the work sheet is completed to determine net income or net loss. The work sheet provides the data for the adjusting and closing entries and the financial statements.

At the end of the period, before any adjusting or closing entries, the Inventory account still holds the cost of the last period's ending inventory, which becomes the beginning inventory of the current period. It is necessary to remove this beginning balance and replace it with the cost of the inventory on hand at the end of the current period. Various techniques may be used to update the inventory records.

To illustrate a merchandiser's adjusting and closing process under the periodic inventory system, let's use **Austin Sound's** December 31, 20X5, trial balance in Exhibit 5A-4. All the new accounts—Inventory, Freight In, and the contra accounts—are highlighted for emphasis. Additional data item (h) gives the ending inventory figure, $40,200.

Exhibit 5A-4

Trial Balance

Austin Sound Center		
Trial Balance		
December 31, 20X5		
Cash	$ 2,850	
Accounts receivable...............................	4,600	
Note receivable, current	8,000	
Interest receivable		
Inventory	38,600	
Supplies..	650	
Prepaid insurance	1,200	
Furniture and fixtures............................	33,200	
Accumulated depreciation		$ 2,400
Accounts payable.................................		47,000
Unearned sales revenue		2,000
Wages payable		
Interest payable		
Note payable, long-term..........................		12,600
C. Ernest, capital		25,900
C. Ernest, withdrawals	54,100	
Sales revenue....................................		168,000
Sales discounts	1,400	
Sales returns and allowances.....................	2,000	
Interest revenue		600
Purchases	91,400	
Purchase discounts...............................		3,000
Purchase returns and allowances..................		1,200
Freight in..	5,200	
Wage expense....................................	9,800	
Rent expense.....................................	8,400	
Depreciation expense		
Insurance expense		
Supplies expense		
Interest expense	1,300	
Total	$262,700	$262,700

Additional Data at December 31, 20X5:

a. Interest revenue earned but not yet collected, $400

b. Supplies on hand, $100

c. Prepaid insurance expired during the year, $1,000

d. Depreciation, $600

e. Unearned sales revenue earned during the year, $1,300

f. Accrued wage expense, $400

g. Accrued interest expense, $200

h. Inventory on hand, $40,200

Preparing and Using the Work Sheet in a Periodic System The Exhibit 5A-5 work sheet is similar to the work sheets we have seen so far, with a few

This work sheet is slightly different from the one introduced in the Chapter 4 acetates. This work sheet contains four pairs of columns, not five.

→ differences. ← Most accounting systems combine trial balance amounts with the adjustments and extend the adjusted balances directly to the income statement and balance sheet columns. Therefore, the adjusted trial balance columns are omitted.

Account Title Columns. The Trial Balance lists the unadjusted amount for each account. A few accounts without balances are affected by the adjusting process. Examples include Interest Receivable, Wages Payable, and Depreciation Expense. Accounts are listed in the order they appear in the ledger.

Trial Balance Columns. Examine the Inventory account in the Trial Balance. The $38,600 amount is the cost of the beginning inventory. The work sheet is designed to replace this outdated amount with the new ending balance, which in our example is $40,200 [additional data item (h) for Exhibit 5A-4].

Adjustments Columns. The adjustments are similar to those discussed in Chapters 3 and 4. The debit amount of each entry should equal the credit amount, and total debits should equal total credits.

Income Statement Columns. The Income Statement columns in Exhibit 5A-5 show adjusted amounts for the revenues and the expenses. Sales Revenue, for example, has an adjusted balance of $169,300.

The income statement totals indicate whether the business had a net income or a net loss.

■ Net income: Total credits > Total debits   ■ Net loss: Total debits > Total credits

Austin Sound's total credits of $214,700 exceed the total debits of $160,850, so the company earned a net income.

You may be wondering why the two inventory amounts appear in the Income Statement columns. The reason is that both beginning inventory and ending inventory enter the computation of cost of goods sold. *Placement of beginning inventory ($38,600) in the work sheet's Income Statement Debit column has the effect of adding beginning inventory to compute cost of goods sold. Placing ending inventory ($40,200) in the Credit column decreases cost of goods sold.*

Purchases and Freight In are in the Debit column because they are added to compute cost of goods sold. Purchase Discounts and Purchase Returns and Allowances are credits because they are subtracted in computing cost of goods sold—$90,800 on the income statement in Exhibit 5A-3.

Balance Sheet Columns. The only new item in the Balance Sheet columns is Inventory. The $40,200 balance is determined by the physical count at the end of the period.

Exhibit 5A-5   Accounting Work Sheet

Austin Sound Center
Accounting Work Sheet (Periodic Inventory System)
Year Ended December 31, 20X5

Account Title	Trial Balance Debit	Trial Balance Credit	Adjustments Debit	Adjustments Credit	Income Statement Debit	Income Statement Credit	Balance Sheet Debit	Balance Sheet Credit
Cash	2,850						2,850	
Accounts receivable.....	4,600						4,600	
Note receivable, current .	8,000						8,000	
Interest receivable			(a) 400				400	
Inventory.............	38,600				38,600	40,200	40,200	
Supplies	650			(b) 550			100	
Prepaid insurance.......	1,200			(c) 1,000			200	
Furniture and fixtures ...	33,200						33,200	
Accumulated depreciation		2,400		(d) 600				3,000
Accounts payable.......		47,000						47,000
Unearned sales revenue .		2,000	(e) 1,300					700
Wages payable				(f) 400				400
Interest payable				(g) 200				200
Note payable, long-term .		12,600						12,600
C. Ernest, capital........		25,900						25,900
C. Ernest, withdrawals ..	54,100						54,100	
Sales revenue..........		168,000		(e) 1,300		169,300		
Sales discounts	1,400				1,400			
Sales returns and allowances	2,000				2,000			
Interest revenue		600		(a) 400		1,000		
Purchases	91,400				91,400			
Purchase discounts		3,000				3,000		
Purchase returns and allowances		1,200				1,200		
Freight in.............	5,200				5,200			
Wage expense	9,800		(f) 400		10,200			
Rent expense...........	8,400				8,400			
Depreciation expense....			(d) 600		600			
Insurance expense			(c) 1,000		1,000			
Supplies expense			(b) 550		550			
Interest expense	1,300		(g) 200		1,500			
	262,700	262,700	4,450	4,450	160,850	214,700	143,650	89,800
Net income					53,850			53,850
					214,700	214,700	143,650	143,650

Journalizing Adjusting and Closing Entries Exhibit 5A-6 presents Austin Sound's adjusting entries. These entries follow the same pattern illustrated in Chapter 4 for a service entity and can be taken directly from the work sheet.

The exhibit also gives Austin Sound's closing entries. The first closing entry closes the revenue accounts. Closing entries 2 and 3 are new. Entry 2 closes the beginning Inventory balance ($38,600), along with Purchases and Freight In, into the Cost of Goods Sold account. Entry 3 sets up the ending balance of Inventory ($40,200) with a debit. Entry 3 also closes the Purchases contra accounts to Cost of Goods Sold.[1] Now Inventory and Cost of Goods Sold have their correct ending balances shown at the top of the next page.

Exhibit 5A-6

Adjusting and Closing Entries

Journal

Adjusting entries

a.	Dec. 31	Interest Receivable...............................	400	
		Interest Revenue		400
b.	31	Supplies Expense ($650 – $100)...................	550	
		Supplies.....................................		550
c.	31	Insurance Expense..............................	1,000	
		Prepaid Insurance		1,000
d.	31	Depreciation Expense..........................	600	
		Accumulated Depreciation		600
e.	31	Unearned Sales Revenue	1,300	
		Sales Revenue..............................		1,300
f.	31	Wage Expense	400	
		Wages Payable.............................		400
g.	31	Interest Expense...............................	200	
		Interest Payable............................		200

Closing Entries

1.	Dec. 31	Sales Revenue.................................	169,300	
		Interest Revenue	1,000	
		Income Summary		170,300
2.	31	Cost of Goods Sold	135,200	
		Inventory (beginning balance)		38,600
		Purchases		91,400
		Freight In		5,200
3.	31	Inventory (ending balance)	40,200	
		Purchase Discounts..........................	3,000	
		Purchase Returns and Allowances	1,200	
		Cost of Goods Sold		44,400
4.	31	Income Summary	116,450	
		Sales Discounts		1,400
		Sales Returns and Allowances...............		2,000
		Cost of Goods Sold ($135,200 – $44,400)		90,800
		Wage Expense		10,200
		Rent Expense		8,400
		Depreciation Expense......................		600
		Insurance Expense.........................		1,000
		Supplies Expense..........................		550
		Interest Expense..........................		1,500
5.	31	Income Summary ($170,300 – $116,450)...........	53,850	
		C. Ernest, Capital..........................		53,850
6.	31	C. Ernest, Capital.............................	54,100	
		C. Ernest, Withdrawals....................		54,100

---

[1]Some accountants make the inventory entries as adjustments rather than as part of the closing process. The adjusting-entry approach adds these adjustments (shifted out of the closing entries):

Adjusting Entries

Dec. 31	Cost of Goods Sold	38,600	
	Inventory (beginning balance)		38,600
31	Inventory (ending balance)	40,200	
	Cost of Goods Sold		40,200

When these entries are posted, the Inventory account will look exactly as shown at the top of page 239, except that the journal references will be "Adj." instead of "Clo." The financial statements are unaffected by the approach used for these entries.

Inventory						
Jan. 1	Bal.	38,600	Dec. 31	Clo.	38,600	
Dec. 31	Clo.	40,200				

Cost of Goods Sold			
Beg. Inventory	38,600	Pur. discounts	3,000
Purchases	91,400	Pur. returns and	
Freight in	5,200	allowances	1,200
		End. inventory	40,200
Bal.	90,800		

Closing entry 4 then closes the Sales contra accounts and Cost of Goods Sold along with the other expense accounts into Income Summary. Closing entries 5 and 6 complete the closing process. All data for the closing entries are taken from the income statement columns of the work sheet.

Study Exhibits 5A-5 and 5A-6 carefully because they illustrate the entire end-of-period process that leads to the financial statements. As you progress through this book, you may want to refer to these exhibits to refresh your understanding of the adjusting and closing process for a merchandising business.

Preparing a Merchandiser's Financial Statements Exhibit 5A-7 presents Austin Sound's financial statements. The *income statement* through gross profit repeats Exhibit 5A-3. This information is followed by the *operating expenses,*

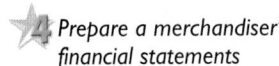

Prepare a merchandiser's financial statements

Exhibit 5A-7   Financial Statements of Austin Sound Center

Austin Sound Center
Income Statement
Year Ended December 31, 20X5

Sales revenue			$169,300	
Less: Sales discounts		$(1,400)		
Sales returns and allowances		(2,000)	(3,400)	
Net sales revenue				$165,900
Cost of goods sold:				
Beginning inventory			$ 38,600	
Purchases		$91,400		
Less: Purchase discounts	$(3,000)			
Purchase returns and allowances	(1,200)	(4,200)		
Net purchases			87,200	
Freight in			5,200	
Cost of goods available for sale			131,000	
Less: Ending inventory			(40,200)	
Cost of goods sold				90,800
Gross profit				75,100
Operating expenses:				
Wage expense			10,200	
Rent expense			8,400	
Insurance expense			1,000	
Depreciation expense			600	
Supplies expense			550	20,750
Income from operations				54,350
Other revenue and (expense):				
Interest revenue			1,000	
Interest expense			(1,500)	(500)
Net income				$ 53,850

(continued)

Austin Sound Center

Statement of Owner's Equity
Year Ended December 31, 20X5

C. Ernest, capital, December 31, 20X4	$25,900
Add: Net income.	53,850
	79,750
Less: Withdrawals.	(54,100)
C. Ernest, capital, December 31, 20X5	$25,650

Austin Sound Center

Balance Sheet
December 31, 20X5

Assets			Liabilities		
Current:			Current:		
Cash.		$ 2,850	Accounts payable		$47,000
Accounts receivable.		4,600	Unearned sales revenue.		700
Note receivable.		8,000	Wages payable.		400
Interest receivable		400	Interest payable.		200
Inventory.		40,200	Total current liabilities		48,300
Prepaid insurance		200	Long-term:		
Supplies.		100	Note payable		12,600
Total current assets		56,350	Total liabilities		60,900
Plant:					
Furniture and fixtures.	$33,200		**Owner's Equity**		
Less: Accumulated			C. Ernest, capital		25,650
depreciation	(3,000)	30,200	Total liabilities and		
Total assets		$86,550	owner's equity.		$86,550

expenses other than cost of goods sold that occur in the entity's major line of business. Many companies report their operating expenses in two categories.

- *Selling expenses* relate to marketing the company's products—sales salaries, sales commissions, advertising, depreciation, rent, utilities, delivery expense, and so on.

- *General expenses* include office expenses, such as the salaries of office employees, and depreciation, rent, and other expenses on the home office building.

Gross profit minus operating expenses and plus any other operating revenues equals *operating income*, or *income from operations*. The last section of Austin Sound's income statement is *other revenue and expense*. This category reports revenues and expenses that are outside the company's main line of business.

Appendix Assignments
Exercises

E5A-1 Journalize, without explanations, the following transactions of Hunter Gift Shop during June. Use the periodic system.

Journalizing purchase and sale transactions
(Obj. A1)

June 3 Purchased $700 of inventory under terms of 2/10 n/eom (end of month) and FOB shipping point.

7 Returned $300 of defective merchandise purchased on June 3.

9 Paid freight bill of $30 on June 3 purchase.

10 Sold inventory for $3,200. Payment terms were 2/15 n/30.

12 Paid amount owed on credit purchase of June 3, less the discount and the return.

16 Granted a sales allowance of $800 on the June 10 sale.

23 Received cash from June 10 customer in full settlement of her debt, less the allowance and the discount.

E5A-2 As the proprietor of Davis Tire Company, you receive the following invoice from a supplier:

Journalizing transactions from a purchase invoice
(Obj. A1)

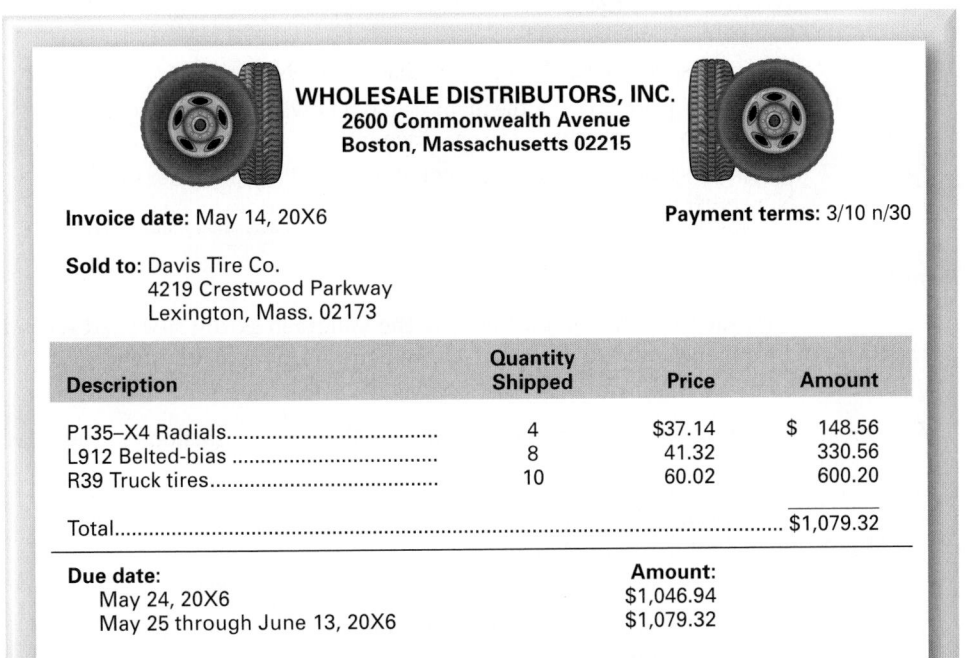

WHOLESALE DISTRIBUTORS, INC.
2600 Commonwealth Avenue
Boston, Massachusetts 02215

Invoice date: May 14, 20X6   **Payment terms:** 3/10 n/30

Sold to: Davis Tire Co.
4219 Crestwood Parkway
Lexington, Mass. 02173

Description	Quantity Shipped	Price	Amount
P135–X4 Radials..	4	$37.14	$ 148.56
L912 Belted-bias	8	41.32	330.56
R39 Truck tires..	10	60.02	600.20
Total..			$1,079.32

Due date:	Amount:
May 24, 20X6	$1,046.94
May 25 through June 13, 20X6	$1,079.32

Required

1. Davis received the invoice on May 15. Record the May 15 purchase on account. Carry amounts to the nearest cent throughout.

2. The R39 truck tires were ordered by mistake and were therefore returned to Wholesale Distributors. Journalize the return on May 19.

3. Record the May 22 payment of the amount owed.

E5A-3 On April 30, Stanley & Weaver Jewelers purchased inventory of $8,000 on account from Intergem Jewels, a jewelry importer. Terms were 3/15 net 45. On receiving the goods, Stanley & Weaver checked the order and found $1,000 of unsuitable merchandise. Therefore, Stanley & Weaver returned $1,000 of merchandise to Intergem on May 4.

Journalizing purchase transactions
(Obj. A1)

To pay the remaining amount owed, Stanley & Weaver borrowed the net amount of the invoice from the bank. On May 14, Stanley & Weaver signed a short-term note payable to the bank and immediately paid the borrowed funds to Intergem. On June 14, Stanley & Weaver paid the bank the net amount of the invoice, which Stanley & Weaver had borrowed, plus 1% monthly interest (round to the nearest dollar).

Required

Record the indicated transactions in the journal of Stanley & Weaver Jewelers. Use the periodic inventory system. Explanations are not required.

Journalizing sales transactions
(Obj.AI)

E5A-4 Refer to the business situation in Exercise 5A-3. Journalize the transactions of Intergem Jewels. Explanations are not required.

Problems

Accounting for the purchase and sale of inventory
(Obj.AI)

P5A-I Assume that the following transactions occurred between Providence Medical Supply and a **Walgreen's** drug store during November of the current year:

Nov. 6	Providence Medical Supply sold $6,200 worth of merchandise to Walgreen's on terms of 2/10 n/30, FOB shipping point. Walgreen's also paid freight-in of $300.
10	Walgreen's returned $900 of the merchandise on November 6.
15	Walgreen's paid $3,000 of the invoice amount owed to Providence for the November 6 purchase, less the discount.
27	Walgreen's paid the remaining amount owed to Providence for the November 6 purchase.

Required

Journalize these transactions, first on the books of the Walgreen's drug store and second on the books of Providence Medical Supply. Use the periodic inventory system.

P5A-2 Preakness Wholesale Grocery engaged in the following transactions during May of the current year:

May 3	Purchased office supplies for cash, $300.
7	Purchased inventory on credit terms of 3/10 net 30, $2,000.
8	Returned half the inventory purchased on May 7. It was not the inventory ordered.
10	Sold goods for cash, $450.
13	Sold inventory on credit terms of 2/15 n/45, $3,900.
16	Paid the amount owed on account from the purchase of May 7, less the discount and the return.
17	Received defective inventory returned from the May 13 sale, $900.
18	Purchased inventory of $4,000 on account. Payment terms were 2/10 net 30.
26	Paid supplier for goods purchased on May 18, less the discount.
28	Received cash in full settlement of the account from the customer who purchased inventory on May 13, less the discount and the return.

Required

Journalize the preceding transactions. Use the periodic inventory system. Explanations are not required.

P5A-3 The year-end trial balance of Latham Sales Company pertains to March 31, 20X4.

Preparing a merchandiser's accounting work sheet, financial statements, and adjusting and closing entries
(Obj. A2, A3, A4)

Latham Sales Company
Trial Balance
March 31, 20X4

Cash	$ 7,880	
Note receivable, current	12,400	
Interest receivable		
Inventory	130,050	
Prepaid insurance	3,600	
Notes receivable, long-term	62,000	
Furniture	6,000	
Accumulated depreciation		$ 4,000
Accounts payable		12,220
Sales commission payable		
Salary payable		
Unearned sales revenue		9,610
Ben Latham, capital		172,780
Ben Latham, withdrawals	66,040	
Sales revenue		440,000
Sales discounts	4,800	
Sales returns and allowances	11,300	
Interest revenue		8,600
Purchases	233,000	
Purchase discounts		3,100
Purchase returns and allowances		7,600
Freight in	10,000	
Sales commission expense	78,300	
Salary expense	24,700	
Rent expense	6,000	
Utilities expense	1,840	
Depreciation expense		
Insurance expense		
Total	$657,910	$657,910

Additional Data at March 31, 20X4:

a. Accrued interest revenue, $1,030.
b. Insurance expense for the year, $3,000.
c. Furniture has an estimated useful life of six years. Its value is expected to be zero when it is retired from service.
d. Unearned sales revenue still unearned, $7,400.
e. Accrued salary expense, $1,200.
f. Accrued sales commission expense, $1,700.
g. Inventory on hand, $133,200.

Required

1. Enter the trial balance on an accounting work sheet, and complete the work sheet for the year ended March 31, 20X4.
2. Journalize the adjusting and closing entries at March 31, 20X4.

3. Post to the Ben Latham, Capital account and to the Income Summary account as an accuracy check on the adjusting and closing process.

4. Prepare the company's multi-step income statement and statement of owner's equity for the year ended March 31, 20X4. Also prepare its classified balance sheet at that date. Long-term notes receivable should be reported on the balance sheet between current assets and plant assets in a separate section labeled Investments.

Comprehensive Problem for Chapters 1–5

COMPLETING A MERCHANDISER'S ACCOUNTING CYCLE

The end-of-month trial balance of St. James Technology at January 31 of the current year follows. Additional data at January 31, 20XX:

a. Supplies consumed during the month, $1,500. Half is selling expense, and the other half is general expense.

b. Depreciation for the month: building, $4,000; fixtures, $4,800. One-fourth of depreciation is selling expense, and three-fourths is general expense.

c. Unearned sales revenue still unearned, $1,200.

d. Accrued salaries, a general expense, $1,150.

e. Accrued interest expense, $780.

f. Inventory on hand, $63,720. St. James uses the perpetual inventory system.

1. Using four-column accounts, open the accounts listed on the trial balance, inserting their unadjusted balances. Date the balances of the following accounts January 1: Supplies; Building; Accumulated Depreciation—Building; Fixtures; Accumulated Depreciation—Fixtures; Unearned Sales Revenue; and Dirk St. James, Capital. Date the balance of Dirk St. James, Withdrawals, January 31. Also open the Income Summary, account number 33.

2. Enter the trial balance on an accounting work sheet, and complete the work sheet for the month ended January 31 of the current year. St. James Technology groups all operating expenses under two accounts, Selling Expense and General Expense. Leave two blank lines under Selling Expense and three blank lines under General Expense.

3. Prepare the company's multi-step income statement and statement of owner's equity for the month ended January 31 of the current year. Also prepare the balance sheet at that date in report form.

Journalizing purchase and sales transactions
(Obj. A1)

St. James Technology
Trial Balance
January 31, 20XX

Account Number	Account	Balance Debit	Balance Credit
11	Cash	$ 16,430	
12	Accounts receivable..................	19,090	
13	Inventory..........................	65,400	
14	Supplies...........................	2,700	
15	Building...........................	188,170	
16	Accumulated depreciation—building ..		$ 36,000
17	Fixtures	45,600	
18	Accumulated depreciation—fixtures ...		5,800
21	Accounts payable...................		28,300
22	Salary payable......................		
23	Interest payable		
24	Unearned sales revenue		6,560
25	Note payable, long-term..............		87,000
31	Dirk St. James, capital		144,980

(*continued*)

32	Dirk St. James, withdrawals............	9,200	
41	Sales revenue		187,970
42	Sales discounts	7,300	
43	Sales returns and allowances	8,140	
51	Cost of goods sold	103,000	
54	Selling expense.....................	21,520	
55	General expense....................	10,060	
56	Interest expense		
	Total	$496,610	$496,610

4. Journalize the adjusting and closing entries at January 31, using page 3 of the journal.

5. Post the adjusting and closing entries, using dates and posting references.

CHAPTER 6

Merchandise Inventory

TIPS CHECK YOUR RESOURCES

- Visit the www.prenhall.com/horngren **Web site** for self-study quizzes, video clips, and other resources

- Try the **Quick Check** exercise at the end of the chapter to test your knowledge

- Learn the **key terms**

- Do the **Starter** exercises keyed in the margins

- Work the **mid-** and **end-of-chapter summary problems**

- Use the **Concept Links** to review material in other chapters

- Search the **CD** for review materials by chapter or by key word

- Watch the **tutorial videos** to review key concepts

- Watch the **On Location Teva Sports Sandals** video to review inventory and e-commerce issues

LEARNING OBJECTIVES

1. Compute perpetual inventory amounts under FIFO, LIFO, and average cost

2. Record perpetual inventory transactions

3. Compare the effects of FIFO, LIFO, and average cost

4. Compute periodic inventory amounts under FIFO, LIFO, and average cost

5. Apply the lower-of-cost-or-market rule to inventory

6. Measure the effects of inventory errors

7. Estimate ending inventory by the gross profit method

Columbia Sportswear Company® serves as the official outerwear supplier to the annual Kodak Albuquerque International Balloon Fiesta® in Albuquerque, New Mexico. Ballooning's largest and most spectacular event now hosts close to a thousand balloons and more than a million spectators. How do pilots and passengers stay warm at the higher altitudes?

For the eighth consecutive year, Columbia is outfitting pilots, sponsor guests, media personalities, and event staff with a special parka. "Columbia is very proud of its relationship with the . . .

Columbia Sportswear Company

celebration . . . ," said Chrisanthi Hatzantonis, Columbia Sportswear promotions manager. "This festival is . . . one of the most . . . visually stunning events I've attended."

Source: "Columbia Sportswear Takes Flight at World-Renowned Albuquerque Balloon Festival," press release, October 2, 2002. ■

■ Sitemap

Columbia makes and markets over 50 different parkas and jackets for men, women, and children. Its line also includes specialized sports products like camouflaged hunting jackets, so how Columbia deals with inventory is vital to its success.

This chapter shows how Columbia Sportswear and other merchandisers apply various methods to account for their inventory. They can use the perpetual system, which we covered in Chapter 5, or the periodic system, which we introduce in this chapter.

But first let's review how merchandise inventory affects a company. Exhibit 6-1 gives the merchandising section of Columbia Sportswear's balance sheet and income statement. Inventories, cost of goods sold, and gross profit are highlighted. These amounts (X, Y, and Z) are left blank to indicate that throughout the chapter we will be computing them using various accounting methods.

Exhibit 6-1

Columbia Sportswear: Merchandising Sections of the Financial Statements

Columbia Sportswear Company
Balance Sheet (partial; adapted)
December 31, 20X1

	Millions
Assets	
Current assets:	
Cash	$ 79
Accounts receivable	155
Inventories	X
Prepaid expenses	18

Columbia Sportswear Company
Income Statement (partial; adapted)
Year Ended December 31, 20X1

	Millions
Net sales	$ 780
Cost of goods sold	Y
Gross profit	Z

The remainder of the chapter explores the various ways a company can determine the amounts of

- Ending inventory (X) in Exhibit 6-1
- Cost of goods sold (Y) and gross profit (Z) in Exhibit 6-1

Inventory Costing Methods

As we saw in Chapter 5,

$$\text{Ending inventory} = \text{Number of units on hand} \times \text{Unit cost}$$

$$\text{Cost of goods sold} = \text{Number of units sold} \times \text{Unit cost}$$

Companies determine the number of units from perpetual inventory records backed up by a physical count.

$$\text{Unit cost} = \text{Purchase price} - \text{Purchase discounts}$$

Exhibit 6-2 gives assumed inventory data for a line of Columbia Sportswear ski parkas.

Student Resource CD

average cost method, inventory costing, FIFO, LIFO

Exhibit 6-2

Perpetual Inventory Record—
Quantities Only—
Columbia Sportswear

Item: Sunrise Ski Parkas

Date	Quantity Purchased	Quantity Sold	Quantity on Hand
Nov. 1			1
5	6		7
15		4	3
26	7		10
30		8	2
Totals	13	12	2

In this illustration, Columbia began November with 1 parka on hand. After buying and selling, Columbia had 2 parkas at the end of the month.

Assume that Columbia Sportswear's cost of each ski parka is $40. In this case,

$$\text{Ending inventory} = \text{Number of units on hand (Exhibit 6-2)} \times \text{Unit Cost}$$
$$2 \times \$40 = \$80$$

$$\text{Cost of goods sold} = \text{Number of units sold (Exhibit 6-2)} \times \text{Unit cost}$$
$$12 \times \$40 = \$480$$

What would Columbia's ending inventory and cost of goods sold be if the cost of ski parkas increased from $40 to $50 during the period? Companies face price increases during periods of inflation. To measure inventory amounts during such periods, the accounting profession has developed several costing methods.

Measuring the cost of inventory is easy when prices are constant. But the unit cost often changes. A ski parka that cost Columbia $40 in January may cost $45 or $50 later in the year. Suppose Columbia sells 10,000 ski parkas in November. How many of the parkas cost $40? How many cost $45 or $50? To compute ending inventory and cost of goods sold, Columbia must assign a cost to each item. The four costing methods GAAP allows are

1. Specific unit cost
2. Average cost
3. First-in, first-out (FIFO) cost
4. Last-in, first-out (LIFO) cost

A company can use any of these methods to account for its inventory.

Specific-Unit-Cost Method
Inventory cost method based on the specific cost of particular units of inventory. Also called the **specific-identification method**.

Exhibit 6-3

Cost Flows for the Three Most Popular Inventory Methods

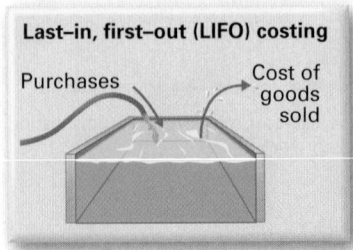

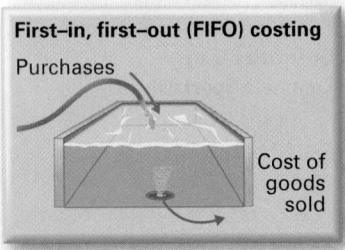

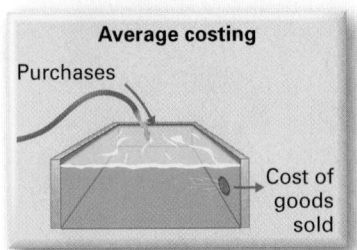

The **specific-unit-cost** method is also called the **specific-identification method**. This method uses the specific cost of each unit of inventory. Some businesses deal in items that differ from unit to unit, such as automobiles, jewels, and real estate. For instance, a Chevrolet dealer may have two vehicles—a "stripped-down" model that cost $16,000 and a "loaded" model that cost $19,000. If the dealer sells the loaded model, cost of goods sold is $19,000, the cost of the specific unit. Suppose the stripped-down auto is the only unit left in inventory at the end of the period; ending inventory is $16,000, the dealer's cost of that particular car.

Amazon.com uses the specific-unit-cost method to account for its inventory. But very few other companies use this method, so we shift to the more popular inventory costing methods.

The other three methods are very different. First-in, first-out (FIFO) and last-in, first-out (LIFO) are exact opposites, and the average-cost method falls between the extremes of FIFO and LIFO. Exhibit 6-3 illustrates how each method works.

- Under the FIFO method, the cost of goods sold is based on the oldest purchases. This is illustrated by the Cost of goods sold coming from the *bottom* of the container.

- Under the LIFO method, the cost of goods sold is based on the most recent purchases. This is illustrated by the Cost of goods sold coming from the *top* of the container.

- Under the average method, the cost of goods sold is based on an average cost for the period. This is illustrated by the Cost of goods sold coming from the *middle* of the container.

Now let's see how to compute inventory amounts under the FIFO, LIFO, and average costing methods. The amounts we compute will complete Columbia's financial statements in Exhibit 6-1. We use the following transaction data for all the illustrations:

Columbia Sportswear Sunrise Ski Parka		Number of Units	Unit Cost
Nov. 1	Beginning inventory	1	$40
5	Purchase	6	45
15	Sale	4	
26	Purchase	7	50
30	Sale	8	

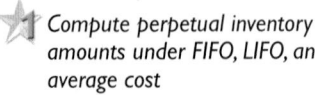
Student ResourceCD

average-cost method, cost of goods sold, FIFO, inventory turnover, LIFO, perpetual method, sales revenue

⭐ *Compute perpetual inventory amounts under FIFO, LIFO, and average cost*

We begin with inventory costing in a perpetual system.

Inventory Costing in a Perpetual System

As we shall see, the various inventory costing methods produce different amounts for ending inventory and cost of goods sold. Let's begin with the FIFO method.

First-In, First-Out (FIFO) Method

Columbia Sportswear actually uses the **FIFO method** to account for its inventory. FIFO costing is consistent with the physical movement of inventory for most companies. Under FIFO, the first costs incurred by Columbia each period are the first costs to be assigned to cost of goods sold. FIFO leaves in ending inventory the last—the most recent—costs incurred during the period. This is illustrated in the FIFO perpetual inventory record in Exhibit 6-4.

Sunrise Ski Parkas

Exhibit 6-4

Perpetual Inventory Record: FIFO and Journal Entries for the Related Transactions

Date	Purchases			Cost of Goods Sold			Inventory on Hand		
	Quantity	Unit Cost	Total Cost	Quantity	Unit Cost	Total Cost	Quantity	Unit Cost	Total Cost
Nov. 1							1	$40	$ 40
5	6	$45	$270				1	40	40
							6	45	270
15				1	$40	$ 40			
				3	45	135	3	45	135
26	7	50	350				3	45	135
							7	50	350
30				3	45	135			
				5	50	250	2	50	100
30	13		$620	12		$560	2		$100

Journal Entries: (All purchases and sales on account.
The sale price of a ski parka is $80 per unit.)

Nov. 5	Inventory	270		
	Accounts Payable		270	
15	Accounts Receivable (4 × $80)	320		
	Sales Revenue		320	
15	Cost of Goods Sold ($40 + $135)	175		
	Inventory.........................		175	
26	Inventory	350		
	Accounts Payable		350	
30	Accounts Receivable (8 × $80)	640		
	Sales Revenue		640	
30	Cost of Goods Sold ($135 + $250)	385		
	Inventory.........................		385	

2 Record perpetual inventory transactions

Columbia began November with one ski parka that cost $40. After the November 5 purchase, the inventory on hand consists of 7 units (1 @ $40 plus 6 @ $45). On November 15, Columbia sold 4 units. Under FIFO, the first unit sold is costed at the oldest cost ($40 per unit). The next 3 units sold come from the group that cost $45 per unit. That leaves 3 units in inventory on hand, and those units cost $45 each. The remainder of the inventory record follows the same pattern.

The FIFO monthly summary at November 30 is

- Cost of goods sold: 12 units that cost a total of $560
- Ending inventory: 2 units that cost a total of $100

Columbia measured cost of goods sold and inventory in this manner to prepare its financial statements in Exhibit 6-1.

First-In, First-Out (FIFO) Inventory Costing Method
Inventory costing method: the first costs into inventory are the first costs out to cost of goods sold. Ending inventory is based on the costs of the most recent purchases.

✔ Starter 6-1

Stop & Think

How does the perpetual inventory record in Exhibit 6-4 help **Columbia Sportswear** manage its business? How will Columbia use the information in the perpetual inventory record? (To answer this question, consider how you would manage your inventory if you did *not* have any perpetual inventory records.) Explain your reasoning.

Answer: Columbia Sportswear uses perpetual inventory records to:

a. *Meet customer demand* for ski parkas. When a customer orders 10 parkas, Columbia can use the perpetual inventory records to determine whether the goods are available for sale.

b. *Prepare financial statements.* Each month Columbia gets inventory and cost of goods sold information from its inventory records, and uses this data to prepare monthly financial statements that managers use to operate the business.

c. *Keep track of merchandise* in order to keep from losing it to spoilage or theft.

Last-In, First-Out (LIFO) Inventory Costing Method
Inventory costing method: the last costs into inventory are the first costs out to cost of goods sold. Leaves the oldest costs—those of beginning inventory and the earliest purchases of the period—in ending inventory.

Last-In, First-Out (LIFO) Method

LIFO is the opposite of FIFO. Under the **LIFO method**, cost of goods sold comes from the latest—the most recent—purchases. Ending inventory's cost comes from the oldest costs of the period. LIFO costing does not follow the flow of goods for most companies. LIFO often results in the highest cost of goods sold—and the lowest income tax. Low taxes are LIFO's main advantage. Exhibit 6-5 gives a perpetual inventory record for the LIFO method.

Exhibit 6-5

Perpetual Inventory Record: LIFO and Journal Entries for the Related Transactions

Sunrise Ski Parkas

	Purchases			Cost of Goods Sold			Inventory on Hand		
Date	Quantity	Unit Cost	Total Cost	Quantity	Unit Cost	Total Cost	Quantity	Unit Cost	Total Cost
Nov. 1							1	$40	$40
5	6	$45	$270				1	40	40
							6	45	270
15				4	$45	$180	1	40	40
							2	45	90
26	7	50	350				1	40	40
							2	45	90
							7	50	350
30				7	50	350			
				1	45	45	1	40	40
							1	45	45
30	13		$620	12		$575	2		$85

Journal Entries: **(All purchases and sales on account. The sale price of a ski parka is $80 per unit.)**

Nov. 5	Inventory	270	
	Accounts Payable		270
15	Accounts Receivable (4 × $80)	320	
	Sales Revenue		320
15	Cost of Goods Sold	180	
	Inventory..........................		180
26	Inventory	350	
	Accounts Payable		350
30	Accounts Receivable (8 × $80)	640	
	Sales Revenue		640
30	Cost of Goods Sold ($350 + $45)	395	
	Inventory..........................		395

Again, Columbia had 1 ski parka at the beginning of November. After the purchase on November 5, Columbia holds 7 units of inventory (1 @ $40 plus 6 @ $45). Columbia then sells 4 units on November 15. Under LIFO, the cost of goods sold always comes from the latest purchase. That leaves 3 ski parkas in inventory on November 15 (1 @ $40 plus 2 @ $45). The purchase of 7 units on November 26 adds a new $50 layer to inventory. Then the sale of 8 units on November 30 peels back units in LIFO order.

The LIFO monthly summary at November 30 is

- Cost of goods sold: 12 units that cost a total of $575
- Ending inventory: 2 units that cost a total of $85

If Columbia used the LIFO method, it could measure cost of goods sold and inventory in this manner to prepare its financial statements in Exhibit 6-1.

 **Starter 6-2**

Examine Exhibit 6-4 (FIFO) and Exhibit 6-5 (LIFO). Focus on the sale of goods on November 15. Why is cost of goods sold different between FIFO costing and LIFO costing? Explain.

Answer: Cost of goods sold differs dramatically between FIFO costing and LIFO costing. The two methods make opposite assumptions about the timing of when costs leave inventory (an asset) and move into cost of goods sold (an expense).

- Under FIFO, the first costs into inventory are the first costs out to cost of goods sold. Under FIFO, the *oldest* costs are expensed first.
- Under LIFO, the last costs into inventory are the first costs out to cost of goods sold. The *newest* costs are expensed first.

FIFO and LIFO are opposites!

Average-Cost Method

Suppose Columbia Sportswear uses the **average-cost method** to account for its inventory of ski parkas. With this method, the business computes a new average cost per unit after each purchase. Ending inventory and cost of goods sold are then based on the average cost per unit. Exhibit 6-6 shows a perpetual inventory record for the average-cost method. We round average unit cost to the nearest cent and total cost to the nearest dollar.

Average-Cost Method
Inventory costing method based on the average cost of inventory during the period. Average cost is determined by dividing the cost of goods available for sale by the number of units available.

Exhibit 6-6

Perpetual Inventory Record: Average Cost and Journal Entries for the Related Transactions

Sunrise Ski Parkas

	Purchases			Cost of Goods Sold			Inventory on Hand		
Date	Quantity	Unit Cost	Total Cost	Quantity	Unit Cost	Total Cost	Quantity	Unit Cost	Total Cost
Nov. 1							1	$40.00	$ 40
5	6	$45	$270				7	44.29	310
15				4	$44.29	$177	3	44.29	133
26	7	50	350				10	48.30	483
30				8	48.30	386	2	48.30	97
30	13		$620	12		$563	2		$ 97

Journal Entries: (All purchases and sales on account. The sale price of a ski parka is $80 per unit.)

Nov. 5	Inventory		270	
	Accounts Payable			270
15	Accounts Receivable (4 × $80)		320	
	Sales Revenue			320
15	Cost of Goods Sold		177	
	Inventory			177
26	Inventory		350	
	Accounts Payable			350
30	Accounts Receivable (8 × $80)		640	
	Sales Revenue			640
30	Cost of Goods Sold		386	
	Inventory			386

After each purchase, Columbia computes a new average cost per unit. The new average unit cost on November 5 is:

	Total cost of inventory on hand		Number of units on hand		Average cost per unit
Nov. 5	$310	÷	7 units	=	$ 44.29

The goods sold on November 15 are then costed out at $44.29 per unit. Columbia then computes a new average cost after the November 26 purchase.

The average-cost summary at November 30 is

- Cost of goods sold: 12 units that cost a total of $563
- Ending inventory: 2 units that cost a total of $97

✔ Starter 6-3

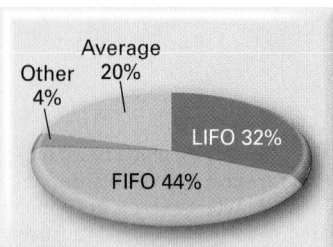

3 *Compare the effects of FIFO, LIFO, and average cost*

Exhibit 6-7

Use of the Various Inventory Methods

If Columbia used the average-cost method, it would use these amounts to prepare its financial statements in Exhibit 6-1.

Comparing FIFO, LIFO, and Average Cost

Exhibit 6-7 shows that FIFO is the most popular inventory costing method. LIFO is next most popular and average cost ranks third.

What leads Columbia Sportswear to select the FIFO method, Lands' End to use LIFO, and Fossil (the watch company) to use average cost? The different methods have different benefits.

Exhibit 6-8 summarizes the results for the three inventory methods for Columbia Sportswear. It shows sales revenue, cost of goods sold, and gross profit for FIFO, LIFO, and average cost. All data come from Exhibits 6-4, 6-5, and 6-6.

Exhibit 6-8 shows that FIFO produces the lowest cost of goods sold and the highest gross profit. Net income is also the highest under FIFO when inventory costs are rising. Many companies wish to report high income in order to attract investors and borrow on good terms. FIFO offers this benefit.

LIFO results in the highest cost of goods sold and the lowest gross profit. That lets companies pay the lowest income taxes when inventory costs are rising. Low tax payments conserve a company's cash, but the downside of LIFO is that the company reports low net income.

The average-cost method generates gross profit, income tax, and net income amounts that fall between the extremes of FIFO and LIFO. Companies that seek a "middle-ground" solution, therefore, use the average-cost method for inventory.

✔ Starter 6-4
✔ Starter 6-5
✔ Starter 6-6

Exhibit 6-8   **Comparative Results for FIFO, LIFO, and Average Cost**

	FIFO	LIFO	Average
Sales revenue	$ 960	$ 960	$ 960
Cost of goods sold	560	575	563
Gross profit	$ 400	$ 385	$ 397

● MID-CHAPTER *Summary Problem*

TIPS

CHECK YOUR RESOURCES

Fossil specializes in designer watches and leather goods. Assume Fossil began June holding 10 wristwatches that cost $50 each. Fossil sells these watches for $100 each. During June, Fossil bought and sold inventory as follows:

June 3	Sold 8 units for $100 each
16	Purchased 10 units @ $55 each
23	Sold 8 units for $100 each

Required

1. Prepare a perpetual inventory record for Fossil under
   - FIFO
   - LIFO
   - Average-Cost
2. Journalize all of Fossil's inventory transactions for June under all three costing methods.
3. Show the computation of gross profit for each method.
4. Which method maximizes net income? Which method minimizes income taxes?

Solution

1. Perpetual inventory records:

FIFO

Wristwatches

Date	Purchases			Cost of Goods Sold			Inventory on Hand		
	Quantity	Unit Cost	Total Cost	Quantity	Unit Cost	Total Cost	Quantity	Unit Cost	Total Cost
June 1							10	$50	$500
3				8	$50	$400	2	50	100
16	10	$55	$550				2	50	100
							10	55	550
23				2	50	100			
				6	55	330	4	55	220
30				16		$830	4		$220

LIFO

Wristwatches

Date	Purchases			Cost of Goods Sold			Inventory on Hand		
	Quantity	Unit Cost	Total Cost	Quantity	Unit Cost	Total Cost	Quantity	Unit Cost	Total Cost
June 1							10	$50	$500
3				8	$50	$400	2	50	100
16	10	$55	$550				2	50	100
							10	55	550
23				8	55	440	2	50	100
							2	55	110
30				16		$840	4		$210

AVERAGE COST

Wristwatches

Date	Purchases			Cost of Goods Sold			Inventory on Hand		
	Quantity	Unit Cost	Total Cost	Quantity	Unit Cost	Total Cost	Quantity	Unit Cost	Total Cost
June 1							10	$50.00	$500
3				8	$50.00	$400	2	50.00	100
16	10	$55	$550				12	54.17	650
23				8	54.17	433	4	54.17	217
30				16		$833	4		217

2. Journal Entries:

			FIFO		LIFO		Average	
June 3	Accounts Receivable		800		800		800	
	Sales Revenue			800		800		800
3	Cost of Goods Sold.		400		400		400	
	Inventory			400		400		400
16	Inventory		550		550		550	
	Accounts Payable			550		550		550
23	Accounts Receivable		800		800		800	
	Sales Revenue			800		800		800
23	Cost of Goods Sold							
	($100 + $330)		430		440		433	
	Inventory			430		440		433

		FIFO	LIFO	Average
3.	Sales revenue ($800 + $800)	$1,600	$1,600	$1,600
	Cost of goods sold ($400 + $430)	830		
	($400 + $440)		840	
	($400 + $433)			833
	Gross profit	$ 770	$ 760	$ 767

4. FIFO maximizes net income.
   LIFO minimizes income taxes.

Student ResourceCD

average-cost method, cost of goods sold, FIFO, inventory costing, LIFO, periodic method, sales revenue

Inventory Costing in a Periodic System

We described the periodic inventory system briefly in Chapter 5. Accounting is simpler in a periodic system because the company keeps no daily running record of inventory on hand. The only way to determine the ending inventory and cost of goods sold in a periodic system is to count the goods—usually at the end of the year. The periodic system works well for a small business, in which the owner can control inventory by visual inspection.

The chapter appendix illustrates how the periodic system works. Journal entries in a periodic system are similar to journal entries in a perpetual system, except:

1. The periodic system uses four additional accounts. In the periodic system we record the purchase of inventory with a debit to the Purchases account, not to the Inventory account. Purchase discounts are credited to the Purchase Discount account, and purchase returns and allowances are credited to the Purchase Returns and Allowances account. Transportation charges on inventory purchases are debited to the Transportation-In account.

2. The end-of-period entries are more extensive in the periodic system because we must close out the beginning inventory balance and set up the cost of the ending inventory. The chapter appendix illustrates this process.

Cost of goods sold in a periodic inventory system is computed by the following formula (using assumed amounts for this illustration):

Beginning inventory (the inventory on hand at the end of the preceding period)......	$ 5,000
Net purchases (often abbreviated as Purchases)	20,000*
Cost of goods available for sale.............................	25,000
Less: Ending inventory (the inventory on hand at the end of the current period)......	(7,000)
Cost of goods sold..	$18,000

*Net purchases is determined as follows (all amounts assumed):	
Purchases	$21,000
Less: Purchase discounts	(2,000)
Purchase returns and allowances	(5,000)
Add: Transportation-in...................................	6,000
Net purchases	$20,000

The application of the various costing methods (FIFO, LIFO, and average cost) in a periodic inventory system follows the pattern illustrated earlier for the perpetual system. To show how the periodic inventory system works, we use the same Columbia Sportswear data as we used for the perpetual system, as follows:

Columbia Sportswear Sunrise Ski Parka		Number of Units	Unit Cost
Nov. 1	Beginning inventory	1	$ 40
5	Purchase	6	45
15	Sale	4	
26	Purchase	7	50
30	Sale	8	
30	Ending inventory	2	?

4 *Compute periodic inventory amounts under FIFO, LIFO, and average cost*

First-In, First-Out (FIFO) Method

Columbia Sportswear could use the FIFO costing method with a periodic inventory system. The FIFO computations follow:

Beginning inventory (1 unit @ $40).....................	$ 40
Purchases (6 units @ $45 + 7 units @ $50)	620
Cost of goods available for sale (14 units)..............	660
Less: Ending inventory (2 units @ $50)	(100)
Cost of goods sold (12 units)	$560

Cost of goods available is always the sum of beginning inventory plus purchases. Under FIFO, the ending inventory comes from the latest—the most recent—purchases, which cost $50 per unit. Ending inventory is therefore $100, and cost of goods sold is $560. These amounts are exactly the same as we saw for FIFO in the perpetual system in Exhibit 6-4.

There are fewer journal entries in the periodic system because Columbia would record a sale with only a single entry. For example, Columbia's sale of 4 ski parkas for $80 each is recorded as follows:

Nov. 15	Accounts Receivable (4 × $80).........	320	
	Sales Revenue		320

There is no cost of goods sold entry in the periodic system.

Last-In, First-Out (LIFO) Method

The LIFO method fits well with a periodic inventory system. Columbia's LIFO computations follow:

Beginning inventory (1 unit @ $40).........................	$ 40
Purchases (6 units @ $45 + 7 units @ $50).....................	620
Cost of goods available for sale (14 units)	660
Less: Ending inventory (1 unit @ $40 + 1 unit @ $45)..........	(85)
Cost of goods sold (12 units)	$575

✔ **Starter 6-7**

Under LIFO, the ending inventory comes from the earliest units obtained—the single beginning unit that cost $40 plus 1 of the units purchased for $45. Ending inventory is therefore $85, and cost of goods sold is $575. These amounts are the same as we saw for the perpetual system in Exhibit 6-5. In some cases, the LIFO amounts can differ between the perpetual and the periodic systems.

Average-Cost Method

In the average method, we compute a single average cost per unit for the entire period as follows:

Cost of goods available for sale		Number of units available for sale		Average cost per unit for the entire period
$660	÷	14 units	=	$47.14

This average cost per unit is then used to compute the ending inventory and cost of goods sold as follows:

Beginning inventory (1 unit @ $40)	$ 40
Purchases (6 units @ $45 + 7 units @ $50)	620
Cost of goods available for sale	
(14 units @ average cost of $47.14)	660
Less: Ending inventory (2 units @ $47.14)	(94)
Cost of goods sold (12 units @ $47.14)	$566

Ending inventory and cost of goods sold under the periodic system differ from the amounts in a perpetual system. Why? Because under the perpetual system, a new average cost is computed after each purchase. But the periodic system uses a single average cost that is determined at the end of the period.

Accounting Principles and Inventories

Several accounting principles have special relevance to inventories. Among them are consistency, disclosure, materiality, and accounting conservatism.

CONSISTENCY PRINCIPLE   The **consistency principle** states that businesses should use the same accounting methods and procedures from period to period. Consistency helps investors compare a company's financial statements from one period to the next.

Suppose you are analyzing a company's net income pattern over a two-year period. The company switched from LIFO to FIFO during that time. Its net income increased dramatically but only as a result of the change in inventory method. If you did not know of the change, you might believe that the company's income increased because of improved operations. Therefore, companies must report any changes in the accounting methods they use. Investors need this information to make wise decisions about the company.

DISCLOSURE PRINCIPLE   The **disclosure principle** holds that a company's financial statements should report enough information for outsiders to make knowledgeable decisions about the company. In short, the company should report *relevant*, *reliable*, and *comparable* information about its economic affairs. With respect to inventories, the disclosure principle means disclosing the method being used to value inventories. Suppose a banker is comparing two companies—one using LIFO and the other FIFO. The FIFO company reports higher net income, but only because it uses the FIFO inventory method. Without knowledge of the accounting methods the companies are using, the banker could lend money to the wrong business.

MATERIALITY CONCEPT   The **materiality concept** states that a company must perform strictly proper accounting *only* for items that are significant for the business's financial statements. Information is significant—or, in accounting terminology, *material*—when its presentation in the financial statements would cause someone to change a decision. The materiality concept frees accountants from having to report every last item in strict accordance with GAAP.

ACCOUNTING CONSERVATISM   **Conservatism** in accounting means reporting items in the financial statements at amounts that lead to the most cautious immediate results. Conservatism appears in accounting guidelines such as

- "Anticipate no gains, but provide for all probable losses."
- "If in doubt, record an asset at the lowest reasonable amount and a liability at the highest reasonable amount."
- "When there's a question, record an expense rather than an asset."

Student ResourceCD
accounting principles

Consistency Principle
A business should use the same accounting methods and procedures from period to period.

Disclosure Principle
A business's financial statements must report enough information for outsiders to make knowledgeable decisions about the company.

Materiality Concept
A company must perform strictly proper accounting only for items that are significant to the business's financial statements.

Conservatism
Reporting the least favorable figures in the financial statements.

The goal is for financial statements to report realistic figures. The lower-of-cost-or-market rule is an example of accounting conservatism.

Other Inventory Issues

In addition to the basic inventory costing methods, accountants face other inventory issues. This section covers those topics, which include

- The lower-of-cost-or-market rule
- Effects of inventory errors
- Ethical issues
- Estimating inventory amounts

Lower-of-Cost-or-Market Rule

The **lower-of-cost-or-market rule** (abbreviated as **LCM**) shows accounting conservatism in action. LCM requires that inventory be reported in the financial statements at whichever is lower—the inventory's historical cost or its market value. For inventories, *market value* generally means *current replacement cost* (that is, the cost to replace the inventory on hand). If the replacement cost of inventory falls below its historical cost, the business must write down the value of its goods. The business reports ending inventory at its LCM value on the balance sheet.

Suppose Columbia Sportswear paid $3,000 for inventory on September 26. By December 31, the inventory can now be replaced for $2,200, and the decline in value appears permanent. Market value is below FIFO cost, and the entry to write down the inventory to LCM follows:

Cost of Goods Sold		
(cost, $3,000 – market, $2,200)...................	800	
Inventory................................		800

In this case, Columbia's balance sheet would report this inventory as follows:

Balance Sheet	
Current assets:	
Inventory, at market	
(which is lower than FIFO cost)	$ 2,200

Companies often disclose LCM in notes to their financial statements, as shown here for Columbia Sportswear:

NOTE 2: STATEMENT OF SIGNIFICANT ACCOUNTING POLICIES
Inventories. Inventories are carried at the *lower of cost or market*. Cost is determined using the first-in, first-out method.

Effects of Inventory Errors

Businesses count their inventories at the end of the period. As the period 1 segment of Exhibit 6-9 shows, an error in the ending inventory creates errors in cost of goods sold and gross profit. Compare period 1's ending inventory, which is overstated, with period 3, which is correct. Period 1 *should* look exactly like period 3.

Recall that one period's ending inventory becomes the next period's beginning inventory. Thus, the error in ending inventory carries over into the next period; note the amounts highlighted in Exhibit 6-9.

Student ResourceCD
ethics, gross profit method, inventory errors, lower of cost or market

5 Apply the lower-of-cost-or-market rule to inventory

Lower-of-Cost-or-Market (LCM) Rule
Rule that an asset should be reported in the financial statements at whichever is lower—its historical cost or its market value.

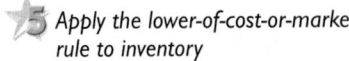 **Starter 6-9**

 Starter 6-10

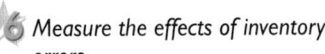 6 Measure the effects of inventory errors

Exhibit 6-9 Inventory Errors: An Example

	Period 1 Ending Inventory Overstated by $5,000	Period 2 Beginning Inventory Overstated by $5,000	Period 3 Correct
Sales revenue	$100,000	$100,000	$100,000
Cost of goods sold:			
Beginning inventory	$10,000	$ 15,000	$10,000
Net purchases.........................	50,000	50,000	50,000
Cost of goods available			
for sale	60,000	65,000	60,000
Ending inventory.......................	(15,000)	(10,000)	(10,000)
Cost of goods sold	45,000	55,000	50,000
Gross profit............................	$ 55,000	$ 45,000	$ 50,000
		$100,000	

The correct gross profit is $50,000 for each period.

Source: The authors thank Carl High for this example.

Because ending inventory is *subtracted* to compute cost of goods sold in one period and the same amount is *added* as beginning inventory the next period, the error cancels out after two periods. The overstatement of cost of goods sold in period 2 counterbalances the understatement for period 1. Thus, total gross profit for the two periods combined is correct. These effects are summarized in Exhibit 6-10.

✔ **Starter 6-11**

Exhibit 6-10

Effects of Inventory Errors

✔ **Starter 6-12**

	Period 1		Period 2	
Inventory Error	Cost of Goods Sold	Gross Profit and Net Income	Cost of Goods Sold	Gross Profit and Net Income
Period 1 Ending inventory *overstated*	Understated	Overstated	Overstated	Understated
Period 1 Ending inventory *understated*	Overstated	Understated	Understated	Overstated

Online retailers try to avoid errors in accounting for their inventory. See the Accounting.com box titled, "Online Category Managers: The New B2B Force Behind Those Huge E-Tailer Inventories," on the next page.

Ethical Issues

No area of accounting has a deeper ethical dimension than inventory. Owners and managers of companies whose profits are lagging are sometimes tempted to "cook the books." The increase in reported income may lead investors and creditors to think the business is more successful than it really is.

There are two main schemes for cooking the books. The easiest way is simply to overstate ending inventory. In Exhibit 6-10, we saw how an error in ending inventory affects net income. A company can intentionally overstate its ending inventory. Such an error overstates assets and owner's equity, as shown in the accounting equation. The upward-pointing arrows indicate an overstatement—reporting more assets and equity than are actually present:

Effect of overstating ending inventory:	ASSETS	=	LIABILITIES	+	OWNER'S EQUITY
	↑	=	0	+	↑

Online Category Managers: The New B2B Force Behind Those Huge E-Tailer Inventories

A big advantage e-tailers have over brick-and-mortar concerns is a much wider selection of goods. Even big-box merchandisers like **Circuit City** have limited floor space. But for Circuitcity.com, cyberspace is the limit. And Circuitcity.com and other dot.com merchants don't have to pay for the goods! Their secret: the online "category manager."

Online category managers are third-party distributors that specialize in a specific product, like DVDs, sporting goods, jewelry, or electronic equipment. They ship directly to customers using e-tailing clients' labels. E-tailers pay a fee to integrate their e-commerce systems and then receive between 10% and 35% of the profit on each item sold—much less than if they owned the inventory themselves. But this is a small price to pay to avoid the risk of inventory ownership and headaches from accounting for the merchandise.

These behind-the-scenes inventory managers are growing faster than their clients. For example, 50% of online sales volume for struggling retailer **Kmart** comes through vendor partners. **GSI Commerce, Inc.**, a sporting goods manager, serves **Sports Authority** and **Athlete's Foot**. In 2001 GSI's sales more than doubled over 2000. Even e-commerce giant **Amazon.com** has tried to get a slice of the pie by becoming a vendor partner. "We created this business [inventory management] years ago, when people said it didn't make any sense," said Michael G. Rubin, chief executive of GSI. "[Now we've] proven what an opportunity this is."

Based on: Miguel Helft, "Still Alive and Growing Online, Without Fanfare," *The New York Times*, January 6, 2002, Sec. 3, p. 4. Bob Sechler, "E-Commerce (A Special Report): B2B—Inventories—Behind the Curtain: How Can Online Retailers Maintain Such Huge Inventories? Here's Their Secret," *The Wall Street Journal*, July 15, 2002, p. R12. Brian Garrity, "The State of E-Commerce," *Billboard*, March 17, 2001, pp. 60–62.

HealthSouth Corp faces civil and criminal charges for overstating the company's inventory and other assets. However, the company's deft handling of its balance sheet made it practically impossible for investors to detect the scheme before it was too late.[1]

The second way of using inventory to cook the books involves sales. Sales schemes are more complex than simple inventory overstatements. **Datapoint Corporation** and **MiniScribe**, both computer-related concerns, were charged with creating fictitious sales to boost reported profits.

Datapoint is alleged to have hired drivers to transport its inventory around San Antonio so that the goods could *not* be physically counted. Datapoint's plan seemed to be that excluding goods from ending inventory would mean they had been sold. The scheme broke down when the trucks returned the goods to Datapoint. What would you think of a company with $10 million in sales and $4 million of sales returns?

MiniScribe is alleged to have cooked its books by shipping boxes of bricks labeled as computer parts to its distributors right before year-end. The scheme affected MiniScribe's reported assets and equity (assuming sales of $10 million and cost of goods sold of $6 million) as follows:

ASSETS	=	LIABILITIES	+	OWNER'S EQUITY
↑	=	0	+	↑

[1]Jonathan Weil, "Accounting Scheme Was Straightforward But Hard to Detect," *The Wall Street Journal*, March 20, 2003, p. C.1.

The bogus transactions increased MiniScribe's assets and equity by $4 million—but only temporarily. The scheme boomeranged when MiniScribe had to record the sales returns. In virtually every area, accounting imposes a discipline that brings out the facts sooner or later.

Estimating Inventory

Estimate ending inventory by the gross profit method

Often a business must *estimate* the value of its inventory. Suppose the company suffers a fire loss and must estimate the value of the inventory destroyed.

The **gross profit method** provides a way to estimate inventory as follows (amounts assumed for illustration):

Gross Profit Method
A way to estimate inventory on the basis of the cost-of-goods-sold model: Beginning inventory + Net purchases = Cost of goods available for sale. Cost of goods available for sale – Cost of goods sold = Ending inventory.

> Beginning inventory
> + Purchases
> = Cost of goods available for sale
> – Ending inventory
> = Cost of goods sold

Rearranging *ending inventory* and *cost of goods sold* helps to estimate ending inventory (amounts assumed for illustration):

> Beginning inventory
> + Purchases
> = Cost of goods available for sale
> – Cost of goods sold (Sales – Gross Profit = COGS)
> = Ending inventory

Suppose a fire destroys your inventory. To collect insurance, you must estimate the cost of the inventory destroyed—that is, the ending inventory. Using your normal *gross profit percent* (that is, gross profit divided by net sales revenue), you can estimate cost of goods sold. Then subtract cost of goods sold from goods available to estimate ending inventory. Exhibit 6-11 illustrates the gross profit method.

Exhibit 6-11

Gross Profit Method of Estimating Inventory (amounts assumed)

Beginning inventory..............................		$14,000
Purchases...		66,000
Cost of goods available for sale		80,000
Estimated cost of goods sold:		
Sales revenue....................................	$100,000	
Less: Estimated gross profit of 40%	(40,000)	
Estimated cost of goods sold		(60,000)
Estimated cost of *ending inventory*		$20,000

Beginning inventory is $70,000, net purchases total $298,000, and net sales are $500,000. With a normal gross profit rate of 40% of sales, how much is ending inventory?

Answer:

Beginning inventory		$ 70,000
Net purchases		298,000
Cost of goods available for sale		368,000
Estimated cost of goods sold:		
Net sales revenue	$500,000	
Less: Estimated gross profit of 40%	(200,000)	
Estimated cost of goods sold		(300,000)
Estimated cost of ending inventory		$ 68,000

Decision Guidelines

GUIDELINES FOR INVENTORY MANAGEMENT

Assume you are starting a business to sell school supplies to your college friends. You'll need to stock computer disks, notebooks, and other inventory items. To manage the business, you'll also need some accounting records. Here are some of the decisions you'll face.

Decision	Guidelines	System or Method
Which inventory system to use?	• Expensive merchandise • Cannot control inventory by visual inspection	→ Perpetual system
	• Can control inventory by visual inspection	→ Periodic system
Which costing method to use?	• Unique inventory items	→ Specific unit cost
	• The most current cost of ending inventory • Maximizes reported income when costs are rising	→ FIFO
	• The most current measure of cost of goods sold and net income • Minimizes income tax when costs are rising	→ LIFO
	• Middle-of-the-road approach for income tax and net income	→ Average-cost
How to estimate the cost of ending inventory?	• The cost-of-goods-sold model provides the framework	→ Gross profit method

Excel Application Exercise

Goal: Create an Excel spreadsheet that will compare gross profit, ending inventory, and cost of goods sold under the LIFO, FIFO, and average-cost methods of inventory valuation.

Scenario: Assume that during the first month of operating your school supplies business, you stock only 100 MB Zip disks. Your task is to create a spreadsheet and embedded graph that compare gross profit, ending inventory, and cost of goods sold under three methods: average cost, FIFO, and LIFO. For the first month of business, you have collected the following data for use in creating the spreadsheet:

August 1	Beginning inventory	50 units @ $4.00 cost per unit
10	Purchase	60 units @ $4.40 cost per unit
17	Purchase	100 units @ $4.75 cost per unit
31	Purchase	100 units @ $5.10 cost per unit
Sales for August:		*200 disks sold @ $10.00 each*

After you have prepared your spreadsheet, answer these questions:

1. Which method produces the lowest cost of goods sold? Why?
2. Which method produces the lowest ending inventory? Why?
3. If you want to maximize gross profit, which method should you choose? Does this method do a good job of matching inventory expense (cost of goods sold) to sales revenue?

Step-by-Step:

1. Open a new Excel spreadsheet.
2. Create a heading for your spreadsheet that contains the following:
   a. Chapter 6 Excel Application Exercise
   b. Inventory Management
   c. Today's date
3. At the top of your spreadsheet, create a "Data Section" for the August data. Set up columns for Date, Activity ("Beginning Inventory," "Purchases," "Goods Available for Sale," "Sales," and "Ending Inventory"), Units, Unit Cost, and Total Cost. Compute goods available for sale and ending inventory.
4. Include the calculation for "average unit cost" on a separate row in this section.
5. Next, create a section titled "Inventory Method Comparison" in bold print and underlined. Include one column for each method (average cost, FIFO, and LIFO). Include rows for Ending Inventory, Cost of Goods Sold, and Gross Profit. Format as necessary. Be sure your calculations are based on the "Data Section" figures. Do not "hard code" any amounts in this section.
6. When finished, create an embedded bar chart underneath the "Inventory Method Comparison" section that compares Gross Profit, Ending Inventory, and Cost of Goods Sold for all three methods. (*Hint:* Use the Chart Wizard button on the standard Excel toolbar.)
7. Save your spreadsheet, and print a copy for your files.

END-OF-CHAPTER *Summary Problem*

CHECK YOUR RESOURCES

Suppose a division of **IBM Corporation** that handles computer components has these inventory records for January 20X6:

Date	Item	Quantity	Unit Cost	Sale Price
Jan. 1	Beginning inventory	100 units	$ 8	
6	Purchase	60 units	9	
13	Sale	70 units		$20
21	Purchase	150 units	9	
24	Sale	210 units		22
27	Purchase	90 units	10	
30	Sale	30 units		25

Company accounting records reveal that operating expense for January was $1,900.

Required

Prepare the January income statement, showing amounts for FIFO, LIFO, and average cost. Label the bottom line "Operating income." (Round the average cost per unit to three decimal places and all other figures to whole-dollar amounts.) Show your computations, and use the periodic inventory model from pages 256–258 to compute cost of goods sold.

Solution

IBM Corporation

Income Statement for Computer Components
Month Ended January 31, 20X6

	FIFO		LIFO		Average Cost	
Sales revenue............................		$6,770		$6,770		$6,770
Cost of goods sold:						
Beginning inventory	$ 800		$ 800		$ 800	
Net purchases	2,790		2,790		2,790	
Cost of goods						
available for sale.....................	3,590		3,590		3,590	
Ending inventory	(900)		(720)		(808)	
Cost of goods sold		2,690		2,870		2,782
Gross profit		4,080		3,900		3,988
Operating expenses		1,900		1,900		1,900
Operating income........................		$2,180		$2,000		$2,088

Computations

Sales revenue:	$(70 \times \$20) + (210 \times \$22) + (30 \times \$25)$	$= \$6,770$
Beginning inventory:	$100 \times \$8$	$= \$800$
Purchases:	$(60 \times \$9) + (150 \times \$9) + (90 \times \$10)$	$= \$2,790$
Ending inventory		
FIFO	$90^* \times \$10$	$= \$900$
LIFO	$90 \times \$8$	$= \$720$
Average cost:	$90 \times \$8.975^{**}$	$= \$808$ (rounded from $807.75)

*Number of units in ending inventory = $100 + 60 - 70 + 150 - 210 + 90 - 30 = 90$.
**$3,590/400 units† = $8.975 per unit.
†Number of units available = $100 + 60 + 150 + 90 = 400$.

REVIEW *Accounting for Merchandise Inventory* ⬤

Quick Check

1. The chain store, **The Limited, Inc.**, made sales of $9,363 million and ended the year with inventories totaling $966 million. Cost of goods sold was $6,110 million. Total operating expenses were $2,734 million. How much net income did The Limited earn for the year?

   a. $519 million

   b. $3,253 million

   c. $5,663 million

   d. $6,629 million

2. Which inventory costing method assigns to ending inventory the latest—the most recent—costs incurred during the period?

   a. Specific unit cost

   b. First-in, first-out (FIFO)

   c. Last-in, first-out (LIFO)

   d. Average cost

3. Assume **Amazon.com** began June with 10 units of inventory that cost a total of $190. During June, Amazon purchased and sold goods as follows:

June 8	Purchase	30 units @ $20
14	Sale	25 units @ $40
22	Purchase	20 units @ $22
27	Sale	30 units @ $40

   Assume Amazon uses the FIFO inventory method and the perpetual inventory system. How much is Amazon's cost of goods sold for the transaction on June 14?

   a. $790

   b. $1,000

   c. $500

   d. $490

4. After the purchase on June 22, what is Amazon's cost of the inventory on hand?

   a. $300

   b. $440

   c. $740

   d. $720

5. Amazon's journal entry (entries) on June 14 is (are)

   a. Accounts Receivable 490

          Inventory 490

   b. Accounts Receivable 1,000

          Sales Revenue...................... 1,000

   c. Cost of Goods Sold 490

          Inventory 490

   d. Both b and c

6. Which inventory costing method results in the lowest net income during a period of rising inventory costs?

   a. Specific unit cost

   b. First-in, first-out (FIFO)

   c. Last-in, first-out (LIFO)

   d. Average cost

7. Suppose Amazon.com used the average-cost method and the periodic inventory system. Use the Amazon data in question 3 to compute the cost of the company's inventory on hand at June 30. Round unit cost to the nearest cent.

   a. $102.50

   b. $105.20

   c. $205.00

   d. $210.40

8. Which of the following is most closely tied to accounting conservatism?

   a. Consistency principle

   b. Disclosure principle

   c. Materiality concept

   d. Lower-of-cost-or-market rule

9. At December 31, 20X5, McAdam Company overstated ending inventory by $40,000. How does this error affect cost of goods sold and net income for 20X5?

   a. Overstates cost of goods sold
   Understates net income

   b. Understates cost of goods sold
   Overstates net income

   c. Overstates both cost of goods sold
   and net income

   d. Leaves both cost of goods sold and net income
   correct because the errors cancel each other

10. Suppose **Columbia Sportswear** suffered a fire loss and needs to estimate the cost of the goods destroyed. Beginning inventory was $100,000, purchases totaled $600,000, and sales came to $1,000,000. Columbia's normal gross profit percentage is 45%. Use the gross profit method to estimate the cost of the inventory lost in the fire.

a. $150,000

b. $250,000

c. $300,000

d. $350,000

Accounting Vocabulary

average-cost method (p. 253)

conservatism (p. 258)

consistency principle (p. 258)

disclosure principle (p. 258)

first-in, first-out (FIFO) inventory costing method (p. 251)

gross profit method (p. 262)

last-in, first-out (LIFO) inventory costing method (p. 252)

lower-of-cost-or-market (LCM) rule (p. 259)

materiality concept (p. 258)

specific identification method (p. 250)

specific-unit-cost method (p. 250)

●ASSESS *Your Progress*

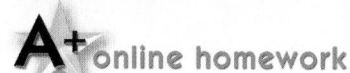
online homework

See *www.prenhall.com/horngren* for selected Starters, Exercises, and Problems.

Measuring FIFO amounts in a perpetual system
(Obj. 1)

Recording LIFO amounts in a perpetual system
(Obj. 1, 2)

Measuring average-cost amounts in a perpetual system
(Obj. 1)

Using a perpetual inventory system
(Obj. 1, 2)

Comparing cost of goods sold under FIFO and LIFO
(Obj. 3)

Comparing ending inventory under FIFO and LIFO
(Obj. 3)

Starters

S6-1 Refer to **Columbia Sportswear's** perpetual inventory record, at FIFO cost, in Exhibit 6-4, page 251. Assume that Columbia began November with 5 ski parkas (instead of 1). Keep all other factors unchanged, and compute these FIFO amounts for Columbia:

a. Cost of goods sold for the November 15 transaction

b. Inventory on hand at November 15

S6-2 Use the LIFO perpetual inventory record of **Columbia Sportswear** in Exhibit 6-5, page 252. Assume that Columbia purchased 10 units (instead of 7) on November 26, and keep all other factors unchanged. Journalize Columbia's transactions under LIFO on November 30. The sale was half for cash and half on account. The sale price of the ski parkas was $70 each.

S6-3 The average-cost perpetual record of **Columbia Sportswear** appears in Exhibit 6-6, page 253. Suppose Columbia purchased 9 ski parkas (instead of 6) on November 5, and keep all other factors unchanged. Compute the cost of Columbia's inventory on hand at November 15.

S6-4 Use the FIFO inventory record in Exhibit 6-4, page 251, to prepare a T-account for the inventory. Show all dates and label each item in the T-account.

S6-5 Study Exhibit 6-8, page 254, and answer these questions in your own words:

1. Why does FIFO produce the lowest cost of goods sold during a period of rising prices?

2. Why does LIFO produce the highest cost of goods sold during a period of rising prices?

S6-6 Explain in your own words which inventory method results in the highest, and the lowest, cost of ending inventory. Prices are rising. The data in Exhibits 6-4, page 251, and 6-5, page 252, may help.

S6-7 St. Louis Dry Goods uses a periodic inventory system. St. Louis completed the following inventory transactions during April:

April 1	Purchased 10 shirts @ $40
7	Sold 6 shirts for $70 each
13	Sold 2 shirts for $80 each
21	Purchased 3 shirts @ $50

Compute St. Louis's ending inventory and cost of goods sold under both LIFO and FIFO. Compute gross profit under both methods. Which method results in more gross profit?

S6-8 St. Louis Dry Goods uses a periodic inventory system. Use the St. Louis Dry Goods data in Starter 6-7 to compute ending inventory and cost of goods sold under the average-cost method. Round average unit cost to the nearest cent.

S6-9 Assume **Columbia Sportswear** prepared the FIFO perpetual inventory record in Exhibit 6-4, page 251. It is now November 30 and Columbia is preparing monthly financial statements. Assume that Columbia's chief financial officer determines that the current replacement cost (market value) of the ending inventory is $90.

Make any adjusting entry that Columbia needs in order to apply the lower-of-cost-or-market rule at November 30. Then report the inventory on the balance sheet.

S6-10 Suppose **Columbia Sportswear** uses the average-cost method and prepares the perpetual inventory record in Exhibit 6-6, page 253. It is now November 30, and Columbia is preparing monthly financial statements. Assume that Columbia's chief financial officer determines that the current market value of the ending inventory is $98.

What journal entry should Columbia make in order to apply the lower-of-cost-or-market rule at November 30? Explain. Then report the inventory on the balance sheet.

S6-11 **Target Corporation's** inventory data for the year ended January 31, 2002, as adapted, follow (in millions):

Beginning inventory	$ 4,248
Purchases	27,447
Cost of goods available	31,695
Less: Ending inventory	(4,449)
Cost of goods sold	$27,246

Assume that the ending inventory figure was accidentally overstated by $100 million. How would this error affect cost of goods sold and gross profit?

S6-12 Refer back to **Target Corporation's** inventory data in Starter 6-11. How would the inventory error affect Target's cost of goods sold and gross profit for the year ended January 31, 2003?

S6-13 Asamax Insulation Company began the year with inventory of $350,000. Inventory purchases for the year totaled $1,600,000. Asamax managers estimate that cost of goods sold for the year will be $1,800,000. How much is Asamax's estimated cost of ending inventory? Use the gross profit method.

S6-14 Cyrus Roofing began the year with inventory of $50,000 and purchased $160,000 of goods during the year. Sales for the year are $300,000, and Cyrus's gross profit percentage is 40% of sales. Compute Cyrus's estimated cost of ending inventory by the gross profit method.

Measuring ending inventory and cost of goods sold in a perpetual system—FIFO
(Obj. 1)

Recording perpetual inventory transactions
(Obj. 2)

Measuring ending inventory and cost of goods sold in a perpetual system—LIFO
(Obj. 1)

Applying the average-cost method in a perpetual inventory system
(Obj. 1)

Recording perpetual inventory transactions
(Obj. 2)

Comparing FIFO and LIFO amounts for ending inventory
(Obj. 3)

Exercises

E6-1 Picker Paradise carries a large inventory of guitars and other musical instruments. Picker uses the FIFO method and a perpetual inventory system. Company records indicate the following for a particular line of Honeydew guitars:

Date	Item	Quantity	Unit Cost
May 1	Balance	5	$70
6	Sale	3	
8	Purchase	10	80
17	Sale	4	
30	Sale	5	

Required

Prepare a perpetual inventory record for the guitars. Then determine the amounts Picker should report for ending inventory and cost of goods sold by the FIFO method.

E6-2 After preparing the FIFO perpetual inventory record in Exercise 6-1, journalize Picker Paradise's May 8 purchase of inventory on account and cash sale on May 17 (sale price of each guitar was $140).

E6-3 Refer to the Picker Paradise inventory data in Exercise 6-1. Assume that Picker Paradise uses the LIFO cost method. Prepare Picker's perpetual inventory record for the guitars on the LIFO basis. Then identify the cost of ending inventory and cost of goods sold for the month.

E6-4 Refer to the Picker Paradise inventory data in Exercise 6-1. Assume that Picker uses the average-cost method. Prepare Picker's perpetual inventory record for the guitars on the average-cost basis. Round average cost per unit to the nearest cent and all other amounts to the nearest dollar.

E6-5 Accounting records for Durall Luggage yield the following data for the year ended December 31, 20X5 (amounts in thousands):

Inventory, December 31, 20X4	$ 370
Purchases of inventory (on account)............................	3,105
Sales of inventory—80% on account; 20% for cash (cost $2,821)	4,395
Inventory, December 31, 20X5	?

Required

1. Journalize Durall's inventory transactions in the perpetual system. Show all amounts in thousands.
2. Report ending inventory on the balance sheet, and sales, cost of goods sold, and gross profit on the income statement (amounts in thousands).

E6-6 Assume that a **Toys "Я" Us** store bought and sold a video game (inventory) during December as follows:

Beginning inventory..........................	10 units @ $20
Sale	6 units
Purchase....................................	15 units @ $22
Sale	14 units

Toys "Я" Us uses the perpetual inventory system. Compute the cost of ending inventory under (a) FIFO and (b) LIFO. Which method results in higher cost of ending inventory? higher cost of goods sold?

E6-7 Use the data in Exercise 6-6 to compute the cost of goods sold under (a) FIFO and (b) LIFO. You will need a complete perpetual inventory record for LIFO.

Comparing FIFO and LIFO amounts for cost of goods sold
(Obj. 3)

E6-8 Assume that a **Home Depot** store completed the following perpetual inventory transactions for a line of carpet.

Comparing FIFO, LIFO, and average-cost amounts
(Obj. 3)

Beginning inventory	20 rolls @ $200
Purchase	8 rolls @ $300
Sale.	15 rolls @ $500

Compute cost of goods sold and gross profit under (a) FIFO, (b) LIFO, and (c) average cost (round average cost per unit to the nearest cent).

E6-9 The periodic inventory records of Flexon Prosthetics indicate the following at October 31:

Determining ending inventory and cost of goods sold by four methods: periodic system
(Obj. 4)

Student ResourceCD
spreadsheet

Oct. 1	Beginning inventory	9 units @ $160
8	Purchase	4 units @ 160
15	Purchase	12 units @ 170
26	Purchase	3 units @ 176

The physical inventory at October 31 counts 8 units on hand.

Required

Compute ending inventory and cost of goods sold, using each of the following methods.

1. Specific unit cost, assuming four $170 units and four $160 units are on hand
2. Average cost (round average unit cost to three decimal places)
3. First-in, first-out   4. Last-in, first-out

E6-10 Supply the missing amounts for each of the following companies:

Determining amounts for the income statement; periodic system
(Obj. 4)

Company	Net Sales	Beginning Inventory	Net Purchases	Ending Inventory	Cost of Goods Sold	Gross Profit
Maple	$101,800	$21,500	$62,700	$19,400	(a)	$37,000
Walnut	(b)	25,450	93,000	(c)	$94,100	43,200
Pine	94,700	(d)	54,900	22,600	62,500	(e)
Magnolia	84,300	10,700	(f)	8,200	(g)	47,100

Prepare the income statement for Magnolia Company, which uses the periodic inventory system. Include a complete heading and show the full computation of cost of goods sold. Magnolia's operating expenses for the year were $31,600.

E6-11 **Alcoa Enterprises,** which uses the FIFO method, has these account balances at December 31, 20X6, prior to releasing the financial statements for the year:

Applying the lower-of-cost-or-market rule to inventories
(Obj. 5)

Inventory	Cost of Goods Sold	Sales Revenue
Beg. bal. 12,489		
End bal. 18,028	Bal. 113,245	Bal. 225,000

A year ago, when Alcoa prepared its 20X5 financial statements, the replacement cost of ending inventory was $13,051. Alcoa has determined that the replacement cost (current market value) of the December 31, 20X6, ending inventory is $16,840.

Required

Prepare Alcoa Enterprises' 20X6 income statement through gross profit to show how Alcoa would apply the lower-of-cost-or-market rule to its inventories. Include a complete heading for the statement.

Applying the lower-of-cost-or-market rule to inventories
(Obj. 5)

E6-12 Nash-Robin Foods reports inventory at the lower of FIFO cost or market. Prior to releasing its March 20X4 financial statements, Nash-Robin's preliminary income statement appears as follows:

Nash-Robin Foods		
Income Statement (partial)		
Sales revenue		$118,000
Cost of goods sold:		
Beginning inventory	$17,200	
Net purchases.................................	51,700	
Cost of goods available for sale..................	68,900	
Ending inventory..............................	(23,900)	
Cost of goods sold		45,000
Gross profit...................................		$ 73,000

Nash-Robin has determined that the replacement cost of beginning inventory was $16,600, and the replacement cost of ending inventory is $18,300.

Required

Prepare the Nash-Robin income statement to apply the lower-of-cost-or-market rule to the company's beginning and ending inventory. Also show the relevant portion of Nash-Robin's balance sheet at March 31, 20X4.

Measuring the effect of an inventory error
(Obj. 6)

E6-13 Refer to the Nash-Robin income statement in Exercise 6-12, and ignore everything else. Assume that the ending inventory amount was miscounted and the cost ($23,900) is incorrect. Determine the correct amounts of cost of goods sold and gross profit if Nash-Robin's

a. Ending inventory is overstated by $3,000.
b. Ending inventory is understated by $3,000.

Start the computation of cost of goods sold with Cost of goods available for sale.

Correcting an inventory error—two years
(Obj. 6)

E6-14 Lazlo Power Tools reported the following comparative income statement for the years ended September 30, 20X2 and 20X1.

Lazlo Power Tools				
Income Statements				
Years Ended September 30, 20X2 and 20X1				
	20X2		**20X1**	
Sales revenue...............		$137,300		$121,700
Cost of goods sold:				
Beginning inventory.......	$14,000		$12,800	
Net purchases	72,000		66,000	
Cost of goods available ...	86,000		78,800	
Ending inventory	(16,600)		(14,000)	
Cost of goods sold........		69,400		64,800
Gross profit		67,900		56,900
Operating expenses		30,300		26,100
Net income................		$ 37,600		$ 30,800

During 20X2, accountants for the company discovered that ending 20X1 inventory, as reported above, was overstated by $3,500. Prepare the corrected comparative income statement for the two-year period, complete with a heading for the statement. What was the effect of the error on net income for the two years combined? Explain your answer.

E6-15 **General Electric Company (GE)** holds inventory all over the world. Assume that the records for a line of refrigerators show the following:

Estimating ending inventory by the gross profit method
(Obj. 7)

Beginning inventory	$ 150,000
Net purchases.	800,000
Net sales	1,000,000
Gross profit rate	30%

Suppose this inventory, stored in Guatemala, was lost in a hurricane. Estimate the amount of the loss to GE. Use the gross profit method.

E6-16 Lake Huron Marineland uses a periodic inventory system. The company began January with inventory of $47,500. During January, the business made net purchases of $37,600 and had net sales of $60,000. For the past several years, Lake Huron's gross profit has been 40% of sales. Use the gross profit method to estimate the cost of the ending inventory for the monthly financial statements.

Estimating ending inventory by the gross profit method
(Obj. 7)

Student ResourceCD

spreadsheet

Problems

(Group A)

P6-1A **Pier 1 Imports** operates almost 1,000 stores around the world. Assume you are dealing with a Pier 1 store in Dallas. Assume the store began with an inventory of 50 chairs that cost a total of $1,500. The store purchased and sold merchandise on account as follows:

Accounting for inventory in a perpetual system—FIFO
(Obj. 1, 2)

Purchase 1	60 chairs @ $35
Sale 1	100 chairs @ $60
Purchase 2	80 chairs @ $40
Sale 2	70 chairs @ $70

Assume that Pier 1 uses the FIFO cost method. Cash payments on account totaled $5,100. Operating expenses were $2,400; the store paid two-thirds in cash and accrued the rest as Accounts Payable.

Required

1. Prepare a perpetual inventory record, at FIFO cost, for this merchandise.
2. Make journal entries to record the store's transactions.

P6-2A Refer to the **Pier 1 Imports** situation in Problem 6-1A. Keep all the data unchanged, except that Pier 1 actually uses the average-cost method.

Accounting for inventory in a perpetual system—average-cost
(Obj. 1, 3)

Required

1. Prepare a perpetual inventory record at average cost. Round average unit cost to the nearest cent and all other amounts to the nearest dollar.
2. Prepare a multistep income statement for the Pier 1 Imports store for the month of February.

P6-3A Rambler Lawn Supply, which uses the LIFO method, began March with 50 units of inventory that cost $15 each. During March, Rambler completed these inventory transactions:

Using the perpetual inventory system—LIFO
(Obj. 1, 3)

		Units	Unit Cost	Unit Sale Price
March 2	Purchase	12	$20	
8	Sale	40		$36
17	Purchase	24	25	
22	Sale	31		40

Required

1. Prepare a perpetual inventory record for the lawn supply merchandise.

2. Determine Rambler's cost of goods sold for March.

3. Compute gross profit for March.

Computing inventory by three methods—periodic system
(Obj. 3, 4)

P6-4A A Best Yet Electronic Center began December with 140 units of inventory that cost $75 each. During December, the store made the following purchases:

Dec. 3	217 @ $79
12	95 @ 82
18	210 @ 83
24	248 @ 87

The store uses the periodic inventory system, and the physical count at December 31 indicates that 229 units of inventory are on hand.

Required

1. Determine the ending inventory and cost-of-goods-sold amounts for the December financial statements under the average cost, FIFO, and LIFO methods. Round average cost per unit to the nearest cent and all other amounts to the nearest dollar.

2. Sales revenue for December totaled $90,000. Compute Best Yet's gross profit for December under each method.

3. Which method will result in the lowest income taxes for Best Yet? Why? Which method will result in the highest net income for Best Yet? Why?

Using the periodic inventory system— FIFO
(Obj. 4)

P6-5A Mesa Hardware Company, which uses a periodic inventory system, began 20X4 with 6,000 units of inventory that cost a total of $30,000. During 20X4, Mesa purchased merchandise on account as follows:

Purchase 1 (10,000 units costing)	$ 60,000
Purchase 2 (20,000 units costing)	140,000

At year-end, the physical count indicated 5,000 units of inventory on hand.

Required

1. How many units did Mesa sell during the year? The sale price per unit was $10. Determine Mesa's sales revenue for the year.

2. Compute cost of goods sold by the FIFO method. Then determine gross profit for the year.

Applying the lower-of-cost-or-market rule to inventories
(Obj. 5)

P6-6A **Revco Drug** has been plagued with lackluster sales, and some of the company's merchandise is gathering dust. It is now December 31, 20X7. Assume the current replacement cost of Revco's ending inventory is $700,000 below what Revco paid for the goods, which was $3,900,000. Before any adjustments at the end of the period, assume the Cost of Goods Sold account has a balance of $22,400,000.

What action should Revco take in this situation, if any? Give any journal entry required. At what amount should Revco report Inventory on the balance sheet? At what amount should the company report Cost of Goods Sold on the income statement? Discuss the accounting principle or concept that is most relevant to this situation.

P6-7A The accounting records of Treviño's Mexican Restaurant show these data (in thousands):

Correcting inventory errors over a three-year period
(Obj. 6)

	20X3		20X2		20X1	
Net sales revenue.		$210		$165		$170
Cost of goods sold:						
Beginning inventory	$ 15		$ 25		$ 40	
Net purchases.	135		100		90	
Cost of goods available.	150		125		130	
Less: Ending inventory.	(30)		(15)		(25)	
Cost of goods sold		120		110		105
Gross profit.		90		55		65
Operating expenses.		74		38		46
Net income		$ 16		$ 17		$ 19

In early 20X4, internal auditors discovered that the ending inventory for 20X1, as reported here, was understated by $8 thousand and that the ending inventory for 20X3 was overstated by $5 thousand. The ending inventory at December 31, 20X2, was correct.

Required

1. Show corrected income statements for the three years.

2. State whether each year's net income as reported here is understated or overstated. For each incorrect figure, indicate the amount of the understatement or overstatement.

P6-8A **Moss Motors** estimates its inventory by the gross profit method when preparing monthly financial statements. For the past two years, gross profit has averaged 30% of net sales. Assume further that the company's inventory records reveal the following data (amounts in thousands):

Estimating ending inventory by the gross profit method; preparing the income statement
(Obj. 7)

Inventory, March 1.	$ 292
Transactions during March:	
Purchases	6,585
Purchase discounts	149
Purchase returns	8
Sales.	8,657
Sales returns	17

Required

1. Estimate the March 31 inventory using the gross profit method.

2. Prepare the March income statement through gross profit for Moss Motors.

Problems

(Group B)

P6-1B **Toys "Я" Us** purchases inventory in crates of merchandise, so each unit of inventory is a crate of toys. Assume you are dealing with a single department in the Toys "Я" Us store in Santa Barbara, California.

Assume the department began January with an inventory of 20 units that cost a total of $1,200. During the month, the department purchased and sold merchandise on account as follows:

Accounting for inventory using the perpetual system—LIFO
(Obj. 1, 2)

Purchase 1	30 units @ $ 65	Purchase 2	70 units @ $ 70
Sale 1	40 units @ $100	Sale 2	75 units @ $110

Toys "Я" Us uses the LIFO cost method.

Cash payments on account totaled $6,300. Department operating expenses for the month were $3,600. The department paid two-thirds in cash, with the rest accrued as Accounts Payable.

Required

1. Prepare a perpetual inventory record, at LIFO cost, for this merchandise.
2. Make journal entries to record the department's transactions.

Accounting for inventory in a perpetual
system—average-cost
(Obj. 1, 3)

P6-2B Refer to the **Toys " Я " Us** situation in Problem 6-1B. Keep all the data unchanged, except assume that Toys " Я " Us uses the average-cost method.

Required

1. Prepare a perpetual inventory record at average cost. Round average unit cost to the nearest cent and all other amounts to the nearest dollar.
2. Prepare a multistep income statement for the Toys " Я " Us department for the month of January.

P6-3B A **Samsonite** outlet store, which uses the FIFO method, began August with 50 units of inventory that cost $40 each. During August, the store completed these inventory transactions:

		Units	Unit Cost	Unit Sale Price
Aug. 3	Sale	40		$70
8	Purchase	80	44	
21	Sale	70		73
30	Purchase	20	48	

Required

1. Prepare a perpetual inventory record for the luggage inventory.
2. Determine the store's cost of goods sold for August.
3. Compute gross profit for August.

Computing inventory by three
methods—periodic system
(Obj. 3, 4)

P6-4B Nelson Framing Co. began March with 73 units of inventory that cost $23 each. During the month, Nelson made the following purchases:

March 4	....	113 @ $26
12	....	81 @ 30
19	....	167 @ 32
25	....	44 @ 35

The company uses the periodic inventory system, and the physical count at March 31 includes 51 units of inventory on hand.

Required

1. Determine the ending inventory and cost-of-goods-sold amounts for the March financial statements under (a) average cost, (b) FIFO cost, and (c) LIFO cost. Round average cost per unit to the nearest cent and all other amounts to the nearest dollar.
2. Sales revenue for March totaled $20,000. Compute Nelson's gross profit for March under each method.
3. Which method will result in the lowest income taxes for Nelson? Why?
4. Which method will result in the highest net income for Nelson? Why?

P6-5B Louisville Baseball Company, which uses a periodic inventory system, began 20X4 with 6,000 units of inventory that cost a total of $30,000. During 20X4, Louisville purchased merchandise on account as follows:

Purchase 1 (10,000 units costing)	$ 60,000
Purchase 2 (20,000 units costing)	140,000

At year-end, the physical count indicated 15,000 units of inventory on hand.

Required

1. How many units did Louisville sell during the year? The sale price per unit was $18. Determine Louisville's sales revenue for the year.

2. Compute cost of goods sold by the LIFO method. Then determine gross profit for the year.

P6-6B **The Army/Navy Surplus Store** has experienced lackluster sales, and some of the company's merchandise is gathering dust. It is now December 31, 20X5, and the current replacement cost of the ending inventory is $650,000 below what Army/Navy actually paid for the goods, which was $4,900,000. Before any adjustments at the end of the period, the company's Cost of Goods Sold account has a balance of $29,600,000.

Applying the lower-of-cost-or-market rule to inventories
(Obj. 5)

What action should The Army/Navy Surplus Store take in this situation, if any? Give any journal entry required. At what amount should Army/Navy report Inventory on the balance sheet? At what amount should the company report Cost of Goods Sold on the income statement? Discuss the accounting principle or concept that is most relevant to this situation.

P6-7B The Victoria British Company books show the following data (in thousands). In early 20X4, internal auditors found that the ending inventory for 20X1 was overstated by $8 thousand and that the ending inventory for 20X3 was understated by $4 thousand. The ending inventory at December 31, 20X2, was correct.

Correcting inventory errors over a three-year period
(Obj. 6)

(Thousands)	20X3		20X2		20X1	
Net sales revenue............		$360		$285		$244
Cost of goods sold:						
Beginning inventory.......	$ 65		$ 55		$ 70	
Net purchases.............	195		135		130	
Cost of goods available.....	260		190		200	
Less: Ending inventory.....	(70)		(65)		(55)	
Cost of goods sold.........		190		125		145
Gross profit.................		170		160		99
Operating expenses..........		113		109		76
Net income.................		$ 57		$ 51		$ 23

Required

1. Show corrected income statements for the three years.

2. State whether each year's net income is understated or overstated. For each incorrect figure, indicate the amount of the understatement or overstatement.

P6-8B **The Roadster Factory** estimates its inventory by the gross profit method when preparing monthly financial statements. The gross profit has averaged 40% of net sales. Assume that the company's inventory records reveal the following data (amounts in thousands):

Estimating ending inventory by the gross profit method; preparing the income statement
(Obj. 7)

Student ResourceCD

GL, PT, QB

Inventory, July 1....................................	$ 367
Transactions during July:	
Purchases	3,789
Purchase discounts	26
Purchase returns	12
Sales...	6,430
Sales returns	25

Required

1. Estimate the July 31 inventory, using the gross profit method.

2. Prepare the July income statement through gross profit for The Roadster Factory.

APPLY *Your Knowledge*

Increasing net income
(Obj. 3)

Decision Cases

Case 1. Suppose you own a **Chevron** convenience store. Most of your sales come from gasoline, but you also sell fast food, snack items, and drinks. The store's summarized financial statements for 20X4, the most recent year, follow:

Chevron Convenience Store
**Balance Sheet
December 31, 20X4**

Chevron Convenience Store
**Income Statement
Year Ended December 31, 20X4**

(Thousands)	Assets	Liabilities and Capital		Income Statement *(Thousands)*	
Cash	$ 30	Accounts payable	$ 35	Sales	$800
Inventories.	75	Note payable	280	Cost of goods sold	660
Land and buildings, net . . .	360	Total liabilities	315	Gross profit	140
		Owner, capital	150	Operating expenses	100
Total assets.	$465	Total liabilities and capital . . .	$465	Net income	$ 40

Assume that you need to double net income. To accomplish your goal, it will be very difficult to raise the prices you charge because there is a **Texaco** store across the street. Also, you have little control over your cost of goods sold for gasoline because Chevron supplies all your gasoline and Chevron sets the price you must pay.

Identify several strategies for doubling net income.

Making inventory decisions
(Obj. 2, 3)

Case 2. Assume you are opening a clothing store that specializes in women's designer dresses. Each dress costs you anywhere from $200 to $500, and you plan to sell the dresses for $350 to $1,000 each.

To finance the business, you need a $50,000 loan, and your banker requires a set of forecasted financial statements. Assume you are preparing the statements and must make some decisions about how to do the accounting for the business. Answer the following questions (refer back to Chapter 5 if necessary):

1. Which type of inventory system will you use? Give your reason.
2. Show how to compute net purchases and net sales. How will you treat the cost of transportation-in?
3. How often do you plan to do a physical count of inventory on hand? What will the physical count accomplish?
4. Inventory costs are rising. Which inventory costing method will you use in order to:
   a. Maximize net income?
   b. Pay the least amount of income tax?

Ethical Issue

During 20X2, Darden Furniture Company changed to the LIFO method of accounting for inventory. Suppose that during 20X3, Darden changes back to the FIFO method and the following year switches back to LIFO again.

Required

1. What would you think of a company's ethics if it changed accounting methods every year?
2. What accounting principle would changing methods every year violate?
3. Who can be harmed when a company changes its accounting methods too often? How?

Financial Statement Case

Analyzing inventories
(Obj. 3, 4, 5)

The notes are an important part of a company's financial statements, giving valuable details that would clutter the tabular data presented in the statements. This case will help you learn to use a company's inventory notes. Refer to the **Amazon.com** financial statements and related notes in Appendix A and answer the following questions:

Required

1. How much was the Amazon.com merchandise inventory at December 31, 2002? At December 31, 2001?
2. How does Amazon value its inventories? Which cost method does the company use? See Note 1.
3. By rearranging the cost-of-goods-sold formula, you can compute purchases, which are not disclosed in the Amazon statements. How much were the company's inventory purchases during 2002?

Team Project

→ *Link Back to Chapter 5 (Gross Profit Percentage and Inventory Turnover).* Obtain the annual reports of as many companies as you have team members—one company per team member. Most companies post their financial statements on their Web sites.

Required

1. Identify the inventory method used by each company.
2. Compute each company's gross profit percentage and rate of inventory turnover for the most recent two years.
3. For the industries of the companies you are analyzing, obtain the industry averages for gross profit percentage and inventory turnover from Robert Morris Associates, *Annual Statement Studies*; Dun and Bradstreet, *Industry Norms and Key Business Ratios*; or Leo Troy, *Almanac of Business and Industrial Financial Ratios*.
4. How well does each of your companies compare to the average for its industry? What insight about your companies can you glean from these ratios?

For Internet Exercises, go to the Web site www.prenhall.com/horngren.

APPENDIX *to Chapter 6*

Comparing the Perpetual and Periodic Inventory Systems

Exhibit 6A-1 provides a side-by-side comparison of the two inventory accounting systems. It gives the journal entries, the T-accounts, and all financial-statement effects of both inventory systems.

In the periodic system, the purchase of inventory is *not* recorded in the Inventory account. Instead, purchases are recorded in the Purchases account,

Exhibit 6A-1 **Comparing the Perpetual and Periodic Inventory Systems (amounts assumed)**

Panel A—Recording in the Journal and Posting to the Accounts

Perpetual System	Periodic System
1. Credit purchases of $560,000:	**1. Credit purchases of $560,000:**

Inventory 560,000
    Accounts Payable   560,000
	Purchases 560,000
	    Accounts Payable 560,000

2. Credit sales of $900,000 (cost $540,000):	**2. Credit sales of $900,000:**

Accounts Receivable 900,000
    Sales Revenue   900,000
	Accounts Receivable 900,000
	    Sales Revenue 900,000

Cost of Goods Sold .... 540,000 Inventory 540,000	**3. End-of-period entries to update Inventory and record Cost of Goods Sold:** **a.** Transfer the cost of beginning inventory ($100,000) to Cost of Goods Sold:
3. End-of-period entries: No entries required. Both Inventory and Cost of Goods Sold are up-to-date.	Cost of Goods Sold .... 100,000 Inventory (beginning balance) .. 100,000
	b. Record the cost of ending inventory ($120,000) based on a physical count:
	Inventory (ending balance) .... 120,000 Cost of Goods Sold 120,000
	c. Transfer the cost of purchases to Cost of Goods Sold:
	Cost of Goods Sold .... 560,000 Purchases 560,000

INVENTORY AND COST OF GOODS SOLD ACCOUNTS		**INVENTORY AND COST OF GOODS SOLD ACCOUNTS**	
Inventory	**Cost of Goods Sold**	**Inventory**	**Cost of Goods Sold**
100,000* **540,000** **540,000**		**100,000**** **100,000** **100,000** **120,000**	
560,000		**120,000** **560,000**	
120,000		**540,000**	
*Beginning inventory was $100,000.		**Beginning inventory was $100,000.	

Panel B—Reporting in the Financial Statements

Perpetual System	Periodic System
Income Statement (partial)	
Sales revenue.................... $900,000	Sales revenue $900,000
Cost of goods sold.............. 540,000 ◄	Cost of goods sold:
Gross profit $360,000	Beginning inventory $100,000
	Purchases 560,000
	Cost of goods available for sale 660,000
	Less: Ending inventory .... (120,000)
	Cost of goods sold 540,000
	Gross profit $360,000
Balance Sheet (partial)	
Current assets:	Current assets:
Cash .... $ XXX	Cash .... $ XXX
Accounts receivable............. XXX	Accounts receivable XXX
Inventories .... 120,000 ◄──►	Inventories 120,000

which is an expense (see transaction 1 in the exhibit, right column). A sale trans-action includes *no* cost of goods sold entry (transaction 2). How, then, does the business record inventory and cost of goods sold?

Transactions 3a and 3b give the end-of-period entries to update the Inventory account and record Cost of Goods Sold. Transaction 3c closes the Purchases account into Cost of Goods Sold to complete the periodic process.

Panel B of the exhibit shows the financial statements under both systems.

CHAPTER 8

Internal Control and Cash

TIPS CHECK YOUR RESOURCES

- Visit the www.prenhall.com/horngren **Web site** self-study quizzes, video clips, and other resources
- Try the **Quick Check** exercise at the end of the chapter to test your knowledge
- Learn the **key terms**
- Do the **Starter** exercises keyed in the margins
- Work the **mid-** and **end-of-chapter summary problems**
- Use the **Concept Links** to review material in other chapters
- Search the **CD** for review materials by chapter or by key word
- Watch the **tutorial videos** to review key concepts

LEARNING OBJECTIVES

⭐1 Define internal control

⭐2 Tell how to achieve good internal control

⭐3 Prepare a bank reconciliation and the related journal entries

⭐4 Apply internal controls to cash receipts

⭐5 Apply internal controls to cash payments

⭐6 Make ethical business judgments

Darlyne Lopez worked as a cashier for the brokerage firm **Merrill Lynch**. Cashiers handle cash, so they are highly trusted employees. Lopez was so dedicated to the company that she never took a vacation and never missed a day of work. It took an auto accident to reveal that she was embezzling money.

Lopez stole $600,000 by using a well-known scheme. Here's how she did it: Merrill Lynch customers made deposits to their accounts through cashier Lopez, or so they thought. Lopez was quietly transferring customer deposits into her own account—and manipulating the Merrill Lynch customer records. She kept the scheme going for five years. When customers called to ask Lopez whether they got credit for a deposit, she would explain that the missing amount would show up on next month's statement. And it did as long as Lopez could apply Customer B's deposit to cover money stolen from Customer A.

Merrill Lynch

While Lopez was in the hospital, a co-worker took over as cashier. The new cashier couldn't explain the missing amounts. All the evidence pointed toward the missing employee. The Merrill Lynch office manager figured out why Lopez never missed a day of work: She had to be present to cover her tracks. After her stay in the hospital, she also did time in prison. All of this could have been avoided if Merrill Lynch had used some basic internal controls. ∎

∎ Sitemap

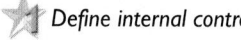

Student Resource CD

e-commerce, internal control

⭐ *Define internal control*

Internal Control
Organizational plan and all the related measures adopted by an entity to safeguard assets, encourage employees to follow company policy, promote operational efficiency, and ensure accurate and reliable accounting records.

✔ **Starter 8-1**

To avoid situations like this, the Foreign Corrupt Practices Act requires companies under SEC jurisdiction to maintain a system of internal control. And the Sarbanes-Oxley Act of 2002 requires managers to give careful attention to internal control in their companies. This chapter discusses *internal control*—the organizational plan companies use to protect their assets. The chapter applies control techniques mainly to cash because cash is the most liquid asset. The chapter also provides a framework for making ethical judgments in business. The material covered is some of the most important in all of business. Unfortunately, it's often overlooked, as in the actual case of the cashier in the Merrill Lynch office.

Internal Control

A key responsibility of managers is to control operations. Owners set goals, managers lead the way, and employees carry out the plan. **Internal control** is the organizational plan and all the related measures that an entity adopts to accomplish four objectives:

1. *Safeguard assets.* A company must safeguard its assets; otherwise it's throwing away resources. Merrill Lynch failed to safeguard customer cash, and Lopez blew the money on clothing, jewelry, and cars. In the end Merrill Lynch had to replace the missing $600,000—a total waste of company resources.

2. *Encourage employees to follow company policy.* Everyone in an organization needs to work toward the same goals. The international accounting firm of Arthur Andersen collapsed soon after a few members of the firm refused to follow its professional standards. They went against company policy and then certified financial statements that held large errors. Andersen fell apart.

3. *Promote operational efficiency.* Companies cannot afford to waste resources. WorldCom, a leading telephone-service provider, lent $366 million to its CEO. Is that an efficient use of WorldCom resources? Not to the company's enraged owners. WorldCom should have spent the money on new technology and better service for customers.

4. *Ensure accurate, reliable accounting records.* Good records are essential. Without reliable records, a manager cannot tell what investments to make or how much to charge for products. Banks cannot determine whether to make a loan. Enron Corporation collapsed when investors decided they couldn't rely on Enron's financial statements.

Exhibit 8-1 diagrams the shield that internal controls provide for an organization. Protected by the wall, people do business safely and securely. How does a business achieve good internal control? The next section identifies the components of internal control.

Exhibit 8-1
The Shield of Internal Control

An Effective Internal Control System

Whether the business is America Online, Merrill Lynch, or an Exxon gas station, an effective internal control system has the following characteristics.

2 Tell how to achieve good internal control

COMPETENT, RELIABLE, AND ETHICAL PERSONNEL Employees should be *competent, reliable,* and *ethical.* Paying good salaries to attract high-quality employees, training them to do the job, and supervising their work builds a competent staff.

ASSIGNED RESPONSIBILITIES In a business with good internal controls, no important duty is overlooked. Each employee has certain responsibilities. A model of *assignment of responsibilities* appears in Exhibit 8-2. This company has a vice president of accounting and finance. Two other officers, the treasurer and the controller, report to that vice president. The treasurer is responsible for cash management. The **controller** is the chief accounting officer.

Within this organization, the controller approves invoices (bills) for payment, and the treasurer signs the checks. Notice that each officer has assigned duties so that all bases are covered.

Controller
The chief accounting officer of a company.

Exhibit 8-2 An Organization Chart Showing Assignment of Responsibilities and Separation of Duties

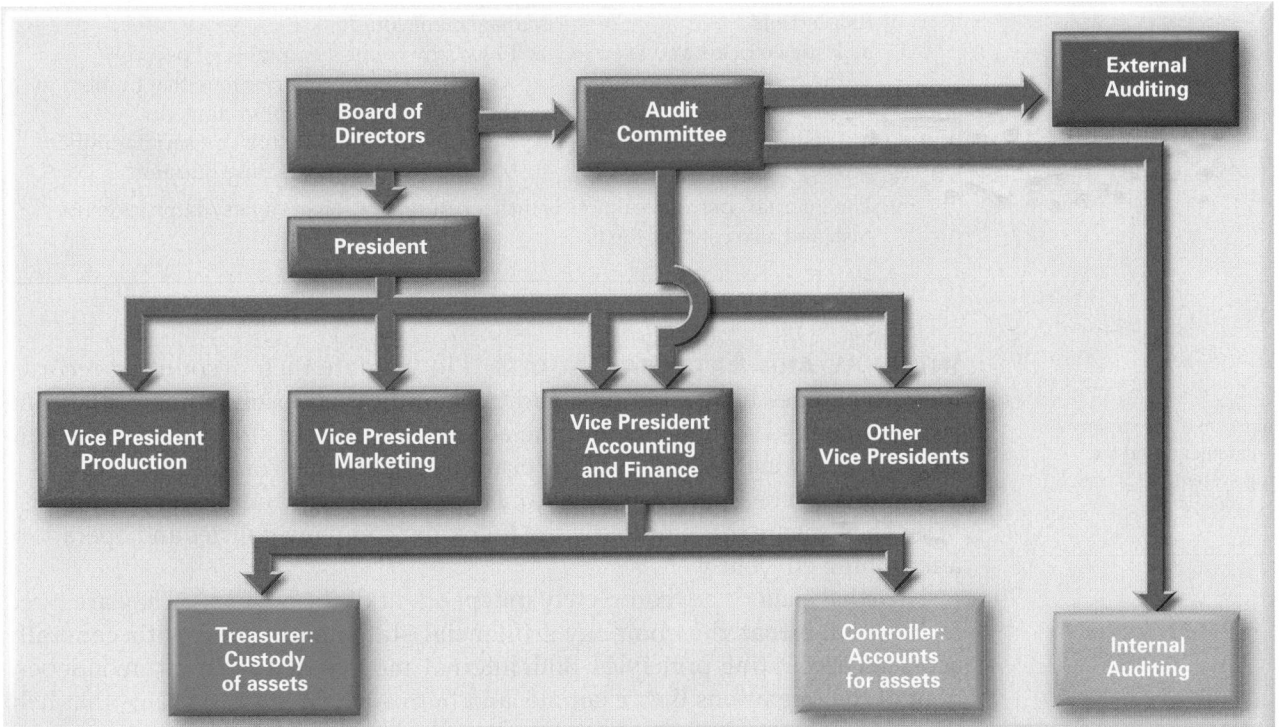

SEPARATION OF DUTIES Smart management divides responsibility between two or more people. *Separation of duties* limits fraud and promotes the accuracy of the accounting records. Separation of duties is illustrated in Exhibit 8-2, with the controller approving payments and the treasurer signing checks.

Separation of duties can be divided into two parts:

1. *Separation of operations from accounting.* Accounting should be completely separate from the operating departments, such as production and marketing. What would happen if sales personnel were to account for the company's revenue? Sales figures would be inflated, and top managers wouldn't know how much the company actually sold. This is why accounting and marketing (sales) are separate in Exhibit 8-2.

2. *Separation of the custody of assets from accounting.* Accountants must not handle cash and cashiers must not have access to the accounting records. If one employee has both cash-handling and accounting duties, that person can steal cash and conceal the theft by making a bogus entry on the books. We see this separation of duties in Exhibit 8-2. The treasurer handles cash, and the controller accounts for the cash. Neither person has both responsibilities. At Merrill Lynch, Darlyne Lopez had access to cash and to the company's accounting records. With both duties, she was able to apply one customer's cash deposit to another's account. The result was a $600,000 loss to the company.

Separation of duties is essential

✔ Starter 8-2

Stop & Think

Ralph works at Galaxy Theater. Occasionally, he must both sell tickets and take tickets as customers enter the theater. Standard procedure requires Ralph to tear each ticket, give half to the customer, and keep the other half. To control cash receipts, the manager compares each night's cash receipts with the number of ticket stubs on hand.

1. How could Ralph steal cash receipts and hide the theft? What additional steps should the manager take to strengthen internal control over cash receipts?

2. What is the internal control weakness in this situation? Explain the weakness.

Answers:

1. Ralph could
   a. Issue no ticket and keep the customer's cash.

   b. Destroy some tickets and keep the customers' cash.

Management could
   a. Physically count the number of people watching a movie and compare that number to the number of ticket stubs retained.

   b. Account for all ticket stubs by serial number. Missing serial numbers raise questions.

2. The internal control weakness is the lack of separation of duties. Ralph receives cash and also controls the tickets.

Audit
An examination of a company's financial statements and the accounting system.

INTERNAL AND EXTERNAL AUDITS To validate their accounting records, most companies have a periodic audit. An **audit** is an examination of the company's financial statements and the accounting system. To evaluate the company's accounting system, auditors examine the internal controls.

Audits can be internal or external. *Internal auditors* are employees of the business. They ensure that employees are following company policies and operations are running efficiently.

External auditors are completely independent of the business. They are hired to determine that the company's financial statements agree with generally accepted accounting principles. Both internal and external auditors are independent of the operations they examine, and both suggest improvements that help the business run efficiently.

✔ Starter 8-3

WorldCom, Inc.: Internal Auditor's Heroism Is Silver Lining in Cloud of Scandal

WorldCom, Inc.'s internal auditor, Cynthia Cooper, met with Controller David Myers on June 17, 2002. This was no ordinary coffee break. Cooper asked some questions that would later cost Myers his job and uncover a huge scandal.

Cooper wondered why WorldCom was counting everyday expenses as long-term assets. A company can boost reported profits by doing this, because expenses of one quarter are spread out over several years. When Cooper finished her audit, she revealed that WorldCom had inflated its income to the tune of $3.9 billion. When all the facts came out, this figure grew to a whopping $9 billion.

The internal audit forced WorldCom into the largest corporate bankruptcy in U.S. history, leaving creditors holding nearly $30 billion in bad receivables. It also turned Cooper into a national heroine. In December 2002, *Time* magazine named Cynthia Cooper, along with two other corporate whistleblowers, a "person of the year" for "doing right by just doing the job rightly."

Documents show how WorldCom's senior management overrode internal controls to hide the company's true financial condition. It turned out that Myers had promised to "do whatever necessary" to improve the company's profit margins. Fortunately, while Myers and other top WorldCom executives were doing what they deemed *necessary*, Internal Auditor Cynthia Cooper was doing what was *right*.

The Decision Guidelines at the end of this chapter outline the sad story of another auditor who did whatever was necessary to keep his client happy.

Based on: Yochi J. Dreazen and Deborah Solomon, "Leading the News: WorldCom Aide Conceded Flaws—Controller Said Company Was Forced to Disguise Expenses, Ignore Warnings," *The Wall Street Journal,* July 16, 2002, p. A3. Karen Kaplan and James S. Granelli, "The Nation; WorldCom Says It Inflated Books by $3.9 Billion," *Los Angeles Times,* June 26, 2002, p. A1. Associated Press, "The Nation; 3 Whistle-Blowers Get *Time* Magazine Honors," *Los Angeles Times,* December 23, 2002, p. A14. Peter Elstrom, "How to Hide $3.8 Billion in Expenses," *Business Week,* July 8, 2002, p. 41.

DOCUMENTS AND RECORDS Business *documents and records* provide the details of business transactions. Documents include invoices and purchase orders, and records include the journals and ledgers. Documents should be prenumbered. A gap in the numbered sequence draws attention.

In a bowling alley a key document is the score sheet. The manager can compare the number of games scored with the amount of cash received. By multiplying the number of games by the price per game and comparing the revenue with cash receipts, the manager can see whether the business is collecting all the revenue.

ELECTRONIC DEVICES AND COMPUTER CONTROLS Accounting systems are relying less on documents and more on digital storage devices. Computers shift the internal controls to the people who write the programs. Programmers then become the focus of internal controls because they can write programs that transfer company assets to themselves.

Businesses use electronic devices to protect assets. Retailers such as **Target Stores, Macy's,** and **Dillard's** control inventory by attaching an electronic sensor to merchandise. The cashier removes the sensor at checkout. If a customer tries to remove an item with the sensor attached, an alarm sounds. According to **Checkpoint Systems,** which manufactures the sensors, these devices reduce theft by as much as 50%.

OTHER CONTROLS   Businesses keep cash and important documents in *fireproof vaults. Burglar alarms* protect buildings and other property.

Retailers receive most of their cash from customers on the spot. To safeguard cash, they use *point-of-sale terminals* that serve as a cash register and also record each transaction. Several times each day, a supervisor deposits the cash in the bank.

Employees who handle cash are in a tempting position. Many businesses purchase *fidelity bonds* on cashiers. The bond is an insurance policy that reimburses the company for any losses due to employee theft. Before issuing a fidelity bond, the insurance company investigates the employee's record.

Mandatory vacations and *job rotation* require that employees be trained to do a variety of jobs. General Electric, Eastman Kodak, and other large companies move employees from job to job. This improves morale by giving employees a broad view of the business. Also, knowing someone else will be doing your job next month also keeps you honest. Had Merrill Lynch required Darlyne Lopez to take a vacation, her embezzlement would have been detected earlier.

✔ **Starter 8-4**

Internal Controls for E-Commerce

E-Commerce creates its own risks. Hackers may gain access to confidential information that's unavailable in face-to-face transactions. To convince people to buy online, Amazon.com and EMusic.com must secure customer data.

PITFALLS   E-Commerce pitfalls include:

- Stolen credit-card numbers
- Computer viruses and Trojan horses
- Impersonation of companies

Stolen Credit-Card Numbers   Suppose you buy several CDs from EMusic.com. To make the purchase, your credit-card number must travel through cyberspace. Amateur hacker Carlos Salgado, Jr., used his home computer to steal 100,000 credit-card numbers with a combined limit exceeding $1 billion. Salgado was caught when he tried to sell the numbers to an undercover FBI agent.

Computer Virus
A malicious program that (a) reproduces itself, (b) enters program code without consent, and (c) performs destructive actions.

Trojan Horse
A malicious program that works like a virus but does not reproduce.

Computer Viruses and Trojan Horses   A **computer virus** is a malicious program that (a) reproduces itself, (b) enters program code without consent, and (c) performs destructive actions. A **Trojan horse** works like a virus, but it does not reproduce. Viruses can destroy or alter data, make bogus calculations, and infect files. The International Computer Security Association reports that virtually all firms have found a virus in their system.

Suppose the U.S. Department of Defense takes bids for a missile defense system, and Raytheon and Lockheed-Martin bid on the contract. A hacker infects Raytheon's system and alters Raytheon's design. In evaluating the bids, Pentagon engineers label the Raytheon design as flawed even though Raytheon's is better and costs less. The American public winds up paying too much.

Impersonation   Hackers sometimes create bogus Web sites, such as AOL4Free.com. The neat-sounding Web site attracts lots of visitors, and the hackers solicit confidential data from unsuspecting people. The hackers then use the data for illicit purposes.

Encryption
Rearranging plain-text messages by a mathematical process; the primary method of achieving confidentiality in e-commerce.

FIREWALLS AND ENCRYPTION   Internet information can be secure, but the server holding the information may not be. Two standard techniques for securing e-commerce data are encryption and firewalls.

Encryption rearranges messages by a mathematical process. The encrypted message cannot be read by one who does not know the process. An accounting example uses check-sum digits for account numbers. Each account number has its last digit equal to the sum of the previous digits. For example, consider Customer Number 2237, where 2 + 2 + 3 = 7. Any account number that fails this test triggers an error message.

Firewalls limit access to a local network. They enable members of the local network to access the Internet but keep nonmembers out of the network. Usually several firewalls are built into the network. Think of a fortress with multiple walls protecting the king's chamber in the center. At the point of entry, passwords, PINs (personal identification numbers) and signatures are used. More-sophisticated firewalls are used deeper in the network.

Firewalls
Devices that enable members of a local network to access the Internet but keep nonmembers out of the network.

The Limitations of Internal Control

Unfortunately, most internal controls can be overcome. Collusion—two or more employees working as a team—can beat internal controls and defraud the firm. Consider Galaxy Theater. Ralph and another employee could design a scheme in which the ticket seller pockets the cash from 10 customers and the ticket taker admits 10 customers without tickets. To prevent this situation, the manager must take additional steps, such as matching the number of people in the theater against the number of ticket stubs retained. But that takes time away from other duties.

The stricter the internal control system, the more it costs. A system of internal control that is too complex can strangle the business with red tape. How tight should controls be? Internal controls must be judged in light of their costs and benefits.

The Bank Account as a Control Device

Cash is the most liquid asset because it is a medium of exchange. Increasingly, cash consists of electronic impulses with no paper checks or deposit slips. Cash is easy to conceal, easy to move, and relatively easy to steal. As a result, most businesses create specific controls for cash.

Keeping cash in a *bank account* helps control cash because banks have established practices for safeguarding customers' money. Banks also provide customers with detailed records of their transactions. To take full advantage, the business should deposit all cash receipts in the bank and make all cash payments through the bank. An exception is a petty cash transaction, which we will examine later.

The documents used to control a bank account include the

- Signature card
- Deposit ticket
- Check
- Bank statement
- Bank reconciliation

Student ResourceCD

bank reconciliation, ethics, internal control

SIGNATURE CARD   Banks require each person authorized to transact business through an account to sign a *signature card*. The bank uses the signature card to protect against forgery.

DEPOSIT TICKET   Banks supply standard forms such as *deposit tickets*. The customer fills in the dollar amount of each deposit. As proof of the transaction, the customer keeps a deposit receipt.

CHECK   To draw money from an account, the depositor writes a **check,** which is the document that tells the bank to pay the designated party a specified amount of money. There are three parties to a check: the *maker*, who signs the check, the *payee*, to whom the check is paid, and the *bank* on which the check is drawn.

Exhibit 8-3 shows a check drawn by Business Research, Inc., the maker. The check has two parts, the check itself and the *remittance advice* below. This is an optional attachment that tells the payee the reason for the payment. Business Research keeps a duplicate copy of the check for its cash payments journal.

Check
Document that instructs a bank to pay the designated person or business a specified amount of money.

Exhibit 8-3

Check with Remittance Advice

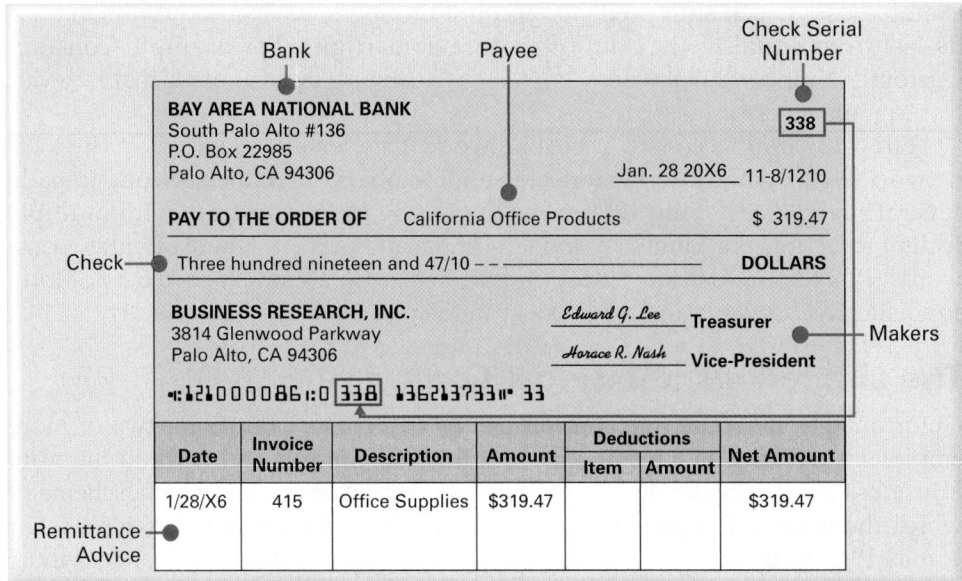

Bank Statement
Document the bank uses to report what it did with the depositor's cash. Shows the bank account's beginning and ending balances and lists the month's cash transactions conducted through the bank.

BANK STATEMENT Banks send monthly statements to customers. A **bank statement** is the document on which the bank reports what it did with the customer's cash. The statement shows the account's beginning and ending balances and lists the cash receipts and payments transacted through the bank. Included with the statement are the maker's *canceled checks* (or photocopies of the paid checks). The statement also lists deposits and other changes in the account. Deposits appear in chronological order, and checks are listed by check number. Exhibit 8-4 is the bank statement of Business Research, Inc., for the month ended January 31, 20X6. The summary at the top shows the beginning balance, plus deposits minus withdrawals, and the ending balance. Details of the transactions follow.

Electronic Funds Transfer (EFT)
System that transfers cash by electronic communication rather than by paper documents.

Electronic funds transfer (EFT) is a system that moves cash by electronic communication. It is cheaper for a company to pay employees by EFT (direct deposit). Many people make mortgage, rent, and insurance payments by EFT and don't have to write checks for those payments. The monthly bank statement lists EFT deposits and payments.

The Bank Reconciliation

There are two records of a business's cash:

1. The Cash account in the company's general ledger (Exhibit 8-5).
2. The bank statement, which shows the cash receipts and payments transacted through the bank.

The books and the bank statement usually show different amounts. Differences arise because of a time lag in recording transactions. When you write a check, you immediately deduct the check in your checkbook. But the bank does not subtract the check from your account until it pays the check. That may take a few days, even weeks, if the payee waits to cash the check. Likewise, you immediately add the cash receipt for all deposits you make to your account. But it may take a day or two for the bank to add these amounts to your balance.

To ensure accurate cash records, you need to update your checkbook often—either online or after you receive your bank statement. All business entities do this. The result of this updating process is a document called the **bank reconciliation,** which is prepared by the company (not by the bank). Properly done, the bank reconciliation explains all differences between the company's cash records and the bank statement figures. It ensures that all cash transactions have been accounted for. It also establishes that bank and book (your own) records of cash are correct.

Bank Reconciliation
Document explaining the reasons for the difference between a depositor's cash records and the depositor's cash balance in its bank account.

Exhibit 8-4   Bank Statement

BAY AREA NATIONAL BANK
SOUTH PALO ALTO #136 P.O. BOX 22985 PALO ALTO, CA 94306

ACCOUNT STATEMENT

Business Research, Inc.
3814 Glenwood Parkway
Palo Alto, CA 94306

CHECKING ACCOUNT 136–213733

CHECKING ACCOUNT SUMMARY AS OF 01/31/X6

BEGINNING BALANCE	TOTAL DEPOSITS	TOTAL WITHDRAWALS	SERVICE CHARGES	ENDING BALANCE
6,556.12	4,352.64	4,963.00	14.25	5,931.51

CHECKING ACCOUNT TRANSACTIONS

DEPOSITS	DATE	AMOUNT
Deposit	01/04	1,000.00
Deposit	01/04	112.00
Deposit	01/08	194.60
EFT—Collection of rent	01/17	904.03
Bank Collection	01/26	2,114.00
Interest	01/31	28.01

CHARGES	DATE	AMOUNT
Service Charge	01/31	14.25

Checks:

CHECKS		DAILY BALANCE			
Number	Amount	Date	Balance	Date	Balance
656	100.00	12/31	6,556.12	01/17	5,264.75
332	3,000.00	01/04	7,616.12	01/20	4,903.75
333	150.00	01/06	7,416.12	01/26	7,017.75
334	100.00	01/08	7,610.72	01/31	5,931.51
335	100.00	01/10	7,510.72		
336	1,100.00	01/12	4,360.72		

OTHER CHARGES	DATE	AMOUNT
NSF	01/04	52.00
EFT—Insurance	01/20	361.00

MONTHLY SUMMARY

Withdrawals: 8   Minimum Balance: 4,360.72   Average Balance: 6,085.19

General Ledger:

ACCOUNT   Cash

Date	Item	Debit	Credit	Balance
20X6				
Jan. 1	Balance			6,556.12
2	Cash receipt	1,112.00		7,668.12
7	Cash receipt	194.60		7,862.72
31	Cash payments		6,160.11	1,702.61
31	Cash receipt	1,591.60		3,294.21

Cash Payments:

Check No.	Amount	Check No.	Amount
332	$3,000.00	338	$ 319.47
333	510.00	339	83.00
334	100.00	340	203.14
335	100.00	341	458.50
336	1,100.00		
337	286.00	Total	$6,160.11

Exhibit 8-5

Cash Records of Business Research, Inc.

 Prepare a bank reconciliation and the related journal entries

Preparing the Bank Reconciliation

Here are some common reconciling items. They all cause differences between the bank balance and the book balance. (We refer to your checkbook record of your cash as the "Book" records.)

1. Items to show on the *Bank* side of the bank reconciliation:
   a. **Deposits in transit** (outstanding deposits). The company has recorded these deposits, but the bank has not.
   b. **Outstanding checks.** The company has issued these checks and recorded them on its books, but the bank has not yet paid them.
   c. **Bank errors.** Correct all bank errors on the Bank side of the reconciliation.
2. Items to show on the *Book* side of the bank reconciliation:
   a. **Bank collections.** Banks sometimes collect money for their depositors. Many businesses have customers pay directly to the company bank account. This practice, called a *lock-box system*, reduces theft and circulates cash faster than if the cash is collected and deposited by company personnel. An example is a bank's collecting cash on a note receivable for the depositor. Bank collections are cash receipts.
   b. **Electronic funds transfers.** The bank may receive or pay cash on behalf of the depositor. An EFT may be a cash receipt or a cash payment.
   c. **Service charge.** This is the bank's fee for processing the depositor's transactions. It is a cash payment.
   d. **Interest revenue on checking account.** Depositors earn interest if they keep enough cash in their account. The bank notifies depositors of this interest on the bank statement. It is a cash receipt.
   e. **Nonsufficient funds (NSF) checks** are cash receipts that turn out to be worthless. NSF checks (sometimes called *hot checks*) should be subtracted on a bank reconciliation.
   f. **The cost of printed checks.** This cash payment is handled like a service charge.
   g. **Book errors.** Correct all book errors on the Book side of the reconciliation.

Deposit in Transit
A deposit recorded by the company but not yet by its bank.

Outstanding Check
A check issued by the company and recorded on its books but not yet paid by its bank.

Bank Collection
Collection of money by the bank on behalf of a depositor.

Nonsufficient Funds (NSF) Check
A "hot" check, one for which the maker's bank account has insufficient money to pay the check.

✔ Starter 8-5

BANK RECONCILIATION ILLUSTRATED   The bank statement in Exhibit 8-4 shows that the January 31 bank balance of Business Research, Inc., is $5,931.51. However, the company's Cash account has a balance of $3,294.21, as shown in Exhibit 8-5. This situation calls for a bank reconciliation. Exhibit 8-6, panel A, lists the reconciling items, and panel B shows the completed reconciliation.

JOURNALIZING TRANSACTIONS FROM THE RECONCILIATION   The bank reconciliation is an accountant's tool separate from the company books. It explains the effects of all cash receipts and all cash payments made through the bank. But it does *not* account for transactions in the journal. To get the transactions into the accounts, we must make journal entries and post to the general ledger. All items on the Book side of the bank reconciliation require journal entries.

Why doesn't the company need to record the reconciling items on the Bank side of the reconciliation?

Answer: Those items have already been recorded on the company books.

Exhibit 8-6 | Bank Reconciliation

PANEL A—Reconciling Items

1. Deposit in transit, $1,591.60
2. Bank error: The bank deducted $100 for a check written by another company. Add $100 to bank balance.
3. Outstanding checks:

Check No.	Amount
337	$286.00
338	319.47
339	83.00
340	203.14
341	458.50

4. EFT receipt of rent revenue, $904.03.
5. Bank collection of a note receivable, $2,114, including interest revenue of $114.
6. Interest revenue earned on bank balance, $28.01.
7. Book error: Check no. 333 for $150 paid to Brown Company on account, was recorded as $510. Add $360 to book balance.
8. Bank service charge, $14.25.
9. NSF check from L. Ross, $52.
10. EFT payment of insurance expense, $361.

PANEL B—Bank Reconciliation

Business Research, Inc.

Bank Reconciliation
January 31, 20X6

Bank			Books		
Balance, January 31		$5,931.51	Balance, January 31		$3,294.21
Add:			Add:		
1. Deposit of January 31 in transit		1,591.60	4. EFT receipt of rent revenue		904.03
2. Correction of bank error		100.00	5. Bank collection of note receivable ($2,000), plus interest revenue of $114		2,114.00
		7,623.11	6. Interest revenue earned on bank balance		28.01
			7. Correction of book error—overstated our check no. 333		360.00
					6,700.25
Less:					
3. Outstanding checks					
No. 337	$286.00		Less:		
No. 338	319.47		8. Service charge	$ 14.25	
No. 339	83.00		9. NSF check	52.00	
No. 340	203.14		10. EFT payment of insurance expense	361.00	(427.25)
No. 341	458.50	(1,350.11)			
Adjusted bank balance		$6,273.00	Adjusted book balance		$6,273.00

These amounts should agree.

Each reconciling item is treated in the same way in every situation. Here is a summary of how to treat the various reconciling items:

BANK BALANCE—ALWAYS	BOOK BALANCE—ALWAYS
• *Add* deposits in transit.	• *Add* bank collections, interest revenue, and EFT receipts.
• *Subtract* outstanding checks.	• *Subtract* service charges, NSF checks, and EFT payments.
• *Add* or *subtract* corrections of bank errors.	• *Add* or *subtract* corrections of book errors.

✔ Starter 8-6

The bank reconciliation in Exhibit 8-6 requires Business Research to make 10 journal entries. They are dated January 31 to bring the Cash account to the correct balance on that date. Numbers in parentheses correspond to the reconciling items listed in Exhibit 8-6, Panel A.

(4) Jan. 31	Cash	904.03		
	Rent Revenue		904.03	
	Receipt of monthly rent.			
(5) 31	Cash	2,114.00		
	Notes Receivable ...		2,000.00	
	Interest Revenue		114.00	
	Note receivable collected by bank.			
(6) 31	Cash	28.01		
	Interest Revenue		28.01	
	Interest earned on bank balance.			
(7) 31	Cash	360.00		
	Accounts Payable —Brown Co.		360.00	
	Correction of check no. 333.			

(8) Jan. 31	Miscellaneous Expense[1] .	14.25		
	Cash		14.25	
	Bank service charge.			
(9) 31	Accounts Receivable —L. Ross	52.00		
	Cash		52.00	
	NSF check returned by bank.			
(10) 31	Insurance Expense	361.00		
	Cash		361.00	
	Payment of monthly insurance.			

These entries update the company's books.

The entry for the NSF check (entry 9) needs explanation. Upon learning that L. Ross's $52 check was not good, Business Research credits Cash to update the Cash account. Business Research still has a receivable from Ross, so the company debits Accounts Receivable—L. Ross.

✔ Starter 8-7

The bank statement balance is $4,500 and shows a service charge of $15, interest earned of $5, and an NSF check for $300. Deposits in transit total $1,200 and outstanding checks are $575. The bookkeeper incorrectly recorded as $152 a check of $125 in payment of an account payable.

1. What is the adjusted balance?
2. Prepare the journal entries needed to update the company's books.

Answers:

1. $5,125 ($4,500 + $1,200 − $575)
2. Journal entries on the books:

Miscellaneous Expense ...	15		Accounts Receivable...	300	
Cash		15	Cash		300
Cash	5		Cash ($152 − $125).....	27	
Interest Revenue		5	Accounts Payable		27

How Owners and Managers Use the Bank Reconciliation

The bank reconciliation can be a powerful control device, as the following example illustrates.

Randy Vaughn is a CPA in Houston, Texas. Vaughn owns apartment complexes that his aunt manages. His accounting practice leaves little time to devote to the properties. Vaughn's aunt signs up tenants, collects the monthly rent, arranges custodial work, hires and fires employees, write the checks, and performs the bank reconciliation. This concentration of duties in one person is terri-

---

[1]Note: Miscellaneous Expense is debited for the bank service charge because the service charge pertains to no particular expense category.

ble from an internal control standpoint. Vaughn's aunt could be stealing from him. As a CPA, he is aware of this possibility.

Vaughn exercises some internal controls over his aunt's activities. Periodically, he drops by his properties to see whether the apartments are in good condition.

To control cash, Vaughn uses a bank reconciliation. On an irregular basis, he examines the bank reconciliations prepared by his aunt. He matches every paid check to the journal entry on the books. Vaughn would know immediately if his aunt were writing checks to herself. Vaughn sometimes prepares his own bank reconciliation to see whether he agrees with his aunt's work. To keep his aunt on her toes, Vaughn lets her know that he periodically audits her work.

Vaughn has a simple method for controlling cash receipts. He knows the occupancy level of his apartments. He also knows the monthly rent he charges. He multiplies the number of apartments—say 100—by the monthly rent (which averages $500 per unit) to arrive at expected monthly rent revenue of $50,000. By tracing the $50,000 revenue to the bank statement, Vaughn can tell that his rent money went into his bank account.

Control activities such as these are critical in small businesses. With only a few employees, a separation of duties may not be feasible. The owner must oversee the operations of the business, or the assets will slip away, as they did for Merrill Lynch in the chapter-opening story.

MID-CHAPTER *Summary Problem*

The cash account of Baylor Associates at February 28, 20X6, is as follows:

TIPS
CHECK YOUR RESOURCES

Cash

Feb. 1	Bal. 3,995	Feb. 3	400
6	800	12	3,100
15	1,800	19	1,100
23	1,100	25	500
28	2,400	27	900
Feb. 28	Bal. 4,095		

Baylor Associates received the bank statement on February 28, 20X6 (as always, negative amounts are in parentheses):

Bank Statement for February 20X6

Beginning balance		$3,995
Deposits:		
Feb. 7	$ 800	
15	1,800	
24	1,100	3,700
Checks (total per day):		
Feb. 8	$ 400	
16	3,100	
23	1,100	(4,600)
Other items:		
Service charge		(10)
NSF check from M. E. Crown		(700)
Bank collection of note receivable for the company		1,000*
EFT—monthly rent expense		(330)
Interest on account balance		15
Ending balance		$3,070

*Includes principal of $881, plus interest of $119.

Additional data:

Baylor deposits all cash receipts in the bank and makes all payments by check.

Required

1. Prepare the bank reconciliation of Baylor Associates at February 28, 20X6.
2. Journalize the entries based on the bank reconciliation.

Solution

Requirement 1

Baylor Associates

Bank Reconciliation
February 28, 20X6

Bank:

Balance, February 28, 20X6............................		$3,070
Add: Deposit of February 28 in transit................		2,400
		5,470
Less: Outstanding checks issued on Feb. 25 ($500)		
and Feb. 27 ($900)		(1,400)
Adjusted bank balance, February 28, 20X6		$4,070

Books:

Balance, February 28, 20X6...........................			$4,095
Add: Bank collection of note receivable, including			
interest of $119			1,000
Interest earned on bank balance			15
			5,110
Less: Service charge...............................	$ 10		
NSF check	700		
EFT—Rent expense	330	(1,040)	
Adjusted book balance, February 28, 20X6			$4,070

Requirement 2

Feb. 28	Cash	1,000	
	Note Receivable		
	($1,000 − $119)		881
	Interest Revenue		119
	Note receivable collected by bank.		
28	Cash	15	
	Interest Revenue		15
	Interest earned on bank balance.		
28	Miscellaneous Expense	10	
	Cash		10
	Bank service charge.		

Feb. 28	Accounts Receivable—		
	M. E. Crown	700	
	Cash		700
	NSF check returned by bank.		
28	Rent Expense	330	
	Cash		330
	Monthly rent expense.		

Student Resource**CD**

cash receipts, internal control

Internal Control over Cash Receipts

Internal controls over cash receipts ensure that all cash receipts are deposited for safekeeping in the bank. Companies receive cash over the counter and through the mail. Each source of cash calls for its own security measures.

CASH RECEIPTS OVER THE COUNTER Exhibit 8-7 illustrates a cash receipt over the counter in a department store. The point-of-sale terminal (cash register) provides control over the cash receipts. Consider a Macy's store.

Company policy requires issuance of a receipt to ensure that each sale is recorded correctly. The cash drawer opens only when the clerk enters an amount on the keypad, and the machine records each transaction. At the end of the day, a manager proves the cash by comparing the total amount in the cash drawer against the machine's record of sales. This step helps prevent outright theft by the clerk.

At the end of the day, the cashier or other employee with cash-handling duties deposits the cash in the bank. The machine tape then goes to the accounting department as the basis for the journal entry to record sales revenue. These security measures, coupled with oversight by a manager, discourage theft.

CASH RECEIPTS BY MAIL   Many companies receive cash by mail. Exhibit 8-8 shows how companies control cash received by mail. All incoming mail is opened by a mailroom employee. The mailroom then sends all customer checks to the treasurer, who deposits the money in the bank. The remittance advices go to the accounting department for the journal entries to Cash and customer accounts. As a final step, the controller compares the records of the day's cash receipts, as follows. Compare the

1. Bank deposit amount from the treasurer
2. Debit to Cash from the accounting department

This comparison ensures that the debit to Cash is for the amount actually deposited in the bank.

Exhibit 8-7

Cash Receipts Over the Counter

🎯 *Apply internal controls to cash receipts*

✔ Starter 8-8

Exhibit 8-8   **Cash Receipts by Mail**

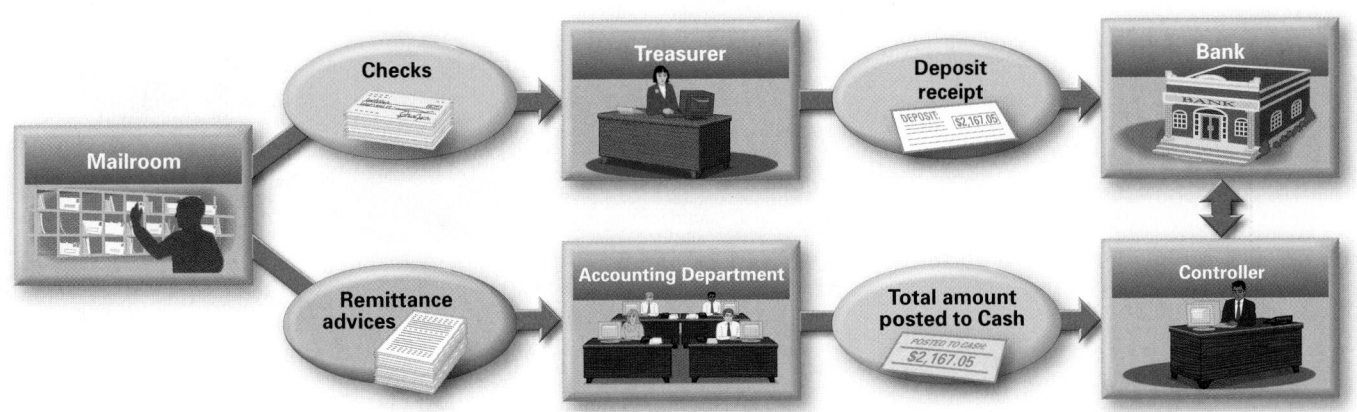

What keeps the mailroom employee from pocketing a customer check and destroying the remittance advice?

Answer: If a customer gets billed a second time, the customer can show the paid check to prove he/she has already paid. That will point to the dishonest mailroom employee.

✔ Starter 8-9

Many companies use a lock-box system to separate cash duties and establish control over cash receipts. Customers send their checks directly to the company's bank account. Internal control is tight because company personnel never touch incoming cash. The lock-box system improves efficiency because cash goes to work immediately.

Student ResourceCD

cash payments, internal control

 Apply internal controls to cash payments

We introduced the invoice in Chapter 5. ➡

Internal Control over Cash Payments

Cash payments are as important as cash receipts. It is therefore critical to control cash payments. Companies make most payments by check. They also pay small amounts from a petty cash fund. Let's begin with cash payments by check.

Controls over Payment by Check

Payment by check is an important internal control. First, the check provides a record of the payment. Second, to be valid, the check must be signed by an authorized official. Before signing the check, the manager should study the evidence supporting the payment. To illustrate the internal control over cash payments, let's suppose the business is paying for merchandise inventory.

CONTROLS OVER PURCHASE AND PAYMENT   The purchasing and payment process—outlined in Exhibit 8-9—starts when the company sends a *purchase order* to the supplier. When the supplier ships the merchandise, the supplier also mails the *invoice*, or bill. ← The goods arrive, and the receiving department checks the goods for damage and prepares a list of the goods received on a *receiving report*. The accounting department combines all the foregoing documents and forwards this *payment packet* to officers for approval. Exhibit 8-10 shows the documents that make up the payment packet.

Exhibit 8-9

Cash Payments by Check

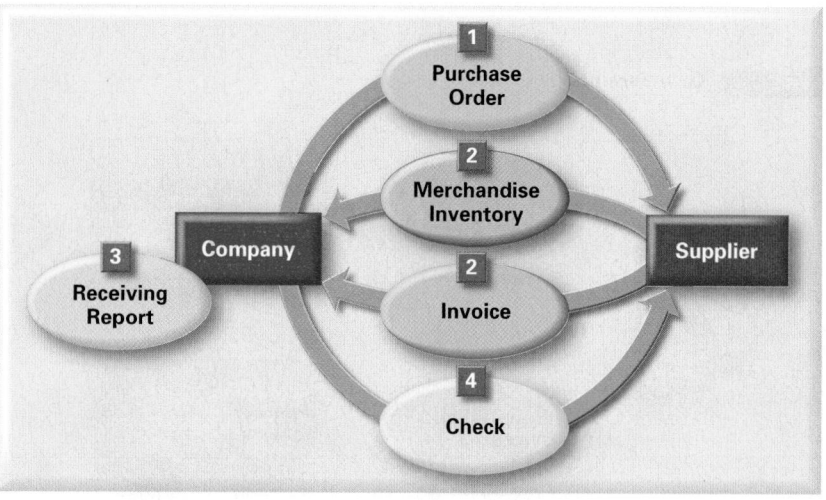

Before signing the check for payment, the controller or the treasurer should examine the packet to prove that all the documents agree. Only then does the company know that

1. It received the goods ordered.
2. It is paying only for the goods received.

These two proofs are needed for good internal control over cash payments by check.

After payment, the check signer punches a hole through the payment packet. Dishonest people have been known to run a bill through for cash payment two or more times. This hole alerts the company that it has paid the bill.

Exhibit 8-10

Payment Packet

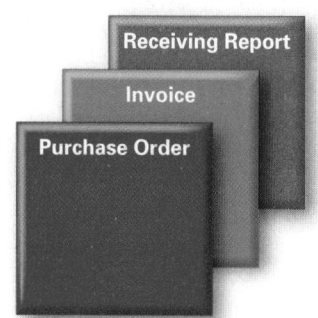

STREAMLINED PROCEDURES   Technology is streamlining payment procedures. Evaluated Receipts Settlement (ERS) compresses the approval process into a single step: compare the receiving report to the purchase order. If those documents match, that proves Kinko's received the paper it ordered, and then Kinko's pays Hammermill Paper, the supplier.

An even more streamlined process bypasses people and documents altogether. In Electronic Data Interchange (EDI), Wal-Mart's computers communicate directly with the computers of suppliers like Hershey Foods and Procter & Gamble. When Wal-Mart's inventory of Hershey chocolate candy reaches a low level, the computer sends a purchase order to Hershey. Hershey ships the candy and invoices to Wal-Mart electronically. Then an electronic fund transfer (EFT) sends Wal-Mart's payment to Hershey.

✔ Starter 8-10

Controlling Petty Cash Payments

It is wasteful to get approval and write a check for an executive's taxi fare or the delivery of a package across town. To meet these needs, companies keep cash on hand to pay small amounts. This fund is called **petty cash**.

Even though petty cash payments are small, the business needs to set up controls such as the following:

Petty Cash
Fund containing a small amount of cash that is used to pay for minor expenditures.

1. Designate an employee to serve as custodian of the petty cash fund.
2. Keep a specific amount of cash on hand.
3. Support all fund payments with a petty cash ticket.

The petty cash fund is opened when a check for the designated amount is issued to Petty Cash. Assume that on February 28, the business creates a petty cash fund of $200. The custodian cashes a $200 check and places the money in the fund. Starting the fund is recorded as follows:

Feb. 28	Petty Cash	200	
	Cash in Bank		200
	To open the petty cash fund.		

For each petty cash payment, the custodian prepares a *petty cash ticket* like the one in Exhibit 8-11.

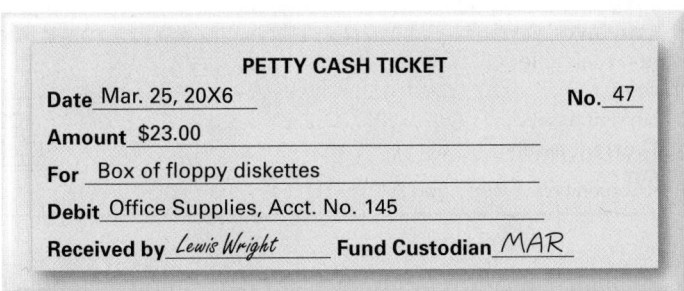

Exhibit 8-11

Petty Cash Ticket

Signatures (or initials) identify the recipient of the cash (Lewis Wright) and the fund custodian (MAR). Requiring both signatures reduces fraudulent payments. The custodian keeps all the petty cash tickets in the fund. The sum of the cash plus the total of the ticket amounts should equal the opening balance ($200) at all times. Also, the Petty Cash account keeps its $200 balance at all times.

Maintaining the Petty Cash account at its designated balance is the nature of an **imprest system**. This clearly identifies the amount of cash for which the custodian is responsible, and that is the system's main internal control feature.

Payments reduce the cash in the fund, so periodically the fund must be replenished. On March 31 this fund has $118 in cash and $82 in tickets. A check for $82 is issued to replenish the fund. The check is made payable to Petty Cash. The fund custodian cashes this check and puts $82 in the fund to return its actual cash to $200.

The petty cash tickets identify the accounts to be debited, as shown in the entry to replenish the fund:

Imprest System
A way to account for petty cash by maintaining a constant balance in the petty cash account, supported by the fund (cash plus payment tickets) totaling the same amount.

Mar. 31	Office Supplies.........................	23	
	Delivery Expense	17	
	Miscellaneous Selling Expense	42	
	Cash in Bank		82
	To replenish the petty cash fund.		

The Petty Cash account keeps its $200 balance at all times. Petty Cash is debited only when the fund is started (see the February 28 entry) or when its amount is changed. If the business raises the fund amount from $200 to $250, this would require a $50 debit to Petty Cash.

Reporting Cash on the Balance Sheet

Cash is the first asset listed on the balance sheet because it's the most liquid asset. Businesses often have many bank accounts and several petty cash funds, but they combine all cash amounts into a single total called "Cash and Cash Equivalents."

Cash equivalents include liquid assets such as time deposits. These are interest-bearing accounts that can be withdrawn with no penalty. These assets are sufficiently liquid to be reported along with cash. The balance sheet of Intel Corporation reported the following current assets:

✔ **Starter 8-11**

☐ Internal Control
☐ The Bank Account
☐ Managing Cash Receipts
☐ Managing Cash Payments
■ **Cash on the Balance Sheet**
☐ Ethics and Accounting
☐ Appendix: Vouchers

Student ResourceCD
balance sheet

Intel Corporation

Balance Sheet (Adapted)
December 31, 2001

	(In millions)
Assets	
Current assets:	
Cash and cash equivalents..............................	$ 7,970
Short-term investments	3,580
Accounts receivable	2,607
Inventories...	2,253
Other current assets	1,223
Total current assets.................................	$17,633

Source: Intel Corporation. *Annual Report 2001*, p. 21.

Intel's cash balance means that Intel has $7,970 million available for immediate use. Cash that is restricted should not be reported as a current asset. For example, banks require customers to keep a *compensating balance* on deposit in order to borrow from the bank. The compensating balance is not included in the cash amount on the balance sheet.

Ethics and Accounting

☐ Internal Control
☐ The Bank Account
☐ Managing Cash Receipts
☐ Managing Cash Payments
☐ Cash on the Balance Sheet
■ **Ethics and Accounting**
☐ Appendix: Vouchers

Student ResourceCD
ethics

A *Wall Street Journal* article described a Russian entrepreneur who was getting ahead in business by breaking laws. "Older people have an ethics problem," he said. "By that I mean they *have* ethics." Conversely, Roger Smith, the former chairman of General Motors, said, "Ethical practice is [. . .] good business." Smith has been around long enough to know that unethical behavior doesn't work. Sooner or later unethical conduct comes to light. Moreover, ethical behavior wins out in the long run because it is the right thing to do.

Corporate and Professional Codes of Ethics

Most large companies have a code of ethics to encourage employees to behave ethically. But codes of ethics are not enough by themselves. Senior management must set a high ethical tone. They must make it clear that the company will not tolerate unethical conduct.

As professionals, accountants are expected to maintain higher standards than society in general. Their ability to do business depends entirely on their reputation. Most independent accountants are members of the American Institute of Certified Public Accountants and must abide by the *AICPA Code of Professional Conduct*. Accountants who are members of the Institute of Management Accountants are bound by the *Standards of Ethical Conduct for Management Accountants*. →

← *See Chapter 19, p. 774.*

Ethical Issues in Accounting

6 *Make ethical business judgments*

In many situations, the ethical choice is easy. For example, stealing cash is both unethical and illegal. In our chapter-opening story, the cashier's actions landed her in prison. In other cases, the choices are more difficult. But in every instance, ethical judgments boil down to a personal decision: What should I do in a given situation? Let's consider three ethical issues in accounting.

Situation 1 Sonja Kleberg is preparing the income tax return of a client who has earned more income than expected. On January 2, the client pays for advertising and asks Sonja to backdate the expense to the preceding year. The tax deduction would help the client more in the year just ended than in the current year. Backdating would decrease taxable income of the earlier year and lower the client's tax payments. After all, there is a difference of only two days between January 2 and December 31. This client is important to Kleberg. What should she do?

She should refuse the request because the transaction took place in January of the new year.

What control device could prove that Kleberg behaved unethically if she backdated the transaction in the accounting records? An IRS audit could prove that the expense occurred in January rather than in December. Falsifying IRS documents is both unethical and illegal.

Situation 2 Jack Mellichamp's software company owes $40,000 to Bank of America. The loan agreement requires Mellichamp's company to maintain a current ratio (current assets divided by current liabilities) of 1.50 or higher. → At present, the company's current ratio is 1.40. At this level, Mellichamp is in violation of his loan agreement. He can increase the current ratio to 1.53 by paying off some current liabilities right before year-end. Is it ethical to do so?

← *For a review of the current ratio, see Chapter 4.*

Yes, because the action is a real business transaction.

Mellichamp should be aware that paying off the liabilities is only a delaying tactic. It will hold off the creditors for now, but the business still must improve in order to keep from violating the agreement.

Situation 3 David Duncan, the lead auditor of Enron Corporation, thinks Enron may be understating the liabilities on its balance sheet. Enron's transactions are very complex, and no one may ever figure this out. Duncan asks his firm's Standards Committee how he should handle the situation. They reply, "Require Enron to report all its liabilities." Enron is Duncan's most important client, and Enron is pressuring him to certify the liabilities. Duncan can rationalize that Enron's reported amounts are okay. What should Duncan do? To make his decision, Duncan could follow the framework outlined in the following Decision Guidelines feature.

Decision Guidelines

FRAMEWORK FOR MAKING ETHICAL JUDGMENTS

Weighing tough ethical judgments requires a decision framework. Answering these four questions will guide you through tough decisions. Let's apply them to David Duncan's situation.

Question	Decision Guideline
1. What is the ethical issue?	1. *Identify the ethical issue.* The root word of ethical is *ethics*, which Webster's dictionary defines as "the discipline dealing with what is good and bad and with moral duty and obligation." Duncan's ethical dilemma is to decide what he should do with the information he has uncovered.
2. What are Duncan's options?	2. *Specify the alternatives.* For David Duncan, the alternatives include (a) go along with Enron's liabilities **as** reported or (b) force Enron to report higher amounts of liabilities.
3. What are the possible consequences?	3. *Assess the possible outcomes.* a. If Duncan certifies Enron's present level of liabilities—and if no one ever objects—Duncan will keep this valuable client. But if Enron's actual liabilities turn out to be higher than reported, Enron investors may lose money and take Duncan to court. That would damage his reputation as an auditor and hurt his firm. b. If Duncan follows his company policy, he must force Enron to increase its reported liabilities. That will anger the company, and Enron may fire Duncan as its auditor. In this case, Duncan will save his reputation, but it will cost him some business in the short run.
4. What shall I do?	4. *Make the decision.* In the end Duncan went along with Enron and certified the company's liabilities. He went directly against his firm's policies. Enron later admitted understating its liabilities, Duncan had to retract his audit opinion, and Duncan's firm, **Arthur Andersen**, collapsed quickly. Duncan should have followed company policy, as we discuss on page 324. Rarely is one person smarter than a team of experts. Duncan got out from under his firm's umbrella of protection, and it cost him and many others dearly.

Excel Application Exercise

Goal: Create an Excel spreadsheet to help evaluate various options for an ethical dilemma.

Scenario: Consider the dilemma of Paul Van Allen, in textbook problem P8-7A. In addition to the facts in the problem, Van Allen's board is considering additional options. First, there is a comparable site in the same general area with an appraised value of $3.9 million. But this location is home to a woodland fungus that may aid in the treatment of diabetes. Second, the board is considering expanding the existing location's square footage by 25%. The board has received a bid of $3.2 million on the new construction from Van Allen's brother-in-law.

Assume the following: If the board makes an offer on Fletcher's property, it will propose a price of $3.5 million. If an offer is made on the comparable site, it will be $3.4 million. If

the board chooses to remodel and expand the current location, the bid price will be accepted.

Your task is to create a spreadsheet that weights the issues associated with each scenario option and calculates the best choice.

After you have prepared your spreadsheet, answer these questions:

1. What additional issues did you include in your list?
2. Which option does your spreadsheet suggest the board choose?
3. For each option, which issue did you weigh the most (in other words, which issue was most important)?
4. If you were Van Allen, which option would you recommend to the board, and why?

Excel Application Exercise *(continued)*

Step-by-Step:

1. Open a new Excel worksheet.
2. Create a bold-faced heading for your spreadsheet that contains the following:
   a. Chapter 8 Excel Application Exercise
   b. Ethical Dilemma
   c. Today's Date
3. In row 5, create the following column headings:
   a. Issues
   b. Option 1 (Fletcher)
   c. Option 2 (Comp Site)
   d. Option 3 (Remodel)
   e. Option 4 (Do Nothing)
4. In the Issues column, list the issues that should be considered in making a decision. Add as many issues as you believe are relevant. Here's a starter list:
   a. Cost
   b. No potential environmental issues

   c. Absence of conflict of interest
   d. No exploitation of seller's circumstances
   e. Local community support
5. Next, using a range of 1 to 10, assign a score to each issue for each option. The higher the number, the more desirable it is for Van Allen and the board. For example, if the local community response for Option 1 is unimportant, the score should be close to 1 or 2. If the local community response to Option 2 is expected to be negative, it could be given a higher score to reflect the expected lack of support.
6. Underneath your last row of issues, create a "Total" row, and sum up the numbers for each column. This number represents the score for the option. Assuming all relevant issues have been appropriately ranked, the option with the highest score indicates the best choice.

END-OF-CHAPTER *Summary Problem*

Abbey Company established a $300 petty cash fund. James C. Brown (JCB) is the fund custodian. At the end of the week, the petty cash fund contains the following:

a. Cash: $171

b. Petty cash tickets, as follows:

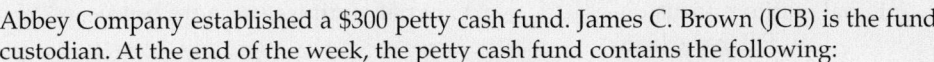

No.	Amount	Issued to	Signed by	Account Debited
44	$14	B. Jarvis	B. Jarvis and JCB	Office Supplies
45	39	S. Bell	S. Bell	Delivery Expense
47	43	R. Tate	R. Tate and JCB	—
48	33	L. Blair	L. Blair and JCB	Travel Expense

CHECK YOUR RESOURCES

Required

1. Identify three internal control weaknesses revealed in the given data.
2. Prepare the general journal entries to record:
   a. Establishment of the petty cash fund.
   b. Replenishment of the fund. Assume that petty cash ticket no. 47 was issued for the purchase of office supplies.
3. What is the balance in the Petty Cash account immediately before replenishment? Immediately after replenishment?

Solution

Requirement 1

The three internal control weaknesses are

1. Petty cash ticket no. 46 is missing. There is no indication of what happened to this ticket. The company should investigate.
2. The petty cash custodian (JCB) did not sign petty cash ticket no. 45. This omission may have been an oversight on his part. However, it raises the question of whether he authorized the payment. Both the fund custodian and the recipient of cash should sign the ticket.
3. Petty cash ticket no. 47 does not indicate which account to debit. What did Tate do with the money, and what account should be debited? See 2b above.

Requirement 2

Petty cash journal entries:

a. Entry to establish the petty cash fund:

Petty Cash	300	
Cash in Bank		300

b. Entry to replenish the fund:

Office Supplies ($14 + $43) ...	57	
Delivery Expense	39	
Travel Expense	33	
Cash in Bank		129

Requirement 3

The balance in Petty Cash is *always* its specified balance, in this case $300.

REVIEW *Internal Control and Cash*

Quick Check

1. Which of the following is not part of the definition of internal control?
   a. Safeguard assets
   b. Encourage employees to follow company policy
   c. Promote operational efficiency
   d. Separation of duties

2. Internal auditors focus on _____; external auditors are more concerned with _____. Fill in the blanks.
   a. operations; financial statements
   b. e-commerce; fraud
   c. documents; records
   d. cash receipts; cash payments

3. Darice Goodrich receives cash from customers. Her other assigned job is to post the collections to customer accounts receivable. Her company has weak
   a. Ethics
   b. Separation of duties
   c. Assignment of responsibilities
   d. Computer controls

4. Encryption
   a. Creates firewalls to protect data
   b. Cannot be broken by hackers
   c. Avoids the need for separation of duties
   d. Rearranges messages by a special process

5. The document that explains all differences between the company's cash records and the bank's figures is called a
   a. Bank statement
   b. Bank reconciliation
   c. Bank collection
   d. Electronic fund transfer

6. Which items appear on the Book side of a bank reconciliation?
   a. Outstanding checks
   b. Deposits in transit
   c. Both a and b
   d. None of the above

7. Which items appear on the Bank side of a bank reconciliation?
   a. Outstanding checks
   b. Deposits in transit
   c. Both a and b
   d. None of the above

8. Navarro Company's Cash account shows an ending balance of $800. There are also a $20 service charge and an NSF check for $100. A $250 deposit is in transit, and outstanding checks total $400. What is Navarro's adjusted cash balance?
   a. $530
   b. $650
   c. $680
   d. $1,050

9. After performing a bank reconciliation, we need to journalize
   a. All items on the book side of the reconciliation
   b. All items on the bank side of the reconciliation
   c. All items on the reconciliation
   d. No items from the reconciliation because all cash transactions have already been recorded

10. Separation of duties is important for internal control of
   a. Cash receipts   **c.** Both of the above
   b. Cash payments   **d.** Neither of the above

Accounting Vocabulary

audit (p. 326)	**controller** (p. 325)	**internal control** (p. 324)
bank collection (p. 332)	**deposit in transit** (p. 332)	**nonsufficient funds (NSF) check** (p. 332)
bank reconciliation (p. 330)	**electronic funds transfer (EFT)** (p. 330)	**outstanding check** (p. 332)
bank statement (p. 330)	**encryption** (p. 328)	**petty cash** (p. 339)
check (p. 329)	**firewalls** (p. 329)	**Trojan horse** (p. 328)
computer virus (p. 328)	**imprest system** (p. 339)	**voucher** (p. 358)

ASSESS *Your Progress*

Starters

Definition of internal control
(Obj. 1)

A⁺online homework

See *www.prenhall.com/horngren* for selected Starters, Exercises, and Problems.

S8-1 Internal controls are designed to safeguard assets, encourage employees to follow company policies, promote operational efficiency, and ensure accurate records. Which goal is most important? Which goal must the internal controls accomplish for the business to survive? Give your reason.

Applying the definition of internal control
(Obj. 1)

S8-2 Explain in your own words why separation of duties is often described as the cornerstone of internal control for safeguarding assets. Describe what can happen if the same person has custody of an asset and also accounts for the asset.

S8-3 How do external auditors differ from internal auditors? How does an external audit differ from an internal audit? How are the two types of audits similar?

Characteristics of an effective system of internal control
(Obj. 2)

S8-4 Review the characteristics of an effective system of internal control that begin on page 324. Then identify two things that **Merrill Lynch** in the chapter-opening story could have done to make it harder for cashier Darlyne Lopez to steal from the company and hide the theft. Explain how each new measure taken by Merrill Lynch would have accomplished its goal.

Characteristics of an effective system of internal control
(Obj. 2)

S8-5 Answer the following questions about the bank reconciliation:

1. What is the difference between a bank statement and a bank reconciliation?
2. Is the bank reconciliation a journal, a ledger, an account, or a financial statement? If none of these, what is it?

Aspects of a bank reconciliation
(Obj. 3)

S8-6 The Cash account of Good Times Video Productions reported a balance of $2,280 at May 31. Included were outstanding checks totaling $900 and a May 31 deposit in transit of $200. The bank statement, which came from Park Cities Bank, listed a May 31 balance of $3,600. Included in the bank balance was a May 30 collection of $630 on account from Kelly Brooks, a Good Times customer who pays the bank directly. The bank statement also shows a $20 service charge and $10 of interest revenue that Good times earned on its bank balance. *Prepare Good Times' bank reconciliation at May 31.*

Preparing a bank reconciliation
(Obj. 3)

S8-7 After preparing Good Times Video's bank reconciliation in Starter 8-6, journalize the company's transactions that arise from the bank reconciliation. Include an explanation with each entry.

Recording transactions from a bank reconciliation
(Obj. 3)

Control over cash receipts
(Obj. 4)

S8-8 Les Albrecht sells furniture for Lane's Interiors in Destin, Florida. Company procedure requires Albrecht to write a customer receipt for all sales. The receipt forms are prenumbered. Albrecht is having personal financial problems and takes $500 that he received from a customer. To hide his theft, Albrecht simply destroys the company copy of the sales receipt he gave the customer. What will alert Monica Lane, the owner, that something is wrong? What will this knowledge lead Lane to do?

Control over cash receipts by mail
(Obj. 4)

S8-9 Review the internal controls over cash receipts by mail, discussed on page 337. Exactly what is accomplished by the final step in the process, performed by the controller? What does a lock-box system accomplish?

Internal control over payments by check
(Obj. 5)

S8-10 Answer the following questions about internal control over cash payments.

1. A purchasing agent for Eastwood Company receives the goods that he purchases and also approves payment for the goods. How could this purchasing agent cheat his company? How could Eastwood avoid this internal control weakness?
2. Payment of cash payments by check carries two basic controls over cash. What are they?

Petty cash
(Obj. 5)

S8-11 Record the following selected transactions of Rosetree Florist in general journal format (explanations are not required):

April 1	Established a petty cash fund with a $200 balance.
30	The petty cash fund has $19 in cash and $181 in petty cash tickets that were issued to pay for Office Supplies ($111), Delivery Expense ($33), and Entertainment Expense ($37). Replenished the fund and recorded the expenses.

Making an ethical judgment
(Obj. 6)

S8-12 Nancy Allen, an accountant for Chinatown Express, discovers that her supervisor, Lee Kwan, made several errors last year. Overall, the errors overstated Chinatown's net income by 20%. It is not clear whether the errors were deliberate or accidental. What should Allen do?

A⁺online homework

Identifying internal control strengths and weaknesses
(Obj. 2)

Exercises

E8-1 The following situations describe two equipment purchases and two cash receipts. In each pair, one situation's internal controls are much better than the other's. Evaluate the internal controls in each situation as strong or weak, and give the reason for your answers.

Equipment Purchases:

a. Centennial Homes policy calls for construction supervisors to request the equipment needed for construction jobs. The home office then purchases the equipment and has it shipped to the construction site.
b. Wayside Construction Company policy calls for project supervisors to purchase the equipment needed for construction jobs. The supervisors then submit the paid receipts to the home office for reimbursement. This policy enables supervisors to get the equipment they need quickly and keep construction jobs moving along.

Cash Receipts:

a. Cash received by mail goes straight to the accountant, who debits Cash and credits Accounts Receivable to record collections from customers. The accountant then deposits the cash in the bank.
b. Cash received by mail goes to the mail room, where a mail clerk opens envelopes and totals the cash receipts for the day. The mail clerk forwards customer checks to the treasurer for deposit in the bank and forwards the remittance slips to the accounting department for posting credits to customer accounts.

E8-2 The following situations suggest a strength or a weakness in internal control. Identify each as *strength* or *weakness*, and give the reason for your answer.

Identifying internal control strengths and weaknesses
(Obj. 2)

a. Top managers delegate all internal control measures to the accounting department.
b. The accounting department orders merchandise and approves invoices for payment.
c. The operator of a computer has no other accounting or cash-handling duties.
d. Cash received over the counter is controlled by the sales clerk, who rings up the sale and places the cash in the register. The sales clerk matches the total recorded on the control tape stored in the register to each day's cash sales.
e. The officer who signs checks need not examine the payment packet because he is confident the amounts are correct.

E8-3 Identify the missing internal control in the following situations. Select from these characteristics:

Identifying internal controls
(Obj. 2)

- Competent, reliable personnel
- Assignment of responsibilities
- Separation of duties
- Audits
- Electronic and computer controls
- Other controls (specify)

a. The same trusted employee has served as cashier for 10 years.
b. Grocery stores such as **Safeway** and **Meier's** purchase most merchandise from a few suppliers. At another grocery store, the manager decides to reduce paperwork. He eliminates the requirement that the receiving department prepare a receiving report, which lists the quantities of items actually received from the supplier.
c. When business is brisk, Stop-n-Go deposits cash in the bank several times during the day. The manager at one store wants to reduce the time employees spend delivering cash to the bank, so he starts a new policy. Cash will build up over Saturdays and Sundays, and the total two-day amount will be deposited on Sunday evening.
d. While reviewing the records of Discount Pharmacy, you find that the same employee orders merchandise and approves invoices for payment.
e. Business is slow at Fun City Amusement Park on Tuesday, Wednesday, and Thursday nights. To reduce expenses, the owner decides not to use a ticket taker on those nights. The ticket seller (cashier) is told to keep the tickets as a record of the number sold.

E8-4 The following items could appear on a bank reconciliation:

Classifying bank reconciliation items
(Obj. 3)

a. Service charge
b. Deposits in transit
c. NSF check
d. Bank collection of a note receivable for us
e. Interest earned on bank balance
f. Book error: We credited Cash for $200. The correct amount was $2,000
g. Outstanding checks
h. Bank error: The bank decreased our account for a check written by another customer

Required

Classify each item as (1) an addition to the book balance, (2) a subtraction from the book balance, (3) an addition to the bank balance, or (4) a subtraction from the bank balance.

E8-5 Jason Coe's checkbook lists the following:

Preparing a bank reconciliation
(Obj. 3)

Date	Check No.	Item	Check	Deposit	Balance
9/1					$ 525
4	622	JD's Art Café	$ 19		506
9		Dividends received		$ 116	622
13	623	General Tire Co.	43		579
14	624	ExxonMobil	58		521
18	625	Cash	50		471
26	626	Woodway Baptist Church	75		396
28	627	Bent Tree Apartments	275		121
30		Paycheck		1,500	1,621

Coe's September bank statement shows the following:

Balance			$525
Add: Deposits			116
Debit checks:	No.	Amount	
	622	$19	
	623	43	
	624	68*	
	625	50	(180)
Other charges:			
Printed checks		$18	
Service charge		12	(30)
Balance			$431

*This is the correct amount for check number 624.

Required

Prepare Coe's bank reconciliation at September 30. How much cash does Coe actually have on September 30?

Preparing a bank reconciliation
(Obj. 3)

E8-6 Zane Grey operates four Quik Pak convenience stores. He has just received the monthly bank statement at October 31 from City National Bank, and the statement shows an ending balance of $2,050. Listed on the statement are an EFT rent collection of $400, a service charge of $12, two NSF checks totaling $74, and a $9 charge for printed checks. In reviewing his cash records, Grey identifies outstanding checks totaling $467 and an October 31 deposit in transit of $1,788. During October, he recorded a $290 check by debiting Salary Expense and crediting Cash for $29. Grey's Cash account shows an October 31 balance of $3,327. *Prepare the bank reconciliation at October 31.*

Making journal entries from a bank reconciliation
(Obj. 3)

E8-7 Using the data from Exercise 8-6, make the journal entries Grey should record on October 31. Include an explanation for each entry.

Using a bank reconciliation as a control device
(Obj. 3)

E8-8 Barry Cruse owns Cruse Vacations. He fears that a trusted employee has been stealing from the company. This employee receives cash from customers and also prepares the monthly bank reconciliation. To check up on the employee, Cruse prepares his own bank reconciliation, as follows:

Cruse Vacations
Bank Reconciliation
August 31, 20X7

Bank		**Books**	
Balance, August 31	$3,000	Balance, August 31	$2,500
Add: Deposit in transit	400	Add: Bank collection	820
		Interest revenue	10
Less: Outstanding checks . .	(1,100)	Less: Service charge	(30)
Adjusted bank balance	$2,300	Adjusted book balance	$3,300

Which side of the reconciliation shows the true cash balance? What is Cruse's true cash balance? Does it appear that the employee has stolen from the company? If so, how much? Explain your answer.

Evaluating internal control over cash receipts
(Obj. 4)

E8-9 When you check out at a **Best Buy** store, the cash register displays the amount of the sale, the cash received from the customer, and any change returned to the customer. Suppose the register also produces a customer receipt but keeps no internal record of transactions. At the end of the day, the clerk counts the cash in the register and gives it to the cashier for deposit in the company bank account.

Write a memo to the store manager. Identify the internal control weakness over cash receipts, and explain how the weakness gives an employee the opportunity to steal cash. State how to prevent such a theft.

E8-10 Leather Goods Company created a $300 imprest petty cash fund. During the month, the fund custodian authorized and signed petty cash tickets as follows:

Accounting for petty cash
(Obj. 5)
Student ResourceCD
General Ledger, Peachtree, QuickBooks

Petty Cash Ticket No.	Item	Account Debited	Amount
1	Delivery of goods to customers	Delivery Expense	$22
2	Mail package	Postage Expense	52
3	Newsletter	Supplies Expense	34
4	Key to closet	Miscellaneous Expense	3
5	Wastebasket	Miscellaneous Expense	13
6	Computer diskettes	Supplies Expense	85

Required

1. Make the general journal entries to (a) create the petty cash fund and (b) record its replenishment. Include explanations.
2. Describe the items in the fund both before and after replenishment.

E8-11

1. Explain how an *imprest* petty cash system works. What is the main control feature of an imprest system?
2. Atlantic Press maintains an imprest petty cash fund of $400 which is under the control of Brenda Montague. At November 30, the fund holds $220 cash and petty cash tickets for travel expense, $80; office supplies, $60; and delivery expense, $40.

   Journalize **(a)** establishment of the petty cash fund on November 1 and **(b)** replenishment of the fund on November 30.
3. Prepare a T-account for the Petty Cash account of Atlantic Press, and post to the account. What is Petty Cash's balance at all times?

Control over petty cash
(Obj. 5)

E8-12 Approximately 300 current and former members of the U.S. House of Representatives—on a regular basis—wrote a quarter million dollars of checks on the House bank without having the cash in their accounts. In effect, the delinquent check writers were borrowing money from each other on an interest-free, no-service-charge basis. The House closed its bank after the events became public.

Evaluating the ethics of conduct by government legislators
(Obj. 6)

Required

Suppose you are a new congressional representative from your state. Apply the ethical judgment framework outlined in the Decision Guidelines feature on page 342 to decide whether you would write NSF checks on a regular basis through the House bank.

Problems

(Group A)

P8-1A San Marino Foreign Cars prospered during the recent economic expansion. Business was so good that the company used very few internal controls. A recent decline in automobile sales caused San Marino to experience a cash shortage. Mike Key, the company owner, is looking for ways to save money.

As a consultant for San Marino, write a memo to convince Key of the company's need for a system of internal control. Be specific in explaining how an internal control system could save the company money. Include the definition of internal control, and

Identifying the characteristics of an effective internal control system
(Obj. 1, 2)

briefly discuss the characteristics of an effective internal control system, beginning with competent, reliable, and ethical personnel.

Correcting internal control weaknesses
(Obj. 2, 4, 5)

P8-2A Each of the following situations has an internal control weakness.

a. Computer programmers for Internet Solutions work under intense pressure. Facing tight deadlines, they sometimes bypass company policies and write programs without securing customer accounts receivable data.

b. Law firms use paraprofessional employees to perform routine tasks. For example, a legal paraprofessional might prepare first drafts of documents to assist a lawyer. In the law firm of Lee & Dunham, Joseph Lee, the senior partner, turns over most of his legal research to new members of his paraprofessional staff.

c. In evaluating internal control over cash payments, an auditor learns that the purchasing agent is responsible for purchasing diamonds for use in the company's manufacturing process. The purchasing agent also approves the invoices for payment and signs the checks.

d. Blake Lemmon owns an engineering firm. His staff consists of 12 engineers, and he manages the office. Often, his work requires him to travel. He notes that when he returns from business trips, the engineering jobs in the office have not progressed much. When he is away, his senior employees take over office management and neglect their engineering duties. One employee could manage the office.

e. Aimee Atkins has worked for Michael Riggs, MD, for many years. Atkins performs all accounting duties, including opening the mail, making the bank deposits, writing checks, and preparing the bank reconciliation. Riggs trusts Atkins completely.

Required

1. Identify the missing internal control characteristic in each situation.

2. Identify the possible problem caused by each control weakness.

3. Propose a solution to each internal control problem.

Preparing a bank reconciliation
(Obj. 3)

Student Resource **CD**
spreadsheet

P8-3A The cash records of Silver Maple Art Gallery for April 20X4 follows.

Cash Receipts (CR)		Cash Payments (CP)	
Date	**Cash Debit**	**Check No.**	**Cash Credit**
Apr. 2	$ 4,174	3113	$ 891
8	501	3114	147
10	559	3115	1,930
16	2,187	3116	664
22	1,854	3117	1,472
29	1,060	3118	1,000
30	337	3119	632
Total	$10,672	3120	1,675
		3121	100
		3122	2,413
		Total	$10,924

The Cash account of Silver Maple Art Gallery shows the following at April 30, 20X4:

Cash					
Date	**Item**	**Jrnl. Ref.**	**Debit**	**Credit**	**Balance**
Apr. 1	Balance				13,911
30		CR. 6	10,672		24,583
30		CP. 11		10,924	13,659

On April 30, 20X4, Silver Maple Art Gallery received the following bank statement:

Bank Statement for April 20X4			
Beginning balance.			$13,911
Deposits and other Credits:			
Apr. 1	$ 300 EFT		
4	4,174		
9	501		
12	559		
17	2,187		
22	1,300 BC		
23	1,854	10,875	
Checks and other Debits:			
Apr. 7 (check no. 3113)	$ 891		
13 (check no. 3115)	1,390		
14	900 US		
15 (check no. 3114)	147		
18 (check no. 3116)	664		
21	200 EFT		
26 (check no. 3117)	1,472		
30 (check no. 3118)	1,000		
30	20 SC	(6,684)	
Ending balance		$18,102	

Explanations: EFT—electronic funds transfer; BC—bank collection; US—unauthorized
signature; SC—service charge.

Additional data for the bank reconciliation:

a. The EFT deposit was a receipt of rent. The EFT debit was an insurance payment.
b. The unauthorized-signature check was received from a customer.
c. The $1,300 bank collection was for a note receivable.
d. The correct amount of check number 3115 is $1,390. (Silver Maple Art Gallery's accountant mistakenly recorded the check for $1,930.)

Required

Prepare the Silver Maple Art Gallery bank reconciliation at April 30, 20X4.

P8-4A The August 31 bank statement of Stop-n-Shop Food Mart has just arrived from United Bank. To prepare the Stop-n-Shop bank reconciliation, you gather the following data:

Preparing a bank reconciliation and the related journal entries
(Obj. 3)

Student Resource**CD**
spreadsheet

a. Stop-n-Shop's Cash account shows a balance of $6,409.31 on August 31.
b. The bank statement includes two charges for returned checks from customers. One is a $395.00 check received from Lakeland Express and returned due to "Unauthorized Signature." The other is an NSF check for $147.17 received from Veracruz, Inc.
c. Stop-n-Shop pays rent expense ($750) and insurance expense ($290) each month by EFT.
d. The Stop-n-Shop checks below are outstanding at August 31.

Check No.	Amount
237	$ 46.10
288	141.00
291	578.05
293	11.87
294	609.51
295	8.88
296	101.63

e. The bank statement includes a deposit of $1,191, collected by the bank on behalf of Stop-n-Shop Food Mart. Of the total, $1,000 is collection of a note receivable, and the remainder is interest revenue.
f. The bank statement shows that Stop-n-Shop earned $38.19 of interest on its bank balance during August. This amount was added to Stop-n-Shop's account by the bank.
g. The bank statement lists a $10 subtraction for the bank service charge.

h. On August 31, Stop-n-Shop deposited $316.15, but this deposit does not appear on the bank statement.

i. The bank statement includes a $300 deposit that Stop-n-Shop did not make. The bank erroneously credited the Stop-n-Shop account for another bank customer's deposit.

j. The August 31 bank balance is $7,527.22.

Required

1. Prepare the bank reconciliation for Stop-n-Shop Food Mart at August 31.

2. Record the journal entries necessary to bring the book balance of Cash into agreement with the adjusted book balance on the reconciliation. Include an explanation for each entry.

Identifying internal control weakness in cash receipts
(Obj. 4)

P8-5A Koala Bear Software makes all sales of its spreadsheet software on credit. Cash receipts arrive by mail. Nick Vaughn opens envelopes and separates the checks from the accompanying remittance advices. Vaughn forwards the checks to another employee, who makes the daily bank deposit but has no access to the accounting records. Vaughn sends the remittance advices, which show the cash received, to the accounting department for entry in the accounts. Vaughn's only other duty is to grant sales allowances to customers. (Recall that a *sales allowance* decreases the amount receivable.) When he receives a customer check for less than the full amount of the invoice, he records the sales allowance and forwards the document to the accounting department.

Required

You are a new employee of Koala Bear Software. Write a memo to the company president identifying the internal control weakness in this situation. State how to correct the weakness.

Accounting for petty cash transactions
(Obj. 5)

Student Resource**CD**

GL, PT, QB

P8-6A Suppose that on June 1, Reyna & Reyna, Consulting Engineers, opens a district office in Omaha and creates a petty cash fund with an imprest balance of $350. During June, Carol McColgin, fund custodian, signs the following petty cash tickets:

Petty Cash Ticket Number	Item	Amount
1	Postage for package received	$ 18
2	Decorations and refreshments for office party	13
3	Two boxes of floppy disks	20
4	Printer cartridges	27
5	Dinner money for sales manager entertaining a customer	50
6	Plane ticket for executive business trip to Chicago	169
7	Delivery of package across town	6

On June 30, prior to replenishment, the fund contains these tickets plus cash. The accounts affected by petty cash payments are Office Supplies Expense, Travel Expense, Delivery Expense, Entertainment Expense, and Postage Expense.

Required

1. Explain the characteristics and the internal control features of an imprest fund.

2. How much cash does this petty cash fund hold before it's replenished?

3. Make general journal entries to **(a)** create the fund and **(b)** replenish it. Include explanations. Also, briefly describe what the custodian does on these dates.

4. Make the entry on July 1 to increase the fund balance to $500. Include an explanation, and briefly describe what the custodian does.

Making an ethical judgment
(Obj. 7)

P8-7A Paul Van Allen is vice president of Tri-Cities Bank in Bristol, Virginia. Active in community affairs, Van Allen serves on the board of directors of Baker Publishing Company. Baker is expanding and relocating its plant. At a recent meeting, board members decided to buy 15 acres of land on the edge of town. The owner of the property, Jack Fletcher, is a customer of Tri-Cities Bank. Fletcher is completing a divorce, and Van Allen knows that Fletcher is eager to sell his property. In view of Fletcher's difficult situation, Van Allen believes he would accept almost any offer for the land. Realtors have appraised the property at $5 million.

Apply the ethical judgment framework from the Decision Guidelines (page 342) to help Van Allen decide what his role should be in Baker's attempt to buy the land from Fletcher.

Problems

(Group B)

P8-1B An employee of a Meyer's Department Store stole thousands of dollars from the company. Suppose Meyer's has installed a new system of internal controls. As a consultant for Meyer's Department Store, write a memo to the president explaining how internal controls safeguard assets.

Identifying the characteristics of an effective internal control system
(Obj. 1, 2)

P8-2B Each of the following situations has an internal control weakness.

Correcting internal control weaknesses
(Obj. 2, 4, 5)

a. MiniScribe Corporation, a private company, has never had an audit. MiniScribe's accountants falsified sales and inventory figures in order to get an important loan. The loan went through, but MiniScribe later went bankrupt and couldn't repay the bank.

b. Discount stores such as **Target** and **Sam's** receive a large portion of their sales revenue in cash, with the remainder in credit-card sales. To reduce expenses, one store manager ceases purchasing fidelity bonds on the cashiers.

c. The office supply company where Champs Sporting Goods purchases cash receipt forms recently notified Champs that their receipt forms were not prenumbered. Alex Champ, the owner, replied that he never uses the receipt numbers.

d. Centex Software specializes in programs with accounting applications. The company's most popular program prepares the journal, accounts receivable subsidiary ledger, and general ledger. In the company's early days, the owner and eight employees wrote the computer programs, sold the products to stores such as ComputerWorld, and performed the accounting. As the company has grown, the number of employees has increased dramatically. Recently, development of a new software program stopped while the programmers redesigned Centex's accounting system. Centex's accountants could have performed this task.

e. Lana Turner, a widow with no known sources of outside income, has been a trusted employee of Stone Products Company for 15 years. She performs all cash-handling and accounting duties, including opening the mail, preparing the bank deposit, accounting for all aspects of cash and accounts receivable, and preparing the bank reconciliation. She has just purchased a new Mercedes and a new home in an expensive suburb. Jeremy Stone, owner of the company, wonders how Turner can afford these luxuries.

Required

1. Identify the missing internal control characteristics in each situation.
2. Identify the possible problem caused by each control weakness.
3. Propose a solution to each internal control problem.

P8-3B The cash records of **Mailboxes Etc.** for March 20X5 follow.

Preparing a bank reconciliation
(Obj. 3)

Student ResourceCD

Cash Receipts (CR)		Cash Payments (CP)	
Date	Cash Debit	Check No.	Cash Credit
Mar. 4	$2,716	1413	$ 465
9	544	1414	1,004
11	1,655	1415	450
14	896	1416	8
17	367	1417	775
25	890	1418	88
31	2,038	1419	126
Total	$9,106	1420	970
		1421	200
		1422	2,267
		Total	$6,353

The Cash account of Mailboxes shows the following on March 31, 20X5:

Cash					
Date	Item	Jrnl. Ref.	Debit	Credit	Balance
Mar. 1	Balance				12,188
31		CR. 10	9,106		21,294
31		CP. 16		6,353	14,941

On March 31, 20X5, Mailboxes received the bank statement that follows.

Bank Statement for March 20X5

Beginning balance		$12,188
Deposits and other Credits:		
Mar. 1	$ 625 EFT	
5	2,716	
10	544	
11	1,655	
15	896	
18	367	
25	890	
31	1,000 BC	8,693
Checks and other Debits:		
Mar. 8	$ 441 NSF	
9 (check no. 1413)	465	
13 (check no. 1414)	1,004	
14 (check no. 1415)	450	
15 (check no. 1416)	8	
19	340 EFT	
22 (check no. 1417)	775	
29 (check no. 1418)	88	
31 (check no. 1419)	216	
31	25 SC	(3,812)
Ending balance		$17,069

Explanations: BC—bank collection; EFT—electronic funds transfer; NSF—nonsufficient funds check; SC—service charge.

Additional data for the bank reconciliation:

a. The EFT deposit was a receipt of rent. The EFT debit was payment of insurance.
b. The NSF check was received from a customer.
c. The $1,000 bank collection was for a note receivable.
d. The correct amount of check 1419 is $216. Mailboxes Etc. mistakenly recorded the check for $126.

Required

Prepare the bank reconciliation of Mailboxes Etc. at March 31, 20X5.

Preparing a bank reconciliation and the related journal entries
(Obj. 3)

P8-4B The May 31 bank statement of Marlow Furniture Co. has just arrived from First State Bank. To prepare the bank reconciliation, you gather the following data.

a. The May 31 bank balance is $19,209.82.
b. The bank statement includes two charges for returned checks from customers. One is a $67.50 NSF check received from Sarah Batten and deposited on May 19. The other is a $195.03 check received from Lena Masters and deposited on May 21. It was returned due to "Unauthorized Signature."
c. The following Marlow checks are outstanding at May 31:

Check No.	Amount
616	$403.00
802	74.25
806	36.60
809	161.38
810	229.05
811	48.91

d. Marlow collects from a few customers by EFT. The May bank statement lists a $200 deposit for a collection on account from customer Jack Oates.

e. The bank statement includes two special deposits: $899.14, for dividend revenue, and $16.86, the interest revenue Marlow earned on its bank balance during May.

f. The bank statement lists a $6.25 subtraction for the bank service charge.

g. On May 31, the Marlow treasurer deposited $381.14, but this deposit does not appear on the bank statement.

h. The bank statement includes a $410.00 deduction for a check drawn by Marimont Freight Company. Marlow notified the bank of this bank error.

i. Marlow's Cash account shows a balance of $18,200.55 on May 31.

Required

1. Prepare the bank reconciliation for Marlow Furniture at May 31.

2. Record the entries called for by the reconciliation. Include an explanation for each entry.

P8-5B Yamaha Marineland makes all sales on credit. Cash receipts arrive by mail. Kenneth Sartain in the mailroom opens envelopes and separates the checks from the accompanying remittance advices. Sartain forwards the checks to another employee, who makes the daily bank deposit but has no access to the accounting records. Sartain sends the remittance advices, which show cash received, to the accounting department for entry in the accounts. Sartain's only other duty is to grant sales allowances to customers. (Recall that a *sales allowance* decreases the amount receivable.) When Sartain receives a customer check for less than the full amount of the invoice, he records the sales allowance and forwards the document to the accounting department.

Identifying internal control weakness in cash receipts
(Obj. 4)

Required

You are a new employee of Yamaha Marineland. Write a memo to the company president identifying the internal control weakness in this situation. State how to correct the weakness.

P8-6B On April 1, City of Buena Vista, Arizona, creates a petty cash fund with an imprest balance of $400. During April, Elise Nelson, the fund custodian, signs the following petty cash tickets:

Accounting for petty cash transactions
(Obj. 5)

Student ResourceCD
GL, PT, QB

Petty Cash Ticket Number	Item	Amount
101	Office supplies	$86
102	Cab fare for executive	25
103	Delivery of package across town	37
104	Dinner money for city manager to entertain the governor	80
105	Inventory	85
106	Decorations for office party	19
107	Six boxes of floppy disks	44

On April 30, prior to replenishment, the fund contains these tickets plus cash. The accounts affected by petty cash payments are Office Supplies Expense, Travel Expense, Delivery Expense, Entertainment Expense, and Inventory.

Required

1. Explain the characteristics and the internal control features of an imprest fund.
2. How much cash does the petty cash fund hold before it's replenished?
3. Make general journal entries to **(a)** create the fund and **(b)** replenish it. Include explanations. Also, briefly describe what the custodian does on April 1 and April 30.
4. Make the May 1 entry to increase the fund balance to $500. Include an explanation, and briefly describe what the custodian does.

Making an ethical judgment
(Obj. 6)

P8-7B Tri State Bank in Cairo, Illinois, has a loan receivable from Cortez Manufacturing Company. Cortez is six months late in making payments to the bank, and Milton Reed, a Tri State vice president, is helping Cortez restructure its debt. Reed learns that Cortez is depending on landing a manufacturing contract from Peters & Sons, another Tri State client. Reed also serves as Peters' loan officer at the bank. In this capacity, he is aware that Peters is considering declaring bankruptcy. No one else outside Peters & Sons knows this. Reed has been a great help to Cortez Manufacturing, and Cortez's owner is counting on him to carry the company through this difficult restructuring. To help the bank collect on this large loan, Reed has a strong motivation to help Cortez survive.

Apply the ethical judgment framework from the chapter to help Reed plan his next action.

APPLY *Your Knowledge*

Decision Cases

Correcting an internal control weakness
(Obj. 1, 5)

Case 1. This case is based on an actual situation. A-1 Construction Company, headquartered in Terre Haute, Indiana, built a Rest Easy Motel 35 miles east of Terre Haute. The construction foreman, whose name was Monty, hired the 40 workers needed to complete the project. Monty had the construction workers fill out the necessary tax forms, and he sent the employment documents to the home office, which opened a payroll file for each employee.

Work on the motel began on April 1 and ended September 1. Each week, Monty filled out a time card of the hours worked by each employee during the week. Monty faxed the time sheets to the home office, which prepared the payroll checks on Friday morning. Monty drove to the home office after lunch on Friday, picked up the payroll checks, and returned to the construction site. At 5 P.M. on Friday, Monty distributed the payroll checks to the workers.

a. Describe in detail the main internal control weakness in this situation. Specify what negative result(s) could occur because of the internal control weakness.
b. Describe what you would do to correct the internal control weakness.

Using the bank reconciliation to detect a theft
(Obj. 3)

Case 2. Diamondback's Restaurant has poor internal control over its cash transactions. Genevieve Gilbreath, the owner, suspects Sam Knicks, the cashier, of stealing. Here are some details of the business's cash position at September 30.

a. The Cash account shows a balance of $6,502. This amount includes a September 30 deposit of $3,794 that does not appear on the September 30 bank statement.

b. The September 30 bank statement shows a balance of $3,124. The bank statement lists a $200 credit for a bank collection, an $8 debit for the service charge, and a $36 debit for an NSF check. The Diamondback's accountant has not recorded any of these items on the books.

c. At September 30, the following checks are outstanding:

Check No.	Amount
154	$116
256	150
278	353
291	190
292	206
293	245

d. The cashier handles all incoming cash and makes bank deposits. He also reconciles the monthly bank statement. Here is his September 30 reconciliation:

Balance per books, September 30..........			$17,502
Add: Outstanding checks...............			260
Bank collection...................			200
			17,962
Less: Deposits in transit		$3,794	
Service charge....................		8	
NSF check		36	3,838
Balance per bank, September 30...........			$14,124

Gilbreath asks you to determine whether the cashier has stolen cash from the business and, if so, how much. She also asks how the cashier concealed the theft. Perform your own bank reconciliation using the format illustrated in the chapter. There are no bank or book errors. Gilbreath also wants your input on changes that will improve Diamondback's internal controls.

Ethical Issue

Pam Dilley owns rental properties in Michigan. Each property has a manager who collects rent, arranges for repairs, and runs advertisements in the local newspaper. The property managers transfer cash to Dilley monthly and prepare their own bank reconciliations. The manager in Lansing has been stealing from the company. To cover the theft, he understates the amount of the outstanding checks on the monthly bank reconciliation. As a result, each monthly bank reconciliation appears to balance. However, the balance sheet reports more cash than Dilley actually has in the bank. In negotiating the sale of the Lansing property, Dilley is showing the balance sheet to prospective investors.

Internal control over cash payments; ethical considerations **(Obj. 5, 6)**

Required

1. Identify two parties other than Dilley who can be harmed by this theft. In what ways can they be harmed?
2. Discuss the role accounting plays in this situation.

Financial Statement Case

Study the audit opinion (labeled Report of Independent Auditors) of **Amazon.com** and the Amazon financial statements given at the end of Appendix A. Answer the following questions about the company.

Internal controls and cash **(Obj. 1, 3)**

Required

1. What is the name of Amazon.com's outside auditing firm (independent auditors)? What office of this firm signed the audit report? How long after the Amazon year-end did the auditors issue their opinion?

2. Who bears primary responsibility for the financial statements? How can you tell?

3. Does it appear that the Amazon internal controls are adequate? How can you tell?

4. What standard of auditing did the outside auditors use in examining the Amazon financial statements? By what accounting standards were the statements evaluated?

5. By how much did Amazon's cash balance (including cash equivalent) change during 2002? What were the beginning and ending cash balances?

Team Project

You are promoting a rock concert in your area. Each member of your team will invest $10,000 of their hard-earned money in this venture. It is April 1, and the concert is scheduled for June 30. Your promotional activities begin immediately, and ticket sales start on May 1. You expect to sell all the business's assets, pay all the liabilities, and distribute all remaining cash to the group members by July 31.

Required

Write an internal control manual that will help safeguard the assets of the business. The starting point of the manual is to assign responsibilities among the group members. Authorize individuals, including group members and any outsiders that you need to hire, to perform specific jobs. Separate duties among the group and any employees.

For Internet Exercises, go to the Web site www.prenhall.com/horngren.

APPENDIX *to Chapter 8*

Voucher
Instrument authorizing a cash payment.

The Voucher System

The voucher system for recording cash payments improves internal control over cash payments by formalizing the process of approving and recording invoices for payment.

A **voucher** is a document authorizing a cash payment. The accounting department prepares vouchers.

The voucher system uses (1) vouchers, (2) a voucher register (similar to a purchases journal), (3) an unpaid voucher file, (4) a check register (similar to a cash payments journal), and (5) a paid voucher file. The improvement in internal control comes from recording all payments through the voucher register. In a voucher system, all expenditures must be approved before payment can be made. This approval takes the form of a voucher. The larger the business, the more likely it is to need strict control over payments. The voucher system provides this control.

Exhibit 8A-I   Voucher

		Voucher No. 326
	BLISS WHOLESALE COMPANY	
Payee	Van Heusen, Inc.	
Address	4619 Shotwell Avenue	
	Brooklyn, NY 10564	
Due Date	March 7	
Terms	2/10, n/30	

Date	Invoice No.	Description	Amount
Mar. 1	6380	144 men's shirts stock no. X14	$1,764

Approved *Jane Trent* Controller   **Approved** *Bob Kraft* Treasurer

Front of Voucher

Voucher No. 326
Payee Van Heusen, Inc.
Invoice Amount $1,800
Discount 36
Net Amount $1,764

Due Date Mar. 7
Date Paid Mar. 6
Check No. 694

Account Distribution

Account Debited	Acct. No.	Amount
Inventory	105	$1,764
Store Supplies	145	
Salary Expense	538	
Advertising Expense	542	
Utilities Expense	548	
Delivery Expense	544	
Total		$1,764

Back of Voucher

Exhibit 8A-1 illustrates the voucher of Bliss Wholesale Company. In addition to the *payee, due date, terms, description,* and *invoice amount,* the voucher includes a section for designated officers to sign their approval for payment. The back of the voucher has places for recording the *account debited, date paid,* and *check number.* You should locate these eight items in Exhibit 8A-1.

CHAPTER 9

Receivables

A+ TIPS CHECK YOUR RESOURCES

- Visit the www.prenhall.com/horngren **Web site** for self-study quizzes, video clips, and other resources

- Try the **Quick Check** exercise at the end of the chapter to test your knowledge

- Learn the **key terms**

- Do the **Starter** exercises keyed in the margins

- Work the **mid-** and **end-of-chapter summary problems**

- Use the **Concept Links** to review material in other chapters

- Search the **CD** for review materials by chapter or by key word

- Watch the **tutorial videos** to review key concepts

- Watch the **On Location Oracle** video to review importance of receivables to a business

LEARNING OBJECTIVES

1. Design internal controls for receivables

2. Use the allowance method to account for uncollectibles by the percent-of-sales and aging-of-accounts methods

3. Use the direct write-off method to account for uncollectibles

4. Account for notes receivable

5. Report receivables on the balance sheet

6. Use the acid-test ratio and days' sales in receivables to evaluate a company

W hat do a pro football team and a software company have in common? More than you might think. A New York Jets lineman must learn which opposing player to block, and that depends on the formation of the other team. In the information age, the Jets use software, not X and O diagrams, to map out plays. Oracle Corporation, the software company, has created an interactive multimedia show that turns football formations into live animation.

Carl Banks, director of player development for the Jets, uses the Oracle program as a teaching model. Says Banks, "By the time [players] hit the practice field, [they can't] visualize X's and O's as actual plays. Oracle has helped create [a] learning environment that increases [players'] retention by as much as 250%."

New York Jets and Oracle Corp.

Oracle is one of the world's largest software companies, offering products and services to clients around the world. Accounts receivable are a significant asset for Oracle and most other businesses. Receivables present an accounting challenge: How much of a company's receivables can it collect? How much will be uncollectible? This chapter shows how to answer these and other questions about receivables. ■

■ Sitemap

Creditor
The party to a credit transaction who sells goods or a service and obtains a receivable.

Debtor
The party to a credit transaction who makes a purchase and has a payable.

Student ResourceCD

accounts receivable, internal control, notes receivable, receivables

Receivables
Monetary claims against a business or an individual.

Chapter 7 introduced special journals and subsidiary ledgers, pp. 287–299. →

As Oracle grows, so do its revenues and receivables. Accounts receivable are Oracle's second-largest asset. This chapter shows how to predict how much of Oracle's receivables the company will collect in cash. The chapter also covers notes receivable, a more formal arrangement that includes a written promise and a stated interest rate.

A *receivable* arises when a company sells goods or services to another party on credit. The receivable is the seller's claim for the amount of the transaction. Each credit transaction involves two parties:

- ■ The **creditor**, who sells something and obtains a receivable (an asset)
- ■ The **debtor**, who makes the purchase and has a payable (a liability)

A receivable also arises when one person loans money to another. Here's an example: Suppose your best friend runs out of cash and needs $100 to make it to the end of the month. You lend $100 to your friend, and he promises to pay you back on May 31. You gave up your cash and got a $100 receivable from your friend. The receivable is an asset to you, just as the cash was. But the receivable is a slightly different asset: It's very close to cash, but it's not cash yet. In this situation, you are the creditor and your friend is the debtor.

This chapter focuses on accounting for receivables by the seller (the creditor).

Receivables: An Introduction

Types of Receivables

Receivables are monetary claims against businesses and individuals. The two major types of receivables are accounts receivable and notes receivable. A business's *accounts receivable* are the amounts to be collected from customers. Accounts receivable, which are *current assets*, are also called *trade receivables*.

Accounts Receivable in the general ledger serves as a *control account* because it summarizes the total of the receivables from all customers. As we saw in Chapter 7, companies also keep a *subsidiary ledger* of the receivable from each customer ←. This is illustrated on the following page.

Notes receivable are more formal than accounts receivable. The debtor promises in writing to pay the creditor a definite sum at a future date—the *maturity* date. A written document known as a *promissory note* serves as the evidence. Notes receivable due within one year or less are *current assets*. Notes due beyond one year are *long-term*. Some notes receivable are collected in periodic installments. The portion due within one year is a current asset, and the remainder is a long-term asset. **General Motors** may hold a $6,000 note receivable from you, but only the $2,000 you owe this year is a current asset to GM. The remaining $4,000 is a long-term receivable.

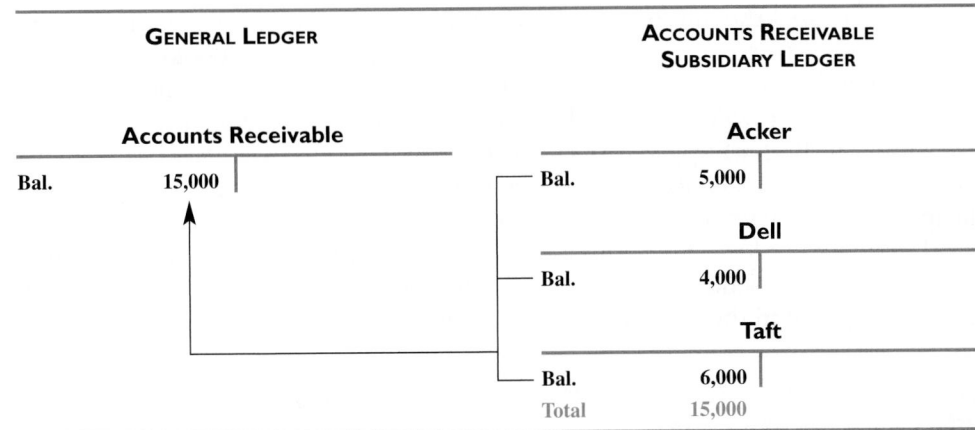

GENERAL LEDGER	ACCOUNTS RECEIVABLE SUBSIDIARY LEDGER

Other receivables is a miscellaneous category that may include loans to employees. Usually, these are long-term receivables, but they are current assets if due within one year or less. Long-term receivables are often reported as shown in Exhibit 9-1. Receivables are highlighted for emphasis.

Exhibit 9-1

Assets, with Receivables Highlighted

Example Company
Assets
Date

Assets		
Current:		
Cash		$X,XXX
Accounts receivable	$X,XXX	
Less: Allowance for		
uncollectible accounts	(XXX)	X,XXX
Notes receivable, short-term		X,XXX
Inventories		X,XXX
Prepaid expenses		X,XXX
Total		X,XXX
Investments and long-term receivables:		
Investments..............................		X,XXX
Notes receivable, long-term		X,XXX
Other receivables		X,XXX
Total		X,XXX
Plant assets:		
Property, plant, and equipment		X,XXX
Total assets		$X,XXX

Establishing Internal Control over Collection of Receivables

 Design internal controls for receivables

Businesses that sell on credit receive most cash receipts by mail. Internal control over collections is very important. → A critical element of internal control is the separation of cash-handling and cash-accounting duties. Consider the following case.

 We introduced internal controls in Chapter 8.

Butler Supply Co. is family-owned and takes pride in the loyalty of its workers. Most company employees have been with the Butlers for years. The company makes 90% of its sales on account.

The office staff consists of a bookkeeper and a supervisor. The bookkeeper maintains the accounts receivable subsidiary ledger. He also makes the daily bank deposit. The supervisor prepares monthly financial statements and special reports.

✔ Starter 9-1

Can you spot the internal control weakness here? The bookkeeper has access to the accounts receivable and also has custody of the cash. The bookkeeper could steal a customer check and write off the customer's account as uncollectible.[1] Unless someone reviews the bookkeeper's work, the theft may go undetected.

How can Butler Supply correct this control weakness? *The bookkeeper should not be allowed to handle cash.* Only the remittance advices should go to the bookkeeper to indicate which customer accounts to credit.

We examined the lock-box system in detail in Chapter 8, p. 332.

Using a bank lock box could achieve the same result. In a lock-box system, customers would send cash directly to Butler Supply's bank, which would then deposit the cash in the company's bank account. ←

Managing the Collection of Receivables: The Credit Department

Most companies have a credit department to evaluate customers. The extension of credit requires a balancing act. The company doesn't want to lose sales to good customers, but it also wants to avoid uncollectible receivables.

✔ Starter 9-2

For good internal control over cash collections, the credit department should have no access to cash. For example, if a credit employee handles cash, he might pocket money received from a customer. He could then label the customer's account as uncollectible, and the company would write off the account receivable, as discussed in the next section. The company would stop billing that customer, and the employee would have covered his theft. For this reason, a sharp separation of duties is important.

The Decision Guidelines feature identifies the main issues in controlling and managing receivables. These guidelines serve as a framework for the remainder of the chapter.

Decision Guidelines

CONTROLLING, MANAGING, AND ACCOUNTING FOR RECEIVABLES

Butler Supply, Oracle Corporation, and all other companies that sell on credit face the same accounting challenges. The main issues in *controlling* and *managing* receivables, plus a plan of action, are as follows:

Issue	Action
Extend credit only to customers most likely to pay.	Run a credit check on prospective customers.
Separate cash-handing, credit, and accounting duties to keep employees from stealing cash collected from customers.	Design the internal control system to separate duties.
Pursue collection from customers to maximize cash flow.	Keep a close eye on collections from customers.

The main issues in *accounting* for receivables, and the related plan of action, are as follows:

Issue	Action
Report receivables at their *net realizable value*, the amount we expect to collect.	Estimate the amount of uncollectible receivables.
	The balance sheet reports receivables at net realizable value (accounts receivable minus the allowance for uncollectibles).
Report the expense associated with failure to collect receivables. This expense is called uncollectible-account expense.	The income statement reports the expense of failing to collect from customers.

---

[1]The bookkeeper would need to forge the endorsement on the check and deposit it in a bank account he controls.

Accounting for Uncollectibles (Bad Debts)

Selling on credit creates both a benefit and a cost.

- *The benefit:* The business increases revenues and profits by making sales to a wide range of customers.

- *The cost:* The company will be unable to collect from some customers, and that creates an expense. The expense is called **uncollectible-account expense**, **doubtful-account expense**, or **bad-debt expense**.

Uncollectible-account expense varies from company to company. The older the receivable, the less valuable it is because of the decreasing likelihood of collection. For Oracle Corporation, each $1 of accounts receivable is worth 86 cents. Uncollectible-account expense is an operating expense in the same way as salary expense and utilities expense. To account for uncollectible receivables, accountants use the allowance method or, in certain limited cases, the direct write-off method.

The Allowance Method

Most companies use the **allowance method** to measure bad debts. They record uncollectible-account expense in the same period in which sales are made on account. The business doesn't wait to see which customers will not pay. Instead, it records an expense on the basis of estimates developed from past experience.

The business records Uncollectible-Account Expense for the estimated amount and sets up **Allowance for Uncollectible Accounts** (or **Allowance for Doubtful Accounts**), a contra account to Accounts Receivable. This allowance account shows the amount of receivables the business expects *not* to collect.

Subtracting the allowance from Accounts Receivable yields the net amount that the company does expect to collect. Here are Oracle Corporation's figures, adapted and in millions:

Balance sheet (partial):	
Accounts receivable	$2,800
Less: Allowance for uncollectible accounts	(400)
Accounts receivable, net.	$2,400

Customers owe Oracle $2,800 million, of which Oracle expects to collect $2,400 million. Oracle estimates it will not collect $400 million of these accounts receivable.

Another way to report receivables follows (in millions):

Accounts receivable, net of allowance for uncollectible accounts of $400 . .	$2,400

The income statement can report Uncollectible-Account Expense (Doubtful-Account Expense) among the operating expenses, as follows (assumed figures in millions):

Income statement (partial):	
Expenses:	
Uncollectible-account expense	$5,000

Estimating Uncollectibles

How are bad debts estimated? Companies use their past experience. There are two basic methods to estimate uncollectibles:

- Percent-of-sales
- Aging-of-accounts

Both approaches work with the allowance method.

Student Resource CD

direct write-off, uncollectibles

Uncollectible-Account Expense
Cost to the seller of extending credit. Arises from the failure to collect from credit customers. Also called **doubtful-account expense**, or **bad-debt expense**.

Allowance Method
A method of recording collection losses on the basis of estimates, instead of waiting to see which customers the company will not collect from.

Allowance for Uncollectible Accounts
A contra account, related to accounts receivable, that holds the estimated amount of collection losses. Also called **Allowance for Doubtful Accounts**.

2 Use the allowance method to account for uncollectibles by the percent-of-sales and aging-of-accounts methods

Percent-of-Sales Method
A method of estimating uncollectible receivables that calculates uncollectible-account expense. Also called the **income-statement approach**.

PERCENT-OF-SALES METHOD The **percent-of-sales method** computes uncollectible-account expense as a percentage of net credit sales. This method is also called the **income-statement approach** because it focuses on the amount of expense. Uncollectible-account expense is recorded as an adjusting entry at the end of the period. Assume it is December 31, 20X6, and the accounts have these balances *before the year-end adjustments*:

Accounts Receivable	Allowance for Uncollectible Accounts
120,000	500

Prior to any adjustments, net receivables total $119,500 ($120,000 – $500). This is more than the business expects to collect from customers. Based on prior experience, the credit department estimates that uncollectible-account expense is 2% of net credit sales, which were $500,000 for 20X6. The adjusting entry to record uncollectible-account expense for 20X6 and to update the allowance is

```
20X6
Dec. 31  Uncollectible-Account Expense
           ($500,000 × 0.02) ....................  10,000
              Allowance for Uncollectible
              Accounts......................              10,000
           Recorded expense for the year.
```

The accounting equation shows that the transaction to record the expense decreases the business's assets by the amount of the expense:

ASSETS	=	LIABILITIES	+	OWNER'S EQUITY	–	EXPENSES
–10,000	=	0			–	10,000

Now the accounts are ready for reporting in the 20X6 financial statements.

✔ Starter 9-3

Accounts Receivable	Allowance for Uncollectible Accounts		
120,000			500
	Adj.		10,000
	End. Bal.		10,500

Customers owe the business $120,000, and now the allowance for uncollectible accounts is realistic. The balance sheet will report accounts receivable at the net amount of $109,500 ($120,000 – $10,500). The income statement will report 20X6's uncollectible-account expense of $10,000, along with the other operating expenses for the period.

AGING-OF-ACCOUNTS The second popular approach for estimating uncollectibles is the **aging-of-accounts method**. This method is also called the **balance-sheet approach** because it focuses on accounts receivable. In the aging approach, individual accounts receivable are grouped according to how long they have been receivable from the customer. The computer sorts customer accounts by their age. For example, Schmidt Builders Supply groups its accounts receivable into 30-day periods, as Exhibit 9-2 shows.

Aging-of-Accounts Method
A way to estimate bad debts by analyzing individual accounts receivable according to the length of time they have been receivable from the customer. Also called the **balance-sheet approach**.

Schmidt's accounts receivable total of $143,000 is shown at the far right of the exhibit. Of this amount, the aging schedule estimates that Schmidt will *not* collect $3,800. The following allowance for uncollectible accounts is not up-to-date *before the year-end adjustment*:

Accounts Receivable	Allowance for Uncollectible Accounts
143,000	1,100

Exhibit 9-2 Aging the Accounts Receivable of Schmidt Builders Supply

Customer Name	1–30 Days	31–60 Days	61–90 Days	Over 90 Days	Total Balance
T-Bar-M Co.	$ 20,000				$ 20,000
Chicago Pneumatic Parts	10,000				10,000
Sarasota Pipe Corp.		$13,000	$10,000		23,000
Oneida, Inc.			3,000	$1,000	4,000
Other accounts	70,000	12,000	2,000	2,000	86,000
Totals	$100,000	$25,000	$15,000	$3,000	143,000
Estimated percentage uncollectible	× 0.1%	× 1%	× 5%	× 90%	
Allowance for Uncollectible Accounts balance	$ 100 +	$ 250 +	$ 750 +	$2,700 =	$ 3,800

The aging method brings the balance of the allowance account to the needed amount as determined by the aging schedule. In Exhibit 9-2, see the lower-right corner for the final result—a needed credit balance of $3,800.

To update the allowance, Schmidt makes this adjusting entry:

```
20X6
Dec. 31   Uncollectible-Account Expense........ 2,700
              Allowance for Uncollectible Accounts
              ($3,800 – $1,100)................          2,700
          Recorded expense for the year.
```

The expense decreases total assets and owner's equity. The accounting equation for the expense is

ASSETS	=	LIABILITIES	+	OWNER'S EQUITY	−	EXPENSES
−2,700	=	0			−	2,700

Now the balance sheet can report receivables at the amount that Schmidt expects to collect from customers, $139,200 ($143,000 – $3,800), as follows:

Accounts Receivable		Allowance for Uncollectible Accounts	
143,000			1,100
		Adj.	2,700
		End. bal.	3,800

Net accounts receivable, 139,200

The *net* amount of accounts receivable—$139,200—is called *net realizable value* because it is the amount Schmidt expects to realize (collect in cash).

USING PERCENT-OF-SALES AND AGING TOGETHER In practice, companies use the percent-of-sales and the aging-of-accounts methods together.

- For *interim statements* (monthly or quarterly), companies use the percent-of-sales method because it is easier. This method focuses on the amount of uncollectible-account *expense*.
- At the end of the year, companies use the aging method to ensure that Accounts Receivable is reported at *net realizable value*. The aging method focuses on the amount of the receivables—the *asset*—that is uncollectible.
- Using the two methods together provides good measures of both the expense and the asset. Exhibit 9-3 summarizes and compares the two methods.

Exhibit 9-3

Comparing the Percent-of-Sales and Aging Methods

✔ Starter 9-4

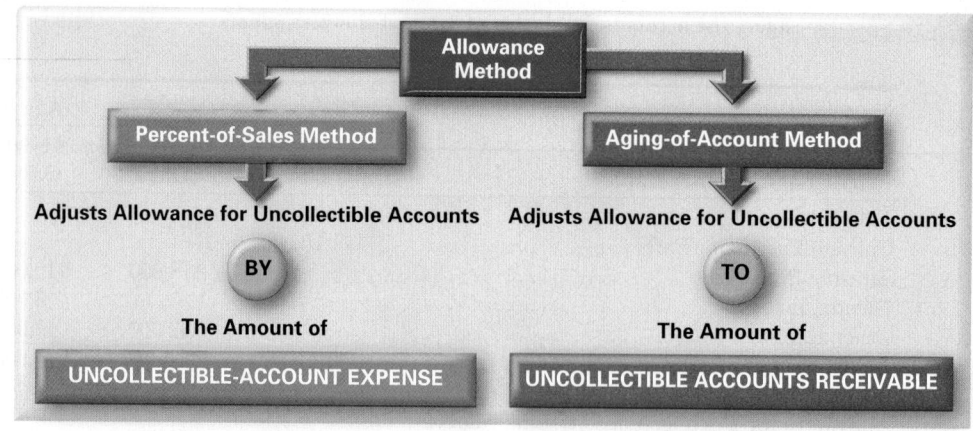

Writing Off Uncollectible Accounts

Early in 20X7, Schmidt Builders Supply collects on most of its $143,000 accounts receivable and records the cash receipts as follows (amount assumed):

```
20X7
Jan.–Mar.   Cash ....................   123,000
                Accounts Receivable ....            123,000
            Collected on account.
```

Suppose that, after repeated attempts to collect, Schmidt's credit department determines that Schmidt cannot collect a total of $1,200 from customers Andrews ($900) and Jones ($300). Schmidt then writes off the receivables from these delinquent customers:

```
20X7
Mar. 31   Allowance for Uncollectible Accounts .... 1,200
              Accounts Receivable—Andrews ....           900
              Accounts Receivable—Jones........           300
          Wrote off uncollectible accounts.
```

The write-off of uncollectible receivables has no impact on total assets, liabilities, or equity.

✔ Starter 9-5

✔ Starter 9-6

ASSETS	=	LIABILITIES	+	OWNER'S EQUITY
+1,200				
−1,200	=	0	+	0

3 Use the direct write-off method to account for uncollectibles

Direct Write-Off Method
A method of accounting for uncollectible receivables, in which the company waits until the credit department decides that a customer's account receivable is uncollectible, and then debits Uncollectible-Account Expense and credits the customer's Account Receivable.

> If the write-off of uncollectible accounts affects no expense or *net* receivables, then why write off the uncollectible account of customer Jones?
>
> *Answer:* The business has decided that it will never collect from Jones. Therefore, eliminate Jones's account from the receivable records. That alerts the credit department not to waste time pursuing collection from Jones.

The Direct Write-Off Method

There is another way to account for uncollectible receivables that is not acceptable for most companies. Under the **direct write-off method**, Schmidt Builders would wait until it decides that it will never collect from the customer. Then Schmidt would write off the customer's account receivable by debiting

Uncollectible-Account Expense and crediting the customer's Account Receivable, as follows (using assumed data):

```
20X7
Jan. 2   Uncollectible-Account Expense . . . . . . . .   2,000
                Accounts Receivable—Smith . . . .              2,000
         Wrote off a bad account.
```

The direct write-off method is defective for two reasons:

1. It does not set up an allowance for uncollectibles. As a result, the direct write-off method always reports the receivables at their full amount. Assets are overstated on the balance sheet because the business does not expect to collect the full amount.

2. It does not match uncollectible-account expense against revenue very well. In this example, Schmidt made the sale to Smith in 20X6 and should have recorded the uncollectible-account expense during 20X6. That's the only way to measure net income properly. By recording the uncollectible-account expense in 20X7, Schmidt overstates net income in 20X6 and understates net income in 20X7.

✔ **Starter 9-7**

Don't confuse the direct write-off method with the allowance method. The two methods of accounting for uncollectible receivables are opposites. A company uses one method or the other. The direct write-off method is acceptable only when the amount of uncollectible receivables is very low. It works well for retailers such as **Wal-Mart, Lands' End**, and **Gap**, because those companies carry almost no receivables.

Recovery of Accounts Previously Written Off

When an account receivable is written off as uncollectible, the receivable does not die: The customer still owes the money. However, the company stops pursuing collection and writes off the account as uncollectible.

Some companies turn delinquent receivables over to an attorney and recover some of the cash. This is called *recovery of a bad account*. Let's see how to record the recovery of an account that we wrote off earlier. Recall that on March 31, 20X7, Schmidt Builders Supply wrote off the $900 receivable from customer Andrews (see page 368). It is now January 4, 20X8, and Schmidt unexpectedly receives $900 from Andrews. To account for this recovery, Schmidt makes two journal entries to (1) reverse the earlier write-off and (2) record the cash collection, as follows:

```
(1) Accounts Receivable—Andrews . . . . . . . . . . . . . .   900
          Allowance for Uncollectible Accounts . . . . . .        900
        Reinstated Andrews' account receivable.

(2) Cash . . . . . . . . . . . . . . . . . . . . . . . . . . . . . . . . . . .   900
          Accounts Receivable—Andrews . . . . . . . . .            900
        Collected on account.
```

Credit-Card, Bankcard, and Debit-Card Sales

Credit-Card Sales

Credit-card sales are common in both traditional and online retailing. Customers present credit cards like **American Express** and **Discover** to pay for purchases. The credit-card company then pays the seller and bills the customer, who pays the credit-card company.

Customer pays $100

Retailer collects $97

Credit-card company collects $3

Credit cards offer customers the convenience of buying without having to pay cash immediately. An American Express customer receives a monthly statement from American Express, detailing each transaction. The customer can write one check to cover the entire month's purchases.

Retailers also benefit from credit-card sales. They do not have to check a customer's credit rating. The credit-card company has already done so. Retailers do not have to keep accounts receivable records, and they do not have to collect cash from customers. These benefits do not come free. The seller receives less than 100% of the face value of the sale. The credit-card company takes a fee of 1 to 5% on the sale. Suppose you and your family have lunch at a Red Lobster restaurant. You pay the bill—$100—with a Discover card. Red Lobster's entry to record the $100 sale, subject to the credit-card company's 3% discount, is

Accounts Receivable—Discover	97	
Credit-Card Discount Expense	3	
Sales Revenue		100
Recorded credit-card sales.		

On collection of the cash, Red Lobster records the following:

Cash	97	
Accounts Receivable—Discover		97
Collected from Discover.		

Bankcard Sales

Most banks issue their own cards, known as *bankcards*, which operate much like credit cards. VISA and MasterCard are the two main bankcards. When an Exxon station makes a sale and takes a VISA card, the station receives cash at the point of sale. The cash received is less than the full amount of the sale because the bank deducts its fee. Suppose the Exxon station sells $150 of fuel to a family vacationing in its motor home. The station takes a VISA card, and the bank that issued the card charges a 2% fee. The Exxon station records the bankcard sale as follows:

Cash	147	
Bankcard Discount Expense ($150 × 0.02)	3	
Sales Revenue		150
Recorded a bankcard sale.		

✔ Starter 9-8

Debit-Card Sales

Debit cards are fundamentally different from credit cards and bankcards. Using a debit card to buy groceries is like paying with cash, except that you don't have to carry cash or write a check.

At Target (or Kroger or Wal-Mart), the buyer "swipes" the card through a special terminal, and the buyer's bank balance is automatically decreased. **Target's** Cash account is increased immediately—without having to deposit a check and wonder if it will clear the bank. With a debit card there is no third party, such as VISA or MasterCard, so there is no Credit-Card Discount Expense.

Merchant Beware: Credit Cards Boom with Online Sales . . . But So Does Fraud

About 97% of all Web payments are made with credit cards. At the end of every month, e-tailers send up to 2.5% of their revenues to credit-card companies. **VISA**, **MasterCard**, **American Express**, and their cousins earn millions in transaction fees.

Who takes the hit when customers deny credit-card charges they actually made (*chargebacks*) or when criminals make purchases with stolen card numbers (*identity theft*)? The online merchants.

The anonymity of online transactions paves the way for both chargebacks and identity theft. It's harder to cheat in a face-to-face transaction. Industry analyst Gartner, Inc., reports that fraud costs online retailers more than $700 million in one year. Gartner's report also notes that credit-card fraud causes e-tailers to lose about 1% of their sales revenue. This is 19 times higher than the losses at traditional stores. Online theft puts a big dent in the bottom line and can even cause companies to go bankrupt. Case in point: **Flooz.com** sold online currency for electronic gift certificates. The company filed for bankruptcy after it was hit by $300,000 in credit-card fraud.

Source: Marcia Savage, "Online Fraud: New Twist on Old Issue," *Computer Reseller News*, March 27, 2000, p. 28. Leslie Beyer, "The Internet Revolution," *Credit Card Management*, November 1999, Mercedes M. Caroona, "VISA Teams Up with E-Tailers to Acquire Online Dominance," *Advertising Age*, December 6, 1999, p. 4. Patricia A. Murphy, "The Murky World of 'Net Chargebacks,'" *Credit Card Management*, February 2000, pp. 54–60. Amy Winn, "Business Online," *Atlanta Journal-Constitution*, March 5, 2002, p. D2. Sharon Gaudin, "Online Fraud Growing in Scale, Sophistication," *internetnews.com*, December 5, 2002.

MID-CHAPTER *Summary Problem*

CPC International, Inc., produces Skippy peanut butter, Hellmann's mayonnaise, and Mazola corn oil. Suppose CPC's balance sheet at December 31, 20X5, reported the following:

	Millions
Notes and accounts receivable [total]	$549.9
Allowance for uncollectible accounts	(12.5)

Required

1. How much of the December 31, 20X5, balance of the receivable did CPC expect to collect? Stated differently, what was the net realizable value of these receivables?
2. Journalize, without explanations, 20X6 entries for CPC International, assuming:
   a. Total estimated Uncollectible-Account Expense was $19.2 million for the first three quarters of the year, based on the percent-of-sales method.
   b. Write-offs of accounts receivable totaled $23.6 million.
   c. December 31, 20X6, aging of receivables, which indicates that $15.3 million of the total receivables of $582.7 million is uncollectible. Post all three entries to Allowance for Uncollectible Accounts.
3. Show how CPC International's receivables and related allowance will appear on the December 31, 20X6, balance sheet.
      What is the net realizable value of receivables at December 31, 20X6? How much is uncollectible-account expense for 20X6?

Solution

Requirement 1

	(In millions)
Net realizable value of receivables ($549.9 – $12.5)	$537.4

Requirement 2

	(In millions)
(a) Uncollectible-Account Expense.	19.2
Allowance for Uncollectible Accounts.	19.2
(b) Allowance for Uncollectible Accounts	23.6
Accounts Receivable.	23.6
(c) Uncollectible-Account Expense ($15.3 – $8.1).	7.2
Allowance for Uncollectible Accounts.	7.2

Allowance for Uncollectible Accounts

20X6 Write-offs	23.6	Dec. 31, 20X5 Bal.	12.5
		20X6 Expense	19.2
		Bal. before adj.	8.1
		Dec. 31, 20X6 Adj.	7.2
		Dec. 31, 20X6 Bal.	15.3

Requirement 3

	(In millions)
Notes and accounts receivable	$582.7
Less: Allowance for uncollectible accounts.	(15.3)
Notes and accounts receivable, net.	$567.4
Uncollectible-account expense for 20X6 ($19.2 + $7.2)	$26.4

Student ResourceCD

notes receivable

Notes Receivable: An Overview

Notes receivable are more formal than accounts receivable. The debtor signs a promissory note as evidence of the debt. Before launching into the accounting, let's define the special terms used for notes receivable.

- **Promissory note:** A written promise to pay a specified amount of money at a particular future date.
- **Maker of the note (debtor):** The entity that signs the note and promises to pay the required amount; the maker of the note is the *debtor*.
- **Payee of the note (creditor):** The entity to whom the maker promises future payment; the payee of the note is the *creditor*.
- **Principal amount, or principal:** The amount loaned out by the payee and borrowed by the maker of the note.
- **Interest:** The revenue to the payee for loaning money; the expense to the debtor.
- **Interest period:** The period of time during which interest is computed. It extends from the original date of the note to the maturity date. Also called **note term**, or simply **time**.

- **Interest rate:** The percentage rate of interest specified by the note. Interest rates are almost always stated for a period of one year. A 9% note means that the amount of interest for *one year* is 9% of the note's principal amount.
- **Maturity date:** The date when final payment of the note is due. Also called the **due date**.
- **Maturity value:** The sum of the principal plus interest due at maturity.

Exhibit 9-4 illustrates a promissory note. Study it carefully.

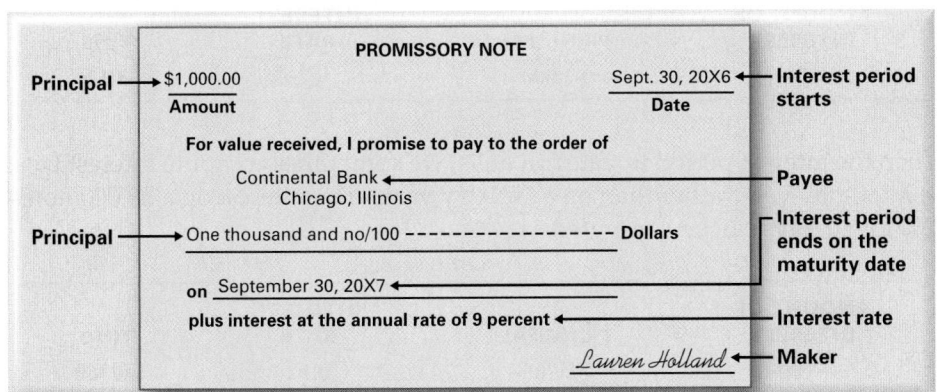

A Promissory Note

Identifying Maturity Date

Some notes specify the maturity date, as shown in Exhibit 9-4. Other notes state the period of the note in days or months. When the period is given in months, the note's maturity date falls on the same day of the month as the date the note was issued. A six-month note dated February 16 matures on August 16.

When the period is given in days, the maturity date is determined by counting the days from the date of issue. A 120-day note dated September 14, 20X6, matures on January 12, 20X7, as shown here:

Month	Number of Days	Cumulative Total
Sep. 20X6	30 – 14 = 16	16
Oct. 20X6	31	47
Nov. 20X6	30	77
Dec. 20X6	31	108
Jan. 20X7	12	120

In counting the days remaining for a note, remember to count the maturity date and to omit the date the note was issued.

Computing Interest on a Note

The formula for computing the interest on a note is

AMOUNT OF INTEREST	=	PRINCIPAL	×	INTEREST RATE	×	TIME

Using the data in Exhibit 9-4, Continental Bank computes interest revenue for one year as

AMOUNT OF INTEREST	=	PRINCIPAL	×	INTEREST RATE	×	TIME
$90		$1,000		0.09		1 yr

The maturity value of the note is $1,090 ($1,000 principal + $90 interest). The time element is 1 because the note's term is 1 year.

When the term of a note is stated in months, we compute the interest based on the 12-month year. Interest on a $2,000 note at 15% for three months is computed as

AMOUNT OF INTEREST	=	PRINCIPAL	×	INTEREST RATE	×	TIME
$75		$2,000		0.15		3/12

When the interest period is stated in days, we sometimes compute interest based on a 360-day year rather than on a 365-day year.[2] The interest on a $5,000 note at 12% for 60 days can be computed as

✔ **Starter 9-9**

AMOUNT OF INTEREST	=	PRINCIPAL	×	INTEREST RATE	×	TIME
$100		$5,000		0.12		60/360

Keep in mind that interest rates are stated as an annual rate. Therefore, the time in the interest formula should also be expressed in terms of a year.

Practice calculating interest on
1. A $30,000, 12 1/2%, 180-day note
2. An $8,000, 9%, 6-month note

Answers:
1. ($30,000 × 0.125 × 180/360) = $1,875   2. ($8,000 × 0.09 × 6/12) = $360

☐ Receivables: An Introduction
☐ Uncollectibles (Bad Debts)
☐ Card (Credit, Bank, Debit) Sales
☐ Notes Receivable
■ **Accounting for Notes Receivable**
☐ Decision Making Ratios
☐ Appendix: Discounting Notes Receivable

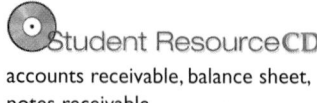

accounts receivable, balance sheet, notes receivable

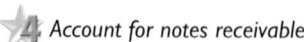

Account for notes receivable

✔ **Starter 9-10**

Accounting for Notes Receivable

Recording Notes Receivable

Consider the loan agreement shown in Exhibit 9-4. After Lauren Holland signs the note, Continental Bank gives her $1,000 cash. At maturity, Holland pays the bank $1,090 ($1,000 principal plus $90 interest). The bank's entries are

Sep. 30, 20X6	Note Receivable—L. Holland 1,000	
	Cash	1,000
	Loaned out money.	
Sep. 30, 20X7	Cash 1,090	
	Note Receivable—L. Holland . . .	1,000
	Interest Revenue ($1,000 × 0.09 × 1)	90
	Collected note receivable.	

Some companies sell merchandise in exchange for notes receivable. Suppose that on October 20, 20X8, **General Electric** sells household appliances for $15,000

---
[2]A 360-day year eliminates some rounding, which is consistent with our use of whole-dollar amounts throughout this book.

to Dorman Builders. Dorman signs a 90-day promissory note at 10% annual interest. General Electric's entries to record the sale and collection from Dorman are

Oct. 20, 20X8	Note Receivable—		
	Dorman Builders	15,000	
	Sales Revenue		15,000
	Made a sale.		
Jan. 18, 20X9	Cash	15,375	
	Note Receivable—		
	Dorman Builders		15,000
	Interest Revenue		
	($15,000 \times 0.10 \times 90/360$)		375
	Collected note receivable.		

A company may accept a note receivable from a trade customer who fails to pay an account receivable. The customer signs a promissory note—that is, becomes the **maker of the note**—and gives it to the creditor, who becomes the **payee**. Suppose Sports Club cannot pay Hoffman Supply. Hoffman may accept a one-year, $2,400 note receivable, with 9% interest, from Sports Club on October 1, 20X8. Hoffman's entry is

Maker of a Note
The person or business that signs the note and promises to pay the amount required by the note agreement; the debtor.

Payee of a Note
The person or business to whom the maker of a note promises future payment; the creditor.

Oct. 1, 20X8	Note Receivable—Sports Club ...	2,400	
	Accounts Receivable—		
	Sports Club................		2,400
	Received a note on account.		

Accruing Interest Revenue

A note receivable may be outstanding at the end of an accounting period. The interest revenue earned on the note up to year-end is part of that year's earnings. Recall that interest revenue is earned over time, not just when cash is received. →

← We saw in Chapter 3 on p. 104 that accrued revenue creates an asset because the revenue has been earned but not received.

Let's continue with the Hoffman Supply note receivable from Sports Club. Hoffman Supply's accounting period ends December 31. How much of the total interest revenue does Hoffman earn in 20X8? How much does it earn in 20X9?

Hoffman will earn three months' interest in 20X8—for October, November, and December. In 20X9, Hoffman will earn nine months' interest—for January through September. At December 31, 20X8, Hoffman will make the following adjusting entry to accrue interest revenue:

Dec. 31, 20X8	Interest Receivable		
	($2,400 \times 0.09 \times 3/12$)	54	
	Interest Revenue.................		54
	Accrued interest revenue.		

Then, on the maturity date, Hoffman collects the principal and interest as follows:

Sep. 30, 20X9	Cash [$2,400 + ($2,400 \times 0.09$)] ...	2,616	
	Note Receivable—Sports Club ..		2,400
	Interest Receivable		
	($2,400 \times 0.09 \times 3/12$)		54
	Interest Revenue		
	($2,400 \times 0.09 \times 9/12$)		162
	Collected note receivable plus interest.		

The entries for accrued interest at December 31, 20X8, and for collection in 20X9 assign the correct amount of interest to each year.

✔ **Starter 9-11**

A company holding a note may need cash before the note matures. A procedure for selling the note, called discounting a note receivable, appears in the chapter appendix.

Dishonored Notes Receivable

Dishonor of a Note
Failure of a note's maker to pay a note receivable at maturity. Also called **default on a note**.

If the maker of a note does not pay at maturity, the maker **dishonors**, or **defaults on**, the note. Because the term of the note has expired, the note agreement is no longer in force. But the payee still has a claim against the debtor. In this case, the payee will transfer the note receivable amount to Accounts Receivable. Suppose Rubinstein Jewelers has a 6-month, 10% note receivable for $1,200 from Mark Adair, and on the February 3 maturity date, Adair defaulted. Rubinstein Jewelers will record the default as follows:

Feb. 3	Accounts Receivable—M. Adair	1,260	
	Note Receivable—M. Adair.		1,200
	Interest Revenue ($1,200 × 0.10 × 6/12) . . .		60
	Recorded a dishonored note receivable.		

Rubinstein will then pursue collection from Adair as an account receivable.

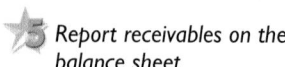 *Report receivables on the balance sheet*

Reporting Receivables on the Balance Sheet

Let's look at how some well-known companies report their receivables on the balance sheet. Terminology may vary. Intel Corporation, maker of the Pentium® processor, reports accounts receivable under Current Assets (in millions):

Accounts receivable, net of allowance for doubtful accounts of $67 . . .	$3,700

The net realizable value of Intel's accounts receivable is $3,700 million. To compute Intel's total amount receivable, add the allowance to the net receivable: $67 + $3,700 = $3,767. Customers actually owe Intel $3,767 million, but Intel expects to collect only $3,700 million.

General Electric Company reports a single amount—net realizable value—for receivables in the balance sheet and uses an explanatory note to give the details (adapted, with amounts in millions):

 **Starter 9-12**

Current receivables (note 10)	$8,740
Note 10: Current Receivables.	$9,060
Less: Allowance for losses.	(320)
	$8,740

1. How much did customers owe **General Electric (GE)**, as adapted?
2. How much did GE expect to collect?
3. How much did GE expect *not* to collect?

Answers:

  1. $9,060 million   2. $8,740 million   3. $320 million

Computers and Accounts Receivable

Accounting for receivables by a large company like Oracle Corporation or M&M Mars requires thousands of postings for credit sales and cash collections. Manual accounting methods cannot keep up.

As we saw in Chapter 7, Accounts Receivable can be computerized. The order entry, shipping, and billing departments at M&M Mars work together to meet customer demand and ensure that Mars collects on its receivables, as shown in Exhibit 9-5.

Exhibit 9-5

The Integration of Order Entry, Shipping, and Billing

Order entry — Orders come in to M&M Mars

Shipping — M&M Mars ships 1,000 cases of Snickers to Wal-Mart

Billing — M&M Mars sends the bill (invoice) to Wal-Mart

Using Accounting Information for Decision Making

The balance sheet lists assets in order of liquidity (closeness to cash):

- Cash comes first because it is the liquid asset.
- Short-term investments come next because they are almost as liquid as cash.
- Current receivables are less liquid than short-term investments because the company must collect the receivables.
- Merchandise inventory is less liquid than receivables because the goods must first be sold.

The balance sheet of Oracle Corporation, as adapted, provides an example in Exhibit 9-6. Focus on the current assets at May 31, 2001. Oracle reports no inventory because the company earns revenue by providing services, not by selling products.

☐ Receivables: An Introduction
☐ Uncollectibles (Bad Debts)
☐ Card (Credit, Bank, Debit) Sales
☐ Notes Receivable
☐ Accounting for Notes Receivable
■ Decision Making Ratios
☐ Appendix: Discounting Notes Receivable

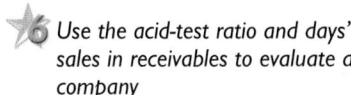

Student ResourceCD
acid-test ratio, balance sheet, days' sales, quick ratio

6 *Use the acid-test ratio and days' sales in receivables to evaluate a company*

Exhibit 9-6

Oracle Corporation Balance Sheet

Oracle Corporation Balance Sheet (Partial, adapted) May 31, 2001 and May 31, 2000	(In millions) May 31,	
Assets	2001	2000
Current assets:		
Cash and cash equivalents	$4,400	$ 7,400
Short-term investments	1,400	300
Trade receivables net of allowance for doubtful accounts of $400 in 2001 and $300 in 2000	2,400	2,500
Prepaid expenses and other current assets	800	700
Total current assets	$9,000	$10,900
Liabilities		
Current liabilities:		
Total current liabilities	$3,900	$5,900

Oracle's balance-sheet data become more useful by showing the relationships among assets, liabilities, and revenues. Let's examine two important ratios.

Acid-Test (or Quick) Ratio

In Chapter 4, we discussed the current ratio, which measures ability to pay current liabilities with current assets. A more stringent measure of ability to pay current liabilities is the **acid-test** (or **quick) ratio**. The acid-test ratio reveals whether the entity can pay all its current liabilities if they come due immediately:

**FOR ORACLE CORPORATION (EXHIBIT 9-6)
(DOLLAR AMOUNTS IN MILLIONS)**

$$\text{Acid-test ratio} = \frac{\text{Cash} + \begin{array}{c}\text{Short-term}\\\text{investments}\end{array} + \begin{array}{c}\text{Net current}\\\text{receivables}\end{array}}{\text{Total current liabilities}} \qquad \frac{\$4,400 + \$1,400 + \$2,400}{\$3,900} = 2.10$$

Acid-Test Ratio
Ratio of the sum of cash plus short-term investments plus net current receivables, to total current liabilities. Tells whether the entity could pay all its current liabilities if they came due immediately. Also called the **quick ratio**.

The higher the acid-test ratio, the more able the business is to pay its current liabilities. Oracle's acid-test ratio of 2.10 means that Oracle has $2.10 of quick assets to pay each $1 of current liabilities. This is an extremely strong position.

What is an acceptable acid-test ratio? That depends on the industry. **Wal-Mart** operates smoothly with an acid-test ratio of less than 0.20. Several things make this possible: Wal-Mart collects cash rapidly and has almost no receivables. The acid-test ratios for most department stores cluster about 0.80, while travel agencies average 1.10. In general, an acid-test ratio of 1.00 is considered safe.

> Use the data in Exhibit 9-6 to compute **Oracle Corporation's** current ratio at May 31, 2001. Then compare Oracle's current ratio and acid-test ratio. Why is the current ratio higher?
>
> *Answer:*
> $$\text{Current ratio} = \frac{\text{Total current assets}}{\text{Total current liabilities}} = \frac{\$9,000}{\$3,900} = 2.31$$
> $$\text{Acid-test ratio} = \qquad\qquad 2.10$$
> The current ratio is higher because it includes all current assets and not just cash, short-term investments, and receivables.

Days' Sales in Receivables

Days' Sales in Receivables
Ratio of average net accounts receivable to one day's sales. Tells how many days' sales it takes to collect the average level of receivables. Also called the **collection period**.

After making a credit sale, the next step is to collect the receivable. **Days' sales in receivables**, also called the **collection period**, indicates how many days it takes to collect the average level of receivables. The shorter the collection period, the more quickly the organization can use its cash. The longer the collection period, the less cash is available for operations. Days' sales in receivables can be computed in two steps, as follows:[3]

FOR ORACLE CORPORATION (EXHIBIT 9-6)
(DOLLAR AMOUNTS IN MILLIONS)

1. $$\text{One day's sales} = \frac{\begin{array}{c}\text{Net sales}\\\text{(or Total revenues)}\end{array}}{365 \text{ days}} = \qquad \frac{\$10,800^*}{365} = \$29.6 \text{ per day}$$

2. $$\text{Days' sales in average accounts receivable} = \frac{\text{Average net accounts receivable}}{\text{One day's sales}} = \frac{\left(\begin{array}{c}\text{Beginning net} \\ \text{receivables}\end{array} + \begin{array}{c}\text{Ending net} \\ \text{receivables}\end{array}\right) \div 2}{\text{One day's sales}}$$

$$= \frac{(\$2,500 + \$2,400)/2}{\$29.6} = 83 \text{ days}$$

* Adapted from Oracle Corporation's 2001 income statement, which is not reproduced here.

The length of the collection period depends on the credit terms of the sale. For example, sales on net 30 terms should be collected within approximately 30 days. When there is a discount, such as 2/10 net 30, the collection period may be shorter. Credit terms of net 45 result in a longer collection period. ←

We discussed sales discounts in Chapter 5, p. 187.

Investors and creditors do not evaluate a company on the basis of one or two ratios. Instead, they analyze all the information available. Then they stand back and ask, "What is our overall impression of this company?"

---

[3]Days' sales in average receivables can also be computed in this one step:

$$\frac{\text{Days' sales in}}{\text{average receivables}} = \frac{\text{Average net receivables}}{\text{Net sales}} \times 365$$

Wal-Mart has a collection period of only 3 days. Why is it so short?

Answer: Wal-Mart sells for cash or credit cards and therefore has very low receivables. This makes the collection period very short.

✔ **Starter 9-13**

✔ **Starter 9-14**

The Decision Guidelines feature summarizes some key decisions for receivables.

Decision Guidelines

ACCOUNTING FOR RECEIVABLES

Accounting for receivables is the same for your own start-up business as it is for a large company like **Oracle Coporation**. Suppose you open a business to maintain Web sites for local companies and you bill them monthly for your services. How should you account for your receivables? These guidelines show the way.

Decision	Guidelines
Accounts Receivable	
How much of our receivables will we collect?	Less than the full amount of the receivables because we cannot collect from some customers.
How to report receivables at their net realizable value?	1. Use the *allowance method* to account for uncollectible receivables. Set up the allowance for Uncollectible Accounts.
	2. Estimate uncollectibles by the
	a. *Percent-of-sales method* (income-statement approach)
	b. *Aging-of-accounts method* (balance-sheet approach)
	3. Write off uncollectible receivables as they prove uncollectible.
	4. $\dfrac{\text{Net accounts}}{\text{receivable}} = \dfrac{\text{Accounts}}{\text{Receivable}} - \dfrac{\text{Allowance for}}{\text{Uncollectible Accounts}}$
Is there another way to account for uncollectible receivables?	The *direct write-off method* uses no Allowance for Uncollectibles. It simply debits Uncollectible-Account Expense and credits a customer's Account Receivable to write it off when it has proved uncollectible. This method is acceptable only when uncollectibles are insignficant.
Notes Receivable	
What two other accounts are related to notes receivable?	Notes receivable are related to:
	• *Interest Revenue.*
	• *Interest Receivable* (Interest revenue earned but not yet collected).
How to compute the interest on a note receivable?	Amount of interest = Principal × Interest rate × Time
Receivables in General	
What two decision aids use receivables to evaluate a company's financial position?	• Acid-test ratio $= \dfrac{\text{Cash} + \text{investments} + \dfrac{\text{Short-term}\ \text{Net current}}{\text{receivables}}}{\text{Total current liabilities}}$
	• $\dfrac{\text{Day's sales in}}{\text{average receivables}} = \dfrac{\dfrac{\text{Average net}}{\text{accounts receivable}}}{\text{One day's sales}}$
How to report receivables on the balance sheet?	Accounts (or Notes) Receivable . . . . $XXX
	Less: Allowance for uncollectible accounts . . . . (X)
	Accounts (or notes) receivable, net . . . . $ XX

Excel Application Exercise

Goal: Create a worksheet that shows accounts receivable activity for a company.

Scenario: You are the summer intern at **Amazon.com** headquarters in Seattle, Washington. Assume that shortly into your employment, your supervisor asks you to prepare an Excel spreadsheet that breaks down the month's accounts receivable by customer. She gives you the following partial data (all dollars are in thousands):

Customer ID	Customer Name	May 31 Balance	Sales	Collections
F01-235-00	Bookfair	$20,469	$22,500	$24,500
F07-988-45	Author Source	$18,752	$11,592	$12,980
W40-860-91	Instore Service Co.	$12,287	$14,765	$14,000

Assume Amazon's credit terms are net 30.

When you have completed your worksheet, answer the following questions:

1. How much cash did Amazon collect from these three customers during June?
2. How much do these three customers still owe Amazon at the end of June?
3. What are the days' sales in average accounts receivable from these three customers?

Step-by-Step:

1. Open a new Excel spreadsheet.
2. Create a bold-faced heading for your spreadsheet that contains the following:
   a. Chapter 9 Excel Application Exercise
   b. Amazon Accounts Receivable (in 000's)
   c. Today's Date
3. Two rows down from your heading, create a row containing the following column headings:
   a. Customer ID   d. Sales
   b. Customer Name   e. Collections
   c. Beginning Balance   f. Ending Balance
4. Enter the data from the scenario into the spreadsheet. At the end of the entries, create a row for "Totals" and calculate totals for all financial columns.
5. Two rows beneath the scenario data, calculate the days' sales in average accounts receivable. Include a row for net sales underneath this calculation so that the net sales amount can be included as a variable in the days' sales in average accounts receivable.
6. Format your work. Experiment with the AutoFormat feature found by clicking "Format" on the menu bar (be sure to highlight the entire chart before doing so).
7. Save your worksheet and print a copy for your files.

● END-OF-CHAPTER *Summary Problem*

CHECK YOUR RESOURCES

Suppose First Fidelity, Inc., engaged in the following transactions:

20X4		
Apr. 1	Loaned out $8,000 to Bland Co. Received a six-month, 10% note.	
Oct. 1	Collected the Bland note at maturity.	
Dec. 1	Loaned $6,000 to Flores, Inc., on a 180-day, 12% note.	
Dec. 31	Accrued interest revenue on the Flores note.	
20X5		
May 30	Collected the Flores note at maturity.	

First Fidelity's accounting period ends on December 31.

Required

Explanations are not needed.

1. Record the 20X4 transactions on April 1 through December 1 on First Fidelity's books.
2. Make the adjusting entry needed on December 31, 20X4.
3. Record the May 30, 20X5, collection of the Flores note.

Solution

Requirement 1

20X4				
Apr. 1	Note Receivable—Bland Co.	8,000	
	Cash		8,000
Oct. 1	Cash ($8,000 + $400)	8,400	
	Note Receivable—Bland Co.		8,000
	Interest Revenue ($8,000 × 0.10 × 6/12) . . .		400

Requirement 2

20X4

Dec. 1	Note Receivable—Flores, Inc.		6,000	
	Cash			6,000
31	Interest Receivable.		60	
	Interest Revenue ($6,000 × 0.12 × 30/360).			60

Requirement 3

20X5

May 30	Cash ($6,000 + $360)		6,360	
	Note Receivable—Flores, Inc..			6,000
	Interest Receivable			60
	Interest Revenue ($6,000 × 0.12 × 150/360)			300

REVIEW *Receivables*

Quick Check

1. With good internal controls, the person who handles cash can also
   a. Account for cash receipts from customers
   b. Account for cash payments
   c. Issue credits to customers for merchandise returned to us
   d. None of the above

2. "Bad debts" are the same as
   a. Uncollectible accounts   **c.** Both a and b
   b. Doubtful accounts   **d.** None of the above

3. Which method of estimating uncollectible receivables focuses on Uncollectible Account Expense for the income statement?
   a. Aging-of-accounts approach   **c.** Net-realizable-value approach
   b. Percent-of-sales approach   **d.** All of the above.

4. Your company uses the allowance method to account for uncollectible receivables. At the beginning of the year, Allowance for Uncollectibles had a credit balance of $1,100. During the year you recorded Uncollectible-Account Expense of $2,000 and wrote off bad receivables of $2,100. What is your year-end balance in Allowance for Uncollectibles?
   a. $1,000   **c.** $3,100
   b. $2,000   **d.** $3,200

[Handwritten margin notes:]
AUA
Credit balance 1,100
Credit
UAE 2000
3100
2100
10000

5. Your ending balance of Accounts Receivable is $20,000. Use the data in the preceding question to compute the net realizable value of Accounts Receivable at year-end. Or, stated differently, determine the net receivables to report on your year-end balance sheet.
   a. $18,000   **c.** $20,000
   b. $19,000   **d.** $21,000

6. What is wrong with the direct write-off method of accounting for uncollectibles?
   a. The direct write-off method does not set up an allowance for uncollectibles.
   b. The direct write-off method overstates assets on the balance sheet.
   c. The direct write-off method does not match expenses against revenue very well.
   d. All of the above.

7. At December 31, you have a $10,000 note receivable from a customer. Interest of 8% has also accrued for 6 months on the note. What will your financial statements report for this situation?
   a. Nothing, because you haven't received the cash yet.
   b. Balance sheet will report the note receivable of $10,000.
   c. Balance sheet will report the note receivable of $10,000 and interest receivable of $400.
   d. Income statement will report a note receivable of $10,000.

8. Return to the data in the preceding question. What will the income statement report for this situation?
   a. Nothing, because you haven't received the cash yet   **c.** Note receivable of $10,000
   b. Interest revenue of $400   **d.** Both b and c

9. At year-end, your company has cash of $10,000, receivables of $40,000, inventory of $50,000, and prepaid expenses totaling $5,000. Liabilities of $60,000 must be paid next year. What is your acid-test ratio?
   a. 0.83   **c.** 1.75
   b. 1.67   **d.** Cannot be determined from the data given

10. Return to the data in the preceding question. A year ago receivables stood at $60,000, and sales for the current year total $730,000. How many days did it take you to collect your average level of receivables?
    a. 45   **c.** 25
    b. 35   **d.** 20

Accounting Vocabulary

acid-test ratio (p. 377)
aging-of-accounts method (p. 366)
Allowance for Doubtful Accounts (p. 365)
Allowance for Uncollectible Accounts (p. 365)
allowance method (p. 365)
bad-debt expense (p. 365)
balance-sheet approach (p. 366)
collection period (p. 378)
creditor (p. 362)
days' sales in receivables (p. 378)

debtor (p. 362)
default on a note (p. 376)
direct write-off method (p. 368)
discounting a note receivable (p. 396)
dishonor of a note (p. 376)
doubtful-account expense (p. 365)
due date (p. 373)
income-statement approach (p. 366)
interest (p. 372)
interest period (p. 372)
interest rate (p. 373)
maker of a note (p. 375)

maturity date (p. 373)
maturity value (p. 373)
note term (p. 372)
payee of a note (p. 375)
percent-of-sales method (p. 366)
principal (p. 372)
principal amount (p. 372)
promissory note (p. 372)
quick ratio (p. 377)
receivables (p. 362)
time (p. 372)
uncollectible-account expense (p. 365)

● ASSESS *Your Progress*

See *www.prenhall.com/horngren* for selected Starters, Exercises, and Problems.

Internal control over the collection of receivables
(Obj. 1)

Internal control over the credit department
(Obj. 1)

Applying the allowance method (percent-of-sales) to account for uncollectibles
(Obj. 2)

Starters

S9-1 Return to the Accounts Receivable T-accounts on page 363. Suppose Melanie Snyder is the accountant responsible for these records. What duty will a good internal control system withhold from Snyder? Why?

S9-2 What duty must be withheld from a company's credit department in order to safeguard its cash? If the credit department does this job, what can a dishonest credit department employee do to hurt the company?

S9-3 During its first year of operations, Spring Break Travel earned revenue of $500,000 on account. Industry experience suggests that Spring Break's bad debts will amount to 2% of revenues. At December 31, 20X3, accounts receivable total $90,000. The company uses the allowance method to account for uncollectibles.

1. Journalize Spring Break Travel's uncollectible-account expense using the percent-of-sales method.

2. Show how Spring Break should report accounts receivable on its balance sheet at December 31, 20X3. Follow the reporting format illustrated in the middle of page 365.

Applying the allowance method (percent-of-sales) to account for uncollectibles
(Obj. 2)

S9-4 ← *Link Back to Chapter 2 (Recording Service Revenue Transactions).* This exercise continues the situation of Starter 9-3, in which Spring Break Travel ended 20X3 with accounts receivable of $90,000 and an allowance for uncollectible accounts of $10,000.

During 20X4, Spring Break Travel completed these transactions:

1. Service revenue, $700,000 (ignore cost of goods sold).
2. Collections on account, $690,000.
3. Write-offs of uncollectibles, $15,000.
4. Uncollectible-account expense, 2% of service revenue.

Journalize Spring Break Travel's 20X4 transactions.

Applying the allowance method (aging-of-accounts) to account for uncollectibles
(Obj. 2)

S9-5 ← *Link Back to Chapter 5 (Recording Sales Transactions).* Guardian Medical Group started 20X0 with accounts receivable of $120,000 and an allowance for uncollectible accounts with a $6,000 credit balance. Credit sales for 20X0 were $500,000, and cash collections on account totaled $420,000. During 20X0, Guardian wrote off uncollectible accounts receivable of $12,000. At December 31, 20X0, the aging of accounts receivable showed that Guardian will probably *not* collect $5,000 of its accounts receivable.

Journalize Guardian's (a) credit sales (ignore cost of goods sold), (b) cash collections on account, (c) write-offs of uncollectible receivables, and (d) uncollectible-account expense for the year. Prepare a T-account for Allowance for Uncollectible Accounts to show your computation of uncollectible-account expense for the year.

Applying the allowance method (aging-of-accounts) to account for uncollectibles
(Obj. 2)

S9-6 Hot Button.com had the following balances at December 31, 20X1, before the year-end adjustments:

Accounts Receivable	Allowance for Uncollectible Accounts
104,000	1,300

The aging of accounts receivable yields these data:

	Age of Accounts Receivable				
	0–30 Days	31–60 Days	61–90 Days	Over 90 Days	Total Receivables
Accounts receivable	$70,000	$20,000	$10,000	$4,000	$104,000
Percent uncollectible	× 1%	× 2%	× 5%	× 50%	

Journalize Hot Button's entry to adjust the allowance account to its correct balance at December 31, 20X1.

Applying the direct write-off method to account for uncollectibles
(Obj. 3)

S9-7 Diane Feinstein is an attorney in San Francisco. Feinstein uses the direct write-off method to account for uncollectible receivables.

At May 31, Feinstein's accounts receivable were $8,000. During June, she earned service revenue of $20,000 on account and collected $22,000 from clients on account. She also wrote off uncollectible receivables of $1,000. What is Feinstein's balance of Accounts Receivable at June 30? Does she expect to collect all of this amount? Why or why not?

Recording credit-card sales
(Obj. 3)

S9-8 Gas stations do a large volume of business by customer credit cards and bankcards. Suppose the **BP Amoco** station near Lenox Square in Atlanta, Georgia, had these transactions on a busy Saturday in July:

American Express credit-card sales	$10,000
VISA bankcard sales	8,000

Suppose **American Express** charges merchants 4% and **VISA** charges 3%. Record these sale transactions for the BP Amoco station.

Computing interest amounts on notes receivable
(Obj. 4)

S9-9 For each of the following notes receivable, compute the amount of interest revenue earned during 20X5. Use a 360-day year, and round to the nearest dollar.

	Principal	Interest Rate	Interest Period During 20X5
Note 1	$100,000	8%	6 months
Note 2	15,000	12%	75 days
Note 3	10,000	9%	60 days
Note 4	50,000	10%	3 months

Accounting for a note receivable
(Obj. 4)

S9-10 **Deutsche Bank** lent $100,000 to Johann Schroeder on a 90-day, 8% note. Record the following transactions for Deutsche Bank (explanations are not required):

a. Lending the money on June 12.
b. Collecting the principal and interest at maturity. Specify the date. For the computation of interest, use a 360-day year.

Accruing interest receivable and collecting a note receivable
(Obj. 4)

S9-11 Return to the promissory note in Exhibit 9-4, page 373. The accounting year of Continental Bank ends on December 31, 20X6. Journalize Continental Bank's (a) lending money on September 30, 20X6 and (b) accrual of interest revenue at December 31, 20X6. Carry amounts to the nearest cent.

Reporting receivables and other accounts in the financial statements
(Obj. 5)

S9-12 ← *Link Back to Chapters 1–3 (Debit/Credit Balances; Income Statement).* **Sprint Corporation**, the telecommunications company, included the following items in its financial statements (adapted, in millions):

Allowance for doubtful accounts	$ 117	Service revenue	$14,045
Cash	1,151	Other assets	355
Accounts receivable	2,581	Cost of services sold and other expenses	12,861
Accounts payable	1,027	Notes payable	3,281

1. How much net income did Sprint earn for the year?
2. Show how Sprint reported receivables on its classified balance sheet. Follow the reporting format shown in the middle of page 365.

Using the acid-test ratio and days' sales in receivables to evaluate a company
(Obj. 6)

S9-13 Vision Equipment, which makes VCRs, reported the following items at February 28, 20X6 (amounts in thousands, with last year's—20X5—amounts also given as needed):

Accounts payable	$ 449	Accounts receivable, net:	
Cash	215	February 28, 20X6	$ 220
Inventories:		February 28, 20X5	150
February 28, 20X6	190	Cost of goods sold	1,200
February 28, 20X5	160	Short-term investments	165
Net sales revenue	1,930	Other current assets	90
Long-term assets	410	Other current liabilities	145
Long-term liabilities	10		

Compute Vision Equipment's (a) acid-test ratio and (b) days' sales in average receivables for 20X6. Evaluate each ratio value as strong or weak. Assume Vision Equipment sells on terms of net 30.

Computing key ratios for a company
(Obj. 6)

S9-14 ← *Link Back to Chapter 4 (Current Ratio and Debt Ratio) and Chapter 5 (Gross Profit Percentage and Inventory Turnover).* Use the data in Starter 9-13 to compute the following 20X6 ratios for Vision Equipment:

a. Current ratio
b. Debt ratio
c. Gross profit percentage
d. Rate of inventory turnover

Exercises

E9-1 ← *Link Back to Chapter 8 (Internal Control Over Cash Receipts).* Suppose **Eastman Kodak** is opening an office in Little Rock, Arkansas. Anita Mills, the office manager, is designing the internal control system. Mills proposes the following procedures for credit checks on new customers, sales on account, cash collections, and write-offs of uncollectible receivables:

Identifying and correcting an internal control weakness
(Obj. 1)

- The credit department runs a credit check on all customers who apply for credit. When an account proves uncollectible, the credit department authorizes the write-off of the account receivable.
- Cash receipts come into the credit department, which separates the cash received from the customer remittance slips. The credit department lists all cash receipts by customer name and amount of cash received.
- The cash goes to the treasurer for deposit in the bank. The remittance slips go to the accounting department for posting to customer accounts.
- The controller compares the daily deposit slip to the total amount posted to customer accounts. Both amounts must agree.

Identify the internal control weakness in this situation, and propose a way to correct it.

E9-2 During October, German Imports had sales of $180,000, which included $120,000 in credit sales. October collections were $90,000. Other data include

Using the allowance method for bad debts
(Obj. 2, 5)

- September 30 debit balance in Accounts Receivable, $28,000
- September 30 credit balance in Allowance for Uncollectible Accounts, $1,000
- Uncollectible-account expense, estimated as 2% of credit sales
- Write-offs of uncollectible receivables totaled $1,200

Required

1. Prepare journal entries to record sales, collections, uncollectible-account expense by the allowance method (percent-of-sales method), and write-offs of uncollectibles during October.
2. Show the ending balances in Accounts Receivable, Allowance for Uncollectible Accounts, and *net* accounts receivable at October 31. How much does German Imports expect to collect?

E9-3 Refer to Exercise 9-2.

Using the direct write-off method for bad debts
(Obj. 3)

Required

1. Record uncollectible-account expense for October using the direct write-off method.
2. What accounts receivable amount does German Imports report on its Oct. 31 balance sheet under the direct write-off method? Does it expect to collect the full amount?

E9-4 At December 31, 20X7, the Accounts Receivable balance of VISA Express is $300,000. The Allowance for Doubtful Accounts has a $3,900 credit balance. VISA prepares the following aging schedule for its accounts receivable:

Using the aging method to estimate bad debts
(Obj. 2, 5)

spreadsheet

| | Age of Accounts | | | |
Total Balance	1–30 Days	31–60 Days	61–90 Days	Over 90 Days
$300,000	$140,000	$80,000	$70,000	$10,000
Estimated percent uncollectible	0.5%	1.0%	6.0%	50%

Required

1. Journalize the year-end adjusting entry for doubtful accounts on the basis of the aging schedule. Show the T-account for the Allowance at December 31, 20X7.
2. Show how VISA Express will report Accounts Receivable on its December 31, 20X7 balance sheet.

Reporting bad debts by the allowance method
(Obj. 2, 5)

E9-5 Circuit Software made credit sales of $500,000 during 20X8. Experience indicates that uncollectible-account expense is 1/2 of 1% of credit sales.

At December 31, 20X8, Circuit Software's Accounts Receivable balance is $130,000, and Allowance for Uncollectibles stands at $1,600 before the year-end adjustment.

Record uncollectible-account expense for 20X8. Then report Circuit Software's receivables, net of the allowance, at December 31, 20X8.

Computing notes receivable amounts
(Obj. 4)

E9-6 On April 30, 20X7, First National Bank of Santa Fe, New Mexico, loaned $100,000 to Grant Thompson on a one-year, 9% note.

Required

1. Compute the interest for the years ended December 31, 20X7 and 20X8 for the Thompson note.
2. Which party has a
   a. Note receivable?   c. Interest revenue?
   b. Note payable?   d. Interest expense?
3. How much in total would Thompson pay the bank if he pays off the note early—say, on November 30, 20X7?

Recording notes receivable and accruing interest revenue
(Obj. 4)

Student Resource**CD**
General Ledger, Peachtree, QuickBooks

E9-7 Journalize the following transactions of Motor Sports Company, which ends its accounting year on June 30:

Apr. 1	Loaned $20,000 cash to Ahmed Fadal on a one-year, 8% note.
June 6	Sold goods to Lennox Corp., receiving a 90-day, 10% note for $3,000.
30	Made a single compound entry to accrue interest revenue on both notes. Use a 360-day year for interest computations.

Recording bankcard sales and a note receivable, and accruing interest revenue
(Obj. 4)

Student Resource**CD**
GL, PT, QB

E9-8 Record the following transactions in the journal of Spaceage Jewelry:

20X8	
Feb. 12	Recorded VISA bankcard sales of $60,000, less a 2% discount.
May 1	Loaned $20,000 to Peter Liu on a one-year, 12% note.
Dec. 31	Accrued interest revenue on the Liu note.
20X9	
May 1	Collected the maturity value of the Liu note.

Recording notes receivable transactions
(Obj. 4)

Student Resource**CD**
GL, PT, QB

E9-9 Acura Enterprises sells on account. When a customer account becomes four months old, Acura converts the account to a note receivable. During 20X6, Acura completed these transactions:

June 29	Sold goods on account to J. Lafferty, $10,000.
Nov. 1	Received a $10,000, 60-day, 9% note from J. Lafferty in satisfaction of his past-due account receivable.
Dec. 31	Collected the Lafferty note at maturity.

Required

Record the transactions in Acura's journal.

Evaluating ratio data
(Obj. 6)

E9-10 **Warnaco** reported the following amounts in its 20X9 financial statements. The 20X8 figures are given for comparison.

		20X9		20X8
Current assets:				
Cash....................		$ 3,000		$ 10,000
Short-term investments		23,000		11,000
Accounts receivable	$80,000		$74,000	
Less: Allowance for uncollectibles	(7,000)	73,000	(6,000)	68,000
Inventory		192,000		189,000
Prepaid insurance		2,000		2,000
Total current assets		293,000		280,000
Total current liabilities		$104,000		$107,000
Net sales		$805,000		$732,000

Required

1. Determine whether Warnaco's acid-test ratio improved or deteriorated from 20X8 to 20X9. How does Warnaco's acid-test ratio compare with the industry average of 0.80?

2. Compare the days' sales in receivables for 20X9 with Warnaco's credit terms of net 30.

E9-11 **Dell Computer** sells on account. Recently, Dell reported these figures (in millions of dollars):

Analyzing an actual company's financial statements
(Obj. 6)

Student ResourceCD

spreadsheet

	2002	2001
Net sales	$31,168	$31,188
Receivables at end of year	2,269	2,424

Required

1. Compute Dell's average collection period on receivables during 2002.

2. Suppose Dell's normal credit terms for a sale on account are "net 30 days." How well does Dell's collection period compare to the company's credit terms? Is this good or bad for Dell? Explain.

E9-12 Navigation Systems sells on store credit and manages its own receivables. Average experience for the past three years has been as follows:

Evaluating credit-card sales for profitability
(Obj. 2)

Student ResourceCD

spreadsheet

	Total
Sales	$350,000
Cost of goods sold	210,000
Bad-debt expense	4,000
Other expenses	61,000

Bruce Slazenger, the owner, is considering whether to accept bankcards (**VISA, MasterCard**). Typically, accepting bankcards increases total sales and cost of goods sold by 10%. But VISA and MasterCard charge approximately 2% of bankcard sales. If Slazenger switches to bankcards, he'll no longer have bad-debt expense. He can also save $5,000 on other expenses. After the switchover to bankcards, Slazenger expects cash sales of $200,000.

Required

Should Slazenger start accepting bankcards? Show the computations of net income under his present arrangement and under the bankcard plan.

Problems

(Group A)

P9-1A Prism Imaging converts hard-copy documents to CD and DVD media. All work is performed on account, with regular monthly billing to customers. Eve Nations, the accountant for Prism, opens the mail. Company procedure requires her to separate customer checks from the remittance slips and then post collections to customer accounts. Nations deposits the checks in the bank. She computes each day's total amount posted to customer accounts and matches this total to the bank deposit slip. This procedure is intended to ensure that all receipts are deposited in the bank.

Controlling cash receipts from customers
(Obj. 1)

Required

As a consultant hired by Prism Imaging, write a memo to management evaluating the company's internal controls over cash receipts from customers. If the system is effective, identify its strong features. If the system has flaws, propose a way to strengthen the controls. Use the memorandum format that follows.

Date: _____	
To:	
From:	
Subject:	

Accounting for uncollectibles by the direct write-off and allowance methods
(Obj. 2, 3, 5)

P9-2A On May 31, Scuba Dive Equipment had a $210,000 debit balance in Accounts Receivable. During June, Scuba made sales of $560,000, all on credit. Other data for June include

- Collections on account, $567,400.
- Write-offs of uncollectible receivables, $8,900.

Required

1. Record sales and collections on account. Then record uncollectible-account expense and write-offs of customer accounts for June using the *allowance* method. Show all June activity in Accounts Receivable, Allowance for Uncollectible Accounts, and Uncollectible-Account Expense (post to these T-accounts). The May 31 unadjusted balance in Allowance for Uncollectible Accounts was $2,800 (credit). Uncollectible-account expense was estimated at 2% of credit sales.

2. Suppose Scuba Dive Equipment used a different method to account for uncollectible receivables. Record sales and collections on account. Then record uncollectible-account expense for June using the *direct write-off* method. Post to Accounts Receivable and Uncollectible-Account Expense and show their balances at June 30.

3. What amount of uncollectible-account expense would Scuba Dive Equipment report on its June income statement under each of the two methods? Which amount better matches expense with revenue? Give your reason.

4. What amount of *net* accounts receivable would Scuba Dive Equipment report on its June 30 balance sheet under each of the two methods? Which amount is more realistic? Give your reason.

Using the percent-of-sales and aging methods for uncollectibles
(Obj. 2, 5)

P9-3A The June 30, 20X7, balance sheet of Texas Golf Carts reports the following:

Accounts Receivable.	$143,000
Allowance for Uncollectible Accounts (credit balance)	3,200

At the end of each quarter, Texas Golf Carts estimates uncollectible-account expense to be 1 1/2% of credit sales. At the end of the year, the company ages its accounts receivable and adjusts the balance in Allowance for Uncollectible Accounts to correspond to the aging schedule. During July through December of 20X7, Texas Golf Carts completed the following transactions:

Aug. 9	Made a compound entry to write off uncollectible accounts: J. Aguilar, $200; Seaton Co., $100; and T. Taylor, $700.
Sep. 30	Recorded uncollectible-account expense equal to 1 1/2% of credit sales of $140,000.
Oct. 18	Wrote off as uncollectible the $500 account receivable from Lintz Co. and the $400 account receivable from Navisor Corp.
Dec. 31	Recorded uncollectible-account expense based on the aging of accounts receivable, which follows:

	Age of Accounts			
Total	1–30 Days	31–60 Days	61–90 Days	Over 90 Days
$163,000	$100,000	$40,000	$14,000	$9,000
Estimated percent uncollectible	0.1%	0.5%	5%	30%

Required

1. Record the transactions in the journal.
2. Open the Allowance for Uncollectible Accounts, and post entries affecting that account. Keep a running balance.
3. Show how Texas Golf Carts should report accounts receivable on its balance sheet at December 31, 20X7.

P9-4A ← *Link Back to Chapter 4 (Closing Entries).* Providence Medical Supply completed the following transactions during 20X4 and 20X5:

Using the percent-of-sales method for uncollectibles
(Obj. 2, 5)

Student ResourceCD
GL, PT, QB

20X4	
Dec. 31	Estimated that uncollectible-account expense for the year was 3/4 of 1% on credit sales of $400,000, and recorded that amount as expense.
31	Made the closing entry for uncollectible-account expense.
20X5	
Jan. 17	Sold inventory to Mitch Vanez, $600, on account. Ignore cost of goods sold.
June 29	Wrote off the Mitch Vanez account as uncollectible after repeated efforts to collect from him.
Aug. 6	Received $200 from Mitch Vanez, along with a letter stating his intention to pay within 30 days. Reinstated his account in full.
Sept. 4	Received the balance due from Mitch Vanez.
Dec. 31	Made a compound entry to write off the following accounts as uncollectible: Bernard Klaus, $700; Marie Monet, $300; and Terry Fuhrman, $600.
31	Estimated that uncollectible-account expense for the year was 2/3 of 1% on credit sales of $480,000, and recorded that amount as expense.
31	Made the closing entry for uncollectible-account expense.

Required

1. Open general ledger accounts for Allowance for Uncollectible Accounts and Uncollectible-Account Expense. Keep running balances. All accounts begin with a zero balance.
2. Record the transactions in the general journal, and post to the two ledger accounts.
3. The December 31, 20X5, balance of Accounts Receivable is $139,000. Show how Accounts Receivable would be reported on the balance sheet at that date.

P9-5A The Bailey Insurance Agency received the following notes during 20X8.

Accounting for notes receivable, including accruing interest revenue
(Obj. 4)

Note	Date	Principal Amount	Interest Rate	Term
(1)	Dec. 23	$13,000	9%	1 year
(2)	Nov. 30	12,000	12%	6 months
(3)	Dec. 7	9,000	10%	30 days

Required

Identify each note by number, compute interest using a 360-day year for those notes with terms specified in days or years, and present entries in general journal form. Explanations are not required.

1. Determine the due date and maturity value of each note.
2. Journalize a single adjusting entry at December 31, 20X8, to record accrued interest revenue on all three notes.
3. For note (1), journalize the collection of principal and interest at maturity.

P9-6A ← *Link Back to Chapter 4 (Closing Entries).* Record the following transactions in the general journal of Triumph Auto Accessories. Explanations are not required.

Accounting for notes receivable, dishonored notes, and accrued interest revenue
(Obj. 4)

20X4

Dec. 19 Received a $3,000, 60-day, 12% note on account from Arnold Cohen.
31 Made an adjusting entry to accrue interest on the Cohen note.
31 Made a closing entry for interest revenue.

20X5

Feb. 17 Collected the maturity value of the Cohen note.
June 1 Loaned $10,000 cash to Blues Brothers, receiving a 6-month, 11% note.
Oct. 31 Received a $1,500, 60-day, 12% note from Mark Phipps on his past-due account receivable.
Dec. 1 Collected the maturity value of the Blues Brothers note.
30 Mark Phipps dishonored his note at maturity; wrote off the note receivable as uncollectible, debiting Allowance for Uncollectible Accounts.

Journalizing uncollectibles, notes receivable, and accrued interest revenue
(Obj. 4)

P9-7A Assume that **Pepperidge Farms**, famous for cookies, crackers, and other baked goods, completed the following selected transactions:

20X6

Nov. 1 Sold goods to **Kroger**, receiving a $40,000, three-month, 9% note. Ignore cost of goods sold.
Dec. 31 Made an adjusting entry to accrue interest on the Kroger note.
31 Made an adjusting entry to record uncollectible-account expense based on an aging of accounts receivable. The aging analysis indicates that $57,400 of accounts receivable will not be collected. Prior to this adjustment, the credit balance in Allowance for Uncollectible Accounts is $42,600.

20X7

Feb. 1 Collected the maturity value of the Kroger note.
June 23 Sold merchandise to Artesian Corp., receiving a 60-day, 10% note for $9,000. Ignore cost of goods sold.
Aug. 22 Artesian Corp. dishonored (failed to pay) its note at maturity; we converted the maturity value of the note to an account receivable.
Nov. 16 Loaned $6,000 cash to Crane, Inc., receiving a 90-day, 12% note.
Dec. 5 Collected in full on account from Artesian Corp.
31 Accrued the interest on the Crane, Inc., note.

Required

Record the transactions in the journal of Pepperidge Farms. Explanations are not required.

Using ratio data to evaluate a company's financial position
(Obj. 6)

P9-8A ← *Link Back to Chapter 4 (Current Ratio).* The comparative financial statements of Pizza Express Delis for 20X6, 20X5, and 20X4 include the following selected data:

	(In thousands)		
	20X6	20X5	20X4
Balance sheet			
Current assets:			
Cash......................................	$ 82	$ 80	$ 60
Short-term investments	140	174	122
Receivables, net of allowance for doubtful accounts of $6, $6, and $5, respectively	257	265	218
Inventories...............................	429	341	302
Prepaid expenses..........................	21	27	46
Total current assets	929	887	748
Total current liabilities	$ 680	$ 700	$ 660
Income statement			
Sales revenue.............................	$5,189	$4,995	$4,206
Cost of sales	2,734	2,636	2,418

Required

1. Compute these ratios for 20X6 and 20X5:
   a. Current ratio   **b.** Acid-test ratio   **c.** Days' sales in receivables
2. Write a memo explaining to the company owner which ratios improved from 20X5 to 20X6 and which ratios deteriorated. Which item in the financial statements increased and caused some ratios to improve and others to deteriorate? Discuss whether this factor conveys a favorable or an unfavorable impression about the company.

Problems

(Group B)

P9-1B Downslope Ski Supply distributes ski gear to sporting goods stores. All sales are on credit, so virtually all cash receipts arrive in the mail. William Yang, the company owner, has just returned from a meeting with new ideas for the business. Among other things, Yang plans to institute stronger internal controls over cash receipts from customers.

Controlling cash receipts from customers
(Obj. 1)

Required

Assume you are William Yang. Write a memo to outline a set of procedures to ensure that (1) all cash receipts are deposited in the bank and (2) all cash receipts are posted as credits to customer accounts receivable. Use the memorandum format given in Problem 9-1A, page 388.

P9-2B On February 28, Hourglass Computers had a $75,000 debit balance in Accounts Receivable. During March, Hourglass made sales of $445,000, all on credit. Other data for March include

Accounting for uncollectibles by the direct write-off and allowance methods
(Obj. 2, 3, 5)

- Collections on account, $422,600.
- Write-offs of uncollectible receivables, $3,500.

Required

1. Record sales and collections on account. Then record uncollectible-account expense and write-offs of customer accounts using the *allowance* method. Show all March activity in Accounts Receivable, Allowance for Uncollectible Accounts, and Uncollectible-Account Expense (post to these T-accounts). The February 28 unadjusted balance in Allowance for Uncollectible Accounts was $800 (credit). Uncollectible-account expense was estimated at 2% of credit sales.
2. Suppose Hourglass Computers used a different method to account for uncollectible receivables. Record sales and collections on account. Then record uncollectible-account expense for March using the *direct write-off* method. Post to Accounts Receivable and Uncollectible-Account Expense and show their balances at March 31.
3. What amount of uncollectible-account expense would Hourglass Computers report on its March income statement under each of the two methods? Which amount better matches expense with revenue? Give your reason.
4. What amount of *net* accounts receivable would Hourglass Computers report on its March 31 balance sheet under each of the two methods? Which amount is more realistic? Give your reason.

P9-3B The June 30, 20X9, balance sheet of RAM Technologies reports the following:

Using the percent-of-sales and aging methods for uncollectibles
(Obj. 2, 5)

Accounts Receivable..	$265,000
Allowance for Uncollectible Accounts (credit balance)............	7,100

At the end of each quarter, RAM estimates uncollectible-account expense to be 2% of credit sales. At the end of the year, RAM ages its accounts receivable. RAM then adjusts the balance in Allowance for Uncollectible Accounts to correspond to the aging schedule. During the second half of 20X9, RAM completed the following transactions:

July 14   Made a compound entry to write off uncollectible accounts:
T. J. Dooley, $700; Design Works, $2,400; and S. DeWitt, $100.

Sep. 30   Recorded uncollectible-account expense equal to 2% of credit sales of $140,000.

Nov. 22   Wrote off accounts receivable as uncollectible:
Transnet, $1,300; **Webvan**, $2,100; and Alpha Group, $700.

Dec. 31   Recorded uncollectible-account expense based on the aging of receivables.

| | Age of Accounts | | | |
Total	1–30 Days	31–60 Days	61–90 Days	Over 90 Days
$255,000	$120,000	$80,000	$40,000	$15,000
Estimated percent uncollectible....................	0.5%	1.0%	4%	50%

Required

1. Record the transactions in the journal.

2. Open the Allowance for Uncollectible Accounts, and post entries affecting that account. Keep a running balance.

3. Show how RAM Technologies should report accounts receivable on its December 31, 20X9, balance sheet.

Using the percent-of-sales method for uncollectibles
(Obj, 2, 5)

Student ResourceCD
GL, PT, QB

P9-4B ← *Link Back to Chapter 4 (Closing Entries).* Mach-1 Sound Systems completed the following selected transactions during 20X1 and 20X2:

20X1

Dec. 31   Estimated that uncollectible-account expense for the year was 2/3 of 1% on credit sales of $450,000 and recorded that amount as expense.

31   Made the closing entry for uncollectible-account expense.

20X2

Feb. 4   Sold inventory to Marian Holt, $1,500 on account. Ignore cost of goods sold.

July 1   Wrote off Marian Holt's account as uncollectible after repeated efforts to collect from her.

Oct. 19   Received $500 from Marian Holt, along with a letter stating her intention to pay within 30 days. Reinstated Holt's account in full.

Nov. 15   Received the balance due from Marian Holt.

Dec. 31   Made a compound entry to write off the following accounts as uncollectible: Kaycee Britt, $800; Tim Sands, $500; and Anna Chin, $1,200.

31   Estimated that uncollectible-account expense for the year was 2/3 of 1% on credit sales of $585,000 and recorded the expense.

31   Made the closing entry for uncollectible-account expense.

Required

1. Open general ledger accounts for Allowance for Uncollectible Accounts and Uncollectible-Account Expense. Keep running balances. All accounts begin with a zero balance.

2. Record the transactions in the general journal, and post to the two ledger accounts.

3. The December 31, 20X2, balance of Accounts Receivable is $164,500. Show how Accounts Receivable would be reported on the balance sheet at that date.

Accounting for notes receivable, including accruing interest revenue
(Obj. 4)

P9-5B Metro Bank loaned money and received the following notes during 20X8.

Note	Date	Principal Amount	Interest Rate	Term
(1)	Dec. 1	$12,000	9%	1 year
(2)	Oct. 31	11,000	12%	3 months
(3)	Nov. 19	15,000	10%	60 days

Required

Identify each note by number, compute interest using a 360-day year, and present entries in general journal form. Explanations are not required.

1. Determine the due date and maturity value of each note.
2. Journalize a single adjusting entry at December 31, 20X8, to record accrued interest revenue on all three notes.
3. For note (1), journalize the collection of principal and interest at maturity.

P9-6B ← *Link Back to Chapter 4 (Closing Entries).* Record the following transactions in the general journal of Recognition Systems. Round all amounts to the nearest dollar. Explanations are not required.

Accounting for notes receivable, dishonored notes, and accrued interest revenue
(Obj. 4)

⊙ Student ResourceCD
GL, PT, QB

20X6	
Dec. 21	Received a $2,800, 30-day, 10% note on account from Joe Fitzhugh.
31	Made an adjusting entry to accrue interest on the Fitzhugh note.
31	Made a closing entry for interest revenue.
20X7	
Jan. 20	Collected the maturity value of the Fitzhugh note.
Sept. 14	Loaned $6,000 cash to Bullseye Investors, receiving a three-month, 13% note.
30	Received a $1,600, 60-day, 16% note from Chuck Powers on his past-due account receivable.
Nov. 29	Chuck Powers dishonored his note at maturity; wrote off the note as uncollectible, debiting Allowance for Uncollectible Accounts.
Dec. 14	Collected the maturity value of the Bullseye Investors note.

P9-7B Assume that **Jones-Blair**, the paint manufacturer, completed the following selected transactions:

Journalizing uncollectibles, notes receivable, and accrued interest revenue
(Obj. 4)

⊙ Student ResourceCD
GL, PT, QB

20X4	
Dec. 1	Sold goods to Kelly Paint Supply, receiving a $12,000, three-month, 10% note. Ignore cost of goods sold.
31	Made an adjusting entry to accrue interest on the Kelly note.
31	Made an adjusting entry to record uncollectible-account expense based on an aging of accounts receivable. The aging analysis indicates that $39,800 of accounts receivable will not be collected. Prior to this adjustment, the credit balance in Allowance for Uncollectible Accounts is $24,100.
20X5	
Mar. 1	Collected the maturity value of the Kelly Paint Supply note.
July 21	Sold merchandise to Mellon Co., receiving a 60-day, 9% note for $4,000. Ignore cost of goods sold.
Sep. 19	Mellon Co. dishonored its note (failed to pay) at maturity; we converted the maturity value of the note to an account receivable.
Nov. 21	Loaned $40,000 cash to Thermo Control, Inc., receiving a 90-day, 9% note.
Dec. 2	Collected in full on account from Mellon Co.
31	Accrued the interest on the Thermo Control note.

Using ratio data to evaluate a company's financial position
(Obj. 6)

Required

Record the transactions in the journal of Jones-Blair. Explanations are not required.

P9-8B ← *Link Back to Chapter 4 (Current Ratio).* The comparative financial statements of Crispy Cream Pastries for 20X8, 20X7, and 20X6 include the data shown here:

⊙ Student ResourceCD
spreadsheet

	(In millions)		
	20X8	**20X7**	**20X6**
Balance sheet			
Current assets:			
Cash..................................	$ 27	$ 26	$ 22
Short-term investments...................	93	101	69
Receivables, net of allowance for doubtful			
accounts of $7, $6, and $4, respectively	146	154	127
Inventories	454	383	341
Prepaid expenses.......................	32	31	25
Total current assets	752	695	584
Total current liabilities....................	$ 400	$ 416	$ 388
Income statement			
Sales revenue	$2,671	$2,505	$1,944
Cost of sales	1,380	1,360	963

Required

1. Compute these ratios for 20X8 and 20X7:

   a. Current ratio   **b.** Acid-test ratio   **c.** Days' sales in receivables

2. Write a memo explaining to the company owner which ratios improved from 20X7 to 20X8 and which ratios deteriorated. Which item in the financial statements increased and caused some ratios to improve and others to deteriorate? Discuss whether this factor conveys a favorable or an unfavorable sign about the company.

APPLY *Your Knowledge*

Decision Cases

Comparing the allowance and direct write-off methods for uncollectibles
(Obj. 2, 3)

Case 1. Pappa Rollo Advertising has always used the direct write-off method to account for uncollectibles. The company's revenues, bad-debt write-offs, and year-end receivables for the most recent year follow.

Year	Revenues	Write-Offs	Receivables at Year-End
20X6	$170,000	$3,000	$20,0000

Pappa Rollo is applying for a bank loan, and the loan officer requires figures based on the allowance method of accounting for bad debts. Pappa Rollo estimates that bad debts run about 4% of revenues each year.

Required

Pappa Rollo must give the banker the following information:

1. How much more or less would net income be for 20X6 if Pappa Rollo were to use the allowance method for bad debts?

2. How much of the receivables balance at the end of 20X6 does Pappa Rollo expect to collect?

Compute these amounts, and then explain for Pappa Rollo why net income is more or less for 20X6 using the allowance method versus the direct write-off method for uncollectibles.

Uncollectible accounts and evaluating a business
(Obj. 2, 3)

Case 2. Heartland Cable Network performs service either for cash or on notes receivable. The business uses the direct write-off method to account for bad debts. Dan Pavlicek, the owner, has prepared the company's financial statements. Summary comparative income statements for 20X6 and 20X5 follow.

	20X6	20X5
Total revenue.........................	$220,000	$195,000
Total expenses.......................	107,000	103,000
Net income	$113,000	$ 92,000

On the basis of the increase in net income, Pavlicek wants to expand operations. He asks you to invest $50,000 in the business. You and Pavlicek have several meetings and you learn that notes receivable from customers were $200,000 at the end of 20X4 and $400,000 at the end of 20X5. Also, total revenues for 20X6 and 20X5 include interest at 13% on the year's beginning notes receivable balance. Total expenses include uncollectible-account expense of $2,000 each year, based on the direct write-off method. Pavlicek estimates that uncollectible-account expense would be 5% of sales revenue if the allowance method were used.

Required

1. Prepare for Heartland Cable a comparative single-step income statement for 20X6 and 20X5 that identifies service revenue, interest revenue, uncollectible-account expense, and other expenses, all computed in accordance with generally accepted accounting principles.
2. Is Heartland Cable's future as promising as Pavlicek's income statement makes it appear? Give the reason for your answer.

Ethical Issue

Show Biz Autos sells cars. Show Biz's bank requires Show Biz to submit quarterly financial statements in order to keep its line of credit. Show Biz's main asset is Notes Receivable. Therefore, Uncollectible-Account Expense and Allowance for Uncollectible Accounts are important accounts.

Lance Van Houten, the owner of Show Biz Autos, wants net income to increase in a smooth pattern, rather than increase in some periods and decrease in others. To report smoothly increasing net income, Van Houten underestimates Uncollectible-Account Expense in some periods. In other periods, Van Houten overestimates the expense. He reasons that over time the income overstatements roughly offset the income understatements.

Required

Is Van Houten's practice of smoothing income ethical? Why or why not?

Financial Statement Case

Use the balance sheet and income statement (statement of operations) of **Amazon.com** in Appendix A.

Analyzing accounts receivable and uncollectibles
(Obj. 2, 6)

1. Do accounts receivable appear to be an important asset for Amazon.com? What about Amazon's business affects the importance of accounts receivable?
2. Assume that all of "Accounts Receivable, Net and Other Current Assets" is accounts receivable. Further assume that gross receivables at December 31, 2002, were $118,000 thousand. Answer the following questions based on these data, plus what's reported on the balance sheet:
   a. How much did customers owe Amazon.com at December 31, 2002?
   b. How much did Amazon expect to collect from customers after December 31, 2002?
   c. Of the total receivable amount at December 31, 2002, how much did Amazon expect *not* to collect?
3. Compute Amazon.com's acid-test ratio at the end of 2002 and at the end of 2001. Marketable securities are short-term investments. Assume that other current assets are zero. If all the current liabilities came due immediately, could Amazon pay them?

Team Project

Notes Receivable of the Bank.
Bob Opper and Denise Shapp worked for several years as sales representatives for **Xerox Corporation**. During this time, they became close friends as they acquired expertise with the company's full range of copier equipment. Now they see an opportunity to put their experience to work and fulfill lifelong desires to establish their own business. Lakeside College, located in their city, is expanding, and there is no copy center within five miles of the campus. Business in the area is booming, and the population in this section of the city is growing.

Opper and Shapp want to open a copy center, similar to a **Kinko's**, near the campus. A small shopping center across the street from the college has a vacancy that would fit their needs. Opper and Shapp each have $20,000 to invest in the business, and they forecast the need for $30,000 to renovate the store. Xerox Corporation will lease two large copiers to them at a total monthly rental of $4,000. With enough cash to see them through the first six months of operation, they are confident they can make the business succeed. The two work very well together, and both have excellent credit ratings. Opper and Shapp must borrow $80,000 to start the business, advertise its opening, and keep it running for its first six months.

Assume the role of Opper and Shapp, the partners who will own Lakeside Copy Center.

1. As a group, visit a copy center to familiarize yourselves with its operations. If possible, interview the manager or another employee. Then write a loan request that Opper and Shapp will submit to a bank with the intent of borrowing $80,000 to be paid back over three years. The loan will be a personal loan to the partnership of Opper and Shapp, not to Lakeside Copy Center. The request should specify all the details of Opper's and Shapp's plan that will motivate the bank to grant the loan. Include a budgeted income statement for the first six months of the copy center's operation.

2. As a group, interview a loan officer in a bank. Have the loan officer evaluate your loan request. Write a report, or make a presentation to your class—as directed by your instructor—to reveal the loan officer's decision.

For Internet exercises, go to the Web site www.prenhall.com/horngren.

APPENDIX *to Chapter 9*

We discuss these concepts in Chapter 15.

Discounting a Note Receivable
Selling a note receivable before its maturity date.

Discounting a Note Receivable

A payee of a note receivable may need cash before the maturity date of the note. When this occurs, the payee may sell the note, a practice called **discounting a note receivable**. The price to be received for the note is determined by present-value concepts. ← But the transaction between the seller and the buyer of the note can take any form agreeable to the two parties. Here we illustrate one procedure used for discounting short-term notes receivable. To receive cash immediately, the seller accepts a lower price than the note's maturity value.

To illustrate discounting a note receivable, suppose **General Electric** loaned $15,000 to Dorman Builders on October 20, 20X8. GE took a note receivable from Dorman. The maturity date of the 90-day 10% Dorman note is January 18, 20X9. Suppose GE discounts the Dorman note at First City Bank on December 9, 20X8, when the note is 50 days old. The bank applies a 12% annual interest rate to determine the discounted value of the note. The bank will use a discount rate that is higher than the note's interest rate in order to earn some interest on the transaction. The discounted value, called the *proceeds*, is the amount GE receives from the bank. The proceeds can be computed in five steps, as shown in Exhibit 9A-1. GE's entry to record discounting (selling) the note on December 9, 20X8, is

Dec. 9, 20X8 Cash	15,170	
Note Receivable—Dorman Builders . .		15,000
Interest Revenue ($15,170 − $15,000) . .		170
Discounted a note receivable.		

When the proceeds from discounting a note receivable are less than the principal amount of the note, the payee records a debit to Interest Expense for the amount of the difference. For example, GE could discount the note receivable for cash proceeds of $14,980. The entry to record this discounting transaction is

Dec. 9, 20X8 Cash	14,980	
Interest Expense	20	
Note Receivable—Dorman Builders . .		15,000
Discounted a note receivable.		

Step	Computation	
1. Compute the original amount of interest on the note receivable.	$15,000 × 0.10 × 90/360	= $375
2. Maturity value of the note = Principal + Interest	$15,000 + $375	= $15,375
3. Determine the period (number of days, months, or years) the *bank* will hold the note (the discount period).	Dec. 9, 20X8 to Jan. 18, 20X9 = 40 days	
4. Compute the bank's discount on the note. This is the bank's interest revenue from holding the note.	$15,375 × 0.12 × 40/360	= $205
5. Seller's proceeds from discounting the note receivable = Maturity value of the note − Bank's discount on the note.	$15,375 − $205	= $15,170

The authors thank Doug Hamilton for suggesting this exhibit.

Exhibit 9A-1
Discounting (Selling) a Note Receivable: GE Discounts the Dorman Builders Note

Appendix Assignments

Exercise

E9A-1 Rider Systems, Inc., sells on account. When a customer account becomes three months old, Rider converts the account to a note receivable and immediately discounts the note to a bank. During 20X4, Rider completed these transactions:

Recording notes receivable and discounting a note
(Obj. 4)

Aug. 29	Sold goods on account to V. Moyer, $3,900.
Dec. 1	Received a $3,900, 60-day, 10% note from V. Moyer in satisfaction of his past-due account receivable.
1	Sold the Moyer note by discounting it to a bank for $3,600.

Required

Record the transactions in Rider Systems' journal.

Problem

P9A-1 A company received the following notes during 20X5. Notes (1), (2), and (3) were discounted on the dates and at the rates indicated.

Discounting notes receivable
(Obj. 4)

Note	Date	Principal Amount	Interest Rate	Term	Date Discounted	Discount Rate
(1)	July 15	$6,000	6%	6 months	Oct. 15	8%
(2)	Aug. 19	9,000	8%	90 days	Aug. 30	10%
(3)	Sept. 1	8,000	9%	120 days	Nov. 2	12%

Required

Identify each note by number, compute interest using a 360-day year for those notes with terms specified in days, round all interest amounts to the nearest dollar, and present entries in general journal form. Explanations are not required.

1. Determine the due date and maturity value of each note.
2. Determine the discount and proceeds from the sale (discounting) of each note.
3. Journalize the discounting of notes (1) and (2).

CHAPTER 10

Plant Assets and Intangibles

TIPS CHECK YOUR RESOURCES

- Visit the www.prenhall.com/horngren **Web site** for self-study quizzes, video clips, and other resources

- Try the **Quick Check** exercise at the end of the chapter to test your knowledge

- Learn the **key terms**

- Do the **Starter** exercises keyed in the margins

- Work the **mid- and end-of-chapter summary problems**

- Use the **Concept Links** to review material in other chapters

- Search the **CD** for review materials by chapter or by key word

- Watch the **tutorial videos** to review key concepts

LEARNING OBJECTIVES

1 Measure the cost of a plant asset

2 Account for depreciation

3 Select the best depreciation method for tax purposes

4 Account for the disposal of a plant asset

5 Account for natural resources

6 Account for intangible assets

Have you ever taken a flight on a commercial airline? Companies like American, Delta, or United have some of the most interesting assets in the world: Boeing and McDonnell-Douglas airplanes.

How long can a commercial airplane keep flying safely and efficiently? American and Delta use their planes for about 20 years. The airlines want to use a plane like a Boeing 737 for a long time because it keeps them from having to come up with the cash to buy new planes. Top managers walk a tightrope between getting the good out of a plane and using one that consumes less fuel.

How do the airlines account for the use of an airplane? They record depreciation over the plane's useful life. Managers also have to consider how much they can sell a plane for when it's taken out of service. The airlines don't depreciate this residual value because they get it back when they sell a plane. ■

American/Delta/United Airlines

This chapter covers these and other topics about plant assets. **Plant assets** are the long-term tangible assets a business uses to operate, such as airplanes for American, copy equipment for Kinko's, and automobiles for Hertz. The chapter also shows how to account for natural resources, such as oil and timber, and **intangibles**—those assets with no physical form, such as trademarks, copyrights, and goodwill.

Chapter 10 concludes our coverage of assets, except for investments. After completing this chapter, you should understand the various assets of a business and how to account for them. Let's begin with an example that is familiar to you.

You probably own an automobile—maybe a Chevy or a Honda. Your car is a plant asset if you use it for day-to-day operations. But if you bought the car to resell it, then it would not be a plant asset; it would be part of your inventory. As your car wears out, it depreciates in usefulness. You should record depreciation on all the plant assets used in a business, except for land.

Plant assets have their own terminology. Exhibit 10-1 shows which expense account applies to each category of plant asset.

Exhibit 10-1

Plant Assets and Their Related Expenses

Plant Assets
Long-lived tangible assets, such as land, buildings, and equipment, used to operate a business.

Intangibles
Assets with no physical form. Valuable because of the special rights they carry. Examples are patents and copyrights.

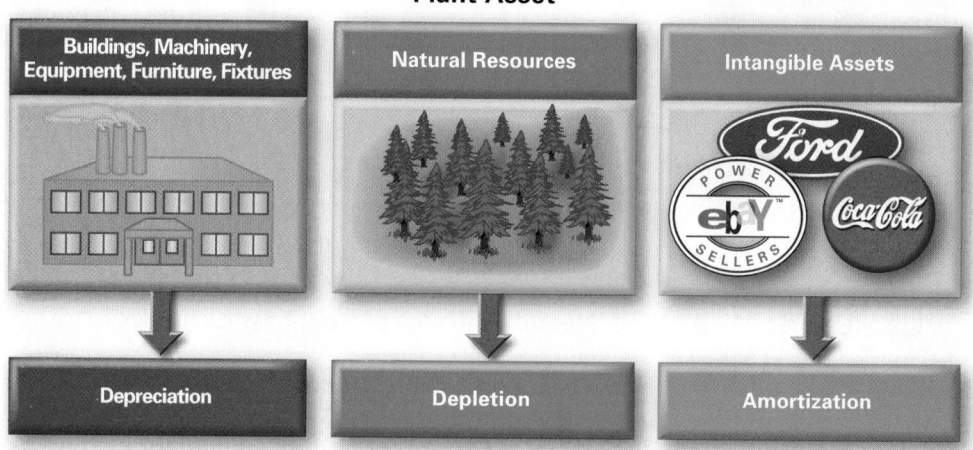

Plant Asset

| Buildings, Machinery, Equipment, Furniture, Fixtures | Natural Resources | Intangible Assets |

| Depreciation | Depletion | Amortization |

Related Expense

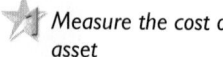Student ResourceCD

capital expenditure, plant asset

⭐ *Measure the cost of a plant asset*

Measuring the Cost of Plant Assets

The *cost principle* says to carry an asset on the balance sheet at its cost—the amount paid for the asset. The general rule for measuring cost is

$$\text{Cost of an asset} = \frac{\text{Sum of all the costs incurred to bring the asset}}{\text{to its intended purpose, net of all discounts}}$$

The *cost of a plant asset* is its purchase price plus applicable taxes, purchase commissions, and all other amounts paid to acquire the asset and make it ready for its intended use. In Chapter 6, we applied this principle to inventory. The types of costs differ for the various plant assets, so we discuss each asset individually.

Land and Land Improvements

The cost of land includes its purchase price, brokerage commission, survey and legal fees, and any back property taxes the purchaser pays. The cost also includes the cost of clearing the land and removing any unwanted buildings. The cost of land is not depreciated.

The cost does *not* include fencing, paving, sprinkler systems, and lighting. These separate plant assets—called *land improvements*—are subject to depreciation.

Suppose American Airlines signs a $500,000 note payable to purchase land. American also pays $40,000 in back property taxes, $8,000 in transfer taxes, $5,000 to remove an old building, and a $1,000 survey fee. What is the cost of this land? Exhibit 10-2 shows that all the costs incurred to bring the land to its intended use are part of the land's cost.

Purchase price of land		$500,000
Add related costs:		
Back property taxes	$40,000	
Transfer taxes	8,000	
Removal of building	5,000	
Survey fee	1,000	
Total related costs.		54,000
Total cost of land		$554,000

Exhibit 10-2

Measuring the Cost of a Plant Asset

American Airlines' entry to record purchase of the land follows.

Land	554,000	
Note Payable.		500,000
Cash		54,000

We would say that American Airlines *capitalized* the cost of the land at $554,000. This means that the company debited an asset account (Land) for $554,000.

Suppose American then pays $260,000 for fences, paving, lighting, and signs. The following entry records the cost of these land improvements.

Land Improvements	260,000	
Cash		260,000

Land and Land Improvements are two entirely separate asset accounts. The cost of land improvements is depreciated over the asset's useful life.

✔ **Starter 10-1**

Buildings

The cost of a building includes architectural fees, building permits, contractors' charges, and payments for material, labor, and overhead. The time to complete a building can be months, even years.

If the company constructs its own assets, the cost of the building may include the cost of interest on borrowed money. When an existing building is purchased, its cost includes all the usual items, plus all costs to repair and renovate the building for its intended use.

Machinery and Equipment

The cost of machinery and equipment includes its purchase price (less any discounts), plus transportation charges, insurance while in transit, sales and other taxes, purchase commission, installation costs, and the cost of testing the asset before it is used. After the asset is up and running, we no longer capitalize these costs to the Equipment account. Thereafter, insurance, taxes, and maintenance costs are recorded as expenses. American Airlines has an account for flight equipment, Kinko's has copy equipment, and Home Depot has delivery equipment for company trucks. All businesses have computer equipment.

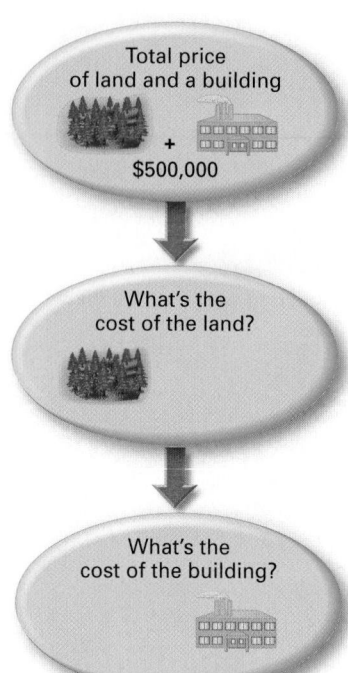

Furniture and Fixtures

Furniture and fixtures include desks, chairs, file cabinets, and display racks. The cost of furniture and fixtures includes the basic cost of each asset (less any discounts), plus all other costs to get the assets ready for use. All companies have furniture and fixtures.

A Lump-Sum (Basket) Purchase of Assets

A company may purchase several assets as a group—in a "basket purchase"—for a single price. For example, Delta Airlines may pay one price for land and a building. For accounting purposes, Delta must identify the cost of each asset, as shown in the margin diagram. The total cost (100%) is divided among the assets according to their relative sales values. This allocation technique is called the *relative-sales-value method*.

Suppose Delta Airlines purchases land and a building in Kansas City for a communication center. The combined purchase price of land and building is $2,800,000. An appraisal indicates that the land's market (sales) value is $300,000 and that the building's market (sales) value is $2,700,000.

First, figure the ratio of each asset's market value to the total market value of both assets combined. Suppose the total appraised value is $2,700,000 + $300,000 = $3,000,000. Thus, the land, valued at $300,000, is 10% of the total market value. The building's appraised value is 90% of the total. The cost of each asset is determined as follows:

Asset	Market (Sales) Value	Percentage of Total Value			Total Purchase Price		Cost of Each Asset
Land	$ 300,000	$300,000/$3,000,000	=	10% ×	$2,800,000	=	$ 280,000
Building	2,700,000	$2,700,000/$3,000,000	=	90% ×	2,800,000	=	2,520,000
Total	$3,000,000			100%			$2,800,000

Suppose Delta pays cash. The entry to record the purchase of the land and building is

Land	280,000	
Building	2,520,000	
Cash		2,800,000

Stop & Think

How would **Kinko's** divide a $120,000 lump-sum purchase price for land, building, and equipment with estimated market values of $40,000, $95,000, and $15,000, respectively? Round decimals to three places.

Answer:

Asset	Market (Sales) Value	Percentage of Total Value			Total Purchase Price		Cost of Each Asset
Land	$ 40,000	$40,000/$150,000	=	26.7% ×	$120,000	=	$ 32,040
Building	95,000	$95,000/$150,000	=	63.3% ×	120,000	=	75,960
Equipment . .	15,000	$15,000/$150,000	=	10.0% ×	120,000	=	12,000
Total	$150,000			100.0%			$120,000

Capital Expenditures

When a company spends money on a plant asset, it must decide whether to debit an asset account or an expense account. Examples of such expenditures range from General Motors buying robots for an assembly plant to you replacing the windshield on your automobile.

Expenditures that increase the asset's capacity or efficiency or that extend the asset's useful life are called **capital expenditures**. For example, GM's purchase of a robot and American Airlines' purchase of a Boeing 767 are capital expenditures. Also, the cost of a major overhaul that extends an asset's useful life is a capital expenditure. Repair work that generates a capital expenditure is called an **extraordinary repair**. Capital expenditures are debited to an asset account. For an extraordinary repair on a delivery truck, we would debit the Delivery Trucks account.

Other expenditures do not extend an asset's capacity, but merely maintain the asset in working order. These costs are *expenses* and are immediately subtracted from revenue. Examples include the costs of repainting a truck, repairing a fender, and replacing tires. These costs for **ordinary repairs** are debited to Repair Expense.

The distinction between capital and maintenance expenditures requires judgment. Does the cost extend the life of the asset (a capital expenditure), or does it only maintain the asset in good order (an expense)? Exhibit 10-3 illustrates the distinction between (a) capital expenditures and (b) expenses for several delivery-truck expenditures.

Capital Expenditure
Expenditure that increases the capacity or efficiency of an asset or extends its useful life. Capital expenditures are debited to an asset account.

Extraordinary Repair
Repair work that generates a capital expenditure.

Ordinary Repair
Repair work that is debited to an expense account.

CAPITAL EXPENDITURE: Debit an Asset Account	EXPENSE: Debit Repair and Maintenance Expense
Extraordinary repairs:	*Ordinary repairs:*
Major engine overhaul	Repair of transmission or engine
Modification for new use	Oil change, lubrication, and so on
Addition to storage capacity	Replacement of tires or windshield
	Paint job

Exhibit 10-3

Delivery-Truck Expenditures— Capital Expenditure or Expense?

Treating a capital expenditure as an expense, or vice versa, creates an accounting error. Suppose a company makes a capital expenditure and expenses this cost. This is an accounting error because the cost should have been debited to an asset account. This error overstates expenses and understates net income. On the balance sheet, the Equipment account is understated. Capitalizing an expense creates the opposite error. Expenses are understated, and net income is overstated. The balance sheet overstates assets.

✔ **Starter 10-3**

☐ Cost of Plant Assets
■ Plant Asset Depreciation
☐ Accounting for Plant Assets
☐ Natural Resources
☐ Intangibles
☐ Ethical Issues

Measuring Plant Asset Depreciation

As we've seen previously, *depreciation* is the allocation of a plant asset's cost to expense over its useful life. Depreciation matches the asset's cost (expense) against the revenue earned by the asset. → Exhibit 10-4 shows depreciation for the purchase of a Boeing 737 jet by United Airlines.

◉ Student Resource CD

accelerated depreciation, depreciation, double-declining balance, plant asset, straight-line depreciation, units-of-production

← See Chapter 3, page 95, for a discussion of the matching principle.

Exhibit 10-4

Depreciation and the Matching of Expense with Revenue

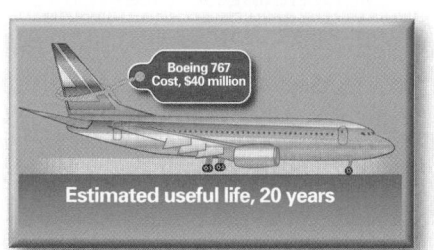

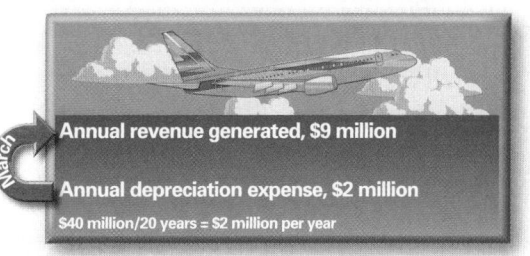

Suppose United Airlines buys a computer for use in its accounting system. United believes it will get four years of service from the computer, and it will then be worthless. Using the straight-line depreciation method, United expenses one-quarter of the asset's cost in each of its four years of use.

Let's contrast what depreciation is with what it is *not*.

1. *Depreciation is not a process of valuation.* Businesses do not record depreciation based on the market (sales) value of their plant assets.

2. *Depreciation does not mean that the business sets aside cash to replace an asset when it is used up.* Depreciation has nothing to do with establishing a cash fund.

Causes of Depreciation

All assets except land wear out. For some plant assets, *wear and tear* causes depreciation. For example, physical deterioration wears out the airplanes that American, Delta, and United fly. The store fixtures used to display merchandise in a Home Depot store are also subject to physical wear and tear.

Assets such as computers, software, and other electronic equipment may become *obsolete* before they wear out. An asset is obsolete when another asset can do the job more efficiently. Thus, an asset's useful life may be shorter than its physical life. Accountants usually depreciate computers over a short period—perhaps two to four years—even though the computers can continue working much longer. In all cases, the asset's cost is depreciated over its useful life.

Measuring Depreciation

Depreciation of a plant asset is based on three factors about an asset:

1. Cost   2. Estimated useful life   3. Estimated residual value

Cost is known. The other two factors are estimates.

Estimated useful life is the length of the service period expected from the asset. Useful life may be expressed in years, units of output, miles, or another measure. For example, a building's life is stated in years, a bookbinding machine in the number of books it can bind, and a delivery truck in miles.

Estimated residual value—also called **salvage value**—is the expected cash value of an asset at the end of its useful life. A machine's useful life may be seven years. After seven years, the company expects to sell the machine as scrap metal. The expected cash receipt is the machine's estimated residual value. Estimated residual value is *not* depreciated because the business expects to receive this amount at the end. If there's no residual value, then the business depreciates the full cost of the asset. Cost minus residual value is called **depreciable cost**.

Estimated Useful Life
Length of the service period expected from an asset. May be expressed in years, units of output, miles, or another measure.

Estimated Residual Value
Expected cash value of an asset at the end of its useful life. Also called **salvage value**.

Depreciable Cost
The cost of a plant asset minus its estimated residual value.

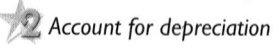 Account for depreciation

Depreciation Methods

Three major methods exist for computing depreciation:

■ Straight-line   ■ Units-of-production   ■ Declining-balance

These methods allocate different amounts of depreciation to each period. But they all result in the same total depreciation for the asset. Exhibit 10-5 gives the data we will use to illustrate depreciation for an American Airlines baggage-handling truck. We cover the three most widely used methods.[1]

---

[1]We omit the sum-of-years'-digits method because only 7 of 600 companies in a recent poll used it.

Data Item	Amount
Cost of truck...................................	$41,000
Less: Estimated residual value	(1,000)
Depreciable cost	$40,000
Estimated useful life:	
Years	5 years
Units of production........................	100,000 miles

Exhibit 10-5

Data for Recording Depreciation on a Truck

STRAIGHT-LINE METHOD   The **straight-line (SL) method** allocates an equal amount of depreciation to each year of asset use. Depreciable cost is divided by useful life in years to determine annual depreciation. The equation for SL depreciation, applied to the American Airlines truck from Exhibit 10-5, is

Straight-Line (SL) Depreciation Method
Depreciation method in which an equal amount of depreciation expense is assigned to each year of asset use.

$$\text{Straight-line depreciation} = \frac{\text{Cost} - \text{Residual value}}{\text{Useful life, in years}} = \frac{\$41,000 - \$1,000}{5}$$

$$= \$8,000 \text{ per year}$$

The entry to record each year's depreciation is

Depreciation Expense.......................	8,000	
Accumulated Depreciation		8,000

This truck was purchased on January 1, 20X1, and a *straight-line depreciation schedule* is given in Exhibit 10-6. The final column in the exhibit shows the asset's *book value*, which is cost less accumulated depreciation. →

As an asset is used, accumulated depreciation increases and the asset's book value decreases. See the Accumulated Depreciation and Book Value columns in Exhibit 10-6. An asset's final book value is *residual value* ($1,000 in Exhibit 10-6). At the end, the asset is said to be *fully depreciated*.

← *We introduced book value in Chapter 3, page 101.*

Exhibit 10-6   **Straight-Line Depreciation for a Truck**

Date	Asset Cost	Depreciation for the Year				Accumulated Depreciation	Book Value
		Depreciation Rate		Depreciable Cost	Depreciation Expense		
1-1-20X1	$41,000						$41,000
12-31-20X1		0.20*	×	$40,000	=	$8,000	$ 8,000	33,000
12-31-20X2		0.20	×	40,000	=	8,000	16,000	25,000
12-31-20X3		0.20	×	40,000	=	8,000	24,000	17,000
12-31-20X4		0.20	×	40,000	=	8,000	32,000	9,000
12-31-20X5		0.20	×	40,000	=	8,000	40,000	1,000

* 1/5 year = 0.20 per year

An asset with cost of $10,000, useful life of five years, and residual value of $2,000 was purchased on January 1. What is the SL depreciation for the first year? For the second year? For the fifth year?

Answer:
$$\frac{\text{SL}}{\text{depreciation}} = \frac{\text{Cost} - \text{Residual value}}{\text{Useful life, in years}} = \frac{\$10,000 - \$2,000}{5}$$

$$= \$1,600 \text{ per year}$$
$$\text{every year}$$

Units-of-Production (UOP) Depreciation Method
Depreciation method by which a fixed amount of depreciation is assigned to each unit of output produced by an asset.

UNITS-OF-PRODUCTION (UOP) METHOD   The **units-of-production (UOP) method** allocates a fixed amount of depreciation to each *unit of output* produced by the asset, as illustrated in Exhibit 10-7:

$$\text{Units-of-production depreciation per unit of output} = \frac{\text{Cost} - \text{Residual value}}{\text{Useful life, in units of production}} = \frac{\$41,000 - \$1,000}{100,000 \text{ miles}}$$

$$= \$0.40 \text{ per mile}$$

Assume that this truck is likely to be driven 20,000 miles the first year, 30,000 the second, 25,000 the third, 15,000 the fourth, and 10,000 during the fifth. The amount of UOP depreciation each period varies with the number of units the asset produces. Exhibit 10-7 shows the UOP schedule for this asset.

Exhibit 10-7   Units-of-Production Depreciation Schedule for a Truck

| | | Depreciation for the Year | | | | |
Date	Asset Cost	Depreciation Per Unit	Number of Units	Depreciation Expense	Accumulated Depreciation	Book Value
1-1-20X1	$41,000					$41,000
12-31-20X1		$0.40 ×	20,000 =	$ 8,000	$ 8,000	33,000
12-31-20X2		0.40 ×	30,000 =	12,000	20,000	21,000
12-31-20X3		0.40 ×	25,000 =	10,000	30,000	11,000
12-31-20X4		0.40 ×	15,000 =	6,000	36,000	5,000
12-31-20X5		0.40 ×	10,000 =	4,000	40,000	1,000

The asset in the preceding Stop & Think produced 3,000 units in the first year, 4,000 in the second, 4,500 in the third, 2,500 in the fourth, and 2,000 units in the last year. Its total estimated useful life is 16,000 miles. What is UOP depreciation for each year?

Answer:

$$\frac{\text{Depreciation}}{\text{per unit}} = \frac{\text{Cost} - \text{Residual value}}{\text{Useful life, in units of production}} = \frac{\$10,000 - \$2,000}{16,000 \text{ miles}} = \$0.50 \text{ per mile}$$

Yr. 1: $1,500 (3,000 miles × $0.50)   Yr. 4: $1,250 (2,500 miles × $0.50)
Yr. 2: $2,000 (4,000 miles × $0.50)   Yr. 5: $1,000 (2,000 miles × $0.50)
Yr. 3: $2,250 (4,500 miles × $0.50)

Accelerated Depreciation Method
A depreciation method that writes off more of the asset's cost near the start of its useful life than the straight-line method does.

Double-Declining-Balance (DDB) Depreciation Method
An accelerated depreciation method that computes annual depreciation by multiplying the asset's decreasing book value by a constant percent that is two times the straight-line rate.

DOUBLE-DECLINING BALANCE METHOD   Double-declining-balance depreciation is *accelerated*. An **accelerated depreciation method** writes off more depreciation near the start of an asset's life than the straight-line method does. The main accelerated depreciation method is **double-declining-balance (DDB)**. This method multiplies the asset's decreasing book value by a constant percentage that is 2 times the straight-line depreciation rate. DDB amounts can be computed in two steps:

1. Compute the straight-line depreciation rate per year. A 5-year asset has a straight-line rate of 1/5, or 20% per year. A 10-year asset has a straight-line rate of 1/10, or 10% per year, and so on.
   Multiply the straight-line rate by 2. The DDB rate for a 5-year asset is 40% per year (20% × 2 = 40%). For a 10-year asset, the DDB rate is 20% (10% × 2 = 20%).

2. Compute DDB depreciation for each year. Multiply the asset's book value (cost less accumulated depreciation) at the beginning of each year by the

DDB rate. Ignore residual value, except for the last year. The first-year depreciation for the truck in Exhibit 10-5 is

$$\begin{array}{ccc} \text{DDB depreciation} \\ \text{for the first year} \end{array} = \begin{array}{c} \text{Asset book value} \\ \text{at the beginning} \\ \text{of the year} \end{array} \times \text{ DDB rate}$$

$$\$16,400 \quad = \quad \$41,000 \quad \times \quad 0.40$$

The same approach is used to compute DDB depreciation for all later years, except for the final year, as follows.

Final-year depreciation is the amount needed to bring the asset to its residual value. In the DDB schedule (Exhibit 10-8), final-year depreciation is $4,314—book value of $5,314 less the $1,000 residual value.

Exhibit 10-8 Double-Declining-Balance Depreciation Schedule for a Truck

		Depreciation for the Year				
Date	Asset Cost	DDB Rate	Book Value	Depreciation Expense	Accumulated Depreciation	Book Value
1-1-20X1	$41,000					$41,000
12-31-20X1		0.40 ×	$41,000 =	$16,400	$16,400	24,600
12-31-20X2		0.40 ×	24,600 =	9,840	26,240	14,760
12-31-20X3		0.40 ×	14,760 =	5,904	32,144	8,856
12-31-20X4		0.40 ×	8,856 =	3,542	35,686	5,314
12-31-20X5				4,314*	40,000	1,000

* Last-year depreciation is the amount needed to reduce book value to the residual amount ($5,314 – $1,000 = $4,314).

The DDB method differs from the other methods in two ways:

- Residual value is ignored at the start. In the first year, depreciation is computed on the asset's full cost.
- Final-year depreciation is the amount needed to bring the asset to residual value. Final-year depreciation is a "plug" figure.

Many companies change to the straight-line method during the next-to-last year of the asset's life. Let's use this plan to compute annual depreciation for 20X4 and 20X5. In Exhibit 10-8, book value at the end of 20X3 is $8,856, so depreciable cost is $7,856 after subtracting residual value of $1,000. Depreciable cost can be spread evenly over the last two years ($7,856 ÷ 2 remaining years = $3,928 per year).

What is DDB depreciation for each year for the asset in the Stop & Think on page 405?

Answer: DDB rate = 1/5 × 2 = 40%

    Yr. 1: $4,000 ($10,000 × 40%)
    Yr. 2: $2,400 [($10,000 – $4,000 = $6,000) × 40%]
    Yr. 3: $1,440 [($6,000 – $2,400 = $3,600) × 40%]
    Yr. 4: $160 ($3,600 – $1,440 – $2,000*)

*Asset cost is not depreciated below residual value.

Stop & Think

Comparing Depreciation Methods

Let's compare the depreciation methods we've just discussed. Annual amounts vary by method, but total depreciation is the same for all methods: $40,000.

✔ **Starter 10-4**

✔ **Starter 10-5**

		Amount of Depreciation per Year	
			Accelerated Method
Year	Straight-Line	Units-of-Production	Double-Declining-Balance
1	$ 8,000	$ 8,000	$16,400
2	8,000	12,000	9,840
3	8,000	10,000	5,904
4	8,000	6,000	3,542
5	8,000	4,000	4,314
Total	$40,000	$40,000	$40,000

STRAIGHT-LINE   Which method is best? That depends on the asset and the company's situation. A business should match an asset's expense against the revenue that the asset produces. For an asset that generates revenue evenly over time, the straight-line method follows the matching principle. Each period the asset is used, an equal amount of depreciation is recorded.

UNITS-OF-PRODUCTION   The units-of-production method best fits an asset that depreciates due to wear and tear, rather than obsolescence. Depreciation is recorded only when the asset is used, and more use causes greater depreciation.

DOUBLE-DECLINING-BALANCE   The accelerated method (DDB) works best for assets that produce more revenue in their early years. Higher depreciation in the early years is matched against those periods' greater revenue. This is the mark of an accelerated method.

COMPARISONS   Exhibit 10-9 graphs annual depreciation for the three methods.

- The graph of straight-line depreciation is flat because annual depreciation is the same in all periods.

- Units-of-production depreciation follows no pattern because annual depreciation varies depending on the use of the asset.

- Accelerated depreciation is greater in the first year and less in the later years.

Exhibit 10-9

Depreciation Patterns for the Various Methods

A recent survey of 600 companies, conducted by the American Institute of CPAs, indicated that the straight-line method is most popular. Exhibit 10-10 shows the percentages of companies that use each depreciation method.

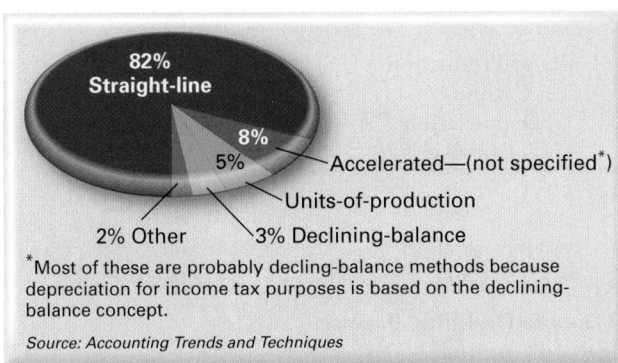

Source: Accounting Trends and Techniques

Exhibit 10-10

Use of Depreciation Methods

MID-CHAPTER *Summary Problem*

Quicker Copies purchased equipment on January 1, 20X5, for $44,000. Expected useful life is 10 years or 100,000 units of production, and residual value is $4,000. Under three depreciation methods, annual depreciation and total accumulated depreciation at the end of 20X5 and 20X6 are as follows:

CHECK YOUR RESOURCES

	Method A		Method B		Method C	
Year	Annual Depreciation Expense	Accumulated Depreciation	Annual Depreciation Expense	Accumulated Depreciation	Annual Depreciation Expense	Accumulated Depreciation
20X5	$1,200	$1,200	$8,800	$ 8,800	$4,000	$4,000
20X6	5,600	6,800	7,040	15,840	4,000	8,000

Required

1. Identify the depreciation method used in each instance, and show the equation and computation for each. (Round amounts to the nearest dollar.)
2. Assume continued use of the same method through 20X7. Determine the annual depreciation expense, accumulated depreciation, and book value of the equipment for 20X5 through 20X7 under each method, assuming 12,000 units of production in 20X7.

Solution

Requirement 1

Method A: Units-of-Production

$$\text{Depreciation per unit} = \frac{\$44,000 - \$4,000}{100,000 \text{ units}} = \$0.40$$

20X5: $0.40 × 3,000 units = $1,200
20X6: $0.40 × 14,000 units = $5,600

Method B: Double-Declining-Balance

$$\text{Rate} = \frac{1}{10 \text{ years}} \times 2 = 10\% \times 2 = 20\%$$

20X5: 0.20 × $44,000 = $8,800
20X6: 0.20 × ($44,000 − $8,800) = $7,040

Method C: Straight-Line

Depreciable cost = $44,000 − $4,000 = $40,000
Each year: $40,000/10 years = $4,000

Requirement 2

Method A: Units-of-Production

Year	Annual Depreciation Expense	Accumulated Depreciation	Book Value
Start			$44,000
20X5	$1,200	$ 1,200	42,800
20X6	5,600	6,800	37,200
20X7	4,800	11,600	32,400

Method B: Double-Declining-Balance

Year	Annual Depreciation Expense	Accumulated Depreciation	Book Value
Start			$44,000
20X5	$8,800	$ 8,800	35,200
20X6	7,040	15,840	28,160
20X7	5,632	21,472	22,528

Method C: Straight-Line

Year	Annual Depreciation Expense	Accumulated Depreciation	Book Value
Start			$44,000
20X5	$4,000	$ 4,000	40,000
20X6	4,000	8,000	36,000
20X7	4,000	12,000	32,000

Computations for 20X7:

Units-of-production	$0.40 × 12,000 units = $4,800
Double-declining-balance	0.20 × $28,160 = $5,632
Straight-line	$40,000 / 10 years = $4,000

☐ Cost of Plant Assets
☐ Plant Asset Depreciation
■ **Accounting for Plant Assets**
☐ Natural Resources
☐ Intangibles
☐ Ethical Issues

Student ResourceCD

depreciation, plant asset, MACRS

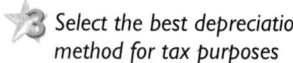

Select the best depreciation method for tax purposes

✔ Starter 10-6

Other Issues in Accounting for Plant Assets

Depreciation affects income taxes, and companies may have gains or losses when they sell plant assets.

Depreciation and Income Taxes

Most companies use straight-line depreciation for their financial statements. But they use a different depreciation method for income taxes. For tax purposes, most companies use an accelerated method.

Suppose you manage the United Airlines operation at Chicago's O'Hare airport. The IRS allows the DDB depreciation method, and you prefer accelerated to straight-line depreciation. Why? Because it provides the most depreciation expense as quickly as possible. The accelerated depreciation decreases your immediate tax payments and conserves your cash. You can then invest the cash and earn more income. This is a common strategy.

To understand how depreciation affects cash flow, recall our earlier depreciation of the American Airlines truck: First-year depreciation is $8,000 under straight-line and $16,400 under double-declining-balance. Which tax deduction would you prefer? You would choose DDB depreciation because it gives you a greater tax deduction and saves cash.

A special depreciation method called the *modified accelerated cost recovery system (MACRS)* is used for income tax purposes. Under MACRS, assets are divided into classes by asset life, as shown in Exhibit 10-11. MACRS depreciation is computed by the double-declining-balance method, the 150%-declining-balance method, or the straight-line method. Under 150% DB, the annual depreciation rate is computed by multiplying the straight-line rate by 1.50 (rather than by 2, as for DDB). For a 20-year asset, the straight-line rate is 0.05 (1/20 = 0.05), so the annual MACRS depreciation rate is 0.075 (0.05 × 1.50 = 0.075).

Class Identified by Asset Life (Years)	Representative Assets	Depreciation Method
3	Racehorses	DDB
5	Automobiles, light trucks	DDB
10	Equipment	DDB
20	Certain real estate	150% DB
27 1/2	Residential rental property	SL
39	Nonresidential rental property	SL

Exhibit 10-11

Selected Details of the Modified Accelerated Cost Recovery System (MACRS) Depreciation Method

Depreciation for Partial Years

Companies purchase plant assets whenever they need them. They don't wait until the beginning of a period. Therefore, companies develop policies to compute depreciation for partial years. Suppose Linens 'n Things purchases a building on *April 1* for $500,000. The building's estimated life is 20 years, with estimated residual value of $80,000. How does Linens 'n Things compute depreciation for the year ended December 31?

Many companies compute partial-year depreciation by first calculating a full year's depreciation. They then multiply full-year depreciation by the fraction of the year that they used the asset. Under the straight-line method, the year's depreciation for the Linens 'n Things building is $15,750, computed as follows:

Full-year depreciation: $\dfrac{\$500,000 - \$80,000}{20 \text{ years}} = \$21,000$

Partial-year depreciation: $\$21,000 \times 9/12 = \$15,750$

What if the company bought the asset on April 18? One policy is to record no depreciation on assets purchased after the 15th of the month. This policy also records a full month's depreciation on an asset bought on or before the 15th. In that case, the year's depreciation would be $14,000 for eight months ($21,000 × 8/12 = $14,000).

Partial-year depreciation is computed under the other depreciation methods in the same way—by applying the appropriate percentage of the year that the asset is used. Most companies use computerized systems to account for fixed assets. Such systems will automatically calculate the depreciation expense for each period.

✔ Starter 10-7

Changing the Useful Life of a Depreciable Asset

Estimating the useful life of a plant asset poses an accounting challenge. As the asset is used, the business may change its estimated useful life based on experience and new information. Walt Disney Company made such a change, called a *change in accounting estimate*. Disney refigured depreciation for theme-park assets. The following note in Disney's financial statements reports this change in accounting estimate:

Note 5

. . . [T]he Company extended the estimated useful lives of certain theme park . . . assets based upon . . . engineering studies. The effect of this change was to decrease depreciation by approximately $8 million. . . .

Accounting changes like these are common because no one has perfect foresight. When a company makes an accounting change, generally accepted accounting principles require the business to report the nature, reason, and effect of the accounting change. The Disney example reports this information.

For a change in accounting estimate, the remaining book value of the asset is spread over the asset's remaining life. Assume that a Disney World hot dog stand cost $40,000. Suppose Disney originally believed the asset had an eight-year life with no residual value. Using the straight-line method, Disney would record depreciation of $5,000 each year ($40,000/8 years = $5,000).

Suppose Disney used the asset for two years. Accumulated depreciation reached $10,000. The asset's remaining depreciable book value (cost *less* accumulated depreciation *less* residual value) is $30,000 ($40,000 − $10,000). Suppose Disney management believes the hot dog stand will remain useful for 10 more years. The company would recompute depreciation as follows:

Asset's Remaining Depreciable Book Value	÷	(New) Estimated Useful Life Remaining	=	(New) Annual Depreciation
$30,000	÷	10 years	=	$3,000

 Starter 10-8

The yearly depreciation entry based on the new useful life is

Depreciation Expense—Hot Dog Stand.........	3,000	
Accumulated Depreciation—		
Hot Dog Stand........................		3,000

Revised straight-line depreciation is computed as follows:

$$\text{Revised SL depreciation} = \frac{\text{Cost} - \text{Accumulated depreciation} - \text{New residual value}}{\text{Estimated remaining useful life in years}}$$

Using Fully Depreciated Assets

A *fully depreciated asset* is one that has reached the end of its *estimated* useful life. No more depreciation is recorded for the asset. If the asset is no longer useful, it is disposed of. But the asset may still be useful, and the company may continue using this fully depreciated asset. The asset account and its accumulated depreciation remain on the books, but no additional depreciation is recorded.

Stop & Think

> A fully depreciated asset has a cost of $80,000 and zero residual value. What is the asset's accumulated depreciation?
>
> *Answer:* $80,000 (same as the asset's cost).
>
> Now suppose the asset's residual value is $10,000. How much is accumulated depreciation?
>
> *Answer:* $70,000 ($80,000 − $10,000).

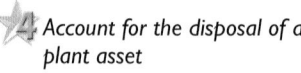 Account for the disposal of a plant asset

Disposing of a Plant Asset

Eventually, an asset no longer serves its purpose. The asset may be worn out or obsolete. The owner may sell the asset or exchange it. If the asset cannot be sold or exchanged, then it is junked. Whatever the method of disposal, the business should bring depreciation up to date. That helps to measure the asset's final book value properly.

To record the disposal of a plant asset, credit the asset account and debit its accumulated depreciation. That removes the asset from the books. Suppose the final year's depreciation expense has just been recorded for a machine. Its cost was $6,000, and there is no residual value. The machine's accumulated depreciation thus totals $6,000. This asset cannot be sold or exchanged, so it is junked. The entry to record its disposal is

Accumulated Depreciation—Machinery . . .	6,000	
Machinery		6,000
To dispose of fully depreciated machine.		

Machinery	
6,000	6,000

Accumulated Depreciation—Machinery	
6,000	6,000

Now both accounts have a zero balance, as shown in the T-accounts at the right.

If assets are junked before being fully depreciated, the company records a loss equal to the asset's book value. Suppose Home Depot fixtures that cost $4,000 are junked at a loss. Accumulated depreciation is $3,000, and book value is therefore $1,000. Disposal of these store fixtures generates a loss, as follows:

Accumulated Depreciation—Store Fixtures	3,000	
Loss on Disposal of Store Fixtures	1,000	
Store Fixtures		4,000
To dispose of store fixtures.		

All losses, including this Loss on Disposal of Store Fixtures, decrease net income. Losses are reported along with expenses on the income statement.

SELLING A PLANT ASSET Suppose a Kinko's store sells furniture on September 30, 20X4, for $5,000 cash. The furniture cost $10,000 when purchased on January 1, 20X1, and has been depreciated on a straight-line basis. Kinko's estimated a 10-year life and no residual value. Prior to selling the furniture, Kinko's must update its depreciation. Partial-year depreciation must be recorded for nine months—from January 1, 20X4, to the sale date on September 30. The straight-line depreciation entry at September 30, 20X4, is

Sep. 30	Depreciation Expense ($10,000/10 years × 9/12) . . 750	
	Accumulated Depreciation—Furniture . . .	750
	To update depreciation.	

Now the Furniture and the Accumulated Depreciation—Furniture accounts appear as follows.

Furniture	
Jan. 1, 20X1 10,000	

Accumulated Depreciation—Furniture	
	Dec. 31, 20X1 1,000
	Dec. 31, 20X2 1,000
	Dec. 31, 20X3 1,000
	Sep. 30, 20X4 750
	Balance 3,750

Book Value = $6,250

Book value of the furniture is $6,250. Suppose Kinko's sells the furniture for $5,000 cash. The loss on the sale is $1,250, computed as follows:

Cash received from selling the asset		$5,000
Book value of asset sold:		
Cost	$10,000	
Less: Accumulated depreciation up to date of sale . . .	(3,750)	6,250
Gain (loss) on sale of the asset		($1,250)

Kinko's entry to sell the furniture is

Sep. 30 Cash	....	5,000	
	Accumulated Depreciation—Furniture	3,750	
	Loss on Sale of Furniture	1,250	
	Furniture		10,000
	To sell furniture.		

When recording the sale of a plant asset, the business must:

- Remove the balances in the asset account (Furniture, in this case) and its accumulated depreciation account
- Record a gain or loss if the cash received differs from the asset's book value.

In our example, cash of $5,000 is less than book value of $6,250. The result is a loss of $1,250.

If the sale price had been $7,000, Kinko's would have had a gain of $750 (Cash, $7,000 – asset book value, $6,250). The entry to record this gain would be

Sep. 30 Cash	....	7,000	
	Accumulated Depreciation—Furniture	3,750	
	Furniture		10,000
	Gain on Sale of Furniture		750
	To sell furniture.		

✔ **Starter 10-9**

A gain is recorded when an asset is sold for more than book value. A loss is recorded when the sale price is less than book value.

Gain (credit) = Sale proceeds > Book value

Loss (debit) = Sale proceeds < Book value

Gains increase net income, and losses decrease net income. All gains and losses are reported on the income statement.

EXCHANGING PLANT ASSETS Businesses often exchange old plant assets for newer, more-efficient assets. The most common exchange transaction is a trade-in. For example, Domino's Pizza may trade in a five-year-old delivery car for a newer model. To record the exchange, Domino's must write off the old asset and its accumulated depreciation exactly as we just did for Kinko's disposal of furniture.

For most trade-ins, the business carries forward the book value of the old asset plus any cash payment as the cost of the new asset. For example, assume Domino's old delivery car cost $9,000 and has accumulated depreciation of $8,000. Book value is $1,000. Domino's trades in the old auto and pays cash of $10,000. Domino's records the trade-in with this journal entry:

Delivery Auto (new)	....	11,000	
Accumulated Depreciation (old)	....	8,000	
Delivery Auto (old)	....		9,000
Cash	....		10,000
Traded in old delivery car for new auto.			

Domino's cost of the new car is $11,000 (cash paid $10,000, plus the book value of the old auto, $1,000).

Accounting for Natural Resources

☐ Cost of Plant Assets
☐ Plant Asset Depreciation
☐ Accounting for Plant Assets
■ **Natural Resources**
☐ Intangibles
☐ Ethical Issues

Natural resources are plant assets. Examples include iron ore, oil, natural gas, and timber. Natural resources are like inventories in the ground (oil) or on top of the ground (timber). Natural resources are expensed through *depletion*. **Depletion expense** is that portion of the cost of natural resources that is used up in a particular period. Depletion expense is computed by the units-of-production formula:

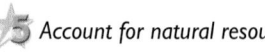

Student ResourceCD

depletion

⭐ **5** *Account for natural resources*

$$\frac{\text{Depletion}}{\text{expense}} = \frac{\text{Cost} - \text{Residual value}}{\text{Estimated total units of natural resource}} \times \textbf{Number of units removed}$$

Depletion Expense
Portion of a natural resource's cost used up in a particular period. Computed in the same way as units-of-production depreciation.

An oil well may cost $100,000 and hold 10,000 barrels of oil. Natural resources usually have no residual value. The depletion rate thus would be $10 per barrel ($100,000/10,000 barrels). If 3,000 barrels are extracted during the year, then depletion is $30,000 (3,000 barrels × $10 per barrel). The depletion entry for the year is

Depletion Expense (3,000 barrels × $10)	30,000	
Accumulated Depletion—Oil		30,000

If 4,500 barrels are removed next year, depletion is $45,000 (4,500 barrels × $10 per barrel).

Accumulated Depletion is a contra account similar to Accumulated Depreciation. Natural resources can be reported on the balance sheet as shown for oil in the following example:

Property, Plant, and Equipment:		
Land..		$120,000
Buildings....................................	$800,000	
Equipment	160,000	
	960,000	
Less: Accumulated depreciation...................	(410,000)	550,000
Oil..	$380,000	
Less: Accumulated depletion......................	(80,000)	300,000
Property, plant, and equipment, net................		$970,000

✔ **Starter 10-10**

Ladue Paper Products pays $500,000 for land that holds 500,000 board feet of lumber. The land can be sold for $100,000 after the timber has been cut. If Ladue Paper harvests 200,000 board feet of lumber, how much depletion should be recorded?

Answer:

(Cost – Residual)	÷	Total output	=	Depletion rate	×	Production	=	Depletion
($500,000 – $100,000)	÷	500,000	=	$0.80 per foot	×	200,000	=	$160,000

☐ Cost of Plant Assets
☐ Plant Asset Depreciation
☐ Accounting for Plant Assets
☐ Natural Resources
■ **Intangibles**
☐ Ethical Issues

Student ResourceCD

amortization, goodwill, intangibles

⭐ **6** *Account for intangible assets*

Accounting for Intangible Assets

As we saw earlier in the chapter, *intangible assets* have no physical form. Instead, these assets convey special rights from patents, copyrights, trademarks, and so on.

In our technology-driven economy, intangibles rival tangible assets in value. Customer loyalty is all-important. Consider online pioneer eBay. The company has no physical products or equipment, but it helps people buy and sell everything from Batman toys to bathroom tiles. Each month eBay serves millions of customers. In a sense, eBay is a company of intangibles.

The intellectual capital of eBay or Intel is difficult to measure. But when one company buys another, we get a glimpse of the value of the acquired company. For example, America Online announced it would acquire Time Warner. AOL said it would give $146 billion of AOL stock for Time Warner's net tangible assets of only $9 billion. Why so much for so little? Because Time Warner's intangible assets were worth $190 billion. Intangibles can account for most of a company's market value, so companies are finding ways to value their intangibles, just as they do inventory and equipment.

A *patent* is an intangible asset that protects a secret process or formula. The acquisition cost of a patent is debited to the Patents account. The intangible is expensed through **amortization**, the systematic reduction of the asset's carrying value on the books. Amortization applies to intangibles exactly as depreciation applies to plant assets. Depreciation, depletion, and amortization are conceptually the same.

Amortization is computed over the asset's estimated useful life—usually by the straight-line method. Obsolescence often shortens an intangible's useful life. Amortization expense for an intangible asset can be written off directly against the asset account with no accumulated amortization account. The residual value of most intangibles is zero.

Some intangibles have indefinite lives. For them, the company records no systematic amortization each period. Instead, it accounts for any decrease in the value of the intangible, as we shall see for goodwill.

Specific Intangibles

PATENTS   A **patent** is a federal government grant conveying an exclusive 20-year right to produce and sell an invention. The invention may be a product or a process—for example, the Dolby noise-reduction process. Like any other asset, a patent may be purchased. Suppose General Electric Company (GE) pays $200,000 to acquire a patent on January 1. GE believes this patent's useful life is five years. Amortization expense is $40,000 per year ($200,000/5 years). Acquisition and amortization entries for this patent are

Jan.	1	Patents.......................... 200,000	
		Cash.......................	200,000
		To acquire a patent.	
Dec.	31	Amortization Expense—Patents	
		($200,000/5) 40,000	
		Patents.....................	40,000
		To amortize the cost of a patent.	

At the end of the first year, GE will report this patent at $160,000 ($200,000 minus the first year's amortization of $40,000), next year at $120,000, and so on.

COPYRIGHTS   A **copyright** is the exclusive right to reproduce and sell a book, musical composition, film, or other work of art or intellectual property. Copyrights also protect computer software programs, such as Microsoft Windows® and the Excel spreadsheet. Issued by the federal government, a copyright extends 70 years beyond the author's life.

A company may pay a large sum to purchase an existing copyright. For example, the publisher Simon & Schuster may pay $1 million for the copyright on a popular novel. Most copyrights have short useful lives.

TRADEMARKS, BRAND NAMES   Trademarks and **trade names** are assets that represent distinctive products or services, such as the CBS "eye" and

---

Amortization
Systematic reduction of the asset's carrying value on the books. Expense that applies to intangibles in the same way depreciation applies to plant assets and depletion to natural resources.

Patent
A federal government grant giving the holder the exclusive right to produce and sell an invention for 20 years.

Copyright
Exclusive right to reproduce and sell a book, musical composition, film, other work of art, or computer program. Issued by the federal government, copyrights extend 70 years beyond the author's life.

Trademarks, Trade Names, or Brand Names
Assets that represent distinctive identifications of a product or service.

NBC's peacock. Legally protected slogans include Chevrolet's "Like a Rock" and Avis Rent A Car's "We try harder." The cost of a trademark or trade name is amortized over its useful life.

FRANCHISES, LICENSES   **Franchises** and **licenses** are privileges granted by a private business or a government to sell products or services under specified conditions. The Green Bay Packers football organization is a franchise granted by the National Football League. McDonald's restaurants and Holiday Inns are popular business franchises. The acquisition cost of a franchise or license is amortized over its useful life.

Franchises, Licenses
Privileges granted by a private business or a government to sell a product or service under specified conditions.

GOODWILL   The term *goodwill* in accounting has a very different meaning from the everyday term, "goodwill among men." In accounting, **goodwill** is the excess of the cost to purchase another company over the market value of its net assets (assets minus liabilities).

Wal-Mart has expanded into Mexico. Suppose Wal-Mart acquired Mexana Company at a cost of $10 million. The sum of the market values of Mexana's assets was $9 million and its liabilities totaled $1 million, so Mexana's net assets totaled $8 million. In this case, Wal-Mart paid $2 million for goodwill, computed as follows:

Goodwill
Excess of the cost of an acquired company over the sum of the market values of its net assets (assets minus liabilities).

Purchase price to acquire Mexana Company		$10 million
Market value of Mexana Company's assets	$ 9 million	
Less: Mexana Company's liabilities	(1 million)	
Market value of Mexana Company's net assets . . .		8 million
Excess, called *goodwill*		$ 2 million

Wal-Mart's entry to record the purchase of Mexana Company, including the goodwill that Wal-Mart purchased, would be

Assets (Cash, Receivables, Inventories,		
Plant Assets, all at market value)	9,000,000	
Goodwill	2,000,000	
Liabilities		1,000,000
Cash		10,000,000
Purchased Mexana Company.		

Goodwill has some special features:

1. Goodwill is recorded only by a company that purchases another company. An outstanding reputation may create goodwill for a company, but that company never records goodwill for its own business. Instead, goodwill is recorded *only* by the acquiring entity when it buys another company.

2. According to generally accepted accounting principles (GAAP), goodwill is *not* amortized. Instead, the company measures the current value of its purchased goodwill each year. If the goodwill has increased in value, there is nothing to record. But if goodwill's value has decreased, then the company records a loss and writes the goodwill down. For example, suppose Wal-Mart's goodwill—purchased above—is worth only $1,500,000 at the end of the first year. In that case, Wal-Mart would make this entry:

✔ Starter 10-11

Loss on Goodwill	500,000	
Goodwill ($2,000,000 − $1,500,000) . .		500,000
Recorded loss on goodwill.		

Wal-Mart would then report this goodwill at its current value of $1,500,000.

When Business Marriages Go Bust

Most partners enter a marriage with high expectations. It's the same with mergers and acquisitions (M&As). But in M&As, those expectations appear on a balance sheet in the form of *goodwill*, which is the excess of the cost to buy another company over the market value of its net assets. Accounting forces companies to measure their losses when M&As go sour.

The FASB used to require companies to write off goodwill evenly over a 40-year period (a process called *amortization*). Now the FASB requires companies to write goodwill down whenever it loses value. That means companies must revalue goodwill each year. Investors first saw the results of the new accounting rule at the start of 2002, when billions of dollars of goodwill evaporated. The huge write-offs reveal that many 1990s megamergers haven't lived up to expectations.

- **Qwest's** merger with **USWest** resulted in a $30 billion write-down.
- **America Online's** $54 billion write-down was an admission that its merger with **Time Warner** never lived up to the hype.

What effects do the huge write-offs have? Most analysts say goodwill write-offs hurt reported profits and depress stock prices. Others see them as one-time events that have little bearing on a company's future. For instance, the day after AOL's $54 billion write-off, the stock actually rose a little. Some companies will benefit from the rule change, for example, those who no longer have to record amortization. This new accounting rule might make companies think twice before getting hitched in the first place.

Based on: Joellen Perry, "The New Math of Mergers; Companies Are Writing Off the 'Goodwill' from Their Not-So-Good Deals," *U.S. News & World Report*, November 11, 2002, p. 40. Jeffrey Krasner, "Biotech Firms Wrestle with New Rules Accounting for Goodwill," *Boston Globe*, August 21, 2002, p. C1. Anne Tergesen, "How Much Is the Goodwill Worth? It Pays to Do the Math Before Your Stock Takes a Hit," *Business Week*, September 16, 2002, p. 83. Jonathan Weil, "Another Write-Off May Loom for AOL—Despite Stock's Recent Recovery, Investors Aren't Likely to Agree with Values Assigned to Assets," *The Wall Street Journal*, August 23, 2002, p. C1. Anonymous, "Qwest Sets Billions in Charges Related to Goodwill Value," *The Wall Street Journal*, October 29, 2002, p. A18.

Accounting for Research and Development Costs

Accounting for research and development (R&D) costs is one of the toughest issues the accounting profession has faced. R&D is the lifeblood of companies such as Procter & Gamble, General Electric, Intel, and Boeing because it is vital to the development of new products and processes. But, in general, they do not report R&D assets on their balance sheets because GAAP requires companies to expense R&D costs as they incur those costs.

Ethical Issues

The main ethical issue in accounting for plant assets is whether to capitalize or to expense a particular cost. In this area, companies have split personalities. On the one hand, they all want to save on taxes. This motivates them to expense all costs to decrease taxable income. But they also want to look as good as possible, with high net income and high amounts for assets.

In most cases, a cost that is capitalized or expensed for tax purposes must be treated the same way in the financial statements. What, then, is the ethical path? Accountants should follow the general guidelines for capitalizing a cost:

Capitalize all costs that provide a future benefit for the business, and expense all other costs, as outlined in the Decision Guidelines box that follows.

Many companies have gotten into trouble by capitalizing costs that were really expenses. They made their financial statements look better than the facts warranted. But there are very few cases of companies getting into trouble by following the general guidelines, or even by erring on the side of expensing questionable costs. This is another example of accounting conservatism. It works. →

← *We discussed accounting conservatism in Chapter 6, p. 258.*

Decision Guidelines

ACCOUNTING FOR PLANT ASSETS AND RELATED EXPENSES

Suppose you buy a **Curves International** franchise and invest in Nautilus and other fitness equipment. You have some decisions to make about how to account for the franchise and the equipment. The Decision Guidelines will help you maximize your cash flow and do the accounting properly.

Decision	Guidelines
Capitalize or expense a cost?	General rule: Capitalize all costs that provide *future benefit*. Expense all costs that provide *no future benefit*.
Capitalize or expense: • Cost associated with a new asset? • Cost associated with an existing asset?	Capitalize all costs that bring the asset to its intended use. Capitalize only those costs that add to the asset's usefulness or its useful life. Expense all other costs as maintenance or repairs.
Which depreciation method to use: • For financial reporting?	Use the method that best matches depreciation expense against the revenues produced by the asset.
• For income tax?	Use the method that produces the fastest tax deductions (MACRS). A company can use different depreciation methods for financial reporting and for income tax purposes. In the United States, this practice is considered both legal and ethical.

Excel Application Exercise

Goal: To create an Excel worksheet that calculates a proposed plant-asset investment's net income using different depreciation methods.

Scenario: Suppose the owner of the local **Curves International** franchise is considering investing in a new multistation weight machine. The following information is related to the acquisition and operation of the machine:

Initial investment	$100,000
Salvage value	$10,000
Useful life	6 years
Annual revenue attributable to the investment	$42,000
Annual operating expenses, excluding depreciation, associated with the investment	$14,000

The machine will be in use for 2,880 hours in year one; 2,550 hours each in years two and four; 2,190 hours in year five; and 1,460 hours each in years three and six.

When finished with your worksheet, answer these questions:

1. Which depreciation method produces the highest net income in year 1? In year 6? If it's not the same method for each year, why not?
2. Which method would Curves choose for tax purposes? Why?
3. Which method would Curves choose for reporting to bankers and creditors? Why? What if the company wanted to change methods after two years?

Step-by-Step:

1. Open a new Excel worksheet.
2. Prepare a bold-faced heading with the following information:
   a. Chapter 10 Excel Application Exercise
   b. Curves Depreciation Schedule
   c. Today's Date

Excel Application Exercise *(continued)*

3. Two rows under your heading, prepare four sections in your worksheet:

   Section I needs to contain the information listed in the table above, plus a line item for depreciation per unit.

   Section 2 will calculate net income from the investment using straight-line depreciation calculated using the SLN spreadsheet function. This section will have the following format:

   Section 2 Straight-Line Depreciation

			Year				
0	1	2	3	4	5	6	
Revenue							
Expenses							
Depreciation							
Net income							

Section 3 will calculate net income from the investment using double-declining-balance depreciation (calculated using the DDB spreadsheet function). This section will have a format like that of Section 2.

Section 4 will calculate net income from the investment using units-of-production depreciation (there is no Excel formula for this method). This section will have a format like that of Section 2, with the addition of a row for the annual units of production.

4. Format all cells appropriately, save your worksheet, and print a copy for your files.

● END-OF-CHAPTER *Summary Problem*

TIPS

CHECK YOUR RESOURCES

The following figures appear in the Answers to the Mid-Chapter Summary Problem, requirement 2, on page 410.

	Method B: Double-Declining-Balance				Method C: Straight-Line		
Year	Annual Depreciation Expense	Accumulated Depreciation	Book Value		Annual Depreciation Expense	Accumulated Depreciation	Book Value
Start			$44,000				$44,000
20X5	$8,800	$ 8,800	35,200		$4,000	$ 4,000	40,000
20X6	7,040	15,840	28,160		4,000	8,000	36,000
20X7	5,632	21,472	22,528		4,000	12,000	32,000

Quicker Copies purchased equipment on January 1, 20X5. Management has depreciated the equipment by using the double-declining-balance method. On July 1, 20X7, the company sold the equipment for $27,000 cash.

Required

1. Suppose the income tax authorities permit a choice between the two depreciation methods shown. Which method would you select for income tax purposes? Why?
2. Record Quicker Copies' depreciation for 20X7 and the sale of the equipment on July 1, 20X7.

Solution

Requirement 1

For tax purposes, most companies select the accelerated method because it results in the most depreciation in the earliest years of the equipment's life. Accelerated depreciation minimizes taxable income and income tax payments in the early years of the asset's life, thereby maximizing the business's cash at the earliest possible time.

Requirement 2

To record depreciation to date of sale and sale of Quicker Copies' equipment:

20X7

July 1 Depreciation Expense—Equipment
           ($5,632 × 1/2 year)   2,816
                   Accumulated Depreciation—Equipment . .   2,816
           To update depreciation.

July 1 Cash 27,000
           Accumulated Depreciation—Equipment
           ($15,840 + $2,816) 18,656
                   Equipment.   44,000
                   Gain on Sale of Equipment.   1,656
           To record sale of equipment.

REVIEW *Plant Assets and Intangibles*

Quick Check

1. Which cost is not recorded as part of the cost of a building?
   a. Construction materials and labor
   b. Annual building maintenance
   c. Real Estate commission paid to buy the building
   d. Earth-moving for the building's foundation

2. **FedEx** bought two used **Boeing** 707 airplanes. Each plane was worth $35 million, but the owner sold the combination for $60 million. How much is FedEx's cost of each plane?
   a. $30 million   c. $60 million
   b. $35 million   d. $70 million

3. How should you record a capital expenditure?
   a. Debit capital   c. Debit a liability
   b. Debit an expense   d. Debit an asset

4. Which depreciation method always produces the most depreciation in the first year?
   a. Straight-line   c. Double-declining-balance
   b. Units-of-production   d. All produce the same total depreciation

5. A FedEx airplane costs $50 million and is expected to fly 500 million miles during its 10-year life. Residual value is expected to be zero because the plane was used when acquired. If the plane travels 20 million miles the first year, how much depreciation should FedEx record under the units-of-production method?
   a. $2 million   c. $10 million
   b. $5 million   d. Cannot be determined from the data given

6. Which depreciation method would you prefer to use for income tax purposes? Why?
   a. Straight-line because it is simplest
   b. Units-of-production because it best tracks the asset's use
   c. Double-declining-balance because it gives the most total depreciation over the asset's life
   d. Double-declining-balance because it gives the fastest tax deductions for depreciation

7. A copy machine cost $40,000 when new and has accumulated depreciation of $37,000. Suppose **Kinko's** junks this machine, receiving nothing. What is the result of the disposal transaction?
   a. Gain of $3,000   c. Gain of $37,000
   b. Loss of $3,000   d. Loss of $40,000

8. Suppose Kinko's in the preceding question sold the machine for $5,000. What is the result of this disposal transaction?
   a. Gain of $2,000   c. Gain of $3,000
   b. Loss of $2,000   d. Gain of $5,000

9. Which method is used to compute depletion?
   a. Depletion method   c. Units-of-production method
   b. Straight-line method   d. Double-declining-balance method

10. Which intangible asset is recorded only as part of the acquisition of another company?
    a. Copyright   c. Franchise
    b. Patent   d. Goodwill

Accounting Vocabulary

accelerated depreciation method (p. 406)
amortization (p. 416)
brand names (p. 416)
capital expenditure (p. 403)
copyright (p. 416)
depletion expense (p. 415)
depreciable cost (p. 404)
double-declining-balance (DDB)
    depreciation method (p. 406)

estimated residual value (p. 404)
estimated useful life (p. 404)
extraordinary repair (p. 403)
franchises (p. 417)
goodwill (p. 417)
intangibles (p. 400)
licenses (p. 417)
ordinary repair (p. 403)
patent (p. 416)

plant assets (p. 400)
salvage value (p. 404)
straight-line (SL) depreciation method
    (p. 405)
trademark (p. 416)
trade name (p. 416)
units-of-production (UOP)
    depreciation method (p. 406)

● ASSESS *Your Progress*

A⁺ online homework

See *www.prenhall.com/horngren* for selected Starters, Exercises, and Problems.

Measuring the cost of a plant asset
(Obj. 1)

Lump-sum purchase of assets
(Obj. 1)

Capitalizing versus expensing plant-asset costs
(Obj. 1)

Computing depreciation by three methods—first year only
(Obj. 2)

Starters

S10-1 Page 401 of this chapter lists the costs included for the acquisition of land. First is the purchase price of the land, which is obviously included in the cost of the land. The reasons for including the other costs are not so obvious. For example, the removal of a building looks more like an expense. State why the costs listed are included as part of the cost of the land. After the land is ready for use, will these costs be capitalized or expensed?

S10-2 Return to the Stop & Think feature on page 402. Suppose at the time of your acquisition, the land has a current market value of $80,000, the building's market value is $60,000, and the equipment's market value is $20,000. Journalize the lump-sum purchase of the three assets for a total cost of $120,000. You sign a note payable for this amount.

S10-3 JetQuick Airways repaired one of its **Boeing** 767 aircraft at a cost of $800,000, which JetQuick paid in cash. JetQuick erroneously capitalized this cost as part of the cost of the plane.

1. Journalize both the incorrect entry the accountant made to record this transaction and the correct entry that the accountant should have made.
2. How will this accounting error affect JetQuick's net income? Ignore depreciation.

S10-4 At the beginning of the year, JetQuick Airways purchased a used **Boeing** aircraft at a cost of $42,000,000. JetQuick expects the plane to remain useful for five years (6 million miles) and to have a residual value of $6,000,000. JetQuick expects the plane to be flown 750,000 miles the first year.

1. Compute JetQuick's first-year depreciation on the plane using the following methods:
   a. Straight-line   b. Units-of-production   c. Double-declining-balance
2. Show the airplane's book value at the end of the first year under the straight-line method.

S10-5 At the beginning of 20X1, JetQuick Airways purchased a used **Boeing** aircraft at a cost of $42,000,000. JetQuick expects the plane to remain useful for five years (6 million miles) and to have a residual value of $6,000,000. JetQuick expects the plane to be flown 750,000 miles the first year and 1.5 million miles the second year. Compute second-year depreciation on the plane using the following methods:

a. Straight-line   b. Units-of-production   c. Double-declining-balance

Computing depreciation by three methods—second year
(Obj. 2)

S10-6 This exercise uses the JetQuick Airways data from Starter 10-4. JetQuick is deciding which depreciation method to use for income tax purposes.

1. Which depreciation method offers the tax advantage for the first year? Describe the nature of the tax advantage.
2. How much extra depreciation will JetQuick get to deduct for the first year as compared with using the straight-line method?

Selecting the best depreciation method for income tax purposes
(Obj. 3)

S10-7 On March 31, 20X2, JetQuick Airways purchased a used **Boeing** aircraft at a cost of $42,000,000. JetQuick expects to fly the plane for five years and to have a residual value of $6,000,000. Compute JetQuick's depreciation on the plane for the year ended December 31, 20X2, using the straight-line method.

Partial-year depreciation
(Obj. 2)

S10-8 Return to the example of the **Disney World** hot dog stand on pages 411–412. Suppose that after using the hot dog stand for four years, the company determines that the asset will remain useful for only two more years. Record Disney's depreciation on the hot dog stand for year 5 by the straight-line method.

Computing and recording depreciation after a change in useful life
(Obj. 2)

S10-9 Return to the **American Airlines** baggage-handling truck in Exhibits 10-6 and 10-8. Suppose American sold the truck on December 31, 20X2, for $28,000 cash, after using the truck for two full years. Depreciation for 20X2 has already been recorded. Make the journal entry to record American's sale of the truck under straight-line depreciation (Exhibit 10-6).

Recording a gain or loss on disposal under two depreciation methods
(Obj. 4)

S10-10 **Chevron**, the giant oil company, holds huge reserves of oil and gas assets. Assume that at the end of 20X6, Chevron's cost of mineral assets totaled approximately $18 billion, representing 2.4 billion barrels of oil and gas reserves in the ground.

1. Which depreciation method does Chevron use to compute its annual depletion expense for the minerals removed from the ground?
2. Suppose Chevron removed 0.8 billion barrels of oil during 20X7. Record Chevron's depletion expense for 20X7.

Accounting for the depletion of natural resources
(Obj. 5)

S10-11 Media-related companies have little in the way of tangible plant assets. Instead, their main asset is goodwill. When one media company buys another, goodwill is often the most costly asset acquired. Media Watch paid $700,000 to acquire *The Thrifty Nickel*, a weekly advertising paper. At the time of the acquisition, *The Thrifty Nickel's* balance sheet reported total assets of $1,200,000 and liabilities of $600,000. The fair market value of *The Thrifty Nickel's* assets was $800,000.

1. How much goodwill did Media Watch purchase as part of the acquisition of *The Thrifty Nickel?*
2. Journalize Media Watch's acquisition of *The Thrifty Nickel*.

Accounting for goodwill
(Obj. 6)

S10-12 This exercise summarizes the accounting for patents and research and development costs.

Questor Applications paid $800,000 to research and develop a new software program. Questor also paid $500,000 to acquire a patent on other software. After readying the software for production, Questor's sales revenue for the first year totaled $1,700,000. Cost of goods sold was $200,000, and selling expenses were $400,000. All these transactions occurred during 20X5. Questor expects the patent to have a useful life of five years. Prepare Questor Applications' income statement for the year ended December 31, 20X5, complete with a heading.

Accounting for patents and research and development cost
(Obj. 6)

Exercises

E10-1 Lone Star Lighting Systems purchased land, paying $80,000 cash as a down payment and signing a $120,000 note payable for the balance. In addition, Lone Star paid delinquent property tax of $2,100, title insurance costing $2,500, and a $5,400 charge for leveling the land and removing an unwanted building. The company constructed an office building on the land at a cost of $800,000. It also paid $51,000 for a fence around the property, $10,400 for the company sign near the entrance, and $6,000 for special lighting of the grounds. Determine the cost of the company's land, land improvements, and building. Which of the assets will Lone Star depreciate?

E10-2 Dicorte Brothers manufactures conveyor belts. Early in January 20X7, Dicorte constructed its own building with borrowed money. The 6% loan was for $900,000. During the year, Dicorte spent the loan amount on construction of the building. At year-end, Dicorte paid the interest for one year.

Required

1. How much should Dicorte record as the cost of the building in 20X7?
2. Record all of Dicorte's transactions during 20X7.

E10-3 Perry's Tanning Salon bought three tanning beds in a $10,000 lump-sum purchase. An independent appraiser valued the tanning beds as follows:

Tanning Bed	Appraised Value
1	$3,000
2	5,000
3	4,000

Perry's paid $5,000 in cash and signed a note payable for $5,000. Record the purchase in the journal, identifying each tanning bed's cost in a separate Tanning Bed account. Round decimals to three places.

E10-4 Classify each of the following expenditures as a capital expenditure or an expense related to machinery: (a) purchase price; (b) ordinary recurring repairs to keep the machinery in good working order; (c) lubrication of the machinery before it is placed in service; (d) periodic lubrication after the machinery is placed in service; (e) major overhaul to extend useful life by three years; (f) sales tax paid on the purchase price; (g) transportation and insurance while machinery is in transit from seller to buyer; (h) installation; (i) training of personnel for initial operation of the machinery; and (j) income tax paid on income earned from the sale of products manufactured by the machinery.

E10-5 Jessica Brooks has just slept through the class in which Professor Dominguez explained the concept of depreciation. Because the next test is scheduled for Wednesday, Brooks telephones Hanna Svensen to get her notes from the lecture. Svensen's notes are concise: "Depreciation—Sounds like Greek to me." Brooks next tries Tim Lake, who says he thinks depreciation is what happens when an asset wears out. David Coe is confident that depreciation is the process of building up a cash fund to replace an asset at the end of its useful life. Explain the concept of depreciation for Brooks. Evaluate the explanations of Lake and Coe. Be specific.

E10-6 Providence Medical Center bought equipment on January 2, 20X6, for $15,000. The equipment was expected to remain in service four years and to perform 1,000 operations. At the end of the equipment's useful life, Providence estimates that its residual value will be $3,000. The equipment performed 100 operations the first year, 300 the second year, 400 the third year, and 200 the fourth year. Prepare a schedule of *depreciation expense* per year for the equipment under the three depreciation methods.

After two years under double-declining-balance depreciation, the company switched to the straight-line method. Show your computations.

Which method tracks the wear and tear on the equipment most closely? Which method would Providence prefer to use for income-tax purposes? Explain in detail why a taxpayer prefers this method.

E10-7 Jazzy Power Chair Co. paid $165,000 for equipment that is expected to have a seven-year life. The residual value of equipment is 10% of the asset's cost.

Selecting the best depreciation method for income tax purposes
(Obj. 3)

Select the appropriate MACRS depreciation method for income tax purposes. Then determine the extra amount of depreciation that Jazzy Power Chair Co. can deduct by using MACRS depreciation, versus straight-line, during the first two years of the equipment's life.

E10-8 Stagecoach Van Lines purchased a building for $700,000 and depreciated it on a straight-line basis over a 40-year period. The estimated residual value was $100,000. After using the building for 15 years, Stagecoach realized that wear and tear on the building would force the company to replace it before 40 years. Starting with the 16th year, Stagecoach began depreciating the building over a revised total life of 30 years and increased the estimated residual value to $175,000. Record depreciation expense on the building for years 15 and 16.

Changing a plant asset's useful life
(Obj. 2)

E10-9 On January 2, 20X6, Amy's Party Supplies purchased showroom fixtures for $10,000 cash, expecting the fixtures to remain in service five years. Amy's has depreciated the fixtures on a double-declining-balance basis, with zero residual value. On September 30, 20X7, Amy's sold the fixtures for $5,000 cash. Record both the depreciation expense on the fixtures for 20X7 and the sale of the fixtures on September 30, 20X7.

Analyzing the sale of a plant asset; DDB depreciation
(Obj. 4)

E10-10 J. B. Hunt is a large trucking company. Hunt uses the units-of-production (UOP) method to depreciate trucks because UOP depreciation best measures wear and tear. Hunt trades in used trucks often to keep driver morale high and to maximize fuel efficiency. Consider these facts about one Mack truck in the company's fleet.

Measuring a plant asset's cost, using UOP depreciation, and trading in an asset
(Obj. 1, 2, 4)

When acquired in 20X1, the tractor/trailer rig cost $350,000 and was expected to remain in service for 10 years or 1,000,000 miles. Estimated residual value was $100,000. The truck was driven 80,000 miles in 20X1, 120,000 miles in 20X2, and 160,000 miles in 20X3. After 40,000 miles in 20X4, the company traded in the Mack truck for a less-expensive Freightliner. Hunt paid cash of $50,000. Determine Hunt's cost of the new truck. Journal entries are not required.

E10-11 Tesoro Mining paid $398,500 for the right to extract mineral assets from a 200,000-ton mineral deposit. In addition to the purchase price, Tesoro also paid a $500 filing fee, a $1,000 license fee to the state of Colorado, and $60,000 for a geological survey of the property. Because the company purchased the rights to the minerals only, the company expected the asset to have zero residual value when fully depleted. During the first year, Tesoro removed 40,000 tons of the minerals. Make journal entries to record (a) purchase of the minerals (debit Mineral Asset), (b) payment of fees and other costs, and (c) depletion for the first year.

Recording natural resource assets and depletion
(Obj. 5)

E10-12 *Part 1.* Advantage Press manufactures high-speed printers. Advantage recently paid $1 million for a patent on a new laser printer. Although it gives legal protection for 20 years, the patent is expected to provide a competitive advantage for only 8 years. Assuming the straight-line method of amortization, make journal entries to record (a) the purchase of the patent and (b) amortization for year 1.

Recording a patent, amortization, and a change in the asset's useful life
(Obj. 6)

Part 2. After using the patent for 4 years, Advantage learns at an industry trade show that another company is designing a more-efficient printer. On the basis of this new information, Advantage decides, starting with year 5, to amortize the remaining cost of the patent over 2 remaining years, giving the patent a total useful life of 6 years. Record amortization for year 5.

E10-13 **PepsiCo, Inc.,** has aggressively acquired other companies. Assume that PepsiCo purchased Kettle Chips Co. for $11 million cash. The market value of Kettle Chips' assets is $15 million, and it has liabilities of $10 million.

Required

1. Compute the cost of the goodwill purchased by PepsiCo.
2. Record the purchase of Kettle Chips by PepsiCo.

E10-14 Papillon is a catalog merchant in France similar to **Lands' End** in the United States. Papillon uses automated shipping equipment. Assume that early in year 1, Papillon purchased equipment at a cost of 5 million euros (€5 million). Management expects the equipment to remain in service five years, with zero residual value. Papillon uses the straight-line depreciation method. Through an accounting error, Papillon accidentally expensed the entire cost of the equipment at the time of purchase.

Required

Prepare a schedule to show the overstatement or understatement in the following items at the end of each year over the five-year life of the equipment.

1. Equipment, net   2. Net income

E10-15 Assume that **General Motors Corporation's** comparative balance sheet reported these amounts:

	(In millions)	
	December 31	
	20X2	**20X1**
Property:		
Land, plant, and equipment......................	$ 59,777	$ 59,565
Less accumulated depreciation	(34,363)	(34,641)
Net land, plant, and equipment	25,414	24,924

Required

Assume that on January 2, 20X3, GM sold 1/10 of its land, plant, and equipment for $3,000 million. Journalize this transaction for GM. Round to the nearest $1 million.

Problems

(Group A)

P10-1A Triumph Motorcycles incurred the following costs in acquiring land, making land improvements, and constructing and furnishing a new building.

a.	Purchase price of four acres of land	$200,000
b.	Landscaping (additional dirt and earthmoving)..............	8,100
c.	Fence around the boundary of the property	17,600
d.	Attorney fee for title search on the land	1,000
e.	Delinquent real estate taxes on the land to be paid by Triumph	5,900
f.	Company signs at front of the property	4,400
g.	Building permit for the building	500
h.	Architect's fee for the design of the building................	22,500
i.	Labor to construct the building	709,000
j.	Materials used to construct the building	215,000
k.	Interest cost on construction loan for the building	9,000
l.	Landscaping (trees and shrubs)..........................	6,400
m.	Parking lot and concrete walks	29,700
n.	Lights for the parking lot and walkways	10,300
o.	Salary of construction supervisor (85% to building; 15% to parking lot and concrete walks)......	40,000
p.	Furniture for the building................................	107,100
q.	Transportation and installation of furniture	2,200

Triumph depreciates buildings over 40 years, land improvements over 20 years, and furniture over 8 years, all on a straight-line basis with zero residual value.

Required

1. Set up columns for Land, Land Improvements, Building, and Furniture. Show how to account for each cost by listing the cost under the correct account. Determine the total cost of each asset.

2. All construction was complete and the assets were placed in service on May 1. Record partial-year depreciation for the year ended December 31. Round to the nearest dollar.

P10-2A Nelson Lewis provides freight service in Missouri, Kansas, and Illinois. The company's balance sheet includes Land, Buildings, and Motor-Carrier Equipment. Lewis has a separate accumulated depreciation account for each depreciable asset. During 20X7, Lewis completed the following transactions:

Recording plant-asset transactions, exchange, and disposal
(Obj. 1, 2, 4)

Student Resource **CD**

General Ledger, Peachtree, QuickBooks

Jan.	1	Traded in motor-carrier equipment with accumulated depreciation of $90,000 (cost of $130,000) for similar new equipment with a cash cost of $176,000. Lewis received a trade-in allowance of $70,000 on the old equipment and paid the remainder in cash.
July	1	Sold a building that cost $550,000 and that had accumulated depreciation of $250,000 through December 31 of the preceding year. Depreciation is computed on a straight-line basis. The building has a 40-year useful life and a residual value of $50,000. Lewis received $100,000 cash and a $600,000 note receivable.
Oct. 31		Purchased land and a building for a cash payment of $300,000. An independent appraisal valued the land at $115,000 and the building at $230,000.
Dec. 31		Recorded depreciation as follows:

      Motor-carrier equipment has an expected useful life of 1,000,000 miles and an estimated residual value of $26,000. Depreciation is units-of-production. During the year, Lewis drove his truck 150,000 miles.

      Depreciation on buildings is straight-line. The new building has a 40-year useful life and a residual value equal to $20,000.

Required

Record the transactions in Nelson Lewis's journal.

P10-3A The board of directors of Ink Jet Products is reviewing the 20X6 annual report. A new board member—a professor—questions the company accountant about the depreciation amounts. The professor wonders why depreciation expense has decreased from $200,000 in 20X4 to $184,000 in 20X5 to $172,000 in 20X6. She states that she could understand the decreasing annual amounts if the company had been selling properties each year, but that has not occurred. Further, growth in the city is increasing the values of property. Why is the company recording depreciation when property values are increasing?

Explaining the concept of depreciation
(Obj. 2)

Required

Write a paragraph or two to explain the concept of depreciation and answer the professor's questions. Which depreciation method does Ink Jet Products appear to be using?

Computing depreciation by three methods and the advantage of accelerated depreciation for tax purposes
(Obj. 2, 3)

P10-4A On January 3, 20X4, Tim Flanagan, Inc., paid $224,000 for equipment used in manufacturing automotive supplies. In addition to the basic purchase price, the company paid $700 transportation charges, $100 insurance for the equipment while in transit, $12,100 sales tax, and $3,100 for a special platform on which to place the equipment in the plant. Flanagan management estimates that the equipment will remain in service five years and have a residual value of $20,000. The equipment will produce 50,000 units the

Student Resource **CD**
spreadsheet

first year, with annual production decreasing by 5,000 units during each of the next four years (that is, 45,000 units in year 2; 40,000 units in year 3; and so on—a total of 200,000 units). In trying to decide which depreciation method to use, Flanagan has requested a depreciation schedule for each of three depreciation methods (straight-line, units-of-production, and double-declining-balance).

Required

1. For each depreciation method, prepare a depreciation schedule showing asset cost, depreciation expense, accumulated depreciation, and asset book value. For the units-of-production method, round depreciation per unit to three decimal places.

2. Flanagan prepares financial statements using the depreciation method that reports the highest income in the early years of asset use. For income tax purposes, the company uses the depreciation method that minimizes income taxes in the early years. Consider the first year Flanagan uses the equipment. Identify the depreciation methods that meet Flanagan's objectives, assuming the income tax authorities permit the use of any of the methods.

Accounting for intangibles, natural resources, and the related expenses
(Obj. 5, 6)

P10-5A *Part 1.* **Collins Foods International, Inc.,** is the majority owner of Sizzler Restaurants. Collins' balance sheet reports goodwill. Assume that Collins purchased this goodwill as part of the acquisition of another company, which carried these figures:

Book value of assets	$2.4 million
Market value of assets	2.7 million
Liabilities	2.2 million

Required

1. Make the journal entry to record Collins's purchase of the other company for $3.0 million cash.

2. How should Collins account for this goodwill after acquiring the other company? Explain in detail.

Part 2. **Georgia-Pacific's** balance sheet includes three assets: Natural Gas; Oil; and Coal. Suppose Georgia-Pacific paid $2.8 million cash for the right to work a mine with an estimated 100,000 tons of coal. Assume the company paid $60,000 to remove unwanted buildings from the land and $45,000 to prepare the surface for mining. Further, assume that Georgia-Pacific signed a $30,000 note payable to a company that will return the land surface to its original condition after the mining ends. During the first year, Georgia-Pacific removed 40,000 tons of coal, which it sold on account for $39 per ton. Operating expenses for the first year totaled $252,000, all paid in cash.

Required

1. Record all of Georgia-Pacific's transactions, including depletion, for the year.

2. Prepare the company's income statement for its coal operations for the year.

Reporting plant-asset transactions in the financial statements—a review
(Obj. 1, 2, 4)

P10-6A At the end of 2002, **The Coca-Cola Company** had total assets of $24.5 billion and total liabilities of $12.7 billion. Included among the assets were property, plant, and equipment with a cost of $9.0 billion and accumulated depreciation of $3.1 billion. During 2002, Coca-Cola earned total revenues of $20.2 billion and had total expenses of $17.1 billion.

Required

1. Show how Coca-Cola reported property, plant, and equipment on its balance sheet at December 31, 2002. What was the book value of property, plant, and equipment on that date?

2. How much was Coca-Cola's owners' equity at December 31, 2002?

3. Did Coca-Cola report net income or net loss on its 2002 income statement? Compute the amount.

Problems

(Group B)

P10-1B Carmel Apartments incurred the following costs to acquire land, make land improvements, and construct and furnish an apartment building:

Identifying the elements of a plant asset's cost
(Obj. 1, 2)

a.	Purchase price of 3 acres of land	$150,000
b.	Delinquent real estate taxes on the land to be paid by Carmel	3,700
c.	Additional dirt and earthmoving	5,100
d.	Title insurance on the land acquisition	1,000
e.	Fence around the boundary of the property	44,200
f.	Building permit for the apartment building	200
g.	Architect's fee for the design of the building	32,000
h.	Signs near the approaches to the property	20,900
i.	Materials used to construct the building	814,000
j.	Labor to construct the building	734,000
k.	Interest cost on construction loan for the building	3,400
l.	Parking lots and concrete walks on the property	17,500
m.	Lights for the parking lot and walkways	8,900
n.	Salary of construction supervisor (90% to building; 10% to parking lot and concrete walks)	55,000
o.	Furniture	123,500
p.	Transportation of furniture from seller to the building	1,100
q.	Landscaping (trees and shrubs)	9,000

Carmel depreciates buildings over 40 years, land improvements over 20 years, and furniture over 8 years, all on a straight-line basis with zero residual value.

Required

1. Set up columns for Land, Land Improvements, Apartment Building, and Furniture. Show how to account for each cost by listing the cost under the correct account. Determine the total cost of each asset.

2. All construction was complete and the assets were placed in service on March 31. Record partial-year depreciation for the year ended December 31. Round to the nearest dollar.

P10-2B Shepherd Smith Associates surveys American television-viewing trends. The company's balance sheet reports Land, Buildings, Office Equipment, Communication Equipment, and Televideo Equipment, with a separate accumulated depreciation account for each depreciable asset. During 20X6, Smith completed the following transactions:

Recording plant-asset transactions, exchange, and disposal
(Obj. 1, 2, 4)

GL, PT, QB

May 1   Purchased communication and televideo equipment from the **Gallup** polling organization. Total cost was $80,000 paid in cash. An independent appraisal valued the communication equipment at $90,000 and the televideo equipment at $10,000.

July 30   Traded in old office equipment with book value of $11,000 (cost of $96,000 and accumulated depreciation of $85,000) for new equipment with a cash cost of $88,000. The seller gave Smith a trade-in allowance of $20,000 on the old equipment, and Smith paid the remainder in cash.

Sep. 1   Sold a building that had cost $475,000 (accumulated depreciation of $350,000 through December 31 of the preceding year). Depreciation is computed on a straight-line basis. The building has a 30-year useful life and a residual value of $47,500. Smith received $200,000 cash.

Dec. 31   Recorded depreciation as follows:
Communication equipment and televideo equipment are depreciated by the straight-line method over a five-year life with zero residual value.
Office equipment is depreciated straight-line over seven years with $9,000 residual value. Make separate depreciation entries for the equipment acquired on May 1 and on July 30.

Required

Record the transactions in the journal of Shepherd Smith Associates.

Explaining the concept of depreciation
(Obj. 2)

P10-3B The board of directors of Austin Healey Motor Company is having its regular quarterly meeting. Accounting policies are on the agenda, and depreciation is being discussed. A new board member, an attorney, has some strong opinions about two aspects of depreciation policy. Lance Lott argues that depreciation must be coupled with a fund to replace company assets. Otherwise, there is no substance to depreciation, he argues. Lott also challenges the three-year depreciable life of company computers. He states that the computers will last much longer and should be depreciated over at least five years.

Required

Write a memo to explain the concept of depreciation to Lott and to answer his arguments. Format your memo as follows:

MEMO
To: _____
From: _____
Subject: _____

Computing depreciation by three methods and the advantage of accelerated depreciation for tax purposes
(Obj. 2, 3)

Student Resource**CD**

spreadsheet

P10-4B On January 2, 20X4, McIntosh Speed Co. purchased a used trailer at a cost of $63,000. Before placing the trailer in service, the company spent $2,200 painting it, $800 replacing tires, and $4,000 overhauling the chassis. McIntosh management estimates that the trailer will remain in service for 6 years and have a residual value of $14,200. The trailer's annual mileage is expected to be 18,000 miles in each of the first four years and 14,000 miles in each of the next two years—100,000 miles in total. In deciding which depreciation method to use, Larry McIntosh, the general manager, requests a depreciation schedule for each of the depreciation methods (straight-line, units-of-production, and double-declining-balance).

Required

1. Prepare a depreciation schedule for each depreciation method, showing asset cost, depreciation expense, accumulated depreciation, and asset book value. For the units-of-production method, round depreciation per mile to three decimal places.

2. McIntosh prepares financial statements using the depreciation method that reports the highest net income in the early years of asset use. For income-tax purposes, however, the company uses the depreciation method that minimizes income taxes in the early years. Consider the first year that McIntosh uses the trailer. Identify the depreciation methods that meet the general manager's objectives, assuming the income tax authorities permit the use of any of the methods.

Accounting for intangibles, natural resources, and the related expenses
(Obj. 5, 6)

P10-5B *Part 1.* **United Telecommunications, Inc.** (United Telecom), provides communication services in Florida, New Jersey, Texas, and other states. Assume that United Telecom purchased goodwill as part of the acquisition of Computer Printer Company, which had these figures:

Book value of assets...............................	$575,000
Market value of assets............................	906,000
Liabilities..	406,000

Required

1. Make the journal entry to record United Telecom's purchase of Computer Printer Company for $1,000,000 cash.

2. How should United Telecom account for goodwill after acquiring the other company? Explain in detail. *(continued)*

Part 2. **Continental Pipeline Company** operates a pipeline that provides natural gas to the East Coast of the United States. The company's balance sheet includes the asset Oil and Gas Properties.

Suppose Continental paid $7,000,000 cash for oil and gas reserves with an estimated 500,000 barrels of oil. Assume the company paid $550,000 for additional geological tests of the property and $450,000 to prepare for drilling. During the first year of production, Continental removed 70,000 barrels of oil, which it sold on credit for $20 per barrel. Operating expenses related to this project totaled $185,000, all paid in cash.

Required

1. Record all of Continental's transactions, including depletion, for the year.
2. Prepare the company's income statement for this oil and gas project for the first year.

P10-6B At the end of 2001, **Sprint Corporation**, the telecommunications company, had total assets of $45.8 billion and total liabilities of $33.2 billion. Included among the assets were property, plant, and equipment with a cost of $48.8 billion and accumulated depreciation of $19.8 billion. During 2001, Sprint earned total revenues of $26.1 billion and had total expenses of $27.5 billion.

Reporting plant-asset transactions in the financial statements—a review
(Obj. 1, 2, 4)

Required

1. Show how Sprint Corporation would report property, plant, and equipment on its balance sheet at December 31, 2001.
2. How much was Sprint's owner's equity at December 31, 2001?
3. Did Sprint report net income or net loss on its 2001 income statement? Compute the amount.

⬤ APPLY *Your Knowledge*

Decision Cases

Case 1. → *Link Back to Chapter 6 (Inventory Methods).* Suppose you are considering investing in two businesses, Payne Stewart and Michael Jordan. The two companies are virtually identical, and both began operations at the beginning of the current year. During the year, each company purchased inventory as follows:

Measuring profitability based on different inventory and depreciation methods
(Obj. 2, 3)

Jan.	4	10,000 units at $4 =	$ 40,000
Apr.	6	5,000 units at 5 =	25,000
Aug.	9	7,000 units at 6 =	42,000
Nov.	27	10,000 units at 7 =	70,000
Totals		32,000	$177,000

During the first year, both companies sold 25,000 units of inventory.

In early January, both companies purchased equipment costing $143,000 (10-year estimated useful life and a $20,000 residual value). Stewart uses the inventory and depreciation methods that maximize reported income (FIFO and straight-line). By contrast, Jordan uses the inventory and depreciation methods that minimize income taxes (LIFO and double-declining-balance). Both companies' trial balances at December 31 included the following:

Sales revenue	$385,000
Operating expenses	80,700

Required

1. Prepare both companies' income statements.
2. Write an investment newsletter to address the following questions for your clients: Which company appears to be more profitable? Which company has more cash to invest in promising projects? If prices continue rising in both companies' industries over the long term, which company would you prefer to invest in? Why?

Case 2. The following questions are unrelated except that they all apply to fixed assets and intangible assets:

a. The manager of Ladue Company regularly buys plant assets and debits the cost to Repairs and Maintenance Expense. Why would he do that, since this action violates generally accepted accounting principles (GAAP)?
b. The manager of Clarkson Corporation regularly debits the cost of repairs and maintenance of plant assets to Plant and Equipment. Why would she do that, since she knows she is violating GAAP?
c. It has been suggested that, because many intangible assets have no value except to the company that owns them, they should be valued at $1.00 or zero on the balance sheet. Many accountants disagree with this view. Which view do you support? Why?

Ethical Issue

Ashton Village Apartments purchased land and a building for the lump sum of $4.1 million. To get the maximum tax deduction, Ashton Village's managers allocated 90% of the purchase price to the building and only 10% to the land. A more realistic allocation would have been 70% to the building and 30% to the land.

Required

1. Explain the tax advantage of allocating too much to the building and too little to the land.
2. Was Ashton Village's allocation ethical? If so, state why. If not, why not? Identify who was harmed.

Financial Statement Case

Refer to the **Amazon.com** financial statements, including Notes 1 and 3, in Appendix A, and answer the following questions.

Required

1. Which depreciation method does Amazon.com use for reporting in the financial statements? What type of depreciation method does the company probably use for income tax purposes? Why is this method preferable for tax purposes?
2. Depreciation expense is embedded in the operating expense amounts listed on the income statement. Note 3 gives the amount of depreciation expense. What was the amount of depreciation for 2002? Record Amazon's depreciation expense for 2002.
3. The statement of cash flows reports the purchases of fixed assets. How much were Amazon's fixed asset purchases during 2002? Journalize the company's purchase of fixed assets. Refer to Note 3 to determine the specific types of fixed assets purchased.

Team Project

Required

Visit a local business.

1. List all its plant assets.
2. If possible, interview the manager. Gain as much information as you can about the business's plant assets. For example, try to determine the assets' costs, the depreciation

method the company is using, and the estimated useful life of each asset category. If an interview is impossible, then develop your own estimates of the assets' costs, useful lives, and book values, assuming an appropriate depreciation method.

3. Determine whether the business has any intangible assets. If so, list them and learn as much as possible about their nature, cost, and estimated useful lives.

4. Write a detailed report of your findings and be prepared to present it to the class.

For Internet Exercises, go to the Web site www.prenhall.com/horngren.

CHAPTER 11

Current Liabilities and Payroll

TIPS CHECK YOUR RESOURCES

- Visit the www.prenhall.com/horngren **Web site** for self-study quizzes, video clips, and other resources

- Try the **Quick Check** exercise at the end of the chapter to test your knowledge

- Learn the **key terms**

- Do the **Starter** exercises keyed in the margins

- Work the **mid-** and **end-of-chapter summary problems**

- Use the **Concept Links** to review material in other chapters

- Search the **CD** for review materials by chapter or by key word

- Watch the **tutorial videos** to review key concepts

LEARNING OBJECTIVES

⭐ 1 Account for current liabilities of known amount

⭐ 2 Account for current liabilities that must be estimated

⭐ 3 Compute payroll amounts

⭐ 4 Record basic payroll transactions

⭐ 5 Use a payroll system

⭐ 6 Report current liabilities on the balance sheet

Most products are guaranteed against defects. Computers, video equipment, and automobiles are prime examples. When you buy a Sony camera or a new General Motors car, the manufacturer agrees to repair it if something goes wrong. Do you ever consider the guarantee when you buy a product? That may be what motivates you to select a Honda over a Chevrolet. If not, you should consider the product guarantee because it varies from company to company. Repairs can be expensive.

Product guarantees are called warranties, and warranties are a major liability of companies such as General Motors, Sony, and Goodyear Tire and Rubber Company. Warranties pose an accounting challenge because General Motors doesn't know which Chevrolets or Buicks will have to be recalled or repaired. But it's almost certain that some cars will have problems, so GM goes ahead and records a warranty liability based on estimates. ∎

General Motors

Account for current liabilities of known amount

Student ResourceCD

accrued expense/liability, current liabilities, payroll, short-term notes

In this chapter we will see how GM, Sony, and other companies account for their product warranties. We also will learn about other current liabilities, such as Accounts Payable and payroll. Recall that *current liabilities* are obligations due within one year or within the company's normal operating cycle if it is longer than one year. Obligations due beyond that period are classified as *long-term liabilities*.

Current Liabilities of Known Amount

The amounts of most current liabilities are known. A few must be estimated. Let's begin with current liabilities of known amount.

Accounts Payable

Amounts owed for products or services purchased on open account are *accounts payable*. We have seen many accounts payable illustrations in preceding chapters. For example, most businesses purchase inventory on account. **General Motors Corporation (GM)** reported accounts payable of $18.3 billion at December 31, 20X1 (see line 1 of Exhibit 11-1).

Let's see how GM's accounts payable get onto the company's balance sheet. One of GM's common transactions is the credit purchase of inventory. GM's accounts payable and inventory systems are integrated. When the inventory of a certain auto part dips below a certain level, the computer automatically places an order to buy the goods. GM records the purchase of inventory on account as follows (amount assumed):

Oct. 19	Inventory	. . . .	600	
	Accounts Payable	. . . .		600
	Purchase on account.			

The purchase increases both inventory and Accounts Payable. Then, to pay the liability, the computer debits Accounts Payable and credits Cash, as follows:

Nov. 12	Accounts Payable	. . . .	600	
	Cash	. . . .		600
	Paid on account.			

Exhibit 11-1

How General Motors Reports Its Current Liabilities

General Motors Corporation
Balance Sheet (partial; adapted)
December 31, 2001

	Liabilities	(In billions)
	Current Liabilities	
1	Accounts payable	$18.3
2	Loans payable	2.4
3	Accrued expenses payable	34.1
4	Other current liabilities	1.5
5	Total current liabilities	$56.3

Short-Term Notes Payable

Short-Term Note Payable
Promissory note payable due within one year, a common form of financing.

Short-term notes payable are a common form of financing. General Motors refers to this liability as Loans Payable (see Exhibit 11-1, line 2). Short-term notes payable are promissory notes that must be paid within one year. The following entries are typical for a short-term note used to purchase inventory:

```
20X6
Sep. 30   Inventory ........................... 8,000
              Note Payable, Short-term.........          8,000
          Purchased inventory on a one-year, 10% note.


Dec. 31   Interest Expense ($8,000 × 0.10 × 3/12) ...  200
              Interest Payable ..................          200
          Accrued interest expense at year-end.
```

The balance sheet at December 31, 20X6, reports the Note Payable of $8,000 and Interest Payable of $200 as current liabilities. The income statement for 20X6 reports interest expense of $200. Both the balance sheet and the income statement are illustrated as follows:

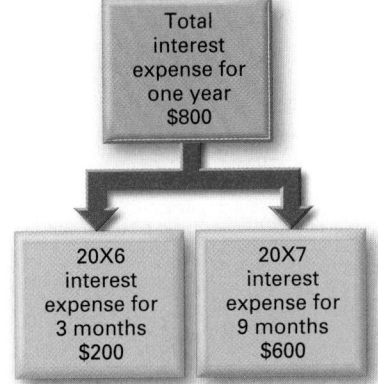

Balance Sheet December 31, 20X6		Income Statement Year Ended December 31, 20X6	
Liabilities		**Expenses**	
Current liabilities............		Interest expense	$200
Note payable, short-term...	$8,000		
Interest payable...........	200		

Interest expense of $200 was correctly allocated to 20X6. GM's interest expense will be $600 for 20X7. At maturity, GM will pay a full year's interest, allocated as shown in the margin diagram.
    GM's entry for payment of the note in 20X7 is

✔ **Starter 11-1**

✔ **Starter 11-2**

```
20X7
Sep. 30   Note Payable, Short-Term .............  8,000
          Interest Payable......................    200
          Interest Expense ($8,000 × 0.10 × 9/12) ..  600
              Cash [$8,000 + ($8,000 × 0.10)].....        8,800
          Paid note and interest at maturity.
```

Sales Tax Payable

Most states levy sales tax on retail sales. Retailers collect the sales tax in addition to the price of the item sold. The retailers then owe the state the sales tax, so Sales Tax Payable is a current liability. For example, **ShowBiz Pizza Time, Inc.,** operator of Chuck E. Cheese pizza and entertainment centers, reports sales tax payable as a current liability.
    Suppose one Saturday's sales at a ShowBiz Pizza Time totaled $10,000. The business collected an additional 5% in sales tax, which would equal $500 ($10,000 × 0.05). The business would record that day's sales as follows:

```
Cash ($10,000 × 1.05).......................  10,500
    Sales Revenue ......................          10,000
    Sales Tax Payable ($10,000 × 0.05).......        500
To record cash sales and the related sales tax.
```

Sales Tax Payable
500

Companies forward the sales tax to the state at regular intervals. To pay the tax, they debit Sales Tax Payable and credit Cash.

A Taxing Dilemma: Sales Tax Liability and the Internet

E-commerce offers two big pluses: shopping from home in your pajamas and no sales tax. Say you live in New York City and purchase a CD from a music store. You pay the

retail price of $15.99, plus sales tax of 8.625%. A purchase of the same CD from **Amazon.com** will be $1.38 cheaper. Fortunately for online (and mail-order) customers, the U.S. Supreme Court ruled that only the U.S. Congress can require retailers to charge sales taxes if they don't have a physical location in a state.

But the e-commerce sales-tax loophole may not be so sweet after all. According to one study, states missed out on $13.3 billion in revenue from taxes in one year. Those billions could have been used to build schools, repair roads, and pay state and local employees.

With the 50 states projecting a total shortfall of $40 billion to $50 billion—growing to $75 billion in the following year—states are looking for ways to tax online sales. Over 30 states are considering online sales tax legislation as part of the Streamlined Sales Tax Project. Expect to hear more about sales taxes as online sales grow. And if you're starting your own dot.com, see <u>EcommerceTax.com</u> for up-to-the-minute news. How the sales tax is treated may influence how you set up your business.

Based on: Peter Schrag, "Loophole.com," *The Nation*, May 15, 2000, pp. 6–7. Anonymous, "United States: Offline," *The Economist*, March 25, 2000, p. 35. Patrick Thibodeau, "States Push to Require Online Sales Tax Collection," *Computerworld*, November 4, 2002, p. 21. Chris Gaither, "States Circle Net: Budget Woes Force Leaders to Revisit Levies on Online Sales," *Boston Globe*, January 2, 2003, p. C.11.

Current Portion of Long-Term Debt

Current Portion of Long-Term Debt
Amount of the principal that is payable within one year. Also called **current maturity**.

Some long-term notes payable and bonds payable are paid in installments. The **current portion of long-term debt** is the amount of the principal payable within one year—a current liability. The remaining portion of the long-term debt is a long-term liability. At the end of the year, the company may make an adjusting entry to shift the current installment of the long-term debt to a current liability account, as follows (amount assumed):

Dec. 31	Long-Term Debt.	10,000	
	Current Portion of Long-Term Debt. . .		10,000

Stop & Think

Suppose **Dell Computer** owes $600,000 on long-term notes payable at December 31, 20X5. The borrowing agreement requires Dell to pay $200,000 of this debt on September 30, 20X6. Show how Dell will report both current and long-term liabilities on its balance sheet at December 31, 20X5.

Answer:
Current liabilities:
    Current maturities of long-term debt $200,000
Long-term liabilities
    Long-term debt ($600,000 − $200,000)   400,000

Accrued Expenses (Accrued Liabilities)

Accrued Expense
An expense that the business has not yet paid. Also called **accrued liability**.

We introduced accrued expenses in Chapter 3, p. 102. →

An **accrued expense** is an expense that has not yet been paid. Therefore, an accrued expense creates a liability. This explains why accrued expenses are also called **accrued liabilities**. Accrued expenses typically occur with the passage of time, such as interest payable on long-term debt. ←

Like most other companies, General Motors has accrued liabilities for salaries payable, other payroll liabilities, interest payable, and income tax payable. We illustrated accounting for interest payable near the top of page 437. The second half of this chapter covers accounting for payroll liabilities.

Payroll, which is also called **employee compensation**, is a major expense. For service organizations—such as CPA firms and travel agencies—payroll is *the* major expense. Payroll expense for salaries or wages usually causes an accrued liability at year-end. We show how to account for payroll expenses later in the chapter.

Payroll
A major expense. Also called **employee compensation**.

Unearned Revenues

Unearned revenues are also called *deferred revenues*. → The business has received cash from customers before earning the revenue. The company therefore has an obligation to provide goods or services to the customer. Let's consider an example.

← *As we saw in Chapter 3, p. 104, an unearned revenue is a liability because it represents an obligation to provide a good or service.*

Dun & Bradstreet (D&B) Corporation provides credit reports for subscribers and collects cash in advance. By receiving cash before earning the revenue, D&B has a liability for future service. The liability account is called Unearned Subscription Revenue.

Assume that D&B charges $600 for a three-year subscription. D&B's entry to record the receipt of cash in advance would be

20X4			
Jan. 1	Cash	600	
	Unearned Subscription Revenue ...		600
	Received cash in advance.		

After receiving the cash on January 1, 20X4, D&B owes service to its customer over three years. D&B's liability is

Unearned Subscription Revenue

	600

During 20X4, D&B performs one-third of the total service and earns $200 ($600 × 1/3) of the revenue. At December 31, 20X4, D&B makes the following adjusting entry to decrease Unearned Subscription Revenue, the liability, and increase Subscription Revenue:

20X4			
Dec. 31	Unearned Subscription Revenue	200	
	Subscription Revenue ($600 × 1/3)..		200
	Earned revenue that was collected in advance.		

After posting, D&B still owes its subscribers $400 in services. D&B has earned $200 of the revenue, as follows:

Unearned Subscription Revenue

Dec. 31	200	Jan. 1	600
		Bal.	400

Subscription Revenue

		Dec. 31	200

Current Liabilities That Must Be Estimated

A business may know that a liability exists but not know the exact amount. It cannot simply ignore the liability. This liability must be reported on the balance sheet. A prime example is Estimated Warranty Payable, which is common for companies like General Motors and Sony. Another example is a contingent liability.

Student ResourceCD

contingent liability, current liabilities

2 *Account for current liabilities that must be estimated*

Estimated Warranty Payable

Many companies guarantee their products against defects under *warranty* agreements. Ninety-day warranties and one-year warranties are common.

The matching principle says to record the *warranty expense* in the same period that we record the revenue. The expense occurs when you make a sale, not when you pay warranty claims. ← At the time of the sale, the company does not know the exact amount of warranty expense. But the business must estimate its warranty expense and the related liability.

For a review of the matching principle, see Chapter 3, p. 95. →

Assume that Whirlpool Corporation, which manufactures appliances for Sears, made sales of $200,000, subject to product warranties. Whirlpool estimates that 3% of its products will require warranty payments. The company would record the sales and the warranty expense in the same period, as follows:

June 20	Accounts Receivable................	200,000		
	Sales Revenue		200,000	
	Sales on account.			
June 20	Warranty Expense ($200,000 × 0.03)..	6,000		
	Estimated Warranty Payable...		6,000	
	To accrue warranty expense.			

Assume that Whirlpool's warranty payments total $5,800. Whirlpool repairs the defective appliances and makes this journal entry:

Dec. 11	Estimated Warranty Payable	5,800		
	Cash		5,800	
	To *repair* defective products sold under warranty.			

Whirlpool's expense on the income statement is the estimated amount of $6,000, not the $5,800 actually paid. After paying for these warranties, Whirlpool's liability account has a credit balance of $200.

Estimated Warranty Payable

5,800	6,000
	Bal. 200

Maxim Company, a new company, made sales of $400,000 on account. The company estimated warranty repairs at 5% of the sales. Actual warranty payments were $19,000. Record sales, warranty expense, and warranty payments. How much is Maxim's estimated warranty payable at the end of the period?

Answer:

Accounts Receivable	400,000	
Sales Revenue................................		400,000
Warranty Expense ($400,000 × 0.05)	20,000	
Estimated Warranty Payable		20,000
Estimated Warranty Payable	19,000	
Cash.....................................		19,000

Estimated Warranty Payable

19,000	20,000
	Bal. 1,000

✔ Starter 11-3

✔ Starter 11-4

Contingent Liabilities

A *contingent liability* is not an actual liability. Instead, it is a potential liability that depends on a *future* event. For example, suppose General Motors is sued because of auto accidents involving Chevy trucks. GM thus faces a contingent liability, which may or may not become an actual liability. If this lawsuit's outcome could hurt GM, it would be unethical for GM to withhold knowledge of the lawsuit. Another contingent liability arises when Company A *cosigns a note payable* for Company B. Company A has a contingent liability until the note comes due. If Company B pays off the note, the contingent liability ceases to exist. If not, Company A must pay Company B's debt, and Company A's liability becomes real.

The accounting profession divides contingent liabilities into three categories. Each category shows a likelihood that the contingency will cause a loss and a liability. The three categories of contingent liabilities, along with how to report them, are shown in Exhibit 11-2.

Likelihood of an Actual Loss	How to Report the Contingency
Remote	Ignore. Example: A frivolous lawsuit.
Reasonably possible	Describe the situation in a note to the financial statements. Example: The company is the defendant in a significant lawsuit and the outcome could go either way.
Probable, and the amount of the loss can be estimated	Record an expense (or loss) and an actual liability, based on estimated amounts. Example: Warranty expense and payable, as illustrated in the preceding section, beginning on page 439.

Exhibit 11-2

Contingent Liabilities: Three Categories

✔ **Starter 11-5**

At this halfway point in the chapter, review what you have learned by studying the Decision Guidelines.

Decision Guidelines

ACCOUNTING FOR CURRENT LIABILITIES

Suppose you're in charge of accounting for your student service club. The club decides to borrow $1,000 for a **Habitat for Humanity** project. The bank requires a balance sheet. These Decision Guidelines will help you report current liabilities accurately.

Decision	Guidelines
What are the two main issues in accounting for current liabilities?	• *Recording* the liability and the asset acquired or the expense incurred • *Reporting* the liability on the balance sheet

What are the two basic categories of current liabilities?	• Current liabilities of *known amount*:
	  Accounts payable Accrued expenses
	  Short-term notes payable (accrued liabilities)
	  Sales tax payable Payroll liabilities
	  Current portion of long-term Salary, wages, commission,
	    debt and bonus payable
	  Unearned revenues
	• Current liabilities that *must be estimated*:
	  Estimated warranty payable

MID-CHAPTER *Summary Problem*

TIPS

CHECK YOUR RESOURCES

Answer each question independently.

Required

1. A **Wendy's** hamburger restaurant made cash sales of $4,000 subject to a 5% sales tax. Record the sales and the related sales tax. Also record Wendy's payment of the tax to the state government.

2. Assume that at December 31, 20X6, **H. J. Heinz Company** reported its 6% long-term debt as follows:

Current Liabilities (In part)	Thousands
Portion of long-term debt payable within one year	$ 10,000
Interest payable ($200,000,000 × 0.06 × 6/12)	6,000
Long-Term Debt and Other Liabilities (In part)	
Long-term debt	$190,000

Assume that Heinz pays interest on June 30 each year.

Show how Heinz would report its liabilities on the year-end balance sheet one year later—December 31, 20X7. The current maturity of the long-term debt is $10 million each year until the liability is paid off.

3. How does a contingent liability differ from an actual liability?

Solution

1.

Cash ($4,000 × 1.05)	4,200	
Sales Revenue		4,000
Sales Tax Payable ($4,000 × 0.05)		200
To record cash sales and sales tax.		
Sales Tax Payable	200	
Cash		200
To pay sales tax.		

2. H. J. Heinz Company balance sheet at December 31, 20X7:

Current Liabilities (In part)	Thousands
Portion of long-term debt payable within one year	$ 10,000
Interest payable ($190,000,000 × 0.06 × 6/12)	5,700
Long-Term Debt and Other Liabilities (In part)	
Long-term debt	$180,000

3. A contingent liability is a *potential* liability; the contingency may or may not become an actual liability.

☐ Liabilities of Known Amount
☐ Estimated Liabilities
■ **Accounting for Payroll**
☐ The Payroll System
☐ Reporting Liabilities
☐ Ethical Issues

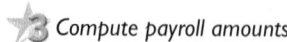

Student ResourceCD

payroll, payroll taxes, withholding taxes

⭐3 *Compute payroll amounts*

Accounting for Payroll

Salaries and wages are so important that most businesses develop a special payroll system to account for labor costs.

Businesses pay employees at a base rate for a set number of hours—called *straight time*. For additional hours—called *overtime*—the employee may get a higher rate of pay.

Lucy Childres is an accountant for Bobby Jones Golf Company. Lucy earns $600 per week for straight time (40 hours), so her hourly pay rate is $15 ($600/40). The company pays *time and a half* for overtime. That rate is 150% (1.5 times) the straight-time rate. Thus, Lucy earns $22.50 for each hour of overtime ($15.00 × 1.5 = $22.50). For working 42 hours during a week, she earns $645, computed as follows:

Straight-time pay for 40 hours............................	$600
Overtime pay for 2 overtime hours: 2 × $22.50...........	45
Total pay	$645

Gross Pay and Net Pay

The federal government requires employers to act as the collection agents for employee taxes. Employers deduct the taxes from employee checks. Insurance companies, labor unions, and other organizations may also receive pieces of employees' pay. Amounts withheld from an employee's check are called *deductions*.

Gross pay is the total amount of salary or wages, before taxes and other deductions. **Net pay**—or "take-home pay"—equals gross pay minus all deductions. Accounting for payroll is complex. Many companies also pay employee *benefits*, which are another form of compensation. Examples include health and life insurance.

Payroll Deductions

Payroll deductions fall into two categories:

- *Required deductions*, such as employee income tax and Social Security tax
- *Optional deductions*, including union dues, insurance premiums, charitable contributions, and other amounts withheld at the employee's request

After withholding, payroll deductions become the liability of the employer, who then pays the outside party—taxes to the government and charitable contributions to United Way or another charity.

REQUIRED DEDUCTIONS: EMPLOYEE INCOME TAX   U.S. law requires companies to withhold income tax from employees' pay checks. The amount of income tax deducted from gross pay is called **withheld income tax**. The withholding depends on the amount of gross pay and on the number of *withholding allowances* the employee claims.

An employee files a Form W-4 with his employer to indicate the number of allowances claimed for withholding purposes. Each allowance lowers the amount of tax withheld. An unmarried taxpayer usually claims one allowance; a childless married couple, two allowances; a married couple with one child, three allowances; and so on. Exhibit 11-3 shows a W-4 for R. C. Dean, who claims four allowances (line 5).

Gross Pay
Total amount of salary, wages, commissions, or any other employee compensation before taxes and other deductions.

Net Pay
Gross pay minus all deductions. The amount of compensation that the employee actually takes home.

Withheld Income Tax
Income tax deducted from employees' gross pay.

Exhibit 11-3

Form W-4

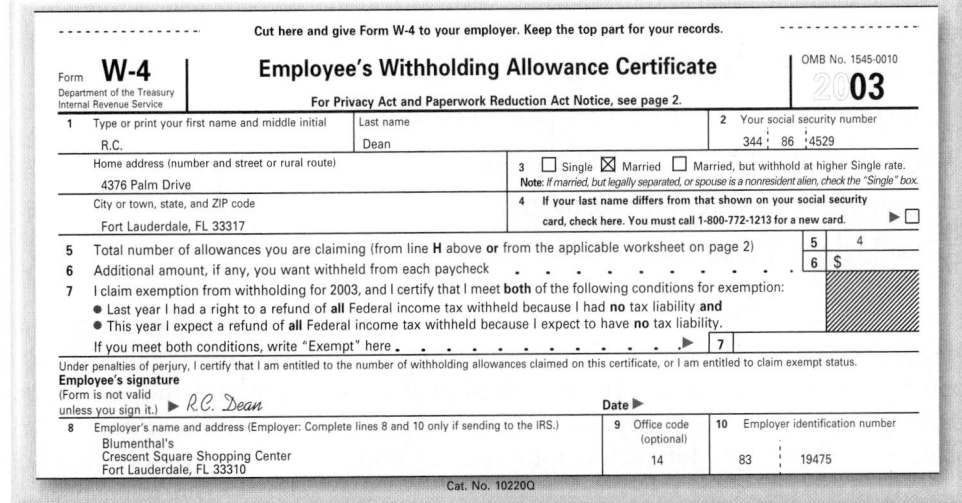

Social Security Tax
Federal Insurance Contributions Act (FICA) tax, which is withheld from employees' pay. Also called **FICA tax**.

REQUIRED DEDUCTIONS: EMPLOYEE SOCIAL SECURITY (FICA) TAX The *Federal Insurance Contributions Act (FICA)*, also known as the Social Security Act, created the Social Security Tax. The Social Security program provides retirement, disability, and medical benefits. The law requires employers to withhold **Social Security (FICA) tax** from employees' pay. The FICA tax has two components:

1. Old age, survivors', and disability insurance (OASDI)
2. Health insurance (Medicare)

The amount of tax withheld varies from year to year. For 2003, the OASDI tax applies to the first $87,000 of employee earnings in a year. The taxable amount of earnings is adjusted annually. The OASDI tax rate is 6.2%. Therefore, the maximum OASDI tax that an employee paid in 2003 was $5,394 ($87,000 × 0.062).

The Medicare portion of the FICA tax applies to all employee earnings. This tax rate is 1.45%. An employee thus pays a combined FICA tax rate of 7.65% (6.2% + 1.45%) of the first $87,000 of annual earnings, plus 1.45% of earnings above $87,000.

To ease the computational burden and focus on the concepts, we assume that the FICA tax is 8% of the first $87,000 of employee earnings each year. (Use these numbers when you complete this chapter's assignment material, unless instructed otherwise.) For each employee who earns $87,000 or more, the employer withholds $6,960 ($87,000 × 0.08) and sends that amount to the federal government.

Assume that Rex Jennings, an employee, earned $80,000 prior to December. Jennings' salary for December is $7,000. How much FICA tax will be withheld from Jennings' December paycheck? The computation follows.

Employee earnings subject to the tax in one year	$87,000
Employee earnings prior to the current month	−80,000
Current pay subject to FICA tax	$ 7,000
FICA tax rate	×0.08
FICA tax to be withheld from current pay check	$ 560

OPTIONAL DEDUCTIONS As a convenience to employees, many companies make payroll deductions and disburse cash according to employee instructions. Union dues, insurance payments, retirement savings plans, and gifts to charities such as United Way and Habitat for Humanity are examples.

✔ **Starter 11-6**

Many employers offer *cafeteria plans* that allow workers to select from a menu of insurance coverage. Suppose Ford Motor Company provides each employee with $500 of insurance coverage each month. One employee may use the monthly allowance to purchase life insurance. Another may select disability coverage. A third worker may choose a combination of life insurance and disability coverage.

Employer Payroll Taxes

Employers must pay at least three payroll taxes:

1. Employer **Social Security (FICA) tax**
2. State **unemployment compensation tax**
3. Federal **unemployment compensation tax**.

Unemployment Compensation Tax
Payroll tax paid by employers to the government, which uses the money to pay unemployment benefits to people who are out of work.

EMPLOYER FICA TAX In addition to the employee's Social Security tax, the employer must pay an equal amount into the program. The Social Security system is funded by equal contributions from the employee and the employer. Using our 8% Social Security tax rate, the employer's maximum annual tax is $6,960 ($87,000 × 0.08) for each employee. The employer records this payroll tax liability in the FICA Tax Payable account.

STATE AND FEDERAL UNEMPLOYMENT COMPENSATION TAXES

State and federal unemployment taxes finance workmen's compensation for people laid off from work. *In recent years, employers have paid a combined tax of 6.2% on the first $7,000 of each employee's annual earnings.* The proportion paid to the state is 5.4%, plus 0.8% to the federal government. The employer uses the accounts Federal Unemployment Tax Payable and State Unemployment Tax Payable. Exhibit 11-4 shows a typical distribution of payroll costs for an employer company.

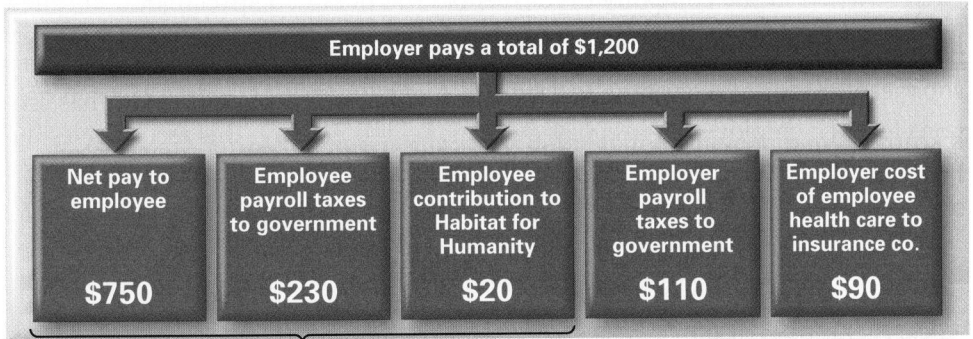

Exhibit 11-4

Typical Breakdown of Payroll Costs for One Employee

✔ Starter 11-7

Payroll Entries

✦ Record basic payroll transactions

Exhibit 11-5 summarizes an employer's entries to record a monthly payroll of $10,000. All amounts are assumed for illustration only. Entry A records *salary expense. Gross salary* is $10,000, and net take-home pay is $7,860. There is a payable to Habitat for Humanity because several employees specify this charitable deduction. Entry B records *payroll tax expense*, which includes the $800 FICA tax plus state and federal unemployment taxes. Entry C records *benefits* paid by the employer. This company pays for health and life insurance on its employees, a common practice. The employer also pays cash into a pension plan for the benefit of employees after they retire.

Exhibit 11-5

Payroll Accounting by the Employer

A. **Salary Expense**

Salary Expense (or Wage Expense or Commission Expense)	10,000	
Employee Income Tax Payable		1,200
FICA Tax Payable ($10,000 × 0.08)		800
Payable to Habitat for Humanity		140
Salary Payable to Employees (take-home pay)		7,860
To record *salary expense.*		

B. **Payroll Tax Expense**

Payroll Tax Expense	1,420	
FICA Tax Payable ($10,000 × 0.08)		800
State Unemployment Tax Payable ($10,000 × 0.054)		540
Federal Unemployment Tax Payable ($10,000 × 0.008)		80
To record employer's *payroll taxes.*		

C. **Benefits Expense**

Health Insurance Expense	800	
Life Insurance Expense	200	
Pension Expense	500	
Employee Benefits Payable		1,500
To record employee benefits payable by employer.		

✔ Starter 11-8

✔ Starter 11-9

What is the employer's total payroll expense in Exhibit 11-5?

Answer: $12,920 ($10,000 + $1,420 + $1,500)

Stop & Think

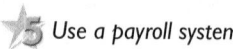

Student ResourceCD

payroll, payroll taxes, withholding taxes

Use a payroll system

We introduced the cash payments journal in Chapter 7, p. 295.

✔ **Starter 11-10**

The Payroll System

Good business means paying employees accurately and on time. A payroll system accomplishes these goals. The components of the payroll system are

- A payroll record
- Payroll checks
- Employee earnings record

Payroll Record

Each pay period the company organizes payroll data in a special journal called the *payroll record*. The payroll record resembles the cash payments journal and serves as a check register for recording payroll checks. ←

Exhibit 11-6 is a payroll record for Blumenthal's. The payroll record has sections for each employee's gross pay, deductions, and net pay. This record gives the employer the information needed to record salary expense for the week, as follows:

Dec. 31	Salary Expense	14,654.00	
	Employee Income Tax Payable		3,367.76
	FICA Tax Payable		861.94
	Payable to Habitat for Humanity		155.00
	Salary Payable		10,269.30

Exhibit 11-6   Blumenthal's Payroll Record (Partial)

Week Ended December 31, 2003

Employee Name	Hours	Gross Pay			Deductions				Net Pay	
		Straight-Time	Overtime	Total Salary Expense	Federal Income Tax	FICA Tax	Habitat for Humanity	Total	Amount	Check No.
Chen, W. L.*	40	500.00		500.00	71.05	40.00	2.50	113.55	386.45	1621
Dean, R. C.	46	400.00	90.00	490.00	59.94	39.20	2.00	101.14	388.86	1622
Ellis, M.	41	560.00	21.00	581.00	86.14	46.48		132.62	448.38	1623
Trimble, E. A.†	40	2,360.00		2,360.00	663.22		15.00	678.22	1,681.78	1641
Total		13,940.00	714.00	14,654.00	3,367.76	861.94	155.00	4,384.70	10,269.30	

*W. L. Chen earned gross pay of $500. His net pay was $386.45, paid with check number 1621.
† The business deducted no FICA tax from E. A. Trimble. She has already earned more than $87,000.
Note: For simplicity we ignore the additional tax for Medicare benefits.

Payroll Checks

Most companies pay employees by check or by electronic fund transfer (EFT). A *paycheck* has an attachment that details the payroll amounts. These figures come

Exhibit 11-7

Payroll Check

Blumenthal's Payroll Account Fort Lauderdale, FL			1622
		12/31 2003	
Pay to the Order of R.C. Dean			$ 388.86
Three hundred eighty-eight & 86/100 .... **Dollars**			
Republic Bank Fort Lauderdale Florida 33310		*Anna Figaro*	
•A111900031A 0787C50000454C			**Treasurer**

Pay			Deductions				Net Pay	Check No.
Straight time	Overtime	Gross	Income tax	FICA	United Way	Total		
400.00	90.00	490.00	59.94	39.20	2.00	101.14	388.86	1622

from the payroll record in Exhibit 11-6. Exhibit 11-7 shows payroll check number 1622, issued to R. C. Dean for net pay of $388.86. To enhance your ability to use payroll data, trace all amounts on the check attachment to Dean's payroll record in Exhibit 11-6.

Many companies pay employees by electronic funds transfer. The employee can authorize the company to make deposits directly to his or her own bank account. This procedure saves time and money.

Earnings Record

The employer must file a payroll tax return with the federal and state governments. Exhibit 11-8 is the Form 941 that Blumenthal's filed with the Internal Revenue Service for the quarter ended December 31, 2003. These forms must be filed no later than one month after the end of a quarter.

The employer must also provide the employee with a wage and tax statement, Form W-2, at the end of the year. Exhibit 11-9 (on page 448) shows the earnings record of R. C. Dean for the last two weeks of 2003.

Exhibit 11-8

Payroll Tax Return

Form 941 (Rev. January 2003)
Department of the Treasury
Internal Revenue Service

Employer's Quarterly Federal Tax Return

► See separate instructions revised January 2002 for information on completing this return.

Please type or print.

OMB No. 1545-0029

Enter state code for state in which deposits were made only if different from state in address to the right (see page 2 of instructions).

Name (as distinguished from trade name)   Date quarter ended

Trade name, if any   Employer identification number
Blumenthal's

Address (number and street)   City, state, and ZIP code
Crescent Square Shopping Center
Fort Lauderdale, FL 33310-1234

If address is different from prior return, check here ►

If you do not have to file returns in the future, check here ► ☐ and enter date final wages paid ►
If you are a seasonal employer, see **Seasonal employers** on page 1 of the instructions and check here ►

1	Number of employees in the pay period that includes March 12th . . . ► 1		19
2	Total wages and tips, plus other compensation	2	113,654
3	Total income tax withheld from wages, tips, and sick pay	3	18,168
4	Adjustment of withheld income tax for preceding quarters of calendar year	4	—
5	Adjusted total of income tax withheld (line 3 as adjusted by line 4—see instructions) . . .	5	18,168
6	Taxable social security wages . . . . . 6a 110,774 × 12.4% (.124) =	6b	13,736
	Taxable social security tips . . . . . . 6c × 12.4% (.124) =	6d	
7	Taxable Medicare wages and tips . . . . 7a 113,654 × 2.9% (.029) =	7b	3,296
8	Total social security and Medicare taxes (add lines 6b, 6d, and 7b). Check here if wages are not subject to social security and/or Medicare tax . . . . ► ☐	8	17,032
9	Adjustment of social security and Medicare taxes (see instructions for required explanation) Sick Pay $ _____ ± Fractions of Cents $ _____ ± Other $ _____ =	9	—
10	Adjusted total of social security and Medicare taxes (line 8 as adjusted by line 9—see instructions)	10	17,032
11	**Total taxes** (add lines 5 and 10)	11	35,200
12	Advance earned income credit (EIC) payments made to employees	12	—
13	Net taxes (subtract line 12 from line 11). **If $2,500 or more, this must equal line 17, column (d) below (or line D of Schedule B (Form 941))**	13	35,200
14	Total deposits for quarter, including overpayment applied from a prior quarter.	14	35,200
15	Balance due (subtract line 14 from line 13). See instructions	15	-0-
16	Overpayment. If line 14 is more than line 13, enter excess here ► $ _____ and check if to be: ☐ Applied to next return **or** ☐ Refunded.		

• All filers: If line 13 is less than $2,500, you need not complete line 17 or Schedule B (Form 941).
• Semiweekly schedule depositors: Complete Schedule B (Form 941) and check here . . . . ► ☐
• Monthly schedule depositors: Complete line 17, columns (a) through (d), and check here . . . . ► ☐

17	Monthly Summary of Federal Tax Liability. Do not complete if you were a semiweekly schedule depositor.			
	(a) First month liability	**(b)** Second month liability	**(c)** Third month liability	**(d)** Total liability for quarter
	35,017	35,336	34,967	35,200

Sign Here

Under penalties of perjury, I declare that I have examined this return, including accompanying schedules and statements, and to the best of my knowledge and belief, it is true, correct, and complete.

Signature ► *Anna Figaro*   Print Your Name and Title ► Anna Figaro, Treasurer   Date ► 1/30/03

For Privacy Act and Paperwork Reduction Act Notice, see back of Payment Voucher.   Cat. No. 17001Z   Form **941** (Rev. 1-2003)

Exhibit 11-9

Employee Earnings Record for 2003

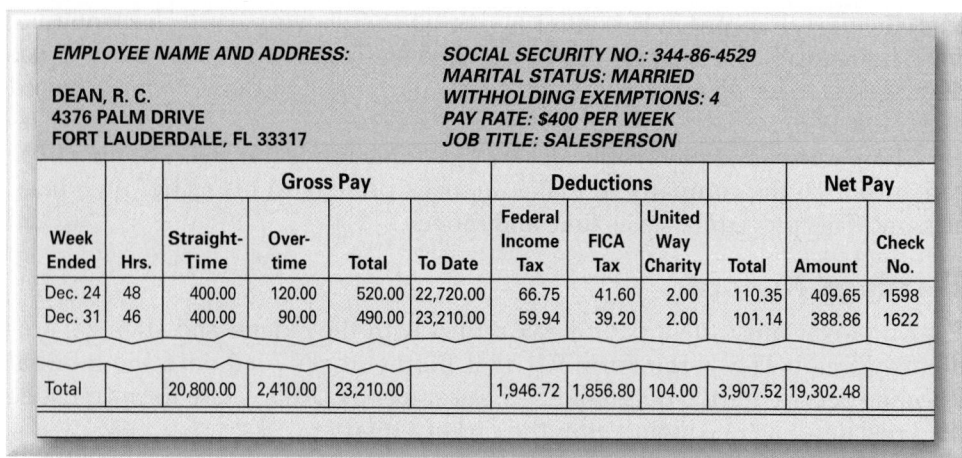

EMPLOYEE NAME AND ADDRESS:					SOCIAL SECURITY NO.: 344-86-4529					
DEAN, R. C. 4376 PALM DRIVE FORT LAUDERDALE, FL 33317					MARITAL STATUS: MARRIED WITHHOLDING EXEMPTIONS: 4 PAY RATE: $400 PER WEEK JOB TITLE: SALESPERSON					

		Gross Pay				Deductions				Net Pay	
Week Ended	Hrs.	Straight- Time	Over- time	Total	To Date	Federal Income Tax	FICA Tax	United Way Charity	Total	Amount	Check No.
Dec. 24	48	400.00	120.00	520.00	22,720.00	66.75	41.60	2.00	110.35	409.65	1598
Dec. 31	46	400.00	90.00	490.00	23,210.00	59.94	39.20	2.00	101.14	388.86	1622
Total		20,800.00	2,410.00	23,210.00		1,946.72	1,856.80	104.00	3,907.52	19,302.48	

The employee earnings record is not a journal or a ledger, and it is not required by law. It is an accounting tool—like the work sheet—that the employer uses to prepare payroll tax reports to the Internal Revenue Service.

Exhibit 11-10 is the Wage and Tax Statement, Form W-2, for employee R. C. Dean. The employer prepares this statement and gives copies to the employee and to the Internal Revenue Service (IRS). Dean uses the W-2 to prepare his income tax return. To ensure that Dean is paying income tax on all his income from that job, the IRS matches Dean's income as reported on his tax return with his earnings as reported on the W-2.

Exhibit 11-10

Employee Wage and Tax Statement, Form W-2

a Control number	2222	Void ☐	For Official Use Only ▶ OMB No. 1545-0008		
b Employer identification number 83-19475				1 Wages, tips, other compensation 23,210.00	2 Federal income tax withheld 1,946.72
c Employer's name, address, and ZIP code Blumenthal's Crescent Square Shopping Center Fort Lauderdale, FL 33310-1234				3 Social security wages 23,210.00	4 Social security tax withheld 1,439.02
				5 Medicare wages and tips 23,210.00	6 Medicare tax withheld 417.78
				7 Social security tips	8 Allocated tips
d Employee's social security number 344-86-4529				9 Advance EIC payment	10 Dependent care benefits
e Employee's name (first, middle initial, last) R.C. Dean 4376 Palm Drive Fort Lauderdale, FL 33317				11 Nonqualified plans	12 Benefits included in box 1
				13 See instrs. for box 13	14 Other
				15 Statutory employee ☐ Deceased ☐ Pension plan ☐ Legal rep. ☐ Deferred compensation ☐	
f Employee's address and ZIP code					

16 State Employer's state ID no.	17 Sate wages, tips, etc	18 State income tax	19 Locality name	20 Local wages, tips, etc	21 Local income tax

Form **W-2** Wage and Tax Statement **2003**	Department of the Treasury—Internal Revenue Service **For Privacy Act and Paperwork Reduction Act Notice, see separate instructions.**
Copy A For Social Security Administration—Send this entire page with Form W-3 to the Social Security Administration; photocopies are **not** acceptable. Cat. No. 10134D	

Paying the Payroll

Up to this point, we have talked only about *recording* payroll expenses and liabilities. We now turn to the *payment* of these liabilities. Most employers must record at least three cash payments for payrolls:

- Net pay to employees
- Payroll taxes and other payroll deductions
- Employee benefits

NET PAY TO EMPLOYEES   When the company pays employees, it debits Salary Payable and credits Cash. Using the data in Exhibit 11-6, the company would make the following entry to record the cash payment (net pay) for the December 31 weekly payroll:

Dec. 31	Salary Payable	10,269.30	
	Cash		10,269.30

PAYROLL TAXES AND OTHER DEDUCTIONS   The employer must send the government two sets of payroll taxes: those withheld from employees' pay and those paid by the employer. Based on the data in Exhibit 11-6, the business would record cash payments that can be summarized as follows (the unemployment tax amounts are assumed):

Dec. 31	Employee Income Tax Payable	3,367.76	
	FICA Tax Payable ($861.94 × 2)	1,723.88	
	Payable to Habitat for Humanity	155.00	
	State Unemployment Tax Payable	104.62	
	Federal Unemployment Tax Payable	15.50	
	Cash		5,366.76

BENEFITS   The employer might pay for employees' insurance coverage and their pension plan. If the total cash payment for these benefits is $1,927.00, the entry is

Dec. 31	Employee Benefits Payable	1,927.00	
	Cash		1,927.00

Internal Control over Payroll

There are two main types of internal controls for payroll: controls for efficiency and controls to safeguard cash payments. →

Chapter 8 discusses internal controls over cash payments.

EFFICIENCY   Reconciling the bank account can be time-consuming because of the large number of paychecks. There may be many outstanding checks. To limit the number of outstanding checks, many companies use two payroll bank accounts. They pay the payroll from one bank account one month and from the other payroll account the next month. This way they can reconcile each account every other month, and that decreases accounting expense.

Payroll transactions are ideal for computer processing. Employee payroll data are stored in a file. The computer makes all calculations, prints the payroll record and the paychecks, and updates employee earnings records electronically.

SAFEGUARDING PAYROLL DISBURSEMENTS   Owners and managers of small businesses can monitor their payrolls by personal contact with employees. Large corporations cannot. A particular risk is that a paycheck may be written to a fictitious person and cashed by a dishonest employee. To guard against this and other crimes, large businesses adopt strict internal control policies for payrolls.

The duties of hiring and firing employees should be separated from payroll accounting and from passing out paychecks. Issuing paychecks to employees with a photo ID ensures that only actual employees receive pay. A formal time-keeping system helps ensure that employees actually worked the number of hours claimed. Employees may punch time cards at the start and end of the workday to prove their attendance and number of hours worked.

✔ Starter 11-11

As we saw in Chapter 8, the foundation for good internal control is separation of duties. This is why companies have separate departments for the following payroll functions:

- Human Resources hires and fires employees
- Payroll maintains employee earnings records
- Accounting records all transactions
- Treasurer (or bursar) distributes paychecks to employees

Centurion Homes of Omaha, Nebraska, builds houses with four construction crews. The foremen hire—and fire—workers and keep their hourly records. Each Friday morning, the foremen telephone their workers' hours to the home office, where accountants prepare the weekly paychecks. Around noon, the foremen pick up the paychecks. They return to the construction site and pay the workers at day's end. What is the internal control weakness in this situation? Propose a way to improve the internal controls.

Answer: The foremen control most of the payroll information, so they can forge the payroll records of fictitious employees and pocket their pay. To improve internal control, Centurion could hire and fire all workers through the home office. This would prove that all workers actually exist. Another way to improve the internal controls would be to have a home-office employee distribute paychecks on a surprise basis. Any unclaimed checks would arouse suspicion. This system would probably prevent foremen from cheating the company.

☐ Liabilities of Known Amount
☐ Estimated Liabilities
☐ Accounting for Payroll
☐ The Payroll System
■ **Reporting Liabilities**
☐ Ethical Issues

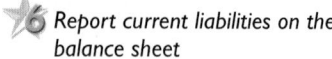
Student Resource**CD**

current liabilities

⭐ *Report current liabilities on the balance sheet*

✔ Starter 11-12

Exhibit 11-11

Current Liabilities on the Balance Sheet

☐ Liabilities of Known Amount
☐ Estimated Liabilities
☐ Accounting for Payroll
☐ The Payroll System
☐ Reporting Liabilities
■ **Ethical Issues**

Student Resource**CD**

contingent liabilities

Reporting Payroll Expense and Liabilities

At the end of each period, the company reports all of its current liabilities on the balance sheet. At December 31, 20X6, Centurion Homes had the current liabilities shown in Exhibit 11-11. Centurion combines all payroll liabilities under a single heading: Compensation and Benefits Payable.

Current Liabilities	
Accounts payable	$ 6,400
Compensation and benefits payable	3,800
Unearned revenue	4,500
Other accrued expenses and liabilities	5,700
Total current liabilities	$20,400

Ethical Issues in Reporting Liabilities

Accounting for liabilities poses an ethical challenge. Businesses want to look as successful as possible. They like to show high levels of net income because that makes the company look successful. High income also helps raise money from investors. And high asset values and low liabilities make the company look safe to lenders.

Owners and managers may be tempted to overlook some expenses and liabilities at the end of the accounting period. For example, a company can fail to accrue warranty expense. This will cause total expenses to be understated and net income to be overstated on the income statement.

Contingent liabilities also pose an ethical challenge. Because contingencies are not real liabilities, they are easy to overlook. But a contingent liability can be very important. Ethical business people do not play games with their accounting. Falsifying financial statements can ruin a reputation. It can also land a person in prison.

Decision Guidelines

ACCOUNTING FOR PAYROLL

CompUSA is a leading computer equipment chain. Suppose you manage a CompUSA store near your college and employ 10 people. What decisions must you make to account for payroll properly? The Decision Guidelines provide an outline for your actions.

Decision	Guidelines
What are the key elements of a payroll accounting system?	• Employee's Withholding Allowance Certificate, Form W-4 • Payroll record • Payroll checks • Employer's quarterly tax returns, such as Form 941 • Employee earnings record • Employee wage and tax statement, Form W-2
What are the key terms in the payroll area?	Gross pay (Total amount earned by the employee) – *Payroll deductions* a. Withheld income tax b. FICA (Social Security) tax—equal amount also payable by employer c. Optional deductions (insurance, savings, charitable contributions, union dues) = *Net (take-home) pay*
What is the employer's total payroll expense?	Gross pay + *Employer's payroll taxes* a. FICA (Social Security) tax—equal amount also payable by employee b. State and federal unemployment taxes + *Benefits for employees* a. Insurance (health, life, and disability) b. Pension (and other retirement) benefits c. Club memberships and other = *Employer's total payroll costs*
Where to report payroll costs?	• Payroll expenses on the income statement • Payroll liabilities on the balance sheet

Excel Application Exercise

Goal: Create a simple spreadsheet for computing payroll for a small company.

Scenario: Romano Service Co. has three employees for whom payroll must be calculated every two weeks. Hourly pay rates for each employee are as follows: J. Smith, $12.00; A. Jackson, $14.00; and B. Allen, $10.00. Overtime is paid at 1.5 times the hourly rate. Tax and withholding rates are as follows: Income tax, 11%; FICA, 8%; and pension plan, 10% of gross pay. Income tax, FICA, and pension are withheld from employee paychecks. During the current pay period, Smith worked 40 regular hours, Jackson worked 40 regular hours and 4 overtime hours, and Allen worked 38 hours.

Romano also must pay the employer portion for FICA (8%), plus state unemployment tax (5.4%) and federal unemployment tax (0.8%).

For each employee, calculate regular pay, overtime pay, gross pay, income tax withholding, FICA, pension plan amount, and net pay. Also calculate state and federal unemployment. When you have completed your work sheet, answer the following questions:

1. What is the net pay for each person?
2. What journal entries are required to record payroll expense for this period?
3. What is Romano's total payroll expense this period?

Excel Application Exercise *(continued)*

Step-by-Step:

1. Open a new Excel spreadsheet.
2. In column 1, create a bold-faced heading as follows:
   a. Chapter 11 Excel Application Exercise
   b. Romano Service Co.
   c. Pay Period Ending April 25, 20X5
3. Two rows down in column A, create a bold-faced heading titled, "Employee." In column B, create the same for "Pay Rate." In column C, enter the heading, "Regular Hours Worked," and in column D, enter "Overtime Hours Worked." Underline all four headings.
4. Enter the data for each employee under the appropriate headings.
5. Underneath the employee data in column A, enter titles for the overtime rate and all taxes/withholdings, one per row. In column B, enter the amount or percentage given in the exercise.
6. Below the employee and tax/withholding data, prepare the payroll calculations. Start with Employee Name in column A, and then enter titles for Regular Pay, Overtime Pay, Gross Pay, Income Tax Withholding, FICA, State Unemployment, Federal Unemployment, Pension Plan, and Net Pay. In the two columns after net pay, calculate state unemployment and federal unemployment taxes. These are not withheld from employee paychecks but are required to be paid by the employer.
7. Enter each employee name. Then create formulas for the calculation of all payroll items. At the end of each column, prepare a total.
8. Save your work sheet and print a copy for your files.

● END-OF-CHAPTER *Summary Problem*

CHECK YOUR RESOURCES

Beth Denius, a clothing store, employs one salesperson, Alan Kingsley. His straight-time salary is $360 per week, with time-and-a-half pay for hours above 40 per week. Beth Denius withholds income tax (11.0%) and FICA tax (8.0%) from Kingsley's pay. She also pays payroll taxes for FICA (8.0%) and state and federal unemployment (5.4% and 0.8%, respectively). In addition, Denius contributes 10% of Kingsley's gross pay into his pension plan.

During the week ended December 26, 20X4, Kingsley worked 48 hours. Prior to this week, Kingsley had earned $5,470.

Required

1. Compute Kingsley's gross pay and net pay for the week.
2. Record the following payroll entries that Denius would make for:
   a. Kingsley's salary, including overtime   d. Payment of cash to Kingsley
   b. Employer payroll taxes   e. Payment of all payroll taxes
   c. Expense for employee benefits   f. Payment for employee benefits
3. How much was Denius's total payroll expense for the week?

Solutions

Requirement 1

Gross pay:	Straight-time pay for 40 hours		$360.00
	Overtime pay:		
	Rate per hour ($360/40 × 1.5)	$13.50	
	Hours (48 − 40)	8	108.00
	Total gross pay.		$468.00
Net pay:	Gross pay		$468.00
	Less: Withheld income tax ($468 × 0.11) . .	$51.48	
	Withheld FICA tax ($468 × 0.08)	37.44	88.92
	Net pay		$379.08

Requirement 2

a.	Sales Salary Expense	468.00	
	Employee Income Tax Payable.		51.48
	FICA Tax Payable		37.44
	Salary Payable.		379.08
b.	Payroll Tax Expense	66.45	
	FICA Tax Payable ($468 × 0.08)		37.44
	State Unemployment Tax Payable ($468 × 0.054) . . .		25.27
	Federal Unemployment Tax Payable ($468 × 0.008) .		3.74

c.	Pension Expense ($468 × 0.10)...............	46.80	
	Employee Benefits Payable		46.80
d.	Salary Payable................................	379.08	
	Cash..		379.08
e.	Employee Income Tax Payable	51.48	
	FICA Tax Payable ($37.44 × 2).............	74.88	
	State Unemployment Tax Payable	25.27	
	Federal Unemployment Tax Payable........	3.74	
	Cash..		155.37
f.	Employee Benefits Payable	46.80	
	Cash..		46.80

Requirement 3

Denius incurred *total payroll expense* of $581.25 (gross salary of $468.00 + payroll taxes of $66.45 + benefits of $46.80). See entries (**a**) through (**c**).

REVIEW *Current Liabilities and Payroll*

Quick Check

1. Known liabilities of uncertain amounts should be
   a. Estimated and accrued when they occur
   b. Ignored (Record them when paid.)
   c. Reported on the income statement
   d. Described in the notes to the financial statements

2. On January 1, 20X5, you borrowed $10,000 on a five-year, 8% note payable. At December 31, 20X6, you should record
   a. Note receivable of $10,000
   b. Nothing (The note is already on the books.)
   c. Interest payable of $800
   d. Cash receipt of $10,000

3. Your company sells $100,000 of goods and you collect sales tax of 3%. What current liability does the sale create?
   a. Accounts payable of $3,000
   b. Unearned revenue of $3,000
   c. Sales revenue of $103,000
   d. Sales tax payable of $3,000

4. At December 31, your company owes employees for three days of the five-day work-week. The total payroll for the week is $8,000. What journal entry should you make at December 31?
   a. Nothing, because you will pay the employees on Friday

b.	Salary Expense..........................	8,000	
	Salary Payable		8,000
c.	Salary Expense..........................	4,800	
	Salary Payable		4,800
d.	Salary Expense..........................	3,200	
	Cash................................		3,200

5. What is unearned revenue?
   a. Receivable
   b. Current liability
   c. Revenue
   d. Current asset

6. **Sony** owed Estimated Warranty Payable of $1,000 at the end of 20X3. During 20X4, Sony made sales of $100,000 and expects product warranties to cost the company 3% of the sales. During 20X4, Sony paid $2,500 for warranties. What is Sony's Estimated Warranty Payable at the end of 20X4?
   a. $1,500
   b. $2,500
   c. $3,000
   d. $3,500

7. Payroll expenses include
  a. Salaries and wages
  b. Employee benefits
  c. Payroll taxes
  d. All of the above

8. What is the most that an employee paid the federal government for old age, survivors', and disability insurance (FICA tax) during 2003?
  a. $5,394.
  b. $87,000.
  c. Nothing. The employer paid it.
  d. There is no upper limit.

9. The document that an employer gives each employee at the end of the year to report annual earnings and taxes paid is the
  a. Payroll record
  b. Form 941
  c. Form W-2
  d. Form W-4

10. The foundation of internal control over payrolls is
  a. Paying the correct amount of payroll tax
  b. Accurately computing gross pay, deductions, and net pay
  c. Filing government tax forms on time
  d. Separating payroll duties

Accounting Vocabulary

accrued expense (p. 438)
accrued liability (p. 438)
current portion of long-term debt (p. 438)
current maturity (p. 438)

employee compensation (p. 439)
FICA tax (p. 444)
gross pay (p. 443)
net pay (p. 443)
payroll (p. 439)

short-term note payable (p. 436)
Social Security tax (p. 444)
unemployment compensation tax (p. 444)
withheld income tax (p. 443)

●ASSESS *Your Progress*

online homework

See *www.prenhall.com/horngren* for selected Starters, Exercises, and Problems.

Accounting for a note payable
(Obj. 1)

Reporting a short-term note payable and the related interest
(Obj. 1)

Accounting for warranty expense and warranty payable
(Obj. 2)

Applying GAAP; reporting warranties in the financial statements
(Obj. 2)

Starters

S11-1 Return to the $8,000 purchase of inventory on a short-term note payable that begins on page 436. Assume that the purchase of inventory occurred on June 30, 20X6, instead of September 30, 20X6. Journalize the company's (a) accrual of interest expense on December 31, 20X6 and (b) payment of the note plus interest on June 30, 20X7.

S11-2 Refer to the data in Starter 11-1. Show what the company would report for the note payable and related interest payable on its balance sheet at December 31, 20X6, and on its income statement for the year ended on that date.

S11-3 **Ford**, the automaker, guarantees its automobiles for three years or 36,000 miles, whichever comes first. Suppose Ford's experience indicates that the company can expect warranty costs to add up to 5% of sales.
  Assume that Friendly Ford in Atlanta made sales totaling $600,000 during March 20X7, its first month of operations. The company received cash for 30% of the sales and notes receivable for the remainder. Payments to satisfy customer warranty claims totaled $25,000 during 20X7.

1. Record the sales, warranty expense, and warranty payments for Friendly Ford.
2. Post to the Estimated Warranty Payable T-account. At the end of 20X7, how much in estimated warranty payable does Friendly Ford owe its customers?

S11-4 Refer to the data given in Starter 11-3.
  What amount of warranty expense will Friendly Ford report during 20X7? Does the warranty expense for the year equal the year's cash payments for warranties? Which accounting principle addresses this situation? Explain how the accounting principle works for measuring warranty expense.

S11-5 **Harley-Davidson, Inc.**, the motorcycle manufacturer, included the following note (adapted) in its annual report:

Notes to Consolidated Financial Statements

7 (in Part): Commitments and Contingencies (Adapted)

The Company self-insures its product liability losses in the United States up to $3 million.

Catastrophic coverage is maintained for individual claims in excess of $3 million up to $25 million.

---

1. Why are these *contingent* (versus real) liabilities?
2. How can a contingent liability become a real liability for Harley-Davidson? What are the limits to the company's product liabilities in the United States?

Starter 11-6 begins a sequence of exercises that ends with Starter 11-8.

S11-6 Examine the payroll situation of Lucy Childres on pages 442–443.

1. Compute Childres's total pay for working 50 hours during the first week of February.
2. Childres is single, and her income tax withholding is 10% of total pay. Her only payroll deductions are payroll taxes. Compute Childres's net pay for the week. (Use an 8% FICA tax rate.)

S11-7 Return to the Lucy Childres payroll situation in Starter 11-6. Childres's employer, Bobby Jones Golf Company, pays all the standard payroll taxes plus benefits for employee pensions (5% of total pay), health insurance ($60 per employee per month), and disability insurance ($8 per employee per month).

Compute Bobby Jones's total expense of employing Lucy Childres for the 50 hours that she worked during the first week of February. Carry amounts to the nearest cent.

S11-8 After solving Starters 11-6 and 11-7, journalize for Bobby Jones Golf Company the following expenses related to the employment of Lucy Childres:

a. Salary expense   **b.** Employer payroll taxes   **c.** Benefits

Use Exhibit 11-5 (p. 445) to format your journal entries. Carry all amounts to the nearest cent.

S11-9 Suppose you work for an accounting firm all year and earn a monthly salary of $8,000. There is no overtime pay. Your withheld income taxes consume 15% of gross pay. In addition to payroll taxes, you elect to contribute 5% monthly to your pension plan. Your employer also deducts $200 monthly for your co-pay of the health insurance premium.

Compute your net pay for November. Use an 8% FICA tax rate on the first $87,000 of income.

S11-10 Refer to the payroll record in Exhibit 11-6, page 446.

1. How much was the company's total salary expense for the week?
2. How much cash did the employees take home for their work?
3. How much did *employees* pay this week for
   a. Federal income tax?
   b. FICA tax?
4. How much expense did the *employer* have this week for
   a. Employee federal income tax?
   b. FICA tax?

S11-11 ←*Link Back to Chapter 8 (Internal Controls).* What are some of the important elements of good internal control to safeguard payroll disbursements?

Reporting current liabilities
(Obj. 6)

S11-12 Study the payroll record of **Blumenthal's** in Exhibit 11-6, page 446. Assume Blumenthal's will pay this payroll on January 2, 2004. In addition to the payroll liabilities shown in the exhibit, Blumenthal's has the following current liabilities at December 31, 2003.

Accounts payable..............................	$44,100
Employer FICA tax payable......................	862
Interest payable	1,110

Prepare the current liabilities section of Blumenthal's balance sheet at December 31, 2003. List current liabilities in descending order, starting with the largest first. Also list each of the payroll liabilities from Exhibit 11-6, rounded to the nearest dollar. Show total current liabilities.

online homework

Exercises

Recording sales tax
(Obj. 1)

E11-1 Make general journal entries to record the following transactions of Club Havasu Vacations for a two-month period. Explanations are not required.

March 31	Recorded cash sales of $200,000 for the month, plus sales tax of 4% collected on behalf of the state of Arizona.
April 6	Sent March sales tax to the state.

Recording and reporting current liabilities
(Obj. 1)

E11-2 Assume the **Chicago Tribune** publishing company completed the following transactions during 20X8:

Nov. 1	Sold a six-month subscription, collecting cash of $180, plus sales tax of 5%.
Dec. 15	Remitted (paid) the sales tax to the state of Illinois.
31	Made the necessary adjustment at year-end to record the amount of subscription revenue earned during the year.

Journalize these transactions (explanations are not required). Then report the liability on the company's balance sheet at December 31, 20X8.

Accounting for warranty expense and warranty payable
(Obj. 2)

E11-3 The accounting records of Grafton Tire Company included the following at December 31, 20X5:

Estimated Warranty Payable

	Balance 3,000

In the past, Grafton's warranty expense has been 6% of sales. During 20X6, Grafton made sales of $200,000 and paid $10,000 to satisfy warranty claims.

Required

1. Journalize Grafton's warranty expense and cash payments to satisfy warranty claims during 20X6. Explanations are not required.
2. What balance of Estimated Warranty Payable will Grafton report on its balance sheet at December 31, 20X6?

Recording note payable transactions
(Obj. 1)

E11-4 Record the following note payable transactions of MG Publishing, Inc., in the company's general journal. Explanations are not required.

20X2	
May 1	Purchased equipment costing $15,000 by issuing a one-year, 6% note payable.
Dec. 31	Accrued interest on the note payable.
20X3	
May 1	Paid the note payable at maturity.

EI I-5 Lana Gautier is manager of the women's sportswear department of Parisian Department Store in High Point, North Carolina. She earns a base monthly salary of $750 plus a 10% commission on her personal sales. Through payroll deductions, Gautier donates $25 per month to a charitable organization, and she authorizes Parisian to deduct $20 monthly for her health insurance. Tax rates on Gautier's earnings are 10% for income tax and 8% of the first $87,000 for FICA. During the first 11 months of the year, she earned $82,000.

Computing net pay
(Obj. 3)

spreadsheet

Required

Compute Gautier's gross pay and net pay for December, assuming her sales for the month are $80,000.

EI I-6 Mel O'Conner works as a cook for a **Steak 'n Shake** diner. His straight-time pay is $10 per hour, with time and a half for hours in excess of 40 per week. O'Conner's payroll deductions include withheld income tax of 7% of total earnings, FICA tax of 8% of total earnings, and a weekly deduction of $5 for a charitable contribution to United Fund.

Computing and recording gross pay and net pay
(Obj. 3, 4)

spreadsheet

Required

Assuming O'Conner worked 50 hours during the week, (a) compute his gross pay and net pay for the week and (b) make a general journal entry to record the store's wage expense for O'Conner's work, including payroll deductions. Explanations are not required.

EI I-7 Mill Creek Golf Course incurred salary expense of $92,000 for December. The pro shop's payroll expense includes employer FICA tax of 8% in addition to state unemployment tax of 5.4% and federal unemployment tax of 0.8%. Of the total salaries, $88,400 is subject to FICA tax, and $9,000 is subject to unemployment tax. Also, the store provides the following benefits for employees: health insurance (cost to the store, $2,060), life insurance (cost to the store, $350), and pension benefits (cost to the store, 6% of salary expense).

Recording a payroll
(Obj. 3, 4)

Required

Record Mill Creek's payroll taxes and its expenses for employee benefits. Explanations are not required.

EI I-8 Jupiter Technologies has annual salary expense of $600,000. In addition, Jupiter incurs payroll tax expense equal to 9% of the total payroll. At December 31, Jupiter owes salaries of $4,000 and FICA and other payroll taxes of $1,000. Jupiter will pay these amounts early next year.

Reporting payroll expense and liabilities
(Obj. 6)

Required

Show what Jupiter will report for these facts on its income statement and year-end balance sheet.

EI I-9 Unity Medical Group borrowed $3,000,000 on January 2, 20X1, by issuing a 9% long-term note payable that must be paid in three equal annual installments plus interest each January 2.

Reporting current and long-term liabilities
(Obj. 6)

Required

Insert the appropriate amounts to show how Unity would report its current and long-term liabilities.

	December 31		
	20X1	20X2	20X3
Current liabilities:			
Current portion of long-term note payable ..	$_____	$_____	$_____
Interest payable	_____	_____	_____
Long-term liabilities:			
Long-term note payable	_____	_____	_____

Reporting current and long-term liabilities
(Obj. 6)

E11-10 Assume that **Wilson Sporting Goods** completed these selected transactions during December 20X4.

a. Sales of $500,000 are subject to estimated warranty cost of 3%.
b. **Champs**, a chain of sporting goods stores, ordered $9,000 of tennis and golf equipment. With its order, Champs sent a check for $9,000 in advance. Wilson will ship the goods on January 3, 20X5.
c. The December payroll of $200,000 is subject to employee withheld income tax of 9%, FICA tax of 8% (employee and employer), state unemployment tax of 5.4%, and federal unemployment tax of 0.8%. On December 31, Wilson pays employees but accrues all tax amounts.

Required

Report each item at its correct amount on Wilson's balance sheet at December 31, 20X4. Show total current liabilities.

Analyzing current liabilities; using the current ratio
(Obj. 1, 6)

E11-11 ←*Link Back to Chapter 4 (Current Ratio).* The balance sheets of **PepsiCo, Inc.,** for two years reported these figures:

	Billions	
	20X2	**20X1**
Total current assets............................	$ 4.6	$ 4.1
Noncurrent assets............................	14.2	13.0
	$18.8	$17.1
Total current liabilities.........................	$ 3.7	$ 4.8
Noncurrent liabilities..........................	9.5	7.4
Stockholders' equity	5.6	4.9
	$18.8	$17.1

Compute PepsiCo's current ratio and debt ratio for both years. Did the ratios improve or deteriorate in 20X2? Compute the debt ratio to 3 decimal places, and use Chapter 4 if necessary.

Recording current liabilities
(Obj. 1, 6)

E11-12 **PepsiCo, Inc.,** reported short-term notes payable and salary payable (adapted, in millions), as follows:

	December 31	
	20X2	**20X1**
Current liabilities (partial):		
Short-term notes payable	$707	$228
Salary payable............................	327	334

Assume that during 20X2, PepsiCo paid off both current liabilities that were left over from 20X1. Also assume that PepsiCo borrowed money on short-term notes payable and accrued salary expense during 20X2.

Required

Journalize all four of PepsiCo's transactions during 20X2.

Problems

Journalizing liability transactions
(Obj. 1, 2)

(Group A)

P11-1A The following transactions of SuperValue stores occurred during 20X5 and 20X6.

20X5		
Feb.	3	Purchased equipment for $10,000, signing a six-month, 9% note payable.
	28	Recorded the week's sales of $51,000, one-third for cash, and two-thirds on credit. All sales amounts are subject to a 5% sales tax.
Mar.	7	Sent last week's sales tax to the state.
Apr.	30	Borrowed $100,000 on a four-year, 9% note payable that calls for annual payment of interest each April 30.
Aug.	3	Paid the six-month, 9% note at maturity.
Nov.	30	Purchased inventory at a cost of $7,200, signing a three-month, 8% note payable for that amount.
Dec.	31	Accrued warranty expense, which is estimated at 3% of sales of $260,000.
	31	Accrued interest on all outstanding notes payable. Made a separate interest accrual entry for each note payable.
20X6		
Feb.	28	Paid off the 8% inventory note, plus interest, at maturity.
Apr.	30	Paid the interest for one year on the long-term note payable.

Required

Record the transactions in the company's general journal. Explanations are not required.

P11-2A The records of Excel Food Service show the following figures:

Computing and recording a payroll
(Obj. 3, 4)

Employee Earnings		
(a)	Straight-time earnings	$?
(b)	Overtime pay	5,109
(c)	Total employee earnings	?
Deductions and Net Pay		
(d)	Withheld income tax	$ 9,293
(e)	FICA tax	6,052
(f)	Charitable contributions	?
(g)	Medical insurance	1,373
(h)	Total deductions	18,880
(i)	Net pay	64,813
Account Debited		
(j)	Salary Expense	$?

Required

1. Determine the missing amounts on lines (a), (c), (f), and (j).

2. Journalize Excel's payroll for the month. No explanation is required.

P11-3A Jan Summers is a vice president at Harbor State Bank in Boston. During 20X5, she worked for the bank all year at a $6,500 monthly salary. She also earned a year-end bonus equal to 15% of her annual salary.

Summers' federal income tax withheld during 20X5 was $820 per month, plus $2,480 on her bonus check. State income tax withheld came to $60 per month, plus $80 on the bonus. The FICA tax withheld was 8% of the first $87,000 of annual earnings. Summers authorized the following payroll deductions: United Fund contribution of 1% of total earnings and life insurance of $20 per month.

Harbor State Bank incurred payroll tax expense on Summers for FICA tax of 8% of the first $87,000 in total annual earnings. The bank also paid state unemployment tax of 5.4% and federal unemployment tax of 0.8% on the first $7,000 in annual earnings. The bank provided Summers with the following benefits: health insurance at a cost of $40 per month, and pension benefits to be paid to Summers during her retirement. During 20X5, the bank's cost of Summers' pension program was $4,000.

Computing and recording payroll amounts
(Obj. 3, 4)

Student ResourceCD
spreadsheet

Required

1. Compute Summers' gross pay, payroll deductions, and net pay during 20X5. Round all amounts to the nearest dollar.

2. Compute the bank's total 20X5 payroll cost for Summers.

3. Prepare the bank's summary general journal entries to record its expense for:

    a. Summers' total earnings for the year, her payroll deductions, and her net pay. Debit Salary Expense and Executive Bonus Compensation as appropriate. Credit liability accounts for the payroll deductions and Cash for net pay.

    b. Employer payroll taxes for Summers. Credit liability accounts.

    c. Benefits provided to Summers. Credit a liability account.

Explanations are not required.

Journalizing, posting, and reporting liabilities
(Obj. 1, 2, 3, 4, 5, 6)

Student ResourceCD

GL, PT, QB

P11-4A The Emerson Technology general ledger at September 30, 20X8, the end of the company's fiscal year, includes the following account balances before adjusting entries.

Accounts Payable	$ 88,200
Current Portion of Long-Term Debt	
Interest Payable	
Salary Payable	
Employee Payroll Taxes Payable	
Employer Payroll Taxes Payable	
Unearned Rent Revenue	3,900
Long-Term Debt	100,000

The additional data needed to develop the adjusting entries at September 30 are as follows:

a. The long-term debt is payable in annual installments of $50,000, with the next installment due on January 31, 20X9. On that date, Emerson will also pay one year's interest at 6.6%. Interest was last paid on January 31. Make the adjusting entry to shift the current installment of the long-term debt to a current liability. Also accrue interest expense at year end.

b. Gross salaries for the last payroll of the fiscal year were $4,300. Of this amount, employee payroll taxes payable were $950.

c. Employer payroll taxes payable were $890.

d. On August 1, the company collected six months' rent of $3,900 in advance.

Required

1. Open the listed accounts, inserting their unadjusted September 30 balances.

2. Journalize and post the September 30 adjusting entries to the accounts opened. Key adjusting entries by letter.

3. Prepare the liabilities section of Emerson Technology's balance sheet at September 30, 20X8. Show total current liabilities and total liabilities.

Using a payroll record; recording a payroll
(Obj. 5)

P11-5A The payroll records of a Nissan Motor Systems' district office provided the following information for the weekly pay period ended December 29, 20X3:

Employee	Hours Worked	Weekly Earnings Rate	Federal Income Tax	Health Insurance	Earnings Through Previous Week
Clay Cooper	43	$ 400	$ 74	$ 16	$17,060
Tim LeMann	46	480	90	10	22,300
Lena Marx	48	1,400	319	46	86,200
Karen York	40	240	32	6	3,410

All employees are paid time and a half for hours worked in excess of 40 per week.

Required

For convenience, round all amounts to the nearest dollar. Show your computations. Explanations are not required for journal entries.

1. Enter the appropriate information in a payroll record similar to Exhibit 11-6, page 446. In addition to the deductions listed, the employer also withholds FICA tax: 8% of the first $87,000 of each employee's annual earnings.

2. Record the payroll information in the general journal.

3. Assume that the first payroll check is number 178, paid to Cooper. Record the check numbers in the payroll record. Also, prepare the general journal entry to record payment of net pay to the employees.

4. The employer's payroll taxes include FICA of 8% of the first $87,000 of each employee's annual earnings. The employer also pays unemployment taxes of 6.2% (5.4% for the state and 0.8% for the federal government) on the first $7,000 of each employee's annual earnings. Record the employer's payroll taxes in the general journal.

P11-6A Following are pertinent facts about events during the current year at Marineland Boats.

Reporting current liabilities
(Obj. 6)

a. December sales totaled $404,000, and Marineland collected sales tax of 5%. The sales tax will be sent to the state of Washington early in January.

b. Marineland owes $75,000 on a long-term note payable. At December 31, 6% interest for the year plus $25,000 of this principal are payable within one year.

c. On August 31, Marineland signed a six-month, 6% note payable to purchase a machine costing $80,000. The note requires payment of principal and interest at maturity.

d. Sales of $909,000 were covered by the Marineland product warranty. At January 1, estimated warranty payable was $11,300. During the year, Marineland recorded warranty expense of $27,900 and paid warranty claims of $30,100.

e. On October 31, Marineland received cash of $2,400 in advance for the rent on a building. This rent will be earned evenly over six months.

Required

For each item, indicate the account and the related amount to be reported as a current liability on Marineland's December 31 balance sheet.

Problems

(Group B)

P11-1B The following transactions of Transocean Shipping occurred during 20X4 and 20X5:

Journalizing liability transactions
(Obj. 1, 2)

Student ResourceCD
GL, PT, QB

20X4		
Jan.	9	Purchased equipment at a cost of $20,000, signing a six-month, 8% note payable for that amount.
	29	Recorded the week's sales of $40,000, three-fourths on credit, and one-fourth for cash. Sales amounts are subject to an additional 6% state sales tax.
Feb.	5	Sent the last week's sales tax to the state.
	28	Borrowed $200,000 on a four-year, 9% note payable that calls for annual installment payments of $50,000 principal plus interest. Record the short-term and the long-term portions of the note payable in two separate accounts.
July	9	Paid the six-month, 8% note at maturity.
Nov.	30	Purchased inventory for $3,000, signing a six-month, 10% note payable.
Dec.	31	Accrued warranty expense, which is estimated at 3% of sales of $650,000.
	31	Accrued interest on all outstanding notes payable. Made a separate interest accrual entry for each note payable.

(*continued*)

20X5

Feb. 28	Paid the first installment and interest for one year on the long-term note payable.
May 31	Paid off the 10% note plus interest on maturity.

Required

Record the transactions in the company's general journal. Explanations are not required.

Computing and recording a payroll
(Obj. 3, 4)

P11-2B The records of Collegiate Specialties show the following figures:

Employee Earnings		
(a)	Straight-time earnings	$16,431
(b)	Overtime pay	?
(c)	Total employee earnings	?
Deductions and Net Pay		
(d)	Withheld income tax	$ 2,300
(e)	FICA tax	?
(f)	Charitable contributions	340
(g)	Medical insurance	668
(h)	Total deductions	5,409
(i)	Net pay	18,540
Accounts Debited		
(j)	Salary Expense	$?

Required

1. Determine the missing amounts on lines (b), (c), (e), and (j).

2. Journalize this payroll for the month. No explanation is required.

Computing and recording payroll amounts
(Obj. 3, 4)

Student Resource**CD**

spreadsheet

P11-3B Brenda Gates is vice president of finance for Transco Leasing. During 20X5, she worked for the company all year at a $6,625 monthly salary. She also earned a year-end bonus equal to 10% of her salary.

Gates's federal income tax withheld during 20X5 was $737 per month, plus $1,007 on her bonus check. State income tax withheld came to $43 per month, plus $27 on the bonus. The FICA tax withheld was 8% of the first $87,000 in annual earnings. Gates authorized the following payroll deductions: United Fund contribution of 1% of total earnings and life insurance of $19 per month.

Transco incurred payroll tax expense on Gates for FICA tax of 8% of the first $87,000 in annual earnings. The company also paid state unemployment tax of 5.4% and federal unemployment tax of 0.8% on the first $7,000 in annual earnings. In addition, Transco provides Gates with health insurance at a cost of $35 per month and pension benefits. During 20X5, Transco paid $7,000 into Gates's pension program.

Required

1. Compute Gates's gross pay, payroll deductions, and net pay for the full year 20X5. Round all amounts to the nearest dollar.

2. Compute Transco's total 20X5 payroll cost for Brenda Gates.

3. Prepare Transco's summary general journal entries to record its expense for the following:
   a. Gates's total earnings for the year, her payroll deductions, and her net pay. Debit Salary Expense and Executive Bonus Compensation as appropriate. Credit liability accounts for the payroll deductions and Cash for net pay.
   b. Employer payroll taxes on Gates. Credit liability accounts.
   c. Benefits provided to Gates. Credit a liability account. Explanations are not required.

Journalizing, posting, and reporting liabilities
(Obj. 1, 2, 3, 4, 5, 6)

Student Resource**CD**

GL, PT, QB

P11-4B The general ledger of Red Brick Investments at June 30, 20X8, the end of the company's fiscal year, includes the following account balances before adjusting entries.

Accounts Payable..	$105,520
Current Portion of Long-Term Debt	_____
Interest Payable	_____
Salary Payable	_____
Employee Payroll Taxes Payable.....................	_____
Employer Payroll Taxes Payable	_____
Unearned Rent Revenue.............................	6,000
Long-Term Debt......................................	200,000

The additional data needed to develop the adjusting entries at June 30 are as follows:

a. The long-term debt is payable in annual installments of $40,000 with the next installment due on July 31. On that date, Red Brick will also pay one year's interest at 9%. Interest was last paid on July 31 of the preceding year. Make the adjusting entry to shift the current installment of the long-term debt to a current liability. Also accrue interest expense at year end.

b. Gross salaries for the last payroll of the fiscal year were $5,044. Of this amount, employee payroll taxes payable were $1,088, and salary payable was $3,956.

c. Employer payroll taxes payable were $876.

d. On February 1, the company collected one year's rent of $6,000 in advance.

Required

1. Open the listed accounts, inserting the unadjusted June 30 balances.

2. Journalize and post the June 30 adjusting entries to the accounts opened. Key adjusting entries by letter.

3. Prepare the liabilities section of the balance sheet at June 30, 20X8. Show total current liabilities and total liabilities.

P11-5B Assume that the payroll records of a district sales office of **Spalding Sporting Goods** provided the following information for the weekly pay period ended December 29, 20X6.

Using a payroll record; recording a payroll
(Obj. 5)

Employee	Hours Worked	Hourly Earnings Rate	Federal Income Tax	United Way Contributions	Earnings Through Previous Week
Larry Fisher	42	$40	$278	$35	$87,474
Felicia Jones	47	8	87	4	23,154
Joe Opper	40	11	64	4	4,880
Sara Tate	46	35	288	8	86,600

Employees are paid time and a half for hours over 40/week. Round all amounts to the nearest dollar. Show your computations. Explanations are not required for journal entries.

Required

1. Enter the appropriate information in a payroll record similar to Exhibit 11-6, page 446. In addition to the deductions listed, the employer also takes out FICA tax: 8% of the first $87,000 of each employee's annual earnings.

2. Record the payroll information in the general journal.

3. Assume that the first payroll check is number 319, paid to Larry Fisher. Record the check numbers in the payroll record. Also, prepare the general journal entry to record payment of net pay to the employees.

4. The employer's payroll taxes include FICA tax of 8% of the first $87,000 of each employee's earnings. The employer also pays unemployment taxes of 6.2% (5.4% for the state and 0.8% for the federal government) on the first $7,000 of each employee's annual earnings. Record the employer's payroll taxes in the general journal.

Reporting current liabilities
(Obj. 6)

P11-6B Following are pertinent facts about Falcon Jet's transactions during the current year.

a. On November 30, Falcon received cash of $6,000 in advance for the rent on a building. This rent will be earned evenly over three months.

b. December sales totaled $110,000, and Falcon collected an additional state sales tax of 7%. This amount will be sent to the state of Tennessee early in January.

c. Falcon owes $100,000 on a long-term note payable. At December 31, 6% interest on the full note and $20,000 of this principal are payable within one year.

d. Sales of $400,000 were covered by Falcon's product warranty. At January 1, estimated warranty payable was $8,000. During the year, Falcon recorded warranty expense of $22,000 and paid warranty claims of $24,000.

e. On September 30, Falcon signed a six-month, 9% note payable to purchase equipment costing $30,000. The note requires payment of principal and interest at maturity.

Required

For each item, indicate the account and the related amount to be reported as a current liability on Falcon's December 31 balance sheet.

APPLY *Your Knowledge*

Decision Cases

Identifying internal control weaknesses and their solution
(Obj. 5)

Case 1. Bluegrass Construction Co. operates throughout Kentucky. The owner, Art Waverly, oversees company operations and employs 15 work crews. Construction supervisors report directly to Waverly. Most supervisors are longtime employees, so Waverly trusts them. Waverly's office staff consists of an accountant and an office manager.

Because employee turnover is high in the construction industry, supervisors hire and fire their own crew members. Supervisors notify the office of all personnel changes. Also, supervisors forward to the office the employee W-4 forms. Each Thursday, the supervisors submit weekly time sheets for their crews, and the accountant prepares the payroll. At noon on Friday, the supervisors come to the office to get paychecks for distribution to the workers at 5 p.m.

The company accountant prepares the payroll, including the payroll checks. Waverly signs all payroll checks. To verify that each construction worker is a bona fide employee, the accountant matches the employee's endorsement signature on the back of the canceled payroll check with the signature on that employee's W-4 form.

Required

1. Identify one way that a supervisor can defraud Bluegrass Construction under the present system.

2. Discuss a control feature that Bluegrass can use to *safeguard* against the fraud you identified in requirement 1.

Contingent liabilities
(Obj. 1, 2)

Case 2. **Microsoft Corporation** is the defendant in numerous lawsuits claiming unfair trade practices. Microsoft has strong incentives not to disclose these contingent liabilities. However, GAAP requires that companies report their contingent liabilities.

Required

1. Why would a company prefer *not* to disclose its contingent liabilities?

2. Describe how a bank could be harmed if a company seeking a loan did not disclose its contingent liabilities.

3. What ethical tightrope must companies walk when they report contingent liabilities?

Ethical Issue

LTV, manufacturer of aircraft and aircraft-related electronic devices, has at times borrowed heavily to finance operations. Often LTV is able to earn operating income much higher than its interest expense and is therefore quite profitable. However, when the business cycle turns down, LTV's debt burden has pushed the company to the brink of bankruptcy. Operating income is sometimes less than interest expense.

Required

Is it unethical for managers to saddle a company with a high level of debt? Or is it just risky? Who can get hurt when a company takes on too much debt? Discuss.

Financial Statement Case

Details about a company's current liabilities appear in a number of places in the annual report. Use **Amazon.com's** financial statements to answer the following questions.

Current liabilities
(Obj. 1, 6)

Required

1. Give the breakdown of Amazon.com's current liabilities at December 31, 2002. Give the January 2003 entry to record the payment of accounts payable that Amazon owed at December 31, 2002.
2. How much was Amazon's long-term debt at December 31, 2002? Of this amount, how much was due within one year? How much was payable beyond one year in the future?
3. The balance sheet lists no liability for Income Tax Payable. Why is this liability omitted?

Team Projects

Project 1. In recent years, the airline industry has dominated headlines. Consumers are shopping **Priceline.com** and other Internet sites for the lowest rates. The airlines have also lured customers with frequent-flyer programs, which award free flights to passengers who accumulate specified miles of travel. Unredeemed frequent-flyer mileage represents a liability that airlines must report on their balance sheets, usually as Air Traffic Liability.

 Southwest Airlines, a profitable, no-frills carrier based in Dallas, has been rated near the top of the industry. Southwest controls costs by flying to smaller, less-expensive airports; using only one model of aircraft; serving no meals; increasing staff efficiency; and having a shorter turnaround time on the ground between flights. The fact that most of the cities served by Southwest have predictable weather maximizes its on-time arrival record.

Required

With a partner or group, lead your class in a discussion of the following questions, or write a report as directed by your instructor.

1. Frequent-flyer programs have grown into significant obligations for airlines. Why should a liability be recorded for those programs? Discuss how you might calculate the amount of this liability. Can you think of other industries that offer similar incentives that create a liability?
2. One of Southwest Airlines' strategies for success is shortening stops at airport gates between flights. The company's chairman has stated, "What [you] produce is lower fares for the customers because you generate more revenue from the same fixed cost in that airplane." Look up *fixed cost* in the index of this book. What are some of the "fixed costs" of an airline? How can better utilization of assets improve a company's profits?

Project 2. Consider three different businesses:

a. A bank   **b.** A magazine publisher   **c.** A department store

Required

For each business, list all of its liabilities—both current and long-term. If necessary, study Chapter 15 on long-term liabilities. Then compare your lists to identify what liabilities the three businesses have in common. Also identify the liabilities that are unique to each type of business.

For Internet Exercises, go to the Web site www.prenhall.com/horngren.

Comprehensive Problem for Chapters 8–11

COMPARING TWO BUSINESSES

Suppose you created a software package, sold the business, and now are ready to invest in a small resort property. Several locations look promising: Jekyll Island, Georgia; Bar Harbor, Maine; and Palm Springs, California. Each place has its appeal, but Jekyll Island wins out. Two small resorts are available. The property owners provide the following data:

	Island Resorts	Ocean Hideaway
Cash	$ 34,100	$ 63,800
Accounts receivable	20,500	18,300
Inventory	74,200	68,400
Land	270,600	669,200
Buildings	1,800,000	1,960,000
Accumulated depreciation—buildings	(105,000)	(822,600)
Furniture and fixtures	750,000	933,000
Accumulated depreciation—furniture and fixtures	(225,000)	(535,300)
Total assets	$2,619,400	$2,354,800
Total liabilities	$1,124,300	$1,008,500
Owners' equity	1,495,100	1,346,300
Total liabilities and owners' equity	$2,619,400	$2,354,800

Income statements for the last three years report total net income of $531,000 for Island Resorts and $283,000 for Ocean Hideaway.

INVENTORIES   Island Resorts uses the FIFO inventory method, and Ocean Hideaway uses the LIFO method. If Island Resorts had used LIFO, its reported inventory would have been $7,000 lower. Three years ago, there was little difference between the LIFO and FIFO amounts for each company.

PLANT ASSETS   Island Resorts uses the straight-line depreciation method and an estimated useful life of 40 years for buildings and 10 years for furniture and fixtures. Estimated residual values are $400,000 for buildings and $0 for furniture and fixtures. Island's buildings are 3 years old.

Ocean Hideaway uses the double-declining-balance method and depreciates buildings over 30 years. The furniture and fixtures, now 3 years old, are being depreciated over 10 years.

ACCOUNTS RECEIVABLE   Island Resorts uses the direct write-off method for uncollectibles. Ocean Hideaway uses the allowance method. The Island Resorts owner estimates that $2,000 of the company's receivables are doubtful. Prior to the current year, uncollectibles were insignificant. Ocean Hideaway receivables are already reported at net realizable value.

Required

1. To compare the two resorts, convert Island Resorts' balance sheet to the accounting methods and the estimated useful lives used by Ocean Hideaway. Round all depreciation amounts to the nearest $100. The necessary revisions will not affect Island's total liabilities.

2. Convert Island Resorts' total net income for the last 3 years to reflect the accounting methods used by Ocean Hideaway. Round all depreciation amounts to the nearest $100.

3. Compare the two resorts' finances after you have revised Island Resorts' figures. Which resort looked better at the outset? Which looks better when they are placed on equal footing?

CHAPTER 13

Corporations: Paid-in Capital and the Balance Sheet

TIPS CHECK YOUR RESOURCES

- Visit the www.prenhall.com/horngren **Web site** for self-study quizzes, video clips, and other resources

- Try the **Quick Check** exercise at the end of the chapter to test your knowledge

- Learn the **key terms**

- Do the **Starter** exercises keyed in the margins

- Work the **mid-** and **end-of-chapter summary problems**

- Use the **Concept Links** to review material in other chapters

- Search the **CD** for review materials by chapter or by key word

- Watch the **tutorial videos** to review key concepts

- Watch the **Amy's Ice Creams On Location** video for a review of forms of business ownership

LEARNING OBJECTIVES

1 Identify the characteristics of a corporation

2 Record the issuance of stock

3 Prepare the stockholders' equity section of a corporation balance sheet

4 Account for cash dividends

5 Use different stock values in decision making

6 Evaluate return on assets and return on stockholders' equity

7 Account for the income tax of a corporation

Get on any interstate highway, and you'll see the distinctive shape of an IHOP (International House of Pancakes) building. We've all stopped at an IHOP for pancakes—or a sandwich. The restaurants are clean, the food is good, and the prices are right. Ever think about how IHOP swept across the country?

IHOP Corporation began as a small operation in Glendale, California. To grow the company, IHOP *went public*. This means IHOP offered its stock to anyone who would buy it. The initial public offering of IHOP stock was pretty successful: The company offered 6.2 million shares for $10 a share. As it turned out, investors bought 3.2 million shares. The $32 million (3.2 million × $10) IHOP received was used to open new restaurants and upgrade old ones.

IHOP

Today, IHOP operates restaurants throughout the United States and in several foreign countries. The restaurants serve pancakes, sandwiches, and other casual food mainly to college students and families, which is the target market. Thanks to the sale of its stock, IHOP has become a large, well-known corporation. ∎

Sitemap

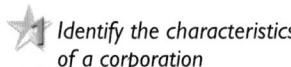
Identify the characteristics of a corporation

Student Resource**CD**

corporation, limited liability, capital stock, stock

Charter
Document that gives the state's permission to form a corporation.

Stockholder
A person who owns the stock of a corporation. Also called **shareholder**.

Stock
Shares into which the owners' equity of a corporation is divided.

This chapter covers the issuance of stock by corporations such as IHOP. Any company—large or small—can sell (issue) its stock to investors. All companies issue stock for the same reasons: to raise money, obtain assets, or pay off debt. Now let's explore how corporations differ from the proprietorships and partnerships we have been studying.

Corporations: An Overview

The corporation is the dominant form of business organization in the United States. IHOP is one example. Proprietorships and partnerships are more numerous, but corporations do much more business and are far larger. Most well-known companies, such as Amazon.com and Intel, are corporations. Their full names include *Corporation* or *Incorporated* (abbreviated *Corp.* and *Inc.*) to show that they are corporations—for example, Intel Corporation and Nike, Inc.

Characteristics of a Corporation

What makes the corporate form of organization so attractive? Several things. We now examine the features of corporations and their advantages and disadvantages.

SEPARATE LEGAL ENTITY   A corporation is a business entity formed under the laws of a particular state. For example, the state of New York may grant a **charter**, a document that gives a business the state's permission to form a corporation. Neither a proprietorship nor a partnership requires a charter, because in the eyes of the law those businesses are the same as their owner(s).

A corporation is totally separate from its owners, who are called **stockholders** or **shareholders**. A corporation has many of the rights of a person. For example, a corporation may buy, own, and sell property. The assets and liabilities of IHOP belong to the corporation, not to its owners. The corporation may enter into contracts, sue, and be sued, just like an individual.

CONTINUOUS LIFE AND TRANSFERABILITY OF OWNERSHIP   The owners' equity of a corporation is divided into shares of **stock**. Corporations have *continuous lives* regardless of who owns the stock. Stockholders may sell or trade stock to another person, give it away, or bequeath it in a will. Transfer of the stock does not affect the continuity of the corporation. By contrast, proprietorships and partnerships end when their ownership changes.

NO MUTUAL AGENCY   *Mutual agency* means that all owners act as agents of the business. A contract signed by one owner is binding for the whole company. Mutual agency operates in partnerships but *not* in corporations. ← A stockholder of IHOP Corp. cannot commit IHOP to a contract (unless the person is also an officer in the business).

We introduced the idea of mutual agency for partnerships in Chapter 12, page 471. →

LIMITED STOCKHOLDER LIABILITY   Stockholders have **limited liability** for corporation debts. That means they have no personal obligation for the corporation's liabilities. The most that a stockholder can lose on an investment in a corporation is the amount invested. In contrast, proprietors and partners are personally liable for all the debts of their businesses, unless the partnership is a limited liability partnership (LLP).

The combination of limited liability and no mutual agency means that persons can invest in a corporation without fear of losing all their personal wealth if the business fails. This feature enables a corporation to raise more money than proprietorships and partnerships.

SEPARATION OF OWNERSHIP AND MANAGEMENT   Stockholders own a corporation, but a *board of directors*—elected by the stockholders—appoints the officers to manage the business. Stockholders may invest $1,000 or $1 million without having to manage the business.

Management's goal is to maximize the firm's value for the benefit of the stockholders. The separation of stockholders and management can create problems. Corporate officers may manage the business for their own benefit. The distance between the stockholders and management may make it difficult for stockholders to overturn bad management. How can stockholders protest? They can vote their shares on matters that come before them. In the extreme, they can sell their stock.

CORPORATE TAXATION   Corporations are separate taxable entities. They pay several taxes not borne by proprietorships or partnerships, including an annual franchise tax levied by the state. The franchise tax keeps the corporate charter in force and enables the corporation to continue doing business. Corporations also pay federal and state income taxes just as individuals do.

Corporate earnings are subject to **double taxation**. First, corporations pay income taxes on corporate income. Then, stockholders pay personal income tax on the cash dividends they receive from corporations. Proprietorships and partnerships pay no business income tax. Instead, the tax falls solely on the owners.

GOVERNMENT REGULATION   Because stockholders have only limited liability for corporation debts, outsiders can look no further than the corporation for payment of its debts. To protect persons who do business with corporations, government agencies monitor corporations. This *government regulation* creates some expenses not borne by proprietorships or partnerships.

Exhibit 13-1 summarizes the advantages and disadvantages of corporations.

Advantages	Disadvantages
1. Can raise more money than a proprietorship or partnership	1. Separation of ownership and management
2. Continuous life	2. Corporate taxation
3. Easy transfer of ownership	3. Government regulation
4. No mutual agency of the stockholders	
5. Limited liability of the stockholders	

Limited Liability
No personal obligation of a stockholder for corporation debts. A stockholder can lose no more on an investment in a corporation's stock than the cost of the investment.

Double Taxation
Corporations pay their own income taxes on corporate income. Then, the stockholders pay personal income tax on the cash dividends they receive from corporations.

Exhibit 13-1

Advantages and Disadvantages of a Corporation

Organizing a Corporation

The process of organizing a corporation begins when the *incorporators* obtain a charter from the state. The charter **authorizes** the corporation to issue a certain number of shares of stock. The incorporators pay fees, sign the charter, and file documents with the state. The corporation then becomes a legal entity. The stockholders agree to a set of **bylaws**, which act as their constitution.

Authorization of Stock
Provision in a corporate charter that gives the state's permission for the corporation to issue—that is, to sell—a certain number of shares of stock.
Bylaws
Constitution for governing a corporation.

Board of Directors
Group elected by the stockholders to set policy and to appoint the officers.

Chairperson
Elected by a corporation's board of directors, the most powerful person in the corporation.

Ultimate control of the corporation rests with the stockholders as they vote their shares of stock. For example, the stockholders elect the **board of directors**, which sets policy and appoints the officers. The board elects a **chairperson**, who is the most powerful person in the company. The board appoints the **president**, who is in charge of day-to-day operations. Most corporations also have a number of vice presidents. Exhibit 13-2 shows the authority structure in a corporation.

Exhibit 13-2 **Structure of a Corporation**

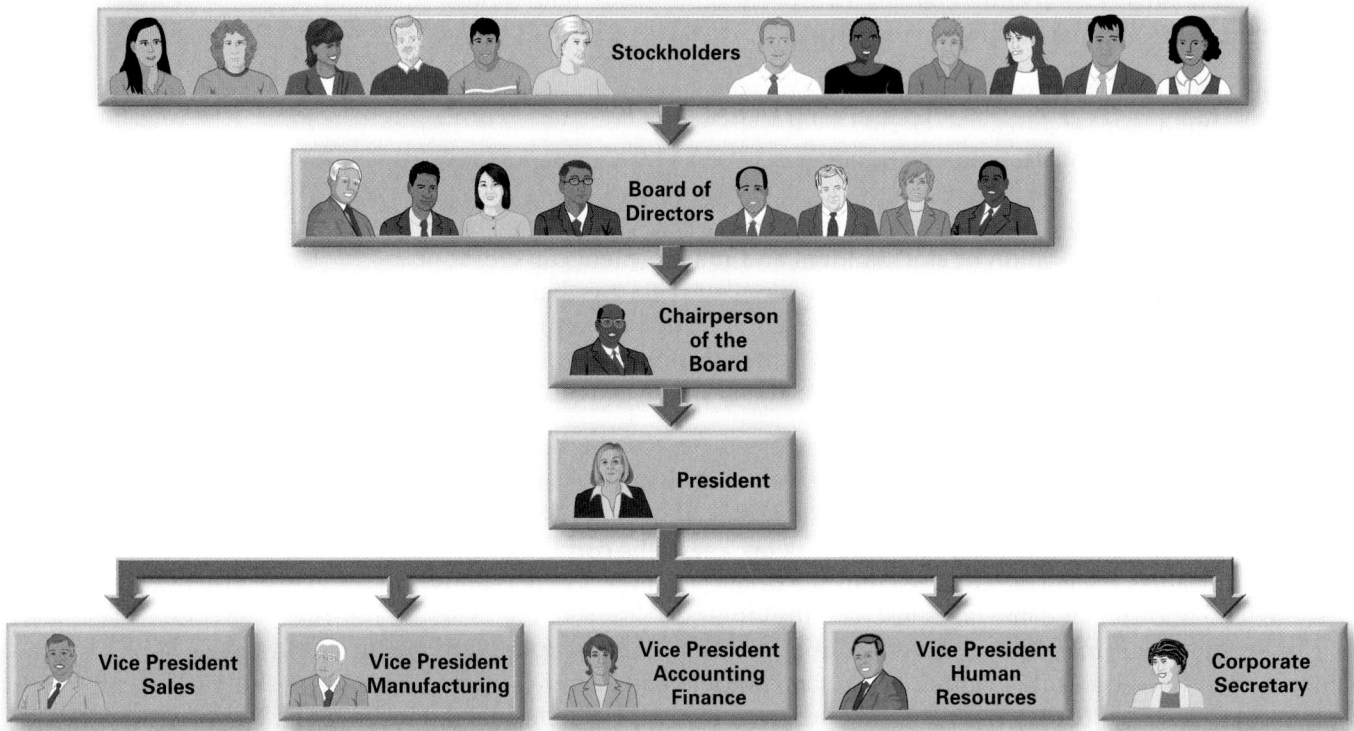

President
Chief operating officer in charge of managing the day-to-day operations of a corporation.

✔ **Starter 13-1**

Capital Stock

A corporation issues *stock certificates* to the stockholders when they invest in the business. The stock represents the corporation's capital, so it is called *capital stock*. The basic unit of stock is a *share*. A corporation may issue a stock certificate for any number of shares. Exhibit 13-3 shows a stock certificate for 288 shares of

Exhibit 13-3

Stock Certificate

Company's name

Stockholder's name

Number of shares held by the stockholder

Central Jersey Bancorp common stock. The certificate shows the company's name, the stockholder's name, and the number of shares.

Stock that is held by the stockholders is said to be **outstanding**. The total shares of stock outstanding represent 100% ownership of the corporation.

Stockholders' Equity: The Basics

The balance sheet of a corporation reports assets and liabilities in the same way as for a proprietorship or a partnership. But the owners' equity of a corporation—called **stockholders' equity**—is reported differently. State laws require corporations to report the sources of their capital. There are two basic sources of capital:

- **Paid-in capital** (also called **contributed capital**) represents amounts received from the stockholders.
- **Retained earnings** is capital earned by profitable operations.

Exhibit 13-4 outlines a summarized version of the stockholders' equity of IHOP Corporation.

Stockholders' Equity	
Paid-in capital:	
Common stock	$ 89
Retained earnings	275
Total stockholders' equity	364

Paid-In Capital Comes from the Stockholders

Common stock is paid-in capital because it comes from the stockholders. Suppose IHOP is issuing common stock. IHOP's entry to record the receipt of $20,000 cash and the issuance of stock is

Oct. 20	Cash	20,000	
	Common Stock		20,000
	Issued stock.		

This entry shows that issuing stock increases both the assets and the stockholders' equity of a corporation.

Retained Earnings Come from Profitable Operations

Profitable operations generate income, which increases stockholders' equity through a separate account called Retained Earnings. As we've just seen, a corporation needs more capital accounts than a proprietorship: A corporation uses a Common Stock account and a Retained Earnings account. Corporations close their revenues and expenses into Income Summary, and then they close net income to Retained Earnings. To illustrate, assume IHOP's revenues were $500,000 and expenses totaled $400,000 for December. The closing entries would be

Dec. 31	Sales Revenue..................	500,000	
	Income Summary		500,000
	To close sales revenue.		
31	Income Summary...............	400,000	
	Expenses (detailed)........		400,000
	To close expenses.		

Outstanding Stock
Stock in the hands of stockholders.

☐ Overview
■ **Stockholders' Equity**
☐ Issuing Stock
☐ Dividends
☐ Stock Values
☐ Evaluating Operations
☐ Income Taxes

Stockholders' Equity
Owners' equity of a corporation.

Paid-in Capital
Capital from investments by the stockholders. Also called **contributed capital**.

Retained Earnings
Capital earned through profitable operation of the business.

Exhibit 13-4

Summarized Stockholders' Equity Sheet of IHOP Corporation (Amounts in Millions)

 Student Resource CD

common stock, dividends, paid-in capital, preferred stock, retained earnings, share, stockholders' equity

✔ **Starter 13-2**

Common Stock
The basic form of capital stock. In a corporation, the common stockholders are the owners of the business.

Now, the Income Summary account holds revenues, expenses, and net income.

Income Summary

Expenses	400,000	Revenues	500,000
		Balance	
		(net income)	100,000

Finally, Income Summary's balance is closed to Retained Earnings.

Dec. 31	Income Summary...............	100,000	
	Retained Earnings.........		100,000
	To close net income to Retained Earnings.		

This closing entry completes the closing process. Income Summary is zeroed out, and Retained Earnings now holds net income, as follows:

Income Summary

Expenses	400,000	Revenues	500,000
Closing	100,000	Net income	100,000

Retained Earnings

	Closing
	(net income) 100,000

If IHOP has a net *loss*, Income Summary will have a debit balance. To close a $60,000 loss, the final closing entry credits Income Summary and debits Retained Earnings as follows:

Dec. 31	Retained Earnings.............	60,000	
	Income Summary.........		60,000
	To close *net loss* to Retained Earnings.		

Deficit
Debit balance in the Retained Earnings account.

A loss may cause a debit balance in the Retained Earnings account. This condition—called a Retained Earnings **deficit**—is reported on the balance sheet as a negative amount in stockholders' equity. **HAL, Inc.**, which owns Hawaiian Airlines, Inc., reported this deficit:

Stockholders' Equity	(In millions)
Paid-in capital: Common stock	$ 50
Deficit	(193)
Total stockholders' equity	$ (143)

Corporations May Pay Dividends to the Stockholders

Dividends
Distributions by a corporation to its stockholders.

If the corporation has been profitable and has sufficient cash, it may distribute cash to the stockholders. Such distributions are called **dividends**. Dividends are similar to the withdrawals made by a proprietor. Dividends decrease both the assets and the retained earnings of the corporation. Most states prohibit using paid-in capital for dividends. Accountants use the term *legal capital* to refer to the portion of stockholders' equity that cannot be used for dividends.

Some people think of Retained Earnings as a fund of cash. It is not, because Retained Earnings is an element of stockholders' equity. Retained earnings has no particular relationship to cash or any other asset. *Remember that cash dividends are paid out of assets, not out of retained earnings.*

Stockholders' Rights

The ownership of stock entitles a stockholder to four basic rights, unless specific rights are withheld by contract:

1. *Vote.* Stockholders participate in management by voting on matters that come before them. This is a stockholder's sole right to manage the corporation. Each share of stock carries one vote.

2. *Dividends.* Stockholders receive a proportionate part of any dividend. Each share of stock receives an equal dividend with every other share of the same class.

3. *Liquidation.* Stockholders receive their proportionate share of any assets remaining after the corporation pays its liabilities in liquidation (goes out of business).

4. *Preemption.* Stockholders can maintain their proportionate ownership in the corporation. Suppose you own 5% of a corporation's stock. If the corporation issues 100,000 new shares of stock, it must offer you the opportunity to buy 5% (5,000) of the new shares. This right, called the *preemptive right*, is usually withheld from the stockholders.

Classes of Stock

Corporations issue different types of stock. The stock of a corporation may be either common or preferred and either par or no-par.

COMMON AND PREFERRED STOCK   Every corporation issues *common stock*, the basic form of capital stock. The owners of a corporation are the common stockholders. Some companies issue Class A common stock, which carries the right to vote. They may also issue Class B common stock, which may be nonvoting. (Classes of stock may also be designated Series A, Series B, and so on.) There is a separate account for each class of stock.

Preferred stock gives its owners certain advantages over the common stockholders. Preferred stockholders receive dividends before the common stockholders, and they receive assets before the common stockholders if the corporation liquidates. Corporations pay a fixed amount of dividends on preferred stock. Investors usually buy preferred stock to earn those fixed dividends.

Owners of preferred stock also have the four basic stockholder rights, unless a right is specifically denied. The right to vote is sometimes withheld from preferred stockholders. Companies may issue different classes of preferred stock (Class A and Class B, or Series A and Series B, for example). Each class of stock is recorded in a separate account. Preferred stock is rarer than you might think. A recent survey of 600 corporations revealed that only 86 of them (14%) had some preferred stock outstanding (Exhibit 13-5).

PAR VALUE, STATED VALUE, AND NO-PAR STOCK   Stock may be par-value stock or no-par stock. **Par value** is an arbitrary amount assigned by a company to a share of its stock. Most companies set par value quite low to avoid legal difficulties from issuing their stock below par. Companies maintain a minimum amount of stockholders' equity for the protection of creditors, and this minimum represents the corporation's legal capital. For corporations with par-value stock, **legal capital** is usually the par value of the shares issued.

The common stock par value of Oracle Corporation, the software giant, is $0.01 (1 cent) per share. Pier 1 Imports' common carries a par value of $1 per share. Par value of preferred stock is often higher; some preferred stocks have par values of $25 or $100. Par value is used to compute dividends on preferred stock, as we shall see.

No-par stock does not have par value. Kimberly Clark, the paper company, has preferred stock with no par value. But some no-par stock has a **stated value**, which makes it similar to par-value stock. The stated value is an arbitrary amount that is similar to par value.

Preferred Stock
Stock that gives its owners certain advantages over common stockholders, such as the right to receive dividends before the common stockholders and the right to receive assets before the common stockholders if the corporation liquidates.

Exhibit 13-5

Preferred Stock

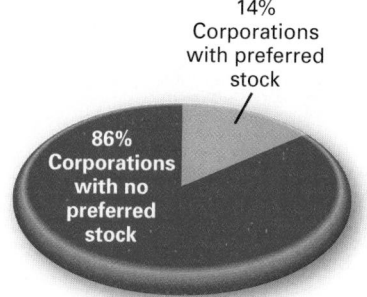

14% Corporations with preferred stock

86% Corporations with no preferred stock

Par Value
Arbitrary amount assigned to a share of stock.

Legal Capital
The portion of stockholders' equity that cannot be used for dividends.

Stated Value
An arbitrary amount that accountants treat as though it were par value.

Record the issuance of stock

Student ResourceCD

common stock, initial public offering, preferred stock

Issuing Stock

Large corporations such as Hewlett-Packard and Coca-Cola use huge quantities of money. They cannot finance all their operations through borrowing, so they raise capital by issuing stock. Corporations may sell the stock directly to stock-holders or use the services of an *underwriter*, such as the brokerage firms Merrill Lynch and Morgan Stanley, Dean Witter. An underwriter agrees to buy all the stock it cannot sell to its clients.

The price that the corporation receives from issuing stock is called the *issue price*. Usually, the issue price exceeds the stock's par value because par value is quite low. In the following sections, we show how to account for the issuance of stock.

Issuing Common Stock

The Wall Street Journal is the most popular medium for advertising stock to attract investors. The ads are called *tombstones*. Exhibit 13-6 reproduces IHOP's tomb-stone, which appeared in *The Wall Street Journal*.

Exhibit 13-6

Announcement of Public Offering of IHOP Stock (Adapted)

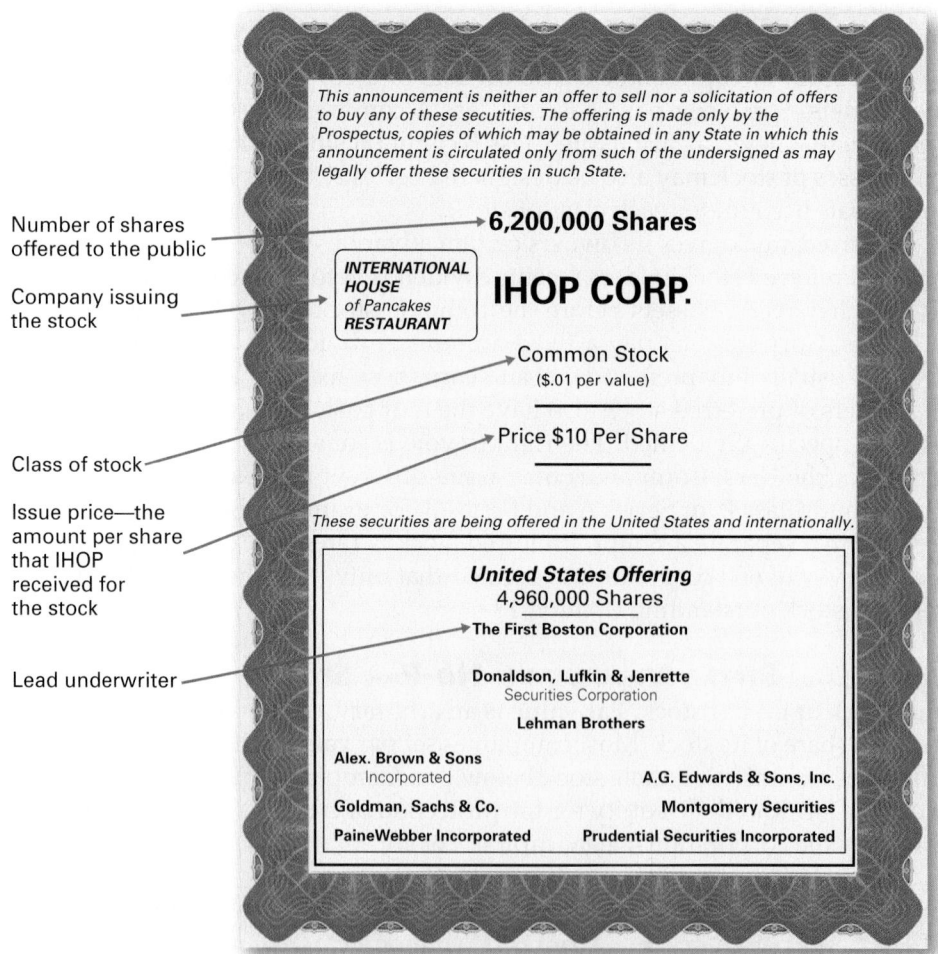

The lead underwriter of IHOP's public offering was The First Boston Corporation. Other brokerage firms and investment bankers also sold IHOP's stock to clients. IHOP's tombstone shows that IHOP hoped to raise approxi-mately $62 million of capital. But in the final analysis, IHOP issued only 3.2 mil-lion of the shares and received cash of approximately $32 million.

COMMON STOCK AT PAR   Suppose IHOP's common stock carried a par value of $10 per share. The stock issuance entry of 3.2 million shares would be

```
Jan. 31   Cash (3,200,000 × $10) ......   32,000,000
              Common Stock. ......                        32,000,000
          Issued common stock at par.
```

Prepare **IHOP's** classified balance sheet immediately after this issuance of stock. Assume zero balances prior to the transaction.

Answer:

IHOP Corporation
Balance Sheet
January 31, 20XX

Assets		Liabilities	
Current:			
Cash	$32,000,000	No liabilities	0
		Stockholders' Equity	
		Common stock	$32,000,000
		Total liabilities and	
Total assets	$32,000,000	stockholders' equity	$32,000,000

COMMON STOCK AT A PREMIUM   Most corporations set par value low and issue common stock for a price above par. The amount above par is called a *premium*. IHOP's common stock has an actual par value of $0.01 (1 cent) per share. The $9.99 difference between issue price ($10) and par ($0.01) is a premium. This sale of stock increases the corporation's paid-in capital by the full $10, total issue price of the stock. Let's see how to account for the premium.

A premium on the sale of stock is not a gain, income, or profit because the entity is dealing with its own stockholders. This situation illustrates one of the fundamentals of accounting: *A company can have no profits or losses when buying or selling its own stock.*

With a par value of $0.01, IHOP's entry to record the issuance of the stock is

```
July 31   Cash (3,200,000 × $10) .................   32,000,000
              Common Stock (3,200,000 × $0.01) ..                 32,000
              Paid-In Capital in Excess of Par—
                 Common (3,200,000 × $9.99). .....            31,968,000
          Issued common stock at a premium.
```

✔ **Starter 13-3**

Paid-In Capital in Excess of Par—Common is also called *Additional Paid-In Capital—Common*. Because both par value and premium amounts increase the corporation's capital, they appear in the stockholders' equity section of the balance sheet.

IHOP Corp. would report stockholders' equity on its balance sheet as follows, assuming that the corporate charter authorizes 40,000,000 shares of common stock and the balance of retained earnings is $26,000,000.

Stockholders' Equity	
Paid-in capital:	
Common stock, $0.01 par, 40 million shares	
authorized, 3.2 million shares issued	$ 32,000
Paid-in capital in excess of par	31,968,000
Total paid-in capital.	32,000,000
Retained earnings	26,000,000
Total stockholders' equity	$58,000,000

Common stock equals the total number of shares *issued* (3.2 million) multiplied by the par value per share ($0.01). The stock *authorization* reports the maximum number of shares the company may issue under its charter.

All transactions recorded in this section include the receipt of cash by the corporation for new stock issued to stockholders. These transactions are different from the vast majority of stock transactions reported each day in the financial press. In those transactions, stockholders are buying and selling stock to each other. The corporation doesn't journalize these transactions because its paid-in capital is unchanged.

NO-PAR COMMON STOCK   When a company issues stock that has no par value, there can be no premium. A recent survey of 600 companies revealed 57 issues of no-par stock.

When a company issues no-par stock, it debits the asset received and credits the stock account. Rocky Mountain Corporation, which manufactures ski equipment, issues 4,000 shares of no-par common stock for $20 per share. The stock-issuance entry is

Aug. 14	Cash (4,000 × $20)	80,000	
	Common Stock		80,000
	Issued no-par common stock.		

Regardless of the stock's price, Cash is debited and Common Stock is credited for the cash received. There is no Paid-In Capital in Excess of Par for no-par stock.

Rocky Mountain's charter authorizes 10,000 shares of no-par stock, and the company has $151,000 in retained earnings. Rocky Mountain reports stockholders' equity on the balance sheet as follows:

Stockholders' Equity	
Paid-in capital:	
Common stock, no par, 10,000 shares	
authorized, 4,000 shares issued	$ 80,000
Retained earnings.	151,000
Total stockholders' equity.	$231,000

UPS Delivers the Dough at Record-Breaking IPO

If you want stock in a company that operates in the global electronic marketplace, what comes to mind? Pioneering dot.coms like Amazon.com or eBay? Think again. There's a 97-year-old business whose workers drive old-fashioned brown trucks and run parcels up to your door. UPS is a business as traditional as apple pie. UPS raised a record-breaking $5.5 billion at its IPO (initial public offering) when it went public. All this money came from investors who saw UPS as a sign of the new economy.

Why would UPS sell its stock to the public? To build a cross-border, USA / European infrastructure, UPS figured it would need to acquire and merge with foreign firms. That required a lot of money. During the first hours of trading in UPS stock, the company's share price soared 40%. By the end of a week, the UPS workforce included 10,000 new millionaires.

Source: Based on Avital Louria Hahn, "Men in Brown: A Growth Story—UPS Recasts Itself for IPO," *The Investment Dealers' Digest: IDD*, December 13, 1999, p. 35. Elise Ackerman, "UPS Delivers as IPO Investors Give the World's No. 1 Package-Delivery Company Full Dot-Com Treatment," *U.S. News & World Report*, November 22, 1999, p. 53. Jenny Anderson, "Up, UPS and Away," *Institutional Investor*, January 2000, pp. 96–98.

Accounting.com

NO-PAR COMMON STOCK WITH A STATED VALUE   Accounting for no-par stock with a stated value is identical to accounting for par-value stock. No-par common stock with a stated value uses an account titled Paid-In Capital in Excess of *Stated* Value—Common.

COMMON STOCK FOR ASSETS OTHER THAN CASH   A corporation may issue stock and receive assets other than cash. It records the assets received at their current market value and credits the capital accounts accordingly. The assets' prior book value is irrelevant because the stockholder will demand stock equal to the market value of the asset given. Kahn Corporation issued 15,000 shares of its $1 par common stock for equipment worth $4,000 and a building worth $120,000. Kahn's entry is

Nov. 30	Equipment...............................	4,000	
	Building.................................	120,000	
	Common Stock (15,000 × $1)...........		15,000
	Paid-In Capital in Excess of Par—		
	Common ($124,000 – $15,000)........		109,000
	Issued common stock in exchange for equipment and a building.		

✔ **Starter 13-4**

Prepare the stockholders' equity section of Kahn's balance sheet immediately after this transaction. Before this issuance of stock, Kahn already had outstanding 10,000 shares of common stock that the company had issued for $8 per share. Kahn's charter authorizes the issuance of 100,000 shares of common stock. Retained earnings is $500,000.

Answer:

Stockholders' Equity	
Paid-in capital:	
Common stock, $1 par, 100,000 shares authorized,	
25,000 (10,000 + 15,000) shares issued	$ 25,000
Paid-in capital in excess of par ($70,000* + $109,000)	179,000
Total paid-in capital	204,000
Retained earnings	500,000
Total stockholders' equity	$704,000
*10,000 shares × ($8 – $1 par) = $70,000	

✔ **Starter 13-5**

✔ **Starter 13-6**

Issuing Preferred Stock

Accounting for preferred stock follows the pattern illustrated for common stock. Chiquita Brands International, Inc., famous for its bananas, has some preferred stock outstanding. Assume Chiquita issued 100,000 shares of preferred stock at par value of $1 per share. The issuance entry is

July 31	Cash	100,000	
	Preferred Stock		
	(100,000 shares × $1).................		100,000
	Issued preferred stock at par.		

✔ **Starter 13-7**

Most preferred stock is issued at par value. Therefore, Paid-In Capital in Excess of Par is rare for preferred stock. For this reason, we do not cover it in this book.

Ethical Considerations

Issuance of stock for *cash* poses no ethical challenge. The company receives cash and issues stock, giving the stockholders certificates as evidence of their ownership.

Issuing stock for assets other than cash can pose an ethical challenge. The company issuing the stock often wishes to record a large amount for the asset received (such as land or a building) and for the stock being issued. Why? Because large asset and equity amounts make the business look successful. The desire to look good can motivate a company to record a high amount for the assets.

A company is supposed to record an asset received at its current market value. But one person's evaluation of a building can differ from another's. One person may appraise the building at a market value of $4 million. Another may honestly believe it is worth only $3 million. A company receiving the building in exchange for its stock must decide whether to record the building at $3 million, $4 million, or some other amount.

The ethical course of action is to record the asset at its current market value, as determined by independent appraisers. Public corporations are rarely found guilty of *understating* the asset values on their balance sheets but companies have been embarrassed by *overstating* asset values.

Review of Accounting for Paid-In Capital

3 Prepare the stockholders' equity section of a corporation balance sheet

Let's review the first half of this chapter by showing the stockholders' equity section of MedTech.com Corporation's balance sheet in Exhibit 13-7.

Exhibit 13-7

Part of MedTech.com Corporation's Balance Sheet

Stockholders' Equity	
Paid-in capital:	
Preferred stock, 5%, $100 par, 5,000 shares	
authorized, 400 shares issued.................	$ 40,000
Common stock, $10 par, 20,000 shares	
authorized, 5,000 shares issued	50,000
Paid-in capital in excess of par—common..........	70,000
Total paid-in capital.........................	160,000
Retained earnings	90,000
Total stockholders' equity.........................	$250,000

✔ **Starter 13-8**

✔ **Starter 13-9**

Note the two sections of stockholders' equity: paid-in capital and retained earnings. Also observe the order of the equity accounts:

- Preferred stock
- Common stock at par value
- Paid-in capital in excess of par—common
- Retained earnings (after the paid-in capital accounts)

Additional Paid-In Capital
The paid-in capital in excess of par, common plus other accounts combined for reporting on the balance sheet.

Many companies label Paid-In Capital in Excess of Par—Common as **Additional Paid-In Capital** on the balance sheet. However, they are careful not to include preferred stock because that paid-in capital belongs to the preferred stockholders.

Review the Decision Guidelines feature to solidify your understanding of stockholders' equity as it is reported on the balance sheet.

Decision Guidelines

STOCKHOLDERS' EQUITY OF A CORPORATION

Suppose you are interested in investing in stock. The following guidelines will help you sort out some of the relevant factors for your decision.

Decision	Guidelines
What are the two main segments of stockholders' equity?	• Paid-in capital • Retained earnings

Decision Guidelines (continued)

Decision	Guidelines
Which is more permanent, paid-in capital or retained earnings?	Paid-in capital is more permanent because corporations can use their retained earnings for dividends.
How are paid-in capital and retained earnings	
• Similar?	• Both represent the stockholders' equity (ownership) in the assets of the corporation.
• Different?	• Paid-in capital and retained earnings come from different sources:
	a. *Paid-in capital* comes from the corporation's stockholders, who invested in the company.
	b. *Retained earnings* comes from profitable operations.
What are the main categories of paid-in capital?	• Preferred stock
	• Common stock, plus paid-in capital in excess of par

MID-CHAPTER *Summary Problem*

1. Test your understanding of the first half of this chapter: Is each of the following statements true or false?
   a. Issuance of 1,000 shares of $5 par-value stock at $12 increases contributed capital by $7,000.
   b. The issuance of no-par stock with a stated value is fundamentally different from issuing par-value stock.
   c. A corporation issues its preferred stock in exchange for land and a building with a combined market value of $200,000. This transaction increases the corporation's owners' equity by $200,000 regardless of the assets' prior book value.
   d. A stockholder may bind the corporation to a contract.
   e. The policy-making body in a corporation is called the board of directors.
   f. The owner of 100 shares of preferred stock has greater voting rights than the owner of 100 shares of common stock.
   g. Par-value stock is worth more than no-par stock.
2. The brewery **Adolph Coors Company** has two classes of common stock. The company's balance sheet included the following (adapted):

TIPS

CHECK YOUR RESOURCES

Stockholders' Equity

Capital stock	
Class A common stock, voting, $1 par value,	
authorized and issued 1,260,000 shares	$ 1,260,000
Additional paid-in capital—Class A common	2,011,000
Class B common stock, nonvoting, no par value,	
authorized and issued 46,200,000 shares	11,000,000
Retained earnings	872,403,000
	$886,674,000

Required

a. Record the issuance of the Class A common stock. The additional paid-in capital is related to the Class A common stock. Use the Coors account titles.
b. Record the issuance of the Class B common stock. Use the Coors account titles.
c. What is the total paid-in capital of the company?

Solutions

1. Answers to true/false statements:

a. False	**c.** True	**e.** True	**g.** False
b. False	**d.** False	**f.** False	

2. Adolph Coors Company:

a. Cash 3,271,000
       Class A Common Stock   1,260,000
       Additional Paid-In Capital   2,011,000
     To record issuance of Class A common stock.

b. Cash 11,000,000
       Class B Common Stock   11,000,000
     To record issuance of Class B common stock.

c. Total paid-in capital is $14,271,000 ($1,260,000 + $2,011,000 + $11,000,000).

Student ResourceCD

dividends

Accounting for Cash Dividends

Corporations share their wealth with the stockholders through dividends. Corporations declare dividends from retained earnings and then pay with cash. The corporation must have enough *retained earnings* to declare the dividend and also have enough *cash* to pay the dividend.

Dividend Dates

A corporation declares a dividend before paying it. The board of directors declares the dividend. The corporation has no obligation to pay a dividend until the board declares one. However, once the dividend is declared, it becomes a legal liability. Three relevant dates for dividends are

1. **Declaration date.** On the declaration date, the board of directors announces the intention to pay the dividend. The declaration creates a liability for the corporation.

2. **Date of record.** Those stockholders holding the stock on the date of record—a week or two after declaration—will receive the dividend when it's paid.

3. **Payment date.** Payment of the dividend usually follows the record date by a week or two.

Dividends on Preferred and Common Stock

Declaration of a cash dividend is recorded by debiting Retained Earnings and crediting Dividends Payable, as follows:[1]

May 1	Retained Earnings....................	XXX
	Dividends Payable..............	XXX
	Declared a cash dividend.	

Payment of the dividend usually follows declaration by a few weeks. Payment is recorded by debiting Dividends Payable and crediting Cash:

May 30	Dividends Payable	XXX
	Cash	XXX
	Paid the cash dividend.	

Dividends Payable is a current liability. When a company has issued both preferred stock and common stock, the preferred stockholders receive their dividends first. The common stockholders receive dividends only if the total dividend is large enough to satisfy the preferred requirement.

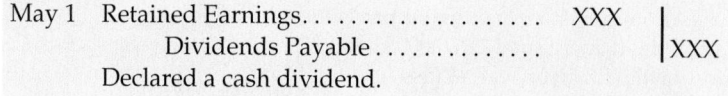 **4** *Account for cash dividends*

✔ **Starter 13-10**

---

[1]Some accountants debit a Dividends account, which is closed to Retained Earnings. But most businesses debit Retained Earnings, as shown here.

Pine Industries, Inc., has 10,000 shares of preferred stock outstanding, plus common stock. Preferred dividends are paid at the annual rate of $1.50 per share. Exhibit 13-8 shows the division of dividends between preferred and common for two situations.

Case A: Total dividend of $8,000:
    Preferred dividend (the full $8,000 goes to preferred
       because the annual preferred dividend is $15,000:
       10,000 shares × $1.50) .... $ 8,000
    Common dividend (none because the total dividend
       did not cover the preferred dividend for the year)   0
    Total dividend .... $ 8,000

Case B: Total dividend of $50,000:
    Preferred dividend (10,000 shares × $1.50 per share)............ $15,000
    Common dividend ($50,000 − $15,000) 35,000
    Total dividend $50,000

Exhibit 13-8

Dividing a Dividend Between Preferred Stock and Common Stock

✔ **Starter 13-11**

If Pine Industries' annual dividend is large enough to cover the preferred dividend for the year (Case B), the preferred stockholders receive their regular dividend, and the common stockholders receive the remainder. But if the year's dividend falls below the amount of the annual preferred dividend (Case A), the preferred stockholders receive the entire dividend, and the common stockholders get nothing that year.

The preferred-stock dividend preference can be stated as a percentage rate or a dollar amount. For example, preferred stock may be "6% preferred," which means that owners of the preferred stock receive an annual dividend of 6% of the par value of the stock. If par value is $100 per share, then the preferred stockholders get an annual dividend of $6 per share (6% of $100). The preferred stock may be "$3 preferred," which means that stockholders get an annual dividend of $3 per share regardless of the preferred stock's par value. The dividend rate on no-par preferred stock is stated in a dollar amount per share.

Dividends on Cumulative and Noncumulative Preferred

The allocation of dividends may be complex if the preferred stock is *cumulative*. Corporations sometimes fail to pay a dividend to their preferred stockholders. This is called *passing the dividend*, and the passed dividends are said to be *in arrears*. The owners of **cumulative preferred stock** must receive all dividends in arrears plus the current year's dividend before the common stockholders get a dividend.

The preferred stock of Pine Industries is cumulative. Suppose the company passed the 20X4 preferred dividend of $15,000. Before paying dividends to its common stockholders in 20X5, the company must first pay preferred dividends of $15,000 for both 20X4 and 20X5, a total of $30,000. *Preferred stock is cumulative in the eyes of the law unless it is labeled as noncumulative.* Most preferred stock is cumulative.

Assume that Pine Industries passes its 20X4 preferred dividend. In 20X5, the company declares a $50,000 dividend. The entry to record the declaration of this dividend is

Cumulative Preferred Stock
Preferred stock whose owners must receive all dividends in arrears before the corporation pays dividends to the common stockholders.

Sep. 6	Retained Earnings................ 50,000	
	Dividends Payable, Preferred	
	($15,000 × 2)...............	30,000
	Dividends Payable, Common	
	($50,000 − $30,000)	20,000
	Declared a cash dividend.	

If the preferred stock is *noncumulative*, the corporation need not pay dividends in arrears. Suppose Pine Industries' preferred stock was noncumulative and the company passed the 20X4 preferred dividend. The preferred stockholders would lose the 20X4 dividend forever. Of course, the common stockholders would not receive a 20X4 dividend either. Before paying any common dividends in 20X5, the company would have to pay the 20X5 preferred dividend of $15,000.

Dividends in arrears are *not* a liability for the corporation. A liability for dividends arises only after the board of directors declares the dividend. Nevertheless, a corporation must report cumulative preferred dividends in arrears. This information alerts common stockholders about how much must be paid before the common stockholders will receive any dividends.

Different Values of Stock

There are several different *stock values* in addition to par value. Market value and book value are used for various investor decisions.

Market Value

A stock's **market value**, or *market price*, is the price for which a person could buy or sell a share of the stock. The corporation's net income, future prospects, and general economic conditions affect market value. The Internet and most newspapers report the market price of many stocks. Log on to any company's Web site to track its stock price. *In almost all cases, stockholders are more concerned about the market value of a stock than about any other value.*

In the chapter-opening story, IHOP's stock had a market price of $10 when it was issued. Shortly thereafter, IHOP's stock shot up to $36, which means that the stock could be bought for $36 per share. The purchase of 100 shares of IHOP stock at $36 would cost $3,600 ($36 × 100), plus a commission. If you were selling 100 shares of IHOP stock, you would receive cash of $3,600 less a commission. The commission is the fee a stockbroker charges for buying or selling the stock. The price of a share of IHOP stock has fluctuated from $10 at issuance to a recent high of $26.

Book Value

The **book value** of a stock is the amount of owners' equity on the company's books for each share of its stock. If the company has only common stock outstanding, divide total stockholders' equity by the number of shares *outstanding*. A company with stockholders' equity of $180,000 and 5,000 shares of common stock has a book value of $36 per share ($180,000/5,000 shares).

If the company has both preferred stock and common stock outstanding, the preferred stockholders have the first claim to owners' equity. Therefore, we subtract preferred equity from total equity to compute book value per share of the common stock. To illustrate, Lille Corporation reports the following amounts:

Stockholders' Equity	
Paid-in capital:	
Preferred stock, 6%, $10 par, 5,000 shares issued......	$ 50,000
Common stock, $1 par, 20,000 shares authorized,	
10,000 shares issued.........................	10,000
Paid-in capital in excess of par—common..........	170,000
Total paid-in capital.........................	230,000
Retained earnings............................	420,000
Total stockholders' equity......................	$650,000

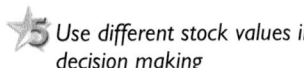
Use different stock values in decision making

Market Value
Price for which a person could buy or sell a share of stock.

Student ResourceCD
book value, market value

Book Value
Amount of owners' equity on the company's books for each share of its stock.

The book-value-per-share computation of common stock follows.

✔ Starter 13-12

Common	
Total stockholders' equity	$650,000
Less stockholders' equity allocated to preferred	(50,000)
Stockholders' equity allocated to common	$600,000
Book value per share ($600,000/10,000 shares)	$ 60.00

Book value is used in decision making. Book value may figure into the price to pay for a closely-held corporation, whose stock is not publicly traded. Also, a company may buy out a stockholder by agreeing to pay the book value of the person's stock.

Some investors compare the book value of a stock with its market value. The idea is that a stock selling below book value is underpriced and thus a good buy. But the relationship between book value and market value is far from clear. Other investors believe that if a stock sells below book value, the company must be experiencing difficulty. Exhibit 13-9 contrasts the book values and market prices for the stocks of three well-known companies. In all three cases, the stock price, which is the market value, exceeds book value—a sign of success. Dell Computer's stock price far exceeds its book value.

✔ Starter 13-13

Exhibit 13-9

Book Value and Market Value for Three Well-Known Companies

	Book Value Per Share	Recent Stock Price
IHOP Corp.	$17.12	$26.00
Fossil	7.34	18.13
Dell Computer	1.80	28.88

Evaluating Operations

Investors and creditors are constantly comparing companies' profits. IHOP's net income may not be comparable with the net income of a new company because IHOP is an established company and the other company is just getting started. IHOP's profits run into the millions, which far exceed a new company's net income. To compare companies, investors use standard profitability ratios. Two key measures are the rate of return on total assets and rate of return on common stockholders' equity.

☐ Overview
☐ Stockholders' Equity
☐ Issuing Stock
☐ Dividends
☐ Stock Values
■ **Evaluating Operations**
☐ Income Taxes

⭐ *Evaluate return on assets and return on stockholders' equity*

◉ Student ResourceCD
rate of return, stockholders' equity

Rate of Return on Total Assets
The sum of net income plus interest expense divided by average total assets. Measures the success a company has in using its assets to earn income for those financing the business. Also called **return on assets**.

Rate of Return on Total Assets

The **rate of return on total assets**, or simply **return on assets**, measures a company's success in using assets to earn income for those who are financing the business.

- Stockholders hold the stock and therefore earn the *net income*.
- Creditors have loaned money to the corporation and thus earn *interest*.

Interest expense and net income are the returns to the two groups that have financed the corporation. The sum of net income plus interest expense is the numerator of the return-on-assets ratio. The denominator is average total assets. Return on assets is computed as follows, using data from the 2002 annual report of IHOP Corp. (dollar amounts in millions):

$$\text{RATE OF RETURN ON TOTAL ASSETS} = \frac{\text{NET INCOME} + \text{INTEREST EXPENSE}}{\text{AVERAGE TOTAL ASSETS}}$$

$$= \frac{\$41 + \$22}{(\$641 + \$820)/2} = \frac{\$63}{\$730.5} = 0.086$$

Net income and interest expense are taken from the income statement. Average total assets comes from the beginning and ending balance sheets.

What is a good rate of return on total assets? There is no single answer because rates of return vary widely by industry. For example, high-tech companies such as Intel and Microsoft earn higher returns than utility companies and manufacturers of consumer goods. In most industries, a return on assets of 10% is considered good.

Rate of Return on Common Stockholders' Equity

Rate of return on common stockholders' equity, often called **return on equity**, shows the relationship between net income available to the common stockholders and average common equity. The numerator is net income minus preferred dividends. Preferred dividends are subtracted because the preferred stockholders have the first claim to dividends from net income. The denominator is average *common stockholders' equity*—total equity minus preferred equity. IHOP's rate of return on common stockholders' equity for 2002 is computed as follows (amounts in millions):

✔ Starter 13-14

✔ Starter 13-15

$$\begin{array}{c}\text{RATE OF RETURN}\\\text{ON COMMON}\\\text{STOCKHOLDERS'}\\\text{EQUITY}\end{array} = \frac{\text{NET INCOME} - \text{PREFERRED DIVIDENDS}}{\text{AVERAGE COMMON STOCKHOLDERS' EQUITY}}$$

$$= \frac{\$41 - \$0}{(\$312 + \$364)/2} = \frac{\$41}{\$338} = 0.121$$

IHOP has no preferred stock, so preferred dividends are zero.

IHOP's return on equity (12.1%) is higher than its return on assets (8.6%). This indicates a healthy company because IHOP is earning more for its stockholders than it is paying for interest expense. Companies borrow at one rate (say, 7%) and try to earn a higher rate (12%) on investments. This is what IHOP did. Borrowing at a lower rate than the return on equity is called *using leverage*.

If a company's return on assets exceeds its return on equity, the company is in trouble. Why?Because interest expense is greater than return on equity. Interest expense should always be lower than the return on equity. Investors and creditors use return on equity in much the same way they use return on total assets—to compare companies. The higher the rate of return, the more successful the company. IHOP's 12% return on common stockholders' equity would be considered fairly good in many industries.

Accounting for Income Taxes by Corporations

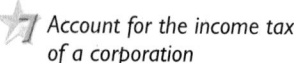
Account for the income tax of a corporation

Corporations pay income tax just as individuals do, but not at the same rates. At this writing, the federal tax rate on most corporate income is 35%. Most states also levy a corporate income tax, so most corporations have a combined federal and state income tax rate of approximately 40%.

To account for income tax, the corporation measures

■ Income tax expense, an expense on the income statement

■ Income tax payable, a liability on the balance sheet

Let's illustrate accounting for income tax with a realistic example. In general, income tax expense and income tax payable can be computed as follows:[2]

Income tax expense	=	Income before tax— from the income statement	×	Income tax rate		Income tax payable	=	Taxable income— from the tax return filed with the IRS	×	Income tax rate

[2]The authors thank Jean Marie Hudson for suggesting this presentation.

The income statement and the income tax return are entirely separate documents. The income statement is the financial statement you've been studying throughout this course. The tax return is used only to report taxes to the IRS.

For most companies, income tax expense and income tax payable differ. The most important difference occurs when a corporation uses straight-line depreciation for the income statement and accelerated depreciation → for the tax return.

Continuing with the IHOP illustration, suppose for 20X6 that IHOP Corp. has

We learned in Chapter 10 that the MACRS depreciation method is used for tax purposes.

- Income before income tax of $70 million (This comes from the income statement.)
- Taxable income of $50 million (This comes from the tax return.)

IHOP will record income tax for 20X6 as follows (dollar amounts in millions and an income tax rate of 40%):

```
20X6
Dec. 31  Income Tax Expense ($70 × 0.40) ............  28
              Income Tax Payable ($50 × 0.40)........        20
              Deferred Tax Liability ...............         8
         Recorded income tax for the year.
```

IHOP will pay the $20 million of Income Tax Payable within a few months. The Deferred Tax Liability account is long-term, so IHOP will pay this debt over a number of years. IHOP's 20X6 financial statements would report these figures (adapted, in millions):

✔ **Starter 13-16**

Income Statement		Balance Sheet	
Income before income tax	$70	Current liabilities:	
Income tax expense	(28)	Income tax payable	$20
Net income	$42	Long-term liabilities:	
		Deferred tax liability	8*

*The beginning balance of Deferred tax liability was zero.

Decision Guidelines

DIVIDENDS, STOCK VALUES, EVALUATING OPERATIONS, & CORPORATE INCOME TAX

Suppose you operate an **IHOP** restaurant near your college. You are naturally interested in how well the company as a whole is doing. Does IHOP pay dividends? What are IHOP's stock values? What are the rates of return on IHOP's assets and equity? The Decision Guidelines will help you evaluate the company.

Decision	Guidelines
Dividends Whether to declare a cash dividend?	• Must have enough retained earnings to declare the dividend. • Must have enough cash to pay the dividend.
What happens with a dividend?	• The corporation's board of directors declares the dividend. Then the dividend becomes a liability of the corporation. • The date of record fixes who will receive the dividend. • Payment of the dividend occurs later.
Who receives the dividend?	• Preferred stockholders receive their dividends first. Preferred dividends have a specified rate. • Common stockholders receive the remainder.

Decision Guidelines (*continued*)

Decision	Guidelines
Stock Values	
How much to pay for a stock?	Its market value.
How is book value used in decision making?	Sometimes used to help determine the market value of a stock that is not traded on a stock exchange.
Evaluating Operations	
How to evaluate the operations of a corporation?	Two measures that relate earnings to the amount stockholders have invested include:
	• Rate of return on assets
	• Rate of return on common stockholders' equity
	For a healthy company, return on stockholders' equity should exceed return on assets.
Accounting for Income Tax	
What are the three main tax accounts?	• Income tax expense
	• Income tax payable, a current liability
	• Deferred tax liability, usually a long-term liability
How to measure	
• Income tax expense?	Income before income tax (from the income statement) × Income tax rate
• Income tax payable?	Taxable income (from the income tax return filed with the Internal Revenue Service) × Income tax rate
• Deferred tax liability?	Difference between income tax expense and income tax payable for any one year

Excel Application Exercise

Goal: To create an Excel worksheet that compares the financial performances of two publicly traded stocks in the restaurant industry.

Scenario: Your task is to create an Excel worksheet that compares the historical performance of **IHOP** and **Cracker Barrel** on two key financial measures. Embedded graphs of each financial dimension also must be created. All data used in your spreadsheet will come from **Morningstar's** Web site.

When finished, answer these questions:

1. Which company has earned a consistently higher return on equity?
2. Which company has earned a consistently higher return on assets?

Step-by-Step:

1. Locate www.morningstar.com on the Web.
2. Under the "Morningstar Quicktake Reports" section, enter the ticker symbol for each company. IHOP's symbol is IHP, and Cracker Barrel's symbol is CBRL. To locate the required information, look under "Financial Statements." (Note: If the Web site differs from these headings, you may have to search

other areas of the Web site.) Print out the pages used for each company.
3. Open a new Excel worksheet.
4. Create a bold-faced heading for your spreadsheet that contains the following:
   a. Chapter 13 Excel Application Exercise
   b. Investing in Stock
   c. Stock Performance Analysis
   d. Today's Date
5. Under the heading, create a bold-faced, underlined section titled "Return on Equity %." Move down one row. Create one column each for the past four years (for example, "2001," "2000," and so on). Create one row each for IHOP and Cracker Barrel.
6. Enter the "Return on Equity %" data for the past five years for each company.
7. Repeat steps 5 and 6 for "Return on Assets %."
8. Using the Excel Chart Wizard, create separate graphs for Return on Equity % and Return on Assets %. Resize and position each graph to the right of the data so that everything appears on one page when you print.
9. Save your work, and print your work sheet in landscape mode (with graphs) for your files.

END-OF-CHAPTER *Summary Problem*

Use the following accounts and related balances to prepare the classified balance sheet of Whitehall, Inc., at September 30, 20X4. Use the account format of the balance sheet.

CHECK YOUR RESOURCES

Common stock, $1 par, 50,000 shares authorized, 25,000 shares issued	$25,000	Long-term note payable	$ 73,000	
		Inventory	85,000	
Dividends payable	4,000	Property, plant, and equipment, net	225,000	
Cash	15,000	Accounts receivable, net	23,000	
Accounts payable	28,000	Preferred stock, $3.50, no-par, 10,000 shares authorized, 2,000 shares issued	20,000	
Retained earnings	80,000			
Paid-in capital in excess of par—common	115,000	Accrued liabilities	3,000	

Compute the book value per share of Whitehall's common stock. No prior-year preferred dividends are in arrears, but Whitehall has not declared the current-year dividend.

Solution

Whitehall, Inc.

Balance Sheet
September 30, 20X4

Assets		Liabilities	
Current:		Current:	
Cash	$ 15,000	Accounts payable	$ 28,000
Accounts receivable, net	23,000	Dividends payable	4,000
Inventory	85,000	Accrued liabilities	3,000
Total current assets	123,000	Total current liabilities	35,000
Property, plant, and equipment, net	225,000	Long-term note payable	73,000
		Total liabilities	108,000

Stockholders' Equity

Paid-in capital:		
Preferred stock, $3.50, no-par, 10,000 shares authorized, 2,000 shares issued	$ 20,000	
Common stock, $1 par, 50,000 shares authorized, 25,000 shares issued	25,000	
Paid-in capital in excess of par—common	115,000	
Total paid-in capital	160,000	
Retained earnings	80,000	
Total stockholders' equity		240,000

Total assets	$348,000	Total liabilities and stockholders' equity $348,000

Preferred equity:	
Carrying value	$ 20,000
Cumulative dividend for current year (2,000 shares × $3.50)	7,000
Stockholders' equity allocated to preferred	$ 27,000
Common:	
Total stockholders' equity	$240,000
Less stockholders' equity allocated to preferred	(27,000)
Stockholders' equity allocated to common	$213,000
Book value per share ($213,000/25,000 shares)	$8.52

REVIEW *Corporations: Paid-In Capital and the Balance Sheet*

Quick Check

1. Which characteristic of a corporation differs from a proprietorship and a partnership?
   a. Separate legal entity
   b. Double taxation
   c. Limited stockholder liability
   d. All of the above

2. Among the corporate characteristics listed in question 1, which is a disadvantage?
   a. Separate legal entity
   b. Double taxation
   c. Limited stockholder liability
   d. None of the above

3. The two basic sources of corporate capital are
   a. Paid-in capital and retained earnings
   b. Stock and bonds
   c. Common stock and preferred stock
   d. Retained earnings and dividends

4. Which class of stockholders takes the greater risk?
   a. Preferred
   b. Common
   c. Neither; bondholders take the most risk
   d. Both preferred and common take equal risk

5. Suppose **IHOP** issued 100,000 shares of its $0.05 par common stock at $1 per share. Which journal entry correctly records the issuance of this stock?

   a. Cash. 100,000
       Common Stock. . | 100,000

   b. Common Stock 100,000
       Cash. . . . . | 5,000
       Paid-In Capital
         in Excess of Par | 95,000

   c. Cash. 100,000
       Common Stock. . | 5,000
       Paid-In Capital
         in Excess of Par | 95,000

   d. Common Stock 100,000
       Cash . . . . | 100,000

6. Suppose IHOP issues common stock to purchase a building. IHOP should record the building at
   a. Its market value
   b. Its book value
   c. The par value of the stock given
   d. A value assigned by the board of directors

7. Chewning Corporation has 10,000 shares of 5%, $10 par preferred stock and 50,000 shares of common stock outstanding. Chewning declared no dividends in 20X5. In 20X6, Chewning declares a total dividend of $25,000. How much of the dividends go to the common stockholders?
   a. $5,000
   b. $10,000
   c. $15,000
   d. None; it all goes to preferred

8. Techster Company has 10,000 shares of $1 par common stock outstanding, which Techster issued at $5 per share. Techster also has retained earnings of $80,000. How much is Techster's total stockholders' equity?
   a. $50,000
   b. $80,000
   c. $90,000
   d. $130,000

9. Dale Corporation has the following data:

Net income.	$22,000	Average total assets	$300,000
Interest expense	8,000	Average common equity . . .	100,000
Preferred dividends	10,000		

Dale's return on common stockholders' equity is
   a. 4%
   b. 10%
   c. 12%
   d. 15%

10. A corporation's income tax expense is computed as follows:
   a. Income before tax × Income tax rate
   b. Taxable income × Income tax rate
   c. Net income × Income tax rate
   d. Return on equity × Income tax rate

Accounting Vocabulary

additional paid-in capital (p. 516)
authorization of stock (p. 507)
board of directors (p. 508)
book value (p. 520)
bylaws (p. 507)
chairperson (p. 508)
charter (p. 506)
common stock (p. 509)
contributed capital (p. 509)
cumulative preferred stock (p. 519)
deficit (p. 510)
dividends (p. 510)

double taxation (p. 507)
legal capital (p. 511)
limited liability (p. 507)
market value (p. 520)
outstanding stock (p. 509)
paid-in capital (p. 509)
par value (p. 511)
preferred stock (p. 511)
president (p. 508)
rate of return on common stockholders'
  equity (p. 522)

rate of return on total assets (p. 521)
retained earnings (p. 509)
return on assets (p. 521)
return on equity (p. 522)
shareholder (p. 506)
stated value (p. 511)
stock (p. 506)
stockholder (p. 506)
stockholders' equity (p. 509)

ASSESS Your Progress

Starters

A⁺ online homework

S13-1 Consider the authority structure in a corporation, as diagrammed in Exhibit 13-2.

1. Who is in charge of day-to-day operations?
2. Who is in charge of accounting?
3. What group holds the ultimate power in a corporation?
4. Who is the most powerful person in the corporation?

See *www.prenhall.com/horngren* for selected Starters, Exercises, and Problems.

Authority structure in a corporation
(Obj. 1)

S13-2 Examine the stockholders' equity of **IHOP Corporation** in Exhibit 13-4. Suppose IHOP were a proprietorship owned by Joe Hopper. How would the IHOP proprietorship balance sheet differ from the one given in Exhibit 13-4? How would the proprietorship balance sheet be similar to the one given in Exhibit 13-4?

The balance sheets of a corporation and a proprietorship
(Obj. 1)

S13-3 Study **IHOP's** July 31 stock issuance entry at a premium on page 513, and answer these questions about the IHOP transaction.

Effect of a stock issuance on net income
(Obj. 2)

1. IHOP received $32,000,000 for the issuance of its stock. The par value of the IHOP stock was only $32,000. Was the excess amount of $31,968,000 a profit to IHOP? Did the excess affect net income? If not, what was it?
2. Suppose the par value of the IHOP stock had been $1 per share, $5 per share, or $10 per share. Would a change in the par value of the company's stock affect IHOP's total paid-in capital? What does affect total paid-in capital?

S13-4 This exercise shows the similarity and the difference between two ways to acquire plant assets.

Issuing stock to finance the purchase of assets
(Obj. 2)

Case A—Issue stock and buy the assets in separate transactions:
  Avisa, Inc., issued 10,000 shares of its $10 par common stock for cash of $700,000. In a separate transaction, Avisa purchased a building for $500,000 and equipment for $200,000. Journalize the two transactions.
Case B—Issue stock to acquire the assets:
  Avisa issued 10,000 shares of its $10 par common stock to acquire a building valued at $500,000 and equipment worth $200,000. Journalize this single transaction.

Compare the balances in all accounts after making both sets of entries. Are the account balances similar or different?

*Issuing stock and interpreting
stockholders' equity*
(Obj. 2)

S13-5 **The Coca-Cola Company** reported the following on its balance sheet at December 31, 2002 (adapted, with amounts in millions, except for par value per share):

Common stock, $0.25 par value	
Authorized: 5,600 shares	
Issued: 3,500 shares	$ 875
Paid-in capital in excess of par.	3,855
Retained earnings.	24,506

1. Assume Coca-Cola issued all of its stock during 2002. Journalize the company's issuance of the stock for cash.
2. Was Coca-Cola's main source of stockholders' equity paid-in capital or profitable operations? How can you tell?

*Issuing stock and analyzing retained
earnings*
(Obj. 2)

S13-6 At December 31, 2002, **The Coca-Cola Company** reported the following on its comparative balance sheet, which included 2001 amounts for comparison (adapted, with all amounts in millions except par value per share):

	December 31,	
	2002	**2001**
Common stock, $0.25 par value		
Authorized: 5,600 shares		
Issued: 3,500 shares in 2002	$ 875	
3,490 shares in 2001		$ 873
Paid-in capital in excess of par	3,855	3,520
Retained earnings	24,506	23,443

1. How much did Coca-Cola's total paid-in capital increase during 2002? What caused total paid-in capital to increase? How can you tell?
2. Did Coca-Cola have a profit or a loss for 2002? How can you tell?

Issuing stock
(Obj. 2)

S13-7 Bruner Corporation has two classes of stock: Common, $1 par: Preferred, $10 par. Journalize Bruner's issuance of

a. 1,000 shares of common stock for $50 per share
b. 1,000 shares of preferred stock for a total of $32,000

Explanations are not required.

*Preparing the stockholders' equity section
of a balance sheet*
(Obj. 3)

S13-8 The financial statements of Manatee Corporation reported the following accounts (in thousands except for par value):

Paid-in capital in excess of par.	$170	Net sales	$1,080
Cost of goods sold	588	Accounts payable.	60
Common stock, $1 par,		Retained earnings	166
400 shares issued	400	Other current liabilities.	52
Cash	240	Operating expenses.	412
Long-term debt.	76	Total assets	?

Prepare the stockholders' equity section of the Manatee balance sheet. Net income has already been closed to Retained Earnings.

Using stockholders' equity data
(Obj. 3)

S13-9 → *Link Back to Chapter 1 (Accounting Equation, Income Statement).* Use the Manatee Corporation data in Starter 13-8 to compute Manatee's

a. Net income   **b.** Total liabilities   **c.** Total assets

S13-10 Colombia Coffee Company earned net income of $85,000 during the year ended December 31, 20X8. On December 15, Colombia declared the annual cash dividend on its 6% preferred stock (par value, $100,000) and a $0.50 per share cash dividend on its common stock (50,000 shares). Colombia then paid the dividends on January 4, 20X9.

Accounting for cash dividends
(Obj. 4)

    Journalize for Colombia Company:

a. Declaring the cash dividends on December 15
b. Paying the cash dividends on January 4, 20X9

S13-11 Refer to the stockholders' equity of MedTech.com Corporation in Exhibit 13-7. Answer these questions about MedTech.com's dividends.

Dividing cash dividends between preferred and common stock
(Obj. 4)

1. How much in dividends must MedTech.com declare each year before the common stockholders get any cash dividends for the year?
2. Suppose MedTech.com declares cash dividends of $20,000 for 20X5. How much of the dividends goes to preferred? How much goes to common?
3. Is MedTech.com's preferred stock cumulative or noncumulative? How can you tell?
4. Suppose MedTech.com passed the preferred dividend in 20X6 and 20X7. In 20X8, the company declares cash dividends of $9,000. How much of the dividends goes to preferred? How much goes to common?

S13-12 Refer to the stockholders' equity of MedTech.com Corporation in Exhibit 13-7. MedTech.com has not declared preferred dividends for three years (including the current year). Compute the book value per share of MedTech.com's common stock.

Book value per share of common stock
(Obj. 5)

S13-13 Answer the following questions about various stock values.

Explaining the use of different stock values for decision making
(Obj. 5)

1. Suppose you are an investor considering the purchase of **Intel** common stock as an investment. You have called your stockbroker to inquire about the stock. Which stock value are you most concerned about? Explain your reasoning.
2. How is the book value of a stock used in decision making?

S13-14 Answer these questions about two rates of return.

1. Give the formula for computing (a) rate of return on common stockholders' equity and (b) rate of return on total assets.

Computing and explaining return on assets and return on equity
(Obj. 6)

2. Why are preferred dividends subtracted from net income to compute return on common stockholders' equity?
3. Why is interest expense added to net income to compute return on assets?

S13-15 **Coca-Cola's** 2002 financial statements reported the following items—with 2001 figures given for comparison (adapted, in millions):

Computing return on assets and return on equity for a leading company
(Obj. 6)

	2002	2001
Balance sheet		
Total assets	$24,501	$22,417
Total liabilities	$12,701	$11,051
Total stockholders' equity (all common)	11,800	11,366
Total liabilities and equity	$24,501	$22,417
Income statement		
Net sales	$19,564	
Cost of goods sold	7,105	
Gross profit	12,459	
Selling, administrative, and general expenses	7,001	
Interest expense	199	
All other expenses, net	2,209	
Net income	$ 3,050	

Compute Coca-Cola's rate of return on total assets and rate of return on common stock-holders' equity for 2002. Do these rates of return look high or low?

Accounting for a corporation's income tax
(Obj. 7)

S13-16 Harry's Hot Dogs had income before income tax of $100,000 and taxable income of $80,000 for 20X4, the company's first year of operations. The income tax rate is 40%.

1. Make the entry to record Harry's income taxes for 20X4.
2. Show what Harry's Hot Dogs will report on its 20X4 income statement, starting with income before income tax.

online homework

Exercises

Organizing a corporation
(Obj. 1)

E13-1 Kyle Dietz and Joe Phipps are opening a limousine service to be named Good Times Limo. They need outside capital, so they plan to organize the business as a corporation. They come to you for advice. Write a memorandum informing them of the steps in forming a corporation. Identify specific documents used in this process, and name the different parties involved in the ownership and management of a corporation.

Issuing stock
(Obj. 2)

General Ledger (GL), QuickBooks (QB), Peachtree (PT)

E13-2 Carolina Systems completed the following stock issuance transactions:

April 19	Issued 1,000 shares of $1 par common stock for cash of $10.50 per share.
May 3	Sold 300 shares of $4.50, no-par preferred stock for $15,000 cash.
11	Received inventory valued at $23,000 and equipment with market value of $11,000. Issued 3,000 shares of the $1 par common stock.

Required

1. Journalize the transactions. Explanations are not required.
2. How much paid-in capital did these transactions generate for Carolina Systems?

Issuing stock and preparing the stockholders' equity section of the balance sheet
(Obj. 2, 3)

GL, QB, PT

E13-3 The charter for Mohammed Rugs, Inc., authorizes the company to issue 100,000 shares of $3, no-par preferred stock and 500,000 shares of common stock with $1 par value. During its start-up phase, Mohammed completed the following transactions:

Aug. 6	Issued 500 shares of common stock to the promoters who organized the corporation, receiving cash of $15,000.
12	Issued 300 shares of preferred stock for cash of $20,000.
14	Issued 1,000 shares of common stock in exchange for land valued at $26,000.
31	Closed net income of $25,000 into Retained Earnings.

Required

1. Record the transactions in the general journal.
2. Prepare the stockholders' equity section of the Mohammed Rugs balance sheet at August 31.

Recording issuance of no-par stock
(Obj. 2)

E13-4 Amalfi Furniture Co., located in Chicago, imports Mediterranean furniture. The corporation issued 5,000 shares of no-par common stock for $10 per share. Record issuance of the stock if the stock (a) is true no-par stock and (b) has stated value of $2 per share. Which type of stock results in more total paid-in capital?

Stockholders' equity section of a balance sheet
(Obj. 3)

E13-5 The charter of Big Bear Corporation authorizes the issuance of 5,000 shares of Class A preferred stock, 1,000 shares of Class B preferred stock, and 10,000 shares of common stock. During a two-month period, Big Bear completed these stock-issuance transactions:

Nov. 23	Issued 2,000 shares of $1 par common stock for cash of $12.50 per share.	
Dec. 2	Sold 300 shares of $4.50, no-par Class A preferred stock for $20,000 cash.	
12	Received inventory valued at $25,000 and equipment with market value of $16,000 for 3,000 shares of the $1 par common stock.	
17	Issued 1,000 shares of 5%, no-par Class B preferred stock with stated value of $50 per share. The issue price was stated value.	

Required

Prepare the stockholders' equity section of the Big Bear Corporation balance sheet for the transactions given in this exercise. Retained Earnings has a balance of $70,000.

E13-6 ReadyTech Co. recently organized. The company issued common stock to an attorney in exchange for his patent with a market value of $40,000. In addition, ReadyTech received cash both for 2,000 shares of its $50 par preferred stock at par value and for 26,000 shares of its no-par common stock at $10 per share. Retained Earnings at the end of the first year was $70,000. Without making journal entries, determine the total paid-in capital created by these transactions.

Paid-in capital for a corporation **(Obj. 2)**

E13-7 Liston Fry Co. has the following selected account balances at June 30, 20X2. Prepare the stockholders' equity section of the company's balance sheet.

Stockholders' equity section of a balance sheet **(Obj. 3)**

Student ResourceCD

spreadsheet

Common stock, no par with $1 stated value, 100,000 shares authorized and issued..............	$100,000	Inventory...................	$112,000
		Machinery and equipment.....	109,000
		Preferred stock, 5%, $20 par, 20,000 shares authorized, 5,000 shares issued.........	100,000
Accumulated depreciation— machinery and equipment................	62,000	Paid-in capital in excess of stated value—common......	90,000
Retained earnings	110,000	Cost of goods sold	81,000

E13-8 Qualcomm Communications has the following stockholders' equity:

Dividing dividends between preferred and common stock **(Obj. 4)**

Preferred stock, 8%, $10 par, 100,000 shares authorized, 20,000 shares issued.................	$ 200,000
Common stock, $0.50 par, 500,000 shares authorized, 300,000 shares issued................	150,000
Paid-in capital in excess of par—common...........	600,000
Total paid-in capital	950,000
Retained earnings	150,000
Total stockholders' equity	$1,100,000

First, determine whether preferred stock is cumulative or noncumulative. Then compute the amount of dividends to preferred and to common for 20X1 and 20X2 if total dividends are $15,000 in 20X1 and $50,000 in 20X2.

E13-9 The following elements of stockholders' equity are adapted from the balance sheet of Bullock Corporation.

Computing dividends on preferred and common stock **(Obj. 4)**

Stockholders' Equity	$ Thousands
Preferred stock, cumulative, $2 par (Note 7), 50,000 shares issued..	$100
Common stock, $0.10 par, 9,000,000 shares issued...............	900

Note 7. Preferred Stock:
Designated Annual Cash Dividend Per Share—$0.40.

Bullock paid no preferred dividends in 20X3.

Required

Compute the dividends to preferred and common for 20X4 if total dividends are $150,000 in 20X4.

Book value per share of common stock
(Obj. 5)

E13-10 The balance sheet of Westview Landscaping reported the following:

Preferred stock, $50 par value, 6%,	
100 shares issued and outstanding	$ 5,000
Common stockholders' equity, 10,000 shares issued	
and outstanding.	222,000
Total stockholders' equity	$227,000

Assume that Westview has paid preferred dividends for the current year and all prior years (no dividends in arrears). Compute the book value per share of the common stock.

Book value per share of common stock;
preferred dividends in arrears
(Obj. 5)

E13-11 Refer to Exercise 13-10. Compute the book value per share of the common stock if three years' preferred dividends (including dividends for the current year) are in arrears. Round book value to the nearest cent.

Evaluating profitability
(Obj. 6)

E13-12 Columbus Furniture, Inc., reported these figures for 20X8 and 20X7:

	20X8	20X7
Income statement:		
Interest expense	$ 2,400,000	$ 7,100,000
Net income	18,000,000	18,700,000
Balance sheet:		
Total assets.	326,000,000	317,000,000
Preferred stock, $1.30, no-par,		
100,000 shares issued and		
outstanding	2,500,000	2,500,000
Common stockholders' equity	164,000,000	157,000,000
Total stockholders' equity	166,500,000	159,500,000

Compute rate of return on total assets and rate of return on common stockholders' equity for 20X8. Do these rates of return suggest strength or weakness? Give your reason.

Accounting for income tax by a
corporation
(Obj. 7)

E13-13 The income statement of **Pier 1 Imports, Inc.**, reported income before income tax of $160 million during a recent year. Assume Pier 1's taxable income for the year was $100 million. The company's income tax rate was close to 40%.

1. Journalize Pier 1's entry to record income tax for the year.
2. Show how Pier 1 would report income tax on its income statement and on its balance sheet. Complete the income statement, starting with income before tax. For the balance sheet, assume all beginning balances were zero.

Accounting for an actual company's
transactions
(Obj. 2, 4)

E13-14 **Wal-Mart Stores, Inc.**, completed many transactions during 20X2, including the following (adapted in billions):

a. Sales revenue—assume all for cash, $218.
b. Total expenses—90% paid in cash; 10% on account, $210.
c. Closing entries for sales revenue and total expenses.
d. Closing entry for net income to Retained Earnings.
e. Total cash dividends declared and then paid later, $1.

Required

Journalize these 20X2 transactions.

Problems

(Group A)

P13-1A Del Chesser and Mark Bailes are opening a **Pier 1 Imports** store in a shopping center in Taos, New Mexico. The area is growing, and no competitors are located nearby. Their basic decision is how to organize the business. Chesser thinks the partnership form is best. Bailes favors the corporate form of organization. They seek your advice.

Organizing a corporation
(Obj. 1)

Required

Write a memo to Chesser and Bailes to make them aware of the advantages and disadvantages of organizing the business as a corporation. Use the following format for your memo:

> **Date:** _____
>
> **To:** Del Chesser and Mark Bailes
>
> **From:** Student Name
>
> **Subject:** Advantages and disadvantages of the corporate form of business organization

P13-2A Partners Craven and Thames wish to avoid the unlimited personal liability of the partnership form of business, so they are incorporating the company as C & T Services, Inc. The charter from the state of Arizona authorizes the corporation to issue 10,000 shares of 6%, $100 par preferred stock and 250,000 shares of no-par common stock. In its first month, C & T Services completed the following transactions:

Journalizing corporation transactions and preparing the stockholders' equity section of the balance sheet
(Obj. 2, 3)

GL, QB, PT

Jan. 3	Issued 6,300 shares of common stock to Craven and 3,800 shares to Thames, both for cash of $10 per share.
12	Issued 1,100 shares of preferred stock to acquire a patent with a market value of $110,000.
22	Issued 1,500 shares of common stock to other investors for $10 cash per share.

Required

1. Record the transactions in the general journal.
2. Prepare the stockholders' equity section of the C & T Services, Inc., balance sheet at January 31. The ending balance of Retained Earnings is $40,000.

P13-3A Delta Corporation was organized in 20X4. At December 31, 20X4, Delta's balance sheet reported the following stockholders' equity:

Issuing stock and preparing the stockholders' equity section of the balance sheet
(Obj. 2, 3)

Preferred stock, 5%, $10 par, 50,000 shares authorized, none issued . .	$ —
Common stock, $2 par, 100,000 shares authorized,	
10,000 shares issued	20,000
Paid-in capital in excess of par—common	30,000
Retained earnings (Deficit)	(5,000)
Total stockholders' equity	$45,000

Required

Answer the following questions, making journal entries as needed.

1. What does the 5% mean for the preferred stock? After Delta issues preferred stock, how much in annual cash dividends will Delta expect to pay on 1,000 shares?
2. At what price per share did Delta issue the common stock during 20X4?
3. Were first-year operations profitable? Give your reason.
4. During 20X5, the company completed the following selected transactions. Journalize each transaction. Explanations are not required.
   a. Issued for cash 5,000 shares of preferred stock at par value.
   b. Issued for cash 1,000 shares of common stock at a price of $7 per share.
   c. Net income for the year was $50,000, and the company declared no dividends. Make the closing entry for net income.

(continued)

5. Prepare the stockholders' equity section of the Delta Corporation balance sheet at December 31, 20X5.

Stockholders' equity section of the balance sheet
(Obj. 3)

P13-4A Stockholders' equity information for two independent companies, Seville Enterprises, Inc., and Madrid Corp., is as follows:

- *Seville Enterprises, Inc.* Seville is authorized to issue 60,000 shares of $5 par common stock. All the stock was issued at $12 per share. The company incurred a net loss of $41,000 in 20X6. It earned net income of $30,000 in 20X7 and $90,000 in 20X8. The company declared no dividends during the three-year period.
- *Madrid Corp.* Madrid's charter authorizes the company to issue 10,000 shares of $2.50 preferred stock with par value of $50 and 120,000 shares of no-par common stock. Madrid issued 1,000 shares of the preferred stock at par. It issued 40,000 shares of the common stock for a total of $220,000. The company's Retained Earnings balance at the beginning of 20X8 was $64,000, and net income for the year was $90,000. During 20X8, the company declared the specified dividend on preferred and a $0.50 per share dividend on common. Preferred dividends for 20X7 were in arrears.

Required

For each company, prepare the stockholders' equity section of its balance sheet at December 31, 20X8. Show the computation of all amounts. Entries are not required.

Analyzing the stockholders' equity of an actual corporation
(Obj. 3, 4)

P13-5A **Radioshack Corp.** operates Radio Shack stores. Radioshack included the following stockholders' equity on its year-end balance sheet at December 31, 20X1, with all dollar amounts, except par value per share, adapted, and in millions:

Stockholders' Equity	($ Millions)
Preferred stock, 6% cumulative.............................	$ 65
Common stock—par value $1 per share; 650,000,000 shares authorized, 236,000,000 shares issued	236
Paid-in capital in excess of par—common.....................	70
Retained earnings	2,003
Other	(1,646)
Total..	$ 728

Required

1. Identify the different issues of stock Radioshack has outstanding.
2. Give two summary entries to record issuance of all the Radioshack stock. Assume that all the stock was issued for cash. Explanations are not required.
3. Assume that preferred dividends are in arrears for 20X0 and 20X1. Record the declaration of a $50 million cash dividend on December 30, 20X2. Use separate Dividends Payable accounts for Preferred and Common. Round to the nearest $1 million. An explanation is not required.

Preparing a corporation balance sheet; measuring profitability
(Obj. 3, 6)

P13-6A → *Link Back to Chapter 1 (Accounting Equation)*. The following accounts and June 30, 20X5, balances of Witt, Inc., are arranged in no particular order:

Property, plant, and equipment, net.............	$ 231,000	Accounts receivable, net	$ 46,000
Common stock, $1 par, 500,000 shares authorized,		Paid-in capital in excess of par—common	19,000
236,000 shares issued........	236,000	Accrued liabilities..............	26,000
Dividends payable...........	9,000	Long-term note payable.........	12,000
Retained earnings	29,000	Inventory	81,000
Preferred stock, $0.10, no-par,		Prepaid expenses...............	10,000
10,000 shares authorized and		Cash.........................	10,000
issued....................	25,000	Accounts payable	31,000
		Trademark, net	9,000

Required

1. Prepare the company's classified balance sheet in the account format at June 30, 20X5.
2. Compute Witt's rate of return on total assets and rate of return on common stockholders' equity for the year ended June 30, 20X5. For the rates of return, you will need these data:

Total assets, June 30, 20X4	$404,000
Common equity, June 30, 20X4	222,000
Net income, 20X5	51,000
Interest expense, 20X5	6,000

3. Do these rates of return suggest strength or weakness? Give your reason.

P13-7A OnPoint Consulting, Inc., has 10,000 shares of $4.50, no-par preferred stock and 50,000 shares of no-par common stock outstanding. OnPoint declared and paid the following dividends during a three-year period: 20X1, $20,000; 20X2, $100,000; and 20X3, $200,000.

Computing dividends on preferred and common stock
(Obj. 4)

Student ResourceCD
spreadsheet

Required

1. Compute the total dividends to preferred stock and to common stock for each of the three years if
   a. Preferred is noncumulative.   b. Preferred is cumulative.
2. For case (1b), journalize the declaration of the 20X3 dividends on December 28, 20X3, and the payment of the dividends on January 17, 20X4. Use separate Dividends Payable accounts for Preferred and Common.

P13-8A The balance sheet of The Lopez Group reported the following:

Analyzing the stockholders' equity of a corporation
(Obj. 4, 5)

Stockholders' Equity	
Nonvoting preferred stock, no-par	$320,000
Common stock, $1.50 par value, authorized	
75,000 shares; issued 30,000 shares	45,000
Additional paid-in capital—common.	240,000
Retained earnings	141,000
Total stockholders' equity.	$746,000

Notes to the financial statements indicate that 8,000 shares of $3.00 preferred stock with a stated value of $40 per share are issued and outstanding. Preferred dividends are in arrears for three years, including the current year. On the balance sheet date, the market value of the Lopez common stock is $10 per share.

Required

1. Is the preferred stock cumulative or noncumulative? How can you tell?
2. What is the amount of the annual preferred dividend?
3. Which class of stockholders controls the company? Give your reason.
4. What is the total paid-in capital of the company?
5. What was the total market value of the common stock?
6. Compute the book value per share of the common stock.

P13-9A The accounting (not the income tax) records of Wolf Security Systems, Inc., provide the income statement for 20X8.

Computing and recording a corporation's income tax
(Obj. 7)

Total revenue	$680,000
Expenses:	
Cost of goods sold.	$290,000
Operating expenses.	180,000
Total expenses before tax	470,000
Income before income tax	$210,000

The operating expenses include depreciation of $50,000 computed under the straight-line method. In calculating taxable income on the tax return, Wolf uses MACRS. MACRS depreciation was $70,000 for 20X8. The corporate income tax rate is 40%.

Required

1. Compute Wolf's taxable income for the year.

2. Journalize the corporation's income tax for 20X8.

3. Prepare the corporation's single-step income statement for 20X8.

Problems

online homework

(Group B)

Organizing a corporation
(Obj. 1)

P13-1B Megan Thomas and Ann Kraft are opening a **Cracker Barrel Restaurant** in Durango, Colorado. There are no competing family restaurants in the immediate vicinity. Their fundamental decision is how to organize the business. Thomas thinks the partnership form is best for their business. Kraft favors the corporate form of organization. They seek your advice.

Required

Write a memo to Thomas and Kraft to make them aware of the advantages and disadvantages of organizing the business as a corporation. Use the following format:

Date: _____
To: Megan Thomas and Ann Kraft
From: Student Name
Subject: Advantages and disadvantages of the corporate form of business organization

Journalizing corporation transactions and preparing the stockholders' equity section of the balance sheet
(Obj. 2, 3)

Student Resource CD

GL, QB, PT

P13-2B The partnership of Duran & Nueces needed additional capital to expand into new markets, so the business incorporated as Ventura, Inc. The charter from the state of Texas authorizes Ventura to issue 50,000 shares of 6%, $100-par preferred stock and 100,000 shares of no-par common stock. To start, Ventura completed the following transactions:

Dec. 2	Issued 9,000 shares of common stock to Duran and 12,000 shares to Nueces, both for cash of $5 per share.
10	Issued 500 shares of preferred stock to acquire a patent with a market value of $50,000.
27	Issued 12,000 shares of common stock to other investors for cash of $60,000.

Required

1. Record the transactions in the general journal.

2. Prepare the stockholders' equity section of the Ventura, Inc., balance sheet at December 31. The ending balance of Retained Earnings is $57,000.

Issuing stock and preparing the stockholders' equity section of the balance sheet
(Obj. 2, 3)

P13-3B Hudson Corporation was organized in 20X8. At December 31, 20X8, Hudson's balance sheet reported the following stockholders' equity:

Preferred stock, 6%, $50 par, 100,000 shares authorized, none issued	$ —
Common stock, $1 par, 500,000 shares authorized, 60,000 shares issued	60,000
Paid-in capital in excess of par—common	40,000
Retained earnings.	25,000
Total stockholders' equity	$125,000

Required

Answer the following questions, making journal entries as needed.

1. What does the 6% mean for the preferred stock? After Hudson issues preferred stock, how much in annual cash dividends will Hudson expect to pay on 1,000 shares?

2. At what price per share did Hudson issue the common stock during 20X8?

3. Were first-year operations profitable? Give your reason.

4. During 20X9, the company completed the following selected transactions. Journalize each transaction. Explanations are not required.
   a. Issued for cash 1,000 shares of preferred stock at par value.
   b. Issued for cash 2,000 shares of common stock at a price of $3 per share.
   c. Net income for the year was $82,000, and the company declared no dividends. Make the closing entry for net income.

5. Prepare the stockholders' equity section of the Hudson Corporation balance sheet at December 31, 20X9.

P13-4B The following summaries for Yurman Jewelry, Inc., and Northern Insurance Company provide the information needed to prepare the stockholders' equity section of each company's balance sheet. The two companies are independent.

Stockholders' equity section of the balance sheet
(Obj. 3)

- *Yurman Jewelry, Inc.* Yurman Jewelry is authorized to issue 40,000 shares of $1 par common stock. All the stock was issued at $10 per share. The company incurred net losses of $50,000 in 20X1 and $14,000 in 20X2. It earned net income of $23,000 in 20X3 and $71,000 in 20X4. The company declared no dividends during the four-year period.

- *Northern Insurance Company.* Northern's charter authorizes the issuance of 50,000 shares of 7%, $15 par preferred stock and 500,000 shares of no-par common stock. Northern issued 1,000 shares of the preferred stock at $15 per share. It issued 100,000 shares of the common stock for $400,000. The company's retained earnings balance at the beginning of 20X4 was $120,000. Net income for 20X4 was $90,000, and the company declared the specified preferred dividend for 20X4. Preferred dividends for 20X3 were in arrears.

Required

For each company, prepare the stockholders' equity section of its balance sheet at December 31, 20X4. Show the computation of all amounts. Entries are not required.

P13-5B The **Procter & Gamble Company** reported the following stockholders' equity, as adapted, on its balance sheet at June 30, 20X3:

Analyzing the stockholders' equity of an actual corporation
(Obj. 3, 4)

Stockholders' Equity	$ Millions
Preferred stock, 6.125%—	
Authorized 600,000,000 shares; issued 1,634,000 shares	$ 1,634
Common stock—$1 stated value—	
Authorized 5,000,000,000 shares; issued 1,301,000,000	1,301
Additional paid-in capital, common........................	2,490
Retained earnings	11,980
Other	(3,699)
Total..	$13,706

Required

1. Identify the different issues of stock Procter & Gamble has outstanding.

2. Make two summary journal entries to record issuance of all the Procter & Gamble stock. Assume all the stock was issued for cash. Explanations are not required.

3. Assume no preferred dividends are in arrears. Journalize the declaration of a $500 million dividend at June 30, 20X3. Use separate Dividends Payable accounts for Preferred and Common. Round to the nearest $1 million. An explanation is not required.

P13-6B → *Link Back to Chapter 1 (Accounting Equation).* The following accounts and November 30, 20X6, balances of Omaha Mutual, Inc., are arranged in no particular order.

Common stock, $5 par,		Retained earnings	$132,000
100,000 shares authorized,		Inventory	101,000
22,000 shares issued.	$110,000	Property, plant, and	
Dividends payable.	3,000	equipment, net.	278,000
Additional paid-in capital—		Prepaid expenses.	13,000
common.	140,000	Goodwill.	37,000
Accounts payable.	31,000	Accrued liabilities	17,000
Preferred stock, 4%, $10 par,		Long-term note payable.	104,000
25,000 shares authorized,		Accounts receivable, net	102,000
3,700 shares issued.	37,000	Cash.	43,000

Required

1. Prepare the company's classified balance sheet in the account format at November 30, 20X6.

2. Compute Omaha Mutual's rate of return on total assets and rate of return on common stockholders' equity for the year ended November 30, 20X6. For the rates of return, you will need these data:

Total assets, Nov. 30, 20X5.	$581,000
Common equity, Nov. 30, 20X5.	383,000
Net income, 20X5	47,200
Interest expense, 20X5	12,800

3. Do these rates of return suggest strength or weakness? Give your reason.

P13-7B Eastern Airlines has 5,000 shares of 5%, $10 par value preferred stock and 100,000 shares of $1.50 par common stock outstanding. During a three-year period, Eastern declared and paid cash dividends as follows: 20X1, $1,500; 20X2, $15,000; and 20X3, $23,000.

Required

1. Compute the total dividends to preferred stock and to common stock for each of the three years if
   a. Preferred is noncumulative.
   b. Preferred is cumulative.

2. For case (1b), journalize the declaration of the 20X3 dividends on December 22, 20X3, and the payment of the dividends on January 14, 20X4. Use separate Dividends Payable accounts for Preferred and Common.

P13-8B The balance sheet of Maple Furniture, Inc., reported the following:

Stockholders' Equity	($ Thousands)
Cumulative preferred stock	$ 45
Common stock, $1 par, authorized 40,000,000 shares;	
issued 16,000,000 shares	16,000
Additional paid-in capital	217,000
Retained earnings (Deficit).	(77,165)
Total stockholders' equity.	$155,880

Notes to the financial statements indicate that 9,000 shares of $1.50 preferred stock with a stated value of $5 per share are issued and outstanding. Preferred dividends are in arrears for two years, including the current year. On the balance sheet date, the market value of the Maple Furniture common stock was $9.50 per share.

Required

1. Is the preferred stock cumulative or noncumulative? How can you tell?

2. What is the amount of the annual preferred dividend?

3. What is the total paid-in capital of the company?

4. What was the total market value of the common stock?

5. Compute the book value per share of the common stock.

P13-9B The accounting (not the income tax) records of Solarex Energy Corporation provide the income statement for 20X4.

Computing and recording a corporation's income tax
(Obj. 7)

Total revenue	$930,000
Expenses:	
Cost of goods sold	$430,000
Operating expenses	270,000
Total expenses before tax	700,000
Income before income tax	$230,000

The operating expenses include depreciation of $50,000 computed on the straight-line method. In calculating taxable income on the tax return, Solarex uses the modified accelerated cost recovery system (MACRS). MACRS depreciation was $80,000 for 20X4. The corporate income tax rate is 35%.

Required

1. Compute taxable income for the year.

2. Journalize the corporation's income tax for 20X4.

3. Prepare the corporation's single-step income statement for 20X4.

APPLY *Your Knowledge*

Decision Cases

Case 1. Ray Link and Sam Chain have written a spreadsheet program (Link Chain) to rival Excel. They need additional capital to market the product, and they plan to incorporate the business. They are considering the capital structure for the corporation. Their primary goal is to raise as much capital as possible without giving up control of the business. Link and Chain plan to invest the software program in the company and receive 100,000 shares of the corporation's common stock. The partners have been offered $100,000 for the rights to the software program.

Evaluating alternative ways to raise capital
(Obj. 2, 3)

The corporation's plans for a charter include an authorization to issue 5,000 shares of preferred stock and 500,000 shares of $1 par common stock. Link and Chain are uncertain about the most desirable features for the preferred stock. Prior to incorporating, the partners are discussing their plans with two investment groups. The corporation can obtain capital from outside investors under either of the following plans:

- *Plan 1.* Group 1 will invest $100,000 to acquire 1,000 shares of $5, no-par preferred stock and $70,000 to acquire 70,000 shares of common stock. Each preferred share receives 50 votes on matters that come before the stockholders.

- *Plan 2.* Group 2 will invest $150,000 to acquire 1,500 shares of 6%, $100 par nonvoting, noncumulative preferred stock.

Required

Assume that the corporation is chartered.

1. Journalize the issuance of common stock to Link and Chain. Explanations are not required.
2. Journalize the issuance of stock to the outsiders under both plans. Explanations are not required.
3. Net income for the first year is $180,000 and total dividends are $30,000. Prepare the stockholders' equity section of the corporation's balance sheet under both plans.
4. Recommend one of the plans to Link and Chain. Give your reasons.

Characteristics of corporations' capital stock
(Obj. 2, 5)

Case 2. Answering the following questions will enhance your understanding of the capital stock of corporations. Consider each question independently of the others.

1. Preferred shares have advantages with respect to dividends and corporate liquidation. Why would investors buy common stock when preferred stock is available?
2. Why are capital stock and retained earnings shown separately in the shareholders' equity section of the balance sheet?
3. Chiu Wang, major shareholder of C-W, Inc., proposes to sell some land she owns to the company for common shares in C-W. What problem does C-W, Inc., face in recording the transaction?
4. If you owned 100 shares of stock in **Dell Computer Corporation** and someone offered to buy the stock for its book value, would you accept the offer? Why or why not?

Ethical Issue

Note: This case is based on an actual situation.

Jeremy Copeland paid $50,000 for a franchise that entitled him to market Success Associates software programs in the countries of the European Union. Copeland intended to sell individual franchises for the major language groups of western Europe—German, French, English, Spanish, and Italian. Naturally, investors considering buying a franchise from Copeland asked to see the financial statements of his business.

Believing the value of the franchise to be greater than $50,000, Copeland sought to capitalize his own franchise at $500,000. The law firm of St. Charles & LaDue helped Copeland form a corporation chartered to issue 500,000 shares of common stock with par value of $1 per share. Attorneys suggested the following chain of transactions:

a. A third party borrows $500,000 and purchases the franchise from Copeland.
b. Copeland pays the corporation $500,000 to acquire all its stock.
c. The corporation buys the franchise from the third party, who repays the loan.

In the final analysis, the third party is debt-free and out of the picture. Copeland owns all the corporation's stock, and the corporation owns the franchise. The corporation's balance sheet lists a franchise acquired at a cost of $500,000. This balance sheet is Copeland's most valuable marketing tool.

Required

1. What is unethical about this situation?
2. Who can be harmed? How can they be harmed? What role does accounting play?

Analyzing stockholders' equity
(Obj. 2, 6, 7)

Financial Statement Case

The **Amazon.com** financial statements appear in Appendix A. Answer the following questions about Amazon's stock.

Required

1. How much of Amazon's preferred stock was outstanding at December 31, 2002? How can you tell?
2. Examine Amazon.com's balance sheet. Which stockholders' equity account increased the most during 2002? What caused this increase? The statement of cash flows answers this question under Financing Activities.
3. Show how to compute the balances in Amazon.com's Common Stock account at the end of both 2002 and 2001.
4. Would it be meaningful to compute Amazon.com's return on equity? Explain your answer.

Team Project

Competitive pressures are the norm in business. **Lexus** automobiles (made in Japan) have cut into the sales of **Mercedes Benz** (a German company), Jaguar (now a division of Ford), **General Motors'** Cadillac Division, and **Ford's** Lincoln Division. **Dell, Gateway,** and **Compaq** computers have siphoned business away from **IBM**. Foreign steelmakers have reduced the once-massive U.S. steel industry to a fraction of its former size.

Indeed, corporate downsizing has occurred on a massive scale. During the past few years, each company or industry mentioned here has pared down plant and equipment, laid off employees, or restructured operations.

Required

1. Identify all the stakeholders of a corporation and the stake each group has in the company. A *stakeholder* is a person or a group who has an interest (that is, a stake) in the success of the organization.
2. Identify several measures by which a corporation may be considered deficient and which may indicate the need for downsizing. How can downsizing help to solve this problem? Discuss how each measure can indicate the need for downsizing.
3. Debate the downsizing issue. One group of students takes the perspective of the company and its stockholders, and another group of students takes the perspective of other stakeholders of the company.

For Internet exercises, go to the Web site www.prenhall.com/horngren.

CHAPTER 14

Retained Earnings, Treasury Stock, and the Income Statement

TIPS CHECK YOUR RESOURCES

- Visit the www.prenhall.com/horngren **Web site** for self-study quizzes, video clips, and other resources

- Try the **Quick Check** exercise at the end of the chapter to test your knowledge

- Learn the **key terms**

- Do the **Starter** exercises keyed in the margins

- Work the **mid-** and **end-of-chapter summary problems**

- Use the **Concept Links** to review material in other chapters

- Search the **CD** for review materials by chapter or by key word

- Watch the **tutorial videos** to review key concepts

LEARNING OBJECTIVES

⭐1 Account for stock dividends

⭐2 Distinguish stock splits from stock dividends

⭐3 Account for treasury stock

⭐4 Report restrictions on retained earnings

⭐5 Analyze a complex income statement

⭐6 Prepare a statement of stockholders' equity

Coca-Cola, Dell Computer, and Pier 1 Imports are all leaders in their respective industries. What do these three companies have in common? A lot, including the fact that all three have bought back large amounts of their own stock. In Chapter 13 we saw how corporations raise capital by issuing their stock. Stock issuance increases stockholders' equity.

Companies also buy their own stock back from the stockholders. A stock repurchase decreases both corporate assets and equity. A company's own stock that it has repurchased is called treasury stock, because the company holds the stock in the corporate treasury. Coca-Cola, Dell, and Pier 1 have spent large sums to buy back their own stock. Coca-Cola's stock buybacks have totaled more than $14 billion—more than the company's total equity. Dell has spent over $2 billion—almost half of its total equity—to reacquire its own stock. ■

Coca-Cola/ Dell/ Pier 1

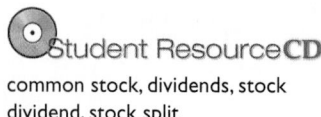

Student ResourceCD

common stock, dividends, stock
dividend, stock split

Why do companies repurchase their own stock? This chapter covers the topic of treasury stock, along with retained earnings, stock dividends, and the corporate income statement. Let's begin with retained earnings.

Retained Earnings, Stock Dividends, and Stock Splits

We have seen that the owners' equity of a corporation is called *stockholders' equity* or *shareholders' equity*. The paid-in capital accounts and retained earnings make up stockholders' equity.

Retained Earnings

Retained Earnings carries the balance of the business's net income less all net losses and less all dividends accumulated over the corporation's lifetime. *Retained* means "held onto." Retained Earnings is the shareholders' stake in total assets that come from profits. A debit balance in Retained Earnings is called a *deficit*. Retained earnings deficits are rare because they can lead to corporate failure and bankruptcy.

When you see a balance sheet, remember these facts about Retained Earnings:

1. *Credits to the Retained Earnings account arise only from net income.* Retained Earnings shows how much net income a corporation has earned and retained in the business. Its balance is the cumulative, lifetime earnings of the company minus all net losses and all dividends.

2. *The Retained Earnings account is not a reservoir of cash.* Retained Earnings represents no asset in particular. In fact, the corporation may have a large balance in Retained Earnings but too little cash to pay a dividend.

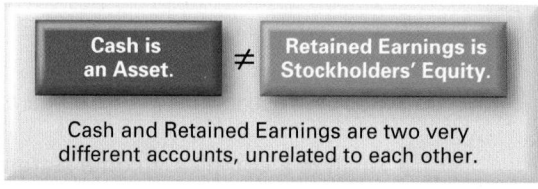

Cash is an Asset. ≠ Retained Earnings is Stockholders' Equity.

Cash and Retained Earnings are two very different accounts, unrelated to each other.

Stop & Think

Assume that the beginning balance of Retained Earnings was $70,000. The net loss for the year was $80,000. What will the Retained Earnings balance be after this net loss?

Answer:

Retained Earnings

		Dec. 31, 20X0 Balance	70,000
Dec. 31, 20X1 Net loss	80,000		
Dec. 31, 20X1 Balance	10,000		

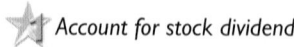
Account for stock dividends

Stock Dividend
A distribution by a corporation of its own stock to its stockholders.

Stock Dividends

A **stock dividend** is a distribution by a corporation of its own stock to its stockholders. Unlike cash dividends, stock dividends do not give any assets to the stockholders. Stock dividends

■ Affect *only* stockholders' equity accounts (including Retained Earnings and Common Stock)

■ Have *no* effect on total stockholders' equity

As Exhibit 14-1 shows, a stock dividend decreases Retained Earnings and increases Common Stock. Both accounts are stockholders' equity, so total equity is unchanged. This is a transfer from Retained Earnings to Common Stock. No asset or liability is affected by a stock dividend.

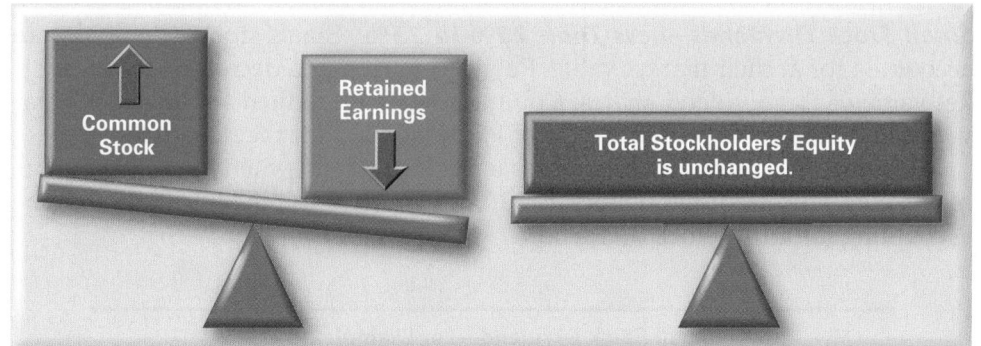

Exhibit 14-1

Effects of a Stock Dividend

The corporation distributes stock dividends to stockholders in proportion to the number of shares they already own. Suppose you own 300 shares of Pier 1 Imports' common stock. If Pier 1 distributes a 10% common stock dividend, you would receive 30 (300 × 0.10) additional shares. You would now own 330 shares of the stock. All other Pier 1 stockholders would also receive additional shares equal to 10% of their prior holdings. You and all the other Pier 1 stockholders would be in the same relative position after the dividend as before it.

WHY ISSUE STOCK DIVIDENDS? A company issues stock dividends for several reasons:

1. *To continue dividends but conserve cash.* A company may want to keep cash in the business. Yet it may also wish to continue dividends in some form.

2. *To reduce the market price of its stock.* A stock dividend may cause the market price of the company's stock to fall because of the increased supply of the stock. A share of Pier 1 Imports stock has traded at $20 recently. Doubling the shares outstanding by issuing a stock dividend would drop the stock's market price by approximately half, to $10 per share. The objective is to make the stock less expensive and thus more attractive to investors.

RECORDING STOCK DIVIDENDS The board of directors announces stock dividends on the declaration date. The date of record and the distribution date then follow. (These are the same dates used for a cash dividend.) The declaration of a stock dividend does *not* create a liability because the corporation is not obligated to pay assets. (Recall that a liability is a claim on *assets*.) Instead, the corporation has declared its intention to distribute its stock. Assume that Pier 1 Imports has the following stockholders' equity prior to a stock dividend:

Pier 1 Imports
Stockholders' Equity (Adapted)

Paid-in capital:	
Common stock, $1 par, 500,000 shares authorized, 100,000 shares issued............................	$100,000
Paid-in capital in excess of par......................	60,000
Total paid-in capital.............................	160,000
Retained earnings	430,000
Total stockholders' equity..........................	$590,000

The entry to record a stock dividend depends on its size. Generally accepted accounting principles distinguish between

- A *small* stock dividend (less than 20% to 25% of issued stock)
- A *large* stock dividend (25% or more of issued stock)

Stock dividends between 20% and 25% are rare.

Small Stock Dividends—Less Than 20% to 25% Small stock dividends are accounted for at their market value. Retained Earnings is decreased for the market value of the dividend shares, Common Stock is credited for the stock's par value, and Paid-In Capital in Excess of Par is credited for the remainder.

Assume Pier 1 Imports distributes a stock dividend when the market value of the company's common stock is $20 per share. Exhibit 14-2 illustrates the accounting for a 10% stock dividend.[1]

Exhibit 14-2

Accounting for Stock Dividends—
Pier 1 Imports

Small Stock Dividend—For Example, 10% (Accounted for at *market* value)		
Retained Earnings		
(100,000 × 0.10 × $20 market value)	200,000	
Common Stock		
(100,000 × 0.10 × $1 par)		10,000
Paid-In Capital in Excess of Par		190,000

A stock dividend does not affect assets, liabilities, or total stockholders' equity. A stock dividend merely rearranges the stockholders' equity accounts, leaving total equity unchanged.

✔ Starter 14-1

✔ Starter 14-2

Large Stock Dividends—25% or More Large stock dividends are rare, so we do not illustrate them. Instead of large stock dividends, companies split their stock, as we illustrate in the next section.

Stock Splits

Stock Split
An increase in the number of outstanding shares of stock coupled with a proportionate reduction in the par value of the stock.

A **stock split** is fundamentally different from a stock dividend. A stock split increases the number of authorized, issued, and outstanding shares of stock. A stock split is also coupled with a proportionate reduction in the stock's par value. For example, if the company splits its stock 2 for 1, the number of outstanding shares is doubled and each share's par value is cut in half. A stock split decreases the market price of the stock—with the intention of making the stock more affordable. Most leading companies in the United States—General Electric, IBM, and many others—have split their stock.

The market price of a share of Pier 1 Imports common stock has been approximately $20. Assume that Pier 1 wishes to decrease the market price to approximately $10. Suppose Pier 1 decides to split the common stock 2 for 1, and the stock's market price drops from $20 to $10. A 2-for-1 stock split means that Pier 1 will have twice as many shares of stock outstanding after the split as before, and each share's par value is cut in half. Assume that Pier 1 had issued 100,000 shares of $1 par common stock before the split. The following table shows how a 2-for-1 split affects Pier 1 Imports' stockholders' equity.

---

[1]A stock dividend can be recorded with two journal entries—for (1) the declaration and (2) the stock distribution. But most companies record stock dividends with a single entry on the date of distribution, as we illustrate here.

Pier 1 Imports' Stockholders' Equity (Adapted) Before 2-for-1 Stock Split		After 2-for-1 Stock Split	
Common stock, $1.00 par,		Common stock, $0.50 par,	
500,000 shares authorized,		1,000,000 shares authorized,	
100,000 shares issued......................	$100,000	200,000 shares issued......................	$100,000
Paid-in capital in excess of par	60,000	Paid-in capital in excess of par	60,000
Retained earnings............................	430,000	Retained earnings............................	430,000
Total stockholders' equity	$590,000	Total stockholders' equity	$590,000

After the 2-for-1 stock split, Pier 1 Imports would have 1 million shares authorized and 200,000 shares (100,000 shares × 2) of $0.50 (50 cents) par ($1.00/2) common stock outstanding. Total stockholders' equity would be exactly as before. Indeed, the balance in the Common Stock account does not even change. Only the par value of the stock and the number of shares change.

Because the stock split affects no account balances, no formal journal entry is needed. Instead, the split is recorded in a *memorandum entry* such as the following:

Aug. 19	Split the common stock 2 for 1. Called in the $1 par common stock and distributed two shares of $0.50 par common stock for each old share previously outstanding.

✔ **Starter 14-3**

Stock Dividends and Stock Splits Compared

2 *Distinguish stock splits from stock dividends*

Both stock dividends and stock splits increase the number of shares of stock owned by each stockholder. Neither stock dividends nor stock splits change investors' cost of the stock they own.

SIMILARITIES   Consider Dell Computer Corporation, the leader in personal computers. Assume you own 100 shares of Dell stock.

- If Dell distributes a stock dividend or a stock split, your 100 shares increase, but your total cost is unchanged.

- Neither a stock dividend nor a stock split creates taxable income for the investor.

DIFFERENCES   Stock dividends and stock splits differ in that

- A stock *dividend* shifts an amount from retained earnings to the stock account. Par value per share is unchanged.

- A stock *split* increases the number of shares of stock authorized, issued, and outstanding. Par value per share decreases.

Exhibit 14-3 summarizes the effects of dividends and stock splits on total stockholders' equity.

Event	Effect on Total Stockholders' Equity
Declaration of *cash* dividend	Decreases total equity
Payment of *cash* dividend	No effect on equity
Distribution of *stock* dividend	No effect on equity
Stock split	No effect on equity

Source: Adapted from material provided by Beverly Terry.

Exhibit 14-3

Effects of Dividends and Stock Splits on Total Stockholders' Equity

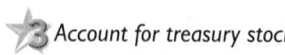
Account for treasury stock

Treasury Stock
A corporation's own stock that it has
issued and later reacquired.

Student ResourceCD

treasury stock

Treasury Stock

A company's own stock that it has issued and later reacquired is called **treasury stock**.[2] In effect, the corporation holds the stock in its treasury. Corporations such as Coca-Cola, Dell Computer, and Pier 1 Imports may purchase their own stock for several reasons:

1. The business is trying to increase net assets by buying its shares low and hoping to sell them for a higher price later.
2. The purchase supports the stock's market price by decreasing the supply of stock available.
3. Management wants to avoid a takeover by an outside party.

When a company buys its own stock back, the company gives up cash and becomes a smaller entity as a result. Now let's see how companies account for their treasury stock.

Purchase of Treasury Stock

We record the purchase of treasury stock by debiting Treasury Stock and crediting Cash. Suppose that Jupiter Cable Company had the following stockholders' equity before purchasing treasury stock:

Jupiter Cable Company
Stockholders' Equity [*Before* Purchase of Treasury Stock]

Common stock, $1 par, 10,000 shares authorized, 9,000 shares issued	$ 9,000
Paid-in capital in excess of par—common	12,000
Retained earnings	14,000
Total stockholders' equity	$35,000

On March 31, Jupiter purchases 1,000 shares of its common as treasury stock, paying cash of $5 per share. Jupiter records the purchase of treasury stock as follows:

Treasury Stock—Common

5,000 |

Mar. 31	Treasury Stock—Common (1,000 × $5)	5,000	
	Cash		5,000
	Purchased treasury stock.		

The Treasury Stock account has a debit balance, which is the opposite of the other owners' equity accounts. Therefore, *Treasury Stock* is *a contra equity account*. Treasury stock is recorded at cost, without reference to par value. The Treasury Stock account is reported beneath Retained Earnings on the balance sheet. Treasury Stock's balance is subtracted from the sum of total paid-in capital and retained earnings, as follows:

Jupiter Cable Company
Stockholders' Equity [*After* Purchase of Treasury Stock]

Common stock, $1 par, 10,000 shares authorized, 9,000 shares issued	$ 9,000
Paid-in capital in excess of par—common	12,000
Retained earnings	14,000
Subtotal	35,000
Less: Treasury stock, 1,000 shares at cost	(5,000)
Total stockholders' equity	$30,000

---
[2]We illustrate the *cost* method of accounting for treasury stock because it is used most widely. Intermediate accounting courses also cover an alternative method.

Total stockholders' equity decreases by $5,000, the cost of the treasury stock. Also, the stock *outstanding* decreases. *Outstanding* shares are computed as follows:

Shares of stock *issued*	9,000
Less: Shares of treasury stock	(1,000)
Shares of stock *outstanding*	8,000

Outstanding shares are important because only outstanding shares have voting rights, receive cash dividends, and receive assets if the corporation liquidates. Treasury stock doesn't carry a vote, receive dividends, or have a claim on assets in liquidation.

Ethical Issue: Treasury stock transactions have a serious ethical and legal dimension. A company such as **Dell Computer** buying its own shares as treasury stock must be careful that its information releases are accurate. What will happen if Dell purchases treasury stock at $17 per share and one day later announces a technological breakthrough that will generate millions of dollars in new business?

Answer: Dell's stock price would likely rise in response to the new information. If it could be proved that Dell management withheld the information, a shareholder selling stock back to Dell could file a lawsuit against the company. The stockholder would claim that with the new information, he would have been able to sell the Dell stock at a higher price.

Sale of Treasury Stock

A company may sell its treasury stock at its cost, above cost, or below cost.

SALE AT COST   If the stock is sold for cost—the same price the corporation paid to reacquire it—the entry debits Cash and credits Treasury Stock for the same amount.

SALE ABOVE COST   If treasury stock is sold for more than its cost, the difference is credited to a new account, Paid-In Capital from Treasury Stock Transactions, because the excess came from the company's stockholders. Suppose Jupiter Cable Company resold its treasury shares for $9 per share (cost was $5). The entry is

Dec. 7	Cash (1,000 × $9)	9,000	
	Treasury Stock—Common (1,000 × $5 cost)		5,000
	Paid-In Capital from Treasury Stock Transactions		4,000
	Sold treasury stock.		

Treasury Stock—Common

5,000	5,000
0	

Paid-In Capital from Treasury Stock Transactions is reported with the other paid-in capital accounts on the balance sheet, beneath the Common Stock and Paid-In Capital in Excess of Par accounts, as shown here:

✔ Starter 14-4

Jupiter Cable Company
Stockholders' Equity [*After* Purchase and Sale of Treasury Stock]

Paid-in capital:	
Common stock, $1 par, 10,000 shares authorized, 9,000 shares issued	$ 9,000
Paid-in capital in excess of par—common	12,000
Paid-in capital from treasury stock transactions	4,000
Retained earnings	14,000
Total stockholders' equity	$39,000

Exhibit 14-4 tracks the stockholders' equity of Jupiter Cable Company to show how treasury stock transactions affect corporate equity.

Exhibit 14-4

Jupiter Cable Stockholders' Equity

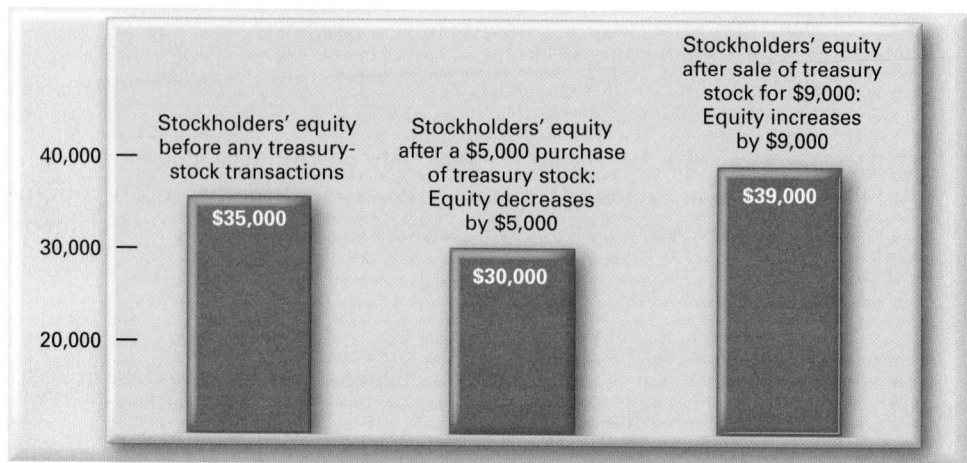

Student ResourceCD

retained earnings, stock buyback

SALE BELOW COST The resale price of treasury stock can be less than cost. The shortfall is debited first to Paid-In Capital from Treasury Stock Transactions. If this account's balance is too small, then debit Retained Earnings for the remaining amount.

Reporting Issues

Companies may retire their stock, restrict retained earnings, and vary the way they report stockholders' equity. This section covers these reporting issues.

Retirement of Stock

A corporation may purchase its own stock and *retire* it by canceling the stock certificates. Retirements of preferred stock are common because companies wish to avoid paying dividends on the preferred stock. The retired stock cannot be reissued.

Retiring stock decreases both the stock issued and the stock outstanding. In retiring stock, the corporation removes all the stock and the paid-in capital accounts related to the retired shares, such as Preferred Stock and Capital in Excess of Par.

Restrictions on Retained Earnings

4 Report restrictions on retained earnings

Dividends, purchases of treasury stock, and retirements of stock require a cash payment. These outlays decrease assets, so the corporation has fewer resources to pay liabilities. A bank may agree to loan $500,000 only if Jupiter Cable Company limits dividend payments and the purchase of treasury stock.

LIMITS ON DIVIDENDS AND TREASURY STOCK PURCHASES To ensure that corporations maintain a minimum level of stockholders' equity, state laws restrict the amount of treasury stock a corporation may purchase. The restriction often focuses on the balance of retained earnings. Companies usually report their retained earnings restrictions in notes to the financial statements. The following disclosure by RTE Corporation, a manufacturer of electronic transformers, is typical:

Notes to Consolidated Financial Statements

Note F—Long-Term Debt The . . . Company's loan agreements . . . restrict cash dividends and similar payments to shareholders. Under the most restrictive of these provisions, retained earnings of $4,000,000 were unrestricted as of December 31, 20X6.

With this restriction, the maximum dividend that RTE Corporation can pay its stockholders is $4,000,000.

Are Stock Buybacks a Value Booster or a PR Gimmick?

What could signal more confidence than a company buying back lots of its own stock? Stock buybacks were a strategy for investing spare cash in the 1990s. Now the buyback has become a strategy for propping up a company's stock prices. For example, the stock of Tenet Healthcare Corporation plunged by 50% in a week, and the health-care giant paid $140 million to buy its own stock. The strategy worked because two weeks later, the stock had risen by 13%.

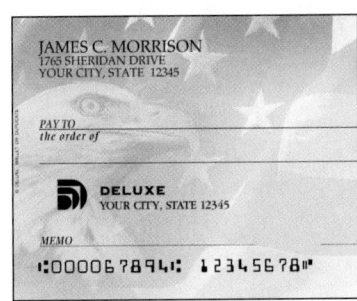

Purchases of a company's own shares reduce the number of outstanding shares, and earnings per share go up. A dramatic example of this occurred when Deluxe, the country's leading check printer, purchased 19 million of its own shares. Deluxe's stock price soared 116% after the buyback.

When the market falls, boosting stock prices becomes a priority, and there's a rush of buyback activity. In the second quarter of 2002, for instance, U.S. companies announced plans to repurchase $24 billion of their own stock. The key words here are "announced plans." Skeptical shareholders point out that buyback announcements aren't always followed by actual stock repurchases. Columnist John Ellis says, "Nothing so perfectly captures the fiber of today's whimpering CEOs than the stock buyback announcement." Ellis complains that CEOs don't always carry through on their buyback announcements: "While many have been announced, probably 6 out of 10 [buybacks] are nothing more than public relations gimmicks."

Dividend announcements are different. Unlike a buyback announcement, a cash dividend, once declared, becomes a real liability. The joke on Wall Street is this: Stock buybacks are like dating. A dividend is more like getting married.

Based on: Tom Petruno, "Stock Buybacks Face Increasing Scrutiny," *Los Angeles Times*, November 24, 2002, p. C.13. Shaheen Pasha, "Stock Buybacks Have Increased as Equities Fall," *The Wall Street Journal*, July 18, 2002, p. C9. John Ellis, "Strategy," *Fast Company*, October 2002, p. 74.

APPROPRIATIONS OF RETAINED EARNINGS **Appropriations** are restrictions on Retained Earnings that are recorded by formal journal entries. A corporation may *appropriate*—segregate in a separate account—a portion of Retained Earnings for a specific use. For example, the board of directors may appropriate part of Retained Earnings for expansion. Appropriated Retained Earnings can be reported as shown near the bottom of Exhibit 14-5.

Retained earnings appropriations are rare. Most companies report any retained earnings restrictions in the notes to the financial statements, as illustrated for RTE Corporation and in the real-world format of Exhibit 14-5.

Appropriation of Retained Earnings
Restriction of retained earnings that is recorded by a formal journal entry.

✔ **Starter 14-5**

Variations in Reporting Stockholders' Equity

Accountants sometimes report stockholders' equity in ways that differ from our examples. We use a detailed format to help you learn the components of stockholders' equity. Companies assume that investors and creditors understand the details.

One of the most important skills you will learn in this course is how to read the financial statements of real companies. In Exhibit 14-5, we present a side-by-side comparison of our general teaching format and the format you are likely to encounter in actual balance sheets. Note the following points in the real-world format:

1. The heading Paid-In Capital does not appear. It is commonly understood that Preferred Stock, Common Stock, and Additional Paid-In Capital are elements of paid-in capital.

2. Preferred stock is often reported in a single amount that combines par value and premium.

3. For presentation in the financial statements, all additional paid-in capital appears as a single amount labeled Additional Paid-In Capital. Additional Paid-In Capital belongs to the common stockholders; therefore it follows Common Stock in the real-world format.

4. Often, total stockholders' equity ($4,000,000 in Exhibit 14-5) is not specifically labeled.

Exhibit 14-5 Formats for Reporting Stockholders' Equity

General Teaching Format		Real-World Format	
Stockholders' equity		**Stockholders' equity**	
Paid-in capital:			
Preferred stock, 8%, $10 par,		Preferred stock, 8%, $10 par,	
30,000 shares authorized and issued	$ 300,000	30,000 shares authorized	
Paid-in capital in excess of par—preferred	10,000	and issued	$ 310,000
Common stock, $1 par, 100,000 shares		Common stock, $1 par,	
authorized, 60,000 shares issued	60,000	100,000 shares authorized,	
Paid-in capital in excess of par—common	2,140,000	60,000 shares issued	60,000
Paid-in capital from treasury stock		Additional paid-in capital	2,160,000
transactions, common	9,000	Retained earnings (Note 7)	1,500,000
Paid-in capital from retirement of		Less: Treasury stock, common	
preferred stock	11,000	(1,000 shares at cost)	(30,000)
Total paid-in capital	2,530,000		$4,000,000
Retained earnings appropriated for		*Note 7—Restriction on retained earnings.*	
contingencies	400,000	At December 31, 20XX, $400,000 of retained	
Retained earnings—unappropriated	1,100,000	earnings is restricted for contingencies	
Total retained earnings	1,500,000	by the company's board of directors.	
Subtotal	4,030,000	Accordingly, dividends are restricted to a	
Less: Treasury stock, common		maximum of $1,100,000.	
(1,000 shares at cost)	(30,000)		
Total stockholders' equity	$4,000,000		

Review the first half of the chapter by studying the following Decision Guidelines feature.

Decision Guidelines

ACCOUNTING FOR RETAINED EARNINGS, DIVIDENDS, AND TREASURY STOCK

Retained earnings, dividends, and treasury stock transactions are unique because they can affect a corporation's equity. The Decision Guidelines provide a foundation for you to understand their effects.

Decision	Guidelines

How to record:

• Distribution of a small stock dividend (20% to 25%)?

Retained Earnings. . . . . Market value
    Common Stock . . . . | Par value
    Paid-In Capital in Excess of Par . . | Excess

• Stock split?

Memorandum only: Split the common stock 2 for 1. Called in the outstanding $10 par common stock and distributed two shares of $5 par for each old share outstanding (amounts assumed).

What are the effects of stock dividends and stock splits on:

	Effects of Stock	
	Dividend	*Split*
• Number of shares issued?	Increase	Increase
• Shares outstanding?	Increase	Increase
• Par value per share?	No effect	Decrease
• Total assets and total liabilities?	No effect	No effect
• Total stockholders' equity?	No effect	No effect
• Common Stock?	Increase	No effect
• Retained Earnings?	Decrease	No effect

How to record:

• Purchase of treasury stock?
• Sale of treasury stock?

Treasury Stock . . . . Cost
    Cash . . . .   Cost

At cost? (Amount received = Cost)

Cash . . . . Amt received
    Treasury Stock . . . .   Cost

Above cost?

Cash . . . . Amt received
    Treasury Stock . . . .   Cost
    Paid-In Capital from Treasury
        Stock Transactions . . . .   Excess

Below cost?

Cash . . . . Amt received
Paid-In Capital from Treasury
    Stock Transactions . . . . Amt up to prior bal
Retained Earnings . . . . Excess
    Treasury Stock . . . .   Cost

What are the effects of the purchase and sale of treasury stock on:

	Effects of	
	Purchase	*Sale*
• Total assets?	Decrease by full amount of payment	Increase by full amount of cash receipt
• Total stockholders' equity?	Decrease by full amount of payment	Increase by full amount of cash receipt

---

MID-CHAPTER *Summary Problem*

Simplicity Graphics, creator of magazine designs, reported shareholders' equity:

Shareholders' Equity	
Preferred stock, $1.00 par value	
Authorized—10,000 shares; Issued—None	$ —
Common Stock, $0.80 par value	
Authorized, 30,000 shares; Issued 14,000 shares	11,200
Capital in excess of par value	48,000
Earnings retained in business	89,000
	148,200
Less: Treasury stock, at cost (1,900 common shares)	(15,200)
	$133,000

TIPS

CHECK YOUR RESOURCES

Required

1. What was the average issue price per share of the common stock?
2. Journalize the issuance of 1,000 shares of common stock at $4 per share. Use Simplicity's account titles.
3. How many shares of Simplicity's common stock are outstanding?
4. How many shares of common stock would be outstanding after Simplicity split its common stock 3 for 1?
5. Using Simplicity account titles, journalize the distribution of a 10% stock dividend when the market price of Simplicity common stock is $5 per share. Simplicity distributes the common stock dividend on the shares outstanding, which were computed in requirement 3.
6. Journalize the following treasury stock transactions, which occur in the order given:
   a. Simplicity purchases 500 shares of treasury stock at $8 per share.
   b. Simplicity sells 100 shares of treasury stock for $9 per share.

Solution

1. Average issue price of common stock was $4.23 per share
   [($11,200 + $48,000)/14,000 shares = $4.23]
2. Cash (1,000 × $4) 4,000

Common Stock (1,000 × $0.80)		800
Capital in Excess of Par Value		3,200

   Issued common stock.

3. Shares outstanding = 12,100 (14,000 shares issued minus 1,900 shares of treasury stock).
4. Shares outstanding after a 3-for-1 stock split = 36,300 (12,100 shares outstanding × 3).
5. Earnings Retained in Business (12,100 × 0.10 × $5) 6,050

Common Stock (12,100 × 0.10 × $0.80)		968
Capital in Excess of Par Value		5,082

   Distributed a 10% common stock dividend.

6. a. Treasury Stock (500 × $8) 4,000

Cash		4,000

   Purchased treasury stock.

   b. Cash (100 × $9) 900

Treasury Stock (100 × $8)		800
Paid-In Capital from Treasury Stock Transactions . .		100

   Sold treasury stock.

☐ Retained Earnings, Stock Dividends & Splits
☐ Treasury Stock
☐ Reporting Issues
■ Corporate Income Statement

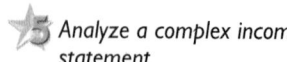 *Analyze a complex income statement*

Student Resource**CD**

comprehensive income, discontinued operations, earnings per share, extraordinary items, income statement, preferred stock, statement of shareholders' equity

The Corporate Income Statement: Analyzing Earnings

Now that we have covered stockholders' equity in detail, we turn to the corporate income statement. Net income (revenues plus gains minus expenses and losses) receives more attention than any other item in the financial statements. In fact, net income is probably the most important piece of information about a company. Net income measures how successfully the company has operated.

Suppose you are considering investing in the stock of Coca-Cola, Dell Computer, or Pier 1 Imports. You would examine these companies' income statements. Of particular interest is the amount of net income they can expect to earn year after year. To understand net income, let's examine Exhibit 14-6, which presents the income statement of Allied Electronics Corporation, a small manufacturer of precision instruments.

Continuing Operations

In Exhibit 14-6, the topmost section reports income from continuing operations. This part of the business should continue from period to period. Income from continuing operations, therefore, helps investors make predictions about future

Exhibit 14-6   Income Statement of Allied Electronics Corporation

Allied Electronics Corporation
Income Statement
Year Ended December 31, 20X5

Continuing operations	Net sales revenue	$500,000
	Cost of goods sold	240,000
	Gross profit	260,000
	Operating expenses (detailed)	181,000
	Operating income	79,000
	Other gains (losses):	
	Gain on sale of machinery	11,000
	Income from continuing operations before income tax	90,000
	Income tax expense	36,000
	Income from continuing operations	54,000
Special items	Discontinued operations, income of $35,000, less income tax of $14,000	21,000
	Income before extraordinary item and cumulative effect of accounting change	75,000
	Extraordinary flood loss, $20,000, less income tax saving of $8,000	(12,000)
	Cumulative effect of accounting change, $10,000, less income tax of $4,000	6,000
	Net income	$ 69,000
Earnings per share	Earnings per share of common stock (20,000 shares outstanding):	
	Income from continuing operations	$2.70
	Income from discontinued operations	1.05
	Income before extraordinary item and cumulative effect of accounting change	3.75
	Extraordinary loss	(0.60)
	Cumulative effect of accounting change	0.30
	Net income	$3.45

earnings. We may use this information to predict that Allied Electronics Corporation will earn approximately $54,000 next year. The continuing operations of Allied Electronics include two items needing explanation.

First, Allied had a gain on the sale of machinery, which is outside the company's core business activity of selling electronics products. This explains why the gain is reported separately from Allied's sales revenue, cost of goods sold, and gross profit.

Second, income tax expense is subtracted to arrive at income from continuing operations. Allied Electronics' income tax rate is 40% ($90,000 × 0.40 = $36,000).

Special Items

After continuing operations, an income statement may include three types of special gains and losses:

- Discontinued operations
- Extraordinary gains and losses
- Cumulative effect of an accounting change

✔ **Starter 14-6**

✔ **Starter 14-7**

DISCONTINUED OPERATIONS   Most large corporations engage in several lines of business. For example, Sears, Roebuck & Co. is best known for its retail stores, but it also has a real-estate development company (Homart) and an insurance company (Allstate). Each identifiable division of a company is called a **segment of the business**. Allstate is the insurance segment of Sears.

Segment of the Business
One of various separate divisions of a company.

A company may sell a segment of its business. For example, May Department Stores, the chain that operates Lord & Taylor and Foley's, sold Payless, its chain of shoe stores. Financial analysts typically do not include discontinued operations to predict a company's future income because the discontinued segments will generate no income in the future.

The income statement reports information on the discontinued segment under the heading Discontinued operations. Income from discontinued operations ($35,000) is taxed at 40% and reported by Allied Electronics Corporation, as shown in Exhibit 14-6. A loss on discontinued operations is reported similarly, with a subtraction for the income tax *savings* on the loss.

Companies dispose of old plant and equipment all the time. Gains and losses on these asset dispositions are *not* reported as discontinued operations. Gains and losses on normal asset dispositions are reported as "Other gains (losses)" up among continuing operations.

EXTRAORDINARY GAINS AND LOSSES (EXTRAORDINARY ITEMS)

Extraordinary Gains and Losses
A gain or loss that is both unusual for the company and infrequent. Also called **extraordinary items**.

Extraordinary gains and losses, also called **extraordinary items**, are both unusual and infrequent. Losses from natural disasters (floods, earthquakes, and tornadoes) and the taking of company assets by a foreign government (expropriation) are extraordinary.

Extraordinary items are reported along with their income tax effect. During 20X5, Allied Electronics Corporation lost $20,000 of inventory in a flood. This flood loss reduced income and also reduced Allied's income tax. The tax effect decreases the net amount of the loss in the same way that the income tax reduces net income. An extraordinary loss can be reported along with its tax effect, as follows:

Extraordinary flood loss..........................	$(20,000)
Less: Income tax saving.........................	8,000
Extraordinary flood loss, net of tax	(12,000)

Trace this item to the income statement in Exhibit 14-6. An extraordinary gain is reported in the same way as a loss, net of the income tax.

Gains and losses due to employee strikes, lawsuits, and the sale of plant assets are *not* extraordinary. These are normal business events. But they are outside the business's central operations, so they are reported on the income statement as other gains and losses. Examples include the gain on sale of machinery reported up in the Other gains (losses) section of Exhibit 14-6.

For a review of depreciation methods, see Chapter 10. For a review of inventory methods, see Chapter 6.

Cumulative Effect of a Change in Accounting Principle

Companies sometimes change accounting methods, such as from double-declining-balance (DDB) to straight-line depreciation, or from first-in, first-out (FIFO) to average cost for inventory. ← An accounting change makes it difficult to compare one period's financial statements with the statements of earlier periods.

Investors and creditors can be misled into thinking that the current year is better when in fact the only difference is a change in accounting method. Investors must separate the effects of business operations from the effects created by accounting. Companies, therefore, report the effect of the accounting change in a special section of the income statement. This section appears after extraordinary items.

Allied Electronics Corporation has changed its method of accounting for depreciation from DDB to straight-line at the beginning of 20X5. If the company had been using straight-line depreciation every year, depreciation expense would have been less in prior years, and net income would have been higher. Exhibit 14-6 reports the $6,000 cumulative effect of this accounting change. A change from straight-line to double-declining-balance depreciation usually produces a negative cumulative effect.

✓ **Starter 14-8**

> Examine all the income tax amounts in Exhibit 14-6. How much was Allied Electronics' *total* income tax expense during 20X5?
>
> *Answer:* $46,000 = $36,000 + $14,000 − $8,000 + $4,000
>
> Note that $36,000 is the company's income tax expense from continuing operations; $46,000 is *total* income tax expense.

Earnings per Share

The final segment of a corporate income statement presents the company's earnings per share, abbreviated as EPS. EPS is the most widely used of all accounting statistics. **Earnings per share (EPS)** reports the amount of net income for each share of the company's *outstanding common stock*. It is a key measure of success in business. EPS is computed as follows:

Earnings Per Share (EPS)
Amount of a company's net income for each share of its outstanding common stock.

$$\text{Earnings per Share} = \frac{\text{Net income − Preferred dividends}}{\text{Average number of Common shares outstanding}}$$

Just as the corporation lists its different sources of income separately—from continuing operations, discontinued operations, and so on—it also shows a separate EPS figure for each element of income. Allied Electronics Corporation's EPS calculations are as follows:

Earnings per share of common stock (20,000 shares outstanding):	
Income from continuing operations ($54,000/20,000)	$2.70
Income from discontinued operations ($21,000/20,000)	1.05
Income before extraordinary item and cumulative effect of	
accounting change ($75,000/20,000)	3.75
Extraordinary loss ($12,000/20,000)	(0.60)
Cumulative effect of accounting change ($6,000/20,000)	0.30
Net income ($69,000/20,000)	$3.45

✔ **Starter 14-9**

The final section of Exhibit 14-6 reports the EPS figures for Allied Electronics.

EFFECT OF PREFERRED DIVIDENDS ON EARNINGS PER SHARE

Preferred dividends also affect EPS. Recall that EPS is earnings per share of *common* stock. Recall also that dividends on preferred stock are paid first. Therefore, preferred dividends must be subtracted from income to compute EPS. Suppose Allied Electronics had 10,000 shares of preferred stock outstanding, each paying a $1.00 dividend. The annual preferred dividend would be $10,000 (10,000 × $1.00). The $10,000 would be subtracted from each of the income subtotals (lines 1, 3, and 6), resulting in the following EPS computations for the company:

← *Chapter 13, p. 511, provides detailed information on preferred stock.*

	Earnings per share of common stock (20,000 shares outstanding):	
1	Income from continuing operations ($54,000 − $10,000)/20,000 . . .	$2.20
2	Income from discontinued operations ($21,000/20,000)	1.05
3	Income before extraordinary item and cumulative	
	effect of accounting change ($75,000 − $10,000)/20,000	3.25
4	Extraordinary loss ($12,000/20,000)	(0.60)
5	Cumulative effect of accounting change ($6,000/20,000)	0.30
6	Net income ($69,000 − $10,000)/20,000	$2.95

✔ **Starter 14-10**

BASIC AND DILUTED EARNINGS PER SHARE   Some corporations must report two sets of EPS figures, as follows:

- EPS based on outstanding common shares (*basic* EPS).
- EPS based on outstanding common shares plus the additional common shares that would arise from conversion of the preferred stock into common stock (*diluted* EPS). Diluted EPS is always lower than basic EPS.

> What makes earnings per share so useful as a business statistic?
>
> *Answer:* Earnings per share is useful because it relates a company's income to one share of stock. Stock prices are quoted at an amount per share, and investors usually consider how much they must pay for a certain number of shares. Earnings per share is used to help determine the value of a share of stock.

Combined Statement of Income and Retained Earnings

Companies can report income and retained earnings on a single statement. Exhibit 14-7 illustrates how Allied Electronics would combine its income statement and its statement of retained earnings.

Exhibit 14-7

Combined Statement of Income and Retained Earnings

Allied Electronics Corporation		
Summarized Statement of Income and Retained Earnings **Year Ended December 31, 20X5**		
Income statement	Sales revenue.........................	$500,000
	Cost of goods sold	240,000
	Gross profit	260,000
	Expenses (listed individually)	191,000
	Net income for 20X5..................	$ 69,000
Statement of retained earnings	Retained earnings, December 31, 20X4 ...	130,000
		199,000
	Dividends for 20X5....................	(54,000)
	Retained earnings, December 31, 20X5 ...	$145,000

Reporting Comprehensive Income

As we have seen, all companies report net income or net loss on the income statement. There is another income figure. **Comprehensive income** is the company's change in total stockholders' equity from all sources other than from its owners. Comprehensive income includes net income plus some specific gains and losses, as follows:

Comprehensive Income
Company's change in total stockholders' equity from all sources other than from the owners.

- Unrealized gains or losses on certain investments
- Foreign-currency translation adjustments

These items do not enter into the determination of net income but instead are reported as other comprehensive income, as shown in Exhibit 14-8. Assumed figures are used for all items.

✔ **Starter 14-11**

Earnings per share applies only to net income and its components, as discussed earlier. Earnings per share is *not* reported for other comprehensive income.

Exhibit 14-8

Reporting Comprehensive Income

National Express Company
Income Statement
Year Ended December 31, 20X2

Revenues	$10,000
Expenses (summarized)	6,000
Net income	4,000
Other comprehensive income:	
Unrealized gain on investments.	1,000
Comprehensive income.	$ 5,000

Prior-Period Adjustments

A company may make an error in recording revenues or expenses. After the revenue and expense accounts are closed, Retained Earnings holds the error. The balance of Retained Earnings is wrong until corrected. Corrections to Retained Earnings for errors of an earlier period are called **prior-period adjustments**. The prior-period adjustment (correction) either increases or decreases the beginning balance of Retained Earnings and appears on that statement.

Prior-Period Adjustment
A correction to retained earnings for an error of an earlier period.

    The year 2003 saw more prior-period adjustments than in the 20 previous years combined. Enron, Worldcom, Xerox, and many other companies restated their net income to correct accounting errors made in earlier years. To illustrate, assume De Graff Corporation recorded $30,000 of income tax expense for 20X7. The correct amount was $40,000. This error

- Understated expenses by $10,000
- Overstated net income by $10,000

In 20X8, the government required De Graff to pay the additional $10,000 in taxes for the prior year. De Graff's prior-period adjustment will decrease retained earnings as follows.

De Graff Corporation
Statement of Retained Earnings
Year Ended December 31, 20X8

✔ Starter 14-12

Retained earnings, December 31, 20X7, as originally reported	$390,000
Prior-period adjustment—To correct error in 20X7	(10,000)
Retained earnings, December 31, 20X7, as adjusted	380,000
Net income for 20X8	100,000
	480,000
Dividends for 20X8	(40,000)
Retained earnings, December 31, 20X8	$440,000

Statement of Stockholders' Equity

 Prepare a statement of stockholders' equity

Most companies report a statement of stockholders' equity, which includes retained earnings. The statement of stockholders' equity is formatted exactly like a statement of retained earnings but with columns for each element of equity. The **statement of stockholders' equity** reports the changes in all categories of equity during the period:

Statement of Stockholders' Equity
Reports the changes in all categories of stockholders' equity during the period.

- Common stock
- Retained earnings
- Additional paid-in capital
- Treasury stock

    Exhibit 14-9 uses assumed figures for Allied Electronics Corporation to illustrate the statement of stockholders' equity. Negative amounts—debits—appear in parentheses. If the company has preferred stock, the statement includes a column for Preferred Stock.

Exhibit 14-9 | Statement of Stockholders' Equity

Allied Electronics Corporation

Statement of Stockholders' Equity
Year Ended December 31, 20X5

	Common Stock	Additional Paid-in Capital	Retained Earnings	Treasury Stock	Total
Balance, December 31, 20X4...............	$ 80,000	$160,000	$130,000	$(25,000)	$345,000
Issuance of stock.........................	20,000	60,000			80,000
Net income			69,000		69,000
Cash dividends.........................			(20,000)		(20,000)
Stock dividends—8%....................	8,000	26,000	(34,000)		0
Purchase of treasury stock				(10,000)	(10,000)
Sale of treasury stock....................		10,000		5,000	15,000
Balance, December 31, 20X5..............	$108,000	$256,000	$145,000	$(30,000)	$479,000

✔ Starter 14-13

Decision Guidelines

ANALYZING A CORPORATE INCOME STATEMENT

Three years out of college, you've saved $5,000 and are ready to start investing. Where do you start? You might begin by analyzing the income statements of **Coca-Cola, Dell Computer**, and **Pier 1 Imports**. These Decision Guidelines will help you understand a corporate income statement.

Decision	Guidelines
What are the main sections of the income statement? See Exhibit 14-6 for an example.	**Continuing operations** { • Continuing operations, including other gains and losses and less income tax expense
	Special items { • Discontinued operations—gain or loss—less the income tax effect • Extraordinary gain or loss, less the income tax effect • Cumulative effect of an accounting change, less the income tax effect • Net income (or net loss) • Other comprehensive income (Exhibit 14-8)
What earnings-per-share (EPS) figures must a corporation report?	• Earnings per share—applies only to net income (or net loss), not to other comprehensive income Separate EPS figures for **Earnings per share** { • Income from continuing operations • Discontinued operations • Income before extraordinary item and cumulative effect of accounting change • Extraordinary gain or loss • Cumulative effect of accounting change • Net income (or net loss)
How to compute EPS for net income?	$$\text{EPS} = \frac{\text{Net income} - \text{Preferred dividends}}{\text{Average number of common shares outstanding}}$$

Excel Application Exercise

Goal: Create an Excel worksheet that charts the earnings-per-share (EPS) trend of a company with extraordinary items and/or changes in accounting principle.

Scenario: You are considering investing $5,000 in your favorite soft drink company, **Coca-Cola.** After taking a financial accounting class, you remember that smart investors investigate the financial performance of companies before investing. One measure of financial performance is earnings (net income) per share of common stock. When finished with your spreadsheet, answer these questions:

1. Why is EPS such a useful business statistic?
2. What is the trend in basic EPS (net income) for Coca-Cola?
3. List the EPS components given in the chapter. Fill in the amounts for Coca-Cola for the most recent year, and calculate EPS. Explain any difference between the amount you calculate and the one reported in the financial statements.
4. Besides EPS, what other financial measures should you examine prior to making an investment decision?

Step-by-Step:

1. Obtain a copy of the most recent annual report for Coca-Cola (online, try www.cocacola.com). Locate the Consolidated Statements of Income and Consolidated Balance Sheets.
2. Open a new Excel worksheet.
3. Create a bold-faced heading for your spreadsheet that contains the following:
   a. Chapter 14 Excel Application Exercise
   b. Coca-Cola Earnings-per-Share Analysis
   c. Today's Date

4. Move down two rows and enter the following title:
   Coca-Cola Company
   Income Statement
   Year Ended December 31, 2002 (or the most recent year)
   (In millions)
5. Copy the Consolidated Statements of Income, following the format used by Coca-Cola (leave out the description "Year Ended . . . "). Include all line items, using formulas where appropriate.
6. Starting with the row containing the three years' titles, highlight all rows of the income statement.
7. Click on the Chart Wizard. Select the line chart type with line markers displayed at each data value. Click next and select "Series in: rows." Then, click on the "Series" tab.
8. Remove from the series all line items except basic net income per share "before accounting change." You'll see lines disappear from your chart as you do this.
9. Then, click the "Add" button. Give the new series the name "EPS, net of changes." Click in the "Values" box, deleting any existing values. On the income statement, select the three amounts underneath the earnings-per-share line item "cumulative effect of accounting change" (these amounts do not have a name in the statement). The cell references should now be in the "Values" box. Click next.
10. Click on the "Titles" tab. For the chart title, enter "Earnings per Share." For the category X axis, enter "Year," and for the category Y axis, enter "EPS."
11. Click on the "Legend" tab, and click to move the legend to the bottom of the chart. Then, click on the "Data Labels" tab. Check "Value," then click "Finish." Position your chart to the right or bottom of your income statement.
12. Save your work, and print your work sheet in landscape mode (with graphs) for your files.

END-OF-CHAPTER *Summary Problem*

The following information was taken from the ledger of **Kraft Corporation** at December 31, 20X6.

CHECK YOUR RESOURCES

Common stock, no-par, 45,000 shares issued	$180,000	Discontinued operations, income	$ 20,000
Sales revenue	620,000	Prior-period adjustment— credit to Retained Earnings	5,000
Extraordinary gain	26,000	Gain on sale of plant assets	21,000
Loss due to lawsuit	11,000	Cost of goods sold	380,000
General expenses	62,000	Income tax expense (saving):	
Preferred stock 8%	50,000	Continuing operations	32,000
Selling expenses	108,000	Discontinued operations	8,000
Retained earnings, beginning, as originally reported	103,000	Extraordinary gain	10,000
Cumulative effect of change in inventory method (debit)	(10,000)	Cumulative effect of change in inventory method	(4,000)
Dividends	16,000	Treasury stock, common (5,000 shares)	25,000

Required

Prepare a single-step income statement and a statement of retained earnings for Kraft Corporation for the year ended December 31, 20X6. Include the EPS presentation and show your computations. Kraft had no changes in its stock accounts during the year.

Solution

Kraft Corporation
Income Statement
Year Ended December 31, 20X6

Revenue and gains:		
Sales revenue		$620,000
Gain on sale of plant assets		21,000
Total revenues and gains		641,000
Expenses and losses:		
Cost of goods sold	$380,000	
Selling expenses	108,000	
General expenses	62,000	
Loss due to lawsuit	11,000	
Income tax expense	32,000	
Total expenses and losses		593,000
Income from continuing operations		48,000
Discontinued operations, income of $20,000, less income tax of $8,000		12,000
Income before extraordinary item and cumulative effect of change in inventory method		60,000
Extraordinary gain, $26,000, less income tax, $10,000		16,000
Cumulative effect of change in inventory method, $10,000, less income tax saving, $4,000		(6,000)
Net income		$ 70,000
Earnings per share:		
Income from continuing operations [($48,000 – $4,000)/40,000 shares]		$1.10
Income from discontinued operations ($12,000/40,000 shares)		0.30
Income before extraordinary item and cumulative effect of change in inventory method [($60,000 – $4,000)/40,000 shares]		1.40
Extraordinary gain ($16,000/40,000 shares)		0.40
Cumulative effect of change in inventory method ($6,000/40,000)		(0.15)
Net income [($70,000 – $4,000)/40,000 shares]		$1.65

Computations:

$$\text{EPS} = \frac{\text{Income} - \text{Preferred dividends}}{\text{Common shares outstanding}}$$

Preferred dividends: $50,000 × 0.08 = $4,000
Common shares outstanding:
   45,000 shares issued – 5,000 treasury shares = 40,000 shares outstanding

Kraft Corporation
Statement of Retained Earnings
Year Ended December 31, 20X6

Retained earnings balance, beginning, as originally reported	$103,000
Prior-period adjustment—credit	5,000
Retained earnings balance, beginning, as adjusted	108,000
Net income for current year	70,000
	178,000
Dividends for current year	(16,000)
Retained earnings balance, ending	$162,000

REVIEW *Retained Earnings, Treasury Stock, and the Income Statement*

Quick Check

1. A company's own stock that it has issued and repurchased is called
   a. Issued stock
   b. Outstanding stock
   c. Stock dividend
   d. Treasury stock

2. A stock dividend
   a. Increases Common Stock
   b. Decreases Retained Earnings
   c. Has no effect on total equity
   d. All of the above

3. In a small stock dividend,
   a. Retained Earnings is debited for the market value of the shares issued.
   b. Common stock is debited for the par value of the shares issued.
   c. Paid-In Capital in Excess of Par is debited for the difference between the debits to Retained Earnings and to Common Stock.
   d. Net income is always decreased.

4. Stock splits
   a. Increase the number of shares of stock issued
   b. Decrease the par value of the stock
   c. Both a and b
   d. None of the above

5. Assume that **Pier 1 Imports** paid $10 per share to purchase 1,000 of its $1 par common as treasury stock. The purchase of treasury stock
   a. Decreased total equity by $1,000
   b. Increased total equity by $1,000
   c. Decreased total equity by $10,000
   d. Increased total equity by $10,000

6. Assume that Pier 1 Imports sold all 1,000 shares of its treasury stock for $15 per share. The sale of treasury stock
   a. Decreased total equity by $15,000
   b. Increased total equity by $15,000
   c. Decreased total equity by $5,000
   d. Increased total equity by $5,000

7. Analyze the income statement of Allied Electronics in Exhibit 14-6, page 555. Suppose you are predicting next year's net income. Allied is most likely to earn net income of $x next year. How much is $x?
   a. $54,000
   b. $75,000
   c. $79,000
   d. $90,000

8. Which of the following events would be an extraordinary loss?
   a. Loss on the sale of equipment
   b. Loss due to an earthquake
   c. Loss on discontinued operations
   d. All of the above are extraordinary items

9. What is the most widely followed statistic in accounting?
   a. Earnings per share
   b. Total assets
   c. Retained earnings
   d. Dividends

10. Earnings per share is *not* computed for
   a. Net income
   b. Discontinued operations
   c. Comprehensive income
   d. Extraordinary items

Accounting Vocabulary

appropriation of retained earnings (p. 551)
comprehensive income (p. 558)
earnings per share (EPS) (p. 557)
extraordinary gains and losses (p. 556)

extraordinary item (p. 556)
prior-period adjustment (p. 559)
segment of the business (p. 555)
statement of stockholders' equity (p. 559)

stock dividend (p. 544)
stock split (p. 546)
treasury stock (p. 548)

ASSESS *Your Progress*

A+ online homework

See *www.prenhall.com/horngren* for selected Starters, Exercises, and Problems.

Recording a small stock dividend
(Obj. 1)

Comparing and contrasting cash dividends and stock dividends
(Obj. 1)

Accounting for a stock split
(Obj. 2)

Accounting for the purchase and sale of treasury stock (above cost)
(Obj. 3)

Interpreting a restriction of retained earnings
(Obj. 4)

Preparing a corporate income statement
(Obj. 5)

Starters

S14-1 Benetech, Inc., has 200,000 shares of $2.50 par common stock outstanding. Benetech distributes a 5% stock dividend when the market value of its stock is $10 per share.

1. Journalize Benetech's distribution of the stock dividend on September 30. An explanation is not required.
2. What is the overall effect of the stock dividend on Benetech's total assets? On total stockholders' equity?

S14-2 → *Link Back to Chapter 13 (Cash Dividends).* Compare and contrast the accounting for cash dividends and stock dividends. In the space provided, insert either "Cash dividends," "Stock dividends," or "Both cash dividends and stock dividends" to complete each of the following statements:

1. ____ increase paid-in capital by the same amount that they decrease Retained Earnings.
2. ____ decrease both total assets and total stockholders' equity, resulting in a decrease in the size of the company.
3. ____ decrease Retained Earnings.
4. ____ have no effect on a liability.

S14-3 Examine **Pier 1 Imports'** stockholders' equity on page 545. Suppose Pier 1 split its common stock 2 for 1 in order to decrease the market price of its stock. The company's stock was trading at $20 immediately before the split.

1. Prepare the stockholders' equity section of Pier 1 Imports' balance sheet after the stock split.
2. Which account balances changed after the stock split? Which account balances were unchanged?

S14-4 Celine Corporation began operations in 20X8. After issuing its common stock to the public, Celine completed the following treasury stock transactions:

a. Purchased 2,000 shares of the company's $1 par common stock as treasury stock, paying cash of $5 per share.
b. Sold 1,000 shares of the treasury stock for cash of $8 per share.

Journalize these transactions. Explanations are not required. Show how Celine will report treasury stock on its December 31, 20X8, balance sheet after completing the two transactions. In reporting the treasury stock, focus solely on the Treasury Stock account. You may ignore all other accounts.

S14-5 Study Exhibit 14-5, page 552. The company's board of directors is preparing to declare a cash dividend.

1. The company has plenty of cash. What is the maximum amount of cash dividends the board of directors can declare? Explain how you arrived at your answer.
2. What is the nature of the retained earnings restriction in the exhibit? Why did the company restrict (appropriate) its retained earnings? Explain.

S14-6 List the major parts of a complex corporate income statement for IMAX Corporation for the year ended December 31, 20X4. Include all the major parts of the income statement, starting with net sales revenue and ending with net income (net loss). You may ignore dollar amounts and earnings per share. Use Exhibit 14-6, page 555, as a guide.

S14-7 Study the income statement of Allied Electronics Corporation in Exhibit 14-6, page 555. Answer these questions about the company's operations:

Explaining the items on a complex corporate income statement
(Obj. 5)

1. How much total gross profit did Allied earn on the sale of its products—before deducting any operating expenses? Name this item and give its amount.
2. Why is the gain on sale of machinery reported as Other gains (losses)?
3. What dollar amount of net income would most sophisticated investors predict for Allied Electronics to earn during 20X6 and beyond? Name this item, give its amount, and state your reason.

S14-8 H&R Young Corporation accounting records include the following items, listed in no particular order, at December 31, 20X3.

Preparing a corporate income statement
(Obj. 5)

Extraordinary gain	$ 5,000	Other gains (losses)	$ (2,000)
Cost of goods sold	71,000	Net sales revenue	182,000
Operating expenses	64,000	Loss on discontinued	
Accounts receivable	19,000	operations	(15,000)

Income tax of 40% applies to all items.

Prepare H&R Young Corporation's income statement for the year ended December 31, 20X3. Use Exhibit 14-6, page 555, as a guide. Omit earnings per share.

S14-9 Return to the H&R Young Corporation data in Starter 14-8. H&R Young had 10,000 shares of common stock outstanding during 20X3. H&R Young declared and paid preferred dividends of $3,000 during 20X3.

Show how H&R Young reported EPS data on its 20X3 income statement.

Reporting earnings per share
(Obj. 5)

S14-10 The **Procter & Gamble Company** has preferred stock outstanding, and the corporation issued additional common stock during the year.

Interpreting earnings-per-share data
(Obj. 5)

1. Give the basic equation to compute earnings per share of common stock for net income.
2. List all the income items for which Procter & Gamble must report EPS data.

S14-11 Use the H&R Young Corporation data in Starter 14-8. In addition, H&R Young had unrealized losses of $4,000 on investments during 20X3. Start with H&R Young's net income from Starter 14-8 and show how the company could report other comprehensive income on its 20X3 income statement.

Should H&R Young report EPS data for other comprehensive income?

Reporting comprehensive income
(Obj. 5)

S14-12 Examine De Graff Corporation's statement of retained earnings on page 559. Suppose instead that De Graff had overpaid 20X7 income tax expense by $10,000. Show how De Graff would report this prior-period adjustment on the statement of retained earnings for 20X8.

Reporting a prior-period adjustment
(Obj. 6)

S14-13 ← *Link Back to Chapter 1 (Accounting Equation).* Use the statement of stockholders' equity in Exhibit 14-9, page 560, to answer the following questions about Allied Electronics Corporation.

Using the statement of stockholders' equity
(Obj. 6)

1. Make a single journal entry to record Allied's declaration and payment of cash dividends during 20X5.
2. How much cash did the issuance of common stock bring in during 20X5?
3. What was the cost of the treasury stock that Allied purchased during 20X5? What was Allied's cost of the treasury stock that Allied sold during the year? For how much did Allied sell the treasury stock during 20X5?

Exercises

E14-1 The stockholders' equity for Clifton, Inc., on December 31, 20X4, follows:

Stockholders' Equity	
Common stock, $1 par, 100,000 shares authorized, 50,000 shares issued...........................	$ 50,000
Paid-in capital in excess of par.....................	400,000
Retained earnings	120,000
Total stockholders' equity.........................	$570,000

On April 30, 20X5, the market price of Clifton's common stock was $16 per share and the company distributed a 10% stock dividend.

Required

1. Journalize the distribution of the stock dividend.
2. Prepare the stockholders' equity section of the balance sheet after the stock dividend.

E14-2 Hunter Racing Motors is authorized to issue 500,000 shares of $1 par common stock. The company issued 80,000 shares at $4 per share, and all 80,000 shares are outstanding. When the market price of common stock was $5 per share, Hunter distributed a 10% stock dividend. Later, Hunter declared and paid a $0.50 per share cash dividend.

Required

1. Journalize the distribution of the stock dividend.
2. Journalize both the declaration and the payment of the cash dividend.

E14-3 Harwood Travel, Inc., had the following stockholders' equity at May 31:

Common stock, $10 par, 200,000 shares authorized, 50,000 shares issued...........................	$500,000
Paid-in capital in excess of par.....................	100,000
Retained earnings	200,000
Total stockholders' equity.........................	$800,000

On June 30, Harwood split its common stock 2 for 1. Make the necessary entry to record the stock split, and prepare the stockholders' equity section of the balance sheet immediately after the split.

E14-4 Identify the effects of the following transactions on total stockholders' equity. Each transaction is independent.

a. Issuance of 50,000 shares of $10 par common at $15.
b. Purchase of 1,000 shares of treasury stock (par value $0.50) at $5 per share.
c. A 10% stock dividend. Before the dividend, 500,000 shares of $1 par common stock were outstanding; market value was $7 at the time of the dividend.
d. Sale of 600 shares of $1 par treasury stock for $5 per share. Cost of the treasury stock was $2 per share.
e. A 3-for-1 stock split. Prior to the split, 60,000 shares of $4 par common were outstanding.

E14-5 Journalize the following transactions of **Foot Locker**, a chain of sports stores:

Feb.	4	Issued 20,000 shares of no-par common stock at $15 per share.
Apr.	22	Purchased 1,000 shares of treasury stock at $14 per share.
Aug.	22	Sold 600 shares of treasury stock at $20 per share.

Journalizing treasury stock transactions and reporting stockholders' equity
(Obj. 3)

E14-6 Far Side, Inc., had the following stockholders' equity on November 30:

Stockholders' Equity	
Common stock, $5 par, 500,000 shares authorized,	
50,000 shares issued............................	$250,000
Paid-in capital in excess of par.....................	150,000
Retained earnings	520,000
Total stockholders' equity.........................	$920,000

On December 30, Far Side purchased 5,000 shares of treasury stock at $10 per share. Journalize the purchase of the treasury stock, and prepare the stockholders' equity section of the balance sheet at December 31.

Reporting a retained earnings restriction
(Obj. 4)

E14-7 The agreement under which Patterson, Inc., issued its long-term debt requires the restriction of $200,000 of the company's retained earnings balance. Total retained earnings is $250,000, and total paid-in capital is $500,000.

Required

Show how to report stockholders' equity on Patterson's balance sheet, assuming the following:

a. Patterson discloses the restriction in a note. Write the note.
b. Patterson appropriates retained earnings in the amount of the restriction and includes no note in its statements.
c. Patterson's cash balance is $100,000. What is the maximum amount of dividends Patterson can declare?

Preparing a multistep income statement
(Obj. 5)

E14-8 Schindler Corporation's accounting records include the following for 20X8:

Student ResourceCD

spreadsheet

Sales revenue...................	$410,000	Income tax expense—	
Operating expenses		extraordinary gain.............	$ 6,000
(including income tax).........	106,000	Income tax expense—change	
Cumulative effect of change in		in depreciation method.........	3,000
depreciation method, a credit...	7,000	Income tax saving—loss	
Cost of goods sold	245,000	on discontinued operations	20,000
Loss on discontinued operations..	50,000	Extraordinary gain	15,000

Required

Prepare a multistep income statement for 20X8. Omit earnings per share.

Computing earnings per share
(Obj. 5)

E14-9 Tyler, Inc. earned net income of $74,000 for 20X6. The ledger reveals the following figures:

Preferred stock, $4.00 per year, no-par, 1,000 shares	
issued and outstanding...........................	$ 50,000
Common stock, $10 par, 52,000 shares issued	520,000
Treasury stock, common, 2,000 shares at cost	36,000

Required

Compute Tyler's EPS for the year.

Computing earnings per share
(Obj. 5)

E14-10 San Marcos, Inc., had 50,000 shares of common stock and 10,000 shares of 5%, $10 par preferred stock outstanding through December 31, 20X5. Income from continuing operations of 20X5 was $110,000, and loss on discontinued operations (net of income tax saving) was $8,000. The company had an extraordinary gain (net of tax) of $50,000.

Required

Compute San Marcos's EPS amounts for 20X5, starting with income from continuing operations.

E14-11 The French Bakery reported a prior-period adjustment in 20X3. An accounting error caused net income of prior years to be understated by $5 million. Retained earnings at December 31, 20X2, as previously reported, stood at $395 million. Net income for 20X3 was $110 million, and dividends totaled $40 million.

Required

Prepare the company's statement of retained earnings for the year ended December 31, 20X3.

E14-12 The Ritz Hotel Company, a large hotel chain, had retained earnings of $410 million at December 31, 20X6. The company reported these figures for 20X7:

	($ Millions)
Net income	$140
Cash dividends—preferred	2
common	88

Required

Beginning with net income, prepare a combined statement of income and retained earnings for The Ritz Hotel Company for the year ended December 31, 20X7.

E14-13 During 20X6, BMW Group earned income from continuing operations of $95,000. The company also sold its land-development segment (discontinued operations) at a gain of $30,000 and had an extraordinary loss of $8,000. At year-end, BMW had an unrealized loss on investments of $3,000.

1. Compute BMW's net income and comprehensive income for 20X6. All amounts are net of income taxes.

2. What would be the final EPS figure that BMW would report for 20X6? Show the amount. BMW had 20,000 shares of common stock (and no preferred stock) outstanding.

E14-14 At December 31, 20X6, Labrador Corp. reported the following stockholders' equity.

Common stock, $5 par, 200,000 shares authorized, 120,000 shares issued.........................	$ 600,000
Additional paid-in capital	100,000
Retained earnings	700,000
Treasury stock, 2,500 shares at cost	(80,000)
	$1,320,000

During 20X7, Labrador completed these transactions and events (listed in chronological order):

a. Sold 1,000 shares of treasury stock for $35 per share (cost of these shares was $30 per share).
b. Issued 500 shares of common stock at $20 per share.
c. Net income for the year was $200,000.
d. Declared and paid cash dividends of $100,000.

Required

Prepare Labrador Corp.'s statement of stockholders' equity for 20X7.

E14-15 Omni Communications, Inc., began 20X5 with 2.9 million shares of $1 par common stock issued and outstanding. Beginning paid-in capital in excess of par was $6 million, and retained earnings was $7 million. In February 20X5, Omni issued 100,000 shares of stock at $11 per share. In September, when the stock's market price was $12 per share, the board of directors distributed a 10% stock dividend.

Required

1. Make the journal entries for the issuance of stock for cash and for the distribution of the 10% stock dividend.

2. Prepare the company's statement of stockholders' equity for the year ended December 31, 20X5.

Problems

(Group A)

P14-1A **Titleist Sports Corporation** completed the following selected transactions during 20X6:

Journalizing stockholders' equity transactions
(Obj. 1, 3)

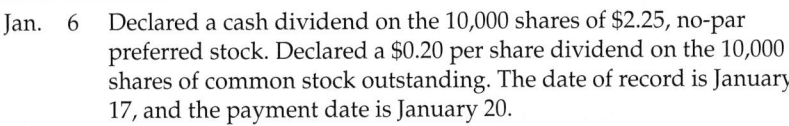

Student Resource CD

General Ledger (GL), QuickBooks (QB), Peachtree (PT)

Jan. 6	Declared a cash dividend on the 10,000 shares of $2.25, no-par preferred stock. Declared a $0.20 per share dividend on the 10,000 shares of common stock outstanding. The date of record is January 17, and the payment date is January 20.
Jan. 20	Paid the cash dividends.
Mar. 21	Split common stock 2 for 1 by calling in the 10,000 shares of $10 par common and issuing new stock in its place.
Apr. 18	Distributed a 10% stock dividend on the common stock. The market value of the common stock was $27 per share.
June 18	Purchased 2,000 shares of treasury common stock at $25 per share.
Dec. 22	Sold 1,000 shares of treasury common stock for $26 per share.

Required

Record the transactions in the general journal.

P14-2A The balance sheet of Quartz, Inc., at December 31, 20X5, reported 500,000 shares of $1 par common stock authorized with 100,000 shares issued. Paid-In Capital in Excess of Par had a balance of $300,000. Retained Earnings had a balance of $101,000. During 20X6, the company completed the following selected transactions:

Journalizing dividend and treasury stock transactions and reporting stockholders' equity
(Obj. 1, 2, 3)

Student Resource CD

GL, QB, PT

Feb. 15	Purchased 5,000 shares of the treasury stock at $4 per share.
Mar. 8	Sold 2,000 shares of treasury stock for $7 per share.
Sep. 28	Distributed a 10% stock dividend on the 97,000 shares of *outstanding* common stock. The market value of Quartz's common stock was $5 per share.
Dec. 31	Earned net income of $73,000 during the year. Closed net income to Retained Earnings.

Required

1. Record the transactions in the general journal. Explanations are not required.

2. Prepare the stockholders' equity section of the balance sheet at December 31, 20X6.

P14-3A Monahans Corporation is well positioned. Located in Tucson, Arizona, Monahans is the only company between Texas and California with reliable sources for its imported gifts. The company does a brisk business with specialty stores such as **Pier 1 Imports**. Monahans' recent success has made the company a prime target for a takeover. An investment group from Hong Kong is attempting to buy 51% of Monahans' outstanding stock against the wishes of Monahans' board of directors. Board members are convinced that the Hong Kong investors would sell the most desirable pieces of the business and leave little of value.

At the most recent board meeting, several suggestions were advanced to fight off the hostile takeover bid. The suggestion with the most promise is to purchase a huge quantity of treasury stock. Monahans has the cash to carry out this plan.

Purchasing treasury stock to fight off a takeover of the corporation
(Obj. 3)

Required

1. As a significant stockholder of Monahans Corporation, write a memorandum to explain to the board how the purchase of treasury stock would make it difficult for the Hong Kong group to take over Monahans. Include a discussion of the effect that purchasing treasury stock would have on stock outstanding and on the size of the corporation.

2. Suppose Monahans' management is successful in fighting off the takeover bid and later sells the treasury stock at prices greater than the purchase price. Explain what effect these sales will have on assets, stockholders' equity, and net income.

Journalizing dividend and treasury stock transactions; reporting retained earnings and stockholders' equity
(Obj. 1, 3)

P14-4A The balance sheet of Swingline, Inc., at December 31, 20X8, presented the following stockholders' equity:

GL, QB, PT

Paid-in capital:	
Common stock, $1 par, 250,000 shares authorized,	
50,000 shares issued	$ 50,000
Paid-in capital in excess of par—common	350,000
Total paid-in capital	400,000
Retained earnings................................	99,000
Total stockholders' equity	$499,000

During 20X9, Swingline completed the following selected transactions:

Mar. 29	Distributed a 5% stock dividend on the common stock. The market value of Swingline common stock was $8 per share.
July 13	Purchased 2,000 shares of treasury stock at $8 per share.
Oct. 4	Sold 1,000 shares of treasury common stock for $9 per share.
Dec. 10	Declared a $0.20 per share cash dividend on the 51,500 shares of common stock outstanding. The date of record is December 17, and the payment date is January 2.
31	Closed the $71,000 net income to Retained Earnings.

Required

1. Record the transactions in the general journal.

2. Prepare the retained earnings statement at December 31, 20X9.

3. Prepare the stockholders' equity section of the balance sheet at December 31, 20X9.

Preparing a detailed income statement
(Obj. 5)

P14-5A The following information was taken from the records of Jeffries Corporation at June 30, 20X5:

Common stock, no-par, 22,000		Selling expenses	$ 120,000
shares authorized and issued	$350,000	General expenses	71,000
Preferred stock, 6%, $25 par,		Gain on discontinued operations........	1,000
4,000 shares issued	100,000	Cost of goods sold	279,000
Retained earnings, beginning	63,000	Dividend revenue	19,000
Income tax expense (tax saving):		Treasury stock, common (2,000 shares)....	28,000
Continuing operations................	28,000	Extraordinary loss	42,000
Gain on discontinued operations.......	400	Net sales revenue......................	567,000
Extraordinary loss (tax saving).........	(15,400)		

Required

Prepare a single-step income statement, including earnings per share, for Jeffries Corporation for the fiscal year ended June 30, 20X5.

Preparing a corrected combined statement of income and retained earnings
(Obj. 5)

P14-6A Eloy Santos, accountant for Airstream, Inc., was injured in an auto accident. Another employee prepared the following income statement for the fiscal year ended June 30, 20X4:

Airstream, Inc.
Income Statement
June 30, 20X4

Revenues and gains:		
Sales		$733,000
Paid-in capital in excess of par—common		111,000
Total revenues and gains		844,000
Expenses and losses:		
Cost of goods sold	$383,000	
Selling expenses	103,000	
General expenses	91,000	
Sales returns	22,000	
Sales discounts	10,000	
Dividends	15,000	
Income tax expense—continuing operations	32,000	
Total expenses and losses		656,000
Income from operations		188,000
Other gains and losses:		
Loss on discontinued operations		(15,000)
Net income		$173,000
Earnings per share		$8.65

The individual *amounts* listed on the income statement are correct. However, some accounts are reported incorrectly, and one doesn't belong on the income statement at all. Also, income tax has not been applied to all appropriate figures. The income tax rate on discontinued operations is 40%. Airstream issued 24,000 shares of common stock in 20X1 and held 4,000 shares as treasury stock during fiscal year 20X4. Retained earnings at June 30, 20X3, was $209,000.

Required

Prepare a corrected combined statement of income and retained earnings for the fiscal year ended June 30, 20X4. Prepare the income statement in single-step format, and include earnings per share.

Computing earnings per share and reporting a retained earnings restriction
(Obj. 4, 5)

P14-7A The capital structure of Avian Company at December 31, 20X7, included 5,000 shares of $2 preferred stock and 120,000 shares of common stock. Common shares outstanding during 20X8 were 120,000. Income from continuing operations during 20X8 was $370,000. The company discontinued a segment of the business at a gain of $60,000 and also had an extraordinary loss of $48,000. Avian's board of directors has restricted $300,000 of retained earnings for expansion of the company's office facilities.

Required

1. Compute Avian's earnings per share for 20X8. Start with income from continuing operations. Income and loss amounts are net of income tax.

2. Show two ways of reporting Avian's retained earnings restriction. Retained earnings at December 31, 20X7, was $120,000, and Avian declared cash dividends of $100,000 during 20X8.

Using a statement of stockholders' equity
(Obj. 6)

P14-8A Business Analysts, Inc., reported the following statement of stockholders' equity for the year ended September 30, 20X9:

		Additional			
(Dollar amounts in thousands)	Common Stock	Paid-in Capital	Retained Earnings	Treasury Stock	Total
Balance, September 30, 20X8	$173	$2,118	$1,706	$(18)	$3,979
Net income			520		520
Cash dividends........................			(117)		(117)
Issuance of stock (5,000 shares)	9	46			55
Stock dividend	18	92	(110)		—
Sale of treasury stock....................		5		11	16
Balance, September 30, 20X9	$200	$2,261	$1,999	$ (7)	$4,453

Business Analysts, Inc.
Statement of Stockholders' Equity
Year Ended September 30, 20X9

Required

1. What is the par value of the company's common stock?

2. At what price per share did the company issue its common stock during the year?

3. What was the cost of treasury stock sold during the year? What was the selling price of the treasury stock sold? What was the increase in total stockholders' equity from selling the treasury stock?

4. What overall effect did the stock dividend have on total stockholders' equity?

online homework

Journalizing stockholders' equity transactions
(Obj. 1,3)

Student Resource CD

GL, QB, PT

Problems

(Group B)

P14-1B Alan Cook Corp. completed the following transactions during 20X9:

Feb. 2	Declared a cash dividend on the 5%, $100 par preferred stock (1,000 shares outstanding). Declared a $0.20 per share dividend on the 100,000 shares of common stock outstanding. The date of record is February 15 and the payment date is February 23.
Feb. 23	Paid the cash dividends.
June 10	Split common stock 2 for 1 by calling in the 100,000 shares of $10 par common and issuing new stock in its place.
July 30	Distributed a 10% stock dividend on the common stock. The market value of the common stock was $15 per share.
Oct. 26	Purchased 2,500 shares of treasury common stock at $14 per share.
Nov. 8	Sold 1,000 shares of treasury common stock for $17 per share.

Required

Record the transactions in Allen Cook's general journal.

Journalizing dividend and treasury stock transactions and reporting stockholders' equity
(Obj. 1, 2, 3)

Student Resource CD

GL, QB, PT

P14-2B The balance sheet of Recreation Concepts, Inc., at December 31, 20X6, reported 100,000 shares of no-par common stock authorized, with 30,000 shares issued and a Common Stock balance of $180,000. Retained Earnings had a balance of $140,000. During 20X7, the company completed the following selected transactions:

Mar. 15	Purchased 5,000 shares of treasury stock at $8 per share.
Apr. 30	Distributed a 20% stock dividend on the 25,000 shares of *outstanding* common stock. The market value of Recreation Concepts common stock was $10 per share.
Oct. 8	Sold 2,000 shares of treasury stock for $12 per share.
31	Earned net income of $110,000 during the year. Closed net income to Retained Earnings.

Required

1. Record the transactions in the general journal. Explanations are not required.
2. Prepare the stockholders' equity section of Recreation Concepts' balance sheet at December 31, 20X7.

P14-3B Cooper Fashions is ideally positioned in the clothing business. Located in Toledo, Ohio, Cooper is the only company with a distribution network for its imported goods. The company does a brisk business with specialty stores such as **Neiman Marcus, Saks Fifth Avenue**, and **Nordstrom**. Cooper's recent success has made the company a prime target for a takeover. Against the wishes of Cooper's board of directors, an investment group from Canada is attempting to buy 51% of Cooper's outstanding stock. Board members are convinced that the Canadian investors would sell off the most desirable pieces of the business and leave little of value.

Increasing dividends to fight off a takeover of the corporation **(Obj. 1)**

At the most recent board meeting, several suggestions were advanced to fight off the hostile takeover bid. One suggestion is to increase the stock outstanding by distributing a 100% stock dividend. The intent is to spread the company's ownership in order to make it harder for the Canadian group to buy a controlling interest.

Required

As a significant stockholder of Cooper Fashions, write a short memo to explain to the board whether distributing the stock dividend would make it more difficult for the investor group to take over Cooper. Include in your memo a discussion of the effect that the stock dividend would have on assets, liabilities, and total stockholders' equity—that is, the dividend's effect on the size of the corporation.

P14-4B The balance sheet of Beta Concepts, Inc., at December 31, 20X6, reported the following stockholders' equity:

Journalizing dividend and treasury stock transactions; reporting retained earnings and stockholders' equity **(Obj. 1, 3)**

Student ResourceCD
GL, QB, PT

Paid-in capital:	
Common stock, $10 par, 100,000 shares authorized,	
20,000 shares issued	$200,000
Paid-in capital in excess of par—common	300,000
Total paid-in capital	500,000
Retained earnings	180,000
Total stockholders' equity	$680,000

During 20X7, Beta Concepts completed the following selected transactions:

Feb. 6 Distributed a 10% stock dividend on the common stock. The market value of Beta Concepts' stock was $24 per share.
July 29 Purchased 2,000 shares of treasury stock at $21 per share.
Nov. 13 Sold 400 shares of treasury stock for $22 per share.
27 Declared a $0.30 per share cash dividend on the 20,400 shares of common stock outstanding. The date of record is December 17, and the payment date is January 7, 20X8.
Dec. 31 Closed the $70,000 net income to Retained Earnings.

Required

1. Record the transactions in the general journal.
2. Prepare a retained earnings statement at December 31, 20X7.
3. Prepare the stockholders' equity section of the balance sheet at December 31, 20X7.

Preparing a detailed income statement **(Obj. 5)**

P14-5B The following information was taken from the records of Courtyard Classics, Inc., at September 30, 20X8.

Cost of goods sold.	$435,000	General expenses	$133,000
Retained earnings, beginning	88,000	Preferred stock, $2, no-par,	
Selling expenses	121,000	5,000 shares issued	200,000
Income from discontinued operations	8,000	Common stock, $10 par, 25,000	
Income tax expense (tax saving):		shares authorized and issued	250,000
Continuing operations	72,000	Net sales revenue	837,000
Income from discontinued operations	2,000	Treasury stock, common (1,000 shares)	11,000
Extraordinary loss (tax saving)	(12,000)	Extraordinary loss	30,000

Required

Prepare a single-step income statement, including earnings per share, for Courtyard Classics, Inc., for the fiscal year ended September 30, 20X8.

Preparing a corrected combined statement of income and retained earnings
(Obj. 5)

P14-6B Quincy Caldwell, accountant for Brooks Furniture Company, was injured in a boating accident. Another employee prepared the accompanying income statement for the year ended December 31, 20X3.

The individual *amounts* listed on the income statement are correct. However, some accounts are reported incorrectly, and one doesn't belong on the income statement at all. Also, income tax has not been applied to all appropriate figures. The income tax rate on discontinued operations was 40%. Brooks Furniture Company issued 52,000 shares of common stock in 20X1 and held 2,000 shares as treasury stock during 20X3. Retained earnings at December 31, 20X2, was $361,000.

Brooks Furniture Company
Income Statement
Year Ended December 31, 20X3

Revenue and gains:		
Sales		$362,000
Paid-in capital in excess of par—common		90,000
Total revenues and gains		452,000
Expenses and losses:		
Cost of goods sold	$105,000	
Selling expenses	67,000	
General expenses	61,000	
Sales returns	11,000	
Sales discounts	6,000	
Dividends	7,000	
Income tax expense	20,000	
Total expenses and losses		277,000
Income from operations		175,000
Other gains and losses:		
Loss on discontinued operations		(3,000)
Net income		$172,000
Earnings per share		$3.44

Required

Prepare a corrected combined statement of income and retained earnings for 20X3; include earnings per share. Prepare the income statement in single-step format.

Computing earnings per share and reporting a retained earnings restriction
(Obj. 4, 5)

P14-7B The capital structure of Smirnoff, Inc., at December 31, 20X6, included 20,000 shares of $1.25 preferred stock and 46,000 shares of common stock. Common stock outstanding during 20X7 totaled 46,000 shares. Income from continuing operations during 20X7 was $94,000. The company discontinued a segment of the business at a gain of $23,000, and also had an extraordinary gain of $11,500. Smirnoff's board of directors restricts $60,000 of retained earnings for contingencies.

Required

1. Compute Smirnoff's earnings per share for 20X7. Start with income from continuing operations. All income and loss amounts are net of income tax.

2. Show two ways of reporting Smirnoff's retained earnings restriction. Retained earnings at December 31, 20X6, was $100,000, and Smirnoff declared cash dividends of $20,000 during 20X7.

P14-8B Public Trust, Inc., reported the following statement of stockholders' equity for the year ended October 31, 20X4:

Using a statement of stockholders' equity
(Obj. 6)

Public Trust, Inc.
Statement of Stockholders' Equity
Year Ended October 31, 20X4

(Dollar amounts in thousands)	Common Stock	Additional Paid-In Capital	Retained Earnings	Treasury Stock	Total
Balance, Oct. 31, 20X3	$427	$1,622	$904	$(117)	$2,836
Net income			336		336
Cash dividends.......................			(194)		(194)
Issuance of stock (60,000 shares)	120	264			384
Stock dividend	22	48	(70)		—
Sale of treasury stock..................		9		19	28
Balance, Oct. 31, 20X4	$569	$1,943	$976	$ (98)	$3,390

Required

Answer these questions about Public Trust's stockholders' equity transactions.

1. What is the par value of the company's common stock?

2. At what price per share did Public Trust issue its common stock during the year?

3. What was the cost of treasury stock sold during the year? What was the selling price of the treasury stock sold? What was the increase in total stockholders' equity from selling the treasury stock?

4. What effect did the stock dividend have on total stockholders' equity?

APPLY *Your Knowledge*

Decision Cases

Case 1. Modem Transmission, Inc., had the following stockholders' equity amounts on June 30, 20X2:

Analyzing cash dividends and stock dividends
(Obj. 1)

Common stock, no-par, 100,000 shares issued	$ 750,000
Retained earnings	790,000
Total stockholders' equity	$1,540,000

In the past, Modem has paid an annual cash dividend of $1 per share. Despite the large retained earnings balance, the board of directors wished to conserve cash for expansion. The board delayed the payment of cash dividends and in July distributed a 10% stock dividend. During August, the company's cash position improved. The board declared and paid a cash dividend of $0.9091 per share in September.

Suppose you owned 5,000 shares of Modem common stock, acquired three years ago, prior to the 10% stock dividend. The market price of the stock was $30 per share before any of these dividends.

Required

1. What amount of cash dividends did you receive last year—before the stock dividend? What amount of cash dividends will you receive after the stock dividend?
2. How does the stock dividend affect your proportionate ownership in Modem Transmission, Inc.? Explain.
3. Immediately after the stock dividend was distributed, the market value of Modem stock decreased from $30 per share to $27.273 per share. Does this decrease represent a loss to you? Explain.

Reporting special items
(Obj. 3, 5)

Case 2. The following accounting issues have arisen at T-Shirts Plus, Inc.:

1. T-Shirts Plus earned a significant profit in the year ended November 30, 20X6, because land that it held was purchased by the State of North Carolina for a new highway. The company proposes to treat the sale of land as operating revenue. Why do you think the company is proposing this plan? Is this disclosure appropriate?
2. Corporations sometimes purchase their own stock. When asked why they do so, T-Shirts Plus management responds that the stock is undervalued. What advantage would T-Shirts Plus gain by buying and selling its own undervalued stock?
3. The treasurer of T-Shirts Plus wants to report a large loss as an extraordinary item because the company produced too much product and cannot sell it. Why do you think the treasurer wants to report the loss as extraordinary? Would that be acceptable?

Ethical Issue

← *Link Back to Chapter 6 (Accounting Principles).* High Plains Production Company is an independent oil producer in Midland, Texas. In February, geologists discovered a pool of oil that tripled the company's proven reserves. Prior to disclosing the new oil to the public, top managers of the company quietly bought most of High Plains' stock for themselves. After the discovery was announced, the High Plains' stock price rose from $7 to $52.

Required

1. Did High Plains managers behave ethically? Explain your answer.
2. Identify the accounting principle relevant to this situation. Review Chapter 6 if necessary.
3. Who was helped and who was harmed by management's action?

Financial Statement Case

Complex income statement, earnings per share
(Obj. 5)

Use the **Amazon.com** financial statements in Appendix A to answer the following questions.

Required

1. Study Amazon.com's income statement, which the company labels "consolidated statement of operations." *Consolidated* means that Amazon owns other companies. Amazon reported one "special" item of income on its income statement. What was the special item, and what was its amount for 2002? Was this special item a gain or a loss? How can you tell?
2. Show how Amazon.com computed earnings per share of $(0.39) for 2002.
3. Prepare a T-account to show the beginning and ending balances and all activity in Retained Earnings (Accumulated Deficit) for 2002.

Team Project

Required

Obtain the annual reports (or annual report data) of five well-known companies. You can get the reports either from your college library or by mailing a request directly to the company (allow two weeks for delivery). Or you can visit the Web site for this book (http://www.prenhall.com/horngren) or the SEC EDGAR database, which includes the financial reports of most well-known companies.

1. After selecting five companies, examine their income statements to search for the following items:
   a. Income from continuing operations
   b. Discontinued operations
   c. Extraordinary gains and losses
   d. Cumulative effects of accounting changes
   e. Net income or net loss
   f. Earnings-per-share data
2. Study the companies' balance sheets to see
   a. What classes of stock each company has issued.
   b. Which item carries a larger balance—the Common Stock account, or Paid-In Capital in Excess of Par (also labeled Additional Paid-In Capital).
   c. What percentage of each company's total stockholders' equity is made up of retained earnings.
   d. Whether the company has treasury stock. If so, how many shares and how much is the cost?
3. Examine each company's statement of stockholders' equity for evidence of
   a. Cash dividends
   b. Stock dividends (Some companies use the term *stock split* to refer to a large stock dividend.)
   c. Treasury stock purchases and sales
4. As directed by your instructor, either write a report or present your findings to your class. You may be unable to understand *everything* you find, but neither can the Wall Street analysts! You will be amazed at how much you have learned.

For Internet exercises, go to the Web site www.prenhall.com/horngren.

CHAPTER 15

Long-Term Liabilities

TIPS CHECK YOUR RESOURCES

- Visit the www.prenhall.com/horngren **Web site** for self-study quizzes, video clips, and other resources

- Try the **Quick Check** exercise at the end of the chapter to test your knowledge

- Learn the **key terms**

- Do the **Starter** exercises keyed in the margins

- Work the **mid-** and **end-of-chapter summary problems**

- Use the **Concept Links** to review material in other chapters

- Search the **CD** for review materials by chapter or by key word

- Watch the **tutorial videos** to review key concepts

LEARNING OBJECTIVES

1. Account for bonds payable transactions

2. Measure interest expense by the effective-interest method

3. Account for retirement and conversion of bonds payable

4. Report liabilities on the balance sheet

5. Show the advantages and disadvantages of borrowing

What's the best way to finance a company—issue stock or borrow the money? When the stock market declines, companies find it hard to sell their stock. They have to look to the bond market for cash to expand. For example, Amazon.com has borrowed by issuing convertible notes payable. Convertible bonds offer advantages for companies that need to borrow and for individuals with money to invest. By issuing convertible bonds, companies can borrow at lower interest rates than if they issued straight bonds. Then if a company's stock goes up, investors can swap the bonds for stock. Amazon gets a lower interest rate and investors can benefit if Amazon's stock price rises. They can convert the bonds into stock.

Accessing bond information has never been easier. You can log on to www.investinginbonds.com for topics such as What Are Bonds? Also,

Amazon.com

www.convertbond.com provides data on convertible bonds plus chat rooms and search functions. These information sources make it easier for companies to borrow and for people to make informed investment decisions.

Sources: Forbes, May 22, 2000, "Best of the Web," p. 86; Jennifer Ablan, "Volume of Convertible Bond Offerings Continues to Rise with Big Deals by Technology Concerns," *The Wall Street Journal*, July 13, 2000, p. C25. ■

■ Sitemap

Chapters 13 and 14 showed two ways to finance operations. Chapter 13 covered the stock accounts and additional paid-in capital, and Chapter 14 discussed profitable operations and retained earnings. This chapter shows the third way to finance a company: borrowing on long-term liabilities. The chapter appendix on the time value of money provides background on the valuation of long-term liabilities.

Before launching into accounting for bonds payable, let's compare stocks and bonds. The following chart shows how stocks and bonds differ.

Stocks	Bonds
1. Stock represents the *ownership* (equity) of the corporation.	1. Bonds represent a *liability* of the corporation.
2. Each shareholder is an *owner* of the corporation.	2. Each bondholder is a *creditor* of the corporation.
3. The corporation *may or may not* pay dividends.	3. The corporation *must* pay interest.
4. Dividends are *not* an expense of the corporation.	4. Interest is a *tax-deductible* expense of the corporation.
5. Corporation is *not* obligated to repay stock amounts to the shareholders.	5. Corporation *must* repay the bonds payable at maturity.

Bonds Payable
Groups of notes payable issued to multiple lenders called bondholders.

◉ Student Resource CD

bonds payable, bond pricing, market interest rate, present value, stated interest rate

Bonds: An Introduction

Well-known companies such as Amazon.com, Inc., and eBay cannot borrow billions from a single lender because no bank will loan that much to a single company. Then how do corporations borrow the huge amounts they need to expand? They issue bonds payable to the public. **Bonds payable** are groups of notes issued to multiple lenders, called bondholders. Amazon can borrow millions of dollars from thousands of individual investors. Each investor buys a modest amount of Amazon bonds.

Purchasers of the bonds each receive a bond certificate, which shows the borrower's name, exactly like a note payable. The certificate states the *principal*, which is the amount the company has borrowed. This figure, typically stated in units of $1,000, is also called the bond's maturity value, or par value. The bond obligates the issuing company to pay the holder the principal amount at a specific future date, called the maturity date.

Bondholders lend their money to earn interest. The bond certificate states the interest rate that the issuer will pay and the dates the interest payments are due (generally twice a year). Exhibit 15-1 shows an actual bond certificate issued by Washington Public Power Supply System (WPPSS).

Exhibit 15-1 Bond Certificate (Adapted)

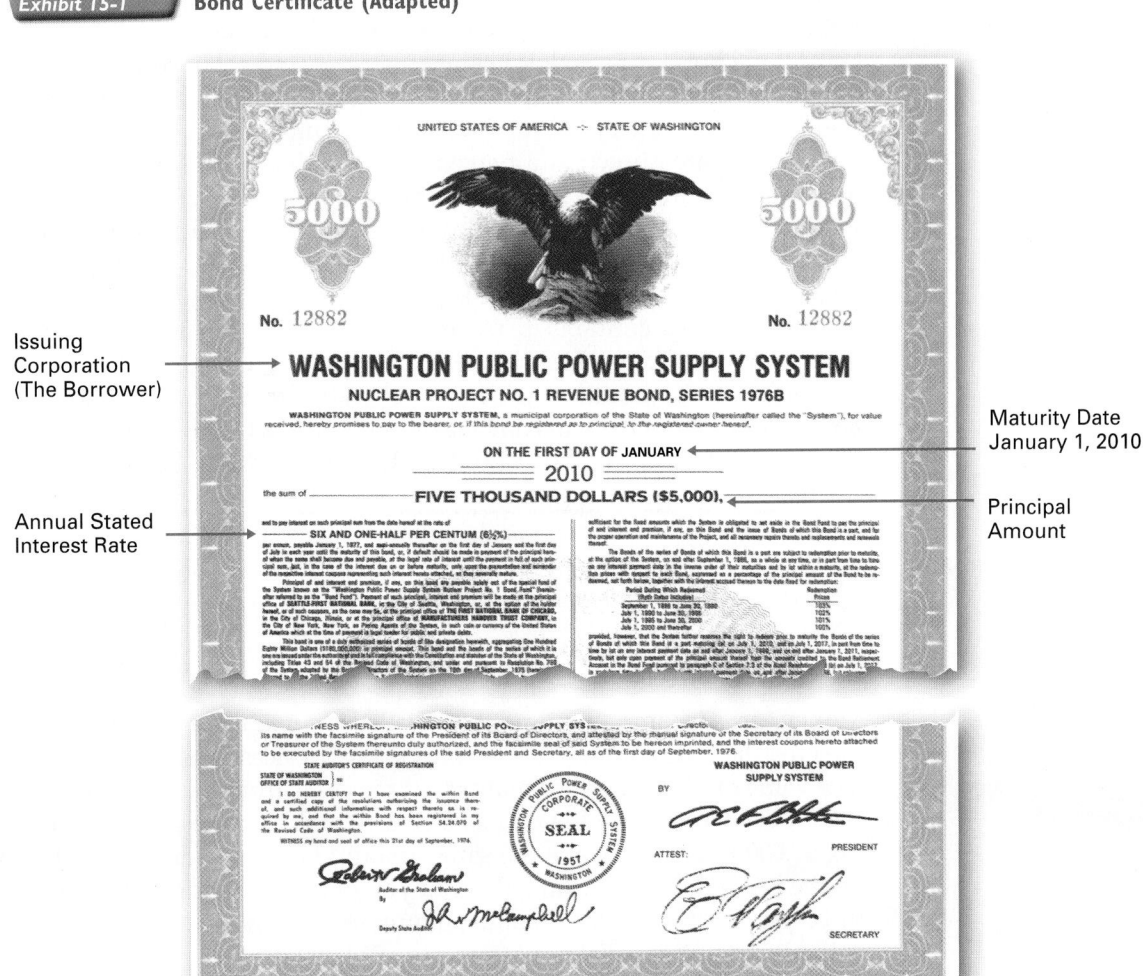

Issuing Corporation (The Borrower)

Maturity Date January 1, 2010

Principal Amount

Annual Stated Interest Rate

Review these bond fundamentals in Exhibit 15-1.

- *Principal amount* (also called maturity value, or par value). The amount the borrower must pay back to the lender.
- *Maturity date* The date on which the borrower must pay the principal amount to the lender.
- *Stated interest rate* The annual rate of interest that the borrower pays the lender.

Types of Bonds

All the bonds in a particular issue may mature at a specified time **(term bonds)**, or they may mature in installments **(serial bonds)**. Serial bonds are like installment notes payable.

Secured, or mortgage, bonds give the bondholder the right to take specified assets of the issuer (called *collateral*) if the company fails to pay interest or principal. A **mortgage** is an example of a secured note or bond. Unsecured bonds, called **debentures**, are backed only by the good faith of the borrower.

Bond Prices

A bond issued at a price above its maturity value is said to be issued at a **premium**, and a bond issued at a price below maturity value has a **discount**. As a bond nears maturity, its market price moves toward maturity value. On the

Term Bonds
Bonds that all mature at the same time for a particular issue.

Serial Bonds
Bonds that mature in installments over a period of time.

Mortgage
Borrower's promise to transfer the legal title to certain assets to the lender if the debt is not paid on schedule.

Debentures
Unsecured bonds backed only by the good faith of the borrower.

Premium
Excess of a bond's issue price over its maturity value. Also called **bond premium**.

Discount (on a Bond)
Excess of a bond's maturity value over its issue price. Also called a **bond discount**.

maturity date, the market value of a bond exactly equals its maturity value because the company pays that amount to retire the bond.

After a bond is issued, investors may buy and sell it through the bond market just as they buy and sell stocks through the stock market. The most famous bond market is the New York Exchange, which lists several thousand bonds. Bond prices are quoted at a percentage of their maturity value. For example, a $1,000 bond quoted at 100 is bought or sold for $1,000, which is 100% of its maturity value. The same bond quoted at 101.5 has a market price of $1,015 (101.5% of maturity value, or $1,000 × 1.015). A $1,000 bond quoted at 88.375 means 88.375% of $1,000, and it is priced at $883.75 ($1,000 × 0.88375).

Exhibit 15-2 contains price information for the bonds of Ohio Edison Company, taken from *The Wall Street Journal*. On this particular day, 12 of Ohio Edison's 9 1/2% bonds maturing in 2006 (indicated by 06) were traded. The bonds' highest price on this day was $795 ($1,000 × 0.795). The lowest price of the day was $784.50 ($1,000 × 0.7845). The closing price (last sale of the day) was $795.

✔ **Starter 15-1**

Exhibit 15-2

Bond Price Information for Ohio Edison Company (OhEd)

Bonds	Volume	High	Low	Close
OhEd 9 1/2 of 06	12	79.5	78.45	79.5

Present Value

The appendix to this chapter covers the time value of money in detail. ➡

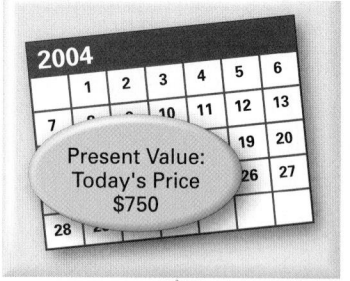

Money earns income over time, a fact called the *time value of money.* ← Let's examine how the time value of money affects bond prices. Assume that a bond with a face value of $1,000 reaches maturity three years from today and carries no interest. As an investor, would you pay $1,000 to purchase the bond? No, because paying $1,000 today to receive the same amount later provides you with no income on the investment. How much would you pay today in order to receive $1,000 in three years? The answer is some amount *less* than $1,000. Suppose $750 is a fair price. By investing $750 now to receive $1,000 later, you will earn $250 over the three years. The company that issued the bonds sees the transaction this way: It pays you $250 interest for the use of your $750 for three years.

The amount that a person would invest *at the present time* to receive a greater amount in the future is called the **present value**. In our example, $750 is the present value, and the $1,000 to be received in three years is the future amount.

Present value is always less than future value. The difference between present value and future value is interest. We show how to compute present value in the chapter appendix. If your instructor so directs you, study the appendix now.

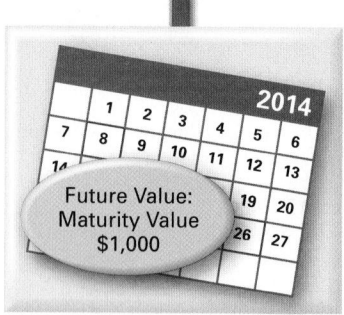

Present value is always less than future value.

Present Value
Amount a person would invest now to receive a greater amount in the future.

Stated Interest Rate
Interest rate that determines the amount of cash interest the borrower pays and the investor receives each year.

Market Interest Rate
Interest rate that investors demand in order to loan their money. Also called the **effective interest rate**.

Bond Interest Rates

Bonds are sold at market price, which is the maximum amount an investor will pay for a bond. Market price is the bond's present value, which is the sum of the present value of the principal payment plus the present value of all the stated interest payments, which may be semiannual, annual, or quarterly.

Two interest rates work together to set the price of a bond:

■ The **stated interest rate** is the interest rate that determines the amount of cash interest the borrower pays each year. The stated rate is printed on the bond and *does not change*. For example, Amazon.com's 10% notes payable have a stated interest rate of 10%. Thus, Amazon pays $1,000 of interest annually on each $10,000 bond. Each semiannual interest payment is $500 ($10,000 × 0.10 × 1/2).

■ The **market interest rate** is the rate investors demand for loaning their money. The market interest rate *varies* daily. A company may issue bonds with a stated interest rate that differs from the market interest rate.

Amazon.com may issue its 10% notes when the market rate has risen to 11%. Will the Amazon notes attract investors in this market? No, because investors can earn 11% on other bonds and notes. Therefore, investors will purchase Amazon notes only at a price less than maturity value. The difference between the lower price and the notes' maturity value is a *discount*.

✔ Starter 15-2

Conversely, if the market interest rate is 8%, Amazon's 10% notes will be so attractive that investors will pay more than maturity value for them. The difference between the higher price and maturity value is a *premium*. Exhibit 15-3 shows how the stated interest rate and the market interest rate work together to determine the price of a bond.

Example: Bond with a Stated Interest Rate of 8%				
Bond's Stated Interest Rate*		Market Interest Rate**		Issue Price of Bonds Payable
8%	=	8%	⇒	Maturity (par) value
8%	<	10%	⇒	Discount [price below maturity (par) value]
8%	>	6%	⇒	Premium [price above maturity (par) value]

*Determines the amount of each cash interest payment.
**Used to set the bond's market price.

Exhibit 15-3

Interaction of the Stated Interest Rate and the Market Interest Rate to Determine the Price of a Bond

✔ Starter 15-3

✔ Starter 15-4

☐ Bonds: Introduction
■ **Issuing Bonds Payable**
☐ Effective-Interest Method
☐ Additional Bond Topics
☐ Bonds versus Stock
☐ Lease Liabilities
☐ Appendix: Time Value of Money

Issuing Bonds Payable to Borrow Money

The basic entry to record issuing bonds payable debits Cash and credits Bonds Payable. The company may issue bonds for three different bond prices:

- At *maturity (par)* value
- At a *discount*
- At a *premium*

We begin with the simplest case: issuing bonds at maturity (par) value.

Issuing Bonds Payable at Maturity (Par) Value

Suppose Amazon.com, Inc., has $50,000 of 8% bonds payable that mature in 5 years. Assume that Amazon issues these bonds at maturity (par) value on January 1, 2002. The issuance entry is

2002			
Jan. 1	Cash	50,000	
	Bonds Payable...............		50,000
	Issued bonds payable.		

Amazon, the borrower, makes this one-time journal entry to record the receipt of cash and the issuance of bonds payable. Interest payments occur each January 1 and July 1. Amazon's entry to record the first semiannual interest payment is

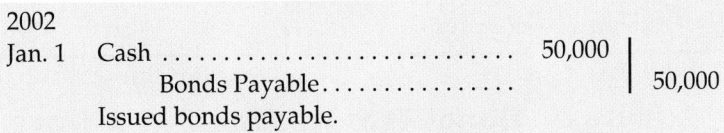

2002			
July 1	Interest Expense ($50,000 × 0.08 × 6/12)	2,000	
	Cash		2,000
	Paid semiannual interest.		

At maturity, Amazon.com will record payment of the bonds as follows:

2007			
Jan. 1	Bonds Payable....................	50,000	
	Cash		50,000
	Paid off bonds payable at maturity.		

Account for bonds payable transactions

Student Resource CD

amortizing bonds, bonds payable, bond discount, bond premium, stated interest rate

✔ Starter 15-5

Now we turn to the issuance of bonds payable at a discount.

Issuing Bonds Payable at a Discount

Bonds are often issued at a discount. We know that market conditions may force the issuing corporation to accept a discount price for its bonds. Suppose Amazon.com, Inc., issues $100,000 of its 9%, five-year bonds when the market interest rate is 9 1/2%. The market price of the bonds drops to 98, which means 98% of par value. Amazon receives $98,000 ($100,000 × 0.98) at issuance and makes the following journal entry:

```
2002
Jan. 1   Cash  ($100,000 × 0.98) . . . . . . . . . . . . .   98,000
         Discount on Bonds Payable. . . . . . . . .    2,000
             Bonds Payable. . . . . . . . . . . . . . .              100,000
         Issued bonds payable at a discount.
```

After posting, the bond accounts have these balances:

Bonds Payable	Discount on Bonds Payable
100,000	2,000

Discount on Bonds Payable is a contra account to Bonds Payable. Bonds Payable minus the discount gives the carrying amount of the bonds. The relationship between Bonds Payable and the Discount account is similar to the relationship between Equipment and Accumulated Depreciation. Amazon would report these bonds payable as follows:

```
Long-term liabilities:
    Bonds payable . . . . . . . . . . . . . . . . . . . . . . . . . . . . . . . .   $100,000
    Less: Discount on bonds payable . . . . . . . . . . . . . . . .     (2,000)    $98,000
```

INTEREST EXPENSE ON BONDS PAYABLE ISSUED AT A DISCOUNT   We saw that the stated interest rate and the market interest rate may differ. The market interest rate was 9 1/2% when Amazon.com issued its 9% bonds. The 1/2% interest-rate difference created the $2,000 discount on the bonds. Investors were willing to pay only $98,000 for a $100,000, 9% bond when they could purchase similar bonds and earn 9 1/2% on them. Amazon thus borrowed $98,000 cash but must pay $100,000 cash when the bonds mature five years later.

What happens to the $2,000 discount? The discount is additional interest expense to Amazon. It raises Amazon's interest expense on the bonds to the market interest rate of 9 1/2%. For each accounting period over the life of the bonds, the discount is accounted for as interest expense through a process called *amortization*. Amortization is the gradual reduction of an item over time.

STRAIGHT-LINE AMORTIZATION OF BOND DISCOUNT   We can amortize a bond discount by dividing it into equal amounts for each interest period. This method is called *straight-line amortization*. In our example, the initial discount is $2,000, and there are 10 semiannual interest periods during the bonds' 5-year life.

Therefore, 1/10 of the $2,000 ($200) of bond discount is amortized each interest period. Amazon.com's first semiannual interest entry is[1]

```
2002
July 1   Interest Expense ...................   4,700
             Cash ($100,000 × 0.09 × 6/12) ...          4,500
             Discount on Bonds Payable
                 ($2,000/10)................              200
         Paid semiannual interest and amortized bond discount.
```

Interest expense of $4,700 for the six-month period is the sum of

- The stated interest ($4,500, which is paid in cash)
- *Plus* the amortization of discount ($200)

 ✔ **Starter 15-6**

Discount on Bonds Payable is credited to amortize its balance. Ten amortization entries will decrease the discount to zero, and the carrying amount of the bonds payable will increase to the maturity value of $100,000.

Finally, the entry to pay off the bonds at maturity is

```
2007
Jan. 1   Bonds Payable....................   100,000
             Cash .....................                100,000
         Paid off bonds payable at maturity.
```

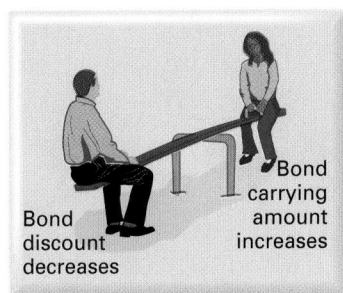

How much interest expense will **Amazon** record each year on these bonds? How much cash interest will Amazon pay each year? What causes the difference?

Answer: Interest expense each year: $9,400 ($4,700 × 2)
           Cash interest paid each year: $9,000 ($4,500 × 2)

The difference is caused by amortization of the bond discount.

Issuing Bonds Payable at a Premium

The issuance of bonds at a premium is rare because companies don't like to pay a stated interest rate higher than the market rate. To illustrate a bond premium, let's change the Amazon.com example. Assume that the market interest rate is 8% when Amazon issues its 9%, five-year bonds. Because 9% bonds are attractive in this market, investors will pay a premium to acquire them. Suppose the bonds are priced at 104 (104% of maturity value). In that case, Amazon receives $104,000 cash upon issuance. The entry to borrow money and issue bonds is

```
2002
Jan. 1   Cash ($100,000 × 1.04) ............   104,000
             Bonds Payable ..............             100,000
             Premium on Bonds Payable ...               4,000
         Issued bonds payable at a premium.
```

---

[1]Some accountants record the payment of interest and the amortization of bond discount in two separate entries, as follows:

```
2002
July 1   Interest Expense.................................   4,500
             Cash ($100,000 × 0.09 × 6/12)...............           4,500
         Paid semiannual interest.

July 1   Interest Expense.................................     200
             Discount on Bonds Payable ($2,000/10).......            200
         Amortized discount on bonds payable.
```

After posting, the bond accounts have the following balances:

Bonds Payable		Premium on Bonds Payable	
	100,000		4,000

Premium on Bonds Payable is added to Bonds Payable to determine the carrying amount of the bonds. Amazon.com would report these bonds payable as follows:

Long-term liabilities:		
Bonds payable	$100,000	
Plus: Premium on bonds payable	4,000	$104,000

INTEREST EXPENSE ON BONDS PAYABLE ISSUED AT A PREMIUM

The 1% difference between the 9% stated interest rate on the bonds and the 8% market interest rate creates the $4,000 premium. Amazon borrows $104,000 cash but must pay only $100,000 at maturity. The premium is like a savings of interest expense to Amazon. The premium cuts Amazon's cost of borrowing and reduces interest expense to 8%, the market rate. We amortize the bond premium as a decrease in interest expense over the life of the bonds.

STRAIGHT-LINE AMORTIZATION OF BOND PREMIUM

In our example, the beginning premium is $4,000, and there are 10 semiannual interest periods during the bonds' 5-year life. Therefore, 1/10 of the $4,000 ($400) of bond premium is amortized each interest period. Amazon.com's first semiannual interest entry is[2]

2002				
July 1	Interest Expense	4,100		
	Premium on Bonds Payable ($4,000/10)..	400		
	Cash ($100,000 × 0.09 × 6/12)		4,500	
	Paid semiannual interest and amortized bond premium.			

✔ Starter 15-7

Interest expense of $4,100 is

- The stated interest ($4,500, which is paid in cash)
- *Minus* the amortization of the premium

Consider bonds issued at a discount. Which will be greater, the cash interest paid per period or the amount of interest expense? Answer the same question for bonds issued at a premium.

Answer: Discount: Interest expense > Stated interest paid
              Premium: Stated interest paid > Interest expense

---

[2]The payment of interest and the amortization of bond premium can be recorded in separate entries as follows:

2002			
July 1	Interest Expense..................................	4,500	
	Cash ($100,000 × 0.09 × 6/12).................		4,500
	Paid semiannual interest.		
July 1	Premium on Bonds Payable ($4,000/10)	400	
	Interest Expense...........................		400
	Amortized premium on bonds payable.		

Reporting Bonds Payable

Bonds payable are reported on the balance sheet at maturity value plus bond premium or minus bond discount. For example, in the preceding example of a bond premium, Amazon.com would report the following on its balance sheet at December 31, 2002:

Long-term liabilities:		
Bonds payable....................................	$100,000	
Plus: Premium on bonds payable [$4,000 − (2 × $400)]...	3,200	$103,200

Over the life of the bonds, 10 amortization entries will decrease the premium to zero. The payment at maturity will debit Bonds Payable and credit cash for $100,000.

Adjusting Entries for Interest Expense

Companies issue bonds when they need cash. The interest payments seldom occur on December 31 (or the end of the fiscal year). So interest expense must be accrued at the end of the period to measure income accurately. → The accrual entry should include the amortization of any bond discount or premium.

Xenon Corporation issued $100,000 of 8%, 10-year bonds at a $2,000 discount on October 1, 2006. The interest payments occur on March 31 and September 30 each year. On December 31, Xenon records interest for three months (October, November, and December) as follows:

The adjusting entry for bond interest expense follows the pattern for the adjusting entries for other accrued liabilities, as in Chapters 3 (p. 105) and 11 (p. 450), except for the addition of the amortization of the premium or discount.

2006			
Dec. 31	Interest Expense	2,050	
	Interest Payable ($100,000 × 0.08 × 3/12)........		2,000
	Discount on Bonds Payable ($2,000/10 × 3/12)..		50
	Accrued three months' interest and amortized bond discount.		

Interest Payable is credited for three months (October, November, and December). Discount on Bonds Payable must also be amortized for these three months.

Xenon's balance sheet at December 31, 2006, reports Interest Payable of $2,000 as a current liability. Bonds Payable are shown as follows:

Long-term liabilities:		
Bonds payable....................................	$100,000	
Less: Discount on bonds payable ($2,000 − $50)	(1,950)	$98,050

Observe that the bonds' carrying amount increases by $50. The bonds' carrying amount continues to increase until it reaches $100,000 at maturity, when the discount will be fully amortized.

The next semiannual interest payment occurs on March 31, 2007:

2007			
Mar. 31	Interest Expense	2,050	
	Interest Payable................................	2,000	
	Cash ($100,000 × 0.08 × 6/12)		4,000
	Discount on Bonds Payable ($2,000/10 × 3/12)..		50
	Paid semiannual interest and amortized bond discount.		

✔ **Starter 15-8**

✔ **Starter 15-9**

Amortization of a bond premium is similar except that Premium on Bonds Payable is debited.

Decision Guidelines

LONG-TERM LIABILITIES—PART A

Amazon.com has borrowed some money by issuing bonds payable. What type of bonds did Amazon issue? How much cash must Amazon pay each interest period? At maturity? The Decision Guidelines address these and other questions.

Decision	Guidelines
When will you pay off the bonds • At maturity? • In installments?	Type of bond to issue: • Term bonds • Serial bonds
Are the bonds secured? • Yes • No	Then they are • Mortgage or secured bonds • Debenture or unsecured bonds
How are bond prices • Quoted? • Determined?	 • As a percentage of maturity value (Example: A $500,000 bond priced at $510,000 would be quoted at 102 ($510,000 ÷ $500,000 = 1.02) • Present value of the future principal amount to pay plus present value of the future interest payments (see chapter appendix)
What are the two interest rates used for bonds?	• The *stated interest rate* determines the amount of cash interest the borrower pays. This interest rate does not change. • The *market interest rate* is the rate investors demand for loaning their money. The market interest rate determines the borrower's true rate of interest expense. This rate varies daily.
What causes a bond to be priced at • Maturity (par) value? • A premium? • A discount?	When the bonds are issued, • The *stated* interest rate on the bond *equals* the *market* interest rate • The *stated* interest rate on the bond is *greater than* the *market* interest rate • The *stated* interest rate on the bond is *less than* the *market* interest rate
What is the relationship between interest expense and interest payments when bonds are issued at • Maturity (par) value? • A premium? • A discount?	 • Interest expense *equals* Interest payment • Interest expense is *less than* Interest payment • Interest expense is *greater than* Interest payment
How to report bonds payable on the balance sheet?	Maturity (par) value $\left\{\begin{array}{c}\text{+ Premium on bonds payable}\\\text{or}\\\text{− Discount on bonds payable}\end{array}\right.$

MID-CHAPTER *Summary Problem*

CHECK YOUR RESOURCES

Assume that Alabama Power Company has an issue of 9% bonds payable that mature on May 1, 2028. The bonds are dated May 1, 2008, and Alabama Power pays interest each April 30 and October 31.

Required

1. Will the bonds be issued at par, at a premium, or at a discount if the market interest rate on the date of issuance is 8%? If the market interest rate is 10%?

2. Assume that Alabama Power issued $1,000,000 of the bonds at 104 on May 1, 2008.
   a. Record issuance of the bonds.
   b. Record the interest payment and amortization of the premium on October 31, 2008. Use the straight-line method of amortization.
   c. Accrue interest and amortize premium on December 31, 2008.
   d. Show how the company would report the bonds on the balance sheet at December 31, 2008.
   e. Record the interest payment and amortization of premium on April 30, 2009.

Solution

Requirement 1

Market Interest Rate	Bond Price
8%	Premium
10%	Discount

Requirement 2

2008
a. May 1   Cash ($1,000,000 × 1.04)..................... $1,040,000
   Bonds Payable........................ 1,000,000
   Premium on Bonds Payable 40,000
   Issued bonds at a premium.

b. Oct. 31   Interest Expense 44,000
   Premium on Bonds Payable ($40,000/40)...... 1,000
   Cash ($1,000,000 × 0.09 × 6/12) 45,000
   Paid semiannual interest and amortized bond premium.

c. Dec. 31   Interest Expense 14,667
   Premium on Bonds Payable
   ($40,000/40 × 2/6) 333
   Interest Payable
   ($1,000,000 × 0.09 × 2/12) 15,000
   Accrued interest and amortized bond premium.

d. Long-term liabilities:
   Bonds payable, 9% $1,000,000
   Premium on bonds payable
   ($40,000 − $1,000 − $333) 38,667 $1,038,667

2009
e. Apr. 30   Interest Expense 29,333
   Interest Payable 15,000
   Premium on Bonds Payable ($40,000/40 × 4/6) 667
   Cash ($1,000,000 × 0.09 × 6/12) 45,000
   Paid semiannual interest and amortized bond premium.

Effective-Interest Method of Amortization

We began with the straight-line amortization method to introduce the concept of amortizing bonds. However, that method has a theoretical weakness. Under the straight-line method, each period's interest expense is the same dollar amount. But over their life, the bonds' carrying amount moves toward maturity. The amount of interest expense should also increase or decrease as the bonds move toward maturity.

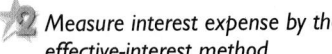 *Measure interest expense by the effective-interest method*

Generally accepted accounting principles require that interest expense be measured using the *effective-interest method* unless the straight-line amounts are similar. In that case, either method is permitted. Total interest expense over the life of the bonds is the same under both methods. We now show how the effective-interest method works.

Effective-Interest Method for a Bond Discount

Assume that eBay Inc. issues $100,000 of 9% bonds at a time when the market rate of interest is 10%. These bonds mature in 5 years and pay interest semiannually, so there are 10 semiannual interest payments. The issue price of the bonds is $96,149,[3] and the discount on these bonds is $3,851 ($100,000 − $96,149). Exhibit 15-4 shows how to measure interest expense by the effective-interest method. (You will need an amortization table to account for bonds by the effective-interest method.)

Exhibit 15-4   Effective-Interest Method for a Bond Discount

PANEL A—Bond Data
Maturity value—$100,000
Stated interest rate—9%
Interest paid—4 1/2% semiannually, $4,500 ($100,000 × 0.045)
Market interest rate at time of issue—10% annually, 5% semiannually
Issue price—$96,149 on January 1, 2005

PANEL B—Amortization Table

	A	B	C	D	E
		Interest *Expense*			
	Interest	(5% of			
End of	*Payment*	preceding			Bond
Semiannual	(4 1/2% of	bond	Discount	Discount	Carrying
Interest	maturity	carrying	Amortization	Balance	Amount
Period	value)	amount)	(B − A)	(D − C)	($100,000 − D)
Jan. 1, 2005				$3,851	$ 96,149
July 1	$4,500	$4,807	$307	3,544	96,456
Jan. 1, 2006	4,500	4,823	323	3,221	96,779
July 1	4,500	4,839	339	2,882	97,118
Jan. 1, 2007	4,500	4,856	356	2,526	97,474
July 1	4,500	4,874	374	2,152	97,848
Jan. 1, 2008	4,500	4,892	392	1,760	98,240
July 1	4,500	4,912	412	1,348	98,652
Jan. 1, 2009	4,500	4,933	433	915	99,085
July 1	4,500	4,954	454	461	99,539
Jan. 1, 2010	4,500	4,961*	461	0	100,000

*Adjusted for effect of rounding.

Notes

- *Column A* The interest payments are constant—fixed by the stated interest rate and the bonds' maturity value.
- *Column B* The interest expense each period is the preceding bond carrying amount multiplied by the market interest rate. Interest expense increases as the bond carrying amount (E) increases.
- *Column C* The excess of interest expense (B) over interest payment (A) is the discount amortization.
- *Column D* The discount decreases by the amount of amortization for the period (C). Balance of discount + Bonds' carrying amount = Bonds' maturity value ($100,000) at all times.
- *Column E* The bonds' carrying amount increases from $96,149 at issuance to $100,000 at maturity.

---

[3]We compute this present value in the chapter appendix.

The *accounts* debited and credited under the effective-interest method and the straight-line method are the same. Only the *amounts* differ.

Exhibit 15-4 gives the amounts for all the bond transactions of eBay. Let's begin with issuance of the bonds payable on January 1, 2005, and the first interest payment on July 1. Entries follow, using amounts from the respective lines of Exhibit 15-4.

2005
Jan. 1 Cash (column E).   96,149
       Discount on Bonds Payable (column D). .   3,851
          Bonds Payable (maturity value).   100,000
       Issued bonds at a discount.

2005
July 1 Interest Expense (column B).   4,807
       Discount on Bonds Payable
          (column C).   307
          Cash (column A).   4,500
       Paid semiannual interest and amortized bond discount.

✔ **Starter 15-10**

Stop & Think

How much interest expense will **eBay** record for 2005 on these bonds? How much cash interest will eBay pay each year? What causes the difference?

Answer: Interest expense for 2005: $9,630 ($4,807 + $4,823)

          Cash interest paid each year: $9,000 ($4,500 × 2)

The difference is caused by amortization of the bond discount.

Exhibit 15-5 diagrams the carrying amount of bonds issued at a discount. Observe how it rises to maturity. All amounts are taken from Exhibit 15-4.

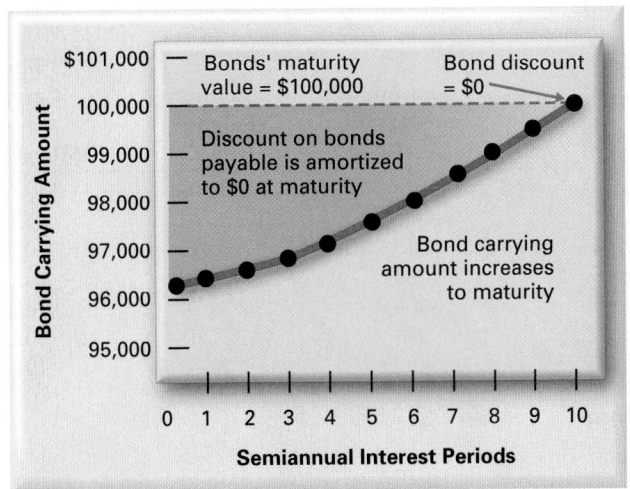

Exhibit 15-5

Carrying Amount for Bonds Payable Issued at a Discount

Effective-Interest Method for a Bond Premium

eBay may issue its bonds payable at a premium. Assume that eBay issues $100,000 of 5-year, 9% bonds when the market interest rate is 8%. The bonds' issue price is $104,100,[4] and the premium is $4,100.

---

[4]Again, we compute the present value of the bonds in the chapter appendix.

Exhibit 15-6 provides the data for all the bond transactions of eBay. Let's begin with issuance of the bonds on January 1, 2005, and the first interest payment on July 1. These entries follow.

```
2005
Jan. 1  Cash (column E)................... $104,100
            Bonds Payable (maturity value)..          100,000
            Premium on Bonds Payable
                (column D)..................           4,100
        Issued bonds at a premium.
```

```
2005
July 1  Interest Expense (column B) ........     4,164
            Premium on Bonds Payable (column C)    336
                Cash (column A)..............           4,500
        Paid semiannual interest and amortized bond premium.
```

Exhibit 15-6   **Effective-Interest Method for a Bond Premium**

PANEL A—Bond Data

Maturity value—$100,000
Stated interest rate—9%
Interest paid—4 1/2% semiannually, $4,500 ($100,000 × 0.045)
Market interest rate at time of issue—8% annually, 4% semiannually
Issue price—$104,100 on January 1, 2005

PANEL B—Amortization Table

	A	B	C	D	E
End of Semiannual Interest Period	**Interest Payment (4 1/2% of maturity value)**	**Interest *Expense* (4% of preceding bond carrying amount)**	**Premium Amortization (A – B)**	**Premium Balance (D – C)**	**Bond Carrying Amount ($100,000 + D)**
Jan. 1, 2005				$4,100	$104,100
July 1	$4,500	$4,164	$336	3,764	103,764
Jan. 1, 2006	4,500	4,151	349	3,415	103,415
July 1	4,500	4,137	363	3,052	103,052
Jan. 1, 2007	4,500	4,122	378	2,674	102,674
July 1	4,500	4,107	393	2,281	102,281
Jan. 1, 2008	4,500	4,091	409	1,872	101,872
July 1	4,500	4,075	425	1,447	101,447
Jan. 1, 2009	4,500	4,058	442	1,005	101,005
July 1	4,500	4,040	460	545	100,545
Jan. 1, 2010	4,500	3,955*	545	0	100,000

*Adjusted for effect of rounding.

Notes

- *Column A* The interest payments are constant—fixed by the stated interest rate and the bonds' maturity value.
- *Column B* The interest expense each period is the preceding bond carrying amount multiplied by the market interest rate. Interest expense decreases as the bond carrying amount decreases.
- *Column C* The excess of interest payment (A) over interest expense (B) is the premium amortization.
- *Column D* The premium balance decreases by the amount of amortization for the period. Bonds' carrying amount – Premium balance = Bonds' maturity value ($100,000) at all times.
- *Column E* The bonds' carrying amount decreases from $104,100 at issuance to $100,000 at maturity.

How much interest expense will **eBay** record for 2005 on these bonds? How much cash interest will eBay pay each year? What causes the difference?

Answer: Interest expense for 2005: $8,315 ($4,164 + $4,151)

Cash interest paid each year: $9,000 ($4,500 × 2)

The difference is caused by amortization of the bond premium.

✔ **Starter 15-11**

Exhibit 15-7 diagrams the carrying amount of the bonds issued at a premium. Observe how it falls to maturity. All amounts are taken from Exhibit 15-6.

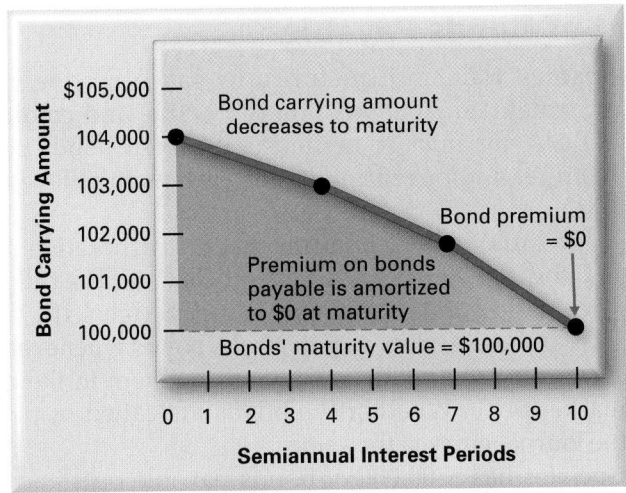

Exhibit 15-7

Carrying Amount for Bonds Payable Issued at a Premium

Additional Bond Topics

Companies that issue bonds payable face additional issues, such as

- Issuance of bonds payable between interest dates
- Retirement of bonds payable
- Convertible bonds payable
- Advantages and disadvantages of issuing bonds versus stock

☐ Bonds: Introduction
☐ Issuing Bonds Payable
☐ Effective-Interest Method
■ **Additional Bond Topics**
☐ Bonds versus Stock
☐ Lease Liabilities
☐ Appendix: Time Value of Money

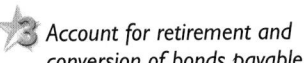
Account for retirement and conversion of bonds payable

Student ResourceCD

callable bonds, convertible bonds, debenture

Issuing Bonds Payable Between Interest Dates

In all the examples we've seen thus far, companies have issued bonds payable on an interest date, such as January 1. Corporations can also issue bonds between interest dates. That creates a complication.

Suppose Intel Corporation has $100,000 of 8% bonds payable that are dated January 1. That means the interest starts accruing on January 1. Suppose Intel issues these bonds on April 1. How should we account for the interest for January, February, and March? At issuance on April 1, Intel collects three months' accrued interest from the bondholder and records the issuance of bonds payable as follows:

2005			
April 1	Cash............................	102,000	
	Bonds Payable		100,000
	Interest Payable		
	($100,000 × 0.08 × 3/12)......		2,000
	Issued bonds two months after the date of the bonds.		

On the next interest date, Intel will pay six months' interest to whoever owns the bonds at that time. But Intel will record interest expense only for the three months the bonds have been outstanding (April, May, and June). To allocate interest expense to the correct months, Intel makes this entry on July 1 for the customary six-month interest payment:

```
2005
July 1  Interest Payable (see entry on April 1) ...   2,000
        Interest Expense (for April, May, June)...     2,000
            Cash ($100,000 × 0.08 × 6/12) .......              4,000
        Paid six months' interest.
```

✔ **Starter 15-12**

Retirement of Bonds Payable

Normally, companies wait until maturity to pay off, or *retire*, their bonds payable. The retirement entry debits Bonds Payable and credits Cash for the maturity value. But companies sometimes retire their bonds payable prior to maturity. The main reason for retiring bonds early is to relieve the pressure of paying interest.

Callable Bonds
Bonds that the issuer may call or pay off at a specified price whenever the issuer wants.

Some bonds are **callable**, which means that the corporation may *call*, or pay off, those bonds at a specified price whenever it chooses. The call price is usually 100 or a few percentage points above par value, perhaps 101 or 102. Callable bonds give the issuer the flexibility to pay off the bonds whenever it is beneficial. An alternative to calling the bonds is to purchase them in the open market at their current market price. Whether the bonds are called or purchased in the open market, the journal entry is the same.

ETrade Associates has $700,000 of bonds payable outstanding with a discount of $30,000. Lower interest rates have convinced management to pay off these bonds now. Assume that the bonds are callable at 103. If the market price of the bonds is 95, will ETrade call the bonds or purchase them in the open market? The market price is lower than the call price, so ETrade will pay off the bonds at their market price. Retiring the bonds at 95 results in a gain of $5,000, computed as follows:

Maturity value of bonds being retired	$700,000
Less: Discount	(30,000)
Carrying amount of bonds payable	670,000
Market price ($700,000 × 0.95).....................	665,000
Gain on retirement of bonds payable..............	$ 5,000

The following entry records retirement of the bonds, immediately after an interest date:

```
June 30  Bonds Payable .................   700,000
             Discount on Bonds Payable ...              30,000
             Cash ($700,000 × 0.95) ........           665,000
             Gain on Retirement
                 of Bonds Payable ..........            5,000
         Retired bonds payable.
```

✔ **Starter 15-13**

The entry removes the bonds payable and the related discount from the accounts and records a gain on retirement. Any existing premium would be removed with a debit. If ETrade Associates retired only half of these bonds, the accountant would remove only half the discount or premium.

When retiring bonds before maturity, follow these steps: (1) Record partial-period amortization of discount or premium if the retirement date does not fall on an interest date. (2) Write off the portion of Discount or Premium that relates to the bonds being retired. (3) Compute gain or loss on retirement.

Convertible Bonds Payable

As the chapter-opening story indicates, convertible bonds and notes are popular. **Convertible bonds** and notes payable may be converted into the common stock of the issuing company at the option of the investor. These bonds, called convertible bonds, combine the benefits of interest and principal on the bonds with the opportunity for a gain on the stock. The conversion feature is so attractive that investors accept a lower interest rate than they would on non-convertible bonds. For example, Amazon.com's convertible bonds payable carry an interest rate of only 4 3/4%. The low cash interest payments benefit Amazon.com.

Convertible Bonds
Bonds that may be converted into the common stock of the issuing company at the option of the investor.

The issuance of convertible bonds payable is recorded like any other debt: Debit Cash and credit Convertible Bonds Payable. Then, if the market price of Amazon's stock gets above the market value of the bonds, the bondholders will convert the bonds into stock. The corporation records conversion by removing the bond accounts and crediting the stock accounts. The carrying amount of the bonds becomes the book value of the newly issued stock. There is no gain or loss.

Assume the Amazon bondholders convert $100,000 of the bonds into 2,000 shares of Amazon's common stock, which has a par value of $0.01 (1 cent) per share. Assume further that the carrying amount of the Amazon bonds is $90,000; thus, there is a discount of $10,000. To record the conversion, Amazon would make this journal entry:

May 14	Bonds Payable...................	100,000	
	Discount on Bonds Payable		
	($100,000 − $90,000).........		10,000
	Common Stock (2,000 × $0.01)...		20
	Paid-in Capital in Excess of		
	Par—Common..............		89,980
	Recorded conversion of bonds payable.		

The entry closes the bonds payable account and its related discount. The carrying amount of the notes ($90,000) becomes the amount of new stockholders' equity ($89,980 + $20).

✔ **Starter 15-14**

Reporting Liabilities on the Balance Sheet

As we have seen, bonds come in all varieties. Companies report their bonds and notes payable among the liabilities on the balance sheet, divided between the current and long-term categories.

 Report liabilities on the balance sheet

Serial bonds are payable in installments. The portion payable within one year is a current liability, and the remaining debt is long-term. For example, assume that Toys "Я" Us has $500,000 of notes payable maturing in various amounts in future years. Assume that the portion payable next year is $200,000. This amount is a current liability, and the remaining $300,000 is a long-term liability. Toys "Я" Us would report the following among its liabilities:

Current liabilities:	
Notes payable, current	$200,000
Long-term liabilities:	
Note payable, long-term.	300,000

Bonds payable are reported in a similar fashion.

Advantages and Disadvantages: Bonds versus Stock

✔ **Starter 15-15**

☐ Bonds: Introduction
☐ Issuing Bonds Payable
☐ Effective-Interest Method
☐ Additional Bond Topics
■ **Bonds versus Stock**
☐ Lease Liabilities
☐ Appendix: Time Value of Money

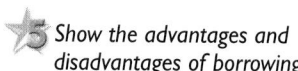
5 *Show the advantages and disadvantages of borrowing*

Earnings per share (EPS) is a company's net income for each share of outstanding common stock (Chapter 14, p. 557). EPS may be the most important figure on the income statement.

Borrowing by issuing bonds payable carries a risk: The company may be unable to pay off the bonds. Why then do companies borrow so heavily? Because bonds are a cheaper source of money than stock. Borrowing can help a company increase its earnings per share of common stock. Companies thus face this decision: How shall we finance the expansion of the company?

Exhibit 15-8 shows the earnings-per-share (EPS) advantage of borrowing. ← Suppose that Vista.com, an Internet startup, has net income of $300,000 and 100,000 shares of common stock outstanding. Earnings per share of common stock is $3.00 ($300,000/100,000 shares). Vista needs $500,000 for expansion and the company is considering two finance plans:

- Plan 1 is to borrow $500,000 at 10% (issue $500,000 of 10% bonds payable).
- Plan 2 is to issue 50,000 shares of common stock for $500,000.

Vista management believes the new cash can be used to earn income of $200,000 before interest and taxes.

EPS is higher if Vista.com borrows. If all goes well, Vista can earn more on the investment ($90,000) than the interest it pays on the bonds ($50,000). Earning more income on borrowed money than the related interest expense increases the earnings for common stockholders and is called using **leverage**. It is widely used to increase earnings per share of common stock.

Exhibit 15-8

Earnings-per-Share Advantage of Borrowing versus Issuing Stock

	Plan 1 Borrow $500,000 at 10%	Plan 2 Issue $500,000 of Common Stock
Net income before expansion.	$300,000	$300,000
Expected income on the new project before		
interest and income tax expenses	$200,000	$200,000
Less: Interest expense ($500,000 × 0.10)	(50,000)	0
Project income before income tax	150,000	200,000
Less: Income tax expense (40%).	(60,000)	(80,000)
Project net income	90,000	120,000
Total company net income	$390,000	$420,000
Earnings per share after expansion:		
Plan 1 ($390,000/100,000 shares).	$3.90	
Plan 2 ($420,000/150,000 shares).		$2.80

✔ **Starter 15-16**

Leverage
Earning more income on borrowed money than the related interest expense, thereby increasing the earnings for the owners of the business.

Borrowing can increase EPS, but borrowing has its disadvantages. Interest expense may be high enough to eliminate net income and lead to a cash shortage or even bankruptcy. This happens to lots of ambitious companies. Borrowing creates liabilities that must be paid during bad years as well as good years.

Lease Liabilities

A **lease** is a rental agreement in which the tenant (**lessee**) obtains the use of an asset by paying rent to the property owner (**lessor**). Leasing can avoid having to make a large initial cash down payment. Accountants divide leases into two types: operating leases and capital leases.

Operating Leases

Operating leases include many apartment leases and car-rental agreements. An operating lease gives the lessee use of an asset but no continuing right to the asset. The lessor keeps the usual rewards and risks of owning the leased asset. To account for an operating lease, the lessee debits Rent Expense and credits Cash for the amount of each lease payment. The lessee's books report no leased asset and no lease liability. This is why lessees prefer operating leases over capital leases. They report no liability.

Capital Leases

A capital lease requires the lessee to record both an asset and a lease liability. Capital leases are both long-term and noncancelable. A **capital lease** meets any *one* of the following criteria:

1. The lease transfers title of the leased asset to the lessee at the end of the lease term. Thus, the lessee becomes the legal owner of the leased asset.
2. The lease contains a *bargain purchase option*. The lessee can be expected to purchase the leased asset and become its legal owner.
3. The lease term is 75% or more of the estimated useful life of the leased asset. The lessee therefore uses up most of the leased asset's service potential.
4. The present value of the lease payments is 90% or more of the market value of the leased asset. In effect, the lease payments operate as installment payments for the leased asset.

Only those leases that meet *none* of these criteria are accounted for as operating leases.

Accounting for a Capital Lease

Accounting for a capital lease is like accounting for a purchase of a long-term asset. The lessee records an asset and a lease liability even though the lessee may never actually own the property.

Safeway, the grocery chain, leases buildings for its stores. Suppose Safeway leases a store building for a 20-year period. This lease is similar to purchasing the building on an installment plan.

Suppose Safeway's liability under this capital lease totals $1,000,000. The lease liability measures Safeway's cost of the building. Safeway makes this entry at the beginning of the lease:

```
2006
Jan. 1   Building ...................  1,000,000
              Lease Liability...........             1,000,000
         Acquired building under a capital lease.
```

During the lease period, Safeway will report both the building and the lease liability on its balance sheet.

Lease
Rental agreement in which the tenant (lessee) agrees to make rent payments to the property owner (lessor) to obtain the use of the asset.

Lessee
Tenant in a lease agreement.

Lessor
Property owner in a lease agreement.

Operating Lease
Usually a short-term or cancelable rental agreement.

Capital Lease
Lease agreement that meets any one of four criteria: (1) The lease transfers title of the leased asset to the lessee. (2) The lease contains a bargain purchase option. (3) The lease term is 75% or more of the estimated useful life of the leased asset. (4) The present value of the lease payments is 90% or more of the market value of the leased asset.

Accounting.com

Qwest: Swapping Bonds to Cut Debt Leaves Bondholders Wary

In the summer of 1998, Baby Bell phone company **USWest** made corporate history with the largest long-term bond issue: $1.5 billion in 30-year bonds. With the company's solid, investment-grade rating and a yield of 6.9 percent for 30 years, the bonds seemed the ideal investment vehicle. Yet individuals and large institutional investors alike are now unsure whether the bonds issued in 1998 will be paid in full at maturity.

USWest was bought by **Qwest Communications**, which sought to create the telecom company of the future. Old-economy USWest and new-economy Qwest never did mesh, and Qwest took on an enormous amount of debt to finance its fiber-optic dreams. Furthermore, the company's attempt to inflate revenue via illegal telecom-capacity swaps and other accounting shenanigans have landed former executives in jail, sunk the stock price, and sparked rumors of impending bankruptcy.

Qwest's capacity swaps were illegal, but a U.S. District judge decided that the company could go ahead with a bond swap to pare down its total debt of $24.5 billion. Qwest came up with a debt-for-debt swap for its institutional investors. It works like this: If a bondholder has a $100 face-value bond now trading at $80, Qwest will issue that holder an $80 face-value bond. In return for giving up the $20 difference, the bondholder gets a better rank among Qwest's creditors—in other words, it's more likely that they will get repaid. Qwest then gets to wipe that $20 off its balance sheet.

For those who bought Qwest's bonds at a discount as the company's troubles mounted, the deal is good. They can exchange bonds they bought at distressed values for little or no loss, get a better interest rate and higher standing among creditors. Those who bought the bonds at full face value are not so happy. In fact, bondholders owning about $4 billion of Qwest's bonds sued to stop the exchange, because those who abstain will be punished. They lost their case. Individual investors aren't even given the option to swap.

But who knows? Those who hold on to their Qwest bonds might benefit in the long run. If Qwest can cut its long-term debt, it becomes less likely that the company will go into bankruptcy, thus boosting the value of its bonds.

Based on: Stephanie N. Mehta, "Joe Nacchio's Dream Has Unraveled," *Fortune,* April 29, 2002, pp. 78–82. Kris Hudson, "Qwest Set to Shuffle Bond Debt," *Denver Post,* November 21, 2002, p. C1. Floyd Norris, "A Bond Swap Available Only to Big Players," *The New York Times,* December 18, 2002, p. C1. Kris Hudson, "Qwest Can Proceed on Bond Plan," *Denver Post,* December 19, 2002, p. C2.

Decision Guidelines

LONG-TERM LIABILITIES—PART B

Suppose **American Airlines** needs $500 million for new **Boeing** aircraft. American issues bonds payable to finance the purchase and now must account for the bonds payable. The Decision Guidelines outline some of the issues American must decide.

Decision

What happens to the bonds' carrying amount when bonds payable are issued at

- Maturity (par) value?
- A premium?
- A discount?

How to account for the retirement of bonds payable?

How to account for the conversion of convertible bonds payable into common stock?

What are the advantages of financing operations with

- Stock

- Bonds (or notes) payable?

Guidelines

- Carrying amount *stays* at maturity (par) value.
- Carrying amount *falls* gradually to maturity value.
- Carrying amount *rises* gradually to maturity value.

At maturity date:

Bonds Payable	Maturity value	
Cash		Maturity value

Before maturity date (assume a discount on the bonds and a gain on retirement):

Bonds Payable	Maturity value	
Discount on Bonds Payable ..		Balance
Cash		Amount Paid
Gain on Retirement of Bonds Payable		Excess

Remove the bonds payable (and related premium or discount) and credit Common Stock at par, plus any excess to Paid-In Capital in Excess of Par.

- Creates no liability or interest expense. Less risky to the issuing corporation.
- Results in higher earnings per share—under normal conditions.

Excel Application Exercise

Goal: Create an Excel worksheet to compare earnings per share under two financing scenarios: borrowing and issuing stock.

Scenario: Suppose **American Airlines** is building a new warehouse to serve its central hub operations. To finance construction of the warehouse, managers must decide whether to borrow the $5 million or issue stock. If borrowing is chosen, long-term bonds payable will be issued at 8%. If stock is chosen, 80,000 shares will be issued. Managers expect income before tax to increase by $700,000. Income tax expense is 40%. Net income before construction is $4 million, and shares outstanding before construction total 500,000.

Your task is to create a spreadsheet that compares earnings per share under the two scenarios described above. After completing the spreadsheet, answer these questions:

1. Which plan generates the higher earnings per share? Why?
2. Under what circumstances would American consider using debt to finance its new warehouse?
3. Under what circumstances would American consider the use of equity to finance its new warehouse?
4. Which option do you recommend? Why? Does your recommendation change if the bond interest rate is 10% rather than 8%?

Step-by-Step:

1. Open a new Excel worksheet.
2. Create a heading for your work sheet that contains the following:
   a. Chapter 15 Excel Application Exercise
   b. Financing with Debt or Stock
   c. American Airlines
   d. Today's date
3. Use Exhibit 15-8 in your textbook as a model for the layout of your spreadsheet. Label the long-term bonds as "Plan 1," and the issuance of common stock as "Plan 2." Be sure to set up the spreadsheet so that you can change variables, such as the interest rate on the bonds, without retyping any formulas in the body of the spreadsheet.
4. When finished, your spreadsheet should show earnings per share under both plans, and be capable of recomputing earnings per share simply by changing the interest rate on the bonds.
5. Save your work and print a copy of the work sheet (in landscape mode) for your files.

END-OF-CHAPTER *Summary Problem*

CHECK YOUR RESOURCES

Trademark, Inc., has outstanding an issue of 8% convertible bonds payable that mature in 2020. Suppose the bonds were dated October 1, 2006, and pay interest each April 1 and October 1.

Required

1. With the bond data below, complete the following effective-interest amortization table through October 1, 2008:
   - Maturity value—$100,000
   - Stated interest rate—8%
   - Interest paid—4% semiannually, $4,000 ($100,000 × 0.04)
   - Market interest rate—9% annually, 4 1/2% semiannually
   - Issue price—90.75 on October 1, 2006

Semiannual Interest Date	A Interest Payment (4% of maturity amount)	B Interest Expense (4 1/2% of preceding bond carrying amount)	C Discount Amortization (B – A)	D Discount Balance (D – C)	E Bond Carrying Amount ($100,000 – D)
10-1-06					
4-1-07					
10-1-07					
4-1-08					
10-1-08					

2. Using the amortization table, record the following transactions:

   a. Issuance of the bonds on October 1, 2006.
   b. Accrual of interest and amortization of discount on December 31, 2006.
   c. Payment of interest and amortization of discount on April 1, 2007.
   d. Conversion of one-third of the bonds payable into no-par common stock on October 2, 2008.
   e. Retirement of two-thirds of the bonds payable on October 2, 2008. Purchase price of the bonds was 102.

Solution

Requirement 1

Semiannual Interest Date	A Interest Payment (4% of maturity amount)	B Interest Expense (4 1/2% of preceding bond carrying amount)	C Discount Amortization (B – A)	D Discount Balance (D – C)	E Bond Carrying Amount ($100,000 – D)
10-1-06				$9,250	$90,750
4-1-07	$4,000	$4,084	$84	9,166	90,834
10-1-07	4,000	4,088	88	9,078	90,922
4-1-08	4,000	4,091	91	8,987	91,013
10-1-08	4,000	4,096	96	8,891	91,109

Requirement 2

2006
a. Oct. 1   Cash ($100,000 × 0.9075)............. 90,750
                Discount on Bonds Payable.......... 9,250
                    Bonds Payable .... | 100,000
                Issued bonds payable at a discount.

b. Dec. 31 Interest Expense ($4,084 × 3/6) 2,042
                    Discount on Bonds Payable
                        ($84 × 3/6) .... | 42
                    Interest Payable ($4,000 × 3/6) ... | 2,000
                Accrued interest and amortized bond discount.

2007
c. Apr. 1   Interest Expense 2,042
                Interest Payable................... 2,000
                    Discount on Bonds Payable
                        ($84 × 3/6) .... | 42
                    Cash....................... | 4,000
                Paid semiannual interest and amortized bond discount.

2008
d. Oct. 2   Bonds Payable ($100,000 × 1/3) 33,333
                    Discount on Bonds Payable
                        ($8,891 × 1/3).............. | 2,964
                    Common Stock ($91,109 × 1/3) .. | 30,369
                Recorded conversion of bonds payable.

e. Oct. 2   Bonds Payable ($100,000 × 2/3) 66,667
                Loss on Retirement Bonds 7,260
                    Discount on Bonds Payable
                        ($8,891 × 2/3).............. | 5,927
                    Cash ($100,000 × 2/3 × 1.02) .... | 68,000
                Retired bonds payable before maturity.

REVIEW *Long-Term Liabilities*

Quick Check

1. Which type of bond is unsecured?
   a. Debenture bond   **c.** Serial bond
   b. Mortgage bond   **d.** Common bond

2. A $100,000 bond priced at 103.5 can be bought or sold for
   a. $100,000 + interest   **c.** $103,500
   b. $3,500   **d.** $103,000 + $500 of interest

3. Which interest rate on a bond determines the amount of the semiannual interest payment?
   a. Market rate   **c.** Semiannual rate
   b. Effective rate   **d.** Stated rate

4. The final journal entry to record for bonds payable is

   a. Interest Expense....   xxx   **c.** Bonds Payable.............. xxx
              Cash........ | xxx   Cash .... | xxx
   b. Cash   xxx   **d.** Discount on Bonds Payable .. xxx
              Bonds Payable | xxx   Interest Expense .... | xxx

5. Lafferty Corporation's bonds payable carry a stated interest rate of 7%, and the market rate of interest is 8%. The price of the Lafferty bonds will be at
   a. Premium
   b. Discount
   c. Par value
   d. Maturity value

6. Bonds issued at a premium always have
   a. Interest expense less than the interest payments
   b. Interest expense greater than the interest payments
   c. Interest expense equal to the interest payments
   d. None of the above

7. Imported Cars of Sarasota has $500,000 of 10-year bonds payable outstanding. These bonds had a discount of $40,000 at issuance, which was 5 years ago. The company uses the straight-line amortization method. The carrying amount of Imported Cars' bonds payable is
   a. $460,000
   b. $480,000
   c. $500,000
   d. $520,000

8. Imported Cars issued its 8% bonds payable at a price of $440,000 (maturity value is $500,000). The market interest rate was 10% when Imported Cars issued its bonds. The company uses the effective-interest method for the bonds. Interest expense for the first year is
   a. $35,200
   b. $40,000
   c. $44,000
   d. $50,000

9. Milton Corporation issued bonds payable on August 1. Milton's bonds were dated July 1. Which statement is true of Milton's journal entry to record issuance of the bonds payable?
   a. Milton must pay one month's accrued interest.
   b. Milton will collect one month's accrued interest in advance.
   c. Milton will collect five months' accrued interest in advance.
   d. Milton will pay five months' interest on the next interest date.

10. Bull & Bear, Inc., retired $100,000 of its bonds payable, paying cash of $103,000. On the retirement date, the bonds payable had a discount of $2,000. The bond retirement created a
   a. Gain of $3,000
   b. Loss of $3,000
   c. Gain of $5,000
   d. Loss of $5,000

Accounting Vocabulary

bond discount (p. 581)
bond premium (p. 581)
bonds payable (p. 580)
callable bonds (p. 594)
capital lease (p. 597)
convertible bonds (p. 595)
debentures (p. 581)

discount (on a bond) (p. 581)
effective interest rate (p. 582)
lease (p. 597)
lessee (p. 597)
lessor (p. 597)
leverage (p. 596)
market interest rate (p. 582)

mortgage (p. 581)
operating lease (p. 597)
premium (p. 581)
present value (p. 582)
serial bonds (p. 581)
stated interest rate (p. 582)
term bonds (p. 581)

● ASSESS *Your Progress*

See *www.prenhall.com/horngren* for selected Starters, Exercises, and Problems.

Pricing bonds
(Obj. 1)

Starters

S15-1 Compute the price of the following 8% bonds:

a. $100,000 quoted at 92.6
b. $100,000 quoted at 102.5
c. $100,000 quoted at 77.75
d. $100,000 quoted at 110.375

Which bond will have the least interest expense over its life?
Which bond will have the most interest expense? Explain.

S15-2 **Washington Public Power Supply System (WPPSS)** borrowed money by issuing the bond payable in Exhibit 15-1. Assume the issue price was 96.5.

Determining bonds payable amounts
(Obj. 1)

1. How much cash did WPPSS receive when it issued the bond payable?
2. How much must WPPSS pay back at maturity? When is the maturity date?
3. How much cash interest will WPPSS pay each six months? Carry the interest amount to the nearest cent.

S15-3 Assume the **WPPSS** bond in Exhibit 15-1 was issued at a price of 96.5. Was the market interest rate at the date of issuance 6 1/2%, above 6 1/2%, or below 6 1/2%? Explain.

Bond interest rates
(Obj. 1)

S15-4 Determine whether the following bonds payable will be issued at maturity value, at a premium, or at a discount:

Determining bond prices at par, discount, or premium
(Obj. 1)

a. The market interest rate is 7%. Chicago Corp. issues bonds payable with a stated rate of 8 1/2%.
b. Phoenix, Inc., issued 7% bonds payable when the market rate was 7 1/2%.
c. Tallahassee Corporation issued 8% bonds when the market interest rate was 8%.
d. Seattle Company issued bonds payable that pay cash interest at the stated rate of 7%. At the date of issuance, the market interest rate was 8 1/4%.

S15-5 Suppose **WPPSS** issued the 10-year bond in Exhibit 15-1 when the market interest rate was 6 1/2%. Assume that the fiscal year of WPPSS ends on December 31. Journalize the following transactions for WPPSS. Include an explanation for each entry.

Journalizing basic bond payable transactions
(Obj. 1)

a. Issuance of the bond payable at par on January 1, 2000.
b. Payment of semiannual cash interest on July 1, 2000. (Round to the nearest dollar.)
c. Payment of the bonds payable at maturity. (Give the date.)

S15-6 Assume **WPPSS** issued the 10-year bond in Exhibit 15-1 at a price of 90 on January 1, 2000. Also assume that the WPPSS fiscal year ends on June 30. Journalize the following transactions for WPPSS. Include an explanation for each entry.

Issuing bonds payable at a discount; paying interest and amortizing discount by the straight-line method
(Obj. 1)

a. Issuance of the bond payable on July 1, 2000.
b. Payment of semiannual interest and amortization of bond discount on July 1, 2000. (Use the straight-line method to amortize the discount. Round interest to the nearest dollar.)

S15-7 Assume **WPPSS** issued the 10-year bond payable in Exhibit 15-1 at a price of 110 on January 1, 2000. Also assume that the WPPSS fiscal year ends on December 31. Journalize the following transactions for WPPSS. Include an explanation for each entry.

Issuing bonds payable at a premium; paying interest and amortizing premium by the straight-line method
(Obj. 1)

a. Issuance of the bond payable on January 1, 2000.
b. Payment of semiannual interest and amortization of bond premium on July 1, 2000. (Use the straight-line method to amortize the premium. Round interest to the nearest dollar.)

S15-8 Return to the **WPPSS** bond in Exhibit 15-1. Assume that WPPSS issued the 10-year bond payable on January 1, 2000, at a price of 90. Also assume that the WPPSS accounting year ends on December 31. Journalize the following transactions for WPPSS. Include an explanation for each entry.

Issuing bonds payable, accruing interest, and amortizing bond discount
(Obj. 1)

a. Issuance of the bonds on July 1, 2000.
b. Accrual of semiannual interest expense and amortization of bond discount on December 31, 2000. Interest will be paid tomorrow, on January 1. (Use the straight-line amortization method, and round interest to the nearest dollar.)
c. Payment of the first semiannual interest amount on January 1, 2001.

Reporting interest payable and bonds payable on the balance sheet
(Obj. 5)

S15-9 Use the situation in Starter 15-8, and show how **WPPSS** would report interest payable and the bond payable on its balance sheet at December 31, 2000.

Issuing bonds payable and amortizing discount by the effective-interest method
(Obj. 2)

S15-10 Clever Path Information Systems issued $600,000 of 7%, 10-year bonds payable at a price of 90 on March 31, 20X3. The market interest rate at the date of issuance was 9%, and the bonds pay interest semiannually.

1. How much cash did Clever Path receive upon issuance of the bonds payable?
2. Prepare an effective-interest amortization table for the bond discount, through the first two interest payments. Use Exhibit 15-4 as a guide, and round amounts to the nearest dollar.
3. Record Clever Path's issuance of the bonds on March 31, 20X3, and on September 30, 20X3, payment of the first semiannual interest amount and amortization of the bond discount. Explanations are not required.

Issuing bonds payable and amortizing premium by the effective-interest method
(Obj. 2)

S15-11 Sandals, Inc., issued $200,000 of 8%, 10-year bonds payable at a price of 110 on May 31, 20X5. The market interest rate at the date of issuance was 6%, and the Sandals bonds pay interest semiannually.

1. How much cash did Sandals receive upon issuance of the bonds payable?
2. Prepare an effective-interest amortization table for the bond premium, through the first two interest payments. Use Exhibit 15-6 as a guide, and round amounts to the nearest dollar.
3. Record Sandals' issuance of the bonds on May 31, 20X5, and, on November 30, 20X5, payment of the first semiannual interest amount and amortization of the bond premium. Explanations are not required.

Issuing bonds payable between interest dates and then paying the interest
(Obj. 1)

S15-12 Assume **WPPSS** issued the 10-year bond in Exhibit 15-1 at par value on May 1, 2000, four months after the bond's original issue date of January 1, 2000. Assume that the fiscal year of WPPSS ends on December 31. Journalize the following transactions for WPPSS. Include an explanation for each entry.

a. Issuance of the bonds payable on May 1, 2000. (Carry amounts to the nearest cent.)
b. Payment of the first semiannual interest amount on July 1, 2000. (Carry amounts to the nearest cent.)

Accounting for the retirement of bonds payable
(Obj. 3)

S15-13 Assume that Pacifica, Inc., issued the bonds payable in Exhibit 15-6. Pacifica has extra cash and wishes to retire the bonds payable on January 1, 2008, immediately after making the sixth semiannual interest payment. The bonds are quoted in the market at a price of 95.

1. What is Pacifica's carrying amount of the bonds payable on the retirement date?
2. How much cash must Pacifica pay to retire the bonds payable?
3. Compute Pacifica's gain or loss on the retirement of the bonds payable.
4. Journalize Pacifica's transaction to retire the bonds payable.

Accounting for the conversion of bonds payable
(Obj. 3)

S15-14 ← *Link Back to Chapter 4 (Debt Ratio)*. New Blue Corp. has $1,000,000 of convertible bonds payable outstanding, with a bond premium of $20,000 also on the books. The bondholders have notified New Blue that they wish to convert the bonds into stock. Specifically, the bonds may be converted into 200,000 shares of New Blue's $1 par common stock.

1. What is New Blue's carrying amount of its convertible bonds payable prior to the conversion?
2. Journalize New Blue's conversion of the bonds payable into common stock. No explanation is required.
3. How will the conversion affect New Blue's debt ratio?

Reporting liabilities
(Obj. 4)

S15-15 Suburban Magazine, Inc., includes the following selected accounts in its general ledger at December 31, 20X8:

Notes payable, long-term........	$100,000	Accounts payable...............	$19,000
Bonds payable	350,000	Discount on bonds	
Interest payable (due next year)..	7,000	payable (all long-term)	6,000

Prepare the liabilities section of Suburban Magazine, Inc.'s balance sheet at December 31, 20X8, to show how the company would report these items. Report a total for current liabilities.

S15-16 Leather Products, Inc. (LPI), needs to raise $1 million to expand company operations. LPI's president is considering two plans:

Earnings-per-share effects of financing with bonds versus stock
(Obj. 5)

- Plan A: $1,000,000 of 8% bonds payable to borrow the money
- Plan B: 100,000 shares of common stock at $10 per share

Before any new financing, LPI expects to earn net income of $500,000, and the company already has 100,000 shares of common stock outstanding. LPI believes the expansion will increase income before interest and income tax by $200,000. LPI's income tax rate is 35%.

Prepare an analysis similar to Exhibit 15-8 to determine which plan is likely to result in the higher earnings per share. Which financing plan would you recommend for LPI?

Exercises

E15-1 Neptune Corporation issued 8%, 20-year bonds payable with a maturity value of $500,000 on March 31. The bonds were issued at 100 and pay interest on March 31 and September 30. Record (a) issuance of the bonds on March 31, (b) payment of interest on September 30, and (c) accrual of interest on December 31.

Issuing bonds payable, paying and accruing interest
(Obj. 1)

E15-2 On January 1, Quest Corp. issues 8%, 20-year bonds payable with a maturity value of $100,000. The bonds sell at 98 and pay interest on January 1 and July 1. Quest amortizes bond discount by the straight-line method. Record (a) issuance of the bonds on January 1, and (b) the semiannual interest payment on July 1.

Issuing bonds payable, paying interest, and amortizing discount by the straight-line method
(Obj. 1)

E15-3 Sandia, Inc., issued $100,000 of 10-year, 6% bonds payable on January 1, 20X6. Sandia pays interest each January 1 and July 1 and amortizes discount or premium by the straight-line method. The company can issue its bonds payable under various conditions:

Bond transactions at par, at a discount, and at a premium
(Obj. 1)

a. Issuance at par (maturity) value
b. Issuance at a price of 95
c. Issuance at a price of 105

Required

1. Journalize Sandia's issuance of the bonds and first semiannual interest payment for each situation. Explanations are not required.
2. Which method results in the most interest expense for Sandia? Explain in detail.

E15-4 All Star Productions is planning to issue long-term bonds payable to borrow for a major expansion. The chief executive, Marty Boyd, asks your advice on some related matters, as follows:

Determining whether the bond price will be at par, at a discount, or at a premium
(Obj. 1)

a. The stated interest rate on the bonds is 7%, and the market interest rate is 8%. What type of price can All Star expect for the bonds?
b. All Star could raise the stated interest rate on the bonds to 9% (market rate is 8%). In that case, what type of price can All Star expect for the bonds?
c. At what type of bond price will All Star have total interest expense equal to the cash interest payments?
d. Under which type of price will All Star's total interest expense be less than the cash interest payments?
e. Under which type of price will All Star's total interest expense be greater than the cash interest payments?

Effective-interest method for bond discount; recording interest payments and interest expense
(Obj. 2)

Student Resource**CD**

spreadsheet

E15-5 Autorama Corp. is authorized to issue 7%, 10-year bonds payable. On January 2, 20X4, when the market interest rate is 8%, the company issues $300,000 of the bonds and receives cash of $279,600. Autorama amortizes bond discount by the effective-interest method. Interest dates are January 2 and July 2.

Required

1. Prepare an amortization table for the first two semiannual interest periods. Follow the format of Exhibit 15-4.
2. Record issuance of the bonds payable and the first semiannual interest payment on July 2.

Effective-interest method for bond premium; recording interest accrual and payment and the related interest expense
(Obj. 2)

Student Resource**CD**

spreadsheet

E15-6 On March 31, 20X2, the market interest rate is 7%. First Federal Bank issues $200,000 of 8%, 20-year bonds payable at 110. The bonds pay interest on March 31 and September 30. First Federal measures interest expense by the effective-interest method.

Required

1. Prepare an amortization table for the first two semiannual interest periods. Follow the format of Exhibit 15-6, Panel B.
2. Record issuance of the bonds on March 31, 20X2, and the semiannual interest payment on September 30.

Debt payment and discount amortization schedule
(Obj. 2)

Student Resource**CD**

spreadsheet

E15-7 Einstein Productions issued $500,000 of 8 3/8% (0.08375), five-year bonds payable when the market interest rate was 9 1/2% (0.095). Einstein pays interest annually at year-end. The issue price of the bonds was $478,402.

Required

Create a spreadsheet model to prepare a schedule to measure interest expense on these bonds. Use the effective-interest method of amortization. Round to the nearest dollar, and format your answer as follows:

	A	B	C	D	E	F
1						
2						Bond
3		Interest	Interest	Discount	Discount	Carrying
4	Date	Payment	Expense	Amortization	Balance	Amount
5	1-1-X1				$ ☐	$478,402
6	12-31-X1	$ ☐	$ ☐	$ ☐		☐
7	12-31-X2					
8	12-31-X3					
9	12-31-X4					
10	12-31-X5					
		500000*.08375	+F5*.095	+C6−B6	500000−F5	+F5+D6

Issuing bonds between interest dates
(Obj. 1)

E15-8 Refer to the data for Neptune Corporation in Exercise 15-1. If Neptune issued the bonds payable on June 30, how much cash would Neptune receive upon issuance of the bonds?

Issuing bonds between interest dates and paying interest
(Obj. 1)

E15-9 Newton, Inc., issues $400,000 of 6%, 20-year bonds payable that are dated April 30. Record (a) issuance of bonds at par on May 31 and (b) the next semiannual interest payment on October 31.

Recording retirement of bonds payable
(Obj. 3)

E15-10 Microdot Printing issued $600,000 of 8% bonds payable at 97 on October 1, 20X0. These bonds mature on October 1, 20X8, and are callable at 102. Microdot pays interest each April 1 and October 1. On October 1, 20X5, when the bonds' market price is 101, Microdot retires the bonds in the most economical way available.

Required

Record the payment of the interest and amortization of bond discount at October 1, 20X5, and the retirement of the bonds on that date. Microdot uses the straight-line amortization method.

E15-11 Jacobs-Cathey Company issued $700,000 of 15-year, 8 1/2% bonds payable on July 31, 20X3, at a price of 98. The bonds may be converted into the company's common stock. Each $1,000 maturity amount of the bonds is convertible into 40 shares of $20 par stock. On July 31, 20X9, bondholders converted bonds into common stock.

Recording conversion of bonds payable
(Obj. 3)

Required

1. What would cause the bondholders to convert their bonds into common stock?
2. Without making journal entries, compute the carrying amount of the bonds payable at July 31, 20X9. Jacobs-Cathey uses the straight-line method to amortize bond discount.
3. All amortization has been recorded properly. Journalize the conversion transaction at July 31, 20X9. No explanation is required.

E15-12 Shaker Village Food Industries reported the following at September 30:

Recording early retirement and conversion of bonds payable
(Obj. 3)

Long-term liabilities:		
Convertible bonds payable	$400,000	
Less: Discount on bonds payable	(12,000)	$388,000

Required

1. Record retirement of half of the bonds on October 1 at the call price of 101.
2. Record conversion of the remainder of the bonds into 10,000 shares of Shaker Village's $5 par common stock on October 1. What would cause the bondholders to convert their bonds into stock?

E15-13 At December 31, Crestview Carpets owes $50,000 on accounts payable, plus salary payable of $14,000 and income tax payable of $8,000. Crestview also has $300,000 of bonds payable that require payment of a $30,000 installment next year and the remainder in later years. The bonds payable also require an interest payment of $7,000 at the end of each year.

Reporting liabilities
(Obj. 4)

Report Crestview's liabilities on its year-end classified balance sheet. List liabilities in descending order (largest first, and so on).

E15-14 OK Copiers is considering two plans for raising $1,000,000 to expand operations. Plan A is to borrow at 9%, and plan B is to issue 100,000 shares of common stock. Before any new financing, OK has net income of $600,000 and 100,000 shares of common stock outstanding. Management believes the company can use the new funds to earn additional income of $420,000 before interest and taxes. The income tax rate is 40%.

Analyzing alternative plans for raising money
(Obj. 5)

Required

Analyze OK Copiers' situation to determine which plan will result in higher earnings per share. Use Exhibit 15-8 as a guide.

Analyzing bond transactions
(Obj. 1, 2)

E15-15 This (partial and adapted) advertisement appeared in *The Wall Street Journal*.

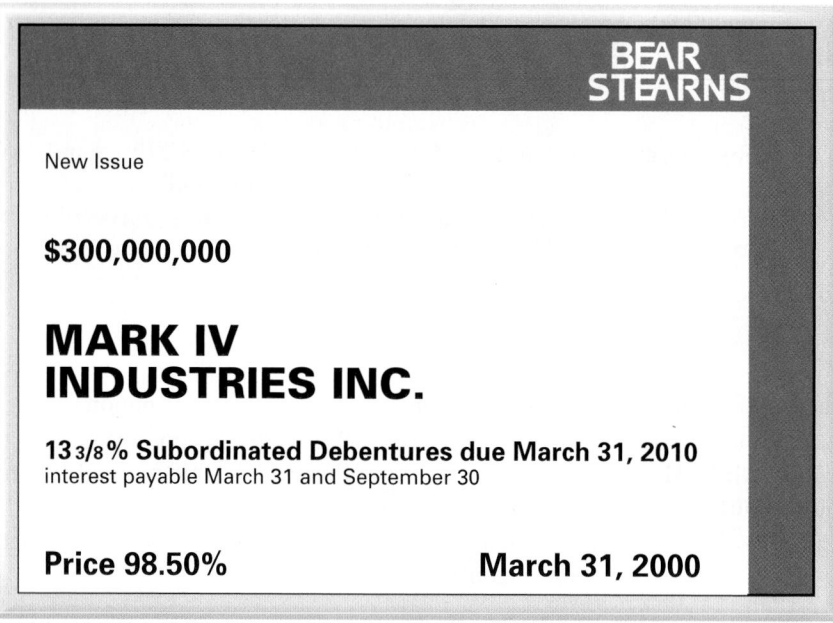

A *subordinated* debenture gives rights to the bondholder that are more restricted than the rights of other bondholders.

Required

Answer these questions about **Mark IV Industries'** debenture bonds payable:

1. Suppose Mark IV Industries issued these bonds payable at their offering price on March 31, 2000. Describe the transaction in detail, indicating who received cash, who paid cash, and how much.
2. Why is the stated interest rate on these bonds so high?
3. Compute Mark IV Industries' annual cash interest payment on the bonds.
4. Compute Mark IV Industries' annual interest expense under the straight-line amortization method.
5. Prepare an effective-interest amortization table for Mark IV Industries' first two interest payments on September 30, 2000, and March 31, 2001. Use Exhibit 15-4 as a guide and show all amounts in thousands. The market rate of interest on the bonds is 13.65% per year.
6. Compute Mark IV Industries interest expense for the first full year ended March 31, 2001, under the effective-interest method. Use the amortization table you prepared for requirement 5.

Analyzing bond transactions
(Obj. 1)

E15-16 Refer to the bond situation of **Mark IV Industries** in Exercise 15-15. Assume Mark IV Industries issued the bonds at the advertised price and that the company uses the straight-line amortization method and reports financial statements on a calendar-year basis.

Required

1. Journalize the following bond transactions of Mark IV Industries. Show all amounts in thousands of dollars. Explanations are not required.

2000
Mar. 31   Issuance of the bonds.
Sep. 30   Payment of interest expense and amortization of discount on bonds payable.

2. What is Mark IV Industries' carrying amount of the bonds payable at
   a. September 30, 2000?   b. March 31, 2001?

Problems

(Group A)

P15-1A Mill Creek Golf Club issued $600,000 of 20-year, 9% bonds payable at maturity (par) value on February 1, 20X3. The bonds pay interest each January 31 and July 31, and the company ends its accounting year on December 31.

1. Fill in the blanks to complete these statements:
   a. Mill Creek's bonds are priced at (express the price as a percentage) ____.
   b. When Mill Creek issued its bonds, the market interest rate was ____%.
   c. The amount of bond discount or premium for Mill Creek to account for is $____ because the bonds were issued at ____.

2. Journalize for Mill Creek
   a. Issuance of the bonds payable on February 1, 20X3.
   b. Payment of interest on July 31, 20X3.
   c. Accrual of interest at December 31, 20X3.
   d. Payment of interest on January 31, 20X4.
   Explanations are not required.

3. Show what Mill Creek Golf Club will report on its income statement for the year ended December 31, 20X3, and on its balance sheet at December 31, 20X3.

P15-2A Assume that on April 1, 20X6, **Goretex Corp.** issues 8%, 10-year notes payable with maturity value of $400,000. The notes pay interest on March 31 and September 30, and Goretex amortizes premium and discount by the straight-line method.

Required

1. If the market interest rate is 7 1/2% when Goretex issues its notes, will the notes be priced at maturity (par) value, at a premium, or at a discount? Explain.

2. If the market interest rate is 9% when Goretex issues its notes, will the notes be priced at par, at a premium, or at a discount? Explain.

3. Assume that the issue price of the notes is 101. Journalize the following note payable transactions:
   a. Issuance of the notes on April 1, 20X6.
   b. Payment of interest and amortization of premium on September 30, 20X6.
   c. Accrual of interest and amortization of premium on December 31, 20X6.
   d. Payment of interest and amortization of premium on March 31, 20X7.

P15-3A Global Positioning System (GPS) finances operations with both bonds and stock. Suppose GPS issued $200,000 of 10-year, 8% bonds payable under various market conditions. Match each market interest rate with the appropriate bond price, as follows:

Market Interest Rate	Bond Price
7%	?
8%	?
9%	?

The three possible bond prices are $187,000; $200,000; and $214,000. GPS pays annual interest each December 31.

After determining the respective bond prices, make the following journal entries for the bond premium situation (explanations are not required):

Dec. 31, 2008	Issuance of the bonds at a premium.
Dec. 31, 2009	Payment of interest and amortization of bond premium by the straight-line method.
Dec. 31, 2018	Payment of interest and amortization of bond premium by the straight-line method.
Dec. 31, 2018	Final payment of the bonds payable.

How much total interest expense will GPS have during the 10-year life of these bonds?

Analyzing a company's long-term debt and journalizing its transactions
(Obj. 2)

P15-4A The balance sheet of Cellular Tracking Company reported the following data on September 30, Year 1, end of the fiscal year:

Long-Term Debt
5% bonds payable, net of
  discount of $55,200 (market interest rate of 8%) $144,800

Cellular Tracking uses the effective-interest amortization method.

Required

1. Answer the following questions about Cellular Tracking's bonds payable:
   a. What is the maturity value of the 5% bonds?
   b. What is the carrying amount of the 5% bonds at September 30, Year 1?
   c. What is Cellular Tracking's annual cash interest payment on the 5% bonds?
2. Prepare an amortization table through September 30, Year 3, for the 5% bonds. Cellular Tracking pays interest annually on September 30.
3. Record the September 30, Year 3, interest payment and amortization of the discount on the 5% bonds.
4. What is the carrying amount of the 5% bonds at September 30, Year 3, immediately after the interest payment?

Recording bonds (at par) and reporting bonds payable on the balance sheet— bonds issued between interest dates
(Obj. 1)

Student Resource CD
GL, PT, QB

P15-5A The board of directors of Alpha Communications authorizes the issuance of $3 million of 9%, 20-year bonds payable. The semiannual interest dates are March 31 and September 30. The bonds are issued on April 30, 20X4, at par plus accrued interest.

Required

1. Journalize the following transactions:
   a. Issuance of the bonds on April 30, 20X4.
   b. Payment of interest on September 30, 20X4.
   c. Accrual of interest on December 31, 20X4.
   d. Payment of interest on March 31, 20X5.
2. Report interest payable and bonds payable as they would appear on the Alpha balance sheet at December 31, 20X4.

Issuing convertible bonds at a discount, using the effective-interest method, retiring bonds early, and reporting on the balance sheet
(Obj. 2, 3, 4)

Student Resource CD
GL, PT, QB

P15-6A On December 31, 20X7, Bible Distributing Company issues 8%, 10-year convertible bonds with a maturity value of $700,000. The semiannual interest dates are June 30 and December 31. The market interest rate is 9%, and the issue price of the bonds is 94. Bible Distributing Company amortizes bond premium and discount by the effective-interest method.

Required

1. Prepare an effective-interest-method amortization table for the first four semiannual interest periods.
2. Journalize the following transactions:
   a. Issuance of the bonds on December 31, 20X7. Credit Convertible Bonds Payable.
   b. Payment of interest on June 30, 20X8.
   c. Payment of interest on December 31, 20X8.
   d. Retirement of bonds with maturity value of $100,000 on December 31, 20X9. Bible Distributing Company purchases the bonds at 98 in the open market.
3. Prepare a balance sheet presentation of the bonds payable that are outstanding at December 31, 20X9.

Reporting liabilities on the balance sheet
(Obj. 4)

P15-7A The accounting records of Far Side Productions, Inc., include the following items:

Salary payable	$32,000	Accounts payable	$ 60,000
Bonds payable, current		Mortgage note payable—	
portion	25,000	long-term	90,000
Discount on bonds payable		Interest payable	19,000
(all long-term)	7,000	Bonds payable, long-term ..	300,000
Income tax payable	16,000		

Required

Report these liabilities on Far Side Productions' balance sheet, including headings and totals for current liabilities and long-term liabilities.

P15-8A Market surveys show that consumers prefer upscale restaurants. To capitalize on this trend, Palomino, Inc., is embarking on a massive expansion. Plans call for opening 20 new restaurants within the next two years. Each restaurant is scheduled to be 30% larger than the company's existing locations and feature upgraded menus. Management estimates that company operations will provide $3 million of the cash needed for expansion. Palomino must raise the remaining $1.5 million from outsiders. The board of directors is considering obtaining the $1.5 million either through borrowing or by issuing common stock.

Financing operations with debt or with stock
(Obj. 5)

Required

1. Write a memo to company management. Discuss the advantages and disadvantages of borrowing and of issuing common stock to raise the needed cash. Use the following format for your memo:

Date: _____
To: Management of Palomino, Inc.
From: Student Name
Subject: Advantages and disadvantages of borrowing versus issuing stock to raise $1.5 million for expansion
Advantages and disadvantages of borrowing:
Advantages and disadvantages of issuing stock:

2. How will what you learned in this problem help you manage a business?

Problems

(Group B)

P15-1B McLaren Ford Sales issued $500,000 of 10-year, 8% bonds payable at maturity (par) value on May 1, 20X5. The bonds pay interest each April 30 and October 31, and the company ends its accounting year on December 31.

Analyzing bonds, recording bonds at par, and reporting on the financial statements
(Obj. 1, 4)

Required

1. Fill in the blanks to complete these statements:
    a. McLaren's bonds are priced at (express the price as a percentage) _____.
    b. When McLaren issued its bonds, the market interest rate was _____%.
    c. The amount of bond discount or premium for McLaren to account for is $ _____ because the bonds were issued at _____.

2. Journalize for McLaren
    a. Issuance of the bonds payable on May 1, 20X5.
    b. Payment of interest on October 31, 20X5.
    c. Accrual of interest at December 31, 20X5.
    d. Payment of interest on April 30, 20X6.
    Explanations are not required.

3. Show what McLaren will report on its income statement for 20X5 and on its balance sheet at December 31, 20X5.

Student Resource CD

GL, PT, QB

Issuing bonds and amortizing discount by the straight-line method
(Obj. 1)

P15-2B On March 1, 20X4, CD Warehouse issues 8 1/4%, 20-year bonds payable with maturity value of $400,000. The bonds pay interest on February 28 and August 31. CD Warehouse amortizes premium and discount by the straight-line method.

Required

1. If the market interest rate is 7 3/8% when CD Warehouse issues its bonds, will the bonds be priced at maturity (par) value, at a premium, or at a discount? Explain.

2. If the market interest rate is 8 7/8% when CD Warehouse issues its bonds, will the bonds be priced at par, at a premium, or at a discount? Explain.

3. The issue price of the bonds is 96. Journalize the following bond transactions:
   a. Issuance of the bonds on March 1, 20X4.
   b. Payment of interest and amortization of discount on August 31, 20X4.
   c. Accrual of interest and amortization of discount on December 31, 20X4.
   d. Payment of interest and amortization of discount on February 28, 20X5.

Determining bond price, recording bond transactions by the straight-line amortization method
(Obj. 1, 3)

P15-3B UPS finances operations with both bonds and stock. Suppose UPS issued $500,000 of 10-year, 7% bonds payable under various market conditions. Match each market interest rate with the appropriate bond price, as follows:

Market Interest Rate	Bond Price
6%	?
7%	?
8%	?

The three possible bond prices are $500,000; $537,000; and $466,000. Assume that UPS pays annual interest each December 31.

After determining the respective bond prices, make the following journal entries for the bond discount situation (explanations are not required):

Dec. 31, 2004	Issuance of the bonds at a discount.
Dec. 31, 2005	Payment of interest and amortization of bond discount by the straight-line method.
Dec. 31, 2014	Payment of interest and amortization of bond discount by the straight-line method.
Dec. 31, 2014	Final payment of the bonds payable.

How much total interest expense will UPS have during the 10-year life of these bonds?

Analyzing a company's long-term debt and journalizing its transactions
(Obj. 2)

P15-4B MUNY Digital's balance sheet reported the following data on September 30, Year 1, end of the fiscal year:

Long-Term Debt:
6.00% bonds payable with a
  market interest rate of 8.00%, net of discount of $35,200 .... $164,800

MUNY Digital uses the effective-interest amortization method.

Required

1. Answer the following questions about MUNY Digital's bonds payable:
   a. What is the maturity value of the 6.00% bonds?
   b. What is the carrying amount of the 6.00% bonds at September 30, Year 1?
   c. What is MUNY's annual cash interest payment on the 6.00% bonds?

2. Prepare an amortization table through September 30, Year 3, for the 6.00% bonds. MUNY pays interest annually on September 30.

3. Record the September 30, Year 3 interest payment and amortization of the discount on the 6.00% bonds.

4. What is the carrying amount of the 6% bonds at September 30, Year 3, immediately after the interest payment?

P15-5B The board of directors of Galaxy Production Company authorizes the issuance of $8 million of 7%, 10-year bonds payable. The semiannual interest dates are May 31 and November 30. The bonds are issued on August 31, 20X5, at par plus accrued interest.

Recording bonds (at par) and reporting bonds payable on the balance sheet—bond issued between interest dates
(Obj. 1)

Student ResourceCD

GL, PT, QB

Required

1. Journalize the following transactions:
   a. Issuance of the bonds on August 31, 20X5.
   b. Payment of interest on November 30, 20X5.
   c. Accrual of interest on December 31, 20X5.
   d. Payment of interest on May 31, 20X6.
2. Report interest payable and bonds payable as they would appear on the Galaxy balance sheet at December 31, 20X5.

P15-6B On December 31, 20X7, Early Bird Wireless, Inc., issues 9%, 10-year convertible bonds with a maturity value of $500,000. The semiannual interest dates are June 30 and December 31. The market interest rate is 8%, and the issue price of the bonds is 106.8. Early Bird measures interest expense by the effective-interest method.

Issuing convertible bonds at a premium, using the effective-interest method, retiring bonds early, and reporting on the balance sheet
(Obj. 2, 3, 4)

Student ResourceCD

GL, PT, QB

Required

1. Prepare an effective-interest-method amortization table for the first four semiannual interest periods.
2. Journalize the following transactions:
   a. Issuance of the bonds on December 31, 20X7. Credit Convertible Bonds Payable.
   b. Payment of interest on June 30, 20X8.
   c. Payment of interest on December 31, 20X8.
   d. Retirement of bonds with maturity value of $100,000 on December 31, 20X9. Early Bird pays the call price of 102.
3. Prepare the balance sheet presentation of the bonds payable that are outstanding at December 31, 20X9.

P15-7B The accounting records of Modern Language Associates include the following items:

Reporting liabilities on the balance sheet
(Obj. 4)

Salary payable	$ 9,000	Mortgage note payable,	
Bonds payable, long-term	160,000	long-term	$116,000
Premium on bonds payable		Accounts payable	54,000
(all long-term)	13,000	Bonds payable, current	
Unearned sales revenue	3,000	installment	20,000
		Interest payable	14,000

Required

Report these liabilities on Modern Language Associates' balance sheet, including headings and totals for current liabilities and long-term liabilities.

P15-8B Two businesses are considering how to raise $10 million.

Jefferson Corporation is having its best year since it began operations in 1980. For each of the past 10 years, earnings per share have increased by at least 15%. The outlook for the future is equally bright, with new markets opening up and competitors unable to manufacture products of Jefferson's quality. Jefferson Corporation is planning a large-scale expansion.

Madison Company has fallen on hard times. Net income has been flat for the last six years, with this year falling by 10% from last year's level of profits. Top management has experienced turnover, and the company lacks leadership. To become competitive again, Madison Company desperately needs $10 million for expansion.

Financing operations with debt or with stock
(Obj. 5)

Required

1. Propose a plan for each company to raise the needed cash. Which company should borrow? Which company should issue stock? Consider the advantages and the disadvantages of raising money by borrowing and by issuing stock, and discuss them in your answer. Use the following memorandum headings to report your plans for the two companies:
   • Plan for Madison Company to raise $10 million
   • Plan for Jefferson Corporation to raise $10 million
2. How will what you learned in this problem help you manage a business?

●APPLY *Your Knowledge*

Decision Cases

Analyzing alternative ways of raising $4 million
(Obj. 5)

Case 1. Business is going well for Email Designers. The board of directors of this family-owned company believes that Email Designers could earn an additional $1,000,000 income before interest and taxes by expanding into new markets. However, the $4,000,000 the business needs for growth cannot be raised within the family. The directors, who strongly wish to retain family control of the company, must issue securities to outsiders. They are considering three financing plans.

Plan A is to borrow at 6%. Plan B is to issue 100,000 shares of common stock. Plan C is to issue 100,000 shares of nonvoting, $2.50 preferred stock ($2.50 is the annual cash dividend for each share of preferred stock). Email Designers currently has net income of $2,000,000 and 400,000 shares of common stock outstanding. The company's income tax rate is 35%.

Required

1. Prepare an analysis similar to Exhibit 15-8 to determine which plan will result in the highest earnings per share of common stock.
2. Recommend one plan to the board of directors. Give your reasons.

Questions about long-term debt
(Obj. 1, 4 and Appendix to Chapter 15)

Case 2. → *Link Back to Chapter 4 (Debt Ratio).* The following questions are not related.

1. **IMAX Theater Corp.** needs to borrow $2 million to open new theaters. IMAX can borrow $2 million by issuing 8%, 20-year bonds at a price of 96. How much will IMAX actually be borrowing under this arrangement? How much must IMAX pay back at maturity? How will IMAX account for the difference between the amount borrowed and the amount paid back?
2. IMAX Corporation likes to borrow for longer periods when interest rates are low and for shorter periods when interest rates are high. Why is this a good business strategy?

Ethical Issue

Python.com owes $6 million on notes payable that will come due for payment in $1.5 million annual installments. The company has used its cash to advertise heavily in the competitive dotcom business environment. The result is that cash is scarce, and Python.com's management doesn't know where next year's note payment will come from. Python.com has prepared its balance sheet at December 31, 20X4, and it reports the following:

Liabilities	
Current:	
Accounts payable	$1,900,000
Salary payable and other accrued liabilities	300,000
Unearned revenue collected in advance	500,000
Income tax payable.	200,000
Total current liabilities	2,900,000
Long-term:	
Notes payable	6,000,000

What is wrong with the way Python.com reported its liabilities? Why did Python.com report its liabilities this way? What is unethical about this way of reporting *these* liabilities? Who can be harmed as a result?

Financial Statement Case

Analyzing long-term debt
(Obj. 1, 2)

The **Amazon.com** balance sheet, income statement (statement of operation's), and Note 6 in Appendix A provide details about the company's long-term debt. Use those data to answer the following questions.

Required

1. How much did Amazon.com owe on long-term debt at December 31, 2002? How much of this debt was payable in the coming year?

2. Journalize in a single entry Amazon's interest expense for 2002. Amazon paid cash of $139,896 thousand for interest.

3. Refer to Note 6 and compute the annual interest on Amazon's 4.75% convertible subordinated notes. Round to the nearest $1 thousand.

Team Project

Note: This project uses the chapter appendix.

Bermuda Corporation leases the equipment that it uses in operations. Bermuda prefers operating leases (versus capital leases) in order to keep the lease liability off its balance sheet and maintain a low debt ratio.

Bermuda is negotiating a 10-year lease on equipment with an expected useful life of 15 years. The lease requires Bermuda to make 10 annual lease payments of $20,000 each, due at the end of each year, plus a down payment that is due at the beginning of the lease term. The interest rate in the lease agreement is 10%. The leased asset has a market value of $160,000. The lease agreement specifies no transfer to title to the lessee and includes no bargain purchase option.

Write a report for Bermuda's management to explain how Bermuda should account for this lease—as an operating lease or as a capital lease. Use the following format for your report:

Date: _____
To: Bermuda Management
From: Student Names
Subject: Accounting for the company's equipment lease

For Internet exercises, go to the Web site www.prenhall.com/horngren.

APPENDIX *to Chapter 15*

Time Value of Money: Future Value and Present Value

This discussion of future value lays the foundation for present value but is not essential. For the valuation of long-term liabilities, some instructors may wish to begin in the middle of page 619.

The term *time value of money* refers to the fact that money earns interest over time. Interest is the cost of using money. To borrowers, interest is the expense of renting money. To lenders, interest is the revenue earned from lending. We must recognize the interest. Otherwise we overlook an important part of the transaction.

Suppose you invest $4,545 in corporate bonds that pay 10% interest each year. After one year, the value of your investment has grown to $5,000. The difference between your original investment ($4,545) and its future value ($5,000) is the amount of interest revenue you will earn ($455). Interest becomes more important as the time period lengthens because the amount of interest depends on how long the money is invested.

Let's consider a second example, but from the borrower's perspective. Suppose you purchase a machine for your business. The cash price of the machine is $8,000, but you cannot pay cash now. To finance the purchase, you sign an $8,000 note payable. The note requires you to pay the $8,000 plus 10% interest one year from the date of purchase. Is your cost of the machine $8,000, or is it $8,800 [$8,000 plus interest of $800 ($8,000 × 0.10)]? The cost is $8,000. The additional $800 is interest expense, which is not part of the cost of the machine.

Future Value

The main application of future value is the accumulated balance of an investment at a future date. In our first example, the investment earned 10% per year. After one year, $4,545 grew to $5,000, as shown in Exhibit 15A-1.

Exhibit 15A-1

Future Value

Present Value		Future Value
Time 0	Roll forward (accumulate) →	1 year
$4,545		$5,000

Present value × (1 + Interest rate) = Future value
$4,545 × 1.10 = $5,000

If the money were invested for five years, you would have to perform five such calculations. You would also have to consider the compound interest your investment is earning. *Compound interest* is the interest you earn not only on your principal amount, but also on the interest to date. Most business applications include compound interest. The following table shows the interest revenue earned each year at 10%:

End of Year	Interest	Future Value
0	—	$4,545
1	$4,545 × 0.10 = $455	5,000
2	5,000 × 0.10 = 500	5,500

Earning 10%, a $4,545 investment grows to $5,000 at the end of one year, to $5,500 at the end of two years, and so on. (Throughout this discussion, we round dollar amounts to the nearest dollar.)

Future-Value Tables The process of computing a future value is called *accumulating* because the future value is *more* than the present value. Mathematical tables ease the computational burden. Exhibit 15A-2, Future Value of $1, gives the future value for a single sum (a present value), $1, invested to earn a particular interest rate for a specific number of periods. Future value depends on three factors: (1) the amount of the investment, (2) the length of time between investment and future accumulation, and (3) the interest rate.

Exhibit 15A-2	Future Value of $1

	Future Value of $1									
Period	4%	5%	6%	7%	8%	9%	10%	12%	14%	16%
1	1.040	1.050	1.060	1.070	1.080	1.090	1.100	1.120	1.140	1.160
2	1.082	1.103	1.124	1.145	1.166	1.188	1.210	1.254	1.300	1.346
3	1.125	1.158	1.191	1.225	1.260	1.295	1.331	1.405	1.482	1.561
4	1.170	1.216	1.262	1.311	1.360	1.412	1.464	1.574	1.689	1.811
5	1.217	1.276	1.338	1.403	1.469	1.539	1.611	1.762	1.925	2.100
6	1.265	1.340	1.419	1.501	1.587	1.677	1.772	1.974	2.195	2.436
7	1.316	1.407	1.504	1.606	1.714	1.828	1.949	2.211	2.502	2.826
8	1.369	1.477	1.594	1.718	1.851	1.993	2.144	2.476	2.853	3.278
9	1.423	1.551	1.689	1.838	1.999	2.172	2.358	2.773	3.252	3.803
10	1.480	1.629	1.791	1.967	2.159	2.367	2.594	3.106	3.707	4.411
11	1.539	1.710	1.898	2.105	2.332	2.580	2.853	3.479	4.226	5.117
12	1.601	1.796	2.012	2.252	2.518	2.813	3.138	3.896	4.818	5.936
13	1.665	1.886	2.133	2.410	2.720	3.066	3.452	4.363	5.492	6.886
14	1.732	1.980	2.261	2.579	2.937	3.342	3.797	4.887	6.261	7.988
15	1.801	2.079	2.397	2.759	3.172	3.642	4.177	5.474	7.138	9.266
16	1.873	2.183	2.540	2.952	3.426	3.970	4.595	6.130	8.137	10.748
17	1.948	2.292	2.693	3.159	3.700	4.328	5.054	6.866	9.276	12.468
18	2.026	2.407	2.854	3.380	3.996	4.717	5.560	7.690	10.575	14.463
19	2.107	2.527	3.026	3.617	4.316	5.142	6.116	8.613	12.056	16.777
20	2.191	2.653	3.207	3.870	4.661	5.604	6.727	9.646	13.743	19.461

The heading in Exhibit 15A-2 states $1. Future-value and present-value tables are based on $1 because unity (the value 1) is so easy to work with. Look at the Period column and the interest-rate columns 4–16%. In business applications, interest rates are always stated for the annual period of one year unless specified otherwise. In fact, an interest rate can be stated for any period, such as 3% per quarter or 5% for a six-month period. The length of the period is arbitrary.

An investment may promise a return (income) of 3% per quarter for six months (two quarters). In that case, you would be working with 3% interest for two periods. It would be incorrect to use 6% for one period because the interest is 3% compounded quarterly, and that amount differs from 6% compounded semi-annually. Take care in studying future-value and present-value problems to align the interest rate with the appropriate number of periods.

Let's use Exhibit 15A-2. The future value of $1.00 invested at 8% for one year is $1.08 ($1.00 × 1.080, which appears at the junction under the 8% column and across from 1 in the Period column). The figure 1.080 includes both the principal (1.000) and the compound interest for one period (0.080).

Suppose you deposit $5,000 in a savings account that pays annual interest of 8%. The account balance at the end of one year will be $5,400. To compute the future value of $5,000 at 8% for one year, multiply $5,000 by 1.080 to get $5,400. Now suppose you invest in a 10-year, 8% certificate of deposit (CD). What will be the future value of the CD at maturity? To compute the future value of $5,000 at 8% for 10 periods, multiply $5,000 by 2.159 (from Exhibit 15A-2) to get $10,795.

This future value of $10,795 indicates that $5,000 earning 8% interest compounded annually grows to $10,795 at the end of 10 years. You can find any present amount's future value at a particular future date.

Future Value of an Annuity In the preceding example, we made an investment of a single amount. Other investments, called annuities, include multiple investments of an equal periodic amount at fixed intervals over the duration of the investment. Consider a family investing for a child's education. The Dietrichs can invest $4,000 annually to accumulate a college fund for 15-year-old Helen. The investment can earn 7% annually until Helen turns 18—a three-year investment. How much will be available for Helen on the date of the last investment? Exhibit 15A-3 shows the accumulation—a total future value of $12,860.

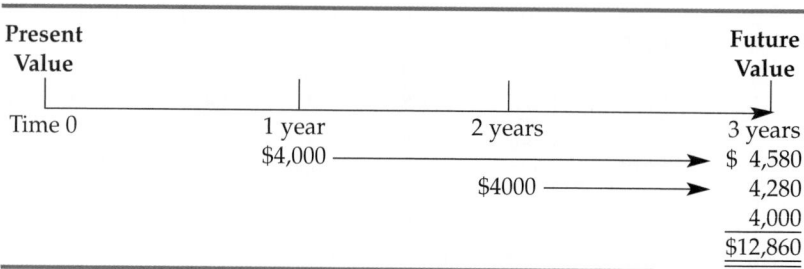

The first $4,000 invested by the Dietrichs grows to $4,580 over the investment period. The second amount grows to $4,280, and the third amount stays at $4,000 because it has no time to earn interest. The sum of the three future values ($4,580 + $4,280 + $4,000) is the future value of the annuity ($12,860), which can be computed as follows:

End of Year	Annual Investment	+	Interest	=	Increase for the Year	Future Value of Annuity
0	—		—		—	0
1	$4,000		—		$4,000	$ 4,000
2	4,000	+	($4,000 × 0.07 = $280)	=	4,280	8,280
3	4,000	+	($8,280 × 0.07 = $580)	=	4,580	12,860

As with the Future Value of $1 table (a lump sum), mathematical tables ease the strain of calculating annuities. Exhibit 15A-4, Future Value of Annuity of $1, gives the future value of a series of investments, each of equal amount, at regular intervals.

What is the future value of an annuity of three investments of $1 each that earn 7%? The answer 3.215 can be found in the 7% column and across from 3 in the Period column of Exhibit 15A-4. This amount can be used to compute the future value of the investment for Helen's education, as follows:

AMOUNT OF EACH PERIODIC INVESTMENT	×	FUTURE VALUE OF ANNUITY OF $1 (EXHIBIT 15A-4)	=	FUTURE VALUE OF INVESTMENT
$4,000	×	3.215	=	$12,860

This one-step calculation is much easier than computing the future value of each annual investment and then summing the individual future values. You can compute the future value of any investment consisting of equal periodic amounts at regular intervals. Businesses make periodic investments to accumulate funds for plant expansion and other uses—an application of the future value of an annuity.

Exhibit 15A-4   **Future Value of Annuity of $1**

Future Value of Annuity of $1

Period	4%	5%	6%	7%	8%	9%	10%	12%	14%	16%
1	1.000	1.000	1.000	1.000	1.000	1.000	1.000	1.000	1.000	1.000
2	2.040	2.050	2.060	2.070	2.080	2.090	2.100	2.120	2.140	2.160
3	3.122	3.153	3.184	3.215	3.246	3.278	3.310	3.374	3.440	3.506
4	4.246	4.310	4.375	4.440	4.506	4.573	4.641	4.779	4.921	5.066
5	5.416	5.526	5.637	5.751	5.867	5.985	6.105	6.353	6.610	6.877
6	6.633	6.802	6.975	7.153	7.336	7.523	7.716	8.115	8.536	8.977
7	7.898	8.142	8.394	8.654	8.923	9.200	9.487	10.089	10.730	11.414
8	9.214	9.549	9.897	10.260	10.637	11.028	11.436	12.300	13.233	14.240
9	10.583	11.027	11.491	11.978	12.488	13.021	13.579	14.776	16.085	17.519
10	12.006	12.578	13.181	13.816	14.487	15.193	15.937	17.549	19.337	21.321
11	13.486	14.207	14.972	15.784	16.645	17.560	18.531	20.655	23.045	25.733
12	15.026	15.917	16.870	17.888	18.977	20.141	21.384	24.133	27.271	30.850
13	16.627	17.713	18.882	20.141	21.495	22.953	24.523	28.029	32.089	36.786
14	18.292	19.599	21.015	22.550	24.215	26.019	27.975	32.393	37.581	43.672
15	20.024	21.579	23.276	25.129	27.152	29.361	31.772	37.280	43.842	51.660
16	21.825	23.657	25.673	27.888	30.324	33.003	35.950	42.753	50.980	60.925
17	23.698	25.840	28.213	30.840	33.750	36.974	40.545	48.884	59.118	71.673
18	25.645	28.132	30.906	33.999	37.450	41.301	45.599	55.750	68.394	84.141
19	27.671	30.539	33.760	37.379	41.446	46.018	51.159	63.440	78.969	98.603
20	29.778	33.066	36.786	40.995	45.762	51.160	57.275	72.052	91.025	115.380

Present Value

Often a person knows a future amount and needs to know the related present value. Recall Exhibit 15A-1, in which present value and future value are on opposite ends of the same time line. Suppose an investment promises to pay you $5,000 at the *end* of one year. How much would you pay *now* to acquire this investment? You would be willing to pay the present value of the $5,000 future amount.

Present value also depends on three factors: (1) the amount of the future payment (or receipt), (2) the time span between investment and future receipt (or payment), and (3) the interest rate. Computing a present value is called *discounting* because the present value is *always less* than the future value.

In our example, the future receipt is $5,000. The investment period is one year. Assume that you demand an annual interest rate of 10% on your investment. With all three factors specified, you can compute the present value of $5,000 at 10% for one year.

$$\frac{\text{Future value}}{(1 + \text{Interest rate})} = \frac{\$5,000}{1.10} = \$4,545$$

By turning the data around into a future-value problem, we verify the present-value computation:

Amount invested (present value).	$4,545
Expected earnings ($4,545 × 0.10).	455
Amount to be received one year from now (future value). .	$5,000

This example illustrates that present value and future value are based on the same equation:

$$\text{Present value} \times (1 + \text{Interest rate}) = \text{Future value}$$

$$\frac{\text{Future value}}{(1 + \text{Interest rate})} = \text{Present value}$$

If the $5,000 is to be received two years from now, you will pay only $4,132 for the investment, as shown in Exhibit 15A-5.

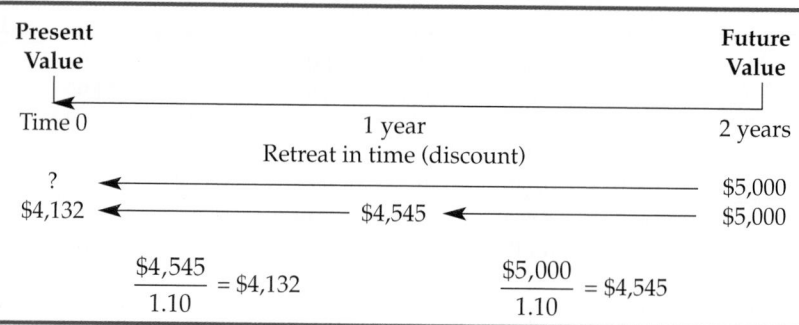

By turning the data around, we verify that $4,132 accumulates to $5,000 at 10% for two years:

Amount invested (present value)................................ $4,132
Expected earnings for first year ($4,132 × 0.10) 413
Value of investment after one year............................. 4,545
Expected earnings for second year ($4,545 × 0.10)................. 455
Amount to be received two years from now (future value).......... $5,000

You would pay $4,132—the present value of $5,000—to receive the $5,000 future amount at the end of two years at 10% per year. The $868 difference between the amount invested ($4,132) and the amount to be received ($5,000) is the return on the investment, the sum of the two interest receipts: $413 + $455 = $868.

Present-Value Tables   We have shown the simple formula for computing present value. However, figuring present value "by hand" for investments spanning many years is burdensome. Present-value tables ease our work. Let's reexamine our examples of present value by using Exhibit 15A-6, Present Value of $1.

Present Value of $1

Period	4%	5%	6%	7%	8%	10%	12%	14%	16%
1	0.962	0.952	0.943	0.935	0.926	0.909	0.893	0.877	0.862
2	0.925	0.907	0.890	0.873	0.857	0.826	0.797	0.769	0.743
3	0.889	0.864	0.840	0.816	0.794	0.751	0.712	0.675	0.641
4	0.855	0.823	0.792	0.763	0.735	0.683	0.636	0.592	0.552
5	0.822	0.784	0.747	0.713	0.681	0.621	0.567	0.519	0.476
6	0.790	0.746	0.705	0.666	0.630	0.564	0.507	0.456	0.410
7	0.760	0.711	0.665	0.623	0.583	0.513	0.452	0.400	0.354
8	0.731	0.677	0.627	0.582	0.540	0.467	0.404	0.351	0.305
9	0.703	0.645	0.592	0.544	0.500	0.424	0.361	0.308	0.263
10	0.676	0.614	0.558	0.508	0.463	0.386	0.322	0.270	0.227
11	0.650	0.585	0.527	0.475	0.429	0.350	0.287	0.237	0.195
12	0.625	0.557	0.497	0.444	0.397	0.319	0.257	0.208	0.168
13	0.601	0.530	0.469	0.415	0.368	0.290	0.229	0.182	0.145
14	0.577	0.505	0.442	0.388	0.340	0.263	0.205	0.160	0.125
15	0.555	0.481	0.417	0.362	0.315	0.239	0.183	0.140	0.108
16	0.534	0.458	0.394	0.339	0.292	0.218	0.163	0.123	0.093
17	0.513	0.436	0.371	0.317	0.270	0.198	0.146	0.108	0.080
18	0.494	0.416	0.350	0.296	0.250	0.180	0.130	0.095	0.069
19	0.475	0.396	0.331	0.277	0.232	0.164	0.116	0.083	0.060
20	0.456	0.377	0.312	0.258	0.215	0.149	0.104	0.073	0.051

For the 10% investment for one year, we find the junction in the 10% column and across from 1 in the Period column. The figure 0.909 is computed as follows: $1/1.10 = 0.909$. This work has been done for us, and only the present values are given in the table. The heading in Exhibit 15A-6 states $1. To figure present value for $5,000, we multiply $5,000 by 0.909. The result is $4,545, which matches the result we obtained by hand.

For the two-year investment, we read down the 10% column and across the Period 2 row. We multiply 0.826 (computed as $0.909/1.10 = 0.826$) by $5,000 and get $4,130, which confirms our earlier computation of $4,132 (the difference is due to rounding in the present-value table). Using the table, we can compute the present value of any single future amount.

Present Value of an Annuity Let's return to the investment example that provided the investor with only a single future receipt ($5,000 at the end of two years). Annuity investments provide multiple receipts of an equal amount at fixed intervals over the investment's duration.

Consider an investment that promises *annual* cash receipts of $10,000 to be received at the end of each of three years. Assume that you demand a 12% return on your investment. What is the investment's present value? What would you pay today to acquire the investment? The investment spans three periods, and you would pay the sum of three present values. The computation follows.

The present value of this annuity is $24,020. By paying this amount today, you will receive $10,000 at the end of each of the three years while earning 12% on your investment.

Year	Annual Cash Receipt	×	Present Value of $1 at 12% (Exhibit 15A-6)	=	Present Value of Annual Cash Receipt
1	$10,000	×	0.893	=	$ 8,930
2	10,000	×	0.797	=	7,970
3	10,000	×	0.712	=	7,120
		Total present value of investment		=	$24,020

The example illustrates repetitive computations of the three future amounts. One way to ease the computational burden is to add the three present values of $1 (0.893 + 0.797 + 0.712) and multiply their sum (2.402) by the annual cash receipt ($10,000) to obtain the present value of the annuity ($10,000 × 2.402 = $24,020).

An easier approach is to use a present value of an annuity table. Exhibit 15A-7 on the next page shows the present value of $1 to be received at the end of each period for a given number of periods. The present value of a three-period annuity at 12% is 2.402 (the junction of the Period 3 row and the 12% column). Thus, $10,000 received annually at the end of each of three years, discounted at 12%, is $24,020 ($10,000 × 2.402), which is the present value.

Present Value of Bonds Payable The present value of a bond—its market price—is the present value of the future principal amount at maturity plus the present value of the future stated interest payments. The principal is a single amount to be paid at maturity. The interest is an annuity because it occurs periodically.

Let's compute the present value of the 9%, five-year bonds of **eBay Inc.** The maturity value of the bonds is $100,000, and they pay 4 1/2% stated (cash) interest semiannually. At issuance, the market interest rate is expressed as 10%, but it is computed at 5% semiannually. Therefore, the market interest rate for each of the 10 semi-

Present Value of Annuity of $1

					Present Value of Annuity of $1				
Period	4%	5%	6%	7%	8%	10%	12%	14%	16%
1	0.962	0.952	0.943	0.935	0.926	0.909	0.893	0.877	0.862
2	1.886	1.859	1.833	1.808	1.783	1.736	1.690	1.647	1.605
3	2.775	2.723	2.673	2.624	2.577	2.487	2.402	2.322	2.246
4	3.630	3.546	3.465	3.387	3.312	3.170	3.037	2.914	2.798
5	4.452	4.329	4.212	4.100	3.993	3.791	3.605	3.433	3.274
6	5.242	5.076	4.917	4.767	4.623	4.355	4.111	3.889	3.685
7	6.002	5.786	5.582	5.389	5.206	4.868	4.564	4.288	4.039
8	6.733	6.463	6.210	5.971	5.747	5.335	4.968	4.639	4.344
9	7.435	7.108	6.802	6.515	6.247	5.759	5.328	4.946	4.607
10	8.111	7.722	7.360	7.024	6.710	6.145	5.650	5.216	4.833
11	8.760	8.306	7.887	7.499	7.139	6.495	5.938	5.453	5.029
12	9.385	8.863	8.384	7.943	7.536	6.814	6.194	5.660	5.197
13	9.986	9.394	8.853	8.358	7.904	7.103	6.424	5.842	5.342
14	10.563	9.899	9.295	8.745	8.244	7.367	6.628	6.002	5.468
15	11.118	10.380	9.712	9.108	8.559	7.606	6.811	6.142	5.575
16	11.652	10.838	10.106	9.447	8.851	7.824	6.974	6.265	5.669
17	12.166	11.274	10.477	9.763	9.122	8.022	7.120	6.373	5.749
18	12.659	11.690	10.828	10.059	9.372	8.201	7.250	6.467	5.818
19	13.134	12.085	11.158	10.336	9.604	8.365	7.366	6.550	5.877
20	13.590	12.462	11.470	10.594	9.818	8.514	7.469	6.623	5.929

annual periods is 5%. We use 5% in computing the present value (PV) of the maturity and of the stated interest. The market price of these bonds is $96,149, as follows:

	Effective Annual Interest Rate ÷ 2	Number of Semiannual Interest Payments	
PV of principal:			
$100,000 × PV of single amount at 5%	↓	for 10 periods	
($100,000 × 0.614—Exhibit 15A-6)		↓	$61,400
PV of stated interest:			
($100,000 × 0.045) × PV of annuity at 5%		for 10 periods	
($4,500 × 7.722—Exhibit 15A-7)			34,749
PV (market price) of bonds			$96,149

The market price of the eBay bonds show a discount because the stated interest rate on the bonds (9%) is less than the market interest rate (10%). We discuss these bonds in more detail on pages 590–591.

Let's consider a premium price for the eBay bonds. Assume that the market interest rate is 8% at issuance. The market rate is 4% for each of the 10 semiannual periods:

	Effective Annual Interest Rate ÷ 2	Number of Semiannual Interest Periods	
PV of principal:			
$100,000 × PV of single amount at 4%	↓	for 10 periods	
($100,000 × 0.676—Exhibit 15A-6)		↓	$ 67,600
PV of stated interest:			
($100,000 × 0.045) × PV of annuity at 4%		for 10 periods	
($4,500 × 8.111—Exhibit 15A-7)			36,500
PV (market price) of bonds			$104,100

We discuss accounting for these bonds on page 591–592.

Appendix Assignments
Problems

P15A-1 Gordon Riley is considering two plans for building an education fund for his children.

Computing future values of investments

Plan A—Invest $2,000 each year to earn 10% annually for six years.

Plan B—Invest $10,000 now, to earn 8% annually for six years.

Which plan provides the larger amount at the end of six years? At the outset, which plan would you expect to provide the larger future amount?

P15A-2 Georgia-Atlantic Corp. needs new manufacturing equipment. Two companies can provide similar equipment but under different payment plans:

Computing present-value amounts

a. **General Electric (GE)** offers to let Georgia-Atlantic pay $60,000 each year for five years. The payments include interest at 12% per year. What is the present value of the payments?
b. **Westinghouse** will let Georgia-Atlantic make a single payment of $400,000 at the end of five years. This payment includes both principal and interest at 12%. What is the present value of this payment?
c. Georgia-Atlantic will purchase the equipment that costs the least, as measured by present value. Which equipment should Georgia-Atlantic select? Why?

P15A-3 This problem demonstrates the relationship between the future value of 1 and the present value of 1.

Relating future-value and present-value amounts

1. Rocky Tanner will need $10,000 at the end of 10 years to cover a business expense due at that time. To meet this future expense, Tanner can invest a sum today. His investment will earn 6% each year over the 10-year period. How much must Tanner invest today (present value)?
2. Now, let's turn this present-value situation around and view it in terms of a future value: Tanner has $5,580 to invest today. He can earn 6% each year over a 10-year period. How much will his investment be worth at the end of 10 years (future value)?

P15A-4 Determine the present value of the following notes and bonds:

Computing the present values of various notes and bonds

a. Ten-year bonds payable with maturity value of $88,000 and stated interest rate of 12%, paid semiannually. The market rate of interest is 12% at issuance.
b. Same bonds payable as in a, but the market interest rate is 14%.
c. Same bonds payable as in a, but the market interest rate is 10%.

P15A-5 For each bond in Problem 15A-4, journalize issuance of the bond and the first semiannual interest payment. The company amortizes bond premium and discount by the straight-line method. Explanations are not required.

Recording bond transactions

P15A-6 On December 31, 20X1, when the market interest rate is 8%, Willis Realty Co. issues $400,000 of 7.25%, 10-year bonds payable. The bonds pay interest semiannually.

Computing a bond's present value, recording its issuance, interest payments, and amortization by the effective-interest method

Required

1. Determine the present value of the bonds at issuance.
2. Assume that the bonds are issued at the price computed in requirement 1. Prepare an effective-interest method amortization table for the first two semiannual interest periods.
3. Using the amortization table prepared in requirement 2, journalize issuance of the bonds and the first two interest payments.

CHAPTER 17

The Statement of Cash Flows

TIPS CHECK YOUR RESOURCES

- Visit the www.prenhall.com/horngren **Web site** for self-study quizzes, video clips, and other resources
- Try the **Quick Check** exercise at the end of the chapter to test your knowledge
- Learn the **key terms**
- Do the **Starter** exercises keyed in the margins
- Work the **mid-** and **end-of-chapter summary problems**
- Use the **Concept Links** to review material in other chapters
- Search the **CD** for review materials by chapter or by key word
- Watch the **tutorial videos** to review key concepts

LEARNING OBJECTIVES

⭐1 Identify the purposes of the statement of cash flows

⭐2 Distinguish among operating, investing, and financing cash flows

⭐3 Prepare a statement of cash flows by the indirect method

⭐4 Prepare a statement of cash flows by the direct method

W hy is cash flow so important? You can probably begin to answer that question from your own experience: It takes cash to pay the bills. You have a certain amount of income, and you have certain expenses: food, gas, entertainment, car insurance, and credit cards. The two have to match in quantity and in timing. You may borrow money for a large purchase, like a car, but if you have to borrow money for everyday living expenses, you are in trouble.

Businesses, including e-businesses, work the same way: They need enough cash flowing in to pay the bills and run their operations. Take eBay, a company that has revolutionized commerce. Lots of dot.coms have come and gone, but eBay is still going strong. One reason is that the company is both profitable and cash-rich. In 2001, eBay's operations provided more than $250 million of cash. In 2002, cash flow almost doubled—to $479 million—

eBay

quite an accomplishment for such a young company. Being cash-rich allows eBay to plan for expansion:

eBay Inc. Outlines Global Business Strategy

eBay Inc., . . . the world's online marketplace, [recently] outlined its strategy for growth. . . . eBay executives highlighted key areas of growth, both domestically and abroad. "The . . . potential of our business gives us great confidence in the future," said Meg Whitman, President and CEO of eBay. "The eBay marketplace is thriving. . . ." [eBay press release] ∎

■Sitemap

- ■ Basic Concepts
- ■ The Indirect Method
- ■ The Direct Method
- ■ Appendix: Work Sheet Approach

This chapter is devoted to analyzing cash flows because understanding cash flows is vital for making good business decisions. We will see how to prepare the statement of cash flows, which is the basis for the analysis, and how to interpret cash-flow information.

We begin by explaining the statement format, called the indirect approach, that is used by the vast majority of companies. We end the chapter with the alternate format of the statement of cash flows, the direct approach. This chapter will prepare you to analyze the cash flows of any company you encounter. It has three distinct sections:

- ■ Introduction
- ■ Preparing the Statement of Cash Flows by the Indirect Method, which begins on page 661
- ■ Preparing the Statement of Cash Flows by the Direct Method, which begins on page 671

The introduction applies to all the cash-flow topics. To cover only the indirect method, instructors can assign the first two parts of the chapter. Those interested only in the direct method can cover the Introduction and proceed to the direct method on page 671.

- ■ **Basic Concepts**
- ☐ The Indirect Method
- ☐ The Direct Method
- ☐ Appendix: Work Sheet Approach

Student Resource CD

direct method, financing activities, indirect method, investing activities, operating activities, statement of cash flows

Basic Concepts: Statement of Cash Flows

A balance sheet reports financial position, and balance sheets for two periods show whether cash increased or decreased. For example, Anchor Corporation's comparative balance sheet reported the following:

	20X5	20X4	Increase (Decrease)
Cash	$22,000	$42,000	$(20,000)

You can see that Anchor's cash decreased by $20,000 during 20X5. But the balance sheet doesn't show *why* cash decreased. We need the cash-flow statement for that.

Statement of Cash Flows
Reports cash receipts and cash payments during the period.

Cash Flows
Cash receipts and cash payments.

The **statement of cash flows** reports **cash flows**—cash receipts and cash payments—during the period. It shows where cash came from and how it was spent. It explains the *causes* of the change in cash during any given time period. The statement of cash flows covers a span of time and therefore is dated "Year Ended December 31, 20X5" or "Month Ended June 30, 20X5." Exhibit 17-1 illustrates the time element of each financial statement.

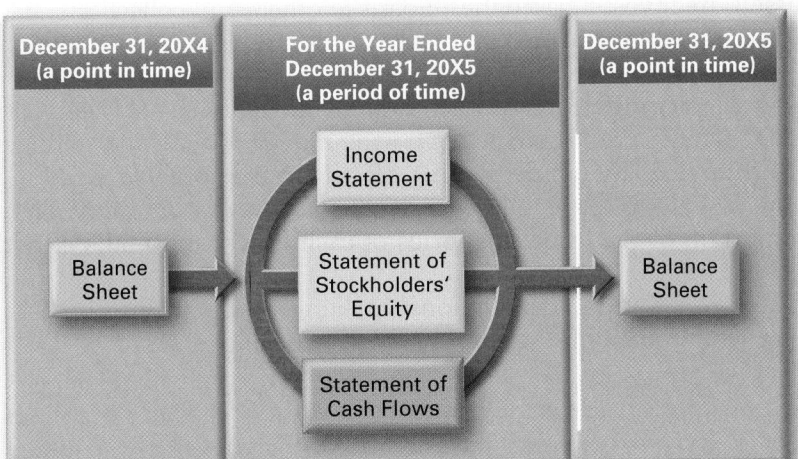

Exhibit 17-1

Timing of the Financial Statements

The statement of cash flows serves several purposes:

1. *Predicts future cash flows.* Past cash receipts and payments are good predictors of future cash flows.

2. *Evaluates management decisions.* If managers make wise investment decisions, the business prospers. If they make unwise investments, the business suffers. The statement of cash flows reports cash flows from operations and also the investments the company is making. Investors and creditors use cash-flow information to evaluate managers' decisions.

3. *Predicts ability to make debt payments to lenders and to pay dividends to stockholders.* Lenders want to collect interest and principal on their loans. Stockholders want dividends on their investments. The statement of cash flows helps predict whether the business can make these payments.

On a statement of cash flows, *Cash* means more than just cash on hand and cash in the bank. It includes **cash equivalents,** which are highly liquid short-term investments that can be readily converted into cash. Examples of cash equivalents are money-market investments and investments in U.S. government securities. Businesses invest cash in liquid assets rather than let the cash remain idle. Throughout this chapter, the term *cash* refers to cash and cash equivalents.

Operating, Investing, and Financing Activities

A business engages in three types of business activities:

- Operating activities
- Investing activities
- Financing activities

Operating activities create revenues, expenses, gains, and losses. They affect *net income* on the income statement, which is a product of accrual accounting. The statement of cash flows reports the cash effects of operating activities. Operating activities also affect *current assets* and *current liabilities* on the balance sheet. Operating activities are the most important of the three categories. A successful business must generate most of its cash from day-to-day operations.

Investing activities increase and decrease *long-term assets,* such as computers and software, land, buildings, and equipment. The purchases and sales of

★ *Identify the purposes of the statement of cash flows*

✔ **Starter 17-1**

Cash Equivalents
Highly liquid short-term investments that can be readily converted into cash.

★2 *Distinguish among operating, investing, and financing cash flows*

Operating Activities
Activities that create revenue or expense in the entity's major line of business; a section of the statement of cash flows. Operating activities affect the income statement.

Investing Activities
Activities that increase or decrease long-term assets; a section of the statement of cash flows.

these assets are investing activities. Loans to others and collections of loans are also investing activities. Investing activities are less critical than operating activities.

Financing activities obtain cash to launch a business and keep it running. Financing includes issuing stock, borrowing money, buying and selling treasury stock, and paying dividends. Paying off a loan is another financing activity. Financing cash flows relate to *long-term liabilities* and *owners' equity*. They are the least important of the three categories of cash flows, and that's why they are reported last.

Exhibit 17-2 shows the relationship between operating, investing, and financing activities and the various parts of the balance sheet.

Financing Activities
Activities that obtain the cash needed to launch and sustain the business; a section of the statement of cash flows.

Exhibit 17-2

Operating, Investing, and Financing Cash Flows and the Balance-Sheet Accounts

Cash and Kisses Meet at Match.com

Who says "Money Can't Buy Me Love"? Match.com, the Internet dating service, is proving that money *can* buy at least the potential for love. Cash flow at the online dating service has surged as it has collected over $15 million a month from clients. For their fees, clients can post photos, contact other members, and receive alerts when potential matches show up.

Ticketmaster, Match.com's parent company, is delighted. Ticketmaster posted its first positive cash flow in 2001, thanks largely to Match.com. Analysts are not surprised: "Online dating [. . .] is one of the few [things] people will [pay] for online, [and. . .] companies are actually upping their prices."

Match.com's only big operating expense is advertising. The company has stayed on top by spending $50 million a year on TV ads. Yet, boasts the Ticketmaster chief executive, 30% to 70% of Match.com's advertising dollars are "instantly recouped."

Cash-rich Internet companies like Match.com can offer vital lessons about what works online. In general, these companies provide services that are information-intensive and require no physical transport of goods. There are no returned goods or other fulfillment costs to deal with.

For Match.com, fulfillment occurs off-screen: To date, the company boasts 1,300 marriages, hundreds of thousands of relationships, and more than 50 babies born of Match.com unions.

Based on: Robert Barker, "Is Ticketmaster Your Perfect Date?" *Business Week*, April 22, 2002, p. 108. Bob Tedeschi, "Online Matchmakers Are Helping to Bolster the Finances of Their Corporate Parents as They Raise the Romantic Hopes of Clients," *The New York Times*, February 4, 2002, p. C6. Julia Angwin, "Net Income: Latest Dot-Com Fad Is a Bit Old-Fashioned: It's Called 'Profitability,'" *The Wall Street Journal*, August 14, 2002, p. A1. Dennis McCafferty, "Hosting in the Name of Love," Hostingtech.com, October 2002.

Two Formats for Operating Activities

There are two ways to format operating activities on the statement of cash flows:

- **Indirect method**, which reconciles from net income to net cash provided by operating activities
- **Direct method**, which reports all cash receipts and cash payments from operating activities

The two methods use different computations but produce the same amount of cash from operations. The indirect and direct methods have no effect on investing or financing activities. The following table summarizes the differences between these approaches for operating activities (all dollar amounts are assumed for the illustration).

Indirect Method		Direct Method	
Net income	$ 300	Collections from customers	$ 900
Adjustments:		*Deductions:*	
Depreciation, etc.	100	Payments to suppliers, etc....	(500)
Net cash provided by		Net cash provided by	
operating activities....	$ 400	operating activities	$ 400

Let's begin with the indirect method because most companies use it.

Preparing the Statement of Cash Flows by the Indirect Method

To prepare the statement of cash flows, you need data from the income statement and the balance sheet. Consider Anchor Corporation, a dealer in older British sports cars such as MG, Triumph, and Austin Healey. To prepare the statement of cash flows by the indirect method,

STEP 1 Lay out the template as shown in Exhibit 17-3. The exhibit is comprehensive. Steps 2 to 4 will complete the statement of cash flows.

STEP 2 Use the comparative balance sheet to determine the increase or decrease in cash. The change in cash is the "check figure" for the statement of cash flows. Exhibit 17-4 gives the comparative balance sheet of Anchor Corporation at December 31, 20X5 and 20X4, with cash highlighted. Anchor's cash decreased by $20,000 during 20X5.

STEP 3 From the income statement, take net income, depreciation, depletion, and amortization expense, and any gains or losses on the sale of assets. Exhibit 17-5 gives the income statement of Anchor Corporation for the year ended December 31, 20X5, with relevant items highlighted.

STEP 4 Use data from the income statement and balance sheet to complete the statement of cash flows. The statement is complete only after you have explained year-to-year changes in all balance-sheet accounts.

Let's apply these steps to prepare the operating activities section of Anchor Corporation's statement of cash flows. Exhibit 17-6 gives the operating activities section of the statement of cash flows.

Indirect Method
Format of the operating activities section of the statement of cash flows; starts with net income and reconciles to net cash provided by operating activities.

Direct Method
Format of the operating activities section of the statement of cash flows; lists the major categories of operating cash receipts and cash payments.

✔ Starter 17-2

☐ Basic Concepts
■ The Indirect Method
☐ The Direct Method
☐ Appendix: Work Sheet Approach

Student ResourceCD

indirect method, financing activities, investing activities, operating activities, financing cash flows, investing cash flows, operating cash flows

Prepare a statement of cash flows by the indirect method

Exhibit 17-3

Template of the Statement
of Cash Flows: Indirect Method

✔ Starter 17-3

Anchor Corporation

Statement of Cash Flows
Year Ended December 31, 20X5

Cash flows from operating activities:
Net income
Adjustments to reconcile net income to net cash provided by
operating activities:
+ Depreciation / amortization expense
+ Loss on sale of long-term assets
– Gain on sale of long-term assets
– Increases in current assets other than cash
+ Decreases in current assets other than cash
+ Increases in current liabilities
– Decreases in current liabilities
Net cash provided by operating activities

Cash flows from investing activities:
Sales of long-term assets (investments, land, building, equipment,
and so on)
– Purchases of long-term assets
Net cash provided by (used for) investing activities

Cash flows from financing activities:
Issuance of stock
+ Sale of treasury stock
– Purchase of treasury stock
+ Issuance of notes or bonds payable (borrowing)
– Payment of notes or bonds payable
– Payment of dividends
Net cash provided by (used for) financing activities

Net increase (decrease) in cash during the year
+ Cash at December 31, 20X4
= Cash at December 31, 20X5

Exhibit 17-4 **Comparative Balance Sheet**

Anchor Corporation

Comparative Balance Sheet
December 31, 20X5 and 20X4

(In thousands)	20X5	20X4	Increase (Decrease)	
Assets				
Current:				
Cash..................................	$ 22	$ 42	$ (20)	Changes in current assets—Operating
Accounts receivable	96	81	15	
Inventory	143	145	(2)	
Plant assets, net of depreciation	464	219	245	Changes in noncurrent assets—Investing
Total................................	$725	$487	$238	
Liabilities				
Current:				
Accounts payable	$ 91	$ 57	$ 34	Changes in current liabilities—Operating
Accrued liabilities	5	9	(4)	
Long-term notes payable	160	77	83	
Stockholders' Equity				Changes in long-term liabilities and common stock—Financing
Common stock........................	359	258	101	
Retained earnings	110	86	24	Change due to net income—Operating / Change due to dividends—Financing
Total................................	$725	$487	$238	

Exhibit 17-5

Income Statement

Anchor Corporation

Income Statement
Year Ended December 31, 20X5

	(In thousands)	
Revenues and gains:		
Sales revenue	$284	
Interest revenue	12	
Dividend revenue	9	
Gain on sale of plant assets	8	
Total revenues and gains		$313
Expenses:		
Cost of goods sold	$150	
Salary and wage expense	56	
Depreciation expense	18	
Other operating expense	17	
Interest expense	16	
Income tax expense	15	
Total expenses		272
Net income		$ 41

Exhibit 17-6

Statement of Cash Flows—
Operating Activities by the
Indirect Method

Anchor Corporation

Statement of Cash Flows
Operating Activities Only
For the Year Ended December 31, 20X5

		(In thousands)	
Cash flows from operating activities:			
	Net income		$41
	Adjustments to reconcile net income to net cash provided by operating activities:		
Ⓐ	Depreciation	$ 18	
Ⓑ	Gain on sale of plant assets	(8)	
Ⓒ	Increase in accounts receivable	(15)	
	Decrease in inventory	2	
	Increase in accounts payable	34	
	Decrease in accrued liabilities	(4)	27
	Net cash provided by operating activities		$68

Cash Flows from Operating Activities

The operating section of the cash-flow statement begins with net income, taken from the income statement (Exhibit 17-5). Additions and subtractions, which follow, are labeled "Adjustments to reconcile net income to net cash provided by operating activities."

Operating Activities Are Related to the Transactions That Make Up Net Income (Revenues, Expenses, Gains, and Losses).[1]

---

[1]The authors thank Alfonso Oddo for suggesting this summary.

Ⓐ **DEPRECIATION, DEPLETION, AND AMORTIZATION EXPENSES**   These expenses are added back to net income to reconcile from net income to cash flow. Let's see why. Depreciation is recorded as follows:

Depreciation Expense	18,000	
Accumulated Depreciation.............		18,000

You can see that depreciation does not affect cash. However, depreciation, like all other expenses, decreases net income. Therefore, in going from net income to cash flows, we add depreciation back to net income. The add-back cancels the earlier deduction.

Example: Suppose you had only two transactions during the period, a $1,000 cash sale and depreciation expense of $300. Net income is $700 ($1,000 − $300). But cash flow from operations is $1,000. To reconcile from net income ($700) to cash flow ($1,000), add back depreciation ($300). Also add back depletion and amortization.

Ⓑ **GAINS AND LOSSES ON THE SALE OF ASSETS**   Sales of long-term assets are *investing* activities. A gain or loss on the sale is included in net income and therefore must be adjusted out of net income on the statement of cash flows. Exhibit 17-6 includes an adjustment for a gain. During 20X5, Anchor sold equipment for $62,000. The equipment's book value was $54,000, so there was a gain of $8,000.

The $62,000 sale is an investing cash flow, and the $8,000 gain on the sale must be removed from operating cash flow. We explain investing activities in the next section.

A loss on the sale of plant assets would be *added back* to net income. The cash received from selling the plant assets is then reported under investing activities.

Ⓒ **CHANGES IN THE CURRENT ASSET AND CURRENT LIABILITY ACCOUNTS**   Most current assets and current liabilities result from operating activities. For example, accounts receivable result from sales, inventory relates to cost of goods sold, and so on. Changes in the current accounts are reported as adjustments to net income on the cash-flow statement. The reasoning follows:

↑ Current assets ⇒ ↓ Cash

1. *An increase in a current asset other than cash means a decrease in cash.* The reason is because it takes cash to acquire assets. If Accounts Receivable, Inventory, or Prepaid Expenses increase during the period, subtract the increase from net income to measure cash flow from operations.

↓ Current assets ⇒ ↑ Cash

2. *A decrease in a current asset other than cash means an increase in cash.* Suppose Anchor's Accounts Receivable decreased by $4,000. Anchor must have collected on the Accounts Receivable. Therefore, add decreases in Accounts Receivable and the other current assets to net income.

↓ Current liabilities ⇒ ↓ Cash

3. *A decrease in a current liability means a decrease in cash.* The payment of a current liability causes cash to decrease. Therefore, subtract decreases in current liabilities from net income.

↑ Current liabilities ⇒ ↑ Cash

The authors thank M. Suzanne Oliver for suggesting these displays.

4. *An increase in a current liability means an increase in cash.* Anchor's Accounts Payable increased. This means that cash was *not* spent to pay this liability, so Anchor has more cash on hand. Thus, increases in current liabilities are *added* to net income.

EVALUATING CASH FLOWS FROM OPERATING ACTIVITIES   During 20X5, Anchor Corporation's operations provided net cash flow of $68,000. This amount exceeds net income, as it should because of the add-back of depreciation. However, to fully evaluate a company's cash flows, you must also examine its investing and financing activities. Let's see how to report those cash flows, as shown in Exhibit 17-7, which gives Anchor's full-blown statement of cash flows.

Exhibit 17-7

Statement of Cash Flows—
Indirect Method

Anchor Corporation

Statement of Cash Flows
For the Year Ended December 31, 20X5

		(In thousands)	
Cash flows from operating activities:			
Net income.		$ 41	
Adjustments to reconcile net income to net cash			
provided by operating activities:			
Ⓐ Depreciation	$ 18		
Ⓑ Gain on sale of plant assets	(8)		
Increase in accounts receivable.	(15)		
Decrease in inventory.	2		
Ⓒ Increase in accounts payable.	34		
Decrease in accrued liabilities.	(4)	27	✔ Starter 17-4
Net cash provided by operating activities		68	
Cash flows from investing activities:			
Acquisition of plant assets.	$ (317)		
Proceeds from sale of plant assets	62		
Net cash used for investing activities		(255)	
Cash flows from financing activities:			
Proceeds from issuance of common stock.	$ 101		
Proceeds from issuance of long-term notes payable . .	94		
Payment of long-term notes payable.	(11)		
Payment of dividends	(17)		
Net cash provided by financing activities.		167	
Net decrease in cash		$ (20)	✔ Starter 17-5
Cash balance, December 31, 20X4		42	
Cash balance, December 31, 20X5		$ 22	✔ Starter 17-6

Cash Flows from Investing Activities

Investing activities affect long-term asset accounts, such as Plant Assets and Investments. Let's see how to compute the investing cash flows.

COMPUTING ACQUISITIONS AND SALES OF PLANT ASSETS Companies keep separate accounts for Land, Buildings, Equipment, and other plant assets. But for computing investing cash flows, it is helpful to combine these accounts into a single Plant Assets account. Also, we subtract accumulated depreciation from the assets' cost and work with a single net figure for plant assets. This simplifies the computations.

To illustrate, observe that Anchor Corporation's

- Balance sheet reports beginning plant assets, net of depreciation, of $219,000 and an ending net amount of $464,000 (Exhibit 17-4).

- Income statement shows depreciation expense of $18,000 and an $8,000 gain on sale of plant assets (Exhibit 17-5).

Further, the acquisitions of plant assets total $317,000 (see Exhibit 17-7). How much, then, are the proceeds from the sale of plant assets? First, we must determine the book value of plant assets sold, as follows:

Plant Assets (Net)									
Beginning balance	+	Acquisitions	−	Depreciation	−	Book value of assets sold	=	Ending balance	
$219,000	+	$317,000	−	$18,000		− X	=	$464,000	
						− X	=	$464,000 − $219,000 − $317,000 + $18,000	
						X	=	$54,000	

Now we can compute the sale proceeds:

Sale proceeds	=	Book value of assets sold	+	Gain	−	Loss
	=	$54,000	+	$8,000	−	$0
	=	$62,000				

Trace the sale proceeds of $62,000 to the statement of cash flows in Exhibit 17-7. If the sale resulted in a loss of $3,000, the sale proceeds would be $51,000 ($54,000 − $3,000), and the statement of cash flows would report $51,000 as a cash receipt from this investing activity.

The Plant Assets T-account provides another look at the computation of the book value of the assets sold.

Plant Assets (Net)

Beginning balance	219,000	Depreciation	18,000
Acquisitions	317,000	Book value of assets sold	54,000
Ending balance	464,000		

✔ **Starter 17-7**

Proceeds from the sale of an asset can be computed as follows:

Proceeds = Book value sold + Gain, or − Loss

The book-value information comes from the balance sheet; the gain or loss comes from the income statement. Exhibit 17-8 summarizes the computation of the investing cash flows.

Exhibit 17-8 | Computing Cash Flows from Investing Activities

Receipts

From sale of plant assets	Beginning plant assets (net)	+	Acquisition cost	−	Depreciation	−	Book value of assets sold	=	Ending plant assets (net)
	Cash received	=	Book value of assets sold	$+$ or $-$	Gain on sale / Loss on sale				

Payments

For acquisition of plant assets	Beginning plant assets (net)	+	Acquisition cost	−	Depreciation	−	Book value of assets sold	=	Ending plant assets (net)

Cash Flows from Financing Activities

Financing activities affect the liability and stockholders' equity accounts, such as Long-Term Notes Payable, Bonds Payable, Common Stock, and Retained Earnings.

COMPUTING ISSUANCES AND PAYMENTS OF LONG-TERM NOTES PAYABLE

The beginning and ending balances of Long-Term Notes Payable or Bonds Payable are taken from the balance sheet. If either the amount of new issuances or the payments is known, the other amount can be computed. For Anchor Corporation, new issuances of notes payable total $94,000 (Exhibit 17-7). The computation of debt payments uses the Long-Term Notes Payable account, with amounts from Anchor Corporation's balance sheet in Exhibit 17-4:

Long-Term Notes Payable

Beginning balance	+	Issuance of new notes payable	−	Payment of notes payable	=	Ending balance
$77,000	+	$94,000		−X	=	$160,000
				−X	=	$160,000 − $77,000 − $94,000
				X	=	$11,000

Another view:

Long-Term Notes Payable

		Beginning balance	77,000
Payments	11,000	Issuance of new notes payable	94,000
		Ending balance	160,000

COMPUTING ISSUANCES OF STOCK AND PURCHASES OF TREASURY STOCK

Cash flows for these financing activities can be determined by analyzing the stock accounts. For example, the amount of a new issuance of common stock is determined from Common Stock. Using data from Exhibits 17-4 and 17-7:

Common Stock

Beginning balance	+	Issuance of new stock	=	Ending balance
$ 258,000	+	$101,000	=	$359,000

Another view:

Common Stock

	Beginning balance	258,000
	Issuance of new stock	101,000
	Ending balance	359,000

Apart from the Anchor Corporation example, cash flows affecting Treasury Stock can be analyzed as follows:

Treasury Stock (Amounts assumed for illustration only)

Beginning balance	+	Purchase of treasury stock	=	Ending balance
$16,000	+	$3,000	=	$19,000

Another view:

Treasury Stock

Beginning balance	16,000	
Purchases of treasury stock	3,000	
Ending balance	19,000	

COMPUTING DIVIDEND PAYMENTS

The amount of dividend payments can be computed by analyzing Retained Earnings. The T-accounts below provide another view.

Retained Earnings

Beginning balance	+	Net income	−	Dividends	=	Ending balance
$86,000	+	$41,000		−X	=	$110,000
				−X	=	$110,000 − $86,000 − $41,000
				X	=	$17,000

Retained Earnings

		Beginning balance	86,000
Dividends	17,000	Net income	41,000
		Ending balance	110,000

✔ Starter 17-8

A stock dividend has *no* effect on Cash and is *not* reported on the cash-flow statement. Exhibit 17-9 summarizes the computation of cash flows from financing activities, highlighted in color.

| Exhibit 17-9 | Computing Cash Flows from Financing Activities |

Receipts

From issuance of long-term notes payable	Beginning notes payable	+	Issuance of notes payable	−	Payment of notes payable	=	Ending long-term notes payable
From issuance of stock	Beginning stock	+	Issuance of new stock			=	Ending stock	

Payments

Of long-term notes payable	Beginning notes payable	+	Issuance of notes payable	−	Payment of notes payable	=	Ending long-term notes payable
To purchase treasury stock	Beginning treasury stock	+	Cost of treasury stock	=	Ending treasury stock			
Of dividends	Beginning retained earnings	+	Net income	−	Dividends	=	Ending retained earnings	

Classify each of the following as an operating activity, an investing activity, or a financing activity:

a. Issuance of stock
b. Borrowing
c. Sales revenue
d. Payment of dividends
e. Purchase of land
f. Purchase of treasury stock

g. Paying bonds payable
h. Interest expense
i. Sale of equipment
j. Cost of goods sold
k. Purchase of another company
l. Making a loan

Answer:

a. Financing
b. Financing
c. Operating
d. Financing

e. Investing
f. Financing
g. Financing
h. Operating

i. Investing
j. Operating
k. Investing
l. Investing

Noncash Investing and Financing Activities

Companies make investments that do not require cash. They also obtain financing other than cash. Our examples thus far have included none of these transactions. Now suppose Anchor Corporation issued common stock of $320,000 to acquire a building. Anchor would journalize this transaction as follows:

Building	320,000	
Common Stock		320,000

This transaction would not be reported on the cash-flow statement because Anchor paid no cash. But the building and the common stock are important. *Noncash investing and financing activities* can be reported in a separate schedule that accompanies the statement of cash flows. Exhibit 17-10 illustrates noncash investing and financing activities (all amounts are assumed). This information follows the cash-flow statement or can be disclosed in a note.

Exhibit 17-10
Noncash Investing and Financing Activities (All amounts assumed)

	Thousands
Noncash Investing and Financing Activities:	
Acquisition of building by issuing common stock	$320
Acquisition of land by issuing note payable	70
Payment of note payable by issuing common stock	100
Total noncash investing and financing activities	$490

Now let's put into practice what you have learned about the statement of cash flows prepared by the indirect method.

MID-CHAPTER *Summary Problem*

CHECK YOUR RESOURCES

Robins Corporation reported the following income statement and comparative balance sheet for 20X5, along with transaction data for 20X5:

Robins Corporation

Income Statement
Year Ended December 31, 20X5

Sales revenue		$662,000
Cost of goods sold		560,000
Gross profit		102,000
Operating expenses:		
Salary expense	$46,000	
Depreciation expense	10,000	
Rent expense	2,000	
Total operating expenses		58,000
Income from operations		44,000
Other items:		
Loss on sale of equipment		(2,000)
Income before income tax		42,000
Income tax expense		16,000
Net income		$ 26,000

Robins Corporation

Balance Sheet
December 31, 20X5 and 20X4

Assets	20X5	20X4	Liabilities	20X5	20X4
Current:			Current:		
Cash and equivalents	$ 22,000	$ 3,000	Accounts payable	$ 35,000	$ 26,000
Accounts receivable	22,000	23,000	Accrued liabilities	7,000	9,000
Inventories	35,000	34,000	Income tax payable	10,000	10,000
Total current assets	79,000	60,000	Total current liabilities	52,000	45,000
Equipment, net	126,000	72,000	Bonds payable	84,000	53,000
			Owners' Equity		
			Common stock	52,000	20,000
			Retained earnings	27,000	19,000
			Less: Treasury stock	(10,000)	(5,000)
Total assets	$205,000	$132,000	Total liabilities and equity	$205,000	$132,000

Transaction Data for 20X5:	
Purchase of equipment	$140,000
Payment of dividends	18,000
Issuance of common stock to retire bonds payable	13,000
Issuance of bonds payable to borrow cash	44,000
Issuance of common stock	19,000
Sale of equipment (book value, $76,000)	74,000
Purchase of treasury stock	5,000

Required

Prepare Robins Corporation's statement of cash flows for the year ended December 31, 20X5. Format operating cash flows by the indirect method. Follow the four steps outlined below.

Requirement 1

STEP 1 Lay out the template of the statement of cash flows.

STEP 2 From the comparative balance sheet, determine the increase in cash during the year, $19,000.

STEP 3 From the income statement, take net income, depreciation, and the loss on sale of equipment to the statement of cash flows.

STEP 4 Complete the statement of cash flows. Account for the year-to-year change in each balance sheet account. Prepare a T-account to show the transaction activity in each long-term balance-sheet account.

Solution

Robins Corporation		
Statement of Cash Flows		
Year Ended December 31, 20X5		
Cash flows from operating activities:		
Net income		$26,000
Adjustments to reconcile net income to		
net cash provided by operating activities:		
Depreciation	$ 10,000	
Loss on sale of equipment	2,000	
Decrease in accounts receivable.............	1,000	
Increase in inventories	(1,000)	
Increase in accounts payable	9,000	
Decrease in accrued liabilities	(2,000)	19,000
Net cash provided by operating activities...		45,000
Cash flows from investing activities:		
Purchase of equipment.......................	$(140,000)	
Sale of equipment	74,000	
Net cash used for investing activities...........		(66,000)
Cash flows from financing activities:		
Issuance of common stock	$ 19,000	
Payment of dividends.........................	(18,000)	
Issuance of bonds payable	44,000	
Purchase of treasury stock	(5,000)	
Net cash provided by financing activities		40,000
Net increase in cash		$19,000
Cash balance, December 31, 20X4		3,000
Cash balance, December 31, 20X5		$22,000
Noncash investing and financing activities:		
Issuance of common stock to retire bonds payable .		$13,000
Total noncash investing and financing activities .		$13,000

Equipment, Net				Bonds Payable		
Bal.	72,000			Bal.	53,000	
	140,000	10,000			13,000	44,000
		76,000			Bal.	84,000
Bal.	126,000					

Common Stock			Retained Earnings			Treasury Stock		
	Bal.	20,000		Bal.	19,000	Bal.	5,000	
		13,000	18,000		26,000		5,000	
		19,000		Bal.	27,000	Bal.	10,000	
	Bal.	52,000						

Excel Application Exercise

Goal: To create an Excel work sheet that computes cash flows from operating activities using the indirect method.

Scenario: As an accountant at Ochoa, Inc., you have been asked to compute the net cash provided by operating activities using the indirect method for the month of March. Accounting records for the company reveal the following:

Cash sales	$ 9,000
Loss on sale of land	5,000
Net income	33,000
Depreciation	12,000
Increase in current assets other than cash	17,000
Acquisition of land	37,000
Decrease in current liabilities	9,000

Using the information provided in this exercise, determine the net cash flows from operating activities. When done, answer these questions:

1. Does Ochoa have net cash provided by (or used by) operating activities?
2. Evaluate Ochoa's operating cash flow as either strong or weak.
3. Based on the Application Exercise for this chapter, what decisions might investors make with this information?

Step-by-Step:
1. Open a new Excel work sheet.
2. Create a heading for your work sheet that contains:
   a. Chapter 17 Excel Application Exercise
   b. Ochoa, Inc.
   c. Statement of Cash Flows - Operating Activities
   d. For the Month Ended March 31, 20X5
3. Follow the statement of cash flows format in Exhibit 17-3 and use formulas for all computations.
4. Save your work and print a copy for your files.

Preparing the Statement of Cash Flows by the Direct Method

- ☐ Basic Concepts
- ☐ The Indirect Method
- ■ The Direct Method
- ☐ Appendix: Work Sheet Approach

The Financial Accounting Standards Board (FASB) has expressed a preference for the direct method of reporting cash flows from operating activities. Unfortunately, very few companies use this method because it takes more computations than the indirect method. But the direct method provides clearer information about the sources and uses of cash. Investing and financing cash flows are unaffected by operating cash flows.

To illustrate the statement of cash flows, we will be using Anchor Corporation, a dealer in older British sports cars such as MG, Triumph, and Austin Healey. To prepare the statement of cash flows by the direct method, proceed as follows:

 Student ResourceCD

direct method, financing activities, investing activities, operating activities, financing cash flows, investing cash flows, operating cash flows

⭐ Prepare a statement of cash flows by the direct method

Step 1 Lay out the template of the statement of cash flows by the direct method, as shown in Exhibit 17-11.

Exhibit 17-11

Template of the Statement
of Cash Flows: Direct Method

Anchor Corporation

Statement of Cash Flows
Year Ended December 31, 20X5

Cash flows from operating activities:
  Receipts:
    Collections from customers
    Interest received
    Dividends received on investments
      Total cash receipts
  Payments:
    To suppliers
    To employees
    For interest and income tax
      Total cash payments
  Net cash provided by operating activities

Cash flows from investing activities:
    Sales of long-term assets (investments, land, building, equipment,
      and so on)
  − Purchases of long-term assets
  Net cash provided by (used for) investing activities

Cash flows from financing activities:
    Issuance of stock
  + Sale of treasury stock
  − Purchase of treasury stock
  + Issuance of notes or bonds payable (borrowing)
  − Payment of notes or bonds payable
  − Payment of dividends
  Net cash provided by (used for) financing activities

Net increase (decrease) in cash during the year
  + Cash at December 31, 20X4
  = Cash at December 31, 20X5

STEP 2 Use the comparative balance sheet to determine the increase or decrease in cash during the period. The change in cash is the "check figure" for the statement of cash flows. The comparative balance sheet of Anchor Corporation at December 31, 20X5 and 20X4 shows that Anchor's cash decreased by $20,000 during 20X5. See Exhibit 17-4.

STEP 3 Use the available data to prepare the statement of cash flows. Suppose Anchor has assembled the summary of 20X5 transactions in Exhibit 17-12. These transactions give the data for both the income statement (Exhibit 17-5) and the statement of cash flows. Some transactions affect one statement and some, the other. For example, sales (item 1) are reported on the income statement, and cash collections (item 2) on the statement of cash flows. Other transactions, such as the cash receipt of dividend revenue (item 4) affect both statements. *The statement of cash flows reports only those transactions with cash effects* (those with an asterisk in Exhibit 17-12). Exhibit 17-13 gives Anchor Corporation's statement of cash flows for 20X5.

Cash Flows from Operating Activities

Operating cash flows are listed first because they are the most important source of cash. Exhibit 17-13 shows that Anchor is sound; its operating activities were the largest source of cash receipts, $290,000. Let's examine the operating cash flows (see page 674).

Exhibit 17-12

Summary of Anchor Corporation's 20X5 Transactions

Operating Activities
1. Sales on account, $284,000
*2. Collections from customers, $269,000
*3. Cash receipt of interest revenue, $12,000
*4. Cash receipt of dividend revenue, $9,000
5. Cost of goods sold, $150,000
* 6. Payments to suppliers, $135,000
* 7. Salary expense and payments, $56,000
8. Depreciation expense, $18,000
9. Other operating expense, $17,000
* 10. Interest expense and payments, $16,000
* 11. Income tax expense and payments, $15,000

Investing Activities
* 12. Cash payments to acquire plant assets, $317,000
* 13. Proceeds from sale of plant assets, $62,000, including $8,000 gain

Financing Activities
* 14. Proceeds from issuance of common stock, $101,000
* 15. Proceeds from issuance of long-term note payable, $94,000
* 16. Payment of long-term note payable, $11,000
* 17. Payment of cash dividends, $17,000

* Indicates a cash flow to be reported on the statement of cash flows
Note: Income statement data are used to prepare Exhibit 17-16, page 676.

Exhibit 17-13

Statement of Cash Flows— Direct Method

Anchor Corporation

Statement of Cash Flows
Year Ended December 31, 20X5

	(In thousands)	
Cash flows from operating activities:		
Receipts:		
Collections from customers......................	$ 269	
Interest received	12	
Dividends received.............................	9	
Total cash receipts............................		$290
Payments:		
To suppliers	$(135)	
To employees...................................	(56)	
For interest....................................	(16)	
For income tax..................................	(15)	
Total cash payments..........................		(222)
Net cash provided by operating activities		68
Cash flows from investing activities:		
Acquisition of plant assets........................	$(317)	
Proceeds from sale of plant assets	62	
Net cash used for investing activities		(255)
Cash flows from financing activities:		
Proceeds from issuance of common stock.............	$ 101	
Proceeds from issuance of long-term notes payable	94	
Payment of long-term note payable..................	(11)	
Payment of dividends	(17)	
Net cash provided by financing activities...........		167
Net decrease in cash		$ (20)
Cash balance, December 31, 20X4.....................		42
Cash balance, December 31, 20X5.....................		$ 22

✔ Starter 17-9

CASH COLLECTIONS FROM CUSTOMERS Cash sales bring in cash immediately; collections of accounts receivable take longer. Both are reported on the statement of cash flows as "Collections from customers . . . $269,000" in Exhibit 17-13.

CASH RECEIPTS OF INTEREST The income statement reports interest revenue. Only the cash receipts of interest appear on the statement of cash flows—$12,000 in Exhibit 17-13.

CASH RECEIPTS OF DIVIDENDS Dividend revenue is reported on the income statement, and this cash receipt is reported on the statement of cash flows—$9,000 in Exhibit 17-13. (Dividends *received* are part of operating activities, but dividends *paid* are a financing activity.)

PAYMENTS TO SUPPLIERS Payments to suppliers include all payments for inventory and operating expenses except employee compensation, interest, and income taxes. *Suppliers* are those entities that provide the business with its inventory and essential services. In Exhibit 17-13, Anchor Corporation reports payments to suppliers of $135,000.

PAYMENTS TO EMPLOYEES This category includes payments for salaries and wages. Accrued amounts are not cash flows because they have not yet been paid. The statement of cash flows in Exhibit 17-13 reports only the cash payments ($56,000).

PAYMENTS FOR INTEREST EXPENSE AND INCOME TAX EXPENSE These cash payments are reported separately from the other expenses. In the Anchor Corporation example, interest ($16,000) and income tax expenses ($15,000) equal their cash payments amounts. Therefore, the same amount appears on the income statement and the statement of cash flows.

DEPRECIATION, DEPLETION, AND AMORTIZATION EXPENSE These expenses are *not* listed on the statement of cash flows because they do not affect cash.

Cash Flows from Investing Activities

Investing is critical because a company's investments determine its future course. Large purchases of plant assets signal expansion. Low levels of investing over a lengthy period indicate that the business is not replenishing assets.

PURCHASES OF PLANT ASSETS AND INVESTMENTS IN OTHER COMPANIES These cash payments acquire a long-term asset. The first investing activity reported by Anchor Corporation in Exhibit 17-13 is the purchase of plant assets ($317,000).

PROCEEDS FROM THE SALE OF PLANT ASSETS AND INVESTMENTS These cash receipts are also investing activities. The sale of plant assets needs explanation. Exhibit 17-13 reports that Anchor Corporation received $62,000 cash from the sale of plant assets. The income statement shows an $8,000 gain on this transaction. What is the appropriate amount to show on the cash-flow statement? Report only the cash proceeds from the sale ($62,000), not the $8,000 gain. Investors and creditors are often critical of a company that sells large amounts of its plant assets. The sale may signal an emergency.

Cash Flows from Financing Activities

Cash flows from financing activities include the following:

PROCEEDS FROM ISSUANCE OF STOCK AND NOTES PAYABLE Readers of financial statements want to know how the entity obtains its financing. Issuing stock and borrowing money are two ways to finance a business. In Exhibit 17-13, Anchor Corporation issued common stock and received cash of $101,000. Anchor also issued long-term notes payable to borrow $94,000.

PAYMENT OF NOTES PAYABLE AND PURCHASES OF TREASURY STOCK The payment of notes payable decreases cash, which is the opposite of borrowing. Anchor Corporation reports long-term note payments of $11,000. Other transactions in this category include the purchase of treasury stock.

✔ **Starter 17-10**

PAYMENT OF CASH DIVIDENDS The payment of dividends decreases cash and is therefore a financing activity, as shown by Anchor's $17,000 payment in Exhibit 17-13. A stock dividend has *no* effect on cash and is *not* reported on the cash-flow statement.

✔ **Starter 17-11**

✔ **Starter 17-12**

Noncash Investing and Financing Activities

Companies make investments that do not require cash. They also obtain financing other than cash. Our examples thus far have included none of these transactions. Now suppose that Anchor Corporation issued common stock of $320,000 to acquire a building. Anchor would journalize this transaction as follows:

Building	320,000	
Common Stock.		320,000

This transaction would not be reported on the cash-flow statement because Anchor paid no cash. But the building and the common stock are important. Noncash investing and financing activities can be reported in a separate schedule that accompanies the statement of cash flows, as Exhibit 17-14 illustrates (all amounts are assumed). This information follows the cash-flow statement or can be disclosed in a note.

	Thousands
Noncash Investing and Financing Activities:	
Acquisition of building by issuing common stock.	$320
Acquisition of land by issuing note payable.	70
Payment of note payable by issuing common stock	100
Total noncash investing and financing activities	$490

Exhibit 17-14

Noncash Investing and Financing Activities (All amounts assumed)

Classify each of the following as an operating activity, an investing activity, or a financing activity. Also identify those items that are not reported on the statement of cash flows prepared by the direct method.

a. Net income	i. Issuance of stock
b. Payment of dividends	j. Purchase of another company
c. Borrowing	k. Payment of a note payable
d. Payment of cash to suppliers	l. Payment of income taxes
e. Making a loan	m. Collections from customers
f. Sale of treasury stock	n. Accrual of interest revenue
g. Depreciation expense	o. Expiration of prepaid expense
h. Purchase of equipment	p. Receipt of cash dividends

Stop & Think

Answer:

a. Not reported	e. Investing	i. Financing	m. Operating
b. Financing	f. Financing	j. Investing	n. Not reported
c. Financing	g. Not reported	k. Financing	o. Not reported
d. Operating	h. Investing	l. Operating	p. Operating

Now let's see how to compute the operating cash flows for the direct method.

Computing Operating Cash Flows by the Direct Method

How do we compute the operating cash flows for the direct method? We can use the income statement and the *changes* in the related balance sheet accounts, as diagrammed in Exhibit 17-15.

Exhibit 17-15 Direct Method: Computing Cash Flows from Operating Activities

Receipts/ Payments	From Income Statement Account	Change in Related Balance Sheet Account
Receipts:		
From customers	Sales Revenue	+ Decrease in Accounts Receivable / − Increase in Accounts Receivable
Payments:		
To suppliers	Cost of Goods Sold	+ Increase in Inventory / − Decrease in Inventory + Decrease in Accounts Payable / − Increase in Accounts Payable
	Operating Expense	+ Increase in Prepaids / − Decrease in Prepaids + Decrease in Accrued Liabilities / − Increase in Accrued Liabilities

We thank Barbara Gerrity for suggesting this exhibit.

Data for computing Anchor Corporation's operating cash flows come from the income statement (Exhibit 17-16) and comparative balance sheet (Exhibit 17-17).

Exhibit 17-16

Income Statement

Anchor Corporation
Income Statement
Year Ended December 31, 20X5

	(In thousands)
Revenues and gains:	
Sales revenue	$284
Interest revenue	12
Dividend revenue	9
Gain on sale of plant assets	8
Total revenues and gains	$313
Expenses:	
Cost of goods sold	$150
Salary and wage expense	56
Depreciation expense	18
Other operating expense	17
Interest expense	16
Income tax expense	15
Total expenses	272
Net income	$ 41

Exhibit 17-17 Comparative Balance Sheet

Anchor Corporation			
Comparative Balance Sheet			
December 31, 20X5 and 20X4			

(In thousands)	20X5	20X4	Increase (Decrease)	
Assets				
Current:				
Cash	$ 22	$ 42	$ (20)	
Accounts receivable	96	81	15	} Changes in current assets—Operating
Inventory	143	145	(2)	
Plant assets, net of depreciation	464	219	245	} Changes in noncurrent assets—Investing
Total.......................	$725	$487	$238	
Liabilities				
Current:				
Accounts payable	$ 91	$ 57	$ 34	} Changes in current liabilities—Operating
Accrued liabilities..................	5	9	(4)	
Long-term notes payable...............	160	77	83	}
Stockholders' Equity				} Changes in long-term liabilities and common stock—Financing
Common stock.......................	359	258	101	}
Retained earnings	110	86	24	} Change due to net income—Operating Change due to dividends—Financing
Total.......................	$725	$487	$238	

COMPUTING CASH COLLECTIONS FROM CUSTOMERS Collections can be computed by converting sales revenue (an accrual-basis amount) to the cash basis. Anchor Corporation's income statement (Exhibit 17-16) reports sales of $284,000. But cash collections are different. Exhibit 17-17 shows that Accounts Receivable increased from $81,000 at the beginning of the year to $96,000 at year-end, a $15,000 increase. Based on those amounts, Cash Collections equal $269,000.

Collections from Customers	=	Sales Revenue	−	Increase in Accounts Receivable
$269,000	=	$284,000	−	$15,000

COMPUTING PAYMENTS TO SUPPLIERS This computation includes two parts:

- Payments for inventory
- Payments for operating expenses (other than interest and income tax)

Payments for inventory are computed by converting cost of goods sold to the cash basis. We must analyze Cost of Goods Sold from the income statement and Inventory and Accounts Payable from the balance sheet. Payments for operating expenses (other than depreciation) use other operating expenses from the income statement and accrued liabilities from the balance sheet. Throughout, all amounts come from Exhibits 17-16 and 17-17.

Payments for Inventory	=	Cost of Goods Sold	−	Decrease in Inventory	−	Increase in Accounts Payable
$114,000	=	$150,000	−	$2,000	−	$34,000

Payments for Operating Expenses	=	Other Operating Expense	+	Decrease in Accrued Liabilities
$21,000	=	$17,000	+	$4,000

Payments to Suppliers	=	Payments for Inventory	+	Payments for Operating Expenses
$135,000	=	$114,000	+	$21,000

Computing Investing and Financing Cash Flows

The computations of investing and financing cash flows are given on pages 665–668.

Viacom, Inc., the company that owns Paramount Pictures, Blockbuster Video, and MTV Music Television, reported the following for 2001 and 2000 (adapted, in millions):

At December 31,	2001	2000
Receivables, net	$ 3,582	$ 3,964
Inventory	5,224	5,035
Accounts payable	945	1,261

Year Ended December 31,	2001	2000
Revenues..........................	$23,223	$20,044
Cost of goods sold	14,137	11,707

Based on these figures, how much cash did Viacom collect from customers during 2001? How much cash did Viacom pay for inventory during 2001?

Answer (In millions):

		Beginning Receivables	+	Revenues	–	Collections	=	Ending Receivables
Collections from customers	= $23,605	$3,964	+	$23,223	–	$23,605	=	$3,582

		Cost of Goods Sold	+	Increase in Inventory	+	Decrease in Accounts Payable	=	Payments
Payments for inventory and related services	= $14,642	$14,137	+	($5,224 – $5,035)	+	($1,261 – $945)	=	$14,642

Decision Guidelines

USING CASH-FLOW AND RELATED INFORMATION TO EVALUATE INVESTMENTS

Ann Browning is a private investor. Through the years, she has devised some guidelines for evaluating investments. Here are some of her guidelines.

Question	Financial Statement	What to Look For
Where is most of the company's cash coming from?	Statement of cash flows	Operating activities → Good sign Investing activities → Bad sign Financing activities → Okay sign
Do high sales and profits translate into more cash?	Statement of cash flows	Usually, but cash flows from *operating* activities must be the main source of cash for long-term success.
If sales and profits are low, how is the company generating cash?	Statement of cash flows	If *investing* activities are generating the cash, the business may be in trouble because it is selling off its long-term assets. If *financing* activities are generating the cash, that cannot go on forever. Sooner or later, investors will demand cash flow from operating activities.
Is the cash balance large enough to provide for expansion?	Balance sheet	The cash balance should be growing over time. If not, the company may be in trouble.
Can the business pay its debts?	Income statement	Increasing trend of net income.
	Statement of cash flows	Cash flows from operating activities should be the main source of cash.
	Balance sheet	Current ratio, debt ratio.

END-OF-CHAPTER *Summary Problem*

CHECK YOUR RESOURCES

Granite Shoals Corporation reported the following comparative balance sheet and income statement for 20X6.

Granite Shoals Corporation

Balance Sheet
December 31, 20X6 and 20X5

	20X6	20X5
Cash	$ 19,000	$ 3,000
Accounts receivable.	22,000	23,000
Inventories	34,000	31,000
Prepaid expenses	1,000	3,000
Equipment (net)	90,000	79,000
Intangible assets.	9,000	9,000
	$175,000	$148,000
Accounts payable.	$ 14,000	$ 9,000
Accrued liabilities	16,000	19,000
Income tax payable	14,000	12,000
Long-term debt.	45,000	50,000
Common stock	31,000	20,000
Retained earnings	64,000	40,000
Treasury stock.	(9,000)	(2,000)
	$175,000	$148,000

Granite Shoals Corporation

Income Statement
Year Ended December 31, 20X6

Sales revenue.	$190,000
Gain on sale of equipment.	6,000
Total revenue and gains.	196,000
Cost of goods sold.	$ 85,000
Depreciation expense	19,000
Other operating expenses	36,000
Total expenses	140,000
Income before income tax	56,000
Income tax expense.	18,000
Net income.	$ 38,000

Required

Assume that **Berkshire Hathaway** is considering buying Granite Shoals Corporation. Berkshire Hathaway analysts need the following Granite Shoals cash-flow data for 20X6. There were no noncash investing and financing activities.

a. Collections from customers
b. Payments for inventory
c. Issuance of common stock
d. Payment of dividends

Solution

a.

Collections from customers	=	Sales revenue	+	Decrease in Accounts Receivable
$191,000	=	$190,000	+	$1,000

b.

Payments for inventory	=	Cost of goods sold	+	Increase in inventory	–	Increase in Accounts Payable
$83,000	=	$85,000	+	$3,000	–	$5,000

c. Analyze Common Stock (let X = issuance)

Beginning	+	Issuance	=	Ending	
$20,000	+	X	=	$31,000	
		X	=		$11,000

d. Analyze Retained Earnings (let X = dividends)

Beginning	+	Net Income	–	Dividends	=	Ending	
$40,000	+	$38,000	–	X	=	$64,000	
				X	=		$14,000

REVIEW *the Statement of Cash Flows*

Quick Check

1. The three main categories of cash-flow activities are
 a. Direct and indirect
 b. Operating, investing, and financing
 c. Noncash investing and financing
 d. Current and long-term

2. The purposes of the cash-flow statement are to
 a. Predict future cash flows
 b. Evaluate management decisions
 c. Determine ability to pay liabilities and dividends
 d. All of the above

3. Financing activities are most closely related to
 a. Current assets and current liabilities
 b. Long-term assets
 c. Long-term liabilities and owners' equity
 d. Net income and dividends

4. Which item does *not* appear on a statement of cash flows prepared by the indirect method?
 a. Collections from customers
 b. Net income
 c. Depreciation
 d. Gain on sale of land

5. Euro Bistro earned net income of $60,000 after deducting depreciation of $4,000 and all other expenses. Current assets increased by $3,000, and current liabilities decreased by $5,000. How much was Euro Bistro's cash provided by operations (indirect method)?
 a. $48,000
 b. $50,000
 c. $52,000
 d. $56,000

6. The Plant Assets account of Canyon Corp. shows the following:

Plant Assets, Net

Beg.	100,000	Depr.	30,000
Purchase	400,000	Sale	?
End.	420,000		

Canyon sold plant assets at a $10,000 gain. Where on the statement of cash flows should Canyon report the sale of plant assets? How much should Canyon report for the sale?
 a. Investing cash flows—sale of $40,000
 b. Investing cash flows—sale of $50,000
 c. Investing cash flows—sale of $60,000
 d. Financing cash flows—sale of $60,000

7. Columbia, Inc., borrowed $15,000, issued common stock of $10,000, and paid dividends of $25,000. What was Columbia's net cash provided (used) by financing activities?
   a. $0
   b. $25,000
   c. $(25,000)
   d. $50,000

8. Which item does *not* appear on a statement of cash flows prepared by the direct method?
   a. Net income
   b. Collections from customers
   c. Payments to suppliers
   d. Payments of income tax

9. Peppertree Copy Center had accounts receivable of $20,000 at the beginning of the year and $50,000 at year-end. Revenue for the year totaled $100,000. How much cash did Peppertree collect from customers?
   a. $170,000
   b. $150,000
   c. $120,000
   d. $70,000

10. Greenlawn Service had operating expense of $40,000. At the beginning of the year, Greenlawn owed $5,000 on accrued liabilities. At year-end, accrued liabilities were $8,000. How much cash did Greenlawn pay for operating expenses?
    a. $35,000
    b. $37,000
    c. $43,000
    d. $45,000

Accounting Vocabulary

cash equivalents (p. 659)
cash flows (p. 658)
direct method (p. 661)

financing activities (p. 660)
indirect method (p. 661)
investing activities (p. 659)

operating activities (p. 659)
statement of cash flows (p. 658)

ASSESS *Your Progress*

Starters

S17-1 Describe how the statement of cash flows helps investors and creditors perform each of the following functions:

1. Predict future cash flows
2. Evaluate management decisions
3. Predict the ability to make debt payments to lenders and pay dividends to stockholders

S17-2 Answer these questions about the statement of cash flows:

a. What is the "check figure" for the statement of cash flows? Where do you get this check figure?
b. List the categories of cash flows in order of importance.
c. What is the first dollar amount to report for the indirect method?
d. What is the first dollar amount to report for the direct method?

S17-3 Post Corporation is preparing its statement of cash flows by the *indirect* method. Post has the following items for you to consider in preparing the statement. Identify each item as

- Operating activity—addition to net income (O+), or subtraction from net income (O–)
- Investing activity (I)
- Financing activity (F)
- Activity that is not used to prepare the cash-flow statement (N)

See *www.prenhall.com/horngren* for selected Starters, Exercises, and Problems.

Purposes of the statement of cash flows
(Obj. 1)

Classifying cash-flow items
(Obj. 1)

Identifying items for reporting cash flows from operations—indirect method
(Obj. 2)

Answer by placing the appropriate symbol in the blank space.

_____ a. Loss on sale of land	_____ f. Increase in accounts
_____ b. Depreciation expense	payable
_____ c. Increase in inventory	_____ g. Payment of dividends
_____ d. Decrease in accounts	_____ h. Decrease in accrued
receivable	liabilities
_____ e. Purchase of equipment	_____ i. Issuance of common stock
	_____ j. Gain on sale of building

Computing cash flows from operating activities—indirect method
(Obj. 3)

S17-4 Vis-à-Vis Printers reported these data for 20X7:

Income Statement	
Net income	$50,000
Depreciation	8,000
Balance sheet	
Increase in Accounts Receivable	6,000
Decrease in Accounts Payable	4,000

Compute Vis-à-Vis Printers' net cash provided by operations—indirect method.

Computing operating cash flows—indirect method
(Obj. 3)

S17-5 (Starter 17-6 is an alternate.) Mid-America Resources, Inc., accountants have assembled the following data for the year ended June 30, 20X5.

Payment of dividends	$ 6,000	Net income	$60,000
Proceeds from issuance		Purchase of equipment..........	40,000
of common stock.............	20,000	Decrease in current liabilities.....	5,000
Increase in current		Payment of note payable	30,000
assets other than cash.........	30,000	Proceeds from sale of land.......	60,000
Purchase of treasury stock.......	5,000	Depreciation expense	15,000

Prepare the *operating* activities section of Mid-America's statement of cash flows for the year ended June 30, 20X5. Mid-America uses the *indirect* method for operating cash flows.

Preparing a statement of cash flows—indirect method
(Obj. 3)

S17-6 Use the data in Starter 17-5 to prepare Mid-America's statement of cash flows for the year ended June 30, 20X5. Mid-America uses the *indirect* method for operating activities. Use Exhibit 17-7 as a guide, but you may stop after determining the net increase (or decrease) in cash.

Computing investing cash flows
(Obj. 3)

S17-7 Grace Chemical Company reported the following financial statements for 20X6:

Grace Chemical Company

Income Statement
Year Ended December 31, 20X6

	(In thousands)
Sales revenue	$710
Cost of goods sold	$340
Depreciation expense..............................	60
Other expenses....................................	200
Total expenses....................................	600
Net income	$110

Grace Chemical Company

Comparative Balance Sheet
December 31, 20X6 and 20X5

(In thousands)

Assets	20X6	20X5	Liabilities	20X6	20X5
Current			Current		
Cash	$ 19	$ 16	Accounts payable	$ 47	$ 42
Accounts receivable	54	48	Salary payable	23	21
Inventory	80	84	Accrued liabilities	8	11
Prepaid expenses	3	2	Long-term notes payable ..	66	68
Long-term investments ...	75	90	**Stockholders' Equity**		
Plant assets, net	225	185	Common stock	40	37
			Retained earnings	272	246
Total	$456	$425	Total	$456	$425

Compute the amount of Grace Chemical's acquisition of plant assets, with Grace selling no plant assets.

S17-8 Use the Grace Chemical Company data in Starter 17-7 to compute

Computing financing cash flows
(Obj. 3)

a. New borrowing or payment of long-term notes payable, with Grace having only one long-term note payable transaction during the year
b. Issuance of common stock, with Grace having only one common stock transaction during the year
c. Payment of cash dividends

S17-9 Wellness Health Laboratories began 20X4 with cash of $104,000. During the year, Wellness earned service revenue of $600,000 and collected $590,000 from customers. Expenses for the year totaled $420,000, of which Wellness paid $410,000 in cash to suppliers and employees. Wellness also paid $140,000 to purchase equipment and a cash dividend of $50,000 to its stockholders during 20X4.

Preparing a statement of cash flows—direct method
(Obj. 4)

    Prepare the company's statement of cash flows for the year ended December 31, 20X4. Format operating activities by the direct method.

S17-10 (Starter 17-11 is an alternate.) Mid-America Resources, Inc., has assembled the following data for the year ended June 30, 20X5.

Computing operating cash flows—direct method
(Obj. 4)

Payment of dividends............................	$ 6,000
Proceeds from issuance of stock	20,000
Collections from customers	200,000
Proceeds from sale of land	60,000
Payments to suppliers............................	80,000
Purchase of equipment...........................	40,000
Payments to employees	70,000
Payment of note payable	30,000

Prepare the *operating* activities section of Mid-America's statement of cash flows for the year ended June 30, 20X5. Mid-America uses the direct method for operating cash flows.

S17-11 Use the data in Starter 17-10 to prepare Mid-America's statement of cash flows for the year ended June 30, 20X5. Mid-America uses the *direct* method for operating activities. Use Exhibit 17-13, page 673, as a guide, but you may stop after determining the net increase (or decrease) in cash.

Preparing a statement of cash flows—direct method
(Obj. 4)

S17-12 Use the Grace Chemical Company data in Starter 17-7 to compute the following:

Computing operating cash flows—direct method
(Obj. 4)

a. Collections from customers   b. Payments for inventory

online homework

Identifying the purposes of the statement of cash flows
(Obj. I)

Exercises

E17-1 Biz Mart Stores, Inc., has experienced an unbroken string of 10 years of growth in net income. Nevertheless, the business is facing bankruptcy. Creditors are calling all of Biz Mart's outstanding loans for immediate payment, and the cash is simply not available. Attempts to explain where Biz Mart went wrong make it clear that managers placed undue emphasis on net income and gave too little attention to cash flows.

Required

Write a brief memo, in your own words, to explain to the managers of Biz Mart Stores the purposes of the statement of cash flows.

Identifying activities for the statement of cash flows—indirect method
(Obj. 2)

E17-2 Identify each of the following transactions as

- Operating activity (O)
- Investing activity (I)
- Financing activity (F)
- Noncash investing and financing activity (NIF)
- Transaction that is not reported on the statement of cash flows (N)

For each cash flow, indicate whether the item increases (+) or decreases (–) cash. The indirect method is used to report cash flows from operating activities.

_____ **a.** Cash sale of land		_____ **j.** Loss on sale of land	
_____ **b.** Issuance of long-term note payable to borrow cash		_____ **k.** Acquisition of equipment by issuance of note payable	
_____ **c.** Depreciation of equipment		_____ **l.** Payment of long-term debt	
_____ **d.** Purchase of treasury stock		_____ **m.** Acquisition of building by issuance of common stock	
_____ **e.** Issuance of common stock			
_____ **f.** Increase in accounts payable		_____ **n.** Accrual of salary expense	
_____ **g.** Net income		_____ **o.** Decrease in inventory	
_____ **h.** Payment of cash dividend		_____ **p.** Increase in prepaid expenses	
_____ **i.** Decrease in accrued liabilities			

Classifying transactions for the statement of cash flows—indirect method
(Obj. 2, 3)

E17-3 Indicate whether each of the following transactions would result in an operating activity, an investing activity, or a financing activity for a statement of cash flows prepared by the *indirect* method and the accompanying schedule of noncash investing and financing activities.

a. Equipment.....................	18,000		**g.** Cash	81,000
Cash		18,000	Common Stock.............	81,000
b. Cash	7,200		**h.** Treasury Stock	13,000
Long-Term Investment		7,200	Cash......................	13,000
c. Bonds Payable.................	45,000		**i.** Cash	60,000
Cash		45,000	Sales Revenue..............	60,000
d. Building......................	164,000		**j.** Land	87,700
Note Payable, Long-Term...		164,000	Cash......................	87,700
e. Loss on Disposal of Equipment ...	1,400		**k.** Depreciation Expense............	9,000
Equipment Net............		1,400	Accumulated Depreciation ..	9,000
f. Dividends Payable..............	16,500			
Cash		16,500		

Computing cash flows from operating activities—indirect method
(Obj. 3)

E17-4 The accounting records of Auto Chef Corporation reveal the following:

Net income	$22,000	Depreciation	$12,000
Sales revenue	9,000	Decrease in current liabilities ..	20,000
Loss on sale of land	5,000	Increase in current assets	
Acquisition of land	37,000	other than cash	27,000

Required

Compute cash flows from operating activities by the indirect method. Use the format of the operating activities section of Exhibit 17-7. Also evaluate the operating cash flow of Auto Chef Corporation. Give the reason for your evaluation.

E17-5 The accounting records of Ochoa, Inc.; include these accounts:

Computing cash flows from operating activities—indirect method
(Obj. 3)

Cash			
Mar. 1	5,000		
Receipts	447,000	Payments	448,000
Mar. 31	4,000		

Accounts Receivable			
Mar. 1	18,000		
Sales	443,000	Collections	447,000
Mar. 31	14,000		

Inventory			
Mar. 1	19,000		
Purchases	337,000	Cost of sales	335,000
Mar. 31	21,000		

Accounts Payable			
		Mar. 1	14,000
Payments	332,000	Purchases	337,000
		Mar. 31	19,000

Accumulated Depreciation—Equipment			
		Mar. 1	52,000
		Depreciation	3,000
		Mar. 31	55,000

Retained Earnings			
		Mar. 1	64,000
Dividend	18,000	Net income	69,000
		Mar. 31	115,000

Compute Ochoa's net cash provided by (used for) operating activities during March. Use the indirect method.

E17-6 The income statement and additional data of Crawford Properties, Inc., follow:

Preparing the statement of cash flows—indirect method
(Obj. 3)

Crawford Properties, Inc.		
Income Statement		
Year Ended June 30, 20X6		
Revenues:		
Sales revenue		$237,000
Expenses:		
Cost of goods sold	$103,000	
Salary expense	58,000	
Depreciation expense	29,000	
Income tax expense	9,000	199,000
Net income		$ 38,000

Additional data:

a. Acquisition of plant assets is $116,000. Of this amount, $101,000 is paid in cash and $15,000 by signing a note payable.
b. Proceeds from sale of land total $24,000.
c. Proceeds from issuance of common stock total $30,000.
d. Payment of long-term note payable is $15,000.
e. Payment of dividends is $11,000.
f. From the balance sheet:

	June 30,	
	20X6	20X5
Current Assets:		
Cash.....................................	$27,000	$20,000
Accounts receivable....................	43,000	58,000
Inventory..............................	92,000	85,000
Current Liabilities:		
Accounts payable......................	$35,000	$22,000
Accrued liabilities	13,000	21,000

Required

1. Prepare Crawford Properties, Inc.'s statement of cash flows for the year ended June 30, 20X6, using the indirect method. Include a separate section for noncash investing and financing activities.

2. Evaluate Crawford Properties' cash flows for the year. In your evaluation, mention all three categories of cash flows and give the reason for your evaluation.

Computing investing and financing amounts for the statement of cash flows
(Obj. 3)

E17-7 Compute the following items for the statement of cash flows:

a. Beginning and ending Retained Earnings are $45,000 and $73,000, respectively. Net income for the period is $62,000. How much are cash dividends?

b. Beginning and ending Plant Assets, net, are $103,000 and $107,000, respectively. Depreciation for the period is $16,000, and acquisitions of new plant assets total $27,000. Plant assets were sold at a $1,000 loss. What were the cash proceeds of the sale?

Identifying activities for the statement of cash flows—direct method
(Obj. 4)

E17-8 Identify each of the following transactions as

- Operating activity (O)
- Investing activity (I)
- Financing activity (F)
- Noncash investing and financing activity (NIF)
- Transaction that is not reported on the statement of cash flows (N)

For each cash flow, indicate whether the item increases (+) or decreases (–) cash. The direct method is used for cash flows from operating activities.

_____	a. Collection of account receivable	_____	i. Sale of land
_____	b. Issuance of long-term note payable to borrow cash	_____	j. Acquisition of equipment by issuance of note payable
_____	c. Depreciation of equipment	_____	k. Payment of long-term debt
_____	d. Purchase of treasury stock	_____	l. Acquisition of building by issuance of common stock
_____	e. Issuance of common stock for cash	_____	m. Purchase of equipment
_____	f. Payment of account payable	_____	n. Payment of wages to employees
_____	g. Issuance of preferred stock for cash	_____	o. Collection of cash interest
_____	h. Payment of cash dividend	_____	p. Sale of building

Classifying transactions for the statement of cash flows—direct method
(Obj. 4)

E17-9 Indicate where, if at all, each of the following transactions would be reported on a statement of cash flows prepared by the *direct* method and the accompanying schedule of noncash investing and financing activities.

a. Equipment	18,000		g. Salary Expense.................	4,300	
Cash......................		18,000	Cash.....................		4,300
b. Cash	7,200		h. Cash	81,000	
Long-Term Investment......		7,200	Common Stock............		81,000
c. Bonds Payable	45,000		i. Treasury Stock	13,000	
Cash......................		45,000	Cash.....................		13,000
d. Building.......................	164,000		j. Cash	2,000	
Note Payable, Long-Term ...		164,000	Interest Revenue		2,000
e. Cash	1,400		k. Land	87,700	
Accounts Receivable........		1,400	Cash.....................		87,700
f. Dividends Payable..............	16,500		l. Accounts Payable	8,300	
Cash......................		16,500	Cash.....................		8,300

E17-10 The accounting records of Auto Chef Corporation reveal the following:

Computing cash flows from operating activities—direct method
(Obj. 4)

Net income	$22,000	Payment of salaries and wages..	$ 34,000
Payment of income tax ..	13,000	Depreciation	12,000
Collection of dividend		Payment of interest.	16,000
revenue	7,000	Payment of dividends	7,000
Payment to suppliers....	54,000	Collections from customers.....	102,000

Required

Compute cash flows from operating activities by the direct method. Use the format of the operating activities section of Exhibit 17-13. Also evaluate the operating cash flow of Auto Chef Corporation. Give the reason for your evaluation.

E17-11 Selected accounts of Crossroads Clinic, Inc., show the following:

Identifying items for the statement of cash flows—direct method
(Obj. 4)

Dividends Receivable

Beginning balance	9,000		
Dividend revenue	40,000	Cash receipts of dividends	38,000
Ending balance	11,000		

Land

Beginning balance	90,000	
Acquisition	18,000	
Ending balance	108,000	

Long-Term Notes Payable

		Beginning balance	273,000
Payments	69,000	Issuance for cash	83,000
		Ending balance	287,000

Required

For each account, identify the item or items that should appear on a statement of cash flows prepared by the direct method. State where to report the item.

E17-12 The income statement and additional data of Crawford Properties, Inc., follow:

Preparing the statement of cash flows—direct method
(Obj. 4)

Crawford Properties, Inc.

Income Statement
Year Ended June 30, 20X6

Revenues:		
Sales revenue	$229,000	
Dividend revenue	8,000	$237,000
Expenses:		
Cost of goods sold	$103,000	
Salary expense	45,000	
Depreciation expense	28,000	
Advertising expense	12,000	
Interest expense	2,000	
Income tax expense	9,000	199,000
Net income		$ 38,000

Additional data:

a. Collections from customers are $15,000 more than sales.
b. Payments to suppliers are the sum of cost of goods sold plus advertising expense.
c. Payments to employees are $1,000 more than salary expense.
d. Dividend revenue, interest expense, and income tax expense equal their cash amounts.
e. Acquisition of plant assets is $101,000.
f. Proceeds from sale of land total $24,000.
g. Proceeds from issuance of common stock total $30,000.
h. Payment of long-term note payable is $15,000.
i. Payment of dividends is $11,000.
j. Cash balance, June 30, 20X5, was $20,000.

Required

1. Prepare Crawford Properties' statement of cash flows for the year ended June 30, 20X6. Use the *direct* method.

2. Evaluate Crawford's cash flows for the year. In your evaluation, mention all three categories of cash flows and give the reason for your evaluation.

Computing amounts for the statement of cash flows—direct method
(Obj. 4)

E17-13 Compute the following items for the statement of cash flows:

a. Beginning and ending Accounts Receivable are $22,000 and $18,000, respectively. Credit sales for the period total $81,000. How much are cash collections?
b. Cost of goods sold is $90,000. Beginning Inventory balance is $25,000, and ending Inventory balance is $21,000. Beginning and ending Accounts Payable are $11,000 and $8,000, respectively. How much are cash payments for inventory?

Computing cash-flow amounts
(Obj. 3, 4)

E17-14 Walgreen Company, the nationwide pharmacy chain, reported the following in its financial statements for the year ended August 31, 20X1 (adapted, in millions):

	20X1	20X0
Income Statement		
Net sales	$24,623	$21,207
Cost of sales	18,048	15,466
Depreciation	269	230
Other operating expenses	4,883	4,248
Income tax expense	537	486
Net income	$ 886	$ 777
Balance Sheet		
Cash and equivalents	$ 17	$ 13
Accounts receivable	798	615
Inventories	3,482	2,831
Property and equipment, net	4,345	3,428
Accounts payable	1,547	1,364
Accrued liabilities	938	848
Long-term liabilities	478	464
Common stock	676	446
Retained earnings	4,531	3,788

Determine the following for Walgreen during 20X1:

a. Collections from customers
b. Payments for inventory
c. Payments of operating expenses
d. Acquisitions of property and equipment (no sales during 20X1)
e. Borrowing, with Walgreen paying no long-term liabilities
f. Proceeds from issuance of common stock
g. Payment of cash dividends

For operating cash flows, follow the approach outlined in Exhibit 17-15.

Problems

(Group A)

P17-1A Top managers of Oasis Water, Inc., are reviewing company performance for 20X7. The income statement reports a 20% increase in net income over 20X6. However, most of the increase resulted from an extraordinary gain on insurance proceeds from storm damage to a building. The balance sheet shows a large increase in receivables. The cash-flow statement, in summarized form, reports the following:

Using cash-flow information to evaluate performance
(Obj. 1, 2)

Net cash used for operating activities	$(80,000)
Net cash provided by investing activities	40,000
Net cash provided by financing activities	50,000
Increase in cash during 20X7	$ 10,000

Required

Write a memo giving Oasis Water managers your assessment of 20X7 operations and your outlook for the future. Focus on the information content of the cash-flow data.

P17-2A Scott Corporation, a furniture store, was formed on January 1, 20X8, when Scott issued common stock for $500,000. Early in January, Scott made the following cash payments:

Preparing an income statement, balance sheet, and statement of cash flows— indirect method
(Obj. 2, 3)

a. $150,000 for equipment
b. $260,000 for inventory (2,000 pieces of furniture)
c. $20,000 for 20X8 rent on a store building

Later in the year, Scott purchased 1,000 units of furniture inventory on account. Cost of this inventory was $120,000. Before year-end, Scott paid $60,000 of this debt. Scott uses the FIFO method to account for inventory.

During 20X8, Scott sold 2,000 units of inventory for $200 each. Before year end, Scott collected 80% of this amount.

The store employs a salesperson whose annual pay is $45,000, of which Scott owes $4,000 at year-end. At the end of the year, Scott paid income tax of $10,000.

Late in 20X8, Scott paid cash dividends of $11,000.

For equipment, Scott uses the straight-line depreciation method, over 5 years, with zero residual value.

Required

1. Prepare Scott Corporation's income statement for the year ended December 31, 20X8. Use the single-step format, with all revenues listed together and all expenses together.
2. Prepare Scott's balance sheet at December 31, 20X8.
3. Prepare Scott's statement of cash flows for the year ended December 31, 20X8. Format cash flows from operating activities by the indirect method.

P17-3A Datex Corporation accountants have assembled the following data for the year ended December 31, 20X7.

Preparing the statement of cash flows— indirect method
(Obj. 2, 3)

Required

Prepare Datex Corporation's statement of cash flows using the *indirect* method to report operating activities. Include an accompanying schedule of noncash investing and financing activities.

Datex Corporation

	December 31,	
	20X7	**20X6**
Current Accounts:		
Current assets:		
Cash and cash equivalents.	$85,000	$22,000
Accounts receivable	69,200	64,200
Inventories	80,000	83,000
Current liabilities:		
Accounts payable	$57,800	$55,800
Income tax payable.	14,700	16,700

Transaction Data for 20X7:			
Net income.	$ 57,000	Purchase of treasury stock	$14,000
Issuance of common stock		Loss on sale of equipment	11,000
for cash.	41,000	Payment of cash dividends	18,000
Depreciation expense.	21,000	Issuance of long-term note	
Purchase of building	125,000	payable to borrow cash	34,000
Retirement of bonds payable		Sale of equipment	58,000
by issuing common stock	65,000		

Preparing the statement of cash flows—indirect method
(Obj. 2, 3)

Student ResourceCD
spreadsheet

P17-4A The comparative balance sheet of Southern Bell Company at March 31, 20X9, reported the following:

	March 31,	
	20X9	**20X8**
Current Assets:		
Cash and cash equivalents.	$ 6,200	$ 4,000
Accounts receivable	14,900	21,700
Inventories	63,200	60,600
Current Liabilities:		
Accounts payable	$30,100	$27,600
Accrued liabilities	10,700	11,100
Income tax payable.	8,000	4,700

Southern Bell's transactions during the year ended March 31, 20X9, included the following:

Payment of cash dividend.	$30,000	Depreciation expense	$ 17,300
Purchase of equipment	78,700	Purchase of building.	47,000
Issuance of long-term note		Net income	70,000
payable to borrow cash	50,000	Issuance of common stock	11,000

Required

1. Prepare Southern Bell's statement of cash flows for the year ended March 31, 20X9, using the *indirect* method to report cash flows from operating activities.
2. Evaluate Southern Bell's cash flows for the year. Mention all three categories of cash flows and give the reason for your evaluation.

Preparing the statement of cash flows—indirect method
(Obj. 2, 3)

Student ResourceCD
spreadsheet

P17-5A The 20X5 comparative balance sheet and income statement of Town East Press follow.

Town East had no noncash investing and financing transactions during 20X5. During the year, there were no sales of land or equipment, no issuances of notes payable, no retirements of stock, and no treasury stock transactions.

Required

1. Prepare the 20X5 statement of cash flows, formatting operating activities by the indirect method.
2. How will what you learned in this problem help you evaluate an investment?

Town East Press
Comparative Balance Sheet

	December 31, 20X5	December 31, 20X4	Increase (Decrease)
Current assets:			
Cash and cash equivalents	$ 6,700	$ 5,300	$ 1,400
Accounts receivable	25,300	26,900	(1,600)
Inventories.	91,800	89,800	2,000
Plant assets:			
Land	89,000	60,000	29,000
Equipment, net	53,500	49,400	4,100
Total assets.	$266,300	$231,400	$34,900
Current liabilities:			
Accounts payable	$ 30,900	$ 35,400	$(4,500)
Accrued liabilities.	30,600	28,600	2,000
Long-term liabilities:			
Notes payable	75,000	100,000	(25,000)
Stockholders' equity:			
Common stock	88,300	64,700	23,600
Retained earnings.	41,500	2,700	38,800
Total liabilities and stockholders' equity . .	$266,300	$231,400	$34,900

Town East Press
Income Statement
Year Ended December 31, 20X5

Revenues:		
Sales revenue		$213,000
Interest revenue		8,600
Total revenues		221,600
Expenses:		
Cost of goods sold.	$70,600	
Salary expense	27,800	
Depreciation expense	4,000	
Other operating expense	10,500	
Interest expense.	11,600	
Income tax expense.	29,100	
Total expenses		153,600
Net income		$ 68,000

P17-6A Accountants for Triad Associates, Inc., have developed the following data from the company's accounting records for the year ended April 30, 20X5:

Preparing the statement of cash flows—direct method
(Obj. 2, 4)

a. Purchase of plant assets, $59,400
b. Proceeds from issuance of common stock, $8,000
c. Payment of dividends, $48,400
d. Collection of interest, $4,400
e. Payments of salaries, $93,600
f. Proceeds from sale of plant assets, $22,400
g. Collections from customers, $620,500
h. Cash receipt of dividend revenue, $4,100

i. Payments to suppliers, $368,500
j. Depreciation expense, $59,900
k. Proceeds from issuance of notes payable, $19,600
l. Payments of notes payable, $50,000
m. Interest expense and payments, $13,300
n. Income tax expense and payments, $37,900
o. Cash balance: April 30, 20X4, $39,300; April 30, 20X5, $47,200

Required

Prepare Triad Associates' statement of cash flows for the year ended April 30, 20X5. Use the direct method for cash flows from operating activities. Follow the format of Exhibit 17-13, but do *not* show amounts in thousands.

Preparing an income statement, balance sheet, and statement of cash flows—direct method
(Obj. 2, 4)

P17-7A Use the Scott Corporation data from Problem 17-2A.

Required

1. Prepare Scott Corporation's income statement for the year ended December 31, 20X8. Use the single-step format, with all revenues listed together and all expenses together.
2. Prepare Scott's balance sheet at December 31, 20X8.
3. Prepare Scott's statement of cash flows for the year ended December 31, 20X8. Format cash flows from operating activities by the direct method.

Preparing the statement of cash flows—direct method
(Obj. 2, 4)

Student ResourceCD

spreadsheet

P17-8A Use the Town East Press data from Problem 17-5A.

Required

1. Prepare the 20X5 statement of cash flows by the direct method.
2. How will what you learned in this problem help you evaluate an investment?

Preparing the statement of cash flows—direct method
(Obj. 3, 4)

P17-9A To prepare the statement of cash flows, accountants for Internet Guide, Inc., have summarized 20X8 activity in the Cash account as follows:

Cash			
Beginning balance	53,600	**Payments on accounts**	
Receipts of interest	17,100	payable	399,100
Collections from		**Payments of dividends**	27,200
customers	673,700	**Payments of salaries**	
Issuance of common stock	47,300	and wages	143,800
		Payments of interest	26,900
		Purchase of equipment	10,200
		Payments of operating	
		expenses	34,300
		Payment of note payable	67,700
		Payment of income tax	18,900
Ending balance	63,600		

Required

Prepare the statement of cash flows of Internet Guide, Inc., for the year ended December 31, 20X8, using the *direct* method for operating activities.

Problems

(Group B)

A⁺online homework

Using cash-flow information to evaluate performance
(Obj. 1, 2)

P17-1B Top managers of Internet Solutions, Inc., are reviewing company performance for 20X4. The income statement reports a 15% increase in net income, the fifth consecutive year with an income increase above 10%. The income statement includes a nonrecurring loss without which net income would have increased by 16%. The balance sheet shows modest increases in assets, liabilities, and stockholders' equity. The assets posting the largest increases are plant and equipment because the company is halfway through a 5-year expansion program. No other assets and no liabilities are increasing dramatically. A summarized version of the cash-flow statement reports the following:

Net cash provided by operating activities	$310,000
Net cash used for investing activities	(290,000)
Net cash provided by financing activities	70,000
Increase in cash during 20X4	$ 90,000

Required

Write a memo giving top managers of Internet Solutions your assessment of 20X4 operations and your outlook for the future. Focus on the information content of the cash-flow data.

P17-2B Dohn Corporation, a discounter of men's suits, was formed on January 1, 20X6, when Dohn issued its common stock for $200,000. Early in January, Dohn made the following cash payments:

Preparing an income statement, balance sheet, and statement of cash flows— indirect method
(Obj. 2, 3)

a. For store fixtures, $50,000
b. For inventory (1,000 men's suits), $100,000
c. For rent on a store building, $10,000

Later in the year, Dohn purchased 2,000 men's suits on account. Cost of each suit was $120, for a total of $240,000. Before year-end, Dohn paid $140,000 of this account payable. Dohn uses the FIFO method to account for inventory.

During 20X6, Dohn sold 2,500 units of inventory for $200 each. Before year end, Dohn collected 90% of this amount.

The store employs three people. The combined annual payroll is $90,000, of which Dohn owes $5,000 at year-end. At the end of the year, Dohn paid income tax of $30,000.

Late in 20X6, Dohn declared and paid cash dividends of $40,000.

For equipment, Dohn uses the straight-line depreciation method, over 5 years, with zero residual value.

Required

1. Prepare Dohn Corporation's income statement for the year ended December 31, 20X6. Use the single-step format, with all revenues listed together and all expenses together.
2. Prepare Dohn's balance sheet at December 31, 20X6.
3. Prepare Dohn's statement of cash flows for the year ended December 31, 20X6. Format cash flows from operating activities by the indirect method.

P17-3B Accountants for WWW.Smart, Inc., have assembled the following data for the year ended December 31, 20X4:

Preparing the statement of cash flows— indirect method
(Obj. 2, 3)

	December 31,	
	20X4	**20X3**
Current Accounts:		
Current assets:		
Cash and cash equivalents.	$56,000	$34,000
Accounts receivable	70,100	73,700
Inventories	90,600	86,600
Current liabilities:		
Accounts payable	71,600	67,500
Income tax payable	5,900	6,800

Transaction Data for 20X4:

Depreciation expense	$30,200	Payment of cash dividends	$48,300
Purchase of equipment	69,000	Issuance of note payable	
Acquisition of land by issuing		to borrow cash	71,000
long-term note payable	118,000	Net income	50,500
Payment of note payable	47,900	Issuance of preferred stock	
Gain on sale of equipment	3,500	for cash	36,200

Required

Prepare WWW.Smart's statement of cash flows using the *indirect* method to report operating activities. Include an accompanying schedule of noncash investing and financing activities.

P17-4B The comparative balance sheet of CNA Leasing, Inc., at December 31, 20X5, reported the following:

Preparing the statement of cash flows—indirect method
(Obj. 2, 3)

	December 31,	
	20X5	**20X4**
Current Assets:		
Cash and cash equivalents........................	$12,500	$22,500
Accounts receivable	26,600	29,300
Inventories....................................	54,600	53,000
Current Liabilities:		
Accounts payable	$29,100	$28,000
Accrued liabilities	14,300	16,800

CNA's transactions during 20X5 included the following:

Payment of cash dividends	$17,000	Purchase of building		$124,000
Purchase of equipment..........	55,000	Net income		31,600
Issuance of long-term note		Issuance of common stock		
payable to borrow cash........	32,000	for cash		105,000
		Depreciation expense		17,700

Required

1. Prepare the statement of cash flows of CNA Leasing, Inc., for the year ended December 31, 20X5. Use the *indirect* method to report cash flows from operating activities.

2. Evaluate CNA's cash flows for the year. Mention all three categories of cash flows and give the reason for your evaluation.

Preparing the statement of cash flows—indirect method
(Obj. 2, 3)

P17-5B The 20X8 comparative balance sheet and income statement of Genie Marketing, Inc., follow.

Genie had no noncash investing and financing transactions during 20X8. During the year, there were no sales of land or equipment, no issuances of notes payable, no retirements of stock, and no treasury stock transactions.

Required

1. Prepare the 20X8 statement of cash flows, formatting operating activities by the indirect method.

2. How will what you learned in this problem help you evaluate an investment?

Genie Marketing, Inc.			
Comparative Balance Sheet			
	December 31,		Increase
	20X8	**20X7**	**(Decrease)**
Current assets:			
Cash and cash equivalents	$ 21,000	$ 18,700	$ 2,300
Accounts receivable	46,500	43,100	3,400
Inventories.........................	84,300	89,900	(5,600)
Plant assets:			
Land	35,100	10,000	25,100
Equipment, net	100,900	93,700	7,200
Total assets.........................	$287,800	$255,400	$ 32,400
Current liabilities:			
Accounts payable....................	$ 31,100	$ 29,800	$ 1,300
Accrued liabilities...................	18,100	18,700	(600)
Long-term liabilities:			
Notes payable	55,000	65,000	(10,000)
Stockholders' equity:			
Common stock	131,100	122,300	8,800
Retained earnings....................	52,500	19,600	32,900
Total liabilities and stockholders' equity ..	$287,800	$255,400	$ 32,400

Genie Marketing, Inc.
Income Statement
Year Ended December 31, 20X8

Revenues:

Sales revenue		$438,000
Interest revenue		11,700
Total revenues.		449,700

Expenses:

Cost of goods sold	$205,200	
Salary expense	76,400	
Depreciation expense.	15,300	
Other operating expense.	49,700	
Interest expense	24,600	
Income tax expense	16,900	
Total expenses.		388,100
Net income		$ 61,600

P17-6B Data Solutions, Inc., accountants have developed the following data from the company's accounting records for the year ended July 31, 20X5:

Preparing the statement of cash flows—direct method
(Obj. 2, 4)

a. Purchase of plant assets, $100,000
b. Proceeds from issuance of notes payable, $44,100
c. Payments of notes payable, $18,800
d. Proceeds from sale of plant assets, $59,700
e. Cash receipt of dividends, $2,700
f. Payments to suppliers, $673,300
g. Interest expense and payments, $37,800
h. Collection of interest revenue, $11,700
i. Payments of salaries, $104,000
j. Income tax expense and payments, $56,400
k. Depreciation expense, $27,700
l. Collections from customers, $827,100
m. Proceeds from issuance of common stock, $116,900
n. Payment of cash dividends, $50,500
o. Cash balance: July 31, 20X4—$53,800; July 31, 20X5—$75,200

Required

Prepare Data Solutions' statement of cash flows for the year ended July 31, 20X5. Use the direct method for cash flows from operating activities. Follow the format of Exhibit 17-13, but do *not* show amounts in thousands.

P17-7B Use the Dohn Corporation data from Problem 17-2B.

Preparing an income statement, balance sheet, and statement of cash flows—direct method
(Obj. 2, 4)

Required

1. Prepare Dohn Corporation's income statement for the year ended December 31, 20X6. Use the single-step format, with all revenues listed together and all expenses together.
2. Prepare Dohn's balance sheet at December 31, 20X6.
3. Prepare Dohn's statement of cash flows for the year ended December 31, 20X6. Format cash flows from operating activities by the direct method.

P17-8B Use the Genie Marketing, Inc., data from Problem 17-5B.

Preparing the statement of cash flows—direct method
(Obj. 2, 4)

Required

1. Prepare the 20X8 statement of cash flows by the direct method.
2. How will what you learned in this problem help you evaluate an investment?

P17-9B To prepare the statement of cash flows, accountants for Rolex Paper Company have summarized 20X8 activity in the cash account as follows:

Cash

Beginning balance	87,100	Payments of operating expenses	46,100
Issuance of common stock	60,800	Payment of note payable	89,300
Receipts of interest revenue	14,100	Payment of income tax	8,000
Collections from customers	308,100	Payments on accounts payable	101,600
		Payment of dividends	1,800
		Payments of salaries and wages	67,500
		Payments of interest	21,800
		Purchase of equipment	51,500
Ending balance	82,500		

Required

Prepare Rolex's statement of cash flows for the year ended December 31, 20X8, using the *direct* method to report operating activities.

APPLY *Your Knowledge*

Decision Cases

Preparing and using the statement of
cash flows to evaluate operations
(Obj. 3)

Case I. The 20X6 comparative income statement and the 20X6 comparative balance sheet of Tennis, Tennis, Tennis! Inc., have just been distributed at a meeting of the company's board of directors. The members of the board of directors raise a fundamental question: Why is the cash balance so low? This question is especially troublesome to the board members because 20X6 showed record profits. As the controller of the company, you must answer the question.

Tennis, Tennis, Tennis! Inc.

Comparative Income Statement
Years Ended December 31, 20X6 and 20X5

(In thousands)	20X6	20X5
Revenues and gains:		
Sales revenue	$444	$310
Gain on sale of equipment (sale price, $33)	—	18
Total revenues and gains	$444	$328
Expenses and losses:		
Cost of goods sold	$221	$162
Salary expense	48	28
Depreciation expense	46	22
Interest expense	13	20
Amortization expense on patent	11	11
Loss on sale of land (sale price, $61)	—	35
Total expenses and losses	339	278
Net income	$105	$ 50

Tennis, Tennis, Tennis! Inc.
Comparative Balance Sheet
December 31, 20X6 and 20X5

(In thousands)	20X6	20X5
Assets		
Cash.	$ 25	$ 63
Accounts receivable, net.	72	61
Inventories	194	181
Long-term investments.	31	0
Property, plant, and equipment.	369	259
Accumulated depreciation.	(244)	(198)
Patents.	177	188
Totals	$624	$554
Liabilities and Owners' Equity		
Accounts payable.	$ 63	$ 56
Accrued liabilities	12	17
Notes payable, long-term.	179	264
Common stock.	149	61
Retained earnings	221	156
Totals	$624	$554

Required

1. Prepare a statement of cash flows for 20X6 in the format that best shows the relationship between net income and operating cash flow. The company sold no plant assets or long-term investments and issued no notes payable during 20X6. There were *no* noncash investing and financing transactions during the year. Show all amounts in thousands.

2. Answer the board members' question: Why is the cash balance so low? In explaining the business's cash flows, identify two significant cash receipts that occurred during 20X5 but not in 20X6. Also point out the two largest cash payments during 20X6.

3. Considering net income and the company's cash flows during 20X6, was it a good year or a bad year? Give your reasons.

Case 2. Carolina Technology, Inc., and Northwest Electric Power Corporation are asking you to recommend their stock to your clients. Because Carolina and Northwest earn about the same net income and have similar financial positions, your decision depends on their cash-flow statements, summarized as follows:

Using cash-flow data to evaluate an investment
(Obj. 1, 2)

	Carolina		Northwest	
Net cash provided by operating activities:		$ 70,000		$ 30,000
Cash provided by (used for) investing activities:				
Purchase of plant assets	$(100,000)		$(20,000)	
Sale of plant assets.	10,000	(90,000)	40,000	20,000
Cash provided by (used for) financing activities:				
Issuance of common stock		30,000		
Paying off long-term debt.		—		(40,000)
Net increase in cash.		$10,000		$ 10,000

Based on their cash flows, which company looks better? Give your reasons.

Ethical Issue

Victoria British Auto Parts is having a bad year. Net income is only $37,000. Also, two important overseas customers are falling behind in their payments to Victoria, and Victoria's accounts receivable are ballooning. The company desperately needs a loan. The Victoria board of directors is considering ways to put the best face on the company's financial statements. Victoria's bank closely examines cash flow from operations. Daniel Peavey, Victoria's controller, suggests reclassifying as long-term the receivables from the slow-paying clients. He explains to the board that removing the $80,000 rise in accounts receivable from current assets will increase net cash provided by operations. This approach may help Victoria get the loan.

Required

1. Using only the amounts given, compute net cash provided by operations, both without and with the reclassification of the receivables. Which reporting makes Victoria look better?
2. Under what condition would the reclassification of the receivables be ethical? Unethical?

Financial Statement Case

Using the statement of cash flows
(Obj. 2, 3, 4)

Use the **Amazon.com** statement of cash flows along with the company's other financial statements, all in Appendix A, to answer the following questions.

Required

1. Which method does Amazon use to report net cash flows from *operating* activities? How can you tell?
2. Amazon suffered a net loss during 2002. Did operations *provide* cash or *use* cash during 2002? Give the amount. How did operating cash during 2002 compare with 2001? Be specific, and state the reason for your answer.
3. Suppose Amazon reported net cash flows from operating activities by the direct method. Compute these amounts for the year ended December 31, 2002.
   a. Collections from customers (Assume that other current assets are zero)
   b. Payments for inventory
4. Evaluate 2002 in terms of net income, cash flows, balance sheet position, and overall results. Be specific.

Team Projects

Project 1. Each member of the team should obtain the annual report of a different company. Select companies in different industries. Evaluate each company's trend of cash flows for the most recent two years. In your evaluation of the companies' cash flows, you may use any other information that is publicly available—for example, the other financial statements (income statement, balance sheet, statement of stockholders' equity, and the related notes) and news stories from magazines and newspapers. Rank the companies' cash flows from best to worst and write a two-page report on your findings.

Project 2. Select a company and obtain its annual report, including all the financial statements. Focus on the statement of cash flows and, in particular, the cash flows from operating activities. Specify whether the company uses the direct method or the indirect method to report operating cash flows. As necessary, use the other financial statements (income statement, balance sheet, and statement of stockholders' equity) and the notes to prepare the company's cash flows from operating activities by the *other* method.

APPENDIX *to Chapter 17*

The Work Sheet Approach to Preparing the Statement of Cash Flows

The body of this chapter discusses the uses of the statement of cash flows in decision making and shows how to prepare the statement using T-accounts. The T-account approach works well as a learning device. In practice, however, most companies face complex situations. In these cases, a work sheet can help in preparing the statement of cash flows. This appendix shows how to prepare the statement using a specially designed work sheet.

The work sheet starts with the beginning balance sheet and concludes with the ending balance sheet. Two middle columns—one for debit amounts and the other for credit amounts—complete the work sheet. These columns, labeled Transaction Analysis, hold the data for the statement of cash flows. Accountants can prepare the statement directly from the lower part of the work sheet. This appendix is based on the Anchor Corporation data used in the chapter. We begin with the indirect method for operating activities.

Preparing the Work Sheet—Indirect Method for Operating Activities

The indirect method reconciles net income to net cash provided by operating activities. Exhibit 17A-1 is the work sheet for preparing the statement of cash flows by the indirect method. Panel A shows the transaction analysis, and Panel B gives the statement of cash flows.

Transaction Analysis on the Work Sheet—Indirect Method Net income, transaction (a), is the first operating cash inflow. Net income is entered on the work sheet (Panel B) as a debit to Net Income under Cash flows from operating activities and as a credit to Retained Earnings. Next come the adjustments to net income, starting with depreciation—transaction (b)—which is debited to Depreciation and credited to Plant Assets, Net. Transaction (c) is the sale of plant assets. The $8,000 gain on the sale is entered as a credit to Gain on Sale of Plant Assets—a subtraction from net income—under operating cash flows. This credit removes the $8,000 gain from operations because the cash proceeds from the sale were $62,000, not $8,000. The $62,000 sale amount is then entered on the work sheet under investing activities. Entry (c) is completed by crediting the plant assets' book value of $54,000 to the Plant Assets, Net account.

Entries (d) through (g) reconcile net income to cash flows from operations for increases and decreases in the other current assets and for increases and decreases in the current liabilities. Entry (d) debits Accounts Receivable for its $15,000 increase during the year. This amount is credited to Increase in Accounts Receivable under operating cash flows. Entries (e), (f), and (g) adjust for the other current accounts.

Entries (h) through (l) account for the investing and financing transactions. Entry (h) debits Plant Assets, Net for their purchase and credits Purchase of plant assets under investing cash flows. Entry (i) debits Proceeds from issuance of common stock under financing cash flows. The offsetting debit is to Common Stock.

The final item in Exhibit 17A-1 is the Net decrease in cash—transaction (m) on the work sheet—a credit to Cash and a debit to Net decrease in cash. To prepare the statement of cash flows, the accountant can rewrite Panel B of the work sheet, adding subtotals for the three categories of activities.

| Exhibit 17A-1 | Work Sheet for Statement of Cash Flows—Indirect Method |

Anchor Corporation
Work Sheet for Statement of Cash Flows (Indirect Method)
Year Ended December 31, 20X5

	In thousands			
	Balances	Transaction Analysis		Balances
	Dec. 31, 20X4	Debit	Credit	Dec. 31, 20X5
PANEL A—Balance-Sheet Accounts				
Cash.....	42		(m) 20	22
Accounts receivable.....	81	(d) 15		96
Inventory.....	145		(e) 2	143
Plant assets, net	219	(h) 317	(b) 18	
			(c) 54	464
Totals	487			725
Accounts payable.....	57		(f) 34	91
Accrued liabilities	9	(g) 4		5
Long-term notes payable	77	(k) 11	(j) 94	160
Common stock.....	258		(i) 101	359
Retained earnings	86	(l) 17	(a) 41	110
Totals	487	364	364	725
PANEL B—Statement of Cash Flows				
Cash flows from operating activities:				
Net income		(a) 41		
Add (subtract) items that affect net income and cash flow differently:				
Depreciation.....		(b) 18		
Gain on sale of plant assets			(c) 8	
Increase in accounts receivable			(d) 15	
Decrease in inventory		(e) 2		
Increase in accounts payable		(f) 34		
Decrease in accured liabilities			(g) 4	
Cash flows from investing activities:				
Purchase of plant assets			(h) 317	
Proceeds from sale of plant assets.....		(c) 62		
Cash flows from financing activities:				
Proceeds from issuance of common stock		(i) 101		
Proceeds from issuance of note payable.....		(j) 94		
Payment of note payable			(k) 11	
Payment of dividends.....			(l) 17	
		352	372	
Net decrease in cash		(m) 20		
Totals		372	372	

Noncash Investing and Financing Activities on the Work Sheet Noncash investing and financing activities can be analyzed on the work sheet. These transactions include both an investing activity and a financing activity, so they require two work-sheet entries. Suppose Anchor Corporation purchased a building by issuing common stock of $300,000. Exhibit 17A-2 illustrates the analysis of this transaction. Cash is unaffected. Work-sheet entry (a) records the purchase of the building, and entry (b) records the issuance of the stock.

| Exhibit 17A-2 | Noncash Investing and Financing Activities on the Work Sheet |

Anchor Corporation
Work Sheet for Statement of Cash Flows
Year Ended December 31, 20X5

	Balances Dec. 31, 20X4	Transaction Analysis Debit	Transaction Analysis Credit	Balances Dec. 31, 20X5
PANEL A—Balance-Sheet Accounts				
Cash				
Building	600,000	(a) 300,000		900,000
Common stock	400,000		(b) 300,000	700,000
PANEL B—Statement of Cash Flows				
Noncash investing and financing transactions:				
Purchase of building by issuing common stock		(b) 300,000	(a) 300,000	

Preparing the Work Sheet—Direct Method for Operating Activities

The direct method separates operating activities into cash receipts and cash payments. Exhibit 17A-3 is the work sheet for the preparation of the statement of cash flows by the direct method.

Transaction Analysis on the Work Sheet—Direct Method For your convenience, we repeat the Anchor Corporation transaction data here.

Operating Activities:
a. Sales on account, $284,000
*b. Collections from customers, $269,000
*c. Cash receipt of interest revenue, $12,000
*d. Cash receipt of dividend revenue, $9,000
e. Purchase of inventory on account, $148,000
f. Cost of goods sold, $150,000

*g. Payments for inventory on account, $114,000
*h. Salary expense and payments, $56,000
i. Depreciation expense, $18,000
j. Accrual of other operating expense, $17,000
*k. Interest expense and payments, $16,000
*l. Income tax expense and payments, $15,000
*m. Payment of accrued liabilities, $21,000

Investing Activities:
*n. Cash payments to acquire plant assets, $317,000

*o. Proceeds from sale of plant assets, $62,000, including $8,000 gain

Financing Activities:
*p. Proceeds from issuance of common stock, $101,000
*q. Proceeds from issuance of long-term note payable, $94,000

*r. Payment of long-term note payable, $11,000
*s. Declaration and payment of cash dividends, $17,000

*Indicates a cash flow to be reported on the statement of cash flows.

The transaction analysis on the work sheet includes journal entries. Only balance-sheet accounts are used on the work sheet. Therefore, revenues are entered as credits to Retained Earnings, and expenses are entered as debits to Retained Earnings. For example, in transaction (a), sales on account are debited to Accounts Receivable and credited to Retained Earnings. Cash is neither debited nor credited because credit sales do not affect cash. But all transactions should be entered on the work sheet to identify all the cash effects of the period's transactions. In transaction (c), the collection of cash for interest revenue is entered by debiting Cash and crediting Retained Earnings.

Exhibit 17A-3 | Work Sheet for Statement of Cash Flows—Direct Method

Anchor Corporation
Work Sheet for Statement of Cash Flows (Direct Method)
Year Ended December 31, 20X5

		(in thousands)			
	Balances	Transaction Analysis			**Balances**
	Dec. 31, 20X4	**Debit**		**Credit**	**Dec. 31, 20X5**
PANEL A—Balance-Sheet Accounts					
Cash....................................	42			(t) 20	22
Accounts receivable.....................................	81	(a) 284		(b) 269	96
Inventory..	145	(e) 148		(f) 150	143
Equipment, net...	219	(n) 317		(i) 18	
				(o) 54	464
Totals	487				725
Accounts payable..	57	(g) 114		(e) 148	91
Accrued liabilities	9	(m) 21		(j) 17	5
Long-term notes payable	77	(r) 11		(q) 94	160
Common stock...	258			(p) 101	359
Retained earnings	86	(f) 150		(a) 284	110
		(h) 56		(c) 12	
		(i) 18		(d) 9	
		(j) 17		(o) 8	
		(k) 16			
		(l) 15			
		(s) 17			
Totals	487	1,184		1,184	725
PANEL B—Statement of Cash Flows					
Cash flows from operating activities:					
Receipts:					
Collections from customers		(b) 269			
Interest received.......................................		(c) 12			
Dividends received		(d) 9			
Payments:					
To suppliers				(g) 114	
				(m) 21	
To employees				(h) 56	
For interest				(k) 16	
For income tax				(l) 15	
Cash flows from investing activities:					
Purchase of plant assets				(n) 317	
Proceeds from sale of plant assets......................		(o) 62			
Cash flows from financing activities:					
Proceeds from issuance of common stock		(p) 101			
Proceeds from issuance of note payable...................		(q) 94			
Payment of note payable				(r) 11	
Payment of dividends.................................				(s) 17	
		547		567	
Net decrease in cash		(t) 20			
Totals		567		567	

Entries (n) through (s) account for the investing and financing transactions. Entry (n) debits Equipment, Net for their purchase and credits Purchase of plant assets under investing cash flows. Entry (p) debits Proceeds from issuance of common stock under financing cash flows. The offsetting credit is to Common stock.

The final item in Exhibit 17A-3 is the Net decrease in cash—transaction (t) on the work sheet—a credit to cash and a debit to Net decrease in cash. To prepare the statement of cash flows, you can rewrite Panel B of the work sheet, adding subtotals for the three categories of activities.

Appendix Assignments
Problems

P17A-1 The 20X8 comparative balance sheet and income statement of Alden Group, Inc., follow. Alden had no noncash investing and financing transactions during 20X8.

Preparing the work sheet for the statement of cash flows—indirect method

Alden Group, Inc.
Comparative Balance Sheet

	December 31, 20X8	December 31, 20X7	Increase (Decrease)
Current assets:			
Cash and cash equivalents	$ 13,700	$ 15,600	$ (1,900)
Accounts receivable	41,500	43,100	(1,600)
Inventories.....................	96,600	93,000	3,600
Plant assets:			
Land	35,100	10,000	25,100
Equipment, net	100,900	93,700	7,200
Total assets.....................	$287,800	$255,400	$32,400
Current liabilities:			
Accounts payable	$ 24,800	$ 26,000	$ (1,200)
Accrued liabilities..............	24,400	22,500	1,900
Long-term liabilities:			
Notes payable	55,000	65,000	(10,000)
Stockholders' equity:			
Common stock	131,100	122,300	8,800
Retained earnings..............	52,500	19,600	32,900
Total liabilities and stockholders' equity	$287,800	$255,400	$32,400

Alden Group, Inc.
Income Statement for Year Ended December 31, 20X8

Revenues:		
Sales revenue.....................		$438,000
Interest revenue...................		11,700
Total revenues		449,700
Expenses:		
Cost of goods sold	$205,200	
Salary expense.................	76,400	
Depreciation expense...........	15,300	
Other operating expense	49,700	
Interest expense................	24,600	
Income tax expense	16,900	
Total expenses		388,100
Net income		$ 61,600

Required

Prepare the work sheet for the 20X8 statement of cash flows. Format cash flows from operating activities by the *indirect* method.

Preparing the work sheet for the statement of cash flows—direct method

P17A-2 Using the Alden Group, Inc., data from Problem 17A-1, prepare the work sheet for Alden's 20X8 statement of cash flows. Format cash flows from operating activities by the *direct* method.

CHAPTER 18

Financial Statement Analysis

TIPS CHECK YOUR RESOURCES

- Visit the www.prenhall.com/horngren **Web site** for self-study quizzes, video clips, and other resources

- Try the **Quick Check** exercise at the end of the chapter to test your knowledge

- Learn the **key terms**

- Do the **Starter** exercises keyed in the margins

- Work the **mid-** and **end-of-chapter summary problems**

- Use the **Concept Links** to review material in other chapters

- Search the **CD** for review materials by chapter or by key word

- Watch the **tutorial videos** to review key concepts

- Watch the **On Location Financial Statement Analysis** video, in which people from three companies talk about how they use financial statements for decision making

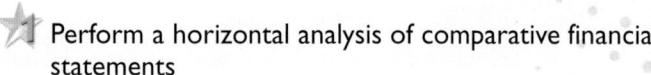

LEARNING OBJECTIVES

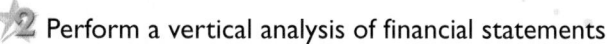

1 Perform a horizontal analysis of comparative financial statements

2 Perform a vertical analysis of financial statements

3 Prepare and use common-size financial statements

4 Compute the standard financial ratios

5 Measure economic value added

Y ou, or people you know, probably invest in stocks. How do you choose those investments? Do you pick large, established companies, or do you look for a new highflier? What kind of information do you use?

Some of the most important information about a company comes from its financial statements. To make an informed decision, you need to be able to analyze those statements, even if the company has been around a long time and is a household name. Take a look at what happened to health-care giant **Bristol-Myers Squibb** (BMS). Study BMS's 2002 income statement:

Bristol-Myers Squibb

Bristol-Myers Squibb Company
Income Statement (Adapted)

(In millions)	Year Ended December 31,	
	2002	2001
Earnings		
1 **Net sales**	$18,119	$17,987
2 **Expenses:**		
3 Cost of goods sold	6,388	5,453
4 Marketing, selling, and administrative	3,923	3,894
5 Advertising and product promotion	1,295	1,299
6 Research and development	2,218	2,183
7 Other expense, net*	1,794	251
8 **Income before income tax**	2,501	4,907
9 Income taxes	435	73
10 **Net income**	$ 2,066	$ 4,834

*Includes discontinued operations.

You can see that 2002 was a tough year for the company. Net income (line 10) was down from 2001, and Wall Street wasn't happy.

Companies have to satisfy lots of people, from individual investors like you and me to Wall Street analysts. What analytical tools do people use to make decisions about a company like Bristol-Myers Squibb? They use many of the techniques we cover in this book. ■

Sitemap

- Horizontal Analysis
- Vertical Analysis
- Benchmarking
- Using Ratios
- Other Evaluation Tools

Investors and creditors can't evaluate a company by examining only one year's data. This is why most financial statements cover at least two periods, like the Bristol-Myers Squibb (BMS) income statement. In fact, most financial analysis covers trends of three to five years. This chapter illustrates some of the analytical tools for charting a company's progress through time.

The graphs in Exhibit 18-1 show some important data about BMS. They depict a three-year trend of net sales and research and development (R&D). Sales and R&D are important drivers of profits.

Exhibit 18-1 Financial Data of Bristol-Myers Squibb Company (Adapted)

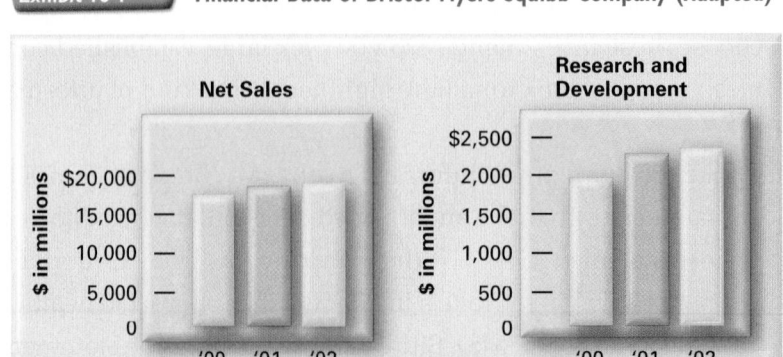

For BMS, both sales and research and development barely grew during 2002. These are not good signs for the future. How can we decide what we really think about BMS's performance in 2002? We need some way to compare that performance

- From one year to another
- With the performance of a competing company, like Procter & Gamble
- With the pharmaceuticals (health-care) industry

Then we will have a better idea of how to judge BMS's situation now and predict what might happen in the near future.

Horizontal analysis provides a direct year-to-year comparison of BMS's performance in 2002 and 2001. Another technique, vertical analysis, is the standard way to compare different companies. Let's begin with horizontal analysis.

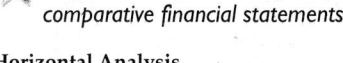

Horizontal Analysis

Many decisions hinge on whether the numbers—in sales, income, and expenses—are increasing or decreasing. Have sales risen from last year? By how much? We may find that sales have increased by $20,000. But considered alone, this fact is not very helpful. The *percentage change* in sales over time aids our understanding. It is more useful to know that sales have increased by 20% than to know that the increase is $20,000.

The study of percentage changes in comparative statements is called **horizontal analysis**. Computing a percentage change in comparative statements requires two steps:

1. Compute the dollar amount of the change from the earlier base period to the later period.
2. Divide the dollar amount of change by the base-period amount.

Illustration: Bristol-Myers Squibb

Horizontal analysis is illustrated for Bristol-Myers Squibb as follows (dollar amounts in millions):

	2002	2001	Increase (Decrease)	
			Amount	Percentage
Net sales	$18,119	$17,987	$132	0.7%

Sales increased by only 7/10 of 1% (0.007) during 2002, computed as follows:

STEP 1 Compute the dollar amount of change in sales from 2001 to 2002:

2002	2001	Increase
$18,119 − $17,987 =		$132

STEP 2 Divide the dollar amount of change by the base-period amount. This computes the percentage change for the period:

$$\text{Percentage change} = \frac{\text{Dollar amount of change}}{\text{Base-year amount}}$$

$$= \frac{\$132}{\$17,987} = 0.007 = 0.7\%$$

Detailed horizontal analyses are shown in the two right-hand columns of Exhibits 18-2 and 18-3, the financial statements of BMS Company. The income statements reveal that net sales increased by 0.7% during 2002. But cost of goods sold grew by 17.1%, so gross profit fell by 6.4%. Net income was down by 57.3%. These results are not encouraging.

■ Horizontal Analysis
☐ Vertical Analysis
☐ Benchmarking
☐ Using Ratios
☐ Other Evaluation Tools

Student ResourceCD
horizontal analysis, trend analysis

Perform a horizontal analysis of comparative financial statements

Horizontal Analysis
Study of percentage changes in comparative financial statements.

✔ **Starter 18-1**

Exhibit 18-2

Comparative Income Statement—
Horizontal Analysis

Bristol-Myers Squibb Company
Income Statement (Adapted)
Years Ended December 31, 2002 and 2001

(Dollar amounts in millions)	2002	2001	Increase (Decrease) Amount	Percentage
Net sales	$18,119	$17,987	$ 132	0.7%
Cost of goods sold	6,388	5,453	935	17.1
Gross profit............................	11,731	12,534	(803)	(6.4)
Operating expenses:				
Marketing, selling, and administrative....	3,923	3,894	29	0.7
Advertising and product promotion......	1,295	1,299	(4)	(0.3)
Research and development..............	2,218	2,183	35	1.6
Other expense, net	1,794	251	1,543	614.7
Income before income tax	2,501	4,907	(2,406)	(49.0)
Income tax expense	435	73	362	495.9
Net income	$ 2,066	$ 4,834	$(2,768)	(57.3)

The comparative balance sheet in Exhibit 18-3 shows that 2002 was not a growth year for BMS. Total assets fell by 10.6%. Fortunately, liabilities decreased by 15.1%, so the drop in stockholders' equity was only 1.2%.

Exhibit 18-3

Comparative Balance Sheet—
Horizontal Analysis

Bristol-Myers Squibb Company
Balance Sheet (Adapted)
December 31, 2002 and 2001

(Dollar amounts in millions)	2002	2001	Increase (Decrease) Amount	Percentage
Assets				
Current Assets:				
Cash and cash equivalents	$ 3,978	$ 5,500	$(1,522)	(27.7)%
Other current assets	5,997	7,749	(1,752)	(22.6)
Total current assets......................	9,975	13,249	(3,274)	(24.7)
Property, plant, and equipment, net	5,321	4,887	434	8.9
Intangible assets, net	6,768	7,203	(435)	(6.0)
Other assets	2,810	2,473	337	13.6
Total assets	$24,874	$27,812	$(2,938)	(10.6)
Liabilities				
Current Liabilities:				
Accounts payable........................	$ 1,553	$ 1,478	$ 75	5.1%
Other current liabilities	6,667	9,631	(2,964)	(30.8)
Total current liabilities..................	8,220	11,109	(2,889)	(26.0)
Long-term liabilities......................	7,687	7,628	59	0.8
Total liabilities.........................	15,907	18,737	(2,830)	(15.1)
Stockholders' Equity				
Common stock	2,711	2,623	88	3.4
Retained earnings and				
other equity..........................	6,256	6,452	(196)	(3.0)
Total stockholders' equity	8,967	9,075	(108)	(1.2)
Total liabilities and equity	$24,874	$27,812	$(2,938)	(10.6)

Trend Percentages

Trend percentages are a form of horizontal analysis. Trends indicate the direction a business is taking. How have sales changed over a five-year period? What trend does net income show? These questions can be answered by trend percentages over a representative period, such as the most recent three to five years.

Trend percentages are computed by selecting a base year whose amounts are set equal to 100%. The amounts for each following year are expressed as a percentage of the base amount. To compute trend percentages, divide each item for following years by the corresponding amount during the base year:

$$\text{Trend \%} = \frac{\text{Any year \$}}{\text{Base year \$}}$$

BMS Company showed the following net sales for the past 6 years:

(In millions)	2002	2001	2000	1999	1998	1997
Net sales	$18,119	$17,987	$17,538	$16,502	$15,007	$13,698
Trend percentages	132%	131%	128%	120%	110%	100%

We want trend percentages for the five-year period 1998 to 2002. The base year is 1997. Trend percentages are computed by dividing each year's amount by the 1997 amount. The trend percentages follow net sales (1997, the base year = 100%).

Net sales increased rapidly through 1999. The rate of growth slowed in 2000 and became a trickle in 2001 and 2002.

You can perform a trend analysis on any item you consider important. We selected net sales because sales drive profits. Trend analysis is widely used to predict the future.

Vertical Analysis

Horizontal analysis highlights changes in an item over time. However, no single technique gives a complete picture of a business.

Vertical analysis of a financial statement shows the relationship of each item to its base amount, which is the 100% figure. Every other item on the statement is then reported as a percentage of that base. For an income statement, net sales is the base. Suppose under normal conditions a company's gross profit is 70% of net sales. A drop to 60% may cause the company to suffer a loss. Investors view a large decline in gross profit with alarm.

Illustration: Bristol-Myers Squibb

Exhibit 18-4 shows the vertical analysis of BMS's income statement. In this case,

$$\text{Vertical analysis \%} = \frac{\text{Each income statement item}}{\text{Net sales}}$$

For example, the vertical-analysis percentage for Cost of goods sold for 2002 is 35.3% ($6,388/$18,119 = 0.353). Unfortunately for BMS, this percentage increased during 2002. Look further. Other expenses' percentages also increased. Consequently, the percentage for net income was down from 2001.

Exhibit 18-5 shows the vertical analysis of BMS's balance sheet. The base amount (100%) is total assets.

Trend Percentages
A form of horizontal analysis in which percentages are computed by selecting a base year as 100% and expressing amounts for following years as a percentage of the base amount.

✔ **Starter 18-2**

☐ Horizontal Analysis
■ **Vertical Analysis**
☐ Benchmarking
☐ Using Ratios
☐ Other Evaluation Tools

Student ResourceCD
common-size statement, vertical analysis

2 *Perform a vertical analysis of financial statements*

Vertical Analysis
Analysis of a financial statement that reveals the relationship of each statement item to a specified base, which is the 100% figure.

Exhibit 18-4

Comparative Income Statement—
Vertical Analysis

Bristol-Myers Squibb Company
Income Statement (Adapted)
Years Ended December 31, 2002 and 2001

(Dollar amounts in millions)	2002 Amount	2002 Percent of Total	2001 Amount	2001 Percent of Total
Net sales	$18,119	100.0%	$17,987	100.0%
Cost of goods sold	6,388	35.3	5,453	30.3
Gross profit	11,731	64.7	12,534	69.7
Operating expenses:				
Marketing, selling, and administrative ..	3,923	21.7	3,894	21.7
Advertising and product promotion.....	1,295	7.1	1,299	7.2
Research and development	2,218	12.2	2,183	12.1
Other expense, net....................	1,794	9.9	251	1.4
Income before income tax................	2,501	13.8	4,907	27.3
Income tax expense	435	2.4	73	0.4
Net income...........................	$ 2,066	11.4%	$ 4,834	26.9%

Note: Percentage may contain slight rounding error.

Exhibit 18-5

Comparative Balance Sheet—
Vertical Analysis

Bristol-Myers Squibb Company
Balance Sheet (Adapted)
December 31, 2002 and 2001

(Dollar amounts in millions)	2002 Amount	2002 Percent of Total	2001 Amount	2001 Percent of Total
Assets				
Current Assets:				
Cash and cash equivalents	$ 3,978	16.0%	$ 5,500	19.8%
Other current assets....................	5,997	24.1	7,749	27.8
Total current assets	9,975	40.1	13,249	47.6
Property, plant, and equipment, net	5,321	21.4	4,887	17.6
Intangible assets, net	6,768	27.2	7,203	25.9
Other assets..........................	2,810	11.3	2,473	8.9
Total assets	$24,874	100.0%	$27,812	100.0%
Liabilities				
Current Liabilities:				
Accounts payable......................	$ 1,553	6.2%	$ 1,478	5.3%
Other current liabilities.................	6,667	26.8	9,631	34.7
Total current liabilities..............	8,220	33.0	11,109	40.0
Long-term liabilities	7,687	30.9	7,628	27.4
Total liabilities.......................	15,907	63.9	18,737	67.4
Stockholders' Equity				
Common stock	2,711	10.9	2,623	9.4
Retained earnings and				
other equity........................	6,256	25.2	6,452	23.2
Total stockholders' equity..............	8,967	36.1	9,075	32.6
Total liabilities and equity	$24,874	100.0%	$27,812	100.0%

Note: Percentages may contain slight rounding error.

✔ **Starter 18-3**

The vertical analysis of BMS's balance sheet reveals several things about the company's financial position:

■ Current assets make up 40.1% of total assets, compared to 47.6% in 2001. A high percentage of current assets can be bad because current assets earn a low rate of return.

■ Intangibles make up 27.2% of total assets. This percentage is high because of the nature of the pharmaceutical business. Lenders dislike a high percentage of intangibles because, in a liquidation of the company, intangibles are often worthless. But in today's technology-driven economy, intangible assets are important.

■ Total liabilities dropped to 63.9%, and stockholders' equity increased to 36.1% of total assets. Overall, BMS's creditworthiness improved a bit in 2002.

How Do We Compare One Company with Another?

⭐3 *Prepare and use common-size financial statements*

The percentages in Exhibits 18-4 and 18-5 can be presented as a separate statement that reports only percentages (no dollar amounts). Such a statement is called a **common-size statement**.

On a common-size income statement, each item is expressed as a percentage of net sales. Net sales is the *common size* to which we relate the other amounts. In the balance sheet, the common size is total assets. A common-size statement eases the comparison of different companies because amounts are stated in percentages.

Common-Size Statement
A financial statement that reports only percentages (no dollar amounts).

Common-size statements may identify the need for corrective action. Exhibit 18-6 gives an example. In 2001, BMS had almost half of its resources tied up in current assets. As we have mentioned, cash, receivables, and inventories earn low rates of return, as compared with long-term assets. It appears that the top management of BMS made a serious shift during 2002. BMS invested in plant and equipment, and the company's long-term assets grew to 59.9% of total resources in 2002.

Exhibit 18-6

Common-Size Analysis of Current Assets

Bristol-Myers Squibb Company
Common-Size Analysis of Current and Long-Term Assets
December 31, 2002 and 2001

	Percent of Total Assets	
	2002	2001
Current assets	40.1%	47.6%
Long-term assets	59.9	52.4
Total assets	100.0%	100.0%

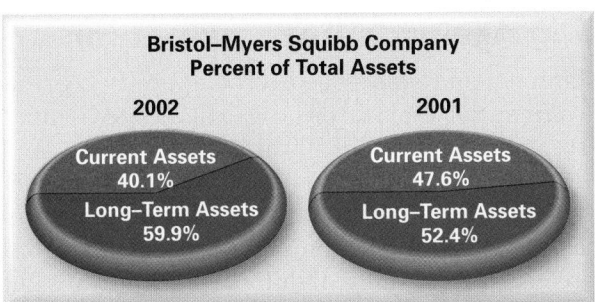

Bristol–Myers Squibb Company
Percent of Total Assets

2002
Current Assets 40.1%
Long–Term Assets 59.9%

2001
Current Assets 47.6%
Long–Term Assets 52.4%

Student ResourceCD

benchmarking

Benchmarking
The practice of comparing a company
with other companies that are leaders.

Benchmarking

Benchmarking is the practice of comparing a company with other companies that are leaders.

Calculate the common-size percentages for the following income statement:

Net sales	$150,000
Cost of goods sold	60,000
Gross profit	90,000
Operating expense	40,000
Operating income	50,000
Income tax expense	15,000
Net income	$ 35,000

Answer:

Net sales	100%	(= $150,000 ÷ $150,000)
Cost of goods sold	40	(= $ 60,000 ÷ $150,000)
Gross profit	60	(= $ 90,000 ÷ $150,000)
Operating expense	27	(= $ 40,000 ÷ $150,000)
Operating income	33	(= $ 50,000 ÷ $150,000)
Income tax expense	10	(= $ 15,000 ÷ $150,000)
Net income	23%	(= $ 35,000 ÷ $150,000)

Benchmarking Against the Industry Average

We study a company to gain insight into past results and future performance. Still, that knowledge is limited to the one company. We may learn that gross profit and net income have increased. This information is helpful, but it does not consider how other companies have fared over the same period. Have competitors profited even more? Investors need to know how a company compares with others in the same line of business. For example, during 2002, Johnson & Johnson and Procter & Gamble increased both sales and profits, while BMS's net income decreased.

Exhibit 18-7 gives the common-size income statement of BMS compared with the average for the pharmaceuticals (health-care) industry. The industry averages were adapted from Risk Management Association's *Annual Statement Studies*. Analysts at Merrill Lynch and Edward Jones & Co. specialize in a particular industry. For example, Merrill Lynch has health-care specialists, airline-industry specialists, and so on. They compare a company with others in the same industry. Exhibit 18-7 shows that BMS compares favorably with competing companies in its industry. BMS's gross profit percentage is much higher than the industry average. Even though 2002 was not a good year, BMS's percentage of net income is still higher than the industry average.

Benchmarking Against a Key Competitor

Common-size statements are also used to compare two or more companies. Suppose you are a financial analyst for Edward Jones & Company. You are considering an investment in the stock of a health-care company, and you are choosing between BMS and P&G. A direct comparison of their financial statements in dollar amounts is not meaningful because the amounts are so different. However, you can convert the two companies' income statements to common size and compare the percentages. Exhibit 18-8 compares the common-size income statements of Bristol-Myers Squibb and Procter & Gamble. The two companies earn similar percentages of net income to sales.

Exhibit 18-7

Common-Size Income Statement Compared with the Industry Average

Bristol-Myers Squibb Company

Common-Size Income Statement for Comparison with Industry Average
Year Ended December 31, 2002

	Bristol-Myers Squibb	Industry Average
Net sales	100.0%	100.0%
Cost of goods sold	35.3	51.6
Gross profit	64.7	48.4
Operating and other expenses	50.9	40.5
Income before income tax	13.8	7.9
Income tax expense	2.4	2.8
Net income	11.4%	5.1%

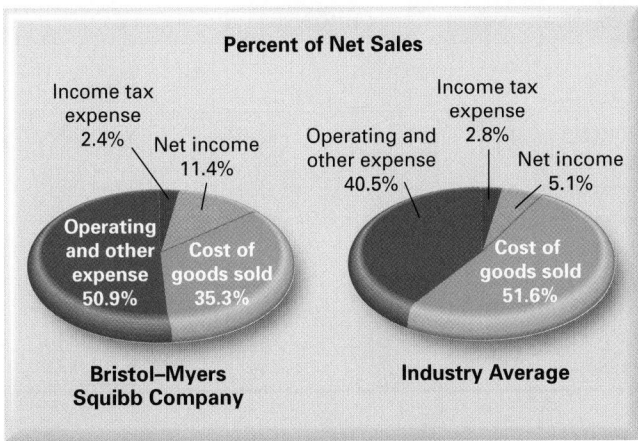

Percent of Net Sales

Bristol–Myers Squibb Company

Industry Average

✔ Starter 18-4

Exhibit 18-8

Common-Size Income Statement Compared with a Key Competitor

Bristol-Myers Squibb Company

Common-Size Income Statement for Comparison with Key Competitor
Year Ended December 31, 2002

	Bristol-Myers Squibb	Procter & Gamble
Net sales	100.0%	100.0%
Cost of goods sold	35.3	52.2
Gross profit	64.7	47.8
Operating and other expenses	50.9	32.0
Income before income tax	13.8	15.8
Income tax expense	2.4	5.0
Net income	11.4%	10.8%

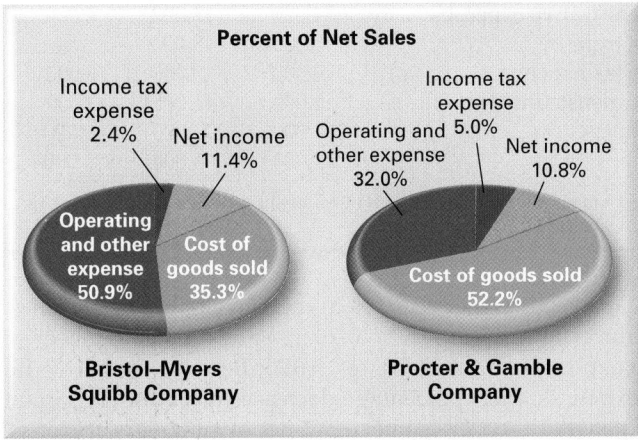

Percent of Net Sales

Bristol–Myers Squibb Company

Procter & Gamble Company

Now let's put your learning to practice. Work the mid-chapter summary problem, which reviews the concepts in the first half of this chapter.

● MID-CHAPTER *Summary Problem*

Perform a horizontal analysis and a vertical analysis of the comparative income statement of TRE Corporation, which makes metal detectors. State whether 20X3 was a good year or a bad year, and give your reasons.

TRE Corporation

Comparative Income Statement
Months Ended December 31, 20X3 and 20X2

	20X3	20X2
Total revenues	$275,000	$225,000
Expenses:		
Cost of products sold	$194,000	$165,000
Engineering, selling, and administrative expenses	54,000	48,000
Interest expense	5,000	5,000
Income tax expense	9,000	3,000
Other expense (income)	1,000	(1,000)
Total expenses	263,000	220,000
Net earnings	$ 12,000	$ 5,000

Solution

The horizontal analysis shows that total revenues increased 22.2%. This was greater than the 19.5% increase in total expenses, resulting in a 140% increase in net earnings.

TRE Corporation

Horizontal Analysis of Comparative Income Statement
Months Ended December 31, 20X3 and 20X2

	20X3	20X2	Increase (Decrease) Amount	Increase (Decrease) Percent
Total revenues	$275,000	$225,000	$50,000	22.2%
Expenses:				
Cost of products sold	$194,000	$165,000	$29,000	17.6
Engineering, selling, and administrative expenses	54,000	48,000	6,000	12.5
Interest expense	5,000	5,000	—	—
Income tax expense	9,000	3,000	6,000	200.0
Other expense (income)	1,000	(1,000)	2,000	—*
Total expenses	263,000	220,000	43,000	19.5
Net earnings	$ 12,000	$ 5,000	$ 7,000	140.0%

*Percentage changes are typically not computed for shifts from a negative to a positive amount, and vice versa.

The vertical analysis shows decreases in the percentages of net sales consumed by the cost of products sold (from 73.3% to 70.5%) and by the engineering, selling, and administrative expenses (from 21.3% to 19.6%). Because these two items are TRE's largest dollar expenses, their percentage decreases are quite important. The relative reduction in expenses raised December 20X3 net earnings to 4.4% of sales, compared with 2.2% the preceding December. The overall analysis indicates that December 20X3 was significantly better than December 20X2.

TRE Corporation				
Vertical Analysis of Comparative Income Statement				
Months Ended December 31, 20X3 and 20X2				

	20X3		20X2	
	Amount	Percent	Amount	Percent
Total revenues................	$275,000	100.0%	$225,000	100.0%
Expenses:				
Cost of products sold.........	$194,000	70.5	$165,000	73.3
Engineering, selling, and				
administrative expenses	54,000	19.6	48,000	21.3
Interest expense	5,000	1.8	5,000	2.2
Income tax expense	9,000	3.3	3,000	1.4**
Other expense (income)	1,000	0.4	(1,000)	(0.4)
Total expenses............	263,000	95.6	220,000	97.8
Net earnings	$ 12,000	4.4%	$ 5,000	2.2%

**Number rounded up.

☐ Horizontal Analysis
☐ Vertical Analysis
☐ Benchmarking
■ Using Ratios
☐ Other Evaluation Tools

Using Ratios to Make Decisions

Online financial databases, such as Lexis/Nexis and the Dow Jones News Retrieval Service, provide financial data on thousands of corporations. Assume that you want to compare some companies' recent earnings histories. You might have the computer compare the companies on the basis of return on stockholders' equity. The computer could then give you the names of the 20 companies with the highest return on equity. A manager, lender, or financial analyst may use any ratio that is relevant to a particular decision.

The ratios we discuss in this chapter may be classified as follows:

1. Measuring ability to pay current liabilities
2. Measuring ability to sell inventory and collect receivables
3. Measuring ability to pay long-term debt
4. Measuring profitability
5. Analyzing stock as an investment

accounts receivable turnover, acid-test ratio, current ratio, day's sales in receivables, debt ratio, dividend yield, earnings per share, inventory turnover ratio, P/E ratio, profitability ratio, return on net sales, return on stockholders' equity, return on total assets, times-interest-earned ratio

Measuring Ability to Pay Current Liabilities

Working capital is defined as

Working capital = Current assets − Current liabilities

Working capital measures the ability to meet short-term obligations with current assets. To use working-capital data in decision making, analysts develop ratios. Two decision tools based on working-capital data are the *current ratio* and the *acid-test ratio*.

CURRENT RATIO   The most widely used ratio is the **current ratio**, which is current assets divided by current liabilities. A company's current assets and current liabilities represent the core of day-to-day operations. The current ratio measures ability to pay current liabilities with current assets.

 Compute the standard financial ratios

Working Capital
Current assets minus current liabilities; measures a business's ability to meet its short-term obligations with its current assets.

Current Ratio
Current assets divided by current liabilities. Measures ability to pay current liabilities with current assets.

Exhibit 18-9 gives the comparative income statement and balance sheet of Palisades Furniture, Inc. The current ratios of Palisades Furniture, Inc., at December 31, 20X5 and 20X4, follow, along with the average for the retail furniture industry:

		Palisades' Current Ratio		Industry Average
	Formula	20X5	20X4	
Current ratio =	$\dfrac{\text{Current assets}}{\text{Current liabilities}}$	$\dfrac{\$262{,}000}{\$142{,}000} = 1.85$	$\dfrac{\$236{,}000}{\$126{,}000} = 1.87$	1.50

Exhibit 18-9 **Comparative Financial Statements**

Palisades Furniture, Inc.
Comparative Income Statement
Years Ended December 31, 20X5 and 20X4

	20X5	20X4
Net sales	$858,000	$803,000
Cost of goods sold.	513,000	509,000
Gross profit	345,000	294,000
Operating expenses:		
Selling expenses	126,000	114,000
General expenses.	118,000	123,000
Total operating expenses	244,000	237,000
Income from operations.	101,000	57,000
Interest revenue.	4,000	—
Interest expense.	24,000	14,000
Income before income taxes	81,000	43,000
Income tax expense.	33,000	17,000
Net income.	$ 48,000	$ 26,000

Palisades Furniture, Inc.
Comparative Balance Sheet
December 31, 20X5 and 20X4

	20X5	20X4
Assets		
Current Assets:		
Cash.	$ 29,000	$ 32,000
Accounts receivable, net.	114,000	85,000
Inventories	113,000	111,000
Prepaid expenses.	6,000	8,000
Total current assets	262,000	236,000
Long-term investments	18,000	9,000
Property, plant, and equipment, net. .	507,000	399,000
Total assets	$787,000	$644,000
Liabilities		
Current Liabilities:		
Notes payable	$ 42,000	$ 27,000
Accounts payable	73,000	68,000
Accrued liabilities.	27,000	31,000
Total current liabilities	142,000	126,000
Long-term debt	289,000	198,000
Total liabilities	431,000	324,000
Stockholders' Equity		
Common stock, no par	186,000	186,000
Retained earnings	170,000	134,000
Total stockholders' equity	356,000	320,000
Total liabilities and equity	$787,000	$644,000

✔ **Starter 18-5**

A high current ratio indicates a strong financial position and that the business has sufficient liquid assets to maintain normal business operations. Compare Palisades Furniture's current ratio of 1.85 with the industry average of 1.50 and with the current ratios of some well-known companies:

Company	Current Ratio
Chesebrough-Pond's Inc..	2.50
Wal-Mart Stores, Inc.	1.51
General Mills, Inc..	1.05

What is an acceptable current ratio? The answer depends on the industry. The norm for companies in most industries is around 1.50, as reported by the Risk Management Association. Palisades Furniture's current ratio of 1.85 is strong. In most industries, a current ratio of 2.0 is very strong.

ACID-TEST RATIO   The **acid-test** (or **quick**) **ratio** tells us whether the entity could pay all its current liabilities if they came due immediately. That is, could the company pass this *acid test*?

To compute the acid-test ratio, we add cash, short-term investments, and net current receivables (accounts and notes receivable, net of allowances) and divide this sum by current liabilities. Inventory and prepaid expenses are the two current assets *not* included in the acid test because they are the least-liquid current assets. Palisades Furniture's acid-test ratios for 20X5 and 20X4 follow.

Acid-Test Ratio
Ratio of the sum of cash plus short-term investments plus net current receivables to total current liabilities. Tells whether the entity can pay all its current liabilities if they come due immediately. Also called the **quick ratio**.

	Formula	Palisades' Acid-Test Ratio		Industry Average
		20X5	20X4	
Acid-test ratio =	Cash + Short-term investments + Net current receivables / Current liabilities	$\dfrac{\$29{,}000 + \$0 + \$114{,}000}{\$142{,}000} = 1.01$	$\dfrac{\$32{,}000 + \$0 + \$85{,}000}{\$126{,}000} = 0.93$	0.40

The company's acid-test ratio improved considerably during 20X5 and is significantly better than the industry average. Palisades' 1.01 acid-test ratio also compares favorably with the acid-test values of some well-known companies.

Company	Acid-Test Ratio
Chesebrough-Pond's Inc..............................	1.25
Wal-Mart Stores, Inc.	0.15
General Motors, Inc....................................	0.91

The norm for the acid-test ratio ranges from 0.20 for shoe retailers to 1.00 for manufacturers of equipment, as reported by the Risk Management Association. An acid-test ratio of 0.90 to 1.00 is acceptable in most industries.

Schlotzky, Inc., has a current ratio of 2.00 and an acid-test ratio of only 0.70. Which account explains the big difference between these two measures of ability to pay current liabilities? Explain.

Answer: Inventory explains the difference. Inventory is included in the current ratio but not in the acid-test ratio. Prepaid expenses may also explain part of the difference, but inventory is more important.

Stop & Think

Measuring Ability to Sell Inventory and Collect Receivables

The ability to sell inventory and collect receivables is fundamental to business success. Recall the operating cycle of a merchandiser: cash to inventory to receivables and back to cash. In this section, we discuss three ratios that measure the company's ability to sell inventory and collect receivables.

INVENTORY TURNOVER   **Inventory turnover** measures the number of times a company sells its average level of inventory during a year. → A high rate of turnover indicates ease in selling inventory; a low rate indicates difficulty in selling. A value of 6 means that the company's average level of inventory has been sold six times during the year.

Inventory Turnover
Ratio of cost of goods sold to average inventory. Indicates how rapidly inventory is sold.

 We introduced inventory turnover in Chapter 6, page 203.

To compute inventory turnover, we divide cost of goods sold by the average inventory for the period. We use the cost of goods sold—not sales—because both cost of goods sold and inventory are stated *at cost*. Sales are stated at the sales value of inventory, which is not comparable with inventory cost.

Palisades Furniture's inventory turnover for 20X5 is

Formula	Palisades' Inventory Turnover	Industry Average
Inventory turnover $= \dfrac{\text{Cost of goods sold}}{\text{Average inventory}}$	$\dfrac{\$513,000}{\$112,000} = 4.6$	3.4

Cost of goods sold comes from the income statement (Exhibit 18-9). Average inventory is figured by averaging the beginning inventory ($111,000) and ending inventory ($113,000). (See the balance sheet, Exhibit 18-9.)

Inventory turnover varies widely with the nature of the business. For example, most manufacturers of farm machinery have an inventory turnover close to three times a year. In contrast, companies that remove natural gas from the ground hold their inventory for a very short period of time and have an average turnover of 30. Palisades Furniture's turnover of 4.6 times a year is high for its industry, which has an average turnover of 3.4.

Accounts Receivable Turnover
Measures a company's ability to collect cash from credit customers. To compute accounts receivable turnover, divide net credit sales by average net accounts receivable.

ACCOUNTS RECEIVABLE TURNOVER **Accounts receivable turnover** measures the ability to collect cash from credit customers. The higher the ratio, the more successfully the business collects cash. However, a receivable turnover that is too high may indicate that credit is too tight, causing the loss of sales to good customers.

To compute the accounts receivable turnover, we divide net credit sales by average net accounts receivable. Palisades Furniture's accounts receivable turnover ratio for 20X5 is computed as follows:

Formula	Palisades' Accounts Receivable Turnover	Industry Average
Accounts receivable turnover $= \dfrac{\text{Net credit sales}}{\text{Average net accounts receivable}}$	$\dfrac{\$858,000}{\$99,500} = 8.6$	51.0

Average net accounts receivable is figured by adding the beginning accounts receivable balance ($85,000) and the ending balance ($114,000), then dividing by 2.

Palisades' receivable turnover of 8.6 times per year is much slower than the industry average. Why the difference? Palisades is a hometown store that sells to local people who tend to pay their bills over time. Many larger furniture stores sell their receivables to other companies called *factors*, a practice that keeps receivables low and receivable turnover high. Palisades Furniture follows a different strategy.

Days' Sales in Receivables
Ratio of average net accounts receivable to one day's sale. Indicates how many days' sales remain in Accounts Receivable awaiting collection. Also called the **collection period**.

Recall from Chapter 9 (page 378) that days' sales in receivables indicates how many days it takes to collect the average level of receivables.

DAYS' SALES IN RECEIVABLES The **days'-sales-in-receivables** ratio also measures the ability to collect receivables. This ratio tells us how many days' sales remain in Accounts Receivable. ← To compute the ratio, we follow a two-step process:

First, divide net sales by 365 days to figure average sales for one day.

Second, divide this average day's sales amount into average net accounts receivable.

The data to compute this ratio for Palisades Furniture, Inc., for 20X5 are taken from the income statement and the balance sheet (Exhibit 18-9):

Formula	Palisades' Days' Sales in Accounts Receivable	Industry Average
Days' Sales in *average* Accounts Receivable:		
1. One day's sales $= \dfrac{\text{Net sales}}{365 \text{ days}}$	$\dfrac{\$858,000}{365 \text{ days}} = \$2,351$	
2. Days' sales in average accounts receivable $= \dfrac{\text{Average net accounts receivable}}{\text{One day's sales}}$	$\dfrac{\$99,500}{\$2,351} = 42 \text{ days}$	7 days

Average accounts receivable of $99,500 = ($85,000 + $114,000)/2.

✔ **Starter 18-6**

Palisades' ratio tells us that 42 average days' sales remain in accounts receivable and need to be collected. Palisades' days' sales in receivables is much higher (worse) than the industry average because Palisades collects its own receivables. Palisades Furniture remains competitive because of its personal relationship with customers. Without their good paying habits, the company's cash flow would suffer.

Measuring Ability to Pay Long-Term Debt

The ratios discussed so far yield insight into current assets and current liabilities. They help us measure ability to sell inventory, collect receivables, and pay current liabilities. Most businesses also have long-term debt. Two key indicators of a business's ability to pay long-term liabilities are the *debt ratio* and the *times-interest-earned ratio*.

DEBT RATIO   Suppose you are a loan officer at a bank and you are evaluating loan applications from two companies with equal sales and total assets. Both companies have asked to borrow $500,000 and have agreed to repay the loan over a 10-year period. The first firm already owes $600,000 to another bank. The second owes only $250,000. Other things being equal, you are more likely to lend money to Company 2 because that company owes less than Company 1.

This relationship between total liabilities and total assets—called the **debt ratio**—shows the proportion of assets financed with debt. → If the debt ratio is 1, then debt has been used to finance all the assets. A debt ratio of 0.50 means that the company has borrowed to finance half its assets; the owners of the business have financed the other half. The higher the debt ratio, the higher the strain of paying off loans.

Debt Ratio
Ratio of total liabilities to total assets. Shows the proportion of a company's assets that is financed with debt.

← *We introduced the debt ratio in Chapter 4, page 155.*

The debt ratios for Palisades Furniture at the end of 20X5 and 20X4 follow:

		Palisades' Debt Ratio		Industry Average
Formula		20X5	20X4	
Debt ratio $= \dfrac{\text{Total liabilities}}{\text{Total assets}}$		$\dfrac{\$431,000}{\$787,000} = 0.55$	$\dfrac{\$324,000}{\$644,000} = 0.50$	0.64

Palisades Furniture's debt ratio of 0.55 is not very high. Risk Management Association reports that the average debt ratio for most companies ranges from 0.57 to 0.67, with relatively little variation from company to company. Palisades' debt ratio indicates a fairly low-risk position compared with the industry average debt ratio of 0.64.

✔ **Starter 18-7**

Times-Interest-Earned Ratio
Ratio of income from operations to interest expense. Measures the number of times that operating income can cover interest expense. Also called the **interest-coverage ratio**.

TIMES-INTEREST-EARNED RATIO The debt ratio says nothing about ability to pay interest expense. Analysts use the **times-interest-earned ratio** to relate income to interest expense. This ratio is also called the **interest-coverage ratio**. It measures the number of times operating income can cover interest expense. A high interest-coverage ratio indicates ease in paying interest expense; a low ratio suggests difficulty.

To compute this ratio, we divide income from operations (operating income) by interest expense. Calculation of Palisades' times-interest-earned ratio follows.

Formula	Palisades' Times-Interest-Earned Ratio		Industry Average
	20X5	20X4	
Times-interest-earned ratio $=\dfrac{\text{Income from operations}}{\text{Interest expense}}$	$\dfrac{\$101,000}{\$24,000} = 4.21$	$\dfrac{\$57,000}{\$14,000} = 4.07$	2.80

The company's times-interest-earned ratio of around 4.00 is significantly better than the average for furniture retailers. The norm for U.S. business, as reported by Risk Management Association, falls in the range of 2.0 to 3.0. Based on its debt ratio and its times-interest-earned ratio, Palisades Furniture appears to have little difficulty *servicing its debt*, that is, paying liabilities.

Measuring Profitability

The fundamental goal of business is to earn a profit. Ratios that measure profitability are reported in the business press and discussed on Money Line. We examine four profitability measures.

Rate of Return on Net Sales
Ratio of net income to net sales. A measure of profitability. Also called **return on sales**.

RATE OF RETURN ON NET SALES In business, the term *return* is used broadly as a measure of profitability. Consider a ratio called the **rate of return on net sales**, or simply **return on sales**. (The word *net* is usually omitted for convenience, even though net sales is used to compute the ratio.) This ratio shows the percentage of each sales dollar earned as net income. Palisades Furniture's rate of return on sales follows.

Formula	Palisades' Rate of Return on Sales		Industry Average
	20X5	20X4	
Rate of return on sales $=\dfrac{\text{Net income}}{\text{Net sales}}$	$\dfrac{\$48,000}{\$858,000} = 0.056$	$\dfrac{\$26,000}{\$803,000} = 0.032$	0.008

Companies strive for a high rate of return on sales. The higher the rate of return, the more sales dollars are providing profit. The increase in Palisades Furniture's return on sales is significant and identifies the company as more successful than the average furniture store. Compare Palisades' rate of return on sales to the rates earned by some leading companies in other industries:

Company	Rate of Return on Sales
eBay..	0.121
Bristol-Myers Squibb	0.114
Wal-Mart.......................................	0.031

RATE OF RETURN ON TOTAL ASSETS The **rate of return on total assets**, or simply **return on assets**, measures success in using assets to earn a profit. → Two groups finance a company's assets. Creditors have loaned money to the company, and they earn interest. Shareholders have invested in stock, and their return is the company's net income.

The sum of interest expense and net income is thus the return to the two groups that have financed the company's assets. Computation of the return-on-assets ratio for Palisades Furniture follows.

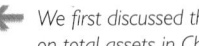
We first discussed the rate of return on total assets in Chapter 13, page 521.

Rate of Return on Total Assets
Net income plus interest expense, divided by average total assets. This ratio measures a company's success in using its assets to earn income for the persons who finance the business. Also called **return on assets**.

Formula	Palisades' 20X5 Rate of Return on Total Assets	Industry Average
$\text{Rate of return on assets} = \dfrac{\text{Net income} + \text{Interest expense}}{\text{Average total assets}}$	$\dfrac{\$48,000 + \$24,000}{\$715,500} = 0.101$	0.078

Average total assets is the average of beginning and ending total assets from the comparative balance sheet: ($644,000 + $787,000)/2 = $715,500. Compare Palisades Furniture's rate of return on assets with the rates of some other companies:

Company	Rate of Return on Assets
General Electric	0.029
Procter & Gamble	0.116
Dell Computer	0.127

RATE OF RETURN ON COMMON STOCKHOLDERS' EQUITY A popular measure of profitability is **rate of return on common stockholders' equity**, often shortened to **return on equity**. → This ratio shows the relationship between net income and common stockholders' equity—how much income is earned for every $1 invested by the common shareholders.

To compute this ratio, we first subtract preferred dividends from net income to get net income available to the common stockholders. We then divide net income available to common stockholders by average common equity during the year. Common equity is total stockholders' equity minus preferred equity. The 20X5 rate of return on common stockholders' equity for Palisades Furniture follows.

We examined this ratio in detail in Chapter 13. For a review, see page 522.

Rate of Return on Common Stockholders' Equity
Net income minus preferred dividends, divided by average common stockholders' equity. A measure of profitability. Also called **return on equity**.

Formula	Palisades' 20X5 Rate of Return on Common Stockholders' Equity	Industry Average
$\text{Rate of return on common stockholders' equity} = \dfrac{\text{Net income} - \text{Preferred dividends}}{\text{Average common stockholders' equity}}$	$\dfrac{\$48,000 - \$0}{\$338,000} = 0.142$	0.121

Average equity is the average of the beginning and ending balances [($356,000 + $320,000)/2 = $338,000]. Observe that Palisades' return on equity (0.142) is higher than its return on assets (0.101). This difference results from borrowing at one rate—say, 8%—and investing the funds to earn a higher rate, such as the firm's 14.2% return on equity. This practice is called **trading on the equity**, or using **leverage**. It is directly related to the debt ratio. The higher the debt ratio, the higher the leverage. Companies that finance operations with debt are said to *leverage* their positions.

Trading on the Equity
Earning more income on borrowed money than the related interest expense, thereby increasing the earnings for the owners of the business. Also called **leverage**.

Leverage usually increases profitability, but not always. Leverage can have a negative impact on profitability. Therefore, leverage is a double-edged sword, increasing profits during good times but compounding losses during bad times. Compare Palisades Furniture's rate of return on common stockholders' equity with the rates of some leading companies.

✔ **Starter 18-8**

Company	Rate of Return on Common Equity
General Electric (GE)	0.26
Procter & Gamble (P&G).	0.65
Dell Computer	0.35

Palisades Furniture is not as profitable as these leading companies. A return on equity of 15% to 20% year after year is considered good in most industries. GE, P&G, and Dell are exceptional performers. Palisades Furniture is okay.

> For an average company, rank the three rates of return from highest to lowest. Palisades Furniture is typical.
>
> *Answer:*
>   1. Rate of return on common stockholders' equity
>   2. Rate of return on assets
>   3. Rate of return on net sales

Chapter 14 provides detailed treatment of EPS.

Earnings per Share (EPS)
Amount of a company's net income for each share of its outstanding common stock.

EARNINGS PER SHARE OF COMMON STOCK   *Earnings per share of common stock,* or simply ← **earnings per share (EPS)**, is perhaps the most widely quoted of all financial statistics. EPS is the only ratio that must appear on the face of the income statement. EPS is the amount of net income earned for each share of the company's outstanding *common* stock.

Earnings per share is computed by dividing net income available to common stockholders by the number of common shares outstanding during the year. Preferred dividends are subtracted from net income because the preferred stockholders have a prior claim to dividends. Palisades Furniture, Inc., has no preferred stock outstanding and no preferred dividends. The firm's EPS for 20X5 and 20X4 follow (Palisades had 10,000 shares of common stock outstanding throughout 20X4 and 20X5).

	Formula	Palisades' Earnings per Share	
		20X5	**20X4**
Earnings per share of common stock	$=\dfrac{\text{Net income} - \text{Preferred dividends}}{\text{Number of shares of common stock outstanding}}$	$\dfrac{\$48,000 - \$0}{10,000} = \$4.80$	$\dfrac{\$26,000 - \$0}{10,000} = \$2.60$

Palisades Furniture's EPS increased 85%. Its stockholders should not expect this big a boost in EPS every year. Most companies strive to increase EPS by 10% to 15% annually, and leading companies do so. But even the most successful companies have an occasional bad year.

Analyzing Stock Investments

Investors purchase stock to earn a return on their investment. This return consists of two parts: (1) gains (or losses) from selling the stock at a price above or below purchase price and (2) dividends. The ratios we examine in this section help analysts evaluate stock in terms of market price or dividends.

PRICE/EARNINGS RATIO The **price/earnings ratio** is the ratio of the market price of a share of common stock to the company's earnings per share. It shows the market price of $1 of earnings. This ratio, abbreviated P/E, appears in *The Wall Street Journal* stock listings. P/E ratios play an important part in decisions to buy, hold, and sell stocks.

Calculations for the P/E ratios of Palisades Furniture, Inc., follow. The market price of its common stock was $60 at the end of 20X5 and $35 at the end of 20X4. These prices can be obtained from a financial publication, a stockbroker, or the company's Web site.

Price/Earnings Ratio
Ratio of the market price of a share of common stock to the company's earnings per share. Measures the value that the stock market places on $1 of a company's earnings.

	Formula	Palisades' Price/Earnings Ratio	
		20X5	**20X4**
P/E ratio =	$\dfrac{\text{Market price per share of common stock}}{\text{Earnings per share}}$	$\dfrac{\$60.00}{\$4.80} = 12.5$	$\dfrac{\$35.00}{\$2.60} = 13.5$

Palisades Furniture's P/E ratio of 12.5 means that the company's stock is selling at 12.5 times earnings. The decline from the 20X4 P/E ratio of 13.5 is no cause for alarm because the market price of the stock is not under Palisades Furniture's control. Net income is more controllable, and net income increased during 20X5.

✔ **Starter 18-9**

DIVIDEND YIELD **Dividend yield** is the ratio of dividends per share to the stock's market price per share. This ratio measures the percentage of a stock's market value that is returned annually as dividends. *Preferred* stockholders, who invest primarily to receive dividends, pay special attention to dividend yield.

Palisades Furniture paid annual cash dividends of $1.20 per share of common stock in 20X5 and $1.00 in 20X4, and market prices of the company's common stock were $60 in 20X5 and $35 in 20X4. The firm's dividend yields on common stock follow.

Dividend Yield
Ratio of dividends per share of stock to the stock's market price per share. Tells the percentage of a stock's market value that the company returns to stockholders annually as dividends.

	Formula	Dividend Yield on Palisades' Common Stock	
		20X5	**20X4**
Dividend yield on common stock* =	$\dfrac{\text{Dividend per share of common stock}}{\text{Market price per share of common stock}}$	$\dfrac{\$1.20}{\$60.00} = .020$	$\dfrac{\$1.00}{\$35.00} = .029$

*Dividend yields may also be calculated for preferred stock.

An investor who buys Palisades Furniture common stock for $60 can expect to receive 2% of the investment annually in the form of cash dividends.

Accounting.com

Expedia.com: Making Investors Happy and Rivals Scared

For an online travel stock, you might turn to the financial pages of a newspaper. The price/earnings (P/E) ratio of online travel giant **Expedia** was 67 in the first quarter of 2003. That means that one share of Expedia stock, valued at $63, was selling at 67 times its earnings per share. A P/E ratio of 67 is very high indeed. By contrast, the P/E ratio of competitor **Sabre Holdings**, Travelocity's owner, was only 10. Why the big difference between these similar companies?

Expedia is doing 55% more business than Travelocity. Why is Expedia so far ahead? Consider the story behind the company's financials: "Our big fat hairy dream is to be the largest seller of travel in the world. . . ," said Richard Barton, Expedia's former CEO.

Profit margins on airline tickets are razor-thin. So, unlike rivals, Expedia doesn't rely on airline bookings. It has expanded into hotel reservations and custom vacation packages, which earn higher profits. In the hotel market, Expedia was not content with the usual 10% commission on reservations. Barton bought hotel rooms at wholesale prices, marked them up as much as 26%, and then sold the rooms to consumers. A 26% markup beats a 10% markup any day.

Based on: Timothy J. Mullaney, "Expedia: Changing Pilots in Mid-Climb," *Business Week*, February 24, 2003, pp. 120–124. Kathy Bergen, "Air-Only Emphasis Trips Up Travel Sites: Online Firms Find Package Deals More Profitable," *Chicago Tribune*, December 1, 2002, p. 5-1. Andrew Chaikivsky, "The Best & Brightest: Business—Richard Barton, CEO, Expedia," *Esquire*, December 2002, p. 177.

Book Value per Share of Common Stock
Common stockholders' equity divided by the number of shares of common stock outstanding. The recorded amount for each share of common stock outstanding.

BOOK VALUE PER SHARE OF COMMON STOCK **Book value per share of common stock** is simply common equity divided by the number of common shares outstanding. Common equity equals total stockholders' equity less preferred equity. Palisades Furniture has no preferred stock outstanding. Its book-value-per-share-of-common-stock ratios follow (10,000 shares of common stock were outstanding).

	Formula	Book Value per Share of Palisades' Common Stock	
		20X5	20X4
Book value per share of common stock	= $\dfrac{\text{Total stockholders' equity} - \text{Preferred equity}}{\text{Number of shares of common stock outstanding}}$	$\dfrac{\$356{,}000 - \$0}{10{,}000} = \$35.60$	$\dfrac{\$320{,}000 - \$0}{10{,}000} = \$32.00$

✔ **Starter 18-10**

✔ **Starter 18-11**

See Chapter 13, page 520, for a discussion of market value and book value. →

Many experts argue that book value is not useful for investment analysis. ← It bears no relationship to market value and provides little information beyond stockholders' equity reported on the balance sheet. But some investors base their investment decisions on book value. For example, some investors rank stocks on the basis of the ratio of market price to book value. To these investors, the lower the ratio, the more attractive the stock.

Other Evaluation Tools

Economic Value Added

Coca-Cola, Quaker Oats, and other leading companies use **economic value added (EVA®)** to evaluate performance. EVA® measures whether operations have increased stockholder wealth. EVA® can be computed as follows:

$$\text{EVA}^® = \text{Net income} + \text{Interest expense} - \text{Capital charge}$$

Student ResourceCD

EVA

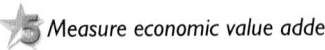

Measure economic value added

where

$$\text{Capital charge} = \left(\frac{\text{Notes}}{\text{payable}} + \frac{\text{Bonds}}{\text{payable}} + \frac{\text{Stockholders'}}{\text{equity}} \right) \times \frac{\text{Cost of}}{\text{capital}}$$

Economic Value Added (EVA®)
EVA = Net income + Interest expense − Capital charge. Used to evaluate a company's operating performance.

Cost of Capital
A weighted average of the returns demanded by the company's stockholders and lenders.

All amounts for the EVA® computation, except the cost of capital, are taken from the financial statements. The **cost of capital** is a weighted average of the returns demanded by the company's stockholders and lenders. The cost of capital varies with the company's level of risk. For example, stockholders and lenders would demand a higher return from a start-up company than from Coca-Cola because the new company is more risky. A new company would thus have a higher cost of capital than Coca-Cola. In the following discussions we assume a value for the cost of capital (such as 10%, 12%, or 15%).

The idea behind EVA® is that the returns to the company's stockholders (net income) and to its creditors (interest expense) should exceed the company's capital charge. The **capital charge** is the amount that investors *charge* for the use of their money. A positive EVA® amount suggests an increase in stockholder wealth, and the company's stock should remain attractive. If EVA® goes negative, stockholders probably will be unhappy and sell the stock, resulting in a decrease in the stock price.

Capital Charge
The amount that stockholders and lenders charge a company for the use of their money. Calculated as (Notes payable + Loans payable + Long-term debt + Stockholders' equity) × Cost of capital.

The Coca-Cola Company is a leading user of EVA.® Coca-Cola's EVA® for 2002 can be computed as follows, assuming a 10% cost of capital for the company (dollar amounts in millions):

Cola-Cola's EVA® =	Net income	+	Interest expense	−	(Loans and notes payable	+	Long-term debt	+	Stockholders' equity	) ×	Cost of capital
=	$3,050	+	$199	−	[($2,475	+	$2,701	+	$11,800)	×	0.10]
=		$3,249		−			$16,976			×	0.10
=		$3,249		−					$1,698		
=				$1,551							

By this measure, Coca-Cola's operations during 2002 added $1.551 billion ($1,551 million) of value to its stockholders' wealth after meeting the company's capital charge. This performance is outstanding.

✔ **Starter 18-12**

Red Flags in Financial Statement Analysis

Another way to analyze a company's situation is to look for *red flags* that may signal financial trouble. Recent accounting scandals highlight the importance of these red flags. If the following conditions are present, the company may be too risky.

- *Earnings Problems.* Have income from continuing operations and net income decreased significantly for several years in a row? Has income turned into a loss? Most companies cannot survive consecutive loss years.

- *Decreased Cash Flow.* Cash flow validates earnings. Is cash flow from operations consistently lower than net income? Are the sales of plant assets a major source of cash? If so, the company may face a cash shortage.

■ *Too Much Debt.* How does the company's debt ratio compare to that of major competitors and to the industry average? If the debt ratio is much higher than average, the company may be unable to pay its debts.

■ *Inability to Collect Receivables.* Are days' sales in receivables growing faster than for other companies in the industry? A cash shortage may be looming.

■ *Buildup of Inventories.* Is inventory turnover slowing down? If so, the company may be unable to sell goods, or it may be overstating inventory. Recall from the cost-of-goods-sold model that one of the easiest ways to overstate net income is to overstate ending inventory.

■ *Movement of Sales, Inventory, and Receivables.* Sales, receivables, and inventory generally move together. Increased sales lead to higher receivables and require more inventory to meet demand. Strange movements among these items may spell trouble.

Do these red flags reveal significant difficulties at Bristol-Myers Squibb (BMS)? Maybe so. Net income took a sharp downturn in 2002. Cash flow from operations was also down a lot. But receivables and inventories weren't up too much, and BMS's debt ratio isn't too high. Overall, we get mixed signals about BMS's financial health. Wall Street doesn't like mixed signals about a company. That's probably why the stock market didn't go for the company's performance in 2002.

Analyzing Nonfinancial Data

There is more to analyzing financial statements than performing horizontal and vertical analysis and computing the standard ratios. The nonquantitative parts of the annual report may hold more important information than the financial statements. For example, the president's letter may describe a turnover of top managers. The management discussion and analysis will reveal management's opinion of the year's results. And the auditor's report may indicate a major problem with the company. Let's consider each of these parts of a corporate annual report.

PRESIDENT'S LETTER TO THE STOCKHOLDERS The president of the company gives his or her view of the year's results and outlines the direction top management is charting for the company. The most recent annual report of Procter & Gamble described the retirement of the company's chairman of the board and the election of a new chairman. A shift in top management or a major change in the company's direction is important to investors.

MANAGEMENT DISCUSSION AND ANALYSIS (MD&A) The people who know the most about a company are its executives. For this reason, stockholders want to know what management thinks about the company's net income (or net loss), cash flows, and financial position. The MD&A section of the annual report discusses *why* net income was up or down, how the company invested the stockholders' money, and plans for future spending. Through the MD&A, investors may learn of the company's plan to discontinue a product line or to expand into new markets. These forward-looking data are not permitted in the historical financial statements, which are based on past transactions.

AUDITOR REPORT Both the president's letter and the MD&A express the views of corporate insiders. The financial statements are also produced by the management of the company. These people naturally want to describe the company in a favorable light. Therefore, all the information coming out of the company could be slanted to make the company look good.

Investors are aware of the possibility for management bias in the financial statements. For this reason, the Securities & Exchange Commission, a federal agency, requires that all financial statements of public corporations be audited by independent accountants. The auditors are not employees of the companies they audit. After auditing the Bristol-Myers Squibb (BMS) financial statements, PricewaterhouseCoopers (PwC), an international accounting firm, issued its professional opinion on the BMS statements. PwC stated that the BMS statements agreed with generally accepted accounting principles. This is how investors in the United States and in other developed countries gain assurance that they can rely on a company's financial statements. If the survival of BMS were in doubt, PwC's audit report would alert investors to the difficulty.

The Decision Guidelines summarize the most widely used ratios. The Excel Application Exercise provides an opportunity to apply your understanding of the ratios.

Decision Guidelines

USING RATIOS IN FINANCIAL STATEMENT ANALYSIS

Lane and Kay Collins operate a financial-services firm. They manage other people's money and do most of their own financial-statement analysis. How do they measure companies' ability to pay bills, sell inventory, collect receivables, and so on? They use the standard ratios we have covered throughout this book.

Ratio	Computation	Information Provided
Measuring ability to pay current liabilities:		
1. Current ratio	$\dfrac{\text{Current assets}}{\text{Current liabilities}}$	Measures ability to pay current liabilities with current assets
2. Acid-test (quick) ratio	$\dfrac{\text{Cash} + \dfrac{\text{Short-term}}{\text{investments}} + \dfrac{\text{Net current}}{\text{receivables}}}{\text{Current liabilities}}$	Shows ability to pay all current liabilities if they come due immediately
Measuring ability to sell inventory and collect receivables:		
3. Inventory turnover	$\dfrac{\text{Cost of goods sold}}{\text{Average inventory}}$	Indicates saleability of inventory— the number of times a company sells its average inventory during a year
4. Accounts receivable turnover	$\dfrac{\text{Net credit sales}}{\text{Average net accounts receivable}}$	Measures ability to collect cash from customers
5. Days' sales in receivables	$\dfrac{\text{Average net accounts receivable}}{\text{One day's sales}}$	Shows how many days' sales remain in Accounts Receivable— how many days it takes to collect the average level of receivables
Measuring ability to pay long-term debt:		
6. Debt ratio	$\dfrac{\text{Total liabilities}}{\text{Total assets}}$	Indicates percentage of assets financed with debt
7. Times-interest-earned ratio	$\dfrac{\text{Income from operations}}{\text{Interest expense}}$	Measures the number of times operating income can cover interest expense
Measuring profitability:		
8. Rate of return on net sales	$\dfrac{\text{Net income}}{\text{Net sales}}$	Shows the percentage of each sales dollar earned as net income
9. Rate of return on total assets	$\dfrac{\text{Net income} + \text{Interest expense}}{\text{Average total assets}}$	Measures how profitably a company uses its assets

Decision Guidelines *(continued)*

Ratio	Computation	Information Provided
10. Rate of return on common stockholders' equity	$$\frac{\text{Net income} - \text{Preferred dividends}}{\text{Average common stockholders' equity}}$$	Gauges how much income is earned for each dollar invested by common shareholders
11. Earnings per share of common stock	$$\frac{\text{Net income} - \text{Preferred dividends}}{\text{Number of shares of common stock outstanding}}$$	Gives the amount of net income earned for each share of the company's common stock
Analyzing stock as an investment:		
12. Price/earnings ratio	$$\frac{\text{Market price per share of common stock}}{\text{Earnings per share}}$$	Indicates the market price of $1 of earnings
13. Dividend yield	$$\frac{\text{Annual dividend per share of common (or preferred) stock}}{\text{Market price per share of common (or preferred) stock}}$$	Shows the percentage of a stock's market value returned as dividends to stockholders each year
14. Book value per share of common stock	$$\frac{\text{Total stockholders' equity} - \text{Preferred equity}}{\text{Number of shares of common stock outstanding}}$$	Indicates the recorded accounting amount for each share of common stock outstanding

Excel Application Exercise

Goal: Create an Excel work sheet that calculates financial ratios to compare PepsiCo and Coca-Cola. Then use the results to determine which company has the stronger financial performance.

Scenario: You've saved $5,000 from your summer internship at PepsiCo. You'd like to invest your savings in the stock of your employer, but your parents think the better investment would be stock in Coca-Cola, their favorite brand of soft drink. Before making your purchase, you decide to create an Excel work sheet that compares both companies on several key financial ratios.

Your task is to create an Excel spreadsheet to compare the following ratios for PepsiCo and Coca-Cola.

1. Acid-test (quick) ratio
2. Inventory turnover
3. Debt ratio
4. Return on net sales
5. Price/earnings ratio

When done with the work sheet, answer the following questions:

1. Which company is in a better position to pay all current liabilities if they come due immediately?
2. Which company's inventory is more "saleable"?
3. Which company is financing more of its assets with debt?
4. Which company earned more profit, as a percentage, on each sales dollar?
5. Which company's earnings have a higher market price per dollar of earnings?

Step-by-Step:

1. Locate the data required for each ratio in the annual reports of PepsiCo (www.pepsico.com) and Coca-Cola (www.cocacola.com). *Note:* For fiscal year-end stock prices, go to www.yahoo.com, and then select "Finance." Enter the ticker symbol (PEP for PepsiCo and KO for Coca-Cola), then select "Performance." You should be able to click on "historical prices" to enter the dates for each fiscal year-end.
2. Open a new Excel work sheet.
3. Create a bold-faced heading for your spreadsheet that contains the following:
   a. Chapter 18 Excel Application Exercise
   b. Using Ratios in Financial Statement Analysis
   c. PepsiCo and Coca-Cola Comparison
   d. Today's date
4. In the first column, enter the names of all five ratios. Skip a row between each ratio name.
5. Create bold-faced, underlined column headings for PepsiCo and Coca-Cola. Underneath, enter the "As of" date for the financial statements used in the analysis. (Fiscal year-ends may not match exactly.)
6. Enter the data located in step 1, using the correct ratio formulas found in the Decision Guidelines. For the P/E ratio, use basic EPS in the denominator. Format all cells as necessary.
7. Save your work, and print a copy for your files.

END-OF-CHAPTER *Summary Problem*

The following financial data are adapted from the annual reports of **Gap Inc.**, which operates Gap, Banana Republic, and Old Navy clothing stores:

CHECK YOUR RESOURCES

Gap Inc.				
Five-Year Selected Financial Data (adapted) **Years Ended January 31,**				
Operating Results*	2002	2001	2000	1999
Net sales	$13,848	$13,673	$11,635	$9,054
Cost of goods sold	9,704	8,599	6,775	5,318
Interest expense	109	75	45	46
Income from operations	338	1,455	1,817	1,333
Net earnings (net loss)	(8)	877	1,127	824
Cash dividends	76	75	76	77
Financial Position				
Merchandise inventory............	1,677	1,904	1,462	1,056
Total assets	7,591	7,012	5,189	3,963
Current ratio....................	1.48:1	0.95:1	1.25:1	1.20:1
Stockholders' equity	3,010	2,928	2,630	1,574
Average number of shares of common stock outstanding (in thousands).................	860	879	895	576

*Dollar amounts are in thousands.

Required

Compute the following ratios for 2000 through 2002, and evaluate Gap's operating results. Are operating results strong or weak? Did they improve or deteriorate during the four-year period? Your analysis will reveal a clear trend.

1. Gross profit percentage
2. Net income as a percentage of sales
3. Earnings per share
4. Inventory turnover
5. Times-interest-earned ratio
6. Rate of return on stockholders' equity

Solution

	2002	2001	2000
1. Gross profit percentage	$\dfrac{\$13,848 - \$9,704}{\$13,848} = 29.9\%$	$\dfrac{\$13,673 - \$8,599}{\$13,673} = 37.1\%$	$\dfrac{\$11,635 - \$6,775}{\$11,635} = 41.8\%$
2. Net income as a percentage of sales	$\dfrac{\$(8)}{\$13,848} = (.06\%)$	$\dfrac{\$877}{\$13,673} = 6.4\%$	$\dfrac{\$1,127}{\$11,635} = 9.7\%$
3. Earnings per share	$\dfrac{\$(8)}{860} = \$(0.01)$	$\dfrac{\$877}{879} = \$1.00$	$\dfrac{\$1,127}{895} = \$1.26$
4. Inventory turnover	$\dfrac{\$9,704}{(\$1,677 + \$1,904)/2} = 5.4 \text{ times}$	$\dfrac{\$8,599}{(\$1,904 + \$1,462)/2} = 5.1 \text{ times}$	$\dfrac{\$6,775}{(\$1,462 + \$1,056)/2} = 5.4 \text{ times}$
5. Times-interest-earned ratio	$\dfrac{\$338}{\$109} = 3.1 \text{ times}$	$\dfrac{\$1,455}{\$75} = 19.4 \text{ times}$	$\dfrac{\$1,817}{\$45} = 40.4 \text{ times}$
6. Rate of return on stockholders' equity	$\dfrac{\$(8)}{(\$3,010 + \$2,928)/2} = (0.3\%)$	$\dfrac{\$877}{(\$2,928 + \$2,630)/2} = 31.6\%$	$\dfrac{\$1,127}{(\$2,630 + \$1,574)/2} = 53.6\%$

Evaluation: During this period, Gap's operating results deteriorated on all these measures except inventory turnover. The gross profit percentage is down sharply, as are the times-interest-earned ratio and all the return measures. From these data it is clear that Gap could sell its merchandise, but not at the markups the company enjoyed in the past. The final result, in 2002, was a net loss for the year.

●REVIEW *Financial Statement Analysis*

Quick Check

The **Coca-Cola Company** reported these figures (adapted and in millions):

	2002	2001		2002
Cash and equivalents	$ 2,345	$ 1,934	Sales	$19,564
Receivables.	2,097	1,882	Cost of sales	7,105
Inventory	1,294	1,055	Operating expenses	7,001
Prepaid expenses.	1,616	2,300	Operating income	5,458
Total current assets	7,352	7,171	Interest expense	199
Other assets	17,149	15,246	Other expense.	2,209
Total assets	$24,501	$22,417	Net income	$ 3,050
Total current liabilities	$ 7,341	$ 8,429		
Long-term liabilities	5,360	2,622		
Common equity.	11,800	11,366		
Total liabilities and equity	$24,501	$22,417		

1. Horizontal analysis of Coca-Cola's balance sheet for 2002 would report
   - **a.** 21% increase in Cash
   - **b.** Cash as 9.6% of total assets
   - **c.** Current ratio of 1.00
   - **d.** Inventory turnover of 6 times

2. Vertical analysis of Coca-Cola's balance sheet for 2002 would report
   - **a.** 21% increase in Cash
   - **b.** Cash as 9.6% of total assets
   - **c.** Current ratio of 1.00
   - **d.** Inventory turnover of 6 times

3. A common-size income statement for Coca-Cola would report (amounts rounded)
   - **a.** Sales of 100%
   - **b.** Cost of sales at 36%
   - **c.** Net income of 16%
   - **d.** All the above

4. Which statement best describes Coca-Cola's acid-test ratio?
   - **a.** Greater than 1
   - **b.** Equal to 1
   - **c.** Less than 1
   - **d.** None of the above

5. Coca-Cola's inventory turnover during 2002 was
   - **a.** 5 times
   - **b.** 6 times
   - **c.** 7 times
   - **d.** Not determinable from the data given

6. During 2002, Coca-Cola's days' sales in receivables ratio was
   - **a.** 30 days
   - **b.** 35 days
   - **c.** 37 days
   - **d.** 39 days

7. Which measure expresses Coca-Cola's times-interest-earned ratio?
   - **a.** 15 times
   - **b.** 20 times
   - **c.** 27 times
   - **d.** 51.8%

8. Coca-Cola's return on common stockholders' equity can be described as
   - **a.** Strong
   - **b.** Good
   - **c.** Average
   - **d.** Weak

9. The company has 2,500 million shares of common stock outstanding. What is Coca-Cola's earnings per share?
   - **a.** 2.04
   - **b.** 3.6 times
   - **c.** $3.05
   - **d.** $1.22

10. Coca-Cola's stock has traded recently around $44 per share. Use your answer to question 9 to measure the company's price/earnings ratio.
    - **a.** 69
    - **b.** 44
    - **c.** 1.00
    - **d.** 36

Accounting Vocabulary

accounts receivable turnover (p. 718)
acid-test ratio (p. 717)
benchmarking (p. 712)
book value per share of common stock
    (p. 724)
capital charge (p. 725)
collection period (p. 718)
common-size statement (p. 711)
cost of capital (p. 725)
current ratio (p. 715)
days' sales in receivables (p. 718)
debt ratio (p. 719)

dividend yield (p. 723)
earnings per share (EPS) (p. 722)
economic value added (EVA)® (p. 725)
horizontal analysis (p. 707)
interest-coverage ratio (p. 720)
inventory turnover (p. 717)
leverage (p. 721)
price/earnings ratio (p. 723)
quick ratio (p. 717)
rate of return on common stockholders'
    equity (p. 721)
rate of return on net sales (p. 720)

return on assets (p. 721)
return on equity (p. 721)
return on sales (p. 720)
rate of return on total assets (p. 721)
return on stockholders' equity (p. 721)
times-interest-earned ratio (p. 720)
trading on the equity (p. 721)
trend percentages (p. 709)
vertical analysis (p. 709)
working capital (p. 715)

ASSESS *Your Progress*

Starters

S18-1 **Nike, Inc.,** reported the following on its 2002 comparative income statement:

See *www.prenhall.com/horngren*
for selected Starters, Exercises,
and Problems.

*Horizontal analysis of revenues and gross
profit*
(Obj. 1)

(in millions)	2002	2001	2000
Revenues	$9,893	$9,489	$8,995
Cost of sales	6,005	5,785	5,404

Perform a horizontal analysis of revenues and gross profit—both in dollar amounts and in percentages—for 2002 and 2001.

S18-2 **Nike, Inc.,** reported the following revenues and net income amounts:

*Trend analysis of revenues and net
income*
(Obj. 1)

(in millions)	2002	2001	2000	1999
Revenues	$9,893	$9,489	$8,995	$8,777
Net income	664	590	579	451

1. Show Nike's trend percentages for revenues and net income. Use 1999 as the base year.
2. Which measure increased faster during 2000–2002?

S18-3 Perfect 10 Sporting Goods reported the following amounts on its balance sheets at December 31, 20X6, 20X5, and 20X4:

*Vertical analysis to correct a cash
shortage*
(Obj. 2)

	20X6	20X5	20X4
Cash and receivables	$ 38,000	$ 30,000	$ 25,000
Inventory	48,000	36,000	24,000
Property, plant, and equipment, net	96,000	88,000	87,000
Total assets	$182,000	$154,000	$136,000

Sales and profits are high. Nevertheless, the company is experiencing a cash shortage. Perform a vertical analysis of Perfect 10 assets at the end of years 20X6, 20X5, and 20X4. Use the analysis to explain the reason for the cash shortage.

S18-4 **Nike, Inc.**, and **Home Depot** are leaders in their respective industries. Compare the two companies by converting their income statements (adapted) to common size.

(in millions)	Nike	Home Depot
Net sales	$9,489	$19,536
Cost of goods sold	5,785	14,101
Other expense	3,114	4,497
Net income	$ 590	$ 938

Which company earns more net income? Which company's net income is a higher percentage of its net sales? Which company is more profitable? Explain your answer.

S18-5 Use the **Bristol-Myers Squibb** balance sheet data in Exhibit 18-3, page 708.

1. Compute the company's current ratio at December 31, 2002 and 2001.
2. Did Bristol-Myers Squibb's current ratio value improve, deteriorate, or hold steady during 2002?

S18-6 Use the **Bristol-Myers Squibb** 2002 income statement (page 708) and balance sheet (page 708) to compute the following (amounts in millions):

a. The rate of inventory turnover for 2002. Inventory was $1,573 at the end of 2002 and $1,699 at the end of 2001.
b. Days' sales in average receivables during 2002. All sales are made on account. Receivables were $2,968 at the end of 2002 and $3,992 at the end of 2001. (Round dollar amounts to one decimal place.)

S18-7 Use the financial statements of **Bristol-Myers Squibb Company** (page 708).

1. Compute the debt ratio at December 31, 2002.
2. Is Bristol-Myers Squibb's ability to pay its liabilities strong or weak? Explain your reasoning.

S18-8 Use the financial statements of **Bristol-Myers Squibb Company** (page 710) to determine or, if necessary, to compute these profitability measures for 2002.

a. Rate of return on net sales.
b. Rate of return on total assets. Interest expense for 2002 was $410 million.
c. Rate of return on common stockholders' equity.

Are these rates of return strong or weak? Explain.

S18-9 The annual report of **Dell Computer Corporation** for fiscal year 2002 included the following items (in millions):

Preferred stock outstanding	$0
Net income	$1,246
Number of shares of common stock outstanding	2,602

1. Compute earnings per share (EPS) for Dell. Round to the nearest cent.
2. Compute Dell's price/earnings ratio. The price of a share of Dell stock is $26.85.

S18-10 A skeleton of **Campbell Soup Company's** income statement (as adapted) appears as follows (amounts in millions):

Using ratio data to reconstruct an income statement
(Obj. 4)

Income Statement

Net sales.......................................	$7,278
Cost of goods sold	(a)
Selling and administrative expenses.................	1,716
Interest expense	(b)
Other expenses	151
Income before taxes	1,042
Income tax expense	(c)
Net income.......................................	$ (d)

Use the following ratio data to complete Campbell Soup's income statement:

a. Inventory turnover was 5.53 (beginning inventory was $787; ending inventory was $755).
b. Rate of return on sales is 0.0959.

S18-11 A skeleton of **Campbell Soup Company's** balance sheet (as adapted) appears as follows (amounts in millions):

Using ratio data to reconstruct a balance sheet
(Obj. 4)

Balance Sheet

Cash.....................	$ 53	Total current liabilities	$2,164
Receivables..............	(a)	Long-term debt	(e)
Inventories	755	Other long-term liabilities ..	826
Prepaid expenses.........	(b)		
Total current assets	(c)		
Plant assets, net	(d)		
Other assets	2,150	Stockholders' equity.......	2,468
Total assets	$6,315	Total liabilities and equity ..	$ (f)

Use the following ratio data to complete Campbell Soup's balance sheet:

a. Current ratio is 0.7306.
b. Acid-test ratio is 0.3161.

S18-12 Use the financial statements of **Bristol-Myers Squibb** (page 710).

Measuring economic value added
(Obj. 5)

1. Compute economic value added (EVA®) by the company's operations during 2002. Use beginning-of-year amounts to compute the capital charge. Interest expense was $410 million, and interest-bearing debt totaled $6,411 million. Assume that the company's cost of capital is 12%. Round all amounts to the nearest million dollars.
2. Should the company's stockholders be happy with the EVA® for 2002?

Exercises

E18-1 What were the dollar amount of change and the percentage of change in Micron Electronics' working capital during 2005 and 2006? Is this trend favorable or unfavorable?

Computing year-to-year changes in working capital
(Obj. 1)

	2006	2005	2004
Total current assets....................	$302,000	$290,000	$280,000
Total current liabilities...............	150,000	157,000	140,000

Horizontal analysis of an income statement
(Obj. 1)

Student ResourceCD

spreadsheet

E18-2 Prepare a horizontal analysis of the following comparative income statement of Newsletter E-Mail, Inc. Round percentage changes to the nearest one-tenth percent (three decimal places):

	Newsletter E-Mail, Inc.	
	Comparative Income Statement **Years Ended December 31, 2005 and 2004**	
	2005	**2004**
Total revenue	$430,000	$373,000
Expenses:		
Cost of goods sold	$202,000	$188,000
Selling and general expenses	98,000	93,000
Interest expense	7,000	4,000
Income tax expense	42,000	37,000
Total expenses	349,000	322,000
Net income	$ 81,000	$ 51,000

Why did net income increase by a higher percentage than total revenues during 2005?

Computing trend percentages
(Obj. 1)

E18-3 Compute trend percentages for Metro Graphics' net revenues and net income for the following 5-year period, using year 1 as the base year. Round to the nearest full percent.

(in thousands)	Year 5	Year 4	Year 3	Year 2	Year 1
Total revenue	$1,418	$1,187	$1,106	$1,009	$1,043
Net income	132	114	83	71	85

Which grew faster during the period, total revenue or net income?

Vertical analysis of a balance sheet
(Obj. 2)

E18-4 Consolidated Water System of Sierra, Nevada, has requested that you perform a vertical analysis of its balance sheet to determine the component percentages of its assets, liabilities, and stockholders' equity.

Consolidated Water System of Sierra, Nevada	
Balance Sheet **December 31, 20X5**	
Assets	
Total current assets	$ 42,000
Property, plant, and equipment, net	247,000
Other assets	35,000
Total assets	$324,000
Liabilities	
Total current liabilities	$ 48,000
Long-term debt	108,000
Total liabilities	156,000
Stockholders' Equity	
Total stockholders' equity	168,000
Total liabilities and stockholders' equity	$324,000

Preparing a common-size income statement
(Obj. 3)

Student ResourceCD

spreadsheet

E18-5 Prepare a comparative common-size income statement for Newsletter E-Mail, Inc., using the 2005 and 2004 data of Exercise 18-2 and rounding percentages to one-tenth percent (three decimal places). To an investor, how does 2005 compare with 2004? Explain your reasoning.

E18-6 The financial statements of Cunningham Financial Group include the following items:

Computing five ratios
(Obj. 4)

tudent ResourceCD

spreadsheet

	Current Year	Preceding Year
Balance sheet:		
Cash	$ 17,000	$ 22,000
Short-term investments.	11,000	26,000
Net receivables	64,000	73,000
Inventory.	77,000	71,000
Prepaid expenses	16,000	8,000
Total current assets.	$185,000	$200,000
Total current liabilities.	$131,000	$ 91,000
Income statement:		
Net credit sales	$454,000	
Cost of goods sold	297,000	

Required

Compute the following ratios for the current year:

a. Current ratio   **c.** Inventory turnover
b. Acid-test ratio   **d.** Days' sales in average receivables

E18-7 Pinnacle Market Research Corporation has asked you to determine whether the company's ability to pay current liabilities and long-term debts improved or deteriorated during 20X4. To answer this question, compute ratios for 20X4 and 20X3:

Analyzing the ability to pay current liabilities
(Obj. 4)

tudent ResourceCD

spreadsheet

a. Current ratio   **c.** Debt ratio
b. Acid-test ratio   **d.** Times-interest-earned ratio

Summarize the results of your analysis in a written report.

	20X4	20X3
Cash	$ 61,000	$ 47,000
Short-term investments	28,000	—
Net receivables	102,000	116,000
Inventory	237,000	272,000
Total assets.	543,000	489,000
Total current liabilities	275,000	221,000
Long-term debt	46,000	52,000
Income from operations.	165,000	158,000
Interest expense.	48,000	39,000

E18-8 Compute four ratios that measure ability to earn profits for Save the Planet's Air, Inc., whose comparative income statement follows:

Analyzing profitability
(Obj. 4)

Save the Planet's Air, Inc.		
Comparative Income Statement		
Years Ended December 31, 20X6 and 20X5		
Dollars in Thousands	**20X6**	**20X5**
Net sales.	$174,000	$158,000
Cost of goods sold	93,000	86,000
Gross profit	81,000	72,000
Selling and general expenses	46,000	41,000
Income from operations.	35,000	31,000
Interest expense.	9,000	10,000
Income before income tax	26,000	21,000
Income tax expense	8,000	8,000
Net income.	$ 18,000	$ 13,000

(continued)

Additional data:

	20X6	20X5	20X4
Total assets..........................	$204,000	$191,000	$171,000
Common stockholders' equity.........	$ 96,000	$ 89,000	$ 79,000
Preferred dividends..................	$ 3,000	$ 3,000	$ 0
Common shares outstanding during the year....................	20,000	20,000	18,000

Did the company's operating performance improve or deteriorate during 20X6?

Evaluating a stock as an investment
(Obj. 4)

E18-9 Evaluate the common stock of Friedman Energy Company as an investment. Specifically, use the three stock ratios to determine whether the common stock has increased or decreased in attractiveness during the past year.

	20X4	20X3
Net income......................................	$ 58,000	$ 55,000
Dividends—common...............................	20,000	20,000
Dividends—preferred	12,000	12,000
Total stockholders' equity at year-end (includes 80,000 shares of common stock)	580,000	500,000
Preferred stock, 6%..............................	200,000	200,000
Market price per share of common stock	$ 11.50	$ 7.75

Using economic value added to measure corporate performance
(Obj. 5)

E18-10 Two companies with very different economic-value-added (EVA®) profiles are **Oracle Corporation**, the world's second-largest software company, and **Wells Fargo & Company**, the nationwide banking conglomerate. Adapted versions of the two companies' financial statements are presented here (in millions):

	Oracle	Wells Fargo
Balance sheet data:		
Total assets	$11,030	$307,569
Interest-bearing debt.........................	$ 304	$195,781
All other liabilities	4,448	84,574
Stockholders' equity	6,278	27,214
Total liabilities and equity	$11,030	$307,569
Income statement data:		
Total revenue	$10,860	$ 26,891
Interest expense	24	6,741
All other expenses	8,275	16,727
Net income	$ 2,561	$ 3,423

Required

Compute the EVA® for each company and then decide which company's stock you would rather hold as an investment. Assume Oracle's cost of capital is 15%, and Wells Fargo's is 5%. Round to the nearest $1 million.

Using ratio data to reconstruct a company's balance sheet
(Obj. 4)

E18-11 The following data (dollar amounts in millions) are adapted from the financial statements of **Wal-Mart Stores, Inc.**

Total current assets.............................	$ 10,196
Accumulated depreciation.......................	$ 1,448
Total liabilities.................................	$ 11,806
Preferred stock	$ 0
Debt ratio.....................................	60.342%
Current ratio...................................	1.51

Required

Complete the following condensed balance sheet. Report amounts to the nearest $1 million.

Current assets.	$?
Property, plant, and equipment. . . . . $?	
Less Accumulated depreciation. . . . . (?)	?
Total assets	$?
Current liabilities.	$?
Long-term liabilities	?
Stockholders' equity	?
Total liabilities and stockholders' equity	$?

Problems

(Group A)

P18-1A Net sales, net income, and total assets for XT Communications, Inc., for a four-year period follow:

Trend percentages, return on sales, and comparison with the industry
(Obj. 1, 4)

(in thousands)	20X8	20X7	20X6	20X5
Net sales.	$357	$313	$266	$281
Net income	29	21	11	18
Total assets.	286	254	209	197

Required

1. Compute trend percentages for each item for 20X6 through 20X8. Use 20X5 as the base year and round to the nearest percentage.
2. Compute the rate of return on net sales for 20X6 through 20X8, rounding to three decimal places. In the telecommunications industry, rates above 5% are considered good, and rates above 7% are outstanding.
3. How does XT Communications' return on net sales compare with that of the industry?

P18-2A Top managers of Escalade Technology Corporation have asked your help in comparing the company's profit performance and financial position with the average for the cell phone industry. The accountant has given you the company's income statement and balance sheet and also the following data for the industry:

Common-size statements, analysis of profitability, and comparison with the industry
(Obj. 2, 3, 4)

Escalade Technology Corporation		
Income Statement Compared with Industry Average		
Year Ended December 31, 20X5		
	Escalade	Industry Average
Net sales	$957,000	100.0%
Cost of goods sold	652,000	65.9
Gross profit	305,000	34.1
Operating expenses	204,000	28.1
Operating income	101,000	6.0
Other expenses	13,000	0.4
Net income	$ 88,000	5.6%

Escalade Technology Corporation		
Balance Sheet Compared with Industry Average		
December 31, 20X5		
	Escalade	Industry Average
Current assets	$486,000	74.4%
Fixed assets, net	117,000	20.0
Intangible assets, net	24,000	0.6
Other assets	3,000	5.0
Total	$630,000	100.0%
Current liabilities	$246,000	45.6%
Long-term liabilities	136,000	19.0
Stockholders' equity	248,000	35.4
Total	$630,000	100.0%

Required

1. Prepare a common-size income statement and balance sheet for Escalade. The first column of each statement should present Escalade's common-size statement, and the second column should show the industry averages.

2. For the profitability analysis, compute Escalade's (a) ratio of gross profit to net sales, (b) ratio of operating income to net sales, and (c) ratio of net income to net sales. Compare these figures with the industry averages. Is Escalade's profit performance better or worse than the average for the industry?

3. For the analysis of financial position, compute Escalade's (a) ratios of current assets and current liabilities to total assets and (b) ratio of stockholders' equity to total assets. Compare these ratios with the industry averages. Is Escalade's financial position better or worse than average for the industry?

Effects of business transactions on selected ratios
(Obj. 4)

P18-3A Financial statement data on Thunderbird Medical Supply include the following:

Cash	$ 47,000	Accounts payable	$ 96,000
Accounts receivable, net	123,000	Accrued liabilities.............	50,000
Inventories..................	289,000	Long-term liabilities...........	224,000
Total assets..................	933,000	Net income...................	119,000
Short-term notes payable.......	72,000	Common shares outstanding...	22,000

Required

1. Compute Thunderbird's current ratio, debt ratio, and earnings per share. Use the following format for your answer:

Requirement 1

Current Ratio	Debt Ratio	Earnings per Share

2. Compute the three ratios after evaluating the effect of each transaction that follows. Consider each transaction *separately*.
   a. Borrowed $27,000 on a long-term note payable.
   b. Issued 10,000 shares of common stock, receiving cash of $108,000.
   c. Purchased merchandise of $48,000 on account, debiting Inventory.
   d. Received cash on account, $6,000.

Format your answer as follows:

Requirement 2

Transaction Letter	Current Ratio	Debt Ratio	Earnings per Share

Using ratios to evaluate a stock investment
(Obj. 4)

P18-4A Comparative financial statement data of Advanced Automotive Company follow:

Advanced Automotive Company		
Comparative Income Statement		
Years Ended December 31, 20X6 and 20X5		
	20X6	**20X5**
Net sales.......................................	$667,000	$599,000
Cost of goods sold	378,000	283,000
Gross profit	289,000	316,000
Operating expenses	129,000	147,000
Income from operations	160,000	169,000
Interest expense	57,000	41,000
Income before income tax	103,000	128,000
Income tax expense	34,000	53,000
Net income	$ 69,000	$ 75,000

Advanced Automotive Company
Comparative Balance Sheet
December 31, 20X6 and 20X5

	20X6	20X5	20X4*
Current assets:			
Cash...	$ 37,000	$ 40,000	
Current receivables, net	208,000	151,000	$138,000
Inventories	352,000	286,000	184,000
Prepaid expenses................................	5,000	20,000	
Total current assets	602,000	497,000	
Property, plant, and equipment, net..................	287,000	276,000	
Total assets	$889,000	$773,000	707,000
Total current liabilities	$286,000	$267,000	
Long-term liabilities	245,000	235,000	
Total liabilities	531,000	502,000	
Preferred stockholders' equity, 4%, $20 par...........	50,000	50,000	
Common stockholders' equity, no par	308,000	221,000	148,000
Total liabilities and stockholders' equity	$889,000	$773,000	

*Selected 20X4 amounts.

Other Information:

1. Market price of Advanced Automotive's common stock: $36.75 at December 31, 20X6, and $50.50 at December 31, 20X5.

2. Common shares outstanding: 15,000 during 20X6 and 14,000 during 20X5.

3. All sales on credit.

Required

1. Compute the following ratios for 20X6 and 20X5:
  a. Current ratio
  b. Inventory turnover
  c. Times-interest-earned ratio
  d. Return on common stockholders' equity
  e. Earnings per share of common stock
  f. Price/earnings ratio

2. Decide whether (a) Advanced's financial position improved or deteriorated during 20X6 and (b) the investment attractiveness of its common stock appears to have increased or decreased.

3. How will what you learned in this problem help you evaluate an investment?

P18-5A Assume that you are considering purchasing stock in a company in the music industry. You have narrowed the choice to Blues, Inc., and Sonic Sound Corporation and have assembled the following data:

Using ratios to decide between two stock investments; measuring economic value added
(Obj. 4, 5)

Selected income-statement data for the current year:

	Blues	Sonic
Net sales (all on credit)	$603,000	$519,000
Cost of goods sold	484,000	387,000
Interest expense	—	8,000
Net income	56,000	38,000

Selected balance-sheet and market-price data at the *end* of the current year:

	Blues	Sonic
Current assets:		
Cash......................................	$ 45,000	$ 39,000
Short-term investments	6,000	13,000
Current receivables, net	169,000	164,000
Inventories	211,000	183,000
Prepaid expenses..........................	19,000	15,000
Total current assets	450,000	414,000
Total assets	974,000	938,000
Total current liabilities	366,000	338,000
Total liabilities	667,000*	691,000*
Common stock, $1 par (150,000 shares)..........	150,000	
$5 par (20,000 shares)		100,000
Total stockholders' equity	307,000	247,000
Market price per share of common stock..........	$ 8	$ 47.50

*Includes bonds payable: Blues, $3,000, and Sonic, $303,000.

Selected balance-sheet data at the *beginning* of the current year:

	Blues	Sonic
Current receivables, net............................	$142,000	$193,000
Inventories.......................................	209,000	197,000
Total assets......................................	842,000	909,000
Common stock, $1 par (150,000 shares)	150,000	
$5 par (20,000 shares)............................		100,000

Your strategy is to invest in companies that have low price/earnings ratios but appear to be in good shape financially. Assume that you have analyzed all other factors and that your decision depends on the results of ratio analysis.

Required

1. Compute the following ratios for both companies for the current year and decide which company's stock better fits your investment strategy.

    a. Acid-test ratio   **d.** Debt ratio

    b. Inventory turnover   **e.** Earnings per share of common stock

    c. Days' sales in average receivables   **f.** Price/earnings ratio

2. Compute each company's economic-value-added (EVA®) measure and determine whether their EVA®s confirm or alter your investment decision. Each company's cost of capital is 10%. Round all amounts to the nearest $1,000.

Analyzing a company based on its ratios
(Obj. 4)

P18-6A Take the role of an investment analyst at **Edward Jones Company**. It is your job to recommend investments for your client. The only information you have are the ratio values for two companies in the graphics software industry.

Ratio	GraphTech, Inc.	Core Software Company
Days' sales in receivables	51	43
Inventory turnover	9	7
Gross profit percentage.........	62%	71%
Net income as a percent of sales .	16%	14%
Times-interest earned	12	18
Return on equity..............	29%	36%
Return on assets	19%	14%

Write a report to the Edward Jones investment committee. Recommend one company's stock over the other. State the reasons for your recommendation.

Problems

(Group B)

online homework

P18-1B Net revenues, net income, and common stockholders' equity for xCel Corporation, a manufacturer of contact lenses, for a four-year period follow.

Trend percentages, return on common equity, and comparison with the industry **(Obj. 1, 4)**

(in thousands)	2008	2007	2006	2005
Net revenues....................	$781	$714	$641	$662
Net income	51	45	32	48
Ending common stockholders' equity.............	366	354	330	296

Required

1. Compute trend percentages for each item for 2006 through 2008. Use 2005 as the base year. Round to the nearest percent.
2. Compute the rate of return on common stockholders' equity for 2006 through 2008, rounding to three decimal places. In the contact lens industry, rates of 13% are average, rates above 16% are good, and rates above 20% are outstanding. xCel has no preferred stock outstanding.
3. How does xCel's return on common stockholders' equity compare with the industry?

P18-2B Bose Stereo Shops has asked you to compare the company's profit performance and financial position with the average for the stereo industry. The proprietor has given you the company's income statement and balance sheet, as well as the industry average data for retailers.

Common-size statements, analysis of profitability, and comparison with the industry **(Obj. 2, 3, 4)**

Bose Stereo Shops		
Income Statement Compared with Industry Average Year Ended December 31, 20X6		
	Bose	Industry Average
Net sales	$781,000	100.0%
Cost of goods sold	497,000	65.8
Gross profit	284,000	34.2
Operating expenses	163,000	19.7
Operating income	121,000	14.5
Other expenses	6,000	0.4
Net income.................	$115,000	14.1%

Bose Stereo Shops		
Balance Sheet Compared with Industry Average December 31, 20X6		
	Bose	Industry Average
Current assets	$350,000	70.9%
Fixed assets, net	74,000	23.6
Intangible assets, net	4,000	0.8
Other assets	22,000	4.7
Total	$450,000	100.0%
Current liabilities	$207,000	48.1%
Long-term liabilities	62,000	16.6
Stockholders' equity	181,000	35.3
Total	$450,000	100.0%

Required

1. Prepare a common-size income statement and balance sheet for Bose. The first column of each statement should present Bose's common-size statement, and the second column, the industry averages.
2. For the profitability analysis, compute Bose's (a) ratio of gross profit to net sales, (b) ratio of operating income to net sales, and (c) ratio of net income to net sales. Compare these figures with the industry averages. Is Bose's profit performance better or worse than the industry average?

3. For the analysis of financial position, compute Bose's (a) ratio of current assets to total assets and (b) ratio of stockholders' equity to total assets. Compare these ratios with the industry averages. Is Bose's financial position better or worse than the industry averages?

Effects of business transactions on selected ratios
(Obj. 4)

P18-3B Financial statement data of Biz Mart Discount Center include the following items (dollars in thousands):

Cash	$ 22,000
Accounts receivable, net	102,000
Inventories	149,000
Total assets	657,000
Short-term notes payable	49,000
Accounts payable.	103,000
Accrued liabilities	38,000
Long-term liabilities	191,000
Net income	71,000
Common shares outstanding	40,000

Required

1. Compute Biz Mart's current ratio, debt ratio, and earnings per share. Use the following format for your answer:

Requirement 1

Current Ratio	Debt Ratio	Earnings per Share

2. Compute the three ratios after evaluating the effect of each transaction that follows. Consider each transaction *separately*.
   a. Purchased store supplies of $46,000 on account.
   b. Borrowed $125,000 on a long-term note payable.
   c. Issued 5,000 shares of common stock, receiving cash of $120,000.
   d. Received cash on account, $19,000.
   Format your answer as follows:

Requirement 2

Transaction (Letter)	Current Ratio	Debt Ratio	Earnings per Share

Using ratios to evaluate a stock investment
(Obj. 4)

P18-4B Comparative financial-statement data of i2 Networks, Inc., follow.

i2 Networks, Inc.
Comparative Income Statement
Years Ended December 31, 20X9 and 20X8

	20X9	20X8
Net sales.	$462,000	$427,000
Cost of goods sold	229,000	218,000
Gross profit	233,000	209,000
Operating expenses	136,000	134,000
Income from operations	97,000	75,000
Interest expense	11,000	12,000
Income before income tax	86,000	63,000
Income tax expense	30,000	27,000
Net income	$ 56,000	$ 36,000

i2 Networks, Inc.
Comparative Balance Sheet
December 31, 20X9 and 20X8

	20X9	20X8	20X7*
Current assets:			
Cash..	$ 96,000	$ 97,000	
Current receivables, net	112,000	116,000	$103,000
Inventories	147,000	162,000	207,000
Prepaid expenses................................	16,000	7,000	
Total current assets	371,000	382,000	
Property, plant, and equipment, net...................	214,000	178,000	
Total assets	$585,000	$560,000	598,000
Total current liabilities	$206,000	$223,000	
Long-term liabilities	119,000	117,000	
Total liabilities	325,000	340,000	
Preferred stockholders'			
equity, 6%, $100 par............................	100,000	100,000	
Common stockholders' equity, no par	160,000	120,000	90,000
Total liabilities and stockholders' equity	$585,000	$560,000	

*Selected 20X7 amounts.

Other information:

1. Market price of i2 Networks' common stock: $53 at December 31, 20X9, and $32.50 at December 31, 20X8.

2. Common shares outstanding: 10,000 during 20X9 and 9,000 during 20X8.

3. All sales on credit.

Required

1. Compute the following ratios for 20X9 and 20X8:
   - **a.** Current ratio
   - **b.** Inventory turnover
   - **c.** Times-interest-earned ratio
   - **d.** Return on common stockholders' equity
   - **e.** Earnings per share of common stock
   - **f.** Price/earnings ratio

2. Decide (a) whether i2 Networks' financial position improved or deteriorated during 20X9 and (b) whether the investment attractiveness of its common stock appears to have increased or decreased.

3. How will what you learned in this problem help you evaluate an investment?

P18-5B Assume that you are purchasing an investment and have decided to invest in a company in the air-conditioning/heating business. You have narrowed the choice to Caremark Laboratories and AmeriCorp, Inc., and have assembled the following data:

Using ratios to decide between two stock investments; measuring economic value added
(Obj. 4, 5)

Selected income-statement data for the current year:

	Caremark	AmeriCorp
Net sales (all on credit).......................	$371,000	$497,000
Cost of goods sold	209,000	258,000
Interest expense	—	19,000
Net income	48,000	72,000

Selected balance-sheet data at the *beginning* of the current year:

	Caremark	AmeriCorp
Current receivables, net	$ 40,000	$ 48,000
Inventories	93,000	88,000
Total assets	259,000	270,000
Common stock, $1 par (10,000 shares)	10,000	
$2.50 par (5,000 shares).....................		12,500

Selected balance-sheet and market-price data at the *end* of the current year:

	Caremark	AmeriCorp
Current assets:		
Cash	$ 22,000	$ 19,000
Short-term investments	20,000	18,000
Current receivables, net	42,000	46,000
Inventories	87,000	100,000
Prepaid expenses	2,000	3,000
Total current assets	173,000	186,000
Total assets	265,000	328,000
Total current liabilities	108,000	98,000
Total liabilities	108,000*	131,000*
Common stock, $1 par (10,000 shares)	10,000	
$2.50 par (5,000 shares)		12,500
Total stockholders' equity	157,000	197,000
Market price per share of common stock	$ 51	$ 112

*Includes notes payable: Caremark, $1,000, and AmeriCorp, $86,000.

Your strategy is to invest in companies that have low price/earnings ratios but appear to be in good shape financially. Assume that you have analyzed all other factors and that your decision depends on the results of ratio analysis.

Required

1. Compute the following ratios for both companies for the current year, and decide which company's stock better fits your investment strategy.

   a. Acid-test ratio   **d.** Debt ratio

   b. Inventory turnover   **e.** Earnings per share of common stock

   c. Days' sales in average receivables   **f.** Price/earnings ratio

2. Compute each company's economic-value-added (EVA®) measure and determine whether their EVA®s confirm or alter your investment decision. Each company's cost of capital is 12%. Round all amounts to the nearest $1,000.

Analyzing a company based on its ratios
(Obj. 4)

P18-6B Take the role of an investment analyst at **Goldman Sachs**. It is your job to recommend investments for your clients. The only information you have are ratio values for two companies in the pharmaceuticals industry.

Ratio	Pratt Corp.	Jacobs, Inc.
Days' sales in receivables.	36	42
Inventory turnover	6	8
Gross profit percentage	49%	51%
Net income as a percentage of sales.	7.2%	8.3%
Times-interest-earned.	16	9
Return on equity	32.3%	21.5%
Return on assets	12.1%	16.4%

Write a report to Goldman Sachs' investment committee. Recommend one company's stock over the other. State the reasons for your recommendation.

APPLY *Your Knowledge*

Decision Cases

Assessing the effects of transactions on a company
(Obj. 4)

Case 1. **AOL Time Warner, Inc.,** had a bad year in 2001; the company suffered a net loss. The loss pushed most of the return measures into the negative column, and the current ratio dropped below 1.0. The company's debt ratio is still only 0.27. Assume top management of AOL Time Warner is pondering ways to improve the company's ratios. In particular, management is considering the following transactions:

1. Borrow $100 million of long-term debt.
2. Purchase treasury stock for $500 million cash.
3. Expense one-fourth of goodwill carried on the books at $128 million.
4. Sell advertising, and the advertisements will run immediately.
5. Purchase trademarks from **NBC**, paying $20 million cash.

Required

Top management wants to know the effects of these transactions (increase, decrease, or no effect) on the following ratios of AOL Time Warner:

a. Current ratio   **b.** Debt ratio   **c.** Return on equity

Case 2. Consider the following business situations:

Understanding the components of accounting ratios
(Obj. 4)

a. Pinehurst Corporation's owners are concerned because the number of days' sales in receivables has increased over the previous two years. Explain why the ratio might have increased.
b. Sara Fulton has asked you about the stock of a particular company. She finds it attractive because it has a high dividend yield relative to another stock she is also considering. Explain to her the meaning of the ratio and the danger of making a decision based on dividend yield alone. Suggest other information (ratios) Sara should consider as she makes her investment decision.
c. Nathanael Smith is the controller of Saturn Ltd., a dance club whose year-end is December 31. Smith prepares checks for suppliers in December and posts them to the appropriate accounts in that month. However, he holds on to the checks and mails them to the suppliers in January. What financial ratio(s) are most affected by the action? What is Smith's purpose in undertaking this activity?

Ethical Issue

Balmoral Golf Corporation's long-term debt agreements make certain demands on the business. For example, Balmoral may not purchase treasury stock in excess of the balance of retained earnings. Also, long-term debt may not exceed stockholders' equity, and the current ratio may not fall below 1.50. If Balmoral fails to meet any of these requirements, the company's lenders have the authority to take over management of the company.

   Changes in consumer demand have made it hard for Balmoral to attract customers. Current liabilities have mounted faster than current assets, causing the current ratio to fall to 1.47. Before releasing financial statements, Balmoral management is scrambling to improve the current ratio. The controller points out that an investment can be classified as either long-term or short-term, depending on management's intention. By deciding to convert an investment to cash within one year, Balmoral can classify the investment as short-term—a current asset. On the controller's recommendation, Balmoral's board of directors votes to reclassify long-term investments as short-term.

Required

1. What effect will reclassifying the investments have on the current ratio? Is Balmoral's true financial position stronger as a result of reclassifying the investments?
2. Shortly after the financial statements are released, sales improve; so, too, does the current ratio. As a result, Balmoral management decides not to sell the investments it had reclassified as short-term. Accordingly, the company reclassifies the investments as long-term. Has management behaved unethically? Give the reasoning underlying your answer.

Financial Statement Case

Amazon.com's financial statements in Appendix A reveal some unusual relationships for a company with a bright future. Answer these questions about Amazon.com.

Measuring profitability and analyzing stock as an investment
(Obj. 4)

1. What is most unusual about the balance sheet?
2. What is most unusual about the income statement (statement of operations)?

3. Consider Amazon's profitability ratios, ratios that measure the ability to pay long-term debt, and ratios for analyzing stock as an investment. What about Amazon makes these ratios meaningless? How can Amazon.com continue as a going business? The statement of cash flows helps to answer this critical question.

Team Projects

Project 1. Select an industry you are interested in, and use the leading company in that industry as the benchmark. Then select two other companies in the same industry. For each category of ratios in the Decision Guidelines on pages 727 and 728, compute at least two ratios for all three companies. Write a two-page report that compares the two companies with the benchmark company.

Project 2. Select a company and obtain its financial statements. Convert the income statement and the balance sheet to common size, and compare the company you selected to the industry average. Risk Management Association's *Annual Statement Studies*, **Dun & Bradstreet's** *Industry Norms & Key Business Ratios*, and Prentice Hall's *Almanac of Business and Industrial Financial Ratios*, by Leo Troy, publish common-size statements for most industries.

For Internet exercises, go to the Web site www.prenhall.com/horngren.

Comprehensive Problem for Chapters 17 and 18

ANALYZING A COMPANY FOR ITS INVESTMENT POTENTIAL

In its 2003 annual report, **Wal-Mart Stores, Inc.**, includes an 11-year financial summary (see pp. 748–749). Analyze the company's financial summary for the fiscal years 1999 to 2003 to decide whether to invest in the common stock of Wal-Mart. Include the following sections in your analysis, and fully explain your final decision.

1. Trend analysis for net sales and net income (use 1999 as the base year)
2. Profitability analysis
3. Measuring ability to sell inventory (Wal-Mart uses the LIFO method)
4. Measuring ability to pay debts
5. Measuring dividends

Wal-Mart Stores, Inc.

11-Year Financial Summary (Partial; adapted)

(Dollar Amounts in Millions Except per Share Data)	2003	2002	2001
Net sales	$244,524	$217,799	$191,329
Net sales increase	12%	14%	16%
Domestic comparative store sales increase	5%	6%	5%
Other income—net	2,001	1,873	1,787
Cost of sales	191,838	171,562	150,255
Operating, selling, and general and administrative expenses	41,043	36,173	31,550
Interest costs:			
Debt	803	1,083	1,104
Capital leases	260	274	279
Interest income	(138)	(171)	(188)
Provision for income taxes	4,487	3,897	3,692
Minority interest and equity in unconsolidated subsidiaries	(193)	(183)	(129)
Cumulative effect of accounting change, net of tax	—	—	—
Net income	8,039	6,671	6,295
Per share of common stock:			
Basic net income	1.81	1.49	1.41
Diluted net income	1.81	1.49	1.40
Dividends	0.30	0.28	0.24
Financial Position			
Current assets	$ 30,483	$ 27,878	$ 26,555
Inventories at LIFO cost	24,891	22,614	21,442
Net property, plant, and equipment and capital leases	51,904	45,750	40,934
Total assets	94,685	83,527	78,130
Current liabilities	32,617	27,282	28,949
Long-term debt	16,607	15,687	12,501
Long-term obligations under capital leases	3,001	3,045	3,154
Shareholders' equity	39,337	35,102	31,343
Financial Ratios			
Current ratio	0.9	1.0	0.9
Inventories/working capital	(11.7)	38.2	(9.0)
Return on assets	9.2%	8.5%	8.7%
Return on shareholders' equity	21.6%	20.1%	22.0%

2000	1999	1998	1997	1996	1995	1994	1993
$165,013	$137,634	$117,958	$104,859	$93,627	$82,494	$67,344	$55,484
20%	17%	12%	12%	13%	22%	21%	26%
8%	9%	6%	5%	4%	7%	6%	11%
1,615	1,391	1,290	1,293	1,138	904	633	490
129,664	108,725	93,438	83,510	74,505	65,586	53,444	44,175
27,040	22,363	19,358	16,946	15,021	12,858	10,333	8,321
779	535	558	629	693	520	331	143
266	268	229	216	196	186	186	180
(204)	(189)	(54)	(26)	(9)	(10)	(12)	(7)
3,338	2,740	2,115	1,794	1,606	1,581	1,358	1,171
(170)	(153)	(78)	(27)	(13)	4	(4)	4
(198)	—	—	—	—	—	—	—
5,377	4,430	3,526	3,056	2,740	2,681	2,333	1,995
1.21	0.99	0.78	0.67	0.60	0.59	0.51	0.44
1.20	0.99	0.78	0.67	0.60	0.59	0.51	0.44
0.20	0.16	0.14	0.11	0.10	0.09	0.07	0.05
$ 24,356	$ 21,132	$ 19,352	$ 17,993	$17,331	$15,338	$12,114	$10,198
19,793	17,076	16,497	15,897	15,989	14,064	11,014	9,268
35,969	25,973	23,606	20,324	18,894	15,874	13,176	9,793
70,349	49,996	45,384	39,604	37,541	32,819	26,441	20,565
25,803	16,762	14,460	10,957	11,454	9,973	7,406	6,754
13,672	6,908	7,191	7,709	8,508	7,871	6,156	3,073
3,002	2,699	2,483	2,307	2,092	1,838	1,804	1,772
25,834	21,112	18,503	17,143	14,756	12,726	10,753	8,759
0.9	1.3	1.3	1.6	1.5	1.5	1.6	1.5
(13.7)	3.9	3.4	2.3	2.7	2.6	2.3	2.7
9.5%	9.6%	8.5%	7.9%	7.8%	9.0%	9.9%	11.1%
22.9%	22.4%	19.8%	19.2%	19.9%	22.8%	23.9%	25.3%

CHAPTER 19

Introduction to Management Accounting

A+ TIPS CHECK YOUR RESOURCES

- Visit the www.prenhall.com/horngren **Web site** for self-study quizzes, video clips, other resources

- Try the **Quick Check** exercise at end of chapter to test your knowledge

- Learn the **key terms**

- Do the **Starter** exercises keyed in the margins

- Work the **mid-** and **end-of-chapter summary problems**

- Use the **Concept Links** to review material in other chapters

- Search the **CD** for review materials by chapter or by key word

- Watch the **tutorial videos** to review **key concepts**

- Watch the **On Location Regal Marine** video for an overview of management accounting in a real setting.

LEARNING OBJECTIVES

⭐1 Distinguish financial accounting from management accounting

⭐2 Describe service, merchandising, and manufacturing companies, and classify their costs by value-chain element

⭐3 Distinguish among (a) direct costs and indirect costs; and (b) full product costs, inventoriable product costs, and period costs

⭐4 Prepare the financial statements of a manufacturing company

⭐5 Identify trends in the business environment and use cost-benefit analysis to make business decisions

⭐6 Use reasonable standards to make ethical judgments

Y ou are relaxing in your new 1800 LSR Regal sport boat after a day on the lake. As you sit there, you ask yourself how **Regal Marine** can make a profit selling these boats at such low prices.

The answer: Regal's managers use management accounting information. It enables them to give you the best-performing boat for your hard-earned dollar. Regal's engineers pioneered the FasTrac hull, which maximizes performance and fuel efficiency while holding down costs. Scientists identified the most durable fiberglass, gelcoats, and upholstery fabrics. Then Regal's purchasing managers worked closely with the makers of

Regal Marine

these materials to keep prices down. The goal is to ensure that suppliers can deliver "just in time" to Regal's plant, so Regal does not have to hold a large inventory. Expert craftsmen cut materials to minimize waste. Others assemble the parts with precision and speed. The efficiency reduces Regal's cost, and Regal passes the savings on to customers.

In addition to controlling production costs, Regal Marine uses accounting information to make other strategic decisions:

- **Which products to emphasize:** Which of Regal's 22 boat models are the most profitable and deserve the most sales emphasis?
- **Which new products to launch:** Would a proposed new jet boat be profitable?
- **Which customers are most important:** Which of Regal's worldwide network of dealers contribute the most to the company's profitability and thus deserve the most attention and support?
- **What marketing strategy to use:** Should Regal continue selling only through its dealer network, or should it also sell direct to consumers?

By using management accounting information to help run its business, Orlando-based Regal Marine has become one of the most successful companies in the marine industry, with more than $100 million in sales each year. ■

■Sitemap

★ *Distinguish financial accounting from management accounting*

So far, we have focused on reporting accounting information for decision makers outside the organization: investors, creditors, and government authorities. We analyzed *financial accounting* reports—the income statement, the balance sheet, and the statement of cash flows—that report *past* performance and financial position.

Now we shift our focus to how accounting information helps managers shape the company's future. You'll see how managers such as those at Regal Marine use *management accounting* reports to make business decisions that increase profits and, in turn, shareholder value.

How Is Management Accounting Different?

Financial and management accounting both use the accrual basis, and both reflect the same underlying economic transactions. However, their focus differs. Financial accounting leads to financial statements that allow stockholders and creditors to make investment decisions. These highly summarized reports are constrained by GAAP and focus on past performance. What you will learn in management accounting is very different from what you learned in financial accounting, because company managers need detailed and timely information to run the company efficiently and effectively day by day.

To understand the kind of information managers need to carry out these responsibilities, let's look first at their main responsibilities.

Managers' Main Responsibilities

Managers have two main responsibilities: planning and controlling (Exhibit 19-1). **Planning** means choosing goals and deciding how to achieve them. For example, one of Regal Marine's goals is to increase operating income. The company's managers could

1. Raise sales prices
2. Increase advertising to stimulate sales
3. Redesign the boats for faster production and servicing

Suppose Regal's managers choose alternative 3. Regal's engineers, purchasing officer, and production, marketing, and service managers work together to redesign the 1800 LSR 18-foot sport boat to speed assembly and servicing. Managers use the new design to budget the cost of the 1800 LSR, considering both the cost per boat and the number they expect to sell. The **budget** is a quantitative expression of a plan that helps managers coordinate and implement the plan.

Regal's purchasing officer uses the new design and the number of boats Regal expects to sell to decide how many component parts to order. The production manager alerts plant workers to the design changes before they begin assembling the new model. After they implement the plan, controlling begins. **Controlling** means evaluating the results of business operations by comparing the actual results to the plan. Regal's accounting system records the number of boats produced and the purchase prices and number of components used to assemble them.

Student Resource CD
budget, management accounting

planning
Choosing goals and deciding how to achieve them.

budget
Quantitative expression of a plan that helps managers coordinate and implement the plan.

controlling
Evaluating the results of business operations by comparing the actual results to the plan.

Exhibit 19-1 Managers' Main Responsibilities

After completing production, managers can compare actual to budgeted costs to evaluate employees' performance. If actual costs fall below budgeted costs, that is good news. But if actual costs exceed the budget, managers may need to act. Costs provide feedback that helps managers decide whether their decision to redesign the 1800 LSR increased or decreased profits.

Management versus Financial Accounting

✔ Starter 19-1

Exhibit 19-2 summarizes the differences between

- What you'll learn in management accounting—to help managers plan and control business operations
- What you already learned in financial accounting—to help external users make investment decisions

Exhibit 19-2

Management Accounting versus
Financial Accounting

	Management Accounting	**Financial Accounting**
1. Primary users	Internal—the company's managers	External—investors, creditors, and government authorities such as the IRS and SEC
2. Purpose of information	Help managers plan and control business operations	Help investors, creditors, and others make investment, credit, and other decisions
3. Focus and time dimension	Relevance and focus on the future—example: 2007 budget prepared in 2006	Reliability, objectivity, and focus on the past—example: 2004 actual performance reported in 2005.
4. Type of report	Internal reports not restricted by GAAP—determined by cost-benefit analysis	Financial statements restricted by GAAP
5. Verification	No independent audit	Annual independent audit by certified public accountant
6. Scope of information	Detailed reports on parts of the company (products, departments, territories), often on a daily or weekly basis	Summary reports primarily on the company as a whole, usually on a quarterly or annual basis
7. Behavioral implications	Concern about how reports will affect employee behavior	Concern about adequacy of disclosure; behavioral implications are secondary

Let's apply points 1, 2, and 3 to Regal. Deciding whether to build a new production plant in Michigan relates to Regal Marine's future, and its managers are the decision makers. Regal will budget (predict) the plant's future income and cash inflows. Its managers then will compare these inflows against the costs of operating the plant. Even if the result is a net inflow, Regal will compare it to net inflows from other investments, like developing a new jet boat. Management accounting helps Regal executives identify which investment has the greatest expected net benefit.

Both management accounting reports and financial accounting reports share the same foundation—the accrual basis of accounting. But managers enjoy more leeway in preparing management accounting reports. Point 4 of Exhibit 19-2 shows that there are no GAAP-type standards for the information managers need to run the business. Managers tailor the company's management accounting system to provide the information they need to help them make better decisions. Managers weigh the *benefits* of the system (information that helps managers make decisions that increase profits) against the *costs* to develop and run the system.

cost-benefit analysis
Weighing costs against benefits to help make decisions.

Weighing the costs against benefits is called **cost-benefit analysis**. The costs and benefits of any particular management accounting system differ from one company to another. Different companies create different systems. In contrast, *all* companies follow GAAP for external reporting. Point 5 of Exhibit 19-2 shows that independent certified public accountants audit the company's financial statements each year, but not the internal management accounting reports.

Point 6 indicates that management accounting provides more detailed and timely information than does financial accounting. Managers use this information to identify ways to cut costs, set prices that will be competitive and yet yield profits, identify the most profitable products and customers so the sales force can focus on key profitmakers, and evaluate employees' job performance. Technology, from Web-based company Intranets to handheld computers, lets managers access this information with the click of a mouse.

Point 7 reminds us that management accounting reports affect employees' behavior. "You get what you measure," because employees try to perform well on the parts of their jobs that the accounting system measures. If the manager of a Regal Marine production plant is evaluated only on her ability to control costs, she may use cheaper raw materials or hire less experienced workers. Although these actions cut costs, they can hurt profits if the quality of the product drops and sales decline as a result.

Service, Merchandising, and Manufacturing Companies, and the Value Chain

Service companies, such as **eBay** (online auction), **H&R Block** (tax return preparation), and **Randstad** (temporary personnel services), sell intangible services, so labor often makes up 70% of their costs. Service companies incur other costs to develop new services, for marketing, and for customer service such as dispute resolution.

Merchandisers and manufacturers sell tangible products. **Merchandising companies**, such as **Amazon.com**, **Wal-Mart**, and **Footlocker**, resell products they buy from suppliers. Amazon.com, for example, buys goods such as books, CDs, and DVDs for resale to customers. Amazon's cost in inventory is simply the price it pays for an item plus freight-in costs. → Because all of the inventory is ready for sale, a merchandiser's balance sheet usually reports just one category of inventory. Of course, merchandisers also incur other costs to research new products and locations for new stores, to market their products, and to provide customer service.

Manufacturing companies use labor, plant, and equipment to convert raw materials into new finished products. For example, **Regal Marine's** production workers use the company's plant and equipment to transform raw materials such as plywood and fiberglass into high-performance powerboats.

Because of their broader range of activities, manufacturers have three kinds of inventory:

1. **Materials inventory**: *Raw materials used in manufacturing.* Regal Marine's materials include plywood, fiberglass, engines, wiring, glass, carpeting, and upholstery fabric.
2. **Work in process inventory**: *Goods that are partway through the manufacturing process but not yet complete.* At Regal Marine, partly completed boats are the work in process inventory.
3. **Finished goods inventory**: *Completed goods that have not yet been sold.* Finished goods are what the manufacturer sells to a merchandiser (or to other customers). Regal Marine sells its completed boats to retail dealers/distributors such as **The Boat Tree**. Regal's finished goods inventory becomes the inventory of The Boat Tree, which then sells the boats to individual customers.

Exhibit 19-3 summarizes the differences among service, merchandising, and manufacturing companies.

service company
A company that sells intangible services, rather than tangible products.

merchandising company
A company that resells products previously bought from suppliers.

manufacturing company
A company that uses labor, plant, and equipment to convert raw materials into new finished products.

☐ What Is Management Accounting?
■ **The Value Chain**
☐ Determining Costs
☐ Costs in Financial Statements
☐ Today's Business Environment
☐ Ethical Standards

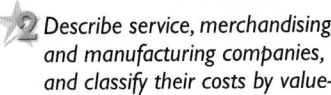 *Describe service, merchandising, and manufacturing companies, and classify their costs by value-chain element.*

Student Resource CD

direct materials inventory, finished goods inventory, supply chain management, value chain, work in progress inventory

← *See Chapter 5, pages 186–187, for a review of inventory in merchandising firms.*

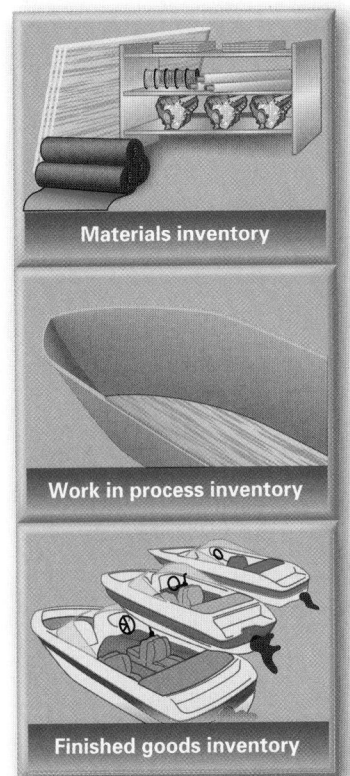

Materials inventory

Work in process inventory

Finished goods inventory

Exhibit 19-3 Service, Merchandising, and Manufacturing Companies

	Service Companies	Merchandising Companies	Manufacturing Companies
Examples	Advertising agencies eBay Law firms Merrill Lynch	Amazon.com Kroger Wal-Mart Wholesalers	Procter & Gamble DaimlerChrysler Dell Computer Regal Marine
Primary Output	Intangible services (auctions or advice)	Tangible products purchased from suppliers	New tangible products made as workers and equipment convert raw materials into new finished products
Type(s) of Inventory	None	Inventory	Materials inventory Work in process inventory Finished goods inventory

materials inventory
Raw materials for use in manufacturing.

work in process inventory
Goods that are partway through the manufacturing process but not yet complete.

finished goods inventory
Completed goods that have not yet been sold.

value chain
The activities that add value to a firm's products and services. Includes R&D, design, production or purchases, marketing, distribution, and customer service.

Which Business Activities Make Up the Value Chain?

Many people describe Regal Marine, Dell Computer, and General Motors as manufacturing companies. But it would be more accurate to say these are companies that do manufacturing. Why? Because companies that do manufacturing also do many other things. Regal Marine also conducts research to determine how to improve next year's models. Regal designs the new models based on its research and then produces, markets, and distributes the boats. These activities form Regal's **value chain**—the activities that add value to its products and services.

To set a selling price or to determine how profitable the 1800 LSR sport boat is, Regal must know how much it costs to develop, produce, market, distribute, and service the product. To figure the full cost of the 1800 LSR, Regal totals the costs incurred across all six elements of the value chain in Exhibit 19-4.

Exhibit 19-4 The Value Chain

✔ Starter 19-2

✔ Starter 19-3

research and development (R&D)
Researching and developing new or improved products or services, or the processes for producing them.

design
Detailed engineering of products and services, or processes for producing them.

production or purchases
Resources used to produce a product or service, or to purchase finished merchandise.

- **Research and development (R&D):** Researching and developing new or improved products or services, or the processes for producing them. Regal Marine invested heavily to create its unique FasTrac Hull, which maximizes performance and fuel efficiency.

- **Design:** Detailed engineering of products and services, or the processes for producing them. Regal's engineers transformed the FasTrac Hull concept into reality by designing hull molds to use in production.

- **Production or purchases:** Resources used to produce a product or service, or to purchase finished merchandise. For a manufacturer such as Regal Marine, this category includes the actual costs incurred to make the products, including materials, labor, and the cost of the equipment. For a merchandiser like The Boat Tree, this category includes the purchase cost of inventory, such as boats and jet skis (and their freight in), that The Boat Tree buys to resell to customers.

- **Marketing**: Promotion of products or services, such as the costs of Regal's print ads and the costs of attending boat shows.

- **Distribution**: Delivery of products or services to customers. For Regal, this category includes the costs of trucking its finished boats to retailers like The Boat Tree.

- **Customer service**: Support provided for customers after the sale. This includes warranty service work.

Managers do not proceed step by step in this exact order through the value chain. Instead, a project team works on R&D, design, production, marketing, and customer service simultaneously.

Controlling Costs Through the Value Chain

The value chain in Exhibit 19-4 also reminds managers to control costs over the value chain as a whole. For example, Regal Marine spends more in R&D and product design to increase the quality of its boats, which in turn reduces customer service costs. Even though R&D and design costs are higher, the total cost of the boat—as measured throughout the entire value chain—is lower as a result of this tradeoff.

The value chain applies to service and merchandising firms, as well as manufacturing firms. For example, an advertising agency such as Saatchi & Saatchi incurs

- *Marketing* costs to obtain a new client
- *Design* costs to develop the client's ad campaign
- *Customer service* costs to address the new client's concerns
- *Distribution* costs to get the ads to the media

Determining the Costs to Serve a Customer or to Make a Product

How do companies like eBay, Amazon.com, and Regal Marine determine how much it costs to serve a customer, fill an order, or produce a sport boat? Before we can answer this question, let's first consider the specialized language accountants use when referring to costs.

Cost Objects, Direct Costs, and Indirect Costs

A **cost object** is anything for which managers want a separate measurement of costs. Regal Marine's cost objects may include:

- Individual products (the 1800 LSR sport boat or the Commodore 4260 yacht)
- Alternative marketing strategies (sales through retailers versus direct-to-customer sales)
- Geographic segments of the business (United States, Europe, the Middle East)
- Departments (personnel, accounting, production)

Suppose the manager of a Regal Marine plant wants to know how much it costs to produce a product—an 1800 LSR sport boat. We can trace the engine directly to the cost object—a particular 1800 LSR boat—so the cost of the engine

marketing
Promotion of products or services.

distribution
Delivery of products or services to customers.

customer service
Support provided for customers after the sale.

☐ What Is Management Accounting?
☐ The Value Chain
■ Determining Costs
☐ Costs in Financial Statements
☐ Today's Business Environment
☐ Ethical Standards

3 Distinguish among (a) direct costs and indirect costs; and (b) full product costs, inventoriable product costs, and period costs.

Student ResourceCD

direct costs, direct materials inventory, indirect costs, inventoriable product cost, manufacturing overhead

cost object
Anything for which managers want a separate measurement of costs.

direct cost
A cost that can be specifically traced to a cost object.

indirect cost
A cost that cannot be specifically traced to a cost object.

is a **direct cost**. We cannot trace the plant manager's salary to any individual boat, so the salary is an **indirect cost**.

Now let's look more carefully at how companies determine the costs of one of the most common cost objects: products.

Product Costs

As a manager, you'll want to focus on the products that are most profitable. But which products are these? To determine the profit a product provides, you start with its selling price and then subtract the cost of the product. But how do you figure the cost of the product? The rest of this section explains how you do it.

Most companies use two different definitions of product costs: (1) full product costs for internal decision-making, and (2) inventoriable product costs for external reporting. Let's see what they are and how managers use each type of cost.

full product costs
The costs of all resources used throughout the value chain for a product.

FULL PRODUCT COSTS   **Full product costs** are the costs of all resources used throughout the value chain. For Regal Marine, the full product cost of a particular boat model is the total cost to research, design, manufacture, market, and distribute the model, as well as to service the customers who buy it. Before launching a new model, managers predict the full product costs of the boat to set a selling price that will cover all costs plus return a profit. Regal also compares each model's sale price to its full cost to determine which models are the most profitable. Marketing can then focus on selling the more profitable models.

inventoriable product costs
All costs of a product that GAAP requires companies to treat as an asset for external financial reporting. These costs are not expensed until the product is sold.

INVENTORIABLE PRODUCT COSTS FOR EXTERNAL REPORTING   GAAP does not regulate the product costs companies use for internal reporting. But for *external* reporting, GAAP requires companies to treat **inventoriable product costs** as an asset until the product is sold, at which time the costs are expensed. GAAP requires specific inventoriable product costs that include only a *portion* of full product costs. Thus, inventoriable costs do not include costs from all elements of the value chain.

Which costs are inventoriable under GAAP? The answer depends on whether the company is a merchandiser or a manufacturer.

MERCHANDISING COMPANIES' INVENTORIABLE PRODUCT COSTS
Merchandising companies' inventoriable costs include *only* the cost of purchasing the inventory from suppliers (for example, the price The Boat Tree pays Regal Marine for boats) plus freight in. These are the costs in the third element of the value chain in Exhibit 19-4. ← The Boat Tree's inventoriable cost (purchase price plus freight in) of boats is an asset—Inventory—in its accounting records. This inventoriable cost remains an asset (Inventory) until the boats are *sold*. Then it becomes an expense—Cost of Goods Sold.

Chapter 6 explains how merchandisers compute inventoriable costs. →

period costs
Operating costs that are expensed in the period in which they are incurred.

Costs incurred in other elements of the value chain—such as The Boat Tree's employee salaries, commissions paid to sales staff, and distribution costs—are not inventoriable product costs. Instead, these are **period costs**, operating costs that are always expensed in the period in which they are incurred. Period costs are never part of the Inventory asset account.

Exhibit 19-5 shows the difference between full product costs and the inventoriable product costs GAAP requires for external reporting. Study the exhibit carefully to make sure you understand how the two components of full product costs—inventoriable product costs and period costs—affect the income statement and balance sheet.

Exhibit 19-5   Full Product Costs, Inventoriable Product Costs, and Period Costs

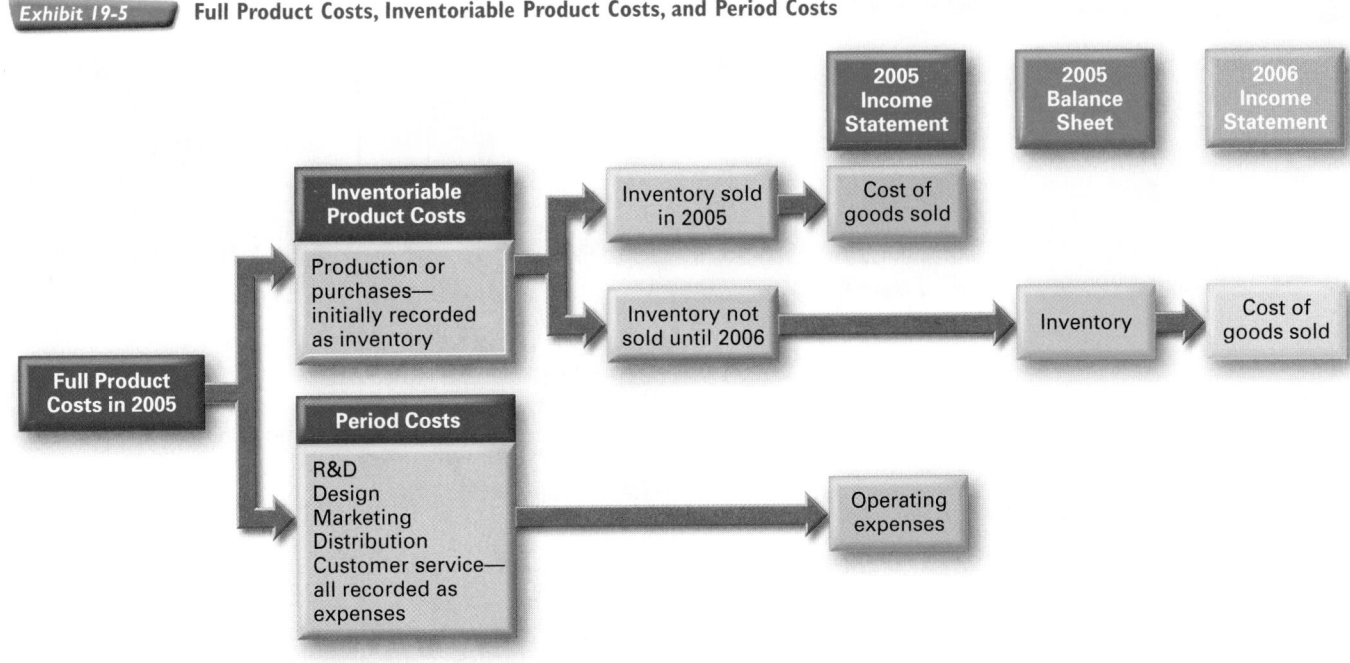

What are the inventoriable costs for a service firm such as **H&R Block**?

Answer: Service firms like H&R Block have no inventory of products for sale. Services cannot be produced today and stored up to sell later. Because service firms have no inventory, they have no inventoriable costs. Instead, they have only period costs that are expensed as incurred.

MANUFACTURING COMPANIES' INVENTORIABLE PRODUCT COSTS

✔ Starter 19-4

Manufacturing companies like Regal Marine figure their inventoriable product costs by totaling three components of manufacturing costs: direct materials, direct labor, and manufacturing overhead.

Direct Materials   **Direct materials** (1) must become a physical part of the finished product, and (2) their costs (invoice cost plus freight in) must be traceable to the finished product. For Regal Marine's 1800 LSR, direct materials include the wood used to fashion the hull, the gel coat that creates a waterproof seal throughout the exterior, the engine, and dashboard instruments like the speedometer and the depth finder.

direct materials
Materials that become a physical part of a finished product and whose costs are traceable to the finished product.

Direct Labor   **Direct labor** is the compensation of employees who physically convert materials into the company's products. For Regal, direct labor includes the wages of different craftsmen who build the hulls, apply the gel coat sealant, and sew the seat cushions; the wages of technicians who wire the electronics; and the wages of workers who assemble the parts to build the completed boat. Their effort can be traced *directly* to the finished products.

direct labor
The compensation of employees who physically convert materials into the company's products; labor costs that are directly traceable to finished products.

Manufacturing Overhead   **Manufacturing overhead** includes all manufacturing costs other than direct materials and direct labor. Examples include indirect materials; indirect labor; plant repairs and maintenance; plant utilities, rent, insurance, and property taxes; and depreciation on plant buildings and equipment. Manufacturing overhead also is called **factory overhead** or **indirect manufacturing cost**.

Exhibit 19-6 summarizes Regal's inventoriable product costs.

manufacturing overhead
All manufacturing costs other than direct materials and direct labor. Also called **factory overhead** or **indirect manufacturing cost**.

| Exhibit 19-6 | A Manufacturer's Inventoriable Product Costs |

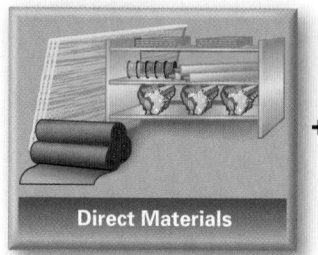

Direct Materials

+

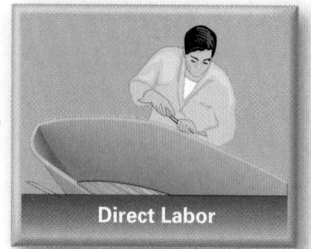

Direct Labor

+

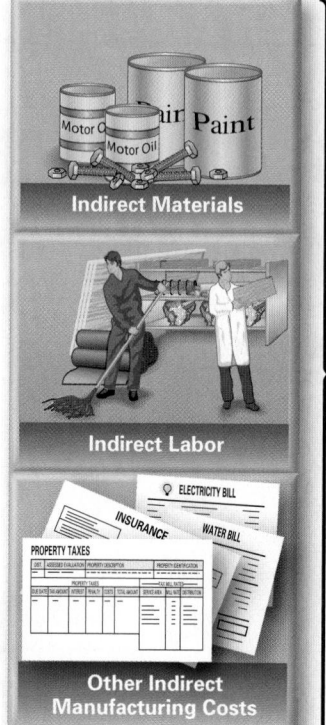

Indirect Materials

Indirect Labor

Other Indirect Manufacturing Costs

} Manufacturing overhead

=

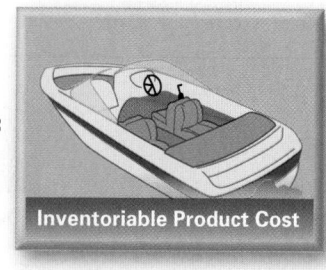

Inventoriable Product Cost

Now look back at Exhibit 19-5. Regal Marine's 2005 income statement reports as Cost of Goods Sold the inventoriable costs of the boats the company sold during 2005. Regal's 2005 balance sheet reports the inventoriable costs of the finished boats still on hand at the end of 2005 (direct materials, direct labor, and manufacturing overhead) as an asset—inventory. If Regal sells the boats in this inventory in 2006, the costs will be included as part of Cost of Goods Sold on Regal's 2006 income statement.

✔ **Starter 19-5**

A CLOSER LOOK AT MANUFACTURING OVERHEAD *Manufacturing overhead includes only those indirect costs that are related to the manufacturing plant.* Insurance and depreciation on the *plant's* building and equipment are indirect manufacturing costs, so they are part of manufacturing overhead. In contrast, depreciation on *delivery trucks* is not a manufacturing cost. Delivery is part of the distribution element of the value chain (see Exhibit 19-4), so its cost is part of distribution expense (a period expense), not manufacturing overhead. Similarly, auto insurance for the sales force is part of the marketing element of the value chain, so it is part of marketing expense (a period expense), not manufacturing overhead.

Manufacturing overhead also includes indirect materials and indirect labor. The bolts and screws used to build the boat become physical parts of the finished product. But, compared with the engine and hull, the costs of bolts and screws are minor. It is hard to measure the costs of those low-priced materials in a particular boat. Materials whose costs cannot conveniently be directly traced to particular finished products are called **indirect materials** and are part of manufacturing overhead.

Like indirect materials, **indirect labor** is difficult to trace to specific products so it is part of manufacturing overhead. Examples include the pay of forklift operators in the plant, plant janitors, and plant managers.

indirect materials
Materials whose costs cannot conveniently be directly traced to particular finished products.

indirect labor
Labor costs that are difficult to trace to specific products.

Inventoriable Product Costs or Period Costs?

Exhibit 19-7 summarizes the differences between inventoriable and period costs for service, merchandising, and manufacturing companies. Study this exhibit carefully. When are costs like depreciation, insurance, utilities, and property taxes inventoriable product costs? *Only* when those costs are related to the manufacturing plant. When those costs are related to nonmanufacturing activities like R&D or marketing, they are treated as period costs. Service companies and merchandisers do no manufacturing, so they always treat depreciation, insurance, utilities, and property taxes as period costs.

Exhibit 19-7 Inventoriable Product Costs and Period Costs for Service, Merchandising, and Manufacturing Companies

Type of Company	Inventoriable Product Costs—Initially an asset (Inventory), and not expensed (Cost of Goods Sold) until inventory is sold	Period Costs—Expensed in period incurred; never considered an asset
Service company	None	Salaries, depreciation expense, utilities, insurance, property taxes, advertising
Merchandising company	Purchases plus freight in	Salaries, depreciation expense, utilities, insurance, property taxes, advertising, freight out
Manufacturing company	Direct materials, plus direct labor, plus manufacturing overhead (including indirect materials; indirect labor; depreciation on plant and equipment; plant insurance, utilities, and property taxes)	R&D; freight out; depreciation expense, utilities, insurance, and property taxes on executive headquarters (separate from plant); advertising; CEO's salary

Inventoriable Product Costs and Period Costs in Financial Statements

The difference between inventoriable product costs and period costs is important because they are treated differently in the financial statements. We begin with a short review to help you see how a manufacturer's financial statements differ from those of service and merchandising companies.

Service Companies

Service companies have the simplest accounting. Exhibit 19-8 (on page 762) shows the income statement of eNow!, a group of e-commerce consultants. → The firm has no inventory and thus no inventoriable costs, so eNow!'s income statement has no Cost of Goods Sold. The statement groups all expenses (period costs) together. eNow!'s largest expense is for the salaries of employees who perform the services.

Merchandising Companies

In contrast with service companies, merchandisers' income statements feature Cost of Goods Sold as the major expense. Consider Apex Showrooms, a

☐ What Is Management Accounting?
☐ The Value Chain
☐ Determining Costs
■ **Costs in Financial Statements**
☐ Today's Business Environment
☐ Ethical Standards

Prepare the financial statements of a manufacturing company

Student Resource CD
cost of goods sold, cost of goods manufactured, inventoriable product cost

← *Chapter 1, p. 6, introduced income statements for service companies.*

Exhibit 19-8

Service Company Income
Statement

eNow!
Income Statement **Month Ended December 31, 20X5**

Revenues...		$160,000
Expenses:		
Salary expense	$106,000	
Office rent expense	18,000	
Depreciation expense—furniture and equipment ...	3,500	
Marketing expense	2,500	(130,000)
Operating Income		$ 30,000

merchandiser of lighting fixtures. Apex's *only* inventoriable costs are for the purchase of chandeliers and track lights that it buys to resell, plus freight in. Merchandisers like Apex compute the Cost of Goods Sold as follows: [1]

	Beginning inventory	$ 9,500	What Apex had at the beginning of the period
+	Purchases and freight in	110,000	What Apex bought during the period
=	Cost of goods available for sale	119,500	Total available for sale during the period
−	Ending inventory	13,000	What Apex had left at the end of the period
=	Cost of goods sold	$106,500	What Apex sold

Panel A of Exhibit 19-9 shows Apex's complete income statement.

Manufacturing Companies

Panel B of Exhibit 19-9 shows the income statement of Top-Flight, a manufacturer of golf equipment and athletic shoes. Compare its income statement with the merchandiser's income statement in Panel A. The only difference is that the merchandiser (Apex) uses *purchases* in computing cost of goods sold, while the manufacturer (Top-Flight) uses the *cost of goods manufactured*. Notice that the term **cost of goods manufactured** is in the past tense. It is the manufacturing (or plant-related) cost of the goods that Top-Flight *finished producing during 20X5*. This is the manufacturer's cost to obtain new *finished goods* that are ready to sell (only finished goods are sold), so it is the manufacturer's counterpart to the merchandiser's *purchases*.

cost of goods manufactured
The manufacturing (or plant-related) cost of the goods that *finished* the production process this period.

CALCULATING THE COST OF GOODS MANUFACTURED   The cost of goods manufactured summarizes the activities that take place in a manufacturing plant over the period (and their associated costs). Let's begin by reviewing these activities. Exhibit 19-10 reminds us that the manufacturer starts by buying materials. Then it uses direct labor and plant and equipment (whose costs are part of manufacturing overhead) to transform these materials into work in process inventory. When the work in process inventory is completed, it becomes finished goods inventory. These are all inventoriable product costs because they are plant-related.

---

[1]To highlight the roles of beginning inventory, purchases, and ending inventory, we assume that Apex uses a periodic inventory system. However, the concepts in this chapter apply equally to companies that use perpetual inventory systems.

PANEL A: Merchandiser's Income Statement

Exhibit 19-9

Comparing a Merchandiser's and a Manufacturer's Income Statements

✔ Starter 19-6

Apex Showrooms
Income Statement
Month Ended December 31, 20X5

Sales revenue.		$150,000
Cost of goods sold:		
Beginning inventory	$ 9,500	
Purchases and freight in	110,000	
Cost of goods available for sale	119,500	
Ending inventory	(13,000)	
Cost of goods sold		106,500
Gross profit		43,500
Operating expenses:		
Showroom rent expense	5,000	
Sales salary expense.	4,000	9,000
Operating income.		$ 34,500

PANEL B: Manufacturer's Income Statement

Top-Flight
Income Statement
Year Ended December 31, 20X5

Sales revenue.		$65,000
Cost of goods sold:		
Beginning finished goods inventory	$ 6,000	
Cost of goods manufactured*	42,000	
Cost of goods available for sale	48,000	
Ending finished goods inventory	(8,000)	
Cost of goods sold		40,000
Gross profit		25,000
Operating expenses:		
Sales salary expense.	3,000	
Delivery expense	7,000	10,000
Operating income.		$15,000

*From the Schedule of Cost of Goods Manufactured in Exhibit 19-11.

Finished goods are the only inventory that is ready to sell. The cost of the finished goods that the manufacturer sells becomes its Cost of Goods Sold on the income statement. Costs the manufacturer incurs in other (nonmanufacturing) elements of the value chain are operating expenses, or period costs that are expensed in the period incurred. Exhibit 19-10 shows that these operating costs are deducted from gross profit to obtain operating income.

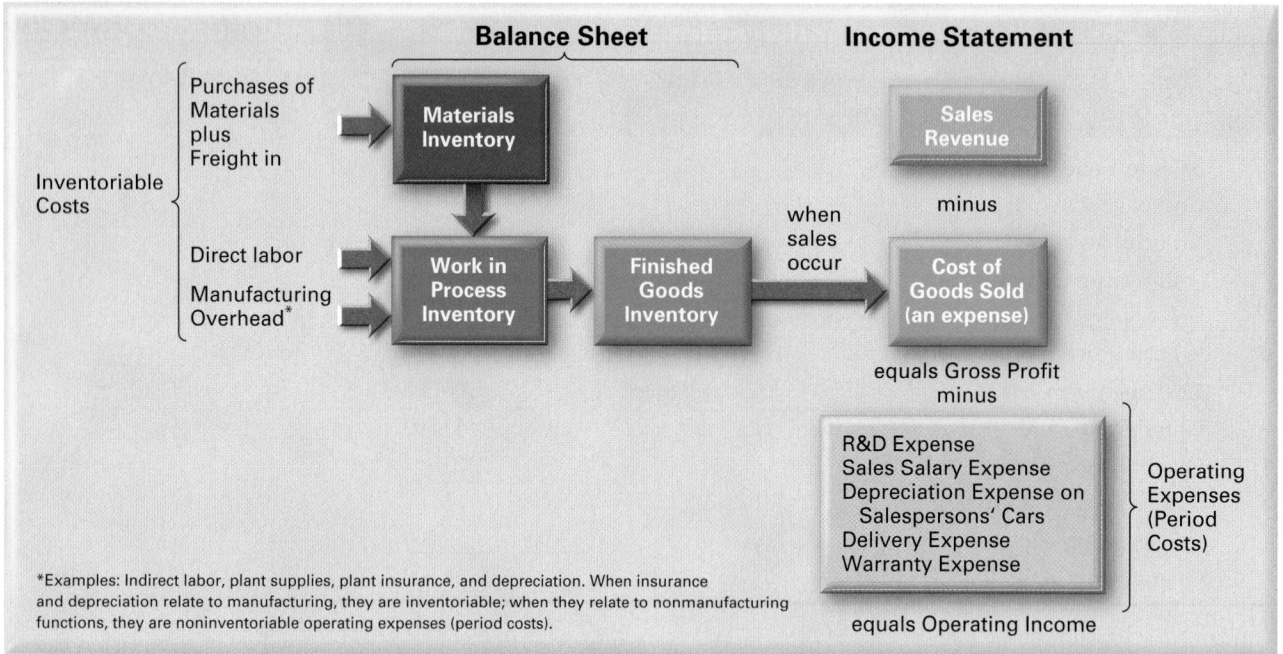

Exhibit 19-10 Manufacturing Company: Inventoriable Costs and Period Costs

*Examples: Indirect labor, plant supplies, plant insurance, and depreciation. When insurance and depreciation relate to manufacturing, they are inventoriable; when they relate to nonmanufacturing functions, they are noninventoriable operating expenses (period costs).

You now have a clear understanding of the flow of activities and costs in the plant, and you're ready to figure the cost of goods manufactured. Exhibit 19-11 shows how Top-Flight computes its cost of goods manufactured—the cost of the goods the plant *finished* during 20X5.

Exhibit 19-11

Schedule of Cost of Goods Manufactured

Top-Flight		
Schedule of Cost of Goods Manufactured **Year Ended December 31, 20X5**		
Beginning work in process inventory		**$ 2,000**
Add: Direct materials used		
Beginning materials inventory	$ 9,000	
Purchases of direct materials		
plus freight in	27,000	
Available for use	36,000	
Ending materials inventory.	(22,000)	
Direct materials used		$14,000
Direct labor.		19,000
Manufacturing overhead:		
Indirect materials	$ 1,500	
Indirect labor	3,500	
Depreciation—plant and equipment	3,000	
Plant utilities, insurance, and		
property taxes	4,000	12,000
Total manufacturing costs incurred **during year**		45,000
Total manufacturing costs to account for		47,000
Less: Ending work in process inventory		(5,000)
Costs of goods manufactured		$42,000

✔ Starter 19-7

✔ Starter 19-8

✔ Starter 19-9

The computation of the cost of goods manufactured summarizes the activities and related costs incurred on Top-Flight's plant floor throughout 20X5. By the end of 20X4, Top-Flight had spent a total of $2,000 to partially complete the golf clubs and shoes that remained on the plant floor at the close of business on December 31, 20X4. This ending work in process inventory for 20X4 is Top-Flight's beginning work in process inventory for 20X5.

Exhibit 19-11 shows that during 20X5, Top-Flight's production plant used $14,000 of direct materials, $19,000 of direct labor, and $12,000 of manufacturing overhead. Adding the sum of these three costs ($45,000) to the beginning Work in Process Inventory balance of $2,000 gives the total cost assigned to goods the plant worked on during the year: $47,000. The plant finished most of these goods and sent them to Finished Goods Inventory, but some were not finished. By the close of business on December 31, 20X5, Top-Flight had spent $5,000 on ending work in process inventory that lay partially complete on the plant floor.

The final step is to figure the *cost of goods manufactured during 20X5*—that is, the cost of the goods that Top-Flight *finished* during 20X5. Take the $47,000 total cost of goods worked on during the year and subtract the $5,000 cost of the goods that were not finished (the ending work in process inventory at December 31, 20X5). Top-Flight's cost of goods manufactured for 20X5 is $42,000 ($47,000 − $5,000).

FLOW OF COSTS THROUGH INVENTORY ACCOUNTS Exhibit 19-12 diagrams the flow of costs through Top-Flight's inventory accounts. The format is the same for all three stages: direct materials, work in process, and finished goods. The final amount at each stage flows into the next stage. Take time to see how the schedule of cost of goods manufactured in Exhibit 19-11 uses the flows of the direct materials and work in process stages, while the income statement in Panel B of Exhibit 19-9 uses the flows for the finished goods inventory.

| Exhibit 19-12 | Flow of Costs Through a Manufacturer's Inventory Accounts |

Direct Materials Inventory		Work in Process Inventory		Finished Goods Inventory	
Beginning inventory	$ 9,000	Beginning inventory	$ 2,000	Beginning inventory	$ 6,000
+ Purchases and freight in.............	27,000	+ Direct materials used ..... $14,000 + Direct labor .... 19,000 + Manufacturing overhead .... 12,000 Total manufacturing costs incurred during the year 45,000		+ Cost of goods manufactured	42,000
= Direct materials available for use	36,000	= Total manufacturing costs to account for.......	47,000	= Cost of goods available for sale.....	48,000
− Ending inventory	(22,000)	− Ending inventory	(5,000)	− Ending inventory	(8,000)
= Direct materials used	$14,000	= Cost of goods manufactured	$42,000	= Cost of goods sold ...	$40,000

Source: The authors are indebted to Judith Cassidy for this presentation.

Effects on the Balance Sheet

The only difference in the balance sheets of service, merchandising, and manufacturing companies relates to inventories. Exhibit 19-13 shows how the current asset sections of eNOW! (service company), Apex Showrooms (merchandising company), and Top-Flight (manufacturing company) might differ at the end of 20X5. eNOW! has no inventory at all, Apex has a single category of inventory, and Top-Flight has three categories of inventory (materials, work in process, and finished goods).

✔ Starter 19-10

Exhibit 19-13	Current Asset Sections of Balance Sheets

eNOW! (Service Company)		Apex Showrooms (Merchandising Company)		Top-Flight (Manufacturing Company)		
Cash...................	$ 4,000	Cash	$ 4,000	Cash...................		$ 4,000
Accounts receivable	5,000	Accounts receivable	5,000	Accounts receivable		5,000
		Inventory (Exhibit 19-9, Panel A).........	13,000	Materials inventory (Exhibit 19-11)	$22,000	
				Work in process inventory (Exhibit 19-11)	5,000	
				Finished goods inventory (Exhibit 19-9, Panel B)....	8,000	35,000
Prepaid expenses...........	1,000	Prepaid expenses	1,000	Prepaid expenses		1,000
Total current assets	$10,000	Total current assets	$23,000	Total current assets........		$45,000

Take time to review the following Decision Guidelines. Make sure you have a solid understanding of all these concepts before you read further.

Decision Guidelines

BUILDING BLOCKS OF MANAGEMENT ACCOUNTING

HP engages in *manufacturing* when it assembles its computers, *merchandising* when it sells them on its Web site, and support *services* such as start-up and implementation services. HP had to make the following decisions in designing its management accounting system to provide managers with the information they need to run the manufacturing, merchandising, and service operations efficiently and effectively.

Decision	Guidelines
What information should management accountants provide? What is the primary focus of management accounting?	Management accounting provides information that helps managers make better decisions; it has a • *Future* orientation • Focus on *relevance* to business decisions
How do you decide on a company's management accounting system, which is not regulated by GAAP?	Use cost-benefit analysis: Design the management accounting system so that benefits (from helping managers make wiser decisions) outweigh the costs of the system.

How do you distinguish among service, merchandising, and manufacturing companies? How do their balance sheets differ?	*Service companies:*
	
	• Provide customers with intangible services
	• Have no inventories on the balance sheet
	
	Merchandising companies:
	
	• Resell tangible products purchased ready-made from suppliers
	• Have only one category of inventory
	
	Manufacturing companies:
	
	• Use labor, plant, and equipment to transform raw materials into new finished products
	• Have three categories of inventory:
	    Materials inventory
	    Work in process inventory
	    Finished goods inventory

Decision Guidelines *(continued)*

Decision	Guidelines
How do you compute cost of goods sold?	• *Service companies:* No cost of goods sold, because they don't sell tangible goods

Merchandising companies:

Beginning inventory
+ Purchases and freight in
– Ending inventory
= Cost of goods sold

Manufacturing companies:

Beginning finished goods inventory
+ Cost of goods manufactured
– Ending finished goods inventory
= Cost of goods sold

How do you compute the cost of goods manufactured for a manufacturer?

Beginning work in process inventory
+ Current period manufacturing costs (direct materials used + direct labor + manufacturing overhead)
– Ending work in process inventory
= Cost of goods manufactured

Which costs are initially treated as assets for external reporting? When are these costs expensed?

Inventoriable product costs are initially treated as assets (Inventory); these costs are not expensed (as Cost of Goods Sold) until the products are sold.

What costs are inventoriable under GAAP?

• *Service companies:* No inventoriable product costs
• *Merchandising companies:* Purchases and freight in
• *Manufacturing companies:* Direct materials used, direct labor, and manufacturing overhead

MID-CHAPTER *Summary Problem*

1. Show how to compute cost of goods manufactured. Use the following amounts: direct materials used ($24,000); direct labor ($9,000); manufacturing overhead ($17,000); beginning work in process inventory ($5,000); and ending work in process inventory ($4,000).
2. For a manufacturing company, identify the following as either an inventoriable product cost or a period cost:
   a. Depreciation on plant equipment
   b. Depreciation on salespersons' automobiles
   c. Insurance on plant building
   d. Marketing manager's salary

CHECK YOUR RESOURCES

Solution

Requirement 1

Cost of goods manufactured:

Beginning work in process inventory......................		$ 5,000
Add: Direct materials used.............................	$24,000	
Direct labor	9,000	
Manufacturing overhead	17,000	
Total manufacturing costs incurred during the period .		50,000
Total manufacturing costs to account for..................		55,000
Less: Ending work in process inventory		(4,000)
Cost of goods manufactured		$51,000

Requirement 2

(a) Inventoriable product cost; (b) Period cost; (c) Inventoriable product cost; (d) Period cost

 Identify trends in the business environment and use cost-benefit analysis to make business decisions

Student Resource CD

enterprise resource planning, JIT, total quality management

Today's Business Environment

The following chapters describe management accounting tools that managers use to make business decisions. Before we turn to these tools, let's first consider recent trends that affect managers' decisions and the management accounting systems that support them. These trends include the shift toward a service economy; the rise of the global marketplace; time-based competition (including changes in information systems, electronic commerce, and just-in-time management); and total quality management.

Shift Toward a Service Economy

Service companies provide health care, communication, transportation, banking, and other important benefits to society. In the last century, North American economies shifted focus from manufacturing to service. Service companies now make up the largest sector of the U.S. economy and employ 55% of the workforce. The U.S. Bureau of the Census expects services, especially technology and health-care services, to be among the fastest growing industries over the next decade. Even companies that do manufacturing, such as General Electric (GE), are shifting to selling more services. It's easy to see why. In GE's jet engine business, services contribute only 30% of the revenues but generate two-thirds of the profit.

Service company managers need cost information to make decisions. For example, banks must include the cost of servicing checking and savings accounts in the fees they charge customers. Hospitals need to know the cost of performing appendectomies to justify reimbursement from insurance companies and from Medicare.

Competing in the Global Marketplace

The costs of international trade have plummeted over the last decade, allowing foreign companies to compete with local firms. Firms that are not world-class competitors will vanish from the global market. However, global markets provide competitive companies with great potential: Foreign operations account for over 25% of Regal Marine's and Amazon.com's revenues, and over 40% of General Electric's revenues. McDonald's has expanded in Russia and China, two countries with billions of consumers.

Manufacturers often move operations to other countries to be closer to new markets and less expensive labor. For example, Thomson SA, maker of GE television sets, closed the world's largest TV factory in Bloomington, Indiana, and moved the work to Mexico to save an estimated $75 million a year in labor costs. Ford, General Motors, and DaimlerChrysler all built plants in Brazil to feed Brazil's car-hungry middle class. The same week Alcoa announced it was closing two plants in the United States, it spelled out plans to build a $1 billion plant in Iceland. Alcoa will go ahead with the plan if the benefits (less expensive energy and labor) outweigh the costs of building the new plant.

Globalization has several implications for management accounting:

1. Stiffer competition means managers need more accurate information to make wise decisions. If Nokia overestimates the cost of its new cell phone, it may set prices too high and lose business to competitors.

2. Companies must decide whether to expand sales and/or production into foreign countries. Managers need estimates of the costs and benefits of international expansion.

3. Globalization fosters the transfer of management philosophy across international borders. Many U.S. companies now follow the just-in-time philosophy developed in Japan.

Time-Based Competition

Question: When did you need that order?
Response: Yesterday, of course!

The Internet, electronic commerce (e-commerce), e-mail, and express delivery speed the pace of business. Customers who surf the Web and Instant Message with people all over the world will not wait four weeks to receive their purchases. Time is the latest competitive turf for world-class business.

Dell Computer commits to delivering your desktop computer within a week of receiving your order. Toyota says it can make a car within five days of receiving a custom order. Sweden's Ericsson Radio Systems has increased on-time delivery from 20% to 99.98%—nearly perfect. How do they do it? By using advanced information systems, e-commerce, and just-in-time management.

ADVANCED INFORMATION SYSTEMS   Many small businesses use QuickBooks or Peachtree software to track their costs and develop the information owners and managers need to run the business. But large companies such as Fujitsu and Allstate Insurance are turning to **enterprise resource planning (ERP) systems** that can integrate all of a company's worldwide functions, departments, and data. ERP systems such as SAP, Oracle, and Peoplesoft gather company data into a centralized data warehouse. The system feeds these data into software for all of the company's business activities, from budgeting and purchasing to production and customer service.

ERP
Software systems that can integrate all of a company's worldwide functions, departments, and data into a single system.

Advantages of ERP systems include:

- Companies streamline their operations before mapping them into ERP software. Streamlining operations saves money.

- ERP helps companies respond to changes. A change in sales instantly ripples through the ERP's purchases, production, shipping, and accounting systems.

- An ERP system can replace hundreds of separate software systems, such as different software in different regions, or different payroll, shipping, and production software.

ERP is expensive: Major installations cost Fujitsu and Allstate over $40 million. ERP also requires a large commitment of time and people. For example, Hershey Foods tried to shrink a four-year ERP project into two and a half years. The result? The software did not map into Hershey's operations, and disrupted deliveries hurt profits in the critical Halloween season.

E-COMMERCE   To survive in a competitive globally wired economy, companies use the Internet in everyday operations such as budgeting, planning, selling, and customer service. Imagine a sales clerk who can sell to thousands of customers at once. This clerk instantly provides every product, option, and price the company offers. It works 24 hours a day, 365 days a year, and never takes a break or vacation. This sales clerk is an e-commerce Web site!

Business-to-business e-commerce takes this speed and efficiency to new levels. Imagine sitting in your office, anywhere in the world. You enter Dell's Web site and customize the new computer you're buying. After you fill your virtual shopping cart, business-to-business software automates ordering, approval, and delivery.

Electronic purchases below specified dollar limits are often untouched by human hands, generate little if any paper, and avoid the time and cost of

Accounting.com

Refining Dining with Data Mining

As chefs in the kitchen slice and dice meat and veggies, managers back at headquarters are asking accountants to "slice and dice" the data. Using the latest in data mining technology from Digital Equipment Corp. and Informix, large restaurant operators now analyze a dizzying amount of data that extend well beyond sales, cash management, and inventory.

- **AFC**, operator and franchiser of more than 3,300 Church's, Popeye's Chicken & Biscuits, Seattle Coffee Company, and Torrefazione Italia outlets worldwide, collects customer-purchase data by item, item combination, day, and location. Sophisticated data mining software ferrets out patterns, trends, and even challenges and problems. Managers get information on how factors such as location affect the profitability of sales promotions and which patrons respond to which offers.
- **Red Robin International**, a 135-unit casual-dining chain based in Englewood, Colorado, relies on patterns revealed by its data warehouse to hone menus. "We do a lot of menu changes, with new items and specials," explains Howard Jenkins, Red Robin's Vice President of Information Systems. "With data mining in place, we can ask ourselves, 'If we put the items with the high margin in the middle of the menu, do we sell more versus putting [them] at the top or bottom . . . ?'"
- **Pizzeria Uno** uses a more economical decision-support system to define and analyze data in response to specific queries, such as take-out versus eat-in pizza sales. A nifty tool called "80/20" identifies the 20% of customers who contribute 80% of sales, so management can adjust menus and promos to suit top patrons' preferences.

Source: Based on "Mining the data of dining," *Nation's Restaurant News*, May 22, 2000, pp. S22–S24.

processing this paperwork. Even the federal government is on the e-bandwagon. An electronic marketplace, E-Mall, allows buyers in the Department of Defense and other federal agencies access to 17 million items online. Orders on E-Mall cost about $11 to process, while those placed by hand cost around $150.

Electronically billing customers is also becoming more popular. Analysts estimate that

1. Companies save $7 per invoice by billing customers electronically
2. The average large company issues 800,000 invoices a year
3. The average cost of installing an e-billing system is $500,000

Should companies that issue 800,000 invoices a year consider e-billing?

Answer: Yes, these companies should consider e-billing. Comparing expected benefits to costs reveals significant expected net benefits from e-billing:

Expected benefits:
800,000 invoices × $7 savings per invoice $5,600,000
Expected costs:
Installation of e-billing system . . . .   (500,000)
Net expected benefits $5,100,000

Managers of Krispy Kreme stores use the company's customized Web portal to plan production and order supplies. Weather news appears on the opening screen. Why? Because Krispy Kreme found that people buy more coffee and donuts when the weather is bad. This simple innovation helps managers forecast how many donuts to make. "I've seen a good 2 to 3 percent increase in profitability just from the portal," says the manager of a Miami-based store.[2]

Firms also use the Internet to tap into other companies' business processes. Companies that supply component parts to Dell use the Internet to look into Dell's production process through a customized virtual window. Each supplier sees the current demand for, and inventory levels of, the parts it supplies Dell. Access to real-time information that lets suppliers automate the size of the next day's order helps Dell cut order-to-delivery times and control costs.

E-commerce is thus an important means of **supply-chain management**, where companies exchange information with suppliers and customers to reduce costs, improve quality, and speed delivery of goods and services from suppliers, through the company itself, and on to customers. E-commerce also increases firms' ability (and need) to use just-in-time management.

supply-chain management
Exchange of information with suppliers and customers to reduce costs, improve quality, and speed delivery of goods and services from suppliers, through the company itself, and on to customers.

JUST-IN-TIME MANAGEMENT   Costs of holding inventory can add up to 25% of the inventory's value. Money tied up in inventory cannot be used for other purposes. Inventory held too long becomes obsolete. Storing inventory takes space that could be used to increase production. The just-in-time philosophy helps managers cut these costs by speeding the transformation of raw materials into new finished products. Let's see how.

Toyota generally gets credit for pioneering the **just-in-time (JIT)** philosophy, which means producing *just in time* to satisfy needs. Ideally, suppliers deliver materials for today's production in exactly the right quantities *just in time* to begin production, and finished units are completed *just in time* for delivery to customers.

Firms adopting JIT report sharp reductions in inventory. Reducing inventory and speeding the production process reduce **throughput time**, the time between

✔ **Starter 19-11**

just-in-time (JIT)
A system in which a company produces just in time to satisfy needs. Suppliers deliver materials just in time to begin production, and finished units are completed just in time for delivery to customers.

throughput time
The time between buying raw materials and selling finished products.

---

[2]Catherine Skip, "Hot Bytes, by the Dozen," *Newsweek*, April 28, 2003, page 42.

buying raw materials and selling finished products. For example, Dell Computer recently cut its throughput time from 17 to fewer than 5 days. Why is this important? *The Wall Street Journal* estimates that new technologies reduce the value of a completed PC by 1% *per week*.[3] Moving inventory quickly means that Dell can cut prices immediately when component part costs decline. Less inventory means that Dell can quickly incorporate new technologies and that more plant space is available for production.

Manufacturers adopting just-in-time have limited safety stock of raw materials, so they depend on their suppliers to make on-time deliveries of perfect-quality materials. As we noted earlier, Dell designed special Web pages for its major suppliers that give them a "virtual window" into the Dell operations they supply. Suppliers use these windows to decide when and how much raw material to deliver to Dell. As another example, one of Regal Marine's suppliers goes to Regal's production floor, takes orders from Regal's assembly-line workers, and then delivers the materials directly to the production floor two days later.

Companies that adopt JIT strive for perfect quality because defects stop production lines. Firms that adopt JIT also commit to total quality management.

Total Quality Management

total quality management (TQM)
A philosophy of delighting customers by providing them with superior products and services. Requires improving quality and eliminating defects and waste throughout the value chain.

Companies must deliver high-quality goods and services to remain competitive. Hewlett-Packard and Ford in the United States, British Telecom in the United Kingdom, and Toyota in Japan view **total quality management (TQM)** as key to succeeding in the global economy. The goal of total quality management is to delight customers by providing them with superior products and services. Companies achieve this goal by improving quality and eliminating defects and waste throughout the value chain.

In TQM, each business function examines its own activities and works to improve performance by setting higher and higher goals. For example, Motorola wanted to reduce the time required to issue a purchase order. Motorola's purchasing department TQM team reduced the number of steps in handling a purchase order from 17 to 6, slashing average processing time from 30 minutes to 3. Service organizations also strive to improve quality. For example, the American Institute of Certified Public Accountants was the first professional membership organization in the United States to earn the ISO 9001 international certification for quality management and assurance.

Quality improvement programs cost money today, but the benefits accrue over time. In deciding whether to undertake such projects, managers compare the project's cost to the present value today of the project's future benefits. (This is called *discounting* the future amounts to their *present values*.)← Also, because no one can foresee the future, the exact amount of the future benefits is not known. Let's see how managers adjust for this uncertainty.

The Appendix to Chapter 15 ➡️
discusses present-value computations; we cover this subject in more detail in Chapter 26.

GE recently started nearly 3,000 quality-related projects at a cost of more than $200 million. The first-year cost savings from these projects totaled only $170 million. Does this mean that GE made a bad decision? Not necessarily. GE expects these projects to continue yielding benefits in the future.

✔ **Starter 19-12**

Suppose GE managers predict these projects will be either moderately successful or extremely successful. Assume that if the projects are moderately successful, they will yield additional benefits (cost savings) with a present value of $20 million. If the projects are extremely successful, they will yield extra benefits with a present value of $100 million. GE managers think the projects are more likely to be extremely successful. Suppose they estimate a 60% chance that the

---

[3]"Compaq Stumbles as PCs Weather New Blow," *Wall Street Journal*, March 9, 1998, page B1.

projects will be extremely successful and a 40% chance that they will be moderately successful.

In an uncertain environment, managers make decisions based on expected values. We compute expected values by multiplying the dollar value of each possible outcome by the probability of that outcome, and then adding the results:

Outcome	Benefit	×	Probability	=	Expected Value (of Additional Benefit)
Extremely successful	$100 million	×	60% chance	=	$60 million
Moderately successful	20 million	×	40% chance	=	8 million
Total expected value of benefits					$68 million

What does this $68 million mean? If GE faced this exact situation ten times, it would expect to get $100 million in extra benefits six times and only $20 million of additional benefits four times. The *average* extra benefits across the ten situations is $68 million.

Thus, the total benefits expected from GE's quality projects ($238 million—calculated as $170 million initial benefits + $68 million additional expected benefits) exceed the $200 million cost of the projects. This analysis suggests that GE's quality initiative was worthwhile.

Even after adopting quality programs, companies cannot rest on their laurels. TQM requires that companies (and individual employees) continually look for ways to improve performance. This is the **continuous improvement** philosophy.

How do companies improve? Many businesses find that investments in higher quality earlier in the value chain (R&D and design) generate savings in later stages (production, marketing, and customer service). Successful companies design and build quality into their products and services rather than depending on finding and fixing defects later. For example, by increasing the proportion of vehicles built right the first time from 50% to 70%, General Motors cut average warranty costs from roughly $1,600 to $1,000 per vehicle, in addition to reducing costs of rework and inspections.

continuous improvement
A philosophy requiring employees to continually look for ways to improve performance.

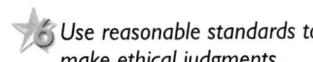 Use reasonable standards to make ethical judgments.

Ethical Standards

As is evident from the accounting scandals that felled multinational giants like Enron and WorldCom, ethical behavior is a critical component of quality. Unfortunately, the ethical path is not always clear. You may want to act ethically and do the right thing, but the consequences can make it difficult to decide what to do. Consider the following examples:

■ Sarah Baker is examining the expense reports of her staff, who counted inventory at Top-Flight's warehouses in Arizona. She discovers that Mike Flinders has claimed but not included hotel receipts for over $1,000 of accommodation expenses. Other staff, who also claimed $1,000, did attach hotel receipts. When asked about the receipt, Mike admits that he stayed with an old friend, not in the hotel, but he believes he deserves the money he saved. After all, the company would have paid his hotel bill.

■ As the accountant of Entreé Computer Co., you are aware of your company's weak financial condition. Entreé is close to signing a lucrative contract that should ensure its future. To do so, the controller states that the company *must* report a profit this year (ending December 31). He suggests: "Two customers have placed orders that are really not supposed to be shipped until early January. Ask production to fill and ship those orders on December 31, so we can record them in this year's sales."

The Institute of Management Accountants (IMA) has developed standards to help management accountants deal with these situations. The standards remind us that society expects professional accountants to exhibit the highest level of ethical behavior. An excerpt from the *Standards of Ethical Conduct for Management Accountants* appears in Exhibit 19-14. These standards require management accountants to

- Maintain their professional competence
- Preserve the confidentiality of the information they handle
- Act with integrity and objectivity

Exhibit 19-14

IMA Standards of Ethical Conduct for Management Accountants (excerpt)

✔ Starter 19-13

✔ Starter 19-14

Management accountants have an obligation to maintain the highest standards of ethical conduct. These standards include

Competence

- Maintain professional competence by ongoing development of knowledge and skills.
- Perform professional duties in accordance with relevant laws, regulations, and technical standards.

Confidentiality

- Refrain from disclosing confidential information acquired in the course of work except when authorized, unless legally obligated to do so.

Integrity

- Avoid actual or apparent conflicts of interest and advise all appropriate parties of any potential conflict.
- Refuse any gift, favor, or hospitality that would influence or would appear to influence actions.
- Communicate unfavorable as well as favorable information and professional judgments or opinions.

Objectivity

- Communicate information fairly and objectively.

Source: Adapted from Institute of Management Accountants, *Standards of Ethical Conduct for Management Accountants* (Montvale, N.J.).

To resolve ethical dilemmas, the IMA also suggests discussing ethical situations with your immediate supervisor, or with an objective adviser.

Let's return to the two ethical dilemmas. By asking to be reimbursed for hotel expenses he did not incur, Mike Flinders violated the IMA's integrity standards (conflict of interest in which he tried to enrich himself at company expense). Because Sarah Baker discovered the inflated expense report, she would not be fulfilling her ethical responsibilities (integrity and objectivity) if she allowed the reimbursement and did not take disciplinary action.

The second dilemma, in which the controller asked you to accelerate the shipments, is less clear-cut. You should discuss the available alternatives and their consequences with others. Many people believe that following the controllers' suggestion to manipulate the company's income would violate the standards of competence, integrity, and objectivity. Others would argue that because Entreé Computer already has the customer order, shipping the goods and recording the sale in December is still ethical behavior. If you refuse to ship the goods in December and you simply resign without attempting to find an alternative solution, you might only hurt yourself and your family.

Weighing costs against benefits to make the best decision comes up again and again in management accounting. Study the Cost-Benefit Analysis Decision Guidelines to make sure you understand this important concept.

Decision Guidelines

COST-BENEFIT ANALYSIS

The company in the chapter-opening story, **Regal Marine**, has responded to changes in the business environment by developing a worldwide network of dealers and a stunning Web site, and by using supply-chain management, JIT, and TQM. Here are some of the key decisions Regal's managers considered to ensure that the company thrives in the future.

Decision	Guidelines
How to compete in a globally wired economy?	Update information systems, embrace e-commerce, and use supply-chain management, JIT, and TQM to compete more effectively.
How to decide whether to undertake new projects such as international expansion, ERP, JIT, and TQM?	Cost-benefit analysis: Compute the benefits of the project and compare with the costs. Undertake the project if benefits exceed costs. Abandon the project if costs exceed benefits.
How to adjust the cost-benefit analysis if the exact amount of the benefit (or cost) is not known?	Compute the *expected value* of the benefits (or costs) of each outcome as follows: $$\text{Estimated amount} \times \text{Probability of occurrence} = \text{Expected value}$$ Then add the expected values across all possible outcomes.
How to resolve an ethical dilemma?	Weigh the costs and benefits of alternative courses of action. Consult the IMA's *Standards of Ethical Conduct for Management Accountants* (Exhibit 19-14). Also consult the Framework for Ethical Judgments in Chapter 8.

Excel Application Exercise

Goal: Create a spreadsheet to assess the costs and benefits of a new project, and use the results to answer questions about the decision.

Scenario: Dennis Popper of EZ-Rider Motorcycles has asked you to prepare an Excel spreadsheet that calculates the net benefits (expected value of benefits minus total costs) of expansion into Germany. The background data for EZ-Rider's expansion project appears in the End-of-Chapter Summary Problem, which follows.

When you have completed your worksheet, answer the following questions:

1. What is the expected value of the benefits of the expansion project? What are the total costs? Does the expected value of the benefits exceed the total costs? If so, what is the expected value of the net benefits?
2. What is the minimum probability of a gas price increase that would justify the expansion? What is the expected value of the net benefits at this point?

(continued on the next page)

Excel Application Exercise *(continued)*

Step-by-Step:

1. Open a new Excel spreadsheet.
2. Create a boldfaced heading as follows:
   a. Chapter 19 Excel Application Exercise
   b. Cost-Benefit Analysis
   c. EZ-Rider Motorcycles
   d. Today's Date
3. Two rows down, enter the heading "Cost Data" in column A. Under the heading, enter the data (with descriptions) needed to calculate total costs. Compute total costs. (For help in formatting currency in euros, click "Help," then search for "euro symbol.")
4. Move down three rows. In the first column, enter the boldfaced and underlined heading "PV If Stable Gas Price."
5. Under this heading, enter the present value of the project if gas prices remain stable. Copy the cell contents down 10 more rows.
6. In the next column, enter the boldfaced and underlined heading, "Probability of Stable Gas Price." Spread the heading over two rows.

7. Under this heading, enter a probability of 100%. In the next 10 rows, decrement 100% by 10% each row, so that the probability is zero at the bottom.
8. In the next column, enter the boldfaced and underlined heading, "PV If Gas Price Increases."
9. Under this heading, enter the present value of the project if gas prices increase. Copy the cell contents down 10 more rows.
10. In the next column, enter the boldfaced and underlined heading, "Probability of Gas Price Increase." Spread the heading over two rows.
11. Under this heading, enter a probability of 0%. In the next 10 rows, increment the percentage by 10% each row, so that the probability is 100% at the bottom.
12. In the next column, enter the boldfaced and underlined heading, "Expected Value of Benefits." Spread the heading over two rows. Compute the expected value for all combinations of percentages for each row.
13. In the last column, enter the boldfaced and underlined heading, "Expected Value of Net Benefits." Spread the heading over two rows. Compute the net benefits for all rows.
14. Save your file to disk and print a copy for your files.

● END-OF-CHAPTER *Summary Problem*

CHECK YOUR RESOURCES

This summary review problem shows how you can apply cost-benefit analysis to a decision about international expansion.

EZ-Rider Motorcycles is considering whether to expand into Germany. If gas prices increase, EZ-Rider expects more interest in fuel-efficient transportation such as motorcycles. EZ-Rider is considering setting up a motorcycle-assembly plant on the outskirts of Berlin.

EZ-Rider estimates it will cost €850,000 (850,000 euros) to convert an existing building to motorcycle production. Workers will need training, at a total cost of €65,000. The CEO of EZ-Rider, Dennis Popper, would have to spend a month in Berlin to organize the business and to establish relationships. He estimates the cost of this travel at €43,000.

Popper sees a 60% chance that the price of gasoline in Germany will increase significantly. If this increase occurs, he believes EZ-Rider can earn profits (before considering the costs in the preceding paragraph) with a present value of €1,624,000. However, if gas prices remain stable, Popper expects to earn profits of only about €812,000. He believes there is a 40% chance that gas prices will remain stable.

Required

1. What are the total costs of EZ-Rider's proposed expansion into Germany?
2. Compute the *expected value* of the benefits if EZ-Rider expands into Germany.
3. Do the benefits outweigh the costs of expanding into Germany?

Solution

Requirement 1

The total costs are as follows:

Conversion of manufacturing plant	€850,000
Workforce training.	65,000
Popper's trip to Berlin	43,000
Total costs	€958,000

Requirement 2

Expected value of the benefits is computed as follows:

Benefit	×	Probability	=	Expected Value
€1,624,000	×	0.60	=	€ 974,400
812,000	×	0.40	=	324,800
				€1,299,200

The *expected value* of the benefits, or profits is €1,299,200. This means that should EZ-Rider find itself in this exact situation many times, its average profits across all the situations would be €1,299,200.

Requirement 3

Yes, the total expected benefits outweigh the costs of the expansion:

Total expected benefits of expansion (from requirement 2)	€1,299,200
Total costs of expansion (from requirement 1)	958,000
Net benefits of expansion.....................................	€ 341,200

●REVIEW *Introduction to Management Accounting*

Quick Check

1. Which is *not* a characteristic of management accounting information?
   a. Emphasizes relevance
   b. Focuses on the future
   c. Provides detailed information about parts of the company, not just the company as a whole
   d. Emphasizes reliability

2. Which is *not* an element of **Regal Marine's** value chain?
   a. Administrative costs
   b. Cost of trucking boats to customers
   c. Salaries of engineers who update boat design
   d. Cost of print ads and attending boat shows

3. For Regal, which is a direct cost with respect to the LSR 1800 sportboat?
   a. Depreciation on plant and equipment
   b. Cost of boat engine
   c. Salary of engineer who rearranges plant layout
   d. Cost of customer hotline

4. Which of the following is *not* part of Regal Marine's manufacturing overhead?
   a. Insurance on plant and equipment
   b. Depreciation on delivery trucks
   c. Plant property taxes
   d. Plant utilities

5. In computing cost of goods sold, which of the following is the manufacturer's counterpart to the merchandiser's purchases?
   a. Direct materials used
   b. Total manufacturing costs incurred during the period
   c. Total manufacturing costs to account for
   d. Cost of goods manufactured

Questions 6, 7, and 8 refer to the list that follows. Suppose Regal Marine reports this information (in hundreds of thousands of dollars):

Beginning materials inventory.	$ 6
Ending materials inventory	5
Beginning work in process inventory	2
Ending work in process inventory	1
Beginning finished goods inventory	3
Ending finished goods inventory	5
Direct labor	30
Purchases of direct materials	100
Manufacturing overhead	20

6. What is the cost of the direct materials that Regal used?
   a. $99
   b. $100
   c. $101
   d. $106

7. What is the cost of goods manufactured?
   a. $149
   b. $150
   c. $151
   d. $152

8. What is the cost of goods sold?
   a. $150
   b. $152
   c. $153
   d. $154

9. Suppose Regal Marine is considering buying an ERP system for $800,000. Regal would spend another $600,000 implementing the system. Management estimates there is a 40% chance that Regal could implement the system on its own, but a 60% chance that it will have to purchase assistance from **Accenture** at an additional cost of $500,000. Regal expects the ERP system to lead to savings with a present value of $1,800,000. What is the net benefit (or cost) of implementing the ERP system?
   a. $100,000 net benefit
   b. $400,000 net benefit
   c. $100,000 net cost
   d. $300,000 net cost

10. A management accountant who refuses an expensive gift from a software salesman meets the ethical standard of
    a. Objectivity
    b. Confidentiality
    c. Integrity
    d. Competence

Accounting Vocabulary

budget (p. 753)
continuous improvement (p. 773)
controlling (p. 753)
cost-benefit analysis (p. 754)
cost object (p. 757)
cost of goods manufactured (p. 762)
customer service (p. 757)
design (p. 756)
direct cost (p. 758)
direct labor (p. 759)
direct materials (p. 759)
distribution (p. 757)
enterprise resource planning (ERP) (p. 769)

factory overhead (p. 759)
finished goods inventory (p. 756)
full product costs (p. 758)
indirect cost (p. 758)
indirect labor (p. 760)
indirect manufacturing cost (p. 759)
indirect materials (p. 760)
inventoriable product costs (p. 758)
just-in-time (JIT) (p. 771)
manufacturing company (p. 755)
manufacturing overhead (p. 759)
marketing (p. 757)
materials inventory (p. 756)

merchandising company (p. 755)
period costs (p. 758)
planning (p. 753)
production or purchases (p. 756)
research and development (R&D) (p. 756)
service company (p. 755)
supply-chain management (p. 771)
throughput time (p. 771)
total quality management (TQM) (p. 772)
value chain (p. 756)
work in process inventory (p. 756)

● ASSESS *Your Progress*

Starters

See *www.prenhall.com/horngren* for selected Starters, Exercises, and Problems.

S19-1 Your roommate, who plans to specialize in international business, is considering whether to enroll in the second principles of accounting course. She says, "I don't want to be an accountant, so why do I need a second accounting course? I just spent a whole term on financial accounting. Most of this second course focuses on management accounting, but how can that be so different from what I already learned in financial accounting?" Respond.

Distinguishing financial from management accounting
(Obj. 1)

S19-2 Give an example of costs that **E*TRADE** (an online brokerage firm) might incur in each of the six business functions in the value chain. Provide another example that shows how E*TRADE might deliberately decide to spend more money on one of the six business functions in order to reduce the costs in other business functions.

Classifying costs by value-chain function
(Obj. 2)

S19-3 Classify each of **Hewlett-Packard's** costs as one of the six business functions in the value chain.

Classifying costs by value-chain function
(Obj. 2)

a. Depreciation on Roseville, California, plant.
b. Costs of a customer support center Web site.
c. Transportation costs to deliver laser printers to retailers, like **Best Buy**.
d. Depreciation on research lab.
e. Cost of a prime-time TV ad featuring the new Hewlett-Packard logo.
f. Salary of scientists at Hewlett-Packard Laboratories who are developing new printer technologies.
g. Purchase of plastic used in printer casings.
h. Salary of engineers who are redesigning the printer's on–off switch.
i. Depreciation on delivery vehicles.
j. Plant manager's salary.

S19-4 Consider **Marvin Windows'** manufacturing plant. Give two examples of

Distinguishing between direct and indirect costs
(Obj. 3)

a. Direct materials
b. Direct labor
c. Indirect materials
d. Indirect labor
e. Other manufacturing overhead

S19-5 Classify each of **Georgia-Pacific's** costs as either inventoriable or period costs:

Inventoriable vs. period costs
(Obj. 3)

a. Depreciation on the gypsum board plant.
b. Purchase of lumber to be cut into boards.
c. Life insurance on CEO.
d. Salaries of scientists studying ways to speed forest growth.
e. Cost of a new software package to track inventory.
f. Cost of electricity at one of Georgia-Pacific's paper mills.
g. Salaries of Georgia-Pacific's top executives.
h. Cost of mold inhibitor applied to treated lumber.
i. Cost of TV ads promoting environmental awareness.

S19-6 ← *Link Back to Chapter 5.* Given the following information for Circuits Plus, an electronics e-tailer, compute the cost of goods sold.

Preparing the cost-of-goods-sold section of a merchandiser's income statement
(Obj. 4)

Web site maintenance	$7,000
Delivery expenses	1,000
Freight in	3,000
Purchases	40,000
Ending inventory	5,500
Revenues	60,000
Marketing expenses	10,000
Beginning inventory	3,500

Computing the cost of goods manufactured
(Obj. 4)

S19-7 Turn to Exhibit 19-11 (page 764). If direct material purchases were $20,000 rather than $27,000, what would be the cost of direct materials used and the cost of goods manufactured? (Other costs remain the same as in Exhibit 19-11.)

Computing manufacturing overhead
(Obj. 4)

S19-8 Snap's manufactures disposable cameras. Suppose the company's March records include the following items. What is Snap's total manufacturing overhead cost in March?

Glue for camera frames	$ 250	Company president's salary ..	$25,000
Depreciation expense on company cars used by sales force	3,000	Plant foreman's salary	4,000
		Plant janitor's salary.........	1,000
Plant depreciation expense ..	10,000	Oil for manufacturing equipment	25
Interest expense..........	2,000	Flash bulbs...............	50,000

Computing direct materials used
(Obj. 4)

S19-9 You are a new accounting intern at Sunny's Bikes, Inc. Your boss gives you the following information and asks you to compute direct materials used.

Purchases of direct materials	$17,000
Freight in.......................................	200
Freight out	1,000
Ending inventory of direct materials	1,500
Beginning inventory of direct materials..............	4,000

Differences among service, merchandising, and manufacturing companies' balance sheets
(Obj. 4)

S19-10 The current asset sections of the balance sheets of three companies follow. Which company is a service company? Which is a merchandiser? Which is a manufacturer? How can you tell?

X-Treme		Y-Not?		Zesto	
Cash	$ 2,500	Cash	$3,000	Cash....................	$ 2,000
Accounts receivable.......	5,500	Accounts receivable	6,000	Accounts receivable.......	5,000
Inventory................	8,000	Prepaid expenses	500	Materials inventory.......	1,000
Prepaid expenses	300	Total	$9,500	Work in process inventory .	800
Total	$16,300			Finished goods inventory..	4,000
				Total....................	$12,800

Understanding JIT
(Obj. 5)

S19-11 Is JIT more appropriate for **Amazon.com**, a book, music, and electronics e-tailer, or **Mouton-Rothschild**, a French winemaker specializing in fine red wines? Explain.

Expected value of the benefits of a quality program
(Obj. 5)

S19-12 Consider the cost-benefit analysis for the **GE** quality program discussed on pages 772 and 773. Suppose GE's managers now estimate an 85% chance that the projects will yield an extra $20 million in benefits, and a 15% chance that the projects will yield an extra $80 million. What is the expected value of the additional benefits *now*? Assuming total costs remain $200 million, does this change your mind about whether the quality program was a worthwhile investment? (Hint: Remember the initial cost savings given on page 772.)

Understanding ethics
(Obj. 6)

S19-13 Explain why each of the four broad ethical standards in the Institute of Management Accountants' *Standards of Ethical Conduct for Management Accountants* (Exhibit 19-14, page 774) is necessary.

S19-14 The Institute of Management Accountants' *Standards of Ethical Conduct for Management Accountants* (Exhibit 19-14, page 774) require management accountants to meet standards regarding

Making ethical decisions
(Obj. 6)

- Competence
- Confidentiality
- Integrity
- Objectivity

Consider the following situations. Which guidelines are violated in each situation?

a. You tell your brother that your company will report earnings significantly above financial analysts' estimates.

b. You see that others take home office supplies for personal use. As an intern, you do the same thing, assuming that this is a "perk."

c. At a conference on e-commerce, you skip the afternoon session and go sightseeing.

d. You failed to read the detailed specifications of a new general ledger package that you asked your company to purchase. After it is installed, you are surprised that it is incompatible with some of your company's older accounting software.

e. You do not provide top management with the detailed job descriptions they requested because you fear they may use this information to cut a position from your department.

Exercises

E19-1 Complete the following statements with one of the terms listed here. You may use a term more than once, and some terms may not be used at all.

Management vs. financial accounting and managers' use of information
(Obj. 1)

Budget	Creditors	Managers	Planning
Controlling	Financial accounting	Management accounting	Shareholders

a. Companies must follow GAAP in their _____ systems.

b. Financial accounting develops reports for external parties, such as _____ and _____.

c. When managers evaluate the company's performance compared to the plan, they are performing the _____ role of management.

d. _____ are decision makers inside a company.

e. _____ provides information on a company's past performance.

f. _____ systems are not restricted by GAAP but are chosen by comparing the costs versus the benefits of the system.

g. Choosing goals and the means to achieve them is the _____ function of management.

E19-2 Suppose the cell phone manufacturer **Samsung Electronics** provides the following information for its costs last month (in hundreds of thousands):

Value chain, direct and indirect costs, inventoriable costs
(Obj. 2, 3)

Salaries of telephone salespeople	$ 5	Transmitters	$61
Depreciation on plant and equipment	65	Rearrange production process to accommodate new robot	2
Exterior case for phone	6	Assembly-line workers' wages	10
Salaries of scientists who developed new model	12	Technical customer-support hotline	3
Delivery expense via **Airborne Express**	7	1-800 (toll-free) line for customer orders	1

(continued on next page)

Required

1. Use the following format to classify each cost according to its place in the value chain. (*Hint:* You should have at least one cost in each value-chain function.)

R&D	Design of Products, Services, or Processes	Production			Marketing	Distribution	Customer Service
		Direct Materials	Direct Labor	Manufacturing Overhead			

2. Compute the total costs for each value-chain category.
3. How much are the total inventoriable product costs?

Value chain, inventoriable costs
(Obj. 2, 3)

E19-3 Suppose **Radio Shack** incurred the following costs at its Charleston, South Carolina, store.

Research on whether store should sell satellite radio service......	$ 400	Payment to consultant for advice on location of new store..................	$2,500
Purchases of merchandise ...	30,000	Freight in	3,000
Rearranging store layout	750	Salespersons' salaries	4,000
Newspaper advertisements	5,000	Customer complaint department.............	800
Depreciation expense on delivery trucks...........	1,000		

Required

1. Use the following format to classify each cost according to its place in the value chain.

R&D	Design of Products, Services, or Processes	Purchases of Merchandise Inventory	Marketing	Distribution	Customer Service

2. Compute the total costs for each value-chain category.
3. How much are the total inventoriable product costs?

Service, merchandising, and manufacturing companies and their inventories
(Obj. 4)

E19-4 Complete the following statements with one of the terms listed here. You may use a term more than once, and some terms may not be used at all.

Finished goods inventory	Inventory (merchandise)	Service companies
Manufacturing companies	Merchandising companies	Work in process inventory
Materials inventory		

a. _____ produce their own inventory.
b. _____ typically have a single category of inventory.
c. _____ do not have tangible products intended for sale.
d. _____ resell products they previously purchased ready-made from suppliers.
e. _____ use their workforce and equipment to transform raw materials into new finished products.

(*continued on next page*)

f. Swaim, a company based in North Carolina, makes furniture. Partially completed sofas are _____. Completed sofas that remain unsold in the warehouse are _____. Fabric and wood are _____.

g. For **Kellogg's**, corn, cardboard boxes, and waxed-paper liners are classified as _____.

E19-5 Consider the following selected amounts and account balances of Lords:

Reporting current assets
(Obj. 4)

Cost of goods sold	$104,000	Prepaid expenses	$ 6,000
Direct labor	47,000	Marketing expense	30,000
Direct materials used	20,000	Work in process inventory	40,000
Accounts receivable	80,000	Manufacturing overhead	26,000
Cash	15,000	Finished goods inventory	63,000
Cost of goods manufactured	94,000	Materials inventory	10,000

Show how Lords reports current assets on the balance sheet. Not all data are used. Is Lords a service company, a merchandiser, or a manufacturer? How do you know?

Student ResourceCD
spreadsheet

E19-6 Compute the 20X5 cost of goods manufactured and cost of goods sold for Strike Marine Company using the following amounts: *Computing CGM and CGS* **(Obj. 3, 4)**

	Beginning of Year	End of Year		End of Year
Materials inventory	$25,000	$28,000	Insurance on plant	$ 9,000
Work in process inventory	50,000	35,000	Depreciation—plant building and equipment	13,000
Finished goods inventory	18,000	25,000	Repairs and maintenance—plant	4,000
Purchases of raw materials		78,000	Marketing expenses	77,000
Direct labor		82,000	General and administrative expenses	29,000
Indirect labor		15,000	Income tax expense	23,000

E19-7 Prepare the 20X5 income statement for the Strike Marine Company in Exercise 19-6. Assume that it sold 32,000 units of its product at a price of $12 during 20X5.

Preparing a manufacturer's I/S
(Obj.4)

E19-8 Smooth Sounds manufactures and sells a new line of MP-3 players. Unfortunately, Smooth Sounds suffered serious fire damage at its home office. As a result, the accounting records for October were partially destroyed—and completely jumbled. Smooth Sounds has hired you to help figure out the missing pieces of the accounting puzzle.

Student ResourceCD
spreadsheet

Flow of costs through manufacturing companies
(Obj. 3, 4)

Work in process inventory, October 31	$ 1,500	Accounts payable, October 1	$3,000
Finished goods inventory, October 1	4,300	Direct materials used in October	8,000
Direct labor in October	3,000	Accounts payable, October 31	5,200
Purchases of direct materials in October	9,000	Accounts receivable, October 31	6,500
Work in process inventory, October 1	0	Direct materials inventory, October 31	3,000
Revenues in October	27,000		
Accounts receivable, October 1	2,000	Manufacturing overhead in October	6,300
Gross profit in October	12,000		

(continued on next page)

Required Find the following amounts:

a. Cost of goods sold in October
b. Beginning direct materials inventory
c. Ending finished goods inventory

(*Hint:* You may find Exhibit 19-12 helpful.)

Understanding today's business environment
(Obj. 5)

E19-9 Complete the following statements with one of the terms listed here. You may use a term more than once, and some terms may not be used at all.

E-commerce	Future value	Shift to service economy
ERP	JIT	Throughput time
Expected value	Present	TQM
Future	Present value	

a. To account for uncertainty in the amounts of future costs and benefits, we compute the _____ by multiplying the probability of each outcome by the dollar value of that outcome.
b. To make a cost-benefit decision today, we must find the _____ of the costs and benefits that are incurred in the future.
c. The goal of _____ is to delight customers by providing them with superior products and services by eliminating defects and waste throughout the value chain.
d. Most of the costs of adopting ERP, JIT, expanding into a foreign market, or improving quality are incurred in the _____, but most of the benefits occur in the _____.
e. _____ is the time between buying raw materials and selling the finished products.
f. _____ serves the information needs of people in accounting, as well as people in marketing and in the warehouse.
g. Firms adopt _____ to conduct business on the Internet.

Comparing costs and benefits of adopting JIT
(Obj. 5)

E19-10 Wild Rides manufactures snowboards. Shawn Mobbs, the CEO, is trying to decide whether to adopt just-in-time (JIT). He expects that in present-value terms, adopting JIT would save $97,000 in warehousing expenses and $46,000 in spoilage costs.

Adopting JIT will require several one-time up-front expenditures: (1) $13,500 for an employee training program, (2) $37,000 to streamline the plant's production process, and (3) $8,000 to identify suppliers that will guarantee zero defects and on-time delivery.

Required

1. What are the total costs of adopting JIT?
2. What are the total benefits of adopting JIT?
3. Should Wild Rides adopt JIT? Why or why not?

Making ethical decisions
(Obj. 6)

E19-11 Mary Gonzales is the controller at Automax, a car dealership. Cory Loftus has recently been hired as bookkeeper. Cory wanted to attend a class on Excel spreadsheets, so Mary temporarily took over Cory's duties, including overseeing a fund for topping up a car's gas before a test drive. Mary found a shortage in this fund and confronted Cory when he returned to work. Cory admitted that he occasionally uses this fund to pay for his own gas. Mary estimated that the amount involved is close to $300.

Required

1. What should Mary Gonzales do?
2. Would you change your answer to the previous question if Mary Gonzales was the one recently hired as controller and Cory Loftus was a well-liked longtime employee who indicated that he always eventually repaid the fund?

Problems

(Group A)

Value chain, direct vs. indirect costs, inventoriable costs
(Obj. 2, 3)

P19-1A ShaZam Cola produces a lemon-lime soda. The production process starts with workers mixing the lemon syrup and lime flavors in a secret recipe. The combined syrup is enhanced with caffeine. Finally, the mixture is diluted with carbonated water.

ShaZam Cola incurs the following costs (in thousands):

Plant utilities	$ 750	Production costs of "cents-off"	
Depreciation on plant and		store coupons for customers....	$ 600
equipment	3,000	Delivery-truck drivers' wages	250
Payment for new recipe.............	1,000	Bottles	1,300
Salt..........................	25	Sales commissions..............	400
Replace products with expired dates		Plant janitors' wages...........	1,000
upon customer complaint.........	50	Wages of workers who	
Rearranging plant layout	1,100	mix syrup	8,000
Lemon syrup	18,000	Customer hotline...............	200
Lime flavoring....................	1,000	Depreciation on delivery	
		trucks......................	150
		Freight in.....................	1,500
		Total	$38,325

Required

1. Use the following format to classify each of these costs according to its place in the value chain. (*Hint:* You should have at least one cost in each value-chain function.)

R&D	Design of Products or Processes	Production			Marketing	Distribution	Customer Service
		Direct Materials	Direct Labor	Manufacturing Overhead			

2. Compute the total costs for each value-chain category.
3. How much are the total inventoriable product costs?
4. Suppose the managers of the R&D and design functions receive year-end bonuses based on meeting their own unit's target cost reductions. What are they likely to do? How might this affect costs incurred in other elements of the value chain?

P19-2A *Part One:* In 20X7, Hannah Summit opened Hannah's Pets, a small retail shop selling pet supplies. On December 31, 20X7, her accounting records show the following:

Preparing financial statements for merchandising and manufacturing companies
(Obj. 3, 4)

Inventory on December 31, 20X7	$10,250
Inventory on January 1, 20X7	15,000
Sales revenue..................................	54,000
Utilities for shop..............................	2,450
Rent for shop.................................	4,000
Sales commissions	2,300
Purchases of merchandise.......................	27,000

Required
Prepare an income statement for Hannah's Pets, a merchandiser, for the year ended December 31, 20X7.

(continued on next page)

Part Two: Hannah's Pets succeeded so well that Hannah decided to manufacture her own brand of pet toys—Best Friends. At the end of December 20X8, her accounting records show the following:

Work in process inventory, December 31, 20X8	$ 720	Plant janitorial services	$ 1,250
Finished goods inventory, December 31, 20X7	0	Direct labor	18,300
Finished goods inventory, December 31, 20X8	5,700	Direct material purchases	31,000
Sales revenue	105,000	Rent on manufacturing plant	9,000
Customer service hotline expense	1,000	Direct materials inventory, December 31, 20X7	13,500
Utilities for plant	4,600	Direct materials inventory, December 31, 20X8	9,275
Delivery expense	1,500	Work in process inventory, December 31, 20X7. . . .	0
Sales salaries expense	5,000		

Required

1. Prepare a schedule of cost of goods manufactured for Best Friends Manufacturing for the year ended December 31, 20X8.

2. Prepare an income statement for Best Friends Manufacturing for the year ended December 31, 20X8.

3. How does the format of the income statement for Best Friends Manufacturing differ from the income statement of Hannah's Pets?

Part Three: Show the ending inventories that would appear on these balance sheets:

1. Hannah's Pets at December 31, 20X7.

2. Best Friends Manufacturing at December 31, 20X8.

Preparing financial statements for a manufacturer
(Obj. 4)

P19-3A Certain item descriptions and amounts are missing from the monthly schedule of cost of goods manufactured and the income statement of Tretinik Manufacturing Company. Fill in the missing items.

_____ **Manufacturing Company**

_____ **June 30, 20X6**

Beginning _____			$21,000
Direct _____ :			
Beginning materials inventory	$ X		
Purchases of materials	51,000		
_____	78,000		
Ending materials inventory	(23,000)		
Direct _____		$ X	
Direct _____		X	
Manufacturing overhead.		40,000	
Total _____ costs _____			166,000
Total _____ costs _____			X
Ending _____			(25,000)
_____			$ X

(continued on next page)

_____ Manufacturing Company		
_____ June 30, 20X6		

Sales revenue		$ X
Cost of goods sold:		
Beginning _____	$115,000	
_____	X	
Cost of goods _____	X	
Ending _____	X	
Cost of goods sold		209,000
Gross profit		254,000
_____ expenses:		
Marketing expense	99,000	
Administrative expense	X	154,000
_____ income		$ X

P19-4A As CEO of SeaSpray Marine, Ron Greenwood knows it is important to control costs and to respond quickly to changes in the highly competitive boat-building industry. When IDG Consulting proposes that SeaSpray invest in an ERP system, he forms a team to evaluate the proposal: the plant engineer, the plant foreman, the systems specialist, the human resources director, the marketing director, and the management accountant.

Using cost-benefit analysis to compute the expected value of an ERP installation **(Obj. 5)**

A month later, management accountant Mike Cobalt reports that the team and IDG estimate that if SeaSpray implements the ERP system, it will incur the following costs:

a. $350,000 in software costs
b. $80,000 to customize the ERP software and load SeaSpray's data into the new ERP system
c. $125,000 for employee training

The team estimates that the ERP system should provide several benefits:

a. More-efficient order processing should lead to savings with a present value of $185,000.
b. Streamlining the manufacturing process so that it maps into the ERP system will create savings with a present value of $275,000.
c. Integrating purchasing, production, marketing, and distribution into a single system will allow SeaSpray to reduce inventories, saving $220,000.
d. Higher customer satisfaction should increase sales, which in turn should increase the present value of profits by $150,000.

The team knows that because of complexity, some ERP installations are not successful. If SeaSpray's fails, there will be no cost savings and no additional sales. The team predicts that there is an 80% chance that the ERP installation will succeed and a 20% chance that it will fail.

Required

1. If the ERP installation succeeds, what is the dollar amount of the benefits?
2. Should SeaSpray install the ERP system? Why or why not? Show your calculations.

P19-5A Problem 19-4A asked you to perform a quantitative analysis to help SeaSpray's managers decide whether to install an ERP system. Now consider some qualitative factors.

ERP, expected value **(Obj. 5)**

Required

1. Why did Ron Greenwood create a team to evaluate IDG's proposal? Consider each piece of cost-benefit information that management accountant Mike Cobalt reported. Which person on the team is most likely to have contributed each item? (*Hint:* Which team member is likely to have the most information about each cost or benefit?)

(*continued on next page*)

2. Quantifying ERP benefits can be difficult. After further discussion, the team predicts that there is a 60% chance that the ERP installation will succeed and a 40% chance that it will fail. Should SeaSpray still install the new ERP system?

Using cost-benefit analysis to evaluate an e-commerce project
(Obj. 5)

P19-6A Sun Gas Corporation wants to move its sales-order system to the Web. Under the proposed system, gas stations and other merchants will use a Web browser and, after typing in a password for the Sun Gas Web page, will be able to check the availability and current price of various products and place an order. Currently, customer service representatives take dealers' orders over the phone; they record the information on a paper form, then manually enter it into the firm's computer system.

CFO Carrie Smith believes that dealers will not adopt the new Web system unless Sun Gas provides financial assistance to help them purchase or upgrade their PCs. Smith estimates this one-time cost at $750,000. Sun Gas will also have to invest $150,000 in upgrading its own computer hardware. The cost of the software and the consulting fee for installing the system will be $230,000. The Web system will enable Sun Gas to eliminate 25 clerical positions. Smith estimates that the benefits of the new system's lower labor costs will have a present value of $1,357,000.

Required

Use a cost-benefit analysis to recommend to Carrie Smith whether Sun Gas should proceed with the Web-based ordering system. Give your reasons, showing supporting calculations.

Using cost-benefit analysis to compute the expected value of an e-commerce project
(Obj. 5)

P19-7A Consider the Sun Gas proposed entry into e-commerce in Problem 19-6A. Carrie Smith revises her estimates of the benefits from the new system's lower labor costs. She now thinks there is a 40% chance of receiving the $1,357,000 in benefits and a 60% chance the benefits will only be $933,000.

Required

1. Compute the expected benefits of the Web-based ordering system.
2. Would you recommend Sun Gas accept the proposal?
3. Before Carrie Smith makes a final decision, what other factors should she consider?

Making ethical decisions
(Obj. 6)

P19-8A Kate Royer is the new controller for ED Software, Inc., which develops and sells education software. Shortly before the December 31 fiscal year-end, Matt Adams, the company president, asks Royer how things look for the year-end numbers. He is not happy to learn that earnings growth may be below 15% for the first time in the company's five-year history. Adams explains that financial analysts have again predicted a 15% earnings growth for the company and that he does not intend to disappoint them. He suggests that Royer talk to the assistant controller, who can explain how the previous controller dealt with this situation. The assistant controller suggests the following strategies:

a. Persuade suppliers to postpone billing until January 1.
b. Record as sales certain software awaiting sale that is held in a public warehouse.
c. Delay the year-end closing a few days into January of the next year, so that some of next year's sales are included as this year's sales.
d. Reduce the allowance for bad debts (and bad debts expense), given the company's continued strong performance.
e. Postpone routine monthly maintenance expenditures from December to January.

Which of these suggested strategies are inconsistent with IMA standards? What should Royer do if Adams insists that she follow all of these suggestions?

Problems

(Group B)

P19-1B Suppose Apple Computer reported the following costs last month. (All costs are in millions.)

(continued on next page)

Payment to UPS for delivering PCs to customers	$ 300
Cost of hard drives used	4,700
Cost of Internet banner ads	650
Plant janitors' wages	10
Wages of workers who assemble the PCs	1,500
Cost of customer hotline for troubleshooting problems	40
Wages of forklift drivers on the plant floor	25
Plant utilities	35
Cost of software loaded on computers	30
Depreciation on plant and equipment	300
Salaries of scientists working on next generation laptops	45
Insurance and taxes on plant property	40
Cost of oil used for conveyor belt and other plant equipment	5
Payment to engineers redesigning the exterior case	20
Wages of sales associates taking phone orders	50
Cost of circuit boards used	5,500
Total	$13,250

Value chain, direct vs. indirect costs, inventoriable costs
(Obj. 2, 3)

Required

1. Use the following format to classify each of these costs according to its place in the value chain. (*Hint:* You should have at least one cost in each value-chain function.)

R&D	Design of Products or Processes	Production			Marketing	Distribution	Customer Service
		Direct Materials	Direct Labor	Manufacturing Overhead			

2. Compute the total costs for each category.
3. How much are the total inventoriable product costs?
4. Suppose the managers of the R&D and design departments receive year-end bonuses based on meeting their own department's target cost reductions. What are they likely to do? How might this affect costs incurred in other elements of the value chain?

P19-2B *Part One:* On January 1, 2005, Terri Shaw opened Precious Memories, a small retail store dedicated to selling picture frames, crafts, and art. On December 31, 2005, her accounting records show the following:

Preparing financial statements for merchandising and manufacturing companies
(Obj. 3, 4)

Store rent	$7,000	Sales revenue	$90,000
Sales salaries	4,500	Store utilities	1,950
Freight in	550	Purchases of merchandise	36,000
Inventory on December 31, 2005	8,750	Inventory on January 1, 2005	12,700
		Advertising expense	2,300

(continued on next page)

Required

Prepare an income statement for Precious Memories, a merchandiser, for the year ended December 31, 20X5.

Part Two: Precious Memories succeeded so well that Terri Shaw decided to manufacture her own special brand of picture frames, to be called Forever. At the end of December 20X7, her accounting records show the following:

Finished goods inventory, December 31, 20X7	$ 2,000	Rent on plant	$ 11,000
Work in process inventory, December 31, 20X7	1,750	Finished goods inventory, December 31, 20X6	0
Direct materials inventory, December 31, 20X7	7,750	Depreciation expense on delivery truck	2,500
R&D for graphic designs	3,700	Depreciation expense on plant	
Sales commissions	4,000	equipment	3,500
Utilities for plant	2,000	Work in process inventory, December 31, 20X6	0
Plant janitorial services	750	Sales revenue	126,450
Direct labor	20,000	Customer warranty refunds	1,500
Direct material purchases	32,000	Direct materials inventory, December 31, 20X6	13,000

Required

1. Prepare a schedule of cost of goods manufactured for Forever Manufacturing, for the year ended December 31, 20X7.
2. Prepare an income statement for Forever Manufacturing, for the year ended December 31, 20X7.
3. How does the format of the income statement for Forever Manufacturing differ from the income statement of Precious Memories?

Part Three: Show the ending inventories that would appear on these balance sheets:

1. Precious Memories at December 31, 2005.
2. Forever Manufacturing at December 31, 20X7.

Preparing financial statements for a manufacturer
(Obj. 4)

P19-3B Certain item descriptions and amounts are missing from the monthly schedule of cost of goods manufactured and income statement of Pacific Manufacturing Company. Fill in the missing items in the financial statement here and at the top of the next page.

_____ **Manufacturing Company**		
_____ **April 30, 20X6**		
_____ work in process inventory		$ 15,000
Direct materials used:		
_____ materials _____	$ X	
_____ of materials	65,000	
_____	75,000	
_____ materials _____	(23,000)	
Direct _____		$ X
Direct _____		68,000
Manufacturing overhead		X
Total _____ costs _____		X
Total _____ costs _____		175,000
_____ work in process inventory		X
_____		$150,000

_____ **Manufacturing Company**		
_____ **April 30, 20X6**		
_____ revenue		$450,000
_____:		
Beginning _____	$ X	
_____	X	
Cost of goods _____	X	
Ending _____	(67,000)	
Cost of goods sold.........................		X
_____		243,000
_____ expenses:		
Marketing expenses	X	
Administrative expenses	$64,000	X
_____		$ 76,000

P19-4B CRM, Inc., manufactures computer disk drives. It sells these disk drives to other manufacturers, which use them in assembling computers. CRM is having trouble with its new DVD drive. About half the time, CRM employees find defects while the disk drive is still on the production line. These drives are immediately reworked in the plant. Otherwise, CRM's customers do not identify the problem until they install the disk drives they've purchased. Customers return defective drives for replacement under warranty, and they have also complained that after they install the disk drive, the drive's connector (which plugs into the computer system board) often shakes loose while the computer is being assembled. The customer must then reassemble the computer after fixing the loose connection.

Using cost-benefit analysis to compute the expected value of a TQM program **(Obj. 5)**

CRM CEO Jay Rich has just returned from a seminar on total quality management (TQM). He forms a team to address these quality problems. The team includes the plant engineer, the production foreman, a customer service representative, the marketing director, and the management accountant.

Three months later, the team proposes a major project to *prevent* these quality problems. CRM's accountant Anna Crowe reports that implementing the team's proposal will require CRM to incur the following costs over the next three months:

- $180,500 for CRM scientists to develop a completely new disk drive.
- $70,000 for company engineers to redesign the connector so that it better tolerates rough treatment.

The project team is unsure whether this investment will pay off. If the effort fixes the problem, Crowe expects that

- A reputation for higher quality will increase sales, which in turn will increase the present value of profits by $200,000.
- Fewer disk drives will fail. The present value of the savings from fewer warranty repairs is $170,300.
- The plant will have fewer defective disk drives to rework. The present value of this savings is $100,200.

However, if this project is not successful, there will be no cost savings and no additional sales. The team predicts a 70% chance that the project will succeed and a 30% chance that it will fail.

Required
1. If the quality improvement project succeeds, what is the dollar amount of the benefits?
2. Should CRM undertake this project? Why or why not? Show supporting calculations.

Value chain, TQM
(Obj. 2, 5)

P19-5B Problem 19-4B asked you to perform a *quantitative* analysis to help CRM's managers decide whether to embark on the project. Now consider some *qualitative* factors in CRM's quality improvement project.

Required

1. Why did Jay Rich create a team to address this quality problem, rather than assigning the task to one person? Consider each piece of cost/benefit information reported by management accountant Anna Crowe. Which person on the team is most likely to have contributed each item? (*Hint:* Which team member is likely to have the most information about each cost or benefit?)
2. Classify the following amounts into one of the six value-chain business functions.
   a. $180,500 cost to develop the new disk drive
   b. $70,000 cost to redesign the connector
   c. $170,300 for warranty repairs on disk drives
   d. $100,200 to rework disk drives identified as defective while still in the factory
3. This problem illustrates how CRM can make trade-offs across business functions in the value chain. Which of the six value-chain functions are involved in the trade-offs proposed by the quality improvement team? What specific trade-offs do they propose?

Using cost-benefit analysis to evaluate an e-commerce project
(Obj. 5)

P19-6B Smart Bank processes checks for smaller banks and insurance companies. When a customer complains that a check was not deposited to its account, a Smart Bank clerk takes the complaint over the phone and fills out a paper form. The complaint form triggers a long search through piles of canceled checks in a warehouse to find the check in question. Smart Bank then compares this check to its computer and paper records.

Smart Bank is considering moving this process to the Web. When a customer has a question, an employee simply uses a Web browser and a password to access Smart Bank's databases. The customer's employee pulls up a computerized image of the check in question to verify the amount and then queries Smart Bank's databases to locate the mistake. If required, a credit to the customer's account can be issued immediately.

The Web-based system will require the bank to invest $83,000 in a new server and check-scanning equipment. eNow! consultants will charge $110,000 for the software and consulting fees to get the system running. The system will also require increasing the bank's Internet capacity. The present value of this cost is $20,000.

Smart Bank has identified two benefits of this project. First, several bank clerks freed from searching through stacks of canceled checks will be reassigned, which will lead to cost savings with a present value of $173,000. Second, the new system's additional capacity will enable Smart Bank to accept more check-processing business, which should lead to additional profits with a present value of $43,200.

Required

Does a cost-benefit analysis justify the Web-based system? Explain why, showing supporting calculations.

Using cost-benefit analysis to compute the expected value of an e-commerce project
(Obj. 5)

P19-7B Consider the Smart Bank project described in Problem 19-6B. Smart Bank has revised its estimates of additional profits the bank is likely to earn. There is an 80% chance that the bank will earn $43,200 in extra profits, but also a 20% chance the bank will earn $75,000.

Required

1. Compute the expected value of the benefits from the additional business.
2. Would you recommend that Smart Bank accept the proposal? Give your reason, showing supporting calculations.
3. Are there other potential benefits not listed in Problems 19-6B or 19-7B that may make the proposal more attractive to Smart Bank?

PI9-8B Kara Williams is the new controller for Colors, a designer and manufacturer of sportswear. Shortly before the December 31 fiscal year-end, Lashea Lucas (the company president) asks Kara how things look for the year-end numbers. Lashea is not happy to learn that earnings growth may be below 10% for the first time in the company's five-year history. Lashea explains that financial analysts have again predicted a 12% earnings growth for the company and that she does not intend to disappoint them. She suggests that Kara talk to the assistant controller, who can explain how the previous controller dealt with this situation. The assistant controller suggests the following strategies:

Making ethical decisions
(Obj. 6)

a. Postpone planned advertising expenditures from December to January.
b. Do not record sales returns and allowances on the basis that they are individually immaterial.
c. Persuade retail customers to accelerate January orders to December.
d. Reduce the allowance for bad debts, given the company's continued strong performance.
e. Colors ships finished goods to public warehouses across the country for temporary storage, until it receives firm orders from customers. As Colors receives orders, it directs the warehouse to ship the goods to the nearby customer. The assistant controller suggests recording goods sent to the public warehouses as sales.

Which of these suggested strategies are inconsistent with IMA standards? What should Kara Williams do if Lashea Lucas insists that she follow all of these suggestions?

●APPLY *Your Knowledge*

Decision Cases

Case I. PowerBox, Inc., designs and manufactures switches used in telecommunications. Serious flooding throughout North Carolina affected PowerBox's facilities. Inventory was completely ruined, and the company's computer system, including all accounting records, was destroyed.

Working backward, using the flow of costs through manufacturing companies to file an insurance claim
(Obj. 4)

Before the disaster recovery specialists clean the buildings, Annette Plum, the company controller, is anxious to salvage whatever records she can to support an insurance claim for the destroyed inventory. She is standing in what is left of the accounting department with Paul Lopez, the cost accountant.

"I didn't know mud could smell so bad," Paul says. "What should I be looking for?"

"Don't worry about beginning inventory numbers," responds Annette, "we'll get them from last year's annual report. We need first-quarter cost data."

"I was working on the first-quarter results just before the storm hit," Paul says. "Look, my report's still in my desk drawer. But all I can make out is that for the first quarter, material purchases were $476,000 and that direct labor, manufacturing overhead, and total manufacturing costs to account for were $505,000, $245,000, and $1,425,000, respectively. Wait, and cost of goods available for sale was $1,340,000."

"Great," says Annette. "I remember that sales for the period were approximately $1.7 million. Given our gross profit of 30%, that's all you should need."

Paul is not sure about that, but decides to see what he can do with this information. The beginning inventory numbers are

- Direct materials, $113,000
- Work in process, $229,000
- Finished goods, $154,000

He remembers a schedule he learned in college that may help him get started.

(continued on next page)

Required

1. Exhibit 19-12 resembles the schedule Paul has in mind. Use it to determine the ending inventories of direct materials, work in process, and finished goods.

2. Draft an insurance claim letter for the controller, seeking reimbursement for the flood damage to inventory. PowerBox's insurance representative is Gary Streer, at Industrial Insurance Co., 1122 Main Street, Hartford, CT 06268. The policy number is #3454340-23. PowerBox's address is 5 Research Triangle Way, Raleigh, NC 27698.

Applying ethical standards in daily life
(Obj. 6)

Case 2. The IMA's *Standards of Ethical Conduct for Management Accountants* can be applied to more than just management accounting. They are also relevant to college students. Explain at least one situation that shows how each IMA standard in Exhibit 19-14 is relevant to your experiences as a student. For example, the ethical standard of competence would suggest not cutting classes!

Ethical Issue

Making ethical decisions
(Obj. 6)

← *Link Back to Chapter 8.* Ricardo Valencia recently resigned his position as controller for Tom White Automotive, a small, struggling foreign car dealer in Austin, Texas. Ricardo has just started a new job as controller for Mueller Imports, a much larger dealer for the same car manufacturer. Demand for this particular make of car is exploding, and the manufacturer cannot produce enough to satisfy demand. The manufacturer's regional sales managers are each given a certain number of cars. Each sales manager then decides how to divide the cars among the independently owned dealerships in the region. Because most dealerships can sell every car they receive, the key is getting a large number of cars from the manufacturer's regional sales manager.

Ricardo's former employer, White Automotive, received only about 25 cars a month. Consequently, the dealership was not very profitable.

Ricardo is surprised to learn that his new employer, Mueller Imports, receives over 200 cars a month. Ricardo soon gets another surprise. Every couple of months, a local jeweler bills the dealer $5,000 for "miscellaneous services." Franz Mueller, the owner of the dealership, personally approves payment of these invoices, noting that each invoice is a "selling expense." From casual conversations with a salesperson, Ricardo learns that Mueller frequently gives Rolex watches to the manufacturer's regional sales manager and other sales executives. Before talking to anyone about this, Ricardo decides to work through his ethical dilemma using the framework from Chapter 8. Put yourself in Ricardo's place and complete the framework.

1. What is the ethical issue?

2. What are my options?

3. What are the possible consequences?

4. What shall I do?

Financial Statement Case

Identifying type of company and its cost objects, and analyzing its response to time-based competition
(Obj. 3, 5)

To help determine whether current profits will continue and grow in the future, investors need information on management's plans. Investors are especially interested in how management plans to compete in today's business environment. Let's use **Amazon.com's** annual report to consider the company's operations and management's plans. To answer the following questions, refer to the CEO's letter to shareholders in the company's 2002 annual report, the financial statements, and the notes to the financial statements.

Required

1. Is Amazon.com a service company, a merchandiser, or a manufacturer? What financial statement information supports your answer? What information outside the financial statements supports your answer?

(continued on next page)

2. What costs would Amazon.com classify as inventoriable?

3. Use notes 1 and 15 to the financial statements to identify some of the company's cost objects.

4. Does Amazon.com's management see time-based competition as critical to the company's success? What specific steps is it taking to meet this challenge? Identify an example of how Amazon.com uses advanced information systems, e-commerce, and JIT management to engage in time-based competition. (*Hint:* see the CEOs letter to shareholders.)

Team Project

Search the Internet for a nearby company that also has a Web page. Arrange an interview with a management accountant, a controller, or other accounting/finance officer of the company. Before you conduct the interview, answer the following questions:

Investigating management accounting, e-commerce, and information systems in the real world
(Obj. 1, 5)

1. Is this a service, merchandising, or manufacturing company? What is its primary product or service?

2. Is the primary purpose of the company's Web site to provide information about the company and its products, to sell online, or to provide financial information for investors?

3. Are parts of the company's Web site restricted so that you need password authorization to enter? What appears to be the purpose of limiting access?

4. Does the Web site provide an e-mail link for contacting the company?

At the interview, begin by clarifying your answers to questions 1 through 4, and ask the following additional questions:

5. If the company sells over the Web, what benefits has the company derived? Did the company perform a cost-benefit analysis before deciding to begin Web sales?

Or

If the company does not sell over the Web, why not? Has the company performed a cost-benefit analysis and decided not to sell over the Web?

6. What is the biggest cost of operating the Web site?

7. Does the company make any purchases over the Internet? What percentage?

8. How has e-commerce affected the company's management accounting system? Have the management accountant's responsibilities become more or less complex? More or less interesting?

9. Does the company use Web-based accounting applications, such as accounts receivable or accounts payable?

10. Does the company use an ERP system? If so, do they view the system as a success? What have been the benefits? The costs?

Prepare a report describing the results of your interview.

For an Internet Exercise, go to the Web site www.prenhall.com/horngren.

CHAPTER 20

Job Costing

TIPS CHECK YOUR RESOURCES

- Visit the www.prenhall.com/horngren **Web site** for self-study quizzes, video clips, other resources
- Try the **Quick Check** exercise at end of chapter to test your knowledge
- Learn the **key terms**
- Do the **Starter** exercises keyed in the margins
- Work the **mid-** and **end-of-chapter summary problems**
- Use the **Concept Links** to review material in other chapters
- Search the **CD** for review materials by chapter or by key word
- Watch the **tutorial videos** to review key concepts
- Watch the **On Location Dell Computer** video to see how Dell handles job costing

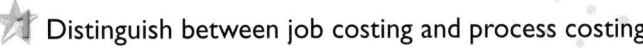

LEARNING OBJECTIVES

⭐ 1 Distinguish between job costing and process costing

⭐ 2 Trace materials and labor in a manufacturer's job costing system

⭐ 3 Allocate manufacturing overhead in a manufacturer's job costing system

⭐ 4 Account for completion and sales of finished goods and adjust for under- or overallocated manufacturing overhead

⭐ 5 Assign noninventoriable costs in job costing

Despite intense competition in the technology sector, Dell Computer continues to gain market share and increase profits while rivals like IBM struggle. How does Dell do it? Cutting costs is one way. Using management accounting information to decide how to cut costs gives Dell a 10% to 15% cost advantage over its competitors.

To pinpoint cost-cutting opportunities, Dell first figures out how much it costs to assemble a computer. Dell's workers build each computer to a specific customer order, which is called a *job*. Dell's *job costing* system traces direct materials (such as CD-ROMs and hard drives) and direct labor (such as assembly-line labor) to each job. Then Dell allocates indirect manufacturing overhead costs (such as depreciation on the plant) to each job. The sum of the job's direct materials, direct labor, and overhead is its total manufacturing cost.

Dell Computer

Dell compiles this cost information for each product into a *cost package* spreadsheet that is available online to all Dell managers. Managers throughout the company need to know how much it costs to assemble desktops, laptops, and servers to make vital business decisions, such as:

- Identifying opportunities to cut costs of different products

- Setting selling prices that will lead to profits for each product

- Determining which products are the most profitable, and therefore, deserve the most sales emphasis

They also need costs to prepare Dell's financial statements:

- Cost of goods manufactured and cost of goods sold for the income statement

- Inventory for the balance sheet

Sources: Lohr, S. "Dell's Results Match Those of a Year Ago," *The New York Times*, May 17, 2002, p. C5; McWilliams, G. "Lean Machine: How Dell Fine-Tunes Its PC Pricing to Gain Edge in Slow Market," *The Wall Street Journal*, June 8, 2001, p. A1; and McWilliams, G. "Mimicking Dell, Compaq to Sell Its PCs Directly," *The Wall Street Journal*, November 11, 1998, p. B1.

Sitemap

- **Full Product Costs**

- **Costing a Product**

- **Accounting for Materials and Labor**

- **Allocating Manufacturing Overhead**

- **Accounting for Finished Goods**

- **Assigning Noninventoriable Costs**

- **Full Product Costs**
  - ☐ Costing a Product
  - ☐ Accounting for Materials and Labor
  - ☐ Allocating Manufacturing Overhead
  - ☐ Accounting for Finished Goods
  - ☐ Assigning Noninventoriable Costs

For a review of the value chain, see ➡ *Chapter 19.*

Student Resource CD

inventoriable product costs, noninventoriable product costs

The Dell story shows why you need to know how much it costs to produce a product, whether you plan a career in marketing, engineering, production, general management, or finance. Dell's marketing team needs to know how much it costs to assemble a computer to set the selling price high enough to cover costs. Engineers study the materials, labor, and overhead that go into each computer to pinpoint new cost-cutting opportunities. Production managers who know how much it costs to assemble a motherboard can decide whether it is more profitable for Dell to assemble motherboards itself or to *outsource* (or buy) them from a supplier. General managers who know Dell's cost to make desktops, laptops, and servers can identify the most profitable products and guide marketing to boost sales of those products. And the finance department uses product costs to figure the cost of goods sold and inventory for the financial statements.

Because it is so important for managers in all areas of the business to know how much it costs to make each product, in this chapter and the next we show you how to figure these costs.

Full Product Costs: A Brief Overview

First, though, let's review some key points about product costs. In Chapter 19, you learned that managers make certain decisions (like setting sale prices) based on *full product costs* from all elements of the value chain: R&D, design, production, marketing, distribution, and customer service.

Recall that full product costs have two components: inventoriable product costs and period costs (also called noninventoriable costs). Inventoriable product costs are from the third element of the value chain in Exhibit 20-1: production for manufacturers and purchases for merchandisers. ⬅ They are called inventoriable costs because in addition to serving as one of the six building blocks for computing full product costs, these are the costs GAAP requires companies to use in computing inventory and cost of goods sold for the balance sheet and income statement. Most of Chapter 20 focuses on how companies determine these inventoriable product costs. The chapter concludes with a discussion of assigning noninventoriable costs (period costs from the other five elements of the value chain) to products and services. By adding noninventoriable costs to inventoriable costs, managers can build up full product costs to make their internal decisions.

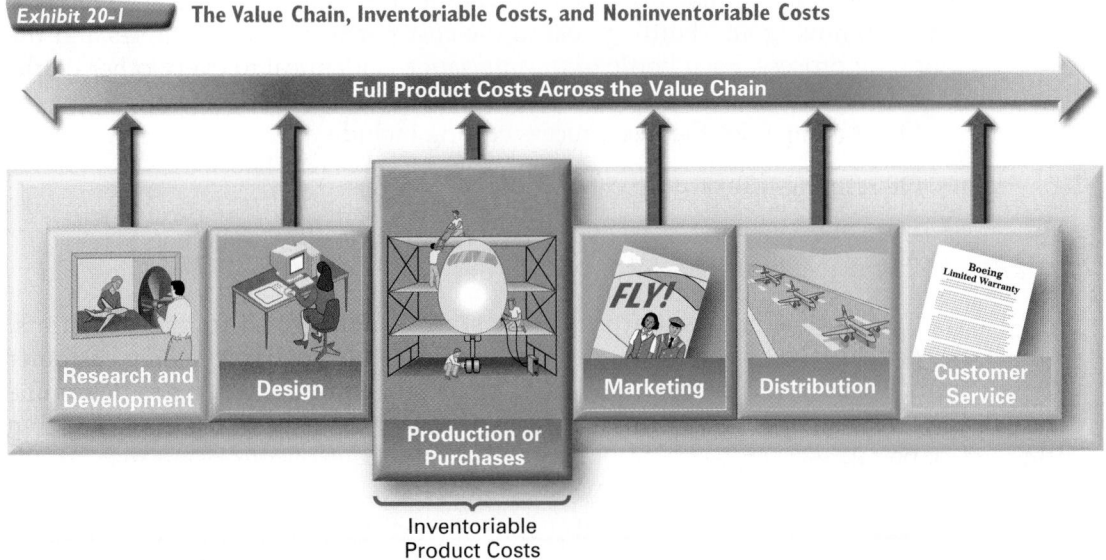

Exhibit 20-1 The Value Chain, Inventoriable Costs, and Noninventoriable Costs

With this big picture in mind, let's see how companies like Dell, Boeing, and Kellogg's figure the costs of making computers, airplanes, and cornflakes.

How Much Does It Cost to Make a Product? Two Approaches

Dell traces the cost of direct materials like hard drives to the computers in which they are installed. But indirect costs such as depreciation on the plant cannot be traced directly to an individual computer because Dell cannot determine exactly how much depreciation a particular computer "caused." → The existence of these indirect costs means that we cannot determine the precise cost of a specific product. Instead, companies use one of two product costing systems that *average* costs across products:

- Process costing
- Job costing

As the name suggests, *process costing* focuses on accumulating costs for each production process. *Job costing* accumulates costs for each individual job. Let's see how each works.

Process Costing

Process costing is used by companies that produce large numbers of identical units in a continuous fashion through a series of uniform production steps or processes. For example, Pace Foods uses two processes to make picante sauce: (1) chopping vegetables and (2) mixing and bottling. Pace separately accumulates the costs for each of the two processes. Next, the company averages the costs of the chopping process over all units passing through the process. Then it averages the costs of the mixing and bottling process over all units passing

☐ Full Product Costs
■ Costing a Product
☐ Accounting for Materials and Labor
☐ Allocating Manufacturing Overhead
☐ Accounting for Finished Goods
☐ Assigning Noninventoriable Costs

← We discussed direct and indirect costs in Chapter 19.

Student Resource CD
job costing, process costing

Distinguish between job costing and process costing

process costing
System for assigning costs to large numbers of identical units that usually proceed in a continuous fashion through a series of uniform production steps or processes.

through that process. If Pace spent $50,000 to mix and bottle 100,000 bottles of picante sauce, the mixing and bottling cost per bottle would be

$$\text{Cost per bottle of mixing and bottling picante sauce} = \frac{\$50,000}{100,000 \text{ bottles}} = \$0.50$$

✔ **Starter 20-1**

To get the total manufacturing cost of a bottle of picante sauce, Pace would add the $0.50 mixing and bottling cost to the cost per bottle of vegetables and the chopping process. Each bottle of picante sauce is identical to every other bottle, so each bears the same average cost.

Other companies that use process costing include:

- Oil refining—Texaco
- Food and beverages—Kellogg's
- Pharmaceuticals—Bayer

Exhibit 20-2 shows that process costing is not limited to manufacturers. Service companies like banks use it to determine the cost of processing customer transactions. Merchandisers such as granaries use process costing to determine the storage cost for each bushel of grain. We consider process costing in detail in Chapter 21.

Exhibit 20-2

Job and Process Costing in Service, Merchandising, and Manufacturing Companies

	Service	Merchandising	Manufacturing
Job Costing	Law firms (cases) Health care (diagnoses, procedures, or patients) Public relations (campaigns)	E-Tailers such as Amazon.com Mail-order catalog companies such as L.L. Bean	Commercial building construction Custom furniture Aircraft manufacturers
Process Costing	Banks (processing customer deposit transactions)	Granaries (distribute tons of identical grains)	Paper mills Mining operations Textile mills

Job Costing

job costing
System for assigning costs to a specific unit or to a small batch of products or services that (1) pass through production steps as a distinct identifiable job and (2) can vary considerably in materials, labor, and overhead costs.

Job costing assigns costs to a specific unit or to a small batch of products or services that passes through production steps as a distinct identifiable job. Different jobs can vary considerably in materials, labor, and overhead costs, so job costing accumulates costs separately for each individual job. We focus on job costing in this chapter.

Job costing is common in industries that produce goods to meet customer specifications. Dell Computer's assembly process is one example. Another is contract manufacturing, in which manufacturing plants (often in Mexico and Asia) produce electronic goods for a variety of customers, including Cisco Systems, HP, and Sony. For example, Singapore-based Flextronics International makes X-box game consoles for Microsoft, cell phones for Sony-Ericsson and Siemens, and printers for HP and Epson. Clearly, Flextronics must carefully track the costs of each of these separate jobs.

Job costing is not confined to manufacturers. Exhibit 20-2 shows that service organizations such as hospitals and physicians also use job costing. A hospital might consider each medical procedure a different job, while a doctor considers each individual patient a job. Architects, accountants, and attorneys use job costing to determine the cost of jobs for individual clients. Merchandisers like Amazon.com use job costing to determine the cost of meeting each customer order.

Companies use job costing when different jobs vary widely in:

- The resources and time required
- The complexity of the production process

Because the jobs are so different, it would not be reasonable to assign them equal costs. It is worth the trouble to compile the costs for each job.

Exhibit 20-3 summarizes key differences between job and process costing.

	Job Costing	Process Costing
Cost object	Job	Process
Outputs	Single units or small batches, with large differences between jobs	Large quantities of identical units
Extent of averaging	Less averaging—costs are averaged over the small number of units in a batch (often 1 unit)	More averaging—costs are averaged over the many identical units in the large batch

Exhibit 20-3

Differences Between Job and Process Costing

HOW JOB COSTS FLOW THROUGH THE ACCOUNTS: AN OVERVIEW
Let's consider how a manufacturer, E-Z-Boy Furniture, uses job costing. For E-Z-Boy, each customer order is a separate job. E-Z-Boy uses a **job cost record** to accumulate the direct materials, direct labor, and manufacturing overhead costs assigned to each individual job. The company starts the job cost record when work begins on the job.

As E-Z-Boy incurs costs for the job, it adds them to the job cost record. For jobs that the company has started but not yet finished, the job cost records form the subsidiary ledger for the general ledger account Work in Process Inventory. →

When E-Z-Boy finishes the job, it totals the costs and transfers them out of Work in Process Inventory and into Finished Goods Inventory.

When the job's units are sold, E-Z-Boy's job costing system moves the costs of the job out of Finished Goods Inventory and into Cost of Goods Sold. Exhibit 20-4 summarizes how the costs of the jobs flow from Work in Process Inventory into Finished Goods Inventory and finally into Cost of Goods Sold.

job cost record
Document that accumulates the direct materials, direct labor, and manufacturing overhead costs assigned to each individual job.

← *For a review of ledgers and subsidiary ledgers, see Chapter 7.*

Exhibit 20-4   Flow of Costs Through the Accounts in a Job Costing System

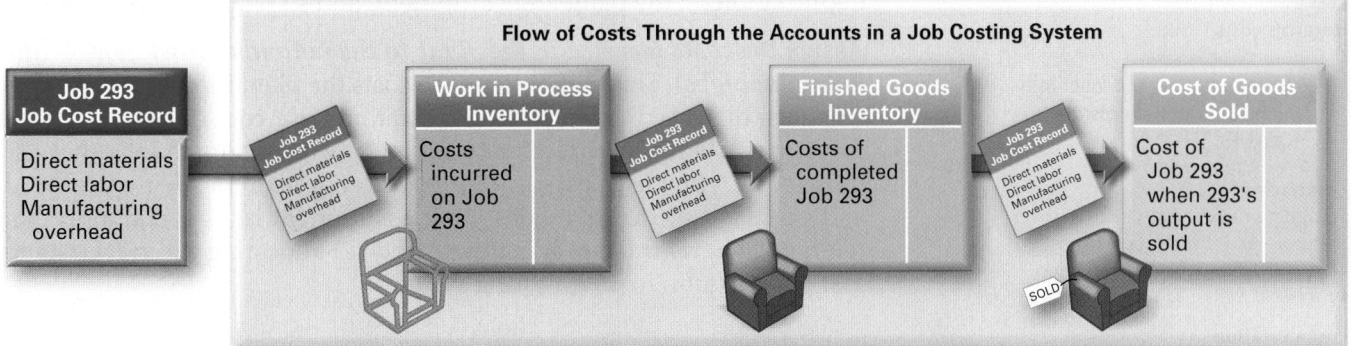

INFORMATION FOR E-Z-BOY JOB COSTING ILLUSTRATION
Let's look at E-Z-Boy's job costing system in more detail. We'll see how E-Z-Boy:

✔ **Starter 20-2**

1. *Accumulates* total direct material costs, direct labor costs, and manufacturing overhead costs incurred during the period for all jobs.
2. *Assigns* appropriate amounts of these costs to individual jobs.

On December 31, 20X8, E-Z-Boy reports the following inventories:

Materials inventory (many kinds)	$20,000
Work in process inventory (5 jobs)	29,000
Finished goods inventory (unsold recliners from 2 completed jobs) . . .	12,000

The following data summarize transactions for 20X9. We will explain the accounting for these transactions, step by step. (For simplicity, we will show summary journal entries for the entire year 20X9. In practice, however, companies record these transactions much more frequently.)

1. Materials purchased on account.	$320,000
2. Direct materials used for manufacturing	285,000
Indirect materials used for manufacturing.	40,000
3. Manufacturing wages incurred	335,000
4. Direct labor on jobs.	250,000
Indirect labor to support manufacturing	85,000
5. Depreciation on plant and equipment.	50,000
6. Plant utilities	20,000
7. Plant insurance	5,000
8. Property taxes—plant	10,000
9. Manufacturing overhead allocated to jobs	200,000
10. Cost of goods manufactured.	740,000
11. Sales on account	996,000
Cost of goods sold.	734,000

Student Resource**CD**

cost assignment, labor costs, materials costs

Trace materials and labor in a manufacturer's job costing system

cost tracing
Assigning direct costs (such as direct materials and direct labor) to cost objects (such as jobs or production processes) that used those costs.

cost allocation
Assigning indirect costs (such as manufacturing overhead) to cost objects (such as jobs or production processes).

cost assignment
A general term that refers to both tracing direct costs and allocating indirect costs to cost objects.

Job Costing: Accounting for Materials and Labor

Managers want to know the costs incurred in each job. There are two steps to obtaining this information.

STEP 1 *Accumulate the costs the plant incurred for all jobs.* Accumulate total purchases of materials, labor, and overhead items such as utilities, depreciation on the plant and equipment, and so on.

STEP 2 *Assign the costs incurred in the plant to the individual cost objects (the individual jobs).* This step assigns the costs the plant incurred to the specific jobs that used those costs. Accountants use **cost tracing** to assign direct costs (such as direct material and direct labor) to jobs that *use* those costs. They use **cost allocation** to assign manufacturing overhead and other indirect costs to jobs. **Cost assignment** is a general term that refers to *both* (1) tracing direct costs and (2) allocating indirect costs to cost objects (jobs, in a job costing system).

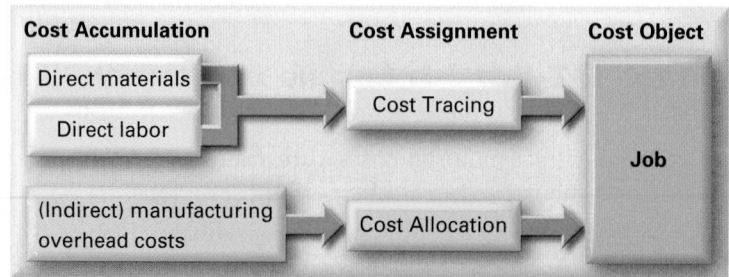

Accounting for Materials

PURCHASING MATERIALS   The job costing system *accumulates* the total material costs and then *traces* or *assigns* the costs to each individual job based on its usage of the materials. We begin by making the journal entry to *accumulate* the costs of all the materials E-Z-Boy purchased (data from page 802):

(1) Materials Inventory................... 320,000
         Accounts Payable .... | 320,000

Entry (1) is similar to the way a merchandiser like Amazon.com records purchases (under the perpetual method). The entry *accumulates* materials costs but does not *assign* them. E-Z-Boy cannot assign the costs to specific jobs until it *uses* the materials on those jobs.

Materials Inventory is a general ledger account. The subsidiary materials ledger includes a separate record for each type of material. The lumber record in Exhibit 20-5 shows that E-Z-Boy received 20 units of lumber at $9 each on July 23.

Exhibit 20-5

Subsidary Materials Ledger Record

SUBSIDIARY MATERIALS LEDGER RECORD   E-Z-Boy

Item No. B–220   Description Lumber / Recliner chairs

	Received			Used				Balance		
Date	Units	Cost	Total Cost	Mat. Req. No.	Units	Cost	Total Cost	Units	Cost	Total Cost
20X9										
7–20								30	$9.00	$270
7–23	20	$9.00	$180					50	9.00	450
7–24				334	10	$9.00	$90	40	9.00	360

Exhibit 20-6 shows the Materials Inventory general ledger account and the subsidiary ledger for all the materials E-Z-Boy uses. The balance of Materials Inventory in the general ledger ($1,170) equals the sum of the balances in the subsidiary materials ledger.

Exhibit 20-6   Materials Inventory Subsidary Ledger and General Ledger

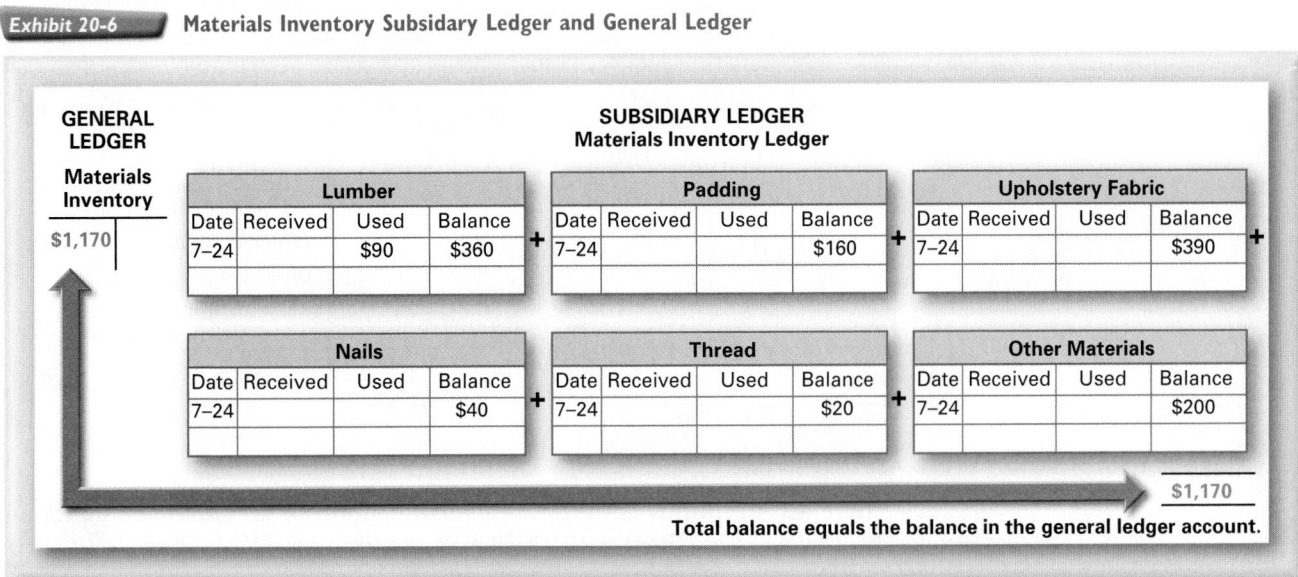

GENERAL LEDGER | SUBSIDIARY LEDGER — Materials Inventory Ledger

Materials Inventory $1,170

Lumber

Date	Received	Used	Balance
7–24		$90	$360

Padding

Date	Received	Used	Balance
7–24			$160

Upholstery Fabric

Date	Received	Used	Balance
7–24			$390

Nails

Date	Received	Used	Balance
7–24			$40

Thread

Date	Received	Used	Balance
7–24			$20

Other Materials

Date	Received	Used	Balance
7–24			$200

$1,170

Total balance equals the balance in the general ledger account.

materials requisition
Request for the transfer of materials to the production floor, prepared by the production team.

USING MATERIALS   Now that you've seen how to *accumulate* the total cost of all the direct and indirect materials that E-Z-Boy purchased, let's see how to *assign* the cost of the materials E-Z-Boy actually used. For both direct and indirect materials, the production team completes a **materials requisition** to request the transfer of materials to the production floor so work can begin. Exhibit 20-7 shows E-Z-Boy's materials requisition for the 10 units of lumber needed to make 10 recliner chairs for Job 293.

Exhibit 20-7

Materials Requisition

MATERIALS REQUISITION NO. _334_

E-Z-Boy

Date _7–24–X9_

Job No. _293_

Item no.	Item	Quantity	Unit cost	Amount
B – 220	Lumber / Recliner Chairs	10	$9.00	$90

To assign, or trace, the cost of the direct material (lumber) to Job 293, Exhibit 20-8 shows how E-Z-Boy posts the costs of lumber used from the materials requisition to the "Direct Materials" section of the job cost record for Job 293. Follow the $90 cost of the lumber from the materials inventory subsidiary ledger record (Exhibit 20-5), to the materials requisition (Exhibit 20-7), to the job cost record in Exhibit 20-8. Of course, all the dollar amounts in these exhibits show E-Z-Boy's *costs*—not the prices at which E-Z-Boy sells its products.

Exhibit 20-8

Direct Materials Entry on Job Cost Record

JOB COST RECORD

E-Z-Boy

Job No. _293_
Customer Name and Address _Macy's New York City_
Job Description _10 Recliner Chairs_

Date Promised		7–31	Date Started	7–24	Date Completed		
	Direct Materials		Direct Labor		Manufacturing Overhead Allocated		
Date	Requisition Numbers	Amount	Labor Time Record Numbers	Amount	Date	Rate	Amount
7–24	334	$90					
					Overall Cost Summary		
					Direct Materials.................$		
					Direct Labor		
					Manufacturing Overhead Allocated...................		
Totals					Total Job Cost ....$		

Technology simplifies both the *accumulation* and the *assignment* of materials costs. As explained in Chapter 19, Dell creates specialized Web pages for each of its key suppliers. Suppliers use these pages, which contain information on Dell's production schedule, to decide how much material to deliver to Dell's production floor. Upon receipt of the materials, Dell's information system can trigger the *accumulation* of material costs. Dell's workers then scan electronic bar codes on materials to *assign* individual computers the cost of materials such as hard drives and CD-ROMs as they are installed.

DIRECT AND INDIRECT MATERIALS   Journal entry (1) debited Materials Inventory for the costs of all materials E-Z-Boy purchased—whether direct or indirect. Thus, when E-Z-Boy *uses* materials (whether direct or indirect), it credits Materials Inventory.

But what account does E-Z-Boy debit? The answer depends on the type of material used. To *assign* the cost of *direct materials* used, such as lumber and upholstery fabric, E-Z-Boy:

- Debits Work in Process Inventory in the general ledger for the total cost of the direct materials used
- Records the total cost of the direct materials used on the specific job cost records in the subsidiary ledger, as shown in Exhibit 20-8

However, E-Z-Boy cannot trace the costs of *indirect materials* like nails and thread to a specific job (otherwise, these would be *direct* materials). This means that E-Z-Boy cannot record indirect materials on any of the specific job cost records in the subsidiary ledger that underlies the general ledger Work in Process Inventory account. So it cannot debit Work in Process Inventory. Instead, it debits indirect materials costs to a separate account, Manufacturing Overhead, in the general ledger. (Recall from Chapter 19 that manufacturing overhead includes all manufacturing costs *other than* direct materials and direct labor.)

Keep this distinction in mind: *Indirect manufacturing costs, such as indirect materials used, are not debited directly to Work in Process Inventory. Instead, they are accumulated in the (separate) Manufacturing Overhead account.*

E-Z-Boy works on many jobs during the year. The summary entry to assign the cost of the direct and indirect materials that E-Z-Boy used in all of its jobs during 20X9 is (data from page 802):

(2) Work in Process Inventory (for direct materials)	285,000	
Manufacturing Overhead (for indirect materials)	40,000	
Materials Inventory		325,000

✔ **Starter 20-3**

We can summarize the flow of materials costs through the T-accounts as follows:

✔ **Starter 20-4**

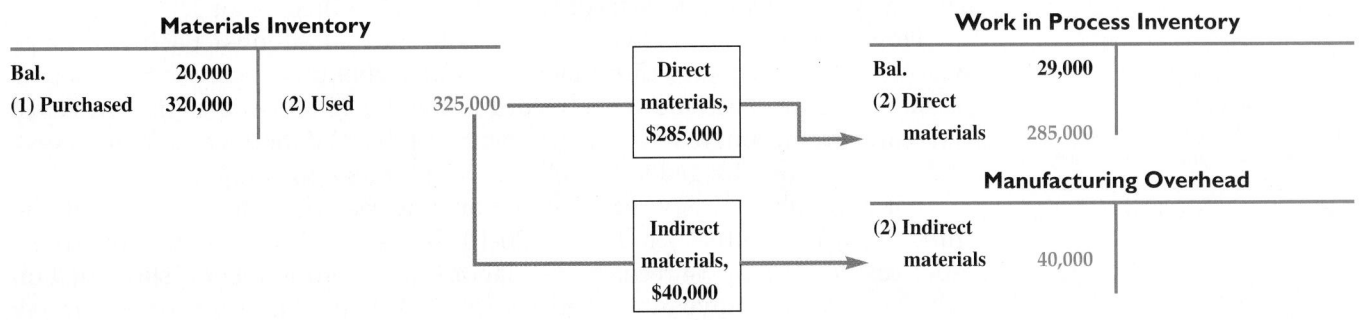

Accounting.com

Beyond the Bar Code: Radio-Frequency Identification Systems

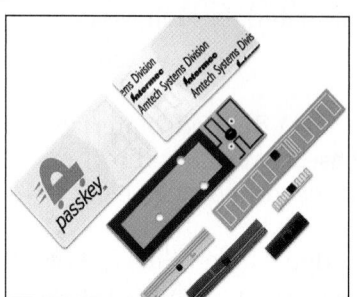

For the past 25 years, companies have used bar codes to identify and follow components in the factory. But if the contents or the destination of an industrial part or product change, someone must print and attach a new bar code label. Even in automated identification systems, as many as 60% of warehouse workers spend time checking bar codes and lining up each item for scanning.

Now there is a better method. Radio-frequency identification (RFID), uses electromagnetic waves to identify, track, and sort objects. An RFID system has two major components: the reader and the card/tag. Radio-frequency waves between the two make the identification. The plastic tag has a memory chip the size of a pinhead, yet it contains far more information than a bar code. And because it relies on radio waves, workers don't have to waste time aligning tagged products for scanning. The Gap uses RFID to trace each item of merchandise from the point of manufacture to the point of sale. Coca-Cola uses RFID to improve the efficiency of workers who refill and maintain vending machines. In the United Kingdom, Marks & Spencer uses RFID to track frozen foods.

The sophisticated "read–write" version of RFID has even more advantages. Employees can change tag information without touching the tag. They can change the route of a component on the factory floor or the destination of a shipment. The read–write tag is a small database that the company can synchronize with its other databases—and now with customers who have RFID technology. The fashion house Prada, for instance, gives customers RFID identification cards which, when combined with tagged merchandise, provide them with product information, videos of the clothing being shown on the runway, and even size and color options.

Based on: Gene Bylinsky, "Hot New Technologies for American Factories," *Fortune,* June 26, 2000, pp. 288A–288K. John Mesenbrink, "Shopping for RFID," *Security,* October 2002, pp. 10–16. Anonymous, "Top 100 2002: Top 10 Companies," *Frontline Solutions,* November 2002, pp. 17–30.

Accounting for Labor

Chapter 11 defined the payroll record as a special journal that lists each employee and the data to record payroll amounts.

Using the payroll record, E-Z-Boy *accumulates* the actual labor costs incurred during 20X9 (data from page 802): ←

(3) Manufacturing Wages	335,000	
Wages Payable		335,000

This entry *accumulates* the costs of both direct and indirect labor.

How does E-Z-Boy *assign* labor costs to individual jobs? Each employee whose work is considered direct labor fills out a labor time record for each job he or she works on. The **labor time record** in Exhibit 20-9 identifies the employee (Jay Barlow), the amount of time he spent on Job 293 (7 hours and 30 minutes), and the labor cost charged to the job ($60 = 7½ hours × $8 per hour).

labor time record
Identifies the employee, the amount of time spent on a particular job, and the labor cost charged to the job; a record used to assign direct labor cost to specific jobs.

For each job, E-Z-Boy totals the labor time records to trace, or *assign*, the direct labor cost to that job. Exhibit 20-10 shows how E-Z-Boy adds the direct labor cost to the job cost record. The "labor time record numbers" show that on July 24, three employees worked on Job 293. Labor time record 251 is Jay

Exhibit 20-9

Labor Time Record

```
                    LABOR TIME RECORD              No. _251_
                                                   Date _7–24_
   Employee _Jay Barlow_
   Job _293_

   ┌─────────────────────────────────────────────────────────┐
   │ TIME:                                                     │
   │                                                           │
   │   Started ___1:00___      Rate ___$8.00___                │
   │   Stopped ___8:30___      Cost of Labor                   │
   │   Elapsed ___7:30___      Charged to Job __$60.00__       │
   │   ─────────────────────────────────────────────────────  │
   │                                                           │
   │     Employee _JB_         Supervisor _GDC_                │
   └─────────────────────────────────────────────────────────┘
```

Barlow's, from Exhibit 20-9. Labor time records 236 and 258 (not shown) indicate that two other employees also worked on Job 293. The job cost record shows that E-Z-Boy assigned Job 293 a total of $150 of direct labor costs for the three employees' work ($60 from Jay Barlow's labor time record and the remainder from the other two employees' records).

Exhibit 20-10

Direct Labor Entry on Job Cost Record

JOB COST RECORD — E-Z-Boy

Job No. 293
Customer Name and Address Macy's New York City
Job Description 10 Recliner Chairs

Date Promised		7–31	Date Started	7–24	Date Completed		
	Direct Materials		Direct Labor		Manufacturing Overhead Allocated		
Date	Requisition Numbers	Amount	Labor Time Record Numbers	Amount	Date	Rate	Amount
7–24	334	$90	236, 251, 258	$150			
					Overall Cost Summary		
					Direct Materials ....$		
					Direct Labor		
					Manufacturing Overhead Allocated		
Totals					Total Job Cost ....$		

Recall that the job cost records form the subsidiary ledger for the general ledger account Work in Process Inventory. Therefore, the total direct labor costs traced to all the individual jobs E-Z-Boy worked on during the period (as recorded on job cost records like Exhibit 20-10) must equal the total direct labor debits to Work in Process Inventory.

The rest of the labor cost is for indirect labor, such as maintenance and janitorial services. Indirect labor cannot be traced to any specific job. Therefore, indirect labor, like indirect materials, is debited to Manufacturing Overhead.

The entry to *assign* total direct and indirect labor costs that E-Z-Boy incurred during 20X9 (data from page 802) is:

✔ Starter 20-5

(4) Work in Process Inventory (for direct labor)...............	250,000	
Manufacturing Overhead (for indirect labor).............	85,000	
Manufacturing Wages.............................		335,000

This entry brings the balance in Manufacturing Wages to zero, because its transferred balance is now divided between Work in Process Inventory (direct labor) and Manufacturing Overhead (indirect labor), as shown in the following T-accounts:

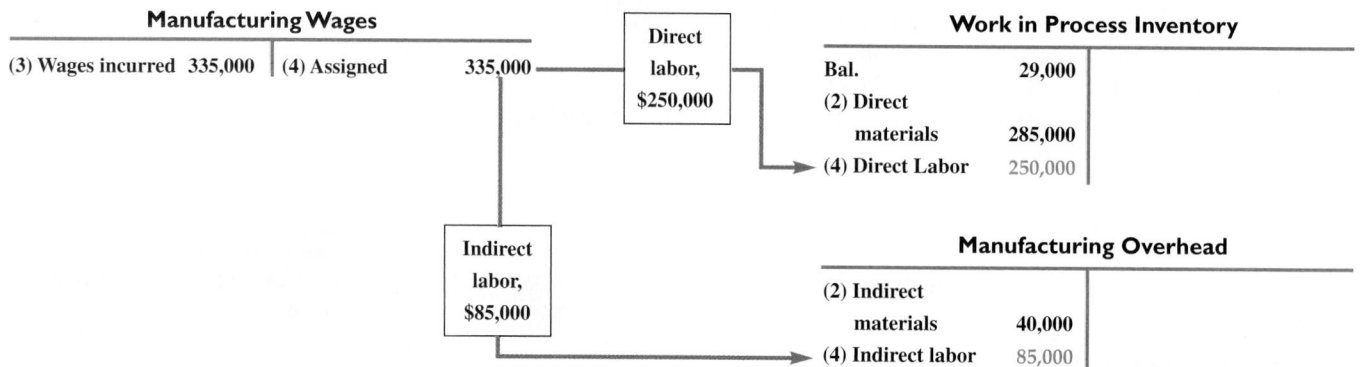

E-Z-Boy uses traditional source documents like the labor time record in Exhibit 20-9 to identify the direct labor cost of each specific job. But many companies have automated this process. For example, at various stages in the production of Saturn automobiles, employees insert their identification cards into computer terminals set up on the plant floor. This system captures direct labor time and cost without using documents.

How can E-Z-Boy managers use the materials inventory subsidiary ledger (Exhibit 20-6), labor time records (Exhibit 20-9), and job cost records (Exhibit 20-10) to run the company more effectively and efficiently?

Answer: Managers can use the *materials inventory subsidiary ledger* to see when lumber, nails, thread, and other materials are running low, so they can reorder.

Managers use *labor time records* to control labor costs. Suppose E-Z-Boy pays an employee for 7½ hours of work per day. Summing the time recorded on all her labor time records for the day should yield a total of 7½ hours worked. If not, the manager should find out how the employee spent any time unaccounted for. By showing how much time employees spend on each job, labor time records and job cost records help managers determine whether employees are working efficiently. If they spend longer than expected on a job, that job may not yield a profit.

Engineers study the detailed materials and labor charges on the *job cost records* to see if they can use materials and labor more efficiently. If a job's costs exceed its budget, E-Z-Boy may be able to use the job cost record to negotiate a price increase with the customer. E-Z-Boy's managers must do a better job controlling costs on future jobs, or raise the sale price on similar jobs, to ensure that the company remains profitable.

Decision Guidelines

JOB COSTING: TRACING DIRECT MATERIALS AND DIRECT LABOR

Dell Computer uses a job costing system that assigns manufacturing costs to each individual computer Dell assembles. These guidelines explain some of the decisions Dell made in designing its system to trace direct materials and labor.

Decision	Guidelines
Should we use job or process costing?	Dell uses *job costing* because the company produces unique products (custom-tailored computers) in small batches (usually a "batch" contains one computer). Dell does not use *process costing*, because that is appropriate for companies like oil refineries, which produce identical products in large batches, often in a continuous flow.

How to record:

• Purchase and use of materials?

Purchase:
Materials Inventory XX
     Accounts Payable (or Cash). XX

Use:
Work in Process Inventory (direct materials). XX
Manufacturing Overhead (indirect materials) XX
     Materials Inventory XX

• Incurrence and assignment of labor?

Incurred:
Manufacturing Wages XX
     Wages Payable (or Cash). XX

Assigned:
Work in Process Inventory (direct labor). XX
Manufacturing Overhead (indirect labor) XX
     Manufacturing Wages XX

MID-CHAPTER *Summary Problem*

Ecosphere Associates, Ltd. in Tucson, Arizona, produces ecospheres—self-sustaining enclosed glass spheres that include water, algae, tiny shrimp, and snails. Suppose Ecosphere has the following transactions:

CHECK YOUR RESOURCES

a. Purchased raw materials on account, $35,000.
b. Materials costing $30,000 were requisitioned for production. Of this total, $3,000 were indirect materials.
c. Labor time records show that direct labor of $22,000 and indirect labor of $4,000 were incurred (but not yet paid).

Required

Prepare journal entries for each transaction.

Solution

a. Materials Inventory.   35,000
     Accounts Payable . . . . | 35,000

When materials are purchased on account:

■ Debit (increase) Materials Inventory for the *cost* of the materials
■ Credit (increase) Accounts Payable to record the liability for the cost of the materials

b. Work in Process Inventory...............	27,000	
Manufacturing Overhead................	3,000	
Materials Inventory................		30,000

When materials are requisitioned (used) in production, we record the movement of materials out of materials inventory and into production:

■ Debit (increase) Work in Process Inventory for the cost of the *direct* materials (in this case, $27,000—the $30,000 total materials requisitioned less the $3,000 indirect materials)
■ Debit (increase) Manufacturing Overhead for the cost of the *indirect* materials
■ Credit (decrease) Materials Inventory for the cost of both direct and indirect materials moved out of the materials storage area and into production

c. Manufacturing Wages...................	26,000	
Wages Payable....................		26,000

To record total labor costs actually incurred ($22,000 + 4,000):

■ Debit (increase) Manufacturing Wages
■ Credit (increase) Wages Payable to record the liability for wages incurred, but not paid

Work in Process Inventory...............	22,000	
Manufacturing Overhead................	4,000	
Manufacturing Wages..............		26,000

To assign the labor costs:

■ Debit (increase) Work in Process Inventory for the cost of the *direct* labor
■ Debit (increase) Manufacturing Overhead for the cost of the *indirect* labor
■ Credit (decrease) Manufacturing Wages for the cost of both direct and indirect labor

Student ResourceCD

allocation base, cost driver, manufacturing overhead

3 *Allocate manufacturing overhead in a manufacturer's job costing system*

✔ **Starter 20-6**

Job Costing: Allocating Manufacturing Overhead

All manufacturing overhead costs are *accumulated* as debits to a single general ledger account—Manufacturing Overhead. We have already recorded the indirect materials (entry 2) and indirect labor (entry 4) manufacturing overhead costs. Entries 5 through 8 record the other manufacturing overhead costs E-Z-Boy incurred, as given on page 802. The account titles in parentheses indicate the specific records debited in the overhead subsidiary ledger.

(5) Manufacturing Overhead (Depreciation—Plant and Equipment).....	50,000	
Accumulated Depreciation—Plant and Equipment		50,000
(6) Manufacturing Overhead (Plant Utilities).......................	20,000	
Cash		20,000
(7) Manufacturing Overhead (Plant Insurance).....................	5,000	
Prepaid Insurance—Plant		5,000
(8) Manufacturing Overhead (Property Taxes—Plant)................	10,000	
Property Taxes Payable		10,000

The actual manufacturing overhead costs (such as indirect materials, indirect labor, and depreciation, utilities, insurance and property taxes related to the plant) are debited to Manufacturing Overhead as they occur throughout the year. By the end of the year, the Manufacturing Overhead account has accumulated all the actual overhead costs as debits:

Manufacturing Overhead

(2) Indirect materials	40,000
(4) Indirect labor	85,000
(5) Depreciation—plant and equipment	50,000
(6) Plant utilities	20,000
(7) Plant insurance	5,000
(8) Property taxes—plant	10,000
Total overhead cost	210,000

How can E-Z-Boy's managers use the Manufacturing Overhead subsidiary ledger to control overhead costs?

Answer: Managers plan the amount of each manufacturing overhead item, such as plant-related depreciation, utilities, and insurance. If actual costs differ from planned costs, they find out why. For example, why are plant utilities higher than expected? Did utility rates increase? Did workers waste electricity or water? Was there a delay in installing more energy-efficient machinery? Answers to these questions may help managers control (reduce) utility costs. On the other hand, if utility costs have increased for reasons beyond the company's control, management may have to increase selling prices to cover the higher utility costs.

Now you have seen how E-Z-Boy *accumulates* overhead costs in the accounting records. But how does it *assign* overhead costs to individual jobs? As you can see from the manufacturing overhead T-account, overhead includes a variety of costs that E-Z-Boy cannot trace to individual jobs. For example, it is impossible to say how much of the cost incurred to cool the plant is related to Job 293. Yet manufacturing overhead costs are as essential as direct materials and direct labor, so E-Z-Boy must find some way to assign these costs to specific jobs.

Allocating Manufacturing Overhead to Jobs

E-Z-Boy traces direct material and direct labor costs directly to each job, as we've seen. Now let's see how it allocates each job its share of the wide variety of indirect manufacturing costs like depreciation and insurance on plant and equipment, indirect materials, and indirect labor.

HOW TO CHOOSE AN ALLOCATION BASE The key to assigning indirect manufacturing costs to jobs is to identify a manufacturing overhead allocation base. The **allocation base** is a common denominator that links indirect manufacturing overhead costs to the cost objects. Ideally, the allocation base is the primary cost driver of manufacturing overhead costs. As the phrase implies, a **cost driver** is the primary factor that causes a cost. For example, in many companies, manufacturing overhead costs rise and fall with direct labor costs. In this case, accountants use direct labor costs or direct labor hours as the allocation base. The more direct labor a job uses, the more manufacturing overhead cost the job is allocated.

But labor is less important in companies that use automated production, like Saturn. Equipment depreciation, maintenance, and utilities change with the number of machine hours used. These companies often use machine hours as the

allocation base
A common denominator that links indirect costs to cost objects. Ideally, the allocation base is the primary cost driver of the indirect cost.

cost driver
The primary factor that causes a cost.

allocation base. The important point is that the cost allocation base should be the primary driver of the manufacturing overhead costs.

For simplicity, we'll assume E-Z-Boy uses only one allocation base to assign manufacturing overhead costs to jobs. Chapter 25 relaxes this assumption. There, we'll see how companies use a method called *activity-based costing* to identify different allocation bases that more accurately link indirect costs with the jobs that caused those costs. Because activity-based costing is a straightforward extension of the single allocation base method, it is important to develop a solid understanding of the simpler system we describe here.

HOW TO ESTIMATE A MANUFACTURING OVERHEAD RATE   The most accurate allocation can be made only when the total amount of the manufacturing overhead cost is known, at the end of the year. But managers making decisions today cannot wait that long for product cost information. So E-Z-Boy develops an estimated manufacturing overhead allocation rate at the beginning of the year. This **predetermined manufacturing overhead rate** (sometimes called the **budgeted manufacturing overhead rate**) is computed as follows:

predetermined manufacturing overhead rate
Estimated manufacturing overhead allocation rate computed at the beginning of the year, calculated as the total estimated manufacturing overhead costs divided by the total estimated quantity of the manufacturing overhead allocation base. Also called the **budgeted manufacturing overhead rate**.

$$\text{Predetermined manufacturing overhead rate} = \frac{\text{Total estimated manufacturing overhead costs}}{\text{Total estimated quantity of the manufacturing overhead allocation base}}$$

A key point is that both the numerator and the denominator are estimated *before* the year begins. (Actual overhead costs and the actual quantity of the allocation base are not known until after the end of the period.) Throughout the year, companies use this predetermined rate to allocate overhead to individual jobs.

Six Steps in Allocating Manufacturing Overhead

Companies follow six steps in allocating manufacturing overhead cost to jobs:

1. Estimate the total overhead cost for the planning period, which is usually a year. In 20X8, E-Z-Boy predicted overhead costs for 20X9 of $220,000.
2. Identify the manufacturing overhead (cost) allocation base. E-Z-Boy uses direct labor cost as the allocation base.
3. Estimate the total quantity of the overhead allocation base. E-Z-Boy expects to incur $275,000 of direct labor cost during 20X9.
4. Compute the predetermined manufacturing overhead rate as follows:

$$\text{Predetermined manufacturing overhead rate} = \frac{\text{Total estimated manufacturing overhead costs (from Step 1)}}{\text{Total estimated quantity of the manufacturing overhead allocation base (from Step 3)}}$$

$$= \frac{\text{Total estimated manufacturing overhead costs (from Step 1)}}{\text{Total estimated direct labor costs (from Step 3)}}$$

$$= \frac{\$220,000}{\$275,000} = 0.80, \text{ or } 80\%$$

This overhead rate is *predetermined* because the numerator and the denominator are both *estimated before* the year starts.

5. Obtain *actual* quantities of the overhead allocation base used by individual jobs as the year unfolds. The total actual direct labor cost of Job 293 is $400, as Exhibit 20-11 shows.
6. Allocate manufacturing overhead cost to jobs by multiplying the *predetermined* manufacturing overhead rate (computed in step 4) by the *actual* quantity of the allocation base used by each job (from step 5). E-Z-Boy uses the same predeter-

mined rate (80% of direct labor cost) to allocate manufacturing overhead to all jobs worked on throughout the year. Because the total direct labor cost for Job 293 is $400 and the predetermined overhead allocation rate is 80% of direct labor cost, E-Z-Boy allocates $320 ($400 × 0.80) of manufacturing overhead to Job 293.

The completed job cost record for Macy's order of 10 recliner chairs (Exhibit 20-11) shows that the job cost E-Z-Boy a total of $1,220: $500 in direct materials, $400 in direct labor, and $320 of allocated manufacturing overhead. The job cost record also shows that a job can include more than a single unit of product. In this case, the Macy's job includes 10 recliners, so E-Z-Boy's cost per recliner is $122 ($1,220 ÷ 10).

Exhibit 20-11

Manufacturing Overhead Entry on Job Cost Record

✔ Starter 20-7

JOB COST RECORD

E-Z-Boy

Job No. 293
Customer Name and Address Macy's New York City
Job Description 10 Recliner Chairs

Date Promised		7–31	Date Started	7–24	Date Completed		7-29
	Direct Materials		Direct Labor		Manufacturing Overhead Allocated		
Date	Requisition Numbers	Amount	Labor Time Record Numbers	Amount	Date	Rate	Amount
7–24	334	$ 90	236, 251, 258	$150	7–29	80% of Direct Labor Cost	$320
25	338	180	264, 269, 273, 291	200			
28	347	230	305	50	Overall Cost Summary		
					Direct Materials ....$ 500		
					Direct Labor 400		
					Manufacturing Overhead Allocated 320		
Totals		$500		$400	Total Job Cost $1,220		

Knowing that the manufacturing cost is $122 per recliner can help E-Z-Boy's management make what kinds of decisions?

Answer

1. *Pricing*—Marketing must price the recliners considerably above the $122 manufacturing cost to cover R&D, design, marketing, distribution, and customer service costs, as well as profits.

2. *Product emphasis*—Using profit calculations (selling price minus cost), E-Z-Boy's top management can design operations and marketing strategy to focus on the most profitable products.

3. *Cost control*—Engineers can study the detailed cost information to identify opportunities to cut costs below $122. Production managers can compare the $122 cost per recliner with the budgeted cost to evaluate worker efficiency.

4. *Outsourcing*—Management can compare the $122 cost to make the recliner versus the cost of buying a similar recliner from a subcontractor. (For example, **Teva** outsources production of its footwear to companies in China; Teva's management focuses on design and marketing.)

5. *Valuing inventory*—Finance and accounting can use the $122 per recliner to value the job as inventory (before it is sold) and as cost of goods sold (after the sale).

Of course, E-Z-Boy also allocated manufacturing overhead to each of the other jobs worked on during 20X9. The total overhead allocated to all jobs is 80% of the total $250,000 direct labor cost, or $200,000 (data from page 802). The journal entry to allocate manufacturing overhead costs to Work in Process Inventory is

(9) Work in Process Inventory	200,000	
Manufacturing Overhead		200,000

The flow of manufacturing overhead though the T-accounts follows:

Manufacturing Overhead				
(2) Indirect materials	40,000	(9) Allocated	200,000	
(4) Indirect labor	85,000			
(5) Depreciation—plant and equipment	50,000			
(6) Plant utilities	20,000			
(7) Plant insurance	5,000			
(8) Property taxes—plant	10,000			
Actual overhead cost	210,000			
Bal.	10,000			

Manufacturing overhead allocated →

Work in Process Inventory		
Bal.	29,000	
(2) Direct materials	285,000	
(4) Direct labor	250,000	
(9) Manufacturing overhead allocated	200,000	

✔ **Starter 20-9**

■ **Accounting for Finished Goods**

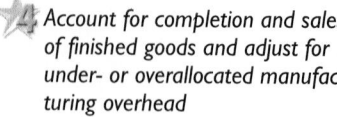

labor costs, manufacturing overhead, materials costs

After allocation, a $10,000 debit balance remains in the Manufacturing Overhead account. This means that E-Z-Boy's actual overhead costs exceed the overhead allocated to Work in Process Inventory. We say that E-Z-Boy's Manufacturing Overhead is *underallocated*. We'll discuss how to correct this problem on pages 815 and 816.

Accounting for Completion and Sale of Finished Goods and Adjusting Manufacturing Overhead

Now you know how to accumulate and assign direct materials, direct labor, and manufacturing overhead to jobs. To complete the process, we must account for the completion and sale of finished goods and then adjust manufacturing overhead at the end of the period.

4 Account for completion and sales of finished goods and adjust for under- or overallocated manufacturing overhead

Accounting for Completion and Sale of Finished Goods

Look at Exhibit 20-4 on page 801 to review the flow of costs as a job goes from work in process, to finished goods, to cost of goods sold. For E-Z-Boy, the $740,000 cost of goods manufactured (from the data on page 802) is the cost of the jobs E-Z-Boy finished this year. E-Z-Boy credits Work in Process Inventory as the jobs leave the plant floor. The debit is to Finished Goods Inventory because the completed products move into the finished goods storage area. A summary entry for E-Z-Boy's goods completed in 20X9 is as follows:

(10) Finished Goods Inventory	740,000	
Work in Process Inventory.		740,000

In turn, E-Z-Boy makes the usual entries for sales and cost of goods sold (data from page 802):

(11) Accounts Receivable..................	996,000	
Sales Revenue..................		996,000
Cost of Goods Sold	734,000	
Finished Goods Inventory		734,000

The key T-accounts for E-Z-Boy's manufacturing costs now show

Work in Process Inventory

Bal.	29,000	(10)	740,000→
(2)	285,000		
(4)	250,000		
(9)	200,000		
Bal.	24,000		

Cost of goods manufactured (completed this period)

Finished Goods Inventory

Bal.	12,000	(11)	734,000→
→(10)	740,000		
Bal.	18,000		

Cost of goods sold this period

Cost of Goods Sold

(11)	734,000

The Work in Process Inventory T-account summarizes what happens on the manufacturing plant floor. Notice that the Work in Process T-account also summarizes the Schedule of Cost of Goods Manufactured: → E-Z-Boy starts the period with beginning inventory of jobs that were started but not finished last period ($29,000). During the current period, the plant uses direct materials ($285,000) and direct labor ($250,000) and manufacturing overhead is allocated to the jobs passing through the plant floor ($200,000). Some jobs are completed, and their costs are transferred out to Finished Goods Inventory ($740,000). We end the period with other jobs started but not finished during this period ($24,000).

 **Starter 20-8**

See Exhibit 19-11 to review the schedule of Cost of Goods Manufactured. Compare the schedule to the entries in the Work in Process Inventory T-account.

Adjusting Underallocated or Overallocated Manufacturing Overhead at Period's End

During the year, E-Z-Boy debits Manufacturing Overhead for the overhead costs the company actually incurred and credits Manufacturing Overhead for amounts allocated to Work in Process Inventory. The total debits rarely equal the total credits. Why? Because E-Z-Boy allocates overhead to jobs using a *predetermined* allocation rate that represents the *expected* relation between overhead costs and the allocation base. In our example, the $10,000 debit balance of Manufacturing Overhead shown on page 814 is called **underallocated manufacturing overhead** (or simply **underallocated overhead**) because the manufacturing overhead allocated to Work in Process Inventory is *less* than the amount actually incurred. (**Overallocated manufacturing overhead** is just the opposite.)

Accountants adjust underallocated and overallocated overhead at year-end, when closing the Manufacturing Overhead account. When overhead is underallocated, as in our example, a credit to Manufacturing Overhead brings the account balance to zero. What account is debited?

To see the answer you need to understand why E-Z-Boy underallocated manufacturing overhead. E-Z-Boy *expected* to incur 20X9 manufacturing overhead at the predetermined rate of

$$\frac{\$220,000 \text{ } expected \text{ manufacturing overhead costs}}{\$275,000 \text{ } expected \text{ direct labor cost}} = 80\%$$

Without a crystal ball to tell the future, it would be surprising indeed if *actual* costs and *actual* quantities of the allocation base—which are not known until the end of the year—exactly match the expected amounts that E-Z-Boy used to

underallocated (manufacturing) overhead
The manufacturing overhead allocated to Work in Process Inventory is *less* than the amount of manufacturing overhead costs actually incurred.

overallocated (manufacturing) overhead
The manufacturing overhead allocated to Work in Process Inventory is *more* than the amount of manufacturing overhead costs actually incurred.

compute the predetermined rate at the beginning of the year. At the end of 20X9, E-Z-Boy's actual manufacturing overhead rate turns out to be

$$\frac{\$210,000 \text{ } \textit{actual} \text{ manufacturing overhead costs}}{\$250,000 \text{ } \textit{actual} \text{ direct labor cost}} = 84\%$$

At the beginning of the year, E-Z-Boy *underestimated* the manufacturing overhead rate, expecting it to be only 80%.

Because the predetermined rate was *less* than the actual rate, E-Z-Boy allocated too *little* manufacturing overhead to every job. In other words, every job worked on in 20X9 was *undercosted*. To correct this error, E-Z-Boy should *increase* the cost of these jobs.

Many companies use software that automatically corrects each job at the end of the year. In companies without such software, accountants usually close the balance in the Manufacturing Overhead account to Cost of Goods Sold, because most of the jobs have been sold.

Because E-Z-Boy *undercosted* jobs during the year, the correction should increase (debit) Cost of Goods Sold:

✔ Starter 20-10

✔ Starter 20-11

(12) Cost of Goods Sold	10,000	
Manufacturing Overhead..........		10,000

The T-accounts show that the Manufacturing Overhead balance is now zero:

Manufacturing Overhead				Cost of Goods Sold	
Actual	210,000	Allocated	200,000	734,000	
		Closed	10,000 ⟶	10,000	

Exhibit 20-12 summarizes the accounting for manufacturing overhead:

- Before the period
- During the period
- At the end of the period

Exhibit 20-12

Summary of Accounting for Manufacturing Overhead

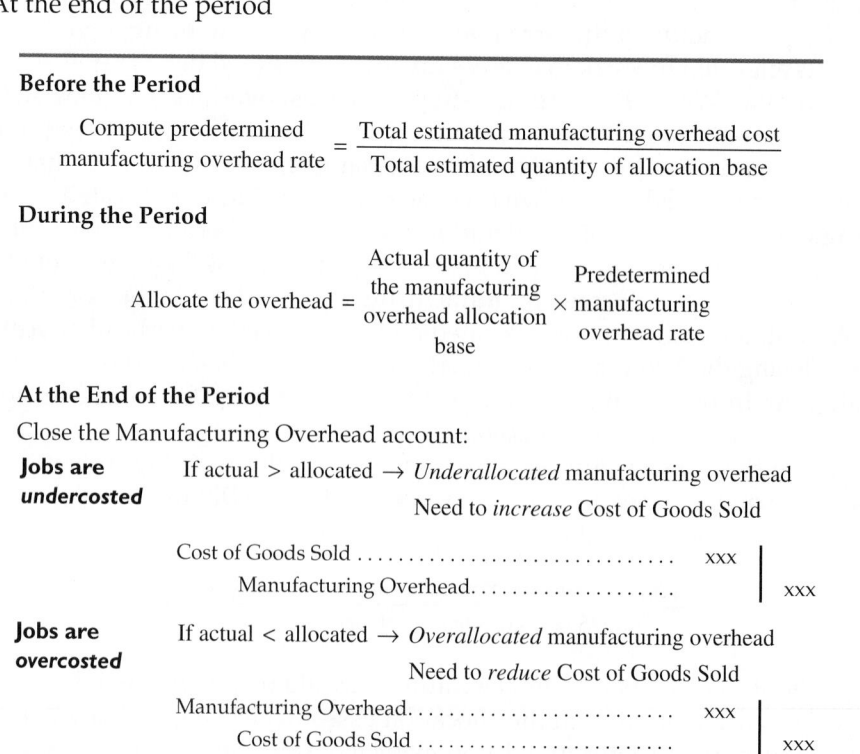

Before the Period

$$\text{Compute predetermined} \atop \text{manufacturing overhead rate} = \frac{\text{Total estimated manufacturing overhead cost}}{\text{Total estimated quantity of allocation base}}$$

During the Period

$$\text{Allocate the overhead} = {\text{Actual quantity of} \atop \text{the manufacturing} \atop \text{overhead allocation} \atop \text{base}} \times {\text{Predetermined} \atop \text{manufacturing} \atop \text{overhead rate}}$$

At the End of the Period

Close the Manufacturing Overhead account:

Jobs are undercosted   If actual > allocated → *Underallocated* manufacturing overhead

Need to *increase* Cost of Goods Sold

Cost of Goods Sold	xxx	
Manufacturing Overhead..................		xxx

Jobs are overcosted   If actual < allocated → *Overallocated* manufacturing overhead

Need to *reduce* Cost of Goods Sold

Manufacturing Overhead.........................	xxx	
Cost of Goods Sold		xxx

Suppose E-Z-Boy's actual manufacturing overhead costs were $180,000 rather than $210,000.

Questions

1. What would the actual overhead rate have been?
2. Would manufacturing overhead have been underallocated or overallocated?
3. What journal entry would you make to close the Manufacturing Overhead account?

Answers

1. The actual manufacturing overhead rate would have been

$$\frac{\$180,000 \; actual \; \text{manufacturing overhead costs}}{\$250,000 \; actual \; \text{direct labor cost}} = 72\%$$

2. The predetermined manufacturing overhead rate (80%) is *higher* than the actual manufacturing overhead rate (72%). In this case, each job would be *overcosted*. And Manufacturing Overhead would be *overallocated* by $20,000, as shown in this T-account:

Manufacturing Overhead

Actual	180,000	Allocated 200,000

3. The jobs E-Z-Boy worked on during the year were allocated too much manufacturing overhead. Accordingly, jobs in Cost of Goods Sold were *overcosted*, so the correction should decrease (credit) Cost of Goods Sold, as shown in the following journal entry:

Manufacturing Overhead	20,000	
Cost of Goods Sold		20,000

Overview of Job Costing in a Manufacturing Company

Exhibit 20-13 provides an overview of E-Z-Boy's job costing system. Each entry is keyed to 1 of the 12 transactions described on pages 803–816 (amounts in thousands). Study this exhibit carefully.

Review the flow of costs through the general ledger accounts:

- Material and labor costs are split between direct costs (traced directly to specific jobs in Work in Process Inventory) and indirect costs (accumulated in Manufacturing Overhead and then allocated to Work in Process Inventory).
- The Work in Process Inventory account summarizes the transactions that occurred on the floor of the manufacturing plant.
- The $740,000 credit to Work in Process Inventory (debit to Finished Goods Inventory) is the cost of goods manufactured—the cost of goods completed and ready for sale—which is the manufacturer's counterpart to merchandise purchases.

In the Manufacturing Overhead account, actual overhead costs are recorded as debits as they occur throughout the period. Credits to the account represent allocated overhead. E-Z-Boy also closed the $10,000 underallocated Manufacturing Overhead to Cost of Goods Sold.

The T-accounts shown in Exhibit 20-13 are general ledger control accounts. Behind each general ledger account appears three examples of subsidiary accounts that underlie the general ledger control account.

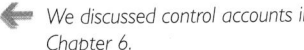

We discussed control accounts in Chapter 6.

Exhibit 20-13 Job Costing—Flow of Costs Through E-Z-Boy's Accounts (amounts in thousands)

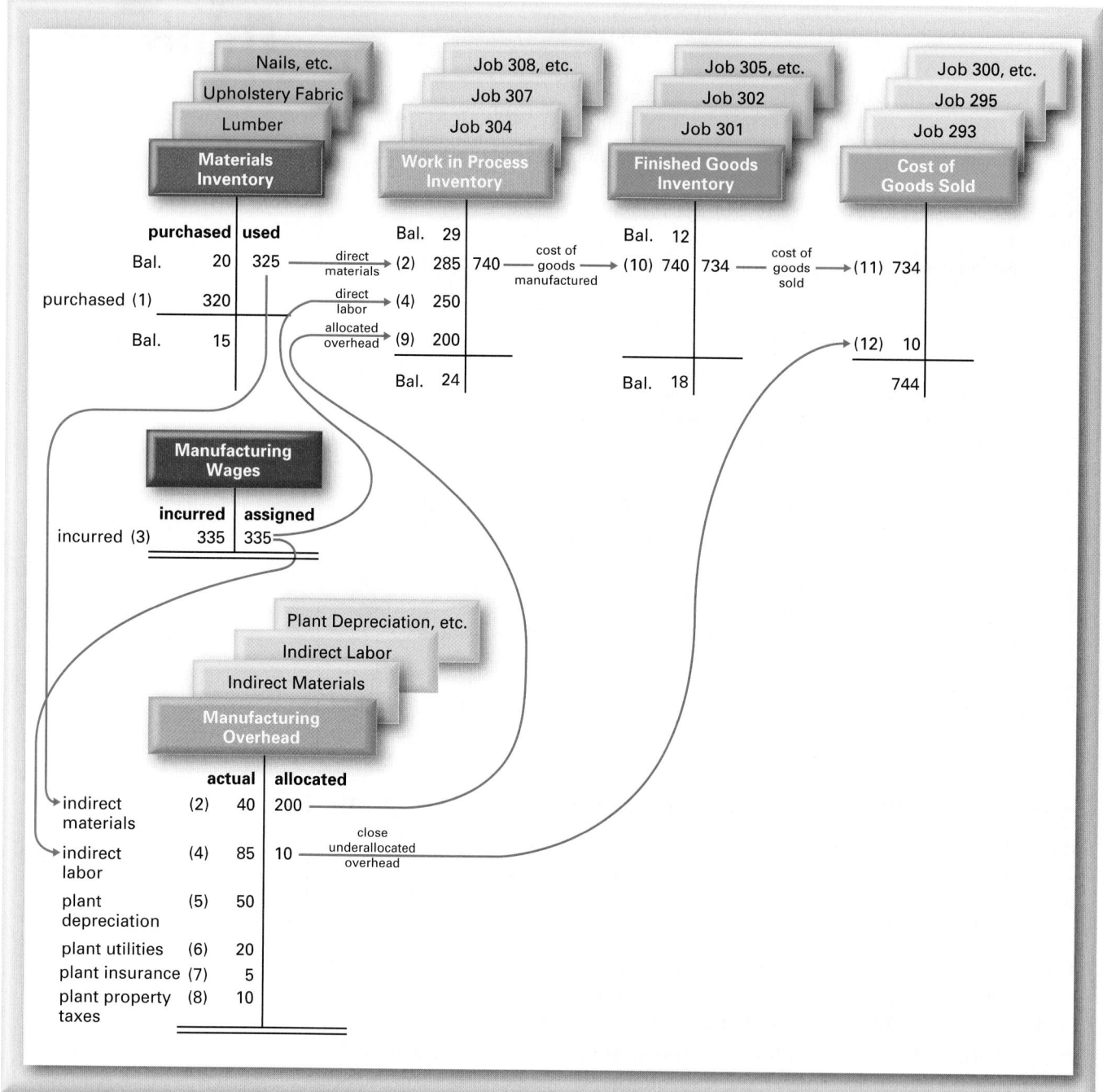

How Information Technology Has Changed Job Costing

The flow of costs through the T-accounts and the journal entries applies to systems ranging from simple manual costing to sophisticated ERP systems. The main difference is the source of data. In traditional systems, sources include material requisitions, labor time records, and job cost records like those we have described. These documents can be paper-based or automated.

In contrast, highly automated systems may have no physical source documents. Employees use bar codes to record materials used and scan identification cards to record their labor time. The software immediately tracks these material and labor costs to the specific job and updates the general ledger accounts (for example, Materials Inventory, Work in Process Inventory, Manufacturing Wages, and Manufacturing Overhead). ERP systems may not store data in the form of separate job cost records. But when employees enter the job number, the system quickly tallies costs assigned to the job so far. Even in sophisticated ERP systems, however, the cost flows and journal entries are identical to those we've described for E-Z-Boy.

Assigning Noninventoriable Costs

So far, we've explained how companies assign inventoriable costs to jobs. But for internal decision-making, many companies also assign noninventoriable costs (R&D, design, marketing, distribution, and customer service) to jobs. Let's see why and how.

Noninventoriable Costs in Manufacturing Companies

Job costing in manufacturing companies has traditionally focused on assigning *manufacturing* costs (*inventoriable* costs) to jobs. This is why our E-Z-Boy illustration focuses on assigning only manufacturing costs. The focus on manufacturing costs arises because generally accepted accounting principles require that the accounting records treat only inventoriable costs (manufacturing costs, for a manufacturer) as assets. Costs incurred in other elements of the value chain are not assigned to products for external reporting, but instead are treated as expenses (or period costs).

As we noted in Chapter 19, managers often want to know the full (total) cost of a product or a job, not just the inventoriable cost. The same principles of tracing direct costs and allocating indirect costs (using predetermined allocation rates) apply to noninventoriable period costs incurred in other elements of the value chain: R&D, design, marketing, distribution, and customer service. Managers can add these noninventoriable (period) costs to inventoriable costs to build the full cost of the product or job to guide internal decisions, such as setting long-run average sale prices. However, these noninventoriable costs are assigned to products (or jobs) *only for internal decision making*. Noninventoriable costs are not assigned to products for external reporting.

Noninventoriable Costs and Job Costing in Nonmanufacturing Companies

Because they have no inventory, service firms incur only noninventoriable costs. But their managers still need to know the costs of different jobs to make decisions. We now illustrate how service firms assign noninventoriable costs to jobs. (A manufacturer such as E-Z-Boy or a merchandiser such as Amazon.com could use the same approach to assign noninventoriable costs to individual jobs.)

The law firm of Barnett Associates considers each client a separate job. Barnett's most significant cost is direct labor—attorney time spent on clients' cases. How do service firms trace direct labor to individual jobs?

For automated services like Web site design, information technology consulting, and external auditing, employees simply enter the client number when they start on the client's job. Software records the time elapsed until the employee signs off that job. When the service is not automated, employees typically fill out a weekly **time record**. Software tallies the weekly total time spent on each job. Attorney Teresa Fox's time record in Exhibit 20-14 shows that she devoted 14 hours to client 367 during the week of June 10, 20X9.

Student ResourceCD
inventoriable costs, noninventoriable costs

5 Assign noninventoriable costs in job costing

time record
Source document used to trace direct labor to specific jobs.

Exhibit 20-14

Employee Time Record

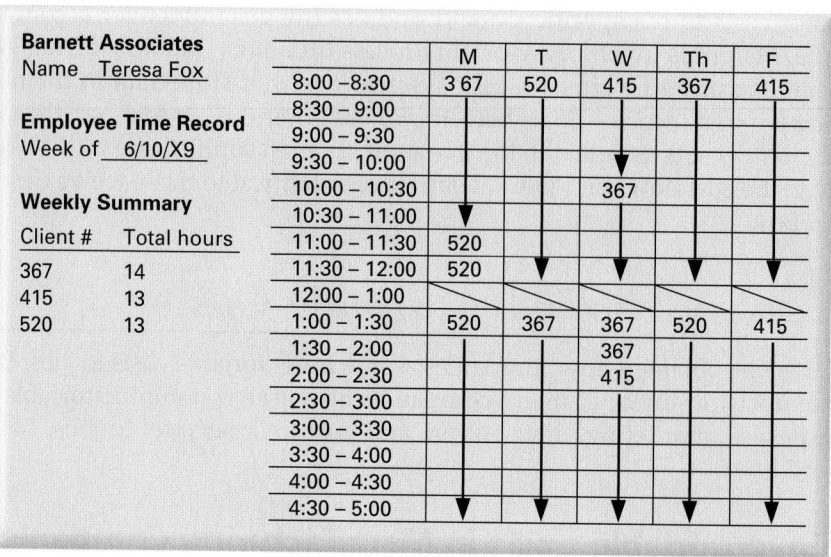

Barnett Associates		M	T	W	Th	F
Name Teresa Fox	8:00 –8:30	3 67	520	415	367	415
	8:30 – 9:00					
Employee Time Record	9:00 – 9:30					
Week of 6/10/X9	9:30 – 10:00					
	10:00 – 10:30			367		
Weekly Summary	10:30 – 11:00					
Client # Total hours	11:00 – 11:30	520				
367 14	11:30 – 12:00	520				
415 13	12:00 – 1:00					
520 13	1:00 – 1:30	520	367	367	520	415
	1:30 – 2:00			367		
	2:00 – 2:30			415		
	2:30 – 3:00					
	3:00 – 3:30					
	3:30 – 4:00					
	4:00 – 4:30					
	4:30 – 5:00					

✔ Starter 20-12

Fox's salary and benefits total $100,000 per year. Assuming a 40-hour work-week and 50 workweeks in each year, Fox has 2,000 available work hours per year (50 weeks × 40 hours per week). Barnett Associates' hourly cost rate of employing Teresa Fox is

$$\text{Hourly cost rate to the employer} = \frac{\$100,000 \text{ per year}}{2,000 \text{ hours per year}} = \$50 \text{ per hour}$$

Fox is the only attorney who served client 367, so the direct labor cost traced to the client is 14 hours × $50 per hour = $700.

Founding partner John Barnett wants to know the total costs of serving clients, not just the direct labor cost. Barnett Associates also allocates indirect costs to individual jobs (clients). The law firm develops a predetermined indirect cost allocation rate, following the same six-step approach that E-Z-Boy (pages 812–813) used.

1. **Estimate the total indirect costs.** In December 20X8, Barnett estimates that the following indirect costs will be incurred in 20X9:

Office rent...	$200,000
Office support staff	70,000
Maintaining and updating law library for case research	25,000
Advertisements in the yellow pages	3,000
Sponsorship of the symphony...........................	2,000
Total indirect costs.....................................	$300,000

2. **Identify a cost allocation base.** Barnett uses direct labor hours as the allocation base, because the number of hours that attorneys work on clients' cases is the main driver of indirect costs.

3. **Estimate the total quantity of the indirect cost allocation base.** Barnett estimates that its attorneys will work 10,000 direct labor hours in 20X9.

4. **Compute the predetermined indirect cost allocation rate. (Divide step 1 by step 3.)**

$$\text{Predetermined indirect cost allocation rate} = \frac{\$300,000 \text{ expected indirect costs}}{10,000 \text{ expected direct labor hours}}$$

$$= \$30 \text{ per direct labor hour}$$

✔ **Starter 20-13**

5. **Obtain the actual quantity of the indirect cost allocation base used by individual jobs as the year unfolds.** Exhibit 20-14 shows that client 367 required 14 direct labor hours.

6. **Allocate indirect costs to jobs by multiplying the predetermined indirect cost rate (step 4) by the actual quantity of the allocation base used by each job (step 5).** Client 367 is allocated indirect costs as follows:

$$14 \text{ direct labor hours} \times \$30/\text{hour} = \$420$$

To summarize, the total costs assigned to client 367 are

Direct labor: 14 hours × $50/hour	$ 700
Indirect costs: 14 hours × $30/hour	420
Total costs	$1,120

You have learned how to use a job cost system to assign costs to jobs. Review the Job Costing Decision Guidelines to solidify your understanding.

Decision Guidelines

JOB COSTING

Dell Computer pioneered the assemble-to-order PC production process. To figure the cost of its computers, Dell uses a job costing system that treats each individual computer as a separate cost object. In designing its job costing system, Dell made decisions like these, in addition to those listed in the mid-chapter Decision Guidelines on page 809:

Decision	Guidelines
Who should have access to product cost information?	All Dell's managers have access to product cost information. *Marketing* uses it to set selling prices that cover costs and contribute to profits. *Top management* uses it to identify the most profitable products, so it can focus on increasing sales of those products. *Engineers* study product costs to identify opportunities for further cost cuts. *Production* managers use product cost information to evaluate how efficiently assembly-line employees are working. *Finance and accounting* use product costs to figure inventory for the balance sheet and cost of goods sold for the income statement.

Decision Guidelines *(continued)*

Decision	Guidelines

Decision

Are utilities, insurance, property taxes, and depreciation
• Manufacturing overhead?

• Or operating expenses?

How to record *actual* manufacturing overhead costs?

How to compute a predetermined manufacturing overhead rate?

How to record allocation of manufacturing overhead?

What is the *amount* of the allocated manufacturing overhead?

How to close Manufacturing Overhead at the end of the period?

When providing services, how to trace employees' direct labor to individual jobs?

Why allocate noninventoriable costs to jobs?

Guidelines

These costs are part of manufacturing overhead *only* if they are incurred in the manufacturing plant.

If not related to manufacturing, they are operating expenses. For example, if related to the research lab, they are R&D expenses. If related to executive headquarters, they are administrative expenses. If related to distribution centers, they are distribution expenses. These are all operating expenses, not manufacturing overhead.

Manufacturing Overhead XXX
    Accumulated Depreciation—
      Plant and Equipment XX
    Prepaid Insurance—Plant and Equipment. . XX
    Utilities Payable (or Cash) XX
    and so on XX

$$\frac{\text{Total estimated manufacturing overhead cost}}{\text{Total estimated quantity of allocation base}}$$

Work in Process Inventory XX
    Manufacturing Overhead XX

Actual quantity of the manufacturing overhead allocation base $\times$ Predetermined manufacturing overhead rate

Close directly to Cost of Goods Sold.

Either automated software directly captures time employees spend on a client's job, or employees fill out a time record.

Managers need total product costs for internal decisions (such as setting selling prices). For external reporting, assign only inventoriable costs to jobs.

Excel Application Exercise

Goal: Create a spreadsheet to compute a predetermined manufacturing overhead rate and to allocate manufacturing overhead.

Scenario: You've just signed on as one of Dell Computer's new accounting interns. The plant manager is working on next year's budget and asks you to answer some key questions about the plant's manufacturing overhead:

1. What is the plant's predetermined manufacturing overhead rate?
2. What is the total amount of allocated manufacturing overhead?
3. What is the total actual overhead?

4. How much is left in the manufacturing overhead account at year-end? Is overhead under- or overallocated?

To get started, you have some figures available: total estimated manufacturing overhead cost, $500,000; total estimated quantity of allocation base, 200,000 direct labor hours; and actual quantity of allocation base, 195,000 direct labor hours. You've also gathered actual overhead costs: depreciation on plant and equipment, $240,000; insurance on plant and equipment, $24,000; plant utilities, $22,000; property taxes on plant and equipment, $20,000; production manager's salary, $90,000; and maintenance and repair costs for plant and equipment, $85,000.

Step-by-Step:
1. Open a new Excel spreadsheet.
2. In column 1, create a bold-faced heading as follows:
   a. Chapter 20 Excel Application Exercise
   b. Dell Computer Manufacturing Overhead
   c. Today's date
3. Two rows down, create a bold-faced heading, "Estimated and Actual Data for 200X."
4. In the next three rows, enter labels and values for total estimated manufacturing overhead cost, total estimated quantity of allocation base, and actual quantity of allocation base.
5. Two rows down, create a bold-faced heading, "Actual Overhead Costs."
6. Underneath the heading, enter labels and values for the remaining data (six rows total).
7. Two rows down, create a bold-faced heading, "Calculations for 200X."
8. Underneath the heading, enter labels for the four items to be calculated. Then, use formulas to compute the values.
9. Format all cells appropriately, save your work, and print a copy for your files.

END-OF-CHAPTER *Summary Problem*

StarZ, Ltd., manufactures skateboards. The company has a highly automated production process, so it allocates manufacturing overhead based on machine hours. StarZ expects to incur $240,000 of manufacturing overhead costs and to use 4,000 machine hours during 20X9.

At the end of 20X8, StarZ reported the following inventories:

Materials Inventory.	$20,000
Work in Process Inventory	17,000
Finished Goods Inventory	11,000

CHECK YOUR RESOURCES

During January 20X9, StarZ actually used 300 machine hours and recorded the following transactions:

a. Purchased materials on account, $31,000.
b. Used direct materials, $39,000.
c. Manufacturing labor cost incurred was $40,000.
d. Manufacturing labor was 90% direct labor and 10% indirect labor.
e. Used indirect materials, $3,000.
f. Incurred other manufacturing overhead, $13,000 (credit Accounts Payable).
g. Allocated manufacturing overhead for January 20X9.
h. Cost of completed skateboards, $99,000.
i. Sold skateboards on account, $172,000; cost of skateboards sold, $91,400.

Required

1. Compute StarZ's predetermined manufacturing overhead rate for 20X9.
2. Record the transactions in the general journal.
3. Post the transactions and inventory balances to the following accounts:

Materials Inventory	Work in Process Inventory	Finished Goods Inventory	Cost of Goods Sold

Manufacturing Wages	Manufacturing Overhead

4. Record the journal entry to close the ending balance of Manufacturing Overhead. Post your entry to the T-accounts.
5. What are the ending balances in the three inventory accounts and Cost of Goods Sold?

Solution

Requirement 1

$$\text{Predetermined manufacturing overhead rate} = \frac{\text{Total estimated manufacturing overhead cost}}{\text{Total estimated quantity of allocation base}}$$

$$= \frac{\$240,000}{4,000 \text{ machine hours}}$$

$$= \$60/\text{machine hour}$$

Requirement 2

Journal entries:

a. Materials Inventory......................	31,000	
Accounts Payable		31,000
b. Work in Process Inventory...............	39,000	
Materials Inventory.................		39,000
c. Manufacturing Wages.....................	40,000	
Wages Payable......................		40,000
d. Work in Process Inventory ($40,000 × 0.90)..	36,000	
Manufacturing Overhead ($40,000 × 0.10)...	4,000	
Manufacturing Wages...............		40,000
e. Manufacturing Overhead.................	3,000	
Materials Inventory.................		3,000
f. Manufacturing Overhead.................	13,000	
Accounts Payable		13,000
g. Work in Process Inventory (300 × $60)......	18,000	
Manufacturing Overhead............		18,000
h. Finished Goods Inventory	99,000	
Work in Process Inventory...........		99,000
i. Accounts Receivable.....................	172,000	
Sales Revenue......................		172,000
Cost of Goods Sold	91,400	
Finished Goods Inventory		91,400

Requirement 3

Post the transactions:

Materials Inventory

Bal.	20,000	(b)	39,000
(a)	31,000	(e)	3,000
Bal.	9,000		

Work in Process Inventory

Bal.	17,000	(h)	99,000
(b)	39,000		
(d)	36,000		
(g)	18,000		
Bal.	11,000		

Finished Goods Inventory

Bal.	11,000	(i)	91,400
(h)	99,000		
Bal.	18,600		

Cost of Goods Sold

(i)	91,400		

Manufacturing Wages

(c)	40,000	(d)	40,000

Manufacturing Overhead

(d)	4,000	(g)	18,000
(e)	3,000		
(f)	13,000		
Bal.	2,000		

Requirement 4

Close Manufacturing Overhead:		
Cost of Goods Sold	2,000	
Manufacturing Overhead............		2,000

Manufacturing Overhead				Cost of Goods Sold		
(d)	4,000	(g)	18,000	(i)	91,400	
(e)	3,000		2,000		2,000	
(f)	13,000					
				Bal.	93,400	

Requirement 5

Ending Balances:

Materials Inventory (from requirement 3)	$ 9,000
Work in Process Inventory (from requirement 3)	11,000
Finished Goods Inventory (from requirement 3).	18,600
Cost of Goods Sold (from requirement 4)	93,400

●REVIEW *Job Costing*

Quick Check

1. Would the advertising agency **Saatchi and Saatchi** use job or process costing? What about a **Georgia-Pacific** paper mill?
   - **a.** Saatchi and Saatchi—job costing
     Georgia-Pacific—job costing
   - **b.** Saatchi and Saatchi—job costing
     Georgia-Pacific—process costing
   - **c.** Saatchi and Saatchi—process costing
     Georgia-Pacific—job costing
   - **d.** Saatchi and Saatchi—process costing
     Georgia-Pacific—process costing

2. When **Dell Computer** *uses* direct materials, it *traces* the cost by debiting:
   - **a.** Materials Inventory
   - **b.** Direct Materials
   - **c.** Manufacturing Overhead
   - **d.** Work in Process Inventory

3. When Dell Computer *uses* indirect materials, it *assigns* the cost by debiting:
   - **a.** Materials Inventory
   - **b.** Indirect Materials
   - **c.** Manufacturing Overhead
   - **d.** Work in Process Inventory

4. When Dell Computer *uses* direct labor, it *traces* the cost by debiting:
   - **a.** Direct Labor
   - **b.** Manufacturing Wages
   - **c.** Manufacturing Overhead
   - **d.** Work in Process Inventory

Questions 5, 6, 7, and 8 are based on the following information. Assume that Dell's Austin, Texas, plant allocates manufacturing overhead based on machine hours. Suppose Dell budgeted 10 million machine hours and $90 million of manufacturing overhead costs. Finally, assume that Dell actually used 12 million machine hours and incurred the following actual costs (in millions):

Indirect labor	$10
Depreciation on plant	47
Machinery repair	15
Direct labor	75
Plant supplies	5
Plant utilities	8
Advertising	35
Sales commissions	25

(continued)

5. What is Dell's predetermined manufacturing overhead rate?
   a. $9.00/machine hour
   b. $7.50/machine hour
   c. $0.13/machine hour
   d. $0.11/machine hour

6. What is Dell's actual manufacturing overhead cost?
   a. $85
   b. $120
   c. $160
   d. $220

7. How much manufacturing overhead would Dell allocate?
   a. $85
   b. $90
   c. $108
   d. $220

8. What entry would Dell make to close the manufacturing overhead account?

   a. Manufacturing Overhead 5
       Cost of Goods Sold .... | 5

   b. Manufacturing Overhead 23
       Cost of Goods Sold .... | 23

   c. Cost of Goods Sold 5
       Manufacturing Overhead .... | 5

   d. Cost of Goods Sold 23
       Manufacturing Overhead .... | 23

9. Dell's management uses product cost information to:
   a. Set prices of its products
   b. Decide which products to emphasize
   c. Identify ways to cut production costs
   d. All of the above

10. For which of the following reasons would John Barnett, owner of the Barnett Associates law firm, want to know the total costs of a job (serving a particular client)?
    a. To determine the fees charged to the client
    b. For inventory valuation
    c. For external reporting
    d. For all of the above

Accounting Vocabulary

allocation base (p. 811)

budgeted manufacturing overhead rate (p. 812)

cost allocation (p. 802)

cost assignment (p. 802)

cost driver (p. 811)

cost tracing (p. 802)

job cost record (p. 801)

job costing (p. 800)

labor time record (p. 806)

materials requisition (p. 804)

overallocated (manufacturing) overhead (p. 815)

predetermined manufacturing overhead rate (p. 812)

process costing (p. 799)

time record (p. 819)

underallocated (manufacturing) overhead (p. 815)

ASSESS *Your Progress*

online homework

See *www.prenhall.com/horngren* for selected Starters, Exercises, and Problems.

Distinguishing between job and process costing
(Obj. 1)

Flow of costs in job costing
(Obj. 2, 3, 4)

Starters

S20-1 Would the following companies use job costing or process costing?

A manufacturer of plywood
A manufacturer of wakeboards
A manufacturer of luxury yachts
A professional services firm
A landscape garden contractor

S20-2 For a manufacturer that uses job costing, diagram the flow of costs through the accounts. Label each transaction. Include the following accounts in your diagram: Finished Goods Inventory, Manufacturing Wages, Cost of Goods Sold, Work in Process Inventory, Materials Inventory, and Manufacturing Overhead.

S20-3 Trekker manufactures backpacks. Its plant records include the following materials-related transactions:

Accounting for materials
(Obj. 2)

Purchases of canvas (on account).....................	$70,000
Purchases of thread (on account).....................	1,100
Material requisitions:	
Canvas	63,000
Thread	280

What journal entries record these transactions? Post these transactions to the Materials Inventory account. If the company had $35,680 of Materials Inventory at the beginning of the period, what is the ending balance of Materials Inventory?

S20-4 Use the following T-accounts to determine direct materials used and indirect materials used.

Accounting for materials
(Obj. 2)

Materials Inventory		
Bal.	16	
Purchases	230	X
Bal.	24	

Work in Process Inventory			
Bal.	32		
Direct materials	Y	Cost of goods	
Direct labor	320	manufactured	744
Manufacturing			
overhead	200		
Bal.	8		

S20-5 Art Glass reports the following labor-related transactions at its plant in Seattle, Washington.

Accounting for labor
(Obj. 2)

Plant janitor's wages	600
Furnace operator's wages..........................	900
Glass blowers' wages..............................	76,000

Record the journal entries for the incurrence and assignment of these wages.

S20-6 Classic Outdoor Furniture manufactures wood patio furniture. The company reports the following costs for June 20X7. What is the balance in the Manufacturing Overhead account?

Accounting for overhead
(Obj. 3)

Wood...	$230,000
Nails and glue....................................	12,000
Wood preserving stain............................	9,000
Depreciation on saws..............................	5,000
Depreciation on delivery truck......................	2,200
Assembly-line workers' wages......................	56,000
Salesman's auto lease.............................	1,400
Indirect manufacturing labor	39,000

S20-7 In the E-Z-Boy job cost record (Exhibit 20-11), how much manufacturing overhead cost would be allocated to Job 293 if the predetermined manufacturing overhead allocation rate is 70% of direct labor cost rather than 80%? What would be the total cost assigned to Job 293?

Allocating overhead
(Obj. 3)

Accounting for materials, labor, and completed goods
(Obj. 2, 4)

S20-8 Touch Enterprises produces LCD touch screen products. The company reports the following information at December 31, 20X6. Touch began operations on January 30, 20X6.

Work in Process Inventory		Manufacturing Wages		Manufacturing Overhead		Finished Goods Inventory		Materials Inventory	
30,000	123,000	70,000	70,000	2,000	48,000	123,000	111,000	52,000	32,000
60,000				10,000					
48,000				37,000					

1. What is the cost of direct materials used? The cost of indirect materials used?
2. What is the cost of direct labor? The cost of indirect labor?
3. What is the cost of goods manufactured?
4. What is cost of goods sold (before adjusting for any under- or overallocated manufacturing overhead)?

Allocating overhead
(Obj. 3)

S20-9 Refer to S20-8.

1. What is the actual manufacturing overhead? Allocated manufacturing overhead?
2. What is the predetermined manufacturing overhead rate as a percentage of direct labor cost?
3. Is manufacturing overhead underallocated or overallocated? By how much?

Under/overallocated overhead
(Obj. 4)

S20-10 In the E-Z-Boy illustration on pages 810–817, actual manufacturing overhead was $210,000. Suppose instead that the actual manufacturing overhead was $225,000.

1. What would be the actual manufacturing overhead rate?
2. Is manufacturing overhead underallocated or overallocated? By how much?
3. Is Cost of Goods Sold too high or too low?

Closing out under/overallocated overhead
(Obj. 4)

S20-11 Refer to S20-10. Make the journal entry to close out E-Z-Boy's Manufacturing Overhead account.

Job costing in a service company
(Obj. 5)

S20-12 In the Barnett Associates example on page 819–821, suppose Teresa Fox's annual salary is $110,000 rather than $100,000.

1. What would be the hourly (cost) rate to Barnett Associates of employing Fox?
2. What direct labor cost would be traced to client 367?

Job costing in a service company
(Obj. 5)

S20-13 Return to the original data in the Barnett Associates example on pages 819–821. Suppose the Barnett attorneys expected to work a total of 12,000 direct labor hours rather than 10,000 direct labor hours.

1. What is the indirect cost allocation rate?
2. What indirect costs will be allocated to client 367?

A⁺online homework

Exercises

Distinguishing job and process costing
(Obj. 1)

E20-1 Listed below are several terms. Complete the following statements with one of these terms. You may use a term more than once, and some terms may not be used at all.

Cost allocation	Cost driver	Job costing	Process costing
Cost tracing	Job cost record	Materials requisition	

a. A _____ accumulates the costs of an individual job.
b. _____ is used by companies that produce small quantities of many different products.

(continued)

c. A _____ is any factor that affects costs.
d. **Georgia-Pacific** pulverizes wood into pulp to manufacture cardboard. The company would use a _____ system.
e. To record costs of maintaining thousands of identical mortgage files, financial institutions like **Money Tree** would use a _____ system.
f. _____ is assigning direct costs to cost objects.
g. Companies that produce large numbers of identical products use _____ systems for product costing.
h. The computer repair service that visits your home and repairs your computer would use a _____ system.
i. A _____ is manufacturing personnel's request that materials be moved to the production floor.
j. _____ is assigning indirect costs to cost objects.

E20-2 Thrifty Trailers' job cost records yielded the following information:

Accounting for job costs
(Obj. 2, 3, 4)

Job No.	Started		Finished		Sold		Total Cost of Job at March 31
1	February	21	March	16	March	17	$ 3,800
2	February	29	March	21	March	26	13,000
3	March	3	April	11	April	13	6,400
4	March	7	March	29	April	1	4,000
5	March	9	March	30	April	2	7,120
6	March	22	April	11	April	13	2,000

Required

Compute Thrifty's cost of (a) work in process inventory at March 31, (b) finished goods inventory at March 31, and (c) cost of goods sold for March.

E20-3 Record the following transactions in Micro Speakers' general journal.

Job costing journal entries
(Obj. 2, 3, 4)

a. Incurred and paid Web site expenses, $3,400.
b. Incurred and paid manufacturing wages, $16,000.
c. Purchased materials on account, $14,750.
d. Used in production: direct materials, $7,000; indirect materials, $3,000.
e. Assigned $15,000 of manufacturing labor to jobs, 70% of which was direct labor and 30% of which was indirect labor.
f. Recorded manufacturing overhead: depreciation on plant, $13,000; plant insurance, $1,700; plant property tax, $4,200 (credit Property Tax Payable).
g. Allocated manufacturing overhead to jobs, 200% of direct labor costs.
h. Completed production, $33,000.
i. Sold inventory on account, $23,000; cost of goods sold, $11,000.

E20-4 Describe the lettered transactions in the following manufacturing accounts:

Identifying job costing journal entries
(Obj. 2, 3, 4)

Manufacturing Wages		Manufacturing Overhead		Cost of Goods Sold	
(a)	(b)	(b)	(e)	(g)	
		(c)	(f)	(f)	
		(d)			

Materials Inventory		Work in Process Inventory		Finished Goods Inventory	
(h)	(i)	(i)	(j)	(j)	(g)
	(c)	(b)			
		(e)			

E20-5 September production generated the following activity in Digital Connection's Work in Process Inventory:

Work in Process Inventory

September 1 Bal.	16,000
Direct materials used	29,000
Direct labor assigned to jobs	32,000
Manufacturing overhead	
allocated to jobs	12,000

Completed production, not yet recorded, consists of Jobs B-78 and G-65, with total costs of $41,000 and $37,000, respectively.

Required

1. Compute the cost of work in process at September 30.
2. Prepare the journal entry for production completed in September.
3. Prepare the journal entry to record the sale (on credit) of Job G-65 for $45,000. Also make the cost-of-goods-sold entry.
4. What is the gross profit of Job G-65? What other costs must this gross profit cover?

E20-6 Selected cost data for Star Poster Co. are as follows:

Expected manufacturing overhead cost for the year ...	$ 97,800
Expected direct labor cost for the year	61,125
Actual manufacturing overhead cost for the year......	104,600
Actual direct labor cost for the year	63,900

Required

1. Compute the predetermined manufacturing overhead rate per direct labor dollar.
2. Prepare the journal entry to allocate overhead cost for the year.
3. Use a T-account to determine the amount of overallocated or underallocated manufacturing overhead.
4. Prepare the journal entry to close the balance of the manufacturing overhead account.

E20-7 Freeman Foundry in Charleston, South Carolina, uses a predetermined manufacturing overhead rate to allocate overhead to individual jobs, based on the machine hours required. At the beginning of 20X6, the company expected to incur the following:

Manufacturing overhead costs.....................	$ 600,000
Direct labor cost	1,500,000
Machine hours	75,000

At the end of 20X6, the company had actually incurred:

Direct labor cost	$1,210,000
Depreciation on manufacturing property, plant, and equipment	480,000
Property taxes on plant	20,000
Sales salaries	25,000
Delivery drivers' wages.....................	15,000
Plant janitors' wages	10,000
Machine hours	55,000 hours

(continued)

Required

1. Compute Freeman's predetermined manufacturing overhead rate.
2. Record the summary journal entry for *allocating* manufacturing overhead.
3. Post the manufacturing overhead transactions to the Manufacturing Overhead T-account. Is manufacturing overhead underallocated or overallocated? By how much?
4. Close the Manufacturing Overhead account to Cost of Goods Sold. Does your entry increase or decrease cost of goods sold?

E20-8 Refer to the data in Exercise 20-7. Freeman's accountant found an error in her 20X6 expense records. Depreciation on manufacturing property, plant, and equipment was actually $400,000, not the $480,000 she had originally reported. Unadjusted balances at the end of 20X6 include

Allocating manufacturing overhead
(Obj. 3, 4)

Finished Goods Inventory..........................	$130,000
Cost of Goods Sold..............................	600,000

Required

1. Use a T-account to determine whether manufacturing overhead is underallocated or overallocated, and by how much.
2. Record the entry to close out the underallocated or overallocated manufacturing overhead.
3. What is the adjusted ending balance of Cost of Goods Sold?

E20-9 Land Resources, a real estate consulting firm, specializes in advising companies on potential new plant sites. Land Resources uses a job cost system with a predetermined indirect cost allocation rate, computed as a percentage of expected direct labor costs.

At the beginning of 20X5, managing partner Tony Black prepared the following plan, or budget, for 20X5:

Job costing in a service company
(Obj. 5)

Student ResourceCD
spreadsheet

Direct labor hours (professionals)	17,000 hours
Direct labor costs (professionals)	$2,669,000
Office rent	350,000
Support staff salaries	1,194,300
Utilities....................................	324,000

Auto Supplies, Inc., is inviting several consultants to bid for work. Tony Black estimates that this job will require about 220 direct labor hours.

Required

1. Compute Land Resources' (a) hourly direct labor cost rate and (b) indirect cost allocation rate.
2. Compute the predicted cost of the Auto Supplies job.
3. If Black wants to earn a profit that equals 50% of the job's cost, how much should he bid for the Auto Supplies job?

E20-10 At the end of the 20X7 fiscal year, Rave Kayaks' manufacturing records show the following unadjusted ending account balances:

	Work in Process Inventory	Finished Goods Inventory	Cost of Goods Sold
Direct materials	$100,000	$170,000	$ 360,000
Direct labor	80,000	250,000	600,000
Manufacturing overhead ..	70,000	300,000	440,000
Total	$250,000	720,000	$1,400,000

Rave's accountants allocated overhead during the year using a predetermined rate of $40 per machine hour. At year-end, they computed the actual rate of $52 per machine hour. The beginning balances of both Work in Process Inventory and Finished Goods Inventory were zero.

Required

1. How many machine hours did Rave Kayaks use in 20X7?
2. Was manufacturing overhead over- or underallocated for the year? By how much?
3. Record the entry to close out the over- or underallocated overhead.

Problems

(Group A)

P20-1A CarNut, Inc., reconditions engines. Its job cost records yield the following information. CarNut uses a perpetual inventory system.

Job No.	Date Started	Date Finished	Sold	Total Cost of Job at March 31	Total Manufacturing Cost Added in April
1	2/26	3/7	3/9	$1,400	
2	2/3	3/12	3/13	1,600	
3	3/29	3/31	4/3	1,300	
4	3/31	4/1	4/1	500	$ 400
5	4/8	4/12	4/14		700
6	4/23	5/6	5/9		1,200

Required

1. Compute CarNut's cost of (a) work in process inventory at March 31 and April 30, (b) finished goods inventory at March 31 and April 30, and (c) cost of goods sold for March and April.
2. Make summary journal entries to record the transfer of completed jobs from work in process to finished goods for March and April.
3. Record the sale of Job 5 for $1,600.
4. Compute the gross profit for Job 5. What costs must the gross profit cover?

P20-2A Getaway Homes manufactures prefabricated chalets in Colorado. The company uses a perpetual inventory system and a job cost system in which each chalet is a job. The following events occurred during May.

a. Purchased materials on account, $405,000.

b. Incurred manufacturing wages of $111,600. Requisitioned direct materials and used direct labor in manufacturing:

	Direct Materials	Direct Labor
Chalet 13	$41,100	$14,800
Chalet 14	56,800	28,500
Chalet 15	62,100	19,200
Chalet 16	66,000	21,000

c. Depreciation of manufacturing equipment used on different chalets, $20,000.

d. Other overhead costs incurred on chalets 13 through 16:

Indirect labor......................................	$28,100
Equipment rentals paid in cash	10,400
Plant insurance expired............................	6,000

e. Allocated overhead to jobs at the predetermined rate of 60% of direct labor cost.

f. Chalets completed: 13, 15, 16.

g. Chalets sold: 13 for $99,000; 16 for $141,900.

Required

1. Record the preceding events in the general journal.

2. Open T-accounts for Work in Process Inventory and Finished Goods Inventory. Post the appropriate entries to these accounts, identifying each entry by letter. Determine the ending account balances, assuming that the beginning balances were zero.

3. Add the costs of the unfinished chalet, and show that this equals the ending balance in Work in Process Inventory.

4. Add the cost of the completed chalet that has not yet been sold, and show that this equals the ending balance in Finished Goods Inventory.

5. Compute the gross profit on each chalet that was sold. What costs must the gross profit cover for Getaway Homes?

P20-3A Geolander Co. manufactures tires for all-terrain vehicles. Geolander uses job costing and has a perpetual inventory system.

Preparing and using a job cost record **(Obj. 2, 3, 4)**

On September 22, Geolander received an order for 100 TX tires from ATV Corporation at a price of $55 each. The job, assigned number 298, was promised for October 10. After purchasing the materials, Geolander began production on September 30 and incurred the following costs in completing the order:

Date	Labor Time Record No.	Description	Amount
9/30	1896	12 hours @ $20	$240
10/3	1904	30 hours @ $19	570

Date	Materials Requisition No.	Description	Amount
9/30	437	60 lb. rubber @ $18	$1,080
10/2	439	40 meters polyester fabric @ $12	480
10/3	501	100 meters steel cord @ $10	1,000

(continued)

Geolander allocates manufacturing overhead to jobs on the basis of the relation between expected overhead ($420,000) and expected direct labor cost ($300,000). Job 298 was completed on October 3 and shipped to ATV on October 5.

Required

1. Prepare a job cost record similar to Exhibit 20-8 for Job 298.
2. Journalize in summary form the requisition of direct materials and the assignment of direct labor and manufacturing overhead to Job 298.
3. Journalize completion of the job and sale of the goods.

Accounting for manufacturing overhead
(Obj. 3, 4)

P20-4A Suit Up produces uniforms. The company allocates manufacturing overhead based on the machine hours each job uses. Suit Up reports the following cost data for 20X6:

	Budget	**Actual**
Direct labor hours	7,000 hours	6,200 hours
Machine hours	6,920 hours	6,400 hours
Depreciation on salespersons' autos	$22,000	$22,000
Indirect materials	50,000	52,000
Depreciation on trucks used to deliver uniforms to customers	14,000	12,000
Depreciation on plant and equipment	65,000	67,000
Indirect manufacturing labor	40,000	43,000
Customer service hotline	19,000	21,000
Plant utilities	18,000	20,000
Direct labor cost	70,000	85,000

Required

1. Compute the predetermined manufacturing overhead rate.
2. Post actual and allocated manufacturing overhead to the Manufacturing Overhead T-account.
3. Close the under- or overallocated overhead to cost of goods sold.
4. How can managers use accounting information to help control manufacturing overhead costs?

Comprehensive accounting for manufacturing transactions
(Obj. 2, 3, 4)

P20-5A ← *Link Back to Chapters 2 and 19.* UbiquiTel manufactures specialized parts used in wireless communication. Initially, the company manufactured the parts for its own use, but it gradually began selling them to wireless companies as well. The trial balance of UbiquiTel's manufacturing operations on January 1 is as follows:

UbiquiTel—Manufacturing Operations

Trial Balance
January 1, 20XX

Cash...	$146,550	
Accounts receivable	87,880	
Inventories:		
Materials.....................................	16,680	
Work in process	44,480	
Finished goods................................	60,550	
Plant assets....................................	352,890	
Accumulated depreciation.......................		$157,070

(continued)

Accounts payable		84,120
Wages payable..................................		5,600
Common stock.................................		225,000
Retained earnings		237,240
Sales revenues		—
Cost of goods sold.............................	—	
Manufacturing wages...........................	—	
Manufacturing overhead	—	
Marketing and general expenses	—	
	709,030	709,030

January 1 balances in the subsidiary ledgers were

- Materials ledger: amplifiers, $6,280; electronic parts, $8,800; indirect materials, $1,600.
- Work in process ledger: Job 86, $44,480.
- Finished goods ledger: transmitters, $37,800; power supplies, $22,750.

January transactions are summarized as follows:

a. Payments on account, $81,430.
b. Marketing and general expenses incurred and paid, $22,400.
c. Collections on account, $194,880.
d. Materials purchased on credit: amplifiers, $20,160; electronic parts, $28,930; indirect materials, $6,690.
e. Materials used in production (requisitioned):
  - Job 86: amplifiers, $4,200.
  - Job 88: amplifiers, $8,080; electronic parts, $30,290.
  - Indirect materials, $6,940.
f. Manufacturing wages incurred during January, $54,060, of which $50,490 was paid. Wages payable at December 31 were paid during January, $5,600.
g. Labor time records for the month: Job 86, $6,600; Job 88, $27,600; indirect labor, $19,860.
h. Depreciation on manufacturing plant and equipment, $7,610.
i. Manufacturing overhead was allocated at the predetermined rate of 120% of direct labor cost.
j. Jobs completed during the month: Job 86, 1,000 transmitters at total cost of $63,200.
k. Credit sales on account: All of Job 86 for $124,690 (cost $63,200).
l. Close Manufacturing Overhead account to Cost of Goods Sold.

Required

1. Open T-accounts for the general ledger, the materials ledger, the work in process ledger, and the finished goods ledger. Insert each account balance as given, and use the reference *Bal.*

2. Record the January transactions directly in the accounts, using the letters as references. UbiquiTel uses a perpetual inventory system.

3. Prepare a trial balance at January 31.

4. Use the work in process T-account to prepare a schedule of cost of goods manufactured for the month of January. (You may want to review Exhibit 19-11.)

5. Prepare an income statement for the month of January. To calculate cost of goods sold, you may want to review Exhibit 19-9. (*Hint:* In transaction l, you closed any under/overallocated manufacturing overhead to Cost of Goods Sold. In the income statement, show this correction as an adjustment to Cost of Goods Sold. If manufacturing overhead is underallocated, the adjustment will increase Cost of Goods Sold. If overhead is overallocated, the adjustment will reduce Cost of Goods Sold.)

P20-6A Adnet.com is an Internet advertising agency. The firm uses a job cost system in which each client is a different "job." Adnet.com traces direct labor, software licensing costs, and travel costs directly to each job (client). The company allocates indirect costs to jobs based on a predetermined indirect cost allocation rate, computed as a percentage of direct labor costs.

At the beginning of 20X5, managing partner Ricky Buena prepared a budget:

Direct labor hours (professional).............	17,500 hours
Direct labor costs (professional)..............	$1,750,000
Support staff salaries......................	305,000
Rent and utilities	95,000
Supplies.................................	15,000
Leased computer hardware	285,000

In January 20X5, Adnet.com served several clients. Records for two clients appear here:

	GoVacation.com	Port Armour Golf Resort
Direct labor hours	460 hours	32 hours
Software licensing costs	$1,490	$280
Travel costs	9,000	—

Required

1. Compute Adnet.com's predetermined indirect cost allocation rate for 20X5.
2. Compute the total cost of each job.
3. If Adnet.com wants to earn profits equal to 20% of sales revenue, how much (what total fee) should it charge each of these two clients?
4. Why does Adnet.com assign costs to jobs?

Problems

(Group B)

P20-1B Serenity Manufacturing makes headphones for portable electronic devices. Its job cost records yield the following information.

Job No.	Date Started	Date Finished	Sold	Total Cost of Job at November 30	Total Manufacturing Costs Added in December
1	11/3	11/12	11/13	$1,400	
2	11/3	11/30	12/1	1,900	
3	11/17	12/24	12/27	300	$ 700
4	11/29	12/29	1/3	500	1,600
5	12/8	12/12	12/14		750
6	12/23	1/6	1/9		500

Required

1. Compute Serenity's cost of (a) work in process inventory at November 30 and December 31, (b) finished goods inventory at November 30 and December 31, and (c) cost of goods sold for November and December.

2. Record summary journal entries for the transfer of completed units from work in process to finished goods for November and December.

3. Record the sale of Job 3 for $1,400.

4. What is the gross profit for Job 3? What other costs must this gross profit cover?

P20-2B Aloha Construction, Inc., is a home builder in Hawaii. Aloha uses a perpetual inventory system and a job cost system in which each house is a job. Because it constructs houses, the company uses accounts titled Construction Wages and Construction Overhead. The following events occurred during August:

Accounting for construction transactions
(Obj. 2, 3, 4)

a. Purchased materials on account, $480,400.

b. Incurred construction wages of $219,800. Requisitioned direct materials and used direct labor in construction:

	Direct Materials	Direct Labor
House 302.....................................	$58,400	$42,300
House 303.....................................	69,000	32,800
House 304.....................................	67,600	50,400
House 305.....................................	84,200	52,700

c. Depreciation of construction equipment, $6,400.

d. Other construction overhead costs incurred on houses 302 through 305:

Indirect labor.......................................	$41,600
Equipment rentals paid in cash	37,300
Worker liability insurance expired	7,100

e. Allocated overhead to jobs at the predetermined overhead rate of 40% of direct labor cost.

f. Houses completed: 302, 304.

g. House sold: 304 for $189,500.

Required

1. Record the events in the general journal.

2. Open T-accounts for Work in Process Inventory and Finished Goods Inventory. Post the appropriate entries to these accounts, identifying each entry by letter. Determine the ending account balances, assuming that the beginning balances were zero.

3. Add the costs of the unfinished houses, and show that this total amount equals the ending balance in the Work in Process Inventory account.

4. Add the cost of the completed house that has not yet been sold, and show that this equals the ending balance in Finished Goods Inventory.

5. Compute gross profit on the house that was sold. What costs must gross profit cover for Aloha Construction?

P20-3B Guandong Technology Co. manufactures CDs and DVDs for computer software and entertainment companies. Guandong uses job costing and has a perpetual inventory system.

Preparing and using a job cost record
(Obj. 2, 3, 4)

On November 2, Guandong began production of 5,000 DVDs, Job 423, for Lion Pictures for $1.10 each. Guandong promised to deliver the DVDs to Lion by November 5. Guandong incurred the following costs:

(continued)

Date	Labor Time Record No.	Description	Amount
11-2	655	10 hours @ $22	$220
11-3	656	20 hours @ $16	320

Date	Materials Requisition No.	Description	Amount
11-2	63	31 lb. polycarbonate plastic @ $11	$341
11-2	64	25 lb. acrylic plastic @ $28	700
11-3	74	3 lb. refined aluminum @ $48	144

Guandong Technology allocates manufacturing overhead to jobs based on the relation between expected overhead ($537,600) and expected direct labor costs ($448,000). Job 423 was completed and shipped on November 3.

Required

1. Prepare a job cost record similar to Exhibit 20-8 for Job 423.
2. Journalize in summary form the requisition of direct materials and the assignment of direct labor and manufacturing overhead to Job 423.
3. Journalize completion of the job and the sale of the 5,000 DVDs.

Accounting for manufacturing overhead
(Obj. 3, 4)

P20-4B Precious Treasures manufactures jewelry boxes. The primary materials (wood, brass, and glass) and direct labor are traced directly to the products. Manufacturing overhead costs are allocated based on machine hours. Data for 20X7 follow:

	Budget	Actual
Machine hours	28,000 hours	32,800 hours
Direct labor hours	42,000 hours	40,000 hours
Wood	$150,000	$148,000
Maintenance labor (repairs to equipment) ..	9,000	22,500
Plant supervisor's wages	40,000	44,000
Screws, nails, and glue	20,400	41,000
Plant utilities	45,600	90,850
Brass	75,000	70,500
Glass	125,000	126,275
Freight out	35,000	44,500
Direct labor	65,000	63,000
Depreciation on plant and equipment	81,000	81,000
Advertising expenses	40,000	55,000

Required

1. Compute the predetermined manufacturing overhead rate.
2. Post actual and allocated manufacturing overhead to the Manufacturing Overhead T-account.
3. Close the under- or overallocated overhead to cost of goods sold.
4. The predetermined manufacturing overhead rate usually turns out to be inaccurate. Why don't accountants just use the actual manufacturing overhead rate?

Comprehensive accounting for manufacturing transactions
(Obj. 2, 3, 4)

P20-5B → *Link Back to Chapters 2 and 19.* Flextronix produces components for telecommunication systems. Initially the company manufactured the parts for its own networks, but it gradually began selling them to other companies as well. Flextronix's trial balance on April 1 follows.

Flextronix		
Trial Balance		
April 1, 20XX		
Cash	$ 17,980	
Accounts receivable..........................	170,360	
Inventories:		
Materials	5,290	
Work in process	41,280	
Finished goods	21,280	
Plant assets	249,570	
Accumulated depreciation		$ 68,400
Accounts payable...........................		129,360
Wages payable		2,800
Common stock		140,000
Retained earnings..........................		165,200
Sales revenues..............................		—
Cost of goods sold	—	
Manufacturing wages	—	
Manufacturing overhead	—	
Marketing and general expenses..............	—	
	$505,760	$505,760

April 1 balances in the subsidiary ledgers were

- Materials ledger: glass substrate, $2,080; multiplexers, $2,660; indirect materials, $550.
- Work in process ledger: Job 145, $41,280.
- Finished goods ledger: fiber optic cable, $9,010; laser diodes, $12,270.

April transactions are summarized as follows:

a. Collections on account, $148,270.
b. Marketing and general expenses incurred and paid, $25,740.
c. Payments on account, $37,890.
d. Materials purchased on credit: glass substrate, $7,640; multiplexers, $16,980; indirect materials, $4,600.
e. Materials used in production (requisitioned):
  - Job 145: glass substrate, $740.
  - Job 146: glass substrate, $2,180; multiplexers, $5,640.
  - Indirect materials, $2,010.
f. Manufacturing wages incurred during April, $38,420, of which $36,200 was paid. Wages payable at March 31 were paid during April, $2,800.
g. Labor time records for the month: Job 145, $4,200; Job 146, $17,800; indirect labor, $16,420.
h. Depreciation on plant and equipment, $2,340.

(continued)

i. Manufacturing overhead was allocated at the predetermined rate of 70% of direct labor cost.

j. Jobs completed during the month: Job 145, 400 fiber optic cables at total cost of $49,160.

k. Credit sales on account: all of Job 145 for $110,460 (cost $49,160).

l. Closed the Manufacturing Overhead account to Cost of Goods Sold.

Required

1. Open T-accounts for the general ledger, the materials ledger, the work in process ledger, and the finished goods ledger. Insert each account balance as given, and use the reference *Bal.*

2. Record the April transactions directly in the accounts, using the letters as references. Flextronix uses a perpetual inventory system.

3. Prepare a trial balance at April 30.

4. Use the work in process T-account to prepare a schedule of cost of goods manufactured for the month of April. (You may want to review Exhibit 19-11.)

5. Prepare an income statement for the month of April. To calculate cost of goods sold, you may want to review Exhibit 19-9. (*Hint:* In transaction l you closed any under/overallocated manufacturing overhead to Cost of Goods Sold. In the income statement, show this correction as an adjustment to Cost of Goods Sold. If manufacturing overhead is underallocated, the adjustment will increase Cost of Goods Sold. If overhead is overallocated, the adjustment will reduce Cost of Goods Sold.)

Job costing in a service company
(Obj. 5)

Student ResourceCD

spreadsheet

P20-6B WB Design, Inc., is a Web site design and consulting firm. The firm uses a job cost system, in which each client is a different "job." WB Design traces direct labor, licensing costs, and travel costs directly to each job (client). It allocates indirect costs to jobs based on a predetermined indirect cost allocation rate, computed as a percentage of direct labor costs.

At the beginning of 20X7, managing partner Mary Milici prepared the following budget:

Direct labor hours (professional).............	8,000 hours
Direct labor costs (professional)	$1,000,000
Support staff salaries......................	80,000
Computer leases...........................	46,000
Office supplies	25,000
Office rent	49,000

In November 20X7, WB Design served several clients. Records for two clients appear here:

	Organic Foods	SunNow.com
Direct labor hours	750 hours	50 hours
Licensing costs	$ 1,850	$160
Travel costs	14,150	—

Required

1. Compute WB Design's predetermined indirect cost allocation rate for 20X7.

2. Compute the total cost of each job.

3. If Milici wants to earn profits equal to 20% of sales revenue, how much (what total fee) should she charge each of these two clients?

4. Why does WB Design assign costs to jobs?

APPLY *Your Knowledge*

Decision Cases

Costing and pricing identical products
(Obj. 2, 3)

Case 1. Hegy Chocolate Ltd. is located in Cleveland. The company prepares gift boxes of chocolates for private parties and corporate promotions. Each order contains a selection of chocolates determined by the customer, and the box is designed to the customer's specifications. Accordingly, Hegy uses a job cost system and allocates manufacturing overhead based on direct labor cost.

One of Hegy's largest customers is the Bailey and Choi law firm. This organization sends chocolates to its clients each Christmas and also provides them to employees at the firm's gatherings. The law firm's managing partner, Peter Bailey, placed the client gift order in September for 500 boxes of cream-filled dark chocolates. But Bailey and Choi did not place its December staff-party order until the last week of November. This order was for an additional 100 boxes of chocolates identical to the ones to be distributed to clients.

Hegy budgeted the cost per box for the original 500-box order as follows:

Chocolate, filling, wrappers, box	$14.00
Employee time to fill and wrap the box (10 min.)	2.00
Manufacturing overhead	1.00
Total manufacturing cost	$17.00

Ben Hegy, president of Hegy Chocolate Ltd., priced the order at $20 per box.

In the past few months, Hegy Chocolate Ltd. has experienced price increases for both dark chocolate and direct labor. *All other costs have remained the same.* Hegy budgeted the cost per box for the second order as:

Chocolate, filling, wrappers, box	$15.00
Employee time to fill and wrap the box (10 min.)	2.20
Manufacturing overhead	1.10
Total manufacturing cost	$18.30

1. Do you agree with the cost analysis for the second order? Explain your answer.
2. Should the two orders be accounted for as one job or two in Hegy's system?
3. What sale price per box should Ben Hegy set for the second order? What are the advantages and disadvantages of this price?

Accounting for manufacturing overhead
(Obj. 3)

Case 2. All Natural manufactures organic fruit preserves sold primarily through health food stores and on the Web. The company closes for two weeks each December to allow employees to spend time with their families over the holiday season. All Natural's manufacturing overhead is mostly straight-line depreciation on its plant and air-conditioning costs for keeping the berries cool during the summer months. The company uses direct labor hours as the allocation base. President Kara Wise has just approved new accounting software and is telling Controller Melissa Powers about her decision.

"I think this new software will be great," Wise says. "It will save you time in preparing all those reports."

"Yes, and having so much more information just a click away will help us make better decisions and help control costs," replies Powers. "We need to consider how we can use the new system to improve our business practices."

"And I know just where to start," says Wise. "You complain each year about having to predict the weather months in advance for estimating air-conditioning costs and direct labor hours for the denominator of the predetermined manufacturing overhead rate, when professional meteorologists can't even get tomorrow's forecast right! I think we should calculate the predetermined overhead rate on a monthly basis."

Controller Powers is not so sure this is a good idea.

Required

1. What are the advantages and disadvantages of Wise's proposal?
2. Should All Natural compute its predetermined manufacturing overhead rate on an annual basis or monthly basis? Explain.

Ethical Issue

Ethics
(Obj. 4, 5)

←*Link back to Chapter 19.* Micro Tek is a contract manufacturer that produces customized computer components for several well-known computer-assembly companies. Micro Tek's latest contract with CompNow.com calls for Micro Tek to deliver sound cards that simulate surround sound from two speakers. Micro Tek spent several hundred thousand dollars to design the sound card to meet CompNow.com's specifications.

Micro Tek's president, Isabel Wang, has stipulated a pricing policy that requires bids (selling prices) for new contracts to be based on Micro Tek's estimated full product cost from all elements of the value chain, plus a profit margin. Upon reviewing the contract figures, Micro Tek's controller, Pennie Bagley, was startled to find that the cost estimates developed by Micro Tek's cost accountant, Anthony Haywood, for the CompNow.com bid were based on only the *inventoriable* costs. Bagley is upset with Haywood. She is not sure what to do next.

Required

1. How did using inventoriable cost rather than full product cost affect the amount of Micro Tek's bid for the CompNow.com job?
2. Identify the parties involved in Pennie Bagley's ethical dilemma. What are her alternatives? How would each party be affected by each alternative? What should Bagley do next?

Team Project

Comparing job costs across airlines, evaluating strategic alternatives
(Obj. 2, 3)

Major airlines like **American**, **Delta**, and **Continental** are struggling to meet the challenges of budget carriers such as **Southwest** and **JetBlue**. Suppose Delta CFO M. Michele Burns has just returned from a meeting on strategies for responding to competition from budget carriers. The vice-president of operations suggested doing nothing: "We just need to wait until these new airlines run out of money. They cannot be making money with their low fares." In contrast, the vice-president of marketing, not wanting to lose marketing share, suggests cutting Delta's fares to match the competition. "If JetBlue charges only $75 for that flight from New York, so must we!" Others, including CFO Burns, emphasized the potential for cutting costs. Another possibility is starting a new budget airline within Delta. Imagine that CEO Leo Mullin cut the meeting short, and directed Burns to "get some hard data."

As a start, Burns decides to collect cost and revenue data for a typical Delta flight, and then compare it to the data for a competitor. Assume she prepares the following schedule:

	Delta	JetBlue
Route: New York to Tampa	Flight 1247	Flight 53
Distance	1,011 miles	1,011 miles
Seats per plane............................	142	162
One-way ticket price......................	$80–$621*	$75
Food and beverage	Meal	Snack

*The highest price is first class airfare

Excluding food and beverage, Burns estimates that the cost per available seat mile is 8.4 cents for Delta, compared to 5.3 cents for JetBlue. (That is, the cost of flying a seat for one mile—whether or not the seat is occupied—is 8.4 cents for Delta, and 5.3 cents for JetBlue.) Assume the average cost of food and beverage is $5 per passenger for snacks and $10 for a meal.

Split your team into two groups. Group 1 should prepare its response to Requirement 1 and group 2 should prepare its response to Requirement 2 before the entire team meets to consider Requirements 3 through 6.

Required

1. Group 1 uses the data to determine for Delta:
   a. the total cost of Flight 1247, assuming a full plane (100% load factor)
   b. the revenue generated by Flight 1247, assuming a 100% load factor and average revenue per one-way ticket of $102
   c. the profit per Flight 1247, given the responses to a. and b.

2. Group 2 uses the data to determine for JetBlue:
   a. the total cost of Flight 53, assuming a full plane (100% load factor)
   b. the revenue generated by Flight 53, assuming a 100% load factor
   c. the profit per Flight 53, given the responses to a. and b.

3. The entire team meets, and both groups combine their analyses. Based on the responses to Requirements 1 and 2, carefully evaluate each of the four alternative strategies discussed in Delta's executive meeting.

4. CFO Burns wants additional data before she meets again with Delta's CEO. Each group should repeat the analyses in *both* Requirements 1 and 2, using another Delta route in Requirement 1, and a budget airline other than JetBlue in Requirement 2 (other budget airlines include **America West**, with a cost per available seat mile of about 6.5 cents, or **Southwest Airlines**, with a cost per available seat mile of about 6.3 cents). Information on flights, available seats, airfares, and mileage are available on airline Web sites.

5. The analysis in this project is based on several simplifying assumptions. As a team, brainstorm factors that your quantitative evaluation does not include, but that may affect a comparison of Delta's operations against budget carriers.

6. Prepare a memo from CFO Burns addressed to Delta CEO Mullin, summarizing the results of your analyses. Be sure to include the limitations of your analyses identified in Requirement 5. Use the following format for your memo.

Date:	_____
To:	CEO Leo F. Mullin
From:	CFO M. Michele Burns
Subject:	Delta's Response to Competition from Budget Airlines

For Internet Exercises, go to the Web site www.prenhall.com/horngren.

CHAPTER 21

Process Costing

TIPS CHECK YOUR RESOURCES

- Visit the www.prenhall.com/horngren **Web site** for self-study quizzes, video clips, and other resources

- Try the **Quick Check** exercise at the end of the chapter to test your knowledge

- Learn the **key terms**

- Do the **Starter** exercises keyed in the margins

- Work the **mid-** and **end-of-chapter summary problems**

- Use the **Concept Links** to review material in other chapters

- Search the **CD** for review materials by chapter or by key word

- Watch the **On Location Jelly Belly** video to review process costing

LEARNING OBJECTIVES

1 Distinguish between the flow of costs in process costing and job costing

2 Compute equivalent units

3 Use process costing to assign costs to units completed and to units in ending work in process inventory

4 Use the weighted-average method to assign costs to units completed and to units in ending work in process inventory in a second department

What's your favorite Jelly Belly flavor? Chocolate Pudding? Very Cherry? Lemon Drop? Peanut Butter? Or maybe Piña Colada? Have you ever wondered how they make these tasty gems?

Each tiny Jelly Belly jelly bean spends 7 to 10 days going through eight different processes:

- Cooking the centers
- Shaping hot liquid centers into jelly beans
- Drying
- Sugar shower
- Shell-building
- Polishing
- Stamping (name of the company on each bean)
- Packaging

Jelly Belly Jelly Beans

The family that owns Jelly Belly needs to know how much it costs to make each batch. That helps them set selling prices and measure profits. They also want to know how efficiently each process is operating. That helps them control costs. The owners use accounting information to answer these questions.

Jelly Belly mass produces its jelly beans in a sequence of processes and accumulates costs for each *process*. Then the company spreads these costs over the pounds of jelly beans passing through each process. This *process costing* approach differs from the job costing approach that Dell Computer uses for its computers. Why the difference? Because Jelly Belly mass produces its products, while Dell custom builds each computer to a specific order. It certainly would not be practical to use job cost records to compile the cost of individual jelly beans! ■

■ Sitemap

- ■ **Overview**
- ■ **Building Blocks**
- ■ **Illustrating Process Costing**
- ■ **Costing in a Second Department**
- ■ **Appendix: FIFO**

Student ResourceCD

job costing, process costing, work in process inventory

As the chapter-opening story explains, managers need to know how much it costs to make their products. Why? So they can control costs, set selling prices, and identify their most profitable products.

Process Costing: An Overview

Let's start by contrasting the two basic types of costing systems: *job costing* and *process costing*.

Distinguish between the flow of costs in process costing and job costing

Two Basic Costing Systems: Job Costing and Process Costing

We saw in Chapter 20 that Dell Computer, Boeing, and PricewaterhouseCoopers use job costing to determine the cost of producing custom goods and services. Job cost records accumulate the cost of each individual job, like each computer Dell custom-builds to a customer order. In contrast, companies like Jelly Belly, Shell Oil, and Sony use a series of steps (called *processes*) to make large quantities of similar products. These companies typically use *process costing* systems.

For the rest of our discussion, we'll simplify Jelly Belly's processes. We'll combine cooking, shaping, and drying the jelly bean centers into a single process called Centers. We'll also combine the sugar shower, shell-building, polishing, and stamping steps into a second process called Shells. The third process is Packaging.

Jelly Belly *accumulates* the costs of each process and then *assigns* these costs to the units (pounds of jelly beans) passing through that process.

Suppose the Centers process incurs $1,350,000 of costs to produce centers for 1,000,000 pounds of jelly beans, the Shells process incurs $800,000, and Packaging incurs $700,000. The total cost to produce a pound of jelly beans is the sum of the cost per pound for each of the three processes:

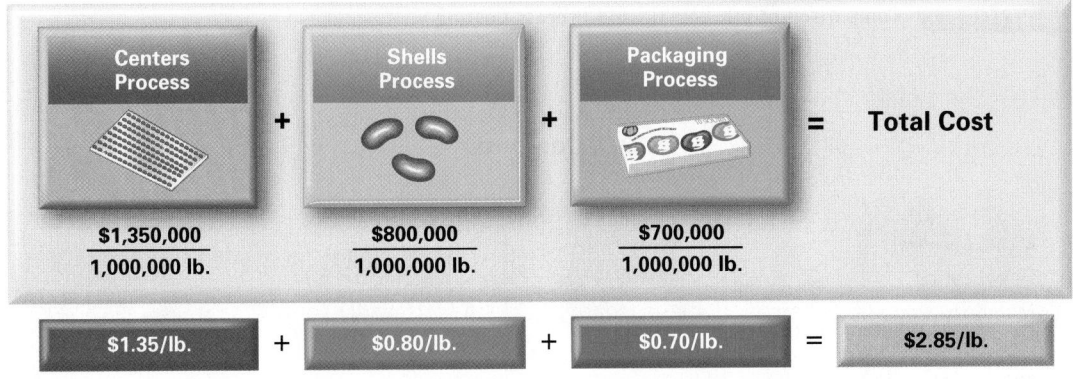

Jelly Belly's owners use the cost per unit of each process to help control costs. For example, they can compare the actual cost of producing centers for a pound of jelly beans (assumed to be $1.35 in our example) to the budget or plan. If the actual cost of the Centers process exceeds the budget, they can look for ways to cut costs in that process. Jelly Belly's owners also consider the total cost of making a pound of jelly beans (assumed to be $2.85 in our example) when setting selling prices. Of course, the price should be high enough to cover costs *and* to return a profit. Jelly Belly also uses the total cost of making a pound of jelly beans for financial reporting:

- To value the ending inventory of jelly beans for the balance sheet
- To value cost of goods sold for the income statement

The simple computation of the cost to make a pound of jelly beans is correct only if there are no work in process inventories. But it takes 7 to 10 days to complete all the processes. So Jelly Belly does have inventories of partially complete jelly beans. These inventories make the costing more complicated. In the rest of this chapter, you'll learn how to do process costing when there are work in process inventories.

How Does the Flow of Costs Differ Between Job and Process Costing?

Exhibit 21-1 compares the flow of costs in

- A job costing system for **Dell Computer**
- A process costing system for **Jelly Belly**

Panel A shows that Dell's job costing system has a single Work in Process Inventory control account, supported by individual subsidiary job cost records for each job in process (that is, each custom-built computer). Dell assigns direct materials, direct labor, and manufacturing overhead to individual jobs, as explained in Chapter 20. When a job is finished, its costs flow directly into Finished Goods Inventory, *not* from one Work in Process Inventory account into another.

In contrast to Dell's individual jobs, Jelly Belly uses a series of *manufacturing processes* to produce jelly beans. Exhibit 21-2 shows that in the Centers process, Jelly Belly uses labor and equipment to cook flavorings and sugar into jelly bean centers. In the Shells process, Jelly Belly uses labor and equipment to coat the centers with syrup and glaze to form the crunchy shells. Finally, the Packaging process uses labor and other equipment to package the finished jelly beans into various boxes and bags.

✔ Starter 21-1

Exhibit 21-1 Comparison of Job Costing and Process Costing

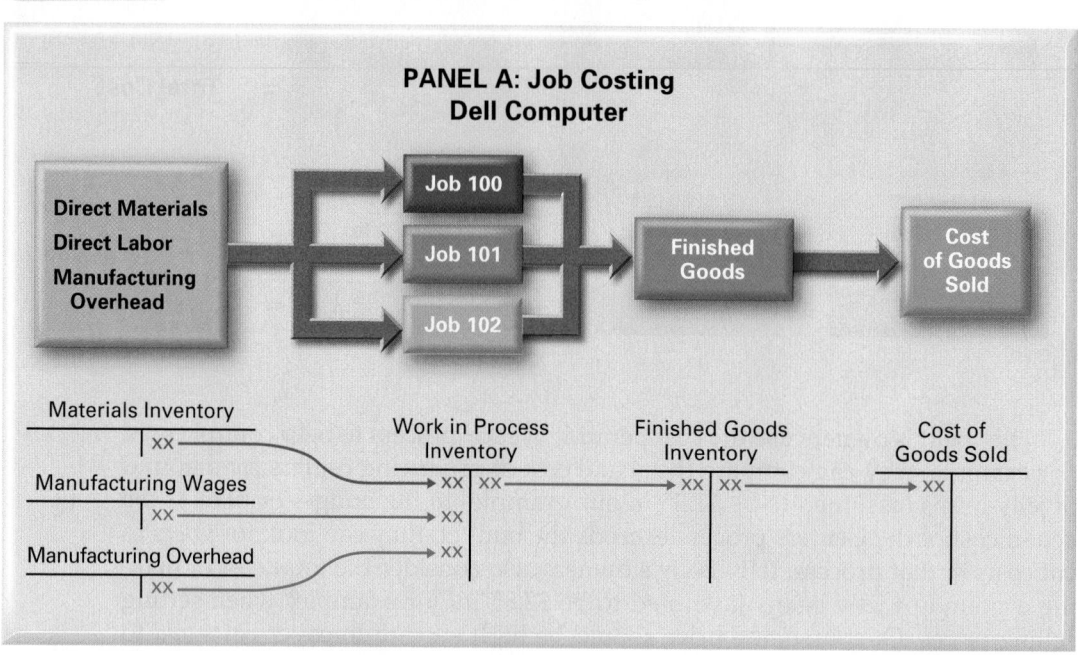

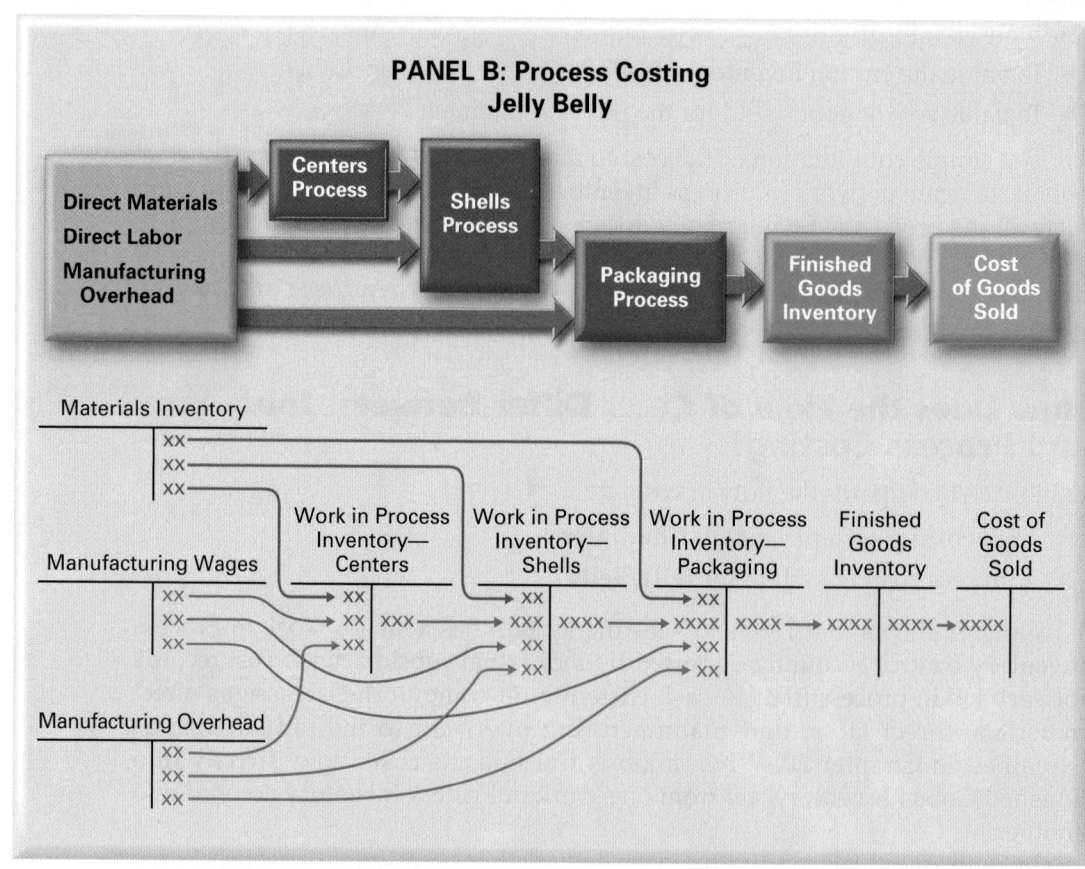

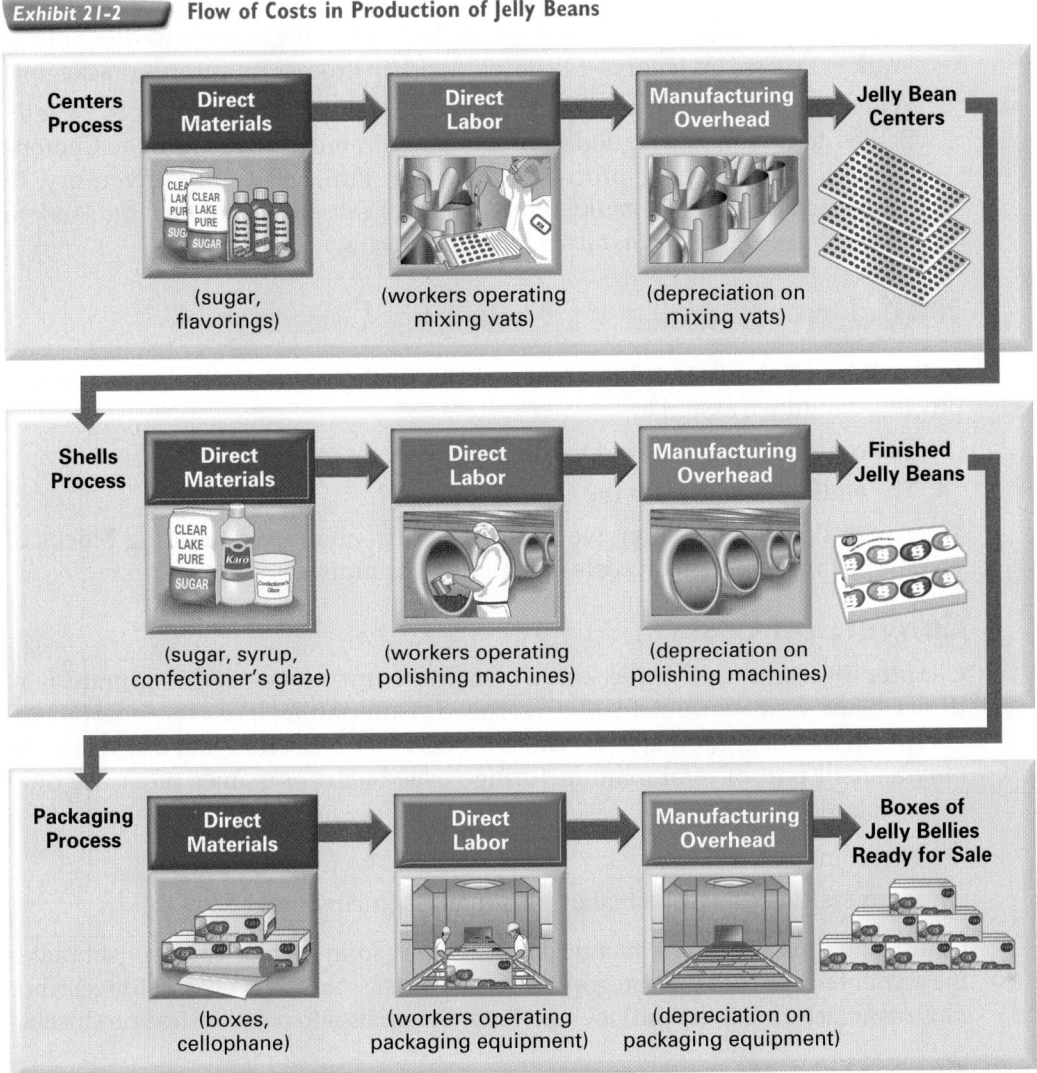

Exhibit 21-2 Flow of Costs in Production of Jelly Beans

Panel B of Exhibit 21-1 summarizes the flow of costs through this process costing system. Study the exhibit carefully, paying particular attention to the following key points.

1. Each process (Centers, Shells, and Packaging) has its own separate Work in Process Inventory account.
2. Direct materials, direct labor, and manufacturing overhead are assigned to the Work in Process Inventory accounts for each process. For example:

	Work in Process Inventory—Centers	Work in Process Inventory—Shells	Work in Process Inventory—Packaging
Direct materials	Sugar, flavorings	Sugar, syrup, confectioners' glaze	Boxes, cellophane
Direct labor	Mixing-vat operators' wages	Polishing-machine operators' wages	Packaging-equipment operators' wages
Manufacturing overhead	Depreciation on mixing vat	Depreciation on polishing machine	Depreciation on packaging equipment

3. When the Centers process is complete, the jelly bean centers move out of this process and into the Shells process. The cost of the centers is also transferred out of Work in Process Inventory—Centers into Work in Process Inventory—Shells.

4. When the Shells process is complete, the finished jelly beans move out of this process and into the Packaging process. The cost of the jelly beans flows out of Work in Process Inventory—Shells into Work in Process Inventory—Packaging.

5. When the Packaging process is complete, the finished packages of Jelly Bellies go into finished goods storage. The combined costs from the Centers, Shells, and Packaging processes flow into Finished Goods Inventory. In process costing *costs flow into Finished Goods Inventory only from the Work in Process Inventory of the **last** manufacturing process.*

Student ResourceCD

conversion costs, cost assignment, equivalent unit costs

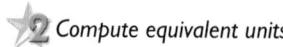

Compute equivalent units

Building Blocks of Process Costing

In Panel B of Exhibit 21-1, how much of the total costs incurred in the Centers process should we assign to:

- The centers transferred out to the Shells process versus
- The ending inventory in the Centers process?

To answer this key question, we must first learn about two building blocks of process costing: conversion costs and equivalent units.

Conversion Costs

Chapter 19 introduced three kinds of manufacturing costs: direct materials, direct labor, and manufacturing overhead. Companies like **HP** and **Harley-Davidson** that use automated production processes often find that direct labor is only a small part of total manufacturing costs. Such companies often use only two categories:

- Direct materials
- **Conversion costs** (direct labor plus manufacturing overhead)

Combining direct labor and manufacturing overhead in a single category simplifies the accounting. We call this category *conversion costs* because it is the cost (direct labor plus manufacturing overhead) to *convert* raw materials into new finished products.

Conversion Costs
Direct labor plus manufacturing overhead.

Equivalent Units

When a company has work in process inventories of partially completed goods, we use equivalent units to measure the amount of work done during a period. **Equivalent units** express the amount of work done during a period in terms of fully complete units of output. Assume **Calloway's** golf ball production plant has 5,000 balls in ending work in process inventory. Each ball is 80% of the way through the production process. If conversion costs are incurred evenly throughout the process, then getting 5,000 balls each 80% of the way through the process takes about the same amount of work as getting 4,000 balls (5,000 × 80%) all the way through. Thus, ending work in process inventory has 4,000 equivalent units.

Equivalent Units
Express the amount of work done during a period in terms of fully complete units of output.

For costs that are incurred evenly throughout the production process:

NUMBER OF PARTIALLY COMPLETE UNITS	×	PERCENTAGE OF PROCESS COMPLETED	=	NUMBER OF EQUIVALENT UNITS
5,000	×	80%	=	4,000

This formula holds only for costs that are incurred evenly throughout production. This is usually true for conversion costs (direct labor and manufacturing overhead). However, direct materials are often added at a particular point in the process. Rubber is added at the beginning of the production process, and packaging materials are not added until the end. How many equivalent units of rubber and packaging materials are in the ending inventory of 5,000 balls?

Look at the time line in Exhibit 21-3:   ✔ Starter 21-2

Exhibit 21-3   Calloway Production Plant Time Line

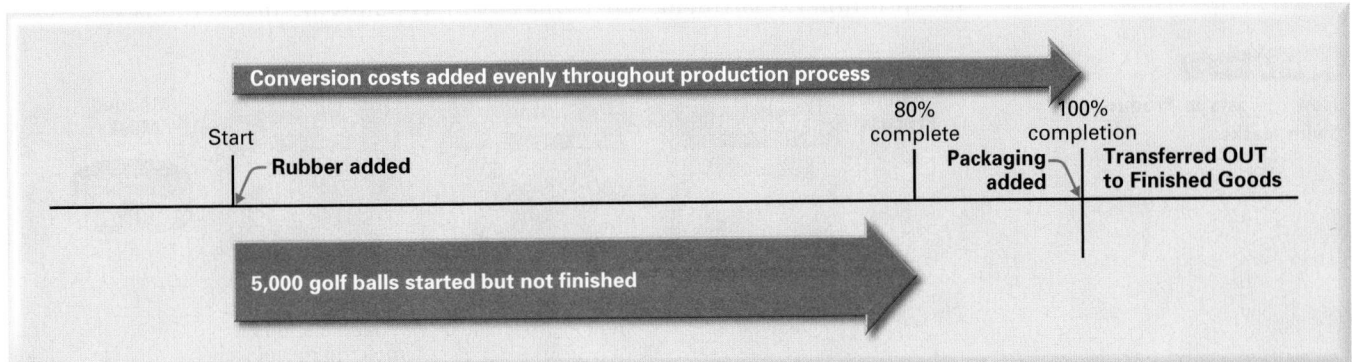

All 5,000 balls are 80% complete, so they all have passed the point at which rubber is added. Each ball has its full share of rubber, so the balls have 5,000 equivalent units of rubber. In contrast, the time line shows that *none* of the 5,000 balls has made it to the end of the process, where the packaging materials are added. The ending inventory therefore has *zero* equivalent units of packaging materials.

To summarize, the 5,000 balls in ending work in process inventory have

- 5,000 equivalent units of rubber
- 0 equivalent units of packaging materials
- 4,000 equivalent units of conversion costs

Be careful to distinguish the *end of the production process* from the *end of the accounting period*. Goods at the end of the production process are transferred to the next process or to finished goods. For example, Calloway's completed golf balls proceed to the finished goods warehouse. By contrast, at the end of the accounting period, goods that are only partway through the production process are the ending work in process inventory. Calloway's ending work in process inventory includes 5,000 golf balls that have their rubber cores but no packaging.

Colleges and universities use the equivalent-unit concept to describe the number of faculty as well as the number of students. The **University of Georgia** has about 2,000 full-time faculty and 400 part-time faculty. Assume the following:

1. A full-time faculty member teaches six courses per year
2. 100 part-time faculty teach three courses per year
3. 300 part-time faculty teach two courses per year

What is the "full-time equivalent" faculty—the number of equivalent units of faculty?

Answer: Compute the full-time equivalent faculty as follows:

Full-time faculty	$2,000 \times 6/6 = 2,000$
Half-time faculty	$100 \times 3/6 = 50$
One-third time faculty	$300 \times 2/6 = 100$
Full-time equivalent faculty	$\underline{\underline{2,150}}$

☐ Overview
☐ Building Blocks
■ Illustrating Process Costing
☐ Costing in a Second Department
☐ Appendix: FIFO

conversion costs, cost assignment, equivalent unit costs, transferred-in costs, work in process inventory

 Use process costing to assign costs to units completed and to units in ending work in process inventory

Illustrating Process Costing

Let's see how SeaView, a sporting goods company, uses process costing to measure (1) its cost of producing swim masks and (2) the cost of the two major processes it uses to make the masks. Exhibit 21-4 illustrates SeaView's production process. The Shaping Department begins with direct materials (including plastic) that labor and equipment transform into shaped masks. The direct materials are added at the beginning but conversion costs are incurred evenly throughout the process. After shaping, the partially completed masks move to the Insertion Department, where the clear faceplates are inserted.

Exhibit 21-4

Flow of Costs in Producing Swim Masks

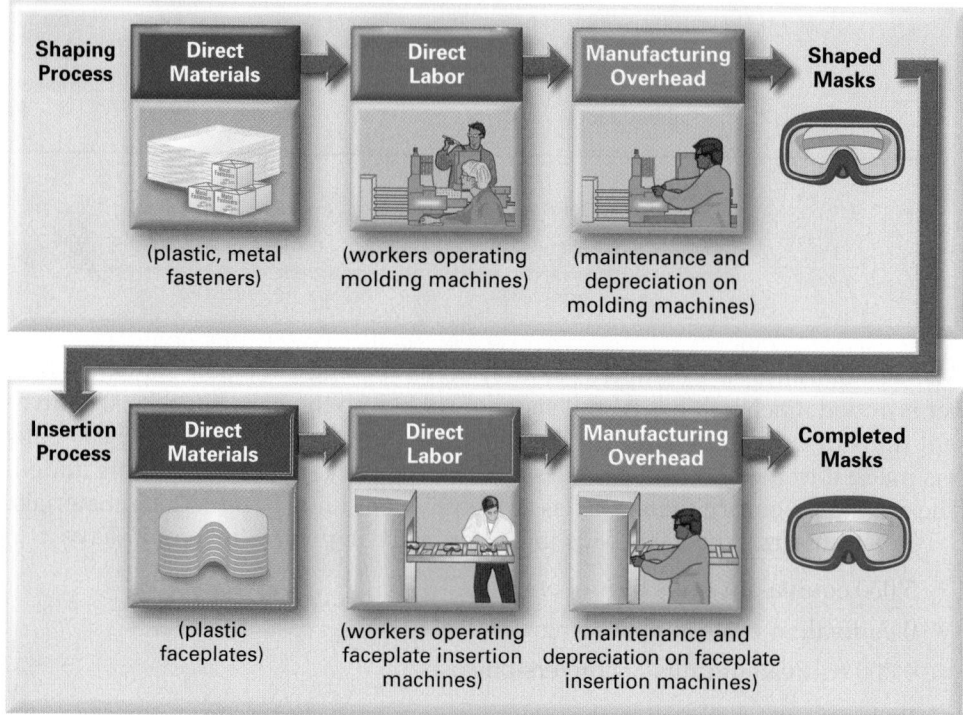

During October, the Shaping Department incurs the following costs for 50,000 masks:

Direct materials		$140,000
Conversion costs:		
Direct labor	$21,250	
Manufacturing overhead	46,750	68,000
Costs to account for		$208,000

If shaping is complete for all 50,000 masks, the costs transferred to Work in Process Inventory—Insertion are the full $208,000. The unit cost is $4.16 ($208,000/50,000 masks).

But what if only 40,000 masks are completely through the shaping process? At October 31, the Shaping Department still has 10,000 masks that are only one-quarter of the way through. How do we split the $208,000 between

- 40,000 completely shaped masks transferred to the Insertion Department
- 10,000 partially shaped masks remaining in the Shaping Department's ending work in process inventory

The answer lies in a five-step process costing procedure.

Step 1: Summarize the Flow of Physical Units

Exhibit 21-5 tracks the movement of swim masks into and out of the Shaping Department. We assume work began October 1, so Work in Process Inventory had a zero balance at September 30. This simplifies the computations so you can more easily learn basic process costing. But the simplification is realistic for firms that have little or no work in process inventory, such as food processors, and financial institutions that clear transactions daily. In the second half of the chapter, you'll see how beginning work in process inventory affects the analysis.

Of the 50,000 masks started in October, 40,000 were completed and transferred out to the Insertion Department during the month. The remaining 10,000 partially shaped masks are the Shaping Department's ending work in process inventory on October 31.

Exhibit 21-5   Step 1: Summarize the Flow of Physical Units; Step 2: Compute Output in Terms of Equivalent Units

SeaView Shaping Department			
Month Ended October 31, 20XX			
	Step 1	Step 2: Equivalent Units	
Flow of Production	Flow of Physical Units	Direct Materials	Conversion Costs
Units to account for:			
Beginning work in process, September 30	—		
Started in production during October..................	50,000		
Total physical units to account for	50,000		
Units accounted for:			
Completed and transferred out during October	40,000	40,000	40,000
Ending work in process, October 31	10,000	10,000	2,500*
Total physical units accounted for	50,000		
Equivalent units		50,000	42,500

*10,000 units each 25% complete = 2,500 equivalent units

Step 2: Compute Output in Terms of Equivalent Units

The Shaping Department time line in Exhibit 21-6 shows that all direct materials are added at the beginning of the process. In contrast, conversion costs are incurred evenly throughout the process. Thus, we must compute equivalent units separately for direct materials and conversion costs.

✔ **Starter 21-3**

✔ **Starter 21-4**

Exhibit 21-6   SeaView's Shaping Department Time Line

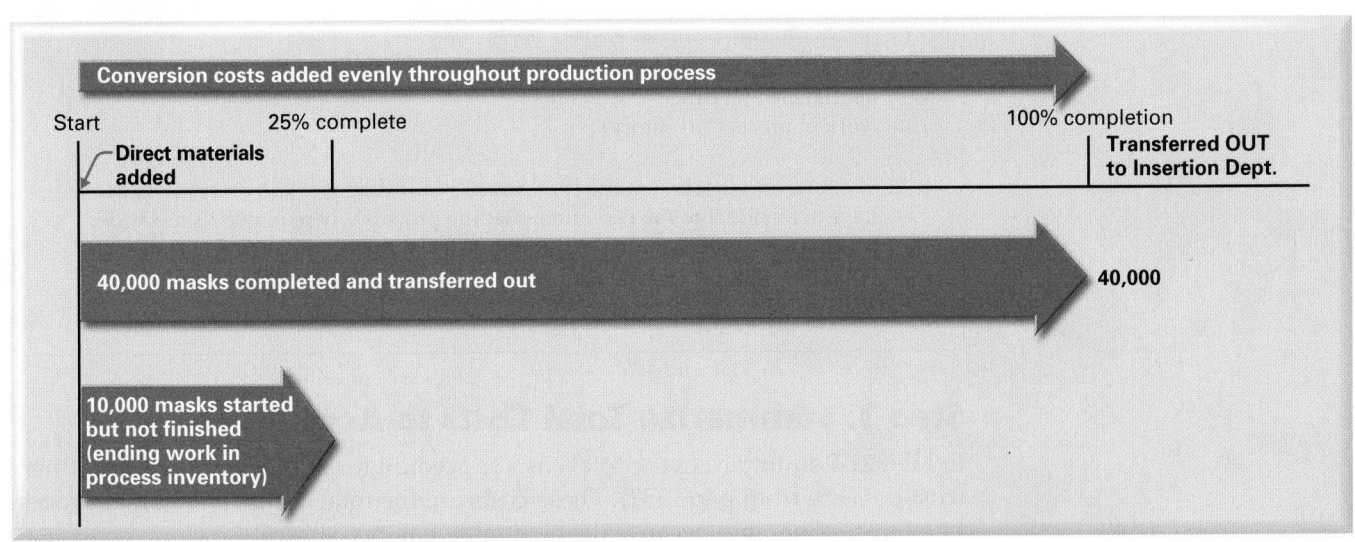

As Exhibit 21-6 shows, 40,000 masks are complete as to both materials and conversion costs. These completed masks have incurred 40,000 equivalent units of direct materials and 40,000 equivalent units of conversion costs.

The Shaping Department has another 10,000 masks that are only 25% of the way through the process on October 31. The time line shows that all the direct materials have been added to these 10,000 masks. The total equivalent units of direct materials include the 40,000 finished masks plus the 10,000 masks in ending (work in process) inventory that are complete as to direct materials, as shown in step 2 of Exhibit 21-5.

Shaping Department conversion costs are incurred evenly throughout the process. The time line shows that for each of the 10,000 partially completed masks, 25% of the conversion costs have been incurred by October 31. The equivalent units of conversion costs are:

$$10,000 \times 25\% = 2,500 \text{ equivalent units}$$

The total equivalent units of conversion costs include the 40,000 finished masks plus the 2,500 equivalent units of conversion costs from the masks in ending work in process inventory that are only partially completed on October 31. See step 2 of Exhibit 21-5.

Suppose that direct materials were added at the *end* of SeaView's shaping process rather than at the beginning.

1. Draw a new time line similar to Exhibit 21-6.
2. Use the time line to determine the number of equivalent units of direct materials.

Answers

1. Conversion costs added evenly throughout process

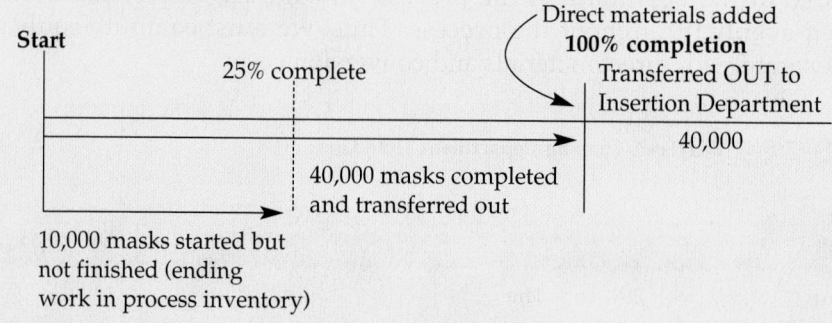

2. The time line shows that the 10,000 masks in ending work in process inventory have not made it to the end of the shaping process where materials are added. Materials have been added *only* to the 40,000 masks completed and transferred out. Thus, there are 40,000 equivalent units of direct materials.

Step 3: Summarize Total Costs to Account For

Exhibit 21-7 summarizes the total costs to account for in the Shaping Department (cost data are from page 852). These costs are the total debits in Work in Process Inventory—Shaping, because the beginning balance is zero.

Exhibit 21-7

Step 3: Summarize Total Costs to Account For

SeaView Shaping Department
Month Ended October 31, 20XX

Work in Process Inventory—Shaping

	Physical Units	Dollars		Physical Units	Dollars
Beginning inventory, September 30	-0-	$ -0-	Transferred out	40,000	$?
Production started:	50,000				
Direct materials		140,000			
Conversion costs:					
Direct labor		21,250			
Manufacturing overhead		46,750			
Total to account for	50,000	$208,000			
Ending inventory, October 31	10,000	$?			

The Shaping Department has 50,000 physical units and $208,000 of costs to account for. Our next task is to split these costs between the 40,000 shaped masks transferred out to the Insertion Department and the 10,000 masks that remain in the Shaping Department's ending work in process inventory.

Step 4: Compute the Cost per Equivalent Unit

In step 2, we computed the total number of equivalent units for direct materials (50,000) and conversion costs (42,500). Because the equivalent units differ, we must compute a separate cost per unit for each category. Exhibit 21-7 shows that the direct materials cost is $140,000. Conversion cost is $68,000, which is the sum of direct labor ($21,250) and manufacturing overhead ($46,750).

To compute the cost per equivalent unit, remember that the word *per* means "divided by." So the cost *per* equivalent unit is the cost *divided by* the number of equivalent units, as shown in Exhibit 21-8.

✔ Starter 21-5

✔ Starter 21-6

Exhibit 21-8

Step 4: Compute the Cost per Equivalent Unit

SeaView Shaping Department
Month Ended October 31, 20XX

	Direct Materials	Conversion Costs
Beginning work in process, September 30	$ 0	$ 0
Costs added during October (from Exhibit 21-7) ..	$140,000	$68,000
Divide by equivalent units (from Exhibit 21-5)	÷ 50,000	÷42,500
Cost per equivalent unit	$2.80	$1.60

In addition to using the cost per equivalent unit in the five-step process costing procedure, managers also use this information to determine how well they have controlled costs. If the cost per equivalent unit of conversion (or direct materials) meets or beats the budgeted target cost per equivalent unit, the manager has successfully controlled the conversion (or direct materials) costs.

Step 5: Assign Costs to Units Completed and to Units in Ending Work in Process Inventory

Exhibit 21-9 shows how the equivalent units computed in step 2 (Exhibit 21-5) are costed at the cost per equivalent unit computed in step 4 (Exhibit 21-8). The goal of Exhibit 21-9 is to determine how much of the $208,000 total costs incurred by the Shaping Department should be assigned to (1) the 40,000 completely shaped masks that have been transferred out to the Insertion Department and (2) the 10,000 partially shaped masks remaining in Shaping's ending work in process inventory.

✔ Starter 21-7

Exhibit 21-9   Step 5: Assign Costs to Units Completed and to Units in Ending Work in Process Inventory

SeaView Shaping Department
Month Ended October 31, 20XX

	Direct Materials	Conversion Costs	Total
Completed and transferred out (40,000)	[40,000 × ($2.80 + $1.60)]		= $176,000
Ending work in process inventory (10,000):			
Direct materials	[10,000 × $2.80]		= $ 28,000
Conversion costs		[2,500 × $1.60]	= 4,000
Total cost of ending work in process inventory			$ 32,000
Total costs accounted for			$208,000

First consider the 40,000 masks completed and transferred out. Exhibit 21-5 reveals 40,000 equivalent units of work for both direct materials and conversion costs. Thus, the total cost of these completed masks is 40,000 × ($2.80 + $1.60) = $176,000, as shown in Exhibit 21-9.

Next consider the 10,000 masks still being shaped at the end of the month. These masks have 10,000 equivalent units of direct materials (at $2.80 per unit), so the direct material cost is 10,000 × $2.80 = $28,000. The 2,500 equivalent units of conversion work in the ending inventory at $1.60 per equivalent unit yields conversion costs of $4,000 (2,500 × $1.60). As Exhibit 21-9 shows, the total cost of the 10,000 partially completed masks in Shaping's ending (work in process) inventory is the sum of these direct material and conversion costs: $28,000 + $4,000 = $32,000.

Exhibit 21-9 has accomplished our goal of splitting the $208,000 total cost identified in step 3 (Exhibit 21-7) between

The 40,000 masks completed and transferred out to the Insertion Department.	$176,000
The 10,000 masks remaining in the Shaping Department's ending work in process inventory on October 31	32,000
Total costs of the Shaping Department	$208,000

Journal entries to record October production in the Shaping Department follow (data from Exhibit 21-7):

Work in Process Inventory—Shaping........	208,000	
Materials Inventory............		140,000
Manufacturing Wages...........		21,250
Manufacturing Overhead........		46,750

To requisition materials and assign labor and overhead cost to the Shaping Department.

The entry to transfer the cost of the 40,000 completed masks out of the Shaping Department and into the Insertion Department is as follows (data from Exhibit 21-9):

Work in Process Inventory—Insertion	176,000	
Work in Process Inventory—Shaping ..		176,000

After these entries are posted, the Work in Process Inventory—Shaping account appears as follows:

Work in Process Inventory—Shaping

Balance, September 30	—	Transferred to Insertion	176,000
Direct materials	140,000		
Direct labor	21,250		
Manufacturing overhead	46,750		
Balance, October 31	32,000		

✔ **Starter 21-8**

What is the shaping cost per mask for each of the 40,000 masks completed and transferred out of the Shaping Department and into the Insertion Department? Why would SeaView's managers want this information?

Answer: Shaping's cost per mask is $4.40 ($2.80 + $1.60)—the $176,000 total Shaping Department cost assigned to the masks completed and transferred out (from Exhibit 21-9) divided by the total number of masks completed and transferred out of Shaping and into Insertion (40,000).

SeaView's managers would compare the cost per mask of the shaping process in October against the planned cost per mask to evaluate the efficiency of the Shaping Department's October operations. Also, the costs of the shaped masks will flow into the Insertion Department and will become part of the total cost of the completed masks. Management can use the total cost of the masks to set selling prices and to determine which products are most profitable.

Before continuing, review the Process Costing Decision Guidelines to make sure you understand equivalent units and the flow of costs in process costing.

Decision Guidelines

PROCESS COSTING—FIRST PROCESS (NO BEGINNING INVENTORY)

Here are some of the key decisions SeaView made in setting up its process costing system.

Decision	Guidelines
Should SeaView use job or process costing?	SeaView mass-produces large quantities of identical swim masks using two production processes: shaping and insertion. It uses *process costing* to: 1. *Accumulate* the cost of each process 2. *Assign* these costs to the masks passing through that process

Decision Guidelines *(continued)*

Decision	Guidelines
How do costs flow from Work in Process Inventory to Finished Goods Inventory in SeaView's process costing system?	In SeaView's process costing system, costs flow from: Work in Process Inventory—Shaping ↓ Work in Process Inventory—Insertion ↓ Finished Goods Inventory More generally, costs flow from one Work in Process Inventory account to the next until the last process, after which they flow into Finished Goods Inventory.
How many Work in Process Inventory accounts does SeaView's process costing system have?	SeaView uses a separate Work in Process Inventory account for each of its two major processes: Shaping and Insertion.
How to account for partially completed products?	Use equivalent units.
Which costs require separate equivalent-unit computations?	Compute equivalent units separately for each input added at a different point in the production process. SeaView computes equivalent units separately for materials and conversion costs because materials are added at a particular point in the production process, but conversion costs are added evenly throughout the process.
How to compute equivalent units?	SeaView's *conversion costs* are incurred evenly throughout the production process, so the equivalent units are computed as follows: $$\begin{array}{c} \text{Equivalent} \\ \text{units} \end{array} = \begin{array}{c} \text{Number of} \\ \text{partially} \\ \text{complete} \\ \text{units} \end{array} \times \begin{array}{c} \text{Percentage} \\ \text{of} \\ \text{process} \\ \text{completed} \end{array}$$ SeaView's *materials* are added at specific points in the production process, so the equivalent units are computed as follows: • If physical units have passed the point at which materials are added → units are complete with respect to materials, so equivalent units of materials = physical units • If physical units have *not* passed the point at which materials are added → units have not incurred any materials, so equivalent units of materials = 0
How to compute the cost per equivalent unit?	Divide the cost by the number of equivalent units.
How to split the costs of the shaping process between • Swim masks completed and transferred out? • Partially complete swim masks in ending work in process inventory?	Multiply the cost per equivalent unit by • Number of equivalent units of work in the physical units completed and transferred out • Number of equivalent units of work in the ending work in process inventory
How well did the manager of the Shaping Department control the department's costs?	If direct material and conversion cost per equivalent unit meets or beats target unit costs, the manager has done a good job controlling costs.

MID-CHAPTER *Summary Problem*

Use the five steps of process costing to identify the missing amounts X and Y in the following report prepared by Florida Tile Industries for May.

Tile-Forming Department
Month Ended May 31, 20XX

	Physical Units	Total Costs
Beginning work in process, April 30	—	$ —
Started in production during May	20,000	43,200*
Total to account for	20,000	$43,200
Completed and transferred to Finishing Department during May.	16,000	$ X
Ending work in process, May 31 (25% complete as to direct materials, 55% complete as to conversion cost).	4,000	Y
Total accounted for	20,000	$43,200

*Includes direct materials of $6,800 and conversion costs of $36,400

Solution

STEP 1 Summarize the flow of physical units.

STEP 2 Compute output in terms of equivalent units.

Tile-Forming Department
Month Ended May 31, 20XX

	Step 1	Step 2: Equivalent Units	
Flow of Production	Flow of Physical Units	Direct Materials	Conversion Costs
Units to account for:			
Beginning work in process, April 30	—		
Started in production during May.	20,000		
Total physical units to account for	20,000		
Units accounted for:			
Completed and transferred out in May	16,000	16,000	16,000
Ending work in process, May 31	4,000	1,000*	2,200*
Total physical units accounted for	20,000		
Equivalent units		17,000	18,200

*Direct materials: 4,000 units each 25% complete = 1,000 equivalent units
Conversion costs: 4,000 units each 55% complete = 2,200 equivalent units

STEP 3 Summarize total costs to account for.

| **Tile-Forming Department** | | | |
| **Month Ended May 31, 20XX** | | | |
	Direct Materials	Conversion Costs	Total
Beginning work in process, April 30...	$ 0	$ 0	$ 0
Costs added during May*	6,800	36,400	43,200
Total costs to account for	$6,800	$36,400	$43,200

*From the first report in the Mid-Chapter Summary Problem.

STEP 4 Compute the cost per equivalent unit.

| **Tile-Forming Department** | | |
| **Month Ended May 31, 20XX** | | |
	Direct Materials	Conversion Costs
Beginning work in process, April 30	$ 0	$ 0
Costs added during May	$ 6,800	$36,400
Divide by equivalent units	÷17,000	÷18,200
Cost per equivalent unit	$0.40	$2.00

STEP 5 Assign costs to units completed and to units in ending work in process inventory.

| **Tile-Forming Department** | | | |
| **Month Ended May 31, 20XX** | | | |
	Direct Materials	Conversion Costs	Total
X: Units completed and transferred out (16,000)	[16,000 × ($0.40 + $2.00)]		= $38,400
Units in ending work in process inventory (4,000):			
Direct materials.............	[1,000 × $0.40]		= 400
Conversion costs............		[2,200 × $2.00] =	4,400
Y: Total cost of ending work in process inventory			4,800
Total costs accounted for			$43,200

Student ResourceCD

conversion costs, cost assignment, equivalent unit costs, weighted-average costing method

Use the weighted-average method to assign costs to units completed and to units in ending work in process inventory in a second department.

Process Costing in a Second Department

Most products require a series of processing steps. In this section, we consider a second department—SeaView's Insertion Department—to complete the picture of process costing.

The Insertion Department receives the shaped masks and polishes them before inserting the faceplates at the end of the process. Exhibit 21-10 shows that

- Shaped masks are transferred in from Shaping at the beginning of Insertion's process.
- Insertion's conversion costs are added evenly throughout the process.
- Insertion's direct materials (faceplates) are not added until the end of the process.

Keep in mind that *direct materials* in the Insertion Department refers to the faceplates added *in that department* and not to the materials (the plastic) added in the Shaping Department. Likewise, *conversion cost* in the Insertion Department refers to all manufacturing costs (other than direct materials) incurred only in Insertion.

Exhibit 21-10	SeaView's Insertion Department Time Line (Weighted-Average)

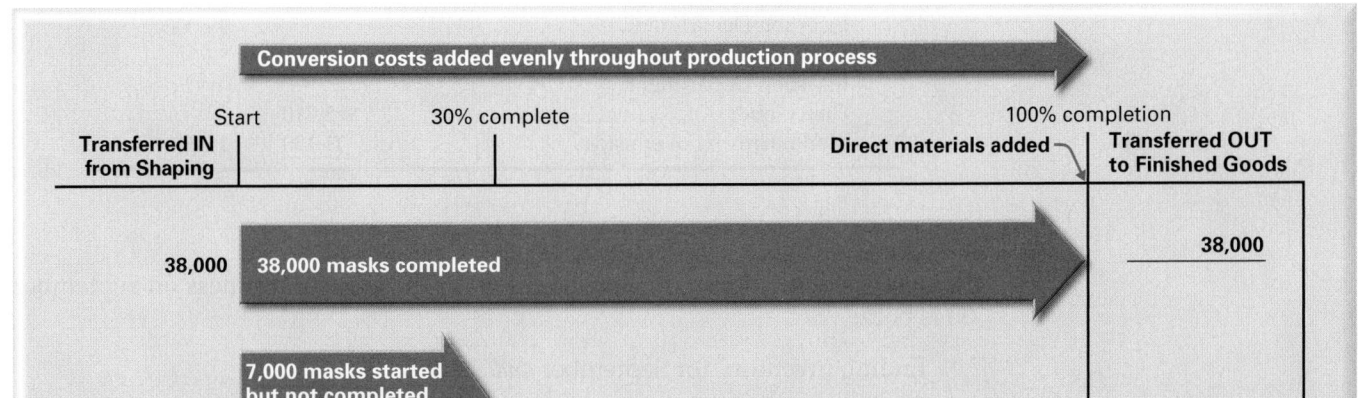

The Weighted-Average Process Costing Method

Here we consider the weighted-average method of accounting for process costs. → The appendix to this chapter covers the FIFO method. Both the weighted-average and the FIFO methods rely on the five-step process costing procedure. The only difference between the two methods lies in how they treat beginning inventory. We focus on the weighted-average method because

← Chapter 6 introduced the weighted-average method of inventory costing.

- It is simpler.
- Differences between the two methods' results are usually insignificant.

Because SeaView's Shaping Department had no beginning work in process inventory, we did not need to specify whether that department used the weighted-average or FIFO method. By contrast, SeaView's Insertion Department does have beginning work in process inventory. Let's see how this beginning inventory affects the process costing computations.

Exhibit 21-11 lists October information for SeaView's Insertion Department. Study this information carefully and think about what each item means.

Exhibit 21-11

SeaView's Insertion Department
Data for October

Units:		
Beginning work in process, September 30		
(0% complete as to direct materials,		
60% complete as to conversion work)		5,000 masks
Transferred in from Shaping Department		
during October (Exhibit 21-6)		40,000 masks
Completed and transferred out to Finished		
Goods Inventory during October.		38,000 masks
Ending work in process, October 31		
(0% complete as to direct materials,		
30% complete as to conversion work)		7,000 masks
Costs:		
Beginning work in process, September 30		
(transferred-in costs, $22,900;		
conversion costs, $1,100)		$ 24,000
Transferred in from Shaping Department		
during October (from Exhibit 21-9)		176,000
Direct materials added during October in		
Insertion Department.		19,000
Conversion costs added during October in		
Insertion Department:		
Direct labor	$ 3,710	
Manufacturing overhead.	11,130	14,840

Remember that work in process inventory at the close of business on September 30 is both:

- Ending inventory for September *and*
- Beginning inventory for October

Exhibit 21-11 shows that SeaView's Insertion Department started the October period with 5,000 masks that had made it partway through the insertion process in September. During October, the Insertion Department started work on 40,000 additional masks received from the Shaping Department.

The weighted-average method combines the Insertion Department's:

- Work done in September to start the insertion process on the 5,000 masks in the department's October beginning work in process inventory
- Work done in October to complete the 5,000 masks in beginning inventory and to work on the 40,000 additional masks transferred in from the Shaping Department during October.

Weighted-Average Process Costing Method
A process costing method that costs all equivalent units of work with a weighted average of the previous period's and the current period's cost per equivalent unit.

Thus, the **weighted-average process costing method** costs all of the Insertion Department's equivalent units of work on these 45,000 masks (5,000 beginning work in process inventory + 40,000 transferred in) with a weighted average of the previous period's and the current period's cost per equivalent unit.

Just as we did for the Shaping Department, our goal is to split the total cost in the Insertion Department between:

- The 38,000 masks that the department completed and transferred out to finished goods inventory, and
- The 7,000 partially complete masks remaining in the department's ending work in process inventory at the end of October.

We use the same five-step process costing procedure that we used for the Shaping Department.

Steps 1 and 2: Summarize the Flow of Physical Units and Compute Output in Terms of Equivalent Units

SUMMARIZE THE FLOW OF PHYSICAL UNITS   Exhibit 21-11 shows that the Insertion Department had a beginning work in process inventory of 5,000 masks that were partway through the insertion process at the start of the period. Exhibits 21-6 and 21-11 show that during October, the Shaping Department finished 40,000 masks and transferred them into the Insertion Department. Thus, Exhibit 21-12 shows that the Insertion Department has 45,000 masks to account for (5,000 + 40,000).

✔ Starter 21-9

Exhibit 21-12   Step 1: Summarize the Flow of Physical Units; Step 2: Compute Output in Terms of Equivalent Units

SeaView Insertion Department
Month Ended October 31, 20XX

| | Step 1 | Step 2: Equivalent Units | | |
| | Flow of | Transferred | Direct | Conversion |
Flow of Production	Physical Units	In	Materials	Costs
Units to account for:				
Beginning work in process, September 30	5,000			
Transferred in during October	40,000			
Total physical units to account for.	45,000			
Units accounted for:				
Completed and transferred out during October	38,000	38,000	38,000*	38,000*
Ending work in process, October 31	7,000	7,000	—†	2,100†
Total physical units accounted for.	45,000			
Equivalent units		45,000	38,000	40,100

In the Insertion Department:
*Units completed and transferred out

	Direct materials:	38,000 units each 100% completed	= 38,000 equivalent units
	Conversion costs:	38,000 units each 100% completed	= 38,000 equivalent units

†Ending inventory

	Direct materials:	7,000 units each 0% completed	= 0 equivalent units
	Conversion costs:	7,000 units each 30% completed	= 2,100 equivalent units

Where did these masks go? Exhibits 21-10 and 21-11 show that the Insertion Department completed and transferred 38,000 masks out to finished goods inventory (the 5,000 masks from beginning work in process inventory, plus another 33,000 masks started and completed this period). The Insertion Department's ending work in process inventory consists of 7,000 masks that were partway through the insertion process at the close of business on October 31. Thus, Exhibit 21-12 shows that the department has accounted for all 45,000 masks (38,000 completed and transferred out + 7,000 in ending work in process inventory).

COMPUTE EQUIVALENT UNITS   Exhibit 21-12 uses the flow of physical units from step 1 and the time line in Exhibit 21-10 to compute the Insertion Department's equivalent units of work. Under the weighted-average method, SeaView computes the equivalent units for the total work done to date. This includes all the work done in the current period (October), plus the work done in the prior period (September) to start the insertion process on the masks in the current period's beginning work in process inventory.

The Insertion Department has three categories of equivalent units. In addition to direct materials (faceplates) and conversion costs added in the Insertion

Department, SeaView must also compute equivalent units for the shaped swim masks that are *transferred in* from the Shaping Department. All second and later departments must account for units (and costs) transferred in from preceding departments.

Let's see how to compute the equivalent units for the Insertion Department. This will include all the work ever done on the 45,000 masks that were in process during October, for each of the three categories of costs.

EQUIVALENT UNITS TRANSFERRED IN   After the Shaping Department completes its work on the masks and transfers them out, the Insertion Department receives those masks (and their accumulated costs) for final processing. Exhibit 21-10 shows that transferred-in costs (from Shaping) act like costs that are added at the very beginning of the insertion process.

The time line in Exhibit 21-10 shows that the Insertion Department completed and transferred out 38,000 masks to finished goods inventory. Of course, these masks are complete with respect to transferred-in (shaping) costs; masks must be completely shaped before they can begin the insertion process. Similarly, the 7,000 masks partway through the insertion process at the end of the period are also complete with respect to the transferred-in (shaping) costs. Why? Because the insertion process cannot begin until the shaping process is complete. Exhibit 21-12 shows that the total transferred-in equivalent units sum to 45,000 (38,000 + 7,000).

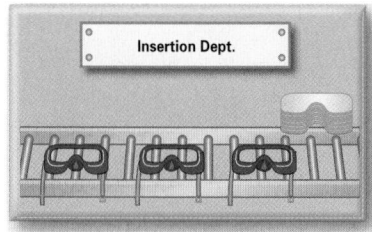

EQUIVALENT UNITS OF DIRECT MATERIALS   Now turn to the direct materials added in the Insertion Department. Workers insert the faceplates at the *end* of the process, as shown in Exhibit 21-10. Exhibit 21-10 also shows that during October, 38,000 masks passed the end of the insertion process. So workers inserted faceplates in all of these 38,000 completed masks. However, the time line shows that ending work in process inventory is only 30% of the way through the process, so it has not yet reached the point at which workers insert the faceplates. Thus, the ending work in process inventory has no faceplates—that is, no Insertion Department direct materials. Exhibit 21-12 summarizes the results, showing that the Insertion Department incurred 38,000 equivalent units of direct materials.

EQUIVALENT UNITS OF CONVERSION COSTS   Finally, consider conversion costs. The time line in Exhibit 21-10 shows that the 38,000 masks completed and transferred out of the Insertion Department are 100% complete with respect to the Insertion Department's conversion costs. Any swim mask transferred to finished goods inventory must have all of the Insertion Department's conversion work completed.

By contrast, the 7,000 masks in the Insertion Department's ending work in process inventory are only 30% of the way through the insertion process on October 31. The Insertion Department has performed $7,000 \times 30\% = 2,100$ equivalent units of conversion work on this ending inventory.

The conversion costs column of Exhibit 21-12 shows that total equivalent units of conversion work include:

38,000	units for the swim masks completed and transferred out to finished goods inventory
2,100	units for the swim masks in the Insertion Department's ending work in process inventory
40,100	total equivalent units of conversion costs

Steps 3 and 4: Summarize Total Costs to Account For and Compute the Cost per Equivalent Unit

Exhibit 21-13 accumulates the Insertion Department's total costs to account for, based on the data in Exhibit 21-11.

Exhibit 21-13 Step 3: Summarize Total Costs to Account For; Step 4: Compute the Cost per Equivalent Unit

	Transferred In	Direct Materials	Conversion Costs	Total
SeaView Insertion Department				
Month Ended October 31, 20XX				
Beginning work in process, September 30 (from Exhibit 21-11)	$ 22,900	$ —	$ 1,100	$ 24,000
Costs added during October (from Exhibit 21-11)	176,000	19,000	14,840	209,840
Total costs	$198,900	$19,000	$15,940	
Divide by equivalent units (from Exhibit 21-12)	÷ 45,000	÷38,000	÷40,100	
Cost per equivalent unit	$4.42	$0.50	$0.3975*	
Total costs to account for				$233,840

*Rounded.

In addition to direct material and conversion costs, the Insertion Department must account for transferred-in costs. **Transferred-in costs** are incurred in a previous process (the Shaping Department, in the SeaView example) and are carried forward as part of the product's cost when it moves to the next process.

Transferred-in costs from a previous process are a special category of costs incurred in second (and later) processes. The Insertion Department can view the masks coming in from the Shaping Department as raw materials introduced at the beginning of the Insertion Department's process. If the Insertion Department had bought these shaped masks from an outside supplier, it would have to account for the costs of purchasing the masks. In this case, Insertion receives the masks from an *internal* supplier—the Shaping Department. Thus, Insertion must account for the costs Shaping incurred to provide the shaped masks (Insertion's transferred-in costs) as well as Insertion's own direct materials (faceplates) and conversion costs (labor and overhead to insert the faceplates).

Exhibit 21-13 shows that in step 3, the Insertion Department's total cost to account for ($233,840) is the sum of:

- The cost incurred in September to start the insertion process on the 5,000 masks in Insertion's beginning work in process inventory ($24,000)
- The costs added to Work in Process Inventory—Insertion during October ($209,840 = $176,000 transferred in from the Shaping Department + $19,000 direct materials incurred in the Insertion Department + $14,840 conversion costs incurred in the Insertion Department)

Exhibit 21-13 also shows the results of step 4—the cost per equivalent unit. For each of the three cost categories, simply divide the total cost of that category by the number of equivalent units of work in that category. Perform this computation for each of the three categories: transferred-in costs, direct materials, and conversion costs.

Transferred-in Costs
Costs incurred in a previous process that are carried forward as part of the product's cost when it moves to the next process.

✔ **Starter 21-10**

Step 5: Assign Total Costs to Units Completed and to Units in Ending Work in Process Inventory

Exhibit 21-14 shows how SeaView assigns the total Insertion Department costs ($233,840, from Exhibit 21-13) to (1) units completed and transferred out to finished goods inventory and (2) units remaining in the Insertion Department's ending work in process inventory. Use the same approach as we used for the Shaping Department in Exhibit 21-9. Multiply the number of equivalent units from step 2 (Exhibit 21-12) by the cost per equivalent unit from step 4 (Exhibit 21-13).

✔ Starter 21-11

Exhibit 21-14 | Step 5: Assign Total Costs to Units Completed and to Units in Ending Work in Process Inventory

SeaView Insertion Department
Month Ended October 31, 20XX

	Transferred In	Direct Materials	Conversion Costs	Total
Units completed and transferred out to Finished Goods Inventory	[38,000 × ($4.42 + $0.50 + $0.3975)]			202,065
Ending work in process, October 31:				
Transferred-in costs	[7,000 × $4.42]			30,940
Direct materials		—		—
Conversion costs			[2,100 × $0.3975]	835*
Total ending work in process, October 31				31,775
Total costs accounted for.				$233,840

*Rounded.

Exhibit 21-15 shows how Exhibit 21-14 assigns the Insertion Department's costs.

Exhibit 21-15

Assigning Insertion Department's Costs to Units Completed and Transferred Out and to Ending Work in Process Inventory

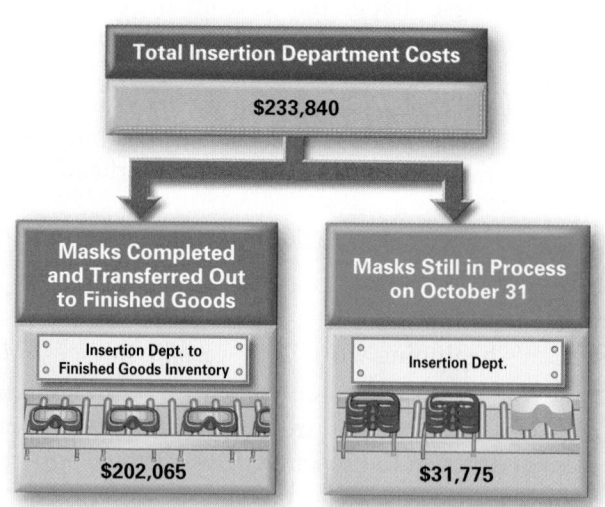

The Insertion Department's journal entries are similar to those of the Shaping Department. First, recall the entry previously made to transfer the cost of shaped swim masks into the Insertion Department (page 857):

| Work in Process Inventory—Insertion . . . . . | 176,000 | |
| Work in Process Inventory—Shaping | | 176,000 |

The following entry records other costs the Insertion Department incurred during October (data from Exhibit 21-11):

Work in Process Inventory—Insertion	33,840	
Materials Inventory.		19,000
Manufacturing Wages.		3,710
Manufacturing Overhead.		11,130

To requisition materials and assign conversion costs to the Insertion Department.

The entry to transfer the cost of completed masks out of the Insertion Department and into Finished Goods Inventory is based on the dollar amount in Exhibit 21-14:

| Finished Goods Inventory . . . . | 202,065 | |
| Work in Process Inventory—Insertion | | 202,065 |

After posting, the key accounts appear as follows:

✔ Starter 21-12

Work in Process Inventory—Shaping

(Exhibit 21-7)		(Exhibit 21-9)	
Balance, September 30	—	Transferred to Insertion	176,000
Direct materials	140,000		
Direct labor	21,250		
Manufacturing overhead	46,750		
Balance, October 31	32,000		

Work in Process Inventory—Insertion

(Exhibit 21-11)		(Exhibit 21-14)	
Balance, September 30	24,000	Transferred to Finished	
Transferred in from Shaping	176,000	Goods Inventory	202,065
Direct materials	19,000		
Direct labor	3,710		
Manufacturing overhead	11,130		
Balance, October 31	31,775		

Finished Goods Inventory

Balance, September 30	—		
Transferred in from Insertion	202,065		

How Managers Use a Production Cost Report

The **production cost report** in Exhibit 21-16 summarizes SeaView's Insertion Department's operations during October. The report combines Exhibit 21-13 and 21-14. It shows the beginning work in process inventory, the cost transferred in from the Shaping Department during October, and the direct material and conversion costs added in the Insertion Department during October.

Production Cost Report
Summarizes a processing department's operations for a period.

Exhibit 21-16 Production Cost Report (Weighted-Average)

SeaView Insertion Department
Production Cost Report (Weighted-Average Method)
Month Ended October 31, 20XX

	Transferred In	Direct Materials	Conversion Costs	Total
Beginning work in process, September 30	$ 22,900	$ —	$ 1,100	$ 24,000
Costs added during October	176,000	19,000	14,840	209,840
Total costs to account for.	$198,900	$19,000	$15,940	$233,840
Equivalent units	÷ 45,000	÷38,000	÷40,100	
Cost per equivalent unit	$4.42	$0.50	$0.3975	
Assignment of total costs:				
Units completed during October.	[38,000 × ($4.42 + $0.50 + $0.3975)]			$202,065
Ending work in process, October 31:				
Transferred-in costs	[7,000 × $4.42]			30,940
Direct materials		—		—
Conversion costs			[2,100 × $0.3975*]	835*
Total ending work in process, October 31				31,775
Total costs accounted for.				$233,840

*Rounded.

The report also shows that the costs of the masks completed and transferred out of the Insertion Department in October ($202,065) and the cost assigned to the Insertion Department's ending work in process inventory ($31,775) sum to the Insertion Department's total costs to account for ($233,840).

How do managers use the production cost report? When faced with economic uncertainty and falling prices for their products, managers carefully monitor product costs to see what they can cut. For example, as the selling prices for its tools continued to decline, Connecticut-based toolmaker Stanley Works decided to use fewer raw material suppliers. By purchasing more from its remaining suppliers, Stanley had the leverage to negotiate better prices.

Similarly, SeaView's managers monitor production costs by comparing the actual direct materials and conversion costs—particularly the equivalent unit costs in Exhibit 21-16—with expected amounts. If actual unit costs are too high, managers look for ways to cut. If actual costs are less than expected (and assuming quality is maintained), the Insertion Department's managers will likely receive good performance evaluations.

SeaView can use these unit costs for making other decisions. Sales managers must set the mask's selling price high enough to cover the unit manufacturing costs shown in Exhibit 21-16 ($5.3175 = $4.42 + $0.50 + $0.3975) plus nonmanufacturing costs from the other elements of the value chain, such as marketing and distribution. Armed with selling price and cost information for each of their many products, SeaView's managers can figure out which products are most profitable. Then they can design sales campaigns to promote those products. Finally, the production cost report supports financial reporting. It provides information for valuing inventory on the balance sheet and cost of goods sold on the income statement.

Overseas Production Cuts Labor Costs

Once it was a matter of pride that our clothing would sport a "Made in the U.S.A." label. Now our clothes are made overseas—wherever labor is cheap and willing.

In the process costing equation, lower manufacturing wages reduce unit costs and increase profit margins. The opportunity to cut costs fueled the exodus of U.S. apparel jobs to low-cost production areas in Asia, Mexico, and Latin America. In 1950, 1.2 million Americans worked in apparel manufacturing. By 2001, that figure had fallen to 566,000, even though the U.S. population had doubled. Consider **Levi Strauss & Co.**, a brand as American as apple pie.

In 2003, Levi's closed its last two U.S. plants, Levi's said it would become a "marketing company" and that future production would be done by contract manufacturers in 50 countries, including Bangladesh and Mexico.

Companies are shifting operations to countries with the lowest costs. Toy maker **Hasbro** closed its Monterrey, Mexico, plant in 2001 and moved to China. Mexico's workers earn $1.47 an hour, compared to the 28 cents a worker makes in China. Labor activists have dubbed this shift to low-cost overseas production a "race to the bottom." However, many major companies now have codes of conduct and monitoring programs to improve working conditions in manufacturing facilities worldwide. In 1991, Levi Strauss & Co. was the first multinational to develop such a code for its contract manufacturers. Called "terms of engagement," it is based on international labor standards.

Based on: Fred Dickey, "Cover Story, Levi Strauss and the Price We Pay," *Los Angeles Times*, December 1, 2002, p. MAG.14. Evelyn Iritani and Richard Boudreux, "Mexico's Factories Shift Gears to Survive," *Los Angeles Times*, January 5, 2003, p. C1. Michael Riley, "High-Tech Industries Meet Low-Cost Labor," *Houston Chronicle*, February 12, 2000, p. C1.

Accounting.com

Decision Guidelines

PROCESS COSTING—SECOND PROCESS (WITH BEGINNING INVENTORY)

Beginning work in process inventory makes process costing a bit more complicated, and second (or later) departments must account for units and costs transferred in from previous departments. Let's use SeaView's Insertion Department to review some of the key process costing decisions that arise in a second (or later) process that has beginning inventory.

Decision	Guidelines
At what point in the insertion process are transferred-in costs (from the shaping process) incurred?	Transferred-in costs are incurred at the *beginning* of the insertion process. The masks must be completely shaped before the insertion process begins.
How to compute equivalent units using the weighted-average method?	Weighted-average equivalent units equal • All work done on units completed and transferred out this period (whether work was done this period or last period), plus • Work done to *start* the ending inventory

Decision Guidelines *(continued)*

Decision	Guidelines
What checks and balances does the five-step process costing procedure provide?	The five-step procedure provides two important checks: **1.** The units to account for (beginning inventory + units started or transferred in) must equal the units accounted for (units completed and transferred out + units in ending inventory). **2.** The total costs to account for (cost of beginning inventory + costs incurred in the current period) must equal the costs accounted for (cost of units completed and transferred out + cost of ending inventory).
What is the main goal of the Insertion Department's process costing?	The main goal is to split total costs between swim masks completed and transferred out to finished goods inventory and the masks that remain in the Insertion Department's ending work in process inventory.
For what kinds of decisions do SeaView's managers use the Insertion Department's production cost report?	Managers use the cost per equivalent unit to control material and conversion costs and to evaluate the performance of the Insertion Department's managers. If actual costs per equivalent unit are higher than the budget, managers try to cut costs. If actual costs are lower than the budget while quality is maintained, Insertion Department managers likely will receive a favorable performance evaluation. SeaView's managers also use the cost per equivalent unit to build the cost of producing a swim mask. These costs provide a basis for setting selling prices, profitability analysis to decide which products to emphasize, and so on. These costs are also the basis for valuing inventory on the balance sheet and cost of goods sold on the income statement.

Excel Application Exercise

Goal: Create an Excel worksheet containing all five steps of the process costing procedure.

Scenario: As assistant to the production manager at work, you are asked to create the production cost report for the Tile-Forming Department for the month ended May 31, 20XX. Using Excel, your worksheet must calculate (1) the total cost of the units completed and transferred out, and (2) the total cost of the units in ending work in process inventory in the last step. When done with your spreadsheet, answer these questions:

1. What are the equivalent units of direct materials and conversion costs for: the units completed and transferred out in May, and ending work in process for May?
2. What is the total cost of units completed and transferred out during the month?

3. What is the total cost of ending work in process inventory for the month?

Step-by-Step:

1. Open a new Excel worksheet.
2. Create a bold-faced heading for your spreadsheet that contains the following:
   a. Chapter 21 Excel Application Exercise
   b. Production Cost Report
   c. Today's date
3. Using the Mid-Chapter Summary Problem on pages 859–860 as your guide, prepare the reports for the five-step process costing procedure. You are re-creating the solution to the Mid-Chapter Summary Problem. Start by creating a data section with the following heading format:

Tile-Forming Department Month Ended May 31, 20XX	Physical Units	Total Costs Direct Materials	Conversion
Beginning work in process, April 30	—	—	—
Started in production during May	20,000	$6,800	$36,400
Total to account for	20,000	$6,800	$36,400
Completed and transferred to Finishing Department during May	16,000		
Ending work in process, May 31 (units):	4,000		
Percentage complete as to:		25%	55%
Total accounted for	20,000		

This data section differs slightly from the way the same information is presented at the beginning of the Mid-Chapter Summary Problem. Your spreadsheet separates Total Costs into the direct materials and conversion components. Separating these two items will allow you to reference these values later.

4. Once finished with the data section, move down two rows and enter the Tile-Forming Department heading as follows:

Tile-Forming Department
Month Ended May 31, 20XX

Format this section as illustrated in the Mid-Chapter Summary Problem report for steps 1 and 2 of the 5-step

process costing procedure (page 859). Use formulas and data section cell references as appropriate.

5. Now re-create the two reports for steps 3 and 4 of the five-step process costing procedure. Use the Mid-Chapter Summary Problem reports on page 860 as your guide. Use formulas and data section cell references as appropriate.

6. Finally, re-create the report for the fifth and final step of the process costing procedure (use the report on page 860 as a guide). Be sure to use formulas instead of the calculations shown in the body of the report on page 860.

7. Save your work, and print a copy for your files.

END-OF-CHAPTER *Summary Problem*

This problem extends the Mid-Chapter Summary problem to a second department. During May, Florida Tile Industries reports the following in its Finishing Department:

CHECK YOUR RESOURCES

Finishing Department Data for May	
Units:	
Beginning work in process, April 30 (20% complete as to direct materials, 70% complete as to conversion work)....	4,000 units
Transferred in from Tile-Forming Department during May..	16,000 units
Completed and transferred out to Finished Goods Inventory during May..	15,000 units
Ending work in process, May 31 (36% complete as to direct materials, 80% complete as to conversion work)	5,000 units
Costs:	
Work in process, April 30 (transferred-in costs, $11,982; direct materials costs, $488; conversion costs, $5,530)	$18,000
Transferred in from Tile-Forming Department during May (page 860)	38,400
Finishing direct materials added during May..............	6,400
Finishing conversion costs added during May.............	24,300

Required

Assign the Finishing Department's May total costs to units completed and to units in ending work in process inventory, using the weighted-average method.

Hint: Don't confuse the Finishing Department with finished goods inventory. The Finishing Department is Florida Tile's second process. The tiles do not become part of finished goods inventory until they have completed the second process, which happens to be called the Finishing Department.

Solution

STEPS 1 AND 2 Summarize the flow of physical units; compute output in terms of equivalent units.

Finishing Department
Month Ended May 31, 20XX

Flow of Production	Step 1 Flow of Physical Units	Step 2: Equivalent Units Transferred In	Direct Materials	Conversion Costs
Units to account for:				
Beginning work in process, April 30	4,000			
Transferred in from Tile-Forming during May . .	16,000			
Total physical units to account for	20,000			
Units accounted for:				
Completed and transferred out during May	15,000	15,000	15,000	15,000
Ending work in process, May 31	5,000	5,000	1,800*	4,000*
Total physical units accounted for	20,000			
Equivalent units		20,000	16,800	19,000

*Start ending inventory

Direct materials: 5,000 units each 36% completed = 1,800 equivalent units
Conversion costs: 5,000 units each 80% completed = 4,000 equivalent units

STEPS 3 AND 4 Summarize total costs to account for; compute the cost per equivalent unit.

Finishing Department
Month Ended May 31, 20XX

	Transferred In	Direct Materials	Conversion Costs	Total
Beginning work in process, April 30 . .	$11,982	$ 488	$ 5,530	$18,000
Costs added during May	38,400	6,400	24,300	69,100
Total costs	$50,382	$ 6,888	$29,830	
Divide by equivalent units	÷20,000	÷16,800	÷19,000	
Cost per equivalent unit	$2.5191	$ 0.41	$ 1.57	
Total costs to account for				$87,100

STEP 5 Assign costs to units completed and to units in ending work in process inventory.

Finishing Department
Month Ended May 31, 20XX

	Transferred In	Direct Materials	Conversion Costs	Total
Units completed and transferred out to Finished Goods Inventory:	[15,000 × ($2.5191 + $0.41 + $1.57)]			$67,486*
Ending work in process, May 31:				
Transferred-in costs	[5,000 × $2.5191]			12,596*
Direct materials		[1,800 × $0.41]		738
Conversion costs			[4,000 × $1.57]	6,280
Total ending work in process, May 31				19,614
Total costs accounted for				$87,100

*Rounded

●REVIEW *Process Costing*

Quick Check

1. Which of these companies would use process costing?
   a. **Saatchi & Saatchi** advertising firm
   b. **Pace Foods**, producer of Pace picante sauce
   c. **Accenture** management consultants
   d. **Amazon.com**

2. Which of the following statements describes **Jelly Belly's** process costing system?
   a. Direct materials and direct labor are traced to each specific order.
   b. Costs flow directly from a single Work in Process Inventory account to Finished Goods Inventory.
   c. Costs flow through a sequence of Work in Process Inventory accounts and then into Finished Goods Inventory from the final Work in Process Inventory account.
   d. The subsidiary Work in Process Inventory accounts consist of separate records for each individual order, detailing the materials, labor, and overhead assigned to that order.

Use the following data to answer questions 3 through 7. Suppose Jelly Belly's Centers process adds sugar at the beginning of the process and flavorings 75% of the way through the process, and conversion costs are incurred evenly throughout the process. Assume there are no beginning inventories, the company started making centers for 10,000 pounds of jelly beans, and the 2,000 pounds in the Centers ending work in process inventory are 65% through the Centers process.

3. Compute the equivalent units of *sugar* used.
   a. 8,000   c. 9,300
   b. 8,700   d. 10,000

4. How many equivalent units of *flavorings* did Jelly Belly use?
   a. 8,000   c. 9,300
   b. 8,700   d. 10,000

5. What are the equivalent units of *conversion costs*?
   a. 8,000   c. 9,300
   b. 8,700   d. 10,000

6. If the cost per equivalent unit is $0.50 for sugar, $1.00 for flavorings, and $0.40 for conversion costs, what is the cost assigned to the Centers ending work in process inventory?
   a. $1,520   c. $2,520
   b. $1,800   d. $3,800

7. Suppose Jelly Belly's second process, Shells, starts out with 3,000 pounds of jelly beans in its beginning work in process inventory. Assume that the Shells process has 1,500 pounds of jelly beans 70% through the process at the end of the period. Start by using the information preceding question 3 to determine how many pounds of jelly beans started in the Shells process this period. Then use this result to compute the number of equivalent units of transferred-in costs that the Shells process will use in computing its weighted-average cost per equivalent unit.
   a. 6,500   c. 9,500
   b. 8,000   d. 11,000

8. In general, transferred-in costs include:
   a. Costs incurred in the previous period
   b. Costs incurred in all prior periods
   c. Costs incurred in only the previous process
   d. Costs incurred in all prior processes

To answer questions 9 and 10, look at the computation of cost per equivalent unit in SeaView's Insertion Department in Exhibit 21-13.

9. Which of the following describes the $22,900 transferred-in costs in beginning inventory?
    a. Costs incurred in October in the Shaping Department
    b. Costs incurred in September in the Shaping Department
    c. Costs incurred in October in the Insertion Department
    d. Costs incurred in September in the Insertion Department

10. Which of the following best describes the swim masks associated with the $22,900 transferred-in costs in the Insertion Department's beginning work in process inventory?
    a. Masks that are partway through the shaping process and have not begun the insertion process by the beginning of October
    b. Masks that moved from the Shaping Department into the Insertion Department in September but have not yet begun the insertion process by the beginning of October
    c. Masks that moved from the Shaping Department into the Insertion Department during October
    d. Masks that moved from the Shaping Department to the Insertion Department in September and are partway through insertion by the beginning of October

Accounting Vocabulary

conversion costs (p. 850)
equivalent units (p. 850)

production cost report (p. 867)
transferred-in costs (p. 865)

weighted-average process costing method (p. 862)

● ASSESS *Your Progress*

See *www.prenhall.com/horngren*
for selected Starters, Exercises,
and Problems.

*Distinguishing between the flow of costs
in job costing and process costing*
(Obj. 1)

*Flow of costs in process costing, cost per
equivalent unit*
(Obj. 1, 2)

Starters

S21-1 Use Exhibit 21-1 to help you describe, in your own words, the major difference in the flow of costs between a job costing system and a process costing system.

S21-2 Polar Spring produces premium bottled water. Polar Spring purchases artesian water, stores the water in large tanks, and then runs the water through two processes:

- Filtration, where workers microfilter *and* ozonate the water
- Bottling, where workers bottle and package the filtered water

During February, the filtration process incurs the following costs in processing 200,000 liters:

Wages of workers operating the filtration equipment. .	$ 11,100
Wages of workers operating ozonation equipment	12,850
Manufacturing overhead allocated to filtration	24,050
Water.	120,000

Polar Spring has no beginning inventory in the Filtration Department.

1. Compute the February conversion costs in the Filtration Department.
2. If the Filtration Department completely processed 200,000 liters, what is the *total* filtration cost per liter?
3. Now assume that the total costs of the filtration process listed in the chart above yield 160,000 liters that are completely filtered and ozonated, while the remaining 40,000 are only partway through the process at the end of February. Is the cost per completely filtered and ozonated liter higher, lower, or the same as in requirement 2? Why?

S21-3 Refer to Starter 21-2. At Polar Spring, water is added at the beginning of the filtration process. Conversion costs are added evenly throughout the process, and in February 160,000 liters have been completed and transferred out of the Filtration Department into the Bottling Department. The 40,000 units remaining in Filtration's ending work in process inventory are 80% of the way through the filtration process. Recall that Polar Spring has no beginning inventories.

Drawing a time line, computing equivalent units
(Obj. 2)

1. Draw a time line for the filtration process, similar to the one in Exhibit 21-6.
2. Compute the equivalent units of direct materials and conversion costs for the Filtration Department. (Refer to Exhibit 21-5 if necessary.)

S21-4 Look at SeaView Shaping Department's equivalent-unit computation in Exhibit 21-5. Suppose the ending work in process inventory is 30% of the way through the shaping process, rather than 25% of the way through. Compute the total equivalent units of direct materials and conversion costs.

Computing equivalent units
(Obj. 2)

S21-5 Return to the original SeaView example. Suppose direct labor is $34,000 rather than $21,250. Now what is the conversion cost per equivalent unit? (Use Exhibit 21-8 to format your answer.)

Computing the cost per equivalent unit
(Obj. 3)

S21-6 Return to Polar Spring's Filtration Department described in Starters 21-2 and 21-3. Using your answers to those exercises, compute the cost per equivalent unit for direct materials and for conversion costs in the Filtration Department. (Recall that there were no beginning inventories.)

Computing the cost per equivalent unit
(Obj. 3)

S21-7 Return to Polar Spring's Filtration Department. Use the information in Starters 21-2, 21-3, and 21-6 to answer the following questions:

Assigning costs to units completed and ending inventory
(Obj. 3)

1. What is the cost of the 160,000 liters completed and transferred out of Polar Spring's Filtration Department?
2. What is the cost of 40,000 liters remaining in Filtration's ending work in process inventory?

S21-8 Use the information in Starters 21-2 and 21-7 to

Preparing a journal entry and posting to a T-account
(Obj. 3)

1. Record the journal entry to transfer the cost of the 160,000 liters completed and transferred out of Filtration and into the Bottling Department.
2. Record all the transactions in the Work in Process Inventory—Filtration T-account. (*Hint:* Use SeaView's Work in Process Inventory—Shaping T-account on page 857 as a guide.)

S21-9 Polar Spring produces premium bottled water. Preceding Starters considered Polar Spring's first process—filtration. We now consider Polar Spring's second process—bottling. In the Bottling Department, workers bottle the filtered water and pack the bottles into boxes. Conversion costs are incurred evenly throughout the bottling process, but packaging materials are not added until the end of the process.

Drawing a time line; computing equivalent units; second department; weighted-average method
(Obj. 1, 4)

February data from the Bottling Department follow:

Beginning work in process inventory (40% of the way through the process)	8,000 liters
Transferred in from Filtration*	160,000 liters
Completed and transferred out to Finished Goods Inventory in February	154,000 liters
Ending work in process inventory (70% of the way through the bottling process)	14,000 liters

(continued)

Costs in beginning work in process inventory		Costs added during February	
Transferred in	$1,760	Transferred in*	$136,000
Direct materials	0	Direct materials	30,800
Direct labor	600	Direct labor	33,726
Manufacturing overhead	520	Manufacturing overhead	22,484
Total beginning work in process inventory as of February 1	$2,880	Total costs added during February	$223,010

*Starter 21-7 showed that Polar Spring's Filtration Department completed and transferred out 160,000 liters at a total cost of $136,000.

1. Draw a time line similar to the one in Exhibit 21-10 using the weighted-average method.
2. Use the time line to help you compute the Bottling Department equivalent units for the month of February, using the weighted-average method.

Computing costs per equivalent unit; second department; weighted average
(Obj. 4)

S21-10 Using data from Polar Spring's Bottling Department and the equivalent units computed in Starter 21-9, compute the cost per equivalent unit for February, using the weighted-average method.

Assigning costs to units completed and ending inventory; second department; weighted-average method
(Obj. 4)

S21-11 Refer to the information on Polar Spring's Bottling Department and the equivalent units and cost per equivalent unit you computed in Starters 21-9 and 21-10. Use these to assign the costs to units completed and transferred out and to ending inventory, using the weighted-average method.

Preparing a journal entry and posting to a T-account; second department; weighted-average method
(Obj. 1, 4)

S21-12 Using data from Polar Spring's Bottling Department in Starter 21-9 and the cost assignments in Starter 21-11:

1. Prepare the journal entry to record the cost of units completed and transferred out under the weighted-average method.
2. Post all transactions from Starters 21-9 and 21-11 to the Work in Process Inventory—Bottling Department T-account. What is the ending balance?

Diagramming flows through a process costing system
(Obj. 1)

Exercises

E21-1 Pule produces kitchen cabinets in a three-stage process that includes milling, assembling, and finishing, in that order. Direct materials are added in the Milling and Finishing Departments. Direct labor and overhead are incurred in all three departments. The company's general ledger includes the following accounts:

Cost of Goods Sold	Work in Process Inventory—Finishing
Manufacturing Wages	Materials Inventory
Work in Process Inventory—Milling	Finished Goods Inventory
Work in Process Inventory—Assembling	Manufacturing Overhead

Outline the flow of costs through the company's accounts, including a brief description of each flow. Include a T-account for each account title given.

Journalizing process costing transactions
(Obj. 1, 3)

E21-2 Record the following process costing transactions in the general journal:

a. Purchase of raw materials on account, $9,000
b. Requisition of direct materials to
 Assembly Department, $4,000
 Finishing Department, $2,000
c. Incurrence and payment of manufacturing labor, $10,800.

(continued)

d. Incurrence of manufacturing overhead costs:
Property taxes—plant, $1,900
Utilities—plant, $4,500
Insurance—plant, $1,100
Depreciation—plant, $3,400

e. Assignment of conversion costs to the Assembly Department:
Direct labor, $4,700
Manufacturing overhead, $2,900

f. Assignment of conversion costs to the Finishing Department:
Direct labor, $4,400
Manufacturing overhead, $6,200

g. Cost of goods completed and transferred out of Assembly and into Finishing, $10,250.

h. Cost of goods completed and transferred out of the Finishing Department into Finished Goods Inventory, $15,600.

E21-3 Color World prepares and packages paint products. Color World has two departments: (1) Blending and (2) Packaging. Direct materials are added at the beginning of the blending process (dyes) and at the end of the packaging process (cans). Conversion costs are added evenly throughout each process. Data from the month of May for the Blending Department are as follows:

Drawing a time line; computing equivalent units and assigning cost to completed units and ending work in process; no beginning inventory or cost transferred in
(Obj. 2, 3)

Gallons:	
Beginning work in process inventory	0
Started production	8,000 gallons
Completed and transferred out to Packaging in May......	6,000 gallons
Ending work in process inventory (30% of the way	
through the blending process)	2,000 gallons
Costs:	
Beginning work in process inventory	$ 0
Costs added during May:	
Direct materials (dyes)...........................	4,800
Direct labor	800
Manufacturing overhead...........................	1,840
Total costs added during May	$7,440

Required

1. Draw a time line for the Blending Department, similar to Exhibit 21-6.

2. Use the time line to help you compute the Blending Department's equivalent units for direct materials and for conversion costs.

3. Compute the total costs of the units (gallons)
   a. Completed and transferred out to the Packaging Department
   b. In the Blending Department ending work in process inventory

E21-4 Return to the Blending Department for Color World in Exercise 21-3.

Preparing journal entries and posting to work in process T-account
(Obj. 1, 3)

Required

1. Present the journal entries to record the use of direct materials and direct labor and the allocation of manufacturing overhead to the Blending Department. Also, give the journal entry to record the costs of the gallons completed and transferred out to the Packaging Department.

2. Post the journal entries to the Work in Process Inventory—Blending T-account. What is the ending balance?

3. What is the average cost per gallon transferred out of Blending into Packaging? Why would Color World's managers want to know this cost?

Computing equivalent units; assigning costs to goods completed and ending work in process inventory; first department, no beginning inventory
(Obj. 2, 3)

E21-5 The Assembly Department of ZAP Surge Protectors began September with no work in process inventory. During the month, production that cost $39,860 (direct materials, $9,900, and conversion costs, $29,960) was started on 23,000 units. ZAP completed and transferred to the Testing Department a total of 15,000 units. The ending work in process inventory was 37.5% complete as to direct materials and 80% complete as to conversion work.

Required

1. Compute the equivalent units for direct materials and conversion costs.
2. Compute the cost per equivalent unit.
3. Assign the costs to units completed and transferred out and ending work in process inventory.
4. Record the journal entry for the costs transferred out of Assembly into Testing.
5. Post all the transactions in the Work in Process Inventory—Assembly Department T-account. What is the ending balance?

Drawing a time line; computing equivalent units; assigning costs to completed units and ending work in process; no beginning inventory or cost transferred in
(Obj. 2, 3)

E21-6 Royal Vine Winery in Kingston, New York, has two departments: Fermenting and Packaging. Direct materials are added at the beginning of the fermenting process (grapes) and at the end of the packaging process (bottles). Conversion costs are added evenly throughout each process. Data from the month of March for the Fermenting Department are as follows:

Gallons:	
Beginning work in process inventory	0
Started production	8,000 gallons
Completed and transferred out to Packaging in March	6,550 gallons
Ending work in process inventory (80% of the way	
through the fermenting process)	1,450 gallons
Costs:	
Beginning work in process inventory	$ 0
Costs added during March:	
Direct materials.	11,600
Direct labor	2,400
Manufacturing overhead.	4,539
Total costs added during May	$18,539

Required

1. Draw a time line for the Fermenting Department, similar to Exhibit 21-6.
2. Use the time line to help you compute the equivalent units for direct materials and for conversion costs.
3. Compute the total costs of the units (gallons)
   a. Completed and transferred out to the Packaging Department
   b. In the Fermenting Department ending work in process inventory

Preparing journal entries and posting to work in process T-account
(Obj. 1, 3)

E21-7 Return to the Fermenting Department for Royal Vine Winery in Exercise 21-6.

Required

1. Present the journal entries to record the use of direct materials and direct labor, and the allocation of manufacturing overhead to the Fermenting Department. Also give the journal entry to record the cost of the gallons completed and transferred out to the Packaging Department.
2. Post the journal entries to the Work in Process Inventory—Fermenting T-account. What is the ending balance?

(continued)

3. What is the average cost per gallon transferred out of Fermenting into Packaging? Why would Royal Vine's managers want to know this cost?

E21-8 The following information was taken from the ledger of Denver Roping. Ending inventory is 60% complete as to direct materials but 20% complete as to conversion work.

Computing equivalent units; assigning costs to goods completed and ending work in process inventory; first department, no beginning inventory
(Obj. 2, 3)

Work in Process—Forming

	Physical Units	Dollars		Physical Units	Dollars
Beginning inventory, September 30	-0-	$ -0-	Transferred to		
Production started:	80,000		Finishing	72,000	$?
Direct materials		215,040			
Conversion costs		195,040			
Ending Inventory	8,000	?			

Required

Journalize the transfer of costs to the Finishing Department. (*Hint:* First compute the number of equivalent units and the cost per equivalent unit.)

E21-9 Selected production and cost data of Martha's Fudge Co. follow for May 20X6.

Computing equivalent units, 2 departments, WA method
(Obj. 4)

	Flow of Physical Units	
	Mixing	Heating
Flow of Production	**Department**	**Department**
Units to account for:		
Beginning work in process, April 30	20,000	6,000
Transferred in during May.	70,000	80,000
Total physical units to account for	90,000	86,000
Units accounted for:		
Completed and transferred out during May. .	80,000	76,000
Ending work in process, May 31.	10,000	10,000
Total physical units accounted for	90,000	86,000

Martha uses weighted-average costing.

Required

1. Fill in the blanks:
   a. On May 31, the Mixing Department ending work in process inventory was 70% complete as to materials and 20% complete as to conversion costs. This means that for the ending inventory _____% of the materials and _____% of the conversion costs were added during May.
   b. On May 31, the Heating Department ending work in process inventory was 65% complete as to materials and 55% complete as to conversion costs. This means that for the ending inventory _____% of the materials and _____% of the conversion costs were added during May.
2. Use the information in the Flow of Production table and the information in Requirement 1 to compute the equivalent units for transferred-in costs, direct materials, and conversion costs for both the Mixing and the Heating Departments.

Computing equivalent units and assigning costs to completed units and to ending work in process inventory; second department, weighted average
(Obj. 4)

E21-10 Alpha Semiconductors, Inc., experienced the following activity in its Photolithography Department during December. Materials are added at the beginning of the photolithography process.

Student ResourceCD
spreadsheet

(continued)

Units:	
Work in process, November 30	
(80% of the way through the process)	8,000 units
Transferred in from the Polishing and Cutting Department	
during December.	27,000 units
Completed during December	26,000 units
Work in process, December 31	
(70% of the way through the process)	9,000 units
Costs:	
Work in process, November 30 (transferred-in costs,	
$20,050; direct materials costs, $20,250; and	
conversion costs, $19,816)	$60,116
Transferred in from the Polishing and Cutting Department	
during December.	97,200
Direct materials added during December	74,250
Conversion costs added during December	90,650

Required

1. Draw a time line for the Photolithography Department using the weighted-average method. (See Exhibit 21-10.)

2. Use the time line to help you compute the number of equivalent units of work for the Photolithography Department in December. Use the weighted-average method.

3. Compute the cost per equivalent unit, and assign total costs to (a) units completed and transferred to Finished Goods Inventory, and (b) units in December 31 work in process inventory.

Problems

(Group A)

Computing equivalent units and assigning costs to completed units and ending work in process; no beginning inventory or cost transferred in
(Obj. 1, 2, 3)

P21-1A Winter Lips produces a lip balm used for cold-weather sports. The balm is manufactured in a single processing department. No lip balm was in process on May 31, and Winter Lips started production on 20,400 lip balm tubes during June. Direct materials are added at the beginning of the process, but conversion costs are incurred evenly throughout the process. Completed production for June totaled 15,200 units. The June 30 work in process was 40% of the way through the production process. Direct materials costing $4,080 were placed in production during June, and direct labor of $3,315 and manufacturing overhead of $1,005 were assigned to the process.

Required

1. Draw a time line for Winter Lips that is similar to Exhibit 21-6.

2. Use the time line to help you compute the number of equivalent units and the cost per equivalent unit for June.

3. Assign total costs to (a) units completed and transferred to finished goods and (b) units still in process at June 30.

4. Prepare a T-account for Work in Process Inventory to show activity during June, including the June 30 balance.

Computing equivalent units; assigning costs to completed units and ending work in process; journalizing transactions; no beginning inventory or cost transferred in
(Obj. 2, 3)

P21-2A The New England Furniture Company produces dining tables in a three-stage process: sawing, assembly, and staining. Costs incurred in the Sawing Department during September are summarized as follows:

(continued)

Work in Process Inventory—Sawing

Sep. 1 balance	0	
Direct materials	1,860,000	
Direct labor	139,100	
Manufacturing overhead	153,400	

Direct materials (lumber) are added at the beginning of the sawing process, while conversion costs are incurred evenly throughout the process. September activity in the Sawing Department included sawing of 11,000 meters of lumber, which were transferred to the Assembly Department. Also, work began on 1,000 meters of lumber, which on September 30 were 70% of the way through the sawing process.

Required

1. Draw a time line for the Sawing Department, similar to Exhibit 21-6.
2. Use the time line to help you compute the number of equivalent units and the cost per equivalent unit in the Sawing Department for September.
3. Show that the sum of (a) cost of goods transferred out of the Sawing Department and (b) ending Work in Process Inventory—Sawing equals the total cost accumulated in the department during September.
4. Journalize all transactions affecting the company's sawing process during September, including those already posted.

EU and assigning costs to completed units and ending WIP; materials added at different points in the production process; no beginning inventory or costs transferred in
(Obj. 1, 2, 3)

P21-3A Kun Pow produces canned chicken à la king. The chicken à la king passes through three departments: (1) Mixing, (2) Retort (sterilization), and (3) Packing. In the Mixing Department, chicken and cream are added at the beginning of the process, the mixture is partly cooked, then chopped green peppers and mushrooms are added at the end of the process. Conversion costs are added evenly throughout the mixing process. November data from the Mixing Department are as follows:

Gallons		Costs	
Beginning work in process inventory........	0 gallons	Beginning work in process inventory	$ 0
Started production......................	15,000 gallons	Costs added during November:	
Completed and transferred out to		Chicken.....................................	12,500
Retort in November....................	12,900 gallons	Cream	4,000
		Green peppers and mushrooms	11,610
Ending work in process inventory		Direct labor................................	11,108
(60% of the way through the		Manufacturing overhead	3,052
mixing process)	2,100 gallons	Total costs	$42,270

Required

1. Draw a time line for the Mixing Department, similar to Exhibit 21-6.
2. Use the time line to help you compute the equivalent units. (*Hint:* Each direct material added at a different point in the production process requires its own equivalent-unit computation.)
3. Compute the total costs of the units (gallons)
   a. Completed and transferred out to the Retort Department
   b. In the Mixing Department's ending work in process inventory
4. Prepare the journal entry to record the cost of the gallons completed and transferred out to the Retort Department.
5. Post the transactions to the Work in Process Inventory—Mixing T-account. What is the ending balance?
6. What is the primary purpose of the work required in steps 1 through 3?

P21-4A Off Road, Inc., manufactures auto roof racks in a two-stage process that includes shaping and plating. Steel alloy is the basic raw material of the shaping process. The steel is molded according to the design specifications of automobile manufacturers (**Ford** and **General Motors**). The Plating Department then adds an anodized finish.

At March 31, before recording the transfer of cost from the Plating Department to Finished Goods Inventory, the Off Road general ledger included the following account:

Work in Process Inventory—Plating

Feb. 28 balance	30,480
Transferred in from Shaping	36,000
Direct materials	24,200
Direct labor	21,732
Manufacturing overhead	35,388

The direct materials (rubber pads) are added at the end of the plating process. Conversion costs are incurred evenly throughout the process. Work in process of the Plating Department on February 28 consisted of 600 racks. The $30,480 beginning balance of Work in Process—Plating includes $18,000 of transferred-in cost and $12,480 of conversion cost. During March, 3,000 racks were transferred in from the Shaping Department. The Plating Department transferred 2,200 racks to Finished Goods Inventory in March, and 1,400 were still in process on March 31. This ending inventory was 50% of the way through the plating process. Off Road uses weighted-average process costing.

Required

1. Draw a time line for the Plating Department, similar to Exhibit 21-10.
2. Use the time line to help you compute the equivalent units, cost per equivalent unit, and total costs to account for in the Plating Department for March.
3. Prepare the March production cost report for the Plating Department.
4. Journalize all transactions affecting the Plating Department during March, including the entries that have already been posted.

P21-5A Sidcrome uses three departments to produce plastic handles for screwdrivers. Forming the handles requires mixing the raw materials, molding, and drying.

Sidcrome's Drying Department requires no direct materials. Conversion costs are incurred evenly throughout the drying process. Other process costing information follows:

Units:	
Beginning work in process	7,000 units
Transferred in from the Molding Department during the period	28,000 units
Completed during the period	16,000 units
Ending work in process (20% complete as to conversion work)	19,000 units
Costs:	
Beginning work in process (transferred-in cost, $140; conversion cost, $231)	$ 371
Transferred in from the Molding Department during the period	4,760
Conversion costs added during the period	1,947

After the drying process, the screwdrivers are completed by assembling the handles and shanks and packaging for shipment to retail outlets. Sidcrome uses weighted-average process costing.

Required

1. Draw a time line of the Drying Department's process, similar to the one in Exhibit 21-10.
2. Use the time line to compute the number of equivalent units of work performed by the Drying Department during the period, the cost per equivalent unit, and the total costs to account for.

(continued)

3. Assign total costs to (a) units completed and transferred to the assembly operation and (b) units in the Drying Department's ending work in process inventory.

Problems

(Group B)

P21-1B E-Z Solutions, Inc., makes electronic personal data assistants (PDAs) in three processes: assembly, programming, and packaging. The Assembly Department had no work in process on May 31. In mid-June, E-Z Solutions started production on 100,000 PDAs. Of this number, 76,400 PDAs were assembled during June. Direct materials are added at the beginning of the assembly process. Conversion costs are incurred evenly throughout the process. The June 30 work in process in the Assembly Department was 60% of the way through the assembly process. Direct materials costing $375,000 were placed in production in Assembly during June, and direct labor of $157,248 and manufacturing overhead of $118,960 were assigned to that department.

Computing equivalent units and assigning costs to completed units and ending work in process; no beginning inventory or cost transferred in
(Obj. 1, 2, 3)

Required

1. Draw a time line for the Assembly Department, similar to Exhibit 21-6.
2. Use the time line to help you compute the number of equivalent units and the cost per equivalent unit in the Assembly Department for June.
3. Assign total costs in the Assembly Department to (a) units completed and transferred to Programming during June and (b) units still in process at June 30.
4. Prepare a T-account for Work in Process Inventory—Assembly to show its activity during June, including the June 30 balance.

P21-2B Papyrus Co. produces the paper used by wallpaper manufacturers. Papyrus's four-stage process includes mixing, cooking, rolling, and cutting. In the Mixing Department, wood pulp and chemicals are blended. The resulting mix is heated in the Cooking Department in much the same way as food is prepared. Then the cooked mix is rolled to produce sheets. The final process, cutting, divides the sheets into large rolled units. The Mixing Department incurred the following costs during August:

Computing equivalent units; assigning costs to completed units and ending work in process; journalizing transactions; no beginning inventory or cost transferred in
(Obj. 2, 3)

Work in Process Inventory—Mixing		
Aug. 1 balance	0	
Direct materials	5,520	
Direct labor	580	
Manufacturing overhead	3,560	

During August, the Mixing Department started and completed mixing for 4,500 rolls of paper. The department started but did not finish the mixing for an additional 500 rolls, which were 20% complete with respect to both direct materials and conversion work at the end of August. Direct materials and conversion costs are incurred evenly throughout the mixing process.

Required

1. Draw a time line for the Mixing Department, similar to Exhibit 21-6.
2. Use the time line to help you compute the number of equivalent units and the cost per equivalent unit in the Mixing Department for August.
3. Show that the sum of (a) cost of goods transferred out of the Mixing Department and (b) ending Work in Process Inventory—Mixing equals the total cost accumulated in the department during August.
4. Journalize all transactions affecting the company's mixing process during August, including those already posted.

EU and assigning costs to completed units and ending WIP inventory; materials added at different points; no beginning inventory or cost transferred in
(Obj. 1, 2, 3)

P21-3B Ply-Wall produces exterior siding for homes. The Preparation Department begins with wood, which is chopped into small bits. At the end of the process, an adhesive is added. Then the wood/adhesive mixture goes on to the Compression Department, where the wood is compressed into sheets. Assume conversion costs are added evenly throughout the preparation process. Suppose that April data for the Preparation Department are as follows (in millions):

Sheets		Costs	
Beginning work in process inventory........	0 sheets	Beginning work in process inventory	$ 0
Started production......................	3,000 sheets	Costs added during April:	
Completed and transferred out to		Wood	2,700
Compression in April	1,950 sheets	Adhesives..................................	1,365
Ending work in process inventory		Direct labor.................................	629
(40% of the way through the		Manufacturing overhead	1,267
preparation process)	1,050 sheets	Total costs	$5,961

Required

1. Draw a time line for the Preparation Department, similar to Exhibit 21-6.

2. Use the time line to help you compute the equivalent units for direct materials and for conversion costs. (*Hint:* Each direct material added at a different point in the production process requires its own equivalent-unit computation.)

3. Compute the total costs of the units (sheets)
   a. Completed and transferred out to the Compression Department
   b. In the Preparation Department's ending work in process inventory

4. Prepare the journal entry to record the cost of the sheets completed and transferred out to the Compression Department.

5. Post the journal entries to the Work in Process Inventory—Preparation T-account. What is the ending balance?

Computing equivalent units for a second department with beginning inventory; preparing a production cost report and recording transactions on the basis of the report's information; WA method
(Obj. 2, 3, 4)

Student ResourceCD
spreadsheet

P21-4B Athena Carpeting manufactures broadloom carpet in seven processes: spinning, dyeing, plying, spooling, tufting, latexing, and shearing. First, fluff nylon purchased from a company such as **DuPont** or **Monsanto** is spun into yarn that is dyed the desired color. Then threads of the yarn are joined together, or plied, for added strength. The plied yarn is spooled for carpet making. Tufting is the process by which yarn is added to burlap backing. After the backing is latexed to hold it together and make it skid-resistant, the carpet is sheared to give it an even appearance and feel.

At March 31, before recording the transfer of costs out of the Dyeing Department, the Athena Carpeting general ledger included the following account for one of its lines of carpet:

Work in Process Inventory—Dyeing

Feb. 28 Balance	11,174
Transferred in from Spinning	21,000
Direct materials	11,760
Direct labor	8,445
Manufacturing overhead	42,900

In the Dyeing Department, direct materials (dye) are added at the beginning of the process. Conversion costs are incurred evenly throughout the process. Work in process inventory of the Dyeing Department on February 28 consisted of 75 rolls. The $11,174 beginning balance of Work in Process—Dyeing includes $4,400 of transferred-in cost, $1,575 of direct materials cost, and $5,199 of conversion cost. During March, 560 rolls were transferred in from the Spinning Department. The Dyeing Department completed and transferred 500 rolls to the Plying Department in March, and 135 rolls were still in process on March 31. The ending inventory was 80% of the way through the dyeing process. Athena uses weighted-average process costing.

(continued)

Required

1. Prepare a time line for the Dyeing Department, similar to Exhibit 21-10.

2. Use the time line to help you compute the equivalent units, cost per equivalent unit, and total costs to account for in the Dyeing Department for March.

3. Prepare the March production cost report for Athena's Dyeing Department.

4. Journalize all transactions affecting the Dyeing Department during March, including the entries that have already been posted.

P21-5B Waterwise uses three processes to manufacture lifts for personal watercraft: forming a lift's parts from galvanized steel, assembling the lift, and testing the completed lifts. The lifts are transferred to finished goods before shipment to marinas across the country.

Computing equivalent units for a second department with beginning inventory; assigning costs to completed units and ending work in process; WA method **(Obj. 2, 3, 4)**

Waterwise's Testing Department requires no direct materials. Conversion costs are incurred evenly throughout the testing process. Other information follows:

Units:	
Beginning work in process......................................	2,000 units
Transferred in from the Assembling Department during the period...	7,000 units
Completed during the period	4,000 units
Ending work in process (40% complete as to conversion work)	5,000 units
Costs:	
Beginning work in process (transferred-in costs, $93,000; conversion costs, $18,000).....................................	$111,000
Transferred in from the Assembling Department during the period...	672,000
Conversion costs added during the period	48,000

The cost transferred into Finished Goods Inventory is the cost of the lifts transferred out of the Testing Department. Waterwise uses weighted-average process costing.

Required

1. Draw a time line for the Testing Department, similar to the one in Exhibit 21-10.

2. Use the time line to compute the number of equivalent units of work performed by the Testing Department during the period, the cost per equivalent unit, and total costs to account for.

3. Assign total costs to (a) units completed and transferred out of Testing and (b) units in Testing's ending work in process inventory.

4. Compute the cost per unit for lifts completed and transferred out to Finished Goods Inventory. Why would management be interested in this cost?

●APPLY *Your Knowledge*

Decision Case

Jimmy Jones operates Jimmy's Cricket Farm in Eatonton, Georgia. Jimmy's raises about 18 million crickets a month. Most are sold to pet stores at $12.60 for a box of 1,000 crickets. Pet stores sell the crickets for 5 to 10 cents each as live feed for reptiles.

Using WA process cost information to evaluate production performance **(Obj. 4)**

Raising crickets requires a two-step process: incubation and brooding. In the first process, incubation employees place cricket eggs on mounds of peat moss to hatch. In the second process, employees move the newly hatched crickets into large boxes filled with cardboard dividers. Depending on the desired size, the crickets spend approximately

(continued)

two weeks in Brooding before shipment to pet stores. In the brooding process, Jimmy's crickets consume about 16 tons of food and produce 12 tons of manure.

Jones has invested $400,000 in the cricket farm and he had hoped to earn a 24% annual rate of return, which works out to a 2% monthly return on his investment. After looking at the farm's bank balance, Jones fears he is not achieving this return. To get more-accurate information on the farm's performance, Jones bought new accounting software that provides weighted-average process cost information. After Jones input data, the software provided the following reports. However, Jones needs help interpreting these reports.

Jones does know that a unit of production is a box of 1,000 crickets. For example, in June's report, the 7,000 physical units of beginning work in process inventory are 7,000 boxes (each one of the 7,000 boxes contains 1,000 immature crickets). The finished goods inventory is zero because the crickets ship out as soon as they reach the required size. Monthly operating expenses total $2,000 (in addition to the costs below).

Jimmy's Cricket Farm
Brooding Department
Month Ended June 30, 20XX

| | | Equivalent Units | | |
| | Flow of | Transferred | Direct | Conversion |
Flow of Production	Physical Units	In	Materials	Costs
Units to account for:				
Beginning work in process inventory......	7,000			
Transferred in during June...............	21,000			
Total units to account for................	28,000			
Units accounted for:				
Completed and shipped out during June...	19,000	19,000	19,000	19,000
Ending work in process, June 30..........	9,000	9,000	7,200	3,600
Total physical units accounted for........	28,000			
Equivalent units.........................		28,000	26,200	22,600

Jimmy's Cricket Farm
Brooding Department
Production Cost Report (Weighted-Average Method)
Month Ended June 30, 20XX

	Transferred In	Direct Materials	Conversion Costs	Total
Unit costs:				
Beginning work in process, May 31	$21,000	$39,940	$ 5,020	$ 65,960
Costs added during June	46,200	156,560	51,480	254,240
Total costs to account for	$67,200	$196,500	$56,500	$320,200
Divide by equivalent units...................	÷28,000	÷26,200	÷22,600	
Cost per equivalent unit.....................	$2.40	$7.50	$2.50	
Assignment of total cost:				
Units completed and shipped out during June...	[19,000 × ($2.40 + $7.50 + $2.50)]			$235,600
Ending work in process, June 30:				
Transferred-in costs......................	[9,000 × $2.40]			21,600
Direct materials		[7,200 × $7.50]		54,000
Conversion costs			[3,600 × $2.50]	9,000
Total ending work in process, June 30				84,600
Total cost accounted for				$320,200

Required

Jimmy Jones has the following questions about the farm's performance during June.

1. What is the cost per box of crickets sold? (*Hint:* This is the cost of the boxes completed and shipped out of brooding.)
2. What is the gross profit per box?
3. How much operating income did Jimmy's Cricket Farm make in June?
4. What is the return on Jones' investment of $400,000 for the month of June? (Compute this as June's operating income divided by Jones' $400,000 investment, expressed as a percentage.)
5. What monthly operating income would provide a 2% monthly rate of return? What price per box would Jimmy's Cricket Farm have had to charge in June to achieve a 2% monthly rate of return?

Ethical Issue

Effect of percentage completion of ending inventory on financial results
(Obj. 1, 2, 3)

Rick Penn and Joe Lopus are the plant managers for Pacific Lumber's particle board division. Pacific Lumber has adopted a just-in-time management philosophy. Each plant combines wood chips with chemical adhesives to produce particle board to order, and all production is sold as soon as it is completed. Laura Green is Pacific Lumber's regional controller. All of Pacific Lumber's plants and divisions send Green their production and cost information. While reviewing the numbers of the two particle board plants, she is surprised that both plants estimate their ending work in process inventories at 80% complete, which is higher than usual. Green calls Lopus, whom she has known for some time. He admits that to ensure their division met its profit goal and that both he and Penn would make their bonus (which is based on division profit), he and Penn agreed to inflate the percentage completion. Lopus explains, "Determining the percent complete always requires judgment. Whatever the percent complete, we'll finish the work in process inventory first thing next year."

Required

1. How would inflating the percentage completion of ending Work in Process Inventory help Penn and Lopus get their bonus?
2. The particle board division is the largest of Pacific Lumber's divisions. If Green does not correct the percentage completion of this year's ending work in process inventory, how will the misstatement affect Pacific Lumber's financial statements?
3. Evaluate Lopus' justification, including the effect, if any, on next year's financial statements.
4. → *Link Back to Chapter 8.* Apply the ethical framework from Chapter 8 (page 342) in considering what Green should do.

Team Project

Computing allowable cost per unit; computing cost per equivalent unit; second process; WA method
(Obj. 3, 4)

Hermiston Food Processors in Hermiston, Oregon, processes potatoes into french fries. Production requires two processes: cutting and cooking. The cutting process begins as scalding steam explodes the potatoes' brown skins. Workers using paring knives gouge out black spots before high pressure water blasts potatoes through a pipe and into blades arranged in a quarter-inch grid. In the cooking process, the raw shoestring fries are cooked in a bleacher, dried, partially fried at 380°F and immediately flash frozen at minus 75°F before being dropped into 5-pound bags. Direct materials are added at the beginning of the cutting process (potatoes) and at the end of the cooking process (bags). Conversion costs are incurred evenly throughout each process. Hermiston uses the weighted-average method of process costing.

Assume that **McDonald's** offers Hermiston $0.40 per pound to supply restaurants in the Far East. If Hermiston accepts McDonald's offer, the cost (per equivalent unit) that Hermiston will incur to fill the McDonald's order equals the April cost per equivalent
(*continued*)

unit. J. R. Simlott, manager of the cooking process, must prepare a report explaining whether Hermiston should accept the offer. Simlott gathers the following information from April's cooking operations:

Hermiston Food Processors
Cooking Department
April 20XX Activity and Costs

Beginning work in process inventory	12,000 pounds
Raw shoestring fries started in April.	129,000 pounds
French fries completed and transferred out	130,000 pounds
Ending work in process inventory (30% of way through process).	11,000 pounds
Costs incurred *within* the Cooking Dept. to start the 12,000 pounds of beginning work in process inventory in March.	$ 576
Costs added during April:	
Direct materials.	6,500
Conversion costs.	15,420

Lola Mendez manages the cutting process. She reports the following data for her department's April operations.

Hermiston Food Processors
Cutting Department
April 20XX Activity and Costs

Beginning work in process inventory	21,000 pounds
Potatoes started in April	121,000 pounds
Raw shoestring fries completed and transferred out	129,000 pounds
Ending work in process inventory (60% of way through process).	13,000 pounds
Costs to start the 21,000 pounds of beginning work in process inventory in March ($1,260 for direct materials and $840 for conversion costs).	$ 2,100
Costs added during April:	
Direct materials.	8,680
Conversion costs.	12,840

Split your team into two groups. Each group should meet separately before a meeting of the entire team.

Required

1. The first group takes the role of J. R. Simlott, manager of the cooking production process. Before meeting with the entire team, determine the maximum transferred-in cost per pound of raw shoestring fries the Cooking Department can incur from the Cutting Department if Hermiston is to make a profit on the McDonald's order. (*Hint:* You may find it helpful to prepare a time line and to use Exhibits 21-10 through 21-13 as a guide to your analysis.)

2. The second group takes the role of Lola Mendez, manager of the cutting process. Before meeting with the entire team, determine the April cost per pound of raw shoestring fries in the cutting process. (*Hint:* You may find it helpful to prepare a time line and to use Exhibits 21-10 through 21-13 as a guide to your analysis.)

3. After each group meets, the entire team should meet to decide whether Hermiston should accept or reject McDonald's offer.

For Internet Exercises, go to the Web site **www.prenhall.com/horngren**.

APPENDIX *to Chapter 21*

The FIFO Process Costing Method

The cost per equivalent unit often changes over time. In the second half of the chapter, we used the weighted-average process costing method in SeaView's Insertion Department. The weighted-average method values both beginning inventory and current production at the same cost per equivalent unit, but that cost is a weighted average of last period's and this period's costs.

In contrast, the **first-in, first-out (FIFO) method** of process costing values each equivalent unit of work at the cost per equivalent unit in effect during the period the work is done. Therefore, FIFO requires us to keep the beginning inventory units and costs (which were incurred *last period*) completely separate from current-period production and costs.[1]

Let's see how SeaView could use FIFO process costing in its Insertion Department. Consider a batch of swim masks transferred out of the Shaping Department and into Insertion at the end of September. These masks did not make it completely through the Insertion Department during September, so the masks are in the Insertion Department's ending (work in process) inventory at the end of September. The masks are not completed until October. Under FIFO, when these masks are completed in October, the total Insertion Department cost of these masks is the sum of

- September's equivalent units of Insertion's work on these masks, costed at September's cost per equivalent unit, *plus*

- October's equivalent units of Insertion's work on these masks, costed at October's cost per equivalent unit

Student Resource CD

cost assignment, equivalent unit costs, FIFO costing method, transferred-in costs, work in process inventory

First-In, First-Out (FIFO) Process Costing Method
A process costing method that values each equivalent unit of work at the cost per equivalent unit in effect during the period the work is done.

Steps 1 and 2: Summarize the Flow of Physical Units and Compute Output in Terms of Equivalent Units

Summarize the Flow of Physical Units Review the October data for SeaView's Insertion Department in Exhibit 21-11. The time line in Exhibit 21A-1 shows that shaped masks are transferred in from Shaping at the beginning of Insertion's process, but Insertion's direct materials (faceplates) are not added until the end of the process.

The FIFO time line that diagrams the Insertion Department's flow of physical units (step 1) is more complex than the weighted-average time line in Exhibit 21-10. Why? Because FIFO costs each equivalent unit of work at the cost per equivalent unit in effect at the time the work was done. Under FIFO, we must separate the work done last period (September) from the work done this period (October). Exhibit 21A-1 identifies work Insertion performed during *October*.

Start with the 38,000 swim masks completed and transferred out of the Insertion Department and into finished goods inventory during October. The time line in Exhibit 21A-1 shows that these include:

---

[1]The FIFO and weighted-average process costing methods differ only in how they treat beginning inventory. Because SeaView's first department, Shaping, had no beginning work in process inventory, we did not need to specify which method that department used.

Exhibit 21A-1   SeaView's Insertion Department Time Line (FIFO)

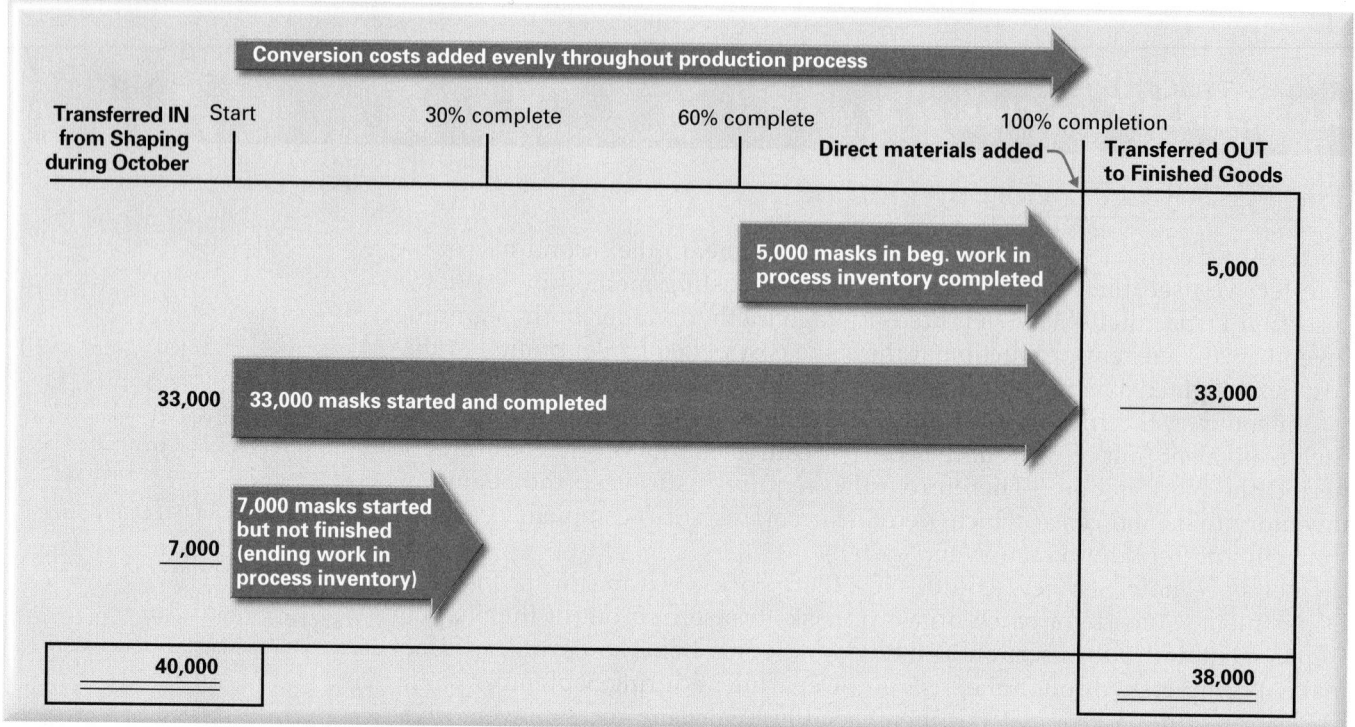

- 5,000 masks that were the Insertion Department's beginning work in process inventory. These masks were *completed* (but not started) in October.
- 33,000 masks that Insertion both *started* and *completed* during October. This number is computed as

38,000	masks completed and transferred out of the Insertion Department in October
(5,000)	masks completed from Insertion's beginning inventory
33,000	masks *started and completed during October*

The time line also shows that the 40,000 masks *transferred into* Insertion from Shaping during October (see Exhibits 21-5 and 21-6) also fall into two categories: (1) 33,000 masks *started and completed* in the Insertion Department during October, plus (2) 7,000 masks *started* in Insertion but not completed in October

Exhibit 21A-2 summarizes the flow of physical units diagrammed in the time line. The Insertion Department starts October with 5,000 masks in beginning inventory and begins work on 40,000 more transferred in from Shaping during the month. Insertion thus must account for 45,000 masks (5,000 + 40,000). Where did these 45,000 masks go? Exhibit 21A-2 shows that 38,000 were completed and transferred out to finished goods inventory (the 5,000 from beginning inventory + 33,000 started and completed during October). The remaining 7,000 masks are still in the Insertion Department's ending inventory.

✔ **Starter 21A-1**

Compute Equivalent Units The Insertion Department has three categories of equivalent units. In addition to direct materials (faceplates) and conversion costs added in the Insertion Department, SeaView must also compute equivalent units for the shaped swim masks that are *transferred in* from the Shaping Department. (All second and later departments must account for units (and costs) transferred in from preceding departments.) Exhibit 21A-1 shows that these transferred-in costs (from Shaping) act like costs that are added at the very beginning of the insertion process.

Exhibit 21A-2   **FIFO, Step 1: Summarize the Flow of Physical Units; Step 2: Compute Output in Terms of Equivalent Units**

	Step 1	Step 2: Equivalent Units		
Flow of Production	**Flow of Physical Units**	**Transferred In**	**Direct Materials**	**Conversion Costs**
SeaView Insertion Department				
Month Ended October 31, 20XX				
Units to account for:				
Beginning work in process, September 30	5,000			
Transferred in during October	40,000			
Total physical units to account for.	45,000			
Units accounted for:				
Completed and transferred out during October:				
From beginning work in process inventory.	5,000	—	5,000*	2,000*
Started and completed during October				
(38,000 − 5,000)	33,000	33,000	33,000	33,000
Ending work in process, October 31	7,000	7,000	— †	2,100†
Total physical units accounted for.	45,000			
Equivalent units.		40,000	38,000	37,100

During October in the Insertion Department:
*Finish beginning inventory
    Direct materials: 5,000 units each 100% completed = 5,000 equivalent units
    Conversion costs: 5,000 units each 40% completed = 2,000 equivalent units
†Start ending inventory
    Direct materials: 7,000 units each 0% completed   = 0 equivalent units
    Conversion costs: 7,000 units each 30% completed = 2,100 equivalent units

To figure out how many equivalent units of work the Insertion Department completed *during October*, look at the time line in Exhibit 21A-1 and add the number of equivalent units of work performed to:

■ *Complete* the 5,000 masks in beginning inventory that were started in September,

■ *Start and complete* an additional 33,000 masks, and

■ *Start* (but not complete) the 7,000 masks that make up the department's work in process inventory at the end of October.

Repeat these computations for each of the three cost categories.

Equivalent Units Transferred In.   Keep in mind that our goal is to figure the number of equivalent units of work performed *during October*. Also recall that transferred-in costs (from Shaping) act like costs that are added at the very beginning of the insertion process. The time line in Exhibit 21A-1 shows that the 5,000 units in Insertion's beginning inventory were *not* transferred in from Shaping *this* month.

Look at the time line again—it shows that the 33,000 masks Insertion started and completed during October and the 7,000 masks in Insertion's ending inventory *were* transferred in during October. Exhibit 21A-2 shows that the total transferred-in equivalent units during October is 40,000 (33,000 + 7,000).

Equivalent Units of Direct Materials.   The time line in Exhibit 21A-1 shows that the Insertion Department's direct materials (faceplates) are not added until the end of the process. Exhibit 21A-1 shows that during October the 5,000 units in beginning inventory were completed, so they reached the end of the production process, where the faceplates are added. The 33,000 units started and completed also reached the end of the process. However, ending inventory has not yet reached the point where workers insert faceplates. Thus, Exhibit 21A-2 shows that Insertion added 5,000 + 33,000 = 38,000 equivalent units of materials (faceplates) during October.

Equivalent Units of Conversion Costs. The time line shows that beginning inventory was 60% complete at the beginning of October. This means that during October these 5,000 masks from the Insertion Department's beginning inventory went through the final 40% of the insertion process. This yields $5,000 \times 0.40 = 2,000$ equivalent units of conversion work during October. The 33,000 masks started and completed during October went through the entire process during October. Finally, the time line shows that the 7,000 masks in ending inventory that were *started* in Insertion during October made it 30% of the way through the process by October 31. Insertion performed $7,000 \times 0.30 = 2,100$ equivalent units of conversion work on this ending inventory during October. Thus, Exhibit 21A-2 shows that the total conversion work performed in Insertion during October includes:

2,000 units to *complete* the beginning inventory

33,000 units from masks started *and* completed during October

2,100 units to *start* the ending inventory

37,100 total equivalent units of conversion costs during October

Steps 3 and 4: Summarize Total Costs to Account For and Compute the Cost per Equivalent Unit

✔ **Starter 21A-2**

Exhibit 21A-3 accumulates the Insertion Department's October costs from Exhibit 21-11. *Under FIFO, the October cost per equivalent unit equals the costs incurred in October divided by the equivalent units of work performed in October.* The $24,000 cost of the beginning inventory is kept separate and is not included in the cost per equivalent unit for work done in October. Why? Because Insertion incurred this $24,000 in *September* to start the 5,000 masks in process on October 1.

Exhibit 21A-3 FIFO, Steps 3 and 4: Summarize Total Costs to Account for and Compute the Cost per Equivalent Unit

	Transferred In	Direct Materials	Conversion Costs	Total
SeaView Insertion Department Month Ended October 31, 20XX				
Beginning work in process, September 30 (Exhibit 21-11).....				$ 24,000
Costs added during October (Exhibit 21-11)...............	$176,000	$ 19,000	$ 14,840	209,840
Divide by equivalent units (Exhibit 21A-2)...............	÷ 40,000	÷ 38,000	÷ 37,100	
Cost per equivalent unit................................	$4.40	$0.50	$0.40	
Total cost to account for				$233,840

Step 5: Assign Total Costs to Units Completed and to Units in Ending Work in Process Inventory

✔ **Starter 21A-3**

Exhibit 21A-4 shows that the Insertion Department uses the same approach as we have used previously to assign its total cost ($233,840 from Exhibit 21A-3) to:

- Units completed and transferred out to Finished Goods Inventory
- Units still in Insertion's ending work in process inventory

Multiply the number of equivalent units from step 2 (Exhibit 21A-2) by the cost per equivalent unit from step 4 (Exhibit 21A-3).

Exhibit 21A-4 shows that when computing the cost of masks completed and transferred out of Insertion, we must remember to include the costs of the beginning inventory:

- $24,000 of Insertion Department beginning inventory costs (incurred in September)
- $3,300 of costs to complete that beginning inventory in October [(5,000 equivalent units of materials added × $0.50) + (2,000 equivalent units of conversion costs added × $0.40)]

| Exhibit 21A-4 | FIFO, Step 5: Assign Total Costs to Units Completed and to Units in Ending Work in Process Inventory |

SeaView Insertion Department
Month Ended October 31, 20XX

	Transferred In	Direct Materials	Conversion Costs	Total
Units completed and transferred out to Finished Goods Inventory:				
From beginning work in process, Sept. 30				$ 24,000
Costs added during October:				
Direct materials		[5,000 × $0.50]		2,500
Conversion costs			[2,000 × $0.40]	800
Total completed from beginning inventory				27,300
Units started and completed during October		[33,000 × ($4.40 + $0.50 + $0.40)]		174,900
Total costs transferred out				202,200
Ending work in process, October 31:				
Transferred-in costs	[7,000 × $4.40]			30,800
Direct materials		—		—
Conversion costs			[2,100 × $0.40]	840
Total ending work in process, October 31				31,640
Total costs accounted for.				$233,840

The entry to transfer the cost of completed masks out of the Insertion Department and into Finished Goods Inventory is based on the dollar amount computed in Exhibit 21A-4:

Finished Goods Inventory.	202,200	
Work in Process Inventory—Insertion . .		202,200

Many companies combine Exhibits 21A-3 and 21A-4 to form a FIFO-based production cost report. (This report is the FIFO-based counterpart to the weighted-average-based production cost report in Exhibit 21-16.)

When will FIFO and weighted average give different results?

Answer: FIFO and weighted average give different results when

1. There is beginning inventory. If there is no beginning inventory, FIFO and weighted average yield identical results. This is why we did not need to specify whether SeaView's Shaping Department used FIFO or weighted average—Shaping had no beginning inventory.
2. The cost per unit changes from one period to the next. If the cost per unit in the current period is the same as in the prior period, then FIFO and weighted average yield identical results.

FIFO and weighted average yield significantly different results only when there are large beginning inventories *and* costs change dramatically from one period to the next. This could happen, for example, in the wine-making industry, in which there are significant work in process inventories and the cost of grapes fluctuates.

Appendix Assignments

Starters

Computing equivalent units under FIFO

S21A-1 Refer to the Polar Spring Bottling process in Starter 21-9.

1. Draw a time line for the Bottling Department under FIFO process costing. Your time line should be similar to Exhibit 21A-1.
2. Use the time line to help you compute the Bottling Department's equivalent units using the FIFO method.

Cost per equivalent unit, FIFO; second department

S21A-2 Consider Polar Spring's Bottling Department, as described in Starter 21-9, and your solution to Starter 21-A1. Compute the cost per equivalent unit using FIFO.

Assigning costs FIFO; second department

S21-A3 Use the information about Polar Spring's Bottling Department in Starters 21-9, 21-A1, and 21-A2 to assign the costs to units completed and transferred out and to ending inventory under FIFO.

Exercises

Computing equivalent units; 2 departments, FIFO method

E21A-1 Zee's Candy uses FIFO process costing. Selected production and cost data follow for May 20X6.

	Flow of Physical Units	
Flow of Production	Mixing Department	Cooking Department
Units to account for:		
Beginning work in process, April 30..........	20,000	6,000
Transferred in during May...................	70,000	80,000
Total physical units to account for...........	90,000	86,000
Units accounted for:		
Completed and transferred out during May		
From beginning work in process inventory..	20,000	6,000
Started and completed during May	60,000	70,000
Ending work in process, May 31	10,000	10,000
Total physical units accounted for.............	90,000	86,000

Required

1. a. On April 30, the Mixing Department beginning work in process inventory was 60% complete as to materials and 75% complete as to conversion costs. This means that for the beginning inventory _____% of the materials and _____% of the conversion costs were added during May.
   b. On May 31, the Mixing Department ending work in process inventory was 70% complete as to materials and 20% complete as to conversion costs. This means that for the ending inventory _____% of the materials and _____% of the conversion costs were added during May.
   c. On April 30, the Cooking Department beginning work in process inventory was 60% complete as to materials and 80% complete as to conversion costs. This means that for the beginning inventory _____% of the materials and _____% of the conversion costs were added during May.
   d. On May 31, the Cooking Department ending work in process inventory was 65% complete as to materials and 55% complete as to conversion costs. This means that for the ending inventory _____% of the materials and _____% of the conversion costs were added during May.
2. Use the information in the Flow of Production table and the information in requirement 1 to compute the equivalent units for transferred-in costs, direct materials, and conversion costs for both the Mixing and the Cooking Departments.

E21A-2 Refer to the Alpha Semiconductors, Inc. information in E21-10.

1. Draw a time line for the Photolithography Department using the FIFO method. (See Exhibit 21A-1.)
2. Use the time line to help you compute the number of equivalent units of work performed by the Photolithography Department during December. Use the FIFO method.
3. Compute the cost per equivalent unit, and assign total costs to (a) units completed and transferred to Finished Goods Inventory and (b) units in December 31 work in process inventory.

Computing equivalent units and assigning costs to completed units and to ending work in process inventory; second department, FIFO

Appendix Problems

P21A-1 Tuff, Inc., manufactures tire tubes in a two-stage process that includes shaping and sealing. The Sealing Department tests the tubes and adds a puncture-resistant coating to each tube to prevent air leaks.

Computing equivalent units for a second department with beginning inventory; assigning costs to completed units and ending work in process; recording transactions, FIFO method

At March 31, before recording the transfer of costs from the Sealing Department to Finished Goods Inventory, the Tuff general ledger included the following account:

Work in Process Inventory—Sealing

Feb. 28 balance	28,100
Transferred in from Shaping	36,000
Direct materials	24,800
Direct labor	23,595
Manufacturing overhead	32,245

The direct materials (coating) are added at the end of the sealing process. Conversion costs are incurred evenly throughout the process. Work in process of the Sealing Department on February 28 consisted of 700 tubes that were 30% of the way through the production process. During March, 3,600 tubes were transferred in from the Shaping Department. The Sealing Department transferred 3,100 tubes to Finished Goods Inventory in March, and 1,200 were still in process on March 31. This ending inventory was 50% of the way through the sealing process. Tuff uses FIFO process costing.

Required

1. Draw a time line for the Sealing Department, similar to Exhibit 21A-1.
2. Use the time line to help you compute the equivalent units, cost per equivalent unit, and total costs to account for in the Sealing Department for March.
3. Assign total Sealing Department costs to (a) goods transferred out of the Sealing Department and (b) Work in Process Inventory—Sealing on March 31.
4. Journalize all transactions affecting the Sealing Department during March, including the entries that have already been posted.

Computing EU for a second department with BI; assigning costs to completed units and ending WIP; FIFO

P21A-2 Do P21-5A using the FIFO method. The Drying Department beginning work in process of 7,000 units is 30% complete as to conversion costs. For requirement 1, use the time line in Exhibit 21A-1 as a guide.

P21A-3 Do P21-4A using the FIFO method. The Plating Department beginning work in process of 600 racks is 30% complete as to conversion costs. For requirement 1, use the time line in Exhibit 21A-1 as a guide. In Requirement 3, prepare a cost assignment report similar to Exhibit 21A-4, instead of a full production cost report.

Computing EU for a second department with BI; assigning costs to completed units and ending WIP; recording transactions; FIFO

CHAPTER 22

Cost-Volume-Profit Analysis

TIPS CHECK YOUR RESOURCES

- Visit the www.prenhall.com/horngren **Web site** for self-study quizzes, video clips, and other resources

- Try the **Quick Check** exercise at the end of the chapter to test your knowledge

- Learn the **key terms**

- Do the **Starter** exercises keyed in the margins

- Work the **mid-** and **end-of-chapter summary problems**

- Use the **Concept Links** to review material in other chapters

- Search the **CD** for review materials by chapter or by key word

- Watch the **tutorial videos** to review key concepts

- Watch the **Grand Canyon Railway On Location video** to review CVP analysis

LEARNING OBJECTIVES

⭐1 Identify how changes in volume affect costs

⭐2 Use CVP analysis to compute breakeven points

⭐3 Use CVP analysis for profit planning, and graph the cost-volume-profit relations

⭐4 Use CVP methods to perform sensitivity analyses

⭐5 Compute income using variable costing and absorption costing

"All aboard!" shouts the conductor of the Grand Canyon Railway as the train departs from the Williams, Arizona, depot. The restored turn-of-the-century train features musicians in period costumes. Passengers have breakfast on the morning trip to the canyon and nibble appetizers on the afternoon trip back to Williams.

Few of the railway's costs vary with the number of passengers because most costs are *fixed*. Track maintenance, insurance, the costs to operate the depot's railway museum, and depreciation on the locomotive and cars stay the same whether 1 or 1,000 passengers travel the scenic 65-mile route. But food and beverage costs are *variable*. They rise and fall with the number of passengers on board.

Grand Canyon Railway

The Railway's managers must set ticket prices high enough to cover costs and earn a profit, but low enough to fill seats. Most costs are fixed, so the extra costs to serve each additional passenger are low. Once fixed costs are covered, most of the revenue from extra guests goes toward profits. ∎

Sitemap

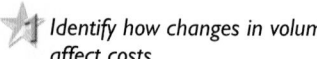

Student ResourceCD

CVP analysis, fixed costs, mixed costs, variable costs

⭐ *Identify how changes in volume affect costs*

Cost-Volume-Profit (CVP) Analysis
Expresses the relationships among costs, volume, and profit or loss.

Cost Behavior
Describes how costs change as volume changes.

Total Variable Costs
Costs that change in total in direct proportion to changes in volume.

Total Fixed Costs
Costs that do not change in total despite wide changes in volume.

How do the railway's managers ensure that revenues cover costs and provide profits? How many seats must the railway fill to cover costs? Grand Canyon's managers perform cost-volume-profit analysis to answer these questions.

Cost-volume-profit (CVP) analysis expresses the relationships among costs, volume, and profit or loss. That is, you use CVP analysis to estimate how changes in volume affect costs and profits. To do this, you first need to understand **cost behavior**: how costs change—if they change at all—as volume changes.

How Do Changes in Volume Affect Costs?

We consider two types of cost behavior:

- **Total variable costs** change in direct proportion to changes in volume. For Grand Canyon Railway, breakfast pastries and afternoon snacks are variable costs because total food costs increase with the number of passengers.

- **Total fixed costs** do not change despite wide changes in volume. For Grand Canyon, depreciation on the tracks and locomotive are fixed costs that will be the same, regardless of the number of passengers carried.

Variable Costs

On the morning trip from Williams, Grand Canyon's passengers enjoy pastries, orange juice, and coffee. Let's assume this breakfast costs the railway $3 per person. On the afternoon return trip, passengers snack on appetizers and sip champagne and soft drinks. Say this costs Grand Canyon $10 per person. Exhibit 22-1 graphs Grand Canyon's $3-per-person breakfast cost and the $10-per-person afternoon snack cost. The vertical axis shows total variable costs, while the horizontal axis plots total volume (thousands of passengers, in this case).

Look at the total variable breakfast costs in Exhibit 22-1(a). If there are no passengers, Grand Canyon incurs no breakfast costs, so the total variable cost line begins at the bottom left corner. This point is called the *origin*, and it represents zero volume and zero cost. The *slope* of the total variable cost line is the change in total variable cost (on the vertical axis) divided by the change in the total volume (on the horizontal axis). This equals the variable cost per unit. In Exhibit 22-1(a), the slope of the breakfast total variable cost line is $3 because the railway spends an additional $3 on breakfast for each additional passenger. If the railroad carries 2,000 passengers, it will spend a total of $6,000 (2,000 passengers × $3 each) for breakfast service. Follow this total variable cost line to the right to see that doubling the number of passengers to 4,000 likewise doubles the total variable cost to $12,000 (4,000 × $3 = $12,000).

Now look at Exhibit 22-1(b), the total variable costs for afternoon snacks and beverages. The slope of the total variable cost line is the $10 cost of providing

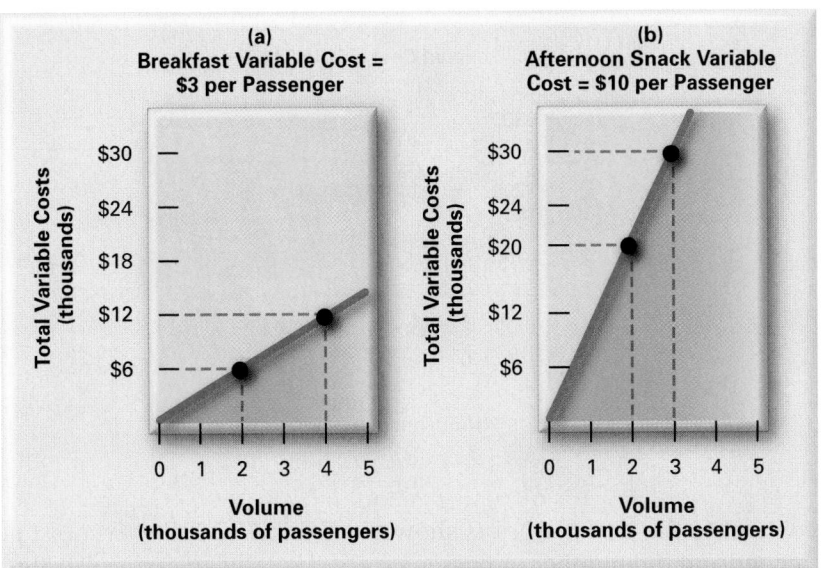

Exhibit 22-1

Variable Costs

afternoon refreshments for each passenger. The total cost of afternoon snacks for 2,000 passengers is $20,000 (2,000 × $10). This is much higher than the breakfast cost for 2,000 passengers ($6,000), so the slope of the afternoon snack's total variable cost line is much steeper than that for breakfast.

The **key point** is

The higher the variable cost per unit, the steeper the slope of the total variable cost line.

Exhibit 22-1 shows how *total variable costs* vary with the number of passengers. *But note that the per-person cost remains constant.* That is, Grand Canyon incurs $3 in breakfast costs and $10 in afternoon snack costs for each passenger, no matter how many passengers the railway carries. The **key point** is

---

Total variable costs fluctuate with changes in volume, but the variable cost per unit remains constant.

Fixed Costs

In contrast to total variable costs, total fixed costs do not change over wide ranges of volume. Most of Grand Canyon's costs are fixed, because the train makes one round-trip each day, regardless of the number of passengers. The railway's fixed costs include

- Salaries of conductors
- Depreciation and maintenance on the track, the locomotive, and the museum
- Entertainment costs (salaries of the strolling musicians)
- Administrative expenses (salaries of managers and accountants)

Suppose Grand Canyon incurs $200,000 of fixed costs each month. Exhibit 22-2 graphs total fixed costs as a flat line that intersects the cost axis at $200,000, because Grand Canyon will incur the same $200,000 of fixed costs regardless of the number of passengers.

Exhibit 22-2

Fixed Costs

✔ **Starter 22-1**

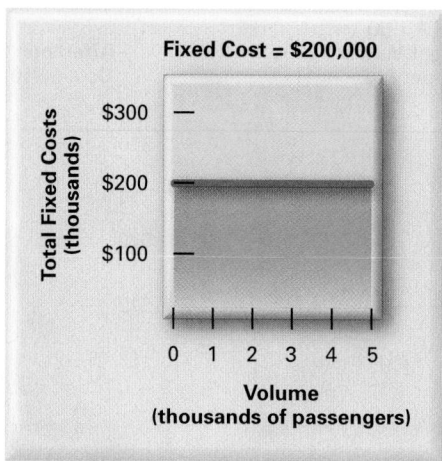

In contrast to the *total fixed costs* shown in Exhibit 22-2, the *fixed cost per passenger* depends on the number of passengers. If the railway carries 2,000 passengers, the fixed cost per passenger is $100 ($200,000 ÷ 2,000 passengers). If the number of passengers doubles to 4,000, the fixed cost per passenger is cut in half to $50 ($200,000 ÷ 4,000 passengers). Thus, the fixed cost per passenger is *inversely* proportional to the number of passengers. The **key point** is

---

Total fixed costs remain constant, but fixed cost per unit is inversely proportional to volume.

World class companies capitalize on this principle to maximize profits. For example, the founder of Europe's budget airline **easyJet** credits the company's success to keeping planes full and flying them hard. "If you have a very expensive fixed asset, you need to make it work for you," he said.[1]

Mixed Costs

Mixed Costs
Costs that have both variable and fixed components.

Costs that have both variable and fixed components are called **mixed costs**. For example, your cell phone company may charge $10 a month to provide the service and $0.15 for each minute you talk. If you talk for 100 minutes, the company will bill you $25 [$10 + (100 × $0.15)].

Exhibit 22-3 shows how you can separate your cell phone bill into fixed and variable components. The $10 monthly charge is a fixed cost because it is the

Exhibit 22-3

Mixed Costs

✔ **Starter 22-2**

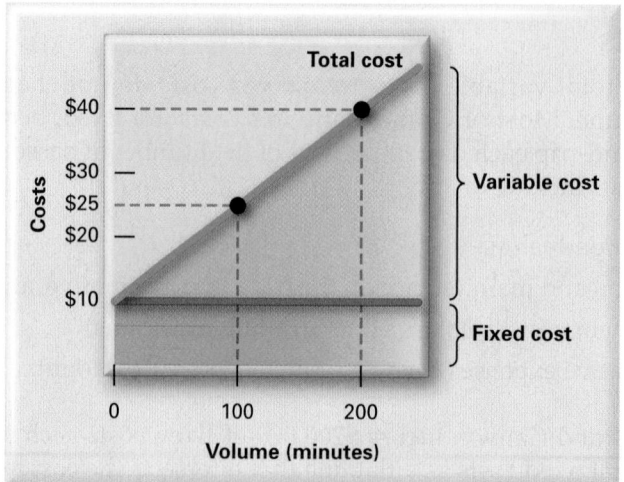

---

[1]Scott Kirsner, "Stelios Makes Growth Look Easy," *Fast Company*, November 2002, pp. 98–104.

same no matter how many minutes you use. The $0.15 a minute charge is a variable cost that increases in direct proportion to the number of minutes you talk. If you talk for 100 minutes, your total variable cost is $15, because each minute costs $0.15. If you double your talking to 200 minutes, total variable cost also doubles to $30 (200 × $0.15), and your total bill is $40 ($10 + $30).

If you double your talk time from 100 to 200 minutes, does your total cell phone bill double? Explain.

Answer: No, your total cell phone bill increases by less than double [($40 − $25) ÷ $25 = 60% increase]. Variable costs double from $15 to $30, but the $10 fixed cost does not change.

Relevant Range

The **relevant range** is the band of volume where total fixed costs remain constant and the variable cost *per unit* remains constant. To estimate costs, managers need to know the relevant range. Why? Because

Relevant Range
The band of volume where total fixed costs remain constant and the variable cost *per unit* remains constant.

- Total "fixed" costs can differ in different relevant ranges, and
- The variable cost *per unit* can differ in different relevant ranges

Exhibit 22-4 shows *fixed costs* for a Footlocker store over three different relevant ranges. If the store expects to sell 15,000 pairs of shoes next year, the relevant range is between 10,000 and 20,000 pairs, and managers budget fixed costs of $80,000.

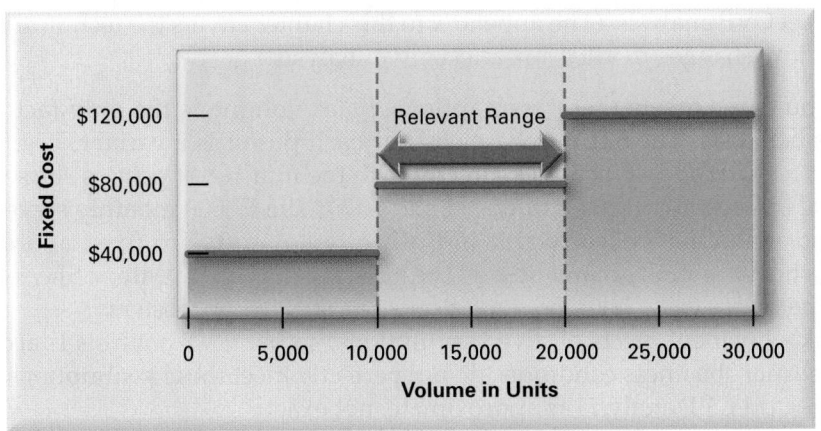

Exhibit 22-4

Relevant Range

To sell 22,000 pairs of shoes, Footlocker will have to expand the store. This will increase rent expense. Exhibit 22-4 shows that total fixed costs increase to $120,000 as the relevant range shifts to this higher band of volume. Conversely, if the store expects to sell only 8,000 pairs of shoes, Exhibit 22-4 shows that the store will budget only $40,000 of fixed costs. Managers will have to cut operating hours, lay off employees, or take other actions to cut fixed costs.

Variable cost per unit also can change outside the relevant range. For example, Footlocker may receive a quantity discount (a lower purchase cost per pair of shoes) if it can sell more than 20,000 pairs of Reeboks.

☐ Changes in Volume and Costs
■ **Basic CVP Analysis**
☐ Using CVP to Plan Profits
☐ Using CVP for Sensitivity Analysis
☐ Variable Costing, Absorption Costing

Basic CVP Analysis: What Must We Sell to Break Even?

Now let's use your understanding of how changes in volume affect costs. Kay Pak is considering starting an e-tail business selling art posters on the Internet. Pak plans to be a "virtual retailer" and carry no inventory. Pak's software will

Student ResourceCD

breakeven point, contribution margin, income statement approach

⭐ *Use CVP analysis to compute breakeven points*

Exhibit 22-5

Components of CVP Analysis

tabulate all customer orders each day and then automatically place Pak's order to buy posters from a wholesaler. Pak buys only what she needs to fulfill the prior day's sales orders. The posters will cost Pak $21 each, and she plans to sell them for $35 each. Monthly fixed costs for server leasing and maintenance, software, and office rental total $7,000.

Armed with this information about the components of CVP analysis, which is illustrated in Exhibit 22-5, you can use CVP analysis to help Kay answer questions such as these: How many posters must she sell to break even? What will profits be if sales double? How will changes in selling price, variable costs, or fixed costs affect profits? Before getting started, we review the assumptions required for CVP analysis to be accurate.

Assumptions

CVP analysis assumes that

1. The only factor that affects costs is change in volume.
2. Managers can classify each cost (or the components of mixed costs) as either variable or fixed.
3. Both costs and revenues are linear throughout the relevant range of volume.
4. Inventory levels will not change.
5. The sales mix of products will not change. **Sales mix** is the combination of products that make up total sales. For example, in 2002, Amazon.com's U.S. retail sales mix was 75% books and music products and 25% electronics and other products. If profits differ across products, then changes in sales mix affect CVP analysis. (The appendix to this chapter covers the technical details of how changes in sales mix affect CVP analysis.)

Pak's business meets these assumptions. Sales volume is the only factor that affects her costs. The $21 purchase cost for each poster is a variable cost. Thus, Pak's *total variable cost* increases directly with the number of posters she sells (an extra $21 in cost for each extra poster she sells). The $7,000 monthly server leasing and maintenance, software, and office rental costs are fixed and do not change no matter how many posters she sells. Pak has no inventory. She sells just one type of poster, so her sales mix is constant at 100% art posters.

Pak's business meets all five assumptions, so her CVP analysis is accurate. Because most business conditions do not perfectly meet these assumptions, managers regard CVP analysis as approximate, not exact.

How Much Must We Sell to Break Even? Three Approaches

The **breakeven point** is the sales level at which operating income is zero: Total revenues equal total expenses. Sales below the breakeven point result in a loss. Sales above the breakeven point provide a profit. Pak does not want to start her business unless it can make a profit, so she wants to know how many posters she must sell to break even.

There are several ways to figure the breakeven point. We start with the most versatile and easiest-to-remember method, which is based on the income statement.

THE INCOME STATEMENT APPROACH Start by expressing income in equation form:

Sales Mix
Combination of products that make up total sales.

Sales revenue –	Total expenses	= Operating income
Sales revenue – Variable expenses – Fixed expenses		= Operating income

Sales revenue equals the unit sale price ($35 per poster in this case) multiplied by the number of units (posters) sold. Variable expenses equal variable cost per unit ($21 in this case) times the number of units sold. Pak's fixed expenses total $7,000. At the breakeven point, operating income is zero. We use this information to solve the income statement equation for the number of posters Pak must sell to break even.

Breakeven Point
The sales level at which operating income is zero: Total revenues equal total expenses.

SALES REVENUE	−	VARIABLE EXPENSES	− FIXED EXPENSES	= OPERATING INCOME
$\left(\dfrac{\text{Sale price}}{\text{per unit}} \times \text{Units sold}\right)$ −		$\left(\dfrac{\text{Variable cost}}{\text{per unit}} \times \text{Units sold}\right)$	− Fixed expenses	= Operating income
($35 × Units sold) −		($21 × Units sold) −	$7,000	= $0
($35 −		$21) × Units sold −	$7,000	= $0
		$14 × Units sold		= $7,000
		Units sold		= $7,000/$14
		Breakeven sales in units		= 500 posters

Kay Pak must sell 500 posters to break even. Her breakeven sales level in dollars is $17,500 (500 posters × $35).

Be sure to check your calculations. "Prove" the breakeven point by substituting the breakeven number of units into the income statement equation and checking that this level of sales results in zero profit.

$$(\$35 \times 500) - (\$21 \times 500) - \$7,000 = \$0$$
$$\$17,500 - \$10,500 - \$7,000 = \$0$$

THE CONTRIBUTION MARGIN APPROACH: A SHORTCUT To use this shortcut method of computing the breakeven point, we first must know Pak's contribution margin. **Contribution margin** is sales revenue minus variable expenses. It is called the *contribution margin* because the excess of sales revenue over variable costs contributes to covering fixed expenses and then to providing operating income. We can refer to contribution margin on a total basis or on a per-unit basis:

Contribution Margin
Sales revenue minus variable expenses.

✔ **Starter 22-3**

Total contribution margin = Total sales revenue − Total variable expenses
Contribution margin per unit = Sales revenue per unit − Variable expense per unit

Now let's rearrange the income statement equation and use the contribution margin to develop a shortcut method for finding the number of posters Pak must sell to break even.

Sales revenue − Variable expenses − Fixed expenses = Operating income

$\left(\dfrac{\text{Sale price}}{\text{per unit}} \times \text{Units sold}\right) - \left(\dfrac{\text{Variable cost}}{\text{per unit}} \times \text{Units sold}\right)$ − Fixed expenses = Operating income

$\left(\dfrac{\text{Sale price}}{\text{per unit}} - \dfrac{\text{Variable cost}}{\text{per unit}}\right) \times \text{Units sold}$ = Fixed expenses + Operating income

Contribution margin per unit × Units sold = Fixed expenses + Operating income

Dividing both sides of the equation by contribution margin per unit yields

$$\text{Units sold} = \frac{\text{Fixed expenses} + \text{Operating income}}{\text{Contribution margin per unit}}$$

Kay Pak can use this contribution margin approach to find her breakeven point. Her fixed expenses total $7,000. Operating income is zero at the breakeven point. Her contribution margin per poster is $14 ($35 sale price − $21 variable cost). Pak's breakeven computation is

$$= \frac{\$7,000 + \$0}{\$14}$$
$$= 500 \text{ posters}$$

Why does this shortcut method work? Each poster Pak sells provides $14 of contribution margin. To break even, Pak must generate enough contribution margin to cover $7,000 of fixed expenses. At the rate of $14 per poster, Pak must sell 500 posters ($7,000/$14) to cover her $7,000 of fixed expenses. Because the contribution margin approach simply rearranges the income statement equation, the breakeven point is the same under both methods (500 posters).

✔ Starter 22-4

USING THE CONTRIBUTION MARGIN RATIO TO COMPUTE THE BREAKEVEN POINT IN SALES DOLLARS It's easy to compute the breakeven point for a simple business like Kay Pak's that has only one product. The sale price and variable cost per poster are available, as are the fixed costs necessary for the business. But what about companies that have thousands of products, like Amazon.com or Sony?

If they don't have detailed information on individual products, companies use the contribution margin ratio to compute breakeven points in terms of *sales dollars*. The **contribution margin ratio** is the ratio of contribution margin to sales revenue. For Kay Pak's poster business, we have:

Contribution Margin Ratio
Ratio of contribution margin to sales revenue.

$$\text{Contribution margin ratio} = \frac{\text{Contribution margin}}{\text{Sales revenue}} = \frac{\$14}{\$35} = 40\%$$

The 40% contribution margin ratio means that each dollar of sales revenue contributes $0.40 toward fixed costs and profit, as shown in Exhibit 22-6.

Exhibit 22-6

Breakdown of $1 of Revenue into Variable Costs and Contribution Margin

The contribution margin *ratio* approach differs from the shortcut contribution margin approach we've just seen in only one way: fixed expenses plus operating income are divided by the contribution margin *ratio* to yield sales in *dollars*:

$$\text{Sales in dollars} = \frac{\text{Fixed expenses + Operating income}}{\text{Contribution margin ratio}}$$

Using this ratio formula, Kay Pak's breakeven point in sales dollars is

$$\text{Sales in dollars} = \frac{\$7,000 + \$0}{0.40}$$
$$= \$17,500$$

This is the same breakeven sales revenue as shown in the proof on page 903.

Why does the contribution margin ratio formula work? Each dollar of Kay Pak's sales contributes $0.40 to fixed expenses and profit. To break even, she must generate enough contribution margin at the rate of $0.40 per sales dollar to cover the $7,000 fixed expenses ($7,000 ÷ 0.40 = $17,500).

> Suppose that **Amazon.com**'s total revenues are $4.5 billion, its variable costs are $3.15 billion, and its fixed costs are $1.1 billion. What is the breakeven point in sales dollars?
>
> *Answer:* The contribution margin ratio is 30% [($4.5 − $3.15) ÷ $4.5].
>
> $$\text{Sales in dollars} = \frac{\text{Fixed expenses} + \text{Operating income}}{\text{Contribution margin ratio}}$$
>
> $$= \frac{\$1.1\text{ billion} + \$0}{0.30}$$
>
> $$= \$3.667\text{ billion (rounded)}$$

We've seen how companies use *contribution margin* to estimate breakeven points in CVP analysis. But managers use the contribution margin for other purposes too, such as motivating the sales force. Salespeople who know the contribution margin of each product can generate more profit by emphasizing high-margin products. This is why many companies base sales commissions on the contribution margins produced by sales rather than on sales revenue alone.

Using CVP to Plan Profits

For established products and services, managers are more interested in the sales level needed to earn a target profit than in the breakeven point. Managers of new business ventures are also interested in the profits they can expect to earn. For example, now that she knows she must sell 500 posters to break even, Kay Pak wants to know how many more posters she must sell to earn $4,900 a month in profit.

How Much Must We Sell to Earn a Profit?

The only difference from our prior analysis is that instead of determining the sales level needed for zero profit, Pak now wants to know how many posters she must sell to earn a $4,900 profit. We can use the income statement approach or the shortcut contribution margin approach to find the answer. Let's use the income statement approach.

☐ Changes in Volume and Costs
☐ Basic CVP Analysis
■ **Using CVP to Plan Profits**
☐ Using CVP for Sensitivity Analysis
☐ Variable Costing, Absorption Costing

breakeven point, income statement approach

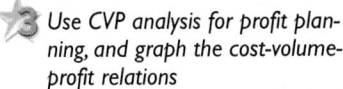

Use CVP analysis for profit planning, and graph the cost-volume-profit relations

✔ Starter 22-5

SALES REVENUE	–	VARIABLE EXPENSES	–	FIXED EXPENSES	=	OPERATING INCOME
($35 × Units sold)	–	($21 × Units sold)	–	$7,000	=	$4,900
($35	–	$21) × Units sold	–	$7,000	=	$4,900
		$14 × Units sold			=	$11,900
				Units sold	=	$11,900/$14
				Units sold	=	850 posters

Proof:

($35 × 850)	–	($21 × 850)	–	$7,000	=	$4,900
$29,750	–	$17,850	–	$7,000	=	$4,900

This analysis shows that Pak must sell 850 posters each month to earn profits of $4,900 a month. This is 850 − 500 = 350 more posters than the breakeven sales level (500 posters).

Webvan.com: How Fixed Costs Kept It from Delivering the Goods

When online grocer Webvan.com opened its virtual doors in April 1999, it seemed to have all the ingredients for an e-commerce success story: financial backing of high-profile financiers and public funding totaling $1.2 billion, an experienced management team led by former Andersen Consulting CEO George Shaheen, and a service custom-made for today's busy professionals.

Shaheen expected the start-up to eventually deliver not just groceries, but everything from CDs to dry cleaning. To handle the huge demand he expected for Webvan's services, Shaheen built 26 state-of-the-art distribution centers in seven cities. They cost the company $25 million each. Each warehouse was equipped with 1,000 expensive servers, 16 employees, and a fleet of top-of-the-line trucks.

Alas, the company's business model turned out to be its undoing. Webvan, like eToys and other failed e-businesses, racked up enormous fixed costs by insourcing distribution. It tanked when the huge sales needed to cover those fixed costs never materialized (Webvan needed 4,000 orders per day at *each* distribution center to break even!). Then, instead of reducing fixed costs by cutting the costs of warehouses and tech support, the company lowered the quality of its produce, further reducing customer demand.

Webvan's approach stands in direct contrast to Amazon.com, which started with more of a variable cost structure. Amazon sold books from its Web site without investing in warehouses or inventory. It did not acquire the books it sold until after it received a customer order. Without warehousing and inventory, Amazon avoided fixed costs if business was slow. Later, as demand grew, it took on more fixed costs—building its own warehouses, for instance.

In 2002, Amazon was finally turning an operating profit, while Webvan was auctioning off its vans and trucks.

Based on: Carrie Kirby, "NEWS ANALYSIS: Webvan's Swan Song: Crash, Burn Calls E-Commerce into Serious Question," *San Francisco Chronicle,* July 10, 2001, p. B.1. Justin Rock, "The Inevitable Crash of Webvan," *Weekly Corporate Growth Report,* July 30, 2001, pp. 11453, 11464. Anonymous, "Digits," *The Wall Street Journal,* May 9, 2002, p. B5. Information about Amazon is from Amazon.com financial statements, stock-analyst reports, and conversations with company management.

The proof shows that Pak needs sales revenues of $29,750 to earn a profit of $4,900. Alternatively, we can compute the dollar sales necessary to earn a $4,900 profit directly, using the contribution margin ratio form of the CVP formula:

$$\text{SALES IN DOLLARS} = \frac{\text{Fixed expenses} + \text{Operating income}}{\text{Contribution margin ratio}}$$

$$= \frac{\$7,000 + \$4,900}{0.40}$$

$$= \frac{\$11,900}{0.40}$$

$$= \$29,750$$

Graphing Cost-Volume-Profit Relations

By graphing the cost-volume-profit relations for her proposed business, Kay Pak can see at a glance how changes in the levels of sales will affect profits. As in the variable-, fixed-, and mixed-cost graphs in Exhibits 22-1 through 22-3, she places the volume of units (posters) on the horizontal axis and dollars on the vertical axis. Then she follows five steps to graph the CVP relations for her business, as illustrated in Exhibit 22-7:

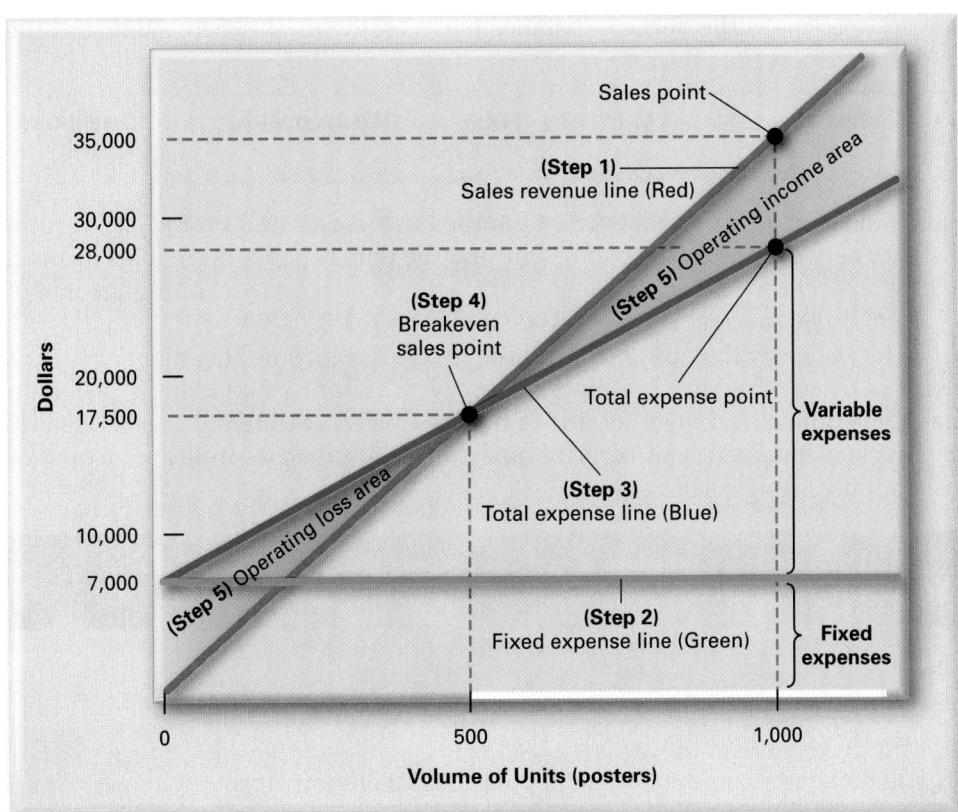

Exhibit 22-7

Cost-Volume-Profit Graph

✔ Starter 22-6

✔ Starter 22-7

STEP 1 Choose a sales volume, such as 1,000 posters. Plot the point for total sales revenue at that volume: 1,000 posters × $35 per poster = sales of $35,000. Draw the *sales revenue line* from the origin (0) through the $35,000 point. Why does the sales revenue line start at the origin? If Pak does not sell any posters, there is no sales revenue.

STEP 2 Draw the *fixed expense line*, a horizontal line that intersects the dollars axis at $7,000. Why is the fixed expense line flat? Because fixed expenses are the same ($7,000) no matter how many posters Pak sells.

STEP 3 Draw the *total expense line*. Total expense is the sum of variable expense plus fixed expense. Thus, total expense is a *mixed* cost. So the total expense line follows the form of the mixed cost line in Exhibit 22-3. Begin by computing variable expense at the chosen sales volume: 1,000 posters × $21 per poster = variable expense of $21,000. Add variable expense to fixed expense: $21,000 + $7,000 = $28,000. Plot the total expense point ($28,000) for 1,000 units. Then draw a line through this point from the $7,000 fixed expense intercept on the dollars axis. This is the *total expense line*. Why does the total expense line start at the fixed expense line? If Pak sells no posters, she still incurs the $7,000 fixed cost for the server leasing, software, and office rental, but she incurs no variable costs.

STEP 4 Identify the *breakeven point*. The breakeven point is the point where the sales revenue line intersects the total expense line. This is the point where sales revenue exactly equals total expenses. Our previous analyses told us that Pak's breakeven point is 500 posters, or $17,500 in sales. The graph shows this information visually.

STEP 5 Mark the *operating income* and the *operating loss* areas on the graph. To the left of the breakeven point, the total expense line lies above the sales revenue line. Expenses exceed sales revenue, leading to an operating loss. If Pak sells only 300 posters, she incurs an operating loss. The amount of the loss is the vertical distance between the total expense line and the sales revenue line:

SALES REVENUE – VARIABLE EXPENSES – FIXED EXPENSES = OPERATING INCOME (LOSS)
(300 × $35) – (300 × $21) – $7,000 = $(2,800)

To the right of the breakeven point, the business earns a profit. The vertical distance between the sales revenue line and the total expense line equals income. Exhibit 22-7 shows that if Pak sells 1,000 posters, she earns operating income of $7,000 ($35,000 sales revenue – $28,000 total expenses).

Why bother with a graph? Why not just use the income statement approach or the shortcut contribution margin approach? Graphs like Exhibit 22-7 help managers quickly estimate the profit or loss earned at different levels of sales. The income statement and contribution margin approaches indicate income or loss for only a single sales amount.

MID-CHAPTER *Summary Problem*

TIPS

CHECK YOUR RESOURCES

Fleet Foot buys hiking socks for $6 a pair and sells them for $10. Management budgets monthly fixed costs of $10,000 for sales volumes between 0 and 12,000 pairs.

Required

1. Use both the income statement approach and the shortcut contribution margin approach to compute the company's monthly breakeven sales in units.
2. Use the contribution margin ratio approach to compute the breakeven point in sales dollars.
3. Compute the monthly sales level (in units) required to earn a target operating income of $14,000. Use either the income statement approach or the shortcut contribution margin approach.
4. Prepare a graph of Fleet Foot's CVP relationships, similar to Exhibit 22-7. Draw the sales revenue line, the fixed expense line, and the total expense line. Label the axes, the breakeven point, the operating income area, and the operating loss area.

Solution

Requirement 1

Income statement approach:

$$\text{Sales revenue} - \text{Variable expenses} - \text{Fixed expenses} = \text{Operating income}$$

$$\left(\begin{array}{c}\text{Sale price}\\ \text{per unit}\end{array} \times \begin{array}{c}\text{Units}\\ \text{sold}\end{array}\right) - \left(\begin{array}{c}\text{Variable}\\ \text{cost per unit}\end{array} \times \begin{array}{c}\text{Units}\\ \text{sold}\end{array}\right) - \begin{array}{c}\text{Fixed}\\ \text{expenses}\end{array} = \begin{array}{c}\text{Operating}\\ \text{income}\end{array}$$

($10 × Units sold) – ($6 × Units sold) – $10,000	=	$0
($10 – $6) × Units sold	=	$10,000
$4 × Units sold	=	$10,000
Units sold	=	$10,000 ÷ $4
Breakeven sales in units	=	2,500 units

Shortcut contribution margin approach:

$$\text{Units sold} = \frac{\text{Fixed expenses} + \text{Operating income}}{\text{Contribution margin per unit}}$$

$$\text{Breakeven sales in units} = \frac{\$10,000 + \$0}{\$10 - \$6}$$

$$= \frac{\$10,000}{\$4}$$

$$= 2,500 \text{ units}$$

Requirement 2

$$\text{Breakeven sales in dollars} = \frac{\text{Fixed expenses} + \text{Operating income}}{\text{Contribution margin ratio}}$$

$$= \frac{\$10,000 + \$0}{0.40*}$$

$$= \$25,000$$

$$* \text{ Contribution margin ratio} = \frac{\text{Contribution margin per unit}}{\text{Sale price per unit}} = \frac{\$4}{\$10} = 0.40$$

Requirement 3

Income statement equation approach:

Sales revenue	−	Variable expenses	−	Fixed expenses	=	Operating income

$$\left(\begin{array}{c}\text{Sale price} \\ \text{per unit}\end{array} \times \begin{array}{c}\text{Units} \\ \text{sold}\end{array}\right) - \left(\begin{array}{c}\text{Variable} \\ \text{cost per unit}\end{array} \times \begin{array}{c}\text{Units} \\ \text{sold}\end{array}\right) - \begin{array}{c}\text{Fixed} \\ \text{expenses}\end{array} = \begin{array}{c}\text{Operating} \\ \text{income}\end{array}$$

($10 × Units sold) − ($6 × Units sold) − $10,000	=	$14,000
($10 − $6) × Units sold	=	$10,000 + $14,000
$4 × Units sold	=	$24,000
Units sold	=	$24,000 ÷ $4
Units sold	=	6,000 units

Shortcut contribution margin approach:

$$\text{Units sold} = \frac{\text{Fixed expenses} + \text{Operating income}}{\text{Contribution margin per unit}}$$

$$= \frac{\$10,000 + \$14,000}{(\$10 - \$6)}$$

$$= \frac{\$24,000}{\$4}$$

$$= 6,000 \text{ units}$$

Requirement 4

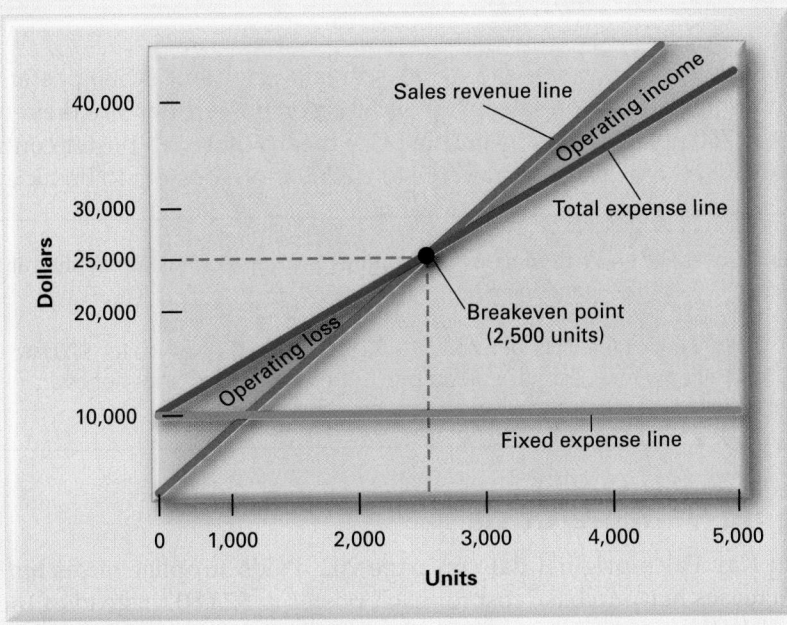

Student ResourceCD
breakeven point, fixed costs, margin of safety, sensitivity analysis, variable costs

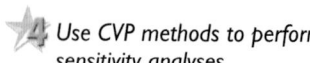
Use CVP methods to perform sensitivity analyses

Sensitivity Analysis
A "what if" technique that asks what results will be if actual prices or costs change, or if an underlying assumption changes.

Using CVP for Sensitivity Analysis

In today's fast-changing business world, managers need to quickly estimate how changes in sale price, costs, or volume affect profits. In a recent drive to increase profitability, Starbucks analyzed the profitability of each product at the store level. Then it realigned prices. For example, coffee mugs and CDs had been money-losers, so it raised the prices of these items.

To predict how raising or lowering prices will affect profits, managers use CVP to conduct **sensitivity analysis**. Sensitivity analysis is a "what if" technique that asks what results will be if actual prices or costs change, or if an underlying assumption changes. Let's see how Kay Pak uses CVP to estimate the effects of important changes in her business environment.

Changing the Sale Price

Competition in the art poster business is so fierce that Kay Pak believes she must cut the sale price to $31 per poster to maintain her market share. If her variable costs remain $21 per poster and her fixed costs stay at $7,000, how will this lower sale price affect her breakeven point?

Using the income statement approach:

SALES REVENUE	– VARIABLE EXPENSES	– FIXED EXPENSES	= OPERATING INCOME
($31 × Units sold) –	($21 × Units sold) –	$7,000	= $0
($31 –	$21) × Units sold –	$7,000	= $0
	$10 × Units sold		= $7,000
		Units sold	= $7,000/$10
		Units sold	= **700 posters**

Proof:

Sales revenue (700 × $31)		$ 21,700
Less: Variable expenses (700 × $21)	$14,700	
Fixed expenses	7,000	(21,700)
Operating income		$ 0

With the original $35 sale price, Pak's breakeven point is 500 posters (page 903). With the new lower sale price of $31 per poster, her breakeven point increases to 700 posters. The lower sale price means that each poster contributes less toward fixed expenses, so Pak must sell 200 more posters to break even.

Kay Pak believes she could dominate the e-commerce art poster business if she cut the sale price to $20. Is this a good idea?

Answer: No. The variable cost per poster is $21. If Pak sells posters for $20 each, she loses $1 on each poster. There can be no profit if the sale price does not even cover variable expenses.

Changing Variable Costs

Return to Kay Pak's original data on page 902. Pak's supplier raises his prices, which increases her purchase cost for each poster to $23.80 (instead of the original $21). Pak does not want to pass this increase on to her customers, so she holds her sale price at the original $35 per poster. Her fixed costs remain at $7,000. How many posters must she sell to break even after her supplier raises his prices?

Using the income statement approach:

SALES REVENUE	– VARIABLE EXPENSES	– FIXED EXPENSES	= OPERATING INCOME
($35 × Units sold) –	($23.80 × Units sold) –	$7,000	= $0
($35 –	$23.80) × Units sold –	$7,000	= $0
	$11.20 × Units sold		= $7,000
		Units sold	= $7,000/$11.20
		Units sold	= 625 posters

✔ Starter 22-8

Higher variable expenses per poster reduce Pak's per-unit contribution margin from $14 per poster to $11.20 per poster. As a result, Pak must sell more posters to break even—625 rather than the original 500 posters. This analysis shows why managers are particularly concerned with controlling costs during an economic downturn. Increases in cost increase the breakeven point, and a higher breakeven point could lead to serious problems if demand falls due to a recession.

Of course, a decrease in variable costs would have just the opposite effect. Lower variable costs increase the contribution each poster provides and, therefore, lower the breakeven point.

Changing Fixed Costs

Return to Kay Pak's original data on page 902. Kay is considering spending an additional $3,500 on Web site banner ads. This would increase her fixed costs from $7,000 to $10,500. If she sells the posters at the original price of $35 each and her variable costs are the original $21 per poster, what is her new breakeven point?

Using the income statement approach:

SALES REVENUE	– VARIABLE EXPENSES	– FIXED EXPENSES	= OPERATING INCOME
($35 × Units sold) –	($21 × Units sold)	– $10,500	= $0
($35 –	$21) × Units sold	– $10,500	= $0
	$14 × Units sold		= $10,500
		Units sold	= $10,500/$14
		Units sold	= 750 posters

✔ Starter 22-9

Higher fixed costs increase the total contribution margin required to break even. In this case, increasing the fixed costs from $7,000 to $10,500 increases the breakeven point to 750 posters (from the original 500 posters).

Managers usually prefer a lower breakeven point to a higher one. But don't overemphasize this one aspect of CVP analysis. Even though investing in the Web banner ads increases her breakeven point, Kay Pak may be willing to pay the extra $3,500 if she expects the ads to stimulate enough extra sales and profits to more than cover the additional advertising expense.

Margin of Safety

The **margin of safety** is the excess of expected sales over breakeven sales. This is the "cushion" or drop in sales the company can absorb without incurring a loss. The higher the margin of safety, the greater the cushion against loss and the less risky the business plan. Managers use the margin of safety to evaluate the risk of current operations, as well as the risk of new plans.

Margin of Safety
Excess of expected sales over breakeven sales. Drop in sales a company can absorb without incurring an operating loss.

Kay Pak's breakeven point in our original data is 500 posters. Suppose she expects to sell 950 posters. Her margin of safety is

✔ **Starter 22-10**

✔ **Starter 22-11**

MARGIN OF SAFETY IN UNITS = EXPECTED SALES IN UNITS − BREAKEVEN SALES IN UNITS

= 950 posters − 500 posters

= 450 posters

MARGIN OF SAFETY IN DOLLARS = MARGIN OF SAFETY IN UNITS × SALE PRICE PER UNIT

= 450 posters × $35

= $15,750

Sales can drop by 450 posters, or $15,750, before Pak incurs a loss. This is a comfortable margin.

Managers can also compute the margin of safety as a percentage for any level of sales. Simply divide the margin of safety by sales. We obtain the same percentage whether we use units or dollars.

In units:

$$\text{MARGIN OF SAFETY AS A PERCENTAGE} = \frac{\textbf{Margin of safety in units}}{\textbf{Expected sales in units}}$$

$$= \frac{450 \text{ posters}}{950 \text{ posters}}$$

= 47.4% (rounded)

In dollars:

$$\text{MARGIN OF SAFETY AS A PERCENTAGE} = \frac{\textbf{Margin of safety in dollars}}{\textbf{Expected sales in dollars}}$$

$$= \frac{450 \text{ units} \times \$35}{950 \text{ units} \times \$35}$$

$$= \frac{\$15,750}{\$33,250}$$

= 47.4% (rounded)

Knowing that she will not incur a loss unless sales fall short of expectations by more than 47.4% should tell Kay Pak that her business plan is not unduly risky.

Information Technology and Sensitivity Analysis

Information technology allows managers to perform a wide array of sensitivity analyses before committing to decisions. Managers of small- to medium-sized companies use Excel spreadsheets to perform sensitivity analyses like those we just did for Kay Pak. Spreadsheets allow managers to estimate how one change (or several changes simultaneously) affects business operations. Managers also use the information the spreadsheets store on basic CVP components (sale price, variable cost, and fixed costs) to display profit-planning graphs similar to Exhibit 22-7.

Many large companies use sophisticated enterprise resource planning software like SAP, Oracle, and Peoplesoft to provide detailed data for CVP analysis. For example, after Sears stores lock their doors at 9:00 P.M., records for each individual transaction flow into a massive database. From a Diehard battery sold in Texas to a Trader Bay polo shirt sold in New Hampshire, the system compiles an average of 1.5 million transactions a day. With the click of a mouse, managers access sale price, variable cost, and sales volume for individual products to conduct breakeven or profit planning analyses.

The next section uses the building blocks of CVP analysis (contribution margin and the distinction between variable and fixed costs) to explain a costing approach many managers use for internal decisions. Before continuing, review the CVP Analysis Decision Guidelines to make sure you understand these basic concepts.

Decision Guidelines

COST-VOLUME-PROFIT ANALYSIS

Take on the role of general manager of **Grand Canyon Railways**, from the chapter opening story. How can you use CVP analysis to make key decisions for the Railway?

Decision	Guidelines
How do changes in the number of passengers affect	
• total costs?	Total variable costs → Change in proportion to changes in volume (number of passengers) Total fixed costs → No change

• cost per passenger?	Variable cost per passenger → No change
	 Fixed cost per passenger:
	     Increases when volume drops (Fixed costs are spread over fewer passengers)
	     Decreases when volume rises (Fixed costs are spread over more passengers)

How to compute sales needed to break even or earn a target operating income	
• in passengers?	*Income Statement Method:*

$$\text{Sales revenue} \quad - \text{ Variable expenses} \quad - \frac{\text{Total fixed}}{\text{expenses}} = \frac{\text{Operating}}{\text{income}}$$

$$\left(\begin{array}{c} \text{Sale price per passenger} \\ \times \text{ Number of passengers} \end{array} \right) - \left(\begin{array}{c} \text{Variable cost per passenger} \\ \times \text{ Number of passengers} \end{array} \right) - \frac{\text{Total fixed}}{\text{expenses}} = \frac{\text{Operating}}{\text{income}}$$

Shortcut Contribution Margin Method:

$$\frac{\text{Fixed expense} + \text{Operating income}}{\text{Contribution margin per passenger}}$$

• in dollars?	*Shortcut Contribution Margin Ratio Method:*

$$\frac{\text{Fixed expense} + \text{Operating income}}{\text{Contribution margin ratio}}$$

How to estimate the effects of changes in sale price, costs, or volume of passengers?	Use CVP methods to perform sensitivity analyses. For example, enter the new sale price, cost, or volume of passengers in the income statement equation:

$$\left(\begin{array}{c} \text{Sale price per passenger} \\ \times \text{ Number of passengers} \end{array} \right) - \left(\begin{array}{c} \text{Variable cost per passenger} \\ \times \text{ Number of passengers} \end{array} \right) - \frac{\text{Total fixed}}{\text{expenses}} = \frac{\text{Operating}}{\text{income}}$$

How to use CVP analysis to measure risk?	Margin of safety = Expected sales − Breakeven sales

Excel Application Exercise

Goal: Create a spreadsheet and graph to show the relationship between costs, volume, and profit and to discover the breakeven point.

Scenario: Phonetronix, Inc., makes telephone and communications devices. Recently, management decided to investigate the profitability of producing cellular phones. The proposed new phone would sell for $99.00. Variable cost per unit is $55.00, and total fixed costs are $110,000.

When you have completed your worksheet, answer the following questions:

Excel Application Exercise *(continued)*

1. How many phones must Phonetronix sell to break even? On the graph in the spreadsheet, point the cursor at the breakeven point. Does the "pop up" value for Total Costs match Total Revenue?
2. What is the breakeven point if Phonetronix raises the price per phone to $129? Note the changes in the graph. Which direction did the breakeven point move?
3. What is the breakeven point if the selling price per phone is $99 but Phonetronix slashes the variable costs per phone to $49? Note the changes in the graph. Which direction did the breakeven point move?

Step-by-Step:

1. Open a new Excel spreadsheet.
2. In column A, create a bold-faced heading as follows:
   a. Chapter 22 Excel Application Exercise
   b. Cost-Volume-Profit Analysis
   c. Phonetronix, Inc.
   d. Today's Date
3. Two rows down, enter the bold-faced and underlined heading, "Data Section" in column A.

4. Move down one row. Starting in column A, enter three rows of data, with these descriptions: price, variable cost per unit, and total fixed costs. Format cells as needed as you work.
5. Move down two rows. Enter the following bold-faced and underlined column headings, in order:
   a. # Units Sold   d. Total Fixed Costs
   b. Total Revenue   e. Total Costs
   c. Total Variable Costs f. Total Profit
6. Enter # Units Sold, in 200-unit increments, starting at 100 units and going up to 3,500 units. (Hint: Use a formula.)
7. Enter the formulas for the remaining five columns.
8. Create your graph by selecting one row of titles and all data except the "Total Profit" column. Then, click on the Chart Wizard. Select the basic line graph without data values or 3D effects.
9. Title your graph "CVP Analysis." Label the x-axis "# Units Sold" and y-axis "Dollars." Click to finish the graph. (Your x-axis values will range from "1" to "17," not the actual unit values. To see the actual values, position your cursor over the x-axis to see a pop-up box containing the values.)
10. Position the graph at the bottom of your data in the spreadsheet and size to fit if necessary.
11. Save your file to disk, and print a copy (in color, if possible) for your files after each scenario change.

Student ResourceCD

absorption costing, contribution margin, fixed costs, variable costs

5 *Compute income using variable costing and absorption costing*

Variable Costing
The costing method that assigns only variable manufacturing costs to products.

Absorption Costing
The costing method that assigns both variable and fixed manufacturing costs to products.

Variable Costing and Absorption Costing

In this chapter, you have seen how managers use contribution margin and CVP analysis to make decisions. Managers often extend this approach to use **variable costing**, which assigns only variable manufacturing costs to products—for internal reporting. Then they use variable costing to prepare special income statements for *internal management decisions*. These variable costing income statements group costs by behavior—variable costs or fixed costs—and highlight the contribution margin. Before we delve into variable costing and how managers use its income statement format to make decisions, let's first review the fundamentals of costing for *external reporting*.

Up to this point, you have focused on the income statements that companies prepare for external reporting under GAAP. GAAP requires that we assign both variable and fixed manufacturing costs to products. This approach is called **absorption costing** because products absorb fixed manufacturing costs as well as variable manufacturing costs. Supporters of absorption costing argue that companies cannot produce products without fixed manufacturing costs, so these costs are an important part of product costs.

For planning and decision making, many managers prefer a different approach. Variable costing assigns only variable manufacturing costs to products. Under variable costing, fixed manufacturing costs are considered period costs and are expensed in the period when they are incurred. Supporters of variable costing argue that fixed manufacturing costs (such as depreciation on the plant) provide the capacity to produce during a period. Because the company incurs these fixed expenses whether or not it produces any products or services, they are period costs, not product costs.

The key difference between absorption costing and variable costing is that absorption costing considers fixed manufacturing costs as inventoriable product costs, while variable costing considers fixed manufacturing costs as period costs (expenses).

All other costs are treated the same way under both absorption and variable costing:

- Variable manufacturing costs are inventoriable products costs.
- All nonmanufacturing costs are period costs.

    Exhibit 22-8 summarizes the difference between variable and absorption costing.

Exhibit 22-8

Differences Between Absorption Costing and Variable Costing

	Absorption Costing	Variable Costing
Product Costs (Capitalized as Inventory until expensed as Cost of Goods Sold)	Direct materials Direct labor Variable manufacturing overhead Fixed manufacturing overhead	Direct materials Direct labor Variable manufacturing overhead
Period Costs (Expensed in period incurred)	Variable nonmanufacturing costs Fixed nonmanufacturing costs	Fixed manufacturing overhead Variable nonmanufacturing costs Fixed nonmanufacturing costs
Focus	External reporting—required by GAAP	Internal reporting only
Income Statement Format	Conventional income statement, as in Chapters 1–19	Contribution margin statement

Variable versus Absorption Costing: Sportade

To see how absorption costing and variable costing differ, let's consider the following example. Sportade incurs the following costs for its powdered sports beverage mix in March 20X5.

Direct material cost per case	$ 6.00
Direct labor cost per case	3.00
Variable manufacturing overhead cost per case	2.00
Sales commission per case	2.50
Total fixed manufacturing overhead expenses	50,000
Total fixed marketing and administrative expenses.....	25,000

   Sportade produced 10,000 cases of powdered mix as planned but sold only 8,000 cases, at a price of $30 per case. There were no beginning inventories, so Sportade has 2,000 cases of powdered mix in ending finished goods inventory (10,000 cases produced – 8,000 cases sold).
   What is Sportade's inventoriable product cost per case under absorption costing and variable costing?

	Absorption Costing	Variable Costing
Direct materials	$ 6.00	$ 6.00
Direct labor..	3.00	3.00
Variable manufacturing overhead	2.00	2.00
Fixed manufacturing overhead	5.00*	
Total cost per case.................................	$16.00	$11.00

* $\dfrac{\$50,000 \text{ fixed manufacturing overhead}}{10,000 \text{ cases}} = \$5 \text{ per case}$

The only difference between absorption and variable costing is that fixed manufacturing overhead is a product cost under absorption costing, but a period cost under variable costing. This is why the cost per case is $5 higher under absorption (total cost of $16) than under variable costing ($11).

Exhibit 22-9 shows that absorption costing income statements use the format we have used in Chapters 1 through 19: Sales minus cost of goods sold equals gross profit.

Exhibit 22-9

Absorption Costing Income Statement

Sportade
Income Statement (Absorption Costing)
Month Ended March 31, 20X5

Sales revenue (8,000 × $30)		$240,000
Deduct: Cost of goods sold:		
Beginning finished goods inventory	$ 0	
Cost of goods manufactured (10,000 × $16)	160,000	
Cost of goods available for sale	160,000	
Ending finished goods inventory (2,000 × $16)	(32,000)	
Cost of goods sold		(128,000)
Gross profit		112,000
Deduct: Operating expenses [(8,000 × $2.50) + $25,000]		(45,000)
Operating income		$ 67,000

Notice that:

- The absorption costing income statement in Exhibit 22-9 groups costs by *function*: manufacturing costs or nonmanufacturing costs. *We subtract manufacturing costs of goods sold* **before** *gross profit, whereas we subtract all nonmanufacturing costs (operating expenses)* **after** *gross profit.*

- Total cost of goods manufactured is the number of cases *produced* multiplied by the $16 total manufacturing cost per case. In contrast, total variable marketing expense (for sales commissions) equals the number of cases *sold* times the sales commission per case.

- Absorption costing holds back as an asset (ending inventory) $32,000 of the manufacturing cost Sportade incurred this period (2,000 cases × $16 total manufacturing cost per case). This $32,000 is not expensed in the month when Sportade incurred these manufacturing costs. Instead, these manufacturing costs are held back as the asset *Inventory* until the related 2,000 cases are sold.

- The absorption costing income statement does not distinguish between variable and fixed costs. This limits the statement's usefulness for managerial decisions. If the CEO of Sportade wants to predict how a 10% increase in sales will affect operating income, the absorption costing income statement is of little help: It does not separate variable costs (which increase with sales) from fixed costs (which will not change).

Contribution Margin Income Statement
Income statement that groups costs by behavior—variable costs or fixed costs—and highlights the contribution margin.

The limitations of absorption costing–based income statements lead many managers to prefer variable costing and contribution margin income statements *for internal reporting and decision making.* Exhibit 22-10 recasts the Sportade information using variable costing and a **contribution margin income statement** that groups costs by behavior—variable costs or fixed costs—and highlights the contribution margin.

Exhibit 22-10

Variable Costing Contribution Margin Income Statement

Sportade		
Contribution Margin Income Statement (Variable Costing) **Month Ended March 31, 20X5**		
Sales revenue (8,000 × $30)		$240,000
Deduct: Variable expenses:		
Variable cost of goods sold:		
Beginning finished goods inventory	$ 0	
Variable cost of goods manufactured (10,000 × $11). . .	110,000	
Variable cost of goods available for sale	110,000	
Ending finished goods inventory (2,000 × $11)	(22,000)	
Variable cost of goods sold	88,000	
Sales commission expense (8,000 × $2.50).	20,000	(108,000)
Contribution margin.		132,000
Deduct: Fixed expenses:		
Fixed manufacturing overhead.	50,000	
Fixed marketing and administrative expenses.	25,000	(75,000)
Operating income		$ 57,000

Compare the general format of the absorption costing income statement in Exhibit 22-9 with the variable costing contribution margin income statement in Exhibit 22-10. The conventional absorption costing income statement subtracts cost of goods sold (including both variable and fixed manufacturing costs) from sales to obtain *gross profit*. In contrast, the contribution margin income statement subtracts all variable costs (both manufacturing and nonmanufacturing) to obtain *contribution margin*. The following chart highlights the differences between gross profit and contribution margin:

✔ **Starter 22-12**

✔ **Starter 22-13**

Conventional Income Statement	**Contribution Margin Income Statement**
Sales revenue	Sales revenue
deduct Cost of Goods Sold:	deduct Variable Expenses:
Variable manufacturing cost of goods sold	Variable manufacturing cost of goods sold
Fixed manufacturing cost of goods sold	Variable nonmanufacturing expenses
= Gross profit	= Contribution margin

The two major differences are

- Fixed manufacturing cost of goods sold is subtracted from sales to compute gross profit, but not to compute contribution margin.
- Variable nonmanufacturing expenses are subtracted from sales to calculate contribution margin, but not to compute gross profit.

Now let's look more closely at the variable costing contribution margin income statement in Exhibit 22-10. First, notice that the details of the (variable) cost of goods sold computation in Exhibit 22-10 parallel those in the absorption costing income statement, *except that we use the $11 variable costing product cost per case rather than the $16 absorption cost per case.* Second, variable costing holds back as an asset (ending inventory) only $22,000 (2,000 cases × $11 variable manufacturing cost per case). Third, the variable costing contribution margin income statement subtracts *all* of the variable costs (*both* the $88,000 manufacturing variable cost of goods sold *and* the $20,000 variable sales commission expense) from sales to get contribution margin. Finally, we subtract fixed costs (both the $50,000 fixed manufacturing overhead and the $25,000 fixed marketing and administrative costs) from contribution margin to get operating income. To summarize, the variable costing contribution margin income statement subtracts all variable costs *before* contribution margin and all fixed costs *after* contribution margin.

By separating variable and fixed costs, the variable costing contribution margin income statement (Exhibit 22-10) allows managers to estimate how changes in sales, costs, or volume will affect profits.

Suppose Sportade can increase the number of cases sold by 10%, using its existing capacity. Compute the likely effect on operating income.

Answer: Because Sportade can accommodate the increased production using existing capacity, fixed costs will be unaffected. Thus, the entire increase in contribution margin flows through to operating income.

A 10% increase in sales is an extra 800 cases (10% × 8,000).

Increase in sales revenue (800 cases × $30/case)	$ 24,000
Increase in variable costs (800 cases × $13.50/case*)	(10,800)
Increase in contribution margin	$ 13,200
Increase in fixed costs	(0)
Increase in operating income	$ 13,200

*Total variable costs per case = $6.00 direct materials + $3.00 direct labor + $2.00 variable manufacturing overhead + $2.50 sales commission. (All variable costs, including the sales commission as well as variable manufacturing costs, must be considered to estimate how the sales increase will affect contribution margin and operating profit.)

Reconciling the Difference in Income

Exhibit 22-9 shows that Sportade's absorption costing operating income is $67,000. Exhibit 22-10 shows that variable costing yields only $57,000 of operating income. Why? To answer this question, we need to understand what happened to the $160,000 ($110,000 variable + $50,000 fixed) total manufacturing costs under each costing method.

Manufacturing costs incurred in March are either

■ Expensed in March, or

■ Held back in inventory (an asset)

Exhibit 22-11 shows that of the $160,000 total manufacturing costs incurred during March, absorption costing holds back $32,000 (2,000 × $16) as inventory. This $32,000 assigned to inventory is not expensed until next month, when the units are sold. Thus, only $160,000 − $32,000 = $128,000 of the manufacturing costs are expensed as cost of goods sold during March.

Variable costing holds back in ending inventory only $22,000 (2,000 × $11) of the total manufacturing costs. This is $10,000 ($22,000 − $32,000) *less* than absorption costing holds back. The difference arises because absorption costing assigns the $5 per case fixed manufacturing overhead costs to the 2,000 cases in ending inventory. In contrast, variable costing does not—it expenses all the fixed manufacturing overhead in the current month.

Costs that are not held back in inventory are expensed in the current period, so variable costing expenses $138,000 ($160,000 − $22,000) of manufacturing costs in March. (This $138,000 also equals the $88,000 variable cost of goods sold plus the $50,000 fixed manufacturing overhead.) This is $10,000 *more* than the $128,000 absorption costing manufacturing expenses during March. *Variable costing has $10,000 more expense in March, so its income is $10,000 lower than absorption costing income.*

Exhibit 22-11 Inventory versus Expenses Under Absorption and Variable Costing

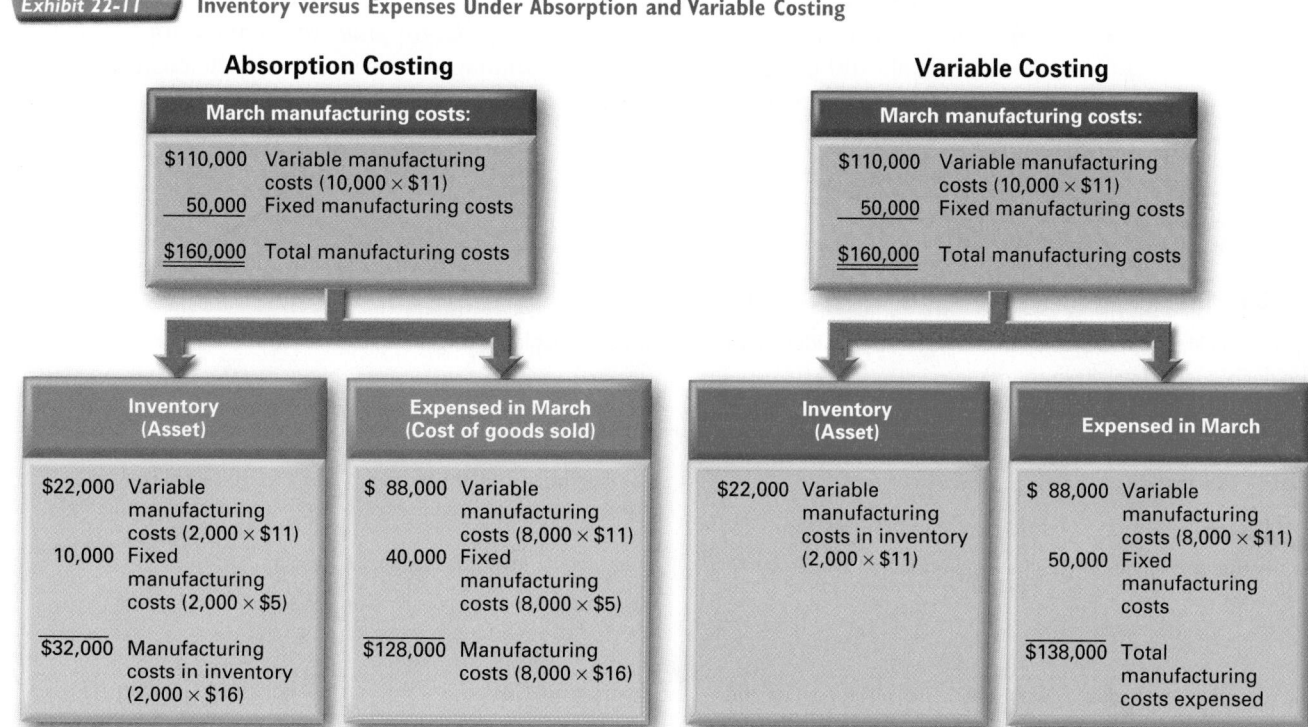

✔ Starter 22-14

Suppose Sportade has no inventory at the end of the next month, April. Will absorption costing report higher or lower operating income than variable costing for the month of April?

Answer: Absorption costing will report lower income than variable costing during April. Ending inventory in March becomes the beginning inventory of April. Absorption costing assigns a higher value to beginning inventory in April. When that beginning inventory is sold, the higher beginning inventory costs increase cost of goods sold for April, which in turn reduces income.

Absorption Costing and Manager's Incentives

The general rule is this: When inventories increase (more units are produced than sold), absorption costing income is higher than variable costing income. When inventories decline (when fewer units are produced than sold), absorption costing income is lower than variable costing income. Suppose the Sportade manager receives a bonus based on absorption costing income. Will the manager want to increase or decrease production?

The manager knows that absorption costing assigns each case of Sportade $5 of fixed manufacturing overhead.

- For every case that is produced but not sold, absorption costing "hides" $5 of fixed overhead in ending inventory (an asset).
- The more cases added to inventory, the more fixed overhead is "hidden" in ending inventory at the end of the month.
- The more fixed overhead in ending inventory, the smaller the cost of goods sold and the higher the operating income.

To maximize the bonus under absorption costing, the manager may try to increase production to build up inventory.

Chapter 19 introduced the just-in-time philosophy. This incentive directly conflicts with the just-in-time philosophy, which emphasizes minimal inventory levels. ← Companies that have adopted just-in-time should either (1) evaluate their managers based on variable costing income or (2) use strict controls to prevent inventory buildup.

Decision Guidelines

ABSORPTION AND VARIABLE COSTING

Suppose you are the CEO of Sportade. You are considering whether to use variable costing. Here are some decisions you will have to make.

Decision	Guideline
When to use absorption costing? Variable costing?	Sportade must use absorption costing for external reporting. Sportade can use variable costing only for internal reporting.
What is the difference between absorption and variable costing?	Fixed manufacturing costs are treated as • inventoriable product costs under absorption costing • period costs under variable costing

How to compute product costs under absorption costing and variable costing?	**Absorption Costing**	**Variable Costing**
	Direct materials	Direct materials
	+ Direct labor	+ Direct labor
	+ Variable overhead	+ Variable overhead
	+ Fixed overhead	
	= Product cost	= Product cost

Decision	Guideline
Will absorption costing income be higher, lower, or the same as variable costing income?	If units produced > units sold: Absorption costing income > Variable costing income If units produced < units sold: Absorption costing income < Variable costing income If units produced = units sold: Absorption costing income = Variable costing income
Why should Sportade use variable costing for internal reporting?	• Sportade managers can use variable costing contribution margin income statements to estimate how changes in sales or costs will affect profits. • Variable costing does not give Sportade's managers incentives to build up inventory.

● END-OF-CHAPTER *Summary Problem*

CHECK YOUR RESOURCES

Continue the Sportade illustration from pages 915–919. In April 20X5, Sportade produces 10,000 cases of the powdered sports beverage and sells 12,000 cases (the 2,000 cases of inventory on March 31, 20X5, plus the 10,000 cases produced during April). The variable costs per case and the total fixed costs are the same as in March.

Required:

1. Prepare an income statement for the month ended April 30, 20X5, using absorption costing.
2. Prepare an income statement for the month ended April 30, 20X5, using variable costing.

(continued)

3. Reconcile (explain the difference between) operating income under absorption versus variable costing.

Solutions

Requirement 1

Sportade		
Income Statement (Absorption Costing)		
Month Ended April 30, 20X5		

Sales revenue (12,000 × $30)...................		$360,000
Deduct: Cost of goods sold		
Beginning finished goods inventory	$ 32,000[1]	
Cost of goods manufactured (10,000 × $16)........	160,000[2]	
Cost of goods available for sale..................	192,000	
Ending finished goods inventory	(0)	
Cost of goods sold............................		192,000
Gross profit....................................		168,000
Deduct: Operating expenses		
[(12,000 × $2.50) + $25,000].....................		(55,000)
Operating income		$113,000

[1]Ending inventory from March 31, 20X5 (Exhibit 22-9).
[2]Absorption costing cost per case = $6.00 + $3.00 + $2.00 + $5.00.

Requirement 2

Sportade		
Contribution Margin Income Statement (Variable Costing)		
Month Ended April 30, 20X5		

Sales revenue (12,000 × $30)........................		$360,000
Deduct: Variable expenses		
Variable cost of goods sold		
Beginning finished goods inventory...............	$ 22,000[3]	
Variable cost of goods manufactured (10,000 × $11)..	110,000[4]	
Variable cost of goods available for sale............	132,000	
Ending finished goods inventory	(0)	
Variable cost of goods sold.......................	132,000	
Sales commission expense (12,000 × $2.50)	30,000	(162,000)
Contribution margin.............................		198,000
Deduct: Fixed expenses		
Fixed manufacturing overhead	50,000	
Fixed marketing and administrative expenses	25,000	(75,000)
Operating income		$123,000

[3]Ending inventory from March 31, 20X5 (Exhibit 22-10).
[4]Variable costing cost per case = $6.00 + $3.00 + $2.00.

Requirement 3

April 20X5 operating income is $10,000 higher under variable costing than under absorption costing. Why? Both methods expense all of April's $160,000 manufacturing costs ($110,000 variable + $50,000 fixed) during April. However, the two methods differ in the amount of *March* manufacturing cost expensed in April. Absorption costing holds $32,000 of March manufacturing costs in inventory and expenses them in April when the goods are sold. Variable costing holds only $22,000 of March manufacturing costs in inventory and expenses them in April.

Thus, absorption costing operating income is

- $10,000 higher than variable costing income in March (because absorption costing defers $10,000 more of March cost to April).
- $10,000 lower than variable costing income in April (because absorption costing expenses $10,000 more of March costs in April).

●REVIEW *CVP Analysis*

Quick Check

1. For **Grand Canyon Railway** in the chapter opening story, straight-line depreciation on the train cars is a:
   a. Variable cost
   b. Fixed cost
   c. Mixed cost

2. Assume **Grand Canyon Railway** is considering hiring a reservations agency to handle its passenger reservations. The agency would charge a flat fee of $10,000 per month, plus $1 per passenger reservation. What is the total reservation cost if 100,000 passengers take the trip next month?
   a. $1.10
   b. $10,000
   c. $100,000
   d. $110,000

3. If **Grand Canyon Railway's** fixed costs total $50,000 per month, the variable cost per passenger is $10, and tickets sell for $60, what is the breakeven point?
   a. 1,000 passengers
   b. 833 passengers
   c. 714 passengers
   d. 100 passengers

4. Suppose **Amazon.com's** total revenues are $5 billion, its variable costs are $3 billion, and its fixed costs are $1 billion. Compute the breakeven point in dollars.
   a. $0.4 billion
   b. $2.5 billion
   c. $4.0 billion
   d. $5.0 billion

5. Assume the same facts about **Grand Canyon Railway** as in Question 3, except that Grand Canyon wants to know how many passengers must buy tickets for the Railway to earn $100,000 in profit per month. The answer is
   a. 1,000 passengers
   b. 3,000 passengers
   c. 30,000 passengers
   d. 31,000 passengers

6. On a CVP graph, the total cost line intersects the vertical (dollars) axis at:
   a. The level of the fixed costs
   b. The level of the variable costs
   c. The breakeven point
   d. The origin

7. Assume the same facts about **Grand Canyon Railway** as in Question 3, except that the Railway is considering cutting its ticket price to $50 per passenger. The new breakeven point is
   a. 100 more passengers than with the original $60 ticket price
   b. 250 more passengers than with the original $60 ticket price
   c. 100 fewer passengers than with the original $60 ticket price
   d. 250 fewer passengers than with the original $60 ticket price

8. Assume the same facts about **Grand Canyon Railway** as in Question 3. If the Railway expects to serve 1,200 passengers next month, what is the margin of safety?
   a. 200 passengers
   b. 1,000 passengers
   c. 1,200 passengers
   d. 2,200 passengers

9. The only difference between variable costing and absorption costing lies in the treatment of:
   a. Fixed manufacturing overhead costs
   b. Variable manufacturing overhead costs
   c. Direct materials and direct labor costs
   d. Variable nonmanufacturing costs

10. When inventories decline, operating income under variable costing is
  a. Lower than operating income under absorption costing
  b. The same as operating income under absorption costing
  c. Higher than operating income under absorption costing

Accounting Vocabulary

absorption costing (p. 914)
breakeven point (p. 903)
contribution margin (p. 903)
contribution margin income statement (p. 916)
contribution margin ratio (p. 904)

cost behavior (p. 898)
cost-volume-profit (CVP) analysis (p. 898)
margin of safety (p. 911)
mixed costs (p. 900)
relevant range (p. 901)

sales mix (p. 902)
sensitivity analysis (p. 910)
total fixed costs (p. 898)
total variable costs (p. 898)
variable costing (p. 914)

ASSESS *Your Progress*

Starters

A+ online homework

See www.prenhall.com/horngren for selected Starters, Exercises, and Problems.

S22-1 Ariel builds innovative loudspeakers for music and home theater. Identify the following costs as variable or fixed:

Variable and fixed costs
(Obj. 1)

  a. Depreciation on routers used to cut wood enclosures
  b. Wood for speaker enclosures
  c. Patents on crossover relays
  d. Crossover relays

  e. Grill cloth
  f. Glue
  g. Quality inspector's salary

S22-2 Suppose World-Link offers an international calling plan that charges $5.00 per month plus $0.35 per minute for calls outside the United States.

Mixed costs
(Obj. 1)

1. Under this plan, what is your monthly international long-distance cost if you call Europe for
  a. 20 minutes?   **b.** 40 minutes?   **c.** 80 minutes?
2. Draw a graph illustrating your total cost under this plan. Label the axes, and show your costs at 20, 40, and 80 minutes.

S22-3 Consider the **Grand Canyon Railway** example from the chapter opening story. Suppose the Railway decides to offer Coach class service at an all-inclusive round-trip ticket price of $60 per passenger. Assume variable expenses of $20 per passenger. If Grand Canyon has $275,000 of fixed expenses per month, compute the number of round-trip tickets it must sell to break even:

Computing breakeven point in units
(Obj. 2)

  a. Using the income statement equation approach
  b. Using the shortcut contribution margin CVP formula

Perform a numerical proof to ensure that your answer is correct.

S22-4 Refer to the information in Starter 22-3.

Computing breakeven point in sales dollars
(Obj. 2)

1. Compute Grand Canyon Railway's contribution margin ratio. Carry your computation to five decimal places.
2. Use the contribution margin ratio CVP formula to determine the sales revenue Grand Canyon Railway needs to break even.

S22-5 If Grand Canyon Railway has a target operating income of $40,000 per month, how many round-trip tickets must the company sell? Use the original data given in Starter 22-3.

Sales needed to earn target income
(Obj. 3)

Graphing cost-volume-profit relationships
(Obj. 3)

S22-6 Using the original information in Starter 22-3, draw a graph of Grand Canyon Railway's cost-volume-profit relationships. Include the sales revenue line, the fixed expense line, and the total expense line. Label the axes, the breakeven point, the income area, and the loss area.

Interpreting a CVP graph
(Obj. 3)

S22-7 Describe what each letter stands for in the cost-volume-profit graph.

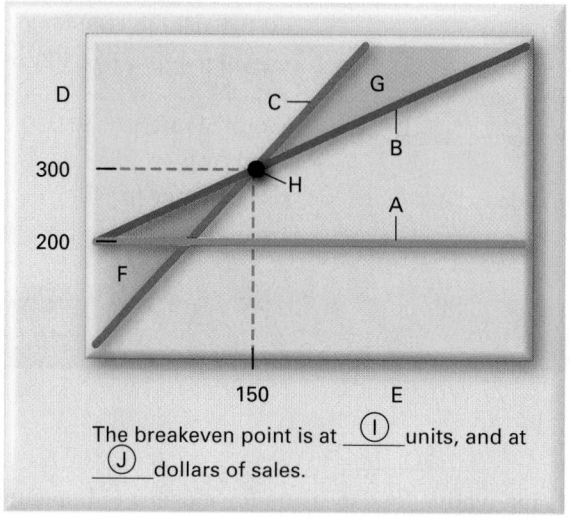

Sensitivity analysis of changing sale price and variable expense on breakeven point
(Obj. 4)

S22-8 Refer to the information in Starter 22-3.

1. Suppose the Railway cuts its round-trip ticket price from $60 to $50 to increase the number of passengers. Compute the new breakeven point in units (passenger round-trips) and in sales dollars. Carry your computations to five decimal places.

2. Return to Starter 22-3. The Railway could reduce its variable costs by cutting champagne from the afternoon beverages. Suppose this reduces the variable expense from $20 to $15 per passenger. Compute the new breakeven point in units (passenger round-trips), and in dollars. Carry your computations to five decimal places.

Sensitivity analysis of changing fixed cost on breakeven point
(Obj. 4)

S22-9 Consider the original Grand Canyon Railway information in Starter 22-3. Suppose Grand Canyon embarks on a cost reduction drive and slashes fixed expenses from $275,000 per month to $200,000 per month.

1. Compute the new breakeven point in units (passenger round-trips) and in sales dollars.
2. Is the breakeven point higher or lower than in Starter 22-3? Explain.

Computing margin of safety
(Obj. 4)

S22-10 Consider the original Grand Canyon Railway information in Starter 22-3. If Grand Canyon expects to sell 7,000 round-trip tickets, compute the margin of safety.

a. In units (round-trip tickets)   **b.** In sales dollars   **c.** As a percentage of expected sales

Computing margin of safety
(Obj. 4)

S22-11 Consider Kay Pak's e-tail poster business. Suppose Pak expects to sell 800 posters. Use the original data on page 902 to compute her margin of safety:

a. In units (posters)   **b.** In sales dollars   **c.** As a percentage of expected sales

Computing variable costing income
(Obj. 5)

S22-12 Consider the Sportade example on pages 915–919. Suppose that during April, the company produces 10,000 cases of powdered drink mix and sells 11,000 cases. Sale price, variable cost per case, and total fixed expenses remain the same as in March. Prepare the April income statement using variable costing.

Comparing variable and absorption costing income
(Obj. 5)

S22-13 Refer to the Sportade example on pages 915–919 and the data and your answer to Starter 22-12.

1. Prepare the April income statement under absorption costing.
2. Is absorption costing income higher or lower than variable costing income? Explain why.

S22-14 For a service company like Grand Canyon Railway, will absorption and variable costing give different operating income figures? Explain.

Absorption and variable costing
(Obj. 5)

Exercises

E22-1 Graph these cost behavior patterns over a relevant range of 0–10,000 units:

a. Variable expenses of $8 per unit
b. Mixed expenses made up of fixed costs of $20,000 and variable costs of $3 per unit
c. Fixed expenses of $15,000

Graphing cost behavior
(Obj. 1)

E22-2 For its top managers, Aussie Travel formats its income statement as follows:

Computing breakeven sales using a contribution margin income statement
(Obj. 2, 5)

Student ResourceCD
spreadsheet

Aussie Travel	
Contribution Margin Income Statement **Three Months Ended March 31, 20XX**	
Sales revenue..	$312,500
Variable expenses	125,000
Contribution margin	187,500
Fixed expenses	170,000
Operating income......................................	$ 17,500

Aussie's relevant range is between sales of $250,000 and $360,000. Prepare contribution margin income statements at those volume levels. (*Hint*: The proportion of each sales dollar that goes toward variable costs is constant within the relevant range. The proportion of each sales dollar that goes toward contribution margin is also constant within the relevant range.) Also, compute breakeven sales in dollars.

E22-3 Big Foot Co. produces sports socks. The company has fixed expenses of $85,000, and variable expenses of $0.85 per package. Each package sells for $1.70.

Computing breakeven sales by the contribution margin approach
(Obj. 2)

Required

1. Compute the contribution margin per package and the contribution margin ratio.
2. Find the breakeven point in units and in dollars, using the contribution margin approach.

Student ResourceCD
spreadsheet

Computing a change in breakeven sales
(Obj. 2)

E22-4 Owner Shan Lo is considering franchising her Happy Wok restaurant concept. She believes people will pay $5 for a large bowl of noodles. Variable costs are $1.50 a bowl. Lo estimates monthly fixed costs for franchisees at $8,400.

Required

1. Use the contribution margin ratio approach to find a franchise's breakeven sales ($).
2. Is franchising a good idea for Lo if franchisees will want a minimum monthly operating income of $8,750, and Lo believes most locations could generate $25,000 in monthly sales?

E22-5 Dave's Steel Parts produces parts for the automobile industry. The company has monthly fixed expenses of $640,000 and a contribution margin of 80% of revenues.

Computing breakeven sales and operating income or loss under different conditions
(Obj. 2, 3, 5)

Required

1. Compute Dave's monthly breakeven sales in dollars. Use the contribution margin ratio approach.
2. Use contribution margin income statements to compute Dave's monthly operating income or operating loss if revenues are $500,000 and if they are $1,000,000.
3. Do the results in Requirement 2 make sense given the breakeven sales you computed in Requirement 1? Explain.

E22-6 Chad Brown is considering starting a Web-based educational business, e-Prep MBA. He plans to offer a short-course review of accounting for students entering MBA programs. The materials would be available on a password-protected Web site and students would complete the course through self-study. Brown would have to grade the course assignments, but most of the work is in developing the course materials, setting up the site, and marketing. Unfortunately, Brown's hard drive crashed before he finished his financial analysis. However, he did recover the following partial CVP chart:

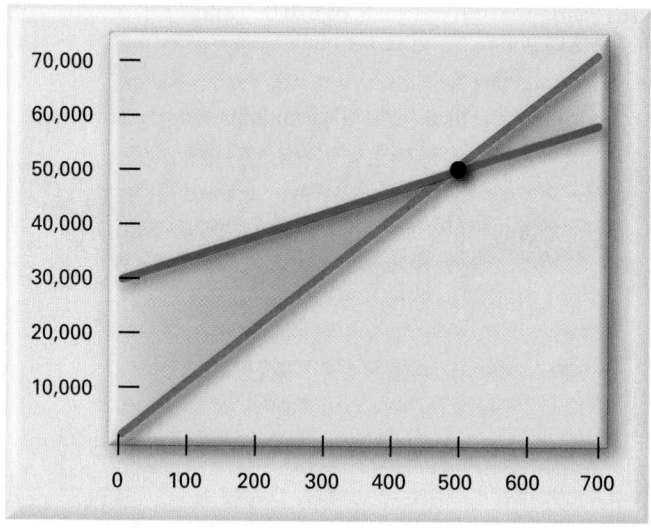

Required

1. Label each axis, sales revenue line, total expenses line, fixed expenses line, operating income area, and operating loss area.
2. If Brown attracts 400 students to take the course, will the venture be profitable?
3. What are the breakeven sales in students and dollars?

E22-7 Suppose that Turner Field, the home of the Atlanta Braves, earns total revenue that averages $24 for every ticket sold. Assume that annual fixed expenses are $24 million, and variable expenses are $4 per ticket.

Required

1. Prepare the ballpark's CVP graph under these assumptions. Label the axes, sales revenue line, fixed expense line, total expense line, the operating loss area, and the operating income area on the graph.
2. Show the breakeven point in dollars and in tickets.

E22-8 Ronnie's Repair Shop has a monthly target operating income of $12,000. Variable expenses are 70% of sales, and monthly fixed expenses are $9,000.

Required

1. Compute the monthly margin of safety in dollars if the shop achieves its income goal.
2. Express Ronnie's margin of safety as a percentage of target sales.

E22-9 The 20X6 data that follow pertain to Rays, a manufacturer of swimming goggles. (Rays has no beginning inventories in January 20X6.)

Sale price............................	$35	Fixed manufacturing		
Variable manufacturing		overhead	$2,000,000
expense per unit	15	Fixed operating expense.......	250,000
Sales commission		Number of goggles produced ..	200,000
expense per unit	5	Number of goggles sold	185,000

(continued)

Required

1. Prepare both conventional (absorption costing) and contribution margin (variable costing) income statements for Rays, for the year ended December 31, 20X6.
2. Which statement shows the higher operating income? Why?
3. Rays' marketing vice president believes a new sales promotion that costs $150,000 would increase sales to 200,000 goggles. Should the company go ahead with the promotion? Give your reason.

Problems

(Group A)

P22-1A Custom Kitchens is opening early next year. Kate Royer, the owner, is considering two plans for obtaining the assets and the sales force needed for operations. Plan 1 calls for purchasing all equipment and paying the sales force straight salaries. Under plan 2, Custom Kitchens would lease equipment month by month and pay the sales force low salaries but give them a big part of their pay in commissions. Discuss the effects of the two plans on variable expenses, fixed expenses, breakeven sales, and likely profits for a new business in the start-up stage. Indicate which plan you favor for Custom Kitchens.

Explaining the effects of different cost behavior patterns on the breakeven point and on likely profits
(Obj. 1)

P22-2A The budgets of four companies yield the following information:

Using CVP analysis to compute contribution margin and breakeven sales
(Obj. 2, 5)

	Company			
	Q	R	S	T
Target sales	$720,000	$300,000	$190,000	$ _____
Variable expenses..............	216,000			260,000
Fixed expenses		156,000	100,000	
Operating income (loss)	$ 30,000	$ _____	$ _____	$ 80,000
Units sold	_____	112,000	12,000	16,000
Contribution margin per unit ...	$ 6		$ 9.50	$ 40
Contribution margin ratio	_____	0.60		

Fill in the blanks for each company. Which company has the lowest breakeven point in sales dollars? What causes the low breakeven point?

P22-3A A traveling production of *The Phantom of the Opera* performs each year. The average show sells 800 tickets at $50 a ticket. There are 100 shows each year. The show has a cast of 40, each earning an average of $260 per show. The cast is paid only after each show. The other variable expense is program printing costs of $6 per guest. Annual fixed expenses total $942,400.

BE sales and sales to earn a target Op. Inc.; CM/IS
(Obj. 2, 3, 5)

Student Resource**CD**
spreadsheet

Required

1. Compute revenue and variable expenses for each show.
2. Use the income statement equation approach to compute the number of shows needed annually to break even.
3. Use the shortcut contribution margin approach to compute the number of shows needed annually to earn a profit of $1,438,400. Is this goal realistic? Give your reason.
4. Prepare *The Phantom of the Opera's* contribution margin income statement for 100 shows each year. Report only two categories of expenses: variable and fixed.

Analyzing CVP relationships
(Obj. 2, 3, 4)

P22-4A Team Spirit imprints calendars with college names. The company has fixed expenses of $1,035,000 each month plus variable expenses of $3.60 per carton of calendars. Team Spirit sells each carton of calendars for $10.50.

(continued)

Required

1. Use the income statement equation approach to compute the number of cartons of calendars Team Spirit must sell each month to break even.

2. Use the contribution margin ratio CVP formula to compute the dollar amount of monthly sales Team Spirit needs to earn $285,000 in operating income. (Round the contribution margin ratio to 2 decimal places.)

3. Prepare Team Spirit's contribution margin income statement for June for sales of 450,000 cartons of calendars. Cost of goods sold is 70% of variable expenses. Operating expenses make up the rest of the variable expenses and all of the fixed expenses.

4. The company is considering an expansion that will increase fixed expenses by 40% and variable expenses by one-fourth. Compute the new breakeven point in units and in dollars. How would this expansion affect Team Spirit's risk? Should Team Spirit expand?

Computing breakeven sales and sales needed to earn a target operating income; graphing CVP relationships
(Obj. 1, 2, 3, 4)

P22-5A Personal Investors is opening an office in Lexington, Kentucky. Fixed monthly expenses are office rent ($2,500), depreciation on office furniture ($260), utilities ($280), special telephone lines ($600), a connection with an online brokerage service ($640), and the salary of a financial planner ($3,400). Variable expenses include payments to the financial planner (10% of revenue), advertising (5% of revenue), supplies and postage (2% of revenue), and usage fees for the telephone lines and computerized brokerage service (3% of revenue).

Required

1. Use the contribution margin ratio CVP formula to compute the investment firm's breakeven revenue in dollars. If the average trade leads to $400 in revenue for Personal Investors, how many trades must be made to break even?

2. Use the income statement equation approach to compute dollar revenues needed to earn monthly operating income of $3,840.

3. Graph Personal Investors' CVP relationships. Assume that an average trade leads to $400 in revenue for Personal Investors. Show the breakeven point, sales revenue line, fixed expense line, total expense line, operating loss area, operating income area, and the sales in units (trades) and dollars when monthly operating income of $3,840 is earned. The graph should range from 0 to 40 units (trades).

4. Assume that the average revenue Personal Investors earns decreases to $300 per trade. How does this affect the breakeven point in number of trades?

Preparing absorption and variable costing income statements and explaining the difference in income
(Obj. 5)

P22-6A ← *Link Back to Chapter 19 (Manufacturing Company Income Statement) and Chapter 20 (Manufacturing Overhead).* Mario's Foods produces frozen meals, which it sells for $7 each. The company uses the FIFO inventory costing method, and it computes a new monthly fixed manufacturing overhead rate based on the actual number of meals produced that month. All costs and production levels are exactly as planned. The following data are from Mario's Foods' first two months in business.

	January 20X7	February 20X7
Sales	1,000 meals	1,200 meals
Production	1,400 meals	1,000 meals
Variable manufacturing expense per meal	$4	$4
Sales commission expense per meal	$1	$1
Total fixed manufacturing overhead	$700	$700
Total fixed marketing and administrative expenses	$600	$600

Required

1. Compute the product cost per meal produced under absorption costing and under variable costing. Do this first for January and then for February.

(continued)

2. Prepare separate monthly income statements for January and for February, using
   a. Absorption costing
   b. Variable costing
3. Is operating income higher under absorption costing or variable costing in January? In February? Explain the pattern of differences in operating income based on absorption costing versus variable costing.

Problems

(Group B)

P22-1B Brooke Miller is in charge of the New York Regional Head Start program. Legislators have just cut the program's funding by 15%. Miller cannot cut total fixed costs like the rent for the program's offices or salaries of the administrative staff. The other main costs are salaries for teachers ($30,000/yr) and teachers' aides ($12,000/yr). Miller cannot cut the salary paid per teacher or teacher's aide.

Explaining the effects of different cost behavior patterns
(Obj. 1)

What alternatives does Miller have to meet the budget? Will the 15% funding cut reduce services provided by more than 15%, less than 15%, or close to 15%? Explain your reasoning.

P22-2B The budgets of four companies yield the following information:

Use CVP analysis to compute contribution margin and breakeven sales
(Obj. 2, 5)

	Company			
	A	B	C	D
Target sales	$680,000	$_____	$550,000	$_____
Variable expenses...............	_____	150,000	280,000	156,000
Fixed expenses	_____	123,000	138,000	
Operating income (loss)	$120,000	$_____	$_____	$ 35,000
Units sold	187,000	10,000		
Contribution margin per unit ...	$ 2	$_____	$ 100	$ 12
Contribution margin ratio	_____	0.20	_____	0.20

Fill in the blanks for each company. Which company has the lowest breakeven point in sales dollars? What causes the low breakeven point?

P22-3B International Productions performs *Cats*, the play. The average show sells 1,000 tickets at $60 a ticket. There are 120 shows a year. *Cats* has a cast of 60, each earning an average of $320 a show. The cast is paid only after each show. The other variable expense is program printing costs of $8 per guest. Annual fixed expenses total $295,200.

BE and sales to earn a target Op. Inc.; CM/IS
(Obj. 2, 3, 5)

spreadsheet

Required

1. Compute revenue and variable expenses for each show.
2. Use the income statement equation approach to compute the number of shows *Cats* must perform each year to break even.
3. Use the shortcut contribution margin approach to compute the number of shows needed each year to earn a profit of $4,264,000. Is this profit goal realistic? Give your reason.
4. Prepare the *Cats* contribution margin income statement for 120 shows for the year. Report only two categories of expenses: variable and fixed.

P22-4B Fanfare sells flags with team logos. Fanfare has fixed expenses of $678,600 per year plus variable expenses of $4.20 per flag. Each flag sells for $12.00.

Analyzing CVP relationships
(Obj. 2, 3, 4)

(continued)

Required

1. Use the income statement equation approach to compute the number of flags Fanfare must sell each year to break even.

2. Use the contribution margin ratio CVP formula to compute the dollar sales Fanfare needs to earn $32,500 in operating income.

3. Prepare Fanfare's contribution margin income statement for the year ended December 31, 20X7, for sales of 70,000 flags. Cost of goods sold is 60% of variable expenses. Operating expenses make up the rest of variable expenses and all of fixed expenses.

4. The company is considering an expansion that will increase fixed expenses by 20% and variable expenses by 30 cents per flag. Compute the new breakeven point in units and in dollars. Should Fanfare undertake the expansion? Give your reason.

Computing breakeven sales and sales needed to earn a target operating income; graphing CVP relationships
(Obj. 1, 2, 3, 4)

P22-5B Money Maker Investment Group is opening an office in Atlanta. Fixed monthly expenses are office rent ($9,100), depreciation on office furniture ($700), utilities ($1,400), special telephone lines ($1,600), a connection with an online brokerage service ($2,000), and the salary of a financial planner ($4,800). Variable expenses include payments to the financial planner (8% of revenue), advertising (12% of revenue), supplies and postage (4% of revenue), and usage fees for the telephone lines and computerized brokerage service (6% of revenue).

Required

1. Use the contribution margin ratio CVP formula to compute Money Maker's breakeven revenue in dollars. If the average trade leads to $700 in revenue for Money Maker, how many trades must be made to break even?

2. Use the income statement equation approach to compute the dollar revenues needed to earn a target monthly operating income of $9,800.

3. Graph Money Maker's CVP relationships. Assume that an average trade leads to $700 in revenue for Money Maker. Show the breakeven point, sales revenue line, fixed expense line, total expense line, operating loss area, operating income area, and the sales in units (trades) and dollars when monthly operating income of $9,800 is earned. The graph should range from 0 to 80 units (trades).

4. Assume that the average revenue Money Maker earns decreases to $560 per trade. Compute the new breakeven point in trades. How does this affect the breakeven point?

Preparing absorption and variable costing income statements and explaining the difference in income
(Obj. 5)

P22-6B ← *Link Back to Chapter 19 (Manufacturing Company Income Statement) and Chapter 20 (Manufacturing Overhead).* Game Source manufactures video games, which it sells for $40 each. The company uses the FIFO inventory costing method, and it computes a new monthly fixed manufacturing overhead rate based on the actual number of games produced that month. All costs and production levels are exactly as planned. The following data are from Game Source's first two months in business during 20X7:

	October	November
Sales.....................................	2,000 units	2,200 units
Production	2,500 units	2,000 units
Variable manufacturing expense per game........	$15	$15
Sales commission per game....................	$8	$8
Total fixed manufacturing overhead	$10,000	$10,000
Total fixed marketing and administrative expenses..	$ 9,000	$ 9,000

Required

1. Compute the product cost per game produced under absorption costing and under variable costing. Do this first for October and then for November.

(continued)

2. Prepare separate monthly income statements for October and for November, using
   a. Absorption costing   **b.** Variable costing

3. Is operating income higher under absorption costing or variable costing in October? In November? Explain the pattern of differences in operating income based on absorption costing versus variable costing.

APPLY *Your Knowledge*

Decision Cases

Case 1. Brian and Nui Soon live in Macon, Georgia. Two years ago, they visited Thailand. Nui, a professional chef, was impressed with the cooking methods and the spices used in the Thai food. Macon does not have a Thai restaurant, and the Soons are contemplating opening one. Nui would supervise the cooking, and Brian would leave his current job to be the maitre d'. The restaurant would serve dinner Tuesday through Saturday.

Using CVP analysis to make business decisions
(Obj. 2, 4)

   Brian has noticed a restaurant for lease. The restaurant has seven tables, each of which can seat four. Tables can be moved together for a large party. Nui is planning two seatings per evening, and the restaurant will be open 50 weeks per year.

   The Soons have drawn up the following estimates:

Average revenue, including beverages and dessert	$40 per meal
Average cost of the food	$12 per meal
Chef's and dishwasher's salaries	$50,400 per *year*
Rent (premises, equipment)	$4,000 per month
Cleaning (linen and premises)	$800 per month
Replacement of dishes, cutlery, glasses	$300 per month
Utilities, advertising, telephone	$1,900 per month

Required

Compute *annual* breakeven number of meals and sales revenue for the restaurant. Also compute the number of meals and the amount of sales revenue needed to earn operating income of $75,600 for the year. How many meals must the Soons serve each night to earn their target income of $75,600? Should the couple open the restaurant?

Case 2. ← *Link Back to Chapter 19 (Just-in-Time Philosophy).* Suppose you serve on the board of directors of American Faucet, a manufacturer of bathroom fixtures that recently adopted just-in-time production. Part of your responsibility is to develop a compensation contract for Toni Moen, the vice president of manufacturing. To give her the incentive to make decisions that will increase the company's profits, the board decides to give Moen a year-end bonus if American Faucet meets a target operating income.

Absorption and variable cost incentives
(Obj. 5)

   Write a memo to the Chairman of the Board, Herbert Kohler, explaining whether the bonus contract should be based on absorption costing or variable costing. Use the following format:

Date:	_____
To:	_____
From:	_____
Subject:	_____

Effect of error on cost-volume-profit analysis
(Obj. 2, 4)

Ethical Issue

You have just begun your summer internship at Tmedic. The company supplies sterilized surgical instruments for physicians. To expand sales, Tmedic is considering paying a commission to its sales force. The controller, Jane Hewitt, asks you to compute (1) the new breakeven sales figure and (2) the operating profit if sales increase 15% under the new sales commission plan. She thinks you can handle this task because you learned CVP analysis in your accounting class.

You spend the next day collecting information from the accounting records, performing the analysis, and writing a memo to explain the results. The company president is pleased with your memo. You report that the new sales commission plan will lead to a significant increase in operating income and only a small increase in breakeven sales.

The following week, you realize that you made an error in the CVP analysis. You overlooked the sales personnel's $2,500 monthly salaries and you did not include this fixed marketing expense in your computations. You are not sure what to do. If you tell Jane Hewitt of your mistake, she will have to tell the president. In this case, you are afraid Tmedic might not offer you permanent employment after your internship.

Required

1. How would your error affect breakeven sales and operating income under the proposed sales commission plan? Could this cause the president to reject the sales commission proposal?
2. Consider your ethical responsibilities. Is there a difference between (a) initially making an error and (b) subsequently failing to inform the controller?
3. Suppose you tell Jane Hewitt of the error in your analysis. Why might the consequences not be as bad as you fear? Should Hewitt take any responsibility for your error? What could Hewitt have done differently?
4. After considering all the factors, should you inform Jane Hewitt or simply keep quiet?

Financial Statement Case

Identifying cost behavior patterns and computing and analyzing breakeven sales
(Obj. 1, 2, 4)

Refer to **Amazon.com's** Consolidated Statements of Operations, and to CEO Jeff Bezos' 2002 letter to shareholders. (Both are included in the financial statements in Appendix A.)

1. Is Amazon.com's cost of sales a fixed cost or a variable cost? Is technology and content a fixed cost or a variable cost? Explain.
2. Look at CEO Jeff Bezos' letter to shareholders. How does the structure of Amazon.com's fixed and variable costs support Bezos' objective to offer both world-leading customer experience and the lowest possible prices?
3. Assume that 90% of Amazon.com's operating expenses are fixed costs. Calculate the contribution margin for each of the last three years.
4. What is the contribution margin ratio for each of the last three years? (Carry your computations to five decimal places.)
5. What is the breakeven sales in dollars for *operations* for each of the last three years? Ignore all items below Income (Loss) from Operations.
6. Refer to your answers to Requirements 3 through 5. Look at the trend in contribution margin, costs, and breakeven sales. Amazon's management has emphasized cost control over the last three years. Has it been successful? Explain.

Variable and absorption costing, bonus contract incentives, using contribution margin statements to make decisions
(Obj. 2, 5)

Team Project

EZPAK Manufacturing produces filament packaging tape. In 20X6, EZPAK produced and sold 15 million rolls of tape. The company has recently expanded its capacity, so it can now produce up to 30 million rolls per year. EZPAK's accounting records show the following results from 20X6:

(continued)

Sale price per roll	$3.00
Variable manufacturing expenses per roll	$2.00
Variable marketing and administrative expenses per roll. . . .	$0.50
Total fixed manufacturing overhead costs.	$8,400,000
Total fixed marketing and administrative expenses.	$600,000
Sales	15 million rolls
Production.	15 million rolls

There were no beginning or ending inventories in 20X6.

In January 20X7, EZPAK hired a new president, Kevin McDaniel. McDaniel has a one-year contract that specifies he will be paid 10% of EZPAK's 20X7 absorption costing operating income, instead of a salary. In 20X7, McDaniel must make two major decisions:

- Should EZPAK undertake a major advertising campaign? This campaign would raise sales to 25 million rolls. This is the maximum level of sales EZPAK can expect to make in the near future. The ad campaign would add an additional $3.5 million in marketing and administrative costs. Without the campaign, sales will be 15 million rolls.
- How many rolls of tape will EZPAK produce?

At the end of the year, EZPAK Manufacturing's Board of Directors will evaluate McDaniel's performance and decide whether to offer him a contract for the following year.

Required

Within your group, form two subgroups. The first subgroup assumes the role of Kevin McDaniel, EZPAK Manufacturing's new president. The second subgroup assumes the role of EZPAK Manufacturing's Board of Directors. McDaniel will meet with the Board of Directors shortly after the end of 20X7 to decide whether he will remain at EZPAK. Most of your effort should be devoted to advance preparation for this meeting. Each subgroup should meet separately to prepare for the meeting between the Board and McDaniel. [*Hint*: Keep computations (other than per-unit amounts) in millions.]

Kevin McDaniel should:

1. Compute EZPAK Manufacturing's 20X6 operating income.
2. Decide whether to adopt the advertising campaign. Prepare a memo to the Board of Directors explaining this decision. Use the memo format outlined in Decision Case 2. Give this memo to the Board of Directors as soon as possible (before the joint meeting).
3. Assume EZPAK adopts the advertising campaign. Decide how many rolls of tape to produce in 20X7.
4. Given your response to Requirement 3, prepare an absorption costing income statement for the year ended December 31, 20X7, ending with operating income before bonus. Then compute your bonus separately. The variable cost per unit and the total fixed expenses (with the exception of the advertising campaign) remain the same as in 20X6. Give this income statement and your bonus computation to the Board of Directors as soon as possible (before your meeting with the Board).
5. Decide whether you wish to remain at EZPAK for another year. You currently have an offer from another company. The contract with the other company is identical to the one you currently have with EZPAK—you will be paid 10% of absorption costing operating income instead of a salary.

The Board of Directors should:

1. Compute EZPAK's 20X6 operating income.
2. Determine whether EZPAK should adopt the advertising campaign.
3. Determine how many rolls of tape EZPAK should produce in 20X7.
4. Evaluate McDaniel's performance, based on his decisions and the information he provided the Board. (*Hint:* You may want to prepare a variable costing income statement.)
5. Evaluate the contract's bonus provision. Are you satisfied with this provision? If so, explain why. If not, recommend how it should be changed.

(continued)

After McDaniel has given the Board his memo and income statement, and after the Board has had a chance to evaluate McDaniel's performance, McDaniel and the Board should meet. The purpose of the meeting is to decide whether it is in their mutual interest for McDaniel to remain with EZPAK, and if so, the terms of the contract EZPAK will offer McDaniel.

For Internet Exercises, go to the Web site, www.prenhall.com/horngren.

APPENDIX *to Chapter 22*

Effect of Sales Mix on CVP Analysis

Our CVP example focused on Kay Pak's e-tail business, which had a single product: art posters. Companies that sell more than one product must consider *sales mix* in figuring CVP relationships. A company earns more income by selling high-margin products than by selling an equal number of low-margin items.

For example, Continental Airlines has focused on attracting more business-people. Business travelers generally pay more for the same flight than leisure travelers. By increasing the proportion of higher-paying business fliers, Continental boosted its sales revenue per available seat-mile (available seats × miles flown) from $0.074 to $0.09. Improving sales mix by selling more high-margin tickets reduced Continental's breakeven point. Before the change, Continental had to fill 63% of its seats to break even. By attracting more business travelers, Continental only has to fill 61%.

We can use the same CVP formulas we used for a company with a single product to perform CVP analysis for a company that sells more than one product. But first, we must compute the *weighted-average contribution margin* of all products. The sales mix provides the weights.

We saw another weighted-average procedure—for inventory costing—in Chapter 6, where it was called the average-cost method, and for process costing in Chapter 21.

→

Continuing the Kay Pak e-tail illustration from the chapter, suppose Pak plans to sell two types of posters. Recall that the regular poster costs $21 and sells for $35. Its contribution margin is $14 ($35 − $21). The second, larger poster costs $40 and sells for $70. Its contribution margin is $30 ($70 − $40). Pak's fixed expenses remain $7,000.

Pak expects to sell 500 regular posters and 300 large posters. This is a 5 : 3 sales mix. For every 5 regular posters, Pak expects to sell 3 large posters, so she expects 5/8 of the sales to be regular posters and 3/8 to be large posters. To compute breakeven sales in units, Pak first computes the weighted-average contribution margin, as follows:

✔ Starter 22A-1

	Regular Posters	Large Posters	Total
Sale price per unit..........................	$ 35	$ 70	
Deduct: Variable expense per unit............	(21)	(40)	
Contribution margin per unit................	$ 14	$ 30	
Sales mix in units	× 5	× 3	8
Contribution margin	$ 70	$ 90	$160
Weighted-average contribution margin per unit ($160/8).................			$ 20

$$\text{SALES IN TOTAL UNITS} = \frac{\text{Fixed expenses} + \text{Operating income}}{\text{Weighted-average contribution margin per unit}}$$

$$= \frac{\$7,000 + \$0}{\$20}$$

$$= 350 \text{ posters}$$

Breakeven sales of regular posters (350 × 5/8)	218.75 regular posters
Breakeven sales of large posters (350 × 3/8)	131.25 large posters

As is often the case in real situations, these computations don't yield round numbers. Since Pak cannot sell partial posters, she must sell 219 regular posters and 132 large posters to avoid a loss. Using these rounded numbers would lead to a small rounding error in our check figures, however, so the rest of our computations will use the exact results: 218.75 regular posters and 131.25 large posters.

✔ **Starter 22A-2**

The overall breakeven point in sales dollars is $16,844 (amounts rounded to the nearest dollar):

218.75 regular posters at $35 each	$ 7,656
131.25 large posters at $70 each	9,188
Total revenues	$16,844

We can prove this breakeven point by preparing a contribution margin income statement (amounts rounded to the nearest dollar):

	Regular	Large	Total
Sales revenue:			
Regular posters (218.75 × $35)	$7,656		
Large posters (131.25 × $70)		$9,188	$16,844
Variable expenses:			
Regular posters (218.75 × $21)	4,594		
Large posters (131.25 × $40)		5,250	9,844
Contribution margin	$3,062	$3,938	$ 7,000
Fixed expenses			(7,000)
Operating income			$ 0

The breakeven proof shows that Pak's breakeven sales are $16,844. Pak could also use the contribution margin ratio approach shown in the chapter body to estimate breakeven sales in dollars. But first, she must estimate her contribution margin ratio:

Total expected contribution margin:		
Regular posters (500 × $14)	$ 7,000	
Large posters (300 × $30)	9,000	$ 16,000
Divided by total expected sales:		
Regular posters (500 × $35)	$17,500	
Large posters (300 × $70)	21,000	÷38,500
Contribution margin ratio		41.558%

Then, Pak uses the contribution margin ratio approach to estimate breakeven sales in dollars:

$$\text{SALES IN DOLLARS} = \frac{\text{Fixed expenses + Operating income}}{\text{Contribution margin ratio}}$$

$$= \frac{\$7,000 + \$0}{0.41558}$$

$$= \$16,844 \text{ (rounded)}$$

If Pak's actual sales mix is not 5 regular posters to 3 large posters, her actual operating income will differ from the planned amount, even if she sells exactly 800 total posters. For each total number of posters sold, there are as many different operating incomes as there are sales mixes. Similarly, there are as many different breakeven points—in total units and in sales dollars—as there are sales mixes.

Suppose Kay Pak plans to sell 800 total posters in the 5 : 3 sales mix (5 regular posters sold for every 3 large posters). She *actually* sells 800 posters—375 regular and 425 large. The unit sale prices and variable expenses are exactly as predicted, and the fixed expense is the budgeted $7,000. Can you tell, without computations, whether Pak's actual operating income is greater than, less than, or equal to her expected income?

Answer: Pak sold more of the higher-margin large posters. This favorable change in the sales mix increased her operating income.

Appendix Assignments

Starters

Sales mix and weighted-average contribution margin
(Appendix)

S22A-1 Consider the **Grand Canyon Railway** example from the chapter opening story. Suppose Grand Canyon decides to offer two classes of service: Coach class and Chief class. Assume Grand Canyon incurs $250,000 of fixed expenses per month and that it has the following ticket prices and variable expenses:

	Coach Class	Chief Class
Sale price per ticket............................	$60.00	$120.00
Variable expense per passenger	12.00	20.00

If Grand Canyon Railway expects to sell seven tickets in Coach class for every four tickets in Chief class, compute the weighted-average contribution margin per unit (round-trip ticket).

Breakeven point and sales mix
(Appendix)

S22A-2 Refer to the Grand Canyon Railway data in Starter 22A-1 and your answer. Compute:

a. The total number of tickets Grand Canyon must sell to break even.
b. The number of Coach class tickets and the number of Chief class tickets the company must sell to break even.

Exercises

CVP analysis with a sales mix
(Appendix)

E22A-1 Racer Scooters plans to sell a standard scooter for $54 and a chrome scooter for $78. Racer purchases the standard scooter for $36, and the chrome scooter for $50. Racer expects to sell two chrome scooters for every three standard scooters. Racer's monthly fixed expenses are $9,680. How many of each type of scooter must Racer sell monthly to break even? To earn $6,600?

Computing contribution margin for one of two products
(Appendix)

E22A-2 Kenisha, Inc., manufactures two styles of watches—the Digital and the Classic. The following data pertain to the Digital:

Variable manufacturing cost............................	$120
Variable operating cost	30
Sale price	200

(continued)

Kenisha's monthly fixed expenses total $190,000. When Digitals and Classics are sold in the mix of 7 : 3, respectively, the sale of 2,000 total watches results in an operating income of $60,000. Compute the contribution margin per watch for the Classic.

Problems

P22A-1 The contribution margin income statement of Extreme Coffee for February 20XX follows:

Using a contribution margin income statement for breakeven analysis; sales mix, margin of safety, and changes in CVP relationships
(Obj. 2, 3, 4, Appendix)

Extreme Coffee
Contribution Margin Income Statement
For the Month of February 20XX

Sales revenue		$90,000
Variable expenses:		
Cost of goods sold	$32,000	
Marketing expense	10,000	
General and administrative expense	3,000	45,000
Contribution margin		45,000
Fixed expenses:		
Marketing expense	16,500	
General and administrative expense	3,500	20,000
Operating income		$25,000

Extreme Coffee sells three small coffees for every large coffee. A small coffee sells for $2, with a variable expense of $1. A large coffee sells for $4, with a variable expense of $2.

Required

1. Determine Extreme Coffee's monthly breakeven point in the numbers of small coffees and large coffees. Prove your answer by preparing a summary contribution margin income statement at the breakeven level of sales. Show only two categories of expenses: variable and fixed.
2. Compute Extreme Coffee's margin of safety in dollars.
3. If Extreme Coffee can increase monthly sales volume by 15%, what will operating income be? (The sales mix remains unchanged.)

CHAPTER **23**

The Master Budget and Responsibility Accounting

A+

TIPS CHECK YOUR RESOURCES

- Visit the www.prenhall.com/horngren **Web site** for self-study quizzes, video clips, and other resources

- Try the **Quick Check** exercise at the end of the chapter to test your knowledge

- Learn the **key terms**

- Do the **Starter** exercises keyed in the margins

- Work the **mid- and end-of-chapter summary problems**

- Use the **Concept Links** to review material in other chapters

- Search the **CD** for review materials by chapter or by key word

LEARNING OBJECTIVES

1 Learn why managers use budgets

2 Prepare an operating budget

3 Prepare a financial budget

4 Use sensitivity analysis in budgeting

5 Prepare performance reports for responsibility centers

Over 20% of sales of books, music, and electronics occur online. If you're one of the millions of customers worldwide who point and click to buy your books and CDs on Amazon.com, then you're part of Amazon's strategy to "get big fast." This strategy increased Amazon's sales, but at a cost. Spending was out of control. There was no budget, and managers spared no expense to help the company grow. As a result, Amazon lost more than half a billion dollars in the fourth quarter of 2000.

Founder and CEO Jeff Bezos had to turn this sea of red ink into income. Bezos set up a *budget* for Amazon's plan of action. Now each division budgets both sales and expenses. In weekly meetings, managers compare actual results to the budget, which helps them correct problems quickly.

The result? Between 2000 and 2002, Amazon.com's sales increased 42%. With such an increase in sales, you'd expect expenses to also increase. But Amazon's new budget helped managers *cut* operating

Amazon.com

expenses. How did they decrease expenses when sales are increasing so dramatically? The budget helped Amazon reduce order-filling and distribution costs by 5%. Switching to lower-cost computer systems reduced "technical and content" operating costs by 20%. The result? Amazon.com reported its first-ever income from operations in 2002.

Sources: Katrina Brooker, "Beautiful Dreamer," *Fortune*, December 18, 2000, pp. 234–239. Fred Vogelstein, "Bezos," *Fortune*, September 2, 2002, pp. 186–187. Fred Vogelstein, "What Went Right 2002," *Fortune*, December 30, 2002, p. 166. Nick Wingfield, "Survival Strategy: Amazon Takes Page from Wal-Mart to Prosper on Web," *The Wall Street Journal*, November 22, 2002, A1. Fred Vogelstein, "Mighty Amazon," *Fortune*, May 26, 2003, pp. 60–74. ∎

∎ Sitemap

Chapter 19 defined a budget as a quantitative expression of a plan that helps managers coordinate and implement the plan.

Student Resource**CD**

benchmarking, budget

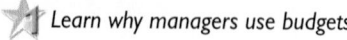

Learn why managers use budgets

Perhaps, like Amazon.com, you've prepared a budget to ensure that you have enough cash to pay your expenses. ← The budget forces you to plan. If your budgeted cash inflow falls short of expenses, you can:

- Increase your cash inflow (by taking on a job or a student loan), or
- Cut your expenses

In addition to planning, your personal budget can help you control expenses. To stay within your grocery budget, you may buy macaroni and cheese instead of shrimp. At the end of the month, if your bank balance is less than expected, you can compare your actual cash inflows and expenses to your budget to see why. You need to know whether cash inflows are lower than expected or expenses are higher than expected to know what corrective action to take.

As Amazon.com learned, it's easy for spending to get out of control if you don't have a budget. That's why everyone, from individuals like you to complex international organizations like Amazon.com, uses budgets. Careful budgeting helps both individuals and businesses stay out of trouble by reducing the risk that they will spend more than they earn.

Why Managers Use Budgets

Let's continue our study of budgets by moving from your personal budget to see how a small service business develops a simple budget. Assume you begin an online service that provides travel itineraries for leisure travelers. You want to earn $550 a month to help with your college expenses. You expect to sell 20 itineraries per month at a price of $30 each. Over the past six months, you paid your Internet service provider an average of $18 a month, and you spent an additional $20 per month on reference materials. You expect these monthly costs to remain about the same. Finally, you spend 5% of your sales revenues for banner ads on other travel Web sites.

Exhibit 23-1 shows how to compute budgeted revenues and then subtract budgeted expenses to arrive at budgeted operating income.

If business goes according to plan, you will not meet your $550 per month operating income goal. You will have to increase revenue (perhaps through word-of-mouth advertising) or cut expenses (perhaps by finding a less-expensive Internet access provider).

Exhibit 23-1

Service Company Budget

Custom Travel Itineraries		
Budget for May 20X9		
Budgeted sales revenue (20 × $30)		$600
Less budgeted expenses:		
Internet-access expense	$18	
Reference-materials expense	20	
Advertising expense (5% × $600)	30	68
Budgeted operating income.............................		$532

Using Budgets to Plan and Control

Large international for-profit companies like Amazon.com and nonprofit organizations like Habitat for Humanity use budgets for the same reasons as you do in your personal life or in your small business—to plan and control actions and the related revenues and expenses. Exhibit 23-2 shows how managers use budgets in fulfilling their major responsibilities. First, they develop strategies—overall business goals like Amazon.com's goal to expand its international operations, or Gateway's to be a value leader in the personal computer market, while diversifying into other markets. Then companies plan and budget for specific actions to achieve those goals. The next step is to act. For example, Amazon.com recently planned for and then added the Marketplace auction feature to its Web sites for the United Kingdom, Germany, and Japan. And Gateway is leaning on its suppliers to cut costs, while at the same time it is pumping out new products like plasma TVs and audio and video gear.

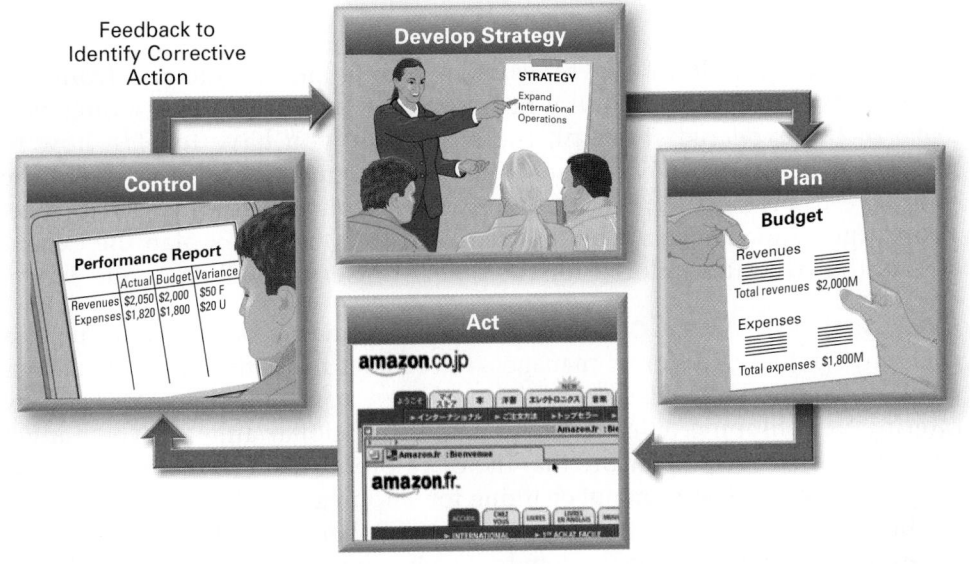

After acting, managers compare actual results with the budget. This feedback allows them to determine what, if any, corrective action to take. If Amazon spent more than expected to add the Marketplace to its international Web sites, managers must cut other costs or increase revenues. These decisions affect the company's future strategies and plans.

Amazon.com has a number of budgets. Its managers develop budgets for their own divisions. Software then "rolls up" the division budgets to create an organization-wide budget for the company as a whole. Managers also prepare both long-term and short-term budgets. Boeing's long-term budget forecasts demand for planes for the next 20 years.

On the other hand, most companies (including Boeing) budget their cash flows monthly, weekly, and even daily to ensure that they have enough cash. They also budget revenues and expenses—and thus operating income—for months, quarters, and years. This chapter focuses on short-term budgets of one year or less. Chapter 26 explains how companies prepare long-term budgets for major capital expenditures on property, plant, and equipment.

Benefits of Budgeting

✔ **Starter 23-1**

Exhibit 23-3 summarizes three key benefits of budgeting. Budgeting forces managers to plan, promotes coordination and communication, and provides a benchmark for evaluating actual performance.

Exhibit 23-3

Benefits of Budgeting

Budgets force managers to plan.

Budgets promote coordination and communication.

Budgets provide a benchmark that motivates employees and helps managers evaluate performance.

PLANNING Exhibit 23-1 shows that your expected income from the online travel itinerary business falls short of the target. The sooner you learn of the expected shortfall, the more time you have to plan how to increase revenues or cut expenses. The better your plan, and the more time you have to act on the plan, the more likely you will find a way to meet your target. Amazon.com's budget required that managers plan the expansion of the Web sites tailored for customers in Germany, France, and Japan.

COORDINATION AND COMMUNICATION The master budget coordinates a company's activities. It forces managers to consider relations among operations across the entire value chain. For example, Amazon.com stimulates sales by offering free shipping on orders over a specified dollar amount. The budget encourages managers to ensure that the extra profits from increased sales outweigh the revenue lost from not charging for shipping.

Budgets also communicate a consistent set of plans throughout the company. For example, the initial Amazon.com budget communicated the message that all employees should help control costs.

BENCHMARKING Budgets provide a benchmark that motivates employees and helps managers evaluate performance. In most companies, part of the manager's performance evaluation depends on how actual results compare to the budget. So, for example, the budgeted expenses for international expansion encourage Amazon.com's employees to increase the efficiency of international warehousing operations and to find less-expensive technology to support the Web sites.

Let's return to your online travel business. Suppose that comparing actual results to the budget in Exhibit 23-1 leads to the performance report in Exhibit 23-4.

Exhibit 23-4

Summary Performance Report

	Actual	Budget	Variance (Actual − Budget)
Sales revenue	$550	$600	$(50)
Total expenses	90	68	(22)
Net income	$460	$532	$(72)

This report should prompt you to investigate why actual sales are $50 less than budgeted ($550 – $600). There are three possibilities:

- The budget was unrealistic.
- You did a poor selling job.
- Uncontrollable factors (such as a sluggish economy) reduced sales.

Of course, all three may have contributed to the poor results.

You will also want to know why expenses are $22 higher than expected ($90 – $68). Did your Internet service provider increase rates? Did you have to buy more reference materials than planned? Did you spend more than 5% of your revenue on Web banner ads? You need to know the answers to these kinds of questions to decide how to get your business back on track.

Preparing the Master Budget

Now that you know *why* managers go to the trouble of developing budgets, let's consider the steps they take to prepare a budget.

Components of the Master Budget

The **master budget** is the set of budgeted financial statements and supporting schedules for the entire organization. Exhibit 23-5 shows the order in which managers prepare the components of the master budget for a merchandiser such as Amazon.com.

Student ResourceCD

budget, budgeted financial statements, capital expenditures budget, financial budget, master budget, operating budget

Exhibit 23-5

Master Budget for a Merchandising Company

✔ **Starter 23-2**

Master Budget
The set of budgeted financial statements and supporting schedules for the entire organization. Includes the operating budget, the capital expenditures budget, and the financial budget.

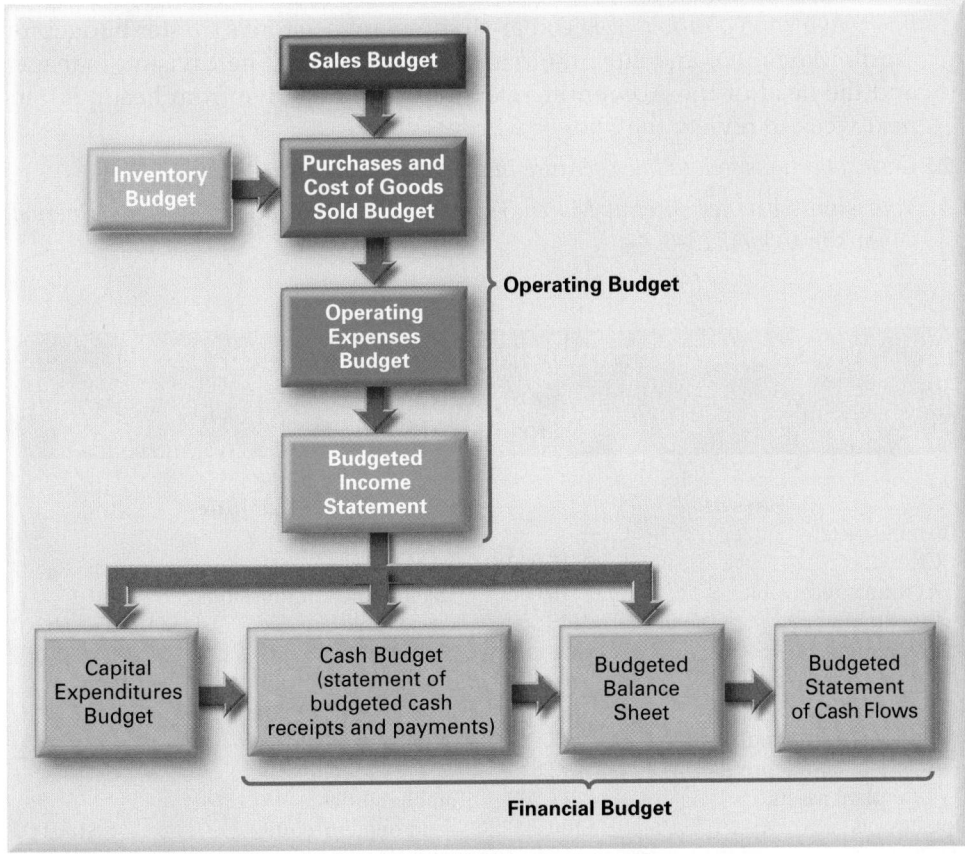

The exhibit shows that the master budget includes three types of budgets:

- The operating budget
- The capital expenditures budget
- The financial budget

Let's consider each in turn.

The first component of the **operating budget** is the sales budget, the cornerstone of the master budget. Why? Because sales affect most other components of the master budget. After projecting sales revenue, cost of goods sold, and operating expenses, management prepares the end result of the operating budget: the budgeted income statement that projects operating income for the period.

The second type of budget is the **capital expenditures budget**. This budget presents the company's plan for purchases of property, plant, equipment, and other long-term assets.

The third type is the **financial budget**. Prior components of the master budget, including the budgeted income statement and the capital expenditures budget, along with plans for raising cash and paying debts, provide information for the first element of the financial budget: the cash budget. The cash budget, which projects cash inflows and outflows, feeds into the budgeted period-end balance sheet, which in turn feeds into the budgeted statement of cash flows. These budgeted financial statements look exactly like ordinary statements. The only difference is that they list budgeted (projected) rather than actual amounts.

Operating Budget
Projects sales revenue, cost of goods sold, and operating expenses, leading to the budgeted income statement that projects operating income for the period.

Capital Expenditures Budget
A company's plan for purchases of property, plant, equipment, and other long-term assets.

Financial Budget
The cash budget (cash inflows and outflows), the budgeted period-end balance sheet, and the budgeted statement of cash flows.

Data for Whitewater Sporting Goods' Master Budget

We'll use Whitewater Sporting Goods Store No. 18 to see how managers prepare operating and financial budgets. (Chapter 26 will explain how to develop the capital expenditures budget.) Here is the information you have.

1. *You manage Whitewater Sporting Goods Store No. 18, which carries a complete line of outdoor recreation gear.* You are to prepare the store's master budget for April, May, June, and July, the main selling season. The division manager and the head of the Accounting Department will arrive from headquarters next week to review the budget with you.

2. *Cash collections follow sales because the company sells on account.*

3. *Your store's balance sheet at March 31, 20X6, the beginning of the budget period, appears in Exhibit 23-6.* ←

We examined the balance sheet in Chapter 5, pages 198–200.

Exhibit 23-6

Balance Sheet

Whitewater Sporting Goods Store No. 18

Balance Sheet
March 31, 20X6

Assets		Liabilities	
Current assets:		Current liabilities:	
Cash	$ 15,000	Accounts payable	$ 16,800
Accounts receivable	16,000	Salary and commissions	
Inventory	48,000	payable	4,250
Prepaid insurance	1,800	Total liabilities	21,050
Total current assets	80,800		
Plant assets:		**Owners' Equity**	
Equipment and fixtures	32,000	Owners' equity	78,950
Accumulated depreciation	(12,800)		
Total plant assets	19,200	Total liabilities	
Total assets	$100,000	and owners' equity	$100,000

4. *Sales in March were $40,000.* The sales force predicts these future monthly sales:

April	$50,000
May	80,000
June	60,000
July	50,000

Sales are 60% cash and 40% on credit. Whitewater collects all credit sales the month after the sale. The $16,000 of accounts receivable at March 31 arose from credit sales in March (40% of $40,000). Uncollectible accounts are insignificant.

5. *Whitewater maintains inventory equal to $20,000 plus 80% of the budgeted cost of goods sold for the following month.* Target ending inventory on July 31 is $42,400. Cost of goods sold averages 70% of sales. Inventory on March 31 is $48,000:

$$\text{March 31 inventory} = \$20,000 + 0.80 \times (0.70 \times \text{April sales of } \$50,000)$$
$$= \$20,000 + (0.80 \times \$35,000)$$
$$= \$20,000 + \$28,000 = \$48,000$$

Whitewater pays for inventory as follows: 50% during the month of purchase and 50% during the next month. Accounts payable consists of inventory purchases only. March purchases were $33,600, so accounts payable at the end of March totals $16,800 ($33,600 × 0.50).

6. *Monthly payroll has two parts: a salary of $2,500 plus sales commissions equal to 15% of sales.* The company pays half this amount during the month and half early in the following month. Therefore, at the end of each month Whitewater reports salary and commissions payable equal to half the month's payroll. The $4,250 liability on the March 31 balance sheet is half the March payroll of $8,500:

$$\text{March payroll} = \text{Salary of } \$2,500$$
$$+ \text{Sales commissions of } \$6,000 \ (0.15 \times \$40,000)$$
$$= \$8,500$$
$$\text{March 31 salary and commissions payable} = 0.50 \times \$8,500 = \$4,250$$

7. *Other monthly expenses are as follows:*

Rent expense	$2,000, paid as incurred
Depreciation expense, including truck	500
Insurance expense	200 expiration of prepaid amount
Miscellaneous expenses	5% of sales, paid as incurred

8. *Whitewater plans to purchase a used delivery truck in April for $3,000 cash.*

9. *Whitewater requires each store to maintain a minimum cash balance of $10,000 at the end of each month.* The store can borrow money on six-month notes payable of $1,000 each at an annual interest rate of 12%. Management borrows no more than the amount needed to maintain the $10,000 minimum. Notes payable require six equal monthly payments of principal, plus monthly interest on the entire unpaid principal. Borrowing and all principal and interest payments occur at the end of the month.

10. *Income taxes are the responsibility of corporate headquarters, so you can ignore tax.*

As you prepare the master budget, remember that you are developing the store's operating and financial plan for the next four months. The steps in this process may seem mechanical, but you must think carefully about pricing, product lines, job assignments, needs for additional equipment, and negotiations with banks. Successful managers use this opportunity to make decisions that affect the future course of business.

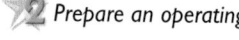

Student ResourceCD

budgeted financial statements, operating budget

⭐ *Prepare an operating budget.*

✔ **Starter 23-3**

✔ **Starter 23-5**

Preparing the Operating Budget

The first three components of the operating budget as shown in Exhibit 23-5, are:

- Sales budget (Exhibit 23-7)
- Inventory, purchases, and cost of goods sold budget (Exhibit 23-8)
- Operating expenses budget (Exhibit 23-9)

The results of these three budgets feed into the fourth element of the operating budget: the budgeted income statement (Exhibit 23-10). We consider each in turn.

The Sales Budget

The forecast of sales revenue is the cornerstone of the master budget because the level of sales affects expenses and almost all other elements of the master budget. Budgeted total sales for each product is the sale price multiplied by the expected number of units sold. The overall sales budget in Exhibit 23-7 is the sum of the budgets for the individual products. Trace the April through July total sales ($240,000) to the budgeted income statement in Exhibit 23-10.

Exhibit 23-7

Sales Budget

		Whitewater Sporting Goods Store No. 18			
		Sales Budget			
	April	**May**	**June**	**July**	**April–July Total**
Cash sales, 60%	$30,000	$48,000	$36,000	$30,000	
Credit sales, 40%	20,000	32,000	24,000	20,000	
Total sales, 100%	$50,000	$80,000	$60,000	$50,000	$240,000

The Inventory, Purchases, and Cost of Goods Sold Budget

This budget determines cost of goods sold for the budgeted income statement, ending inventory for the budgeted balance sheet, and purchases for the cash budget. The familiar cost-of-goods-sold computation specifies the relations among these items:

$$\text{Beginning inventory} + \text{Purchases} - \text{Ending inventory} = \text{Cost of goods sold}$$

Beginning inventory is known from last month's balance sheet; budgeted cost of goods sold is 70% of sales; and budgeted ending inventory is a computed amount. You must solve for the budgeted purchases figure. To do this, rearrange the previous equation to isolate purchases on the left side:

$$\text{Purchases} = \text{Cost of goods sold} + \text{Ending inventory} - \text{Beginning inventory}$$

This equation makes sense. How much does Whitewater have to purchase? Enough to cover sales and desired ending inventory, less the amount of beginning inventory already on hand at the start of the period. Exhibit 23-8 shows Whitewater's inventory, purchases, and cost of goods sold budget.

✔ Starter 23-4

✔ Starter 23-6

Exhibit 23-8 Inventory, Purchases, and Cost of Goods Sold Budget

Whitewater Sporting Goods Store No. 18
Inventory, Purchases, and Cost of Goods Sold Budget

	April	May	June	July	April–July Total
Cost of goods sold (0.70 × sales, from Sales Budget in Exhibit 23-7)	$35,000	$ 56,000	$42,000	$35,000	$168,000
+ Desired ending inventory ($20,000 + 0.80 × Cost of goods sold for the next month)	64,800*	53,600	48,000	42,400‡	
= Total inventory required	99,800	109,600	90,000	77,400	
− Beginning inventory...	(48,000)†	(64,800)	(53,600)	(48,000)	
= Purchases..	$51,800	$ 44,800	$36,400	$29,400	

* $20,000 + (0.80 × $56,000) = $64,800.
† Balance at March 31 (Exhibit 23-6).
‡ Given in item 5 on page 945.

Trace the total budgeted cost of goods sold from Exhibit 23-8 ($168,000) to the budgeted income statement in Exhibit 23-10. We will use the budgeted inventory and purchases amounts later.

The Operating Expenses Budget

Exhibit 23-9 shows the operating expense budget. Study each expense to make sure you know how it is computed. For example, sales commissions fluctuate with sales. Other expenses, such as rent and insurance, are the same each month (fixed).

Trace the April through July totals from the operating expenses budget in Exhibit 23-9 (salary and commissions of $46,000, rent expense of $8,000, and so on) to the budgeted income statement in Exhibit 23-10.

Exhibit 23-9 Operating Expenses Budget

Whitewater Sporting Goods Store No. 18
Operating Expenses Budget

	April	May	June	July	April–July Total
Salary, fixed amount (item 6, page 945)	$ 2,500	$ 2,500	$ 2,500	$ 2,500	
Commission, 15% of sales from Sales Budget (item 6, page 945 and Exhibit 23-7)	7,500	12,000	9,000	7,500	
Total salary and commissions	10,000	14,500	11,500	10,000	$46,000
Rent expense, fixed amount (item 7, page 945)	2,000	2,000	2,000	2,000	8,000
Depreciation expense, fixed amount (item 7, page 945)	500	500	500	500	2,000
Insurance expense, fixed amount (item 7, page 945)	200	200	200	200	800
Miscellaneous expenses, 5% of sales from Sales Budget (item 7, page 945 and Exhibit 23-7)	2,500	4,000	3,000	2,500	12,000
Total operating expenses	$15,200	$21,200	$17,200	$15,200	$68,800

The Budgeted Income Statement

Use the sales budget (Exhibit 23-7); the inventory, purchases, and cost of goods sold budget (Exhibit 23-8); and the operating expenses budget (Exhibit 23-9) to prepare the budgeted income statement in Exhibit 23-10. (We explain the computation of interest expense as part of the cash budget in the next section.)

Exhibit 23-10 | Budgeted Income Statement

Whitewater Sporting Goods Store No. 18

Budgeted Income Statement
Four Months Ending July 31, 20X6

		Amount		Source
Sales revenue		$240,000		Sales Budget (Exhibit 23-7)
Cost of goods sold		168,000		Inventory, Purchases, and Cost of Goods Sold
Gross profit		72,000		Budget (Exhibit 23-8)
Operating expenses:				
Salary and commissions	$46,000			Operating Expenses Budget (Exhibit 23-9)
Rent expense.	8,000			Operating Expenses Budget (Exhibit 23-9)
Depreciation expense	2,000			Operating Expenses Budget (Exhibit 23-9)
Insurance expense	800			Operating Expenses Budget (Exhibit 23-9)
Miscellaneous expenses	12,000	68,800		Operating Expenses Budget (Exhibit 23-9)
Operating income		3,200		
Interest expense		225*		Cash Budget (Exhibit 23-14)
Net income		$ 2,975		

* $90 + $75 + $60

Take this opportunity to solidify your understanding of operating budgets by carefully working the Mid-Chapter Summary Problem.

● MID-CHAPTER *Summary Problem*

TIPS

CHECK YOUR RESOURCES

Review the Whitewater Sporting Goods example. You now think July sales might be $40,000 instead of the projected $50,000 in Exhibit 23-7. You want to see how this change in sales affects the budget.

Required

Revise the sales budget (Exhibit 23-7), the inventory, purchases, and cost of goods sold budget (Exhibit 23-8), and the operating expenses budget (Exhibit 23-9). Prepare a revised budgeted income statement for the four months ended July 31, 20X6.
Note: You need not repeat the parts of the revised schedules that do not change.

Solution

Although not required, this solution repeats the budgeted amounts for April, May, and June. Revised figures appear in color for emphasis.

Whitewater Sporting Goods Store No. 18

Revised—Sales Budget

	April	May	June	July	Total
Cash sales, 60%	$30,000	$48,000	$36,000	$24,000	
Credit sales, 40%	20,000	32,000	24,000	16,000	
Total sales, 100%	$50,000	$80,000	$60,000	$40,000	$230,000

Whitewater Sporting Goods Store No. 18

Revised—Inventory, Purchases, and Cost of Goods Sold Budget

	April	May	June	July	Total
Cost of goods sold (0.70 × sales, from Revised Sales Budget)	$35,000	$56,000	$42,000	$28,000	$161,000
+ Desired ending inventory ($20,000 + 0.80 × cost of goods sold for next month)	64,800	53,600	42,400	42,400[†]	
= Total inventory required	99,800	109,600	84,400	70,400	
− Beginning inventory..	(48,000)*	(64,800)	(53,600)	(42,400)	
= Purchases	$51,800	$44,800	$30,800	$28,000	

* Balance at March 31, Exhibit 23-6.
† Given in item 5 on page 945.

Whitewater Sporting Goods Store No. 18

Revised—Operating Expenses Budget

	April	May	June	July	Total
Salary, fixed amount	$ 2,500	$ 2,500	$ 2,500	$ 2,500	
Commission, 15% of sales from Revised Sales Budget...............	7,500	12,000	9,000	6,000	
Total salary and commissions.......................	10,000	14,500	11,500	8,500	$44,500
Rent expense, fixed amount	2,000	2,000	2,000	2,000	8,000
Depreciation expense, fixed amount.............................	500	500	500	500	2,000
Insurance expense, fixed amount	200	200	200	200	800
Miscellaneous expenses, 5% of sales from Revised Sales Budget.......	2,500	4,000	3,000	2,000	11,500
Total operating expenses..........................	$15,200	$21,200	$17,200	$13,200	$66,800

Whitewater Sporting Goods Store No. 18

Revised Budgeted Income Statement
Four Months Ending July 31, 20X6

	Amount		Source
Sales revenue		$230,000	Revised Sales Budget
Cost of goods sold		161,000	Revised Inventory, Purchases, and Cost of Goods Sold Budget
Gross profit		69,000	
Operating expenses:			
Salary and commissions	$44,500		Revised Operating Expenses Budget
Rent expense...................	8,000		Revised Operating Expenses Budget
Depreciation expense............	2,000		Revised Operating Expenses Budget
Insurance expense	800		Revised Operating Expenses Budget
Miscellaneous expenses	11,500	66,800	Revised Operating Expenses Budget
Operating income..................		2,200	
Interest expense		225	Revised Cash Budget (page 964)
Net income		$ 1,975	

☐ Why Managers Use Budgets
☐ Preparing the Master Budget
☐ Preparing the Operating Budget
■ **Preparing the Financial Budget**
☐ Using Information Technology
☐ Responsibility Accounting
☐ Appendix: Departmental Accounting

Preparing the Financial Budget

Armed with a clear understanding of Whitewater's operating budget, you're now ready to prepare the financial budget. Exhibit 23-5 shows that the financial budget includes the cash budget, the budgeted balance sheet, and the budgeted statement of cash flows. We start with the cash budget.

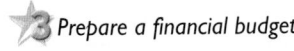
Prepare a financial budget

Preparing the Cash Budget

The **cash budget**, or **statement of budgeted cash receipts and payments**, details how the business expects to go from the beginning cash balance to the desired ending balance. The cash budget has four major parts:

- Cash collections from customers (Exhibit 23-11)
- Cash payments for purchases (Exhibit 23-12)
- Cash payments for operating expenses (Exhibit 23-13)
- Cash payments for capital expenditures (for example, the $3,000 capital expenditure to acquire the delivery truck)

Cash collections and payments depend on revenues and expenses, which appear in the operating budget. This is why you cannot prepare the cash budget until you have finished the operating budget.

BUDGETED CASH COLLECTIONS FROM CUSTOMERS   Exhibit 23-11 shows that April's budgeted cash collections consist of two parts: (1) April's cash sales from the sales budget in Exhibit 23-7 ($30,000) plus (2) collections of March's credit sales ($16,000 from the March 31 balance sheet, Exhibit 23-6). Trace April's $46,000 ($30,000 + $16,000) total cash collections to the cash budget in Exhibit 23-14.

✔ Starter 23-7

✔ Starter 23-9

Exhibit 23-11 | Budgeted Cash Collections

Whitewater Sporting Goods Store No. 18

Budgeted Cash Collections from Customers

	April	May	June	July	April–July Total
Cash sales from Sales Budget (Exhibit 23-7)	$30,000	$48,000	$36,000	$30,000	
Collections of last month's credit sales, from Sales Budget (Exhibit 23-7)	16,000*	20,000	32,000	24,000	
Total collections	$46,000	$68,000	$68,000	$54,000	$236,000

* March 31 accounts receivable, Exhibit 23-6.

BUDGETED CASH PAYMENTS FOR PURCHASES   Exhibit 23-12 uses the inventory, purchases, and cost of goods sold budget from Exhibit 23-8 and payment information from item 5 to compute budgeted cash payments for purchases of inventory. April's cash payments for purchases consist of two parts: (1) payment of 50% of March's purchases ($16,800 accounts payable balance from the March 31 balance sheet, Exhibit 23-6) plus (2) payment for 50% of April's purchases ($25,900 = 50% × $51,800 from Exhibit 23-8). Trace April's $42,700 ($16,800 + $25,900) cash outlay for purchases to the cash budget in Exhibit 23-14.

✔ Starter 23-8

Exhibit 23-12 | Budgeted Cash Payments for Purchases

Whitewater Sporting Goods Store No. 18

Budgeted Cash Payments for Purchases

	April	May	June	July	April–July Total
50% of last month's purchases from Inventory, Purchases, and Cost of Goods Sold Budget (Exhibit 23-8)	$16,800*	$25,900	$22,400	$18,200	
50% of this month's purchases from Inventory, Purchases, and Cost of Goods Sold Budget (Exhibit 23-8)	25,900	22,400	18,200	14,700	
Total payments for purchases	$42,700	$48,300	$40,600	$32,900	$164,500

*March 31 accounts payable, Exhibit 23-6.

Budgeted Cash Payments for Operating Expenses
Exhibit 23-13 uses items 6 and 7 and the operating expenses budget (Exhibit 23-9) to compute cash payments for operating expenses. April's cash payments for operating expenses consist of four items:

Payment of 50% of March's salary and commissions (from March 31 balance sheet, Exhibit 23-6).....................	$ 4,250
Payment of 50% of April's salary and commissions (50% × $10,000, Exhibit 23-9).....................................	5,000
Payment of rent expense (Exhibit 23-9)...........................	2,000
Payment of miscellaneous expenses (Exhibit 23-9).................	2,500
Total April cash payments for operating expenses.................	$13,750

Follow April's $13,750 cash payments for operating expenses from Exhibit 23-13 to the cash budget in Exhibit 23-14.

Exhibit 23-13   Budgeted Cash Payments for Operating Expenses

Whitewater Sporting Goods Store No. 18
Budgeted Cash Payments for Operating Expenses

	April	May	June	July	April–July Total
Salary and commissions:					
50% of last month's expenses, from					
Operating Expenses Budget (Exhibit 23-9)......................	$ 4,250*	$ 5,000	$ 7,250	$ 5,750	
50% of this month's expenses, from					
Operating Expenses Budget (Exhibit 23-9)......................	5,000	7,250	5,750	5,000	
Total salary and commissions	9,250	12,250	13,000	10,750	
Rent expense, from Operating Expenses					
Budget (Exhibit 23-9)...	2,000	2,000	2,000	2,000	
Miscellaneous expenses, from Operating					
Expenses Budget (Exhibit 23-9).................................	2,500	4,000	3,000	2,500	
Total payments for operating expenses	$13,750	$18,250	$18,000	$15,250	$65,250

*March 31 salary and commissions payable, Exhibit 23-6.

> Why are depreciation expense and insurance expense from the operating expenses budget (Exhibit 23-9) *excluded* from the budgeted cash payments for operating expenses in Exhibit 23-13?
>
> *Answer:* These expenses do not require cash outlays in the current period. Depreciation is the periodic write-off of the cost of the equipment and fixtures that Whitewater acquired previously. Insurance expense is the expiration of prepaid insurance.

✔ **Starter 23-10**

The Cash Budget
To prepare the cash budget in Exhibit 23-14, start with the beginning cash balance and add the budgeted cash collections from Exhibit 23-11 to determine the cash available. Then subtract cash payments for purchases (Exhibit 23-12), operating expenses (Exhibit 23-13), and any capital expenditures. This yields the ending cash balance before financing.

Item 9 (on page 945) states that Whitewater requires a minimum cash balance of $10,000. April's $1,550 budgeted cash balance before financing falls $8,450 short of the minimum required ($10,000 – $1,550). Because Whitewater borrows in $1,000 notes, the company will have to borrow $9,000 to cover April's expected shortfall. The budgeted ending cash balance equals the "ending cash balance before financ-

Exhibit 23-14 Cash Budget

Whitewater Sporting Goods Store No. 18				
Cash Budget				
Four Months Ending July 31, 20X6				

	April	May	June	July
Beginning cash balance	$15,000*	$10,550	$10,410	$18,235
Cash collections (Exhibit 23-11)	46,000	68,000	68,000	54,000
Cash available	$61,000	$78,550	$78,410	$72,235
Cash payments:				
Purchases of inventory (Exhibit 23-12)	$42,700	$48,300	$40,600	$32,900
Operating expenses (Exhibit 23-13)	13,750	18,250	18,000	15,250
Purchase of delivery truck (item 8, page 945)	3,000	—	—	—
Total cash payments	59,450	66,550	58,600	48,150
(1) Ending cash balance before financing	1,550	12,000	19,810	24,085
Less: Minimum cash balance desired	(10,000)	(10,000)	(10,000)	(10,000)
Cash excess (deficiency)	$(8,450)	$ 2,000	$ 9,810	$14,085
Financing of cash deficiency (see notes *a–c*):				
Borrowing (at end of month)	$ 9,000			
Principal payments (at end of month)		$ (1,500)	$(1,500)	$(1,500)
Interest expense (at 12% annually)		(90)	(75)	(60)
(2) Total effects of financing	9,000	(1,590)	(1,575)	(1,560)
Ending cash balance (1) + (2)	$10,550	$10,410	$18,235	$22,525

*March 31 cash balance, Exhibit 23-6.
Notes
[a] Borrowing occurs in multiples of $1,000 and only for the amount needed to maintain a minimum cash balance of $10,000.
[b] Monthly principal payments: $9,000 ÷ 6 = $1,500.
[c] Interest expense:
  May: $9,000 × (0.12 × 1/12) = $90
  June: ($9,000 − $1,500) × (0.12 × 1/12) = $75
  July: ($9,000 − $1,500 − $1,500) × (0.12 × 1/12) = $60

ing," adjusted for the total effects of the financing (a $9,000 inflow in April). Exhibit 23-14 shows that Whitewater expects to end April with $10,550 of cash ($1,550 + $9,000). The exhibit also shows the cash balance at the end of May, June, and July.

Item 9 states that Whitewater must repay the notes in six equal installments. Thus, May through July show principal repayments of $1,500 ($9,000 ÷ 6) per month. Whitewater also pays interest expense on the outstanding notes payable, at 12% per year. The June interest expense is $75 [($9,000 principal − $1,500 repayment at the end of May) × 12% × 1/12]. Interest expense for the four months totals $225 ($90 + $75 + $60). This interest expense appears on the budgeted income statement in Exhibit 23-10.

The cash balance at the end of July ($22,525) is the cash balance in the July 31 budgeted balance sheet in Exhibit 23-15.

The Budgeted Balance Sheet

To prepare the budgeted balance sheet, project each asset, liability, and owners' equity account based on the plans outlined in the previous exhibits.

Study the budgeted balance sheet in Exhibit 23-15 to make certain you understand the computation of each figure. For example, on the budgeted balance sheet as of July 31, 20X6, budgeted cash equals the ending cash balance from the cash budget in Exhibit 23-14 ($22,525). Accounts receivable as of July 31 equal July's credit sales of $20,000, shown in the sales budget (Exhibit 23-7). July 31 inventory of $42,400 is July's desired ending inventory in the inventory, purchases, and cost of goods sold budget in Exhibit 23-8. Detailed computations for each of the other accounts appear in Exhibit 23-15.

Exhibit 23-15 Budgeted Balance Sheet

Whitewater Sporting Goods Store No. 18
Budgeted Balance Sheet
July 31, 20X6

Assets

Current assets:

Cash (Exhibit 23-14)	$22,525	
Accounts receivable (Sales Budget, Exhibit 23-7)	20,000	
Inventory (Inventory, Purchases, and Cost of Goods Sold Budget, Exhibit 23-8)	42,400	
Prepaid insurance (beginning balance of $1,800 – $800* for four months' expiration; Operating Expenses Budget, Exhibit 23-9)	1,000	
Total current assets		$ 85,925

Plant assets:

Equipment and fixtures (beginning balance of $32,000* + $3,000 truck acquisition; item 8, page 945)	$35,000	
Accumulated depreciation (beginning balance of $12,800* + $2,000 for four months' depreciation; Operating Expenses Budget, Exhibit 23-9)	(14,800)	
Total plant assets		20,200
Total assets		$106,125

Liabilities

Current liabilities:

Accounts payable (0.50 × July purchases of $29,400; Inventory, Purchases, and Cost of Goods Sold Budget, Exhibit 23-8)	$14,700	
Short-term note payable ($9,000 – $4,500 paid back; Exhibit 23-14)	4,500	
Salary and commissions payable (0.50 × July expenses of $10,000; Operating Expenses Budget, Exhibit 23-9)	5,000	
Total liabilities		$ 24,200

Owners' Equity

Owners' equity (beginning balance of $78,950* + $2,975 net income; Exhibit 23-10)		81,925
Total liabilities and owners' equity		$106,125

*March 31, 20X6, Balance Sheet, Exhibit 23-6

The Budgeted Statement of Cash Flows

The final step is preparing the budgeted statement of cash flows. Use the information from the schedules of cash collections and payments, the cash budget, and the beginning balance of cash to project cash flows from operating, investing, and financing activities. Take time to study Exhibit 23-16, and make sure you understand the origin of each figure.

Getting Employees to Accept the Budget

What is the most important part of Whitewater Sporting Goods' budgeting system? Despite all the numbers we have crunched, it is not the mechanics. It is getting managers and employees to accept the budget, so Whitewater can reap the planning, coordination, and control benefits illustrated in Exhibit 23-3.

Few people enjoy having their work monitored and evaluated. So if managers use the budget as a benchmark to evaluate employees' performance, managers must first motivate employees to accept the budget's goals. Here's how they can do it:

- Managers must support the budget themselves, or no one else will.
- Show employees how budgets can help them achieve better results.
- Have employees participate in developing the budget.

Whitewater Sporting Goods Store No. 18
Budgeted Statement of Cash Flows
Four Months Ending July 31, 20X6

Cash flows from operating activities:		
Receipts:		
Collections from customers (Exhibit 23-11)	$ 236,000	
Total cash receipts.		$236,000
Payments:		
Purchases of inventory (Exhibit 23-12)	$ (164,500)	
Operating expenses (Exhibit 23-13).	(65,250)	
Payment of interest expense (Exhibits 23-14 and 23-10).	(225)	
Total cash payments.		(229,975)
Net cash inflow from operating activities.		6,025
Cash flows from investing activities:		
Acquisition of delivery truck (item 8, page 945)	$ (3,000)	
Net cash outflow from investing activities.		(3,000)
Cash flows from financing activities:		
Proceeds from issuance of notes payable (Exhibit 23-14).	$ 9,000	
Payment of notes payable (Exhibit 23-14).	(4,500)	
Net cash inflow from financing activities.		4,500
Net increase in cash		$ 7,525
Cash balance, April 1, 20X6 (Exhibit 23-6 and 23-14)		15,000
Cash balance, July 31, 20X6 (Exhibits 23-14 and 23-15)		$ 22,525

But these principles alone are not enough. As the manager of Store No. 18, your performance is evaluated by comparing actual results to budget. When you develop your store's budget, you may be tempted to build in *slack*. For example, you might want to budget fewer sales and higher purchases than you expect. This increases the chance that actual performance will be better than the budget and that you will receive a good evaluation. But adding slack into the budget makes it less accurate—and less useful for planning and control. When the division manager and the head of the Accounting Department arrive from headquarters next week, they will scour your budget to find any slack you may have inserted.

Student ResourceCD

Enterprise Resource Planning, master budget, sensitivity analysis

Use sensitivity analysis in budgeting

Using Information Technology for Sensitivity Analysis and Rolling Up Unit Budgets

Exhibits 23-7 through 23-16 show that the manager must prepare many calculations to develop the master budget for just one of the retail stores in the Whitewater Sporting Goods merchandising chain. No wonder managers embrace information technology to help prepare budgets! Let's see how advances in information technology make it more cost-effective for managers to:

- Conduct sensitivity analysis on their own unit's budget
- Roll up individual unit budgets to create the companywide budget

Sensitivity Analysis

The master budget models the company's *planned* activities. Top management pays special attention to ensure that the results of the budgeted income statement (Exhibit 23-10), the cash budget (Exhibit 23-14), and the budgeted balance sheet (Exhibit 23-15) support key strategies.

But actual results often differ from plans, so management wants to know how budgeted income and cash flows would change if key assumptions turned out to be incorrect. Chapter 22 defined *sensitivity analysis* as a *what-if* technique that asks *what* a result will be *if* a predicted amount is not achieved or *if* an underlying assumption changes. → *What if* the stock market crashes? How will this affect Amazon.com's sales? Will it have to postpone the planned expansion in Asia and Europe? *What* will be Whitewater Store No. 18's cash balance on July 31 *if* the period's sales are 45% cash, not 60% cash? Will Whitewater have to borrow more cash?

Sensitivity analysis is introduced in Chapter 22, page 910.

Most companies use computer spreadsheet programs (or special budget software) to prepare master budget schedules and statements. In fact, one of the earliest spreadsheet programs was developed by graduate business students who realized that computers could take the drudgery out of hand-computed master budget sensitivity analyses. Today, managers answer what-if questions simply by changing a number. At the press of a key, the computer screen flashes a revised budget that includes all the effects of the change.

Technology makes it cost-effective to perform more-comprehensive sensitivity analyses. Armed with a better understanding of how changes in sales and costs are likely to affect the company's bottom line, today's managers can react quickly if key assumptions underlying the master budget (such as sales price or quantity) turn out to be wrong.

Rolling Up Individual Unit Budgets into the Companywide Budget

Whitewater Sporting Goods Store No. 18 is just one of the company's many retail stores. As Exhibit 23-17 shows, Whitewater's headquarters must roll up the budget data from Store No. 18, along with budgets for each of the other stores, to prepare the companywide master budget. This roll-up can be difficult for companies whose units use different spreadsheets to prepare the budgets.

Companies like Sunoco turn to budget-management software to solve this problem. Often designed as a component of the company's Enterprise Resource Planning (ERP) system (or data warehouse), this software helps managers develop and analyze budgets.

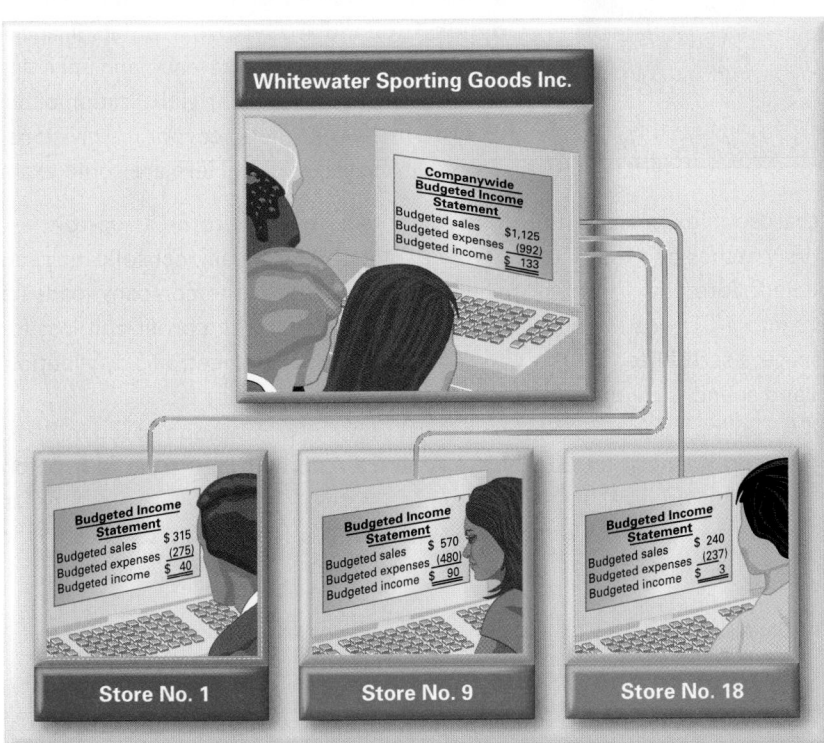

Exhibit 23-17

Rolling Up Individual Unit Budgets into the Companywide Budget

Across the globe, managers sit at their desks, log into the company's budget system, and enter their numbers. The software allows them to conduct sensitivity analyses on their own unit's data. When the manager is satisfied with her budget, she can enter it in the companywide budget with the click of a mouse. Her unit's budget automatically rolls up with budgets from all other units around the world.

Whether at headquarters or on the road, top executives can log into the budget system and conduct their own sensitivity analyses on individual units' budgets or on the companywide budget. Managers can spend less time compiling and summarizing data and more time analyzing it to ensure that the budget leads the company to achieve its key strategic goals.

Consider two budget situations: (1) Whitewater Sporting Goods' marketing analysts produce a near-certain forecast for four-month sales of $4,500,000 for the company's 20 stores. (2) Much uncertainty exists about the period's sales. The most likely amount is $4,500,000, but marketing considers any amount between $3,900,000 and $5,100,000 to be possible. How will the budgeting process differ in these two circumstances?

Answer: Whitewater will prepare a master budget for the expected sales level of $4,500,000 in either case. Because of the uncertainty in situation 2, executives will want a set of budgets covering the entire range of volume rather than a single level. Whitewater's managers may prepare budgets based on sales of, say, $3,900,000, $4,200,000, $4,500,000, $4,800,000, and $5,100,000. These budgets will help managers plan for sales levels throughout the forecasted range.

Enterprise Resource Planning Keeps Fossil's Budget from Becoming a Fossil

Pioneering companies are shelving their Excel spreadsheets in favor of budgeting and planning software integrated into their Enterprise Resource Planning (ERP) systems. The software, from companies such as Cognos, Inc., and Adaytum, Inc., lets financial managers continuously update revenue and spending forecasts. With the ever-increasing globalization of business, ERP systems help far-flung corporate divisions speak the same financial language. Here are some examples:

- Richardson, Texas, based Fossil, Inc., wants its budgets to be as up-to-the-minute as its watches and accessories. Now, rather than manually consolidating sales and spending forecasts from a host of Excel spreadsheets, the company loads its numbers into a Cognos system, which immediately generates a profit-and-loss forecast. Managers scrutinize the report by product line, department, and distribution channel and spend their time analyzing results.
- AXA Corp., a 2,700-employee financial services corporation based in Paris, owns divisions in Western Europe, North America, Asia, and the Pacific Rim. Before ERP, each division used a different accounting system, and multiple spreadsheets were consolidated by hand. With ERP, AXA has reduced the time it takes to close its books to four days from two weeks, and it processes 350 currencies in a single system.

Based on: Russ Banhan, "Better Budgets," *Journal of Accountancy*, February 2000, pp. 37–40. J. W. Dysart, "Planning for Real-Time Information," *Banking Strategies*, May/June 2000, pp. 6–10. Louisa Wah, "Give ERP a Chance," *Management Review*, March 2000, pp. 20–24. Rick Whiting, "Crystal-Ball Glance into Fiscal Future," *Information Week*, July 22, 2002, p. 37. Jennifer Jaroneczyk, "ERP Streamlines Global Finances," *Internet World*, September 2002, pp. 22–24.

Accounting.com

Responsibility Accounting

You've now seen how managers set strategic goals and then develop plans and budget resources for activities that will help reach those goals. Let's look more closely at how managers *use* budgets to control operations.

Each manager is responsible for planning and controlling some part of the firm's activities. A **responsibility center** is a part or subunit of an organization whose manager is accountable for specific activities. Lower-level managers are often responsible for budgeting and controlling costs of a single value-chain function. For example, one manager is responsible for planning and controlling the *production* of Pace picante sauce at the plant, while another is responsible for planning and controlling the *distribution* of the product to customers. Lower-level managers report to higher-level managers, who have broader responsibilities. Managers in charge of production and distribution report to senior managers responsible for profits (revenues minus costs) earned by an entire product line.

Four Types of Responsibility Centers

Responsibility accounting is a system for evaluating the performance of each responsibility center and its manager. Responsibility accounting performance reports compare plans (budgets) with actions (actual results) for each center. Superiors then evaluate how well each manager: (1) used the budgeted resources to achieve the responsibility center's goals and thereby (2) controlled the operations for which he or she was responsible. Exhibit 23-18 illustrates four types of responsibility centers.

 Student ResourceCD

responsibility accounting, responsibility center

5 *Prepare performance reports for responsibility centers*

Responsibility Center
A part or subunit of an organization whose manager is accountable for specific activities.

Responsibility Accounting
A system for evaluating the performance of each responsibility center and its manager.

Exhibit 23-18   Four Types of Responsibility Centers

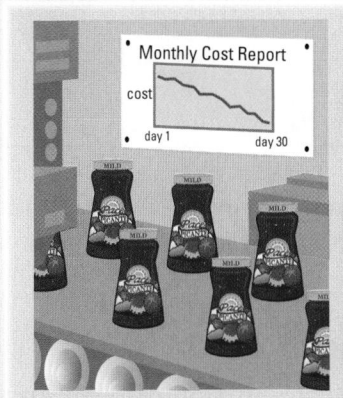

In a **cost center**, such as a production line for Pace picante sauce, managers are responsible for costs.

In a **revenue center**, such as the Midwest sales region, managers are responsible for generating sales revenue.

In a **profit center**, such as a line of products, managers are responsible for generating income.

In an **investment center**, such as Campbell Soups and Sauces division, managers are responsible for income and invested capital.

---

1. *In a cost center, managers are accountable for costs (expenses) only.* Manufacturing operations like the Pace picante sauce production lines are cost centers. The line foreman controls costs by ensuring that employees work efficiently. The foreman is *not* responsible for generating revenues, because he is not involved in selling the product. The plant manager evaluates the foreman on his ability to control *costs* by comparing actual costs to budgeted costs. All else being equal (for example, holding quality constant), the foreman is likely to receive a more favorable evaluation if actual costs are less than budgeted costs.

✔ **Starter 23-11**

2. *In a revenue center, managers are primarily accountable for revenues*. Examples include the Midwest and Southeast sales regions of businesses like Pace Foods and Reebok. Such managers of revenue centers may also be responsible for the costs of their own sales operations. Revenue center performance reports compare actual with budgeted revenues and may include the costs incurred by the revenue center itself. All else being equal, the manager is likely to receive a more-favorable evaluation if actual revenues exceed the budget.

3. *In a profit center, managers are accountable for both revenues and costs (expenses) and, therefore, profits*. The (higher-level) manager responsible for the entire Pace product line would be accountable for increasing sales revenue *and* controlling costs to achieve the profit goals. Profit center reports include both revenues and expenses to show the profit center's income. Superiors evaluate the manager's performance by comparing actual revenues, expenses, and profits to the budget. All else being equal, the manager is likely to receive a more-favorable evaluation if actual profits exceed the budget.

4. *In an investment center, managers are accountable for investments, revenues, and costs (expenses)*. Examples include the Saturn division of General Motors and the North American Sauces and Beverages Division (which includes Pace Foods) of Campbell Soup. Managers of investment centers are responsible for (1) generating sales, (2) controlling expenses, and (3) managing the amount of investment required to earn the income (revenues minus expenses). For example, Bell South Corp considers its information technology (IT) department an investment center. Managers are responsible for keeping IT costs within the budget while using the department's assets to generate revenue from projects such as Bell South's FastAccess DSL service or its e-business operations.

See Chapter 18, p. 721, for discussion of rate of return on total assets. Top management often evaluates investment center managers based on return on investment (ROI). ← When evaluating a division, the return on investment is often computed as:

$$ROI = \frac{\text{Division's operating income}}{\text{Division's average total assets}}$$

All else being equal, the manager will receive a more-favorable evaluation if the division's actual return on investment exceeds the budgeted return on investment.

Responsibility Accounting Performance Reports

Exhibit 23-19 shows how an organization like Campbell Soup Company (the parent company of Pace Foods) may assign responsibility.

At the top level, the CEO oversees each of the four divisions. Division managers generally have broad responsibility, including deciding how to use assets to maximize return on investment. Most companies consider divisions as *investment centers*.

Each division manager supervises all the product lines in that division. Exhibit 23-19 shows that the VP of North American Sauces and Beverages oversees the Prego Italian sauces, Pace Mexican sauces, V8 juice, and Franco-American canned pasta product lines. Product lines are generally considered *profit centers*. Thus, the manager of the Pace product line is responsible for evaluating lower-level managers of both

- *Cost centers* (such as plants that make Pace products) and
- *Revenue centers* (such as managers responsible for selling Pace products).

Exhibit 23-19 Partial Organization Chart

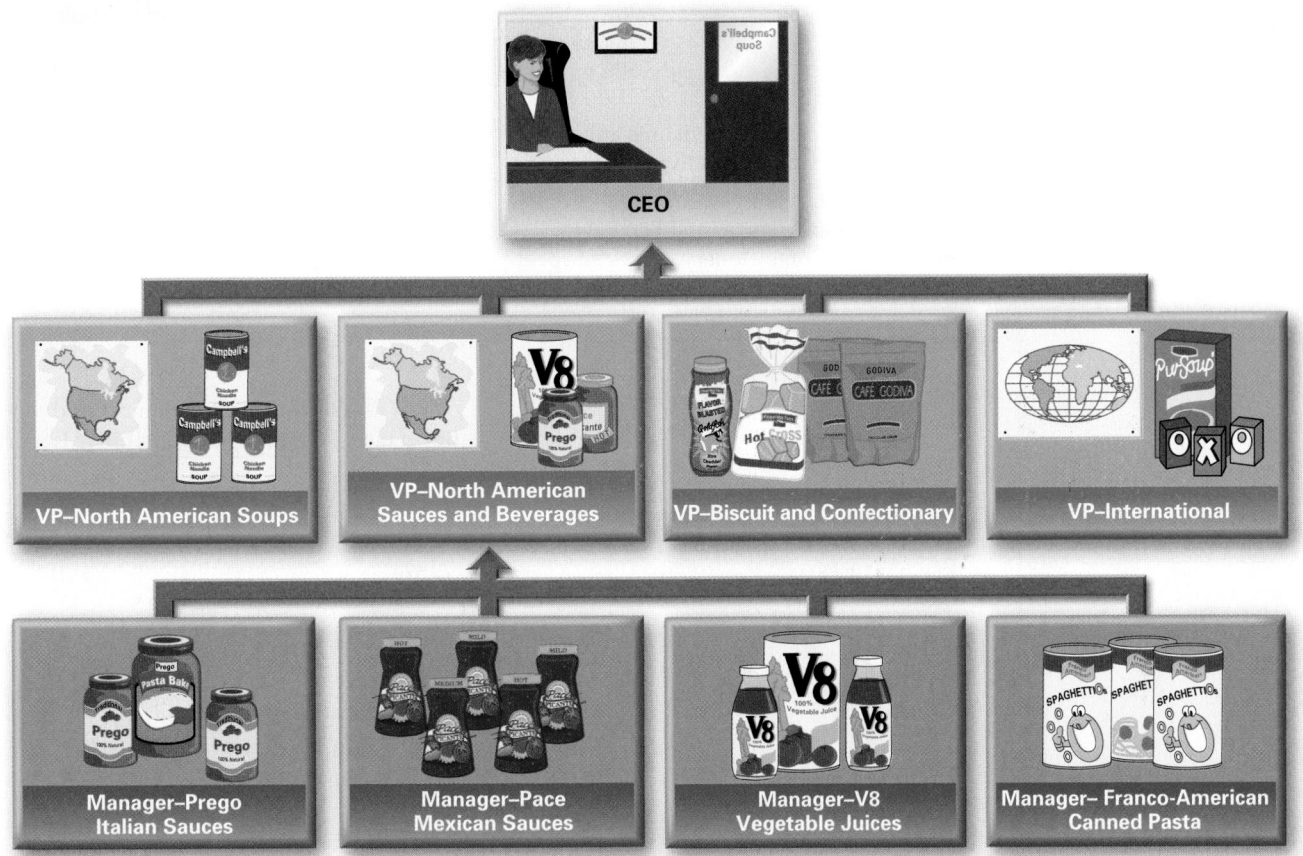

Exhibit 23-20 on the next page illustrates responsibility accounting performance reports for each level of management shown in Exhibit 23-19. Exhibit 23-20 uses assumed numbers to illustrate reports like those

- The CEO may use to evaluate divisions
- The divisional VPs may use to evaluate individual product lines
- The product-line managers may use to evaluate the development, production, marketing, and distribution of their products

At each level, the reports compare actual results with the budget.

Start with the lowest level and move to the top. Follow the $25 million budgeted operating income from the Mexican sauces product-line report to the report of the VP–North American Sauces and Beverages. The VP's report summarizes the budgeted and actual operating incomes for each of the four product lines he supervises.

Now trace the $70 million budgeted operating income from the VP's report to the CEO's report. The CEO's report includes a summary of each division's budgeted and actual profits, as well as the costs incurred by corporate headquarters, which are not assigned to any of the divisions.

MANAGEMENT BY EXCEPTION The variances reported in Exhibit 23-20 aid **management by exception**, which directs executives' attention to important differences between actual and budgeted amounts. Look at the CEO's report. The International Soups and Sauces Division's actual operating income of $34 million is very close to the budgeted $35 million. Unless there are other signs of trouble, the CEO will not waste time investigating such a small variance.

Management by Exception
Directs management's attention to important differences between actual and budgeted amounts.

Exhibit 23-20

Responsibility Accounting Performance Reports

✔ Starter 23-12

✔ Starter 23-13

✔ Starter 23-14

Responsibility Accounting Performance Reports at Various Levels (In Millions of Dollars)

CEO's Quarterly Responsibility Report

Operating Income of Divisions and Corporate Headquarters Expense	Budget	Actual	Variance Favorable/ (Unfavorable)
North American Soups	$218	$209	$ (9)
North American Sauces and Beverages...	70	84	14
Biscuits and Confectionery	79	87	8
International Soups and Sauces	35	34	(1)
Corporate Headquarters Expense	(33)	(29)	4
Operating Income....................	$369	$385	$16

VP—North American Sauces and Beverages, Quarterly Responsibility Report

Operating Income of Product Lines	Budget	Actual	Variance Favorable/ (Unfavorable)
Italian Sauces.........................	$20	$18	$ (2)
Mexican Sauces.......................	25	38	13
Vegetable Juices......................	10	15	5
Canned Pastas........................	15	13	(2)
Operating Income....................	$70	$84	$14

Manager—Mexican Sauces Quarterly Responsibility Report

Revenues and Expenses	Budget	Actual	Variance Favorable/ (Unfavorable)
Sales revenue........................	$ 80	$ 84	$ 4
Cost of goods sold	(36)	(30)	6
Gross profit	44	54	10
Marketing expenses	(12)	(9)	3
Research and development expenses	(2)	(3)	(1)
Other expenses	(5)	(4)	1
Operating income....................	$25	$38	$13

In contrast, the North American Sauces and Beverages Division earned much more profit than budgeted. The CEO will want to know why. Suppose the VP of the division believes a national sales promotion was especially effective. That promotion may be repeated or adapted by other divisions. To identify the reason for exceptional results, so that other parts of the organization may benefit, is one reason why managers investigate large favorable variances (not just large unfavorable ones). Another is to ensure that employees are not skimping on ingredients, marketing, or R&D, which could hurt the company's long-term success.

A CEO who received the report at the top of Exhibit 23-20 would likely concentrate on improving the North American Soups Division, because its actual income fell $9 million below budget. The CEO will want to see which product lines caused the shortfall, so that he or she and the VP of the division can work together to correct any problems.

Exhibit 23-20 also shows how summarized data may hide problems. Although the North American Sauces and Beverages Division as a whole performed well, the Italian sauces and canned pasta lines did not. If the CEO received only the condensed report at the top of the exhibit, he or she would rely on division managers to spot and correct problems in individual product lines.

NOT A QUESTION OF BLAME Responsibility accounting assigns managers responsibility for their unit's actions and provides a way to evaluate both their and the unit's performance. But superiors should not misuse responsibility accounting to find fault or place blame. The question is not "Who is to blame for an unfavorable variance?" Instead, the question is "Who can best explain why a specific variance occurred?" Consider the North American Soups Division in Exhibit 23-20. Suppose a tornado devastated the primary production plant. It may be that the remaining plants operated very efficiently, and this efficiency kept the income variance down to $9 million. If so, the North American Soups Division and its VP may actually have done a good job.

The following Decision Guidelines review budgets and how managers use them in responsibility accounting. Take a moment to study these guidelines before working the summary review problem.

Decision Guidelines

THE MASTER BUDGET AND RESPONSIBILITY ACCOUNTING

Amazon.com's initial strategy was to "get big fast." But without a budget, spending got out of control. So founder and CEO Jeff Bezos added a second strategic goal—to become the world's most cost-efficient high-quality e-tailer. Today, Amazon's managers use budgets to help reach both the growth and cost-efficiency goals. Let's consider some of the decisions Amazon made as it set up its budgeting process.

Decision	Guidelines
What benefits should Amazon.com expect to obtain from developing a budget?	Requires managers to *plan* how to increase sales and how to cut costs
	Promotes *coordination and communication*, such as communicating the importance of the cost-efficiency goal
	Provides a *benchmark* that motivates employees and helps managers evaluate how well employees contributed to the sales growth and cost-efficiency goals
In what order should Amazon's managers prepare the components of the master budget?	Begin with the *operating budget*. • Start with the *sales budget*, which feeds into all other budgets. • The sales and *ending inventory budgets* determine the *purchases and cost of goods sold budget*. • The sales, cost of goods sold, and *operating expense budgets* determine the *budgeted income statement*.
	Next, prepare the *capital expenditures budget*. Finally, prepare the *financial budget*. • Start with the *cash budget*. • The cash budget provides the ending cash balance for the *budgeted balance sheet* and the details for the *budgeted statement of cash flows*.

Decision Guidelines (continued)

Decision	Guidelines
What extra steps should Amazon take given the uncertainty of Internet-based sales forecasts?	Prepare a *sensitivity analysis* and project budgeted results at different sales levels.
How does Amazon compute budgeted purchases?	$$\frac{\text{Beginning}}{\text{inventory}} + \text{Purchases} - \frac{\text{Ending}}{\text{inventory}} = \frac{\text{Cost of}}{\text{goods sold}}$$ so $$\text{Purchases} = \frac{\text{Cost of}}{\text{goods sold}} + \frac{\text{Ending}}{\text{inventory}} - \frac{\text{Beginning}}{\text{inventory}}$$
What kind of a responsibility center does each manager supervise?	Cost center: Manager is responsible for costs. Revenue center: Manager is responsible for revenues. Profit center: Manager is responsible for both revenues and costs, and therefore profits. Investment center: Manager is responsible for revenues, costs, and the amount of the investment required to earn the income.
How to evaluate managers?	Compare actual performance with the budget for the manager's responsibility center. *Management by exception* focuses on large differences between budgeted and actual results.

Excel Application Exercise

Goal: Create a spreadsheet to prepare the sales budget and the inventory, purchases, and cost of goods sold budget for a small business.

Scenario: After reading about how **Amazon** uses budgets to help manage its business, you decide that your own business could use them. You estimate the following *total* sales for the coming year: January, $9,000; February, $9,100; March, $8,900; and April, $8,800. Cash sales represent 80% of your business, and your cost of goods sold is 60% of sales revenue. Ending inventory as of December 31 of last year was $1,620, and your desired ending inventory each month is 30% of the next month's cost of goods sold.

When you have completed your worksheet, answer the following questions:

1. What is the total inventory required (e.g., the third line in Exhibit 23-8) in January, in February, and in March?
2. What is the desired ending inventory for March?
3. What happens to purchases each month if February total sales drop to $8,100?

Step-by-Step:

1. Open a new Excel spreadsheet.
2. In column A, create a bold-faced heading as follows:
   a. Chapter 23 Excel Application Exercise
   b. Sales and Inventory, Purchases, and COGS Budgets
   c. Today's Date
3. Two rows down, enter the label, "Total January Sales." In column B, enter the sales amount. Underneath January sales, enter a row for February sales. Do the same for March and April.
4. Two rows down from the sales line items, enter the label "Cash Sales as a Percentage of Total Sales." In column B, enter the percentage given in the scenario. Then, in column A one row down, enter the label, "Cost of Goods Sold Percentage." In column B, enter the percentage. Two rows down, enter the label "Beginning Inventory as of January 1" in column A. Enter the appropriate amount in column B. One row down in column A enter the label, "Desired Ending Inventory Percentage." In column B, enter the percentage given.
5. Move down two rows. Using Exhibit 23-7 as your guide, create a sales budget for your company. All dollar amounts should be formulas. Format as needed.
6. Move down two rows. Using Exhibit 23-8 as your guide, create an inventory, purchases, and COGS budget for your company. Use formulas for all dollar amounts. Format as needed. *Hint:* The desired ending inventory in March requires the use of the April sales figure.
7. Save your worksheet and print a copy for your files.

END-OF-CHAPTER *Summary Problem*

CHECK YOUR RESOURCES

Continue the revised Whitewater Sporting Goods illustration from the mid-chapter summary problem. Now that you think July sales will be $40,000 instead of $50,000, as projected in Exhibit 23-7, how will this affect the financial budget?

Required:

Revise the schedule of budgeted cash collections (Exhibit 23-11), the schedule of budgeted cash payments for purchases (Exhibit 23-12), and the schedule of budgeted cash payments for operating expenses (Exhibit 23-13). Prepare a revised cash budget, a revised budgeted balance sheet at July 31, 20X6, and a revised budgeted statement of cash flows for the four months ended July 31, 20X6. *Note:* You need not repeat the parts of the revised schedule that do not change.

Solution

Although not required, this solution repeats the budgeted amounts for April, May, and June. Revised figures appear in color for emphasis.

Whitewater Sporting Goods Store No. 18

Revised—Budgeted Cash Collections from Customers

	April	May	June	July	Total
Cash sales, from Revised Sales Budget	$30,000	$48,000	$36,000	$24,000	
Collections of last month's credit sales, from Revised Sales Budget	16,000*	20,000	32,000	24,000	
Total collections	$46,000	$68,000	$68,000	$48,000	$230,000

* March 31 accounts receivable, Exhibit 23-6.

Whitewater Sporting Goods Store No. 18

Revised—Budgeted Cash Payments for Purchases

	April	May	June	July	Total
50% of last month's purchases, from Revised Inventory, Purchases, and Cost of Goods Sold Budget	$16,800*	$25,900	$22,400	$15,400	
50% of this month's purchases, from Revised Inventory, Purchases, and Cost of Goods Sold Budget	25,900	22,400	15,400	14,000	
Total payments for purchases.	$42,700	$48,300	$37,800	$29,400	$158,200

* March 31 accounts payable, Exhibit 23-6.

Whitewater Sporting Goods Store No. 18

Revised—Budgeted Cash Payments for Operating Expenses

	April	May	June	July	Total
Salary and commissions:					
50% of last month's expenses, from Revised Operating Expenses Budget	$ 4,250*	$ 5,000	$ 7,250	$ 5,750	
50% of this month's expenses, from Revised Operating Expenses Budget	5,000	7,250	5,750	4,250	
Total salary and commissions.	9,250	12,250	13,000	10,000	
Rent expense, from Revised Operating Expenses Budget	2,000	2,000	2,000	2,000	
Miscellaneous expenses, from Revised Operating Expenses Budget. . . .	2,500	4,000	3,000	2,000	
Total payments for operating expenses	$13,750	$18,250	$18,000	$14,000	$64,000

* March 31 salary and commissions payable, Exhibit 23-6.

Whitewater Sporting Goods Store No. 18

Revised Cash Budget
Four Months Ending July 31, 20X6

	April	May	June	July
Beginning cash balance	$15,000*	$10,550	$10,410	$21,035
Cash collections (Revised Budgeted Cash Collections)	46,000	68,000	68,000	48,000
Cash available	$61,000	$78,550	$78,410	$69,035
Cash payments:				
Purchases of inventory (Revised Budgeted Cash Payments for Purchases)	$42,700	$48,300	$37,800	$29,400
Operating expenses (Revised Budgeted Cash Payments for Operating Expenses)	13,750	18,250	18,000	14,000
Purchase of delivery truck (item 8, page 945)	3,000	—	—	—
Total cash payments	59,450	66,550	55,800	43,400
(1) Ending cash balance before financing	1,550	12,000	22,610	25,635
Less: Minimum cash balance desired	(10,000)	(10,000)	(10,000)	(10,000)
Cash excess (deficiency)	$(8,450)	$ 2,000	$12,610	$15,635
Financing of cash deficiency (see notes *a–c*):				
Borrowing (at end of month)	$ 9,000			
Principal payments (at end of month)		$(1,500)	$(1,500)	$(1,500)
Interest expense (at 12% annually)		(90)	(75)	(60)
(2) Total effects of financing	9,000	(1,590)	(1,575)	(1,560)
Ending cash balance (1) + (2)	$10,550	$10,410	$21,035	$24,075

* March 31 cash balance, Exhibit 23-6.

Notes

[a] Borrowing occurs in multiples of $1,000 and only for the amount needed to maintain a minimum cash balance of $10,000.

[b] Monthly principal payments: $9,000 \div 6 = \$1,500$.

[c] Interest expense:

May: $\$9,000 \times (0.12 \times 1/12) = \$90$; June: $(\$9,000 - \$1,500) \times (0.12 \times 1/12) = \$75$; July: $(\$9,000 - \$1,500 - \$1,500) \times (0.12 \times 1/12) = \$60$

Whitewater Sporting Goods Store No. 18

Revised Budgeted Balance Sheet
July 31, 20X6

Assets

Current assets:

Cash (Revised Cash budget)	$24,075	
Accounts receivable (Revised Sales Budget)	16,000	
Inventory	42,400	
Prepaid insurance	1,000	
Total current assets		$ 83,475

Plant assets:

Equipment and fixtures	$35,000	
Accumulated depreciation	(14,800)	
Total plant assets		20,200
Total assets		$103,675

Liabilities

Current liabilities:

Accounts payable (0.50 × July purchases of $28,000; Revised Inventory, Purchases, and Cost of Goods Sold Budget)	$14,000	
Short-term note payable	4,500	
Salary and commissions payable (0.50 × July expenses of $8,500; Revised Operating Expenses Budget)	4,250	
Total liabilities		$ 22,750

Owners' Equity

Owners' equity (beginning balance of $78,950* + $1,975 net income, Revised Budgeted Income Statement)	80,925
Total liabilities and owners' equity	$103,675

*March 31, 20X6, Balance Sheet, Exhibit 23-6

Whitewater Sporting Goods Store No. 18
Revised Budgeted Statement of Cash Flows
Four Months Ending July 31, 20X6

Cash flows from operating activities:		
Receipts:		
Collections (Revised Budgeted Cash Collections)	$230,000	
Total cash receipts........................		$230,000
Payments:		
Purchases of inventory (Revised Budgeted Cash		
Payments for Purchases)	(158,200)	
Operating expenses (Revised Budgeted		
Cash Payments for Operating Expenses)	(64,000)	
Payment of interest expense	(225)	
Total cash payments........................		(222,425)
Net cash inflow from operating activities.........		7,575
Cash flows from investing activities:		
Acquisition of delivery truck	$ (3,000)	
Net cash outflow from investing activities........		(3,000)
Cash flows from financing activities:		
Proceeds from issuance of notes payable	$ 9,000	
Payment of notes payable	(4,500)	
Net cash inflow from financing activities.........		4,500
Net increase in cash		$ 9,075
Cash balance, April 1, 20X6 (Exhibit 23-6)		15,000
Cash balance, July 31, 20X6 (Revised Cash Budget) ..		$ 24,075

REVIEW *the Master Budget and Responsibility Accounting*

Quick Check

1. **Amazon.com** expected to receive which of the following benefits when it started its budgeting process?
   a. The planning required to develop the budget helps managers foresee and avoid potential problems before they occur.
   b. The budget helps motivate employees to achieve Amazon's sales growth and cost-reduction goals.
   c. The budget provides Amazon's managers with a benchmark against which to compare actual results for performance evaluation.
   d. All of the above.

2. Which of the following is the cornerstone (or most critical element) of the master budget?
   a. The sales budget   c. The purchases and cost of goods sold budget
   b. The inventory budget   d. The operating expenses budget

3. The income statement is part of which element of Amazon.com's master budget?
   a. The operating budget   c. The financial budget
   b. The capital expenditures budget   d. None of the above

   Use the following information to answer questions 4 through 6. Suppose Amazon.com sells 1 million hardback books a day at an average price of $30 and 1.5 million paperback books a day at an average price of $15. Assume that Amazon's purchase price for the books is 60% of the selling price it charges retail customers. Amazon has no beginning inventory, but it wants to have a three-day supply of ending inventory. Assume that operating expenses are $0.5 million per day.

4. Compute Amazon's budgeted sales for the next (seven-day) week.
   a. $52.5 million   c. $220.5 million
   b. $210 million   d. $367.5 million

5. Determine Amazon's budgeted purchases for the next (seven-day) week.
   a. $220.5 million
   c. $367.5 million
   b. $315 million
   d. $525 million

6. What is Amazon.com's budgeted operating income for a (seven-day) week?
   a. $52.5 million
   c. $143.5 million
   b. $56 million
   d. $147 million

7. Which of the following expenses would *not* appear in Amazon.com's cash budget?
   a. Depreciation expense
   c. Interest expense
   b. Wages expense
   d. Marketing expense

8. Information technology has made it easier for Amazon's managers to perform all of the following tasks *except*:
   a. Sensitivity analyses
   b. Rolling up individual units' budgets into the companywide budget
   c. Removing slack from the budget
   d. Preparing responsibility center performance reports that identify variances between actual and budgeted revenues and costs

9. Which of the following managers is at the highest level of the organization?
   a. Cost center manager
   c. Profit center manager
   b. Revenue center manager
   d. Investment center manager

10. Suppose Amazon.com budgets $5 million for customer service costs but actually spends $4 million.
   a. Because this $1 million variance is favorable, management does not need to investigate further.
   b. Management will investigate this $1 million favorable variance to ensure that the cost savings do not reflect skimping on customer service.
   c. Management will investigate this $1 million unfavorable variance to try to identify and then correct the problem that led to the unfavorable variance.
   d. Management should investigate every variance, especially unfavorable ones.

Accounting Vocabulary

capital expenditures budget (p. 944)
cash budget (p. 950)
financial budget (p. 944)

management by exception (p. 959)
master budget (p. 943)
operating budget (p. 944)

responsibility accounting (p. 957)
responsibility center (p. 957)
statement of budgeted cash receipts and payments (p. 950)

●ASSESS *Your Progress*

See *www.prenhall.com/horngren* for selected Starters, Exercises, and Problems.

Why managers use budgets
(Obj. 1)

Ordering components of the master budget
(Obj. 2, 3)

Starters

S23-1 Consider the budget for your travel itinerary business (page 941). Explain how you benefit from preparing the budget.

S23-2 In what order should you prepare the following components of the master budget?

Budgeted income statement	Operating expense budget	Cash budget
Budgeted statement of cash flows	Purchases and cost of goods sold budget	Capital expenditures budget
Budgeted balance sheet	Sales budget	Inventory budget

Which are components of the operating budget? Which are components of the financial budget?

S23-3 In a series of Starters, you will prepare parts of the master budget for Grippers, which sells its rock-climbing shoes worldwide. We will concentrate on Grippers' budget for January and February.

(continued)

Grippers expects to sell 4,000 pairs of shoes for $185 each in January, and 3,500 pairs of shoes for $220 each in February. All sales are cash only. Prepare the sales budget for January and February.

Preparing a sales budget
(Obj. 2)

S23-4 In Starter 23-3, Grippers expects cost of goods sold to average 65% of sales revenue, and the company expects to sell 4,300 pairs of shoes in March for $240 each. Grippers' target ending inventory is $10,000 plus 50% of the next month's cost of goods sold. Use this information and the sales budget from Starter 23-3 to prepare Grippers' inventory, purchases, and cost of goods sold budget for January and February.

Preparing a purchases, cost of goods sold, and inventory budget
(Obj. 2)

S23-5 Turn to the Whitewater Sporting Goods example on pages 944–954. Suppose June sales are expected to be $40,000 rather than $60,000. Revise Whitewater's sales budget.

What other components of Whitewater's master budget would be affected by this change in the sales budget?

Preparing a sales budget
(Obj. 2, 4)

S23-6 Refer to the original Whitewater Sporting Goods example on pages 944–954. Suppose cost of goods sold averages 75% of sales rather than 70%. Revise Whitewater's inventory, purchases, and cost of goods sold budget for April and May.

What other components of Whitewater's master budget would be affected by the change in the budgeted cost of goods sold?

Preparing a purchases, cost of goods sold, and inventory budget
(Obj. 2, 4)

S23-7 Turn to the original Whitewater Sporting Goods example on pages 944–954. Suppose 70% of sales are cash and 30% are credit. Revise Whitewater's sales budget and budgeted cash collections from customers for April and May.

Preparing a sales budget and cash collections budget
(Obj. 2, 3, 4)

S23-8 Refer to the original Whitewater Sporting Goods example on pages 944–954. Suppose Whitewater pays for 60% of inventory purchases in the month of the purchase and 40% during the next month. Revise Whitewater's budgeted cash payments for purchases of inventory for April and May. (*Hint:* Assume these new percentages also apply to March purchases of $33,600 given in item 5 on page 945).

Preparing a cash payments for purchases budget
(Obj. 3, 4)

S23-9 You prepared Grippers' sales budget in Starter 23-3. Now assume that Grippers' sales are 25% cash and 75% on credit. Grippers' collection history indicates that credit sales are collected as follows:

Budgeting cash collections
(Obj. 3)

30% in the month of the sale	6% two months after the sale
60% in the month after the sale	4% are never collected

November sales totaled $391,500 and December sales were $398,250. Prepare a schedule for the budgeted cash collections for January and February.

S23-10 Refer to Starter 23-9. Grippers has $8,300 cash on hand on January 1. The company requires a minimum cash balance of $7,500. January cash collections are $548,330 (as you calculated in Starter 23-9). Total cash payments for January are $583,200. Prepare a cash budget for January. Will Grippers need to borrow cash by the end of January?

Preparing a cash budget
(Obj. 3)

S23-11 Fill in the blanks with the phrase that best completes the sentence.

Distinguishing among different types of responsibility centers
(Obj. 5)

A cost center	A responsibility center	Lower
An investment center	A revenue center	Higher
A profit center		

a. The Maintenance Department at the **San Diego Zoo** is _____.
b. The concession stand at the San Diego Zoo is _____.
c. The Menswear Department at **Bloomingdale's**, which is responsible for buying and selling merchandise, is _____.
d. A production line at a **Palm Pilot** plant is _____.
e. _____ is any segment of the business whose manager is accountable for specific activities.
f. Gatorade, a division of **Quaker Oats**, is _____.
g. The sales manager in charge of **NIKE's** northwest sales territory oversees _____.
h. Managers of cost and revenue centers are at _____ levels of the organization than are managers of profit and investment centers.

Interpreting a responsibility accounting performance report
(Obj. 5)

Analyzing a performance report, management by exception
(Obj. 5)

Not a question of blame
(Obj. 5)

See *www.prenhall.com/horngren*
for selected Starters, Exercises,
and Problems.

Budgeting and performance evaluation
(Obj. 1)

Budgeting purchases, cost of goods sold, and inventory
(Obj. 2)

Student ResourceCD
spreadsheet

Budgeting quarterly income for a year
(Obj. 2)

Student ResourceCD
spreadsheet

Computing cash receipts and payments
(Obj. 3)

S23-12 In Exhibit 23-20, the next to last line of the CEO's report consists entirely of expenses. Describe the kinds of expenses that would be included in this category.

S23-13 Look at the performance report in Exhibit 23-20. On which variances should the manager of the Mexican sauces product line focus his efforts, according to the management by exception principle? For these variances, compute the variance as a percent of the budgeted amount, and suggest some questions the manager may want to investigate.

S23-14 Exhibit 23-20 shows that the Mexican sauces product line had a favorable marketing expense variance. Does this favorable variance necessarily mean that the manager of the Mexican sauces line is doing a good job? Explain.

Exercises

E23-1 Hanna White owns a chain of travel goods stores. Last year, her sales staff sold 10,000 suitcases at an average sale price of $150. Variable expenses were 80% of sales revenue, and the total fixed expense was $100,000. This year the chain sold more-expensive product lines. Sales were 8,000 suitcases at an average price of $200. The variable expense percentage and the total fixed expense were the same both years. White evaluates the chain manager by comparing this year's income with last year's income.

Prepare a performance report for this year, similar to Exhibit 23-4. How would you improve White's performance evaluation system to better analyze this year's results?

E23-2 Leno Inc. sells tire rims. Its sales budget for the nine months ended September 30 follows:

	Quarter Ended			
	March 31	**June 30**	**Sep. 30**	**Nine-Month Total**
Cash sales, 30%	$ 30,000	$ 45,000	$ 37,500	$112,500
Credit sales, 70%	70,000	105,000	87,500	262,500
Total sales, 100%	$100,000	$150,000	$125,000	$375,000

In the past, cost of goods sold has been 60% of total sales. The director of marketing and the financial vice president agree that each quarter's ending inventory should not be below $20,000 plus 10% of cost of goods sold for the following quarter. The marketing director expects sales of $220,000 during the fourth quarter. The January 1 inventory was $19,000.

Prepare an inventory, purchases, and cost of goods sold budget for each of the first three quarters of the year. Compute cost of goods sold for the entire nine-month period. (Use Exhibit 23-8 as a model.)

E23-3 Wheels, Inc., is an exotic car dealership. Suppose that its Miami office projects that 20X7 quarterly sales will increase by 3% in quarter 1, by 4% in quarter 2, by 6% in quarter 3, and by 5% in quarter 4. Management expects operating expenses to be 80% of revenues during each of the first two quarters, 79% of revenues during the third quarter, and 81% during the fourth. The office manager expects to borrow $100,000 on July 1, with quarterly principal payments of $10,000 beginning on September 30 and interest paid at an annual rate of 13%. Assume that fourth-quarter 20X6 sales were $4,000,000.

Prepare a budgeted income statement for each of the four quarters of 20X7 and for the entire year. Present the 20X7 budget as follows:

Quarter 1	Quarter 2	Quarter 3	Quarter 4	Full Year

E23-4 Aqua Pure is a distributor of bottled water. For each of items a through c, compute the amount of cash receipts or payments Aqua Pure will budget for September. The solution to one item may depend on the answer to an earlier item.

(continued)

a. Management expects to sell equipment that cost $14,000 at a gain of $2,000. Accumulated depreciation on this equipment is $7,000.

b. Management expects to sell 7,500 cases of water in August and 9,200 in September. Each case sells for $12. Cash sales average 30% of total sales, and credit sales make up the rest. Three-fourths of credit sales are collected in the month of sale, with the balance collected the following month.

c. The company pays rent and property taxes of $4,200 each month. Commissions and other selling expenses average 25% of sales. Aqua Pure pays two-thirds of commissions and other selling expenses in the month incurred, with the balance paid in the following month.

E23-5 Battery Power, a family-owned battery store, began October with $10,500 cash. Management forecasts that collections from credit customers will be $11,000 in October and $15,000 in November. The store is scheduled to receive $6,000 cash on a business note receivable in October. Projected cash payments include inventory purchases ($13,000 in October and $13,900 in November) and operating expenses ($3,000 each month).

Preparing a cash budget; sensitivity analysis
(Obj. 3, 4)

Student ResourceCD

spreadsheet

Battery Power's bank requires a $10,000 minimum balance in the store's checking account. At the end of any month when the account balance dips below $10,000, the bank automatically extends credit to the store in multiples of $1,000. Battery Power borrows as little as possible and pays back loans in quarterly installments of $2,000, plus 4% interest on the entire unpaid principal. The first payment occurs three months after the loan.

Required

1. Prepare Battery Power's cash budget for October and November.
2. How much cash will Battery Power borrow in November if collections from customers that month total $12,000 instead of $15,000?

E23-6 You recently began a job as an accounting intern at Outdoor Adventures Ltd. Your first task was to help prepare the cash budget for February and March. Unfortunately, the computer with the budget file crashed, and you did not have a backup or even a hard copy. You ran a program to salvage bits of data from the budget file. After entering the following data in the budget, you may have just enough information to reconstruct the budget.

Preparing a cash budget
(Obj. 3)

Outdoor Adventures eliminates any cash deficiency by borrowing the exact amount needed from State Street Bank, where the current interest rate is 8%. Outdoor Adventures pays interest on its outstanding debt at the end of each month. The company also repays all borrowed amounts at the end of the month, as cash becomes available.

Complete the following cash budget:

Outdoor Adventures Ltd.
Cash Budget
February and March

	February	March
Beginning cash balance	$ 16,900	$?
Cash collections	?	79,600
Cash from sale of plant assets	0	1,800
Cash available	106,900	?
Cash payments:		
Purchase of inventory	$?	$41,000
Operating expenses	47,200	?
Total payments	98,000	?
(1) Ending cash balance before financing	?	25,100
Minimum cash balance desired	20,000	20,000
Cash excess (deficiency)	$?	$?
Financing of cash deficiency:		
Borrowing (at end of month)	$?	$?
Principal repayments (at end of month)	?	?
Interest expense	?	?
(2) Total effects of financing	?	?
Ending cash balance (1) + (2)	$?	$?

Preparing a budgeted balance sheet
(Obj. 3)

E23-7 Use the following to prepare a budgeted balance sheet for Marine.com at March 31, 20X6. Show computations for the cash and owners' equity amounts.

a. March 31 inventory balance, $15,000
b. March payments for inventory, $4,600
c. March payments of accounts payable and accrued liabilities, $8,200
d. March 31 accounts payable balance, $4,300
e. February 28 furniture and fixtures balance, $34,800; accumulated depreciation balance, $29,870
f. February 28 owners' equity, $26,700

g. March depreciation expense, $600
h. Cost of goods sold, 60% of sales
i. Other March expenses, including income tax, total $5,000; paid in cash
j. February 28 cash balance, $11,400
k. March budgeted sales, $12,200
l. March 31 accounts receivable balance, one-fourth of March sales
m. March cash receipts, $14,300

Identifying different types of responsibility centers
(Obj. 5)

E23-8 Identify each responsibility center as a cost center, a revenue center, a profit center, or an investment center.

a. The bakery department of a **Publix** supermarket reports income for the current year.
b. **Pace Foods** is a subsidiary of **Campbell Soup Company**.
c. The personnel department of **State Farm Insurance Companies** prepares its budget and subsequent performance report on the basis of its expected expenses for the year.
d. The shopping section of **Burpee.com** reports both revenues and expenses.
e. Burpee.com's investor relations Web site provides operating and financial information to investors and other interested parties.
f. The manager of a **BP** service station is evaluated based on the station's revenues and expenses.
g. A charter airline records revenues and expenses for each airplane each month. The airplane's performance report shows its ratio of operating income to average book value.
h. The manager of the southwest sales territory is evaluated based on a comparison of current period sales against budgeted sales.

Using responsibility accounting to evaluate profit centers
(Obj. 5)

E23-9   InTouch is a Seattle company that sells cell phones and PDAs on the Web. InTouch has assistant managers for its digital and video cell phone operations. These assistant managers report to the manager of the total cell phone product line, who with the manager of PDAs reports to the manager for all sales of hand-held devices, Beth Beverly. Beverly received the following data for November operations:

	Cell Phones		PDAs
	Digital	**Video**	
Revenues, budget	$204,000	$800,000	$300,000
Expenses, budget	140,000	390,000	225,000
Revenues, actual	214,000	840,000	290,000
Expenses, actual	135,000	400,000	230,000

Arrange the data in a performance report similar to Exhibit 23-20. Show November results, in thousands of dollars, for digital cell phones, for the total cell phone product line, and for all devices. Should Beverly investigate the performance of digital cell phone operations?

Problems

(Group A)

Budgeting income for two months
(Obj. 2)

P23-1A The budget committee of Vinning Office Supply Co. has assembled the following data. As the business manager, you must prepare the budgeted income statements for May and June 20X6.

a. Sales in April were $42,100. You forecast that monthly sales will increase 2.0% in May and 2.4% in June.

(continued)

b. Vinning maintains inventory of $9,000 plus 25% of sales budgeted for the following month. Monthly purchases average 50% of sales revenues in that same month. Actual inventory on April 30 is $14,000. Sales budgeted for July are $42,400.

c. Monthly salaries amount to $4,000. Sales commissions equal 4% of sales for that month. Combine salaries and commissions into a single figure.

d. Other monthly expenses are:

Rent expense...........	$3,000, paid as incurred
Depreciation expense....	$ 600
Insurance expense	$ 200, expiration of prepaid amount
Income tax.............	20% of operating income

Prepare Vinning's budgeted income statements for May and June. Show cost of goods sold computations. Round *all* amounts to the nearest $100. (Round amounts ending in $50 or more upward, and amounts ending in less than $50 downward.) For example, budgeted May sales are $42,900 ($42,100 × 1.02), and June sales are $43,900 ($42,900 × 1.024).

P23-2A Refer to Problem 23-1A. Vinning's sales are 70% cash and 30% credit. (Use the rounded sales on the last line of P23-1A.) Credit sales are collected in the month after sale. Inventory purchases are paid 50% in the month of purchase and 50% the following month. Salaries and sales commissions are also paid half in the month earned and half the next month. Income tax is paid at the end of the year.

Budgeting cash receipts and payments **(Obj. 3)**

The April 30, 20X6, balance sheet showed the following balances:

Cash	$11,000
Accounts payable................................	7,400
Salary and commissions payable....................	2,850

Required

1. Prepare schedules of (a) budgeted cash collections, (b) budgeted cash payments for purchases, and (c) budgeted cash payments for operating expenses. Show amounts for each month and totals for May and June. *Round* your computations to the nearest dollar.

2. Prepare a cash budget similar to Exhibit 23-14. If no financing activity took place, what is the budgeted cash balance on June 30, 20X6?

P23-3A Alliance Printing of Baltimore has applied for a loan. Bank of America has requested a budgeted balance sheet at April 30, 20X7, and a budgeted statement of cash flows for April. As Alliance's controller, you have assembled the following information:

Preparing a budgeted balance sheet and budgeted statement of cash flows **(Obj. 3)**

a. March 31 equipment balance, $52,400; accumulated depreciation, $41,300.

b. April capital expenditures of $42,800 budgeted for cash purchase of equipment.

c. April depreciation expense, $900.

d. Cost of goods sold, 60% of sales.

e. Other April operating expenses, including income tax, total $13,200, 25% of which will be paid in cash and the remainder accrued at April 30.

f. March 31 owners' equity, $93,700.

g. March 31 cash balance, $40,600.

h. April budgeted sales, $90,000, 70% of which is for cash. Of the remaining 30%, half will be collected in April and half in May.

i. April cash collections on March sales, $29,700.

j. April cash payments of March 31 liabilities incurred for March purchases of inventory, $17,300.

k. March 31 inventory balance, $29,600.

l. April purchases of inventory, $10,000 for cash and $36,800 on credit. Half of the credit purchases will be paid in April and half in May.

Required

1. Prepare the budgeted balance sheet for Alliance Printing at April 30, 20X7. Show separate computations for cash, inventory, and owners' equity balances.

2. Prepare the budgeted statement of cash flows for April.

3. Suppose that Alliance Printing has become aware of more efficient (and more expensive) equipment than it budgeted for purchase in April. What is the total amount of

(*continued*)

cash available for equipment purchases in April, before financing, if the minimum desired ending cash balance is $21,000? (For this requirement, disregard the $42,800 initially budgeted for equipment purchases.)

*Preparing a budgeted balance sheet;
sensitivity analysis*
(Obj. 3, 4)

P23-4A Refer to Problem 23-3A. Before granting a loan to Alliance Printing, Bank of America asks for a sensitivity analysis assuming April sales are only $60,000 rather than the $90,000 originally budgeted. (While the cost of goods sold will change, assume that purchases, depreciation, and the other operating expenses will remain the same as in Problem 23-3A.)

Required

1. Prepare a revised budgeted balance sheet for Alliance Printing, showing separate computations for cash, inventory, and owners' equity balances.

2. Suppose Alliance Printing has a minimum desired cash balance of $23,000. Will the company need to borrow cash in April?

3. In this sensitivity analysis, sales declined by $33\frac{1}{3}$% ($30,000 ÷ $90,000). Is the decline in expenses and income more or less than $33\frac{1}{3}$%? Explain why.

*Identifying different types of responsibility
centers*
(Obj. 5)

P23-5A Is each of the following most likely a cost center, a revenue center, a profit center, or an investment center?

a. Shipping department of **Amazon.com**

b. Eastern district of a salesperson's territory

c. Child care department of a church or synagogue

d. Catering operation of **Sonny's BBQ** restaurant

e. Executive headquarters of the **United Way**

f. Accounts payable section of the Accounting Department at **Home Depot**

g. Proposed new office of **Coldwell Banker**, a real-estate firm

h. **Disneyland**

i. The Empire State Building in New York City

j. Branch warehouse of **Dalton Carpets**

k. Information systems department for **Habitat for Humanity**

l. Service Department of Audio Forest stereo shop

m. Investments Department of **Citibank**

n. Assembly-line supervisors at **Dell Computer**

o. American subsidiary of a Japanese manufacturer

p. Surgery unit of a privately owned hospital

q. Research and Development Department of **Cisco Systems**

r. Childrenswear department at a **Target** store

s. Typesetting Department of Northend Press, a printing company

t. Prescription Filling Department of **Drugstore.com**

u. Order-Taking Department at **L.L. Bean**

v. Personnel Department of **Goodyear Tire and Rubber Company**

w. Grounds maintenance department at Augusta National golf course

*Preparing a profit center performance
report for management by exception;
benefits of budgeting*
(Obj. 1, 5)

P23-6A Winnie's World operates a chain of pet stores in the Midwest. The manager of each store reports to the region manager, who in turn reports to headquarters in Milwaukee, Wisconsin. The *actual* income statements for the Dayton store, the Ohio region (including the Dayton store) and the company as a whole (including the Ohio region) for July 20X6 are:

	Dayton	**Ohio**	**Companywide**
Revenue........................	$148,900	$1,647,000	$4,200,000
Expenses:			
Region manager/			
headquarters office	$ —	$ 60,000	$ 116,000
Cost of materials	81,100	871,900	1,807,000
Salary expense	38,300	415,100	1,119,000
Depreciation expense	7,200	91,000	435,000
Utilities expense...............	4,000	46,200	260,000
Rent expense..................	2,400	34,700	178,000
Total expenses..................	133,000	1,518,900	3,915,000
Operating income	$ 15,900	$ 128,100	$ 285,000

(continued)

Budgeted amounts for July were as follows:

	Dayton	Ohio	Companywide
Revenue	$162,400	$1,769,700	$4,450,000
Expenses:			
Region manager/			
headquarters office	$ —	$ 65,600	$ 118,000
Cost of materials	86,400	963,400	1,972,000
Salary expense.............	38,800	442,000	1,095,000
Depreciation expense	7,200	87,800	449,000
Utilities expense	4,400	54,400	271,000
Rent expense	3,600	32,300	174,000
Total expenses	140,400	1,645,500	4,079,000
Operating income	$ 22,000	$ 124,200	$ 371,000

Required

1. Prepare a report for July 20X6 that shows the performance of the Dayton store, the Ohio region, and the company as a whole. Follow the format of Exhibit 23-20.

2. As the Ohio region manager, would you investigate the Dayton store on the basis of this report? Why or why not?

3. Briefly discuss the benefits of budgeting. Base your discussion on Winnie's World's performance report.

Problems

(Group B)

P23-1B Representatives of the various departments of Go Sports have assembled the following data. As the business manager, you must prepare the budgeted income statements for August and September 20X7.

Budgeting income for two months
(Obj. 2)

a. Sales in July were $196,000. You forecast that monthly sales will increase 3% in August and 2% in September.

b. Go Sports tries to maintain inventory of $50,000 plus 20% of sales budgeted for the following month. Monthly purchases average 60% of sales revenue in that same month. Actual inventory on July 31 is $90,000. Sales budgeted for October are $220,000.

c. Monthly salaries amount to $15,000. Sales commissions equal 6% of sales for that month. Combine salaries and commissions into a single figure.

d. Other monthly expenses are

Rent expense...........	$13,000, paid as incurred
Depreciation expense....	$ 4,000
Insurance expense	$ 1,000, expiration of prepaid amount
Income tax.............	30% of operating income

Prepare Go Sports' budgeted income statements for August and September. Show cost-of-goods-sold computations. Round *all* amounts to the nearest $1,000. For example, budgeted August sales are $202,000 ($196,000 × 1.03) and September sales are $206,000 ($202,000 × 1.02).

P23-2B Refer to Problem 23-1B. Go Sports' sales are 50% cash and 50% credit. (Use sales on the last two lines of P23-1B.) Credit sales are collected in the month after the sale. Inventory purchases are paid 60% in the month of purchase and 40% the following month. Salaries and sales commissions are paid three-fourths in the month earned and one-fourth the next month. Income tax is paid at the end of the year.
The July 31, 20X7 balance sheet showed the following balances:

Budgeting cash receipts and payments
(Obj. 3)

Cash	$22,000
Accounts payable....................................	52,000
Salaries and commissions payable	6,750

(continued)

Required

1. Prepare schedules of (a) budgeted cash collections from customers, (b) budgeted cash payments for purchases, and (c) budgeted cash payments for operating expenses. Show amounts for each month and totals for August and September. Round your computations to the *nearest dollar.*

2. Prepare a cash budget similar to Exhibit 23-14. If no financing activity took place, what is the budgeted cash balance on September 30, 20X7?

Preparing a budgeted balance sheet and budgeted statement of cash flows
(Obj. 3)

P23-3B The Music Box has applied for a loan. First Central Bank has requested a budgeted balance sheet at June 30, 20X5, and a budgeted statement of cash flows for June. As the controller (chief accounting officer) of The Music Box, you have assembled the following information:

a. May 31 equipment balance, $80,800; accumulated depreciation, $12,400.
b. June capital expenditures of $16,400 budgeted for cash purchase of equipment.
c. June depreciation expense, $400.
d. Cost of goods sold, 50% of sales.
e. Other June operating expenses, including income tax, total $34,000, 75% of which will be paid in cash and the remainder accrued at June 30.
f. May 31 owners' equity, $137,500.
g. May 31 cash balance, $50,200.
h. June budgeted sales, $85,000, 40% of which is for cash. Of the remaining 60%, half will be collected in June and half in July.
i. June cash collections on May sales, $15,300.
j. June cash payments of liabilities for May inventory purchases on credit, $8,300.
k. May 31 inventory balance, $11,900.
l. June purchases of inventory, $11,000 for cash and $37,200 on credit. Half the credit purchases will be paid in June and half in July.

Required

1. Prepare the budgeted balance sheet for The Music Box at June 30, 20X5. Show separate computations for cash, inventory, and owners' equity balances.

2. Prepare the budgeted statement of cash flows for June.

3. On the basis of this data, if you were a First Central Bank loan officer, would you grant The Music Box a loan? Give your reason.

Preparing a budgeted balance sheet; sensitivity analysis
(Obj. 3, 4)

P23-4B Refer to Problem 23-3B. Before granting a loan to The Music Box, First Central Bank asks for a sensitivity analysis, assuming that June sales are only $65,000 rather than the $85,000 originally budgeted. (While cost of goods sold will change, assume that purchases, depreciation, and the other operating expenses will remain the same as in Problem 23-3B.)

Required

1. Prepare a revised budgeted balance sheet for The Music Box, showing separate computations for cash, inventory, and owners' equity balances.

2. Suppose The Music Box has a minimum desired cash balance of $35,000. Will the company borrow cash in June?

3. How would this sensitivity analysis affect First Central's loan decision?

Identifying different types of responsibility centers
(Obj. 5)

P23-5B Is each of the following most likely a cost center, a revenue center, a profit center, or an investment center?

a. Purchasing Department of **Milliken**, a textile manufacturer
b. Quality Control Department of **Mayfield Dairies**
c. European subsidiary of **Coca-Cola**
d. Payroll Department of the University of Wisconsin
e. Lighting Department in a **Sears** store
f. Children's nursery in a church or synagogue
g. Personnel Department of **E* Trade**, the online broker
h. **igourmet.com,** an e-tailer of gourmet cheeses

(continued)

i. Service Department of an automobile dealership
j. Customer Service Department of **Procter & Gamble Co.**
k. Proposed new office of **Deutsche Bank**
l. Southwest region of **Pizza Inns, Inc.**
m. **Delta Air Lines, Inc.**
n. Order-Taking Department at **Lands' End** mail-order company
o. Editorial Department of **The Wall Street Journal**
p. A **Ford Motor Company** production plant
q. Police Department of Boston
r. **Century 21 Real Estate Co.**
s. A small pet grooming business
t. Northeast sales territory for **Boise-Cascade**
u. Different product lines of **Broyhill**, a furniture manufacturer
v. **McDonald's** restaurants under the supervision of a regional manager
w. Job superintendents of a home builder

P23-6B Etown is a chain of home electronics stores. Each store has a manager who answers to a city manager, who in turn reports to a statewide manager. The actual income statements of Store No. 23, all stores in the Dallas area (including Store No. 23), and all stores in the state of Texas (including all Dallas stores) are summarized as follows for April:

Preparing a profit center performance report for management by exception; benefits of budgeting
(Obj. 1, 5)

	Store No. 23	Dallas	State of Texas
Sales revenue	$43,300	$486,000	$3,228,500
Expenses:			
City/state manager's office expenses	$ —	$ 18,000	$ 44,000
Cost of goods sold	15,000	171,300	1,256,800
Salary expense	4,000	37,500	409,700
Depreciation expense	3,700	13,100	320,000
Utilities expense	1,900	19,300	245,600
Rent expense	700	16,600	186,000
Total expenses	25,300	275,800	2,462,100
Operating income	$18,000	$210,200	$ 766,400

Budgeted amounts for April were as follows:

	Store No. 23	Dallas	State of Texas
Sales revenue	$39,000	$470,000	$3,129,000
Expenses:			
City/state manager's office expenses	$ —	$ 19,000	$ 45,000
Cost of goods sold	12,100	160,800	1,209,000
Salary expense	6,000	37,900	412,000
Depreciation expense	3,200	23,400	320,000
Utilities expense	1,000	15,000	240,000
Rent expense	700	15,700	181,000
Total expenses	23,000	271,800	2,407,000
Operating income	$16,000	$198,200	$ 722,000

Required

1. Prepare a report for April that shows the performance of Store No. 23, all the stores in the Dallas area, and all the stores in Texas. Follow the format of Exhibit 23-20.

2. As the city manager of Dallas, would you investigate Store No. 23 on the basis of this report? Why or why not?

3. Briefly discuss the benefits of budgeting. Base your discussion on Etown's performance report.

APPLY *Your Knowledge*

Decision Cases

Using a budgeted income statement
(Obj. 1)

Case 1. Donna Tse has recently accepted the position of assistant manager at Cycle World, a bicycle store in St. Louis. She has just finished her accounting courses. Cycle World's manager and owner, Jeff Towry, asks Donna to prepare a budgeted income statement for 20X6 based on the information he has collected. Tse's budget follows:

Cycle World		
Budgeted Income Statement **For the Year Ending July 31, 20X6**		
Sales revenue		$244,000
Cost of goods sold		177,000
Gross profit		67,000
Operating expenses:		
Salary and commission expense	$46,000	
Rent expense	8,000	
Depreciation expense	2,000	
Insurance expense	800	
Miscellaneous expenses	12,000	68,800
Operating loss		(1,800)
Interest expense		225
Net loss		$ (2,025)

Required

Tse does not want to give Towry this budget without making constructive suggestions for steps Towry could take to improve expected performance. Write a memo to Towry outlining your suggestions. Your memo should take the following form:

Date: _____	
To:	Mr. Jeff Towry, Manager
	Cycle World
From:	Donna Tse
Subject:	Cycle World's 20X6 budgeted income statement

Budgeting cash flows and financial statements to analyze alternatives
(Obj. 2, 3)

Case 2. Each autumn, as a hobby, Suzanne De Angelo weaves cotton placemats to sell through a local craft shop. The mats sell for $20 per set of four. The shop charges a 10% commission and remits the net proceeds to De Angelo at the end of December. De Angelo has woven and sold 25 sets each of the last two years. She has enough cotton in inventory to make another 25 sets. She paid $7 per set for the cotton. De Angelo uses a four-harness loom that she purchased for cash exactly two years ago. It is depreciated at the rate of $10 per month. The accounts payable relate to the cotton inventory and are payable by September 30.

De Angelo is considering buying an eight-harness loom so that she can weave more-intricate patterns in linen. The new loom costs $1,000; it would be depreciated at $20 per month. Her bank has agreed to lend her $1,000 at 18% interest, with $200 principal plus accrued interest payable each December 31. De Angelo believes she can weave 15 linen placemat sets in time for the Christmas rush if she does not weave any cotton mats. She predicts that each linen set will sell for $50. Linen costs $18 per set. De Angelo's supplier will sell her linen on credit, payable December 31.

(continued)

De Angelo plans to keep her old loom whether or not she buys the new loom. The balance sheet for her weaving business at August 31, 20X7, is as follows:

Suzanne De Angelo, Weaver

Balance Sheet
August 31, 20X7

Current assets:			Current liabilities:		
Cash		$ 25			
Inventory of cotton		175	Accounts payable		$ 74
		200			
Fixed assets:					
Loom		500	Owner's equity		386
Accumulated depreciation		(240)			
		260	Total liabilities		
Total assets		$460	and owner's equity		$460

Required

1. Prepare a cash budget for the four months ending December 31, 20X7, for two alternatives: weaving the placemats in cotton using the existing loom, and weaving the placemats in linen using the new loom. For each alternative, prepare a budgeted income statement for the four months ending December 31, 20X7, and a budgeted balance sheet at December 31, 20X7.

2. On the basis of financial considerations only, what should De Angelo do? Give your reason.

3. What nonfinancial factors might De Angelo consider in her decision?

Ethical Issue

→ *Link Back to Chapter 8, p. 342, for Ethics, Decision Guidelines box.* Residence Suites operates a regional hotel chain. Each hotel is operated by a manager and an assistant manager/controller. Many of the staff who run the front desk, clean the rooms, and prepare the breakfast buffet work part-time or have a second job, so turnover is high.

Budget slack
(Obj. 2, 5)

Assistant manager/controller Terry Dunn asked the new bookkeeper to help prepare the hotel's master budget. The master budget is prepared once a year and submitted to company headquarters for approval. Once approved, the master budget is used to evaluate the hotel's performance. These performance evaluations affect hotel managers' bonuses and they also affect company decisions on which hotels deserve extra funds for capital improvements.

When the budget was almost complete, Dunn asked the bookkeeper to increase amounts budgeted for labor and supplies by 15%. When asked why, Dunn responded that hotel manager Clay Murry told her to do this when she began working at the hotel. Murry explained that this budgetary cushion gave him flexibility in running the hotel. For example, since company headquarters tightly controls capital improvement funds, Murry can use the extra money budgeted for labor and supplies to replace broken televisions or pay "bonuses" to keep valued employees. Dunn initially accepted this explanation because she had observed similar behavior at the hotel where she worked previously.

Put yourself in Dunn's position. Use the ethical judgment decision guidelines in Chapter 8 (page 342) to decide how Dunn should deal with the situation.

Financial Statement Case

Budgets are an important management tool in a large company like **Amazon.com**. Refer to Amazon.com's annual report to answer the following questions:

Budgeting by quarter and segment, types of responsibility centers, performance evaluation
(Obj. 3, 5)

1. When preparing the master budget, would Amazon.com budget approximately the same sales and profit amounts for each quarter? Explain. (*Hint:* Quarterly results appear in footnote 16.)

(continued)

2. **Amazon.com** distinguishes among four segments. Identify these segments. Are these segments cost centers, revenue centers, profit centers, or investment centers? Explain.

3. Prepare a responsibility accounting performance report for 2002 similar to Exhibit 23-20. Show the results, in thousands of dollars, for North America Books, Music, DVD/Video (BMVD); North America; and the company as a whole. (In the report for the company as a whole, combine the two North American segments into a single line item.) Use the 2001 data as the budgeted amounts for 2002. (*Hint:* Business segment data are presented in footnote 15.)

4. CEO Jeff Bezos's 2002 letter to shareholders presents a positive picture of Amazon.com's performance. Does your responsibility accounting performance report support Jeff Bezos's enthusiasm? Explain, considering the results in each level of the responsibility accounting report, starting from the lowest reporting level and working up the organizational hierarchy.

Team Project

Responsibility accounting, return on investment
(Obj. 1, 2, 5)

Xellnet provides e-commerce software for the pharmaceuticals industry. Xellnet is organized into several divisions. A companywide planning committee sets general strategy and goals for the company and its divisions, but each division develops its own budget.

Rick Watson is the new division manager of wireless communications software. His division has two departments: Development and Sales. Carrie Pronai manages the 20 or so programmers and systems specialists typically employed in Development to create and update the division's software applications. Liz Smith manages the sales department.

Xellnet considers the divisions to be investment centers. To earn his bonus next year, Watson must achieve a 30% return on the $3 million invested in his division. Within the Wireless Division, Development is a cost center, while Sales is a revenue center.

Budgeting is in progress. Carrie Pronai met with her staff and is now struggling with two sets of numbers. Alternative A is her best estimate of next year's costs. However, unexpected problems can arise when writing software, and finding competent programmers is an ongoing challenge. She knows that Watson was a programmer before he earned an MBA, so he should be sensitive to this uncertainty. Consequently, she is thinking of increasing her budgeted costs (Alternative B). Her department's bonuses largely depend on whether the department meets its budgeted costs.

Xellnet
Wireless Division
Development Budget 20XX

	Alternative A	Alternative B
Salaries expense		
(including overtime and part-time)	$2,400,000	$2,640,000
Software expense	120,000	132,000
Travel expense	65,000	71,500
Depreciation expense	255,000	255,000
Miscellaneous expense	100,000	110,000
Total expense	$2,940,000	$3,208,500

Liz Smith is also struggling with her sales budget. Companies have made their initial investments in communications software, so it is harder to win new customers. If things go well, she believes her sales team can maintain the level of growth achieved over the last few years. This is Alternative A in the Sales Budget. However, if Smith is too optimistic, sales may fall short of the budget. If this happens, her team will not receive bonuses. Smith is therefore considering reducing the sales numbers and submitting Alternative B.

(*continued*)

	Xellnet	
	Wireless Division **Sales Budget 20XX**	

	Alternative A	Alternative B
Sales revenue	$5,000,000	$4,500,000
Salaries expense	360,000	360,000
Travel expense	240,000	210,500

Split your team into three groups. Each group should meet separately before the entire team meets.

Required

1. The first group plays the role of Development Manager Carrie Pronai. Before meeting with the entire team, determine which set of budget numbers you are going to present to Rick Watson. Write a memo supporting your decision. Use the format shown in Decision Case 1. Give this memo to the third group before the team meeting.

2. The second group plays the role of Sales Manager Liz Smith. Before meeting with the entire team, determine which set of budget numbers you are going to present to Rick Watson. Write a memo supporting your decision. Use the format shown in Decision Case 1. Give this memo to the third group before the team meeting.

3. The third group plays the role of Division Manager Rick Watson. Before meeting with the entire team, use the memos that Pronai and Smith provided you to prepare a division budget based on the sales and development budgets. Your divisional overhead costs (additional costs beyond those incurred by the development and sales departments) are approximately $390,000. Determine whether the Wireless Division can meet its targeted 30% return on assets given the budgeted alternatives submitted by your department managers.

During the meeting of the entire team, the group playing Watson presents the division budget and considers its implications. Each group should take turns discussing its concerns with the proposed budget. The team as a whole should consider whether the division budget must be revised. The team should prepare a report that includes the division budget and a summary of the issues covered in the team meeting.

For Internet Exercises, go to the Web site www.prenhall.com/horngren.

APPENDIX *to Chapter 23*

Departmental Accounting

Responsibility centers are often called *departments*. Consider a retailer such as **Macy's, Lazarus**, or **Nordstrom**. Top managers of a department store want more information than just the net income of the store as a whole. They want to know each department's gross profit (sales minus cost of goods sold). They also usually want to know each department's operating income. These data can help identify the most profitable departments.

It is easy to measure gross profit because each department records sales and cost of goods sold. It is more difficult to measure a department's operating income (gross profit minus operating expenses). Why? Many operating expenses are indirect costs that are not directly traced to the department.

☐ Why Managers Use Budgets
☐ Preparing the Master Budget
☐ Preparing the Operating Budget
☐ Preparing the Financial Budget
☐ Using Information Technology
☐ Responsibility Accounting
■ Appendix: Departmental Accounting

Allocating Indirect Costs

See Chapter 20, pp. 811–813 for a discussion of allocating indirect costs.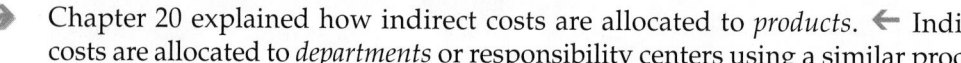

Chapter 20 explained how indirect costs are allocated to *products*. ← Indirect costs are allocated to *departments* or responsibility centers using a similar process.

■ Choose an allocation base for the indirect cost
■ Compute an indirect cost allocation rate:

$$\text{Indirect cost allocation rate} = \frac{\text{Total indirect costs}}{\text{Total quantity of allocation base}}$$

■ Allocate the indirect cost to the department:

$$\text{Allocation of indirect costs} = \frac{\text{Quantity of allocation}}{\text{base used by department}} \times \frac{\text{Indirect cost}}{\text{allocation rate}}$$

As we noted in Chapter 20, the ideal cost allocation base is the cost driver. Suppose Macy's decides that its receiving costs are driven by the number of orders placed to purchase inventory. If 15% of the orders are for the Shoe Department and 20% are for the Menswear Department, then Macy's will allocate 15% of the Receiving Department costs to the Shoe Department and 20% to the Menswear Department. (The remaining Receiving Department costs will be allocated to other departments in proportion to the number of orders each issued.)

Exhibit 23A-1 lists common allocation bases for different indirect costs. Managers use their experience and judgment to choose these bases, but there is no single "correct" allocation base for each indirect cost.

✔ **Starter 23A-1**

Exhibit 23A-1

Bases for Allocating Indirect Costs to Departments

Cost or Expense	Base for Allocating Cost
Supervisors' salaries	Time spent, or number of employees, in each department
Equipment depreciation	Separately traced, or hours used by each department
Building depreciation, property taxes	Square feet of space
Janitorial services	Square feet of space
Advertising	Separately traced if possible; otherwise, in proportion to sales
Materials handling	Number or weight of items handled for each department
Personnel Department	Number of employees in each department
Purchasing Department	Number of purchase orders placed for each department

How to Allocate Indirect Costs to Departments: An Example

Exhibit 23A-2 shows a departmental income statement for WorldPC, a retail computer store. Let's see how the company assigns operating expenses to the store's two departments: Hardware and Software.

Salaries and Wages. WorldPC traces salespersons' salaries and department managers' salaries directly to each department.

Rent. WorldPC allocates the $600,000 rent expense based on the square feet each department occupies. The Hardware and Software departments occupy 20,000 square feet and 5,000 square feet, respectively, so WorldPC allocates rent as follows:

Rent for entire store	$600,000
Total square feet (20,000 + 5,000)	÷ 25,000
Rent per square foot.	$ 24

Hardware Department:	20,000 square feet ¥ $24 per square foot =	$480,000
Software Department:	5,000 square feet ¥ $24 per square foot =	120,000
Total rent expense . . . . =		$600,000

✔ Starter 23A-2

Exhibit 23A-2

Departmental Income Statement

WorldPC

Departmental Income Statement
Year Ended December 31, 20X9
(In Thousands)

		Department	
	Total	Hardware	Software
Sales revenue	$10,000	$7,000	$3,000
Cost of goods sold	6,500	4,500	2,000
Gross profit.	3,500	2,500	1,000
Operating expenses:			
Salaries and wages expense	1,400	660	740
Rent expense.	600	480	120
Purchasing department expense . .	48	36	12
Total operating expenses	2,048	1,176	872
Operating income	$ 1,452	$1,324	$ 128

Purchasing Department. WorldPC found that it takes just as long to complete a purchase order for inexpensive modems as for expensive notebook computers. Consequently, the company allocates the $48,000 costs of the Purchasing Department based on the number of purchase orders processed. Hardware had 300 purchase orders, and Software had 100.

Purchasing Department costs.	$48,000
Total number of purchase orders (300 + 100)	÷ 400
Cost per purchase order	$ 120

Hardware Department:	300 purchase orders × $120 per purchase order =	$36,000
Software Department:	100 purchase orders × $120 per purchase order =	12,000
Total Purchasing Department cost . . . . =		$48,000

WorldPC's top executives can use the departmental income statements in Exhibit 23A-2 to evaluate how well each department and its manager performed in 20X9. Hardware was more profitable than Software. Hardware's profit margin (income divided by sales) was $1,324 ÷ $7,000 = 18.9%, while Software's profit margin was only $128 ÷ $3,000 = 4.3%. However, it is better to compare a department's actual results to its budget rather than to another department's results. For example, if WorldPC has just added the Software Department, performance may have exceeded expectations.

Appendix Assignments
Starters

S23A-1 Listed below are several cost drivers.

Identifying indirect cost allocation bases

Number of loads of materials moved	Number of customer complaints	Number of pages
Number of purchase orders	Number of inches	Number of square feet
Number of shipments received	Number of machine hours	Number of employees

(continued)

Which of these is most likely the driver for the following costs?

a. Photocopying Department costs
b. Maintenance Department costs
c. Receiving Department costs
d. Customer Service Department costs
e. Purchasing Department costs

f. Material handling costs
g. Personnel Department costs
h. Building rent and utilities
i. Newspaper advertising costs

Allocating indirect costs to departments

S23A-2 Consider the WorldPC example on page 981. Suppose the Hardware Department occupies 20,000 square feet and the Software Department occupies 10,000 square feet. How much of the $600,000 rent expense would be allocated to each department?

Exercises

Allocating indirect expenses to departments

E23A-1 Scott Manufacturing incurred the following indirect costs in April:

Indirect labor expense.............................	$18,000
Equipment depreciation expense	24,000
Marketing expense	25,200

Data for cost allocations:

	Department		
	Priming	**Welding**	**Custom Orders**
Sales revenue	$60,000	$30,000	$90,000
Indirect labor hours	500	700	300
Machine hours	550	525	125
Building square feet	11,000	3,500	1,000
Marketing expense—allocated to departments in proportion to sales.			

Required

1. Allocate Scott Manufacturing's April indirect expenses to the three departments.
2. Compute total indirect expenses for each department.

Preparing a departmental income statement

E23A-2 Handsong sells chrome and plastic harmonicas. It has two departments: Chrome and Plastic. The company's income statement for 20X6 appears as follows:

Sales revenue	$372,000
Cost of goods sold	154,000
Gross profit......................................	218,000
Operating expenses:	
Salaries expense	$ 78,000
Depreciation expense..........................	40,000
Advertising expense	6,000
Other expenses................................	12,000
Total operating expenses.......................	136,000
Operating income................................	$ 82,000

Handsong sales are $206,000 of chrome harmonicas and $166,000 of plastic harmonicas. Cost of goods sold is distributed $68,000 to Chrome and $86,000 to Plastic. Salaries are traced directly to departments: Chrome, $36,000; and Plastic, $42,000. The Chrome Department accounts for 70% of advertising. Depreciation is allocated based on the warehouse square footage occupied by each department: Chrome has 20,000 square feet and Plastic has 30,000 square feet. Other expenses are allocated based on

(*continued*)

the number of employees. Each department currently employs an equal number of employees.

Required

1. Prepare departmental income statements that show revenues, expenses, and operating income for each of the two departments.

2. Which of the expenses in the departmental performance report are the most important for evaluating Handsong department managers? Give your reason.

Problem

P23A-1 The Ritz-Carlton Club, an exclusive "hotel within a hotel," provides an even more luxurious atmosphere than the hotel's regular accommodations. Access is limited to guests residing on the hotel's top floors. The Club's private lounge serves complimentary continental breakfast, afternoon snacks, and evening cocktails and chocolates. The Club has its own concierge staff that provides personal service to Club guests. Guests staying in regular accommodations do not receive complimentary snacks and beverages, nor do they have a private concierge.

Allocating indirect expenses to departments, performance evaluation

Ritz-Carlton Club floors are considered one department, and regular accommodations are considered a separate department.

Suppose the general manager of the new Ritz-Carlton hotel in St. Thomas, an island in the Caribbean, wants to know the costs of her hotel's Club Accommodations Department and Regular Accommodations Department. Housekeeping costs are allocated based on the number of occupied room-nights, utilities are allocated based on the number of cubic feet, and building depreciation is allocated based on the number of square feet. Assume each department reports the following information for March:

	Club Accommodations	Regular Accommodations
Number of occupied room-nights....	540	7,560
Cubic feet	192,000	1,440,000
Square feet......................	16,000	144,000

Required

1. Given the following (assumed) total costs, what are the costs assigned to the Club Accommodations and the Regular Accommodations Departments?

Food and beverage expense	$ 12,000
Housekeeping expense	194,400
Utilities expense................................	97,920
Building depreciation expense.....................	480,000
Concierge staff salaries	15,000
Total	$799,320

2. What is the cost per occupied room in Club Accommodations? In Regular Accommodations?

3. Why might the general manager want to know the cost per occupied room for the Club Accommodations and the Regular Accommodations?

CHAPTER 24

Flexible Budgets and Standard Costs

TIPS CHECK YOUR RESOURCES

- Visit the www.prenhall.com/horngren **Web site** for self-study quizzes, video clips, and other resources

- Try the **Quick Check** exercise at the end of the chapter to test your knowledge

- Learn the **key terms**

- Do the **Starter** exercises keyed in the margins

- Work the **mid-** and **end-of-chapter summary problems**

- Use the **Concept Links** to review material in other chapters

- Search the **CD** for review materials by chapter or by key word

- Watch the **tutorial videos** to review key concepts

- Watch the **On Location McDonald's** video for more on flexible budgets.

LEARNING OBJECTIVES

1 Prepare a flexible budget for the income statement

2 Use the flexible budget to show why actual results differ from the static budget

3 Identify the benefits of standard costs and learn how to set standards

4 Compute standard cost variances for direct materials and direct labor

5 Analyze manufacturing overhead in a standard cost system

6 Record transactions at standard cost and prepare a standard cost income statement

How does McDonald's make sure that its 30,000 restaurants deliver quality, service, cleanliness, and value to over 46 million customers worldwide each day? By using budgets, standards, and variances. Managers budget sales for each hour and schedule just enough workers to handle the budgeted level of sales. During the day, the manager computes variances for sales (for example, actual sales minus budgeted sales) and for direct labor. If actual sales fall short of the budget, the manager can send employees home early. This helps control direct labor cost.

McDonald's

McDonald's also sets budgets and standards for direct materials. From Beijing to Miami, the standards for a regular McDonald's hamburger are the same: 1 bun, 1 hamburger patty, 1 pickle slice, 1/8 teaspoon dehydrated onion, 1/8 teaspoon mustard, and 1/3 ounce of ketchup. To control direct materials costs, the manager compares the number of, say, hamburger patties actually used with the number of patties that should have been used, given the store's actual sales.

McDonald's uses budgets, standards, and variances to control costs so prices remain low enough that customers believe McDonald's provides good *value*. McDonald's also uses standards and variances to motivate employees to focus on:

- Quality—sandwiches unsold within 10 minutes are thrown away.
- Service—customers should receive food within 90 seconds of ordering.
- Cleanliness—mystery shoppers score restaurants' cleanliness.

■Sitemap

- **How Managers Use Flexible Budgets**
- **Actual Results versus Static Budget**
- **Standard Costing**
- **Analyzing Flexible Budget Variance**
- **Manufacturing Overhead Variances**
- **Standard Cost Accounting Systems**

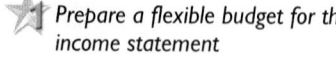

Student ResourceCD

flexible budget, static budget, variances

★ *Prepare a flexible budget for the income statement*

Static Budget
The budget prepared for only one level of sales volume. Also called the **master budget.**

This chapter builds on your knowledge of budgeting (from Chapter 23) to show how managers use variances to learn *why* actual results differ from budgets. Why is this important? Because you must know *why* actual costs differ from the budget to identify problems and to decide what, if any, action to take.

Suppose you buy soft drinks for a party. Your budget is $30, but you actually spend $35. To know how you can avoid exceeding your budget in the future, you must first know *why* you spent more than the $30 budget.

- If the price per can of soft drinks was higher than the price per can in the budget, then you might:
  - Find a cheaper price at a warehouse club like Costco, or watch for sales and buy soft drinks when they are on special.
  - Buy less-expensive store-brand soft drinks.
- If you bought a larger quantity of soft drinks than you budgeted, why did you need this larger quantity?
  - If more than the planned number of guests attended the party, you could restrict the invitation list.
  - If the expected number of guests attended the party but on average each guest drank more soft drinks than you budgeted, perhaps you could cut per-guest consumption by starting the party later or ending earlier, or by reducing the number of salty snacks served.
- If the budget for soft drinks was unrealistically low, in the future you may have to increase the budget.

In this chapter, you'll learn how you—like managers of companies from McDonald's to Dell Computer—can use flexible budgets, standards, and variances to pinpoint exactly *why* actual results differ from the budget. This is the first step in determining how to correct problems.

How Managers Use Flexible Budgets

Kool-Time Pools installs swimming pools. At the beginning of the year, Kool-Time managers prepared a master budget like the one in Chapter 23 for June. The master budget is a **static budget** that is prepared for *one* level of sales volume. This budget does not change after it is developed.

Exhibit 24-1 shows that Kool-Time's actual operating income is $4,000 higher than expected in the static budget. This is a $4,000 favorable variance in Kool-Time's June operating income. A **variance** is the difference between an actual amount and the budget. The variances in the third column of Exhibit 24-1 are favorable (F) if a higher actual amount increases operating income and unfavorable (U) if a higher actual amount decreases operating income. The variance for the number of pools installed is favorable because higher volume (10 rather than 8 pools) tends to increase income.

Variance
The difference between an actual amount and the budget. A variance is labeled as favorable if it increases operating income and unfavorable if it decreases operating income.

Kool-Time Pools			
Comparison of Actual Results with Static Budget			
Month Ended June 30, 20X5			
	Actual Results	**Static Budget**	**Variance**
Output units (pools installed).....	10	8	2 F
Sales revenue..................	$121,000	$96,000	$25,000 F
Expenses	(105,000)	(84,000)	21,000 U
Operating income..............	$ 16,000	$12,000	$ 4,000 F

Exhibit 24-1

Actual Results versus Static Budget

What Is a Flexible Budget?

The report in Exhibit 24-1 is hard to analyze because the static budget is based on 8 pools, but actual results are for 10 pools. Why did the $21,000 unfavorable expense variance occur? Did workers waste materials? Did the cost of materials suddenly increase? How much of the additional expense arose because Kool-Time built 10 rather than 8 pools? Exhibit 24-1's simple comparison of actual results with the static budget does not give managers enough information to answer these questions.

Flexible budgets do answer such questions. Exhibit 24-2 shows that in contrast to the static master budget developed for a single level of sales volume, **flexible budgets** are summarized budgets that managers can easily compute for several different volume levels.

Flexible Budget
A summarized budget that managers can easily compute for several different volume levels. Flexible budgets separate variable costs from fixed costs; it is the variable costs that put the "flex" in the flexible budget.

← Chapter 23, pp. 943–954, discusses the master budget process.

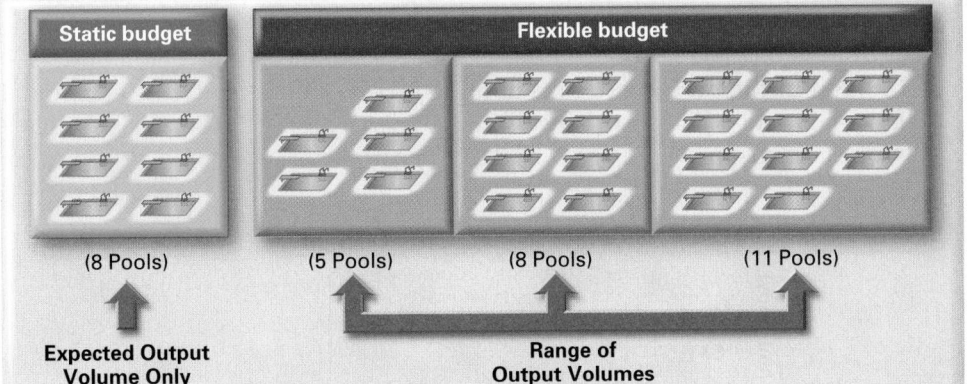

Exhibit 24-2

Static versus Flexible Budgets

Exhibit 24-3 uses flexible budgets to show how Kool-Time's revenues and expenses should vary as sales increase from 5 to 8 to 11 pools. The budgeted sale price per pool is $12,000. → The flexible budget formula for total cost is

← See Chapter 22, pp. 898–899, to review the distinction between variable costs and fixed costs.

$$\text{Flexible budget total cost} = \left(\begin{array}{c} \text{Number of} \\ \text{output units} \end{array} \times \begin{array}{c} \text{Variable cost} \\ \text{per output unit} \end{array} \right) + \text{Total fixed cost}$$

Exhibit 24-3

Flexible Budget

Kool-Time Pools

Flexible Budget
Month Ended June 30, 20X5

	Flexible Budget per Output Unit	Output Units (Pools Installed)		
		5	8	11
Sales revenue	$12,000	$60,000	$96,000	$132,000
Variable expenses.	8,000	40,000	64,000	88,000
Fixed expenses*		20,000	20,000	20,000
Total expenses		60,000	84,000	108,000
Operating income		$ 0	$12,000	$ 24,000

*Fixed expenses are given as a total amount rather than as a cost per unit.

✔ Starter 24-1

Budgeted total variable costs (such as the cost of materials and labor) increase at the rate of $8,000 per pool installed. It is these variable costs that put the "flex" in the flexible budget because budgeted total monthly fixed costs (such as administrative salaries and depreciation on equipment) remain constant at $20,000 throughout the range of 5 to 11 pools.

Managers develop flexible budgets like Exhibit 24-3 for any number of outputs, using a simple Excel spreadsheet or more-sophisticated Web-based budget management software. However, managers must be wary: *The flexible budget total cost formula applies only to a specific relevant range.* Why? Because total monthly fixed costs and the variable cost per pool change outside this range. Kool-Time's relevant range is 0 to 11 pools. If the company installs 12 pools, it will have to rent additional equipment, so fixed costs will exceed $20,000. Kool-Time will also have to pay workers an overtime premium, so the variable cost per pool will be more than $8,000.

Graphing the Flexible Budget

Exhibit 24-4 shows budgeted total costs for the entire relevant range of 0 to 11 pools. The flexible budget total cost line intersects the vertical axis at the amount of the total fixed cost ($20,000) Kool-Time will incur whether it installs 0 pools or 11 pools. ← The flexible budget's total cost line slopes upward at the rate of $8,000 per pool, which is Kool-Time's variable cost per pool. For example, the cost for one pool is $28,000 [(1 pool × $8,000 variable cost per pool) + $20,000 fixed cost]. But the *extra* cost of installing a second pool is only the additional $8,000 variable cost. The cost to install two pools is therefore $36,000 [(2 pools × $8,000 variable cost per pool) + $20,000 fixed cost].

The flexible budget cost line in Exhibit 24-4 follows the same principles as the cost-volume-profit graph's total cost line in Exhibit 22-7, page 907.
→

Exhibit 24-4

Kool-Time Pools Monthly Flexible
Budget Graph

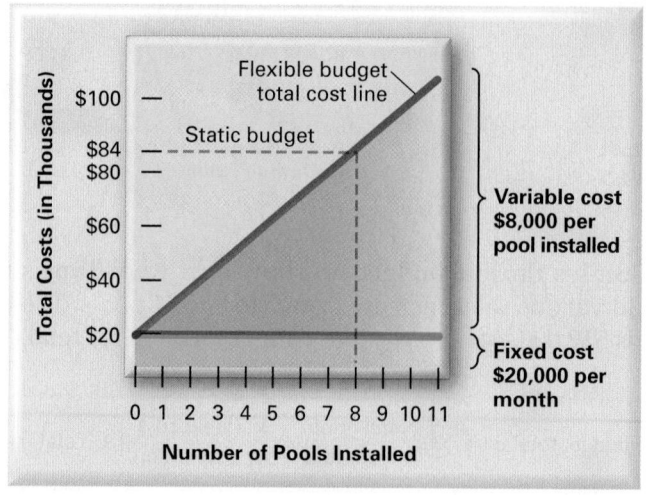

Kool-Time initially expected to install eight pools per month (at a total cost of $84,000). But managers also can use the flexible budget graph in Exhibit 24-4 to *plan costs* for anywhere from 0 to 11 pools.

At the end of the period, managers also can use the flexible budget to help control costs. They plot actual costs on the graph, as shown in Exhibit 24-5. Consider June, when Kool-Time actually installed 10 pools. The flexible budget graphs in Exhibits 24-4 and 24-5 show that *budgeted* total costs for 10 pools are

Variable costs (10 × $8,000)	$ 80,000
Fixed costs......................................	20,000
Total costs	$100,000

June's *actual* costs, or expenses, were $105,000 (Exhibit 24-1). Consequently, Exhibit 24-5 shows that June's actual costs for 10 pools ($105,000) exceed the budget for 10 pools ($100,000). Managers use graphs of actual versus budgeted costs to see at a glance whether actual costs are

- Higher than budgeted for the actual level of output, as in April, June, and August, or
- Lower than budgeted for the actual level of output, as in May and July

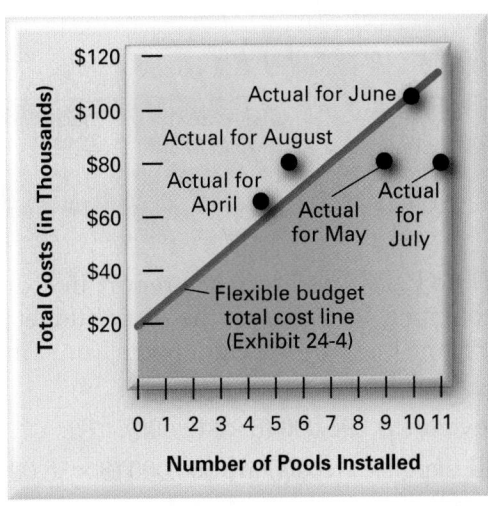

Exhibit 24-5

Kool-Time Pools Graph of Actual and Budgeted Monthly Costs

✔ **Starter 24-2**

Use the graph in Exhibit 24-5 and Kool-Time's flexible budget formula (page 987) to answer the following questions:

1. How many pools did Kool-Time install in July?
2. What were Kool-Time's actual costs in July?
3. Using Kool-Time's flexible budget formula, what is the flexible budget total cost for the month of July?
4. Is Kool-Time's variance for total costs favorable or unfavorable in July?

Answers

1. Exhibit 24-5 shows that Kool-Time installed 11 pools in July.
2. Exhibit 24-5 shows that Kool-Time's actual costs in July were about $80,000.
3. Using Kool-Time's flexible budget total cost formula:

Variable costs (11 × $8,000)	$ 88,000
Fixed costs	20,000
Total costs	$108,000

4. Kool-Time's July variance for total costs is $28,000 ($80,000 − $108,000) favorable, because actual costs are less than the budget.

Use the flexible budget to show why actual results differ from the static budget

Sales Volume Variance
The difference arising only because the number of units actually sold differs from the static budget units. This equals the difference between a static budget amount and a flexible budget amount.

Exhibit 24-6

The Static Budget Variance, the Sales Volume Variance, and the Flexible Budget Variance

Flexible Budget Variance
The difference arising because the company actually earned more or less revenue, or incurred more or less cost, than expected for the actual level of output. This equals the difference between the actual amount and a flexible budget amount.

✔ **Starter 24-3**

Student ResourceCD

flexible budget, flexible budget variance, sales volume variance, static budget

Using the Flexible Budget to See Why Actual Results Differ from the Static Budget

Managers must know *why* a variance occurred to pinpoint problems and to identify corrective action. To analyze variances, managers begin by using the *flexible budget for the number of units actually sold* to divide the static budget variance into two broad categories:

■ **Sales volume variance**—arises only because the number of units actually sold differs from the static budget units.

■ **Flexible budget variance**—arises because the company actually earned more or less revenue, or incurred more or less cost, than expected for the actual level of output.

Exhibit 24-6 shows that the sales volume variance is the difference between

1. The *static* (master) budget—for the number of units *expected* to be sold (8 pools, for Kool-Time), and

2. The *flexible* budget—for the number of units *actually* sold (10 pools in June).

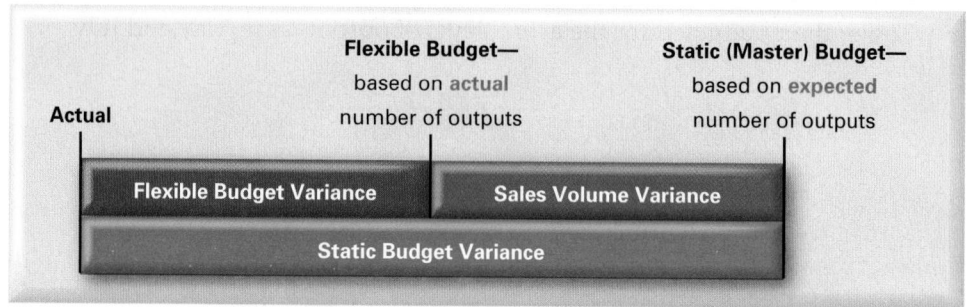

Consider Kool-Time Pool's performance report in Exhibit 24-7. The static budget amounts in column 5 are based on the static budget sales forecast developed at the *beginning* of the period—the eight pools Kool-Time *expected* to install. For these eight pools, Kool-Time's

■ Budgeted sales revenue is $96,000 (8 × $12,000).

■ Budgeted variable expenses (costs) are $64,000 (8 × $8,000).

■ Budgeted fixed expenses (costs) are $20,000.

(Note that this is a slightly more detailed version of Kool-Time's static budget for eight pools shown in Exhibit 24-1.)

In contrast to the static budget, which is developed *before* the period, the flexible budget used in the performance report in Exhibit 24-7 is not developed until the *end* of the period. Why? Because *flexible budgets used in performance reports are based on the actual number of outputs, which is not known until the end of the period.* For Kool-Time, the flexible budget used in the performance report (column 3 of Exhibit 24-7) is based on the 10 pools actually installed:

■ Budgeted sales revenue is $120,000 (10 × $12,000).

■ Budgeted variable expenses are $80,000 (10 × $8,000).

■ Budgeted fixed expenses are $20,000.

The only difference between the static and flexible budgets in the performance report is the number of outputs on which the budget is based (8 pools versus 10 pools). Both budgets use the same

■ Budgeted sale price per unit ($12,000 per pool)

■ Budgeted variable cost per unit ($8,000 per pool)

■ Budgeted total fixed costs ($20,000 per month)

Exhibit 24-7

Income Statement Performance Report

Kool-Time Pools
Income Statement Performance Report
Month Ended June 30, 20X5

	(1)	(2) (1)–(3)	(3)	(4) (3)–(5)	(5)
	Actual Results at Actual Prices	Flexible Budget Variance	Flexible Budget for Actual Number of Output Units*	Sales Volume Variance	Static (Master) Budget*
Output units (pools installed) . .	10	–0–	10	2 F	8
Sales revenue	$121,000	$1,000 F	$120,000	$24,000 F	$96,000
Variable expenses	83,000	3,000 U	80,000	16,000 U	64,000
Fixed expenses.	22,000	2,000 U	20,000	–0–	20,000
Total expenses	105,000	5,000 U	100,000	16,000 U	84,000
Operating income	$ 16,000	$4,000 U	$ 20,000	$ 8,000 F	$12,000

Flexible budget variance,
$4,000 U

Sales volume variance,
$8,000 F

Static budget variance,
$4,000 F

*Budgeted sale price is $12,000 per pool, budgeted variable expense is $8,000 per pool, and budgeted total monthly fixed expenses are $20,000.

Holding selling price per unit, variable cost per unit, and total fixed costs constant highlights the effects of differences in sales volume—the variance in column 4. This variance is typically marketing's responsibility. Exhibit 24-7 shows that by installing two more pools than initially expected, Kool-Time's

Who is responsible for sales volume variance?

Sales Volume
Actual   10
Budgeted 8

Answer: Marketing

- Sales revenue should increase from $96,000 (8 × $12,000) to $120,000 (10 × $12,000)—a $24,000 favorable sales volume variance.

- Variable costs should increase from $64,000 (8 × $8,000) to $80,000 (10 × $8,000)—a $16,000 unfavorable sales volume variance.

Budgeted total fixed expenses are unaffected because 8 pools and 10 pools are within the relevant range where fixed expenses total $20,000 (0 to 11 pools). Consequently, installing two more pools should increase operating income by $8,000 ($24,000 F – $16,000 U). So Kool-Time's June sales volume variance is $8,000 F.

When is there a sales volume variance for fixed expenses?

Answer: Only when the number of units actually sold falls within a different relevant range than the static budget sales volume. When actual and expected number of units sold fall in the same relevant range, there is no sales volume variance for fixed expenses.

Stop & Think

✔ Starter 24-4

✔ Starter 24-5

Exhibits 24-6 and 24-7 show that the second piece of the static budget variance is the flexible budget variance—the difference between

- Actual amounts (column 1 in Exhibit 24-7) and
- Flexible budget amounts that should have been incurred *for the actual number of output units* (column 3 in Exhibit 24-7)

Who is responsible for sales revenue flexible budget variance?

Revenue 10 pools

Actual $ 121,000

Flex budget $ 120,000

Flex budget variance $ 1,000F

Answer: Marketing

Kool-Time actually incurred $83,000 of variable costs to install the 10 pools. This is $3,000 more than the $80,000 (10 pools × $8,000 per pool) budgeted variable cost for 10 pools. The company also spent $2,000 more than budgeted on fixed expenses ($22,000 – $20,000). Consequently, the flexible budget variance for total expenses is $5,000 unfavorable ($3,000 U + $2,000 U). That is, Kool-Time spent $5,000 more than expected for installing 10 pools.

Exhibit 24-7 shows there is also a flexible budget variance for sales revenue. Kool-Time actually received $121,000 for installing 10 pools, which is $1,000 more than the $120,000 flexible budget sales revenue for 10 pools (10 pools × $12,000). This $1,000 sales revenue price variance means the average sale price was $12,100 per pool ($121,000 ÷ 10 pools), which is $100 higher than the budgeted sale price of $12,000 per pool.

How would Kool-Time's managers use these variances? The favorable sales volume variance reveals that strong sales should have increased Kool-Time's income by $8,000. And the sales staff increased sales without discounting prices: The favorable $1,000 sales revenue flexible budget variance shows that the sale price was on average *higher* than budgeted. These favorable variances on the quantity of pools sold (the $8,000 favorable sales volume variance) and the sale price per pool (the $1,000 favorable sales revenue price variance) suggest that Kool-Time's marketing staff did a better-than-expected job in selling pools and maintaining sales prices.

Who is responsible for flexible budget variance?

Actual expense $105,000

Flex budget expense 100,000

Flex budget var. $ 5,000U

Answer: Purchasing, Production, HR

On the other hand, higher-than-expected expenses offset much of these favorable sales variances. Exhibit 24-7 shows a $5,000 unfavorable flexible budget variance for expenses. Management will want to find out why. The reason might be an uncontrollable increase in the cost of materials. Or higher costs might have resulted from more-controllable factors such as employees wasting materials or working inefficiently. If so, managers can take action to reduce waste or inefficiency. The second half of this chapter explains how Kool-Time's managers probe flexible budget variances to identify the reason for the cost overrun so they can decide what action to take to avoid similar overruns in the future.

Decision Guidelines

FLEXIBLE BUDGETS

You and your roommate have started a business printing T-shirts for special customer requests (for example, including school or student organization logos). How can you use flexible budgets to plan and control your costs?

Decision	Guidelines
How to estimate sales revenues, costs, and profits over the range of likely sales (output) levels?	Prepare a set of flexible budgets for different sales levels.
How to prepare a flexible budget for total costs?	$$\text{Flexible budget total cost} = \left(\text{Number of T-shirts} \times \text{Variable cost per T-shirt} \right) + \text{Fixed cost}$$
How to use budgets to help control costs?	• Graph actual costs versus flexible budget costs, as in Exhibit 24-5. • Prepare an income statement performance report, as in Exhibit 24-7.
On which output level is the budget based?	Static (master) budget—*expected* number of T-shirts, estimated before the period
	Flexible budget—*actual* number of T-shirts, not known until the end of the period

Decision Guidelines (continued)

Decision	Guidelines
Why does your actual income differ from budgeted income?	Prepare an income statement performance report comparing actual results, flexible budget for actual number of T-shirts sold, and static (master) budget, as in Exhibit 24-7.
• How much of the difference is because the actual number of T-shirts sold does not equal budgeted sales?	Compute the sales volume variance (SVV) by comparing the flexible budget with the static budget. • Favorable SVV—Income effect if Actual number of T-shirts sold > Expected number of T-shirts sold • Unfavorable SVV—Income effect if Actual number of T-shirts sold < Expected number of T-shirts sold
• How much of the difference occurs because actual revenues and costs are not what they should have been for the actual number of T-shirts sold?	Compute the flexible budget variance (FBV) by comparing actual results with the flexible budget. • Favorable FBV—Income effect if Actual sales revenue > Flexible budget sales revenue Actual expenses < Flexible budget expenses • Unfavorable FBV—Income effect if Actual sales revenue < Flexible budget sales revenue Actual expenses > Flexible budget expenses
What actions can you take to avoid an unfavorable sales volume variance?	• Design more-attractive T-shirts to increase demand. • Provide marketing incentives to increase number of T-shirts sold.
What actions can you take to avoid an unfavorable flexible budget variance?	• Avoid an unfavorable sales revenue price flexible budget variance by maintaining (not discounting) sales prices. • Avoid an unfavorable flexible budget variance for expenses by controlling variable expenses, such as the cost of the plain T-shirts, dye, and labor, and by controlling fixed expenses.

Excel Application Exercise

Goal: Create a spreadsheet and use it to analyze a company's flexible budget.

Scenario: After the first month of operating the T-Shirt Time printing business, you prepare a flexible budget to see how the company did versus your original expectations. When you and your roommate started the business, you expected to sell 1,000 shirts your first month, at $12 each. Your budgeted variable cost per shirt was $6, and budgeted fixed costs were $2,500. At the end of the first month, you had sold 900 shirts at $11 each. Actual variable cost per shirt was $7, and actual fixed expenses were $2,200.

Using Exhibit 24-7 as your guide, prepare an Excel spreadsheet that has two sections: one for budgeted and actual data given above, and one for T-Shirt Time's Income Statement Performance Report. When you have completed your worksheet, answer the following questions:

1. What is T-Shirt Time's sales volume variance? What does this variance mean?
2. What is T-Shirt Time's flexible budget variance? What does this variance mean?
3. How would you and your roommate use these variances?

Step-by-Step:

1. Open a new Excel spreadsheet.

2. In column A, create a bold-faced heading as follows:
   a. Chapter 24 Excel Application Exercise
   b. Flexible Budgets
   c. T-Shirt Time
   d. Today's Date
3. Two rows down, enter "Budgeted Data" in bold. Underneath this heading, create the following four rows:
   a. T-shirts expected to be sold
   b. Budgeted sales price per T-shirt
   c. Budgeted variable cost per T-shirt
   d. Budgeted fixed expenses
4. Two rows down, enter "Actual Data" in bold. Underneath this heading, create the following four rows:
   a. T-shirts actually sold
   b. Actual sales price per T-shirt
   c. Actual variable cost per T-shirt
   d. Actual fixed expenses
5. Across from each description in Budgeted Data and Actual Data, enter the values found in the exercise scenario in column B.
6. Starting two rows down from the Actual Data section, replicate the format of the income statement performance report shown in Exhibit 24-7. Make sure the report consists entirely of formulas based on the budgeted and actual data provided. Format as appropriate.
7. When finished, save your work and print a copy for your files.

TIPS

CHECK YOUR RESOURCES

Exhibit 24-7 indicates that Kool-Time Pools installed 10 swimming pools during June. Now assume that Kool-Time installed 7 pools (instead of 10) and that the actual sale price averaged $12,500 per pool. Actual variable expenses were $57,400, and actual fixed expenses were $19,000.

Required

1. Prepare a revised income statement performance report using Exhibit 24-7 as a guide.
2. Show that the sum of the flexible budget variance and the sales volume variance for operating income equals the static budget variance for operating income.
3. As the company owner, which employees would you praise or criticize after you analyze this performance report?

Solution

Requirements 1 and 2

Kool-Time Pools
Income Statement Performance Report—Revised
Month Ended June 30, 20X5

	(1) Actual Results at Actual Prices	(2) (1)–(3) Flexible Budget Variance	(3) Flexible Budget for Actual Number of Output Units	(4) (3)–(5) Sales Volume Variance	(5) Static (Master) Budget
Output units	7	–0–	7	1 U	8
Sales revenue	$87,500	$3,500 F	$84,000	$12,000 U	$96,000
Variable expenses	57,400	1,400 U	56,000	8,000 F	64,000
Fixed expenses	19,000	1,000 F	20,000	—	20,000
Total expenses	76,400	400 U	76,000	8,000 F	84,000
Operating income	$11,100	$3,100 F	$ 8,000	$ 4,000 U	$12,000

Flexible budget variance, $3,100 F — Sales volume variance, $4,000 U

Static budget variance, $900 U

Requirement 3

As the company owner, you should determine the *causes* of the variances before deciding who deserves praise or criticism. It is especially important to determine who is responsible for the variance and whether the variance is due to factors the manager can control. For example, the unfavorable sales volume variance could be due to an ineffective sales staff. Or it could be due to an uncontrollable long period of heavy rain that brought work to a standstill. Similarly, the $1,000 favorable flexible budget variance for fixed expenses could be due to an employee finding a lower-cost source of rented equipment. Or the savings might have come from delaying a needed overhaul of equipment that could increase the company's costs in the long run. Smart managers use variances to raise questions and direct attention, not to fix blame.

 Student Resource CD

benchmarking, costs, price standard, quantity standard, standard costing

 *Identify the benefits of standard costs and learn how to set standards*

Standard Costing

Most companies use **standard costs** to develop their flexible budgets. Think of a standard cost as a budget for a single unit. For example, Kool-Time Pool's standard variable cost is $8,000 per pool (see Exhibit 24-3). This $8,000 variable cost includes the standard cost of inputs like the direct materials, direct labor, and variable overhead costs necessary to install one pool.

In a standard cost system, each input has both a quantity standard and a price standard. McDonald's has a standard for the amount of beef per hamburger and for the price paid per pound of beef. Kool-Time Pools has a standard for the amount of gunite (a concrete derivative) used per pool and for the price it pays per cubic foot of gunite. Let's see how managers set these price and quantity standards.

Standard Cost
A budget for a single unit.

Price Standards

Accountants help managers set direct material price standards after considering early-payment discounts, freight in, and receiving costs, in addition to base purchase price. World-class businesses expect continuous reductions in direct material standard prices. → For example, Toyota sent its own engineers to one of its bumper suppliers to help the supplier cut costs. Toyota expected the supplier to pass on much of the savings in lower prices. Similarly, suppliers say Dell Computer expects them to push down the prices of their components. When one supplier walked into a meeting carrying cinnamon rolls, Michael Dell reportedly snapped, "Take those back. We don't need food. We want lower prices!"

← *We discuss continuous improvement in Chapter 19, page 773.*

E-commerce helps managers continuously lower direct material price standards. Purchasing managers use the Internet to solicit price quotes from suppliers around the world. Dell uses the Internet to provide its major suppliers with customized virtual windows into Dell's production process. Each supplier sees Dell's production forecast and the inventory of the supplier's parts Dell currently has on hand. The supplier uses this information to decide when to ship more parts to Dell. By sharing information about its operations, Dell helps its suppliers plan their own production, purchasing, and deliveries more precisely, which helps them further cut costs.

For direct labor, accountants work with personnel or human resources managers to determine standard labor rates, taking into account payroll taxes and fringe benefits as well as the hourly wage rate.

For overhead, accountants work with production managers to estimate variable and fixed manufacturing overhead expenses. Production managers then identify an appropriate allocation base that accountants use to compute the standard (predetermined) overhead rates, as you learned in Chapter 20. →

← *See Chapter 20, pages 810–813, to review the computation of overhead rates.*

The manager in charge of purchasing gunite for Kool-Time Pools indicates that the purchase price, net of discounts, is $1.90 per cubic foot of gunite and that delivery, receiving, and inspection costs average $0.10 per cubic foot. Kool-Time's Human Resources Department indicates that the hourly wage rate for workers is $8 and that payroll taxes and fringe benefits total $2.50 per direct labor hour. The production manager estimates that variable and fixed overhead will total $6,400 and $12,000, respectively, and that overhead should be allocated based on 3,200 estimated direct labor hours.

Required: Compute Kool-Time Pools' price standards for direct materials, direct labor, and overhead.

Answer: Direct materials price standard for gunite:

Purchase price, net of discounts	$1.90	per cubic foot
Delivery, receiving, and inspection	0.10	per cubic foot
Total standard cost per cubic foot of gunite . . .	$2.00	per cubic foot

Direct labor price (or rate) standard:

Hourly wage rate	$ 8.00	per direct labor hour
Payroll taxes and fringe benefits	2.50	per direct labor hour
Total standard cost per direct labor hour	$10.50	per direct labor hour

(*continued*)

Variable overhead price (or rate) standard:

$$\frac{\text{Estimated variable overhead cost}}{\text{Estimated quantity of allocation base}} = \frac{\$6,400}{3,200 \text{ direct labor hours}}$$

$$= \underline{\$2} \text{ per direct labor hour}$$

Fixed overhead price (or rate) standard:

$$\frac{\text{Estimated fixed overhead cost}}{\text{Estimated quantity of allocation base}} = \frac{\$12,000}{3,200 \text{ direct labor hours}}$$

$$= \underline{\$3.75} \text{ per direct labor hour}$$

Quantity Standards

Engineers and production managers set direct material and direct labor *quantity standards*, usually allowing for unavoidable waste and spoilage. World-class companies often follow the continuous improvement philosophy for setting quantity standards, just as they do for setting price standards. For example, groups of managers and workers in Westinghouse Air Brake's Chicago plant analyzed every moment in the production of the brakes. The goal was to (1) eliminate unnecessary work, (2) reduce the time and effort required for necessary work, and (3) set a time standard for the work.

To eliminate unnecessary work, the company rearranged machines in tight U-shaped cells. Workers no longer had to move parts all over the plant floor. The team conducted time-and-motion studies to streamline the physical demands of various tasks. For example, the plant installed a conveyer at waist height to minimize bending and lifting. The result? Workers slashed the standard time to produce one component by 90%.

Benchmarking
Using standards based on "best practice." Best practice may be an internal benchmark or an external benchmark from other companies.

Companies from Ritz-Carlton to Federal Express develop quantity standards based on "best practices." This is often called **benchmarking**. The *best practice* may be an internal benchmark from other plants, locations, or divisions within the company or an external benchmark from other companies. Internal benchmarks are easy to obtain, but managers can also purchase external benchmark data. For example, Riverside Hospital in Columbus, Ohio, can compare its cost of performing an appendectomy with the "best practice" cost developed by a consulting firm that compares many different hospitals' costs for the same procedure.

Kool-Time Pools' production staff indicate that each pool installed requires 975 cubic feet of gunite and that unavoidable waste and spoilage from hardened, unused gunite averages 25 cubic feet per pool. Each pool should require 400 direct labor hours to install.

Required: Compute Kool-Time's standard quantity of materials (gunite) and labor per pool.

Answer: Direct materials quantity standard:

Gunite required	975 cubic feet per pool
Unavoidable waste and spoilage	25 cubic feet per pool
Total gunite per pool installed	1,000 cubic feet per pool
Direct labor quantity standard	400 direct labor hours per pool

Exhibit 24-8 shows Kool-Time's standard costs for direct materials, direct labor, variable overhead, and fixed overhead.[1]

Exhibit 24-8

Kool-Time's Standard Materials, Labor, and Overhead Costs of Installing One Pool

Why Do Companies Use Standard Costs?

✔ Starter 24-6

U.S. surveys have shown that more than 80% of responding companies use standard costing. International surveys show that over half of responding companies in the United Kingdom, Ireland, Sweden, and Japan use standard costing. Why? Exhibit 24-9 shows five key reasons.

Exhibit 24-9   **The Benefits of Standard Costs**

Standard cost systems might appear to be expensive. Indeed, the company must invest in developing the standards. But standards can save data-processing costs. It is easier to value all inventories at standard costs rather than at actual costs. With standard costs, accountants avoid the expense of tracking actual unit costs and of making LIFO, FIFO, or average-cost computations.

---

[1]The direct materials ($2,000), direct labor ($4,200), and variable overhead standard costs ($800) sum to $7,000 per pool installed. Exhibit 24-3 showed that the standard variable cost per pool is $8,000. The $1,000 difference is the variable marketing and administrative expense per pool.

Harley-Davidson, Inc.: Revving Up with Innovation and Cost-Cutting

For Milwaukee-based Harley Davidson, Inc., the 1980s were dark days. The market for heavyweight motorcycles was declining. At one point, the company laid off 40% of its workforce.

Fortunately, CEO and part-owner Jeffrey Bluestein "felt compelled to innovate rather than abdicate." Under Bluestein's stewardship, Harley has enjoyed 16 consecutive years of record revenue and earnings. The key has been involving suppliers in the innovation process.

Harley uses pioneering software, DFM Concurrent Costing 2.0, to investigate the cost impact of alternate manufacturing processes, thus minimizing new-product development costs. For instance, the cost of creating a part by sheet metal bending can be compared with the cost of injection molding the same part. Then Harley and the supplier can work together to cut costs of parts during the design process.

Harley-Davidson uses the software with major suppliers who provide bids accompanied by Concurrent Costing 2.0 reports on new parts based on their specific equipment. The goal is to work with vendors to reduce costs in a way that still allows them to maintain their profit margins. Cheryl Wood, a Harley-Davidson new-products cost analyst, says, "real savings come from helping suppliers reduce the cost of materials and improve the manufacturability of their designs."

Based on: Tim Stevens, "Technologies of the Year: DFM Concurrent Costing Version 2.0," *Industry Week*, December 2002, pp. 64–65. John Teresko, "Fuelled by Innovation," *Industry Week*, December 2002, pp. 52–57. Tim Stevens, "Designs in Sync," http://www.ivvaluechain.com, June 12, 2000.

 Student Resource CD
efficiency variance, price variance, standard costing, variances

4 *Compute standard cost variances for direct materials and direct labor*

How Kool-Time Uses Standard Costing: Analyzing the Flexible Budget Variance

Let's return to our Kool-Time Pools example. Exhibit 24-7 showed that the main cause for concern at Kool-Time is the $5,000 unfavorable flexible budget variance for expenses. The first step in identifying the causes of this variance is to identify the variances in the components of the variable and fixed expenses, as shown in Panel A of Exhibit 24-10.

Study Exhibit 24-10 carefully. Panel B shows how to use the price and quantity standards developed in the Stop & Think on pages 995–996 to compute flexible budget amounts. Panel C shows how to compute actual materials and labor costs. Trace the flexible budget amounts in Panel B and the actual costs in Panel C to the computation of the flexible budget variance in Panel A.

Direct Material Variances

The largest single component of the flexible budget variance in Panel A of Exhibit 24-10 is the $3,100 unfavorable variance in direct materials. Recall that the flexible budget variance is the difference between the actual cost incurred and the flexible budget, as shown in Exhibits 24-6 and 24-7. Exhibit 24-11 on page 1000 shows that Kool-Time computes the direct materials flexible budget variance as the difference between (1) the actual amount paid for gunite and (2) the flexible budget amount (*not the static budget amount!*) that Kool-Time should have spent on gunite for the 10 pools that it actually installed.

Exhibit 24-10

Data for Standard Costing
Example

Kool-Time Pools

Data for Standard Costing Example
Month of June 20X5

PANEL A—Comparison of Actual Results with Flexible Budget for 10 Swimming Pools

	Actual Results at Actual Prices	Flexible Budget for 10 Pools	Flexible Budget Variance
Variable expenses:			
Direct materials..............................	$ 23,100*	$ 20,000†	$3,100 U
Direct labor	41,800*	42,000†	200 F
Variable overhead.............................	9,000	8,000†	1,000 U
Marketing and administrative expenses..........	9,100	10,000	900 F
Total variable expenses	83,000	80,000	3,000 U
Fixed expenses:			
Fixed overhead	12,300	12,000‡	300 U
Marketing and administrative expenses..........	9,700	8,000	1,700 U
Total fixed expenses	22,000	20,000	2,000 U
Total expenses...............................	$105,000	$100,000	$5,000 U

*See Panel C.
†See Panel B.
‡Fixed overhead was budgeted at $12,000 per month (Stop & Think on page 995).

PANEL B—Computation of Flexible Budget for Direct Materials, Direct Labor, and Variable Overhead for 10 Swimming Pools

	(1) Standard Quantity of Inputs Allowed for 10 Pools	(2) Standard Price per Unit of Input	(1) × (2) Flexible Budget for 10 Pools
Direct materials	1,000 cubic feet per pool × 10 pools = 10,000 cubic feet	$ 2.00	$20,000
Direct labor.....................	400 hours per pool × 10 pools = 4,000 hours	10.50	42,000
Variable overhead	400 hours per pool × 10 pools = 4,000 hours	2.00	8,000

PANEL C—Computation of Actual Costs for Direct Materials and Direct Labor for 10 Swimming Pools

	(1) Actual Quantity of Inputs Used for 10 Pools	(2) Actual Price per Unit of Input	(1) × (2) Actual Cost for 10 Pools
Direct materials	11,969 cubic feet actually used	$1.93 actual cost/cubic foot	$23,100
Direct labor.....................	3,800 hours actually used	$11.00 actual cost/hour	41,800

Now that Kool-Time knows it spent $3,100 more than it should have on gunite, the next question is why. Did the $3,100 unfavorable variance arise because Kool-Time:

- Did not meet the price standard because it paid too much for each cubic foot of gunite, or

- Did not meet the quantity standard because workers used more gunite than they should have used to install 10 pools?

Exhibit 24-11

Kool-Time Pools Direct Materials Flexible Budget Variance

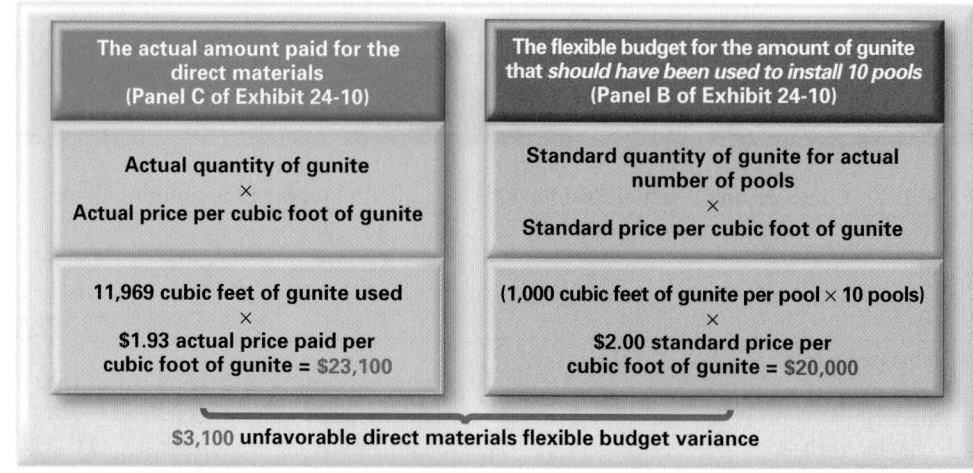

To answer this question, Kool-Time's managers separate the flexible budget variance for direct materials into price and efficiency components, as shown in Exhibit 24-12.

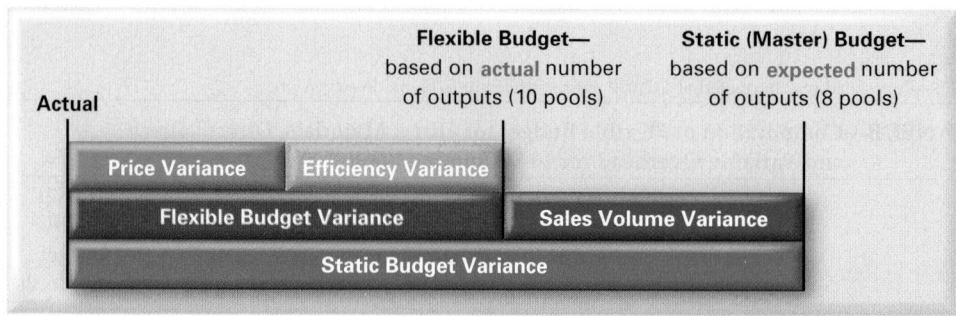

Exhibit 24-12 emphasizes two points. First, the price and efficiency variances sum to the flexible budget variance. Second, *static budgets like column 5 of Exhibit 24-7 play no role in computing the flexible budget variance or how it is split into price and efficiency variances*. The static budget is used *only* in computing the sales volume variance—never in computing the flexible budget variance or its component price and efficiency variances.

DIRECT MATERIALS PRICE VARIANCE   A **price variance** measures how well the business keeps unit prices of material and labor inputs within standards. As the name suggests, the price variance is the *difference in prices* (actual price per unit – standard price per unit) of an input, multiplied by the *actual quantity* of the input:

Price Variance
Measures how well the business keeps unit prices of material and labor inputs within standards. This is computed as the difference in prices (actual price per unit minus standard price per unit) of an input multiplied by the actual quantity of the input.

$$\text{Price variance} = \begin{pmatrix} \text{Difference between} \\ \text{actual and standard} \\ \text{prices per input unit} \end{pmatrix} \times \begin{pmatrix} \text{Actual quantity} \\ \text{of input} \end{pmatrix}$$

$$\text{Price variance} = \begin{pmatrix} \text{Actual} & \text{Standard} \\ \text{price per} - \text{price per} \\ \text{input unit} & \text{input unit} \end{pmatrix} \times \begin{pmatrix} \text{Actual quantity} \\ \text{of input} \end{pmatrix}$$

✔ Starter 24-7

For Kool-Time, the direct materials price variance for gunite is

✔ Starter 24-8

$$\begin{aligned} \text{Direct materials} \atop \text{price variance} &= \left(\frac{\$1.93 \text{ per}}{\text{cubic foot}} - \frac{\$2.00 \text{ per}}{\text{cubic foot}} \right) \times 11{,}969 \text{ cubic feet} \\ &= (\$0.07 \text{ per cubic foot}) \times 11{,}969 \text{ cubic feet} \\ &= \$838 \text{ F (rounded)} \end{aligned}$$

The $838 direct materials price variance is *favorable*, because the purchasing manager spent $0.07 *less* per cubic foot of gunite than budgeted ($1.93 actual price − $2.00 standard price).

The purchasing manager is responsible for the price variance on the *actual quantity* of materials he buys, so we multiply the $0.07 favorable price variance per cubic foot by the 11,969 cubic feet of gunite he *actually purchased*. Thus, Kool-Time's June operating income is $838 higher [($1.93 − $2.00) × 11,969] than the flexible budget because the purchasing manager paid less than the standard price for gunite. (Of course, if the purchasing manager had actually paid *more* than the $2.00 per cubic foot standard price, the direct materials price variance would have been *unfavorable*.)

DIRECT MATERIALS EFFICIENCY VARIANCE

An **efficiency variance** measures whether the firm meets its quantity standards. In other words, it measures whether the quantity of materials or labor actually used to make the *actual number of outputs* is within the standard allowed for that number of outputs. The efficiency variance is the *difference in quantities* (actual quantity of input used − standard quantity of input allowed for the actual number of outputs) multiplied by the *standard price per unit* of the input.

Report
Materials Price Variance
Actual Standard Var.
$1.93 − $2.00 = $0.07 F

Answer: Purchasing

Efficiency Variance
Measures whether the quantity of materials or labor used to make the actual number of outputs is within the standard allowed for that number of outputs. This is computed as the difference in quantities (actual quantity of input used minus standard quantity of input allowed for the actual number of outputs) multiplied by the standard price per unit of the input.

$$\begin{array}{l} \text{Efficiency} \\ \text{variance} \end{array} = \left(\begin{array}{l} \text{Difference between actual quantity of} \\ \text{inputs used and the standard quantity} \\ \text{of inputs that should have been used} \\ \text{for the actual number of outputs} \end{array}\right) \times \left(\begin{array}{l} \text{Standard price} \\ \text{per input unit} \end{array}\right)$$

$$\begin{array}{l} \text{Efficiency} \\ \text{variance} \end{array} = \left(\begin{array}{l} \text{Actual} \\ \text{quantity} - \\ \text{of input} \end{array}\begin{array}{l} \text{Standard} \\ \text{quantity} \\ \text{of input} \end{array}\right) \times \left(\begin{array}{l} \text{Standard price} \\ \text{per input unit} \end{array}\right)$$

The standard quantity of inputs is the *quantity that should have been used*, or the standard quantity of inputs *allowed*, for the actual output. For Kool-Time, the *standard quantity of inputs (gunite) that workers should have used for the actual number of outputs* (10 pools) is

1,000 cubic feet of gunite per pool × 10 pools installed = 10,000 cubic feet of gunite

Thus, the direct materials efficiency variance is

$$\begin{array}{l} \text{Direct materials} \\ \text{efficiency variance} \end{array} = \left(\begin{array}{l} 11,969 \\ \text{cubic feet} - \\ \end{array}\begin{array}{l} 10,000 \\ \text{cubic feet} \end{array}\right) \times \begin{array}{l} \$2.00 \text{ per} \\ \text{cubic foot} \end{array}$$

$$= (1,969 \text{ cubic feet}) \times \$2.00 \text{ per cubic foot}$$

$$= \$3,938 \text{ U}$$

The $3,938 direct materials efficiency variance is *unfavorable*, because workers actually used 1,969 *more* cubic feet of gunite than they should have used to install 10 pools (11,969 actual cubic feet − 10,000 standard cubic feet).

The manager in charge of installing the pools is responsible for the variance in the quantity of the materials (gunite) used—in this case, the extra 1,969 cubic feet of gunite. However, this manager generally is *not* the person who purchases the gunite. The manager who installs the pools often has no control over the actual price paid for the gunite. Thus, we multiply the extra 1,969 cubic feet of gunite his workers used by the *standard price* of $2.00 per cubic foot to obtain the direct materials efficiency variance. Kool-Time's operating income is $3,938 lower [(11,969 − 10,000) × $2.00] than the flexible budget because workers used more gunite than they should have to install the 10 pools in June. (Of course, if workers had used *less* than the standard 10,000 cubic feet to install the 10 pools, the direct materials efficiency variance would have been *favorable*.)

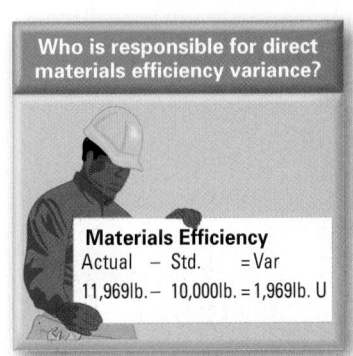

Materials Efficiency
Actual − Std. = Var
11,969lb. − 10,000lb. = 1,969lb. U

Answer: Pool Installation Manager

SUMMARY OF DIRECT MATERIAL VARIANCES Exhibit 24-13 summarizes how Kool-Time splits the $3,100 unfavorable direct materials flexible budget variance first identified in Panel A of Exhibit 24-10 into price and efficiency variances.

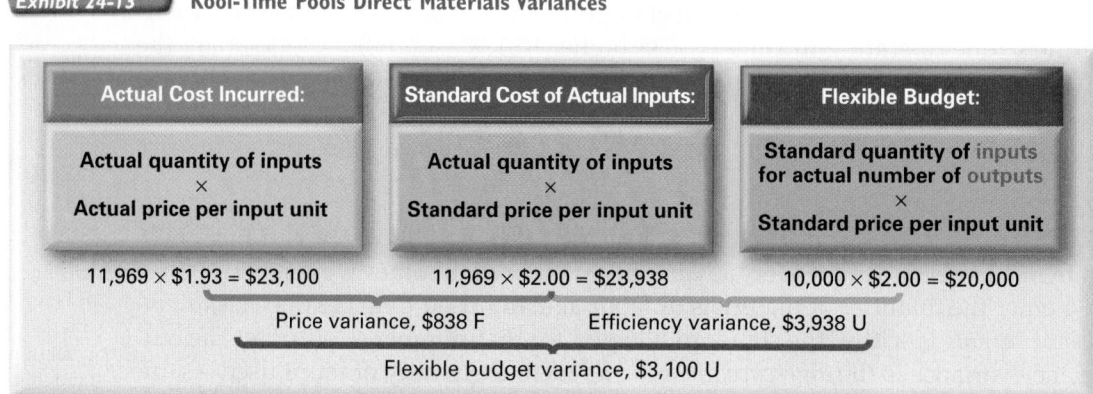

Exhibit 24-13 Kool-Time Pools Direct Materials Variances

Kool-Time actually spent $3,100 more than it should have for gunite because:

- A good price for the gunite increased profits by $838, but
- Inefficient use of the gunite reduced profits by $3,938.

Let's review who is responsible for each of these variances and consider why each variance may have occurred.

1. *Purchasing managers typically are responsible for direct materials price variances* because they should know why the actual price differs from the standard price. Kool-Time's purchasing manager may have negotiated a good price for gunite, or perhaps the supplier did not increase the price of gunite as much as expected when Kool-Time developed its standard cost. In either case, the purchasing manager is in the best position to explain the favorable price variance.

2. *Production managers typically are responsible for direct materials efficiency variances* because they are responsible for ensuring that workers use materials efficiently and effectively. The manager in charge of installing pools should be able to explain why workers used so much more gunite than they should have used to install the 10 pools. Was the gunite of lower quality? Did workers waste materials? Did their equipment malfunction? Kool-Time's top management needs the answers to these questions to decide what corrective action to take. Should they require purchasing to buy higher quality gunite, train and supervise workers more closely to reduce waste, or improve maintenance of equipment?

Smart managers know that these variances raise questions that can help pinpoint problems. But be careful! A favorable variance does not necessarily mean that a manager did a good job, nor does an unfavorable variance mean that a manager did a bad job. Perhaps Kool-Time's purchasing manager obtained a lower price by purchasing inferior-quality gunite, and this in turn led to waste and spoilage. If so, the purchasing manager's decision hurt the company because the $838 favorable price variance is more than offset by the $3,938 unfavorable efficiency variance. This illustrates why good managers (1) use variances as a guide for investigation rather than as a simple tool to assign blame and (2) investigate favorable as well as unfavorable variances.

Direct Labor Variances

Kool-Time uses a similar approach to analyze the direct labor flexible budget variance. Using the information from Panels B and C of Exhibit 24-10, Exhibit 24-14 shows how Kool-Time computes this variance as the difference between the actual amount paid for direct labor and the flexible budget amount that Kool-Time should have spent on direct labor for 10 pools.

Exhibit 24-14

Kool-Time Pools' Direct Labor Flexible Budget Variance

The actual amount paid for the direct labor (Panel C of Exhibit 24-10)	The flexible budget for the direct labor hours that *should have been used to install 10 pools* (Panel B of Exhibit 24-10)
Actual quantity of direct labor hours × Actual price per direct labor hour	Standard quantity of labor for actual number of pools × Standard price per direct labor hour
3,800 direct labor hours actually used × $11.00 actual price paid per direct labor hour = $41,800	(400 direct labor hours per pool × 10 pools) × $10.50 standard price per direct labor hour = $42,000

$200 **favorable direct labor flexible budget variance**

Why did Kool-Time spend $200 less on labor than it should have to install 10 pools? To answer this question, Kool-Time splits the direct labor flexible budget variance into price and efficiency variances, in exactly the same way as it did for direct materials.

DIRECT LABOR PRICE VARIANCE The direct labor price variance is computed exactly the same way as the direct materials price variance:

✔ Starter 24-9

$$\text{Price variance} = \left(\begin{array}{cc} \text{Actual} & \text{Standard} \\ \text{price per} - \text{price per} \\ \text{input unit} & \text{input unit} \end{array} \right) \times \begin{array}{c} \text{Actual quantity} \\ \text{of input} \end{array}$$

$$= \left(\frac{\$11.00 \text{ per}}{\text{hour}} - \frac{\$10.50 \text{ per}}{\text{hour}} \right) \times 3,800 \text{ hours}$$

$$= (\$0.50 \text{ per hour}) \times 3,800 \text{ hours}$$

$$= \$1,900 \text{ U}$$

The $1,900 direct labor price variance is *unfavorable* because the Human Resources (or Personnel) Department hired workers at $0.50 *more* per direct labor hour than budgeted ($11.00 actual price – $10.50 standard price).

The human resources manager is responsible for the price variance on the *actual quantity* of labor she hires, so we multiply the $0.50 unfavorable price variance per direct labor hour by the 3,800 hours of labor she *actually purchased.*

DIRECT LABOR EFFICIENCY VARIANCE The direct labor efficiency variance is computed exactly the same way as the direct materials efficiency variance:

Who is responsible for direct labor price variance?

Labor Price
Actual – Std. = Var
$11.00 – $10.50 = $0.50 U

Answer: HR Department

$$\text{Efficiency variance} = \left(\begin{array}{cc} \text{Actual} & \text{Standard} \\ \text{quantity} - \text{quantity} \\ \text{of input} & \text{of input} \end{array} \right) \times \begin{array}{c} \text{Standard} \\ \text{price per} \\ \text{input unit} \end{array}$$

For Kool-Time, the *standard quantity of direct labor hours that workers should have used for the actual number of outputs* (10 pools) is

400 direct labor hours per pool × 10 pools installed = 4,000 direct labor hours

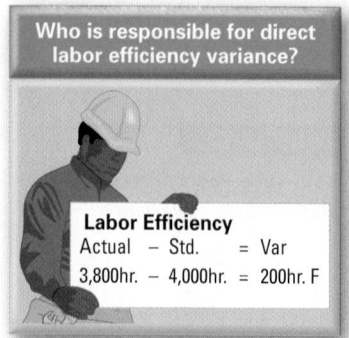

Who is responsible for direct labor efficiency variance?

Labor Efficiency
Actual – Std. = Var
3,800hr. – 4,000hr. = 200hr. F

Answer: Pool Installation Manager

Thus, the direct labor efficiency variance is

$$\begin{aligned}
\text{Direct labor} \\
\text{efficiency variance}
\end{aligned} = (3,800 \text{ hours} - 4,000 \text{ hours}) \times \$10.50 \text{ per hour}$$

$$= (200 \text{ hours}) \times \$10.50 \text{ per hour}$$

$$= \$2,100 \text{ F}$$

The \$2,100 direct labor efficiency variance is *favorable* because installers actually worked 200 *fewer* hours than they should have to install 10 pools (3,800 actual hours – 4,000 standard hours).

The manager in charge of installing the pools is responsible for the variance in the quantity of direct labor hours used—in this case, the 200 fewer hours used. Assuming that this manager is not also responsible for setting employees' pay rates (which is usually the responsibility of the human resources or personnel department), the manager in charge of installing the pools has little control over the actual price paid per labor hour. Thus, we multiply the 200 fewer direct labor hours by the *standard price* of \$10.50 per direct labor hour to obtain the direct labor efficiency variance.

SUMMARY OF DIRECT LABOR VARIANCES Exhibit 24-15 summarizes how Kool-Time splits the \$200 favorable direct labor flexible budget variance into price and efficiency variances.

Exhibit 24-15 Kool-Time Pools Direct Labor Variances

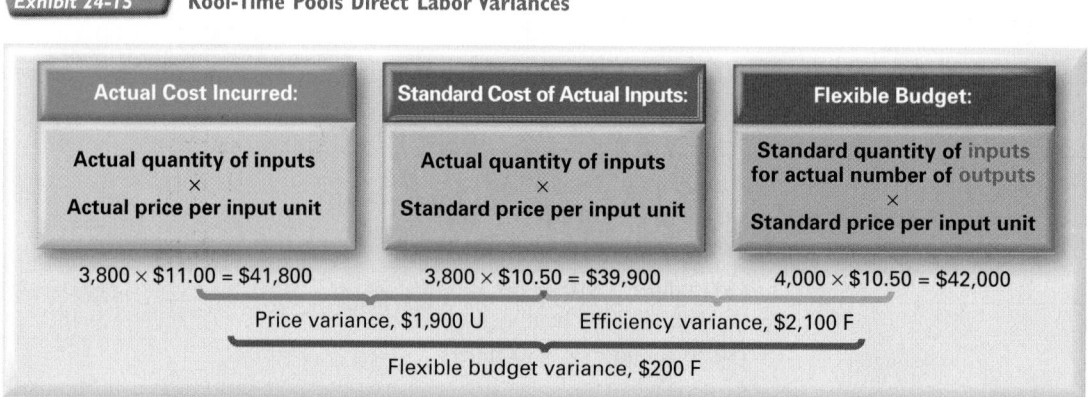

Actual Cost Incurred:	Standard Cost of Actual Inputs:	Flexible Budget:
Actual quantity of inputs × Actual price per input unit	Actual quantity of inputs × Standard price per input unit	Standard quantity of inputs for actual number of outputs × Standard price per input unit
3,800 × \$11.00 = \$41,800	3,800 × \$10.50 = \$39,900	4,000 × \$10.50 = \$42,000

Price variance, \$1,900 U   Efficiency variance, \$2,100 F

Flexible budget variance, \$200 F

Had they looked only at the \$200 favorable direct labor flexible budget variance, Kool-Time's managers might have thought direct labor costs were close to expectations. But this illustrates the danger in ending the analysis after computing only the flexible budget variance. "Peeling the onion" to examine the price and efficiency variances yields more insight:

- The unfavorable direct labor price variance means that Kool-Time's operating income is \$1,900 lower than expected, because the company paid its employees an average of \$11.00 per hour in June instead of the standard rate of \$10.50. But this unfavorable variance was more than offset by

- The favorable direct labor efficiency variance. Kool-Time's operating income is \$2,100 higher than expected because workers installed 10 pools in 3,800 hours instead of the budgeted 4,000 hours.

✔ Starter 24-10

Kool-Time's top management will ask the Human Resources Department to explain the unfavorable labor price variance, and they will ask the manager in charge of installing the pools to explain the favorable labor efficiency variance. Once again, there might have been a tradeoff. Kool-Time might have hired more-experienced (and thus more highly paid) workers and traded off an unfavorable price variance for a favorable efficiency variance. If so, the strategy was successful—the overall effect on profits was favorable. This possibility reminds us that managers should be careful in using variances to evaluate performance.

You have now seen how Kool-Time analyzes flexible budget variances for direct materials and direct labor. Variances for variable marketing and administrative expenses could be calculated in the same way, but for simplicity we limit our detailed analysis to the variances in the production element of the value chain. Before leaving this topic, we need to examine three common pitfalls in computing price and efficiency variances.

Price and Efficiency Variances: Three Common Pitfalls

Here are three common pitfalls to avoid in computing price and efficiency variances for direct materials and direct labor:

1. *Static budgets like column 5 of Exhibit 24-7 play no role in computing the flexible budget variance or how it is split into the price and efficiency variances.* Exhibit 24-12 shows that the static budget is used *only* in computing the sales volume variance—never in computing the flexible budget variance or its component price and efficiency variances.

2. In the efficiency variance, the standard quantity is the *standard quantity of inputs allowed for the actual number of outputs*—the basis for the flexible budget. To compute the standard quantity of inputs allowed, first determine the actual number of outputs. For Kool-Time Pools, the actual number of outputs is 10 pools. Next, compute how many inputs should have been used to produce the actual number of outputs (10 pools). For example, each pool should use 400 direct labor hours, so the standard quantity of direct labor hours allowed for 10 pools is 10×400 hours = 4,000 hours.

Notice that the standard quantity of inputs is *not* based on the budgeted number of outputs (8 pools). That number is the basis for the static budget, which is not used to compute price and efficiency variances.

3. In the direct materials price variance, the difference in prices is multiplied by the *actual quantity* of materials. In the direct materials efficiency variance, the difference in quantities is multiplied by the *standard price* of the materials. The following explanation can help you remember this difference.
- The materials price variance is usually the responsibility of purchasing personnel; they purchase the actual quantity used, not just the amount of materials that should have been used (the standard quantity). So the price variance is the difference in prices multiplied by the *actual quantity* of materials purchased.
- The materials efficiency variance is usually the responsibility of production personnel; they have no influence over the actual price paid. So the efficiency variance is computed as the difference in quantities multiplied by the *standard* price (the price that should have been paid).

Similar logic applies to the direct labor price and efficiency variances.

Using Variances

Let's look at some practical tips for using variances.

HOW OFTEN TO COMPUTE VARIANCES?   Many firms monitor sales volume, direct material efficiency, and direct labor efficiency variances day to day or even hour to hour. **McDonald's** restaurants compute variances for sales and direct labor each hour. Material efficiencies are computed for each shift. The Brass Products Division of **Parker Hannafin** computes efficiency variances for each job the day after workers finish the job. This allows managers to ask questions about any large variances while the job is still fresh in workers' minds.

Technology like bar coding of materials and even labor (through bar-coded identity cards) and computerized data entry allows McDonald's and Parker

Hannafin to quickly compute efficiency variances. In contrast to efficiency variances, monthly computations of material and labor price variances may be sufficient if long-term contracts with suppliers or labor unions make large price variances unlikely.

USING VARIANCES TO EVALUATE EMPLOYEES' PERFORMANCE Good managers use variances to raise questions, not as simple indicators of whether employees performed well or poorly. Why should you take care in using variances to evaluate performance?

- Some variances are caused by factors managers cannot control. For example, perhaps Kool-Time used more gunite than budgeted because workers had to repair cracked foundations resulting from an earthquake.

- Managers often make trade-offs among variances. Chrysler intentionally accepted a large order for customized Dodge vans because it expected the favorable sales volume variance to more than offset the unfavorable direct labor price variance from the overtime premium and the unfavorable sales revenue price variance from extra rebates offered to the customer. Similarly, managers often trade off price variances against efficiency variances. Purchasing personnel may decide to buy higher-quality (but more expensive) direct materials to reduce waste and spoilage. The unfavorable price variance may be more than offset by a favorable efficiency variance.

- Evaluations based primarily on one variance can encourage managers to take actions that make the variance look good but hurt the company in the long run. For example, Kool-Time's managers could:
  - Purchase low-quality gunite or hire less-experienced labor to get favorable price variances
  - Use less gunite or less labor (resulting in lower-quality installed pools) to get favorable efficiency variances

How can upper management discourage such actions? One approach is to base performance evaluation on *nonfinancial* measures as well, such as quality indicators like variances in the grade of gunite or labor used, or customer satisfaction measures. For example, McDonald's discourages skimping on labor by evaluating nonfinancial measures such as the difference between actual and standard time to serve drive-through customers. If the McDonald's shift manager does not have enough workers, drive-through customers may have to wait too long to get their French fries. They may take their business to Wendy's or Burger King.

Why might an auto assembly plant experience a favorable direct labor efficiency variance? Should managers investigate favorable as well as unfavorable efficiency variances? Why?

Answer:

1. The plant may have redesigned the manufacturing process to avoid wasted motion. For example, a **Dodge** van plant in Canada significantly reduced direct labor by reorganizing production so employees reach for raw materials as needed rather than carrying arm-loads of materials across the plant floor.

2. Employees may have worked harder or more intensely than budgeted.

3. Employees may have rushed through the work and skimped on quality.

There are two reasons why managers should investigate favorable efficiency variances. First, managers want to maximize improvements that increase profits. For example, can managers capitalize on 1 and 2 to further improve labor efficiency at this or other plants? Second, managers want to prevent employees from achieving favorable variances at the expense of long-run profits through strategies like 3.

Manufacturing Overhead Variances

The total manufacturing overhead variance is the difference between:

Actual overhead cost	and	**Standard manufacturing overhead allocated to production**

Exhibit 24-10 shows that Kool-Time actually incurred $21,300 of overhead: $9,000 variable and $12,300 fixed. So the next step is to see how Kool-Time allocates overhead using its standard cost system.

Allocating Overhead in a Standard Cost System

In a standard costing system, the manufacturing overhead allocated to production is

$$\text{Manufacturing overhead allocated to production} = \text{Standard predetermined manufacturing overhead rate} \times \text{Standard quantity of the allocation base allowed for the } \textit{actual} \text{ number of outputs}$$

Let's begin by computing the first term on the right-hand side, the standard predetermined overhead rate. Kool-Time allocates overhead based on direct labor hours. As explained in Chapter 20 →:

$$\text{Standard predetermined manufacturing overhead rate} = \frac{\text{Budgeted manufacturing overhead cost}}{\text{Budgeted quantity of the allocation base}}$$

Managers use predetermined overhead rates because they cannot wait until the end of the year to figure the costs of products. *Predetermined* overhead rates use data that are available at the *beginning* of the year. Thus, most companies base their rates on amounts from the static (master) budget, which is known at the beginning of the year. (The predetermined manufacturing overhead rate cannot be based on the flexible budget for actual production because the actual number of outputs is not known until the end of the year.)

The Stop & Think, pages 995–996, and Exhibit 24-16 show that Kool-Time's standard manufacturing overhead rates are:

Variable: $\dfrac{\$6{,}400 \text{ static budget variable manufacturing overhead}}{3{,}200 \text{ static budget direct labor hours}}$

= $\underline{\$2.00}$ per direct labor hour

Fixed: $\dfrac{\$12{,}000 \text{ static budget fixed manufacturing overhead}}{3{,}200 \text{ static budget direct labor hours}}$

= $\underline{\$3.75}$ per direct labor hour

Total: $2.00 variable manufacturing overhead per direct labor hour
$\underline{+\ 3.75}$ fixed manufacturing overhead per direct labor hour
$\underline{\$5.75}$ total manufacturing overhead per direct labor hour

Now that we have computed the standard predetermined manufacturing overhead rate, the next step is to identify the standard quantity of the allocation base allowed for the *actual* number of outputs. Kool-Time actually installed 10 pools during June. Thus, the standard quantity of the allocation base (direct labor hours) allowed for the actual number of outputs (10 pools) is 4,000 direct labor hours (400 direct labor hours per pool × 10 pools actually installed). Notice that 4,000 direct labor hours is the standard number of direct labor hours for the flexible budget at the actual output level of 10 pools in Exhibit 24-16 and in Exhibit 24-10 (Panel B), and for the direct labor efficiency variance (Exhibit 24-15).

 Student ResourceCD

allocation base, flexible budget variance, manufacturing overhead, production volume variance

 Analyze manufacturing overhead in a standard cost system

← *To review the computation of the predetermined overhead rate, see Chapter 20, page 812.*

✔ **Starter 24-11**

Kool-Time Pools
Budget Data for the Month Ended June 30, 20X5

	Flexible Budget for Actual Output	Static Budget for Expected Output
Output units (pools installed)	10	8
Standard direct labor hours (400 hours per pool).	4,000	3,200
Budgeted manufacturing overhead cost:		
Variable	$ 8,000	$ 6,400
Fixed.	12,000	12,000
Total	$20,000	$18,400
Standard variable manufacturing overhead rate per direct labor hour		$ 6,400 ÷ 3,200 = $2.00
Standard fixed manufacturing overhead rate per direct labor hour		$12,000 ÷ 3,200 = $3.75
Standard total manufacturing overhead rate per direct labor hour		$18,400 ÷ 3,200 = $5.75

Thus, Kool-Time allocates manufacturing overhead as follows:

$$\begin{array}{rcl} \text{Manufacturing overhead} \atop \text{allocated to production} & = & \text{Standard predetermined} \atop {\text{manufacturing} \atop \text{overhead rate}} \quad \times \quad {\text{Standard quantity of} \atop {\text{the allocation base} \atop {\text{allowed for the } \textit{actual} \atop \text{number of outputs}}}} \end{array}$$

$$= \text{\$5.75 per hour} \quad \times \quad 4{,}000 \text{ hours}$$
$$= \text{\$23,000}$$

Kool-Time's total manufacturing overhead variance is the difference between:

Actual overhead cost (Exhibit 24-10)	and	Standard manufacturing overhead allocated to production
$21,300		**$23,000**

$1,700 F

Kool-Time actually spent $1,700 less on overhead than it allocated to production. To see why, Kool-Time "drills down" by splitting this total variance into two components:

- The overhead flexible budget variance
- The production volume variance

Overhead Flexible Budget Variance

Overhead Flexible Budget Variance
Shows how well management has controlled overhead costs. It is the difference between the actual overhead cost and the flexible budget overhead for the actual number of outputs.

The **overhead flexible budget variance** shows how well management has controlled overhead costs. It is computed in exactly the same way as the flexible budget variances for direct materials and direct labor. It is the difference between:

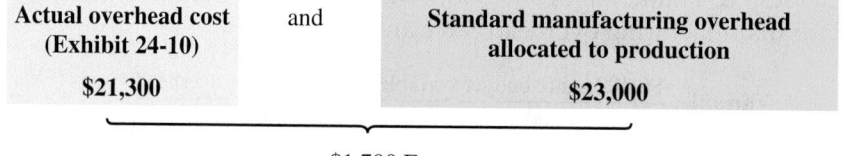

Actual overhead cost	and	Flexible budget overhead for the actual number of outputs

Exhibit 24-10 shows that Kool-Time actually spent $21,300 on overhead items ($9,000 variable + $12,300 fixed) to install the 10 pools. Exhibit 24-16 shows that the flexible budget overhead for the installation of 10 pools is $20,000 ($8,000 variable + $12,000 fixed). So Kool-Time's overhead flexible budget variance is the difference between

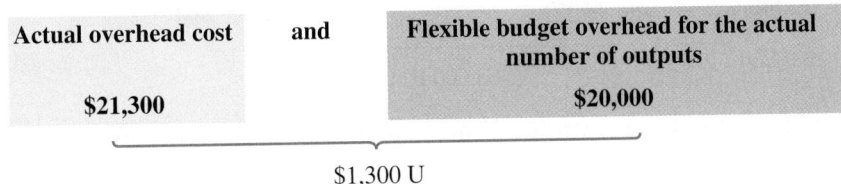

Actual overhead cost	and	Flexible budget overhead for the actual number of outputs
$21,300		$20,000

$1,300 U

Why did Kool-Time spend $1,300 more on overhead items than it should have spent to install the 10 pools in June? You can see from Exhibit 24-17 that $1,000 ($9,000 − $8,000) of the variance is due to higher-than-expected spending on variable overhead items, and the remaining $300 ($12,300 − $12,000) is due to higher spending on fixed overhead items. Kool-Time will investigate the reason for each of these variances.

Exhibit 24-17 Manufacturing Overhead Variances

	Kool-Time Pools		
	Manufacturing Overhead Variances (For the month ended June 30, 20X5)		
	Actual Overhead Cost (Exhibit 24-10)	**Flexible Budget Overhead for Actual Number of Outputs (Exhibits 24-10 and 24-16)**	**Standard Overhead Allocated to Production (Rates from Exhibit 24-16)**
Variable overhead.........	$ 9,000	$ 8,000	$2.00 × 4,000 direct labor hours = $ 8,000
Fixed overhead	12,300	12,000	$3.75 × 4,000 direct labor hours = 15,000
Total overhead............	$21,300	$20,000	$5.75 × 4,000 direct labor hours = $23,000

Overhead flexible budget variance, $1,300 U

Production volume variance, $3,000 F

Total manufacturing overhead variance, $1,700 F

Most companies compile actual and budget cost information for the individual component items that make up overhead, such as indirect materials, indirect labor, utilities, and depreciation on plant and equipment. Managers drill down by comparing actual to budgeted costs for each of these individual items. For example, Kool-Time's drill-down analysis might reveal that variable overhead costs were higher than expected because water rates increased or because workers used more water in mixing the gunite than expected for installing 10 pools. Perhaps spending on fixed overhead increased because Kool-Time purchased new equipment and its depreciation expense increased. (Advanced books on cost accounting explain this drill-down variance analysis in more detail.)

Production Volume Variance

As Exhibit 24-17 shows, the second component of the total manufacturing overhead variance is the **production volume variance**. This variance arises when

✔ **Starter 24-12**

Production Volume Variance
Arises when actual production differs from expected production. It is the difference between (1) the manufacturing overhead cost in the flexible budget for actual outputs and (2) the standard overhead allocated to production.

actual production differs from expected production. You can see from Exhibit 24-17 that it is computed as the difference between:

Flexible budget overhead for actual outputs (10 pools)	and	Standard overhead allocated to (actual) production
$20,000 (Exhibits 24-16 and 24-17)		$23,000 (Exhibit 24-17)

$3,000 F

The production volume variance is favorable whenever actual output (10 pools, for Kool-Time) exceeds expected output (8 pools, Exhibit 24-16). By installing 10 pools instead of 8, Kool-Time used its production capacity more fully than originally planned. If Kool-Time had installed 7 or fewer pools, the production volume variance would have been unfavorable because the company would have used less production capacity than expected.

Exhibit 24-17 reveals that the *variable* overhead cost in the flexible budget for actual outputs is always the same as the standard variable overhead allocated. Both are computed as:

Standard predetermined variable overhead rate	×	Standard quantity of the allocation base allowed for the actual number of outputs

The production volume variance, therefore, is due only to fixed overhead. The $3,000 favorable production volume variance arises because Kool-Time did the following:

- Budgeted fixed overhead of $12,000, but
- Allocated $15,000 of fixed overhead to the 10 pools it installed.

Why did Kool-Time allocate $3,000 more than the budgeted fixed overhead? Exhibit 24-8 shows that the standard fixed overhead cost for each pool is $1,500. Because Kool-Time installed 2 more pools than planned, it allocated $3,000 more fixed overhead (2 pools × $1,500 per pool) than expected when it set the static budget at the beginning of the period.

How did the increase in Kool-Time's "production volume," from 8 pools (the expected static budget amount) to 10 pools (actually installed) affect June's profit? Is this amount equal to the production volume variance?

Answer: Using the contribution margin income statement approach from Chapter 22:

Increase in sales revenue (2 × $12,000)	$24,000
Increase in variable expenses (2 × $8,000)	16,000
Increase in contribution margin	8,000
Increase in fixed expenses	–0–
Increase in operating income	$ 8,000

Installing two more pools increased Kool-Time's profits by $8,000, not by the $3,000 favorable "production volume variance." Thus, the production volume variance does *not* reveal how changes in production volume affect profits. The production volume variance only captures the difference between the flexible budget manufacturing overhead and the allocated manufacturing overhead. Companies use the term *production volume variance* because this variance arises only when actual production differs from expected (static budget) production.

Standard Cost Accounting Systems

Journal Entries

We use Kool-Time Pools' June transactions to demonstrate standard costing in a job costing context. Because management needs to know about variances in a timely manner so they can correct any problem, Kool-Time recognizes variances from standards as soon as possible. This means that Kool-Time records direct materials price variances when materials are purchased. It also means that Work in Process Inventory is debited (swimming pools are costed) at standard input quantities and standard prices. June's entries follow:

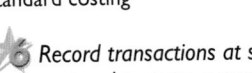

standard costing

🌟 *Record transactions at standard cost and prepare a standard cost income statement*

✔ **Starter 24-13**

1. Materials Inventory (11,969 × $2.00)	23,938	
Direct Materials Price Variance.		838
Accounts Payable (11,969 × $1.93)		23,100
To record purchases of direct materials.		

The credit to Accounts Payable is for the *actual quantity* of gunite purchased (11,969 cubic feet) costed at the *actual price* ($1.93 per cubic foot). In contrast, the debit to Materials Inventory is for the *actual quantity* purchased (11,969 cubic feet) costed at the *standard price* ($2 per cubic foot). Maintaining Materials Inventory at the *standard* price ($2.00) allows Kool-Time to record the direct materials price variance at time of purchase. Recall that Kool-Time's direct materials price variance was $838 favorable (page 1000). A favorable variance has a credit balance and is a contra expense, or a reduction in expense. Consequently, the $838 favorable direct materials price variance is a contra expense that increases Kool-Time's June profits.

2. Work in Process Inventory (10,000 × $2.00) . .	20,000	
Direct Materials Efficiency Variance.	3,938	
Materials Inventory (11,969 × $2.00) . . .		23,938
To record use of direct materials.		

Kool-Time's direct materials efficiency variance was $3,938 unfavorable (page 1001). An unfavorable variance has a debit balance, which increases expense. Kool-Time's $3,938 unfavorable direct materials efficiency variance decreases June profits. Kool-Time debits Work in Process Inventory for the *standard price × standard quantity* of direct materials that should have been used for the actual output of 10 pools. This maintains Work in Process Inventory at standard cost. Of course, Materials Inventory is credited for the *actual quantity* of materials put into production (11,969 cubic feet) costed at the *standard price* at which journal entry 1 entered them into the Materials Inventory account.

3. Manufacturing Wages (3,800 × $10.50).	39,900	
Direct Labor Price Variance	1,900	
Wages Payable (3,800 × $11.00)		41,800
To record direct labor costs incurred.		

By maintaining Manufacturing Wages at the *standard* price for direct labor ($10.50), Kool-Time records the direct labor price variance at the time work is performed. Of course, Wages Payable is credited for the *actual* hours worked at the *actual* wage rate.

4. Work in Process Inventory (4,000 × $10.50) . .	42,000	
Direct Labor Efficiency Variance		2,100
Manufacturing Wages (3,800 × $10.50)		39,900
To assign direct labor costs.		

Kool-Time debits Work in Process Inventory for the standard price × standard quantity of direct labor that should have been used for 10 pools, like direct materials entry 2. This maintains Work in Process Inventory at standard cost.

✔ Starter 24-14

5. Manufacturing Overhead................	21,300	
Accounts Payable, Accumulated		
Depreciation, and so on		21,300
To record actual overhead costs incurred.		
(See Exhibit 24-17.)		

6. Work in Process Inventory (4,000 × $5.75)...	23,000	
Manufacturing Overhead............		23,000
To allocate overhead. (See Exhibit 24-17.)		

In standard costing, the overhead allocated to Work in Process Inventory is computed as the standard predetermined overhead rate × standard quantity of the allocation base that should have been used for the actual output (10 pools).

✔ Starter 24-15

7. Finished Goods Inventory	85,000	
Work in Process Inventory		85,000
To record completion of 10 pools ($20,000 of materials +		
$42,000 of labor + $23,000 of manufacturing overhead).		

8. Cost of Goods Sold	85,000	
Finished Goods Inventory		85,000
To record the cost of sales of 10 pools.		

9. Manufacturing Overhead.................	1,700	
Overhead Flexible Budget Variance	1,300	
Production Volume Variance		3,000
To record overhead variances and close the		
Manufacturing Overhead account. (See Exhibit 24-17.)		

Entry 9 closes Manufacturing Overhead. Many companies wait until the end of the fiscal year to close this account.

Exhibit 24-18 shows selected Kool-Time accounts after posting these entries.

Standard Cost Income Statement for Management

Exhibit 24-19 shows a standard cost income statement that highlights the variances for Kool-Time's management. The statement shows sales revenue at standard, and then adds the favorable flexible budget sales revenue variance to yield actual sales revenue. Next, the statement shows the cost of goods sold at standard cost. Then the statement separately lists each manufacturing cost variance, followed by the cost of goods sold at actual cost. (Recall that since Kool-Time had no raw materials, work in process, or finished goods inventories, all the variances relate to June's sales.) At the end of the period, all the variance accounts are closed to zero out their balances. The net amount is closed to Income Summary.

The income statement shows that the net effect of all the manufacturing cost variances is $1,200 unfavorable. Thus, June's operating income is $1,200 lower than it would have been if all actual costs had been equal to standard amounts. Management can prepare statements with similar detail for research and development, design, marketing, distribution, and customer service costs, if they are subject to standard cost analysis.

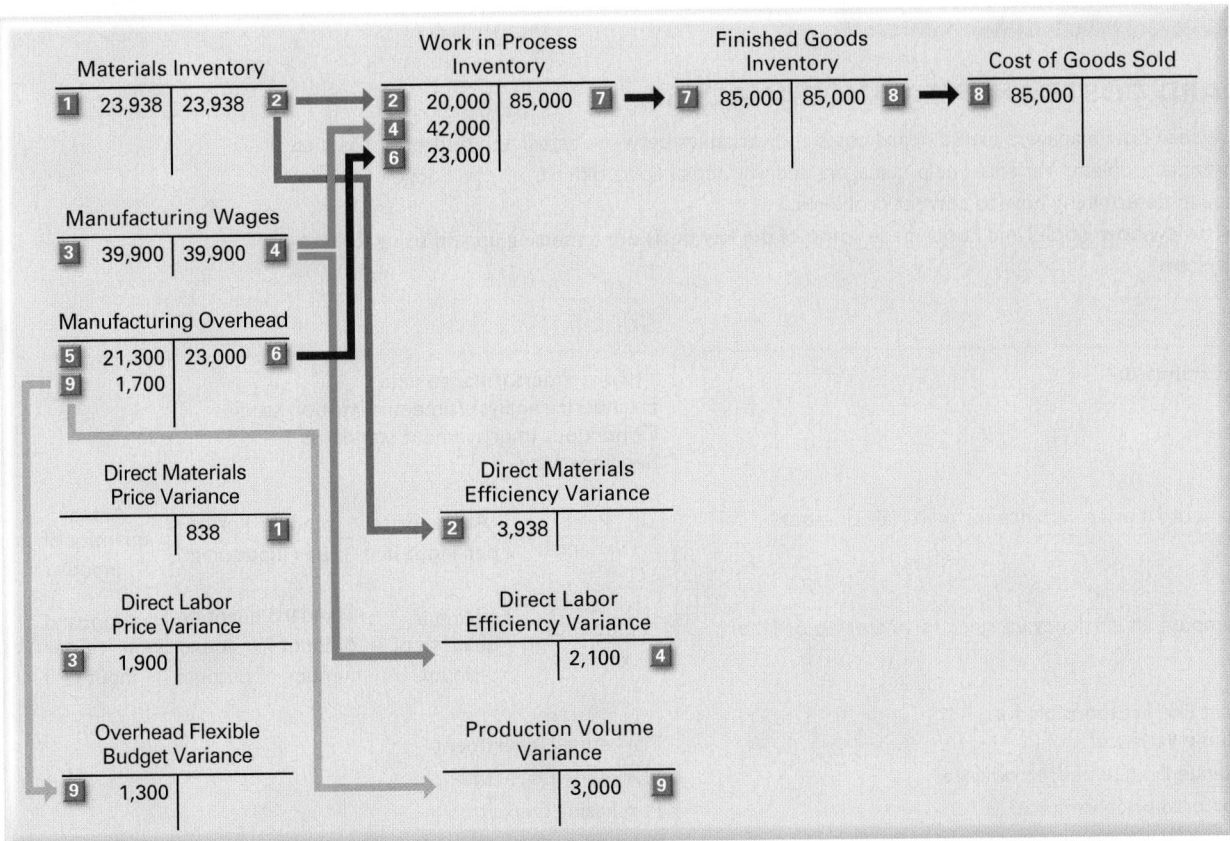

Exhibit 24-18   Kool-Time Pools' Flow of Costs in Standard Costing System

	Kool-Time Pools	Exhibit 24-19

Standard Cost Income Statement

Kool-Time Pools

Standard Cost Income Statement
Month Ended June 30, 20X5

Sales revenue at standard (10 × $12,000)		$120,000
Flexible budget sales revenue variance		$1,000
Sales revenue at actual		121,000
Cost of goods sold at standard cost		85,000
Manufacturing cost variances:		
Direct materials price variance.....................	$ (838)	
Direct materials efficiency variance	3,938	
Direct labor price variance	1,900	
Direct labor efficiency variance....................	(2,100)	
Manufacturing overhead flexible		
budget variance...............................	1,300	
Production volume variance......................	(3,000)	
Total manufacturing variances....................		1,200
Cost of goods sold at actual cost		86,200
Gross profit.......................................		34,800
Marketing and administrative expenses*..............		(18,800)
Operating income		$16,000

✔ Starter 24-16

*$9,100 + $9,700 from Exhibit 24-10.

Decision Guidelines

STANDARD COSTS AND VARIANCE ANALYSIS

Now you've seen how managers use standard costs and variances between actual and budgeted costs to identify potential problems. Variances help managers see *why* actual costs differ from the budget. This is the first step in determining how to correct problems.

Let's review how Kool-Time Pools made some of the key decisions in setting up and using its standard cost system.

Decision	Guidelines
How to set standards?	Historical performance data Engineering analysis/time-and-motion studies Continuous improvement standards Benchmarking
How to compute a price variance for materials or labor?	$$\text{Price variance} = \left(\begin{array}{c} \text{Actual price} \\ \text{per input unit} \end{array} - \begin{array}{c} \text{Standard price} \\ \text{per input unit} \end{array} \right) \times \begin{array}{c} \text{Actual} \\ \text{quantity of} \\ \text{input} \end{array}$$
How to compute an efficiency variance for materials or labor?	$$\text{Efficiency variance} = \left(\begin{array}{c} \text{Actual} \\ \text{quantity of} \\ \text{input} \end{array} - \begin{array}{c} \text{Standard quantity} \\ \text{of input for actual} \\ \text{number of outputs} \end{array} \right) \times \begin{array}{c} \text{Standard} \\ \text{price per} \\ \text{input unit} \end{array}$$
Who is most likely responsible for: Sales volume variance? Sales revenue flexible budget variance? Direct material price variance? Direct material efficiency variance? Direct labor price variance? Direct labor efficiency variance?	Marketing Department Marketing Department Purchasing Department Production Department Human Resources or Personnel Department Production Department
How to allocate manufacturing overhead in a standard costing system?	$$\begin{array}{c} \text{Manufacturing} \\ \text{overhead} \\ \text{allocated} \end{array} = \left(\begin{array}{c} \text{Standard} \\ \text{predetermined} \\ \text{manufacturing} \\ \text{overhead rate} \end{array} \right) \times \left(\begin{array}{c} \text{Standard quantity of} \\ \text{allocation base allowed} \\ \text{for actual outputs} \end{array} \right)$$
How to analyze over- or underallocated manufacturing overhead?	Split over- or underallocated overhead into $$\text{Flexible budget variance} = \begin{array}{c} \text{Actual} \\ \text{overhead} \end{array} - \begin{array}{c} \text{Flexible budget} \\ \text{overhead} \\ \text{for actual outputs} \end{array}$$ $$\begin{array}{c} \text{Production volume} \\ \text{variance} \end{array} = \begin{array}{c} \text{Flexible budget} \\ \text{overhead} \\ \text{for actual outputs} \end{array} - \begin{array}{c} \text{Standard overhead} \\ \text{allocated to} \\ \text{actual outputs} \end{array}$$
How to record standard costs in the accounts?	Materials Inventory: Actual quantity at standard price Work in Process Inventory (and Finished Goods Inventory and Cost of Goods Sold): Standard quantity of inputs allowed for actual outputs, at standard price of inputs

Exhibit 24-10 indicates that Kool-Time Pools installed 10 swimming pools in June. Suppose Kool-Time had installed 7 pools instead of 10 and that actual expenses were

Direct materials (gunite)	7,400 cubic feet @ $2.00 per cubic foot
Direct labor	2,740 hours @ $10.00 per hour
Variable overhead	$5,400
Fixed overhead	$11,900

CHECK YOUR RESOURCES

Required

1. Given these new data, prepare two exhibits similar to Exhibits 24-10 and 24-16. Ignore marketing and administrative expenses in your first exhibit.
2. Compute price and efficiency variances for direct materials and direct labor.
3. Compute the total variance, the flexible budget variance, and the production volume variance for manufacturing overhead.

Solution

Requirement 1

Kool-Time Pools

Revised Data for Standard Costing Example
Month of June 20X5

PANEL A—Comparison of Actual Results with Flexible Budget for 7 Swimming Pools

	Actual Results at Actual Prices	Flexible Budget for 7 Pools	Flexible Budget Variance
Variable expenses:			
Direct materials	$14,800*	$14,000†	$ 800 U
Direct labor	27,400*	29,400†	2,000 F
Variable overhead	5,400	5,600†	200 F
Total variable expenses	47,600	49,000	1,400 F
Fixed expenses:			
Fixed overhead	11,900	12,000‡	100 F
Total expenses	$59,500	$61,000	$1,500 F

*See Panel C.
†See Panel B.
‡Fixed overhead was budgeted at $12,000 per month.

PANEL B—Computation of Flexible Budget for Direct Materials, Direct Labor, and Variable Overhead for 7 Swimming Pools

	(1) Standard Quantity of Inputs Allowed for 7 Pools	(2) Standard Price per Unit of Input	(1) × (2) Flexible Budget for 7 Pools
Direct materials	1,000 cubic feet per pool × 7 pools = 7,000 cubic feet	$ 2.00	$14,000
Direct labor	400 hours per pool × 7 pools = 2,800 hours	10.50	29,400
Variable overhead	400 hours per pool × 7 pools = 2,800 hours	2.00	5,600

(continued)

Kool-Time Pools (continued)

Revised Data for Standard Costing Example
Month of June, 20X5

PANEL C—Computation of Actual Costs for Direct Materials and Direct Labor for 7 Swimming Pools

	(1) Actual Quantity of Inputs Used for 7 Pools	(2) Actual Price per Unit of Input	(1) × (2) Actual Cost for 7 Pools
Direct materials.......	7,400 cubic feet actually used	$ 2.00 actual cost/cubic foot	$14,800
Direct labor	2,740 hours actually used	$10.00 actual cost/hour	27,400

Kool-Time Pools

Revised Budget Data for the Month Ended June 30, 20X5

	Flexible Budget for Actual Output	Static Budget for Expected Output
Output units (pools installed)	7	8
Standard direct labor hours (400 hours per pool)..................	2,800	3,200
Budgeted manufacturing overhead cost:		
Variable	$ 5,600*	$ 6,400
Fixed...............................	12,000†	12,000
Total	$17,600	$18,400
Standard variable manufacturing overhead rate per direct labor hour.......		$ 6,400 ÷ 3,200 = $2.00
Standard fixed manufacturing overhead rate per direct labor hour.......		$12,000 ÷ 3,200 = $3.75
Standard total manufacturing overhead rate per direct labor hour.......		$18,400 ÷ 3,200 = $5.75

*Flexible budget variable overhead is the standard quantity of the allocation base allowed for actual outputs (2,800 direct labor hours = 7 pools × 400 direct labor hours per pool) multiplied by the $2.00 standard variable manufacturing overhead rate per direct labor hour: 2,800 hours × $2.00 per hour = $5,600.
†Budgeted fixed overhead is *fixed* within the relevant range, so flexible budget fixed overhead is $12,000, the same as static budget fixed overhead.

Requirement 2

$$\text{Price variance} = \left(\begin{array}{c}\text{Actual price}\\\text{per input unit}\end{array} - \begin{array}{c}\text{Standard price}\\\text{per input unit}\end{array}\right) \times \begin{array}{c}\text{Actual}\\\text{quantity of}\\\text{input}\end{array}$$

Direct materials:

Price variance = ($2.00 − $2.00) × 7,400 cubic feet = $0

Direct labor:

Price variance = ($10.00 − $10.50) × 2,740 hours = $1,370 F

$$\text{Efficiency variance} = \left(\begin{array}{c}\text{Actual}\\\text{quantity}\\\text{of input}\end{array} - \begin{array}{c}\text{Standard}\\\text{quantity of}\\\text{input}\end{array}\right) \times \begin{array}{c}\text{Standard}\\\text{price per}\\\text{input unit}\end{array}$$

Direct materials:

$$\text{Efficiency variance} = \left(\begin{array}{c}7,400\\\text{cubic feet}\end{array} - \begin{array}{c}7,000\\\text{cubic feet}\end{array}\right) \times \begin{array}{c}\$2.00\text{ per}\\\text{cubic foot}\end{array} = \$800\text{ U}$$

Direct labor:

$$\text{Efficiency variance} = \left(\begin{array}{c}2,740\\\text{hours}\end{array} - \begin{array}{c}2,800\\\text{hours}\end{array}\right) \times \begin{array}{c}\$10.50\text{ per}\\\text{hour}\end{array} = \$630\text{ F}$$

Requirement 3

Total overhead variance:

Actual overhead cost ($5,400 variable + $11,900 fixed)...........	$17,300
Standard overhead allocated to production	
(2,800 standard direct labor hours × $5.75)	16,100
Total overhead variance	$ 1,200 U

Overhead flexible budget variance:

Actual overhead cost ($5,400 + $11,900).......................	$17,300
Flexible budget overhead for actual outputs ($5,600 + $12,000) ...	17,600
Overhead flexible budget variance............................	$ 300 F

Production volume variance:

Flexible budget overhead for actual outputs ($5,600 + $12,000) ...	$17,600
Standard overhead allocated to (actual) production	
(2,800 standard direct labor hours × $5.75)	16,100
Production volume variance	$ 1,500 U

REVIEW *Flexible Budgets and Standard Costing*

Quick Check

Questions 1 through 4 rely on the following data. Digital Systems is a start-up company that makes connectors for high-speed Internet connections. The company has budgeted variable costs of $130 for each connector and fixed costs of $8,000 per month.

Digital's static budget predicted production and sales of 100 connectors in January, but the company actually produced and sold only 75 connectors at a total cost of $23,000.

1. Digital's total flexible budget cost for 75 connectors per month is
- **a.** $17,750
- **b.** $13,000
- **c.** $9,750
- **d.** $8,130

2. Digital's sales volume variance for total costs is
- **a.** $3,250 F
- **b.** $3,250 U
- **c.** $5,250 F
- **d.** $5,250 U

3. Digital's flexible budget variance for total costs is
- **a.** $3,250 F
- **b.** $3,250 U
- **c.** $5,250 F
- **d.** $5,250 U

4. Digital Systems' managers could set direct labor standards based on:
- **a.** Past actual performance
- **b.** Continuous improvement
- **c.** Benchmarking
- **d.** Time-and-motion studies
- **e.** Any of the above

Questions 5 through 7 rely on the following data. Digital Systems has budgeted 3 hours of direct labor per connector, at a standard cost of $15 per hour. During January, technicians actually worked 210 hours completing the 75 connectors. Digital paid the technicians $15.50 per hour.

5. What is Digital's direct labor price variance for January?
- **a.** $37.50 U
- **b.** $105.00 U
- **c.** $112.50 U
- **d.** $120.00 U

6. What is Digital's direct labor efficiency variance for January?
- **a.** $75.00 F
- **b.** $225.00 F
- **c.** $232.50 F
- **d.** $1,350.00 F

7. The journal entry to record Digital's *use* of direct labor in January is

    a. Manufacturing Wages
        Direct Labor Efficiency Variance
            Work in Process Inventory

    b. Manufacturing Wages
            Direct Labor Efficiency Variance
            Work in Process Inventory

    c. Work in Process Inventory
        Direct Labor Efficiency Variance
            Manufacturing Wages

    d. Work in Process Inventory
            Direct Labor Efficiency Variance
            Manufacturing Wages

8. Digital Systems allocates manufacturing overhead based on machine hours. Each connector should require 10 machine hours. According to the static budget, Digital expected to incur:

    1,000 machine hours per month (100 connectors × 10 machine hours per connector)
    $5,250 in variable manufacturing overhead costs
    $8,000 in fixed manufacturing overhead costs

During January, Digital actually used 825 machine hours to make the 75 connectors. Digital's predetermined standard *total* manufacturing overhead rate is

    a. $5.25 per machine hour   **c.** $13.25 per machine hour
    b. $8.00 per machine hour   **d.** $16.06 per machine hour

9. The total manufacturing overhead variance is composed of:
    a. Price variance and efficiency variance
    b. Price variance and production volume variance
    c. Efficiency variance and production volume variance
    d. Flexible budget variance and production volume variance

10. When Digital *uses* direct materials, the amount of the debit to Work in Process Inventory is based on:
    a. Actual quantity of the materials used × Actual price per unit of the materials
    b. Standard quantity of the materials allowed for the actual production of 75 connectors × Actual price per unit of the materials
    c. Standard quantity of the materials allowed for the actual production of 75 connectors × Standard price per unit of the materials
    d. Actual quantity of the materials used × Standard price per unit of the materials

Accounting Vocabulary

benchmarking (p. 996)
efficiency variance (p. 1001)
flexible budget (p. 987)
flexible budget variance (p. 990)

master budget (p. 986)
overhead flexible budget variance (p. 1008)
price variance (p. 1000)
production volume variance (p. 1009)

sales volume variance (p. 990)
standard cost (p. 994)
static budget (p. 986)
variance (p. 987)

●ASSESS *Your Progress*

online homework

See *www.prenhall.com/horngren*
for selected Starters, Exercises,
and Problems.

Preparing and using flexible budgets
(Obj. 1)

Starters

S24-1 Turn to the Kool-Time Pools example on pages 987 to 988.

1. Using the data from Exhibit 24-3 (page 988), develop flexible budgets for four- and nine-pool levels of output.

2. Would Kool-Time's managers use the flexible budgets you developed in requirement 1 for planning or for controlling? What specific insights can Kool-Time's managers gain from the flexible budgets you prepared in requirement 1?

S24-2 Look at Kool-Time Pools' graph of actual and budgeted monthly costs in Exhibit 24-5 on page 989.

Interpreting flexible budget graph and formula
(Obj. 1)

1. How many pools did Kool-Time install in May?
2. How much were Kool-Time's actual expenses in May?
3. Using Kool-Time's flexible budget formula, what is the flexible budget total cost for May?
4. What is Kool-Time's flexible budget variance for total costs? Is the variance favorable or unfavorable in May?

S24-3 Use your results from Starter 24-2 to explain why the actual results differ from the static budget. Prepare an income statement performance report for Kool-Time Pools for May, using Exhibit 24-7 (page 991) as a guide. Assume that the actual sale price per pool is $12,000, actual variable expenses total $61,000, and actual fixed expenses are $19,000 in May. The static budget number of pools remains eight.

Explaining why actual results differ from the static budget **(Obj. 2)**

Explain to Kool-Time's management why May's operating income differs from the static budget operating income.

S24-4 Consider the Kool-Time Pools example on pages 986–992.

Role of fixed costs
(Obj. 1, 2)

1. What is the relevant range for the flexible budget total cost formula?
2. Explain whether Kool-Time would have a sales volume variance for fixed expenses in Exhibit 24-7 (page 991) if
   a. Kool-Time installs 14 pools per month.
   b. Kool-Time installs 7 pools per month.

S24-5 Fill in the blank with the phrase that best completes the sentence.

Static budgets and flexible budgets
(Obj. 2)

Actual number of outputs	Beginning of the period	Static budget variance
Expected number of outputs	End of the period	
Sales volume variance	Flexible budget variance	

a. The static budget is developed at the _____.
b. The flexible budget used in an income statement performance report is based on the

_____.
c. The master budget is based on the _____.
d. The flexible budget used in an income statement performance report is developed at the _____.
e. The difference between actual costs and the costs that should have been incurred for the actual number of outputs is the _____.

S24-6 Lladró is a Spanish manufacturer of porcelain art objects. Raw materials are mixed to form clay, which is shaped into figurines. The pieces are then glazed and fired at high temperatures.

Benefits of standard costs
(Obj. 3)

Explain how the five benefits of standard costs (Exhibit 24-9) apply to Lladró. Be as specific as possible.

S24-7 In a series of Starters, we will compute variances and record journal entries for Watermate, a manufacturer of ceramic bottles. The company has these standards:

Computing materials variances
(Obj. 4)

Direct materials (clay).	1 pound per bottle, at a cost of $0.40 per pound
Direct labor.	1/5 hour per bottle, at a cost of $14 per hour
Static budget variable overhead . . .	$70,000
Static budget fixed overhead.	$30,000
Static budget direct labor hours . . .	10,000 hours
Static budget number of bottles . . .	50,000

(continued)

Watermate allocates manufacturing overhead to production based on standard direct labor hours. Last month, Watermate reported the following actual results for the production of 70,000 bottles:

Direct materials	1.1 pound per bottle, at a cost of $0.50 per pound
Direct labor	1/4 hour per bottle, at a cost of $13 per hour
Actual variable overhead	$104,000
Actual fixed overhead	$28,000

Compute Watermate's variances for materials.

S24-8 As explained in the chapter opening story, the standard direct materials for a regular **McDonald's** hamburger are:

1 bun	1 pickle slice	1/4 teaspoon mustard
1 hamburger patty	1/8 teaspoon dehydrated onion	1/2 ounce ketchup

Assume that a San Diego, California, McDonald's sold 500 hamburgers yesterday and actually used the following materials:

515 buns	480 pickle slices	140 teaspoons mustard
510 hamburger patties	80 teaspoons dehydrated onion	275 ounces ketchup

Compute the direct materials efficiency variances for each material, using the following standard materials prices (all amounts assumed):

Buns	$0.10 each	Dehydrated onion . .	$0.04 per teaspoon
Hamburger patties . .	0.15 each	Mustard	0.02 per teaspoon
Pickle slices	0.01 per slice	Ketchup	0.04 per ounce

S24-9 Refer to the Watermate data in Starter 24-7. Compute the direct labor variances.

S24-10 Refer to Starters 24-7 and 24-9. For each variance, who in Watermate's organization is most likely responsible? Interpret the direct materials and direct labor variances for Watermate's management.

S24-11 Use the Watermate data in Starter 24-7 to compute the standard predetermined variable manufacturing overhead rate and the standard predetermined fixed manufacturing overhead rate.

S24-12 Refer to the Watermate data in Starters 24-7 and 24-11. Compute the overhead variances. (Use Exhibit 24-17 as a guide.)

S24-13 Refer to the information in Starters 24-7 and 24-9. Record Watermate's direct materials and direct labor journal entries.

S24-14 Refer to the information in Starters 24-7 and 24-12. Record Watermate's journal entries for Manufacturing Overhead, including the entry that records the overhead variances and closes the Manufacturing Overhead account.

S24-15 Refer to the information in Starters 24-7, 24-9, and 24-12 through 24-14. Watermate sold on account each of the 70,000 bottles at a sale price of $8.00 each. There were no beginning or ending inventories of any kind.

Record the journal entries for the completion and sale of the 70,000 bottles.

S24-16 Use the information from Starters 24-7, 24-9, and 24-12 through 24-15 to prepare a standard cost income statement for Watermate's management, using Exhibit 24-19 as a guide. Actual marketing and administrative expenses were $76,500.

Exercises

E24-1 Logiclik sells its main product, ergonomic mouse pads, for $11 each. Its variable cost is $5 per pad. Fixed expenses are $200,000 per month for volumes up to 60,000 pads. Above 60,000 pads, monthly fixed expenses are $250,000.

Prepare a monthly flexible budget for the product, showing sales, variable expenses, fixed expenses, and operating income or loss for volume levels of 40,000, 50,000, and 70,000 pads.

Preparing a flexible budget for the income statement (**Obj. 1**)

spreadsheet

E24-2 → *Link Back to Chapter 22, Exhibit 22-7 (page 907).* Graph the flexible budget total cost line for Logiclik in Exercise 24-1. Show total costs for volume levels of 40,000, 50,000, and 70,000 pads.

Graphing cost behavior (**Obj. 1**)

E24-3 Joe Boxer Company managers received the following incomplete performance report:

Completing a performance report (**Obj. 2**)

Joe Boxer Company
Income Statement Performance Report
Year Ended July 31, 20X7

	Actual Results at Actual Prices	Flexible Budget Variance	Flexible Budget for Actual Number of Output Units	Sales Volume Variance	Static (Master) Budget
Output units.............	36,000	____	36,000	4,000 F	____
Sales revenue	$216,000	____	$216,000	$24,000 F	____
Variable expenses.........	84,000	____	81,000	9,000 U	____
Fixed expenses............	106,000	____	100,000	–0–	____
Total expenses...........	190,000	____	181,000	9,000 U	____
Operating income	$ 26,000	____	$ 35,000	$15,000 F	____

Complete the performance report. Identify the employee group that may deserve praise and the group that may be subject to criticism. Give your reasons.

E24-4 Top managers of Manion Industries predicted 20X6 sales of 145,000 units of its product at a unit price of $8. Actual sales for the year were 140,000 units at $9.50 each. Variable expenses were budgeted at $2.20 per unit, and actual variable expenses were $2.30 per unit. Actual fixed expenses of $420,000 exceeded budgeted fixed expenses by $20,000. Prepare Manion's income statement performance report in a format similar to Exercise 24-3. What variance contributed most to the year's favorable results? What caused this variance?

Preparing an income statement performance report (**Obj. 2**)

E24-5 The following direct materials variance computations are incomplete:

Computing price and efficiency variances for direct materials (**Obj. 4**)

$$\text{Price variance} = (\$? - \$10) \times 9,600 \text{ pounds} = \$4,800 \text{ U}$$
$$\text{Efficiency variance} = (? - 10,400 \text{ pounds}) \times \$10 = ? \text{ F}$$
$$\text{Flexible budget variance} = \$?$$

Fill in the missing values, and identify the flexible budget variance as favorable or unfavorable.

Price and efficiency variances for materials and labor (**Obj. 4**)

spreadsheet

E24-6 Dock Guard, which uses a standard cost accounting system, manufactured 200,000 boat fenders during the year, using 1,450,000 feet of extruded vinyl purchased at $1.05 per foot. Production required 4,500 direct labor hours that cost $14.00 per hour. The materials standard was 7 feet of vinyl per fender, at a standard cost of $1.10 per foot. The

(continued)

labor standard was 0.025 direct labor hour per fender, at a standard cost of $13.00 per hour. Compute the price and efficiency variances for direct materials and direct labor. Does the pattern of variances suggest Dock Guard's managers have been making trade-offs? Explain.

Journal entries
(Obj. 6)

E24-7 Make the journal entries to record the purchase and use of direct materials and direct labor in Exercise 24-6.

Explaining standard cost variances
(Obj. 4, 5)

E24-8 The managers of Viewx Co., a contract manufacturer of DVD drives, are seeking explanations for the variances in the following report. Explain the meaning of each of Viewx's materials, labor, and overhead variances.

Viewx Co.
Standard Costing Income Statement
Year Ended December 31, 20X7

Sales revenue		$1,200,000
Cost of goods sold at standard cost		700,000
Manufacturing cost variances:		
Direct materials price variance	$ 8,000 F	
Direct materials efficiency variance	32,000 U	
Direct labor price variance	24,000 F	
Direct labor efficiency variance	10,000 U	
Manufacturing overhead flexible budget variance	28,000 U	
Production volume variance	8,000 F	
Total manufacturing variances		30,000
Cost of goods sold at actual cost		730,000
Gross profit		470,000
Marketing and administrative expenses		418,000
Operating income		$ 52,000

Computing overhead variances
(Obj. 5)

E24-9 Deelux manufactures paint. The company charges the following standard unit costs to production on the basis of static budget volume of 30,000 gallons of paint per month:

Direct materials	$2.50
Direct labor	2.00
Manufacturing overhead	1.50
Standard unit cost	$6.00

Deelux allocates overhead based on standard machine hours, and it uses the following monthly flexible budget for overhead:

	Number of Outputs (gallons)		
	27,000	30,000	33,000
Standard machine hours	2,700	3,000	3,300
Budgeted manufacturing overhead cost:			
Variable	$13,500	$15,000	$16,500
Fixed	30,000	30,000	30,000

Deelux actually produced 33,000 gallons of paint, using 3,100 machine hours. Actual variable overhead was $16,200, and fixed overhead was $32,500. Compute the total overhead variance, the overhead flexible budget variance, and the production volume variance.

E24-10 Western Outfitters, Inc., revenue and expense information for April follows:

Preparing a standard cost income statement for management
(Obj. 6)

Sales revenue	$560,000
Cost of good sold (standard)	342,000
Direct materials price variance	2,000 F
Direct materials efficiency variance	6,000 F
Direct labor price variance	4,000 U
Direct labor efficiency variance	2,000 F
Overhead flexible budget variance	3,500 U
Production volume variance	8,000 F

Prepare a standard cost income statement for management through gross profit. Report all standard cost variances for management's use. Has management done a good or poor job of controlling costs? Explain.

Problems

(Group A)

P24-1A → *Link Back to Chapter 22, Exhibit 22-7 (page 907).* Lasting Bubbles, Inc., produces multicolored bubble solution used for weddings and other events. The company's static budget income statement for August 20X6 follows. It is based on expected sales volume of 55,000 bubble kits.

Preparing a flexible budget income statement and graphing cost behavior
(Obj. 1)

Student Resource CD

spreadsheet

Lasting Bubbles, Inc.	
Static Budget Income Statement	
Month Ended August 31, 20X6	
Sales revenue	$165,000
Variable expenses:	
Cost of goods sold	63,250
Sales commissions	13,750
Utilities expense	6,050
Fixed expenses:	
Salary expense	32,500
Depreciation expense	20,000
Rent expense	11,000
Utilities expense	5,200
Total expenses	151,750
Operating income	$ 13,250

Lasting Bubbles' plant capacity is 62,500 kits. If actual volume exceeds 62,500 kits, the company must expand the plant. In that case, salaries will increase by 10%, depreciation by 15%, and rent by $6,000. Fixed utilities will be unchanged by any volume increase.

Required

1. Prepare flexible budget income statements for the company, showing output levels of 55,000, 60,000, and 65,000 kits.

2. Graph the behavior of the company's total costs.

3. Why might Lasting Bubbles' managers want to see the graph you prepared in requirement 2 as well as the columnar format analysis in requirement 1? What is the disadvantage of the graphic approach?

Preparing an income statement performance report **(Obj. 2)**

P24-2A Refer to Lasting Bubbles, Inc., of Problem 24-1A. The company sold 60,000 bubble kits during August 20X6, and its actual operating income was as follows:

(continued)

Lasting Bubbles, Inc.
Income Statement
Month Ended August 31, 20X6

Sales revenue		$185,000
Variable expenses:		
Cost of goods sold	$ 69,500	
Sales commissions	18,000	
Utilities expense	6,600	
Fixed expenses:		
Salary expense	34,000	
Depreciation expense	20,000	
Rent expense	10,000	
Utilities expense	5,200	
Total expenses		163,300
Operating income		$ 21,700

Required

1. Prepare an income statement performance report for August 20X6.

2. What accounts for most of the difference between actual operating income and static budget operating income?

3. What is Lasting Bubbles' static budget variance? Explain why the income statement performance report provides Lasting Bubbles' managers with more useful information than the simple static budget variance. What insights can Lasting Bubbles' managers draw from this performance report?

Preparing a flexible budget and computing standard cost variances
(Obj. 1, 3, 4, 5)

P24-3A One System Co. assembles PCs and uses flexible budgeting and a standard cost system. One System allocates overhead based on the number of direct materials parts. The company's performance report includes the following selected data:

	Static Budget (20,000 PCs)	Actual Results (22,000 PCs)
Sales (20,000 PCs × $400)	$8,000,000	
(22,000 PCs × $420)		$9,240,000
Variable manufacturing expenses:		
Direct materials (200,000 parts @ $10.00)	2,000,000	
(214,200 parts @ $9.80)		2,099,160
Direct labor (40,000 hr @ $14.00)	560,000	
(42,500 hr @ $14.60)		620,500
Variable overhead (200,000 parts @ $4.00)	800,000	
(214,200 parts @ $4.10)		878,220
Fixed manufacturing expenses:		
Fixed overhead	900,000	930,000
Total cost of goods sold	4,260,000	4,527,880
Gross profit	$3,740,000	$4,712,120

Required

1. Prepare a flexible budget based on the actual number of PCs sold.

2. Compute the price variance and the efficiency variance for direct materials and for direct labor. For manufacturing overhead, compute the total variance, the flexible budget variance, and the production volume variance.

3. What is the total flexible budget variance for One System's manufacturing costs? Show how the total flexible budget variance is divided into materials, labor, and overhead variances.

4. Have One System's managers done a good job or a poor job controlling material and labor costs? Why?

5. Describe how One System's managers can benefit from the standard costing system.

P24-4A Amanda's Music manufactures harmonicas. Amanda uses standard costs to judge performance. Recently, a clerk mistakenly threw away some of the records, and Amanda has only partial data for October. She knows that the direct labor flexible budget variance for the month was $330 F and that the standard labor price was $10 per hour. A recent pay cut caused a favorable labor price variance of $0.50 per hour. The standard direct labor hours for actual October output were 5,600.

Using incomplete cost and variance information to determine the number of direct labor hours worked
(Obj. 4)

Required

1. Find the actual number of direct labor hours worked during October. First, find the actual direct labor price per hour. Then, determine the actual number of direct labor hours worked by setting up the computation of the direct labor flexible budget variance of $330 F.
2. Compute the direct labor price and efficiency variances. Do these variances suggest the manager may have made any trade-offs? Explain.

P24-5A Avanti manufactures embroidered jackets. The company prepares flexible budgets and uses a standard cost system to control manufacturing costs. The following standard unit cost of a jacket is based on the static budget volume of 14,000 jackets per month:

Computing and journalizing, standard cost variances
(Obj. 4, 5, 6)

Direct materials (3.0 sq. ft @ $4.00 per sq. ft).		$ 12.00
Direct labor (2 hours @ $9.40 per hour)		18.80
Manufacturing overhead:		
Variable (2 hours @ $0.65 per hour)	$1.30	
Fixed (2 hours @ $2.20 per hour).	4.40	5.70
Total cost per jacket.		$36.50

Data for November of the current year include the following:

a. Actual production was 13,600 jackets.
b. Actual direct materials usage was 2.70 square feet per jacket, at an actual cost of $4.15 per square foot.
c. Actual direct labor usage of 24,480 hours cost $235,008.
d. Total actual overhead cost was $79,000.

Required

1. Compute the price and efficiency variances for direct materials and direct labor.
2. Journalize the usage of direct materials and the assignment of direct labor, including the related variances.
3. For manufacturing overhead, compute the total variance, the flexible budget variance, and the production volume variance. (*Hint:* Remember that the total fixed overhead in the flexible budget equals the total fixed overhead in the static budget.)
4. Avanti's management intentionally purchased superior materials for November production. How did this decision affect the other cost variances? Overall, was the decision wise?

P24-6A Happ and Sons, Inc., makes ground covers to prevent weed growth. During May, the company produced and sold 44,000 rolls and recorded the following cost data:

Computing standard cost variances and reporting to management
(Obj. 4, 5, 6)

	Standard Unit Cost	Actual Total Cost
Direct materials:		
Standard (3 lb @ $1.10 per lb)	$3.30	
Actual (136,600 lb @ $1.05 per lb)		$143,430
Direct labor:		
Standard (0.1 hr @ $9.00 per hr)	0.90	
Actual (4,600 hr @ $8.80 per hr).		40,480
		(continued)

(continued)

Manufacturing overhead:
 Standard:
  Variable (0.2 machine hr @ $9.00 per hr) $1.80
  Fixed ($96,000 for static budget volume of
   40,000 units and 8,000 machine hours). . . . .   _2.40_   4.20
 Actual   168,800
Total manufacturing costs $8.40 $352,710

Required

1. Compute the price and efficiency variances for direct materials and direct labor.

2. For manufacturing overhead, compute the total variance, the flexible budget variance, and the production volume variance.

3. Prepare a standard cost income statement through gross profit to report all variances to management. Sale price was $10.60 per roll.

4. Happ intentionally purchased cheaper materials during May. Was the decision wise? Discuss the trade-off between the two materials variances.

Problems

online homework

Preparing a flexible budget income statement and graphing cost behavior
(Obj. 1)

Student Resource CD
spreadsheet

(Group B)

P24-1B → *Link Back to Chapter 22, Exhibit 22-7 (page 907).* Digital Technologies manufactures capacitors for cellular base stations and other communications applications. The company's static budget income statement for October 20X7 follows. It is based on expected sales volume of 9,000 units.

Digital Technologies' plant capacity is 9,500 units. If actual volume exceeds 9,500 units, Digital Technologies must rent additional space. In that case, salaries will increase by 15%, rent will double, and insurance expense will increase by $1,000. Depreciation will be unaffected.

Digital Technologies
Static Budget Income Statement   **Month Ended October 31, 20X7**

Sales revenue	$207,000
Variable expenses:	
Cost of goods sold	90,000
Sales commissions	9,900
Shipping expense.	6,300
Fixed expenses:	
Salary expense	30,500
Depreciation expense	12,750
Rent expense.	11,500
Insurance expense	3,750
Total expenses	164,700
Operating income	$ 42,300

Required

1. Prepare flexible budget income statements for 7,500, 9,000, and 11,000 units.

2. Graph the behavior of the company's total costs.

3. Why might Digital Technologies' managers want to see the graph you prepared in requirement 2 as well as the columnar format analysis in requirement 1? What is the disadvantage of the graphic approach in requirement 2?

P24-2B Refer to Digital Technologies, Problem 24-1B. The company sold 11,000 units during October 20X7, and its actual operating income was as follows:

Digital Technologies	
Income Statement	
Month Ended October 31, 20X7	
Sales revenue	$257,000
Variable expenses:	
Cost of goods sold	112,250
Sales commissions	11,800
Shipping expense.	8,950
Fixed expenses:	
Salary expense	36,650
Depreciation expense	12,750
Rent expense.	22,500
Insurance expense	4,700
Total expenses	209,600
Operating income	$ 47,400

Required

1. Prepare an income statement performance report for October.

2. What was the effect on Digital Technologies' operating income of selling 2,000 units more than the static budget level of sales?

3. What is Digital Technologies' static budget variance? Explain why the income statement performance report provides more useful information to Digital Technologies' managers than the simple static budget variance. What insights can Digital Technologies' managers draw from this performance report?

P24-3B Relax-the-Back manufactures leather recliners and uses flexible budgeting and a standard cost system. Relax-the-Back allocates overhead based on yards of direct materials. The company's performance report includes the following selected data:

	Static Budget (1,000 recliners)	Actual Results (980 recliners)
Sales (1,000 recliners × $500)	$500,000	
(980 recliners × $490)		$480,200
Variable manufacturing expenses:		
Direct materials (6,000 yd × $8.90)	53,400	
(6,150 yd × $8.70)		53,505
Direct labor (10,000 hr × $9.00)	90,000	
(9,600 hr × $9.15)		87,840
Variable overhead (6,000 yd × $5.00)	30,000	
(6,150 yd × $6.40)		39,360
Fixed manufacturing expenses:		
Fixed overhead	60,000	66,000
Total cost of goods sold	233,400	246,705
Gross profit	$266,600	$233,495

Required

1. Prepare a flexible budget based on the actual number of recliners sold.

2. Compute the price variance and the efficiency variance for direct materials and for direct labor. For manufacturing overhead, compute the total variance, the flexible budget variance, and the production volume variance.

(continued)

3. What is the total flexible budget variance for Relax-the-Back's manufacturing costs? Show how the total flexible budget variance is divided into materials, labor, and overhead variances.

4. Have Relax-the-Back's managers done a good job or a poor job controlling material and labor costs? Why?

5. Describe how Relax-the-Back's managers can benefit from the standard costing system.

Using incomplete cost and variance information to determine the direct labor hours
(Obj. 4)

P24-4B Adam's Shades manufactures lamp shades. The manager uses standard costs to judge performance. Recently, a clerk mistakenly threw away some of the records, and the manager has only partial data for March. The manager knows that the direct labor flexible budget variance for the month was $1,050 U and that the standard labor price was $9 per hour. The shop experienced an unfavorable labor price variance of $0.50 per hour. The standard direct labor hours for actual March output were 4,000.

Required

1. Find the actual number of direct labor hours worked during March. First, find the actual direct labor price per hour. Then, determine the actual direct labor hours by setting up the computation of the direct labor flexible budget variance of $1,050 U.

2. Compute the direct labor price and efficiency variances. Do these variances suggest the manager may have made any trade-offs? Explain.

Computing and journalizing standard cost variances
(Obj. 4, 5, 6)

P24-5B Alon manufactures paper weights that it sells to other companies for customizing with their own logos. Alon prepares flexible budgets and uses a standard cost system to control manufacturing costs. The standard unit cost of a paper weight is based on static budget volume of 60,000 paper weights per month. The unit cost is computed as follows:

Direct materials (0.2 lb. @ $0.25 per lb.)................		$0.05
Direct labor (3 minutes @ $0.12 per minute).............		0.36
Manufacturing overhead:		
Variable (3 minutes @ $0.06 per minute).............	$0.18	
Fixed (3 minutes @ $0.14 per minute)	0.42	0.60
Total cost per paper weight...........................		$1.01

Transactions during May of the current year included the following:

a. Actual production and sales were 62,700 paper weights.
b. Actual direct materials usage was 0.18 lb. per paper weight, at an actual cost of $0.20 per pound.
c. Actual direct labor usage of 210,000 minutes cost $29,400.
d. Actual overhead cost was $40,800.

Required

1. Compute the price and efficiency variances for direct materials and direct labor.

2. Journalize the usage of direct materials and the assignment of direct labor, including the related variances.

3. For manufacturing overhead, compute the total variance, the flexible budget variance, and the production volume variance. (*Hint:* Remember that the total fixed overhead in the flexible budget equals the total fixed overhead in the static budget.)

4. Alon intentionally hired more skilled workers during May. How did this decision affect the cost variances? Overall, was the decision wise?

Computing standard cost variances and reporting to management
(Obj. 4, 5, 6)

P24-6B Protex Industries manufactures sunglass cases. During August, the company produced and sold 106,000 cases and recorded the following cost data:

(*continued*)

	Standard Unit Cost	Actual Total Cost
Direct materials:		
Standard (2 parts @ $0.16 per part)......................	$0.32	
Actual (218,000 parts @ $0.20 per part)		$43,600
Direct labor:		
Standard (0.02 hr @ $8.00 per hr)	0.16	
Actual (1,650 hr @ $8.20 per hr)........................		13,530
Manufacturing overhead:		
Standard:		
Variable (0.02 machine hr @ $8.00 per hr)	$0.16	
Fixed ($32,000 for static budget volume of		
100,000 units and 2,000 machine hours)..............	0.32 0.48	
Actual		60,500
Total manufacturing costs	$0.96	$117,630

Required

1. Compute the price and efficiency variances for direct materials and direct labor.

2. For manufacturing overhead, compute the total variance, the flexible budget variance, and the production volume variance.

3. Prepare a standard cost income statement through gross profit to report all variances to management. Sale price of the sunglass cases was $1.50 each.

4. Protex's management used more experienced workers during August. Discuss the trade-off between the two direct labor variances.

APPLY *Your Knowledge*

Decision Cases

Case 1. ReelTime, Inc., distributes DVDs to movie retailers, including dot.coms. ReelTime's top management meets monthly to evaluate the company's performance. Controller Terri Lon prepared the following performance report for the meeting.

Preparing a performance report and using it to evaluate performance **(Obj. 1, 2)**

ReelTime, Inc.
Income Statement Performance Report
Month Ended July 31, 2006

	Actual Result	Static Budget	Variance
Sales revenue	$1,640,000	$1,960,000	$320,000 U
Variable expenses:			
Cost of goods sold	773,750	980,000	206,250 F
Sales commissions	77,375	107,800	30,425 F
Shipping expense............	42,850	53,900	11,050 F
Fixed expenses:			
Salary expense	311,450	300,500	10,950 U
Depreciation expense	208,750	214,000	5,250 F
Rent expense................	128,250	108,250	20,000 U
Advertising expense	81,100	68,500	12,600 U
Total expenses................	1,623,525	1,832,950	209,425 F
Operating income	$ 16,475	$ 127,050	$110,575 U

Lon also revealed that the actual sale price of $20 per movie was equal to the budgeted sale price and that there were no changes in inventories for the month.

(continued)

Management is disappointed by the operating income results. CEO Lyle Nesbitt exclaims, "How can actual operating income be roughly 13% of the static budget amount when there are so many favorable variances?"

Required

1. Prepare a more informative performance report. Be sure to include a flexible budget for the actual number of DVDs bought and sold.
2. As a member of ReelTime's management team, which variances would you want investigated? Why?
3. Nesbitt believes that many consumers are postponing purchases of new movies until after the introduction of a new format for recordable DVD players. In light of this information, how would you rate the company's performance?

Efficiency variances and setting
standards
(Obj. 4)

Case 2. Assume you manage your local Marble Slab Creamery ice cream parlor. In addition to selling ice cream cones, you make large batches of a few flavors of milk shakes to sell throughout the day. Your parlor is chosen to test the company's "Made-for-You" system. The system allows patrons to customize their milk shakes by choosing different flavors.

Customers like the new system, and your staff appears to be adapting, but you wonder whether this new made-to-order system is as efficient as the old system where you just made a few large batches. Efficiency is a special concern because your performance is evaluated in part on the restaurant's efficient use of materials and labor. Assume that your superiors consider efficiency variances greater than 5% unacceptable.

You decide to look at your sales for a typical day. You find that the parlor used 390 lbs. of ice cream and 72 hours of direct labor to produce and sell 2,000 shakes. Assume that the standard quantity allowed for a shake is 0.2 pound of ice cream and 0.03 hours (1.8 minutes) of direct labor. Further, assume that standard costs are $1.50 per pound for ice cream and $8 an hour for labor.

Required

1. Compute the efficiency variances for direct labor and direct materials.
2. Provide likely explanations for the variances. Do you have reason to be concerned about your performance evaluation? Explain.
3. Write a memo to Marble Slab Creamery's national office explaining your concern and suggesting a remedy. Your memo should take the following form:

Date:	_____
To:	Marble Slab Creamery's National Office
From:	_____
Subject:	"Made-for-You" system

Ethical Issues

Setting standards
(Obj. 3)

Austin Landers is the accountant for Sun Coast, a manufacturer of outdoor furniture that is sold through specialty stores and Internet companies. Annually, Landers is responsible for reviewing the standard costs for the following year. While reviewing the standard costs for the coming year, two ethical issues arise. Use the IMA's ethical guidelines, page 774, to identify the ethical dilemma in each situation. Identify the relevant factors in each situation and suggest what Landers should recommend to the controller.

Issue 1. Landers has been approached by Kara Willis, a former colleague who worked with Landers when they were both employed by a public accounting firm. Willis has recently started her own firm, Willis Benchmarking Associates, which collects and sells data on industry benchmarks. She offers to provide Landers with benchmarks for the outdoor furniture industry free of charge, if he will provide her with the last

(continued)

three years of Sun Coast's standard and actual costs. Willis explains that this is how she obtains most of her firm's benchmarking data. Landers always has a difficult time with the standard-setting process and believes that the benchmark data would be very useful.

Issue 2. Sun Coast's management is starting a continuous improvement policy that requires a 10% reduction in standard costs each year for the next three years. Dan Jones, manufacturing foreman of the Teak furniture line, asks Landers to set loose standard costs this year before the continuous improvement policy is implemented. Jones argues that there is no other way to meet the tightening standards while maintaining the high quality of the Teak line.

Team Project

*Setting standards
(Obj. 3, 4)*

Pella Corporation is the world's second-largest manufacturer of wood windows and doors. In 1992, Pella entered the national retail market with its ProLine windows and doors, manufactured in Carroll, Iowa. Since then, Pella has introduced many new product lines with manufacturing facilities in several states.

Suppose Pella has been using a standard cost system that bases price and quantity standards on Pella's historical long-run average performance. Assume Pella's controller has engaged your team of management consultants to advise him whether Pella should use some basis other than historical performance for setting standards.

1. List the types of variances you recommend that Pella compute (for example, direct materials price variance for glass). For each variance, what specific standards would Pella need to develop? In addition to cost standards, do you recommend that Pella develop any nonfinancial standards?
2. There are many approaches to setting standards other than simply using long-run average historical prices and quantities.
   a. List three alternative approaches that Pella could use to set standards, and explain how Pella could implement each alternative.
   b. Evaluate each alternative method of setting standards, including the pros and cons of each method.
   c. Write a memo to Pella's controller detailing your recommendations. First, should Pella retain its historical data–based standard cost approach? If not, which of the alternative approaches should it adopt? Use the following format for your memo:

> Date: _____
>
> To: Controller, Pella Corporation
>
> From: _____, Management Consultants
>
> Subject: Standard Costs

For Internet Exercises, go to the Web site www.prenhall.com/horngren.

CHAPTER 25

Activity-Based Costing and Other Cost Management Tools

TIPS CHECK YOUR RESOURCES

- Visit the www.prenhall.com/horngren **Web site** for self-study quizzes, video clips, and other resources

- Try the **Quick Check** exercise at the end of the chapter to test your knowledge

- Learn the **key terms**

- Do the **Starter** exercises keyed in the margins

- Work the **mid-** and **end-of-chapter summary problems**

- Use the **Concept Links** to review material in other chapters

- Search the **CD** for review materials by chapter or by key word

- Watch the **tutorial videos** to review key concepts

- Watch the **On Location Dell** video on activity-based costing

LEARNING OBJECTIVES

1. Develop activity-based costs (ABC)

2. Use activity-based management (ABM) to make business decisions, including achieving target costs

3. Decide when ABC is most likely to pass the cost-benefit test

4. Describe a just-in-time (JIT) production system, and record its manufacturing costs

5. Contrast the four types of quality costs and use them to make decisions

After **Dell Computer** reported its first-ever quarterly loss several years ago, CEO Michael Dell knew he had to focus on the company's most profitable products. But which products were they? The accounting system traced direct materials and direct labor to individual product lines, but it did not do a good job matching indirect costs with the specific products that caused those costs.

Dell needed a more finely tuned cost accounting system: *activity-based costing (ABC)*. Employee teams identified the 10 most important indirect activities—for example, purchases of raw materials, indirect assembly labor, and warranty service. *For each activity*, the teams devel-

Dell Computer

oped a separate indirect cost allocation rate. The goal was to assign the cost of each activity to the product lines that caused that activity's cost. For example:

- Purchasing costs are assigned based on the number of different "part numbers" in a product.
- Indirect assembly labor is assigned based on the number of times the product is "touched."
- Warranty costs are assigned based on the number of service calls for the product line.

ABC assigns costs more accurately than simpler systems that combine the indirect costs of many activities into a single cost pool and then allocate these costs using a single allocation base.

Has ABC worked for Dell? By 2003, Dell was the leader in worldwide PC sales. Given the rapidly changing costs in the computer industry, Dell uses ABC costs for pricing its computers every day. ABC also helps Dell's managers cut costs, especially by highlighting non-value-added activities such as inventory storage. As the controller of Dell Americas Operations says: "Activity-based costing has really allowed Dell to go to the next level of understanding of its profitability for each of the products it sells." ■

■ Sitemap

To thrive in a globally competitive market, Dell Computer must deliver value to the customer by providing goods or services at an attractive price, while managing costs so the company still earns a profit. This chapter will show you several methods today's managers use to deliver value to the customer at a profit:

- Activity-based costing
- Activity-based management and target costing
- Just-in-time systems
- Costs of quality

⭐ *Develop activity-based costs (ABC)*

 Student Resource CD

cost allocation system, indirect costs

Refining Cost Systems

Why Managers Need More Accurate Cost Systems

Organizations from Dell Computer, to Carolina Power and Light, to the U.S. Marine Corps use refined ABC costing systems. Why? Because simple systems that do not match costs with the consumption of resources can assign costs inequitably. An example shows why.

David Larimer, Matt Sewell, and Marc Bryan are three college friends who share an apartment. They agree to split the following monthly costs equally:

Rent and utilities	$570
Cable TV	50
High-speed Internet access..........................	40
Groceries	240
Total monthly costs	$900

Each roommate's share is $300 ($900/3).

Things go smoothly for the first few months. But then David calls a meeting. "Since I started having dinner at Amy's each night, I shouldn't have to chip in for the groceries." Matt then pipes in: "I'm so busy studying and surfing the Net that I never have time to watch TV. I don't want to pay for the cable TV any more. And Marc, since your friend Jennifer eats here most evenings, you should pay a double share of the grocery bill." Marc retorts, "If that's the way you feel, Matt, then you should pay for the Internet access, since you're the only one around here who uses it!"

What happened? The friends originally agreed to share the costs equally. But they are not participating equally in watching cable TV, surfing the Net, and eating. Splitting these costs equally is not equitable.

The roommates could use an approach that better matches costs with the people who participate in each activity. This means splitting the cable TV costs between David and Marc, assigning the Internet access cost to Matt, and allocating the grocery bill 1/3 to Matt and 2/3 to Marc. Exhibit 25-1 compares the results of this refined system with the original system.

| Exhibit 25-1 | More-Refined versus Less-Refined Cost Allocation System |

	David Larimer	Matt Sewell	Marc Bryan	Total
More-refined cost allocation system:				
Rent and utilities......................................	$190	$190	$190	$570
Cable TV..	25	—	25	50
High-speed Internet access	—	40	—	40
Groceries..	—	80	160	240
Total costs allocated	$215	$310	$375	$900
Less-refined original cost allocation system..............	$300	$300	$300	$900
Difference..	$(85)	$ 10	$ 75	$ 0

No wonder David called a meeting! The original system allocated him $300 a month, but the refined system shows that a more-equitable share would be only $215. On the other hand, the new system allocates Marc $375 a month instead of $300. David was paying for resources he did not use (Internet and groceries), while Marc was not paying for all the resources (groceries) he and his guest consumed. David was "overcosted" and Marc was "undercosted."

Total monthly costs are the same ($900) under both systems. The only difference is how that $900 is allocated among the three roommates. The amount by which David is "overcosted" ($85) must exactly equal the amounts by which Matt and Marc are "undercosted" ($10 + $75).

Sharpening the Focus: From Business Functions to Departments to Activities

In today's competitive, globally wired market, Dell needs to know what it costs to assemble and deliver a customized laptop to a buyer in Eugene, Oregon. Why? So Dell can set a price that covers the costs of all the resources required to assemble and deliver that laptop (and provide some profit), yet remain competitive with Gateway and HP prices.

As the chapter-opening story explained, Dell decided it needed to refine its cost system. There is little error in assigning direct costs (like direct materials and direct labor) to computers and servers. So Dell focused on refining the way it allocated *indirect costs*. The goal was to more accurately reflect the cost of the resources each product uses. How? By drilling down from the indirect costs incurred in each of the six functions in the value chain to the indirect costs incurred in each individual department within each value-chain function and, finally, to the indirect costs of the specific activities in each department. Let's look at each step.

The first column of Exhibit 25-2 lists the six value-chain functions: R&D, design, production, marketing, distribution, and customer service. We'll focus on how Dell refined costs in the production element of the value chain, because that is where most companies like Dell and Dow Chemical begin refining their cost systems.

Exhibit 25-2

Sharpening the Focus from Business Functions to Departments to Activities

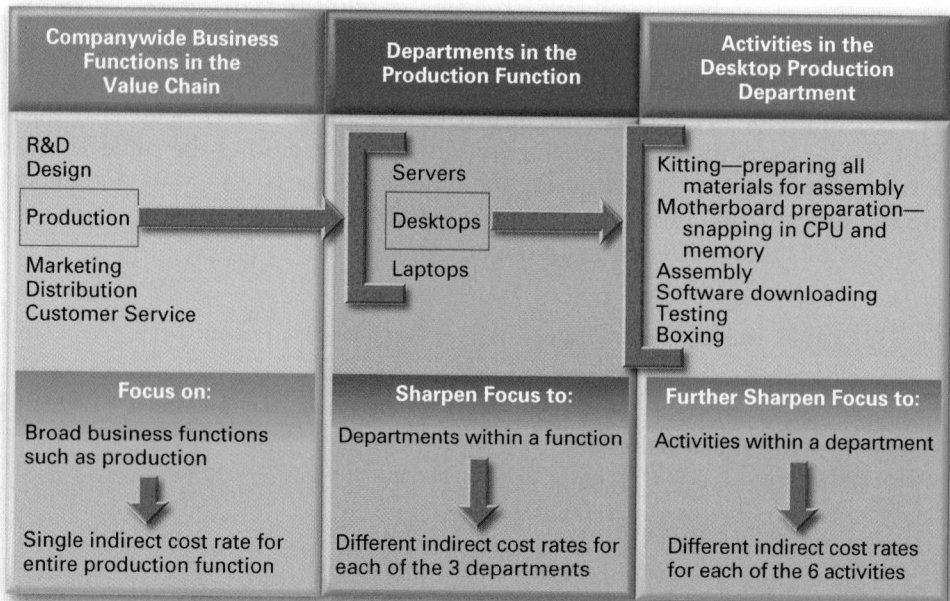

Long ago, when managers could limit their focus to broad business functions, simple cost systems were often good enough. For example, many companies started out with a broad focus on the production function and used a single plantwide indirect cost rate (manufacturing overhead rate), like we did in Chapter 20. ←

See Chapter 20, pp. 811–814, to review the allocation of indirect manufacturing costs (overhead). →

As competition increased, managers needed more-accurate estimates of product costs to set prices and to identify the most profitable products. When broad averages like plantwide overhead rates (or like the three roommates splitting their costs equally) are no longer good enough, managers drill down to focus on the indirect costs incurred by each *department* within the function. Exhibit 25-2 shows that Dell's production function includes separate departments (or production lines) for its three main products: servers, desktops, and laptops. The next step in refining its cost system is to establish separate indirect cost rates for each department—one rate for the server department, another for the desktop department, and a third for the laptop department.

To obtain even more accurate estimates of the resources each product uses, managers drill down deeper yet to analyze the indirect costs of each *activity* in a department. Exhibit 25-2 shows the six activities in the desktop production department. Rather than using a single overhead rate for the entire desktop department, Dell develops separate rates for each of these six activities, from kitting to boxing. This is called activity-based costing.

☐ Refining Cost Systems
■ **Activity-Based Costing**
☐ Activity-Based Management
☐ ABC and Cost-Benefit
☐ JIT Systems
☐ Quality Management

Activity-Based Costing (ABC)
Focuses on *activities* as the fundamental cost objects. The costs of those activities become building blocks for compiling the indirect costs of products, services, and customers.

Activity-Based Costing

Activity-based costing (ABC) focuses on *activities* as the fundamental cost objects. The costs of those activities become building blocks for compiling the indirect costs of products, services, and customers. Companies like Allied

Signal, Coca-Cola, and American Express use ABC to more accurately estimate the cost of resources required to produce different products, to render different services, and to serve different customers.

Companies that use ABC trace direct materials and direct labor to cost objects, as described in Chapter 20. → The only difference is that ABC systems make more effort to allocate *indirect costs*—such as manufacturing overhead—to the products, services, or customers that caused those costs. How? By separately estimating the indirect costs of each activity and then allocating those indirect costs based on what caused them.

Each activity's indirect cost has its own (usually unique) cost driver. For example, Dell allocates indirect assembly costs (such as depreciation on the equipment used in the assembly process) based on the number of times workers touch a computer as it moves through assembly. Computers that require more touches are allocated more costs. Exhibit 25-3 illustrates other common activities and related cost drivers.

See Chapter 20, pp. 802–808, to review how direct materials and direct labor are traced to cost objects.

Student ResourceCD

activity-based costing, cost allocation rate, cost allocation system, cost driver, manufacturing overhead

Exhibit 25-3 **Activities and Cost Drivers**

Data warehouses and other information technology have made detailed ABC systems easier to use. Optical scanning and bar coding reduce the cost of collecting cost driver information. ERP systems like SAP, Oracle, and Peoplesoft have ABC modules. Managers can also buy specialized ABC software. But Dell began its ABC system simply using Excel spreadsheets!

Developing an Activity-Based Costing System

The main difference between ABC and traditional systems is that ABC systems have separate indirect cost allocation rates for each activity. ABC requires seven steps:

1. Identify the activities.
2. Estimate the total indirect costs of each activity.
3. Identify the allocation base for each activity's indirect costs—this is the primary cost driver.
4. Estimate the total quantity of each allocation base.
5. Compute the cost allocation rate for each activity:

$$\frac{\text{Cost allocation rate}}{\text{for activity}} = \frac{\text{Estimated total indirect costs of activity}}{\text{Estimated total quantity of cost allocation base}}$$

6. Obtain the actual quantity of each allocation base used by the cost object (for example, the quantity used by a particular product).
7. Allocate the costs to the cost object:

$$\text{Allocated activity cost} = \frac{\text{Cost allocation rate}}{\text{for activity}} \times \frac{\text{Actual quantity of cost allocation}}{\text{base used by the cost object}}$$

The first step in developing an activity-based costing system is to identify the activities. Analyzing all the activities required to make a product forces managers to think about how each activity might be improved—or whether the activity is necessary at all. Steps 2 through 7 are the same approach used to allocate manufacturing overhead, as explained in Chapter 20. The only difference is that ABC systems repeat steps 2 through 7 for each activity.

Traditional versus Activity-Based Costing Systems: Chemtech

To emphasize the distinctions between ABC systems and traditional costing systems, our example simplifies the process that would occur in a real company, which might identify more than 50 different activities.

Chemtech's Chemical Manufacturing Department produces hundreds of different chemicals. The company has focused on producing mass quantities of "commodity" chemicals for large customers. It also manufactures small quantities of specialty chemicals for individual customers.

Last updated in 1990, the Chemical Manufacturing Department's cost system uses a single indirect cost pool and allocates manufacturing overhead at 200% of direct labor cost. Chemtech's controller, Martha Wise, gathered data for two of the department's many products:

■ Aldehyde—a commodity chemical used in producing plastics
■ Phenylephrine hydrochloride (PH)—a specialty chemical (A single customer uses PH in blood-pressure medications.)

	Aldehyde	Phenylephrine Hydrochloride (PH)
Number of pounds per year	7,000 lb	5 lb
Direct materials cost per pound	$ 5	$20
Direct labor cost per pound	$ 1	$10
Sale price per pound	$10	$70

Wise used this information to compute each product's gross profit, as shown in Exhibit 25-4.

Exhibit 25-4

Chemtech's Traditional Cost System—Product Cost and Gross Profit

 **Starter 25-4**

	Aldehyde	PH
Sale price per pound............................	$10.00	$70.00
Less: Manufacturing cost per pound:		
Direct materials.............................	5.00	20.00
Direct labor	1.00	10.00
Manufacturing overhead		
(at 200% of direct labor cost).................	2.00	20.00
Total manufacturing cost per pound	8.00	50.00
Gross profit per pound.........................	$ 2.00	$20.00

The gross profit for the PH specialty chemical is $20 per pound—10 times as high as the gross profit for the aldehyde commodity chemical ($2). Chemtech CEO Randy Smith is surprised that PH appears so much more profitable (per pound) than aldehyde. He asks Wise to check 50 of the department's other products. Wise confirms that the gross profit per pound is 10 times as high for specialty chemicals as it is for commodity chemicals. Smith wonders whether Chemtech should switch its focus to specialty chemicals.

1. What is the *total* direct labor cost assigned to
   a. Aldehyde?
   b. PH?
2. What is the *total* manufacturing overhead allocated to
   a. Aldehyde?
   b. PH?

Answers

1. Total direct labor cost assigned to aldehyde is 7,000 pounds × $1 per pound = $7,000. Total direct labor cost assigned to PH is 5 pounds × $10 per pound = $50. Thus, Chemtech assigns to aldehyde 140 times as much total direct labor cost as it does to PH ($7,000 ÷ $50 = 140).

2. **Key Point**: Total overhead allocated to aldehyde is 7,000 pounds × $2 per pound = $14,000. Total overhead allocated to PH is 5 pounds × $20 per pound = $100. Thus, because Chemtech uses direct labor cost as its single allocation base, Chemtech also allocates 140 times as much total overhead to aldehyde as to PH ($14,000 ÷ $100). This costing is accurate only if direct labor really is the primary overhead cost driver, and so aldehyde really does cause 140 times as much overhead as PH.

CEO Smith calls a meeting with the department foreman Steve Pronai and controller Wise. Smith is perplexed that the accounting numbers show specialty chemicals are more profitable (on a per-pound basis) than commodity chemicals. He expected the department would be more efficient producing a few commodity chemicals (in a few very large batches) than producing a wide variety of specialty chemicals (in many small batches). Foreman Pronai echoes Smith's concern. Pronai says it takes just as long to mix a small batch of specialty chemicals as a large batch of commodity chemicals. Finally, Smith is puzzled because Chemtech's competitors seem to be earning good profits, even though they usually undercut Chemtech's prices on commodity chemicals.

Wise fears that the problem could be Chemtech's cost accounting system. She suggests that Foreman Pronai and the plant engineer work with her to develop a pilot ABC system. Using a cross-functional team that includes the plant engineer and foreman, as well as the controller, should lead to a more-accurate ABC system because it incorporates a wider variety of perspectives. Also, managers are more likely to believe costs from a system they helped build.

Exhibit 25-5 presents a bird's-eye overview that compares the original direct labor single-allocation-base system (Panel A) to the new ABC system Wise's team developed (Panel B).

Panel B of Exhibit 25-5 shows that Chemtech's ABC team identifies three activities: mixing, processing, and testing. Each activity has its own indirect cost pool and cost driver. But exactly how does this work? The ABC team develops the new system by following the seven steps described earlier. Exhibit 25-6 shows how, with a special focus on computing and assigning the costs of the mixing activity.

Exhibit 25-6 highlights the seven steps in developing Chemtech's ABC system, with a focus on the mixing activity.

Exhibit 25-5   Chemtech's Traditional and ABC Systems

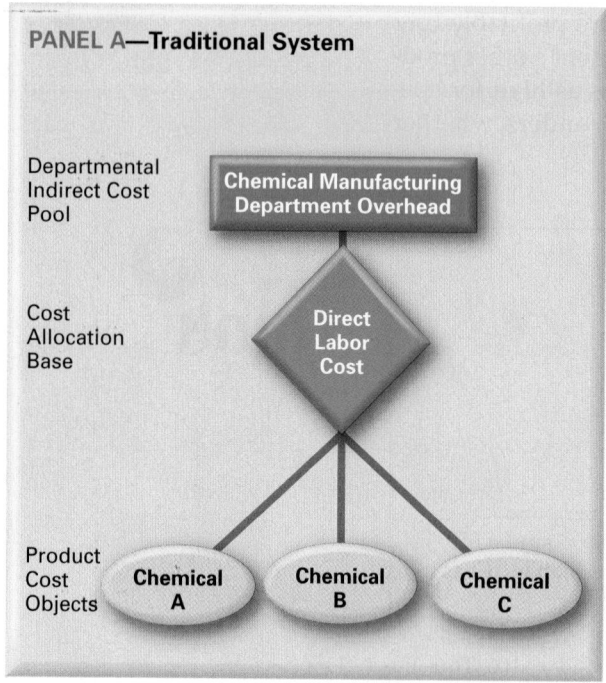

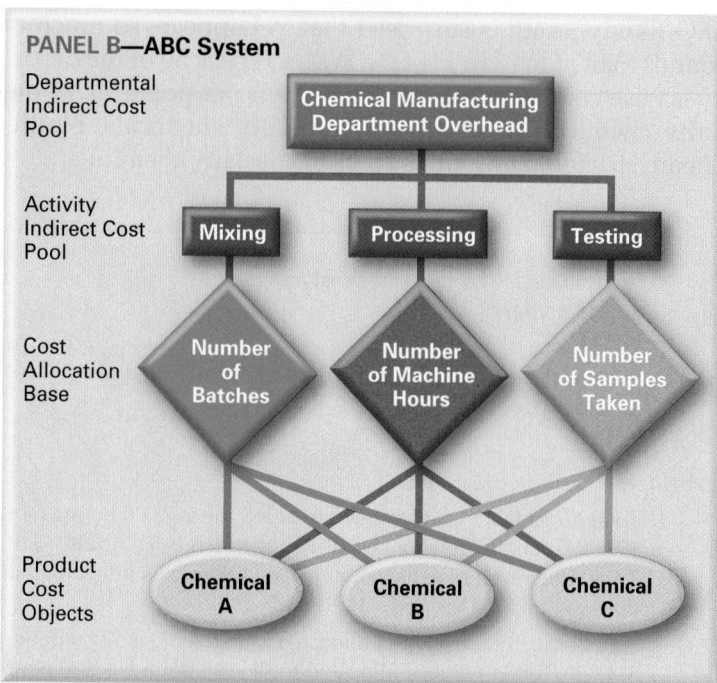

✔ Starter 25-1

✔ Starter 25-7

Follow the details of each step in Exhibit 25-6. Make sure you understand exactly how each ABC step applies to Chemtech's mixing process.

Exhibit 25-7 summarizes the seven steps for all three activities. Study Exhibit 25-7 carefully, following each of the seven steps for the processing and testing activities to make sure you understand how the activity costs are allocated.

Controller Wise then uses the ABC costs allocated to aldehyde and to PH (from column 7 of Exhibit 25-7) to recompute manufacturing overhead costs, as shown in Exhibit 25-8. For each product, Wise adds the total costs of the three activities to obtain the total manufacturing overhead allocated to each product. She then divides each product's total manufacturing overhead cost by the number of pounds Chemtech produced to get the overhead cost per pound.

Compare the overhead cost per pound under the original direct-labor-based system with the ABC costs:

	Overhead Cost per Pound	
	Traditional Direct Labor System (Exhibit 25-4)	**ABC System (Exhibit 25-8)**
Aldehyde	$ 2.00	$ 1.95
PH	20.00	94.00

ABC costs are more accurate because ABC takes into account the resources (mixing costs, machine time, and testing) each product actually uses. Recall that the old direct labor single-allocation-base system allocated 140 times as much overhead to aldehyde as to PH (see the Stop & Think on page 1039).

With more-precise allocations, ABC shifts costs out of aldehyde and into PH, where the costs belong. Why? Exhibit 25-7 shows that aldehyde uses more of each activity's resources than PH, but *not* 140 times as much. Column 6 shows that aldehyde uses 60 times as much mixing, about 15 times as many machine hours (processing costs), and 14 times as much testing as PH.

Exhibit 25-6 Seven Steps in Developing Chemtech's ABC System

Step 1: Identify activities: mixing, processing, testing

Chemtech Controller Wise and her team identify three activities in the Chemical Manufacturing Department: mixing, processing, and testing.

Step 2: Estimate total indirect cost of each activity

Foreman Steve Pronai estimates that total mixing costs for all products will be $600,000. Estimated costs for each activity appear in Exhibit 25-7, column 2.

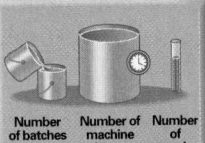

Step 3: Identify allocation base for each activity

The allocation base for each activity should be the primary cost driver. Workers mix ingredients separately for each batch of chemicals, so the number of batches drives mixing costs. Pronai and the plant engineer decide that the number of machine hours is the best allocation base for processing costs, and that number of samples drives testing costs.

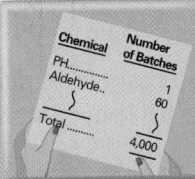

Step 4: Estimate total quantity of each allocation base

Wise and Pronai estimate the department will produce a total of 4,000 batches. Estimated quantities of the cost driver allocation bases appear in column 4 of Exhibit 25-7.

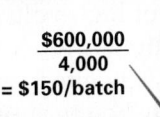

Step 5: Compute allocation rates for each activity

Wise computes the allocation rate for mixing, as follows:

$$\text{Cost allocation rate for mixing} = \frac{\$600,000}{4,000 \text{ batches}} = \$150 \text{ per batch}$$

Column 5 of Exhibit 25-7 shows the cost allocation rate for each activity.

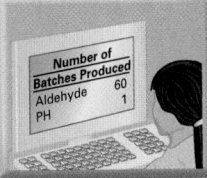

Step 6: Obtain actual quantities of each allocation base used by each product

During the year, Chemtech produces 60 batches of aldehyde and 1 batch of PH. (This total of 61 batches is only a small fraction of the 4,000 total batches Chemtech produces. The remaining batches consist of Chemtech's other chemicals.) Exhibit 25-7, column 6, shows the actual quantities of each activity's allocation base used by aldehyde and PH.

Step 7: Allocate costs to each product

Wise allocates mixing costs as follows:

Aldehyde: 60 batches × $150 per batch = $9,000
PH: 1 batch × $150 per batch = $ 150

Column 7 of Exhibit 25-7 shows the cost allocation for all three activities.

Exhibit 25-7 Summary of Chemtech's Activity-Based Costing System

(1) Activity	(2) Estimated Costs	(3) Cost Allocation Base	(4) Estimated Quantity of Cost Allocation Base	(5) Cost Allocation Rate	(6) Actual Quantity of Cost Allocation Base Used by:		(7) Allocated Activity Cost	
					Aldehyde	PH	Aldehyde	PH
Mixing	$600,000	# Batches	4,000 batches	$\frac{\$600,000}{4,000} = \$150/\text{batch}$	60 batches	1 batch	$150 × 60 = $9,000	$150 × 1 = $150
Processing	$3,000,000	# Machine hours (MH)	50,000 MH	$\frac{\$3,000,000}{50,000} = \$60/\text{MH}$	30 1/2 MH	2 MH	$60 × 30 1/2 = $1,830	$60 × 2 = $120
Testing	$600,000	# Samples	3,000 samples	$\frac{\$600,000}{3,000} = \$200/\text{sample}$	14 samples	1 sample	$200 × 14 = $2,800	$200 × 1 = $200

Exhibit 25-8

Chemtech's Manufacturing
Overhead Costs Under ABC

Manufacturing Overhead Costs	Aldehyde	PH
Mixing (from Exhibit 25-7)...............	$ 9,000	$150
Processing (from Exhibit 25-7)	1,830	120
Testing (from Exhibit 25-7).................	2,800	200
Total manufacturing overhead	$13,630	$470
Divide by number of pounds	÷ 7,000 lb	÷ 5 lb
Manufacturing overhead per pound	$ 1.95/lb*	$ 94/lb

*Rounded

✔ Starter 25-2

✔ Starter 25-8

✔ Starter 25-9

Allocating overhead based on the actual resources *used* generally increases the costs of low-volume products like PH that are produced in small batches. Why? Because costs like mixing and testing are spread over the small number of units in that batch, which can dramatically increase product costs. For example, although Chemtech made only 5 pounds of PH, column 6 of Exhibit 25-7 shows that this product still required

- Workers to mix a batch, at a mixing cost of $150
- 2 machine hours at $60 per hour
- One sample tested at a cost of $200

Spreading these costs over the 5 pounds of PH yields an overhead cost of $94 per pound, as shown in Exhibit 25-8. This is much higher than the $20-per-pound cost under the original system (Exhibit 25-4).

On the other hand, for high-volume products produced in large batches, such as aldehyde, mixing and testing costs are spread over the larger number of units in the batch. So ABC often assigns *fewer* costs to each unit of high-volume products than do single-allocation-base systems. After implementing ABC, companies often realize they were overcosting high-volume products (Chemtech was overcosting aldehyde) and undercosting low-volume products (Chemtech was undercosting PH).

Now that we know the indirect costs of aldehyde and PH under the refined ABC system, let's see how Chemtech's managers *use* this new cost information to make better pricing and product-mix decisions and to find new ways to cut costs.

☐ Refining Cost Systems
☐ Activity-Based Costing
■ Activity-Based Management
☐ ABC and Cost-Benefit
☐ JIT Systems
☐ Quality Management

2 Use activity-based management
(ABM) to make business decisions,
including achieving target costs

Student ResourceCD

activity-based costing, activity-based
management, target cost, target pricing,
value engineering

Activity-Based Management
Using activity-based cost information
to make decisions that increase profits
while satisfying customers' needs.

✔ Starter 25-10

✔ Starter 25-11

Activity-Based Management: Using ABC for Decision Making

Activity-based management (ABM) refers to using activity-based cost information to make decisions that increase profits while satisfying customers' needs. We consider how Chemtech can use ABC information in three kinds of decisions: (1) pricing and product mix, (2) cost cutting, and (3) routine planning and control.

Pricing and Product Mix Decisions

Armed with the ABC manufacturing overhead cost per pound (Exhibit 25-8), Controller Wise recomputes each product's total manufacturing costs and gross profit. Panel A of Exhibit 25-9 shows that the total manufacturing cost per pound of aldehyde is $7.95 under the ABC system. Contrast this with the $8.00 cost per pound under Chemtech's original system, as shown in Panel B. More important, the refined ABC data in Panel A show that specialty chemical PH costs $124 per pound, rather than the $50 per pound indicated by the old system (Panel B). Chemtech has been losing $54 on each pound of PH—and this is *before* nonmanufacturing costs such as R&D, marketing, and distribution! Wise finds that most of Chemtech's other specialty chemicals show similar increases in costs under the ABC system.

PANEL A: Total Manufacturing Cost and Gross Profit Under ABC

	Aldehyde	PH
Sale price per pound	$10.00	$ 70.00
Less: Manufacturing cost per pound:		
Direct materials	$ 5.00	$ 20.00
Direct labor	1.00	10.00
Manufacturing overhead (from Exhibit 25-8)	1.95	94.00
Total manufacturing cost	7.95	124.00
Gross profit (loss) per pound	$ 2.05	$(54.00)

PANEL B: Total Manufacturing Cost and Gross Profit Under Original Cost System (from Exhibit 25-4)

	Aldehyde	PH
Sale price per pound	$10.00	$ 70.00
Less: Manufacturing cost per pound	8.00	50.00
Gross profit per pound	$ 2.00	$ 20.00

Exhibit 25-9

Comparison of Chemtech's Manufacturing Product Costs Under ABC versus Original Systems

✔ Starter 25-3

As you'll see in the next section, Chemtech may be able to use the ABC analysis to find ways to cut costs. If it cannot cut costs enough to earn a profit on PH, then it may have to raise the sale price. If customers will not pay more, Chemtech should consider dropping PH. More generally, if the ABC system shows that commodity chemicals are more profitable than Chemtech thought, and specialty chemicals are less profitable, Chemtech may shift its product mix away from specialty chemicals toward commodity chemicals. *This is the exact opposite of the strategy suggested by cost data from the original system.*

Cutting Costs

Most companies adopt ABC to get more-accurate product costs for pricing and product mix decisions. But they often reap even greater benefits by using ABM to pinpoint opportunities to cut costs. For example, farm machinery maker John Deere uses an enterprisewide Web-based system to track cost changes. The system pulls cost data from companywide purchasing, ABC, and forecasting data warehouses. Managers use the system to see how well they are meeting cost-cutting goals for individual products, suppliers, and locations.

ABC can help organizations use value engineering to cut costs. **Value engineering** means reevaluating activities to reduce costs while satisfying customer needs. Value engineering requires cross-functional teams: marketers to identify customer needs, engineers and production personnel to design more efficient processes and products, and accountants to estimate how proposed changes will affect costs.

Why are managers turning to value engineering to cut costs? Companies like Carrier Corporation and General Motors are following Japanese automakers like Toyota and Nissan and setting sale prices based on **target prices**—what customers are willing to pay for the product or service. Instead of starting with the full product cost from all elements of the value chain (as discussed in Chapter 19) and then adding a profit to determine the sale price, Exhibit 25-10 shows that target pricing does just the opposite. Target pricing starts with the price customers are willing to pay and then subtracts the company's desired profit to determine the **target** (or allowable) **cost** to develop, produce, and deliver the product or service. Target costs are usually less than the (current) full cost of the product or service. The target cost is a goal the company must shoot for.

Value Engineering
Reevaluating activities to reduce costs while satisfying customer needs.

Target Price
What customers are willing to pay for the product or service.

Target Cost
Allowable cost to develop, produce, and deliver the product or service. Equals target price minus desired profit.

Exhibit 25-10

Target Pricing versus Traditional Cost-Based Pricing

Let's return to our Chemtech illustration. After seeing the results of the ABC analysis in Exhibit 25-9, CEO Smith decides to focus on commodity chemicals. The marketing department says the market price of aldehyde is likely to fall to $9.50 per pound. Smith wants to earn a profit equal to 20% of the sale price. In addition to the manufacturing costs in Exhibit 25-9, Chemtech incurs a total of $0.50 per pound in nonmanufacturing costs (R&D, design, marketing, distribution, and customer service).

What is Chemtech's target cost per pound of aldehyde? Do Chemtech's current costs meet this target?

Answer:

Target sale price per pound of aldehyde	$9.50
Desired profit ($9.50 × 20%)	(1.90)
Target cost per pound of aldehyde	$7.60

Chemtech's current costs do not meet the target cost.

Current total manufacturing cost (from Exhibit 25-9) ...	$7.95
Nonmanufacturing costs	0.50
Current full product cost per pound of aldehyde	$8.45

Because Chemtech's current full product costs ($8.45) exceed the target cost of $7.60, Smith assembles a cross-functional value-engineering team to identify opportunities to cut costs. The team includes marketing Manager Liz Smith, plant engineer Edward Michaels, and production foreman Steve Pronai, along with controller Martha Wise. The team analyzes each of Chemtech's three production activities: mixing, processing, and testing. For each activity, the team considers (1) how to cut costs given current production processes and (2) how to redesign the production process to further cut costs.

Of the team's several proposals, Smith chooses three:

1. *Redesign the mixing process to reduce cost per batch mixed.* The proposal is to group raw materials that are used together to reduce time required to assemble them when mixing each batch. Total estimated savings is $150,000, and the plant's total annual number of batches remains unchanged at 4,000.

2. *Redesign the processing activity to reduce the number of machine hours used.* The proposal is to purchase equipment that will cut processing time in half, but it costs $1,000,000. Total machine hours will remain 50,000, but each product will require only half as many hours. (Chemtech will use the extra machine hours to make other profitable products).

3. *Redesign the testing process to reduce* **both** *the cost per sample* **and** *the number of samples.* The recommendation is to improve quality control to reduce the need to test samples of each product. This will cut total testing costs by $375,000 and also will cut the total number of samples tested in half—from 3,000 to just 1,500. Chemtech will now test only 7 rather than 14 samples of aldehyde.

Will these changes allow Chemtech to reach the target cost? Exhibit 25-11 shows how Controller Wise starts with the original data summarized in Exhibit 25-7 and adjusts these data for the value-engineering changes. Wise first recomputes the cost allocation rates for each activity: She incorporates changes in both the numerator (estimated indirect costs of the activity) and the denominator (estimated total quantity of the activity's allocation base). She then uses these new allocation rates to assign the costs of each activity to aldehyde, based on how much of each allocation base aldehyde uses after the value-engineering changes.

Exhibit 25-11 Recomputing Activity Costs for Aldehyde After Value-Engineering Changes

	Mixing	Processing	Testing
Estimated total indirect costs of activity:			
Mixing ($600,000 − $150,000)	$450,000		
Processing ($3,000,000 + $1,000,000)		$4,000,000	
Testing ($600,000 − $375,000)			$225,000
Estimated total quantity of each allocation base	4,000 batches	50,000 MH	1,500 samples
Compute the cost allocation rate for each activity:			
(Divide estimated indirect cost by	$450,000	$4,000,000	$225,000
estimated quantity of the allocation base)	÷ 4,000 batches	÷ 50,000 MH	÷ 1,500 samples
Cost allocation rate for each activity	= $112.50/batch	= $80/MH	= $150/sample
Actual quantity of each allocation base used by aldehyde:			
Mixing	60 batches		
Processing ($30\frac{1}{2} \times 50\%$)		$15\frac{1}{4}$ MH	
Testing			7 samples
Allocate the costs to aldehyde:			
Mixing (60 batches × $112.50)	$6,750		
Processing ($15\frac{1}{4}$ MH × $80)		$1,220	
Testing (7 samples × $150)			$1,050

Exhibit 25-11 shows that value-engineering cuts the total manufacturing overhead costs assigned to aldehyde to $9,020 ($6,750 + $1,220 + $1,050) from $13,630 (in Exhibit 25-8). Spread over 7,000 pounds of aldehyde, this is $1.29 per pound ($9,020 ÷ 7,000, rounded). Now Wise totals the revised cost estimates for aldehyde:

Direct materials (from Exhibit 25-9)	$5.00
Direct labor (from Exhibit 25-9)	1.00
Manufacturing overhead	1.29
Total manufacturing costs	7.29
Nonmanufacturing costs	0.50
Full product cost of aldehyde	$7.79

These changes are quite an improvement from the prior full product cost of $8.45 per pound. But they are *not* enough to meet the $7.60 target cost. Chemtech must conduct more value engineering (or accept less profit) to meet the target sale price.

Routine Planning and Control Decisions

For the master budget, see Chapter 23, pp. 943–954.

Analyzing manufacturing overhead variances; see Chapter 24, pp. 1007–1110.

In addition to pricing, product mix, and cost cutting decisions, Chemtech can use ABC in routine planning and control. In activity-based budgeting, managers budget costs of individual activities to build up the indirect cost schedules in the master budget (discussed in Chapter 23). ← Chemtech can also analyze manufacturing overhead variances (presented in Chapter 24) ← in more detail by computing variances for each of the three individual indirect activities (mixing, processing, and testing). Finally, Chemtech's managers can use ABC information to evaluate workers. For example, Foreman Pronai may receive a bonus if he can cut:

- The cost per sample tested (that is, cut the cost allocation rate for the testing activity) or
- The number of samples tested (that is, cut the consumption of the activity) *while maintaining product quality*.

☐ Refining Cost Systems
☐ Activity-Based Costing
☐ Activity-Based Management
■ ABC and Cost-Benefit
☐ JIT Systems
☐ Quality Management

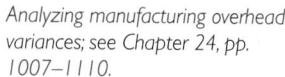 *Decide when ABC is most likely to pass the cost-benefit test*

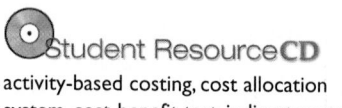 Student Resource CD

activity-based costing, cost allocation system, cost-benefit test, indirect costs

When Does ABC Pass the Cost-Benefit Test?

Like all other management tools, ABC must pass the cost-benefit test. The system should be refined enough to provide accurate product costs, but simple enough for managers to understand. In the Chemtech example, ABC triples the number of allocation bases—from the single allocation base (direct labor) in the original system, to three allocation bases (for mixing, processing, and testing) under ABC. ABC systems are even more complex in real-world companies that have many more activities and cost drivers.

The Cost-Benefit Test

Activity-based costing and activity-based management pass the cost-benefit test when the benefits of adopting ABC/ABM exceed the costs. Benefits of adopting ABC/ABM are higher for companies in competitive markets because:

- Accurate product cost information is essential for setting competitive sale prices that still allow the company to earn a profit.
- ABM can pinpoint opportunities for cost savings, which increase the company's profit or are passed on to customers in lower prices.

ABC's benefits are higher when ABC reports different product costs than under the old system. This is likely to happen when:

- The company produces many different products that use different amounts of resources. (If all products use similar amounts of resources, a simple single-allocation-base system works fine.)
- The company has high indirect costs. (If indirect costs are immaterial, it does not matter how they are allocated.)
- The company produces high volumes of some products and low volumes of other products. (Traditional single-allocation-base systems tend to overcost high-volume products and undercost low-volume products.)

The costs of adopting ABC are lower when the company has:

✔ Starter 25-5

- Accounting and information system expertise to develop the system

✔ Starter 25-6

- Information technology like bar coding, optical scanning, or "data warehouse" systems to record and compile cost driver data

Are real-world companies glad they adopted ABC? Usually, but not always. A recent survey has shown that 89% of the companies using ABC data say it was worth the cost.[1] Adoption is on the rise among financial companies like American Express, utilities like Indianapolis Power and Light, and nonprofits like the U.S. Marine Corps. But ABC is not a cure-all. As the controller for one Midwest manufacturer said, "ABC will not reduce cost, it will only help you understand costs better to know what to correct."

Signs That the Cost System May Be Broken

Broken cars or computers simply stop running. But unlike cars and computers, even broken or outdated product cost systems continue to report "product costs." How can you tell whether a cost system needs repair?

Management accounting expert Robin Cooper and others suggest that a company's product cost system may need repair when

Managers don't understand costs and profits:

- In bidding for jobs, managers lose bids they expected to win and win bids they expected to lose.
- Competitors with similar high-volume products price their products below our costs, but still earn good profits.
- Employees do not believe the cost numbers reported by the accounting system.

The cost system is outdated:

- The company uses a single-allocation-base system developed long ago.
- The company has reengineered its production process but has not changed its accounting system.

Review the Chemtech example on pages 1038–1042. List the symptoms that Chemtech's original cost system may be broken.

Answer:

1. The Chemical Manufacturing Department uses a single allocation base (direct labor cost) in a cost system developed over 15 years ago.

2. Competitors that focused on high-volume commodity chemicals earned good profits, despite undercutting Chemtech's sale prices. This was puzzling because Chemtech should be especially efficient at producing large batches of commodity chemicals.

3. Cost numbers reported by the accounting system were inconsistent with employees' intuition.

Stop & Think

---

[1]K. Krumwiede, "ABC: Why It's Tried and How It Succeeds," *Management Accounting* (April 1998), pp. 32–38.

Decision Guidelines

ACTIVITY-BASED COSTING

Several years ago **Dell** decided it needed to refine its cost system. Starting with an Excel spreadsheet, Dell developed a simple ABC system that focused on the 10 most critical activities. Here are some of the decisions Dell faced as it began refining its cost system.

Decision	Guidelines
How to develop an ABC system?	1. Identify the activities. 2. Estimate total indirect costs of each activity. 3. Identify the allocation base (primary cost driver) for each activity's indirect costs. 4. Estimate the total quantity of each allocation base. 5. Compute the cost allocation rate for each activity. 6. Obtain the actual quantity of each allocation base used by cost object. 7. Allocate costs to cost object.
How to compute a cost allocation rate for an activity?	$$\frac{\text{Estimated total indirect cost of activity}}{\text{Estimated total quantity of allocation base}}$$
How to allocate an activity's cost to the cost object?	$$\begin{array}{c}\text{Cost allocation}\\\text{rate for}\\\text{activity}\end{array} \times \begin{array}{c}\text{Actual quantity of}\\\text{allocation base used by}\\\text{cost object}\end{array}$$
For what kinds of decisions do managers use ABC?	Managers use ABC data in ABM to make decisions on • Pricing and product mix • Cost cutting • Routine planning and control
How to set target costs?	$$\begin{array}{rl}&\text{Target sale price (based on market research)}\\-&\text{minus desired profit}\\\hline=&\text{Target cost}\end{array}$$
How to achieve target costs?	Cross-functional teams use value engineering to cut costs by improving product design or production processes.
What are the main benefits of ABC?	• More-accurate product cost information. • More detailed information on costs of activities and drivers of those costs helps managers control costs.
When is ABC most likely to pass the cost-benefit test?	• Company is in competitive environment and needs accurate product costs. • Company makes different products that use different amounts of resources. • Company has high indirect costs. • Company produces high volumes of some products and lower volumes of other products. • Company has accounting and information technology expertise to implement system. • Old cost system appears "broken."
How to tell when a cost system needs revision?	• Managers lose bids they expected to win and win bids they expected to lose. • Competitors earn profits despite pricing high-volume products below our costs. • Employees do not believe cost numbers. • Company uses a single-allocation-base system developed long ago. • Company has reengineered the production process but not the accounting system.

Excel Application Exercise

Goal: Create a spreadsheet to compare traditional versus activity-based costing.

Scenario: Assume that Circuitech Corporation is one of **Dell's** circuit board suppliers. Circuitech currently uses a traditional costing system that allocates all indirect manufacturing costs based on machine hours, but at Dell's urging, it has decided to move to activity-based costing. You've been asked to compare the two costing methods for the next company board meeting. Your supervisor has given you the following quarterly data for products LP-7310 and PC-33:

	Assembly	Soldering	Inspection
Total indirect costs for the quarter	$630,000	$270,000	$160,000
Allocation base	Machine Hours	Number of Batches	Testing Hours

	LP-7310	PC-33
Direct cost of production (materials, labor)	$162,400	$178,240
Machine hours (assembly)	480	1,080
Number of batches produced (soldering)	60	40
Testing hours (inspection)	6,000	8,000
Number of units per batch	100	100

When you have completed your worksheet, answer the following questions:

1. What is the total manufacturing cost per unit under traditional costing for LP-7310? For PC-33?
2. What is the total manufacturing cost per unit under activity-based costing for LP-7310? For PC-33?
3. What conclusions do you draw from the spreadsheet information?

Step-by-Step:

1. Open a new Excel spreadsheet.
2. In column A, create a bold-faced heading as follows:
   a. Chapter 25 Excel Application Exercise
   b. Traditional vs. Activity-Based Costing
   c. Circuitech Corporation
   d. Today's Date
3. Move down one row. Starting in column C, enter the bold and underlined heading "Assembly." Enter "Soldering" in column D and "Inspection" in column E. In the next row, in column A, enter "Total Indirect Costs for the Quarter." Enter the data from the scenario under each column heading.

4. Two rows under this area, set up three columns: column A for the titles related to the remaining cost data, column D for product LP-7310, and column E for product PC-33. Enter the titles for each data item (from direct costs through the number of units per batch) in column A. Enter the appropriate amounts of each item for LP-7310 and PC-33 in columns D and E, respectively.
5. Two rows down in column A, enter the bold and underlined heading, "Traditional Costing System."
6. Under this heading, enter the description, "Cost Allocation Rate (per machine hour)." In column B, calculate the cost allocation rate.
7. Two rows down, in column A, enter the bold, underlined heading, "Cost per Product." Move over to column D and enter "LP-7310." In column E, enter "PC-33." Make these both bold and underlined.
8. Next, in column A, enter the following descriptions (one per line): "Direct Costs," "Manufacturing Overhead," "Total Manufacturing Cost per Product," "Number of Units," and "Total Manufacturing Cost per Unit." Compute each item for both products.
9. Move down two rows in column A. Enter the bold, underlined heading, "Activity-Based Costing System." In column B, enter the heading, "Cost Allocation Rate." In columns C and D, enter the heading, "Actual Quantity of Cost Allocation Base Used By:." In columns E and F, enter the heading, "Allocated Activity Cost." Make all headings bold.
10. Under the heading "Actual Quantity of Cost Allocation Base Used By:," enter LP-7310 in one column and PC-33 in the next column. Center the heading over the two products.
11. Under the heading "Allocated Activity Cost," enter LP-7310 in one column and PC-33 in the next column. Center the heading over the two products.
12. In column A, list the three activities (assembly, soldering, inspection), one per row. Then, calculate each item for both products.
13. Finally, two rows down, in column A, enter the bold, underlined heading, "Cost per Product." Move over four columns and set up boldfaced and underlined headings for LP-7310 and PC-33. Under the "Cost per Product" heading, enter "Direct Costs," Manufacturing Overhead:," "Assembly," "Soldering," "Inspection," "Total Manufacturing Cost per Product," "Number of Units," and "Total Manufacturing Cost per Unit." Calculate each line item for LP-7310 and PC-33.
14. Save your work and print a copy for your files.

MID-CHAPTER *Summary Problem*

Indianapolis Auto Parts (IAP) has a Seat Manufacturing Department that uses activity-based costing. IAP's system has the following features:

Activity	Allocation Base	Cost Allocation Rate
Purchasing	Number of purchase orders	$60.00 per purchase order
Assembling	Number of parts	0.50 per part
Packaging	Number of finished seats	0.90 per finished seat

(continued)

CHECK YOUR RESOURCES

Each seat has 20 parts; direct materials cost per seat is $11. Suppose **Ford** has asked for a bid on 50,000 built-in baby seats that would be installed as an option on some Ford SUVs. IAP will use a total of 200 purchase orders if Ford accepts IAP's bid.

Required

1. Compute the total cost IAP will incur to purchase the needed materials and then assemble and package 50,000 baby seats. Also compute the average cost per seat.
2. For bidding, IAP adds a 30% markup to total cost. What price will the company bid for the Ford order?
3. Suppose that instead of an ABC system, IAP has a traditional product costing system that allocates all costs other than direct materials at the rate of $65 per direct labor hour. The baby-seat order will require 10,000 direct labor hours. What price will IAP bid using this system's total cost?
4. Use your answers to requirements 2 and 3 to explain how ABC can help IAP make a better decision about the bid price it will offer Ford.

Solution

Requirement 1

Total Cost of Order and Average Cost per Seat:

Direct materials, 50,000 × $11.00	$ 550,000
Activity costs:	
Purchasing, 200 × $60.00	12,000
Assembling, 50,000 × 20 × $0.50	500,000
Packaging, 50,000 × $0.90	45,000
Total cost of order	$1,107,000
Divide by number of seats	÷ 50,000
Average cost per seat	$ 22.14

Requirement 2

Bid Price (ABC System):

Bid price ($1,107,000 × 130%) $1,439,100

Requirement 3

Bid Price (Traditional System):

Direct materials, 50,000 × $11.00	$ 550,000
Other product costs, 10,000 × $65	650,000
Total cost of order	$1,200,000
Bid price ($1,200,000 × 130%)	$1,560,000

Requirement 4

IAP's bid would be $120,900 higher using the direct labor single-allocation-base system than using ABC ($1,560,000 − $1,439,100). Assuming the ABC system more accurately captures the costs caused by the order, the traditional direct labor system overcosts the order. This leads to a higher bid price that reduces IAP's chance of winning the bid. The ABC system shows that IAP can increase its chance of winning the bid by bidding a lower price and still make a profit.

Traditional versus Just-in-Time Systems

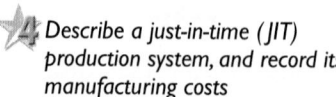

Describe a just-in-time (JIT) production system, and record its manufacturing costs

ABC and ABM often reveal the high costs of (1) buying, storing, and moving inventories, and (2) poor-quality products and services. So it is not surprising that a recent study of "best practices" companies revealed most had linked their ABC/ABM systems to just-in-time (JIT) or quality initiatives. For example,

Carrier Corporation's ABC/ABM system's evidence that materials handling was a major cost driver prompted Carrier to adopt JIT. The rest of this chapter expands on Chapter 19's introduction to JIT and quality. →

We begin by contrasting JIT production systems with traditional systems.

← *Chapter 19, p. 771, introduced JIT.*

Student ResourceCD
just-in-time costing, standard costing system

Traditional Systems

Traditional businesses keep large inventories of raw materials, work in process, and finished goods. Why? First, poor-quality raw materials lead companies to buy more than they need. Also, machine breakdowns and production problems *within* departments prompt managers to keep extra work in process *between* departments. Exhibit 25-12 describes the production of drill bits from bar stock (the raw material). Work in process inventory between the grinding and smoothing operations allows smoothing work to continue even if grinding machines break down.

Exhibit 25-12

Sequence of Operations for Drill-Bit Production

A second reason for large inventories is that companies with long setup times often make products in large batches to spread setup costs over many units. A third reason for stocking large inventories is uncertainty in deliveries from suppliers and orders from customers. Large raw material inventories protect against delayed deliveries. Large inventories of finished goods protect against lost sales if customer demand is higher than expected.

Why are large inventories a problem? First, inventories tie up cash. Companies incur interest expense or forgo interest revenue on that cash. Second, inventories often hide quality problems, production bottlenecks, and obsolescence.

Just-in-Time Systems

Workers read orders off a monitor and assemble a Dell desktop every 3 to 5 minutes. Most days, workers finish more than 25,000 computers, which ship directly to customers. But the plant rarely holds more than two *hours* of inventory![2] How does Dell do it? By complete commitment to the just-in-time philosophy.

Companies with JIT systems buy materials and complete finished goods *just in time* for delivery to customers. This reduces waste. Many managers regard JIT as a *general philosophy of waste elimination*. Companies that follow JIT have several common characteristics:

1. Production activities in self-contained cells. A traditional drill-bit manufacturer would group all the shaping machines in one area, all the grinding machines in another area, and all the smoothing machines in a third area, as illustrated in Panel A of Exhibit 25-13. After switching to JIT, the company would group the machines in self-contained production cells, or production lines, as in Panel B of Exhibit 25-13. The goal is continuous production without interruptions or work in process inventories. Arranging machines in sequential production cells slashes production time. Within six years after adopting JIT, Harley-Davidson reduced the time to produce a motorcycle by 77%.

✔ **Starter 25-12**

---
[2]*Source:* Kathryn Jones, "The Dell Way," *Business 2.0*, February 2003, www.business2.com.

Exhibit 25-13 Equipment Arrangement in Traditional and JIT Production Systems

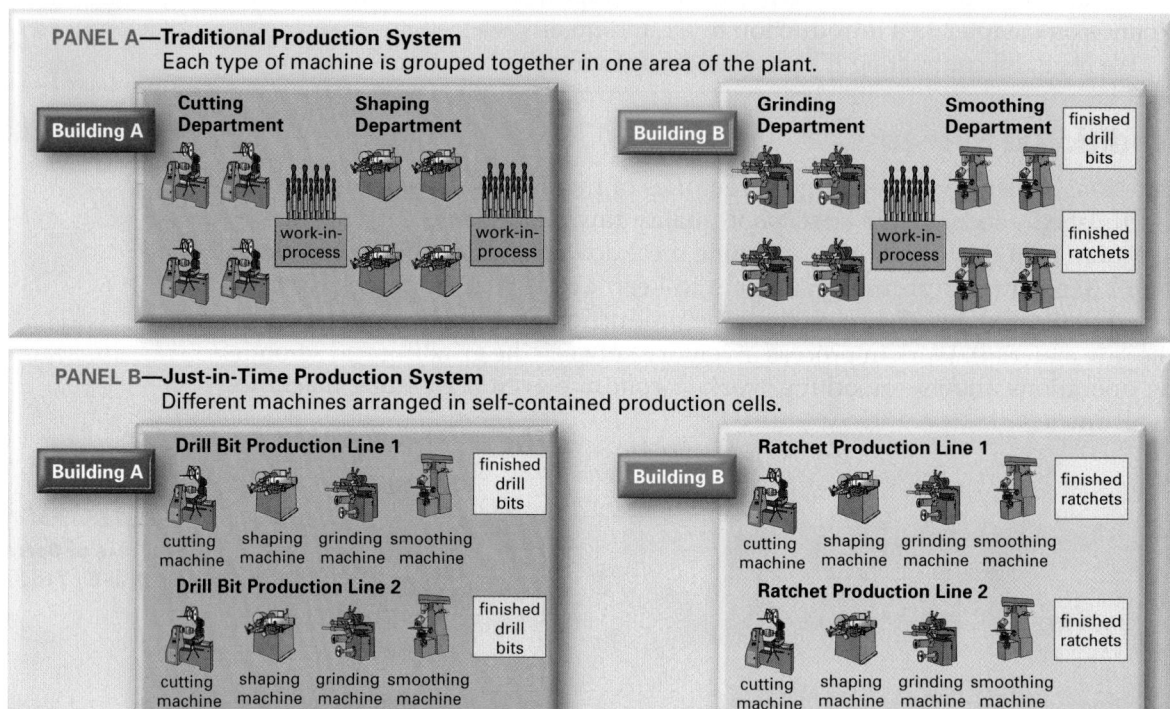

PANEL A—Traditional Production System
Each type of machine is grouped together in one area of the plant.

Building A

Cutting Department   Shaping Department
work-in-process   work-in-process

Building B

Grinding Department   Smoothing Department
finished drill bits
work-in-process
finished ratchets

PANEL B—Just-in-Time Production System
Different machines arranged in self-contained production cells.

Building A

Drill Bit Production Line 1
cutting machine   shaping machine   grinding machine   smoothing machine
finished drill bits

Drill Bit Production Line 2
cutting machine   shaping machine   grinding machine   smoothing machine
finished drill bits

Building B

Ratchet Production Line 1
cutting machine   shaping machine   grinding machine   smoothing machine
finished ratchets

Ratchet Production Line 2
cutting machine   shaping machine   grinding machine   smoothing machine
finished ratchets

2. Short setup times. JIT companies reduce setup times on machines used for more than one product. Employee training and technology helped Toyota cut setup times from several hours to a few minutes. This increases flexibility in scheduling production to meet customer orders, which in turn increases customer satisfaction and company profits.

3. Broad employee roles. Employees in JIT systems do more than operate a single machine. They also conduct maintenance, perform setups, inspect their own work, and operate other machines. This cross-training boosts morale and lowers costs.

4. Small batches produced just in time. JIT businesses schedule production in small batches *just in time* to satisfy needs. A customer order triggers manufacturing. The final operation in the production sequence (smoothing, in our drill-bit example) "pulls" parts from the preceding operation (grinding). The grinding-machine operator pulls shaped parts from shaping, and so on. This "demand–pull" system extends back to suppliers of materials. Suppliers make frequent deliveries of defect-free materials *just in time* for production.

Purchasing and producing only what customers demand reduces inventory. Less inventory frees floor space for more productive use. When HP adopted JIT, the company cut its work-in-process inventory by 82% and its production floor space by 40%.

5. Supply chain management. Because there are no inventory buffers, JIT requires close coordination with suppliers who guarantee on-time delivery of defect-free materials. ← Chapter 19 defined *supply-chain management* as exchanging information with suppliers and customers to reduce costs, improve quality, and speed delivery of goods and services from the company's suppliers, through the company itself, and on to the company's end customers. Consider the following examples.[3]

See Chapter 19, p. 771, for a discussion of supply-chain management.

[3]*Sources:* Gregory L. White, "Chrysler Makes Manufacturing Inroads at Plant in Brazil," *The Wall Street Journal*, Aug. 28, 1998. Emily Nelson, "Wal-Mart Sets Supply Plan as Net Tops Forecasts," *The Wall Street Journal*, Nov. 10, 1999, B12. Joshua Dean, "The Supply Chain's Demands," May 1, 2002. GovExec.com. Joseph Martha, and Sunil Subbakrishna, "When Just-in-Time Becomes Just-in-Case," *The Wall Street Journal*, Oct. 22, 2001, A18.

Chrysler's Brazilian plant, which makes Dakota pickup trucks, buys a partially completed chassis from supplier Dana Corporation's plant 2 miles down the road. Dana assembles 320 parts onto the truck's frame, including axles, brakes, and wheels, within 108 minutes of receiving an electronic order from the Chrysler plant. Dana then delivers each partially complete chassis to the Chrysler production line, in the sequence that Chrysler specifies. Chrysler adds the engines, transmissions, and body to complete each truck.

When Procter & Gamble delivers Crest toothpaste on a just-in-time basis to Wal-Mart's distribution center, Wal-Mart immediately unloads the toothpaste directly onto trucks headed for Wal-Mart stores. On average, the toothpaste is on the Wal-Mart shelf within 4 hours and sold within 24 hours. "It is our objective to sell the merchandise before we pay for it" says a Wal-Mart senior vice president.

Even the U.S. government uses supply-chain management to implement JIT. A flat tire can ground a $20 million jet fighter, and aircraft carriers don't have room to store many spare parts. How does the U.S. Navy ensure that tires and other parts are available when needed? By contracting with Lockheed Martin to manage the supply chain. Sailors simply fill out an online form, and Lockheed Martin must ensure that the Michelin tires are delivered within four days, anywhere in the world.

While companies like Toyota, Carrier, and Dell credit JIT for saving them millions of dollars, the system is not without problems. With no inventory buffers, JIT users are vulnerable when problems strike suppliers or distributors. For example, Ford cut production of its SUVs in response to the tire shortage resulting from the Firestone tire recall. It also had to shut down five of its U.S. plants when engine deliveries from Canadian suppliers were late due to security-related transportation delays in the wake of the World Trade Center attacks.

Continued security-related delays in air, rail, and truck border crossings have stressed DaimlerChrysler's JIT system, which relies on 1,500 daily truckloads of materials crossing the U.S.–Canadian border between Detroit and Windsor, Ontario.

Just-in-Time Costing

After adopting JIT, many companies simplify their accounting systems. **Just-in-time costing**, sometimes called **backflush costing**, is a standard costing system that starts with output completed and then assigns manufacturing costs to units sold and to inventories. There are three major differences between JIT costing and the traditional standard costing system we described in Chapter 24:

Just-in-Time (JIT) Costing
A standard costing system that starts with output completed and then assigns manufacturing costs to units sold and to inventories. Also called **backflush costing**.

1. JIT systems do not track the cost of products from raw materials inventory to work in process inventory to finished goods inventory. Instead, JIT costing systems wait until the units are completed to record the cost of production.

2. Because JIT systems do not track costs attached to units in the production process, JIT systems do not need a separate Work in Process Inventory account. They combine raw materials and work in process inventories into a single account called Raw and In Process Inventory.

3. Under the JIT philosophy, workers perform many tasks. Since little labor is directly traceable to individual finished products, most companies using JIT combine labor and manufacturing overhead costs into an account called Conversion Costs (as we saw in Chapter 21 on process costing). → The Conversion Cost account is a temporary account that works just like the Manufacturing Overhead account described in Chapter 20. Actual conversion costs accumulate as debits in the Conversion Cost account, and the account is credited when conversion costs are allocated to completed units. Accountants close any under- or overallocated conversion costs to Cost of Goods Sold at the end of the year, just like under- or overallocated manufacturing overhead in Chapter 20.

Chapter 21, p. 850, introduced conversion costs.

Point, Click, Buy, Sell: Businesses Cut Costs by Buying and Selling Online

At Minneapolis-based **3M Company**, processing a single invoice used to cost $120. Thanks to purchasing products online, that cost has dropped to under $40. 3M, **Texas Instruments, John Deere,** and **Owens-Corning** are among the hundreds of large U.S. companies who are using e-procurement to achieve incredible cost savings. On average, companies can trim costs by 15 to 20% when they buy online. That's why materials purchased online have ballooned from $75 billion in 2000 to about $3 trillion in 2003.

E-procurement includes: (1) the creation of electronic product catalogs, (2) the exchange of product and purchasing information directly with suppliers via electronic data interchange (EDI), and (3) the use of digital marketplaces or exchanges, such as a "reverse online auction," in which suppliers bid to see who can come in with the lowest price. E-procurement can lead to substantial savings, such as:

- **Mercedes Benz** in Spain has saved between $1.5 million and $3 million, of which 20 to 30% is due to lower transaction-processing costs and the rest due to better price negotiations.
- Toledo, Ohio-based Owens-Corning has cut costs of bottled-water jugs by 60% and stretch wrap by 25%. Overall, the glass and building materials manufacturer has cut 10% on annual purchases of $3.4 billion.
- **HP** cut 30% off the amount it pays for the logos it places on its products.

Yet, these e-procurement success stories do come with some caveats. Most of the companies taking advantage of e-procurement are large companies with at least $750 million in sales. The number of suppliers participating is also limited because they are wary about a technology that cuts their profit margins. For instance, reverse auctions may force suppliers to either bid below their actual costs to get the work or else lose out to competitors. Finally, e-procurement is not just about adopting newfangled software in the purchasing department. All stakeholders—from staff to suppliers—must be convinced of the program's worth and be given the necessary support and training. For some companies, the switch to e-procurement requires a complete organizational change. Yet, judging by the continuing explosion in e-procurement, it's a change many companies find worth making.

Based on: Sarah Perrin, "Business: E-Procurement—Doing It Right," *Accountancy*, September 2002, pp. 59–60. Karen J. Bannan, "The Pulse of the Supply Chain," *Internet World*, January 2003, pp. 22–25. Michael A. Verespej, "E-Procurement Explosion," *Industry Week*, March 2002, pp. 24–28.

Consider Mintel Company, which converts silicon wafers into integrated circuits for computers. Mintel has only one direct manufacturing product cost: silicon wafers, which are labeled "raw." All other manufacturing costs, including labor and various chemicals, are indirect costs of converting the "raw" silicon wafers into the finished integrated circuits. These indirect costs are collected in the "Conversion Costs" account.

Mintel does not use a separate Work in Process Inventory account. Instead, it uses the following two inventory accounts:

- Raw and In Process Inventory, which combines direct materials with work in process
- Finished Goods Inventory

✔ Starter 25-13

Mintel has $100,000 of Raw and In Process Inventory and $900,000 of Finished Goods Inventory at July 31, and it uses JIT costing to record the August transactions.

1. Mintel purchases $3,020,000 of direct materials (silicon wafers) on account.

Raw and In Process Inventory	3,020,000	
Accounts Payable.		3,020,000

2. Mintel spends $18,540,000 on labor and overhead.

Conversion Costs	18,540,000	
Various Accounts (such as wages payable and accumulated depreciation on property, plant, and equipment.)		18,540,000

3. Mintel completed 3,000,000 circuits. The standard cost of the circuit is $7 ($1 direct materials and $6 conversion cost). The debit (increase) to finished goods is $21,000,000 (3,000,000 completed circuits × $7). There is no work in process inventory in JIT costing, so Mintel credits
   - Raw and In Process Inventory, $3,000,000 (3,000,000 completed circuits × $1 standard raw material cost per circuit) for the silicon wafers, and
   - Conversion Costs, $18,000,000 (3,000,000 completed circuits × $6 standard conversion cost per completed circuit) for the labor and other indirect costs allocated to the finished circuits.

Finished Goods Inventory	21,000,000	
Raw and In Process Inventory (3,000,000 × $1).		3,000,000
Conversion Costs (3,000,000 × $6). .		18,000,000

This is the essence of JIT costing. The system does not track costs as the circuits move through manufacturing. Instead, *completion* of the circuits triggers the accounting system to go back and pull costs from Raw and In Process Inventory and to allocate conversion costs to the finished products.

4. Mintel sold 2,930,000 circuits (2,930,000 circuits × $7 per circuit = $20,510,000).

Cost of Goods Sold.	20,510,000	
Finished Goods Inventory		20,510,000

Exhibit 25-14 shows Mintel's major accounts. Combining the raw materials inventory with work in process inventory to form the single Raw and In Process Inventory account eliminates detail. Although Mintel tracks the number of physical units in process, the company does not use material requisitions or time records to assign *costs* to circuits as they flow through the production process. Mintel does not assign costs to physical products until the goods are completed.

 **Mintel's Major JIT Costing Accounts**

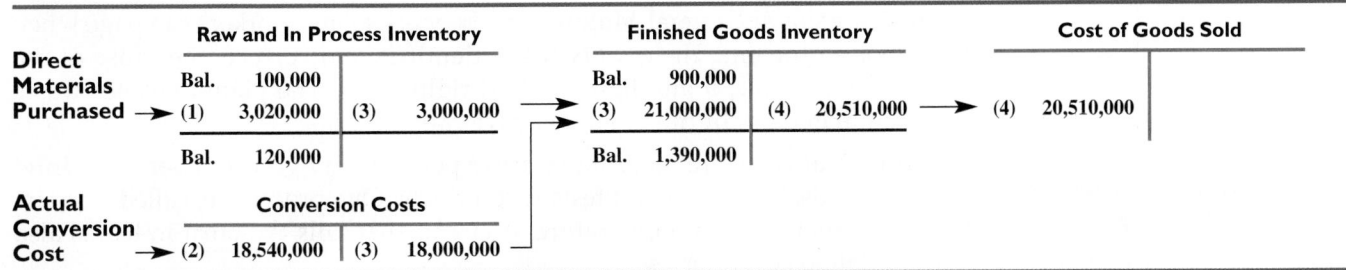

You can see from Exhibit 25-14 that conversion costs are underallocated by $540,000 ($18,540,000 – $18,000,000). Under- and overallocated conversion costs are treated just like under- and overallocated manufacturing overhead and closed to Cost of Goods Sold. ←

See Chapter 20, pp. 815–817, for a review of under- and overallocated manufacturing overhead.

Cost of Goods Sold	540,000	
Conversion Costs...................		540,000

☐ Refining Cost Systems
☐ Activity-Based Costing
☐ Activity-Based Management
☐ ABC and Cost-Benefit
☐ JIT Systems
■ Quality Management

5 *Contrast the four types of quality costs and use them to make decisions*

Student Resource CD

quality costs, total quality management

See TQM discussion in Chapter 19, pp. 772–773. ➡

> Activity-based costing is a detailed costing method that provides more-accurate product costs. Just-in-time costing is simplified and does not track costs through the sequence of manufacturing operations. Are these two costing systems incompatible? Or can they be used together?
>
> *Answer:* ABC and JIT costing can be compatible. Mintel's $6 standard conversion cost per circuit used in JIT costing could be provided by an ABC system.

Continuous Improvement and the Management of Quality

Companies using JIT strive for high-quality production. Because goods are produced only as needed, poor-quality materials or defective manufacturing processes shut down production.

To meet this challenge, many companies adopt *total quality management (TQM)*. ← The goal of TQM is to provide customers with superior products and services. Each business function in the value chain examines its own activities to improve quality and eliminate defects and waste.

Carefully designed products reduce manufacturing time, inspections, rework, and warranty claims. Investing in the front end of the value chain (R&D and design) can generate savings in the back end (production, marketing, and customer service). World-class companies like Toyota and Dell *design* and *build* quality into their products rather than having to *inspect* and *repair* later.

Types of Quality Costs

The four types of quality-related costs include:

Prevention Costs
Costs incurred to *avoid* poor-quality goods or services.

1. Prevention costs incurred to *avoid* poor-quality goods or services. For example, Michael Dell became convinced that reducing human interaction with critical components was key to improving the quality of Dell computers. So Dell reengineered its assembly process to cut in half the number of times humans touch the hard drive. The result? The hard-drive failure rate dropped 40%.

Winemaker Robert Mondavi Corporation's prevention costs include the cost of using satellite imaging and Global Positioning Systems in the vineyard to ensure grapes are uniformly ripe at harvest time. Production workers assigned to quality teams at General Motors carry beepers so line workers can page when they spot a problem. The quality team identifies and corrects the cause of the defect (for example, a misaligned robot) right away. The plant does not waste time and materials churning out defective cars.

Appraisal Costs
Costs incurred to *detect* poor-quality goods or services.

2. Appraisal costs are incurred to *detect* poor-quality goods or services. Intel incurs appraisal costs when it tests its products. One procedure, called burn-in, heats circuits to a high temperature. A circuit that fails the burn-in test is also likely to fail in customer use.

3. Internal failure costs occur when the company detects and corrects poor-quality goods or services *before* delivery to customers. An example is the labor of a BMW mechanic who reworks a faulty brake job after inspection by a supervisor.

4. External failure costs occur when the company does not detect poor-quality goods or services until *after* delivery to customers. If an auto-repair shop does faulty work, the customer will discover the flawed brakes. Then the shop may have to repair the body of the car as well as the brakes. External failures can ruin a company's reputation.

Exhibit 25-15 lists some examples of the four types of quality costs. Most prevention costs occur in the R&D and design stages of the value chain. In contrast, most appraisal and internal failure costs occur in the production element of the value chain. External failure costs occur in the customer-service stage or are opportunity costs of lost sales. Managers make trade-offs among these costs. Many prevention costs are incurred only periodically, while internal and external failure costs are ongoing. One expert estimates that 8¢ spent on prevention saves most manufacturers $1 in failure costs.

Internal Failure Costs
Costs incurred when the company detects and corrects poor-quality goods or services *before* delivery to customers.

External Failure Costs
Costs incurred when the company does not detect poor-quality goods or services until *after* delivery to customers.

✔ Starter 25-14

Exhibit 25-15

Four Types of Quality Costs

Prevention Costs	**Appraisal Costs**
Training personnel	Inspection of incoming materials
Evaluating potential suppliers	Inspection at various stages of production
Improved materials	Inspection of final products or services
Preventive maintenance	Product testing
Improved equipment and processes	
Internal Failure Costs	**External Failure Costs**
Production loss caused by downtime	Lost profits from lost customers
Rework	Warranty costs
Scrap	Service costs at customer sites
Rejected product units	Sales returns and allowances due to quality
Disposal of rejected units	problems
	Product liability claims

Deciding Whether to Adopt a New Quality Program

Let's revisit Chemtech. CEO Randy Smith is considering spending the following amounts on a new quality program:

Inspect raw materials	$100,000
Reengineer the production process to improve product quality	750,000
Inspect finished goods	150,000
Supplier screening and certification.	25,000
Preventive maintenance of plant and equipment	75,000

Chemtech expects this quality program to reduce costs by the following amounts:

Lost profits from lost sales due to disappointed customers	$800,000
Fewer sales returns to be processed	50,000
Lost profits from lost production time due to rework.	250,000
Reduced warranty costs.	125,000

Smith asks Controller Wise to

1. Classify each of these costs into one of the four categories (prevention, appraisal, internal failure, external failure) and total the estimated costs in each category.

2. Recommend whether Chemtech should undertake the quality program. Wise uses the results in Exhibit 25-16 to analyze Chemtech's two alternatives:
   - Incur the prevention and appraisal costs to undertake the quality program
   - Do not undertake the quality program and incur the internal and external failure costs

Exhibit 25-16	Analysis of Chemtech's Proposed Quality Program

Undertake the Quality Program		Do Not Undertake the Quality Program	
Prevention		**Internal Failure**	
Reengineer the production process to improve product quality	$ 750,000	Lost profits from lost production time due to rework	$ 250,000
Supplier screening and certification	25,000	Total internal failure costs	$ 250,000
Preventive maintenance of plant and equipment	75,000	**External Failure**	
Total prevention costs	$ 850,000	Lost profits from lost sales due to disappointed customers	$ 800,000
Appraisal		Sales return processing	50,000
Inspect raw materials	$ 100,000	Warranty costs	125,000
Inspect finished goods	150,000	Total external failure costs	$ 975,000
Total appraisal costs	$ 250,000		
Total costs of undertaking the quality program	$1,100,000	Total costs of not undertaking the quality program	$1,225,000
	Decision: Undertake the Quality Program		

These estimates suggest that Chemtech would save $125,000 ($1,225,000 – $1,100,000) by undertaking the quality program.

Quality costs can be hard to measure. For example, design engineers may spend only part of their time on quality. Allocating their salaries to various activities is subjective. It is especially hard to measure external failure costs. The biggest external failure cost—profits lost because unhappy customers never return ($800,000)—does not even appear in the accounting records! So total quality management programs also emphasize nonfinancial measures such as number of customer complaints.

Decision Guidelines

JUST-IN-TIME AND QUALITY COSTS

Dell Computer, the worldwide leader in PC sales, is famous for its complete commitment to both the just-in-time and total quality management philosophies. Following are several decisions Dell's managers made when adopting these two modern management techniques.

Decision	Guidelines	
How to change a traditional production system to a JIT system?	***Traditional***	***JIT***
	Like machines grouped together	Production cells
	Longer setup times	Short setup times
	Larger batches	Smaller batches
	Higher inventories	Lower inventories
	An individual does fewer tasks	An individual does wider range of tasks
	Many suppliers	Fewer, but well-coordinated suppliers

(continued)

Decision Guidelines *(continued)*

Decision	Guidelines
How to simplify costing after adopting JIT?	Use JIT costing. 1. Summary journal entries are not made until units are completed; costs are not separately tracked as units move through production. 2. Raw materials and work in process are combined into a single Raw and In Process Inventory account. 3. Labor and overhead are combined into a Conversion Cost account.
What are the four types of quality costs?	Prevention costs Appraisal costs Internal failure costs External failure costs
How to make trade-offs among the four types of quality costs?	Investment in prevention costs and appraisal costs reduces internal and external failure costs.

END-OF-CHAPTER *Summary Problem*

CHECK YOUR RESOURCES

The Flores Company manufactures cellular telephones. Flores uses JIT costing. The standard unit cost is $37: $24 direct materials and $13 conversion costs. Direct materials purchased on account during June totaled $2,540,000. Actual conversion costs totaled $1,295,000. Flores completed 102,000 telephones in June and sold 98,000.

Required

1. Prepare the June journal entries for these transactions.
2. Make the entry to close the under- or overallocated conversion costs to Cost of Goods Sold.

Solutions

Requirement 1

Raw and In Process Inventory	2,540,000	
Accounts Payable		2,540,000
Conversion Costs	1,295,000	
Various accounts (such as payables and accumulated depreciation)		1,295,000
Finished Goods Inventory	3,774,000	
Raw and In Process Inventory (102,000 × $24)		2,448,000
Conversion Costs (102,000 × $13)		1,326,000
Cost of Goods Sold (98,000 × $37)	3,626,000	
Finished Goods Inventory		3,626,000

Requirement 2

Conversion Costs	31,000	
Cost of Goods Sold		31,000

●REVIEW _Activity-Based Costing and Other Cost Management Tools_

Quick Check

1. Which of the following is _false_?
   a. The distinguishing feature of ABC is that it focuses on allocating indirect costs.
   b. Advances in information technology have made it feasible for more companies to adopt ABC.
   c. ABC is primarily for manufacturing firms.
   d. A system that uses ABC is more refined than one that uses departmental overhead rates.

   The following data apply to questions 2 through 4. Two of **Dell Computer's** primary production activities are _kitting_ (assembling raw materials needed for a particular computer or server in one kit) and _boxing_ the completed products for shipment to customers. Assume that Dell spends $5 million a month on the kitting activity and $10 million a month on boxing. It allocates kitting activity costs based on the number of parts used in the product and boxing activity costs based on the cubic feet of space the product requires. Suppose Dell estimates it will use 800 million parts a month and ship products with a total volume of 20 million cubic feet.
   Assume that each desktop computer requires 100 parts and has a volume of 5 cubic feet. Assume that each server requires 150 parts and has a volume of 7 cubic feet.

2. What is the activity cost allocation rate for:

	Kitting	Boxing
a.	$0.00625/part	$0.50/cubic foot
b.	$0.0125/part	$0.25/cubic foot
c.	$0.50/part	$40/cubic foot
d.	$160/part	$2/cubic foot

3. What are the kitting and boxing costs assigned to one desktop computer?

	Kitting	Boxing
a.	$0.625	$2.50
b.	$0.9375	$3.50
c.	$1.25	$1.25
d.	$50.00	$200

4. Dell contracts with its suppliers to pre-kit certain component parts before delivering them to Dell. Assume this saves $1.5 million of the kitting activity cost and that it reduces the total number of parts by 400 million (because Dell considers each pre-kit as one part). If a server now uses 80 parts, what is the new kitting cost assigned to one server?
   a. $0.35
   b. $0.70
   c. $0.9375
   d. $1.00

5. Dell can use ABC information for what decisions?
   a. Pricing
   b. Cost cutting
   c. Evaluating managers' performance
   d. All of the above

6. Which of the following is _not_ a good reason for Dell to use ABC?
   a. The computer industry is highly competitive.
   b. Dell produces many more desktops than servers, and servers are more difficult to assemble.
   c. Most costs are direct; indirect costs are a small proportion of total costs.
   d. Dell has advanced information technology, including bar-coded materials and labor.

7. Dell enjoys many benefits from committing to JIT. Which is *not* a benefit of adopting JIT?
   a. Lower inventory carrying costs
   b. More space available for production
   c. Ability to respond more quickly to changes in customer demand
   d. Ability to continue production despite disruptions in deliveries of raw materials

8. The following account is *not* used in JIT costing:
   a. Raw and in process inventory
   b. Conversion costs
   c. Work in process inventory
   d. Finished goods inventory

9. The cost of lost future sales after a customer finds flaws in a product or service is which of the following quality costs?
   a. External failure cost
   b. Internal failure cost
   c. Appraisal cost
   d. Prevention cost

10. Dell's spending on testing its computers before shipment to customers helps *reduce* which of the following costs?
   a. Prevention cost
   b. Appraisal cost
   c. External failure cost
   d. None of the above

Accounting Vocabulary

activity-based costing (ABC) (p. 1036)
activity-based management (ABM) (p. 1042)
appraisal costs (p. 1056)

backflush costing (p. 1053)
external failure costs (p. 1057)
internal failure costs (p. 1057)
just-in-time (JIT) costing (p. 1053)

prevention costs (p. 1056)
target cost (p. 1043)
target price (p. 1043)
value engineering (p. 1043)

ASSESS *Your Progress*

Starters

for selected Starters, Exercises, and Problems.

Developing an activity cost allocation rate
(Obj. 1)

S25-1 Suppose Chemtech's activity-based costing team identifies a fourth activity: machine setup. The foreman estimates that the total setup cost will be $280,000 and that production will require 2,500 setups. (This is less than the 4,000 total batches in Exhibit 25-7. Chemtech often eliminates a setup by running two batches of the same chemical in a row.) Aldehyde will require 30 setups, and PH will require 2 setups.

1. Compute the cost allocation rate for machine setups.
2. Compute the total machine setup costs allocated to aldehyde and to PH.
3. Did Chemtech's original allocation base (200% of direct labor cost) allocate setup costs appropriately? Give your reason.

S25-2 Consider the Chemtech example on pages 1038–1042 and your analysis in Starter 25-1.

Computing activity costs and explaining changes **(Obj. 1)**

1. Compute the machine setup cost per pound for aldehyde and for PH.
2. Use your answer to requirement 1 to explain why switching from a traditional single-allocation-base system to an ABC system usually shifts costs away from high-volume products toward low-volume products.

S25-3 Use the results of Starter 25-1 and the information in Exhibits 25-8 and 25-9 to revise the

Using ABC to allocate indirect costs **(Obj. 1)**

1. Manufacturing overhead cost per pound for aldehyde and for PH
2. Gross profit per pound for aldehyde and for PH

S25-4 Starters 25-4 through 25-10 center on Mission, Inc., a technology consulting firm focused on Web site development and integration of Internet business applications. President Susan Nelson's ear is ringing after an unpleasant call from client Jerry Webb.
(continued)

Allocating indirect costs and computing income
(Obj. 1)

Webb was irate after opening his bill for Mission's redesign of his company's Web site. Webb said that Nelson's major competitor, Delta Applications, charged much lower fees to another company for which Webb serves on the board of directors.

Nelson is puzzled for two reasons. First, she is confident that her firm knows Web site design and support as well as any of Mission's competitors. Nelson cannot understand how Delta Applications can undercut Mission's rates and still make a profit. But Delta Applications is reputed to be very profitable. Second, just yesterday Nelson received a call from client Keith Greg. Greg was happy with the excellent service and reasonable fees Nelson charged him for adding a database-driven job posting feature to his company's Web site. Nelson was surprised by Greg's compliments because this was an unusual job for Mission that required development of complex database management and control applications, and she had felt a little uneasy accepting it.

Like most consulting firms, Mission traces direct labor to individual engagements (jobs). Mission allocated indirect costs to engagements using a budgeted rate based on direct labor hours. Nelson is happy with this system, which she has used since she established Mission in 1995.

Nelson expects to incur $706,000 of indirect costs this year, and she expects her firm to work 5,000 direct labor hours. Nelson and the other systems consultants earn $350 per hour. Clients are billed at 150% of direct labor cost. Last month Mission's consultants spent 100 hours on Webb's engagement. They also spent 100 hours on Greg's engagement.

1. Compute Mission's indirect cost allocation rate.
2. Compute the total costs assigned to the Webb and Greg engagements.
3. Compute the operating income from the Webb and Greg engagements.

Identifying signals of a broken cost system
(Obj. 3)

S25-5 Review Mission's situation in Starter 25-4. List all the signals or clues that indicate Mission's cost system may be "broken."

Deciding whether ABC will pass cost-benefit test
(Obj. 3)

S25-6 Susan Nelson has employed your consulting firm to help her decide whether to develop an activity-based costing system. After reviewing the information in Starters 25-4 and 25-5, draft a memo to Nelson. Make a recommendation whether her firm should develop an ABC system. Be sure to explain the costs and benefits Nelson could expect from adopting ABC. Use the following format for your memo.

Date: _____
To: Ms. Susan Nelson, President, Mission, Inc.
From: Student name
Subject: Cost system recommendation

Computing ABC allocation rates
(Obj. 1)

S25-7 Susan Nelson from Starter 25-4 suspects that her allocation of indirect costs could be giving misleading results, so she decides to develop an ABC system. She identifies three activities: documentation preparation, information technology support, and training. Nelson figures that documentation costs are driven by the number of pages, information technology support costs are driven by the number of software applications used, and training costs are most closely associated with the number of direct labor hours worked. Estimates of the costs and quantities of the allocation bases follow:

Activity	Estimated Cost	Allocation Base	Estimated Quantity of Cost Driver
Documentation preparation.......	$100,000	Pages................	3,125 pages
Information technology support...	156,000	Applications used......	780 applications
Training......................	450,000	Direct labor hours......	5,000 hours
Total indirect costs..............	$706,000		

Compute the cost allocation rate for each activity.

S25-8 Refer to Mission, Inc., in Starters 25-4 and 25-7. The Webb and Greg engagements used the following resources last month:

Using ABC to allocate costs and compute profit
(Obj. 1)

Cost Driver	Webb	Greg
Direct labor hours......................	100	100
Pages.................................	50	300
Applications used.....................	1	78

1. Compute the cost assigned to the Webb engagement and to the Greg engagement, using the ABC system.
2. Compute the operating income from the Webb engagement and from the Greg engagement, using the ABC system.

S25-9 Write a memo to Susan Nelson comparing the costs of the Webb and Greg jobs using the original direct labor single-allocation-base system (Starter 25-4) and the ABC system (Starter 25-8). Be sure to explain:

Explaining results of ABC analysis
(Obj. 1)

- How have the costs changed under the ABC system?
- Why have the costs changed in the direction they changed, rather than in the opposite direction?
- Do the ABC results solve Nelson's puzzle from Starter 25-4?

Your memo should follow the format outlined in Starter 25-6.

S25-10 Write a memo to Susan Nelson (Starters 25-4 through 25-9) explaining how she can use the ABC information to make decisions about her consulting firm. Consider how she could use ABC information in:

Using ABC information to make decisions
(Obj. 2)

- Setting fees (prices)
- Responding to client concerns about fees
- Controlling costs

Your memo should follow the format outlined in Starter 25-6.

S25-11 The vice president of marketing storms into your office, exclaiming:

Activity-based management, Uses of ABC data
(Obj. 2)

> Activity-based costing is worse than useless. It's endangering the future of our company! Because of your ABC cost "information," the CEO is pressuring us to (1) charge customers higher prices for customized products, (2) shift customers from customized products to standard products, and (3) require customers to accept larger deliveries than they would prefer. This completely violates our motto of "delighting the customer." Worse yet, we are being pressured to drop some of the customers we have spent a great deal of effort cultivating. This stupid ABC system will ruin us all!

Reply to your colleague.

S25-12 Indicate whether each of the following is characteristic of a JIT production system or a traditional production system.

Comparing JIT and traditional production systems
(Obj. 4)

a. Management works with suppliers to ensure defect-free raw materials.
b. Products produced in large batches.
c. Large stocks of finished goods protect against lost sales if customer demand is higher than expected.
d. Suppliers make frequent deliveries of small quantities of raw materials.
e. Long setup times.
f. Employees do a variety of jobs, including maintenance and setups as well as operating machines.

(continued)

g. Machines are grouped into self-contained production cells or production lines.

h. Machines are grouped according to function. For example, all cutting machines are located in one area.

i. Suppliers can access the company's intranet.

j. The final operation in the production sequence "pulls" parts from the preceding operation.

k. Each employee is responsible for inspecting his or her own work.

Recording JIT costing journal entries
(Obj. 4)

S25-13 Hamilton Products uses a JIT system to manufacture trading pins for the 2004 Olympic Games in Athens, Greece. The standard cost per pin is $2 for raw materials and $3 for conversion costs. Last month Hamilton recorded the following data:

Number of pins completed....	4,000 pins	Raw material purchases.........	$ 8,800
Number of pins sold	3,500 pins	Conversion costs..............	$12,660

Use JIT costing to prepare journal entries for the month, including the entry to close the Conversion Cost account.

Giving examples of four types of quality costs
(Obj. 5)

S25-14 Bombardier, Inc., manufactures SeaDoo personal watercraft (jet skis). Give examples of costs Bombardier might incur in each of the four categories of quality costs:

- Prevention costs
- Appraisal costs
- Internal failure costs
- External failure costs

Be as specific as possible.

Classifying and using quality costs in decision making
(Obj. 5)

S25-15 Wharfedale manufactures high-quality speakers. Suppose Wharfedale is considering spending the following amounts on a new quality program:

Additional 20 minutes of testing for each speaker	$ 600,000
Negotiating with and training suppliers to obtain higher quality materials and on-time delivery...........................	300,000
Redesigning the speakers to make them easier to manufacture ...	1,400,000

Wharfedale expects this quality program to save costs, as follows:

Reduced warranty repair costs.....................	$200,000
Avoid inspection of raw materials	400,000
Rework avoided because of fewer defective units.....	650,000

It also expects this program to avoid lost profits from:

Lost sales due to disappointed customers............	$850,000
Lost production time due to rework	300,000

1. Classify each of these costs into one of the four categories of quality costs (prevention, appraisal, internal failure, external failure).

2. Should Wharfedale implement the quality program? Give your reasons.

Product costing in an activity-based costing system
(Obj. 1)

Student Resource CD

spreadsheet

Exercises

E25-1 Northstar, Inc., uses activity-based costing to account for its chrome wheel manufacturing process. Company managers have identified four manufacturing activities: materials handling, machine setup, insertion of parts, and finishing. The budgeted activity costs for 20X6 and their allocation bases are as follows:

(continued)

Activity	Total Budgeted Cost	Allocation Base
Materials handling	$ 12,000	Number of parts
Machine setup	3,400	Number of setups
Insertion of parts	48,000	Number of parts
Finishing	80,000	Finishing direct labor hours
Total	$143,400	

Northstar, Inc., expects to produce 1,000 chrome wheels during the year. The wheels are expected to use 3,000 parts, require 10 setups, and consume 2,000 hours of finishing time.

Required

1. Compute the cost allocation rate for each activity.
2. Compute the indirect manufacturing cost of each wheel.

E25-2 Several years after reengineering its production process, Enke, Inc., hired a new controller, Natalie Babin. She developed an ABC system very similar to the one used by Enke's chief rival, Northstar, Inc., of Exercise 25-1. Part of the reason Babin developed the ABC system was that Enke's profits had been declining, even though the company had shifted its product mix toward the product that had appeared most profitable under the old system. Before adopting the new ABC system, Enke had used a direct labor hour single-allocation-base system that was developed 20 years ago.

Product costing in ABC and traditional systems
(Obj. 1)

For 20X6, Enke's budgeted ABC allocation rates are

Activity	Allocation Base	Cost Allocation Rate
Materials handling	Number of parts	$ 3.75 per part
Machine setup	Number of setups	300.00 per setup
Insertion of parts	Number of parts	24.00 per part
Finishing	Finishing direct labor hours	50.00 per hour

The number of parts is now a feasible allocation base because Enke recently purchased bar coding technology. Enke produces two wheel models: standard and deluxe. Budgeted data for 20X6 are as follows:

	Standard	Deluxe
Parts per wheel	4.0	6.0
Setups per 1,000 wheels	15.0	15.0
Finishing direct labor hours per wheel	1.0	2.5
Total direct labor hours per wheel	2.0	3.0

The company's managers expect to produce 1,000 units of each model during the year.

Required

1. Compute the total budgeted indirect manufacturing cost for 20X6.
2. Compute the ABC indirect manufacturing cost per unit of each model.
3. Using Enke's old direct labor hour single-allocation-base system, compute the (single) allocation rate based on direct labor hours. Use this rate to determine the indirect manufacturing cost per wheel for each model under the old single-allocation-base method.

E25-3 Refer to Exercise 25-2. For 20X7 Enke's managers have decided to use the same indirect manufacturing costs per wheel that they computed in 20X6. In addition to the unit indirect manufacturing costs, the following data are budgeted for the company's standard and deluxe models for 20X7:

Using activity-based costing to make decisions
(Obj. 2)

	Standard	Deluxe
Sale price............................	$300.00	$440.00
Direct materials	30.00	46.00
Direct labor...........................	45.00	50.00

(*continued*)

Because of limited machine hour capacity, Enke can produce *either* 2,000 standard wheels *or* 2,000 deluxe wheels.

Required

1. If the managers rely on the ABC unit cost data computed in Exercise 25-2, which model will they produce? (All nonmanufacturing costs are the same for both models.)
2. If the managers rely on the single-allocation-base cost data, which model will they produce?
3. Which course of action will yield more income for Enke?

Activity-based management and target cost
(Obj. 2)

E25-4 Refer to Exercise 25-2. Controller Natalie Babin is surprised by the increase in cost of the deluxe model under ABC. Market research shows that to remain a viable product while still providing a reasonable profit, Enke will have to meet a target cost of $350 for the deluxe wheel. A value engineering study by Enke's employees suggests that modifications to the finishing process could cut finishing cost from $50 to $40 per hour and reduce the finishing direct labor hours per deluxe wheel from 2.5 hour to 2 hour per wheel. Direct materials would remain unchanged at $46 per wheel, as would direct labor at $50 per wheel. The materials handling, machine setups, and insertion of parts activity costs would remain the same as in Exercise 25-2. Would implementing the value engineering recommendation allow Enke to achieve its target ABC-based cost for the deluxe wheel?

Explaining why ABC passes the cost-benefit test
(Obj. 3)

E25-5 Refer to Exercise 25-2. Why might controller Natalie Babin have expected ABC to pass the cost-benefit test? Were there any warning signs that Enke's old direct-labor-based allocation system was "broken"?

Recording manufacturing costs in a JIT costing system
(Obj. 4)

E25-6 Pixel, Inc., produces flat-screen displays. Pixel uses a JIT costing system. One of the company's products has a standard direct materials cost of $8 per unit and a standard conversion cost of $32 per unit.

During 20X5, Pixel produced 500,000 units and sold 480,000. It purchased $4,400,000 of direct materials and incurred actual conversion costs totaling $15,280,000.

Required

1. Prepare summary journal entries for 20X5.
2. The January 1, 20X5, balance of the Raw and In Process Inventory account was $80,000. Use a T-account to find the December 31, 20X5, balance.
3. Use a T-account to determine whether conversion cost is over- or underallocated for the year. By how much? Give the journal entry to close the Conversion Cost account.

Recording manufacturing costs in a JIT costing system
(Obj. 4)

E25-7 Shutterbug produces digital cameras. Suppose Shutterbug's standard cost per camera is $24 for materials and $32 for conversion costs. The following data apply to July production:

Materials purchased.....................	$6,500,000
Conversion costs incurred................	$7,420,000
Number of cameras completed	200,000 cameras
Number of cameras sold	196,000 cameras

Shutterbug uses JIT costing.

Required

1. Prepare summary journal entries for July, including the entry to close the Conversion Costs account.
2. The beginning balance of Finished Goods Inventory was $100,000. Use a T-account to find the ending balance of Finished Goods Inventory.

E25-8 JIT costing is typically used by businesses that (1) assign standard costs to each product and (2) have low inventories. Explain why each of these conditions makes JIT costing more feasible.

Explaining when JIT costing is most likely to be used
(Obj. 4)

E25-9 Millan & Co. makes electronic components. Mike Millan, the president, recently instructed vice president Steve Bensen to develop a total quality control program. "If we don't at least match the quality improvements our competitors are making," he told Bensen, "we'll soon be out of business." Bensen began by listing various "costs of quality" that Millan incurs. The first six items that came to mind were

Classifying quality costs
(Obj. 5)

a. Costs of electronic components returned by customers
b. Costs incurred by Millan customer representatives traveling to customer sites to repair defective products
c. Lost profits from lost sales due to reputation for less-than-perfect products
d. Costs of inspecting components in one of Millan's production processes
e. Salaries of engineers who are designing components to withstand electrical overloads
f. Costs of reworking defective components after discovery by company inspectors

Required

Classify each item as a prevention cost, an appraisal cost, an internal failure cost, or an external failure cost.

E25-10 Chihooli, Inc., manufactures radiation-shielding glass panels. Suppose Chihooli is considering spending the following amounts on a new total quality management (TQM) program:

Classifying quality costs and using these costs to make decisions
(Obj. 5)

Strength-testing one item from each batch of panels..............	$65,000
Training employees in TQM	30,000
Training suppliers in TQM....................................	40,000
Identifying preferred suppliers who commit to on-time delivery of perfect quality materials	60,000

Chihooli expects the new program would save costs through the following:

Avoid lost profits from lost sales due to disappointed customers....	$90,000
Avoid rework and spoilage	55,000
Avoid inspection of raw materials	45,000
Avoid warranty costs	15,000

Required

1. Classify each item as a prevention cost, an appraisal cost, an internal failure cost, or an external failure cost.
2. Should Chihooli implement the new quality program? Give your reason.

E25-11 Channell Fabricators, Inc., completed two jobs in June 20X6. Channell recorded the following costs assigned to the jobs by the company's activity-based costing system:

Using activity-based costing
(Obj. 1, 2)

		Allocated Cost	
Activity	**Allocation Base**	**Job 409**	**Job 622**
Materials handling	Number of parts	$ 500	$ 1,500
Lathe work	Number of lathe turns	5,000	15,000
Milling	Number of machine hours	4,000	28,000
Grinding	Number of parts	300	1,500
Testing	Number of output units	126	2,700

Job 622 required 3,000 parts, 60,000 lathe turns, and 1,400 machine hours. All 300 of the job's output units were tested. All units of Job 409 were tested.

(continued)

Required

1. How do you know that at least one of the costs recorded for the two jobs is inaccurate?

2. Disregard materials-handling costs. How many parts were used for Job 409? How many lathe turns did Job 409 require? How many machine hours? How many units were produced in Job 409?

3. A nearby company has offered to test all product units for $13 each. On the basis of ABC data, should Channell accept or reject the offer? Give your reason.

Problems

(Group A)

Product costing in an ABC system
(Obj. I)

P25-1A Narnia Technology's Cell Phone Department, which assembles and tests digital processors, reports the following data regarding processor G27:

Direct materials cost.	$56.00
Activity costs allocated	?
Manufacturing product cost	$?

The activities required to build the processors are as follows:

Activity	Allocation Base	Cost Allocated to Each Board
Start station	Number of processor boards	$1 \times \$ 0.90 = \$0.90$
Dip insertion	Number of dip insertions	$20 \times \$ 0.25 = $?
Manual insertion	Number of manual insertions	$5 \times \$ $? $ = 2.00$
Wave solder	Number of processor boards soldered	$1 \times \$ 4.50 = 4.50$
Backload	Number of backload insertions	$? \times \$ 0.70 = 2.80$
Test	Standard time each processor board is in test activity (hr.)	$0.15 \times \$90.00 = $?
Defect analysis	Standard time for defect analysis and repair (hr.)	$0.16 \times \$ $? $ = 8.00$
Total		$?

Required

1. Fill in the blanks in both the opening schedule and the list of activities.

2. How is labor cost assigned to products under this product costing system?

3. Why might managers favor this ABC system instead of the older system that allocated all conversion costs on the basis of direct labor?

Product costing in an ABC system
(Obj. I, 2)

spreadsheet

P25-2A Hone's Office Department manufactures computer desks in its Topeka, Kansas, plant. The company uses activity-based costing. Its activities and related data follow.

Activity	Budgeted Cost of Activity	Allocation Base	Cost Allocation Rate
Materials handling	$ 300,000	Number of parts	$ 0.60
Assembling	2,500,000	Direct labor hours	15.00
Painting	170,000	Number of painted desks	5.00

Hone produced two styles of desks in March: The standard desk, and unpainted desk that had fewer parts. Data for each follow:

Product	Total Units Produced	Total Direct Materials Costs	Total Number of Parts	Total Assembling Direct Labor Hours
Standard desk	6,000	$96,000	120,000	6,000
Unpainted desk	1,500	21,000	30,000	900

(continued)

Required

1. Compute the per-unit manufacturing product cost of standard desks and unpainted desks.

2. Premanufacturing activities, such as product design, were assigned to the standard desks at $5 each and to the unpainted desks at $3 each. Similar analyses were conducted of postmanufacturing activities such as distribution, marketing, and customer service. The post-manufacturing costs were $25 per standard and $22 per unpainted desk. Compute the full product costs per desk.

3. Which product costs are reported in the external financial statements? Which costs are used for management decision making? Explain the difference.

4. What price should Hone's managers set for standard desks to earn a $42.00 profit per desk?

P25-3A Xnet, Inc., develops software for Internet applications. The market is very competitive, and Xnet's competitors continue to introduce new products at low prices. Xnet offers a wide variety of different software—from simple programs that enable new users to create personal Web pages, to complex commercial search engines. Like most software companies, Xnet's raw material costs are insignificant.

Comparing costs from ABC versus single-rate systems; clues that ABC passes cost-benefit test
(Obj. 1, 3)

Xnet has just hired Tom Merrell, a recent graduate of State University's accounting program. Merrell asks Software Department manager Jeff Gire to join him in a pilot activity-based costing study. Merrell and Gire identify the following activities, related costs, and cost allocation bases.

Activity	Estimated Indirect Activity Costs	Allocation Base	Estimated Quantity of Allocation Base
Applications development	$1,600,000	New applications	4 new applications
Content production	2,400,000	Lines of code	12 million lines
Testing	288,000	Testing hours	1,800 testing hours
Total indirect costs	$4,288,000		

Xnet is planning to develop the following new applications:

- X-Page—for developing personal Web pages
- X-Secure—commercial security and firewall software

X-Page requires 500,000 lines of code and 100 hours of testing, while X-Secure requires 7.5 million lines of code and 600 hours of testing. Xnet expects to produce and sell 30,000 units of X-Page and 10 units of X-Secure.

Required

1. Compute the cost allocation rate for each activity.

2. Use the activity-based cost allocation rates to compute the activity costs of X-Page and X-Secure. (*Hint:* First compute the total activity costs allocated to each product line, and then compute the cost per unit.)

3. Xnet's original single-allocation-base cost system allocated indirect costs to products at $100 per programmer hour. X-Page requires 10,000 programmer hours, while X-Secure requires 15,000 programmer hours. Compute the total indirect costs allocated to X-Page and X-Secure under the original system. Then compute the indirect cost per unit for each product.

4. Compare the activity-based costs per unit to the costs from the simpler original system. How have the unit costs changed? Explain why the costs changed as they did.

5. What are the clues that Xnet's ABC system is likely to pass the cost-benefit test?

P25-4A Even though Problem 25-3A shows that X-Page's costs are lower under ABC than under the simpler original cost system, Xnet's CEO Jay Wilner is still concerned that the software may be less profitable than expected. Wilner asks Merrell to recommend a sale price that will yield a profit of $8 per unit, after direct production costs of $3 per unit,

Activity-based management, target cost, and value engineering
(Obj. 2)

(continued)

marketing and distribution costs of $5 per unit, and the indirect production costs of $17.20 per unit (from Problem 25-3A). Wilner believes that the sale price must be $30 or less to reach estimated sales of 30,000 units. If Merrell's "cost-plus-based" recommended sale price exceeds $30, Wilner authorizes him to establish a cross-functional value-engineering team to squeeze out cost savings.

Required

1. Determine the sale price that yields a profit of $8 per unit. Will this meet Wilner's target price?

2. Merrell establishes a value-engineering team that finds new software writing routines can cut application development costs for the four new applications from $1.6 million to $1.2 million. This would also save $600,000 in content production and require 10 million instead of 12 million lines of code. Testing would be unaffected. The value-engineering team also finds that improved supply-chain management can cut X-Page's direct production costs from $3 per unit to $2 per unit. However, marketing and distribution costs for X-Page are unchanged.

    Given these cost savings, what are the indirect activity cost allocation rates for application development, content production, and testing?

3. If the value-engineering team's suggestions are implemented, X-Page would require 480,000 lines of code and the same 100 hours of testing. What is the new indirect activity (production) cost per unit (including all three activities) for X-Page?

4. With these changes, can Xnet set a sale price of $30 and still earn a profit of $8 per unit?

Recording manufacturing costs for a JIT costing system
(Obj. 4)

P25-5A Titan produces sports watches. The company has a JIT production system and uses JIT costing.

Titan has two inventory accounts, Raw and In Process Inventory, and Finished Goods Inventory. On August 1, 20X5, the account balances were Raw and In Process Inventory, $12,000; Finished Goods Inventory, $2,000.

Titan's standard cost per watch is $55: $35 direct materials plus $20 conversion costs. The following data pertain to August manufacturing and sales:

Number of watches		Raw material purchased	$305,000
completed................	9,000 watches	Conversion costs	
Number of watches sold	8,800 watches	incurred	$116,000

Required

1. What are the major features of a JIT production system such as Titan's?

2. Prepare summary journal entries for August. Under- and overallocated conversion costs are closed to Cost of Goods Sold at the end of each month.

3. Use a T-account to determine the August 31, 20X5, balance of Raw and In Process Inventory.

Analyzing costs of quality
(Obj. 5)

P25-6A Real Toys is using a costs-of-quality approach to evaluate design engineering efforts for a new toy robot. The company's senior managers expect the engineering work to reduce appraisal, internal failure, and external failure activities. The predicted reductions in activities over the 2-year life of the toy robot follow. Also shown are the cost allocation rates for each activity.

Activity	Predicted Reduction in Activity Units	Activity Cost Allocation Rate Per Unit
Inspection of incoming materials.......	300	$20
Inspection of finished goods...........	300	30
Number of defective units discovered in-house	3,200	15
Number of defective units discovered by customers	900	35
Lost sales to dissatisfied customers	300	55

(continued)

Required

1. Calculate the predicted quality cost savings from the design engineering work.

2. Real Toys spent $60,000 on design engineering for the new toy robot. What is the net benefit of this "preventive" quality activity?

3. What major difficulty would Real Toys' managers have had in implementing this costs-of-quality approach? What alternative approach could they use to measure quality improvement?

Problems

(Group B)

Product costing in an ABC system
(Obj. I)

P25-1B The Electronics Manufacturing Department of Imagine, Inc., in Austin, Texas, assembles and tests electronic components used in hand-held video phones. Consider the following data regarding component T24:

Direct materials cost	$81.00
Activity costs allocated	?
Manufacturing product cost	$?

The activities required to build the component follow.

Activity	Allocation Base	Cost Allocated to Each Unit
Start station	Number of raw component chasses	$2 \times \$1.30 = \$ 2.60$
Dip insertion	Number of dip insertions	$? \times \$0.40 = 12.00$
Manual insertion	Number of manual insertions	$12 \times \$0.80 = ?$
Wave solder	Number of components soldered	$1 \times \$1.40 = 1.40$
Backload	Number of backload insertions	$7 \times \$? = 4.20$
Test	Standard time each component is in test activity	$0.40 \times \$80.00 = ?$
Defect analysis	Standard time for defect analysis and repair	$0.10 \times \$? = 5.00$
Total		$\$?$

Required

1. Fill in the blanks in both the opening schedule and the list of activities.

2. How is labor cost assigned to products under this product costing system?

3. Why might managers favor this ABC system instead of the older system, which allocated all conversion costs on the basis of direct labor?

Product costing in an ABC system
(Obj. 1, 2)

Student ResourceCD

spreadsheet

P25-2B McKinney, Inc., manufactures bookcases and uses an activity-based costing system. McKinney's activity areas and related data follow.

Activity	Budgeted Cost of Activity	Allocation Base	Cost Allocation Rate
Materials handling	$ 200,000	Number of parts	$ 0.80
Assembling	3,000,000	Direct labor hours	15.00
Finishing	160,000	Number of finished units	3.90

McKinney produced two styles of bookcases in April: the standard bookcase and an unfinished bookcase, which has fewer parts per bookcase and requires no finishing. The totals for quantities, direct materials costs, and other data follow.

Product	Total Units Produced	Total Direct Materials Costs	Total Number of Parts	Total Assembling Direct Labor Hours
Standard bookcase	3,000	$26,000	80,000	3,000
Unfinished bookcase	3,600	27,000	84,000	2,000

(continued)

Required

1. Compute the manufacturing product cost per unit of each type of bookcase.

2. Suppose that premanufacturing activities, such as product design, were assigned to the standard bookcases at $4 each and to the unfinished bookcases at $3 each. Similar analyses were conducted of postmanufacturing activities such as distribution, marketing, and customer service. The postmanufacturing costs were $20 per standard bookcase and $15 per unfinished bookcase. Compute the full product costs per unit.

3. Which product costs are reported in the external financial statements? Which costs are used for management decision making? Explain the difference.

4. What price should McKinney's managers set for unfinished bookcases to earn a unit profit of $16?

Comparing costs from ABC versus single-rate systems; clues that ABC passes cost-benefit test
(Obj. 1, 3)

P25-3B HCI Pharmaceuticals manufactures an over-the-counter allergy medication called Breathe. HCI is trying to win market share from Sudafed and Tylenol. HCI has developed several different Breathe products tailored to specific markets. For example, the company sells large commercial containers of 1,000 capsules to health-care facilities and travel packs of 20 capsules to shops in airports, train stations, and hotels.

HCI's controller Sandra Dean has just returned from a conference on activity-based costing. She asks Keith Yeung, foreman of the Breathe product line, to help her develop an activity-based costing system. Dean and Yeung identify the following activities, related costs, and cost allocation bases:

Activity	Estimated Indirect Activity Costs	Allocation Base	Estimated Quantity of Allocation Base
Materials handling	$190,000	Kilos	19,000 kilos
Packaging	400,000	Machine hours	2,000 hours
Quality assurance	112,500	Samples	1,875 samples
Total indirect costs	$702,500		

The commercial-container Breathe product line had a total weight of 8,000 kilos, used 1,200 machine hours, and required 200 samples. The travel-pack line had a total weight of 6,000 kilos, used 400 machine hours, and required 300 samples. HCI produced 2,500 commercial containers of Breathe and 50,000 travel packs.

Required

1. Compute the cost allocation rate for each activity.

2. Use the activity-based cost allocation rates to compute the activity costs of the commercial containers and the travel packs. (*Hint*: First compute the total activity costs allocated to each product line, and then compute the cost per unit.)

3. HCI's original single-allocation-base cost system allocated indirect costs to products at $300 per machine hour. Compute the total indirect costs allocated to the commercial containers and to the travel packs under the original system. Then compute the indirect cost per unit for each product.

4. Compare the activity-based costs per unit to the costs from the original system. How have the unit costs changed? Explain why the costs changed as they did.

5. What clues indicate that HCI's ABC system is likely to pass the cost-benefit test?

Activity-based management, target cost, and value engineering
(Obj. 2)

P25-4B Continuing Problem 25-3B, HCI controller Sandra Dean is surprised that ABC reports such a higher indirect production cost per travel pack. She wonders whether HCI is making the desired profit of $1.25 per unit on this product. The current sale price is $7.25 per travel pack, direct production costs are $2.15 per pack, marketing and distribution costs are $0.90 per pack, and the indirect production costs are $3.16 per pack (from Problem 25-3B). Dean believes that to reach estimated sales of 50,000 units, the sale price cannot exceed $7.25. If the travel pack is not providing the desired profit of $1.25 per unit,

(continued)

Dean decides that the next step should be to establish a cross-functional value-engineering team to identify opportunities for cost savings. If this does not provide the desired profit, Dean doubts it will be possible to increase market share to sales of 50,000 travel packs.

Required

1. Determine the sale price that yields a profit of $1.25 per travel pack. Does this meet the $7.25 target price?

2. Dean establishes a value-engineering team. The value-engineering team finds that improved supply-chain management can cut the travel pack's direct production costs from $2.15 per pack to $2.03 per pack. Further, the team believes it can cut materials-handling costs from $190,000 to $180,500. Changes in the packaging department will save $112,000 in packaging costs and 400 in machine hours. Improvements to quality assurance should reduce costs to $102,000 based on 1,700 samples. Marketing and distribution costs will remain unchanged.

   Given these cost savings, compute the indirect activity cost allocation rates for materials handling, packaging, and quality assurance.

3. If the value-engineering team's suggestions are implemented, the travel pack line would require 6,000 kilos, use 380 machine hours, and require 256 samples. Compute the new indirect production cost per travel pack (including all three activities).

4. With these changes, can HCI set a sale price of $7.25 and still earn a profit of $1.25 per travel pack?

P25-5B North Slope produces fleece jackets. The company uses JIT costing for its JIT production system.

Recording manufacturing costs for a JIT costing system **(Obj. 4)**

North Slope has two inventory accounts: Raw and In Process Inventory and Finished Goods Inventory. On October 1, 20X6, the account balances were Raw and In Process Inventory, $6,000; Finished Goods Inventory, $1,000.

The standard cost of a jacket is $50—$15 direct materials plus $35 conversion costs. Data for October's activity follow.

Number of jackets completed.....	18,000	Direct materials purchased	$265,000
Number of jackets sold	17,600	Conversion costs incurred	551,000

Required

1. What are the major features of a JIT production system such as North Slope?

2. Prepare summary journal entries for October. Under- or overallocated conversion costs are closed to Cost of Goods Sold monthly.

3. Use a T-account to determine the October 31, 20X6, balance of Raw and In Process Inventory.

P25-6B Big Sky, Inc., is using a costs-of-quality approach to evaluate design engineering efforts for a new wakeboard. Big Sky's senior managers expect the engineering work to reduce appraisal, internal failure, and external failure activities. The predicted reductions in activities over the 2-year life of the wakeboards follow. Also shown are the cost allocation rates for each activity.

Analyzing costs of quality **(Obj. 5)**

Activity	Predicted Reduction in Activity Units	Activity Cost Allocation Rate Per Unit
Inspection of incoming materials.......	400	$ 40
Inspection of work in process..........	400	20
Number of defective units discovered in-house	1,100	50
Number of defective units discovered by customers.........................	300	70
Lost sales to dissatisfied customers	100	110

(*continued*)

Required

1. Calculate the predicted quality cost savings from the design engineering work.

2. Big Sky spent $106,000 on design engineering for the new wakeboard. What is the net benefit of this "preventive" quality activity?

3. What major difficulty would Big Sky's managers have in implementing this costs-of-quality approach? What alternative approach could they use to measure quality improvement?

APPLY *Your Knowledge*

Decision Cases

Comparing costs from ABC versus single-rate systems; using these costs to make decisions
(Obj. 1, 2)

Case 1. Axis Systems specializes in servers for workgroup, e-commerce, and ERP applications. The company's original job cost system has two direct cost categories: direct materials and direct labor. Overhead is allocated to jobs at the single rate of $22 per direct labor hour.

A task force headed by Axis's CFO recently designed an ABC system with four activities. The ABC system retains the current system's two direct cost categories. Thus, it budgets only overhead costs for each activity. Pertinent data follow.

Activity	Allocation Base	Cost Allocation Rate
Materials handling	Number of parts	$ 0.85
Machine setup	Number of setups	500.00
Assembling	Assembling hours	80.00
Shipping	Number of shipments	1,500.00

Axis Systems has been awarded two new contracts, which will be produced as Job A and Job B. Budget data relating to the contracts follow.

	Job A	Job B
Number of parts	15,000	2,000
Number of setups	6	4
Number of assembling hours	1,500	200
Number of shipments	1	1
Total direct labor hours	8,000	600
Number of output units	100	10
Direct materials cost	$210,000	$30,000
Direct labor cost	$160,000	$12,000

Required

1. Compute the product cost per unit for each job, using the original costing system (with two direct cost categories and a single overhead allocation rate).

2. Suppose Axis Systems adopts the ABC system. Compute the product cost per unit for each job using ABC.

3. Which costing system more accurately assigns to jobs the costs of the resources consumed to produce them? Explain.

4. A dependable company has offered to produce both jobs for Axis for $5,400 per output unit. Axis may outsource (buy from the outside company) either Job A only, Job B only, or both jobs. Which course of action will Axis's managers take if they base their decision on (a) the original system? (b) ABC system costs? Which course of action will yield more income? Explain.

Activity-based management, target cost, and value engineering
(Obj. 1, 2)

Case 2. To remain competitive, Axis Systems' management believes the company must produce Job B–type servers (from Decision Case 1) at a target cost of $5,400. Axis Systems

(continued)

has just joined a B2B e-market site that management believes will enable the firm to cut direct material costs by 10%. Axis's management also believes that a value-engineering team can reduce assembly time.

Compute the assembly cost savings per Job B–type server required to meet the $5,400 target cost. (*Hint:* Begin by calculating the direct material, direct labor, and allocated activity cost per server.)

Ethical Issue

Mary Lipe is assistant controller at Stone Packaging, Inc., a manufacturer of cardboard boxes and other packaging materials. Lipe has just returned from a packaging industry conference on activity-based costing. She realizes that ABC may help Stone meet its goal of reducing costs by 5% over each of the next three years.

ABC and ethical decisions
(Obj. 1, 2)

Stone Packaging's Order Department is a likely candidate for ABC. While orders are entered into a computer that updates the accounting records, clerks manually check customers' credit history and hand-deliver orders to shipping. This process occurs whether the sales order is for a dozen specialty boxes worth $80, or 10,000 basic boxes worth $8,000.

Lipe believes that identifying the cost of processing a sales order would justify (1) further computerization of the order process and (2) changing the way the company processes small orders. However, the significant cost savings would arise from elimination of two positions in the Order Department. The company's sales order clerks have been with the company many years. Lipe is uncomfortable with the prospect of proposing a change that will likely result in terminating these employees.

Required

Use the IMA's ethical standards (Exhibit 19-14) to consider Lipe's responsibility when cost savings come at the expense of employees' jobs.

Financial Statement Case

In his annual letter to shareholders, Jeff Bezos, founder and chief executive officer of **Amazon.com,** discusses the three pillars of Amazon.com's success: selection, convenience, and lower prices. Bezos and his management team need ABC information to continuously improve Amazon.com's customer experience. They need this information to make decisions like whether to improve selection by increasing the available items in Amazon.com's Electronics Store or by additional alliances with affiliates such as **Circuit City.**

Identifying activities and cost drivers at Amazon.com
(Obj. 1)

Many of Amazon.com's activities and cost drivers are the same as those for retailers like **Wal-Mart** and **Best Buy,** but others are unique to e-tailers. Before answering the following questions, read Jeff Bezos' Letter to Shareholders and Amazon.com's annual report.

Required

1. Activities like purchasing books and DVDs from suppliers, and the associated cost drivers (number of orders), are common to all retailers, including Amazon.com and Best Buy. Identify four other activities and their cost drivers that would be the same for Amazon.com and Best Buy.
2. Other activities are unique to e-tailers. Suppose Amazon.com managers have identified the following 12 specific activities. Because it would be too expensive to track each activity with a separate cost driver, management has identified four general activities (also listed below). Assign each of the 12 specific activities to one of the four general activities.

Specific Activities

- Maintain hardware and software to process customer orders
- Upload and remove images from Web site
- Improve the Web site's design
- Track affiliate sales from Amazon.com's Web site
- Research new hardware and software products

(continued)

- Select product images for the Web site
- Obtain approval to scan and put products on Web site
- Create product information and product reviews for each product
- Maintain the Web site and telephone system for processing customers' orders
- Prepare and maintain affiliate links on the Web site
- Contact Internet businesses to promote new affiliate marketing opportunities
- Research and test new Web site features

General Activities

- Electronic customer-order processing
- Inventory selection and management
- Web site optimization
- Affiliate marketing

3. Identify a cost driver for each of the four general activities.

Team Project

Developing an ABC system; explaining how ABC changes costs; signs of a broken cost system
(Obj. 1, 2, 3)

Lahana Shrimp Farms in Kihei Hawaii, has a Processing Department that processes raw shrimp into two products:

- Headless shrimp
- Peeled and deveined shrimp

Lahana recently submitted bids for two orders: (1) headless shrimp for a cruise line and (2) peeled and deveined shrimp for a restaurant chain. Lahana won the first bid, but lost the second. The production and sales managers are upset. They believe that Lahana's state-of-the-art equipment should have given the company an edge in the peeled and deveined market. Consequently, production managers are starting to keep their own sets of product cost records.

Lahana is reexamining both its production process and its cost system. The company is considering changing its cost accounting system, which has been in place since 1991. The existing system allocates all indirect costs based on direct labor hours. Lahana is considering adopting activity-based costing. Controller Heather Barefield and a team of production managers performed a preliminary study. The team identified six activities, with the following (departmentwide) estimated indirect costs and cost drivers:

Activity	Total Estimated Cost of Activity	Allocation Base
Redesign of production process (costs of changing process and equipment)	$ 5,000	Number of design changes
Production scheduling (production scheduler's salary)	6,000	Number of batches
Chilling (depreciation on refrigerators)	1,500	Weight (in pounds)
Processing (utilities and depreciation on equipment)	21,000	Number of cuts
Packaging (indirect labor and depreciation on equipment)	1,425	Cubic feet of surface exposed
Order filling (order-takers' and shipping clerks' wages)	7,000	Number of orders
Total indirect costs for the entire department	$41,925	

The raw shrimp are chilled and then cut. For headless shrimp, employees remove the heads, then rinse the shrimp. For peeled and deveined shrimp, the headless shrimp are further processed—the shells are removed and the backs are slit for deveining. Both headless shrimp and peeled and deveined shrimp are packaged in foam trays and covered with shrink wrap. The Order-Filling Department assembles orders of headless shrimp as well as peeled and deveined shrimp.

(continued)

Barefield estimates that Lahana will produce 10,000 packages of headless shrimp and 50,000 packages of peeled and deveined shrimp. The two products incur the following costs per package:

	Costs per Package	
	Headless Shrimp	**Peeled and Deveined Shrimp**
Shrimp	$3.50	$4.50
Foam trays	$0.05	$0.05
Shrink wrap	$0.05	$0.02
Number of cuts	12 cuts	48 cuts
Cubic feet of exposed surface	1 cubic foot	0.75 cubic foot
Weight (in pounds)	2.5 pounds	1 pound
Direct labor hours	0.01 hour	0.05 hour

Lahana pays direct laborers $20 per hour. Barefield estimates that each product line will also require the following *total* resources:

	Headless Shrimp			**Peeled and Deveined Shrimp**		
Design changes	1 change	⎫	for all	4 changes	⎫	for all
Batches	40 batches	⎬	10,000	20 batches	⎬	50,000
Sales orders	90 orders	⎭	packages	110 orders	⎭	packages

Required

Form groups of four students. All group members should work together to develop the group's answers to the four requirements. However, the first two students have primary responsibility for writing up the final responses to requirements 1 and 4, while the other two students have primary responsibility for writing up the responses to requirements 2 and 3. (Carry all computations at least four decimal places.)

1. List the clues that Lahana's original cost system may be broken.

2. Using the original cost system with the single indirect cost allocation base (direct labor hours), compute the *total budgeted cost per package* for the headless shrimp and then for the peeled and deveined shrimp. (*Hint:* First compute the indirect cost allocation rate—that is, the predetermined overhead rate. Then compute the total budgeted cost per package for each product.)

3. Use activity-based costing to recompute the *total budgeted cost per package* for the headless shrimp and then for the peeled and deveined shrimp. (*Hint:* First, calculate the budgeted cost allocation rate for each activity. Then calculate the total indirect costs of (a) the entire headless shrimp product line and (b) the entire peeled and deveined shrimp product line. Next compute the indirect cost per package of each product. Finally, calculate the total cost per package of each product.)

4. Write a memo to Lahana CEO Gary Pololu explaining the results of the ABC study. Compare the costs reported by the ABC system with the costs reported by the original system. Point out whether the ABC system shifted costs toward headless shrimp or toward peeled and deveined shrimp, and explain why. Finally, explain whether Pololu should feel more comfortable making decisions using cost data from the original system or from the new ABC system. Use the memo format outlined in Starter 25-6.

For Internet Exercises, go to the Web site www.prenhall.com/horngren.

CHAPTER 26

Special Business Decisions and Capital Budgeting

A+ TIPS CHECK YOUR RESOURCES

- Visit the www.prenhall.com/horngren **Web site** for self-study quizzes, video clips, and other resources

- Try the **Quick Check** exercise at the end of the chapter to test your knowledge

- Learn the **key terms**

- Do the **Starter** exercises keyed in the margins

- Work the **mid-** and **end-of-chapter summary problems**

- Use the **Concept Links** to review material in other chapters

- Search the **CD** for review materials by chapter or by key word

- Watch the **tutorial videos** to review key concepts

- Watch the **On Location Deer Valley** video to see how the company handles capital budgeting

LEARNING OBJECTIVES

⭐ **1** Identify the relevant information for a special business decision

⭐ **2** Make five types of short-term special business decisions

⭐ **3** Use payback and accounting rate of return models to make longer-term capital budgeting decisions

⭐ **4** Use discounted cash flow models to make longer-term capital budgeting decisions

⭐ **5** Compare and contrast the four capital budgeting methods

On the slopes of Deer Valley Ski Resort in Park Valley, Utah—site of the 2002 Winter Olympics slalom competition—management accounting seems a world away. But the counter where you rent your skis, the chairlift that whisks you up the mountain, and the restaurant that serves you dinner are all part of the resort's recent expansion. How did Deer Valley's developers decide to spend $13 million to expand Snow Park Lodge?

Director of Finance Jim Madsen explains that when the resort reaches a target number of skiers per day and a target level of profit, the owners expand. But each expansion must meet two requirements. First, the project must be profitable. Second, Deer Valley must expect to get its money back on the investment in a relatively short time. To figure out which projects

Deer Valley Ski Resort

meet these requirements, Deer Valley's managers compare the amount of the investment needed to expand the resort with the additional revenues expected from expansion. Managers make this comparison using two *capital budgeting* techniques:

- *Net present value*—to predict whether the investment will be profitable
- *Payback period*—to predict how long it will take to "get the money back" ■

In this chapter, we'll see how companies like Deer Valley use net present value, payback period, and other capital budgeting techniques to decide which long-term capital investments to make. Deer Valley's capital expansion project is a *long-term* special decision because it will tie up the company's resources for years. We'll tackle these long-term special decisions in the second half of this chapter. First, we consider *short-term* special decisions.

Relevant Information

In this chapter, you'll see how managers use financial information to guide important decisions about how to maximize profits.

How Managers Make Decisions

Exhibit 26-1 illustrates how managers make decisions among alternative courses of action. Management accountants help with the third step: gathering and analyzing *relevant information* to compare alternatives. The key is to focus on information that is *relevant* to the decision at hand.

Exhibit 26-1 How Managers Make Decisions

Identify the relevant information for a special business decision

✔ **Starter 26-1**

Relevant Information
Expected future data that differs among alternatives.

What Information Is Relevant to a Special Business Decision?

Exhibit 26-2 shows that **relevant information** is expected future data that differs among alternatives.

Suppose you are deciding whether to buy a Toyota or a Saturn car. The cost of the car, the insurance premium on this car, and the cost to maintain the car are all relevant because these costs

- Will be incurred in the *future* (after you decide to buy the car), and
- Will *differ between alternatives* (each car has a different cost, and maintenance and insurance costs will also differ)

Exhibit 26-2

Relevant Information

Relevant Information

Expected future (cost and revenue) data

Sales Forecast

Differs among alternatives

Accept Special Order

Sales Rev. $100 M

Reject Special Order

Sales Rev. $75 M

These costs are *relevant* because they can affect your decision of which car to purchase. Costs that were incurred in the past and costs that do not differ between alternatives are *irrelevant* because they do not affect your decision. For example, a campus parking sticker costs the same whether you buy the Toyota or the Saturn, so that cost is irrelevant to your decision.

The same distinction applies to all situations—*only relevant data affect decisions*. Let's consider another application of this general principle.

Suppose Pendleton Woolen Mills is deciding whether to use pure wool or a wool blend in a new line of sweaters. Assume Pendleton predicts the following costs under the two alternatives:

	Expected Materials and Labor Cost per Sweater		
	Wool	Wool Blend	Cost Difference
Direct materials........................	$10	$6	$4
Direct labor	2	2	0
Total cost of direct materials and direct labor ..	$12	$8	$4

The cost of direct materials is relevant because this cost differs between alternatives (the wool costs $4 more than the wool blend). The labor cost is irrelevant because that cost is the same for both.

Managers base their decisions on expected future data rather than on historical data. Historical data supplied by the accounting system are useful guides for predictions. However, historical data by themselves are irrelevant for making decisions about the future.

> You are considering replacing your Pentium IV computer with the latest model. Is the $1,500 you spent (in 2003) on the Pentium relevant to your decision about buying the new model?
>
> *Answer:* The $1,500 cost of your Pentium is irrelevant. The $1,500 is a *past* (sunk) cost that has already been incurred, so it is the same whether or not you buy the new computer.

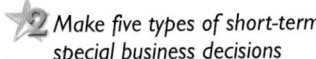

How to Make Short-Term Special Decisions

⭐2 *Make five types of short-term special business decisions*

Our approach to making short-term special decisions is called the *relevant information approach*, or the *incremental analysis approach*. We'll consider five kinds of decisions:

- Special sales orders
- Dropping products, departments, and territories

■ Product mix

■ Outsourcing (make or buy)

■ Selling as is or processing further

As you study these decisions, keep in mind the two keys in analyzing short-term special business decisions shown in Exhibit 26-3. We'll use these two keys in each decision.

Exhibit 26-3

Two Keys to Making Short-Term Special Decisions

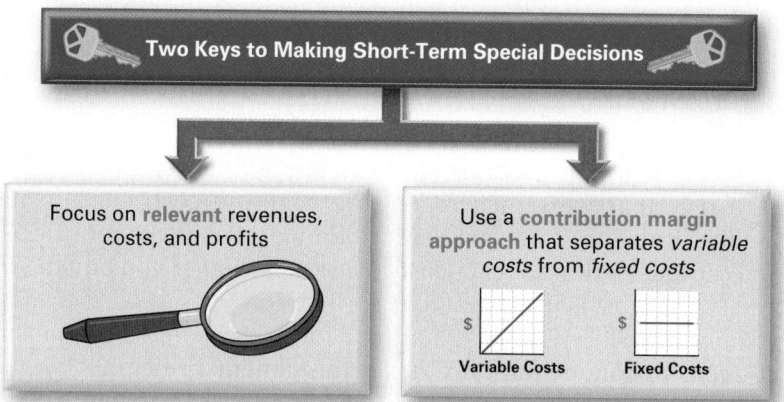

When to Accept a Special Sales Order

Suppose ACDelco sells oil filters for $3.20 each. Assume that a mail-order company has offered ACDelco $35,000 for 20,000 oil filters, or $1.75 per filter ($35,000 ÷ 20,000 = $1.75). This sale will not affect regular business, and it:

■ Will not change fixed costs

■ Will not require any additional variable nonmanufacturing expenses

■ Will use manufacturing capacity that would otherwise be idle

Suppose ACDelco made and sold 250,000 oil filters before considering the special order. Using the conventional (absorption costing) income statement on the left-hand side of Exhibit 26-4, the manufacturing cost per unit is $2 ($500,000 ÷ 250,000). This suggests that ACDelco should *not* accept the special order at a sale price of $1.75, because each oil filter costs $2 to manufacture. But appearances can be deceiving!

Exhibit 26-4 Conventional (Absorption Costing) Format and Contribution Margin Format Income Statements

Income Statement
Year Ended December 31, 20X5

Conventional (Absorption Costing) Format		Contribution Margin Format		
Sales revenue............................	$800,000	Sales revenue...............		$800,000
Less manufacturing cost of goods sold.....	500,000	Less variable expenses:		
Gross profit............................	300,000	Manufacturing	$300,000	
Less marketing and administrative		Marketing and		
expenses............................	200,000	administrative..........	75,000	375,000
		Contribution margin		425,000
		Less fixed expenses:		
		Manufacturing	$200,000	
		Marketing and		
		administrative..........	125,000	325,000
Operating income.....................	$100,000	Operating income...........		$100,000

The right-hand side of Exhibit 26-4 shows the contribution margin income statement that separates variable expenses from fixed expenses. → Managers find this format more useful because it shows how sales volume affects costs and income. The contribution margin income statement allows us to see that the *variable* manufacturing cost per unit is only $1.20 ($300,000 ÷ 250,000).

Chapter 22, page 903, explains that contribution margin equals revenues minus all variable expenses. Chapter 22 also compares conventional and contribution margin income statements.

Now let's reconsider the key question facing ACDelco: How would the special sale affect the company's operating income? The correct analysis in Exhibit 26-5 is an incremental approach that follows the two key guidelines:

1. Focus on relevant revenues, costs, and profits.

2. Use a contribution margin approach.

Exhibit 26-5 shows that this special sale increases revenues by $35,000 (20,000 × $1.75). The only cost that will differ between the alternatives is the variable manufacturing cost, which is expected to increase by $24,000 (20,000 × $1.20). The other costs are irrelevant. Variable marketing and administrative expenses will be the same whether or not ACDelco accepts the special order, because no special efforts were made to get this sale. Fixed expenses are unchanged because ACDelco has enough idle capacity to produce 20,000 extra oil filters without requiring additional facilities.

Expected increase in revenues—	
sale of 20,000 oil filters × $1.75 each.	$35,000
Expected increase in expenses—variable manufacturing costs:	
20,000 oil filters × $1.20 each.	(24,000)
Expected increase in operating income.	$11,000

Exhibit 26-5

Incremental Analysis of Special Sales Order

ACDelco compares the additional (incremental) revenues with the additional (incremental) expenses. If the increase in revenues exceeds the increase in expenses, the sale contributes to profits. Management predicts that the order will increase operating income by $11,000, as shown in Exhibit 26-5, so ACDelco should accept the special order.

✔ **Starter 26-2**

Thus, the decision rule is:

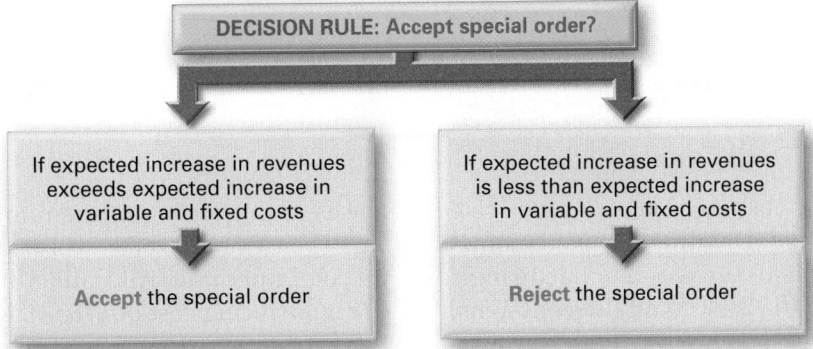

DECISION RULE: Accept special order?

If expected increase in revenues exceeds expected increase in variable and fixed costs	If expected increase in revenues is less than expected increase in variable and fixed costs
Accept the special order	**Reject** the special order

The absorption costing income statement on the left-hand side of Exhibit 26-4 shows that the total cost of manufacturing 250,000 filters is $500,000. What is the flaw in reasoning that ACDelco should accept special orders only if the sale price exceeds $2 each?

Answer: The flaw in this analysis arises from treating a fixed cost as though it changes in total like a variable cost does. Manufacturing one extra oil filter will only cost $1.20—the variable manufacturing cost. *Fixed expenses are irrelevant because ACDelco will incur $200,000 of fixed manufacturing overhead expenses whether or not the company accepts the special order.* Producing 20,000 more oil filters will not increase *total* fixed expenses, so manufacturing costs increase at the rate of $1.20 per unit, not $2.00 per unit.

Our special sales order analysis focused on the short-term expected effect on operating income. We must also consider long-term factors. Will accepting the order at $1.75 hurt ACDelco's ability to sell the oil filter at the regular price of $3.20? Will regular customers find out about the special price and balk at paying more? How will competitors react? Will this sale start a price war?

If the sales manager believes these disadvantages outweigh the extra $11,000 in profit from accepting the order, he will reject the order. The company is better off passing up $11,000 now to protect its long-term market position and customer relations. Rejecting the special sales order may be an $11,000 "investment" in the company's long-term future.

We will use this same approach of analyzing changes in revenues and costs among the different alternatives for the remaining short-term special decisions.

When to Drop Products, Departments, or Territories

Assume that ACDelco is operating at the 270,000-unit level, as shown in Exhibit 26-6. Suppose the company is now considering *dropping* the air cleaner product line with $35,000 (20,000 units) in sales and total variable costs per unit of $1.50. Exhibit 26-6 shows contribution margin income statements by product line.

Exhibit 26-6

Contribution Margin Income Statements by Product Line

		Product Line	
	Total (270,000 units)	**Oil Filters** (250,000 units)	**Air Cleaners** (20,000 units)
Sales revenue	$835,000	$800,000	$ 35,000
Variable expenses.	405,000	375,000	30,000
Contribution margin	430,000	425,000	5,000
Fixed expenses:			
Manufacturing	200,000	185,185*	14,815*
Marketing and administrative.	125,000	115,741†	9,259†
Total fixed expenses.	325,000	300,926	24,074
Operating income (loss)	$105,000	$124,074	$(19,074)

* $200,000 ÷ 270,000 units = $0.74074 per unit; 250,000 units × $0.74074 = $185,185; 20,000 units × $0.74074 = $14,815

† $125,000 ÷ 270,000 units = $0.462963 per unit; 250,000 units × $0.462963 = $115,741; 20,000 units × $0.462963 = $9,259

Suppose ACDelco allocates fixed expenses in proportion to the number of units sold. Dividing the fixed manufacturing expense of $200,000 by 270,000 total units yields a fixed manufacturing cost of $0.74074 per unit. Allocating this unit cost to the 250,000 oil filters assigns fixed manufacturing cost of $185,185 to this product. The same procedure allocates $14,815 to air cleaners. Fixed marketing and administrative expenses are allocated in the same manner.

The result is an operating loss of $19,074 for air cleaners. Should ACDelco drop the air cleaner product line? The answer depends on whether or not fixed costs change.

✔ **Starter 26-3**

FIXED COSTS DO NOT CHANGE   As in the special sales order example, we follow the two key guidelines for special business decisions: (1) focus on relevant data items, and (2) use a contribution margin approach. The relevant items are still the changes in revenues and expenses, but now we are considering a *decrease* in volume rather than an increase. If fixed costs remain the same whether or not the air cleaner product line is dropped, the fixed costs are not relevant to the decision. Only the revenues and variable expenses are relevant.

Exhibit 26-6 shows that the air cleaner product line has a positive contribution margin of $5,000. If this product line is dropped, the company will forgo this $5,000. Exhibit 26-7 verifies that expected revenue decreases by $35,000, and expected variable expenses decrease by $30,000, a net $5,000 decrease in operating income (since fixed costs are unaffected). This analysis suggests that management should *not* drop air cleaners.

Expected decrease in revenues:	
Sale of air cleaners (20,000 × $1.75)............................	$35,000
Expected decrease in expenses:	
Variable manufacturing expenses (20,000 × $1.50)...............	30,000
Expected decrease in operating income.........................	$ 5,000

Exhibit 26-7

Incremental Analysis for Dropping a Product—Fixed Costs Do Not Change

FIXED COSTS CHANGE Don't jump to the conclusion that fixed costs never change and are always irrelevant. Suppose ACDelco employed a part-time foreman to oversee the air cleaner product line. The foreman's $13,000 salary can be avoided if the company stops producing air cleaners.

Exhibit 26-8 shows that in this situation, operating income will increase by $8,000 if ACDelco drops air cleaners. A "fixed" cost *is* relevant, so managers must consider the change in the cost.

✔ **Starter 26-4**

Expected decrease in revenues:		
Sale of air cleaners (20,000 × $1.75)		$35,000
Expected decrease in expenses:		
Variable manufacturing expenses (20,000 × $1.50)	$30,000	
Fixed expenses—foreman's salary...................	13,000	
Expected decrease in total expenses		43,000
Expected increase in operating income................		$ 8,000

Exhibit 26-8

Incremental Analysis for Dropping a Product—Fixed Costs Change

Special decisions should take into account all costs affected by the choice of action. Managers must ask: What total costs—variable *and* fixed—will change? As Exhibits 26-7 and 26-8 show, the key to deciding whether to drop products, departments, or territories is to compare the lost revenue against the costs that can be saved from dropping. The decision rule is:

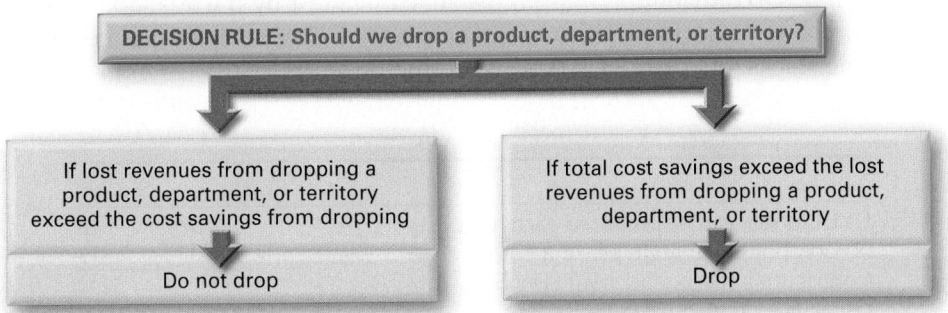

DECISION RULE: Should we drop a product, department, or territory?

If lost revenues from dropping a product, department, or territory exceed the cost savings from dropping

Do not drop

If total cost savings exceed the lost revenues from dropping a product, department, or territory

Drop

Product Mix—Which Product to Emphasize?

Companies do not have unlimited resources. **Constraints** that restrict production or sale of a product vary from company to company. For example, Dell Computer has limited production capacity. For a manufacturer, the production constraint may be labor hours, machine hours, or available materials. For a merchandiser like Wal-Mart, the primary constraint is cubic feet of display space.

Constraint
A factor that restricts production or sale of a product.

Other companies are constrained by sales. Competition may be stiff, and the company may be able to sell only so many units.

Consider Chazz, a manufacturer of shirts and slacks. The following data suggest that shirts are more profitable than slacks:

	Per Unit	
	Shirts	**Slacks**
Sale price	$30	$60
Variable expenses	12	48
Contribution margin	$18	$12
Contribution margin ratio:		
Shirts—$18 ÷ $30......................	60%	
Slacks—$12 ÷ $60		20%

However, an important piece of information is missing—the time it takes to manufacture each product. Chazz can produce either 20 pairs of slacks *or* 10 shirts per machine hour. The company can sell all the shirts and slacks it produces. The company has 2,000 machine hours of capacity. Which product should it emphasize?

To maximize profits, follow the decision rule:

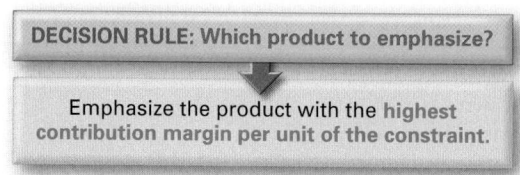

Chazz can sell all the slacks and shirts it makes, so production (machine hours) is the constraint. Thus, Chazz should produce the product with the highest contribution margin per machine hour. Exhibit 26-9 determines the contribution margin per machine hour for each product. Slacks have a higher contribution margin per machine hour ($240 = 20 pairs of slacks × $12 per pair) than shirts ($180 = 10 shirts × $18 per shirt). Chazz will earn more profit by producing slacks. Why? Because even though slacks have a lower contribution margin *per unit*, Chazz can make twice as many slacks as shirts in the available machine hours. Exhibit 26-9 proves that Chazz earns more total profit by making slacks. Multiplying the contribution margin per machine hour by the available number of machine hours shows that Chazz can earn $480,000 of contribution margin by producing slacks, but only $360,000 by producing shirts.

Exhibit 26-9

Product Mix—Which Product to Emphasize

	Shirts	Slacks
(1) Units that can be produced each hour	10	20
(2) Contribution margin per unit	× $18	× $12
Contribution margin per hour (1) × (2)	$180	$240
Capacity—number of hours......................	× 2,000	× 2,000
Total contribution margin at full capacity	$360,000	$480,000

✔ **Starter 26-5**

Notice that the analysis again follows the two guidelines for special business decisions: (1) Focus on relevant data (contribution margin in this example, because only sales revenue and variable costs are relevant), and (2) use a contribution margin approach.

Why are Chazz's fixed expenses irrelevant in the decision to produce slacks or shirts?

Answer: Chazz will use the same property, plant, and equipment to make either slacks or shirts. The fixed expenses will be the same whether the company makes slacks or shirts, so the fixed expenses are irrelevant.

When to Outsource

IBM, the company that invented the dominant type of personal computer, has decided to outsource (or buy from a supplier) most of its desktop models. **Cisco Systems** buys most of its products from low-cost technology manufacturing specialists in Asia. On the other hand, **Nokia** has become the cost leader in cell phone manufacturing using its own plants in high-cost areas like Finland, the United States, and Germany.[1] Make-or-buy decisions are often called **outsourcing** decisions, because managers must decide whether to buy a component product or service or produce it in-house. The heart of these decisions is *how best to use available facilities.*

Outsourcing
A make-or-buy decision: managers decide whether to buy a component product or service or produce it in-house.

Let's see how managers make outsourcing decisions. DefTone, a manufacturer of music CDs, is deciding whether to make the paper liners for the CD jewel boxes in-house or whether to outsource them to Mūz-Art, a company that specializes in producing paper liners. DefTone's cost to produce 250,000 liners is:

	Total Cost (250,000 liners)
Direct materials	$ 40,000
Direct labor.	20,000
Variable overhead	15,000
Fixed overhead	50,000
Total manufacturing cost	$125,000
Cost per liner ($125,000 ÷ 250,000)	$0.50

Mūz-Art offers to sell DefTone the liners for $0.37 each. Should DefTone make the liners or buy them from Mūz-Art? DefTone's $0.50 cost per unit to make the liner is $0.13 higher than the cost of buying it from Mūz-Art. It appears that DefTone should outsource the liners. But the correct answer is not so simple.

To make the best decision, you must compare the difference in expected future costs between the alternatives. Which costs will differ depending on whether DefTone makes or buys the liners?

By purchasing the liners, DefTone can avoid all variable manufacturing costs and reduce its fixed overhead cost by $10,000. (Fixed overhead will decrease to $40,000.) Exhibit 26-10 shows the differences in costs between the make and buy alternatives.

Liner Costs	Make Liners	Buy Liners	Difference
Direct materials	$ 40,000	—	$40,000
Direct labor.	20,000	—	20,000
Variable overhead	15,000	—	15,000
Fixed overhead	50,000	$ 40,000	10,000
Purchase cost from Mūz-Art (250,000 × $0.37).	—	92,500	(92,500)
Total cost of liners	$125,000	$132,500	$(7,500)
Cost per unit—Divide by 250,000 liners	$0.50	$0.53	$(0.03)

Exhibit 26-10

Incremental Analysis for Outsourcing Decision

✔ Starter 26-6

✔ Starter 26-7

[1]*Source*: David Pringle, "How Nokia Thrives by Breaking the Rules," *The Wall Street Journal*, Jan. 3, 2003, A7.

The decision rule is:

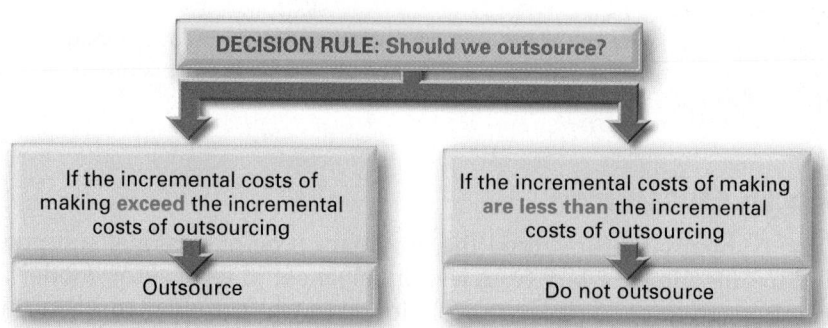

Exhibit 26-10 shows that it would cost DefTone less to make the liners than to buy them from Mūz-Art. The net savings from making 250,000 liners is $7,500, which works out to $0.03 each.

This example shows that *fixed costs are relevant to a special decision when those fixed costs differ between alternatives*. Exhibit 26-10 also shows that outsourcing decisions follow our two guidelines for special business decisions: (1) Focus on relevant data (variable and fixed manufacturing costs in this case), and (2) use a contribution margin approach that separates variable costs from fixed costs. They help answer the fundamental question: What difference does the proposed change make?

The analysis in Exhibit 26-10 assumes there is no other use for the production facilities freed up if DefTone buys the liners from Mūz-Art. But suppose DefTone has an opportunity to use its freed-up facilities to make more CDs, which have an expected profit of $18,000. Now DefTone must consider its **opportunity cost**—the benefit forgone by not choosing an alternative course of action. In this case, DefTone's opportunity cost of making the liners is the $18,000 profit it forgoes if it does not free its production facilities to make the additional CDs.

Opportunity Cost
The benefit forgone by not choosing an alternative course of action.

Let's see how DefTone's managers decide among three alternatives:

1. Use the facilities to make the liners.
2. Buy the liners and leave facilities idle.
3. Buy the liners and use facilities to make more CDs.

The alternative with the lowest *net* cost is the best use of DefTone's facilities. Exhibit 26-11 compares the three alternatives.

		Buy Liners	
	Make Liners	Facilities Idle	Make Additional CDs
Expected cost of obtaining 250,000 liners (from Exhibit 26-10).....................	$125,000	$132,500	$132,500
Expected profit from additional CDs.........	—	—	(18,000)
Expected net cost of obtaining 250,000 liners ..	$125,000	$132,500	$114,500

DefTone should buy the liners from Mūz-Art and use the vacated facilities to make more CDs. If DefTone makes the liners, or if it buys the liners from Mūz-Art but leaves its production facilities idle, it will forgo the opportunity to earn $18,000.

DefTone's managers should consider qualitative factors as well as revenue and cost differences in making their final decision. For example, DefTone managers may believe they can better control quality by making the liners themselves. This argues for making the liners.

Outsourcing decisions are increasingly important in today's globally wired economy. In the past, make-or-buy decisions often ended up as "make" because coordination, information exchange, and paperwork problems made buying from suppliers too inconvenient. Now companies can use the Web to tap into information systems of suppliers and customers located around the world. Paperwork vanishes, and information required to satisfy the strictest just-in-time delivery schedule is available in real time. As a result, companies are focusing on their core competencies and outsourcing more and more other functions.

Like Cisco Systems and Nike, many world-class competitors have discovered that their core competency lies not in manufacturing, but in research and development and in brand marketing. Such companies outsource much of their manufacturing to contract manufacturers like Flextronics and Yue Yuen Industrial Holdings, which operate huge plants in Mexico and Taiwan, where labor is less expensive.

Cisco makes its most sophisticated components, but outside suppliers directly fill many of Cisco's customers' orders. Hewlett-Packard (HP) is a leader in laser printers, but it outsources production of the laser mechanisms to Canon.

Outsourcing doesn't stop at production. Many companies outsource computing and software needs instead of developing information technology in-house. Application service providers, or ASPs, install and maintain software

We Brand It, You Make It: The Outsourcing Trend

Here's a riddle for our times: What makes an IBM computer an IBM computer? Do IBM employees have to assemble the computer, or just design and service it? Increasingly, companies like IBM and Motorola are outsourcing the manufacture of their products to off-shore contract manufacturers. In 2003, IBM signed a $3.6 billion deal with Sanmina-SCI Corp. to manufacture servers and desktop PCs in Guadalajara, Mexico.

The deal with Sanmina is part of IBM's continuing quest to reduce its total supply-chain costs. According to a *Purchasing* magazine survey, 81% of electronics manufacturers cited cost as their reason for outsourcing everything from motherboards and set-top boxes to entire products. Contract manufacturers can produce products more cheaply because orders from multiple clients keep them busy around the clock and cover overhead costs.

Outsourcing manufacturing also allows IBM to concentrate on other activities where it adds more value. As Meta Group analyst Steve Kleyhan puts it, outsourcing "lets IBM focus on design and customer service instead of the bits, bytes, and bolts of making the box, where IBM has no competitive advantage." Yet outsourcing cuts into activities once thought of as core capabilities, such as product development and technical support. The outsourcing of knowledge work has already begun in China, India, eastern Europe, and other countries with an educated white-collar workforce that will do the work for less than their U.S. counterparts. For instance, engineers in India and China who once wrote code for chips designed in the U.S. now develop devices for Texas Instruments, Intel, and others. The savings are considerable: The Indian engineers—with master's degrees and five years' experience—make $1,000 a month. Their U.S. counterparts make $7,000.

Based on: Jeffrey Burt, "Sanmina to Build IBM eServers, IntelliStations," *eWeek*, January 13, 2002, p. 23. Steve Lohr, "IBM in Deal to Farm Out Some PC Jobs," *The New York Times*, January 8, 2003, p. C4. Pete Engardio, Aaron Bernstein, and Manjeet Kripalani, "Is Your Job Next?" *Business Week*, February 3, 2003, pp. 50–60. James Carbone, "What Buyers Look For in Contract Manufacturers," *Purchasing*, March 23, 2000, pp. 32–38.

Accounting.com

ranging from budgeting and activity-based costing applications to e-mail and supply-chain management. The ASP then charges its client companies to access this software through the Internet. The fee charged depends on the time the client is logged on and the specific features of the software that the client uses.

Companies are even outsourcing telemarketing and customer service. GE, American Express, and IBM were among the first to outsource such work to "business process outsourcing" firms, largely located in India. Now half the Fortune 500, including Microsoft and Dell, send work to India. So chances are that the last time you phoned a customer help desk, the voice on the line was in New Delhi![2]

Many outsourcing decisions are short-term but Cisco's decision to subcontract most of its manufacturing is a long-term one. When making decisions with long-term consequences, managers identify and analyze the relevant costs and benefits of different alternatives, as DefTone did in Exhibits 26-10 and 26-11. The only difference is that these cost and benefit calculations may extend many years into the future. Managers discount these costs and benefits to their *present values*, as we explain in the second half of the chapter.

Sell As Is or Process Further?

After processing crude oil into regular gasoline, should Chevron sell the regular gas as is, or should it spend more to process the gas into premium grade? Suppose Chevron spent $48,000 to produce 50,000 gallons of regular gasoline, as shown in Exhibit 26-12. Assume Chevron can sell this regular gasoline for $1.20 per gallon, for a total of $60,000 (50,000 × $1.20). Alternatively Chevron could further process this regular gasoline into premium-grade gas. Suppose the additional cost to process the gas further is $0.11 per gallon, for an additional cost of $5,500 (50,000 gallons × $0.11). Assume the sale price of premium gasoline is $1.40 per gallon, for a total of $70,000 (50,000 × $1.40).

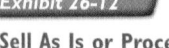

Exhibit 26-12

Sell As Is or Process Further Decision

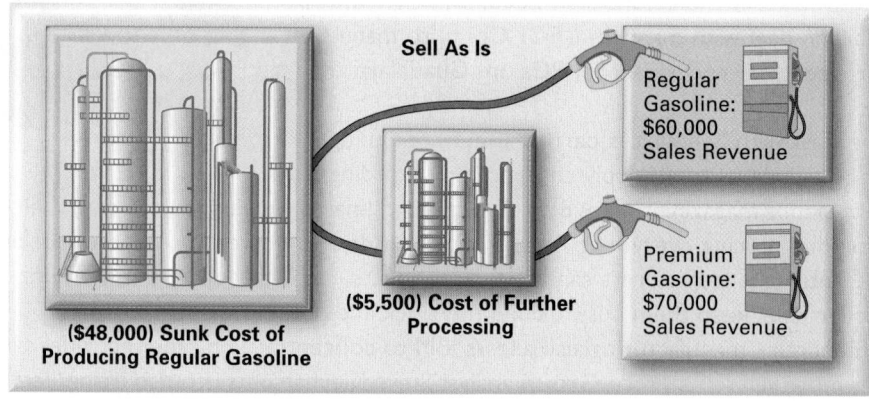

Which items are relevant to the sell-or-process-further decision? The $48,000 cost of producing the 50,000 gallons of regular gasoline is *not* relevant. It is a **sunk cost**—a past cost that cannot be changed regardless of which future action is taken. The $48,000 has been incurred whether Chevron sells the regular gasoline as is or processes it further into premium.

Exhibits 26-12 and 26-13 show that the relevant items that differ between Chevron's (1) sell as is and (2) process further alternatives are

- Expected revenues   - Expected costs of processing further

The $10,000 extra revenue ($70,000 − $60,000) outweighs the $5,500 cost of the extra processing, so Chevron should process the gasoline into the premium grade.

Sunk Cost
A past cost that cannot be changed regardless of which future action is taken.

✔ Starter 26-8

---

[2]Mary Carmichael, "Help from Far Away," *Newsweek*, May 12, 2003, pp. E16–E17.

Exhibit 26-13 | Incremental Analysis for Sell As Is or Process Further Decision

	Sell As Is	Process Further	Difference
Expected revenue from selling 50,000 gallons of regular gasoline at $1.20 per gallon	$60,000		
Expected revenue from selling 50,000 gallons of premium gasoline at $1.40 per gallon		$70,000	$10,000
Additional costs of $0.11 per gallon to convert 50,000 gallons of regular gasoline into premium gasoline		(5,500)	(5,500)
Total net revenue	$60,000	$64,500	
Difference in net revenue			$ 4,500

Thus, the decision rule is:

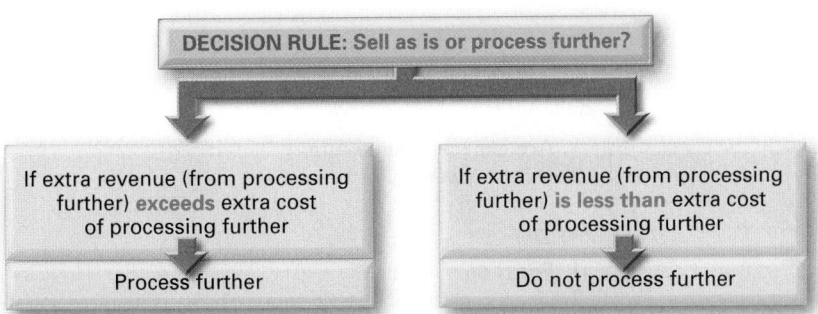

Suppose one of **Chevron's** customers wants to buy the 50,000 gallons, but in the form of regular gasoline, not premium. The customer is willing to pay more than $1.20 a gallon for the regular gas. What is the minimum price Chevron should charge?

Answer: Exhibit 26-13 shows that if Chevron does not process the gas into premium grade, it would give up $64,500 ($70,000 revenues given up – $5,500 further processing cost not incurred). To obtain the same income from selling the gas as regular grade, Chevron must sell the regular gas for at least $1.29 per gallon ($64,500 revenue required ÷ 50,000 gallons of regular gas). If the customer offers to pay more than $1.29 per gallon, Chevron will be better off selling regular gas to this customer. If the customer offers less than $1.29, Chevron will be better off further processing the gas into premium grade.

How Do Short-Term and Long-Term Special Decisions Differ?

The special decisions we reviewed pertain to short periods of time, such as a year. In this time frame:

- Many costs are fixed and do not vary with the volume of goods or services produced. This is why short-term special business decisions use the contribution margin approach, which distinguishes variable from fixed costs.

- There is no need to worry about the time value of money. Managers do not bother computing present values of revenues and expenses for short-term decisions.

In the next half of the chapter, we turn to longer-term special decisions, like Deer Valley's decision to expand Snow Park Lodge. For long-term decisions:

- Few if any costs are fixed.

- Managers often take into account the time value of money.

The approach to long-term decisions will reflect these differences.

But before moving on to long-term special decisions, stop for a moment to review the Decision Guidelines that summarize key points from our discussion of short-term decisions. Then work the mid-chapter summary problems.

Decision Guidelines

SHORT-TERM SPECIAL BUSINESS DECISIONS

Amazon.com has confronted most of the special business decisions we've covered. Of course, Amazon's managers consider qualitative factors as they make each decision, but a quantitative analysis of the decision's immediate effect on profits is a good starting point. Here are key guidelines Amazon.com's managers follow in making their decisions.

Decision	Guideline
What information is relevant to a short-term special business decision?	Relevant data: 1. Are expected *future* data 2. *Differ* between alternatives
What are two key guidelines in making short-term special business decisions?	Key guidelines: 1. Focus on *relevant* data 2. Use a *contribution margin* approach that separates variable costs from fixed costs
Should Amazon.com accept a lower sale price for a large order from a customer in São Paulo, Brazil?	If the revenue from the order exceeds the extra variable and fixed costs incurred to fill the order, then accepting the order will increase operating income.
Should Amazon.com drop its electronics product line?	If the cost savings exceed the lost revenues from dropping the electronics product line, then dropping will increase operating income.
Given limited warehouse space, which products should Amazon.com focus on selling?	Amazon should focus on selling the products with the highest contribution margin per unit of the constraint, which is cubic feet of warehouse space.
Should Amazon.com outsource its warehousing operations?	If the incremental costs of operating its own warehouses exceed the costs of outsourcing, then outsourcing will increase operating income.
How to decide whether to sell a product as is or process further?	Process further only if the extra sales revenue (from processing further) exceeds the extra costs of additional processing.

MID-CHAPTER *Summary Problems*

CHECK YOUR RESOURCES

Problem 1

Aziz, Inc., produces standard and deluxe sunglasses:

	Per Pair	
	Standard	**Deluxe**
Sale price............................	$20	$30
Variable expenses....................	16	21

(continued)

The company has 15,000 machine hours available. In one machine hour, Aziz can produce either 70 pairs of the standard model or 30 pairs of the deluxe model. Which should Aziz emphasize?

Problem 2

Just Do It! incurs the following costs for 20,000 pairs of its high-tech hiking socks:

Direct materials	$ 20,000
Direct labor	80,000
Variable overhead	40,000
Fixed overhead	80,000
Total manufacturing cost	$220,000
Cost per pair ($220,000 ÷ 20,000)	$11

Another manufacturer has offered to sell Just Do It! similar socks for $10, a total purchase cost of $200,000. If Just Do It! outsources *and* leaves its plant idle, it can save $50,000 of fixed overhead cost. Or, the company can use the released facilities to make other products that will contribute $70,000 to profits. Identify and analyze the alternatives. What is the best course of action?

Solutions:

Problem 1

	Style of Sunglasses	
	Standard	Deluxe
Sale price per pair	$ 20	$ 30
Variable expense per pair	(16)	(21)
Contribution margin per pair	$ 4	$ 9
Units produced each machine hour	× 70	× 30
Contribution margin per machine hour	$ 280	$ 270
Capacity—number of machine hours	× 15,000	× 15,000
Total contribution margin at full capacity	$4,200,000	$4,050,000

Decision: Emphasize the standard model because it has the higher contribution margin per unit of the constraint—machine hours.

Problem 2

		Buy Socks	
	Make Socks	Facilities Idle	Make Other Products
Relevant costs:			
Direct materials	$ 20,000	—	
Direct labor	80,000	—	
Variable overhead	40,000	—	
Fixed overhead	80,000	$ 30,000	$ 80,000
Purchase cost from outsider (20,000 × $10)	—	200,000	200,000
Total cost of obtaining socks	220,000	230,000	280,000
Profit from other products	—	—	(70,000)
Net cost of obtaining 20,000 pairs of socks	$220,000	$230,000	$210,000

Decision: Just Do It! should buy the socks from the outside supplier and use the released facilities to make other products.

3 *Use payback and accounting rate of return models to make longer-term capital budgeting decisions.*

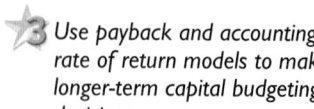
Student Resource CD

accounting rate of return, capital budgeting, payback period, residual value

Capital Budgeting
Budgeting for the acquisition of capital assets—assets used for a long period of time.

We discussed cash flows from operating activities, often the primary source of cash, in Chapter 17, page 659.

Payback
The length of time it takes to recover, in net cash inflows, the dollars of a capital outlay.

✔ Starter 26-9

✔ Starter 26-10

Using Payback and Accounting Rate of Return to Make Capital Budgeting Decisions

Think back to the chapter-opening story. The Deer Valley owners' decision to spend $13 million to expand Snow Park Lodge will tie up resources for years to come. So will Amazon.com's decision to build several highly automated warehouses at over $20 million each. How did management decide that these expansions would be a good investment? By using capital budgeting analysis.

Capital budgeting is budgeting for the acquisition of *capital assets*—assets used for a long period of time. Capital budgeting decisions include expanding the Deer Valley resort, building a new plant, or developing a major commercial Web site.

Capital budgeting is not an exact science. Although the calculations may appear precise, remember that they are based on predictions about an uncertain future. These predictions must consider many unknown factors, such as changing consumer preferences, competition, and government regulations. The further into the future the decision extends, the more likely that actual results will differ from predictions. Long-term decisions are thus riskier than short-term decisions.

We now discuss four popular capital budgeting decision models (or decision methods): payback, accounting rate of return, net present value, and internal rate of return. Three of these models compare the *net cash inflows from operations* each alternative generates. ← Generally accepted accounting principles are based on accrual accounting, but capital budgeting focuses on cash flows. The desirability of a capital asset depends on its ability to generate net cash inflows—that is, inflows in excess of outflows—over the asset's useful life.

Payback Period

Payback is the length of time it takes to recover, in net cash inflows, the dollars of a capital outlay. The payback model measures how quickly managers expect to recover their investment dollars. The shorter the payback period, the more attractive the asset, all else being equal.

Tierra Firma, which makes camping gear, is considering investing $240,000 in hardware and software to develop a portal, or interface, with a business-to-business (B2B) electronic market. Employees throughout the company will use the portal to enter the electronic market of certified suppliers to purchase goods and services appropriate to their jobs. The portal will limit the kinds of goods and services each employee can buy. Accountants will be able to buy office supplies, and maintenance workers will be able to buy parts. Tierra Firma expects the portal to save $60,000 a year for the six years of its useful life. The savings will arise from reducing the number of purchasing personnel the company employs and from lower prices on the goods and services purchased.

When net cash inflows are equal each year, managers compute the payback period as follows:

$$\text{Payback period} = \frac{\text{Amount invested}}{\text{Expected annual net cash inflow}}$$

Net cash inflows arise from an increase in revenues, a decrease in expenses, or both. In Tierra's case, the net cash inflows result from lower expenses. Tierra computes the investment's payback as follows:

$$\text{Payback period for B2B portal} = \frac{\$240,000}{\$60,000} = 4 \text{ years}$$

Exhibit 26-14 verifies that Tierra expects to recoup the $240,000 investment in the B2B portal by the end of year 4, when the accumulated cash inflows (savings) total $240,000.

Tierra Firma is also considering investing $240,000 to develop a Web site. The company expects the Web site to generate $80,000 in cash inflows each year of its three-year life. The payback period is computed as follows:

$$\text{Payback period for Web site development} = \frac{\$240,000}{\$80,000} = 3 \text{ years}$$

Exhibit 26-14 verifies that Tierra Firma will recoup the $240,000 investment for Web site development by the end of year 3, when the accumulated net cash inflows total $240,000. The payback model favors Web site development because it recovers the investment more quickly.

Exhibit 26-14

Payback—Equal Annual Net Cash Inflows

| | | Net Cash Inflows | | | |
| | | B2B Portal | | Web Site Development | |
Year	Amount Invested	Annual	Accumulated	Annual	Accumulated
0	$240,000	—	—	—	
1	—	$60,000	$ 60,000	$80,000	$ 80,000
2	—	60,000	120,000	80,000	160,000
3	—	60,000	180,000	80,000	240,000
4	—	60,000	240,000		
5	—	60,000	300,000		
6	—	60,000	360,000		

Given the fast pace of advances in technology, information technology managers find payback's emphasis on the short term to be useful. For example, Amazon.com considers its software to have a useful life of only two years!

But using the payback method alone can lead to unwise decisions, because payback focuses only on time; it does not consider profitability. The asset's payback period must be shorter than its useful life to provide any profit. In Tierra Firma's decision about developing a B2B portal or Web site, Exhibit 26-14 shows that the Web site's useful life is the same as its payback period—three years. The Web site will merely cover its cost and provide no profit. On the other hand, the B2B portal has a useful life of six years. It will continue to generate net cash inflows for two years after its payback period. This will give the company an additional net cash inflow of $120,000 ($60,000 × 2 years). Unlike the Web site, the B2B portal will be profitable. After considering the assets' useful lives, the B2B portal appears to be the better investment. The key point is that the investment with the shortest payback period is best *only if all other factors are the same*.

This leads to the following decision rule:

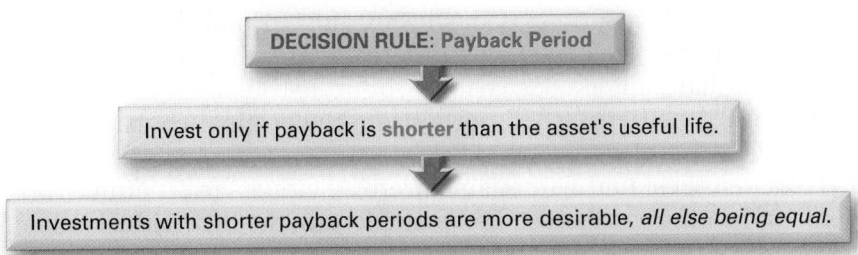

DECISION RULE: Payback Period

Invest only if payback is shorter than the asset's useful life.

Investments with shorter payback periods are more desirable, *all else being equal.*

Managers at Deer Valley Resort use the payback method to eliminate proposals that are too risky—those with long payback periods. But they rarely use payback alone, because it ignores profitability.

✔ Starter 26-11

Accounting Rate of Return

Companies are in business to earn profits. One measure of profitability is the **accounting rate of return** on an asset:

Accounting Rate of Return
A measure of profitability computed by dividing the average annual operating income from an asset by the average amount invested in the asset.

$$\text{Accounting rate of return} = \frac{\text{Average annual operating income from asset}}{\text{Average amount invested in asset}}$$

The accounting rate of return focuses on the operating income an asset generates. Operating income from an asset can be computed as net cash inflow from the asset minus depreciation on the asset. Exhibit 26-15 computes the accounting rate of return for Tierra Firma's B2B portal in the original payback example. Recall that Tierra expects the portal to generate annual net cash inflows of $60,000. The portal's development costs $240,000, and it has a useful life of six years with no residual value. Annual straight-line depreciation is $40,000 ($240,000 ÷ 6 years). ← Exhibit 26-15 shows that Tierra expects the portal to generate average annual operating income of $20,000 ($60,000 − $40,000).

Recall from Chapter 10, page 405,  *that straight-line depreciation assigns an equal amount of depreciation expense to each year of an asset's life.*

Exhibit 26-15

Accounting Rate of Return

$$\text{Accounting rate of return} = \frac{\text{Average annual operating income from asset *}}{\text{Average amount invested in asset}}$$

$$= \frac{\text{Annual net cash inflow from asset} - \text{Annual depreciation on asset}}{(\text{Amount invested in asset} + \text{Residual value}) / 2}$$

$$= \frac{\$60,000 - \$40,000^{\dagger}}{(\$240,000 + \$0)/2}$$

$$= \frac{\$20,000}{\$120,000} = 0.167 = 16.7\%$$

*Operating income can also be computed as revenues minus operating expenses.

$^{\dagger}\$40,000 = \dfrac{\$240,000}{6 \text{ years}}$

The accounting rate of return measures the *average* rate of return over the asset's entire life. First, consider the average annual operating income in the numerator. If operating income varies by year, compute the *total* operating income over the asset's life. Then divide the total by the number of years of life to find the *average* annual operating income from the asset.

Second, consider the average amount invested. The book value of the asset decreases as it is used and depreciated. Thus, the company's investment in the asset declines over time. The *average* amount invested is the amount invested halfway through the asset's useful life. To find the average amount invested, we divide by 2. If the asset's residual value is zero, the average investment is half the asset's cost. Exhibit 26-15 shows that the average amount invested in Tierra's B2B portal from the original payback example is $120,000 ($240,000 ÷ 2).

If the asset's residual value is not zero, the average amount invested is greater than half the asset's cost. For example, assume the residual value of the portal's technology is $30,000. Then annual depreciation declines to $35,000 [($240,000 − $30,000)/6]. The accounting rate of return is

$$\text{Accounting rate of return} = \frac{\$60,000 - \$35,000}{(\$240,000 + \$30,000)/2} = \frac{\$25,000}{\$135,000} = 0.185 = 18.5\%$$

Companies that use the accounting rate of return model set a minimum required rate of return. The decision rule is:

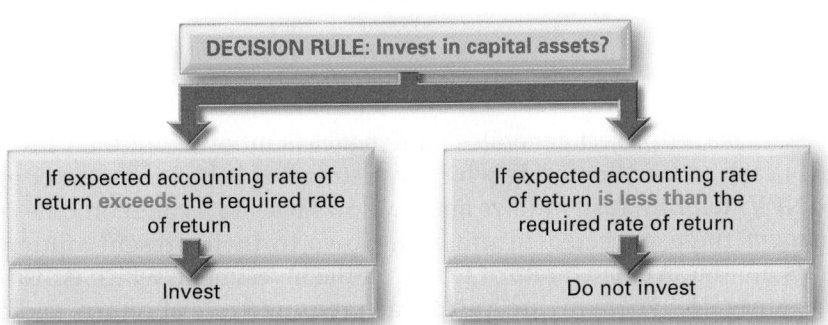

If Tierra Firma requires a rate of return of at least 20%, then its managers would not approve an investment in the B2B portal in Exhibit 26-15, because the average annual return is less than 20%.

Using Discounted Cash-Flow Models to Make Capital Budgeting Decisions

A dollar received today is worth more than a dollar to be received in the future. Why? Because you can invest today's dollar and earn extra income. If you receive $1 today and deposit it in a bank that pays 6% interest, a year from today you will have $1.06 (the original $1 plus $0.06 interest). Presumably, you would rather receive the $1 now, which will grow to $1.06 a year from today, rather than receive $1 a year from today. The fact that money can be invested to earn income over time is called the **time value of money**, and this explains why we would prefer to receive cash sooner rather than later.

The time value of money → means that the timing of capital investments' net cash flows is important. Consider two $10,000 investments that both promise future cash inflows of $11,000. Investment 1 will bring in cash of $5,500 at the end of each of the next two years. Investment 2 will return the full $11,000 at the end of the second year. Which investment is better? Investment 1, because it brings in cash sooner. Its $5,500 net cash inflow at the end of the first year can be reinvested right away to earn additional returns.

Neither the payback period nor the accounting rate of return recognizes the time value of money. That is, these models fail to consider the *timing* of the net cash flows an asset generates. *Discounted cash-flow models*— the net present value and the internal rate of return—overcome this weakness. Over 85% of large industrial firms in the United States use discounted cash-flow methods to make capital budgeting decisions. Companies that provide services, like Deer Valley Resort, also use these models.

Net Present Value

Allegra is considering producing CD players and VCRs. The products require different specialized machines that each cost $1 million. Each machine has a five-

Use discounted cash flow models to make longer-term capital budgeting decisions

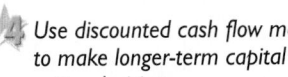

annuity, cash flows, cost of capital, discount rate, internal rate of return, present value, required rate of return, sensitivity analysis, time value of money

Time Value of Money
The fact that money can be invested to earn income over time.

The time value of money is discussed in the Chapter 15 appendix, page 616.

year life and zero residual value. The two products have different patterns of predicted net cash inflows:

	Annual Net Cash Inflows	
Year	CD Players	VCRs
1	$ 305,450	$ 500,000
2	305,450	350,000
3	305,450	300,000
4	305,450	250,000
5	305,450	40,000
Total	$1,527,250	$1,440,000

Net Present Value (NPV)
The decision model that brings cash inflows and outflows back to a common time period by discounting these expected future cash flows to their present value, using a minimum desired rate of return.

Discount Rate
Management's minimum desired rate of return on an investment. Also called the **hurdle rate, required rate of return**, and **cost of capital**.

Annuity
A stream of equal periodic cash flows.

The CD-player project generates more net cash inflows. But the VCR project brings in cash sooner. To decide which investment is better, we use **net present value (NPV)** to bring cash inflows and outflows back to a common time period. We *discount* these expected future cash flows to their present value, using Allegra's minimum desired rate of return on the investment, which is also called the **discount rate**. Synonyms are **hurdle rate, required rate of return**, and **cost of capital**. The discount rate depends on the riskiness of investments. The higher the risk, the higher the discount rate. Allegra's discount rate for these investments is 14%.

NET PRESENT VALUE WITH EQUAL PERIODIC CASH FLOWS (ANNUITY)

Allegra expects the CD-player project to generate $305,450 of new cash inflows each year. This stream of equal periodic cash flows is an **annuity**. The present value of an annuity is:

$$\text{Periodic Cash Flow} \times \text{Present Value of an Annuity of } \$1$$
$$\text{(Exhibit 26-16 and Appendix C-2)}$$

Exhibit 26-16 shows the present value of annuity factors for various interest rates and numbers of periods. (This is an excerpt from the more-comprehensive table in Appendix C-2.) The present value of an annuity of $1 received each year for five years, discounted at 14% per year, is $3.433. That is, the value today of receiving $1 at the end of each year for the next five years, discounted at 14%, is $3.433. Another way to think about this is that if Allegra invested $3.433 today at a 14% annual interest rate, there would be just enough money to pay out $1 at the end of each year for the next five years.

Exhibit 26-16

Present Value of Annuity of $1

	Present Value of Annuity of $1						
Period	4%	6%	8%	10%	12%	14%	16%
1	0.962	0.943	0.926	0.909	0.893	0.877	0.862
2	1.886	1.833	1.783	1.736	1.690	1.647	1.605
3	2.775	2.673	2.577	2.487	2.402	2.322	2.246
4	3.630	3.465	3.312	3.170	3.037	2.914	2.798
5	4.452	4.212	3.993	3.791	3.605	3.433	3.274
6	5.242	4.917	4.623	4.355	4.111	3.889	3.685
7	6.002	5.582	5.206	4.868	4.564	4.288	4.039
8	6.733	6.210	5.747	5.335	4.968	4.639	4.344
9	7.435	6.802	6.247	5.759	5.328	4.946	4.607
10	8.111	7.360	6.710	6.145	5.650	5.216	4.833

Appendix C-2 provides a more-comprehensive table for the present value of an annuity of $1.

The present value of the cash inflows from Allegra's CD-player project is:

Present Value = Periodic Cash Flow × Present Value of an Annuity of $1
= $305,450   × 3.433
= $1,048,610

After subtracting the $1,000,000 investment, the net present value of the CD-player project is $48,610, as shown in Exhibit 26-17.

	Present Value at 14%	Net Cash Inflow	Total Present Value
Present value of annuity of equal annual net cash inflows for 5 years at 14%........	3.433* × $305,450 per year =		$1,048,610
Investment.............................			(1,000,000)
Net present value of the CD-player project ..			$ 48,610

*Present value of an annuity of $1 for 5 years at 14%.

Exhibit 26-17

Net Present Value with Equal Cash Flows—CD-Player Project

A positive net present value means that the project earns more than the required rate of return. A negative net present value means that the project fails to earn the required rate of return. This leads to the following decision rule:

✔ Starter 26-12

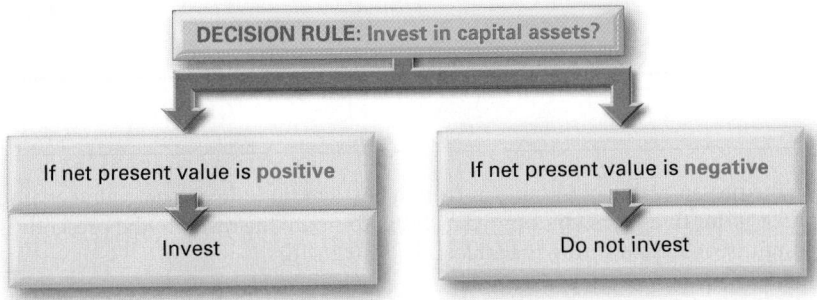

DECISION RULE: Invest in capital assets?

If net present value is positive → Invest

If net present value is negative → Do not invest

In Allegra's case, the $48,610 positive net present value means that the CD-player project earns more than the target 14% rate of return. The project is an attractive investment.

NET PRESENT VALUE WITH UNEQUAL PERIODIC CASH FLOWS In contrast to the CD-player project, the net cash inflows of the VCR project are unequal—$500,000 in year 1, $350,000 in year 2, and so on. Because these amounts vary by year, Allegra's managers cannot use the annuity table in Exhibit 26-16 to compute the present value of the VCR project. They must compute the present value of each individual year's cash flows separately, using the present value of $1 table in Exhibit 26-18 (which is an excerpt from the more-comprehensive table in Appendix C-1).

Present Value of $1							
Period	4%	6%	8%	10%	12%	14%	16%
1	0.962	0.943	0.926	0.909	0.893	0.877	0.862
2	0.925	0.890	0.857	0.826	0.797	0.769	0.743
3	0.889	0.840	0.794	0.751	0.712	0.675	0.641
4	0.855	0.792	0.735	0.683	0.636	0.592	0.552
5	0.822	0.747	0.681	0.621	0.567	0.519	0.476
6	0.790	0.705	0.630	0.564	0.507	0.456	0.410
7	0.760	0.665	0.583	0.513	0.452	0.400	0.354
8	0.731	0.627	0.540	0.467	0.404	0.351	0.305
9	0.703	0.592	0.500	0.424	0.361	0.308	0.263
10	0.676	0.558	0.463	0.386	0.322	0.270	0.227

Appendix C-1 provides a more-comprehensive table for the present value of $1.

Exhibit 26-18

Present Value of $1

Exhibit 26-19 shows that the total present value of the VCR project's net cash inflows is $1,078,910. After subtracting the $1,000,000 investment, the VCR project has a total net present value of $78,910. Allegra expects the VCR project to earn more than the 14% target rate of return, so this is an attractive investment.

| **Exhibit 26-19** | Net Present Value with Unequal Cash Flows—VCR Project |

	Present Value of $1 from Exhibit 26-18, 14% Column		Net Cash Inflow		Present Value of Net Cash Inflow
Present value of each year's net cash inflows discounted at 14%:					
Year 1...	0.877†	×	$500,000	=	$ 438,500
Year 2...	0.769	×	350,000	=	269,150
Year 3...	0.675	×	300,000	=	202,500
Year 4...	0.592	×	250,000	=	148,000
Year 5...	0.519	×	40,000	=	20,760
Total present value of net cash inflows					1,078,910
Investment					(1,000,000)
Net present value of the VCR project.............					$ 78,910

†Present value of $1 in 1 year, 2 years, 3 years, and so on, at 14%, Exhibit 26-18.

Use the present value of $1 table in Exhibit 26-18 to find the present value of an *annuity* of $1 for five years, discounted at 14%. Compare the result to the present value of an annuity of $1 factor from the table in Exhibit 26-16.

Answer: Exhibit 26-18 shows that at a 14% discount rate, the present value of $1 received:

In one year is	$0.877
In two years is	0.769
In three years is	0.675
In four years is	0.592
In five years is	0.519
Total present value of $1 received at the end of each year for five years, discounted at 14% is	$3.432

Except for a slight rounding error, this sum ($3.432) equals the present value of an annuity of $1 for five years discounted at 14%, shown in Exhibit 26-16 ($3.433). This shows how entries in the present value of an annuity table (Exhibit 26-16) are the sums of the present value of $1 factors from Exhibit 26-18.

Exhibits 26-17 and 26-19 show that both projects have positive net present values. Therefore, both are attractive investments. If Allegra wants to pursue only one of the projects, the net present value analysis favors the VCR. This project should earn an additional $78,910 beyond the 14% required rate of return, while the CD-player project returns only an additional $48,610.

This example illustrates an important point. The CD-player project promises more *total* net cash inflows. But the *timing* of the VCR cash flows—loaded near the beginning of the project—gives the VCR investment a higher net present value. The VCR project is more attractive because of the time value of money. Its dollars, which are received sooner, are worth more now than the more-distant dollars of the CD-player project.

SENSITIVITY ANALYSIS   Capital budgeting decisions affect cash flows far into the future. Allegra's managers might want to know whether their decision would be affected by any of their major assumptions. For example:

- Changing the discount rate from 14% to 12% or to 16%
- Changing the net cash flows by 10%

After entering the basic information for net present value analysis into spreadsheet software, managers perform sensitivity analyses with just a few keystrokes. The software quickly recalculates and displays the results.

Suppose Allegra uses a 6% discount rate rather than the 14% rate. Would the net present value of the CD-player project using the 6% rate be higher or lower than the original 14% rate? Why?

Answer: The smaller the discount rate, the higher the present value (today) of dollars to be received in the future. Thus, discounting the cash flows at 6% rather than 14% *increases* the net present value of the CD-player project, as follows:

CD-Player Project	Present Value at 6%		Net Cash Inflow		Total Present Value
Present value of annuity of equal annual net cash inflows for 5 years..........................	4.212*	×	$305,450	=	$1,286,555
Investment...					(1,000,000)
Net present value at 6%.................................					286,555
Net present value at 14% (from Ex. 26-17).....					(48,610)
Difference..					$ 237,945

*Present value of an annuity of $1 for 5 years at 6%, Exhibit 26-16.

Internal Rate of Return

Another discounted cash-flow model for capital budgeting is the internal rate of return. The **internal rate of return (IRR)** is the rate of return (based on discounted cash flows) a company can expect to earn by investing in the project. It is the discount rate that makes the net present value of the project's cash flows equal to zero. The higher the IRR, the more desirable the project.

For projects with equal cash flows each period, like Allegra's CD-player project, use the following three steps to compute the IRR:

1. Identify the expected net cash inflows ($305,450 each year for five years) exactly as in calculating the net present value.

2. Find the discount rate that makes the total present value of the cash inflows equal to the present value of the cash outflows. Work backward to find the discount rate that makes the present value of the annuity of cash inflows equal to the amount of the investment by solving the following equation for the annuity present value (PV) factor:

Internal Rate of Return (IRR)
The rate of return (based on discounted cash flows) that a company can expect to earn by investing in the project. The discount rate that makes the net present value of the project's cash flows equal to zero.

✔ **Starter 26-13**

$$\text{Investment} = \text{Expected annual net cash flow} \times \text{Annuity PV factor}$$

$$\text{Annuity PV factor} = \frac{\text{Investment}}{\text{Expected annual net cash flow}}$$

$$= \frac{\$1,000,000}{\$305,450}$$

$$= 3.274$$

3. Turn to the table presenting the present value of an annuity of $1 (Exhibit 26-16). Scan the row corresponding to the project's expected life—period 5, in our example. Choose the column with the number closest to the annuity PV factor you calculated in step 2. The 3.274 annuity factor is in the 16% column. Therefore, the IRR of the CD-player project is 16%. Allegra expects the project to earn an annual rate of return of 16% over its life. Exhibit 26-20 confirms this result.

| Exhibit 26-20 | Internal Rate of Return, CD-Player Project |

	Present Value at 16%		Net Cash Inflow		Total Present Value
Present value of annuity of equal annual net cash inflows for 5 years at 16%..............	3.274*	×	$305,450	=	$1,000,000†
Investment					(1,000,000)
Net present value of the CD-player project........					$0‡

*Present value of annuity of $1 for 5 years at 16%, Exhibit 26-16.
†Slight rounding error.
‡The zero difference proves that the IRR is 16%.

To decide whether the project is acceptable, compare the IRR with the minimum desired rate of return. The decision rule is:

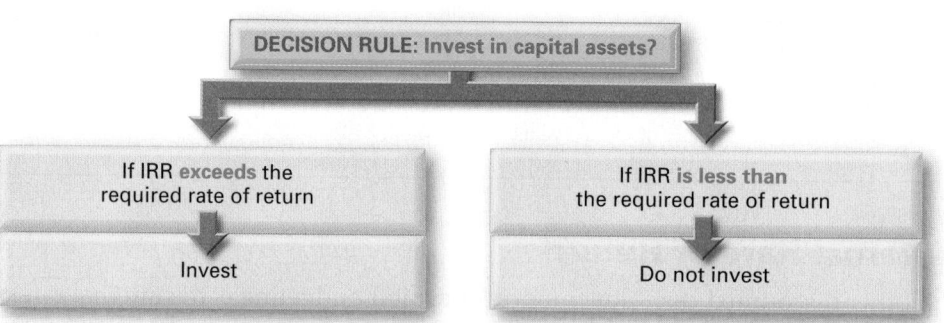

If CD players were the only investment under consideration, Allegra would invest in CD players because their 16% IRR exceeds the 14% discount rate. But recall that the VCR project has a higher net present value. The VCR investment also has a higher IRR. Because the VCR project has unequal cash inflows, however, computation of the VCR's IRR requires a trial-and-error procedure that is covered in more-advanced courses. (Spreadsheet software and even calculators can perform these computations.)

Comparing Capital Budgeting Methods

☐ Relevant Information
☐ Short-Term Special Decisions
☐ Using Payback and ARR
☐ Using Discounted Cash-Flow Models
■ **Comparing Capital Budgeting Methods**

⑤ *Compare and contrast the four capital budgeting methods*

Payback period, net present value, and internal rate of return are all based on *cash inflows and outflows*. Only the accounting rate of return is based on accrual accounting *revenues and expenses*. Payback is the simplest to compute, but it ignores profitability and the time value of money. The accounting rate of return considers profitability, but it also ignores the time value of money. Only net present value and internal rate of return consider the time value of money.

How do the net present value and IRR approaches compare? Net present value indicates the amount of the excess (or deficiency) of a project's present value of net cash inflows over (or under) its cost—at a specified discount rate.

Student ResourceCD

internal rate of return, payback period, present value

But net present value does not show the project's unique rate of return. The internal rate of return shows the project's rate but does not indicate the dollar difference between the project's present value and its investment cost. In many cases, the two discounted cash-flow methods lead to the same investment decision.

The discounted cash-flow methods are superior because they consider both the time value of money and profitability. The time value of money enters the analysis through the discounting of future dollars to present value. Profitability is built into the discounted cash-flow methods because they consider all cash inflows and outflows over the project's life. The payback model considers only the cash flows necessary to recover the initial cash invested.

✔ **Starter 26-14**

Exhibit 26-21 summarizes the strengths and weaknesses of payback, accounting rate of return, and the discounted cash-flow methods. Managers often use more than one method to gain different perspectives on risks and returns. For example, Deer Valley's owners could decide to pursue capital projects with positive net present values, provided that those projects have a payback of four years or less.

Method	Strengths	Weaknesses
Payback	Easy to understand Based on cash flows Highlights risks	Ignores profitability and the time value of money
Accounting rate of return	Based on profitability	Ignores the time value of money
Discounted cash flow: Net present value Internal rate of return	Based on cash flows, profitability, and the time value of money	Difficult to determine discount rate

Exhibit 26-21

Capital Budgeting Methods

A pharmaceutical company is considering two research projects. Project A has a net present value of $232,000 and a 3-year payback period. Project B has a net present value of $237,000 and a payback period of 4.5 years. Which project would you choose?

Answer: Many managers would choose project A. Net present value is a better guide to decision making than payback period. But managers would consider the 2.2% [($237,000 – $232,000)/$232,000] difference between the net present values to be insignificant. In contrast, the 50% [(4.5 years – 3.0 years)/3.0 years] difference between payback periods *is* significant. The uncertainty of receiving operating cash flows increases with each passing year. Managers often forgo small differences in expected cash inflows to decrease the risk of investments.

Decision Guidelines

CAPITAL BUDGETING

Amazon.com started as a virtual retailer. It held no inventory. Instead, it bought books and CDs only as needed to fill customer orders. As the company grew, its managers decided to invest in their own warehouse facilities. Why? Owning warehouse facilities allows Amazon to save money by buying in bulk. Also, shipping all items in the customer's order in one package, from one location, saves shipping costs. Here are some of the guidelines Amazon.com's managers used as they made the major capital budgeting decision to invest in building warehouses.

Decision Guidelines (continued)

Decision	Guideline

Should we make a long-term investment in warehouse facilities?	Investment in warehouse facilities may be worthwhile if:
	
	• Payback period is shorter than warehouse's useful life.
	• Expected accounting rate of return on warehouse exceeds required rate of return.
	• Discounted cash-flow methods:
	   Net present value (NPV) is positive.
	   Internal rate of return (IRR) exceeds required rate of return.

How to compute the payback period?	$$\text{Payback period} = \frac{\text{Amount invested in warehouse}}{\text{Expected annual net cash inflow (from cost savings)}}$$
How to compute the accounting rate of return?	$$\begin{aligned}\text{Accounting rate of return} &= \frac{\text{Average annual operating income (cost savings) from warehouse}}{\text{Average amount invested in warehouse}}\\[2mm] &= \frac{\text{Average annual net cash inflow from warehouse} - \text{Annual depreciation on warehouse}}{(\text{Amount invested in warehouse} + \text{Residual value})/2}\end{aligned}$$
How to compute net present value with • Equal annual cash flows?	$$\begin{array}{c}\text{Present value of}\\\textit{annuity} \text{ of \$1}\\(\text{Exhibit 26-16})\end{array} \times \begin{array}{c}\text{Annual net cash}\\\text{inflow or outflow}\end{array}$$
• Unequal annual cash flows?	Compute the present value of each year's net cash inflow or outflow (present value of \$1 from Exhibit 26-18 × net cash inflow or outflow) and add up yearly present values.
How to compute internal rate of return with • Equal annual cash flows?	$$\begin{array}{c}\text{Annuity PV factor}\\(\text{Use Exhibit 26-16})\end{array} = \frac{\text{Investment in warehouse}}{\text{Expected annual net cash inflow}}$$
• Unequal annual cash flows?	Trial and error, spreadsheet software, or calculator
Which capital budgeting methods are best?	Discounted cash-flow methods (net present value and IRR) are best because they incorporate both profitability and the time value of money.

Excel Application Exercise

Goal: Create a spreadsheet to compute payback period, accounting rate of return, and net present value of a machine.

Scenario: Suppose **Amazon** is considering the purchase of a new bar-coding machine for one of its warehouses. You are asked to prepare a simple analysis to determine whether the machine should be purchased. The summary problem for review at the end of the chapter provides a good outline for completing your analysis.

The bar-coding machine costs \$60,000. It has a five-year useful life with no salvage value. The estimated annual net cash flow from the machine is \$16,000. Assume Amazon's required rate of return is 12%.

When you have completed your worksheet, answer the following questions:

1. What is the machine's payback period?
2. What is the machine's accounting rate of return?
3. What is the machine's net present value (NPV)?
4. Should Amazon purchase the machine? Why or why not?

Step-by-Step:
1. Open a new Excel spreadsheet.
2. In column A, create a bold-faced heading as follows:
   a. Chapter 26 Excel Application Exercise
   b. Capital Budgeting Decision
   c. Amazon
   d. Today's Date

(continued)

3. Two rows down, create a bold-faced and underlined heading titled "Data Section." Enter the data and descriptions provided in the problem under this heading in your spreadsheet.

4. At the end of the Data Section, add a row for "Annual Depreciation on Asset." Use the "SLN" financial function to compute depreciation.

5. Move down two rows. In column A, enter the description "Payback Period (years)." Compute the payback period in column B.

6. Move down one row. In column A, enter the description "Accounting Rate of Return." Compute the accounting rate of return in column B.

7. Move down two rows, and enter "Net Present Value" as a bold-faced and underlined heading.

8. Underneath the heading, use the textbook's Summary Problem format (listed as Requirement 3 on page 1106) to compute net present value. Use the "PV" financial function for the present value of an annuity.

9. Save your file to disk, and print a copy for your files.

END-OF-CHAPTER *Summary Problem*

Zetamax is considering buying a new bar-coding machine for its Austin, Texas, plant. The data for the machine follow:

CHECK YOUR RESOURCES

Cost of machine..	$48,000
Estimated residual value	$ 0
Estimated annual net cash inflow (each year for 5 years)..	$13,000
Estimated useful life.....................................	5 years
Required rate of return.................................	16%

Required

1. Compute the bar-coding machine's payback period.
2. Compute the bar-coding machine's accounting rate of return.
3. Compute the bar-coding machine's net present value.
4. Would you buy the bar-coding machine? Why?

Solution

Requirement 1

$$\text{Payback period} = \frac{\text{Amount invested}}{\text{Expected annual net cash inflow}} = \frac{\$48,000}{\$13,000} = 3.7 \text{ years (rounded)}$$

Requirement 2

$$\text{Accounting rate of return} = \frac{\text{Average annual operating income from asset}}{\text{Average amount invested in asset}}$$

$$= \frac{\text{Average annual net cash inflow from asset} - \text{Annual depreciation on asset}}{(\text{Amount invested in asset} + \text{Residual value})/2}$$

$$= \frac{\$13,000 - \$9,600^*}{(\$48,000 + \$0)/2}$$

$$= \frac{\$3,400}{\$24,000}$$

$$= 0.142 \text{ (rounded)}$$

$$= 14.2\%$$

$$^* \frac{\$48,000}{5 \text{ years}} = \$9,600$$

Requirement 3

Present value of annuity of equal annual net cash inflows at 16% ($13,000 × 3.274†)	$42,562
Investment	(48,000)
Net present value	$(5,438)

†Present value of annuity of $1 for 5 years at 16%, Exhibit 26-16.

Requirement 4

Decision: Do not buy the bar-coding machine because it has a negative net present value. The net present value model considers profitability and the time value of money. The other models ignore at least one of those factors.

REVIEW *Special Business Decisions and Capital Budgeting*

Quick Check

1. In making short-term special decisions, you should:
   a. Focus on total costs
   b. Separate variable from fixed costs
   c. Use a conventional absorption costing approach
   d. Discount cash flows to their present values

2. Which of the following is relevant to **Amazon.com's** decision to accept a special order at a lower sale price from a large customer in China?
   a. The cost of Amazon's warehouses in the United States
   b. Amazon's investment in its Web site
   c. The cost of shipping the order to the customer
   d. Founder Jeff Bezos's salary

3. In deciding whether to drop its electronics product line, Amazon.com would consider:
   a. The costs it could save by dropping the product line
   b. The revenues it would lose from dropping the product line
   c. How dropping the electronics product line would affect sales of its other products like CDs
   d. All of the above

4. In deciding which product lines to emphasize, Amazon.com should focus on the product line that has the highest:
   a. Profit per unit of product
   b. Contribution margin per unit of product
   c. Contribution margin ratio
   d. Contribution margin per unit of the constraining factor

5. Suppose **Deer Valley** is considering whether to (1) bake bread for all its restaurants in-house or (2) buy the bread from a local bakery. The chef estimates that variable costs for each loaf include $0.50 of ingredients and $1.00 of direct labor for kneading and forming the loaves. Allocating fixed overhead (depreciation on the kitchen equipment and building) based on direct labor assigns $1.00 of fixed overhead per loaf. The local bakery charges $1.75 per loaf. Should Deer Valley bake the bread in-house or buy from the local bakery?
   a. There is a $0.25 per loaf advantage to baking the bread in-house.
   b. There is a $1.25 per loaf advantage to baking the bread in-house.
   c. There is a $0.25 per loaf advantage to buying the bread from the local bakery.
   d. There is a $0.75 per loaf advantage to buying the bread from the local bakery.

6. In computing the accounting rate of return on the Snow Park Lodge expansion, Deer Valley would consider all of the following *except*:
   a. Predicted cash inflows over the life of the expansion
   b. The cost of the expansion
   c. Depreciation on the assets built in the expansion
   d. Present value factors

7. Suppose Deer Valley is deciding whether to purchase new accounting software. The payback period for the $30,000 software package is 4 years, and the software's expected life is 6 years. What are the expected annual cash savings from the new software?
   a. $7,500   c. $200
   b. $5,000   d. $130

8. In computing the net present value of the Snow Park Lodge expansion, Deer Valley would consider all of the following *except*:
   a. Predicted cash inflows over the life of the expansion
   b. The cost of the expansion
   c. Depreciation on the assets built in the expansion
   d. The company's required rate of return on investments

9. Suppose Amazon.com is considering investing in warehouse-management software that costs $500,000 and should lead to cost savings of $120,000 a year for its 5-year life. If Amazon has a 12% required rate of return, what is the net present value of the software investment?
   a. ($88,040)   c. $411,960
   b. ($67,400)   d. $432,600

10. Which of the following is the most reliable method for making capital budgeting decisions?
    a. Net present value method   c. Payback method
    b. Accounting rate of return method d. Incremental method

Accounting Vocabulary

accounting rate of return (p. 1096)
annuity (p. 1098)
capital budgeting (p. 1094)
constraint (p. 1085)
cost of capital (p. 1098)
discount rate (p. 1098)

hurdle rate (p. 1098)
internal rate of return (IRR) (p. 1101)
net present value (NPV) (p. 1098)
opportunity cost (p. 1088)
outsourcing (p. 1087)

payback (p. 1094)
relevant information (p. 1080)
required rate of return (p. 1098)
sunk cost (p. 1090)
time value of money (p. 1097)

○ ASSESS *Your Progress*

Starters

S26-1 You are trying to decide whether to trade in your inkjet printer for a more-recent model. Your usage pattern will remain unchanged, but the old and new printers use different ink cartridges. Are the following items relevant or irrelevant to your decision?

a. The price of the new printer
b. The price you paid for the old printer
c. The trade-in value of the old printer
d. Paper costs
e. The difference between ink cartridges' costs

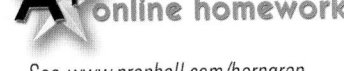

See *www.prenhall.com/horngren* for selected Starters, Exercises, and Problems.

Identifying relevant data
(Obj. 1)

S26-2 Consider the **ACDelco** special sales order example on pages 1082–1084. Suppose that:

a. ACDelco's variable manufacturing cost is $1.35 per oil filter (instead of $1.20).
b. ACDelco would have to buy a special stamping machine that costs $9,000 to mark the customer's logo on the special-order oil filters. The machine would be scrapped when the special order is complete.

Would you recommend that ACDelco accept the special order under these conditions?

Accepting or rejecting a special sales order
(Obj. 2)

Dropping a department
(Obj. 2)

S26-3 Knight Fashion in New York operates three departments: Men's, Women's, and Accessories. Knight Fashion allocates fixed expenses (building depreciation and utilities) based on the square feet occupied by each department. Departmental operating income data for the third quarter of 20X7 are as follows:

| | Department | | | |
	Men's	Women's	Accessories	Total
Sales revenue..................	$105,000	$54,000	$100,000	$259,000
Variable expenses	60,000	30,000	80,000	170,000
Fixed expenses	25,000	20,000	25,000	70,000
Total expenses.................	85,000	50,000	105,000	240,000
Operating income (loss).........	$ 20,000	$ 4,000	$ (5,000)	$ 19,000

Should Knight Fashion drop any of the departments? Give your reason. (The store will remain in the same building regardless of the decision.)

Dropping a department
(Obj. 2)

S26-4 Consider Knight Fashion from Starter 26-3. Assume that the fixed expenses assigned to each department include only:

• Salary of the department's manager

• Cost of advertising directly related to that department

Knight Fashion will not incur these fixed expenses if the department is dropped. Under these circumstances, should Knight Fashion drop any of the departments? Give your reason.

Determining product mix
(Obj. 1, 2)

S26-5 Lifemaster, Inc., produces two types of exercise treadmills: Regular and Deluxe.
   The exercise craze is such that Lifemaster could use all its available machine hours producing either model. The two models are processed through the same production departments.
   What is the constraint? Which model should Lifemaster produce? If both models should be produced, compute the mix that will maximize operating income.

| | Per Unit | |
	Deluxe	Regular
Sale price	$1,000	$550
Costs:		
Direct materials......................	$ 290	$100
Direct labor	80	180
Variable manufacturing overhead*	240	80
Fixed manufacturing overhead*..........	120	40
Variable operating expenses	115	65
Total cost............................	845	465
Operating income......................	$ 155	$ 85

* Allocated on the basis of machine hours.

Outsourcing decision for services
(Obj. 1, 2)

S26-6 U.S. Food Corp. in Lexington, Kentucky, manufactures and markets snack foods. Betsy Gonzalez manages the company's fleet of 200 delivery trucks. Gonzalez has been charged with "reengineering" the fleet-management function. She has an important decision to make.

• Should she continue to manage the fleet in-house with the five employees reporting to her? To do so, she will have to acquire new fleet-management software to streamline U.S. Food's fleet-management process.

• Should she outsource the fleet-management function to Fleet Management Services, a company that specializes in managing fleets of trucks for other companies? Fleet Management Services would take over the maintenance, repair, and scheduling of U.S. Food's fleet (but U.S. Food would retain ownership). This

(continued)

alternative would require Gonzalez to lay off her five employees. However, her own job would be secure as she would be U.S. Food's liaison with Fleet Management Services.

Assume that Gonzalez's records show the following data concerning U.S. Food's fleet:

Book value of U.S. Food's trucks, with an estimated 5-year life....	$3,500,000
Annual leasing fee for new fleet-management software	8,000
Annual maintenance of trucks................................	145,500
Fleet Supervisor Gonzalez's annual salary.....................	60,000
Total annual salaries of U.S. Food's five other fleet-management employees	150,000

Suppose that Fleet Management Services offers to manage U.S. Food's fleet for an annual fee of $290,000.
  Which alternative will maximize U.S. Food's short-term operating income?

S26-7 Refer to U.S. Food Corp. in Starter 26-6. What qualitative factors should Gonzalez consider before making a final decision?

Outsourcing decision for services
(Obj. 2)

S26-8 Auto Components, Inc., has an inventory of 500 obsolete remote entry keys that are carried in inventory at a manufacturing cost of $80,000. Production Supervisor Terri Smith must decide whether to:

- Process the inventory further at a cost of $20,000, with the expectation of selling it for $28,000, or
- Scrap the inventory for a sale price of $6,000

Deciding whether to sell as is or process further **(Obj. 1, 2)**

What should Smith do? Present figures to support your decision.

S26-9 Starters 26-9 through 26-14 consider how **Deer Valley Resort** (from the chapter-opening story) could use capital budgeting methods to decide whether the $13 million Snow Park Lodge expansion would be a good investment.

Computing net cash inflow from project **(Obj. 3)**

  Assume Deer Valley's managers developed the following estimates concerning the expansion (all numbers assumed):

Number of additional skiers per day	120
Average number of days per year that weather conditions allow skiing at Deer Valley....................	150
Useful life of expansion (in years).........................	10
Average cash spent by each skier per day...................	$245
Average variable cost of serving each skier per day	$85
Cost of expansion	$13,000,000
Discount rate	12%

Assume that Deer Valley uses the straight-line depreciation method and expects the lodge expansion to have a residual value of $1 million at the end of its 10-year life.
  Compute the average annual net cash inflow from the expansion.

S26-10 Refer to the Deer Valley Snow Park Lodge expansion project in Starter 26-9. Compute the payback period for the expansion project.

Computing payback period **(Obj. 3)**

S26-11 Refer to the Deer Valley Snow Park Lodge expansion project in Starter 26-9. What is the accounting rate of return?

Computing accounting rate of return **(Obj. 3)**

S26-12 ← *Link Back to Chapter 15 (Present-Value Concepts).* Refer to Starter 26-9. *Assume the expansion has zero residual value.* What is the project's net present value?

Computing net present value **(Obj. 4)**

Computing internal rate of return
(Obj. 4)

S26-13 Refer to Starter 26-9. *Assume the expansion has zero residual value.* What is the project's internal rate of return?

Evaluating results of different capital budgeting methods
(Obj. 5)

S26-14 Use your results from Starters 26-9 through 26-13 to write a memo to Deer Valley Director of Finance Jim Madsen, recommending whether Deer Valley should undertake the expansion. Cover the strengths and weaknesses of each capital budgeting method cited in your memo. Use the following format:

Date: _____
To: Mr. Jim Madsen, Director of Finance
From: _____
Subject: _____

online homework

Exercises

Accepting or rejecting a special sales order
(Obj. 1, 2)

Student Resource**CD**

spreadsheet

E26-1 Suppose the **Baseball Hall of Fame** in Cooperstown, New York, has approached Sports-Cardz, Inc., with a special order. The Hall of Fame wishes to purchase 50,000 baseball card packs for a special promotional campaign and offers $0.40 per pack, a total of $20,000. Sports-Cardz's, total production cost is $0.60 per pack, as follows:

Variable costs:	
Direct materials................................	$0.14
Direct labor	0.08
Variable overhead..............................	0.13
Fixed overhead	0.25
Total cost	$0.60

Sports-Cardz has enough excess capacity to handle the special order.

Required

1. Prepare an incremental analysis to determine whether Sports-Cardz should accept the special sales order.

2. Now assume that the Hall of Fame wants special hologram baseball cards. Sports-Cardz will spend $5,000 to develop this hologram, which will be useless after the special order is completed. Should Sports-Cardz accept the special order under these circumstances?

Deciding on a special sales order
(Obj. 1, 2)

E26-2 Maui Jane sunglasses sell for about $150 per pair. Suppose that the company incurs the following average costs per pair:

Direct materials.......................................	$40
Direct labor	12
Variable manufacturing overhead	8
Variable marketing expenses	4
Fixed manufacturing overhead	20*
Total costs...	$84

$$ * \frac{\$2,000,000 \text{ total fixed manufacturing overhead}}{100,000 \text{ pairs of sunglasses}} $$

Maui Jane has enough idle capacity to accept a one-time-only special order from Lenscrafters for 20,000 pairs of sunglasses at $76 per pair. Maui Jane will not incur any additional variable marketing expenses for the order.

Required

1. How would accepting the order affect Maui Jane's operating income? In addition to the special order's effect on profits, what other (longer-term qualitative) factors should Maui Jane's managers consider in deciding whether to accept the order?

(continued)

2. Maui Jane's marketing manager, Jim Revo, argues against accepting the special order because the offer price of $76 is less than Maui Jane's $84 cost to make the sunglasses. Revo asks you, as one of Maui Jane's staff accountants, to write a memo explaining whether his analysis is correct. Use the format from S26-14.

E26-3 Top managers of Video Avenue are alarmed about their operating losses. They are considering dropping the VCR-tape product line. Company accountants have prepared the following analysis to help make this decision:

Keeping or dropping a product line (fixed costs unchanged)
(Obj. 1, 2)

	Total	DVD Discs	VCR Tapes
Sales revenue	$420,000	$300,000	$120,000
Variable expenses	230,000	150,000	80,000
Contribution margin	190,000	150,000	40,000
Fixed expenses:			
Manufacturing	125,000	70,000	55,000
Marketing and administrative	70,000	55,000	15,000
Total fixed expenses	195,000	125,000	70,000
Operating income (loss)	$ (5,000)	$ 25,000	$ (30,000)

Total fixed costs will not change if the company stops selling VCR tapes.

Prepare an incremental analysis to show whether Video Avenue should drop the VCR-tape product line. Will dropping VCR tapes add $30,000 to operating income? Explain.

E26-4 Refer to Exercise 26-3. Assume that Video Avenue can avoid $30,000 of fixed expenses by dropping the VCR-tape product line. Prepare an incremental analysis to show whether Video Avenue should stop selling VCR tapes.

Keeping or dropping a product line (fixed costs change) **(Obj. 1, 2)**

E26-5 Vivace sells both designer and moderately priced fashion accessories. Top management is deciding which product line to emphasize. Accountants have provided the following data:

Determining product mix
(Obj. 1, 2)

	Per Item	
	Designer	Moderately Priced
Average sale price	$200	$84
Average variable expenses	85	24
Average contribution margin	115	60
Average fixed expenses (allocated)	20	10
Average operating income	$ 95	$50

The Vivace store in Reno, Nevada, has 10,000 square feet of floor space. If it emphasizes moderately priced goods, 650 items can be displayed in the store. If it emphasizes designer wear, only 300 designer items can be displayed. These numbers are also the average monthly sales in units.

Prepare an analysis to show which product to emphasize.

E26-6 Fiber Systems manufactures an optical switch that it uses in its final product. The switch has the following manufacturing costs per unit:

Outsourcing decision
(Obj. 1, 2)

Direct materials	$ 9.00
Direct labor	1.50
Variable overhead	2.00
Fixed overhead	6.50
Manufacturing product cost	$19.00

Student ResourceCD

spreadsheet

Another company has offered to sell Fiber Systems the switch for $14 per unit. If Fiber Systems buys the switch from the outside supplier, the manufacturing facilities that will be idled cannot be used for any other purpose. Should Fiber Systems make or buy the switch?

Determining best use of facilities
(Obj. 1, 2)

Student ResourceCD

spreadsheet

Sell or process further
(Obj. 1, 2)

Computing payback
(Obj. 3)

Determining accounting rate of return
(Obj. 3)

Computing net present value
(Obj. 4)

Student ResourceCD

spreadsheet

Computing internal rate of return
(Obj. 4)

Determining product mix
(Obj. 2)

E26-7 Refer to Exercise 26-6. Fiber Systems needs 80,000 optical switches. By outsourcing them, Fiber Systems can use its idle facilities to manufacture another product that will contribute $220,000 to operating income. Identify the *incremental* costs that Fiber Systems will incur to acquire 80,000 switches under three alternative plans. Which plan makes the best use of Fiber System's facilities? Support your answer.

E26-8 Concert Sounds has damaged some custom speakers that cost the company $10,000 to manufacture. Owner Jim Buffett is considering two options for disposing of this inventory. One plan is to sell the speakers as damaged inventory for $2,500. The alternative is to spend an additional $500 to repair the damage and expect to sell the speakers for $3,100. What should Buffett do? Support your answer with an analysis that shows expected net revenue under each alternative.

E26-9 Quiksilver Co. is considering acquiring a manufacturing plant. The purchase price is $1,236,100. The owners believe the plant will generate net cash inflows of $309,025 annually. It will have to be replaced in 8 years. Use the payback method to determine whether Quiksilver should purchase this plant.

E26-10 Engineered Products is shopping for new equipment. Managers are considering two investments. Equipment manufactured by Atlas, Inc., costs $1,000,000 and will last for five years, with no residual value. The Atlas equipment is expected to generate annual operating income of $160,000. Equipment manufactured by Veras Co. is priced at $1,200,000 and will remain useful for six years. It promises annual operating income of $240,500, and its expected residual value is $100,000.

Which equipment offers the higher accounting rate of return?

E26-11 ← *Link Back to Chapter 15 (Present-Value Concepts).* Use the net present value method to determine whether Salon Products should invest in the following projects:

- *Project A*: Costs $272,000 and offers eight annual net cash inflows of $60,000. Salon Products requires an annual return of 14% on projects like A.

- *Project B*: Costs $380,000 and offers nine annual net cash inflows of $70,000. Salon Products demands an annual return of 12% on investments of this nature.

What is the net present value of each project? What is the maximum acceptable price to pay for each project?

E26-12 Refer to Exercise 26-11. Compute the internal rate of return of each project, and use this information to identify the better investment.

E26-13 Each morning, Max Imery stocks the drink case at Max's Beach Hut in Myrtle Beach, South Carolina. Max's has 100 linear feet of refrigerated display space for cold drinks. Each linear foot can hold either six 12-ounce cans or four 20-ounce plastic or glass bottles. Max's sells three types of cold drinks:

- Coca-Cola in 12-oz. cans, for $1.50 per can
- Coca-Cola in 20-oz. plastic bottles, for $1.75 per bottle
- SoBe in 20-oz. glass bottles, for $2.20 per bottle

Max's pays its suppliers:

- $0.25 per 12-oz. can of Coca-Cola
- $0.40 per 20-oz. bottle of Coca-Cola
- $0.75 per 20-oz. bottle of SoBe

Max's monthly fixed expenses include:

Hut rental	$ 375
Refrigerator rental	75
Max's salary	1,550
Total fixed expenses.	$2,000

(*continued*)

Max's can sell all the drinks stocked in the display case each morning.

1. What is Max's constraining factor? What should Imery stock to maximize profits?
2. Suppose Max's refuses to devote more than 60 linear feet to any individual product. Under this condition, how many linear feet of each drink should Imery stock? How many units of each product will be available for sale each day?

Problems

(Group A)

P26-1A Buoy, Inc. manufactures flotation vests in Tampa, Florida. Buoy's contribution-margin income statement for the most recent month contains the following data:

Accepting or rejecting a special sales order
(Obj. 1, 2)

Sales in units	31,000
Sales revenue.	$434,000
Variable expenses:	
Manufacturing	$ 93,000
Marketing and administrative	107,000
Total variable expenses	200,000
Contribution margin	234,000
Fixed expenses:	
Manufacturing	126,000
Marketing and administrative	90,000
Total fixed expenses.	216,000
Operating income.	$ 18,000

Suppose Overton's wishes to buy 5,000 vests from Buoy. Acceptance of the order will not increase any of Buoy's marketing and administrative expenses. The Buoy plant has enough unused capacity to manufacture the additional vests. Overton's has offered $10.00 per vest, which is below the normal sale price of $14.

Required

1. Prepare an incremental analysis to determine whether Buoy should accept this special sales order.
2. Identify long-term factors Buoy should consider in deciding whether to accept the special sales order.

P26-2A Members of the board of directors of Security Systems, Inc., have received the following operating income data for the year just ended.

Keeping or dropping a product line
(Obj. 1, 2)

	Product Line		
	Industrial Systems	Household Systems	Total
Sales revenue	$300,000	$310,000	$610,000
Cost of goods sold:			
Variable.	$ 38,000	$ 42,000	$ 80,000
Fixed	210,000	69,000	279,000
Total cost of goods sold	248,000	111,000	359,000
Gross profit.	52,000	199,000	251,000
Marketing and administrative expenses:			
Variable.	66,000	71,000	137,000
Fixed	40,000	22,000	62,000
Total marketing and administrative expenses	106,000	93,000	199,000
Operating income (loss).	$(54,000)	$106,000	$ 52,000

Members of the board are surprised that the industrial-systems product line is losing money. They commission a study to determine whether the company should drop the line. Company accountants estimate that dropping industrial systems will decrease fixed cost of goods sold by $80,000 and decrease fixed marketing and administrative expenses by $12,000.

Required

1. Prepare an incremental analysis to show whether Security Systems should drop the industrial-systems product line.

2. Prepare contribution margin income statements to show Security Systems' total operating income under the two alternatives: (a) with the industrial systems line, and (b) without the line. Compare the *difference* between the two alternatives' income numbers to your answer to Requirement 1. What have you learned from this comparison?

Determining product mix
(Obj. 1, 2)

P26-3A Brun Corp., located in St. Cloud, Minnesota, produces two lines of electric toothbrushes: deluxe and standard. Because Brun can sell all the toothbrushes it can produce, the owners are expanding the plant. They are deciding which product line to emphasize. To make this decision, they assemble the following data.

	Per Unit	
	Deluxe Toothbrush	Standard Toothbrush
Sale price.	$80	$48
Variable expenses.	20	18
Contribution margin	$60	$30
Contribution margin ratio	75%	62.5%

After expansion, the factory will have a production capacity of 4,500 machine hours per month. The plant can manufacture either 60 standard electric toothbrushes or 24 deluxe electric toothbrushes per machine hour.

Required

1. Identify the constraining factor for Brun Corp.
2. Prepare an analysis to show which product line to emphasize.

Outsourcing; best use of facilities
(Obj. 1, 2)

P26-4A X-Perience manufactures snow boards. Its cost of making 1,800 bindings is

Direct materials	$17,520
Direct labor.	3,100
Variable overhead	2,080
Fixed overhead	6,800
Total manufacturing costs for 1,800 bindings	$29,500

Suppose O'Brien will sell bindings to X-Perience for $14 each. X-Perience would pay $1 per unit to transport the bindings to its manufacturing plant, where it would add its own logo at a cost of $0.20 per binding.

Required

1. X-Perience's accountants predict that purchasing the bindings from O'Brien will enable the company to avoid $2,200 of fixed overhead. Prepare an analysis to show whether X-Perience should make or buy the bindings.

2. The facilities freed by purchasing bindings from O'Brien can be used to manufacture another product that will contribute $3,100 to profit. Total fixed costs will be the same as if X-Perience had produced the bindings. Show which alternative makes the best use of X-Perience's facilities: (a) make bindings, (b) buy bindings and leave facilities idle, or (c) buy bindings and make another product.

P26-5A Vision Chemical Corporation has spent $240,000 to refine 72,000 gallons of acetone, which can be sold for $2.16 a gallon. Alternatively, Vision can process the acetone further. This processing will yield a total of 60,000 gallons of lacquer thinner that can be sold for $3.20 a gallon. The additional processing will cost $0.62 per gallon of lacquer thinner. To sell the lacquer thinner, Vision must pay shipping of $0.22 a gallon and administrative expenses of $0.10 a gallon on the thinner.

Deciding whether to sell as is or process further
(Obj. 1, 2)

Required

1. Diagram Vision's decision, using Exhibit 26-12 as a guide.

2. Identify the sunk cost. Is the sunk cost relevant to Vision's decision?

3. Should Vision sell the acetone or process it into lacquer thinner? Show the expected net revenue difference between the two alternatives.

P26-6A Water World, Inc. is considering purchasing a water park in San Antonio, Texas, for $1,850,000. The new facility will generate annual net cash inflows of $520,000 for eight years. Engineers estimate that the facility will remain useful for eight years and have no residual value. The company uses straight-line depreciation, and its stockholders demand an annual return of 12% on investments of this nature.

Capital budgeting
(Obj. 3, 4, 5)

Required

1. Compute the payback period, the accounting rate of return, and the net present value of this investment.

2. Make a recommendation whether the company should invest in this project.

P26-7A Locos operates a chain of sandwich shops. The company is considering two possible expansion plans. Plan A would open eight smaller shops at a cost of $8,440,000. Expected annual net cash inflows are $1,600,000, with zero residual value at the end of 10 years. Under plan B, Locos would open three larger shops at a cost of $8,340,000. This plan is expected to generate net cash inflows of $1,100,000 per year for 10 years, the estimated life of the properties. Estimated residual value is $1,000,000. Locos uses straight-line depreciation and requires an annual return of 8%

Capital budgeting
(Obj. 3, 4, 5)

Required

1. Compute the payback period, the accounting rate of return, and the net present value of these two plans. Use the residual value when calculating the accounting rate of return, but *assume a residual value of zero when calculating net present values*. What are the strengths and weaknesses of these capital budgeting models?

2. Which expansion plan should Locos choose? Why?

3. Estimate plan A's internal rate of return (IRR). How does the IRR compare with the company's required rate of return?

Problems

(Group B)

P26-1B United Packaging Co.'s contribution margin income statement follows:

Accepting or rejecting a special sales order
(Obj. 1, 2)

Sales in units	360,000
Sales revenue.	$432,000
Variable expenses:	
Manufacturing	$108,000
Marketing and administrative	53,000
Total variable expenses	161,000
Contribution margin	271,000
Fixed expenses:	
Manufacturing	156,000
Marketing and administrative	40,000
Total fixed expenses.	196,000
Operating income.	$ 75,000

(continued)

Wallace Farms wants to buy 5,000 produce boxes from United. Acceptance of the order will not increase any of United's marketing and administrative expenses. United's plant has enough unused capacity to manufacture the additional boxes. Wallace Farms has offered $0.80 per box, which is considerably below the normal sale price of $1.20.

Required

1. Prepare an incremental analysis to determine whether United Packaging should accept this special sales order.

2. Identify long-term factors that United Packaging should consider in deciding whether to accept the special sales order.

Keeping or dropping a product line
(Obj. 1, 2)

P26-2B The following operating income data of Abalone Seafood highlight the losses of the fresh seafood product line:

| | | Product Line | |
	Total	Fresh Seafood	Frozen Seafood
Sales revenue	$730,500	$190,500	$540,000
Cost of goods sold:			
Variable.	$138,000	$ 44,000	$ 94,000
Fixed	61,000	20,000	41,000
Total cost of goods sold	199,000	64,000	135,000
Gross profit.	531,500	126,500	405,000
Marketing and administrative expenses:			
Variable.	223,000	98,000	125,000
Fixed	93,000	38,000	55,000
Total marketing and administrative expenses	316,000	136,000	180,000
Operating income (loss).	$215,500	$ (9,500)	$225,000

Abalone is considering discontinuing the fresh seafood product line. The company's accountants estimate that dropping the fresh seafood line will decrease fixed cost of goods sold by $16,000 and decrease fixed marketing and administrative expenses by $10,000.

Required

1. Prepare an incremental analysis to show whether Abalone should drop the fresh seafood product line.

2. Prepare contribution margin income statements to compare Abalone's total operating income (a) with the fresh seafood product line, and (b) without it. Compare the *difference* between the two alternatives' income numbers to your answer to Requirement 1. What have you learned from this comparison?

Determining product mix
(Obj. 1, 2)

P26-3B Easy Living of Charlotte, North Carolina, specializes in outdoor furniture and spas. Owner Linda Spring is expanding the store. She is deciding which product line to emphasize. To make this decision, she assembles the following data:

| | Per Unit | |
	Spas	Patio Sets
Sale price.	$1,000	$800
Variable expenses.	480	440
Contribution margin	$ 520	$360
Contribution margin ratio	52%	45%

(*continued*)

After renovation, the store will have 8,000 square feet of floor space. By devoting the new floor space to patio sets, Easy Living can display 60 patio sets. Alternatively, Easy Living could display 30 spas. Spring expects monthly sales to equal the maximum number of units displayed.

Required

1. Identify the constraining factor for Easy Living.

2. Prepare an analysis to show which product line to emphasize.

P26-4B Morning Grain, Inc., makes organic cereal. Cost data for producing 140,000 boxes of cereal each year are as follows:

Outsourcing; best use of facilities
(Obj. 1, 2)

Direct materials	$220,000
Direct labor.	140,000
Variable overhead	60,000
Fixed overhead	440,000
Total manufacturing costs	$860,000

Suppose Kellogg will sell Morning Grain the cereal for $4 a box. Morning Grain would also pay $0.19 a box to transport the cereal to its warehouse.

Required

1. Morning Grain's accountants predict that purchasing the cereal from Kellogg will enable the company to avoid $140,000 of fixed overhead. Prepare an analysis to show whether Morning Grain should make or buy the cereal.

2. Assume that the Morning Grain facilities freed up by purchasing the cereal from Kellogg can be used to manufacture snack bars that will contribute $180,000 to profit. Total fixed costs will be the same as if Morning Grain used the plant to make cereal. Prepare an analysis to show which alternative makes the best use of Morning Grain's facilities: (a) make cereal, (b) buy cereal and leave facilities idle, or (c) buy cereal and make snack bars.

P26-5B Acme Petroleum has spent $200,000 to refine 60,000 gallons of petroleum distillate. Suppose Acme can sell the distillate for $6 a gallon. Alternatively, it can process the distillate further and produce cleaner fluid. The additional processing will cost another $1.75 a gallon and the cleaner can be sold for $8.50 a gallon. To sell cleaner fluid, Acme must pay a sales commission of $0.10 a gallon and a transportation charge of $0.15 a gallon.

Deciding whether to sell as is or process further
(Obj. 1, 2)

Required

1. Diagram Acme's alternatives, using Exhibit 26-12 as a guide.

2. Identify the sunk cost. Is the sunk cost relevant to Acme's decision?

3. Prepare an analysis to indicate whether Acme should sell the distillate or process it into cleaner. Show the expected net revenue difference between the two alternatives.

P26-6B Zippi Co. manufactures motorized scooters in Oakland, California. The company is considering an expansion. The plan calls for a construction cost of $5,200,000. The expansion will generate annual net cash inflows of $675,000 for 10 years. Engineers estimate that the new facilities will remain useful for 10 years and have no residual value. The company uses straight-line depreciation, and its stockholders demand an annual return of 10% on investments of this nature.

Capital budgeting
(Obj. 3, 4, 5)

Required

1. Compute the payback period, the accounting rate of return, and the net present value of this investment.

2. Make a recommendation whether the company should invest in this project.

Capital budgeting
(Obj. 3, 4, 5)

P26-7B Java Café is considering two possible expansion plans. Plan A is to open 8 cafés at a cost of $4,180,000. Expected annual net cash inflows are $780,000, with residual value of $820,000 at the end of seven years. Under plan B, Java Café would open 12 cafés at a cost of $4,200,000. This investment is expected to generate net cash inflows of $994,000 each year for seven years, which is the estimated useful life of the properties. Estimated residual value of the plan B cafés is zero. Java Café uses straight-line depreciation and requires an annual return of 14%.

Required

1. Compute the payback period, the accounting rate of return, and the net present value of each plan. Use the residual value when calculating the accounting rate of return, but *assume a zero residual value when calculating the net present values*. What are the strengths and weaknesses of these capital budgeting models?
2. Which expansion plan should Java Café adopt? Why?
3. Estimate the internal rate of return (IRR) for plan B. How does plan B's IRR compare with Java Café's required rate of return?

APPLY *Your Knowledge*

Decision Cases

Outsourcing e-mail
(Obj. 1, 2)

Case 1. BKFin.com provides banks access to sophisticated financial information and analysis systems over the Web. The company combines these tools with benchmarking data access, including e-mail and wireless communications, so that banks can instantly evaluate individual loan applications and entire loan portfolios.

BKFin.com's CEO Jon Wise is happy with the company's growth. To better focus on client service, Wise is considering outsourcing some functions. CFO Jenny Lee suggests that the company's e-mail may be the place to start. She recently attended a conference and learned that companies like **Continental Airlines, DellNet, GTE**, and **NBC** were outsourcing their e-mail function. Wise asks Lee to identify costs related to BKFin.com's in-house **Microsoft** Exchange mail application, which has 2,300 mailboxes. This information follows:

Variable costs:	
E-mail license	$7 per mailbox per month
Virus protection license	$1 per mailbox per month
Other variable costs	$8 per mailbox per month
Fixed costs:	
Computer hardware costs	$94,300 per month
$8,050 monthly salary for two information technology staff members who work only on e-mail	$16,100 per month

Required

1. Compute the *total cost* per mailbox per month of BKFin.com's current e-mail function.
2. Suppose **Mail.com**, a leading provider of Internet messaging outsourcing services, offers to host BKFin.com's e-mail function for $9 per mailbox per month. If BKFin.com outsources its e-mail to Mail.com, BKFin.com will still need the virus protection software, its computer hardware, and one information technology staff member, who would be responsible for maintaining virus protection, quarantining suspicious e-mail, and managing content (e.g., screening e-mail for objectionable content). Should CEO Wise accept Mail.com's offer?

(continued)

3. Suppose for an additional $5 per mailbox per month, Mail.com will also provide virus protection, quarantine, and content-management services. Outsourcing these additional functions would mean that BKFin.com would not need either an e-mail information technology staff member or the separate virus protection license. Should CEO Wise outsource these extra services to Mail.com?

Case 2. Ted Christensen, a second-year business student at the University of Utah, will graduate in two years with an accounting major and a Spanish minor. Christensen is trying to decide where to work this summer. He has two choices: work full-time for a bottling plant or work part-time in the Accounting Department of a meat-packing plant. He probably will work at the same place next summer as well. He is able to work 12 weeks during the summer.

Analyzing relevant factors in an employment decision
(Obj. 1, 4)

   The bottling plant will pay Christensen $380 per week this year and 7% more next year. At the meat-packing plant, he could work 20 hours per week at $8.75 per hour. By working only part-time, he could take two accounting courses this summer. Tuition is $225 per hour for each of the four-hour courses. Christensen believes that the experience he gains this summer will qualify him for a full-time accounting position with the meat-packing plant next year. That position will pay $550 per week.

   Christensen sees two additional benefits of working part-time this summer. First, he could reduce his workload during the fall and spring semesters by one course each term. Second, he would have the time to work as a grader in the university's Accounting Department during the 15-week fall term. Grading pays $50 per week.

Required

1. Suppose that Ted Christensen ignores the time value of money in decisions that cover this short a time period. Suppose also that his sole goal is to make as much money as possible between now and the end of next summer. What should he do? What would *you* do if you were faced with these alternatives?

2. Now suppose that Christensen considers the time value of money for all cash flows that he expects to receive one year or more in the future. Which alternative does this consideration favor? Why?

Ethical Issue

→ *Link Back to the IMA Ethical Guidelines in Chapter 19.* Mary Tan is the controller for Duck Associates, a property management company in Portland, Oregon. Each year Tan and payroll clerk Toby Stock meet with the external auditors about payroll accounting. This year, the auditors suggest that Tan consider outsourcing Duck Associates' payroll accounting to a company specializing in payroll processing services. This would allow Tan and her staff to focus on their primary responsibility: accounting for the properties under management. At present, payroll requires 1.5 employee positions—payroll clerk Toby Stock and a bookkeeper who spends half her time entering payroll data in the system.

Make or buy decision
(Obj. 1, 2)

   Tan considers this suggestion, and she lists the following items relating to outsourcing payroll accounting:

a. The current payroll software that was purchased for $4,000 three years ago would not be needed if payroll processing were outsourced.
b. Duck's bookkeeper would spend half her time preparing the weekly payroll input form that is given to the payroll processing service. She is paid $450 a week.
c. Duck Associates would no longer need payroll clerk Toby Stock, whose annual salary is $42,000.
d. The payroll processing service would charge $2,000 a month.

Required

1. Would outsourcing the payroll function increase or decrease Duck Associates' operating income?

(continued)

2. Tan believes that outsourcing payroll would simplify her job, but she does not like the prospect of having to lay off Toby Stock, who has become a close personal friend. She does not believe there is another position available for Stock at his current salary. Can you think of other factors that might support keeping Stock, rather than outsourcing payroll processing? How should each of the factors affect Tan's decision if she wants to do what is best for Duck and act ethically?

Financial Statement Case

Computing payback period and NPV of investments
(Obj. 3, 4)

In creating **Amazon.com**, CEO Jeff Bezos realized the importance of investing in technology. Brick and mortar retailers rely on convenient store location to attract shoppers. Bezos saw that technology could create the same competitive edge for Internet shopping. He invested heavily in technology to make Amazon.com a leader in both: (1) Web site design to facilitate customers' purchases, and (2) warehouse operations to deliver those purchases quickly.

Required

1. Notes to the Consolidated Financial Statements in Amazon.com's 2002 Annual Report (in Appendix A of this book) describe the company's accounting policies. Look at notes 1 and 3.
   a. What depreciation method does Amazon.com use?
   b. What is the range of useful lives over which Amazon.com depreciates its fixed assets?
   c. Identify the types of assets Amazon.com includes in fixed assets. For each type of asset, would the useful life fall toward the shorter or longer end of the range?

2. Amazon.com's 2002 Consolidated Financial Statements indicate a cash outflow of $39,163,000 for investment in fixed assets. Assume that these investments have an average useful life of four years and that Amazon.com requires a 14% rate of return on such investments. Compute the minimum average annual net cash inflow that would justify this investment.

3. For the investment of $39,163,000, and using the average annual net cash inflows calculated in Requirement 2, determine the investment's (a) payback period and (b) accounting rate of return. Assume a zero residual value.

4. Compare the average payback period calculated in Requirement 3 to the estimated useful lives of the different assets identified in Requirement 1. When different assets have very different estimated useful lives, what are the implications for using the payback model to make investment decisions?

Team Project

Identifying relevant data, outsourcing, capital budgeting
(Obj. 1, 2, 3, 4)

John Menard is the founder and sole owner of **Menards, Inc.**. Analysts have estimated that his chain of home improvement stores scattered around nine midwestern states generate about $3 billion in annual sales. But how can Menards compete with giant **Home Depot**?

Suppose Menard is trying to decide whether to invest $45 million in a state-of-the-art manufacturing plant in Eau Claire, Wisconsin. Menard expects the plant would operate for 15 years, after which it would have no residual value. The plant would produce Menards' own line of Formica countertops, cabinets, and picnic tables.

Suppose Menards would incur the following unit costs in producing its own product lines:

	Per Unit		
	Countertops	**Cabinets**	**Picnic Tables**
Direct materials..................	$15	$10	$25
Direct labor	10	5	15
Variable manufacturing overhead ..	5	2	6

(continued)

Rather than making these products, assume Menards could buy them from outside suppliers. Suppliers would charge Menards $40 per countertop, $25 per cabinet, and $65 per picnic table.

Whether Menard makes or buys these products, assume that he expects the following annual sales:

- Countertops—487,200 at $130 each
- Picnic tables—100,000 at $225 each
- Cabinets—150,000 at $75 each

If "making" is sufficiently more profitable than outsourcing, Menard will build the new plant. John Menard has asked your consulting group for a recommendation. Menard uses a 14% discount rate and the straight-line depreciation method.

Required

1. Are the following items relevant or irrelevant in Menard's decision to build a new plant that will manufacture his own products?
   a. The unit sale prices of the countertops, cabinets, and picnic tables (the sale prices that Menards charges its customers)
   b. The prices outside suppliers would charge Menards for the three products, if Menards decides to outsource the products rather than make them
   c. The $45 million to build the new plant
   d. The direct materials, direct labor, and variable overhead Menards would incur to manufacture the three product lines
   e. Menard's salary

2. Determine whether Menards should make or outsource the countertops, cabinets, and picnic tables, *assuming that the company has already built the plant and therefore has the manufacturing capacity to produce these products*. In other words, what is the annual difference in cash flows if Menards decides to make rather than outsource each of these three products?

3. In requirement 2, you computed the annual difference in cash flows if Menards decides to make rather than buy the three products. To analyze the investment in the plant relative to the alternative of outsourcing the products, use this *difference* in annual cash flows to compute the following for the investment in the new plant:
   a. Payback period   c. Net present value
   b. Accounting rate of return   d. Internal rate of return
   (*Hint*: Base the benefit side of your computations on the *difference* in annual cash flows you computed in requirement 2, *not* the total expected cash flows from building the plant. Use the present value tables in Appendix C.)

4. Write a memo giving your recommendation to John Menard. The memo should clearly state your recommendation, along with a brief summary of the reasons for your recommendation. Use the memo format outlined in Starter 26-14.

For Internet exercises, go to the Web site www.prenhall.com/horngren.

2 0 0 2

amazon.com®

ANNUAL REPORT (EXCERPTED)

amazon.com.

To our shareholders:

In many ways, Amazon.com is not a normal store. We have deep selection that is unconstrained by shelf space. We turn our inventory 19 times in a year. We personalize the store for each and every customer. We trade real estate for technology (which gets cheaper and more capable every year). We display customer reviews critical of our products. You can make a purchase with a few seconds and one click. We put used products next to new ones so you can choose. We share our prime real estate—our product detail pages—with third parties, and, if they can offer better value, we let them.

One of our most exciting peculiarities is poorly understood. People see that we're determined to offer both world-leading customer experience *and* the lowest possible prices, but to some this dual goal seems paradoxical if not downright quixotic. Traditional stores face a time-tested tradeoff between offering high-touch customer experience on the one hand and the lowest possible prices on the other. How can Amazon.com be trying to do both?

The answer is that we transform much of customer experience—such as unmatched selection, extensive product information, personalized recommendations, and other new software features—into largely a fixed expense. With customer experience costs largely fixed (more like a publishing model than a retailing model), our costs as a percentage of sales can shrink rapidly as we grow our business. Moreover, customer experience costs that remain variable—such as the variable portion of fulfillment costs—improve in our model as we reduce defects. Eliminating defects improves costs and leads to better customer experience.

We believe our ability to lower prices and simultaneously drive customer experience is a big deal, and this past year offers evidence that the strategy is working.

First, we do continue to drive customer experience. The holiday season this year is one example. While delivering a record number of units to customers, we also delivered our best-ever experience. Cycle time, the amount of time taken by our fulfillment centers to process an order, improved 17% compared with last year. And our most sensitive measure of customer satisfaction, contacts per order, saw a 13% improvement.

Inside existing product categories, we've worked hard to increase selection. Electronics selection is up over 40% in the U.S. alone over the prior year, and we now offer 10 times the selection of a typical big box electronics store. Even in U.S. books, where we've been working for 8 years, we increased selection by 15%, mostly in harder-to-find and out-of-print titles. And, of course, we've added new categories. Our Apparel and Accessories store has more than 500 top clothing brands, and in its first 60 days, customers bought 153,000 shirts, 106,000 pairs of pants, and 31,000 pairs of underwear.

In this year's American Customer Satisfaction Index, the most authoritative study of customer satisfaction, Amazon.com scored an 88, the highest score ever recorded—not just online, not just in retailing—but the highest score ever recorded in any service industry. In ACSI's words:

"Amazon.com continues to show remarkably high levels of customer satisfaction. With a score of 88 (up 5%), it is generating satisfaction at a level unheard of in the service industry.... Can customer satisfaction for Amazon climb more? The latest ACSI data suggest that it is indeed possible. Both service and the value proposition offered by Amazon have increased at a steep rate."

Second, while focused on customer experience, we've also been lowering price substantially. We've been doing so broadly across product categories, from books to electronics, and we've eliminated shipping fees with our 365 day-per-year Free Super Saver Shipping on orders over $25. We've been taking similar actions in every country in which we do business.

Our pricing objective is not to discount a small number of products for a limited period of time, but to offer low prices everyday and apply them broadly across our entire product range. To illustrate this point, we recently did a price comparison versus a major well-known chain of book superstores. We did not hand pick a choice group of books against which we wanted to compare. Instead, we used their published list of their 100 bestsellers for 2002. It was a good representation of the kinds of books people buy most, consisting of 45 hardcover titles and 55 paperbacks across many different categories, including Literature, Romance, Mystery and Thrillers, Nonfiction, Children's, Self-Help, and so on.

We priced all 100 titles by visiting their superstores in both Seattle and New York City. It took us six hours in four of their different superstores to find all 100 books on their list. When we added up everything we spent, we discovered that:

- At their stores, these 100 bestselling books cost $1,561. At Amazon.com, the same books cost $1,195 for a total savings of $366, or 23%.

- For 72 of the 100 books, our price was cheaper. On 25 of the books, our price was the same. On 3 of the 100, their prices were better (we subsequently reduced our prices on these three books).

- In these physical-world superstores, only 15 of their 100 titles were discounted—they were selling the other 85 at full list price. At Amazon.com, 76 of the 100 were discounted and 24 were sold at list price.

To be sure, you may find reasons to shop in the physical world—for instance, if you need something immediately—but, if you do so, you'll be paying a premium. If you want to save money and time, you'll do better by shopping at Amazon.com.

Third, our determination to deliver low price *and* customer experience is generating financial results. Net sales this year increased 26% to a record $3.9 billion, and unit sales grew at an even faster 34%. Free cash flow—our most important financial measure—reached $135 million, a $305 million improvement over the prior year.[1]

In short, what's good for customers is good for shareholders.

Once again this year, I attach a copy of our original 1997 letter and encourage current and prospective shareowners to take a look at it. Given how much we've grown and how much the Internet has evolved, it's notable that the fundamentals of how we do business remain the same.

As always, we at Amazon.com are grateful to our customers for their business and trust, to each other for our hard work, and to our shareholders for their support and encouragement.

Jeffrey P. Bezos
Founder and Chief Executive Officer
Amazon.com, Inc.

---

[1] Free cash flow for 2002 of $135 million is net cash provided by operating activities of $174 million less purchases of fixed assets of $39 million. Free cash flow for 2001 of negative $170 million is net cash used in operating activities of $120 million less purchases of fixed assets of $50 million.

REPORT OF ERNST & YOUNG LLP, INDEPENDENT AUDITORS

The Board of Directors and Stockholders
Amazon.com, Inc.

We have audited the accompanying consolidated balance sheets of Amazon.com, Inc. as of December 31, 2002 and 2001, and the related consolidated statements of operations, stockholders' equity (deficit) and cash flows for each of the three years in the period ended December 31, 2002. Our audits also included the financial statement schedule listed at Item 15(a)(2). These financial statements and schedule are the responsibility of the Company's management. Our responsibility is to express an opinion on these financial statements and schedule based on our audits.

We conducted our audits in accordance with auditing standards generally accepted in the United States. Those standards require that we plan and perform the audit to obtain reasonable assurance about whether the financial statements are free of material misstatement. An audit includes examining, on a test basis, evidence supporting the amounts and disclosures in the financial statements. An audit also includes assessing the accounting principles used and significant estimates made by management, as well as evaluating the overall financial statement presentation. We believe that our audits provide a reasonable basis for our opinion.

In our opinion, the financial statements referred to above present fairly, in all material respects, the consolidated financial position of Amazon.com, Inc. at December 31, 2002 and 2001, and the consolidated results of its operations and its cash flows for each of the three years in the period ended December 31, 2002, in conformity with accounting principles generally accepted in the United States. Also, in our opinion, the related financial statement schedule, when considered in relation to the basic financial statements taken as a whole, presents fairly in all material respects the information set forth therein.

As discussed in Note 1 to the consolidated financial statements, the Company adopted the full provisions of Statement of Financial Accounting Standards No. 141, Business Combinations, and No. 142, Goodwill and Other Intangible Assets, effective January 1, 2002. The Company also adopted Statement of Financial Accounting Standards No. 133, Accounting for Derivative Instruments and Hedging Activities, effective January 1, 2001. In addition, as discussed in Note 1 to the consolidated financial statements, effective January 1, 2002, the Company prospectively changed its inventory costing method to the first-in first-out method of accounting.

/s/ ERNST & YOUNG LLP

Seattle, Washington
January 17, 2003

1997 LETTER TO SHAREHOLDERS
(Reprinted from the 1997 Annual Report)

To our shareholders:

Amazon.com passed many milestones in 1997: by year-end, we had served more than 1.5 million customers, yielding 838% revenue growth to $147.8 million, and extended our market leadership despite aggressive competitive entry.

But this is Day 1 for the Internet and, if we execute well, for Amazon.com. Today, online commerce saves customers money and precious time. Tomorrow, through personalization, online commerce will accelerate the very process of discovery. Amazon.com uses the Internet to create real value for its customers and, by doing so, hopes to create an enduring franchise, even in established and large markets.

We have a window of opportunity as larger players marshal the resources to pursue the online opportunity and as customers, new to purchasing online, are receptive to forming new relationships. The competitive landscape has continued to evolve at a fast pace. Many large players have moved online with credible offerings and have devoted substantial energy and resources to building awareness, traffic, and sales. Our goal is to move quickly to solidify and extend our current position while we begin to pursue the online commerce opportunities in other areas. We see substantial opportunity in the large markets we are targeting. This strategy is not without risk: it requires serious investment and crisp execution against established franchise leaders.

It's All About the Long Term

We believe that a fundamental measure of our success will be the shareholder value we create over the *long term*. This value will be a direct result of our ability to extend and solidify our current market leadership position. The stronger our market leadership, the more powerful our economic model. Market leadership can translate directly to higher revenue, higher profitability, greater capital velocity, and correspondingly stronger returns on invested capital.

Our decisions have consistently reflected this focus. We first measure ourselves in terms of the metrics most indicative of our market leadership: customer and revenue growth, the degree to which our customers continue to purchase from us on a repeat basis, and the strength of our brand. We have invested and will continue to invest aggressively to expand and leverage our customer base, brand, and infrastructure as we move to establish an enduring franchise.

Because of our emphasis on the long term, we may make decisions and weigh tradeoffs differently than some companies. Accordingly, we want to share with you our fundamental management and decision-making approach so that you, our shareholders, may confirm that it is consistent with your investment philosophy:

- We will continue to focus relentlessly on our customers.

- We will continue to make investment decisions in light of long-term market leadership considerations rather than short-term profitability considerations or short-term Wall Street reactions.

- We will continue to measure our programs and the effectiveness of our investments analytically, to jettison those that do not provide acceptable returns, and to step up our investment in those that work best. We will continue to learn from both our successes and our failures.

- We will make bold rather than timid investment decisions where we see a sufficient probability of gaining market leadership advantages. Some of these investments will pay off, others will not, and we will have learned another valuable lesson in either case.

- When forced to choose between optimizing the appearance of our GAAP accounting and maximizing the present value of future cash flows, we'll take the cash flows.

- We will share our strategic thought processes with you when we make bold choices (to the extent competitive pressures allow), so that you may evaluate for yourselves whether we are making rational long-term leadership investments.

- We will work hard to spend wisely and maintain our lean culture. We understand the importance of continually reinforcing a cost-conscious culture, particularly in a business incurring net losses.

- We will balance our focus on growth with emphasis on long-term profitability and capital management. At this stage, we choose to prioritize growth because we believe that scale is central to achieving the potential of our business model.

- We will continue to focus on hiring and retaining versatile and talented employees, and continue to weight their compensation to stock options rather than cash. We know our success will be largely affected by our ability to attract and retain a motivated employee base, each of whom must think like, and therefore must actually be, an owner.

We aren't so bold as to claim that the above is the "right" investment philosophy, but it's ours, and we would be remiss if we weren't clear in the approach we have taken and will continue to take.

With this foundation, we would like to turn to a review of our business focus, our progress in 1997, and our outlook for the future.

Obsess Over Customers

From the beginning, our focus has been on offering our customers compelling value. We realized that the Web was, and still is, the World Wide Wait. Therefore, we set out to offer customers something they simply could not get any other way, and began serving them with books. We brought them much more selection than was possible in a physical store (our store would now occupy 6 football fields), and presented it in a useful, easy-to-search, and easy-to-browse format in a store open 365 days a year, 24 hours a day. We maintained a dogged focus on improving the shopping experience, and in 1997 substantially enhanced our store. We now offer customers gift certificates, 1-Click^{SM} shopping, and vastly more reviews, content, browsing options, and recommendation features. We dramatically lowered prices, further increasing customer value. Word of mouth remains the most powerful customer acquisition tool we have, and we are grateful for the trust our customers have placed in us. Repeat purchases and word of mouth have combined to make Amazon.com the market leader in online bookselling.

By many measures, Amazon.com came a long way in 1997:

- Sales grew from $15.7 million in 1996 to $147.8 million—an 838% increase.

- Cumulative customer accounts grew from 180,000 to 1,510,000—a 738% increase.

- The percentage of orders from repeat customers grew from over 46% in the fourth quarter of 1996 to over 58% in the same period in 1997.

- In terms of audience reach, per Media Metrix, our Web site went from a rank of 90th to within the top 20.

- We established long-term relationships with many important strategic partners, including America Online, Yahoo!, Excite, Netscape, GeoCities, AltaVista, @Home, and Prodigy.

Infrastructure

During 1997, we worked hard to expand our business infrastructure to support these greatly increased traffic, sales, and service levels:

- Amazon.com's employee base grew from 158 to 614, and we significantly strengthened our management team.

- Distribution center capacity grew from 50,000 to 285,000 square feet, including a 70% expansion of our Seattle facilities and the launch of our second distribution center in Delaware in November.

- Inventories rose to over 200,000 titles at year-end, enabling us to improve availability for our customers.

- Our cash and investment balances at year-end were $125 million, thanks to our initial public offering in May 1997 and our $75 million loan, affording us substantial strategic flexibility.

Our Employees

The past year's success is the product of a talented, smart, hard-working group, and I take great pride in being a part of this team. Setting the bar high in our approach to hiring has been, and will continue to be, the single most important element of Amazon.com's success.

It's not easy to work here (when I interview people I tell them, "You can work long, hard, or smart, but at Amazon.com you can't choose two out of three"), but we are working to build something important, something that matters to our customers, something that we can all tell our grandchildren about. Such things aren't meant to be easy. We are incredibly fortunate to have this group of dedicated employees whose sacrifices and passion build Amazon.com.

Goals for 1998

We are still in the early stages of learning how to bring new value to our customers through Internet commerce and merchandising. Our goal remains to continue to solidify and extend our brand and customer base. This requires sustained investment in systems and infrastructure to support outstanding customer convenience, selection, and service while we grow. We are planning to add music to our product offering, and over time we believe that other products may be prudent investments. We also believe there are significant opportunities to better serve our customers overseas, such as reducing delivery times and better tailoring the customer experience. To be certain, a big part of the challenge for us will lie not in finding new ways to expand our business, but in prioritizing our investments.

We now know vastly more about online commerce than when Amazon.com was founded, but we still have so much to learn. Though we are optimistic, we must remain vigilant and maintain a sense of urgency. The challenges and hurdles we will face to make our long-term vision for Amazon.com a reality are several: aggressive, capable, well-funded competition; considerable growth challenges and execution risk; the risks of product and geographic expansion; and the need for large continuing investments to meet an expanding market opportunity. However, as we've long said, online bookselling, and online commerce in general, should prove to be a very large market, and it's likely that a number of companies will see significant benefit. We feel good about what we've done, and even more excited about what we want to do.

1997 was indeed an incredible year. We at Amazon.com are grateful to our customers for their business and trust, to each other for our hard work, and to our shareholders for their support and encouragement.

Jeffrey P. Bezos
Founder and Chief Executive Officer
Amazon.com, Inc.

AMAZON.COM, INC.
CONSOLIDATED BALANCE SHEETS

	December 31, 2002	December 31, 2001
	(In thousands, except per share data)	

ASSETS

Current assets:		
Cash and cash equivalents	$ 738,254	$ 540,282
Marketable securities	562,715	456,303
Inventories	202,425	143,722
Accounts receivable, net and other current assets	112,282	67,613
Total current assets	1,615,676	1,207,920
Fixed assets, net	239,398	271,751
Goodwill, net	70,811	45,367
Other intangibles, net	3,460	34,382
Other equity investments	15,442	28,359
Other assets	45,662	49,768
Total assets	$ 1,990,449	$ 1,637,547

LIABILITIES AND STOCKHOLDERS' DEFICIT

Current liabilities:		
Accounts payable	$ 618,128	$ 444,748
Accrued expenses and other current liabilities	314,935	305,064
Unearned revenue	47,916	87,978
Interest payable	71,661	68,632
Current portion of long-term debt and other	13,318	14,992
Total current liabilities	1,065,958	921,414
Long-term debt and other	2,277,305	2,156,133
Commitments and contingencies		
Stockholders' deficit:		
Preferred stock, $0.01 par value:		
Authorized shares — 500,000		
Issued and outstanding shares — none	—	—
Common stock, $0.01 par value:		
Authorized shares — 5,000,000		
Issued and outstanding shares — 387,906 and 373,218 shares, respectively	3,879	3,732
Additional paid-in capital	1,649,946	1,462,769
Deferred stock-based compensation	(6,591)	(9,853)
Accumulated other comprehensive income (loss)	9,662	(36,070)
Accumulated deficit	(3,009,710)	(2,860,578)
Total stockholders' deficit	(1,352,814)	(1,440,000)
Total liabilities and stockholders' deficit	$ 1,990,449	$ 1,637,547

See accompanying notes to consolidated financial statements.

AMAZON.COM, INC.

CONSOLIDATED STATEMENTS OF OPERATIONS (Adapted)

	Years Ended December 31,		
	2002	2001	2000
	(In thousands, except per share data)		
Net sales	$3,932,936	$3,122,433	$ 2,761,983
Cost of sales	2,940,318	2,323,875	2,106,206
Gross profit	992,618	798,558	655,777
Operating expenses:			
Fulfillment	392,467	374,250	414,509
Marketing	125,383	138,283	179,980
Technology and content	215,617	241,165	269,326
General and administrative	79,049	89,862	108,962
Stock-based compensation	68,927	4,637	24,797
Amortization of goodwill and other intangibles	5,478	181,033	321,772
Restructuring-related and other	41,573	181,585	200,311
Total operating expenses	928,494	1,210,815	1,519,657
Income (loss) from operations	64,124	(412,257)	(863,880)
Interest income	23,687	29,103	40,821
Interest expense	(142,925)	(139,232)	(130,921)
Other income (expense), net	5,623	(1,900)	(10,058)
Other gains (losses), net	(96,273)	(2,141)	(142,639)
Total non-operating expenses, net	(209,888)	(114,170)	(242,797)
Loss before equity in losses of equity-method investees	(145,764)	(526,427)	(1,106,677)
Equity in losses of equity-method investees, net	(4,169)	(30,327)	(304,596)
Loss before change in accounting principle	(149,933)	(556,754)	(1,411,273)
Cumulative effect of change in accounting principle	801	(10,523)	—
Net loss	$ (149,132)	$ (567,277)	$(1,411,273)
Basic and diluted loss per share:			
Prior to cumulative effect of change in accounting principle	$ (0.40)	$ (1.53)	$ (4.02)
Cumulative effect of change in accounting principle	0.01	(0.03)	—
	$ (0.39)	$ (1.56)	$ (4.02)
Shares used in computation of loss per share:			
Basic and diluted	378,363	364,211	350,873

•   •   •

See accompanying notes to consolidated financial statements.

AMAZON.COM, INC.

CONSOLIDATED STATEMENTS OF CASH FLOWS

	Years Ended December 31,		
	2002	**2001**	**2000**
	(In thousands)		
CASH AND CASH EQUIVALENTS, BEGINNING OF PERIOD	$ 540,282	$ 822,435	$ 133,309
OPERATING ACTIVITIES:			
Net loss	(149,132)	(567,277)	(1,411,273)
Adjustments to reconcile net loss to net cash provided by (used in) operating activities:			
Depreciation of fixed assets and other amortization	82,274	84,709	84,460
Stock-based compensation	68,927	4,637	24,797
Equity in losses of equity-method investees, net	4,169	30,327	304,596
Amortization of goodwill and other intangibles	5,478	181,033	321,772
Non-cash restructuring-related and other	3,470	73,293	200,311
Gain on sale of marketable securities, net	(5,700)	(1,335)	(280)
Other losses (gains), net	96,273	2,141	142,639
Non-cash interest expense and other	29,586	26,629	24,766
Cumulative effect of change in accounting principle	(801)	10,523	—
Changes in operating assets and liabilities:			
Inventories	(51,303)	30,628	46,083
Accounts receivable, net and other current assets	(32,948)	20,732	(8,585)
Accounts payable	156,542	(44,438)	22,357
Accrued expenses and other current liabilities	4,491	50,031	93,967
Unearned revenue	95,404	114,738	97,818
Amortization of previously unearned revenue	(135,466)	(135,808)	(108,211)
Interest payable	3,027	(345)	34,341
Net cash provided by (used in) operating activities	174,291	(119,782)	(130,442)
INVESTING ACTIVITIES:			
Sales and maturities of marketable securities and other investments	553,289	370,377	545,724
Purchases of marketable securities	(635,810)	(567,152)	(184,455)
Purchases of fixed assets, including internal-use software and Web site development	(39,163)	(50,321)	(134,758)
Investments in equity-method investees and other investments	—	(6,198)	(62,533)
Net cash provided by (used in) investing activities	(121,684)	(253,294)	163,978
FINANCING ACTIVITIES:			
Proceeds from exercise of stock options and other	121,689	16,625	44,697
Proceeds from issuance of common stock, net of issuance costs	—	99,831	—
Proceeds from long-term debt and other	—	10,000	681,499
Repayment of capital lease obligations and other	(14,795)	(19,575)	(16,927)
Financing costs	—	—	(16,122)
Net cash provided by financing activities	106,894	106,881	693,147
Effect of exchange-rate changes on cash and cash equivalents	38,471	(15,958)	(37,557)
Net increase (decrease) in cash and cash equivalents	197,972	(282,153)	689,126
CASH AND CASH EQUIVALENTS, END OF PERIOD	$ 738,254	$ 540,282	$ 822,435
SUPPLEMENTAL CASH FLOW INFORMATION:			
Fixed assets acquired under capital leases and other financing arrangements	$ 3,023	$ 5,597	$ 9,303
Equity securities received for commercial agreements	—	331	106,848
Stock issued in connection with business acquisitions and minority investments	—	5,000	32,130
Cash paid for interest	111,589	112,184	67,252

See accompanying notes to consolidated financial statements.

AMAZON.COM, INC.

CONSOLIDATED STATEMENTS OF STOCKHOLDERS' EQUITY (DEFICIT)

	Common Stock		Additional Paid-In Capital	Deferred Stock-Based Compensation	Accumulated Other Comprehensive Income (Loss)	Accumulated Deficit	Total Stockholders' Equity (Deficit)
	Shares	Amount					
				(In thousands)			
Balance at December 31, 1999	345,155	$3,452	$1,194,369	$(47,806)	$ (1,709)	$ (882,028)	$ 266,278
Net loss	—	—	—	—	—	(1,411,273)	(1,411,273)
Foreign currency translation losses, net...........................	—	—	—	—	(364)	—	(364)
Change in unrealized gain (loss) on available-for-sale securities, net...	—	—	—	—	(303)	—	(303)
Comprehensive loss	—	—	—	—	—	—	(1,411,940)
Issuance of capital stock, net of issuance costs	866	8	30,977	—	—	—	30,985
Exercise of common stock options, net..........................	11,119	111	41,995	—	—	—	42,106
Public offering of equity-method investee	—	—	76,898	—	—	—	76,898
Note receivable for common stock ..	—	—	27	—	—	—	27
Deferred stock-based compensation, net of adjustments	—	—	(5,963)	2,528	—	—	(3,435)
Amortization of deferred stock-based compensation	—	—	—	31,830	—	—	31,830
Balance at December 31, 2000	357,140	3,571	1,338,303	(13,448)	(2,376)	(2,293,301)	(967,251)
Net loss	—	—	—	—	—	(567,277)	(567,277)
Foreign currency translation losses, net..........................	—	—	—	—	(1,257)	—	(1,257)
Change in unrealized gain (loss) on available-for-sale securities, net...	—	—	—	—	7,005	—	7,005
Net unrealized losses on Euro-based currency swap	—	—	—	—	(17,337)	—	(17,337)
Reclassification of currency gains on 6.875% PEACS................	—	—	—	—	(9,811)	—	(9,811)
Cumulative effect of change in accounting principle	—	—	—	—	(12,294)	—	(12,294)
Comprehensive loss	—	—	—	—	—	—	(600,971)
Issuance of capital stock, net of issuance costs	8,989	90	98,716	—	—	—	98,806
Exercise of common stock options, net..........................	6,089	61	14,989	—	—	—	15,050
Repayments of note receivable for common stock	—	—	1,130	—	—	—	1,130
Deferred stock-based compensation, net of adjustments	1,000	10	9,631	(4,797)	—	—	4,844
Amortization of deferred stock-based compensation	—	—	—	8,392	—	—	8,392
Balance at December 31, 2001	373,218	3,732	1,462,769	(9,853)	(36,070)	(2,860,578)	(1,440,000)
Net loss	—	—	—	—	—	(149,132)	(149,132)
Foreign currency translation gains, net..........................	—	—	—	—	16,910	—	16,910
Change in unrealized gain (loss) on available-for-sale securities, net...	—	—	—	—	20,294	—	20,294
Net unrealized gains on Euro-based currency swap	—	—	—	—	8,528	—	8,528
Comprehensive loss	—	—	—	—	—	—	(103,400)
Exercise of common stock options, net..........................	14,728	147	121,542	—	—	—	121,689
Deferred stock-based compensation, net of adjustments	(40)	—	1,592	(2,828)	—	—	(1,236)
Amortization of deferred stock-based compensation	—	—	—	6,090	—	—	6,090
Variable accounting and other stock compensation amortization	—	—	64,043	—	—	—	64,043
Balance at December 31, 2002	387,906	$3,879	$1,649,946	$ (6,591)	$ 9,662	$(3,009,710)	$(1,352,814)

See accompanying notes to consolidated financial statements.

AMAZON.COM, INC.

NOTES TO CONSOLIDATED FINANCIAL STATEMENTS (Excerpts; Adapted)

Note 1 — Description of Business and Accounting Policies (Partial)

Description of Business

Amazon.com, Inc., a Fortune 500 company, commenced operations on the World Wide Web in July 1995. The Company seeks to offer Earth's Biggest Selection and to be Earth's most customer-centric company, where customers can find and discover anything they may want to buy online. The Company and its sellers list new, used and collectible items in categories such as apparel and accessories, electronics, computers, kitchen and housewares, books, music, DVDs, videos, cameras and photo items, office products, toys, baby items and baby registry, software, computer and video games, cell phones and service, tools and hardware, travel services, magazine subscriptions and outdoor living items. Through Amazon Marketplace, the Merchants@ program, zShops and Auctions, participating businesses or individuals can sell their products to Amazon.com's customers.

The Company operates six global Web sites: *www.amazon.com, www.amazon.co.uk, www.amazon.de, www.amazon.fr, www.amazon.co.jp* and *www.amazon.ca*. The Company also owns and operates the Internet Movie Database at *www.imdb.com* ("IMDb"), which is a source of information on movie and entertainment titles and cast and crew members. IMDb offers IMDb Pro, a subscription service designed for the entertainment industry.

Principles of Consolidation

The consolidated financial statements include the accounts of the Company and its wholly owned subsidiaries. All intercompany balances and transactions have been eliminated.

Use of Estimates

The preparation of financial statements in conformity with accounting principles generally accepted in the United States requires estimates and assumptions that affect the reported amounts of assets and liabilities, revenues and expenses, and related disclosures of contingent assets and liabilities in the consolidated financial statements and accompanying notes. Estimates are used for, but not limited to, inventory valuation, depreciable lives, sales returns, receivables valuation, restructuring-related liabilities, incentive discount offers, valuation of investments, taxes and contingencies. Actual results could differ materially from those estimates.

Business Combinations

For business combinations that have been accounted for under the purchase method of accounting, the Company includes the results of operations of the acquired business from the date of acquisition. Net assets of the companies acquired are recorded at their fair value at the date of acquisition. The excess of the purchase price over the fair value of tangible and identifiable intangible net assets acquired is included in goodwill on the accompanying consolidated balance sheets.

Cash and Cash Equivalents

The Company classifies all highly liquid instruments with an original maturity of three months or less at the time of purchase as cash equivalents.

Inventories

Inventories, consisting of products available for sale, are valued at the lower of cost or market value. The Company makes judgments, based on currently-available information, about the likely method of disposition (whether through sales to individual customers, returns to product vendors or liquidations), and expected recoverable values of each disposition category. Based on this evaluation, which is applied consistently from period to period, the Company records a valuation allowance to adjust the carrying amount of its inventories to lower of cost or market value.

Accounting Changes

Inventories

Effective January 1, 2002, the Company prospectively changed its inventory costing method to the first-in first-out ("FIFO") method of accounting. This change resulted in a cumulative increase in inventory of $0.8 million, with a corresponding amount recorded to "Cumulative effect of change in accounting principle" on the consolidated statements of operations. The Company evaluated the effect of the change on each quarter of 2001 and determined such effect to be less than $1.2 million individually and in the aggregate. The Company determined this change to be preferable under accounting principles generally accepted in the United States since, among other reasons, it facilitates the Company's record keeping process, significantly improves its ability to provide cost-efficient fulfillment services to third-party companies as part of its services offering and results in increased consistency with others in the industry. The Company received a letter of preferability for this change in inventory costing from its independent auditors.

· · ·

Fixed Assets

Fixed assets are stated at cost less accumulated depreciation, which includes the amortization of assets recorded under capital leases. Fixed assets, including assets purchased under capital leases, are depreciated on a straight-line basis over the estimated useful lives of the assets (generally two to ten years).

Included in fixed assets is the cost of internal-use software, including software used to upgrade and enhance the Company's Web sites. The Company expenses all costs related to the development of internal-use software other than those incurred during the application development stage. Costs incurred during the application development stage are capitalized and amortized over the estimated useful life of the software (generally two years).

· · ·

Cost of Sales

Cost of sales consists of the purchase price of consumer products sold by the Company, inbound and outbound shipping charges, packaging supplies and certain costs associated with service revenues. Costs associated with service revenues classified as cost of services generally include direct and allocated indirect fulfillment-related costs to ship products on behalf of third-party sellers, costs to provide customer service, credit card fees and other related costs.

Outbound shipping charges and the cost of tangible supplies used to package products for shipment to customers totaled $404 million, $376 million, and $340 million in 2002, 2001 and 2000, respectively.

Fulfillment

Fulfillment costs represent those costs incurred in operating and staffing the Company's fulfillment and customer service centers, including costs attributable to: receiving, inspecting and warehousing inventories; picking, packaging and preparing customers' orders for shipment; credit card fees and bad debt costs; and responding to inquiries from customers. Fulfillment costs also include amounts paid to third-party co-sourcers that assist the Company in fulfillment and customer service operations. Certain Services segment fulfillment-related costs incurred on behalf of other businesses are classified as cost of sales rather than fulfillment.

Marketing

Marketing expenses consist of advertising, promotional, and public relations expenditures, and payroll and related expenses for personnel engaged in marketing and selling activities. The Company expenses general media advertising costs as incurred. The Company enters into certain online promotional agreements with third parties to increase traffic to its Web sites. Costs associated with these promotional agreements consist of fixed payments, variable activity-based payments, or a combination of the two. Fixed payments are amortized ratably over the corresponding agreement term and variable payments are expensed in the period incurred. The Company receives reimbursements from vendors for certain general media and other advertising costs. Such reimbursements are recorded as a reduction of expense. Advertising expense and other promotional costs were $114 million, $125 million and $172 million in 2002, 2001 and 2000, respectively. Prepaid advertising costs were $1 million and $2 million at December 31, 2002 and 2001, respectively.

Technology and Content

Technology and content expenses consist principally of payroll and related expenses for development, editorial, systems, and telecommunications operations personnel; and systems and telecommunications infrastructure.

Technology and content costs are expensed as incurred, except for certain costs relating to the development of internal-use software, including upgrades and enhancements to the Company's Web sites, that are capitalized and depreciated over two years. Fixed assets associated with capitalized internal-use software, net of accumulated depreciation, was $23 million and $24 million at December 31, 2002 and 2001, respectively. Costs capitalized during the application development stage for internal-use software, offset by corresponding amortization, was a net expense of $1 million in 2002, and net deferrals of $3 million and $14 million in 2001 and 2000, respectively.

• • •

Note 2 — Cash, Cash Equivalents and Marketable Securities

The following tables summarize, by major security type, the Company's cash and marketable securities (in thousands):

	December 31, 2002			
	Cost or Amortized Cost	Gross Unrealized Gains	Gross Unrealized Losses	Estimated Fair Value
Cash......................................	$ 302,964	$ —	$ —	$ 302,964
Commercial paper and short-term obligations	429,943	5,347	—	435,290
Cash and cash equivalents..............	732,907	5,347	—	738,254
Certificates of deposit	19,494	2,832	—	22,326
Commercial paper and short-term obligations	2,073	—	—	2,073
Corporate notes and bonds	42,586	355	—	42,941
Asset-backed and agency securities	309,549	7,166	—	316,715
U.S. Treasury notes and bonds............	172,145	2,616	(35)	174,726
Equity securities	3,934	—	—	3,934
Marketable securities..................	549,781	12,969	(35)	562,715
Total	$1,282,688	$18,316	$(35)	$1,300,969

• • •

Note 3 — Fixed Assets

Fixed assets, at cost, consist of the following (in thousands):

	December 31,	
	2002	2001
Furniture, fixtures and leasehold improvements	$ 112,943	$ 109,227
Technology infrastructure and other computer equipment	57,086	58,140
Software purchased or developed for internal use	94,561	70,944
Equipment and other fixed assets acquired under capital leases	218,146	199,832
	482,736	438,143
Less accumulated depreciation	(243,338)	(166,392)
Fixed assets, net	$ 239,398	$ 271,751

Depreciation expense on fixed assets was $77 million, $83 million and $83 million, which includes amortization of fixed assets acquired under capital lease obligations of $7 million, $9 million and $11 million for 2002, 2001 and 2000, respectively.

• • •

Note 6 — Long-Term Debt and Other

The Company's long-term debt and other long-term liabilities are summarized as follows (in thousands):

	December 31,	
	2002	2001
4.75% Convertible Subordinated Notes	$1,249,807	$1,249,807
6.875% PEACS	724,500	608,787
Senior Discount Notes	255,597	231,830
Long-term restructuring liabilities	31,614	20,640
Euro currency swap	12,159	33,265
Capital lease obligations	8,491	16,415
Other long-term debt..	8,456	10,381
	2,290,624	2,171,125
Less current portion of capital lease obligations....................	(7,506)	(9,922)
Less current portion of other long-term debt	(5,813)	(5,070)
	$2,277,305	$2,156,133

• • •

Note 15 — Segment Information

The Company presents information to its chief operating decision maker in four segments: North America Books, Music, and DVD/Video ("BMVD"); North America Electronics, Tools, and Kitchen ("ETK"); International; and Services. Accordingly, the Company discloses its segment financial information along these lines.

• • •

BMVD Segment

The BMVD segment includes retail sales from *www.amazon.com* and *www.amazon.ca* of books, music and DVD/video products and magazine subscription commissions. This segment also includes commissions from sales of these products, new, used or collectible, through Amazon Marketplace, amounts earned from sales of these products by other businesses through the Merchants@ program and product revenues from stores offering these products through the Syndicated Stores program.

ETK Segment

The ETK segment includes *www.amazon.com* retail sales of electronics, home improvement and home and garden products, as well as our mail-order catalog sales. This segment also includes commissions from sales of these products, new, used or collectible, through Amazon Marketplace and amounts earned from sales of these products by other businesses through the Merchants@ program, such as with Office Depot, and will include revenues from stores offering these products, if any, through the Syndicated Stores program.

International Segment

The International segment includes all retail sales of the following internationally-focused Web sites: *www.amazon.co.uk, www.amazon.de, www.amazon.fr* and *www.amazon.co.jp.* These international sites share a common Amazon.com experience, but are localized in terms of language, products, customer service and fulfillment. To the extent available on these sites, this segment includes commissions and other amounts earned from sales of products through Amazon Marketplace and revenues from stores offering products through the Syndicated Stores program, such as *www.waterstones.co.uk* and *www.virginmega.co.jp,* and amounts earned from sales of products by other businesses through the Merchants@ program. The International segment includes export sales from *www.amazon.co.uk, www.amazon.de, www.amazon.fr* and *www.amazon.co.jp* (including export sales from these sites to customers in the U.S. and Canada), but excludes export sales from *www.amazon.com* and *www.amazon.ca.* Operating results for the International segment are affected by movements in foreign exchange rates. During 2002, International segment revenues improved $47 million, and operating results improved $4 million in comparison to the prior year due to changes in foreign exchange rates.

Services Segment

The Services segment consists of commissions, fees and other amounts earned from the services business, including the Merchant.com program (such as *www.target.com*), and to the extent full product categories are not also offered by the Company through its online retail stores, the Merchants@ program, such as the apparel store, Toysrus.com and Babiesrus.com stores, and portions of the Target store at *www.amazon.com,* as well as the commercial agreement with America Online, Inc. This segment also includes Auctions, zShops, Amazon Payments and miscellaneous marketing and promotional agreements.

Included in Services segment revenues are equity-based service revenues of $13 million, $27 million and $79 million for 2002, 2001 and 2000, respectively.

The Company measures the results of operations of its reportable segments using a pro forma measure. Pro forma results from operations, which exclude stock-based compensation, amortization of goodwill and other intangibles, and restructuring-related and other charges, are not in conformity with accounting principles generally accepted in the United States. Stock-based compensation, amortization of goodwill and other intangibles, and restructuring-related and other costs are not allocated to segment results. All other centrally-incurred operating costs are fully allocated to segment results. There are no internal transactions between the Company's reporting segments.

Information on reportable segments and reconciliation to consolidated net loss is as follows (in thousands):

Year Ended 2002:

| | North America | | | | | |
	Books, Music and DVD/Video	Electronics, Tools and Kitchen	Total	International	Services	Consolidated
Net sales	$1,873,291	$645,031	$2,518,322	$1,168,935	$245,679	$3,932,936
Gross profit	527,542	89,863	617,405	249,089	126,124	992,618
Pro forma income (loss) from operations..................	211,363	(73,220)	138,143	(640)	42,599	180,102
Stock-based compensation						(68,927)
Amortization of other intangibles						(5,478)
Restructuring-related and other.......						(41,573)
Total non-operating expenses, net.....						(209,888)
Equity in losses of equity-method investees, net						(4,169)
Cumulative effect of change in accounting principle						801
Net loss						$ (149,132)

Year Ended 2001:

| | North America | | | | | |
	Books. Music and DVD/Video	Electronics, Tools and Kitchen	Total	International	Services	Consolidated
Net sales......................	$1,688,752	$ 547,190	$2,235,942	$ 661,374	$225,117	$3,122,433
Gross profit...................	453,129	78,384	531,513	140,606	126,439	798,558
Pro forma income (loss) from operations	156,753	(140,685)	16,068	(103,112)	42,042	(45,002)
Stock-based compensation						(4,637)
Amortization of goodwill and other intangibles...................						(181,033)
Restructuring-related and other						(181,585)
Total non-operating expenses, net						(114,170)
Equity in losses of equity-method investees, net						(30,327)
Cumulative effect of change in accounting principle.............						(10,523)
Net loss......................						$ (567,277)

Year Ended 2000:

	North America					
	Books, Music and DVD/Video	Electronics, Tools and Kitchen	Total	International	Services	Consolidated
Net sales	$1,698,266	$ 484,151	$2,182,417	$ 381,075	$198,491	$ 2,761,983
Gross profit	417,452	44,655	462,107	77,436	116,234	655,777
Pro forma income (loss) from operations.....................	71,441	(269,890)	(198,449)	(145,070)	26,519	(317,000)
Stock-based compensation..........						(24,797)
Amortization of goodwill and other intangibles						(321,772)
Restructuring-related and other						(200,311)
Total non-operating expenses, net.....						(242,797)
Equity in losses of equity-method investees, net						(304,596)
Net loss						$(1,411,273)

Net sales to customers outside of the U.S. represented approximately 35%, 29% and 22% of net sales for 2002, 2001 and 2000, respectively. Other than sales into the United Kingdom, which represents approximately 11% of total net sales in 2002, no individual foreign country, geographical area or customer accounted for more than 10% of net sales in any of the periods presented.

Depreciation expense, by segment, was as follows (in thousands):

	North America					
Year Ended December 31,	Books, Music and DVD/Video	Electronics, Tools and Kitchen	Total	Services	International	Consolidated
2002	$25,774	$19,051	$44,825	$7,339	$21,194	$73,358
2001	29,317	21,670	50,987	8,349	24,108	83,444
2000	29,501	26,818	56,319	7,649	18,970	82,938

At December 31, 2002 and 2001, fixed assets, net totaled $196 million and $228 million in the United States, respectively, and $43 million and $44 million in other countries, respectively.

Note 16 — Quarterly Results (Unaudited)

The following tables contain selected unaudited statement of operations information for each quarter of 2002, 2001 and 2000. The Company believes that the following information reflects all normal recurring adjustments necessary for a fair presentation of the information for the periods presented. The operating results for any quarter are not necessarily indicative of results for any future period. Unaudited quarterly results were as follows (in thousands, except per share data):

	Year Ended December 31, 2002			
	Fourth Quarter	Third Quarter	Second Quarter	First Quarter
Net sales	$1,428,610	$851,299	$805,605	$847,422
Gross profit	335,159	216,167	218,167	223,125
Income (loss) before change in accounting principle	2,651	(35,080)	(93,553)	(23,951)
Cumulative effect of change in accounting principle	—	—	—	801
Net income (loss)	2,651	(35,080)	(93,553)	(23,150)
Basic income (loss) per share(1):				
Prior to cumulative effect of change in accounting principle	$ 0.01	$ (0.09)	$ (0.25)	$ (0.06)
Cumulative effect of change in accounting principle	—	—	—	—
	$ 0.01	$ (0.09)	$ (0.25)	$ (0.06)
Diluted income (loss) per share(1):				
Prior to cumulative effect of change in accounting principle	$ 0.01	$ (0.09)	$ (0.25)	$ (0.06)
Cumulative effect of change in accounting principle	—	—	—	—
	$ 0.01	$ (0.09)	$ (0.25)	$ (0.06)
Shares used in computation of income (loss) per share:				
Basic	383,702	379,650	376,937	373,031
Diluted	407,056	379,650	376,937	373,031

	Year Ended December 31, 2001			
	Fourth Quarter	Third Quarter	Second Quarter	First Quarter
Net sales	$1,115,171	$ 639,281	$ 667,625	$ 700,356
Gross profit	274,049	162,192	179,720	182,597
Income (loss) before change in accounting principle	5,087	(169,874)	(168,359)	(223,608)
Cumulative effect of change in accounting principle	—	—	—	(10,523)
Net income (loss)	5,087	(169,874)	(168,359)	(234,131)

	Year Ended December 31, 2001			
	Fourth Quarter	**Third Quarter**	**Second Quarter**	**First Quarter**
Basic and diluted income (loss) per share(1):				
Prior to cumulative effect of change in accounting principle	$ 0.01	$ (0.46)	$ (0.47)	$ (0.63)
Cumulative effect of change in accounting principle	—	—	—	(0.03)
	$ 0.01	$ (0.46)	$ (0.47)	$ (0.66)
Shares used in computation of basic income (loss) per share.....................	371,420	368,052	359,752	357,424
Shares used in computation of diluted income (loss) per share	384,045	368,052	359,752	357,424

	Year Ended December 31, 2000			
	Fourth Quarter	**Third Quarter**	**Second Quarter**	**First Quarter**
Net sales	$ 972,360	$ 637,858	$ 577,876	$ 573,889
Gross profit	224,300	167,279	136,064	128,134
Net loss.............................	(545,140)	(240,524)	(317,184)	(308,425)
Basic and diluted loss per share(1)	$ (1.53)	$ (0.68)	$ (0.91)	$ (0.90)
Shares used in computation of basic and diluted loss per share	355,681	353,954	349,886	343,884

(1) The sum of quarterly per share amounts may not equal per share amounts reported for year-to-date periods. This is due to changes in the number of weighted-average shares outstanding and the effects of rounding for each period.

■ Appendix B

Typical Charts of Accounts for Different Types of Businesses

(For Businesses Discussed in Chapters 1–12)

Service Proprietorship

Assets

Cash
Accounts Receivable
Allowance for Uncollectible Accounts
Notes Receivable, Short-Term
Interest Receivable
Supplies
Prepaid Rent
Prepaid Insurance
Notes Receivable, Long-Term
Land
Furniture
Accumulated Depreciation—Furniture
Equipment
Accumulated Depreciation—Equipment
Building
Accumulated Depreciation—Building

Liabilities

Accounts Payable
Notes Payable, Short-Term
Salary Payable
Wage Payable
Employee Income Tax Payable
FICA Tax Payable
State Unemployment Tax Payable
Federal Unemployment Tax Payable
Employee Benefits Payable
Interest Payable
Unearned Service Revenue
Notes Payable, Long-Term

Owner's Equity

Owner, Capital
Owner, Withdrawals

Revenues and Gains

Service Revenue
Interest Revenue
Gain on Sale of Land (or Furniture,
    Equipment, or Building)

Expenses and Losses

Salary Expense
Payroll Tax Expense
Rent Expense
Insurance Expense
Supplies Expense
Uncollectible-Account Expense
Depreciation Expense—Furniture
Depreciation Expense—Equipment
Depreciation Expense—Building
Property Tax Expense
Interest Expense
Miscellaneous Expense
Loss on Sale of Land (Furniture,
    Equipment, or Building)

Service Partnership

Same as Service Proprietorship, except for Owners' Equity:

Owners' Equity

Partner 1, Capital
Partner 2, Capital
Partner N, Capital

Partner 1, Drawing
Partner 2, Drawing
Partner N, Drawing

(For Businesses Discussed in Chapters 13–26)

Merchandising Corporation

Assets	Liabilities	Stockholder's Equity	
Cash	Accounts Payable	Preferred Stock	**Expenses and Losses**
Short-Term Investments (Trading Securities)	Notes Payable, Short-Term	Paid-in Capital in Excess of Par—Preferred	Cost of Goods Sold
Accounts Receivable	Current Portion of Bonds Payable	Common Stock	Salary Expense
Allowance for Uncollectible Accounts	Salary Payable	Paid-in Capital in Excess of Par—Common	Wage Expense
Notes Receivable, Short-Term	Wage Payable	Paid-in Capital from Treasury Stock Transactions	Commission Expense
Interest Receivable	Employee Income Tax Payable	Paid-in Capital from Retirement of Stock	Payroll Tax Expense
Inventory	FICA Tax Payable	Retained Earnings	Rent Expense
Supplies	State Unemployment Tax Payable	Foreign Currency Translation Adjustment	Insurance Expense
Prepaid Rent	Federal Unemployment Tax Payable	Treasury Stock	Supplies Expense

Assets

Cash
Short-Term Investments
   (Trading Securities)
Accounts Receivable
Allowance for Uncollectible
   Accounts
Notes Receivable, Short-Term
Interest Receivable
Inventory
Supplies
Prepaid Rent
Prepaid Insurance
Notes Receivable, Long-Term
Investments in Stock
   (Available-for-Sale
   Securities)
Investments in Bonds (Held-
   to-Maturity Securities)
Other Receivables, Long-Term
Land
Land Improvements
Furniture and Fixtures
Accumulated Depreciation—
   Furniture and Fixtures
Equipment
Accumulated Depreciation—
   Equipment
Buildings
Accumulated Depreciation—
   Buildings
Franchises
Patents
Leaseholds
Goodwill

Liabilities

Accounts Payable
Notes Payable, Short-Term
Current Portion of Bonds
   Payable
Salary Payable
Wage Payable
Employee Income Tax Payable
FICA Tax Payable
State Unemployment Tax
   Payable
Federal Unemployment Tax
   Payable
Employee Benefits Payable
Interest Payable
Income Tax Payable
Unearned Sales Revenue
Notes Payable, Long-Term
Bonds Payable

Stockholder's Equity

Preferred Stock
Paid-in Capital in Excess of
   Par—Preferred
Common Stock
Paid-in Capital in Excess of
   Par—Common
Paid-in Capital from Treasury
   Stock Transactions
Paid-in Capital from
   Retirement of Stock
Retained Earnings
Foreign Currency Translation
   Adjustment
Treasury Stock

Revenues and Gains

Sales Revenue
Interest Revenue
Dividend Revenue
Equity-Method Investment
   Revenue
Unrealized Gain on
   Investments
Gain on Sale of Investments
Gain on Sale of Land
   (Furniture and Fixtures,
   Equipment, or Buildings)
Discontinued Operations—
   Gain
Extraordinary Gains

Expenses and Losses

Cost of Goods Sold
Salary Expense
Wage Expense
Commission Expense
Payroll Tax Expense
Rent Expense
Insurance Expense
Supplies Expense
Uncollectible-Account
   Expense
Depreciation Expense—Land
   Improvements
Depreciation Expense—
   Furniture and Fixtures
Depreciation Expense—
   Equipment
Depreciation Expense—
   Buildings
Amortization Expense—
   Franchises
Amortization Expense—
   Leaseholds
Loss on Goodwill
Income Tax Expense
Unrealized Loss on
   Investments
Loss on Sale of Investments
Loss on Sale of Land
   (Furniture and Fixtures,
   Equipment, or Buildings)
Discontinued Operations—
   Loss
Extraordinary Losses

Manufacturing Corporation

Same as Merchandising Corporation, except for Assets and Expenses:

Assets

Inventories:
   Materials Inventory
   Work in Process Inventory
   Finished Goods Inventory

Expenses (Contra Expenses If Credit Balance)

Direct Materials Price Variance
Direct Materials Efficiency Variance
Direct Labor Price Variance
Direct Labor Efficiency Variance
Manufacturing Overhead Flexible Budget Variance
Manufacturing Overhead Production Volume
   Variance

■ A p p e n d i x C

Present Value Tables and Future Value Tables

This appendix provides present value tables and future value tables (more complete than those in the Chapter 15 appendix and in Chapter 26).

Exhibit C-1

Present Value of $1

Present Value

Periods	1%	2%	3%	4%	5%	6%	7%	8%	9%	10%	12%
1	0.990	0.980	0.971	0.962	0.952	0.943	0.935	0.926	0.917	0.909	0.893
2	0.980	0.961	0.943	0.925	0.907	0.890	0.873	0.857	0.842	0.826	0.797
3	0.971	0.942	0.915	0.889	0.864	0.840	0.816	0.794	0.772	0.751	0.712
4	0.961	0.924	0.888	0.855	0.823	0.792	0.763	0.735	0.708	0.683	0.636
5	0.951	0.906	0.883	0.822	0.784	0.747	0.713	0.681	0.650	0.621	0.567
6	0.942	0.888	0.837	0.790	0.746	0.705	0.666	0.630	0.596	0.564	0.507
7	0.933	0.871	0.813	0.760	0.711	0.665	0.623	0.583	0.547	0.513	0.452
8	0.923	0.853	0.789	0.731	0.677	0.627	0.582	0.540	0.502	0.467	0.404
9	0.914	0.837	0.766	0.703	0.645	0.592	0.544	0.500	0.460	0.424	0.361
10	0.905	0.820	0.744	0.676	0.614	0.558	0.508	0.463	0.422	0.386	0.322
11	0.896	0.804	0.722	0.650	0.585	0.527	0.475	0.429	0.388	0.350	0.287
12	0.887	0.788	0.701	0.625	0.557	0.497	0.444	0.397	0.356	0.319	0.257
13	0.879	0.773	0.681	0.601	0.530	0.469	0.415	0.368	0.326	0.290	0.229
14	0.870	0.758	0.661	0.577	0.505	0.442	0.388	0.340	0.299	0.263	0.205
15	0.861	0.743	0.642	0.555	0.481	0.417	0.362	0.315	0.275	0.239	0.183
16	0.853	0.728	0.623	0.534	0.458	0.394	0.339	0.292	0.252	0.218	0.163
17	0.844	0.714	0.605	0.513	0.436	0.371	0.317	0.270	0.231	0.198	0.146
18	0.836	0.700	0.587	0.494	0.416	0.350	0.296	0.250	0.212	0.180	0.130
19	0.828	0.686	0.570	0.475	0.396	0.331	0.277	0.232	0.194	0.164	0.116
20	0.820	0.673	0.554	0.456	0.377	0.312	0.258	0.215	0.178	0.149	0.104
21	0.811	0.660	0.538	0.439	0.359	0.294	0.242	0.199	0.164	0.135	0.093
22	0.803	0.647	0.522	0.422	0.342	0.278	0.226	0.184	0.150	0.123	0.083
23	0.795	0.634	0.507	0.406	0.326	0.262	0.211	0.170	0.138	0.112	0.074
24	0.788	0.622	0.492	0.390	0.310	0.247	0.197	0.158	0.126	0.102	0.066
25	0.780	0.610	0.478	0.375	0.295	0.233	0.184	0.146	0.116	0.092	0.059
26	0.772	0.598	0.464	0.361	0.281	0.220	0.172	0.135	0.106	0.084	0.053
27	0.764	0.586	0.450	0.347	0.268	0.207	0.161	0.125	0.098	0.076	0.047
28	0.757	0.574	0.437	0.333	0.255	0.196	0.150	0.116	0.090	0.069	0.042
29	0.749	0.563	0.424	0.321	0.243	0.185	0.141	0.107	0.082	0.063	0.037
30	0.742	0.552	0.412	0.308	0.231	0.174	0.131	0.099	0.075	0.057	0.033
40	0.672	0.453	0.307	0.208	0.142	0.097	0.067	0.046	0.032	0.022	0.011
50	0.608	0.372	0.228	0.141	0.087	0.054	0.034	0.021	0.013	0.009	0.003

Exhibit C-1
(cont'd)

Present Value

14%	15%	16%	18%	20%	25%	30%	35%	40%	45%	50%	Periods
0.877	0.870	0.862	0.847	0.833	0.800	0.769	0.741	0.714	0.690	0.667	1
0.769	0.756	0.743	0.718	0.694	0.640	0.592	0.549	0.510	0.476	0.444	2
0.675	0.658	0.641	0.609	0.579	0.512	0.455	0.406	0.364	0.328	0.296	3
0.592	0.572	0.552	0.516	0.482	0.410	0.350	0.301	0.260	0.226	0.198	4
0.519	0.497	0.476	0.437	0.402	0.328	0.269	0.223	0.186	0.156	0.132	5
0.456	0.432	0.410	0.370	0.335	0.262	0.207	0.165	0.133	0.108	0.088	6
0.400	0.376	0.354	0.314	0.279	0.210	0.159	0.122	0.095	0.074	0.059	7
0.351	0.327	0.305	0.266	0.233	0.168	0.123	0.091	0.068	0.051	0.039	8
0.308	0.284	0.263	0.225	0.194	0.134	0.094	0.067	0.048	0.035	0.026	9
0.270	0.247	0.227	0.191	0.162	0.107	0.073	0.050	0.035	0.024	0.017	10
0.237	0.215	0.195	0.162	0.135	0.086	0.056	0.037	0.025	0.017	0.012	11
0.208	0.187	0.168	0.137	0.112	0.069	0.043	0.027	0.018	0.012	0.008	12
0.182	0.163	0.145	0.116	0.093	0.055	0.033	0.020	0.013	0.008	0.005	13
0.160	0.141	0.125	0.099	0.078	0.044	0.025	0.015	0.009	0.006	0.003	14
0.140	0.123	0.108	0.084	0.065	0.035	0.020	0.011	0.006	0.004	0.002	15
0.123	0.107	0.093	0.071	0.054	0.028	0.015	0.008	0.005	0.003	0.002	16
0.108	0.093	0.080	0.060	0.045	0.023	0.012	0.006	0.003	0.002	0.001	17
0.095	0.081	0.069	0.051	0.038	0.018	0.009	0.005	0.002	0.001	0.001	18
0.083	0.070	0.060	0.043	0.031	0.014	0.007	0.003	0.002	0.001		19
0.073	0.061	0.051	0.037	0.026	0.012	0.005	0.002	0.001	0.001		20
0.064	0.053	0.044	0.031	0.022	0.009	0.004	0.002	0.001			21
0.056	0.046	0.038	0.026	0.018	0.007	0.003	0.001	0.001			22
0.049	0.040	0.033	0.022	0.015	0.006	0.002	0.001				23
0.043	0.035	0.028	0.019	0.013	0.005	0.002	0.001				24
0.038	0.030	0.024	0.016	0.010	0.004	0.001	0.001				25
0.033	0.026	0.021	0.014	0.009	0.003	0.001					26
0.029	0.023	0.018	0.011	0.007	0.002	0.001					27
0.026	0.020	0.016	0.010	0.006	0.002	0.001					28
0.022	0.017	0.014	0.008	0.005	0.002						29
0.020	0.015	0.012	0.007	0.004	0.001						30
0.005	0.004	0.003	0.001	0.001							40
0.001	0.001	0.001									50

Exhibit C-2

Present Value of Annuity of $1

Present Value

Periods	1%	2%	3%	4%	5%	6%	7%	8%	9%	10%	12%
1	0.990	0.980	0.971	0.962	0.952	0.943	0.935	0.926	0.917	0.909	0.893
2	1.970	1.942	1.913	1.886	1.859	1.833	1.808	1.783	1.759	1.736	1.690
3	2.941	2.884	2.829	2.775	2.723	2.673	2.624	2.577	2.531	2.487	2.402
4	3.902	3.808	3.717	3.630	3.546	3.465	3.387	3.312	3.240	3.170	3.037
5	4.853	4.713	4.580	4.452	4.329	4.212	4.100	3.993	3.890	3.791	3.605
6	5.795	5.601	5.417	5.242	5.076	4.917	4.767	4.623	4.486	4.355	4.111
7	6.728	6.472	6.230	6.002	5.786	5.582	5.389	5.206	5.033	4.868	4.564
8	7.652	7.325	7.020	6.733	6.463	6.210	5.971	5.747	5.535	5.335	4.968
9	8.566	8.162	7.786	7.435	7.108	6.802	6.515	6.247	5.995	5.759	5.328
10	9.471	8.983	8.530	8.111	7.722	7.360	7.024	6.710	6.418	6.145	5.650
11	10.368	9.787	9.253	8.760	8.306	7.887	7.499	7.139	6.805	6.495	5.938
12	11.255	10.575	9.954	9.385	8.863	8.384	7.943	7.536	7.161	6.814	6.194
13	12.134	11.348	10.635	9.986	9.394	8.853	8.358	7.904	7.487	7.103	6.424
14	13.004	12.106	11.296	10.563	9.899	9.295	8.745	8.244	7.786	7.367	6.628
15	13.865	12.849	11.938	11.118	10.380	9.712	9.108	8.559	8.061	7.606	6.811
16	14.718	13.578	12.561	11.652	10.838	10.106	9.447	8.851	8.313	7.824	6.974
17	15.562	14.292	13.166	12.166	11.274	10.477	9.763	9.122	8.544	8.022	7.120
18	16.398	14.992	13.754	12.659	11.690	10.828	10.059	9.372	8.756	8.201	7.250
19	17.226	15.678	14.324	13.134	12.085	11.158	10.336	9.604	8.950	8.365	7.366
20	18.046	16.351	14.878	13.590	12.462	11.470	10.594	9.818	9.129	8.514	7.469
21	18.857	17.011	15.415	14.029	12.821	11.764	10.836	10.017	9.292	8.649	7.562
22	19.660	17.658	15.937	14.451	13.163	12.042	11.061	10.201	9.442	8.772	7.645
23	20.456	18.292	16.444	14.857	13.489	12.303	11.272	10.371	9.580	8.883	7.718
24	21.243	18.914	16.936	15.247	13.799	12.550	11.469	10.529	9.707	8.985	7.784
25	22.023	19.523	17.413	15.622	14.094	12.783	11.654	10.675	9.823	9.077	7.843
26	22.795	20.121	17.877	15.983	14.375	13.003	11.826	10.810	9.929	9.161	7.896
27	23.560	20.707	18.327	16.330	14.643	13.211	11.987	10.935	10.027	9.237	7.943
28	24.316	21.281	18.764	16.663	14.898	13.406	12.137	11.051	10.116	9.307	7.984
29	25.066	21.844	19.189	16.984	15.141	13.591	12.278	11.158	10.198	9.370	8.022
30	25.808	22.396	19.600	17.292	15.373	13.765	12.409	11.258	10.274	9.427	8.055
40	32.835	27.355	23.115	19.793	17.159	15.046	13.332	11.925	10.757	9.779	8.244
50	39.196	31.424	25.730	21.482	18.256	15.762	13.801	12.234	10.962	9.915	8.305

Exhibit C-2
(cont'd)

Present Value

14%	15%	16%	18%	20%	25%	30%	35%	40%	45%	50%	Periods
0.877	0.870	0.862	0.847	0.833	0.800	0.769	0.741	0.714	0.690	0.667	1
1.647	1.626	1.605	1.566	1.528	1.440	1.361	1.289	1.224	1.165	1.111	2
2.322	2.283	2.246	2.174	2.106	1.952	1.816	1.696	1.589	1.493	1.407	3
2.914	2.855	2.798	2.690	2.589	2.362	2.166	1.997	1.849	1.720	1.605	4
3.433	3.352	3.274	3.127	2.991	2.689	2.436	2.220	2.035	1.876	1.737	5
3.889	3.784	3.685	3.498	3.326	2.951	2.643	2.385	2.168	1.983	1.824	6
4.288	4.160	4.039	3.812	3.605	3.161	2.802	2.508	2.263	2.057	1.883	7
4.639	4.487	4.344	4.078	3.837	3.329	2.925	2.598	2.331	2.109	1.922	8
4.946	4.772	4.607	4.303	4.031	3.463	3.019	2.665	2.379	2.144	1.948	9
5.216	5.019	4.833	4.494	4.192	3.571	3.092	2.715	2.414	2.168	1.965	10
5.553	5.234	5.029	4.656	4.327	3.656	3.147	2.752	2.438	2.185	1.977	11
5.660	5.421	5.197	4.793	4.439	3.725	3.190	2.779	2.456	2.197	1.985	12
5.842	5.583	5.342	4.910	4.533	3.780	3.223	2.799	2.469	2.204	1.990	13
6.002	5.724	5.468	5.008	4.611	3.824	3.249	2.814	2.478	2.210	1.993	14
6.142	5.847	5.575	5.092	4.675	3.859	3.268	2.825	2.484	2.214	1.995	15
6.265	5.954	5.669	5.162	4.730	3.887	3.283	2.834	2.489	2.216	1.997	16
6.373	6.047	5.749	5.222	4.775	3.910	3.295	2.840	2.492	2.218	1.998	17
6.467	6.128	5.818	5.273	4.812	3.928	3.304	2.844	2.494	2.219	1.999	18
6.550	6.198	5.877	5.316	4.844	3.942	3.311	2.848	2.496	2.220	1.999	19
6.623	6.259	5.929	5.353	4.870	3.954	3.316	2.850	2.497	2.221	1.999	20
6.687	6.312	5.973	5.384	4.891	3.963	3.320	2.852	2.498	2.221	2.000	21
6.743	6.359	6.011	5.410	4.909	3.970	3.323	2.853	2.498	2.222	2.000	22
6.792	6.399	6.044	5.432	4.925	3.976	3.325	2.854	2.499	2.222	2.000	23
6.835	6.434	6.073	5.451	4.937	3.981	3.327	2.855	2.499	2.222	2.000	24
6.873	6.464	6.097	5.467	4.948	3.985	3.329	2.856	2.499	2.222	2.000	25
6.906	6.491	6.118	5.480	4.956	3.988	3.330	2.856	2.500	2.222	2.000	26
6.935	6.514	6.136	5.492	4.964	3.990	3.331	2.856	2.500	2.222	2.000	27
6.961	6.534	6.152	5.502	4.970	3.992	3.331	2.857	2.500	2.222	2.000	28
6.983	6.551	6.166	5.510	4.975	3.994	3.332	2.857	2.500	2.222	2.000	29
7.003	6.566	6.177	5.517	4.979	3.995	3.332	2.857	2.500	2.222	2.000	30
7.105	6.642	6.234	5.548	4.997	3.999	3.333	2.857	2.500	2.222	2.000	40
7.133	6.661	6.246	5.554	4.999	4.000	3.333	2.857	2.500	2.222	2.000	50

Exhibit C-3
Future Value of $1

Future Value

Periods	1%	2%	3%	4%	5%	6%	7%	8%	9%	10%	12%	14%	15%
1	1.010	1.020	1.030	1.040	1.050	1.060	1.070	1.080	1.090	1.100	1.120	1.140	1.150
2	1.020	1.040	1.061	1.082	1.103	1.124	1.145	1.166	1.188	1.210	1.254	1.300	1.323
3	1.030	1.061	1.093	1.125	1.158	1.191	1.225	1.260	1.295	1.331	1.405	1.482	1.521
4	1.041	1.082	1.126	1.170	1.216	1.262	1.311	1.360	1.412	1.464	1.574	1.689	1.749
5	1.051	1.104	1.159	1.217	1.276	1.338	1.403	1.469	1.539	1.611	1.762	1.925	2.011
6	1.062	1.126	1.194	1.265	1.340	1.419	1.501	1.587	1.677	1.772	1.974	2.195	2.313
7	1.072	1.149	1.230	1.316	1.407	1.504	1.606	1.714	1.828	1.949	2.211	2.502	2.660
8	1.083	1.172	1.267	1.369	1.477	1.594	1.718	1.851	1.993	2.144	2.476	2.853	3.059
9	1.094	1.195	1.305	1.423	1.551	1.689	1.838	1.999	2.172	2.358	2.773	3.252	3.518
10	1.105	1.219	1.344	1.480	1.629	1.791	1.967	2.159	2.367	2.594	3.106	3.707	4.046
11	1.116	1.243	1.384	1.539	1.710	1.898	2.105	2.332	2.580	2.853	3.479	4.226	4.652
12	1.127	1.268	1.426	1.601	1.796	2.012	2.252	2.518	2.813	3.138	3.896	4.818	5.350
13	1.138	1.294	1.469	1.665	1.886	2.133	2.410	2.720	3.066	3.452	4.363	5.492	6.153
14	1.149	1.319	1.513	1.732	1.980	2.261	2.579	2.937	3.342	3.798	4.887	6.261	7.076
15	1.161	1.346	1.558	1.801	2.079	2.397	2.759	3.172	3.642	4.177	5.474	7.138	8.137
16	1.173	1.373	1.605	1.873	2.183	2.540	2.952	3.426	3.970	4.595	6.130	8.137	9.358
17	1.184	1.400	1.653	1.948	2.292	2.693	3.159	3.700	4.328	5.054	6.866	9.276	10.76
18	1.196	1.428	1.702	2.026	2.407	2.854	3.380	3.996	4.717	5.560	7.690	10.58	12.38
19	1.208	1.457	1.754	2.107	2.527	3.026	3.617	4.316	5.142	6.116	8.613	12.06	14.23
20	1.220	1.486	1.806	2.191	2.653	3.207	3.870	4.661	5.604	6.728	9.646	13.74	16.37
21	1.232	1.516	1.860	2.279	2.786	3.400	4.141	5.034	6.109	7.400	10.80	15.67	18.82
22	1.245	1.546	1.916	2.370	2.925	3.604	4.430	5.437	6.659	8.140	12.10	17.86	21.64
23	1.257	1.577	1.974	2.465	3.072	3.820	4.741	5.871	7.258	8.954	13.55	20.36	24.89
24	1.270	1.608	2.033	2.563	3.225	4.049	5.072	6.341	7.911	9.850	15.18	23.21	28.63
25	1.282	1.641	2.094	2.666	3.386	4.292	5.427	6.848	8.623	10.83	17.00	26.46	32.92
26	1.295	1.673	2.157	2.772	3.556	4.549	5.807	7.396	9.399	11.92	19.04	30.17	37.86
27	1.308	1.707	2.221	2.883	3.733	4.822	6.214	7.988	10.25	13.11	21.32	34.39	43.54
28	1.321	1.741	2.288	2.999	3.920	5.112	6.649	8.627	11.17	14.42	23.88	39.20	50.07
29	1.335	1.776	2.357	3.119	4.116	5.418	7.114	9.317	12.17	15.86	26.75	44.69	57.58
30	1.348	1.811	2.427	3.243	4.322	5.743	7.612	10.06	13.27	17.45	29.96	50.95	66.21
40	1.489	2.208	3.262	4.801	7.040	10.29	14.97	21.72	31.41	45.26	93.05	188.9	267.9
50	1.645	2.692	4.384	7.107	11.47	18.42	29.46	46.90	74.36	117.4	289.0	700.2	1,084

Exhibit C-4

Future Value of Annuity $1

Future Value

Periods	1%	2%	3%	4%	5%	6%	7%	8%	9%	10%	12%	14%	15%
1	1.000	1.000	1.000	1.000	1.000	1.000	1.000	1.000	1.000	1.000	1.000	1.000	1.000
2	2.010	2.020	2.030	2.040	2.050	2.060	2.070	2.080	2.090	2.100	2.120	2.140	2.150
3	3.030	3.060	3.091	3.122	3.153	3.184	3.215	3.246	3.278	3.310	3.374	3.440	3.473
4	4.060	4.122	4.184	4.246	4.310	4.375	4.440	4.506	4.573	4.641	4.779	4.921	4.993
5	5.101	5.204	5.309	5.416	5.526	5.637	5.751	5.867	5.985	6.105	6.353	6.610	6.742
6	6.152	6.308	6.468	6.633	6.802	6.975	7.153	7.336	7.523	7.716	8.115	8.536	8.754
7	7.214	7.434	7.662	7.898	8.142	8.394	8.654	8.923	9.200	9.487	10.09	10.73	11.07
8	8.286	8.583	8.892	9.214	9.549	9.897	10.26	10.64	11.03	11.44	12.30	13.23	13.73
9	9.369	9.755	10.16	10.58	11.03	11.49	11.98	12.49	13.02	13.58	14.78	16.09	16.79
10	10.46	10.95	11.46	12.01	12.58	13.18	13.82	14.49	15.19	15.94	17.55	19.34	20.30
11	11.57	12.17	12.81	13.49	14.21	14.97	15.78	16.65	17.56	18.53	20.65	23.04	24.35
12	12.68	13.41	14.19	15.03	15.92	16.87	17.89	18.98	20.14	21.38	24.13	27.27	29.00
13	13.81	14.68	15.62	16.63	17.71	18.88	20.14	21.50	22.95	24.52	28.03	32.09	34.35
14	14.95	15.97	17.09	18.29	19.60	21.02	22.55	24.21	26.02	27.98	32.39	37.58	40.50
15	16.10	17.29	18.60	20.02	21.58	23.28	25.13	27.15	29.36	31.77	37.28	43.84	47.58
16	17.26	18.64	20.16	21.82	23.66	25.67	27.89	30.32	33.00	35.95	42.75	50.98	55.72
17	18.43	20.01	21.76	23.70	25.84	28.21	30.84	33.75	36.97	40.54	48.88	59.12	65.08
18	19.61	21.41	23.41	25.65	28.13	30.91	34.00	37.45	41.30	45.60	55.75	68.39	75.84
19	20.81	22.84	25.12	27.67	30.54	33.76	37.38	41.45	46.02	51.16	63.44	78.97	88.21
20	22.02	24.30	26.87	29.78	33.07	36.79	41.00	45.76	51.16	57.28	72.05	91.02	102.4
21	23.24	25.78	28.68	31.97	35.72	39.99	44.87	50.42	56.76	64.00	81.70	104.8	118.8
22	24.47	27.30	30.54	34.25	38.51	43.39	49.01	55.46	62.87	71.40	92.50	120.4	137.6
23	25.72	28.85	32.45	36.62	41.43	47.00	53.44	60.89	69.53	79.54	104.6	138.3	159.3
24	26.97	30.42	34.43	39.08	44.50	50.82	58.18	66.76	76.79	88.50	118.2	158.7	184.2
25	28.24	32.03	36.46	41.65	47.73	54.86	63.25	73.11	84.70	98.35	133.3	181.9	212.8
26	29.53	33.67	38.55	44.31	51.11	59.16	68.68	79.95	93.32	109.2	150.3	208.3	245.7
27	30.82	35.34	40.71	47.08	54.67	63.71	74.48	87.35	102.7	121.1	169.4	238.5	283.6
28	32.13	37.05	42.93	49.97	58.40	68.53	80.70	95.34	113.0	134.2	190.7	272.9	327.1
29	33.45	38.79	45.22	52.97	62.32	73.64	87.35	104.0	124.1	148.6	214.6	312.1	377.2
30	34.78	40.57	47.58	56.08	66.44	79.06	94.46	113.3	136.3	164.5	241.3	356.8	434.7
40	48.89	60.40	75.40	95.03	120.8	154.8	199.6	259.1	337.9	442.6	767.1	1,342	1,779
50	64.46	84.58	112.8	152.7	209.3	290.3	406.5	573.8	815.1	1,164	2,400	4,995	7,218

■ A p p e n d i x   D

*Check Figures**

Chapter 1

Quick Check   1 b; 2 c; 3 b; 4 d; 5 a; 6 d;
　　　　　　　7 c; 8 c; 9 a; 10 d
S1-1   NCF
S1-2   NCF
S1-3   NCF
S1-4   NCF
S1-5   Owner, Capital $10,000
S1-6   Briggs, Capital $3,000
S1-7   NCF
S1-8   Gillen, Capital $34,000
S1-9   NCF
S1-10   Owner, Capital:
　　　　(a) $10,000 (b) −$6,000
S1-11   Net income $5,200
　　　　Total assets $35,400
S1-12   NCF
S1-13   Net income $40,000
S1-14   Owner, capital, Dec. 31, 20X8
　　　　$17,000
S1-15   Total assets $25,000
E1-1   NCF
E1-2   NCF
E1-3   NCF
E1-4   NCF
E1-5   Amy's Hallmark Owner's
　　　　Equity $22,900
E1-6   1. Increase in equity $3,000
E1-7   1. Net income $13,000
　　　　3. Net loss $1,000
E1-8   NCF
E1-9   Total assets $64,800
E1-10   2. Net income $1,000
E1-11   2. Total assets $25,000
E1-12   1. Net income $65,200
　　　　2. Capital, ending $27,100
E1-13   1. Net income $0.6 billion
　　　　2. Owner equity, ending $5.9
　　　　billion
E1-14   Net income $45,000
P1-1A   2. a. Total assets $100,600
　　　　d. Net income $1,100
P1-2A   1. Total assets $38,320
　　　　2. Net income $4,240
P1-3A   NCF
P1-4A   a. Net income $37,000
　　　　b. L. Collins, capital $71,000
　　　　c. Total assets $89,000
P1-5A   1. Net income $47,000
　　　　2. Matthew Vail, capital $58,000
　　　　3. Total assets $102,000
P1-6A   1. Total assets $105,000
P1-7A   1. Total assets $50,000
P1-1B   2. a. Total assets $81,000
　　　　d. Net income $4,000
P1-2B   1. Total assets $29,850
　　　　2. Net income $2,100

P1-3B   NCF
P1-4B   a. Net income $46,000
　　　　b. J. Robinson, capital $52,000
　　　　c. Total assets $88,000
P1-5B   1. Net income $64,000
　　　　2. Brian Sartor, capital $174,000
　　　　3. Total assets $279,000
P1-6B   1. Total assets $145,000
P1-7B   1. Total assets $88,000
Case 1 2. Total assets $500,000
Case 2 NCF
Financial Statement Case   2. Total
　　　　assets Dec. 31, 2002
　　　　$1,990,449,000
　　　　4. Net sales increased
　　　　$810,503,000

Chapter 2

Quick Check   1 c; 2 a; 3 d; 4 c; 5 b; 6 b;
　　　　　　　7 c; 8 d; 9 a; 10 a
S2-1   NCF
S2-2   NCF
S2-3   NCF
S2-4   NCF
S2-5   NCF
S2-6   NCF
S2-7   NCF
S2-8   NCF
S2-9   3. a. Earned $6,000
　　　　b. Total assets $6,000
S2-10   3. Trial bal. total $45,000
S2-11   Trial bal. total $74 mil.
S2-12   Incorrect Trial bal. total debits
　　　　$24,200
S2-13   Incorrect Trial bal. total debits
　　　　$13,300
S2-14   Total debits $180,000
E2-1   NCF
E2-2   1. Owners' equity $11 bil.
　　　　2. Net income $4 bil.
E2-3   NCF
E2-4   Total debits $180,600
E2-5   NCF
E2-6   2. Trial bal. total $74,700
E2-7   4. Trial bal. total $47,600
E2-8   NCF
E2-9   Trial bal. total $59,400
E2-10   Trial bal. total $184,100
E2-11   Trial bal. total $74,600
E2-12   Cash bal. $4,300
E2-13   Trial bal. total $22,300
E2-14   3. Total debits $53,000
E2-15   NCF
E2-16   b. Cash paid $75,000
　　　　c. Cash collected $88,000
E2-17   4. Trial bal. total $20,400

P2-1A   1. Total assets $268,000
　　　　Net income $45,000
P2-2A   NCF
P2-3A   3. Trial bal. total $35,500
P2-4A   3. Trial bal. total $33,500
P2-5A   1. Trial bal. total $85,100
　　　　2. Net income $10,140
P2-6A   3. Trial bal. total $61,200
P2-7A   1. Net income $400
　　　　2. Vince Serrano, capital Jan. 31,
　　　　20X7 $28,800
　　　　3. Total assets $54,900
P2-1B   1. Total assets $106,000
　　　　Net income $57,000
P2-2B   NCF
P2-3B   3. Trial bal. total $27,300
P2-4B   3. Trial bal. total $42,000
P2-5B   1. Trial bal. total $200,500
　　　　2. Net income $6,370
P2-6B   3. Trial bal. total $93,600
P2-7B   1. Net income $2,800
　　　　2. Christie Clinton, capital Dec.
　　　　31, 20X3 $50,300
　　　　3. Total assets $82,200
Case 1 3. Trial bal. total $17,500
　　　　4. Net income $5,550
Case 2 NCF
Financial Statement Case   Dec. 5 Debit
　　　　Cash $110,000; Credit Sales
　　　　Revenue $110,000

Chapter 3

Quick Check   1 d; 2 a; 3 b; 4 c; 5 a; 6 c;
　　　　　　　7 a; 8 b; 9 d; 10 c
S3-1   Service revenue:
　　　　Cash basis $900;
　　　　Accrual basis $1,200
S3-2   NCF
S3-3   2. Revenue $375,000
S3-4   Expense $140,000
S3-5   1. Prepaid Rent bal. $2,500
　　　　Rent Expense bal. $500
S3-6   3. Book value $23,000
S3-7   2. Interest Payable at Dec. 31
　　　　$900
S3-8   2. Interest Receivable at Dec. 31
　　　　$900
S3-9   NCF
S3-10   Supplies to report on balance
　　　　sheet $400
S3-11   Income statement reports ser-
　　　　vice revenue $7,400
S3-12   1. Total assets $45,925
　　　　Total liabilities $14,350
S3-13   1. Net income $3,525
E3-1   NCF

E3-2	NCF
E3-3	NCF
E3-4	A. Rent Expense $1,500
	B. Total to account for $1,300
E3-5	NCF
E3-6	Overall, net income is overstated by $7,000
E3-7	NCF
E3-8	Service Revenue bal. $6,900
E3-9	Adjusted trial bal. total $54,400
E3-10	NCF
E3-11	Net income $7,100; S. Perdue, capital $28,400; Total assets $29,300
E3-12	1. Net income $68,500
E3-13	1. Kent Black, capital Dec. 31, 20X5 $126,000
E3-14	Supplies expense $7,800 Salary expense $84,000 Service revenue $182,300
E3-15	7. Net income $1,690; Marsha Walker, capital $14,090; Total assets $18,790
P3-1A	2. Net income $9,150
P3-2A	NCF
P3-3A	a. Insurance Expense $1,800 d. Supplies Expense $6,600
P3-4A	Rental Revenue $700; Interest Revenue $300; Wage Expense $300
P3-5A	3. Adjusted trial bal. total $450,000
P3-6A	1. Net income $40,900; Cindy Sorrel, capital Dec. 31, 20X6 $37,900; Total assets $43,000
P3-7A	2. Net income $10,800; Pat Patillo, capital, July 31, 20X6 $45,900; Total assets $49,500
P3-1B	2. Net income $3,750
P3-2B	NCF
P3-3B	a. Salary Expense $4,000 d. Supplies Expense $6,400
P3-4B	Commission Revenue $8,000; Supplies Expense $900; Salary Expense $1,000
P3-5B	3. Adjusted trial bal. total $62,300
P3-6B	1. Net income $83,470; D. Brooks, capital Dec. 31, 20X8 $67,850; Total assets $134,030
P3-7B	2. Net income $5,400; Jack Dicorte, capital, Oct. 31, 20X7 $132,800; Total assets $136,000
Case 1	1. Your highest price $167,500 2. Wayne's lowest price $139,100
Case 2	Net income $33,540
Financial Statement Case	3. Account balances—all credits: Accum. Depr. $243,338,000; Interest Payable $71,661,000; Unearned Revenue $47,916,000
E3A-1	Supplies bal. $860
E3A-2	Unearned Service Revenue bal. $3,700

E3A-1	Prepaid Rent bal. $2,250; Unearned Service Revenue bal. $2,400

Chapter 4

Quick Check 1 a; 2 a; 3 d; 4 b; 5 b; 6 c; 7 d; 8 b; 9 b; 10 d

S4-1	NCF
S4-2	NCF
S4-3	NCF
S4-4	1. d. Close $3,525 2. Gay Gillen, Capital $31,575
S4-5	1. Gay Gillen, Capital $31,575
S4-6	NCF
S4-7	Income Summary Credit bal. $2,496 mil.
S4-8	Trial bal. total $7,260 mil.
S4-9	NCF
S4-10	c. $826 mil. d. $5,658 mil. e. $1,322 mil.
S4-11	Current ratio 1.71 Debt ratio 0.67
S4-12	1. $1.79 2. 49%
E4-1	Net income $2,200
E4-2	Sep. 30 Close net income of $2,200 to Gail Pfeiffer, Capital
E4-3	Gail Pfeiffer, Capital bal. $36,200
E4-4	Trial bal. total $42,200
E4-5	2. b. Insurance Expense $4,600
E4-6	Ending balances of Insurance Expense and Service Revenue are zero
E4-7	Park Daewoo, Capital bal. $59,800
E4-8	Felix Rohr, Capital bal. $72,700
E4-9	Alvin Chang, Capital, Dec. 31, 20X2 $235,000
E4-10	2. Net income $9,300
E4-11	1. Total assets $61,700 2. Current ratio of current year 1.99
E4-12	Net income $52,300
E4-13	1. Marsha Walker, Capital bal. $14,090; 2. Total assets $18,790 3. Net income $1,690
P4-1A	Net income $15,000
P4-2A	1. Net income $117,000 2. Ross Reagan, capital $104,000; Total assets $164,000
P4-3A	2. Close net income of $33,300
P4-4A	Net income $33,300
P4-5A	2. Net income $12,670 3. Total assets $45,460 5. Postclosing trial bal. total $49,110
P4-6A	1. Total assets $81,400 2. Debt ratio 20X3 0.53
P4-7A	a. Overall, net income is understated by $2,520
P4-1B	Net income $16,400

P4-2B	1. Net income $90,000 2. Betsy Willis, Capital $64,000; Total assets $131,000
P4-3B	2. Close net income of $85,100
P4-4B	Net income $85,100
P4-5B	2. Net income $21,000 3. Total assets $99,320 5. Postclosing trial bal. total $141,220
P4-6B	1. Total assets $124,600 2. Debt ratio 20X6 0.46
P4-7B	a. Overall, net income is understated by $1,060
Case 1	Net income $55,440
Case 2	NCF
Financial Statement Case	3. Current ratio at Dec. 31, 2002 1.52 5. Book value $239,398,000
Team Project	1. Net income $2,750 2. Total assets $2,950
P4A-1	All balances are the same both without and with reversing entries.

Chapter 5

Quick Check 1 d; 2 b; 3 c; 4 a; 5 a; 6 c; 7 d; 8 c; 9 b; 10 d

S5-1	NCF
S5-2	a. $100,000 b. $97,000
S5-3	c. Credit Cash for $97,000
S5-4	Cost of inventory $137,200
S5-5	c. Debit Cash for $137,200
S5-6	Gross profit $6,030
S5-7	b. Gross profit $315,360
S5-8	NCF
S5-9	C. Earnest, Capital bal. $25,650
S5-10	NCF
S5-11	Net income $1,666 mil.
S5-12	Total assets $11,471 mil.
S5-13	Gross profit % 20.7% Invy. turnover 56.4 times
S5-14	b. Excess of collections over payments $641 mil.
E5-1	May 22 Credit Cash for $464.75
E5-2	June 14 Credit Cash for $6,858
E5-3	May 14 Debit Cash for $6,790
E5-4	Sept. 23 Debit Cash for $2,231
E5-5	b. Net income for 2001 $13.7 bil.
E5-6	2. Gross profit for 20X1 $3,541 mil.
E5-7	f. $115,100 g. $112,100
E5-8	2. Owner Capital bal. $10,805 mil.
E5-9	Net income $80,760
E5-10	Net income $80,760
E5-11	1. Net income $31,300 2. Invy. turnover—current year 4.9 times
E5-12	Net income $31,300 Gross profit %—current year 48%

E5-13	Gross profit % 40%
	Invy. turnover 6.6 times
E5-14	3. Net income $4,900
P5-1A	NCF
P5-2A	NCF
P5-3A	2. Receivable $2,200
P5-4A	1. Net income $52,500
P5-5A	Net income $35,000
P5-6A	2. Elaine Lorens, Capital bal. $61,820
P5-7A	1. Net income $10,300
	2. Total assets $374,100
P5-8A	1. Net income $10,300
	2. Total assets $374,100
P5-9A	1. Net income $42,760
	2. Invy. turnover for 20X9 8.5 times
P5-1B	NCF
P5-2B	NCF
P5-3B	2. Belmont was $70 better off as a result of borrowing.
P5-4B	1. Net income $24,200
P5-5B	Net income $48,190
P5-6B	2. Jacob Xiang, Capital bal. $64,560
P5-7B	1. Net income $56,400
	2. Total assets $200,900
P5-8B	1. Net income $56,400
	2. Total assets $200,900
P5-9B	1. Net income $57,310
	2. Invy. turnover for 20X4 2.03 times
Case 1	Net income: Sever's plan $97,000
	Hagins' plan $102,000
Case 2	2. Net income $78,380
	Total assets $104,590
Financial Statement Case	Dec. 31 Credit Income Summary for total revenues of $3,963,047,000. Then debit Income Summary for total expenses of $4,112,179,000. Finally, credit Income Summary for net loss of $149,132,000.

Chapter 5 Appendix

E5A-1	June 23 Debit Cash for $2,352
E5A-2	May 22 Credit Cash for $469.54
E5A-3	May 14 Credit Cash for $6,790
	June 14 Credit Cash for $6,858
E5A-4	May 14 Debit Cash for $6,790
P5A-1	Nov. 27 Walgreen credits Cash for $2,300. Providence debits Cash for $2,300.
P5A-2	May 26 Credit Cash for $3,920.
	May 28 Debit Cash for $2,940.
P5A-3	1. Net income $88,850
	3. Ben Latham, Capital bal. $195,590
	4. Total assets $218,110

Chapter 6

Quick Check	1 a; 2 b; 3 d; 4 c; 5 d; 6 c; 7 a; 8 d; 9 b; 10 a
S6-1	a. COGS $160
	b. Inventory $310
S6-2	COGS $400
S6-3	Inventory $267
S6-4	Inventory bal. $100
S6-5	NCF
S6-6	NCF
S6-7	Gross profit: FIFO $260; LIFO $230
S6-8	COGS $338
S6-9	Report Inventory at $90
S6-10	NCF
S6-11	COGS understated by $100 mil.
S6-12	COGS overstated by $100 mil.
S6-13	Ending invy. $150,000
S6-14	Estimated cost of ending invy. $30,000
E6-1	End. invy. $240; COGS $910
E6-2	May 17 COGS $300
E6-3	End. invy. $220; COGS $930
E6-4	COGS $915; May 31 Invy. $235
E6-5	2. Gross profit $1,574 thou.
E6-6	End. invy.: FIFO $110; LIFO $102
E6-7	COGS: FIFO $420; LIFO $428
E6-8	Gross profit: FIFO $4,500; LIFO $3,700; Avg. $4,071
E6-9	COGS: Avg. $3,320; FIFO $3,270; LIFO $3,368
E6-10	a. $64,800; c. $24,350; d. $30,200; f. $34,700
E6-11	Gross profit $110,567
E6-12	Gross profit $68,000; End. invy. $18,300
E6-13	Gross profit is $70,000 with invy. overstated; $76,000 with invy. understated
E6-14	Net income: 20X2 $41,100; 20X1 $27,300
E6-15	Estimated cost of invy. destroyed $250,000
E6-16	Estimated cost of end. invy. $49,100
P6-1A	1. COGS $6,000; End. invy. $800
P6-2A	1. COGS $6,016; End. invy. $784
	2. Net income $2,484
P6-3A	1. COGS $1,365; End. invy. $225
	3. Gross profit $1,315
P6-4A	2. Gross profit: Avg. $34,293; FIFO $35,484; LIFO $33,092
P6-5A	1. Sales revenue $310,000
	2. COGS $195,000
P6-6A	NCF
P6-7A	1. Net income: 20X3 $11,000; 20X2 $9,000; 20X1 $27,000
P6-8A	1. Estimated cost of end. invy. $672,000
	2. Gross profit $2,592,000
P6-1B	1. COGS $7,750; End. invy. $300
P6-2B	1. COGS $7,705; End. invy. $345
	2. Net income $945
P6-3B	1. COGS $4,640; End. invy. $1,840
	3. Gross profit $3,270
P6-4B	2. Gross profit: Avg. $7,555; FIFO $7,833: LIFO $7,242
P6-5B	1. Sales revenue $378,000
	2. COGS $155,000
P6-6B	NCF
P6-7B	1. Net income: 20X3 $61,000; 20X2 $59,000; 20X1 $15,000
P6-8B	1. Estimated cost of end. invy. $275,000
	2. Gross profit $2,562,000
Case 1	NCF
Case 2	NCF
Financial Statement Case	3. Purchases $2,999,021,000

Chapter 7

Quick Check	1 c; 2 e; 3 a; 4 b; 5 c; 6 a; 7 b; 8 d; 9 d; 10 b
S7-1	NCF
S7-2	NCF
S7-3	NCF
S7-4	NCF
S7-5	NCF
S7-6	NCF
S7-7	NCF
S7-8	NCF
S7-9	2. Decrease in Accounts Receivable $1,235
S7-10	2. Credit Cash $2,876
S7-11	1. Increase in Accounts Payable $2,876
S7-12	2. Net sales revenue $7,456
E7-1	NCF
E7-2	Total assets $107,000
E7-3	NCF
E7-4	NCF
E7-5	Total debit to Cash $450
E7-6	NCF
E7-7	NCF
E7-8	Purchases journal: Total credit to Accounts Payable $18,265
E7-9	3. Total Accounts Payable $3,300
E7-10	Total credit to Cash $11,697
E7-11	Kendrick: Credit Cash for $1,151
E7-12	Gross profit $3,935
P7-1A	NCF
P7-2A	1. Cash receipts journal: Total debit to Cash $53,748
P7-3A	3. Corrected cash receipts journal: Total debit to Cash $24,302
P7-4A	1. Cash payments journal: Total credit to Cash $15,109
P7-5A	6. Total Accounts Receivable $560
	Total Accounts Payable $2,925
P7-1B	NCF
P7-2B	1. Cash receipts journal: Total debit to Cash $35,345

P7-3B	3. Corrected cash receipts journal: Total debit to Cash $10,830	S9-3	Accts. Rec., net $80,000	P9-6B	Jan. 20, 20X7 Debit Cash for $2,823
P7-4B	1. Cash payments journal: Total credit to Cash $17,237	S9-4	Uncollectible-Account Expenses $14,000		Dec. 14, 20X7 Debit Cash for $6,195
P7-5B	6. Total Accounts Receivable $496	S9-5	Allowance for Uncollectible Accts. bal. $5,000	P9-7B	Dec. 31, 20X4 Debit Uncollectible-Acct. Expense for $15,700

P7-5B 6. Total Accounts Receivable $496
Total Accounts Payable $2,692

Case 1 Cash receipts journal: Total debit to Cash $7,749

Case 2 NCF

Chapter 8

Quick Check 1 d; 2 a; 3 b; 4 d; 5 b; 6 d; 7 c; 8 c; 9 a; 10 c

S8-1	NCF
S8-2	NCF
S8-3	NCF
S8-4	NCF
S8-5	NCF
S8-6	Adjusted balance $2,900
S8-7	NCF
S8-8	NCF
S8-9	NCF
S8-10	NCF
S8-11	April 30 Credit Cash for $181
S8-12	NCF
E8-1	NCF
E8-2	NCF
E8-3	NCF
E8-4	NCF
E8-5	Adjusted balance $1,581
E8-6	Adjusted balance $3,371
E8-7	NCF
E8-8	NCF
E8-9	NCF
E8-10	1. Credit Cash in Bank for $209
E8-11	3. Petty Cash balance $400
E8-12	NCF
P8-1A	NCF
P8-2A	NCF
P8-3A	Adjusted balance $14,679
P8-4A	1. Adjusted balance $6,046.33
P8-5A	NCF
P8-6A	3. June 30 Credit Cash in Bank for $303
P8-7A	NCF
P8-1B	NCF
P8-2B	NCF
P8-3B	Adjusted balance $15,670
P8-4B	1. Adjusted balance $19,047.77
P8-5B	NCF
P8-6B	3. April 30 Credit Cash in Bank for $376
P8-7B	NCF
Case 1	NCF
Case 2	Cashier stole $1,000
Financial Statement Case	5. Cash increased by $197,972,000

Chapter 9

Quick Check 1 d; 2 c; 3 b; 4 a; 5 b; 6 d; 7 c; 8 b; 9 a; 10 c

S9-1	NCF
S9-2	NCF
S9-3	Accts. Rec., net $80,000
S9-4	Uncollectible-Account Expenses $14,000
S9-5	Allowance for Uncollectible Accts. bal. $5,000
S9-6	Uncollectible-Account Expense $2,300
S9-7	June 30 Accts. Rec. bal. $5,000
S9-8	Debit Cash for $7,760
S9-9	Note 1 $4,000
	Note 2 $375
S9-10	a. Credit Cash for $100,000
	b. Debit Cash for $102,000
S9-11	b. Debit Interest Receivable for $22.50
S9-12	1. Net income $1,184 mil.
	2. Accts. Rec., net $2,464 mil.
S9-13	a. 1.01 b. 35 days
S9-14	a. 1.48 c. 0.38
	b. 0.47 d. 6.9 times
E9-1	NCF
E9-2	2. Accts. Rec., net $54,600
E9-3	2. Accts. Rec. bal. $56,800
E9-4	2. Accts. Rec., net $289,300
E9-5	Accts. Rec., net $125,900
E9-6	1. Interest for:
	20X7 $6,000
	20X8 $3,000
E9-7	June 30 Debit Interest Receivable for $420
E9-8	May 1, 20X9 Debit Cash for $22,400
E9-9	Dec. 31 Debit Cash for $10,150
E9-10	1. 20X9 0.95
	2. 32 days
E9-11	1. 27 days
E9-12	Net income:
	Without bankcards $75,000;
	With bankcards $94,300
P9-1A	NCF
P9-2A	Uncollectible-Acct. Expense:
	1. $11,200
	2. $8,900
P9-3A	3. Accts. Rec., net $159,300
P9-4A	3. Accts. Rec., net $134,400
P9-5A	1. Note 1 $14,170; Note 2 $12,720; Note 3 $9,075
	3. Debit Cash for $14,170
P9-6A	Feb. 17, 20X5 Debit Cash for $3,060
	Dec. 1, 20X5 Debit Cash for $10,550
P9-7A	Dec. 31, 20X6 Debit Uncollectible-Acct. Expense for $14,800
P9-8A	1. Ratios for 20X6:
	a. 1.37 c. 18 days
	b. 0.70
P9-1B	NCF
P9-2B	Uncollectible-Acct. Expense:
	1. $8,900; 2. $3,500
P9-3B	3. Accts. rec., net $244,500
P9-4B	3. Accts. rec., net $160,100
P9-5B	1. Note 1 $13,080; Note 2 $11,330; Note 3 $15,250
	3. Debit Cash for $13,080

P9-6B	Jan. 20, 20X7 Debit Cash for $2,823
	Dec. 14, 20X7 Debit Cash for $6,195
P9-7B	Dec. 31, 20X4 Debit Uncollectible-Acct. Expense for $15,700
P9-8B	1. Ratios for 20X8:
	a. 1.88 c. 20 days
	b. 0.67
Case 1	2. Expected amount to collect $16,200
Case 2	1. Net income: 20X6 $106,600; 20X5 $85,550
Financial Statement Case	2. b. Expect to collect $112,282,000
	c. Expect not to collect $5,718,000
	3. Acid-test ratio for 2002 1.33

Chapter 10

Quick Check 1 b; 2 a; 3 d; 4 c; 5 a; 6 d; 7 b; 8 a; 9 c; 10 d

S10-1	NCF
S10-2	Land $60,000; Building $45,000; Equipment $15,000
S10-3	2. Net income overstated by $800,000
S10-4	2. Book value $34,800,000
S10-5	2nd-year depreciation:
	b. UOP $9,000,000; DDB $10,080,000
S10-6	2. Extra tax deduction with DDB $9,600,000
S10-7	$5,400,000
S10-8	Depreciation Expense $10,000
S10-9	Gain on Sale $3,000
S10-10	2. Depletion Expense $6.0 bil.
S10-11	Goodwill $500,000
S10-12	Net income $200,000
E10-1	Land $210,000; Land improvements $67,400; Building $800,000
E10-2	1. Cost of building $954,000
E10-3	Bed 1 $2,500; Bed 2 $4,170; Bed 3 $3,330
E10-4	NCF
E10-5	NCF
E10-6	20X9 Depreciation: SL $3,000; UOP $2,400; DDB $375
E10-7	Extra depreciation with DDB $38,388
E10-8	Depreciation for Year 16 $20,000
E10-9	Gain on sale $800
E10-10	Cost of new truck $300,000
E10-11	c. Depletion Expense $92,000
E10-12	Part 2. Amortization Expense for year 5 $250,000
E10-13	Goodwill $6,000,000
E10-14	Year 5: Equipment is correct; Net income is overstated by 1 million euros
E10-15	Gain on sale $458 mil.

P10-1A 2. Depreciation: Land Improvements $2,480; Building $16,500; Furniture $9,108
P10-2A Dec. 31 Depreciation Expense: Motor-Carrier Equip. $18,000; Buildings $750
P10-3A NCF
P10-4A 1. Book value at Dec. 31, 20X7: SL $64,000; UOP $53,000; DDB $31,104
P10-5A Part 1. Goodwill $2,500,000 Part 2. Net income $134,000
P10-6A 1. Book value $5.9 bil.; 2. Owners' equity $11.8 bil.; 3. Net income $3.1 bil.
P10-1B 2. Depreciation: Land Improvements $3,975; Building $30,621; Furniture $11,681
P10-2B Dec. 31 Depreciation Expense: Comm. Equip. $9,600; Televideo Equip. $1,067; Office Equip. $4,167
P10-3B NCF
P10-4B 1. Book value at Dec. 31, 20X8: SL $23,500; UOP $22,012; DDB $14,200
P10-5B Part 1. Goodwill $500,000 Part 2. Net income $95,000
P10-6B 1. Book value $29.0 bil.; 2. Owners' equity $12.6 bil.; 3. Net loss $1.4 bil.
Case 1 1. Net income: Stewart $164,000; Jordan $126,700
Case 2 NCF
Financial Statement Case
2. Depreciation expense $77 mil.
3. Purchases of fixed assets $39,613,000

Chapter 11

Quick Check 1 a; 2 c; 3 d; 4 c; 5 b; 6 a; 7 d; 8 a; 9 c; 10 d
S11-1 b. Credit Cash for $8,800
S11-2 Interest Expense $400
S11-3 2. Estimated Warranty Payable bal. $5,000
S11-4 NCF
S11-5 NCF
S11-6 2. Net pay $676.50
S11-7 Total expense $1,000.40
S11-8 a. Salary Payable $676.50
S11-9 Net pay $5,640
S11-10 1. Total salary expense $14,654; 2. Net pay $10,269.30
S11-11 NCF
S11-12 Total current liabilities $60,726
E11-1 Mar. 31 Debit Cash for $208,000
E11-2 Unearned subscription revenue bal. $120
E11-3 2. Estimated Warranty Payable bal. $5,000
E11-4 May 1, 20X3 Credit Cash for $15,900
E11-5 Net pay $7,430
E11-6 a. Net pay $462.50

E11-7 Payroll Tax Expense $7,630
E11-8 Salary expense $600,000; Salary payable $4,000
E11-9 20X1: Current portion of long-term note payable $1,000,000; Interest payable $270,000
E11-10 Total current liabilities $86,400
E11-11 Ratios for 20X2: Current 1.24; Debt 0.702
E11-12 NCF
P11-1A NCF
P11-2A 1. c. $83,693
P11-3A 1. Net pay $68,483 2. Total cost $101,574
P11-4A 3. Total liabilities $200,390
P11-5A 1. Total net pay $2,334 3. Credit Cash for $2,334 4. Debit Payroll Tax Expense for $181
P11-6A NCF
P11-1B NCF
P11-2B 1. c. $23,949
P11-3B 1. Net pay $68,993
P11-4B 2. Total cost $102,264 3. Total liabilities $331,440
P11-5B 1. Total net pay $3,412 3. Credit Cash for $3,412 4. Debit Payroll Tax Expense for $127
P11-6B NCF
Case 1 NCF
Case 2 NCF
Financial Statement Case
1. Debit Accounts Payable for $618,128,000; Credit Cash for $618,128,000
2. Total long-term debt $2,290,623,000

Chapter 12

Quick Check 1 b; 2 d; 3 b; 4 a; 5 c; 6 b; 7 d; 8 c; 9 d; 10 a
S12-1 NCF
S12-2 Debit Land for $400,000
S12-3 1. Total equity $23 mil.
S12-4 2. Benz, Capital $460,000 Hanna, Capital $95,000
S12-5 Lawson $38,000; Martinez $22,000; Norris $50,000
S12-6 NCF
S12-7 Teal, Capital $80,000
S12-8 Credit Page, Capital $6,667; Franco, Capital $3,333; Neely, Capital $130,000
S12-9 NCF
S12-10 a. Credit Green, Capital $10,000; Henry, Capital $20,000; Isaac, Capital $10,000
S12-11 Pay Akers $37,000; Bloch $19,000; Crane $9,000
S12-12 Final entry: Debit Akers, Capital $37,000; Bloch, Capital $19,000; Crane, Capital $9,000
S12-13 Green, capital $64,000; Henry, capital $63,000

S12-14 Net income: Frost $63,000; Martin $42,000
E12-1 NCF
E12-2 Credit Monteros, Capital for $76,700
E12-3 c. Coe $33,000; Price $65,000
E12-4 Partnership capital increased by $8,000
E12-5 c. Tse, capital $44,000; Graham, capital $108,000; Ott, capital $68,000
E12-6 c. Credit Tse, Capital for $44,000; Graham, Capital for $8,000; Ott, Capital for $8,000
E12-7 1. Echols receives $50,000; 2. Scheffer's equity $60,000
E12-8 b. Debit Augustine, Capital for $46,000; Rye, Capital for $8,400; Bermuda, Capital for $5,600
E12-9 2. Grant gets $20,000, Harris $17,000, and Isbell $8,000
E12-10 Pay Park $26,000, Quade $19,500, Ross $15,500
E12-11 Selling for $140,000: West, Capital $15,500; Young, Capital $43,300; Zeno, Capital $10,200
E12-12 Total assets $283,200; Klatt, capital $90,700; Stover, capital $93,100
P12-1A NCF
P12-2A 2. Total assets $102,100; Ogden, capital $41,500; Croyle, capital $41,500
P12-3A Carter's capital: 2. $60,000 3. $95,000
P12-4A 1. b. Net income to: Lake $79,750 Wood $63,500 Parks $66,750
P12-5A 3. Debit McNut, Capital for $50,000; Black, Capital for $13,548; Tate, Capital for $16,452
P12-6A 1. Pay Parr $19,700, Johnston $35,100, Rake $30,200
P12-7A 2. Capital balances: Vela $27,000 Thomas $16,000 Prago $9,000
P12-1B NCF
P12-2B 2. Total assets $124,740; Dalton, capital $51,220; Sperry, capital $51,220
P12-3B Milano's capital: 2. $50,000 3. $31,250
P12-4B 1. b. Net income to: Trump $33,667 Rivers $28,667 Jetta $23,666
P12-5B 3. Debit Tracy, Capital for $38,000; Mertz, Capital for $1,143; Brucks, Capital for $857
P12-6B 1. Pay Jackson $20,700; Pierce $52,800; Fenner $11,500

P12-7B	2. Capital balances: Alberts $10,250 Beech $12,750 Sumner $17,000
Case 1	NCF
Case 2	NCF

Chapter 13

Quick Check 1 d; 2 b; 3 a; 4 b; 5 c; 6 a; 7 c; 8 d; 9 c; 10 a

S13-1	NCF
S13-2	NCF
S13-3	NCF
S13-4	Balances: Building $500,000; Equip. $200,000
S13-5	1. Paid-in Capital in Excess of Par $3,855
S13-6	1. Total increase in paid-in capital $337 mil.
S13-7	a. Paid-in Capital in Excess—Common $49,000
S13-8	Total stockholders' equity $736,000
S13-9	a. Net income $80,000; c. Total assets $924,000
S13-10	NCF
S13-11	4. Preferred gets $6,000; common gets $3,000
S13-12	Book value per share of common $40.80
S13-13	NCF
S13-14	NCF
S13-15	ROA 13.8% ROE 26.3%
S13-16	2. Net income $60,000
E13-1	NCF
E13-2	2. Total paid-in capital $59,500
E13-3	2. Total stockholders' equity $86,000
E13-4	Both plans result in total paid-in capital of $50,000
E13-5	Total stockholders' equity $206,000
E13-6	Total paid-in capital $400,000
E13-7	Total stockholders' equity $400,000
E13-8	20X2: Preferred gets $17,000; common gets $33,000
E13-9	Preferred gets $40,000; Common gets $110,000
E13-10	Book value per share of common $22.20
E13-11	Book value per share of common $22.11
E13-12	ROA 0.063 ROE 0.111
E13-13	2. Net income $96 mil. Deferred tax liability $24 mil.
E13-14	d. Close net income of $8 mil. to Retained Earnings
P13-1A	NCF
P13-2A	2. Total stockholders' equity $266,000
P13-3A	5. Total stockholders' equity $152,000

P13-4A	Total stockholders' equity: Seville $799,000; Madrid $399,000
P13-5A	3. Dividends Payable: Preferred $12 mil.; Common $38 mil.
P13-6A	1. Total assets $387,000; Total S/E $309,000 2. ROA 0.144; ROE 0.198
P13-7A	1. b. 20X2: Preferred gets $70,000; Common gets $30,000
P13-8A	6. Book value per share of common $11.80
P13-9A	3. Net income $126,000
P13-1B	NCF
P13-2B	2. Total stockholders' equity $272,000
P13-3B	5. Total stockholders' equity $263,000
P13-4B	Total stockholders' equity: Yurman $430,000; Northern $622,900
P13-5B	3. Dividends Payable: Preferred $100 mil.; Common $400 mil.
P13-6B	1. Total assets $574,000; Total S/E $419,000 2. ROA 0.104; ROE 0.120
P13-7B	1. b. 20X2: Preferred gets $3,500; common gets $11,500
P13-8B	5. Book value per share of common $9.74
P13-9B	3. Net income $149,500
Case 1	3. Total stockholders' equity: Plan 1 $420,000; Plan 2 $400,000
Case 2	NCF
Financial Statement Case	3. At Dec. 31, 2002, Common shares issued 387,906,000; Common Stock balance $3,879,000

Chapter 14

Quick Check 1 d; 2 d; 3 a; 4 c; 5 c; 6 b; 7 a; 8 b; 9 a; 10 c

S14-1	Paid-in Capital in Excess of Par $75,000
S14-2	NCF
S14-3	1. Total stockholders' equity $590,000
S14-4	Balance sheet reports Treasury stock $(5,000)
S14-5	NCF
S14-6	NCF
S14-7	NCF
S14-8	Net income $21,000
S14-9	EPS for net income $1.80
S14-10	NCF
S14-11	Comprehensive income $17,000
S14-12	Retained earnings Dec. 31, 20X8 $460,000
S14-13	2. $80,000 3. Sold treasury stock for $15,000
E14-1	2. Total stockholders' equity $570,000
E14-2	NCF

E14-3	Total stockholders' equity $800,000
E14-4	d. Increase stockholders' equity by $3,000
E14-5	Aug. 22 Credit Paid-in Capital from Treasury Stock Transactions for $3,600
E14-6	Total stockholders' equity $870,000
E14-7	b. Total stockholders' equity $750,000
E14-8	Net income $42,000
E14-9	EPS $1.40
E14-10	EPS for net income $2.94
E14-11	Retained earnings Dec. 31, 20X3 $470 mil.
E14-12	Retained earnings Dec. 31, 20X7 $460 mil.
E14-13	1. Comprehensive income $114,000 2. EPS $5.85
E14-14	Total stockholders' equity Dec. 31, 20X7 $1,465,000
E14-15	2. Total stockholders' equity Dec. 31, 20X5 $17,000,000
P14-1A	Dec. 22 Credit Paid-in Capital from Treasury Stock Transactions for $1,000
P14-2A	2. Total stockholders' equity $568,000
P14-3A	NCF
P14-4A	3. Total stockholders' equity $552,700
P14-5A	Net income $62,000; EPS for net income $2.80
P14-6A	Retained earnings June 30, 20X4 $277,000; EPS for net income $4.15
P14-7A	EPS for net income $3.10
P14-8A	1. Par value $1.80 2. Price per share $11.00 3. Increase in equity $16,000
P14-1B	Nov. 8 Credit Paid-in Capital from Treasury Stock Transactions for $3,000
P14-2B	2. Total stockholders' equity $414,000
P14-3B	NCF
P14-4B	3. Total stockholders' equity $710,680
P14-5B	Net income $64,000; EPS for net income $2.25
P14-6B	Retained earnings Dec. 31, 20X3 $444,200; EPS for net income $1.80
P14-7B	1. EPS for net income $2.25
P14-8B	1. Par value $2 2. Price per share $6.40 3. Increase in equity $28,000
Case 1	NCF
Case 2	NCF
Financial Statement Case	2. Basic EPS (loss per share) $(0.39) 3. Accumulated Deficit balance—debit of $3,009,710,000

Chapter 15

Quick Check   1 a; 2 c; 3 d; 4 c; 5 b; 6 a; 7 b; 8 c; 9 b; 10 d

S15-1   c. $77,750
d. $110,375
S15-2   a. $4,825
c. $162.50
S15-3   NCF
S15-4   NCF
S15-5   NCF
S15-6   July 1, 2000 Interest Expense $188
S15-7   July 1, 2000 Interest Expense $138
S15-8   Dec. 31, 2000 Interest Expense $188
S15-9   LT liabilities: Bonds payable, net $4,550
S15-10   2. Bond carrying amount. Mar. 31, 20X4 $546,749
S15-11   2. Bond carrying amount May 31, 20X6 $217,158
S15-12   Interest Expense July 1, 2000 $54.17
S15-13   Gain on retirement of bonds $6,872
S15-14   2. Paid-in Capital in Excess of Par $820,000
S15-15   Total current liabilities $26,000; LT bonds payable, net $344,000
S15-16   EPS: Plan A $5.78; Plan B $3.15
E15-1   c. Dec. 31 Interest Expense $10,000
E15-2   July 1 Interest Expense $4,050
E15-3   At July 1:
b. Credit Discount for $250
c. Debit Premium for $250
E15-4   NCF
E15-5   1. Bond carrying amount 1-2-X5 $280,995
E15-6   1. Bond carrying amount 3-31-X3 $219,390
E15-7   Bond carrying amount 12-31-X5 $500,000
E15-8   Total cash received $510,000
E15-9   b. Oct. 31 Interest Expense $10,000
E15-10   Oct. 1 Loss on Retirement of Bonds $12,750
E15-11   2. Bond carrying amount July 31, 20X9 $691,600
E15-12   2. Oct. 1 Credit Paid-in Capital in Excess of Par for $144,000
E15-13   NCF
E15-14   EPS: Plan A $7.98; Plan B $4.26
E15-15   4. Interest expense $40,575,000
5. Bond carrying amount Mar. 31, 2001 $295,717
6. Interest expense $40,343,000
E15-16   2. a. $295,725
b. $295,950
P15-1A   2. Interest Expense Jan. 31, 20X4 $4,500; 3. Interest expense for 20X3 $49,500; Interest payable $22,500

P15-2A   3. d. Interest Expense Mar. 31, 20X7 $7,900
P15-3A   Interest Expense:
Dec. 31, 2009 $14,600
Dec. 31, 2018 $14,600
P15-4A   2. Bond carrying amount Sep. 30, Year 3 $148,095
P15-5A   1. d. Interest Expense Mar. 31, 20X5 $67,500
2. Interest payable at Dec. 31, 20X4 $67,500
P15-6A   3. Convertible bonds payable, net $569,903
P15-7A   Total current liabilities $152,000
Total LT liabilities $383,000
P15-8A   NCF
P15-1B   2. Interest Expense, Apr. 30, 20X6 $13,333
3. Interest expense $26,667; Interest payable $6,667
P15-2B   3. d. Interest Expense Feb. 28, 20X5 $5,633
P15-3B   Interest Expense:
Dec. 31, 2005 $38,400
Dec. 31, 2014 $38,400
P15-4B   2. Bond carrying amount Sep. 30, Year 3 $167,263
P15-5B   1. d. Interest Expense May 31, 20X6 $233,333
2. Interest payable at Dec. 31, 20X5 $46,667
P15-6B   3. Convertible bonds payable, net $423,327
P15-7B   Total current liabilities $100,000
Total LT liabilities $289,000
P15-8B   NCF
Case 1   EPS: Plan A $6.24; Plan B $5.30; Plan C $6.00
Case 2   NCF
Financial Statement Case
3. Annual interest $59,366,000

Chapter 15 Appendix

P15A-1   Future value:
Plan A $15,432
Plan B $15,870
P15A-2   Present value:
GE $216,300
Westinghouse $226,800
P15A-3   1. Invest $5,580 today
P15A-4   Present value of bonds:
a. $88,018
b. $78,640
c. $98,975
P15A-5   Interest expense for bonds issued at:
12% $5,280
14% $5,748
10% $4,731
P15A-6   2. Bond carrying amount 12-31-X2 $380,838
3. Interest expense Dec. 31, 20X2 $15,205

Chapter 16

Quick Check   1 a; 2 c; 3 b; 4 d; 5 c; 6 c; 7 b; 8 a; 9 b; 10 d

S16-1   a. $3,314
b. $38,304
S16-2   NCF
S16-3   2. Jan. 27, 20X5 Loss on Sale $3,000
S16-4   2. Jan. 16, 20X7 Gain on Sale $1,750
S16-5   2. Gain on sale $1,000
S16-6   2. Unrealized loss $435
S16-7   1. Gain on Sale $510
S16-8   3. LT Equity-Method Investment bal. $104 mil.
S16-9   NCF
S16-10   4. Annual interest revenue $78,000
S16-11   b. Interest Revenue $70,000
c. Interest Revenue $8,000
S16-12   Overall foreign-currency gain $1,000
E16-1   1. Jan. 14, 20X9 Gain on Sale $6,000
E16-2   d. Gain on Sale $800
E16-3   Dec. 4 Loss on Sale $550
E16-4   3. LT available-for-sale investments $205,030; Unrealized loss $15,500
E16-5   b. Equity-Method Investment Revenue $156,000
E16-6   Gain on sale $444,000
E16-7   2. LT Equity-Method Investment bal. $169,000
E16-8   3. LT investment in bonds $27,840
E16-9   Dec. 16 Foreign-Currency Loss $160
Dec. 30 Foreign-Currency Gain $2,400
E16-10   1. Cost $274 mil.
2. Loss on sale $15 mil.
P16-1A   1. Dec. 31 Loss on Trading Investment $3,500
P16-2A   3. LT available-for-sale investments $26,800; LT equity-method investments $431,500
P16-3A   LT Equity-Method Investment bal. $832,000; Unrealized gain $1,100
P16-4A   2. LT investment in bonds $409,600
P16-5A   Investment carrying amount 12-31-X6 $488,051
P16-6A   Income statement reports Foreign-currency loss, net $2,400
P16-1B   1. Dec. 31 Loss on Trading Investment $4,500
P16-2B   3. LT available-for-sale investment $44,100; LT equity-method investments $724,000
P16-3B   LT Equity-Method Investment bal. $920,000; Unrealized loss $2,500
P16-4B   2. LT investment in bonds $744,000

P16-5B   Investment carrying amount
12-31-X7 $388,355

P16-6B   Income statement reports
Foreign-currency loss, net $600

Case 1   NCF

Case 2   NCF

Financial Statement Case   1.a. Market
value $562,715,000

Chapter 17

Quick Check   1 b; 2 d; 3 c; 4 a; 5 d; 6 c;
7 a; 8 a; 9 d; 10 b

S17-1   NCF

S17-2   NCF

S17-3   NCF

S17-4   Net cash from operating
$48,000

S17-5   Net cash from operating
$40,000

S17-6   Net cash from operating
$40,000; Net increase in cash
$39,000

S17-7   Acquisitions of plant assets
$100,000

S17-8   a. $2,000 c. $84,000
b. $3,000

S17-9   Net cash from operating
$180,000; Cash balance ending
$94,000

S17-10   Net cash from operating
$50,000

S17-11   Net cash from operating
$50,000; Net increase in cash
$54,000

S17-12   a. $704,000
b. $331,000

E17-1   NCF

E17-2   NCF

E17-3   NCF

E17-4   Net cash used for operating
$(8,000)

E17-5   Net cash from operating $79,000

E17-6   1. Net cash from operating
$80,000; investing ($77,000);
financing $4,000

E17-7   a. $34,000
b. $6,000

E17-8   NCF

E17-9   NCF

E17-10   Net cash used for operating
$(8,000)

E17-11   NCF

E17-12   Net cash from operating
$80,000; investing ($77,000);
financing $4,000

E17-13   a. $85,000
b. $89,000

E17-14   a. $24,440 mil.
b. $18,516 mil.
c. $4,793 mil.
d. $1,186 mil.
e. $14 mil.
f. $230 mil.
g. $143 mil.

P17-1A   NCF

P17-2A   1. Net income $35,000
2. Total assets $588,000
3. Net cash used for operating
$(71,000); Cash bal., Dec. 31,
20X8 $268,000

P17-3A   Net cash from operating
$87,000; investing $(67,000);
financing $43,000; Total non-
cash investing and financing
$65,000

P17-4A   1. Net cash from operating
$96,900; investing $(125,700);
financing $31,000

P17-5A   1. Net cash from operating
$69,100; investing $(37,000);
financing $(30,600)

P17-6A   Net cash from operating
$115,700; investing $(37,000);
financing $(70,800)

P17-7A   1. Net income $35,000; 2. Total
assets $588,000; 3. Net cash
used for operating $(71,000);
Cash balance Dec. 31, 20X8
$268,000

P17-8A   1. Net cash from operating
$69,100; investing $(37,100);
financing $(30,600)

P17-9A   Net cash from operating
$67,800; investing $(10,200);
financing $(47,600)

P17-1B   NCF

P17-2B   1. Net income $80,000 2. Total
assets $345,000 3. Net cash
from operating $85,000; Cash
bal., Dec. 31, 20X6 $195,000

P17-3B   Net cash from operating
$80,000; investing $(69,000);
financing $11,000; Total non-
cash investing and financing
$118,000

P17-4B   1. Net cash from operating
$49,000; investing $(179,000);
financing $120,000

P17-5B   1. Net cash from operating
$79,800; investing $(47,600);
financing $(29,900)

P17-6B   Net cash from operating
$(30,000); investing $(40,300);
financing $91,700

P17-7B   1. Net income $80,000 2. Total
assets $345,000 3. Net cash
from operating $85,000; Cash
bal., Dec. 31, 20X6 $195,000

P17-8B   1. Net cash from operating
$79,800; investing $(47,600);
financing $(29,900)

P17-9B   Net cash from operating
$77,200; investing $(51,500);
financing $(30,300)

Case 1   1. Net cash from operating
$140,000; investing $(141,000);
financing $(37,000)

Case 2   NCF

Financial Statement Case   3. a.
Collections $3,888,267,000
b. Payments $2,825,641,000

Chapter 17 Appendix

P17A-1   Column totals:
Dec. 31, 20X7 $255,400
Dec. 31, 20X8 $287,800

17A-2   Column totals:
Dec. 31, 20X7 $255,400
Dec. 31, 20X8 $287,800

Chapter 18

Quick Check   1 a; 2 b; 3 d; 4 c; 5 b; 6 c;
7 c; 8 a; 9 d; 10 d

S18-1   2002 Gross profit increase 5.0%

S18-2   1. Trend % for 2002 revenue
113%

S18-3   20X6 Cash 20.9% of total assets

S18-4   Net income % of sales: Nike
6.2%; Home Depot 4.8%

S18-5   1. Current ratio for 2002 1.21

S18-6   a. 3.9 times
b. 70 days

S18-7   1. Debt ratio 0.64

S18-8   a. 11.4% c. 22.9%
b. 9.4%

S18-9   1. $0.48
2. 56 times

S18-10   d. $698 mil.

S18-11   a. $631 mil.
c. $1,581 mil.
f. $6,315 mil.

S18-12   1. EVA® $1,858 mil.

E18-1   2006 Increase in working capital 14.3%

E18-2   Total revenue increased 15.3%;
Net income increased 58.8%

E18-3   Trend % for Year 5:
Total revenue 136%
Net income 155%

E18-4   Total current assets 13.0%;
Long-term debt 33.3%

E18-5   % for 2005: COGS 47.0%; Net
income 18.8%

E18-6   a. 1.41   c. 4.01 times
b. 0.70   d. 55 days

E18-7   Ratios for 20X4:
a. 1.56   c. 0.59
b. 0.69   d. 3.44 times

E18-8   Ratios for 20X6:
a. 0.103   c. 0.162
b. 0.137   d. $0.75

E18-9   Ratios for 20X4:
a. 20   c. $4.75
b. 0.022

E18-10   EVA®: Oracle $1,598 mil.; Wells
Fargo −$986 mil.

E18-11   Total assets $19,565 mil.;
Current liabilities $6,752 mil.

P18-1A 1. Trend % for 20X8: Net sales 127%; Net income 161%; Total assets 145%
2. Return on sales for 20X8 0.081

P18-2A 1. Gross profit 31.9%; Net income 9.2%; Current assets 77.1%; Stockholders' equity 39.4%

P18-3A 2. a. Current ratio 2.23; Debt ratio 0.49; EPS no effect

P18-4A 1. Ratios for 20X6:
a. 2.10   d. 0.253
b. 1.18   e. $4.47
c. 2.81   f. 8.2

P18-5A 1. Blues ratios:
a. 0.66   d. 0.68
b. 2.30   e. $0.37
c. 94 days f. 21.6
2. Blues EVA® $25,000

P18-6A NCF

P18-1B 1. Trend % for 2008: Net revenues 118%; Net income 106%; Common stockholders' equity 124%
2. ROE for 2008 0.142

P18-2B 1. Gross profit 36.4%; Net income 14.7%; Current assets 77.8%; Stockholders' equity 40.2%

P18-3B 2. a. Current ratio 1.35; Debt ratio 0.61; EPS No effect

P18-4B 1. Ratios for 20X9:
a. 1.80   d. 0.357
b. 1.48   e. $5.00
c. 8.82   f. 10.6

P18-5B 1. Caremark ratios:
a. 0.78   d. 0.41
b. 2.32   e. $4.80
c. 40 days f. 10.6
2. Caremark EVA® $29,000

P18-6B NCF
Case 1 NCF
Case 2 NCF
Financial Statement Case   NCF

Chapter 19

Quick Check   1 d; 2 a; 3 b; 4 b; 5 d; 6 c; 7 d; 8 a; 9 a; 10 c
S19-1 NCF
S19-2 NCF
S19-3 NCF
S19-4 NCF
S19-5 NCF
S19-6 CGS $41,000
S19-7 CGM $35,000
S19-8 Total MOH $15,275
S19-9 DM used $19,700
S19-10 NCF
S19-11 NCF
S19-12 Total expected benefits $199 million
S19-13 NCF
S19-14 NCF

E19-1 NCF
E19-2 Total inventoriable product costs $142
E19-3 Total inventoriable product costs $33,000
E19-4 NCF
E19-5 Total current assets $214,000
E19-6 CGM $213,000
E19-7 NI $49,000
E19-8 a. CGS $15,000
b. Beg. Materials inv. $2,000
c. End. FG inv. $5,100
E19-9 NCF
E19-10 Expected benefits exceed costs by $84,500
E19-11 NCF

P19-1A Total MOH $4,775
Total inventoriable product costs $34,575

P19-2A Part One: Hannah's Pets Op. Inc. $13,500
Part Two: Best Friends Manufacturing CGM $67,655; Op. Inc. $35,545
Part Three: Best Friends' Manufacturing total inventories $15,695

P19-3A Direct labor $71,000; CGM $162,000; Op. Inc. $100,000

P19-4A *Req 1:* Total benefits if project succeeds $830,000
Req 2: Expected value of the benefits exceed cost by $109,000

P19-5A *Req 2:* Expected value of the benefits falls short of costs by $57,000

P19-6A Present value of benefits exceeds costs by $227,000

P19-7A *Req 1:* Present value of expected benefits $1,102,600
Req 2: Expected value of benefits falls short of costs by $27,400

P19-8A NCF

P19-1B Total MOH $415
Total inventoriable product costs $12,145

P19-2B Part One: Precious Memories Op. Inc. $33,750
Part Two: Forever Manufacturing CGM $72,750; Op. Inc. $44,000
Part Three: Forever Manufacturing total inventories $11,500

P19-3B Manufacturing overhead $40,000; Beg. FG inv. $124,000

P19-4B *Req 1:* Total benefits if project succeeds $470,500
Req 2: Expected value of the benefits exceeds cost by $78,850

P19-5B NCF

P19-6B Present value of benefits exceeds costs by $3,200

P19-7B *Req 1:* Expected value of benefits from additional business $49,560
Req 2: Present value of expected benefits exceeds cost by $9,560

P19-8B NCF
Case 1 End. Materials inv $143,000; End. WIP inv. $239,000; End FG inv. $150,000
Case 2 NCF
Ethical Issue   NCF
Financial Statement Case   NCF
Team Project   NCF

Chapter 20

Quick Check   1 b; 2 d; 3 c; 4 d; 5 a; 6 a; 7 c; 8 b; 9 d; 10 a
S20-1 NCF
S20-2 NCF
S20-3 Ending Materials Inv., $43,500
S20-4 DM, $200
S20-5 NCF
S20-6 Total MOH, $65,000
S20-7 Total cost, $1,180
S20-8 Indirect materials used, $2,000
S20-9 MOH is $1,000 underallocated
S20-10 MOH is $25,000 underallocated
S20-11 NCF
S20-12 DL for Client 367, $770
S20-13 Indirect cost for Client 367, $350

E20-1 NCF
E20-2 WIP Inv., $8,400
E20-3 MOH allocated, $21,000
E20-4 Item f is closing underallocated MOH
E20-5 1. End. WIP Inv., $11,000
4. GP on G-65, $8,000
E20-6 2. MOH allocated, $102,240
3. Underallocated MOH, $2,360
E20-7 2. MOH allocated, $440,000
3. Underallocated MOH, $70,000
E20-8 1. Overallocated MOH, $10,000
3. Adjusted CGS, $590,000
E20-9 1. b. Indirect cost allocation rate, 70%
2. Total predicted cost, $58,718
E20-10 1. MH used, 20,250
2. Underallocated overhead, $243,000
P20-1A 1. c. March CGS, $3,000
April CGS, $2,900
4. GP for Job 5, $900
P20-2A 2. End. WIP Inv., $102,400
FG Inv., $92,820
5. GP for Chalet 13, $34,220
P20-3A 1. MOH allocated, $1,134
Total job cost, $4,504
P20-4A 1. PMOHR, $25/MH
3. Underallocated MOH, $22,000

P20-5A 2. End. WIP Inv., $99,090
FG Inv., $60,550
4. CGM, $63,200

P20-6A 2. GoVacation.com, $74,890
3. Port Armour, $5,950

P20-1B 1. c. Nov. CGS, $1,400
Dec. CGS, $3,650
2. Transferred to FG in Nov.,
$3,300
Transferred to FG in Dec.,
$3,850

P20-2B 2. End. WIP Inv., $272,900
FG Inv., $117,620
5. GP for House 304, $51,340

P20-3B 1. MOH allocated, $648
Total job cost, $2,373

P20-4B 1. PMOHR, $7/MH
3. Underallocated MOH,
$49,750

P20-5B 2. End. WIP Inv., $38,080
FG Inv., $21,280
4. CGM, $49,160

P20-6B 2. Organic Foods, $128,500
3. SunNow.com, $9,575

Case 1 NCF
Case 2 NCF
Ethical Issue NCF
Team Project 1. Delta's profit per
flight 1247, $1,004.79
2. JetBlue's profit per flight 53,
$2,659.55

Chapter 21

Quick Check 1 b; 2 c; 3 d; 4 a; 5 c; 6 a;
7 d; 8 d; 9 b; 10 d

S21-1 NCF
S21-2 2. Cost per liter, $0.84
S21-3 2. EU of DM, 200,000
EU of CC, 192,000
S21-4 EU of DM, 50,000
EU of CC, 43,000
S21-5 CC/EU, $1.90
S21-6 DM/EU, $0.60; CC/EU, $0.25
S21-7 2. End. WIP Inv., $32,000
S21-8 End. WIP Inv., $32,000
S21-9 2. EU of TI costs, 168,000
EU of DM, 154,000
EU of CC, 163,800
S21-10 TI cost/EU, $0.82; DM/EU,
$0.20; CC/EU, $0.35
S21-11 End. WIP Inv., $14,910
S21-12 End. WIP Inv., $14,910
E21-1 NCF
E21-2 NCF
E21-3 2. EU of DM, 8,000
3. End. WIP Inv., $1,440
E21-4 2. End. WIP Inv., $1,440
3. Avg. Cost/gal. CTO, $1.00
E21-5 1. EU of DM 18,000
2. CC/EU, $1.40
3. End. WIP Inv., $10,610
E21-6 2. EU of CC, 7,710
3. End. WIP Inv., $3,146.50
E21-7 3. Avg. Cost/gal. CTO, $2.35

E21-8 Costs transferred out, $392,400
E21-9 2. Mixing Dep't. EU of TI costs,
90,000
Heating Dep't. EU of TI costs,
86,000
E21-10 2. EU of TI, 35,000
3. End. WIP Inv., $75,996
P21-1A 2. EU of DM, 20,400
CC/EU, $0.25
3b. End. WIP Inv., $1,560
P21-2A 2. EU of CC, 11,700
CC/EU, $25
3b. End. WIP Inv., $172,500
P21-3A 2. EU of CC, 14,160
3. CC/EU, $1
3b. End. WIP Inv., $3,570
P21-4A 2. EU of CC, 2,900
TI cost/EU, $15; CC/EU, $24
3. Costs transferred out,
$110,000
P21-5A 2. EU of CC, 19,800
3. TI cost/EU, $0.14
3b. End. WIP Inv., $3,078
P21-1B 2. EU of CC, 90,560
CC/EU, $3.05
3b. End. WIP Inv., $131,688
P21-2B 2. EU of CC, 4,600
CC/EU, $0.90
3b. End. WIP Inv., $210
P21-3B 2. EU of CC, 2,370
3. CC/EU, $0.80
3b. End. WIP Inv., $1,281
P21-4B 2. EU of CC, 608
TI cost/EU, $40; CC/EU, $93
3. Costs transferred out, $77,000
P21-5B 2. EU of CC, 6,000
3. TI cost/EU, $85
3. b. End. WIP Inv., $447,000
Case 3. Op. Inc., $1,800
5. Selling price per box, $12.93
Ethical Issue NCF
Team Project 1. Max. TI cost/lb., $0.23
2. Cutting Dep't. cost/lb., $0.17

Chapter 21 Appendix

S21A-1 2. EU of TI, 160,000
EU of CC, 160,600
S21A-2 DM/EU, $0.20
S21A-3 End. WIP Inv., $15,330
E21A-1 1a. 40%, 25%
2. Mixing Dep't. EU of DM
75,000
Cooking Dep't. EU of CC
76,700
E21A-2 2. EU of CC, 25,900
3. b. End. WIP Inv., $79,200
P21A-1 2. EU of DM, 3,100
DM/EU, $8; CC/EU, $16
3. Costs transferred out, $123,140
P21A-2 2. EU of CC, 17,700
CC/EU, $0.11
3b. End. WIP Inv., $3,648
P21A-3 2. EU of DM, 2,200
TI cost/EU, $12; DM/EU, $11
3. Costs transferred out, $116,300

Chapter 22

Quick Check 1 b; 2 d; 3 a; 4 b; 5 b; 6 a;
7 b; 8 a; 9 a; 10 c

S22-1 NCF
S22-2 1c. Total cost, $33
S22-3 a. BEP, 6,875 tickets
S22-4 1. CM ratio, 0.66667
S22-5 7,875 tickets
S22-6 NCF
S22-7 B is the total expense line
S22-8 1. 9,167 tickets
2. 6,111 tickets
S22-9 1. BEP, 5,000 tickets
S22-10 a. Margin of safety, 125 tickets
c. Margin of safety, 1.79%
S22-11 b. Margin of safety, $10,500
S22-12 VC Op. Inc., $106,500
S22-13 1. AC Op. Inc., $101,500
S22-14 NCF
E22-1 NCF
E22-2 Op. Loss when sales are
$250,000 = $20,000
BEP, $283,333
E22-3 1. CM ratio, 50%
2. BEP, 100,000 packages
E22-4 1. BEP, $12,000
2. Sales required to earn target
income, $24,500
E22-5 2. Op. Loss when sales are
$500,000 = $240,000
E22-6 3. BEP, 500 students, $50,000
E22-7 2. BEP, 1,200,000 tickets
E22-8 1. Margin of safety, $40,000
E22-9 1. AC Op. Inc., $675,000
VC Op. Inc., $525,000
3. Increase in Op. Inc., $75,000
P22-1A NCF
P22-2A CM ratio:
Q 0.70
S 0.60
T 0.711
P22-3A 1. VE per show, $15,200
2. BEP, 38 shows
3. Target shows, 96 shows
P22-4A 1. BEP, 150,000 cartons
2. Target sales, $2,000,000
3. Op. Inc., $2,070,000
4. BEP, $2,535,750
P22-5A 1. BEP, 24 trades
2. Target sales, $14,400
4. BEP, 32 trades
P22-6A 1. AC product cost/meal
Jan., $4.50
Feb., $4.70
2. a. AC Op. Inc.
Jan., $900
Feb., $1,040
P22-1B NCF
P22-2B A CM ratio, 0.550
B CM per unit, $3.75
C CM ratio, 0.491
P22-3B 1. VE per show, $27,200
2. BEP, 9 shows
3. Target shows, 139 shows

P22-4B 1. BEP, 87,000 flags
2. Target sales, $1,094,000
3. Op. Loss, $132,600
4. BEP, 108,576 flags

P22-5B 1. BEP, 40 trades
2. Target sales, $42,000
4. BEP, 50 trades

P22-6B 1. AC product cost/game
Oct., $19
Nov., $20
2. a. AC Op. Inc.
Oct., $17,000
Nov., $17,900

Case 1 BEP, 4,800 meals
To earn target Op. Inc., 7,500 meals

Case 2 NCF

Ethical Issue NCF

Financial Statement Case
3. 2002 CM, $899,769
4. 2002 CM ratio, 0.22878
5. 2002 BEP, $3,652,614

Team Project 1. Op. Loss in 20X6, $1.5 million
2. Adopting ad campaign will increase Op. Inc. by $1.5 million

Chapter 22 Appendix

S22A-1 WA CM/unit, $66.91
S22A-2 a. 3,737 total tickets
E22A-1 BEP, 264 standard and 176 chrome
E22A-2 WA CM/unit, $125;
CM per Classic, $300
P22A-1 1. BEP, 12,000 small and 4,000 large
3. Op. Inc., $31,750

Chapter 23

Quick Check 1 d; 2 a; 3 a; 4 d; 5 b; 6 c;
7 a; 8 c; 9 d; 10 b

S23-1 NCF
S23-2 NCF
S23-3 Feb. sales, $770,000
S23-4 Jan. purchases, $490,750
Feb. purchases, $585,650
S23-5 June cash sales, $24,000
S23-6 May purchases, $48,000
S23-7 May cash collections, $71,000
S23-8 May cash payments for purchases, $47,600
S23-9 January cash collections, $548,330
S23-10 Grippers must borrow $34,070
S23-11 NCF
S23-12 NCF
S23-13 NCF
S23-14 NCF

E23-1 NI this year, $220,000
E23-2 Purchases, qtr. ended June 30, $88,500
Purchases, qtr. ended Sept. 30, $80,700
E23-3 Qtr. 2 NI, $856,960
Qtr. 3 NI, $950,546
E23-4 b. Sept. cash receipts from customers, $106,830
E23-5 1. Nov. borrowing, $1,000
E23-6 Feb. borrowing, $11,100
March interest paid, $74
E23-7 Total assets, $30,280
Owners' Equity, $25,980
E23-8 NCF
E23-9 Total cell phone Op. Inc. Var., $45,000 F

P23-1A May CGS, $15,500
May NI, $14,300
June NI, $9,500
P23-2A 1a. May cash collections, $42,660
b. May cash payments for purchases, $18,125
c. May cash payments for op. expenses, $8,708
2. May ending cash balance, $26,827
June ending cash balance, $39,991
P23-3A 1. Ending cash balance, $55,000
Total Assets, $143,900
Owners' Equity, $115,600
2. Net increase in cash, $14,400
3. Cash available, $76,800
P23-4A 1. Ending cash balance, $29,500
Total Assets, $131,900
Owners' Equity, $103,600
P23-5A NCF
P23-6A 1. Dayton Op. Inc. Var., $6,100U
Other Ohio stores Op. Inc. Var., $4,400 F
Companywide Op. Inc. Var., $86,000 U
P23-1B Aug. CGS, $120,000
Aug. NI, $26,000
Sept. NI, $28,000
P23-2B 1a. Aug. cash collections, $199,000
b. Aug. cash payments for purchases, $124,720
c. Aug. cash payments for op. expenses, $40,090
2. Aug. ending cash balance, $56,190
Sept. ending cash balance, $97,250
P23-3B 1. Ending cash balance, $45,200
Total Assets, $172,700
Owners' Equity, $145,600
2. Net decrease in cash, $5,000
P23-4B 1. Ending cash balance, $31,200
Total Assets, $162,700
Owners' Equity, $135,600
P23-5B NCF

P23-6B 1. Store No. 23 Op. Inc. Var., $2,000 F
Other Dallas stores Op. Inc. Var., $9,000 F
Texas Op. Inc. Var., $44,400 F
Case 1 NCF
Case 2 1. NI cotton mats, $235
NI linen mats, $225
Ethical Issue NCF
Financial Statement Case
3. Company-wide total Op. Inc. Var., $225,104 F
North American Books, Music, DVD/Video Op. Inc. Var., $54,610 F
Team Project NCF

Chapter 23 Appendix

S23A-1 NCF
S23A-2 Software Dep't., $200,000
E23A-1 Marketing cost allocated to Welding, $4,200
Total indirect costs allocated to Priming, $25,400
E23A-2 1. Chrome Op. Inc., $75,800
P23-A1 1. Housekeeping cost, $24/room
Total Club expense, $99,480
2. Club cost $184.22/room
Regular cost $92.57/room

Chapter 24

Quick Check 1 a; 2 a; 3 d; 4 e; 5 b; 6 b;
7 d; 8 c; 9 d; 10 c

S24-1 1. 4-Pool Op. Loss, $4,000
S24-2 2. Actual expenses, $80,000
4. FB Var., $12,000F
S24-3 Total FB Var., $12,000F; Total SVV, $4,000F
S24-4 1. Relevant range, 0–11 pools
S24-5 NCF
S24-6 NCF
S24-7 DM Eff. Var., $2,800U
S24-8 DM Eff. Var. for onion, $0.70U
S24-9 DL Price Var., $17,500F
S24-10 NCF
S24-11 VMOHR = $7/DLH
S24-12 FB Var., $4,000U; PVV, $12,000F
S24-13 NCF
S24-14 NCF
S24-15 CGS, $364,000
S24-16 Op. Inc., $85,500
E24-1 Op. Inc. at 70,000 units, $170,000
E24-2 NCF
E24-3 Total FB Var., $9,000U;
Static Budget Op. Inc., $20,000
E24-4 Sales Revenue FB Var., $210,000F; Static Budget Op. Inc., $441,000
E24-5 Actual price, $10.50/lb.
E24-6 DM Price Var., $72,500F;
DL Eff. Var., $6,500F
E24-7 NCF
E24-8 NCF

E24-9   MOH FB Var., $2,200U; PVV, $3,000F

E24-10   GP, $228,500

P24-1A   1. 60,000 units: SR, $180,000; CGS, $69,000; Op. Inc., $20,700

P24-2A   1. Total Exp. FB Var., $4,000U; Total Exp. SVV, $7,550U

P24-3A   1. FB Gross Profit, $4,204,000
2. DM Price Var., $42,840F; DM Eff. Var., $58,000F; MOH FB Var., $28,220U
3. Total FB Var., $68,120F

P24-4A   1. DL hrs. worked, 5,860 hrs.
2. DL Price Var., $2,930F

P24-5A   1. DL Price Var., $4,896U; DL Eff. Var., $25,568F
3. PVV, $1,760U

P24-6A   1. DL Price Var., $920F
2. MOH FB Var., $6,400F
3. Total Man. Cost Variances, $16,890F

P24-1B   1. 11,000 units: SR, $253,000; CGS, $110,000; Op. Inc., $47,625

P24-2B   1. Total Exp. FB Var., $4,225U; Total Exp. SVV, $40,675U

P24-3B   1. FB Gross Profit, $260,068
2. DM Price Var., $1,230F; DM Eff. Var., $2,403U; MOH FB Var., $15,960U
3. Total FB Var., $16,773U

P24-4B   1. DL hrs. worked, 3,900 hrs.
2. DL Price Var., $1,950U

P24-5B   1. DL Price Var., $4,200U; DL Eff. Var., $2,628U
3. PVV, $1,134F

P24-6B   1. DL Price Var., $330U
2. MOH FB Var., $11,540U
3. Total Man. Cost Variances, $15,870U

Case 1   Total FB Var., $23,025 F
Total SVV, $133,600U

Case 2   DL Eff. Var., $96U

Ethical Issue   NCF

Team Project   NCF

Chapter 25

Quick Check   1 c; 2 a; 3 a; 4 b; 5 d; 6 c; 7 d; 8 c; 9 a; 10 c

S25-1   2. Aldehyde, $3,360

S25-2   1. Setup cost/lb. of PH, $44.80

S25-3   1. MOH/lb. of PH, $138.80
2. GP/lb. of aldehyde, $1.57

S25-4   2. TC of Webb, $49,120
3. Op. Inc. of Greg, $3,380

S25-5   NCF

S25-6   NCF

S25-7   Doc. Prep., $32/page

S25-8   1. TC of Webb, $45,800
2. Op. Loss of Greg, $16,700

S25-9   NCF

S25-10   NCF

S25-11   NCF

S25-12   NCF

S25-13   CC are $660 underallocated

S25-14   NCF

S25-15   2. Net advantage to implementing quality program, $100,000

E25-1   1. Mat. Handling, $4/part
2. Ind. mfg. cost/wheel, $143.40

E25-2   1. Total budgeted indirect mfg. costs, $461,500
2. ABC indirect cost/Deluxe wheel, $296
3. Original system indirect cost/Deluxe wheel, $276.90

E25-3   1. ABC GP for Standard, $59.50
2. Original system GP for Standard, $40.40

E25-4   Total cost of Deluxe, $347

E25-5   NCF

E25-6   2. EB RIP, $480,000
3. CC, $720,000 overallocated

E25-7   1. CC, $1,020,000 underallocated
2. EB FG, $324,000

E25-8   NCF

E25-9   NCF

E25-10   2. Net advantage to undertaking TQM, $10,000

E25-11   2. Job 409 Lathe turns, 20,000

P25-1A   Mfg. product cost, $92.70

P25-2A   1. Total mfg. cost of Standard, $288,000
2. Full product cost of Standard, $78/unit
4. Sale price, $120

P25-3A   2. X-Secure indirect cost, $199,600/unit
3. X-Page indirect cost, $33.33/unit

P25-4A   1. Total cost, $25.20/unit
3. Indirect cost, $13.41/unit

P25-5A   2. CC, $64,000 overallocated
3. EB RIP, $2,000

P25-6A   2. Net benefit, $51,000

P25-1B   Mfg. product cost, $147.80

P25-2B   1. Total mfg. cost of Standard, $146,700
2. Full product cost of Standard, $72.90/unit
4. Sale price, $68.50

P25-3B   2. Commercial indirect cost, $132.80/unit
3. Travel pack indirect cost, $2.40/unit

P25-4B   1. Total cost, $6.21/unit
3. Indirect cost, $2.82/unit

P25-5B   2. CC, $79,000 overallocated
3. EB RIP, $1,000

P25-6B   2. Net benefit, $5,000

Case 1   1. Original system cost/unit of Job A, $5,460
2. ABC cost/unit of Job A, $5,072.50

Case 2   Savings required, $620

Ethical Issue   NCF

Financial Statement Case   NCF

Team Project   2. Ind. cost allocation rate, $16.125/DLH; Total cost/lb. of Headless shrimp, $3.96125
3. Scheduling, $100/batch; Chilling, $0.02/lb.; Total indirect cost/lb. of Headless shrimp, $0.995; Total cost/lb. of Headless shrimp, $4.795

Chapter 26

Quick Check   1 b; 2 c; 3 d; 4 d; 5 a; 6 d; 7 a; 8 c; 9 b; 10 a

S26-1   NCF

S26-2   Expected decrease in Op. Inc., $1,000

S26-3   NCF

S26-4   NCF

S26-5   Regular CM/unit, $125

S26-6   Advantage to outsourcing, $13,500

S26-7   NCF

S26-8   Advantage to processing further, $2,000

S26-9   Average annual net cash inflow, $2,880,000

S26-10   Payback period, 4.51 years

S26-11   ARR, 24%

S26-12   NPV, $3,272,000

S26-13   IRR, over 16%

S26-14   NCF

E26-1   1. Increase in Op. Inc., $2,500
2. Decrease in Op. Inc., $2,500

E26-2   1. Increase in Op. Inc., $320,000

E26-3   Decrease in Op. Inc., $40,000

E26-4   Decrease in Op. Inc., $10,000

E26-5   Total CM of moderately priced line, $39,000

E26-6   Advantage to making switch, $1.50/unit

E26-7   Advantage to buying and using facilities for other product, $100,000

E26-8   Advantage to processing further, $100

E26-9   Payback period, 4 years

E26-10   ARR Veras, 37%

E26-11   NPV Project B, $(7,040)

E26-12   IRR Project A, between 14% and 16%

E26-13   1. 12 oz. cans of Coca-Cola, CM/linear foot, $7.50
2. 360 12 oz. cans of Coca-Cola

P26-1A   1. Increase in Op. Inc., $35,000

P26-2A   1. Decrease in Op. Inc., $104,000
2b. Operating loss, $52,000

P26-3A   2. Deluxe: CM, $1,440 / MH; Total CM at capacity, $6,480,000

P26-4A   1. Advantage to making, $2,460
2. Net cost to buy and make another product, $31,060

P26-5A 1. Cost of further processing, $56,400
3. Advantage to selling as is, $19,920

P26-6A 1. ARR, 31.2%;
NPV, $733,360

P26-7A 1. Plan B's ARR, 7.8%
Plan B's NPV, $(959,000)
3. IRR, 12%–14%

P26-1B 1. Increase in Op. Inc., $2,500

P26-2B 1. Decrease in Op. Inc., $22,500
2b. Op. Inc. $193,000

P26-3B 2. Spas:
CM, $1.95/sq. ft.;
Total CM at capacity, $15,600

P26-4B 1. Advantage to making, $26,600
2. Net cost to buy and make snack bars, $846,600

P26-5B 1. Cost of further processing, $120,000
3. Advantage to process further, $30,000

P26-6B 1. ARR, 6%;
NPV, $(1,052,125)

P26-7B 1. Plan A's ARR, 12%
Plan A's NPV, $(835,360)
3. IRR, 14%–16%

Case 1 1. Total cost/mailbox per month, $64
2. Total advantage to outsourcing, $21,850
3. Advantage to insourcing extra services, $1,150

Case 2 1. Total earnings if he chooses the meat packing plant, $9,450

Ethical Issue Advantage to outsourcing, $18,000/year

Financial Statement Case 2. Annual net cash inflow, $13,439,602
3.b. ARR, 18.6%

Team Project 2. Annual cash inflow advantage to insourcing, $7,972,000
3.b. ARR, 22.1%
c. NPV, $3,964,024

Glossary

Absorption Costing. The costing method that assigns both variable and fixed manufacturing costs to products.

Accelerated Depreciation Method. A depreciation method that writes off more of the asset's cost near the start of its useful life than the straight-line method does.

Account. The detailed record of the changes in a particular asset, liability, or owner's equity during a period. The basic summary device of accounting.

Account Payable. A liability backed by the general reputation and credit standing of the debtor.

Account Receivable. A promise to receive cash from customers to whom the business has sold goods or for whom the business has performed services.

Accounting. The information system that measures business activities, processes that information into reports, and communicates the results to decision makers.

Accounting Cycle. Process by which companies produce their financial statements for a specific period.

Accounting Equation. The basic tool of accounting, measuring the resources of the business and the claims to those resources: Assets = Liabilities + Owner's Equity.

Accounting Information System. The combination of personnel, records, and procedures that a business uses to provide financial data.

Accounting Rate of Return. A measure of profitability computed by dividing the average annual operating income from an asset by the average amount invested in the asset.

Accounts Receivable Turnover. Measures a company's ability to collect cash from credit customers. To compute accounts receivable turnover, divide net credit sales by average net accounts receivable.

Accrual Accounting. Accounting that records the impact of a business event as it occurs, regardless of whether the transaction affected cash.

Accrued Expense. An expense that the business has not yet paid. Also called **accrued liability**.

Accrued Revenue. A revenue that has been earned but not yet collected in cash.

Accumulated Depreciation. The cumulative sum of all depreciation expense recorded for an asset.

Acid-Test Ratio. Ratio of the sum of cash plus short-term investments plus net current receivables, to total current liabilities.

Tells whether the entity could pay all its current liabilities if they came due immediately. Also called the **quick ratio**.

Activity-Based Costing (ABC). Focuses on *activities* as the fundamental cost objects. The costs of those activities become building blocks for compiling the indirect costs of products, services, and customers.

Activity-Based Management. Using activity-based cost information to make decisions that increase profits while satisfying customers' needs.

Additional Paid-In Capital. The paid-in capital in excess of par, common plus other accounts combined for reporting on the balance sheet.

Adjusted Trial Balance. A list of all the accounts with their adjusted balances.

Adjusting Entry. Entry made at the end of the period to assign revenues to the period in which they are earned and expenses to the period in which they are incurred. Adjusting entries help measure the period's income and bring the related asset and liability accounts to correct balances for the financial statements.

Aging-of-Accounts Method. A way to estimate bad debts by analyzing individual accounts receivable according to the length of time they have been receivable from the customer. Also called the **balance-sheet approach**.

Allocation base. A common denominator that links indirect costs to cost objects. Ideally, the allocation base is the primary cost driver of the indirect cost.

Allowance for Uncollectible Accounts. A contra account, related to accounts receivable, that holds the estimated amount of collection losses. Also called **Allowance for Doubtful Accounts**.

Allowance Method. A method of recording collection losses on the basis of estimates, instead of waiting to see which customers the company will not collect from.

Amortization. Systematic reduction of the asset's carrying value on the books. Expense that applies to intangibles in the same way depreciation applies to plant assets and depletion to natural resources.

Annuity. A stream of equal periodic cash flows.

Appraisal Costs. Costs incurred to *detect* poor-quality goods or services.

Appropriation of Retained Earnings. Restriction of retained earnings that is recorded by a formal journal entry.

Asset. An economic resource that is expected to be of benefit in the future.

Audit. An examination of a company's financial statements and the accounting system.

Authorization of Stock. Provision in a corporate charter that gives the state's permission for the corporation to issue—that is, to sell—a certain number of shares of stock.

Available-for-Sale Investments. All less-than-20% investments other than trading securities.

Average-Cost Method. Inventory costing method based on the average cost of inventory during the period. Average cost is determined by dividing the cost of goods available for sale by the number of units available.

Balance Sheet. An entity's assets, liabilities, and owner's equity as of a specific date. Also called the **statement of financial position**.

Bank Collection. Collection of money by the bank on behalf of a depositor.

Bank Reconciliation. Document explaining the reasons for the difference between a depositor's cash records and the depositor's cash balance in its bank account.

Bank Statement. Document the bank uses to report what it did with the depositor's cash. Shows the bank account's beginning and ending balances and lists the month's cash transactions conducted through the bank.

Batch Processing. Computerized accounting for similar transactions in a group or batch.

Benchmarking. The practice of comparing a company with other companies that are leaders.

Board of Directors. Group elected by the stockholders to set policy and to appoint the officers.

Bonds Payable. Groups of notes payable issued to multiple lenders called bondholders.

Book Value. Amount of owners' equity on the company's books for each share of its stock.

Book Value (of a Plant Asset). The asset's cost minus accumulated depreciation.

Book Value per Share of Common Stock. Common stockholders' equity divided by the number of shares of common stock outstanding. The recorded amount for each share of common stock outstanding.

Breakeven Point. The sales level at which operating income is zero: Total revenues equal total expenses.

Budget. Quantitative expression of a plan that helps managers coordinate and implement the plan.

Bylaws. Constitution for governing a corporation.

Callable Bonds. Bonds that the issuer may call or pay off at a specified price whenever the issuer wants.

Capital Budgeting. Budgeting for the acquisition of capital assets—assets used for a long period of time.

Capital Charge. The amount that stockholders and lenders charge a company for the use of their money. Calculated as (Notes payable + Loans payable + Long-term debt + Stockholders' equity)

Capital Expenditure. Expenditure that increases the capacity or efficiency of an asset or extends its useful life. Capital expenditures are debited to an asset account.

Capital Expenditures Budget. A company's plan for purchases of property, plant, equipment, and other long-term assets.

Capital Lease. Lease agreement that meets any one of four criteria: (1) The lease transfers title of the leased asset to the lessee. (2) The lease contains a bargain purchase option. (3) The lease term is 75% or more of the estimated useful life of the leased asset. (4) The present value of the lease payments is 90% or more of the market value of the leased asset.

Cash Budget. Details how the business expects to go from the beginning cash balance to the desired ending balance. Also called the **statement of budgeted cash receipts and payments**.

Cash Equivalents. Highly liquid short-term investments that can be readily converted into cash.

Cash Flows. Cash receipts and cash payments.

Cash Payments Journal. Special journal used to record cash payments by check. Also called the **check register** or **cash disbursements journal**.

Cash Receipts Journal. Special journal used to record cash receipts.

Cash-Basis Accounting. Accounting that records transactions only when cash is received or paid.

Certified Management Accountant (CMA). A licensed accountant who works for a single company.

Certified Public Accountant (CPA). A licensed accountant who serves the general public rather than one particular company.

Chairperson. Elected by a corporation's board of directors, the most powerful person in the corporation.

Chart of Accounts. List of all the accounts and their account numbers in the ledger.

Charter. Document that gives the state's permission to form a corporation.

Check. Document that instructs a bank to pay the designated person or business a specified amount of money.

Closing Entries. Entries that transfer the revenue, expense, and owner withdrawal balances to the capital account.

Closing the Accounts. Step in the accounting cycle at the end of the period. Closing the accounts consists of journalizing and posting the closing entries to set the balances of the revenue, expense, and withdrawal accounts to zero for the next period.

Common Stock. The basic form of capital stock. In a corporation, the common stockholders are the owners of the business.

Common-Size Statement. A financial statement that reports only percentages (no dollar amounts).

Comprehensive Income. Company's change in total stockholders' equity from all sources other than from the owners.

Computer Virus. A malicious program that (a) reproduces itself, (b) enters program code without consent, and (c) performs destructive actions.

Conservatism. Reporting the least favorable figures in the financial statements.

Consistency Principle. A business should use the same accounting methods and procedures from period to period.

Consolidated Statements. Financial statements of the parent company plus those of majority-owned subsidiaries as if the combination were a single legal entity.

Constraint. A factor that restricts production or sale of a product.

Continuous Improvement. A philosophy requiring employees to continually look for ways to improve performance.

Contra Account. An account that always has a companion account and whose normal balance is opposite that of the companion account.

Contribution Margin. Sales revenue minus variable expenses.

Contribution Margin Income Statement. Income statement that groups costs by behavior —variable costs or fixed costs— and highlights the contribution margin.

Contribution Margin Ratio. Ratio of contribution margin to sales revenue.

Control Account. An account whose balance equals the sum of the balances in a group of related accounts in a subsidiary ledger.

Controller. The chief accounting officer of a company.

Controlling. Evaluating the results of business operations by comparing the actual results to the plan.

Controlling Interest. Ownership of more than 50% of an investee company's voting stock. Also called **majority interest**.

Conversion Costs. Direct labor plus manufacturing overhead.

Convertible Bonds. Bonds that may be converted into the common stock of the issuing company at the option of the investor.

Copyright. Exclusive right to reproduce and sell a book, musical composition, film, other work of art, or computer program. Issued by the federal government, copyrights extend 70 years beyond the author's life.

Corporation. A business owned by stockholders; it begins when the state approves its articles of incorporation. A corporation is a legal entity, an "artificial person," in the eyes of the law.

Cost Allocation. Assigning indirect costs (such as manufacturing overhead) to cost objects (such as jobs or production processes).

Cost Assignment. A general term that refers to both tracing direct costs and allocating indirect costs to cost objects.

Cost Behavior. Describes how costs change as volume changes.

Cost Driver. The primary factor that causes a cost.

Cost Object. Anything for which managers want a separate measurement of costs.

Cost of Capital. A weighted average of the returns demanded by the company's stockholders and lenders.

Cost of Goods Manufactured. The manufacturing (or plant-related) cost of the goods that finished the production process this period.

Cost of Goods Sold. The cost of the inventory that the business has sold to customers. Also called **cost of sales**.

Cost Tracing. Assigning direct costs (such as direct materials and direct labor) to cost objects (such as jobs or production processes) that used those costs.

Cost-Benefit Analysis. Weighing costs against benefits to help make decisions.

Cost-Volume-Profit (CVP) Analysis. Expresses the relationships among costs, volume, and profit or loss.

Credit. The right side of an account.

Credit Memorandum or Credit Memo. A document issued by a seller to credit a customer account for returned merchandise.

Creditor. The party to a credit transaction who sells goods or a service and obtains a receivable.

Cumulative Preferred Stock. Preferred stock whose owners must receive all dividends in arrears before the corporation pays dividends to the common stockholders.

Current Asset. An asset that is expected to be converted to cash, sold, or consumed during the next 12 months, or within the business's normal operating cycle if the cycle is longer than a year.

Current Liability. A debt due to be paid with cash or with goods and services within one year or within the entity's operating cycle if the cycle is longer than a year.

Current Portion of Long-Term Debt. Amount of the principal that is payable within one year. Also called **current maturity**.

Current Ratio. Current assets divided by current liabilities. Measures the company's ability to pay current liabilities from current assets.

Customer Service. Support provided for customers after the sale.

Data Warehouse. A very large database holding data for a number of years and used for analysis rather than for transaction processing.

Database. A computerized storehouse of information.

Days' Sales in Receivables. Ratio of average net accounts receivable to one day's sales. Indicates how many days' sales it takes to collect the average level of receivables. Also called the **collection period**.

Debentures. Unsecured bonds backed only by the good faith of the borrower.

Debit. The left side of an account.

Debit Memorandum or Debit Memo. A document issued by a buyer when returning merchandise. The memo informs the seller that the buyer no longer owes the seller for the amount of the returned purchases.

Debt Ratio. Ratio of total liabilities to total assets. Shows the proportion of a company's assets that it has financed with debt.

Debtor. The party to a credit transaction who makes a purchase and has a payable.

Deficit. Debit balance in the Retained Earnings account.

Depletion Expense. Portion of a natural resource's cost used up in a particular period. Computed in the same way as units-of-production depreciation.

Deposit in Transit. A deposit recorded by the company but not yet by its bank.

Depreciable Cost. The cost of a plant asset minus its estimated residual value.

Depreciation. The allocation of a plant asset's cost to expense over its useful life.

Design. Detailed engineering of products and services, or processes for producing them.

Direct Cost. A cost that can be specifically traced to a cost object.

Direct Labor. The compensation of employees who physically convert materials into the company's products; labor costs that are directly traceable to finished products.

Direct Materials. Materials that become a physical part of a finished product and whose costs are traceable to the finished product.

Direct Method. Format of the operating activities section of the statement of cash flows; lists the major categories of operating cash receipts and cash payments.

Direct Write-Off Method. A method of accounting for uncollectible receivables, in which the company waits until the credit department decides that a customer's account receivable is uncollectible, and then debits Uncollectible-Account Expense and credits the customer's Account Receivable.

Disclosure Principle. A business's financial statements must report enough information for outsiders to make knowledgeable decisions about the company.

Discount (on a Bond). Excess of a bond's maturity value over its issue price. Also called a **bond discount**.

Discount Rate. Management's minimum desired rate of return on an investment. Also called the **hurdle rate, required rate of return**, and **cost of capital**.

Discounting a Note Receivable. Selling a note receivable before its maturity date.

Dishonor of a Note. Failure of a note's maker to pay a note receivable at maturity. Also called **default on a note**.

Dissolution. Ending of a partnership.

Distribution. Delivery of products or services to customers.

Dividend Yield. Ratio of dividends per share of stock to the stock's market price per share. Tells the percentage of a stock's market value that the company returns to stockholders annually as dividends.

Dividends. Distributions by a corporation to its stockholders.

Double Taxation. Corporations pay their own income taxes on corporate income. Then, the stockholders pay personal income tax on the cash dividends they receive from corporations.

Double-Declining-Balance (DDB) Depreciation Method. An accelerated depreciation method that computes annual depreciation by multiplying the asset's decreasing book value by a constant percent that is two times the straight-line rate.

Earnings Per Share (EPS). Amount of a company's net income for each share of its outstanding common stock.

Economic Value Added (EVA). EVA = Net income + Interest expense − Capital charge. Used to evaluate a company's operating performance.

Efficiency Variance. Measures whether the quantity of materials or labor used to make the actual number of outputs is within the standard allowed for that number of outputs. This is computed as the difference in quantities (actual quantity of input used minus standard quantity of input allowed for the actual number of outputs) multiplied by the standard price per unit of the input.

Electronic Funds Transfer (EFT). System that transfers cash by electronic communication rather than by paper documents.

Encryption. Rearranging plain-text messages by a mathematical process; the primary method of achieving confidentiality in e-commerce.

Entity. An organization or a section of an organization that, for accounting purposes, stands apart from other organizations and individuals as a separate economic unit.

Equity Method. Method used to account for investments in which the investor has 20% to 50% of the investee's voting stock and can significantly influence the decisions of the investee.

Equivalent Units. Express the amount of work done during a period in terms of fully complete units of output.

Enterprise Resource Planning (ERP). Software systems that can integrate all of a company's worldwide functions, departments, and data into a single system.

Estimated Residual Value. Expected cash value of an asset at the end of its useful life. Also called **salvage value**.

Estimated Useful Life. Length of the service period expected from an asset. May be expressed in years, units of output, miles, or another measure.

Expense. Decrease in owner's equity that occurs from using assets or increasing liabilities in the course of delivering goods or services to customers.

External Failure Costs. Costs incurred when the company does not detect poor-quality goods or services until *after* delivery to customers.

Extraordinary Gains and Losses. A gain or loss that is both unusual for the company and infrequent. Also called **extraordinary items**.

Extraordinary Repair. Repair work that generates a capital expenditure.

Financial Accounting. The branch of accounting that focuses on information for people outside the firm.

Financial Accounting Standards Board (FASB). The private organization that determines how accounting is practiced in the United States.

Financial Budget. The case budget (cash inflows and outflows), the budgeted period-end balance sheet, and the budgeted statement of cash flows.

Financial Statements. Documents that report on a business in monetary amounts, providing information to help people make informed business decisions.

Financing Activities. Activities that obtain the cash needed to launch and sustain the business; a section of the statement of cash flows.

Finished Goods Inventory. Completed goods that have not yet been sold.

Firewalls. Devices that enable members of a local network to access the Internet but keep nonmembers out of the network.

First-In, First-Out (FIFO) Inventory Costing Method. Inventory costing method: the first costs into inventory are the first costs out to cost of goods sold. Ending inventory is based on the costs of the most recent purchases.

First-In, First-Out (FIFO) Process Costing Method. A process costing method that values each equivalent unit of work at the cost per equivalent unit in effect during the period the work is done.

Flexible Budget. A summarized budget that managers can easily compute for several different volume levels. Flexible budgets separate variable costs from fixed costs; it is the variable costs that put the "flex" in the flexible budget.

Flexible Budget Variance. The difference arising because the company actually earned more or less revenue, or incurred more or less cost, than expected for the actual level of output. This equals the difference between the actual amount and a flexible budget amount.

Foreign-Currency Exchange Rate. The measure of one currency against another currency.

Franchises, Licenses. Privileges granted by a private business or a government to sell a product or service under specified conditions.

Full Product Costs. The costs of all resources used throughout the value chain for a product.

General Ledger. Ledger of accounts that are reported in the financial statements.

General Partnership. A form of partnership in which each partner is an owner of the business, with all the privileges and risks of ownership.

Generally Accepted Accounting Principles (GAAP). Accounting guidelines, formulated by the Financial Accounting Standards Board, that govern how accountants measure, process, and communicate financial information.

Goodwill. Excess of the cost of an acquired company over the sum of the market values of its net assets (assets minus liabilities).

Gross Pay. Total amount of salary, wages, commissions, or any other employee compensation before taxes and other deductions.

Gross Profit. Excess of net sales revenue over cost of goods sold. Also called **gross margin**.

Gross Profit Method. A way to estimate inventory on the basis of the cost-of-goods-sold model: Beginning inventory + Net purchases = Cost of goods available for sale. Cost of goods available for sale − Cost of goods sold = Ending inventory.

Gross Profit Percentage. Gross profit divided by net sales revenue. A measure of profitability. Also called **gross margin percentage**.

Hardware. Electronic equipment that includes computers, disk drives, monitors, printers, and the network that connects them.

Hedging. Protecting oneself from losing money in one transaction by engaging in a counterbalancing transaction.

Held-to-Maturity Investments. Investment in bonds, notes, and other debt securities that the investor expects to hold until their maturity date.

Horizontal Analysis. Study of percentage changes in comparative financial statements.

Imprest System. A way to account for petty cash by maintaining a constant balance in the petty cash account, supported by the fund (cash plus payment tickets) totaling the same amount.

Income Statement. Summary of an entity's revenues, expenses, and net income or net loss for a specific period. Also called the **statement of earnings** or the **statement of operations**.

Income Summary. A temporary "holding tank" account into which revenues and expenses are transferred prior to their final transfer to the capital account.

Indirect Cost. A cost that cannot be specifically traced to a cost object.

Indirect Labor. Labor costs that are difficult to trace to specific products.

Indirect Materials. Materials whose costs cannot conveniently be directly traced to particular finished products.

Indirect Method. Format of the operating activities section of the statement of cash flows; starts with net income and reconciles to net cash provided by operating activities.

Intangibles. Assets with no physical form. Valuable because of the special rights they carry. Examples are patents and copyrights.

Interest. The revenue to the payee for loaning money; the expense to the debtor.

Interest period. The period of time during which interest is computed. It extends from the original date of the note to the maturity date. Also called **note term**, or simply **time**.

Interest rate. The percentage rate of interest specified by the note. Interest rates are almost always stated for a period of one year. A 9% note means that the amount of interest for one year is 9% of the note's principal amount.

Internal Control. Organizational plan and all the related measures adopted by an entity to safeguard assets, encourage employees to follow company policies, promote operational efficiency, and ensure accurate and reliable accounting records.

Internal Failure Costs. Costs incurred when the company detects and corrects poor-quality goods or services *before* delivery to customers.

Internal Rate of Return (IRR). The rate of return (based on discounted cash flows) that a company can expect to earn by investing in the project. The discount rate that makes the net present value of the project's cash flows equal to zero.

Inventoriable Product Costs. All costs of a product that GAAP requires companies to treat as an asset for external financial reporting. These costs are not expensed until the product is sold.

Inventory. All the goods that the company owns and expects to sell in the normal course of operations.

Inventory Turnover. Ratio of cost of goods sold to average inventory. Measures the number of times a company sells its average level of inventory during a year.

Investing Activities. Activities that increase or decrease long-term assets; a section of the statement of cash flows.

Invoice. A seller's request for cash from the purchaser.

Job Cost Record. Document that accumulates the direct materials, direct labor, and manufacturing overhead costs assigned to each individual job.

Job Costing. System for assigning costs to a specific unit or to a small batch of products or services that (1) pass through production steps as a distinct identifiable job and (2) can vary considerably in materials, labor, and overhead costs.

Journal. The chronological accounting record of an entity's transactions.

Just-in-Time (JIT). A system in which a company produces just in time to satisfy needs. Suppliers deliver materials just in time to begin production, and finished units are completed just in time for delivery to customers.

Just-in-Time (JIT) Costing. A standard costing system that starts with output completed and then assigns manufacturing costs to units sold and to inventories. Also called **backflush costing**.

Labor Time Record. Identifies the employee, the amount of time spent on a particular job, and the labor cost charged to the job; a record used to assign direct labor cost to specific jobs.

Last-In, Last-Out (LIFO) Inventory Costing Method. Inventory costing method: the last costs into inventory are the first costs out to cost of goods sold. Leaves the oldest costs—those of beginning inventory and the earliest purchases of the period—in ending inventory.

Lease. Rental agreement in which the tenant (lessee) agrees to make rent payments to the property owner (lessor) to obtain the use of the asset.

Ledger. The record holding all the accounts.

Legal Capital. The portion of stockholders' equity that cannot be used for dividends.

Lessee. Tenant in a lease agreement.

Lessor. Property owner in a lease agreement.

Leverage. Earning more income on borrowed money than the related interest expense, thereby increasing the earnings for the owners of the business.

Liability. An economic obligation (a debt) payable to an individual or an organization outside the business.

Limited Liability. No personal obligation of a stockholder for corporation debts. A stockholder can lose no more on an investment in a corporation's stock than the cost of the investment.

Limited Liability Partnership. A form of partnership in which each partner's personal liability for the business's debts is limited to a certain amount. Also called **LLPs**.

Limited Partnership. A partnership with at least two classes of partners: a general partner and limited partners.

Liquidation. The process of going out of business by selling the entity's assets and paying its liabilities. The final step in liquidation is the distribution of any remaining cash to the owner(s).

Liquidity. Measure of how quickly an item can be converted to cash.

Long-Term Asset. An asset other than a current asset.

Long-Term Investment. A noncurrent asset; a separate asset category reported on the balance sheet between current assets and plant assets.

Long-Term Liability. A liability other than a current liability.

Lower-of-Cost-or-Market (LCM) Rule. Rule that an asset should be reported in the financial statements at whichever is lower—its historical cost or its market value.

Maker of a Note. The person or business that signs the note and promises to pay the amount required by the note agreement; the debtor.

Management Accounting. The branch of accounting that focuses on information for internal decision makers of a business.

Management by Exception. Directs management's attention to important differences between actual and budgeted amounts.

Manufacturing Company. A company that uses labor, plant, and equipment to convert raw materials into new finished products.

Manufacturing Overhead. All manufacturing costs other than direct materials and direct labor. Also called **factory overhead** or **indirect manufacturing cost**.

Margin of Safety. Excess of expected sales over breakeven sales. Drop in sales a company can absorb without incurring an operating loss.

Market Interest Rate. Interest rate that investors demand in order to loan their money. Also called the **effective interest rate**.

Market Value. Price for which a person could buy or sell a share of stock.

Marketing. Promotion of products or services.

Market-Value Method. Used to account for all trading investments. These investments are reported at their current market value.

Master Budget. The set of budgeted financial statements and supporting schedules for the entire organization. Includes the operating budget, the capital expenditures budget, and the financial budget.

Matching Principle. Guide to accounting for expenses. Identify all expenses incurred during the period, measure the expenses, and match them against the revenues earned during that same time period.

Materiality Concept. A company must perform strictly proper accounting only for items that are significant to the business's financial statements.

Materials Inventory. Raw materials for use in manufacturing.

Materials Requisition. Request for the transfer of materials to the production floor, prepared by the production team.

Maturity Date. The date when final payment of the note is due. Also called the **due date**.

Maturity Value. The sum of the principal plus interest due at maturity.

Menu. A list of options for choosing computer functions.

Merchandising Company. A company that resells products previously bought from suppliers.

Minority Interest. A subsidiary company's equity that is held by stockholders other than the parent company.

Mixed Costs. Costs that have both variable and fixed components.

Module. Separate compatible units of an accounting package that are integrated to function together.

Mortgage. Borrower's promise to transfer the legal title to certain assets to the lender if the debt is not paid on schedule.

Multi-Step Income Statement. Format that contains subtotals to highlight significant relationships. In addition to net income, it reports gross profit and operating income.

Mutual Agency. Every partner can bind the business to a contract within the scope of the partnership's regular business operations.

Net Income. Excess of total revenues over total expenses. Also called **net earnings** or **net profit**.

Net Loss. Excess of total expenses over total revenues.

Net Pay. Gross pay minus all deductions. The amount of compensation that the employee actually takes home.

Net Present Value (NPV). The decision model that brings cash inflows and outflows back to a common time period by discounting these expected future cash flows to their present value, using a minimum desired rate of return.

Net Purchases. Purchases less purchase discounts and purchase returns and allowances.

Net Sales Revenue. Sales revenue less sales discounts and sales returns and allowances.

Network. The system of electronic linkages that allows different computers to share the same information.

Nonsufficient Funds (NSF) Check. A "hot" check, one for which the maker's bank account has insufficient money to pay the check.

Normal Balance. The balance that appears on the side of an account—debit or credit—where we record increases.

Note Payable. A written promise of future payment.

Note Receivable. A written promise for future collection of cash.

Online Processing. Computerized processing of related functions, such as the recording and posting of transactions, on a continuous basis.

Operating Activities. Activities that create revenue or expense in the entity's major line of business; a section of the statement of cash flows. Operating activities affect the income statement.

Operating Budget. Projects sales revenue, cost of goods sold, and operating expenses, leading to the budgeted income statement that projects operating income for the period.

Operating Cycle. Time span during which cash is paid for goods and services, which are then sold to customers from whom the business collects cash.

Operating Expenses. Expenses, other than cost of goods sold, that are incurred in the entity's major line of business. Examples include rent, depreciation, salaries, wages, utilities, and supplies expense.

Operating Income. Gross profit minus operating expenses plus any other operating revenues. Also called **income from operations**.

Operating Lease. Usually a short-term or cancelable rental agreement.

Opportunity Cost. The benefit forgone by not choosing an alternative course of action.

Ordinary Repair. Repair work that is debited to an expense account.

Other Expense. Expense that is outside the main operations of a business, such as a loss on the sale of plant assets.

Other Revenue. Revenue that is outside the main operations of a business, such as a gain on the sale of plant assets.

Outsourcing. A make-or-buy decision: managers decide whether to buy a component product or service or produce it in-house.

Outstanding Check. A check issued by the company and recorded on its books but not yet paid by its bank.

Outstanding Stock. Stock in the hands of stockholders.

Overallocated (Manufacturing) Overhead. The manufacturing overhead allocated to Work in Process Inventory is more than the amount of manufacturing overhead costs actually incurred.

Overhead Flexible Budget Variance. Shows how well management has controlled overhead costs. It is the difference between the actual overhead cost and the flexible budget overhead for the actual number of outputs.

Owner Withdrawals. Amounts removed from the business by an owner.

Owner's Equity. The claim of a business owner to the assets of the business. Also called **capital**.

Paid-in Capital. Capital from investments by the stockholders. Also called **contributed capital**.

Par Value. Arbitrary amount assigned to a share of stock.

Parent Company. An investor company that owns more than 50% of the voting stock of a subsidiary company.

Partnership. An association of two or more persons who co-own a business for profit.

Partnership Agreement. The contract between partners that specifies such items as the name, location, and nature of the business; the name, capital investment, and duties of each partner; and the method of sharing profits and losses among the partners. Also called **articles of partnership**.

Patent. A federal government grant giving the holder the exclusive right to produce and sell an invention for 20 years.

Payback. The length of time it takes to recover, in net cash inflows, the dollars of a capital outlay.

Payee of a Note. The person or business to whom the maker of a note promises future payment; the creditor.

Payroll. A major expense. Also called **employee compensation**.

Percent-of-Sales Method. A method of estimating uncollectible receivables that calculates uncollectible-account expense. Also called the **income-statement approach**.

Period Costs. Operating costs that are expensed in the period in which they are incurred.

Periodic Inventory System. A system in which the business does not keep a continuous record of inventory on hand. At the end of the period, it makes a physical count of on-hand inventory and uses this information to prepare the financial statements.

Permanent Accounts. Accounts that are *not* closed at the end of the period—the asset, liability, and capital accounts.

Perpetual Inventory System. The accounting inventory system in which the business keeps a running record of inventory and cost of goods sold.

Petty Cash. Fund containing a small amount of cash that is used to pay for minor expenditures.

Planning. Choosing goals and deciding how to achieve them.

Plant Assets. Long-lived tangible assets, such as land, buildings, and equipment, used to operate a business.

Plant or Fixed Asset. Another name for property, plant, and equipment.

Postclosing Trial Balance. List of the accounts and their balances at the end of the period after journalizing and posting the closing entries. This last step of the accounting cycle ensures that the ledger is in balance to start the next accounting period.

Posting. Copying amounts from the journal to the ledger.

Predetermined Manufacturing Overhead Rate. Estimated manufacturing overhead allocation rate computed at the beginning of the year, calculated as the total estimated manufacturing overhead costs divided by the total estimated quantity of the manufacturing overhead allocation base. Also called the **budgeted manufacturing overhead rate**.

Preferred Stock. Stock that gives its owners certain advantages over common stockholders, such as the right to receive dividends before the common stockholders and the right to receive assets before the common stockholders if the corporation liquidates.

Premium. Excess of a bond's issue price over its maturity value. Also called **bond premium**.

Prepaid Expense. Advance payments of expenses. Examples include prepaid rent, prepaid insurance, and supplies.

Present Value. Amount a person would invest now to receive a greater amount in the future.

President. Chief operating officer in charge of managing the day-to-day operations of a corporation.

Prevention Costs. Costs incurred to *avoid* poor-quality goods or services.

Price Variance. Measures how well the business keeps unit prices of material and labor inputs within standards. This is computed as the difference in prices (actual price per unit minus standard price per unit) of an input multiplied by the actual quantity of the input.

Price/Earnings Ratio. Ratio of the market price of a share of common stock to the company's earnings per share. Measures the value that the stock market places on $1 of a company's earnings.

Principal Amount, or Principal. The amount loaned out by the payee and borrowed by the maker of the note.

Prior-Period Adjustment. A correction to retained earnings for an error of an earlier period.

Process Costing. System for assigning costs to large numbers of identical units that usually proceed in a continuous fash-

ion through a series of uniform production steps or processes.

Production Cost Report. Summarizes a processing department's operations for a period.

Production or Purchases. Resources used to produce a product or service, or to purchase finished merchandise.

Production Volume Variance. Arises when actual production differs from expected production. It is the difference between (1) the manufacturing overhead cost in the flexible budget for actual outputs and (2) the standard overhead allocated to production.

Promissory note. A written promise to pay a specified amount of money at a particular future date.

Proprietorship. A business with a single owner.

Purchases Journal. Special journal used to record all purchases of inventory, supplies, and other assets on account.

Rate of Return on Common Stockholders' Equity. Net income minus preferred dividends, divided by average common stockholders' equity. A measure of profitability. Also called **return on equity**.

Rate of Return on Net Sales. Ratio of net income to net sales. A measure of profitability. Also called **return on sales**.

Rate of Return on Total Assets. Net income plus interest expense, divided by average total assets. Measures the success a company has in using its assets to earn income for those financing the business. Also called **return on assets**.

Receivables. Monetary claims against a business or an individual.

Relevant Information. Expected future data that differs among alternatives.

Relevant Range. The band of volume where total fixed costs remain constant and where the variable cost per unit remains constant.

Research and Development (R&D). Researching and developing new or improved products or services, or the processes for producing them.

Responsibility Accounting. A system for evaluating the performance of each responsibility center and its manager.

Responsibility Center. A part or subunit of an organization whose manager is accountable for specific activities.

Retained Earnings. Capital earned through profitable operation of the business.

Revenue. Amounts earned by delivering goods or services to customers. Revenues increase owner's equity.

Revenue Principle. The basis for recording revenues; tells accountants when to record revenue and the amount of revenue to record.

Reversing Entries. Special journal entries that ease the burden of accounting for transactions in the next period.

S Corporation. A corporation taxed in the same way as a partnership.

Sales Discount. Reduction in the amount receivable from a customer, offered by the seller as an incentive for the customer to pay promptly. A contra account to Sales Revenue.

Sales Journal. Special journal used to record credit sales.

Sales Mix. Combination of products that make up total sales.

Sales Returns and Allowances. Decreases in the seller's receivable from a customer's return of merchandise or from granting the customer an allowance from the amount owed to the seller. A contra account to Sales Revenue.

Sales Revenue. The amount that a merchandiser earns from selling its inventory. Also called **sales**.

Sales Volume Variance. The difference arising only because the number of units actually sold differs from the static budget units. This equals the difference between a static budget amount and a flexible budget amount.

Segment of the Business. One of various separate divisions of a company.

Sensitivity Analysis. A "what if" technique that asks what results will be if actual prices or costs change, or if an underlying assumption changes.

Serial Bonds. Bonds that mature in installments over a period of time.

Server. The main computer in a network, where the program and data are stored.

Service Company. A company that sells intangible services, rather than tangible products.

Short-Term Investment. A current asset; an investment that is readily convertible to cash and that the investor intends either to convert to cash within one year or use to pay a current liability. Also called a **marketable security**.

Short-Term Note Payable. Promissory note payable due within one year, a common form of financing.

Single-Step Income Statement. Format that groups all revenues together and then lists and deducts all expenses together without drawing any subtotals.

Social Security Tax. Federal Insurance Contributions Act (FICA) tax, which is withheld from employees' pay. Also called **FICA tax**.

Software. Set of programs or instructions that drive the computer to perform the work desired.

Specific-Unit-Cost Method. Inventory cost method based on the specific cost of particular units of inventory. Also called the **specific-identification method**.

Spreadsheet. A computer program that links data by means of formulas and functions; an electronic work sheet.

Standard Cost. A budget for a single unit.

Stated Interest Rate. Interest rate that determines the amount of cash interest the borrower pays and the investor receives each year.

Stated Value. An arbitrary amount that accountants treat as though it were par value.

Statement of Cash Flows. Reports cash receipts and cash payments during a period.

Statement of Owner's Equity. Summary of the changes in an entity's owner's equity during a specific period.

Statement of Stockholders' Equity. Reports the changes in all categories of stockholders' equity during the period.

Static Budget. The budget prepared for only one level of sales volume. Also called the **master budget**.

Stock. Shares into which the owners' equity of a corporation is divided.

Stock Dividend. A distribution by a corporation of its own stock to its stockholders.

Stock Split. An increase in the number of outstanding shares of stock coupled with a proportionate reduction in the par value of the stock.

Stockholder. A person who owns the stock of a corporation. Also called **shareholder**.

Stockholders' Equity. Owners' equity of a corporation.

Straight-Line (SL) Depreciation Method. Depreciation method in which an equal amount of depreciation expense is assigned to each year of asset use.

Strong Currency. A currency that is rising relative to other nations' currencies.

Subsidiary Company. A company in which a parent company owns more than 50% of the voting stock.

Subsidiary Ledger. Record of accounts that provides supporting details on individual balances, the total of which appears in a general ledger account.

Sunk Cost. A past cost that cannot be changed regardless of which future action is taken.

Supply-Chain Management. Exchange of information with suppliers and customers to reduce costs, improve quality, and speed delivery of goods and services from suppliers, through the company itself, and on to customers.

Target Cost. Allowable cost to develop, produce, and deliver the product or service. Equals target price minus desired profit.

Target Price. What customers are willing to pay for the product or service.

Temporary Accounts. The revenue and expense accounts that relate to a particular accounting period and are closed at the end of the period. For a proprietorship, the owner withdrawal account is also temporary.

Term Bonds. Bonds that all mature at the same time for a particular issue.

Throughput Time. The time between buying raw materials and selling finished products.

Time Record. Source document used to trace direct labor to specific jobs.

Time Value of Money. The fact that money can be invested to earn income over time.

Time-Period Concept. Ensures that information is reported at regular intervals.

Times-Interest-Earned Ratio. Ratio of income from operations to interest expense. Measures the number of times that operating income can cover interest expense. Also called the **interest-coverage ratio**.

Total Fixed Costs. Costs that do not change in total despite wide changes in volume.

Total Quality Management (TQM). A philosophy of delighting customers by providing them with superior products and services. Requires improving quality and eliminating defects and waste throughout the value chain.

Total Variable Costs. Costs that change in total in direct proportion to changes in volume.

Trademarks, Trade Names, or Brand Names. Assets that represent distinctive identifications of a product or service.

Trading Investments. Investments that are to be sold in the very near future with the intent of generating profits on price changes.

Trading on the Equity. Earning more income on borrowed money than the related interest expense, thereby increasing the earnings for the owners of the business. Also called **leverage**.

Transaction. An event that affects the financial position of a particular entity and can be recorded reliably.

Transferred-in Costs. Costs incurred in a previous process that are carried forward as part of the product's cost when it moves to the next process.

Treasury Stock. A corporation's own stock that it has issued and later reacquired.

Trend Percentages. A form of horizontal analysis in which percentages are computed by selecting a base year as 100% and expressing amounts for following years as a percentage of the base amount.

Trial Balance. A list of all the accounts with their balances.

Trojan Horse. A malicious program that works like a virus but does not reproduce.

Uncollectible-Account Expense. Cost to the seller of extending credit. Arises from the failure to collect from credit customers. Also called **doubtful-account expense**, or **bad-debt expense**.

Underallocated (Manufacturing) Overhead. The manufacturing overhead allocated to Work in Process Inventory is less than the amount of manufacturing overhead costs actually incurred.

Unearned Revenue. A liability created when a business collects cash from customers in advance of doing work. Also called **deferred revenue**.

Unemployment Compensation Tax. Payroll tax paid by employers to the government, which uses the money to pay unemployment benefits to people who are out of work.

Units-of-Production (UOP) Depreciation Method. Depreciation method by which a fixed amount of depreciation is assigned to each unit of output produced by an asset.

Unlimited Personal Liability. When a partnership (or a proprietorship) cannot pay its debts with business assets, the partners (or the proprietor) must use personal assets to meet the debt.

Value Chain. The activities that add value to a firm's products and services. Includes R&D, design, production or purchases, marketing, distribution, and customer service.

Value Engineering. Reevaluating activities to reduce costs while satisfying customer needs.

Variable Costing. The costing method that assigns only variable manufacturing costs to products.

Variance. The difference between an actual amount and the budget. A variance is labeled as favorable if it increases operating income and unfavorable if it decreases operating income.

Vertical Analysis. Analysis of a financial statement that reveals the relationship of each statement item to a specified base, which is the 100% figure.

Voucher. Instrument authorizing a cash payment.

Weak Currency. A currency that is falling relative to other nations' currencies.

Weighted-Average Process Costing Method. A process costing method that costs all equivalent units of work with a weighted average of the previous period's and the current period's cost per equivalent unit.

Withheld Income Tax. Income tax deducted from employees' gross pay.

Work in Process Inventory. Goods that are partway through the manufacturing process but not yet complete.

Work Sheet. A columnar document designed to help move data from the trial balance to the financial statements.

Working Capital. Current assets minus current liabilities; measures a business's ability to meet its short-term obligations with its current assets.

Company Index

*Real companies are in **bold** type.*

I-1